T0301106

LOCAL EXPLORER

CHESHIRE

www.philips-maps.co.uk

Published by Philip's, a division of
Octopus Publishing Group Ltd
www.octopusbooks.co.uk
Carmelite House
50 Victoria Embankment
London EC4Y 0DZ
An Hachette UK Company
www.hachette.co.uk

First edition 2022
CHEFA

ISBN 978-1-84907-600-5

Photographic acknowledgements:
Dreamstime.com: /Kadirlookatme II top;
/Andrew Hamilton III top left; /Christopher
John III top right; /Garryuk III bottom.
iStock: /NicolasMcComber front cover.

Printed in China

CONTENTS

II **Best places to visit**

IV **Key to map pages**

VI **Route planning**

VIII **Key to map symbols**

1 **Street maps** at 3½ inches to 1 mile

237 **Street map of Chester** at 7 inches to 1 mile

238 **Index** of towns, villages, streets, hospitals, industrial estates, railway stations, schools, shopping centres, universities and places of interest

Best places to visit

Chester Beautiful historic city which grew up around a large Roman fort on the River Dee. It became an important Anglo-Saxon settlement, resisting – apart from one brief occupation – Viking raids, and was a wealthy trading port by the Middle Ages. Over the centuries the harbour silted up, but the city continued to be important, and its history can be traced through its extensive Roman remains, medieval Rows and Tudor buildings, as well as elegant Georgian houses and imposing Victorian public architecture, such as the Gothic-style town hall and Eastgate Clock.

The **City Walls** are the oldest, longest and most complete city walls in Britain, built by the Romans between 70 and 80 AD, and developed and extended by both the Saxons and the Normans. Just outside the City Walls lie **Chester Roman Gardens**, next to the Newgate and the partially excavated remains of the Roman amphitheatre.

Chester Cathedral is a large, mainly Gothic cathedral founded as a Benedictine Abbey in 1092. Monastic buildings date from the 11th century, but the Abbey Church – now the cathedral – was largely rebuilt on an impressive scale during the 13th and 14th centuries. The monks' 13th-century dining room serves as the café.

Grosvenor Museum explores the history of Chester, with collections of archaeology, art, silver and natural history. Among its Roman archaeology artefacts are internationally important Roman tombstones. Grosvenor Park is a large ornamental park overlooking the River Dee. Amenities include a play area, miniature railway and open air theatre in the summer.

Chester Rows, medieval shopping streets in the heart of the city, are where shops and cafes can be accessed on two storeys thanks to the mostly black-and-white, half-timbered galleries (or 'rows') at first floor level.

🖳 ww.visitcheshire.com/chester **237**

Outdoors

Abbeywood Gardens A 45-acre estate in the Delamere countryside, with seasonal gardens, both formal and informal, 27 acres of woodland, and an arboretum with many rare tree species. *Delamere* 🖳 www.abbeywoodestate.co.uk **123 E5**

Alderley Edge and Cheshire Countryside Dramatic red sandstone escarpment overlooking the Cheshire plain, owned by the National Trust, offering varied woodland walks and dramatic views over the surrounding countryside. There is evidence of copper mining from the Bronze Age onwards, with many mines still accessible on tours. Among the many myths associated with the area is that of the Wizard of Alderley Edge, whose caves house men and horses ready to defend the country. Restaurants, cafes and shops can be found in the picturesque village of Alderley Edge. **85 D8**

Brereton Heath Nature Reserve Over 50 acres of woodland surrounding a 15-acre

▼ *Lyme Park*

lake, offering a variety of walks as well as an easy access trail and ample opportunities for bird and butterfly spotting. There are also heathland and wetland areas and a wildflower meadow. Activities include an orienteering course. *Congleton* **154 D6**

Delamere Forest Park Cheshire's largest woodland area, once part of a vast Norman hunting forest, offering walking, cycling and orienteering trails as well as a visitor centre with café and cycle hire. Covering over 2,400 acres, the forest is home to many different woodland bird species and includes the reclaimed wetland area of Blakemere Moss, where waterfowl and rare mosses flourish. Several long-distance walking routes pass through the forest. The Old Pale Stones hill provides far-reaching views. 🖳 www.forestryengland.uk/delamere-forest **100 B3**

Grappenhall Heys Walled Garden Ornamental and kitchen gardens established around 1830 by the wealthy banker Thomas Parr alongside his new manor house (demolished in 1975). The gardens are unusual in that both are contained within one

surrounding wall, which also encloses three ponds and eight fully refurbished Victorian glass-houses. *Warrington* 🖳 www.ghwalledgarden.org.uk **27 A8**

Hare Hill National Trust-owned landscaped parkland, surrounding a peaceful wooded garden and a Victorian walled garden. The garden is noted for its rare and exotic rhododendron species, its wide variety of holly plants and the walled garden's equestrian statues and white perennial borders. There is a play area and a permissive path to Alderley Edge. *Over Alderley* 🖳 www.nationaltrust.org.uk **86 B6**

Marbury Country Park Large area of parkland and woodland overlooking Budworth Mere. Its lime avenues and arboretum reflect its past as part of the grand estate of Marbury Hall (now demolished). The country park has an extensive network of paths popular with cyclists, walkers and horse riders. It forms part of Northwich Community Woodlands – nearly 400 acres of woods, country parks and lakes that are being created on formerly industrial land. 🖳 www.visitcheshire.com **78 E5**

Tatton Park National Trust-owned estate, with a neo-classical mansion, medieval hall, working farm and large formal gardens set within 1,000 acres of parkland. The estate is perhaps best known for its gardens, notably the Japanese Garden, which is one of the finest in Europe. The Tudor Old Hall, the original manor house, served as the estate's farmhouse and then cottages for the estate workers. Highlights include the Great Hall and Cruck Barn. The early 18th-century mansion contains an important collection of paintings

and books, as well as ornate state rooms and unusually complete servants' quarters. Within the estate's grounds is a working rare breeds farm, with children's activities and a woodland play area. Deer herds roam the parkland, which together with the woodland and lakes, is a popular place for walking, cycling and horse riding. *Knutsford* 🖳 www.tattonpark.org.uk **56 E8**

Tegg's Nose Country Park Country park on the western edge of the Peak District, a rocky landscape of steep-sided valleys, old sandstone quarries and views across the Cheshire Plain and beyond. Climbing and abseiling are available in the quarry, and the park is a popular area for walking, orienteering and horse riding. There is a geology trail around the summit of Tegg's Nose. *Macclesfield* 🖳 www.teggsnose.co.uk **113 D6**

Walton Hall and Gardens Mature parkland and spacious ornamental gardens surrounding Walton Hall, an early 19th-century manor house built in Gothic revival style. The park's attractions include historic glasshouses, a large pond and woodland walks, as well as a children's zoo and a cycle museum. *Warrington* 🖳 www.waltonhallgardens.co.uk **25 F7**

Towns & villages

Daresbury Picturesque village, birthplace in 1832 of the author Lewis Carroll. **All Saints Church**, where his father was vicar, contains a stained glass window commissioned to celebrate the centenary of Carroll's birth, which features characters from Alice in Wonderland. The Lewis Carroll Centre adjacent to the church provides information on his life and family, and the nearby

Lewis Carroll Centenary Wood has a commemorative tablet. 🖳 www.lewiscarrollcentre.org.uk 🖳 www.woodlandtrust.org.uk **25 B2**

Knutsford Historic market town, with buildings dating from the Tudor, Georgian and Victorian eras, and well known for those by 19th-century designer Richard Watt, who favoured an eccentric Italianate style. Other attractions include a Penny Farthing Museum. **Knutsford Heritage Centre** is based in a 17th-century timber-framed building, previously known as Musgrave's Yard, which had housed an ironmonger and a tinsmith and now contains two galleries, courtyard gardens and the remarkable 40ft-long Millennium Tapestry. 🖳 www.thecourtyardknutsford.co.uk/museum 🖳 www.knutsfordheritage.co.uk **57**

Macclesfield Historic market town on the edge of the Peak District National Park. Known as a centre for silk making from the mid-18th century onwards, it has two museums devoted to its history and manufacture – the **Silk Museum** and **Paradise Mill** the latter housing a collection of Jacquard silk handlooms. Hovis Mill, where the famous flour was originally milled, lies on the Macclesfield Canal. On the banks of the River Bollin is **Macclesfield Riverside Park**, which contains mature woodland and wildflower grasslands grazed by Longhorn cattle. Nearby, **Macclesfield Forest** has a herd of red deer and other wildlife, including a variety of waterfowl on its four reservoirs. 🖳 www.macclesfieldmuseums.co.uk **112**

Nantwich Historic market town on the River Weaver, known for its medieval timbered houses, among them Churche's Mansion,

▲ *Beeston Castle*
◄ *Eastgate Street, Chester*

Queen's Aid House and the Crown Hotel. It was a centre of salt production from Roman times up to the 18th century, and is home to one of the country's few remaining inland brine swimming pools. Nantwich Lake and the riverside area, location of the brine spring 'Old Biot', are popular with walkers. **St Mary's Church** is one of the finest medieval churches in the country, designed on a grand scale and constructed from red sandstone with a striking octagonal tower. A Victorian library, now **Nantwich Museum**, has exhibitions focusing on Nantwich's central role in both the salt-making and cheese-producing industries. There are galleries devoted to clockmaking and to the Great Fire of 1583, with a display of old fire-fighting equipment. The **Cheshire Civil War Centre** explains the importance of Cheshire in the Civil War together with Nantwich's pivotal role. 🖳www.nantwichmuseum. org.uk 🖳www.stmarys nantwich.org.uk **204**

Northwich Town on the River Weaver, site of a Roman settlement and a centre of the salt-making industry until the 19th century, when the method of pumping hot water into the mines resulted in widespread subsidence in the town and its surroundings. The **Weaver Hall Museum** (in the old Victorian Northwich Union Workhouse) details the history and industry of the region as well as life in the workhouse. See also the Lion Salt Works 🖳https://:weaverhall. westcheshiremuseums.co.uk 🖳www.visitnorthwich.co.uk **103**

Buildings

See also Tatton Park

Arley Hall & Gardens Victorian manor house, built in the Elizabethan style, surrounded by gardens and parkland. The Hall has an impressive interior, with detailed oak panelling and stained glass, and the large formal gardens are known for their double herbaceous borders and variety of plants. There is a 15th-century barn, a chapel and a play area. *Northwich* 🖳www.arleyhalland gardens.com **54 D6**

Beeston Castle Medieval castle on a rocky crag overlooking the Cheshire Plain. Next to the substantial ruins is a museum that tells the castle's story. Highlights include one of the deepest castle wells in the country and spectacular views towards the Pennines and the Welsh mountains. 🖳www. english-heritage.org.uk **167 F3**

Cholmondeley Castle Gardens Large ornamental gardens surrounding a private, early 19th-century castle, with many specimen trees and shrubs, including rare magnolias and camellias. Highlights include the Temple and Folly water gardens, a rose garden and a double herbaceous border. *Whitchurch* 🖳www.cholmondeleycastle. com **201 A4**

Gawsworth Hall Timber-framed manor house dating from the late 15th century. The house retains some original Tudor features, including a carved chimneypiece, as well as historic paintings, furniture and sculptures brought to the house more recently. The gardens were once a large Elizabethan Pleasure Garden, complete with a 'tilting ground' used for jousting. *Macclesfield* 🖳www.gawsworthhall.com **134 E8**

Little Moreton Hall National Trust-owned Tudor manor house surrounded by a moat. Built in the 15th century in the traditional timber-framed style, it retains its original great hall and kitchen wing and has been little altered since. It has an unusually irregular appearance, with its impressive Long Gallery giving it a precarious 'top heavy' appearance. Outdoors there is an Elizabethan-style Knot Garden and tea rooms. *Congleton* 🖳www.nationaltrust.org.uk **177 E2**

Lyme Park Imposing manor house, with a substantial Elizabethan core, complete with stained glass and oak panelling, and 18th-century additions in a grand Italianate style. One of the National Trust's most important books – the rare Caxton-printed Lyme Missal – is on display. The house is surrounded by formal gardens and its reflecting lake was famously used in the filming of the BBC's adaptation of Jane Austen's Pride and Prejudice. The surrounding 1,400 acres of deerpark and moorland are popular with walkers and birdwatchers. *Disley* 🖳www. nationaltrust.org.uk **38 B2**

Nether Alderley Mill National Trust-restored water mill housed in the original 16th-century mill buildings. Tours explain the milling process and describe the lives of the millers, and there are regular demonstrations using the mill's 19th-century machinery. *Alderley Edge* 🖳www.national trust.org.uk **85 A5**

Museums & galleries

Anson Engine Museum Museum on the site of an old colliery, with a large collection of gas and oil engines, many in working condition. Displays include the history of the internal combustion engine, the story of engines from cannons to those of the future, and a steam section. There are running engines every day and frequent craft demonstrations. *Poynton* 🖳www.enginemuseum.org **37 C4**

Crewe Heritage Centre Railway museum located on the site of the old Crewe Locomotive Works, with steam, diesel and electric locomotives, signal boxes and a miniature railway, plus an exhibition hall with displays on the history of Crewe and a collection of ice cream vans. 🖳www.crewehc.co.uk **190 D3**

Hack Green Secret Nuclear Bunker Substantial, semi-sunk concrete nuclear bunker, now a museum dedicated to the history of the Cold War and of the bunker itself, which was originally a radar station before being adapted to serve as a Regional Government Headquarters in the event of a nuclear attack. Visitors can see the original blast doors and explore the network of underground rooms and equipment, as well as a collection of nuclear weapons. *Nantwich* 🖳www.hackgreen.co.uk **218 D4**

Jodrell Bank Internationally famous observatory, location of the Lovell Telescope, one of the world's largest radio telescopes. It has been a UNESCO World Heritage Site since 2019. The Discovery Centre has interactive exhibitions, talks and other events. There are outdoor activities, a children's play area, gardens and an arboretum. *Macclesfield* 🖳www.jodrellbank.net **108 C3**

Lion Salt Works Museum on the site of a former open-pan salt works. Renovated stove and pan houses contain some of the original equipment and explain the processes involved in salt-making and extraction. Visitors can also learn about the lives of the managers and workers, the science of salt, and salt-related habitats. *Northwich* 🖳https://lionsaltworks.westcheshire museums.co.uk **79 C3**

National Waterways Museum Museum at Ellesmere Port on the old trans-shipment dock where the Shropshire Union Canal meets the Manchester Ship Canal. The wide-ranging collection covers the history of the waterways and the people who worked on them, a large collection of engines and over 50 traditional boats. There are interactive exhibits and a children's play area. *Ellesmere Port* 🖳www.canalrivertrust.org. uk **70 C7**

Norton Priory Museum and Gardens Extensively excavated remains of a medieval priory, with the original layout clearly visible, and its 12th-century vaulted undercroft. In the extensive grounds are the National Tree Quince Collection and a Georgian walled garden. *Runcorn* 🖳www.nortonpriory. org **24 B3**

Quarry Bank Large estate, owned by the National Trust, with cotton mill and associated buildings from the early years of the Industrial Revolution. The mill has working steam engines and waterwheel, displays on the cotton trade, working conditions at the mill and the engineering involved, with plenty of hands-on children's activities. In Styal village itself is a worker's cottage. *Wilmslow* 🖳www. nationaltrust.org.uk **33 F2**

Warrington Museum and Art Gallery Museum with a wide-ranging collection that covers ethnology, botany, fish and reptiles, geology and local history. Its art galleries display some nationally important paintings. There are changing exhibitions and children's activities. 🖳www.wmag. culturewarrington.org **16 A4**

Family activities

Anderton Boat Lift Impressive boat lift, opened in 1875 and one of only two working boat lifts remaining in the UK. Known as one of the 'Seven Wonders of the Waterways', it lifts barges and boats from the River Weaver Navigation to the Trent and Mersey Canal, 50 feet above. After extensive

▲ *The Lovell Radio Telescope at Jodrell Bank*

restoration in 2000 to 2002, it now runs using a modified version of the original hydraulic system. Activities include boat trips on the lift and further afield, a visitor centre and nature park. *Northwich* 🖳www.canalriver-trust.org.uk **78 D3**

Chester Zoo Largest and most visited zoo in the UK, home to more than 20,000 animals in near-natural enclosures. The zoo does internationally important work to conserve many rare and endangered species, from Asian elephants, Sumatran tigers and Andean bears, to rare Latin American birds, Komodo dragons and butterflies. Many unusual plants can be seen in the award-winning botanical gardens. *Upton-by-Chester* 🖳www.chesterzoo.org **95 E1**

Gauntlet Birds of Prey Park with a large collection of birds of prey, including eagles, vultures, hawks, falcons and owls, as well as more unusual species. Flying demonstrations and handling sessions are available, as well as talks and children's activities. *Knutsford* 🖳www.gauntlet birdsofprey.co.uk **56 D5**

Reaseheath Mini Zoo Small zoo in the grounds of Reaseheath College, usually open to the public at weekends and in school holidays, with a variety of species from around the world. Keeper talks and children's activities are available. *Nantwich* 🖳www. reaseheath.ac.uk/zoo **188 D1**

► *Anderton Boat Lift*

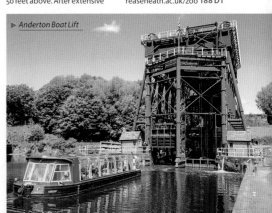

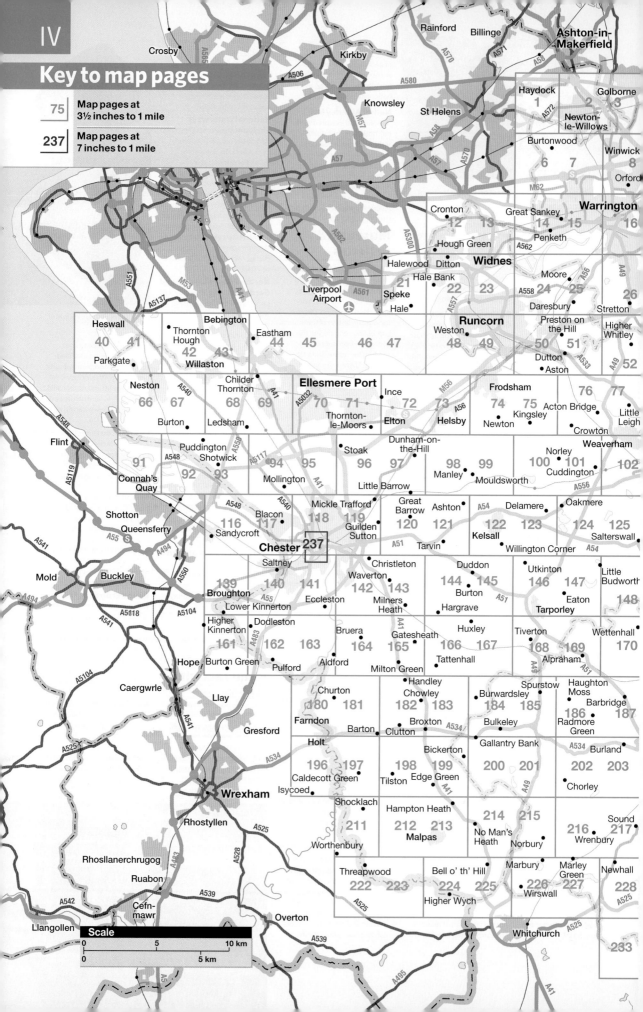

Key to map pages

75	Map pages at 3½ inches to 1 mile
237	Map pages at 7 inches to 1 mile

Crosby

Rainford · Billinge · Ashton-in-Makerfield

Kirkby

Knowsley · St Helens

Haydock **1** · Golborne **2 3**

Newton-le-Willows

Burtonwood **6 7** Winwick **8** Orford

Warrington

Cronton **12 13** Great Sankey **14 15 16**

Hough Green · Penketh

Halewood · Ditton **Widnes**

Liverpool Airport · Hale Bank **21 22 23** Moore **24 25 26**

Speke · Hale · Daresbury · Stretton

Weston **48 49** **Runcorn** Preston on the Hill **50 51** Higher Whitley **52**

Dutton · Aston

Heswall **40 41** Bebington Eastham **44 45 46 47**

Thornton Hough **42 43** Willaston

Parkgate

Neston **66 67** Childer Thornton **68 69** **Ellesmere Port 70 71** Ince **72 73** Frodsham **74 75 76 77**

Burton · Ledsham · Thornton-le-Moors · Elton · Helsby · Newton · Kingsley · Acton Bridge · Little Leigh · Crowton

Flint

Puddington Shotwick **91 92 93 94 95** Stoak **96 97** Dunham-on-the-Hill **98 99** Manley · Mouldsworth **100 101 102** Norley Cuddington Weaverham

Connah's Quay · Mollington · Little Barrow

Shotton · Blacon **116 117 118 119** Great Barrow Ashton **120 121** Delamere **122 123** Oakmere **124 125**

Queensferry · Sandycroft · Mickle Trafford · Guilden Sutton **Kelsall** Salterswall

Chester 237 Tarvin · Willington Corner

Mold · Buckley · Saltney **139 140 141** Christleton Waverton **142 143** Duddon **144 145** Utkinton **146 147** Little Budworth **148**

Broughton · Eccleston · Milners Heath · Burton · Hargrave · Eaton · **Tarporley**

Lower Kinnerton

Higher Kinnerton Dodleston **161 162 163** Bruera **164 165** Gateshealth Huxley **166 167** Tiverton **168 169** Wettenhall **170**

Hope · Burton Green · Pulford · Aldford · Milton Green · Tattenhall · Alpraham

Caergwrle

Llay · Churton **180 181** Handley **182 183** Burwardsley **184 185** Spurstow Haughton Moss **186 187** Barbridge

Gresford · Farndon · Chowley · Radmore Green

Holt · Barton · Broxton · Bulkeley · Gallantry Bank · Burland

Wrexham **196 197** Clutton **198 199 200 201 202 203** Chorley

Caldecott Green · Bickerton

Rhostyllen · Tilston Edge Green

Rhosllanerchrugog · Isycoed · Shocklach **211** Hampton Heath **212 213 214 215** Sound **216 217**

Ruabon · Worthenbury · **Malpas** · No Man's Heath · Norbury · Wrenbury

Cefn-mawr · Threapwood **222 223** Bell o' th' Hill **224 225** Marbury **226 227** Newhall **228**

Llangollen · Higher Wych · Wirswall · Marley Green

Overton · Whitchurch **233**

Scale

0	5	10 km

0	5 km

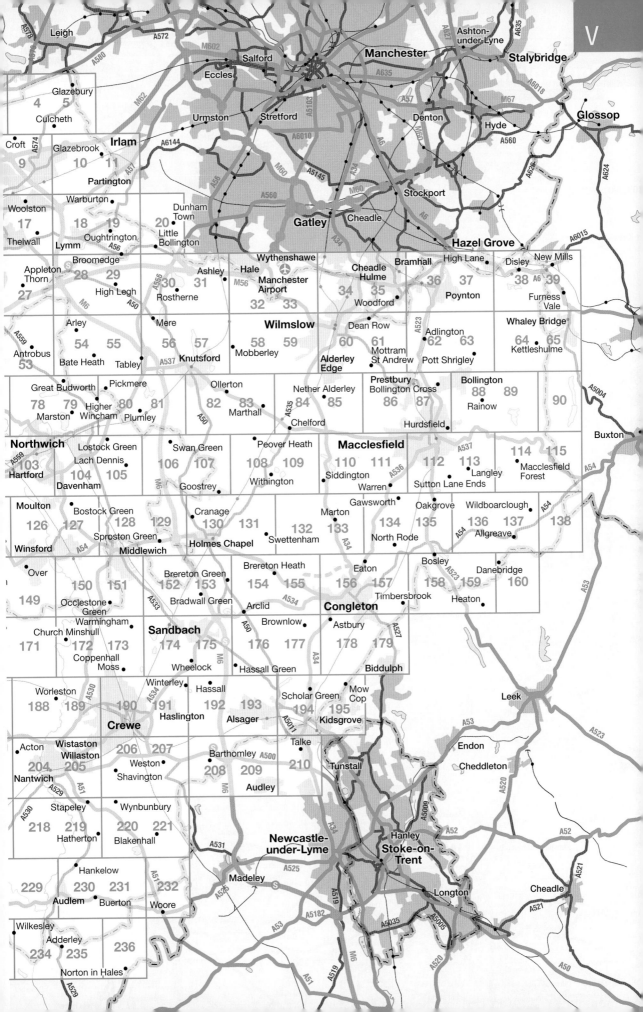

Key to map symbols

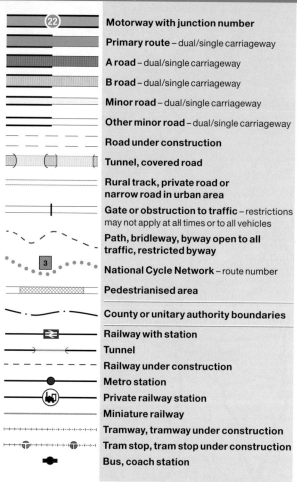

	Motorway with junction number
	Primary route – dual/single carriageway
	A road – dual/single carriageway
	B road – dual/single carriageway
	Minor road – dual/single carriageway
	Other minor road – dual/single carriageway
	Road under construction
	Tunnel, covered road
	Rural track, private road or narrow road in urban area
	Gate or obstruction to traffic – restrictions may not apply at all times or to all vehicles
	Path, bridleway, byway open to all traffic, restricted byway
	National Cycle Network – route number
	Pedestrianised area
	County or unitary authority boundaries
	Railway with station
	Tunnel
	Railway under construction
	Metro station
	Private railway station
	Miniature railway
	Tramway, tramway under construction
	Tram stop, tram stop under construction
	Bus, coach station

	Ambulance station
	Coastguard station
	Fire station
	Police station
	Accident and Emergency entrance to hospital
H	Hospital
+	Place of worship
i	Information centre
P	Shopping centre, parking
P&R / PO	Park and Ride, Post Office
	Camping site, caravan site
	Golf course, picnic site
Church / ROMAN FORT	Non-Roman antiquity, Roman antiquity
Univ	Important buildings, schools, colleges, universities and hospitals
	Woods, built-up area
River Medway	Water name
	River, weir
	Stream
	Canal, lock, tunnel
	Water
	Tidal water

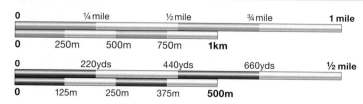

Adjoining page indicators and overlap bands – the colour of the arrow and band indicates the scale of the adjoining or overlapping page (see scales below)

The dark grey border on the inside edge of some pages indicates that the mapping does not continue onto the adjacent page

The small numbers around the edges of the maps identify the 1-kilometre National Grid lines

Abbreviations

Acad	Academy	Meml	Memorial
Allot Gdns	Allotments	Mon	Monument
Cemy	Cemetery	Mus	Museum
C Ctr	Civic centre	Obsy	Observatory
CH	Club house	Pal	Royal palace
Coll	College	PH	Public house
Crem	Crematorium	Recn Gd	Recreation ground
Ent	Enterprise		
Ex H	Exhibition hall	Resr	Reservoir
Ind Est	Industrial Estate	Ret Pk	Retail park
IRB Sta	Inshore rescue boat station	Sch	School
		Sh Ctr	Shopping centre
Inst	Institute	TH	Town hall / house
Ct	Law court	Trad Est	Trading estate
L Ctr	Leisure centre	Univ	University
LC	Level crossing	W Twr	Water tower
Liby	Library	Wks	Works
Mkt	Market	YH	Youth hostel

Enlarged maps only

	Railway or bus station building
	Place of interest
	Parkland

The map scale on the pages numbered in blue is 3½ inches to 1 mile
5.52 cm to 1 km • 1:18 103

0	¼ mile	½ mile	¾ mile	1 mile
0	250m	500m	750m	1km

The map scale on the pages numbered in red is 7 inches to 1 mile
11.04 cm to 1 km • 1:9051

0	220yds	440yds	660yds	½ mile
0	125m	250m	375m	500m

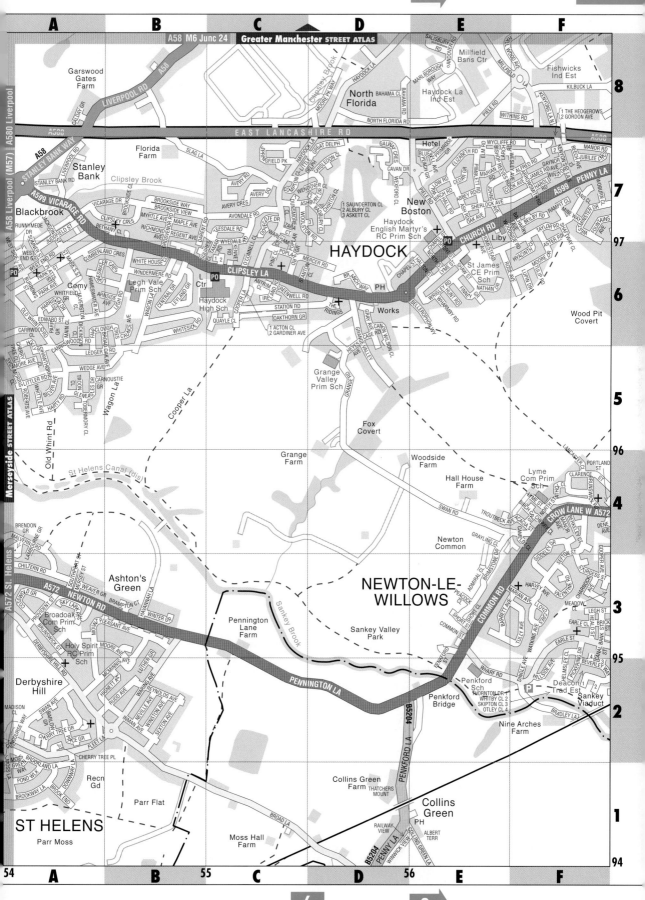

HAYDOCK

M6 Preston A49 Wigan

Greater Manchester STREET ATLAS

Haydock Park Racecourse

GOLBORNE

SPRINGFIELD AVE 1
HIGHFIELD AVE 2
CLIFTONMILL MDWS 3

Yew Tree Farm Trad Est

Old Boston Trad Est

Haydock Park

White Door Covert

White Door Dam

PLANE TREE GR

Hotel

Ladder Hill Plantation

East Lancashire Rd

Haydock Park Farm

Fox Covert

Dean Dam

Dean Dam Farm

Newton-Haydock Bridge

Ellam's Brook

Ellam's Rough

Woodlands Pk

Woodlands Ind Est

Lawson's Farm

Hollows Bridge

Selwyn Jones Sports Ctr

CH

The Hope Acad

Newton Bank Prep Sch

Newton Lake

WATERWORKS COTTS

The Courtyard

Borron Road Ind Est

HIGH ST

SOUTHWORTH RD

St Aelred's RC Tech Coll

St Peter's CE Prim Sch

Stones Crossing

Newton-le-Willows Prim Sch

Newton-le-Willows

Mill Green Sch

Newton Park Farm

NEWTON-LE-WILLOWS

Earlestown

Wargrave

Newton Park Dr

1 PARK VIEW
2 CRABTREE CL
3 OWLSFIELD

Sankey Valley Ind Est

Newton Community

Earlestown

Wargrave CE Prim Sch

Wargrave House Sch

Cemy

1 MALDEN RD
2 VULCAN PK CT
3 LIBERATION RD
4 FRANKLYN DR
5 KIRTLEY CL
6 JACKMAN CL

Red Bank

HAVERTY PREC 1
NOON CT 2
CAUNCE AVE 3
LANGLEY AVE 4
SCOTT WLK 5
THOMPSON CL 6
INGHAM AVE 7
FEARNLEY WAY 8
KENT WAY 9
OLD HEY WLK 10

Sankey Canal (dis)

Vulcan Ind Est

Works

New Hey Farm

D8
1 SARSFIELD AVE
2 FOXGLOVE CL
3 GROSVENOR AVE
4 RIDGEWELL AVE
5 CHAPEL HO MS

E8
1 TURRET HALL DR
2 ROYSTON CL
3 SANDFIELD CL
4 ARIEL WLK
5 BALLANTYNE WAY
6 BUNTING CL

7 REDSTART CL
8 WILD ARUM CL
9 HUDSON GR
10 STONECHAT CL
11 SPEEDWELL CL
12 LUNEHURST
13 CONINGSBY GDNS

F8
1 SCOTIA WLK
2 TYRER WLK
3 ROBSON WAY
4 HORNCASTLE CL
5 HOPWOOD CL
6 BIRCH TREE RD

7 Green Meadow
Ind Prim Sch

4

Greater Manchester STREET ATLAS

GOLBORNE

Lowton

Lowton St Mary's

Bank Heath

Lowton Heath

Lane Head

Town of Lowton

Lowton Heath

Golborne Junction

Golborne Dale Bridge

Highfield Farm

Highfield Moss

Moss Pits

Kenyon

Morris's Farm

Barrow Farm

Lowe's Farm

Parkside Farm

Kenyon Hall

Sandy Bank Farm

Rock House

Oven Back Cottage

Oven Back Farm

Wood Head

St Oswald's Well

Hermitage Farm

Rough Farm

Sandfield Hall

Parkside Manchester Junction

Highfield Farm

Parkside Liverpool Junction

Highfield Farm

Stirrups Farm

Lowton Heath House

Hotel

Five Acres

Dickinson's Farm

Hayes' Farm

Dolly's Bridge

Beard's Battery

Stone Cross Pk

Parkside Bsns Pk

Millingford Ind Est

All Saints Prim Sch

1 HEREFORD AVE
2 GLOUCESTER AVE
3 WORCESTER AVE
4 MILLFIELD PK

BROADLEY AVE 1
BARNTON CL 2
FIELDACRE CL 3
NORTHACRE CL 4
FIELD MDW CL 5
THOMPSON FARM MDW 6
CROFT GN CL 7
LEA GN CL 8
SOUTH MDW CL 9
HEATH FIELD CL 10

PIMBLETT ST 1
WAKEFIELD ST 2
MARYFIELD CL 3
WEARHEAD CL 4
ORFORD CL 5
SUMMERCROFT CL 6
BELTON CL 7
Golborne Cty 8
Prim Sch

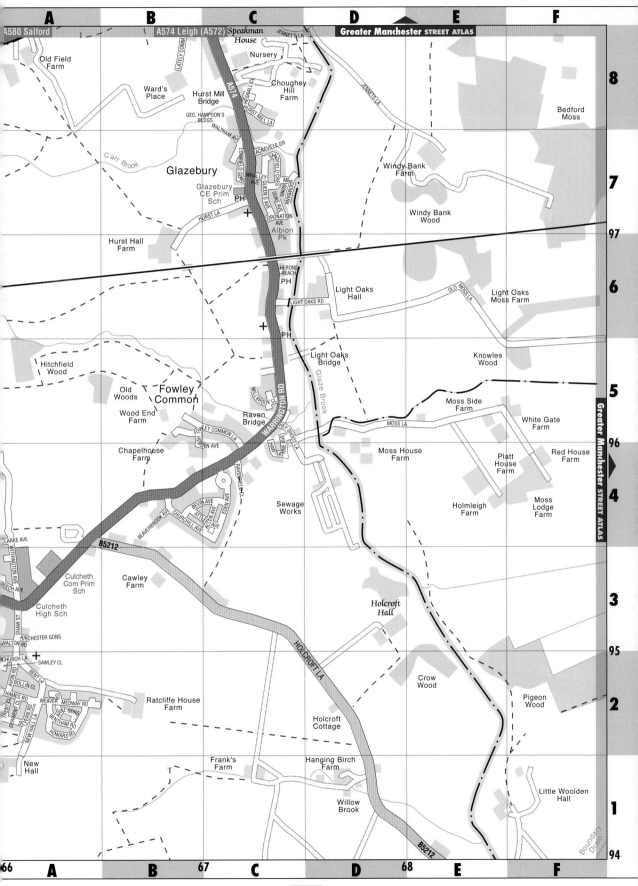

A B C D E F

A580 Salford
A574 Leigh (A572)

Speakman House

Jennet's La

8

Old Field Farm

Ward's Place

Hurst Mill Bridge

GEO. HAMPSON'S BLDGS

Nursery

Choughey Hill Farm

ACREVILLE GR

Bedford Moss

Carr Brook

WALTHAM AVE

LOWEFIELD GDNS

HURST MILL LA

LATELY COMM

THE SMALL LA

Windy Bank Farm

Glazebury

SAYFIELD CRES

WHALLEY AVE

Glazebury CE Prim Sch

QUEEN'S AVE

DUKE AVE

MOSSBANK

7

PH

HURST LA

CORONATION AVE

Windy Bank Wood

Albion Pk

97

Hurst Hall Farm

HERONS REACH PH

Light Oaks Hall

OLD MOSS LA

6

Light Oaks Moss Farm

LIGHT OAKS RD

Light Oaks Bridge

Hitchfield Wood

Glaze Brook

Knowles Wood

PH

Old Woods

Fowley Common

Raven Bridge

WARRINGTON RD

Moss Side Farm

5

Wood End Farm

MILL BROOK CL

FOWLEY COMMON LA

HEY SHOOT LA

MOSS LA

White Gate Farm

Chapelhouse Farm

HEYDEN AVE

HAWTHORNE AVE

96

RAVENFIELD CL

Moss House Farm

Platt House Farm

Red House Farm

BEVIN AVE

ATTLEE AVE

EDEN AVE

Sewage Works

Holmleigh Farm

Moss Lodge Farm

4

BEAVERBROOK AVE

CHURCHILL AVE

ASPELL AVE

WITHINGTON AVE

CLARKE AVE

B5212

Culcheth Com Prim Sch

Cawley Farm

Holcroft Hall

3

BEECH AVE

Culcheth High Sch

1ST AVE

R/BCHESTER GDNS

WALTON RD

95

CHURCH LA

SAWLEY CL

HOLCROFT LA

Crow Wood

Pigeon Wood

BENTLE CL

BOLLIN CL

Ratcliffe House Farm

2

AV LN

THAMES RD

DERWENT CL

SEVERN RD

WEAVER MEDWAY RD

MEDLE GDNS

NEW HALL LA

BENTHAM RD

HOWARD RD

Holcroft Cottage

Little Woolden Hall

Frank's Farm

Hanging Birch Farm

New Hall

Willow Brook

B5212

Boundary Drain

1

94

A B C D E F

66 67 68

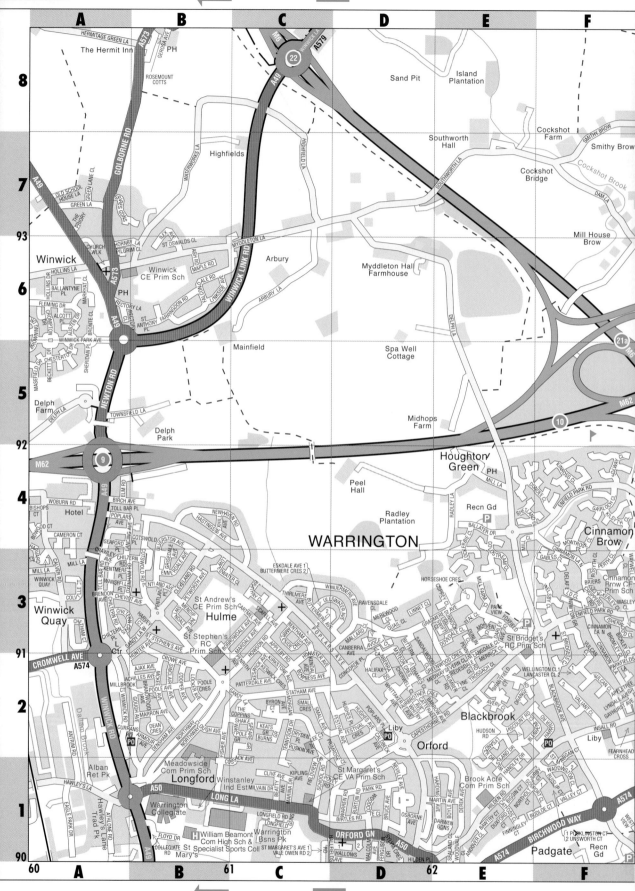

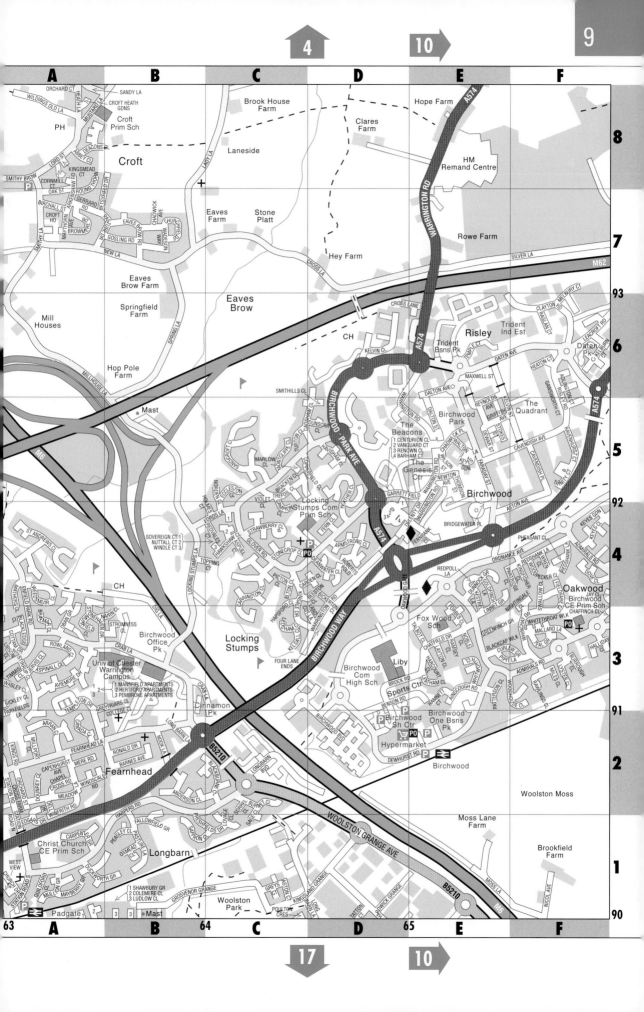

A B C D E F

8

Moss Side Farm

Aikin Knowle's Bridge

Keeper's Cottage

Glaze Brook

HOLCROFT LA

B5212

M62

B5212

7

M62

SILVER LA

11

Holcroft Moss

Ferndale Nurseries

Masts

93

PRESTWOOD CT

LEACROFT RD

Ind Est

Pestfurlong Hill

BIRCHWOOD WAY

A574

Pestfurlong Moss

Glazebrook Moss

6

HAMSTERLEY CL

TALISTONE CL

GORSE COVERT RD

WOOLMERE CL

ROCKINGHAM CL

SILVER LA

Hoyle's Moss Farm

APPLECROSS CL

BRAMSHILL CL

ARDEN CL

DARNAWAY CL

STANMORE CL

FISHERFIELD DR

RENDLESHAM CL

HAZELBOROUGH CL

PO

Gorse Covert Prim Sch

5

WESTHAY CRES 1
WIGMORE CL 2
DUNLEY CL 3
ROSENDALE DR 4
CULBIN CL 5.

MOSS

GORSE COVERT RD

FAILEY CL

LANGWELL

WHITTLE WOOD CL

CHARNWOOD

ASHDOWN CL

ROWLAND CL

RINGWOOD CL

BILDERDALE CL

DALBY CL

KILLINGWORTH

GATE

Gorse Covert

New Hall Farm

SCHOOL LA

Milverton Farm

MOSS LA

Birchwood Forest Park

P

Visitor Ctr

Risley Moss

Omrod Farm

92

KEYES CL

KEYES CL

ORDNANCE AVE

DAM LA

DAM HEAD LA

Bridge Farm

Hollingreave Farm

4

DANIELS CL

MARGARET CL

Birchwood Brook

Risley Moss Nature Reserve

Land Fill Site

Moss Hall Farm

BOUNDARY CL

DE STRATTON CL

MCCARTHY CL

PALLISER CL

PENNANT CL

ASPINMORE CL

Moss Side

Ash Tree Farm

3

CHAFFINCH CL

Prospect Farm

PROSPECT LA

Moss Side Farm No.2

Moss Side LA

Moss Side Farm

Brick Works

Rixton Park Homes

91

Rixton Moss

HOLLY BUSH LA

WOODEND LA

Woodend Farm

2

Woolston Moss

Rixton Clay Pits Nature Reserve

MOAT LA

Works

Works

Mast

CHAPEL LA

A57

1

Marshall's Farm

BROOK LA

Moss Farm

Moss Head

Rixton Firs

MANCHESTER RD

A57

90

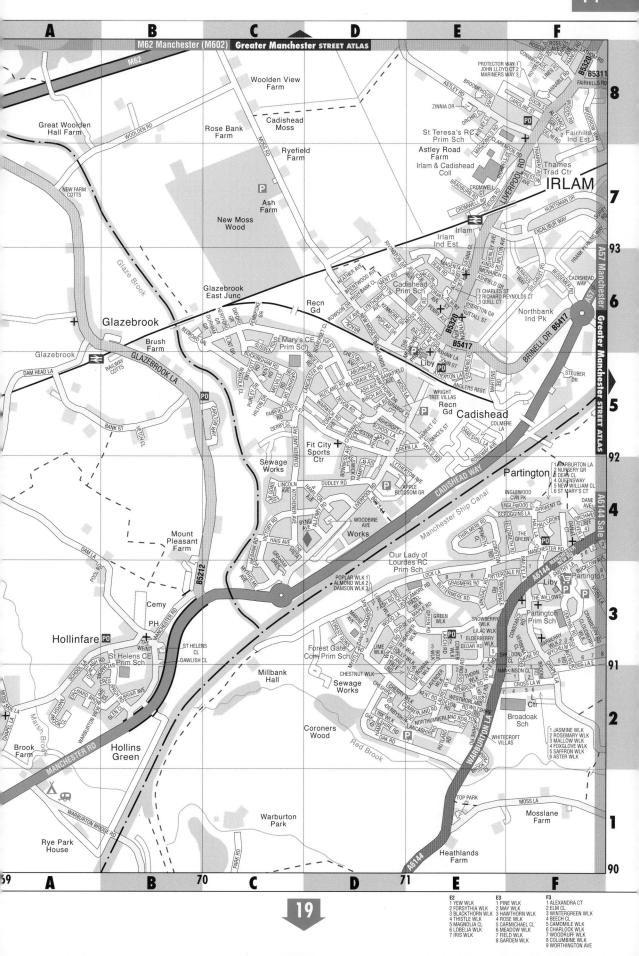

IRLAM

Glazebrook

Cadishead

Partington

Hollinfare

Hollins
Green

E2	E3	F3
1 YEW WLK	1 PINE WLK	1 ALEXANDRA CT
2 FORSYTHIA WLK	2 MAY WLK	2 ELM CL
3 BLACKTHORN WLK	3 HAWTHORN WLK	3 WINTERGREEN WLK
4 THISTLE WLK	4 ROSE WLK	4 BEECH CL
5 MAGNOLIA CL	5 CARMICHAEL CL	5 CAMOMILE WLK
6 LOBELIA WLK	6 MEADOW WLK	6 CHARLOCK WLK
7 IRIS WLK	7 FIELD WLK	7 WOODRUFF WLK
	8 GARDEN WLK	8 COLUMBINE WLK
		9 WORTHINGTON AVE

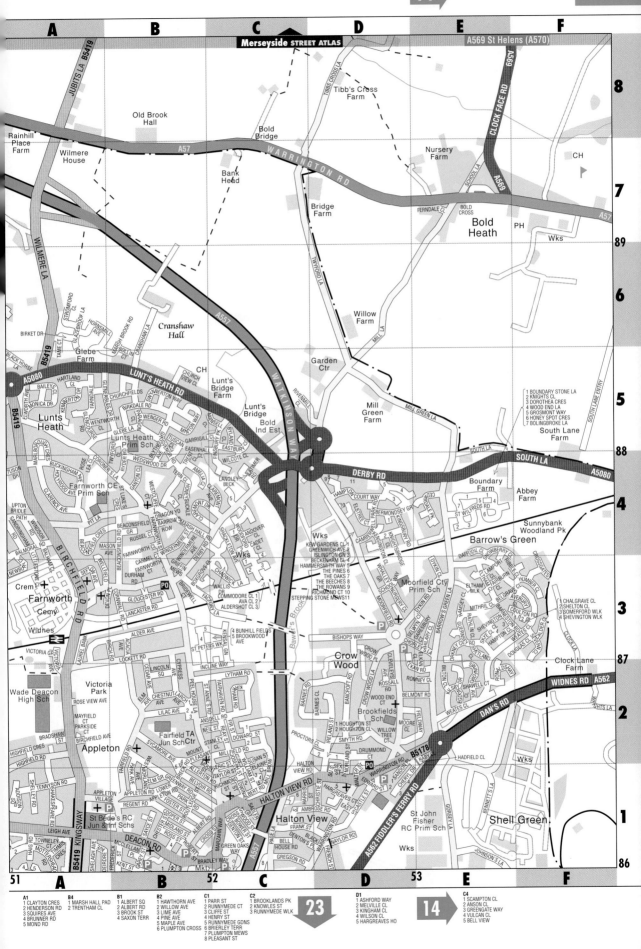

A1
1 CLAYTON CRES
2 HENDERSON RD
3 SQUIRES AVE
4 BRUNNER RD
5 MOND RD

B4
1 MARSH HALL PAD
2 TRENTHAM CL

B1
1 ALBERT SQ
2 ALBERT RD
3 BROOK ST
4 SAXON TERR

B2
1 HAWTHORN AVE
2 WILLOW AVE
3 LIME AVE
4 PINE AVE
5 MAPLE AVE
6 PLUMPTON CROSS

C1
1 PARR ST
2 RUNNYMEDE CT
3 CLIFFE ST
4 HENRY ST
5 RUNNYMEDE GDNS
6 BRIERLEY TERR
7 PLUMPTON MEWS
8 PLEASANT ST

C2
1 BROOKLANDS PK
2 KNOWLES ST
3 RUNNYMEDE WLK

D1
1 ASHFORD WAY
2 MELVILLE CL
3 KINGHAM CL
4 WILSON CL
5 HARGREAVES HO

C4
1 SCAMPTON CL
2 ANSON CL
3 GREENGATE WAY
4 VULCAN CL
5 BELL VIEW

13
6

D8
1 WATERGROVE CRES
2 BROADSTONE CL
3 RUDYARD LAKE
4 DRAYCOTE WATER
5 CASTLESHAW CL

E8
1 WELFORD GDNS
2 MOLESWORTH CL
3 CRANAGE CL
4 ATTLEBRIDGE GDNS
5 RACKHEATH CRES
6 HALESWORTH GDNS
7 BUTTER BROOK
8 CALF HEY
9 TRENTHAM GDNS
10 FOXCOTE GDNS

F8
1 BRAVO WAY
2 ECHO GR
3 SHEPHERDS GR
4 COTTESMORE CL
5 RAMSBURY CT
6 METFIELD GDNS

A
B
C
D
E
F
8
7
89
6
5
88
4
3
87
2
1
86
54
55
56
Eccles Plantation
Finch's Plantation
South Park Plantation
Lingley Mere
Lingley Mere Bsns Pk
Great Sankey L Ctr
Great Sankey High Sch
Barrow Hall Com Prim Sch
Brow Farm
Whittle Brook
Park Farm
Bargyloo
Lingley Green
Dawson House
Hayfield Farm
Greenside Farm
Laburnum Farm
Sandy Lane Farm
1 REDMIRES
2 FERNWORTHY
3 CARSINGTON WATER
4 WINTERBURN
5 HALLINGTON
6 DOVESTONES
PH
A57
WARRINGTON RD
LIVERPOOL RD
SOUTH LANE ENTRY
SANDY LA
LABURNUM LA
Park Road Com Prim Sch
Sankey for Penketh
St Joseph's RC Prim Sch
Penketh Cty High Sch
Liby
PO
Camp (dis)
A5080
SUNNY BANK COTTS
SOUTH LA
FARNWORTH RD
Four Top'd Oak
Brook Farm
Penketh Com Prim Sch
Penketh
Recn Gd
A562
Doe Green
Fowl Farm
MOWCROFT LA
WIDNES RD
Newspaper House
St Vincent's RC Prim Sch
Penketh South Com Prim Sch
Cuerdley Cross
CUERDLEY GN
BACK LA
WRIGHTS LA
TAYLOR'S LA
Cross Lane Farm Cottages
CH
Marsh End Farm
MARSH LA
Power Station
P
LC
Trans Pennine Trail
River Mersey
62
Swing Bridge
Riverside Trad Est
Fiddler's Ferry Reach
Fiddler's Ferry
St Helens Canal (disused)

13
24

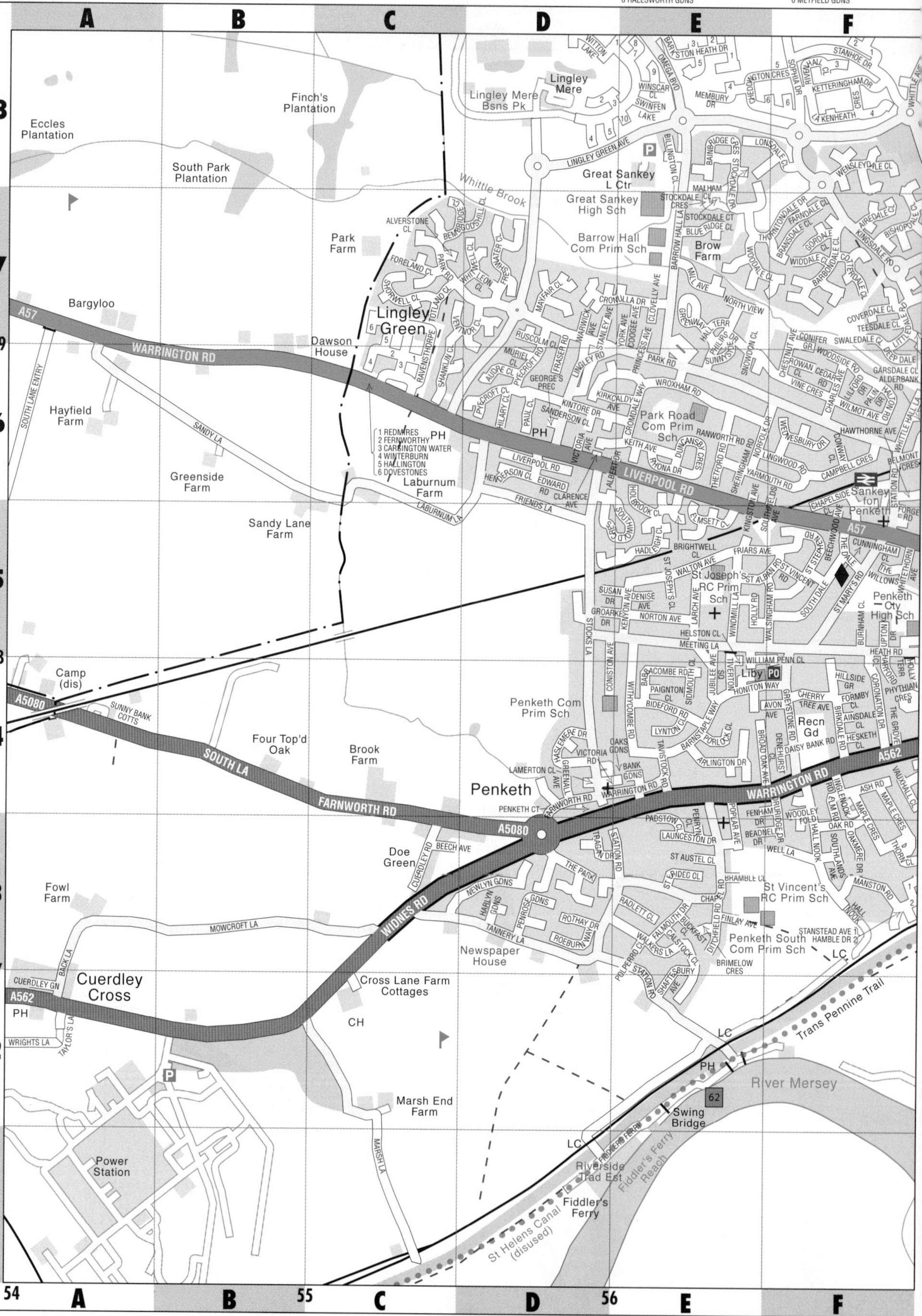

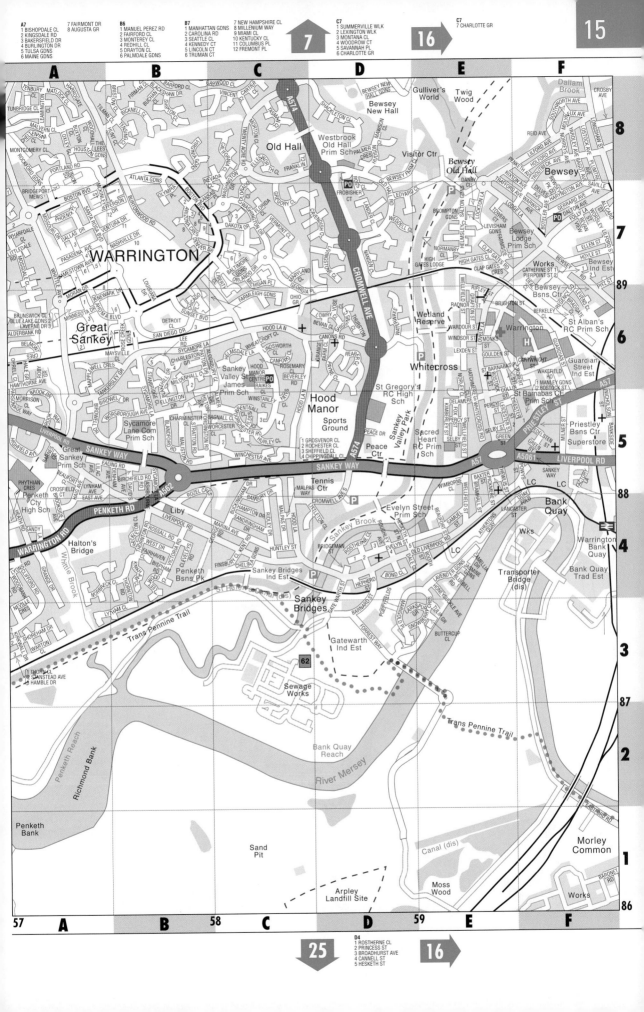

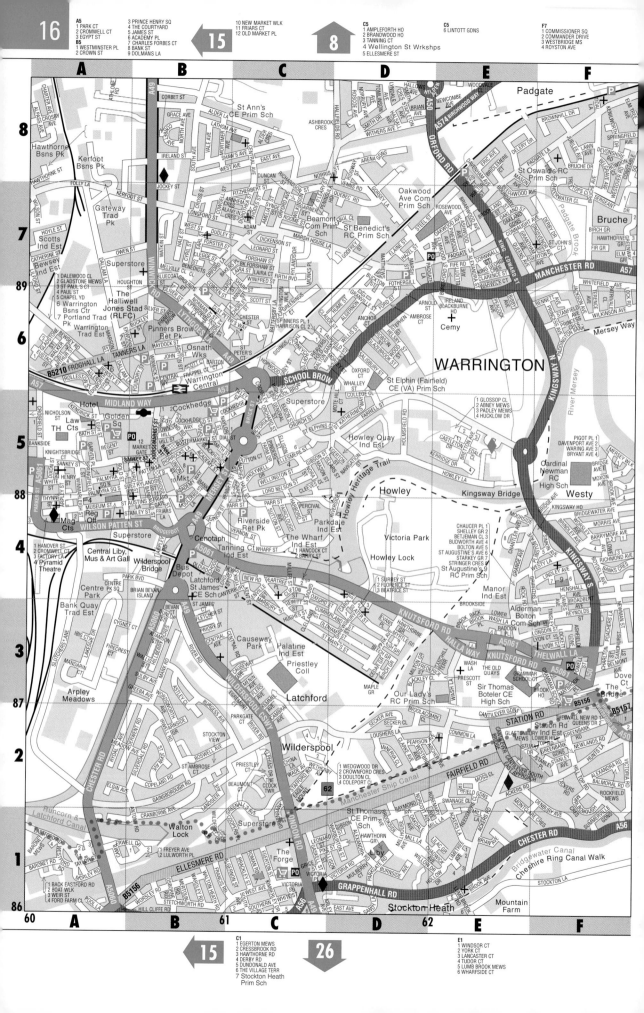

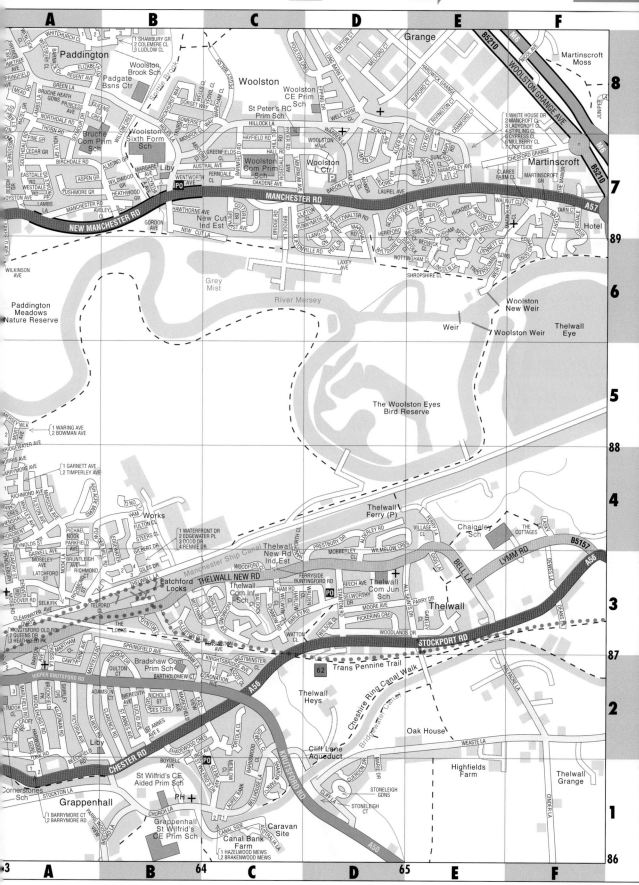

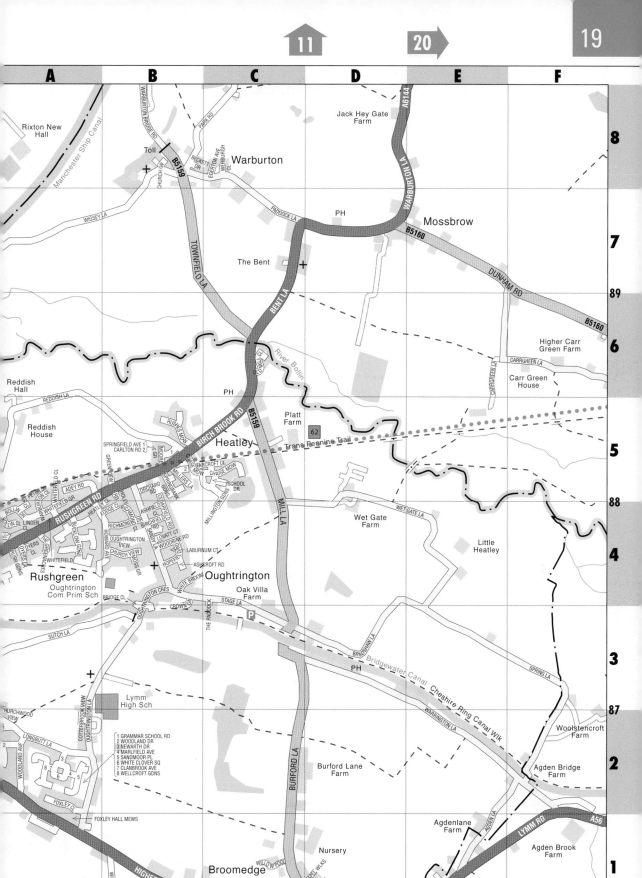

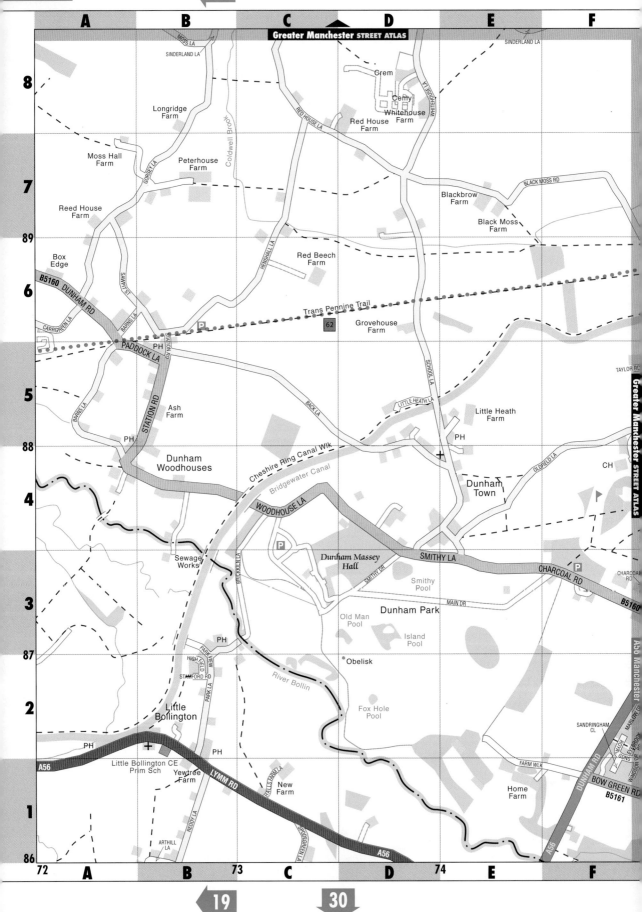

Greater Manchester STREET ATLAS

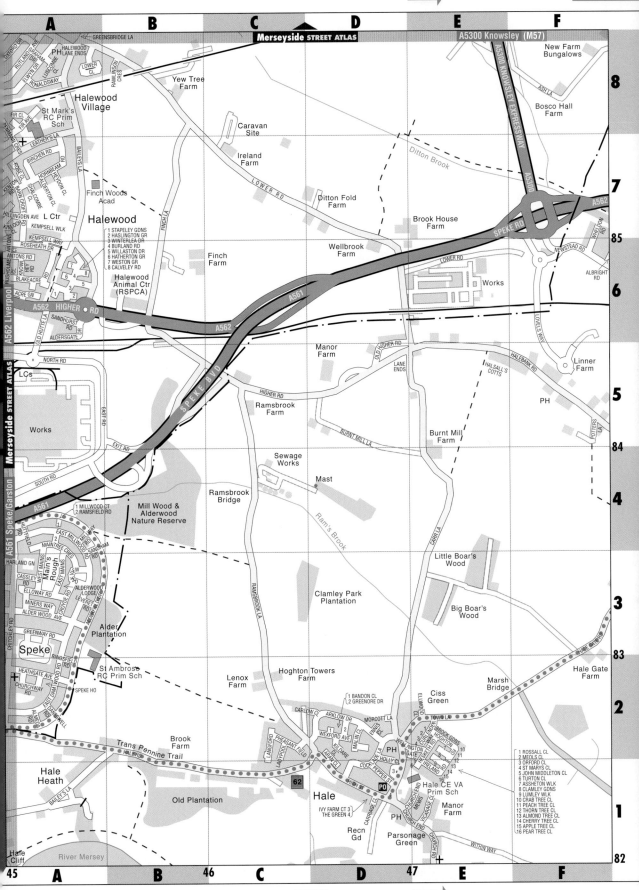

21
12
21
48

C8
1 LEVENS WAY
2 RIDSDALE
3 LONSDALE CL
4 LEIGH GREEN CL
5 APPLEBY WLK
6 AYCLIFFE WLK

F1
1 DELAMARE PL
2 PICOW ST
3 ELAINE PRICE CT
4 HAVERGAL ST
5 CURZON ST
6 LIGHTBURN ST
7 STANLEY VILLAS
8 SOUTHLANDS MEWS
9 SOUTHLANDS CT
10 COTTAGE HOSPITAL CT
11 THE SEASONS

F2
1 RUTLAND ST
2 HANKEY ST
3 WATERLOO RD
4 HIGH ST
5 DARESBURY EXPRESSWAY
6 LOWLANDS RD
7 CAVENDISH ST
8 ARTHUR ST
9 CAMPBELTOWN CL

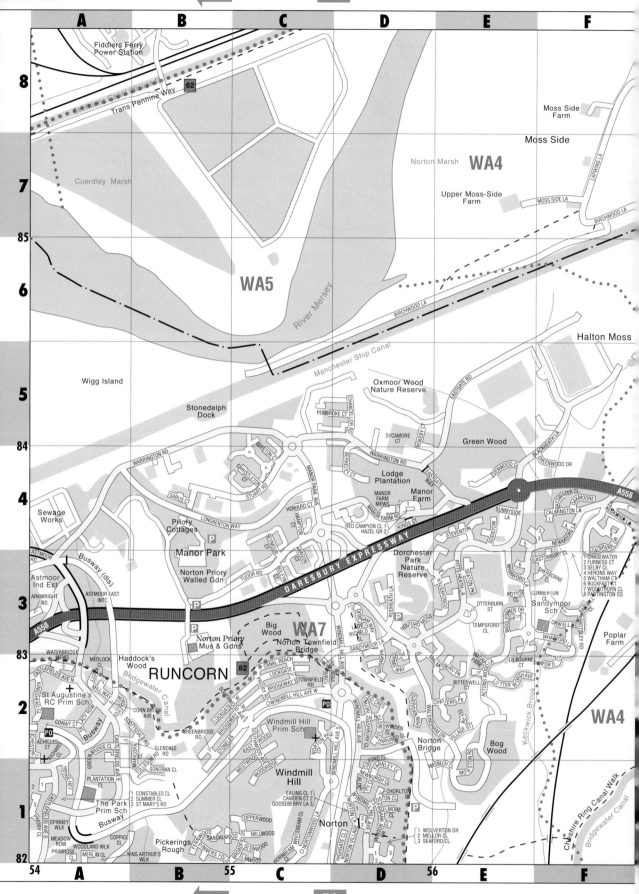

A   B   C   D   E   F

8
7
85
6
85
84
4
83
2
1
82

LAPWING LA

Moore
Reserve

Birch
Wood

Landfill
Site

Works

Acton Grange
Viaduct

BIRCHWOOD LA

Warehouses

Manchester Ship Canal

Sewage
Works

Moor Lane Bridge
(Swing)

Bellhouse
Farm

BELLHOUSE LA

Higher
Walton

MILL LA

Grange Green
Manor

CHESTER NEW RD

CHESTER RD A56

Church
Park

LYCHGATE

OLD CHESTER RD

WALTON LEA RD

PH

CH

Walton
Hall
& Gardens

Walton
Bridge

WARRINGTON RD

CONIFER GR
WILLOW CRES
POPLAR VIEW

MOSS LA

MOORE LA

Porch-house
Farm

RUNCORN RD

Canal
Farm

Bridgewater Canal

Acton
Grange
Bridge

HOLLY HEDGE LA

THOMASONS
BRIDGE LA

UNDERBRIDGE

ROWSWOOD
CTYD

PARK LA

P

Moore

Moore
Prim Sch

GIGG LA

CANAL SIDE

Hollyhedge
Farm

Rowswood
Farm

Rowswood
Farm

SIX ACRE LA

SIX ACRE GDNS

LINDFIELD CL

BEECHMOORE

RUNCORN RD

HOLLYBANK

Moore
Bridge

Hall

HOBB LA

Norton
House

CHESTER RD

Row's
Wood

Outer
Wood

PO PH

Cheshire Ring Canal Walk

New
Farm

WOODTHORN CL

Keckwick

Keckwick
Bridge

KECKWICK LA

EASTERN EXPRESSWAY

A558

Daresbury
Lodge

INNOVATION
WAY

Hatton
Lodge

WARRINGTON RD

Bluecoat
Farm

Hatton
Cottage

Laboratory

Daresbury

DARESBURY BYPASS

PH

B5356

CHESTER RD

Morts
Wood

Common Side
Farm

Hatton
Hall

Hatton

DELPH LA

HATTERS
CL

Daresbury
Prim Sch

Daresbury Firs
Nature Reserve

Hall Lane
Farm

HALL LA

DARESBURY LA

ST EDWIN'S VIEW

GOOSE LA

PH
2

B5356

HATTON LA 1
INNER GOSLING CL 2

Crow's
Nest

THE
BRACKENS

Daresbury Hall

CHESTER RD

A56

Daresbury
Delph

QUEASTYBIRCH

SANKEY LA

SUMMER
LA

57   A   58   B   C   59   D   E   F

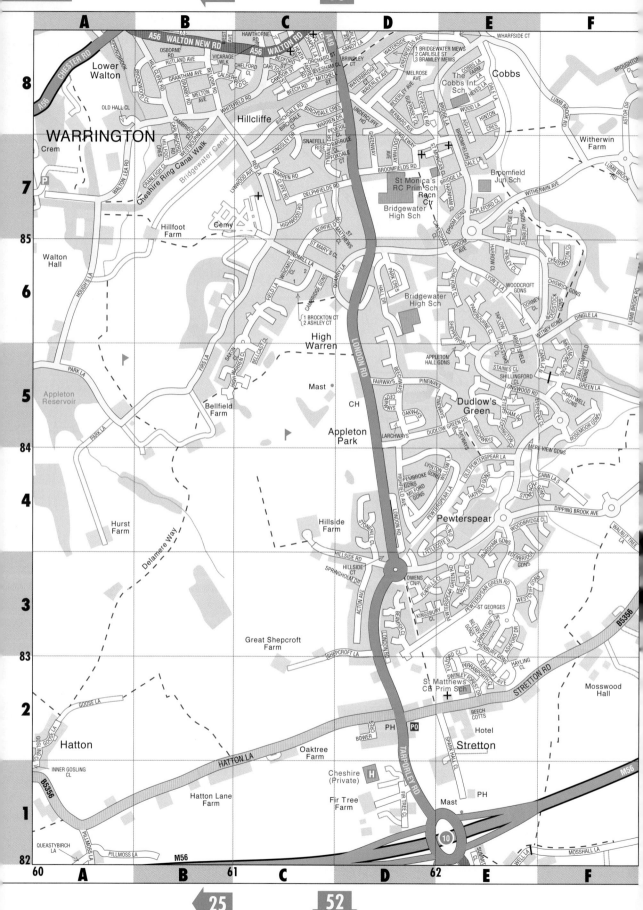

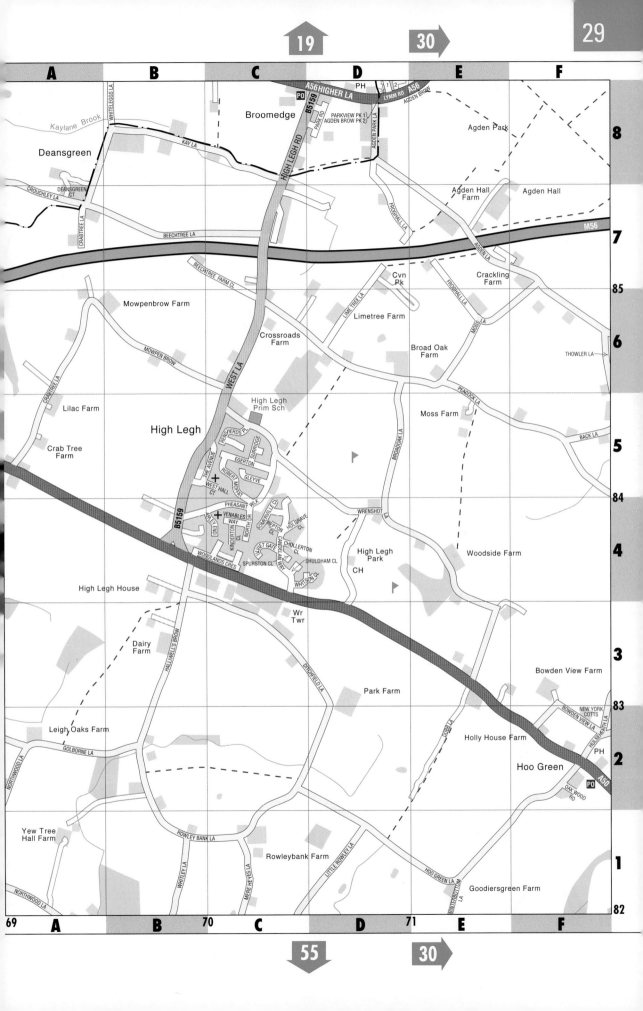

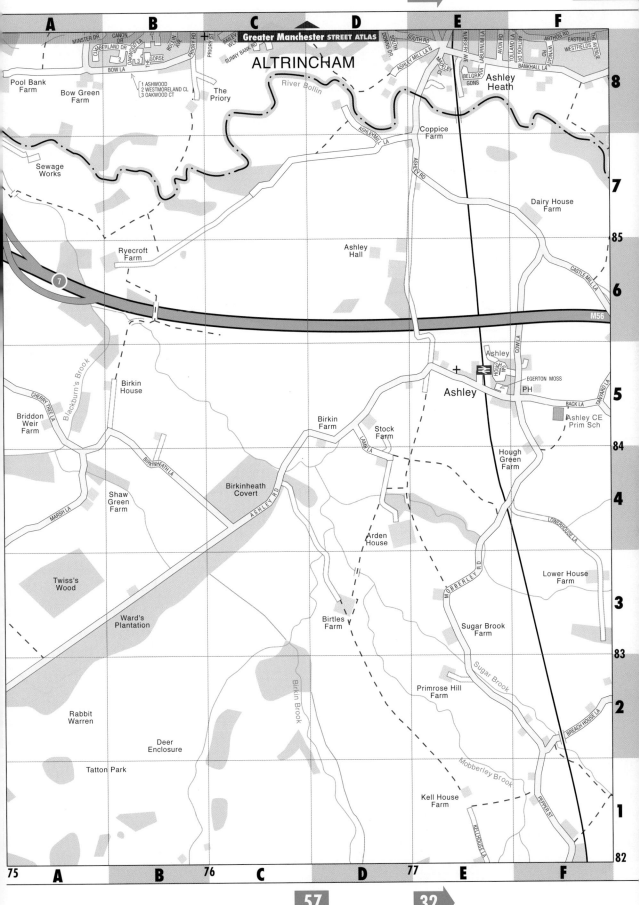

Greater Manchester STREET ATLAS

ALTRINCHAM

Pool Bank Farm

Bow Green Farm

1 ASHWOOD
2 WESTMORELAND CL
3 OAKWOOD CT

The Priory

River Bollin

Ashley Heath

Coppice Farm

Sewage Works

Dairy House Farm

Ashley Hall

Ryecroft Farm

Castle Mill La

M56

Egerton Moss

Ashley

Birkin House

Hough Green Farm

Briddon Weir Farm

Ashley CE Prim Sch

Birkin Farm

Stock Farm

Back La

Blackburn's Brook

Cherry Tree La

Birkinheath La

Shaw Green Farm

Birkinheath Covert

Arden House

Lower House Farm

Ashley Rd

Marsh La

Twiss's Wood

Ward's Plantation

Birtles Farm

Sugar Brook Farm

Sugar Brook

Primrose Hill Farm

Birkin Brook

Rabbit Warren

Deer Enclosure

Tatton Park

Mobberley Brook

Kell House Farm

Breach House La

Pepper St

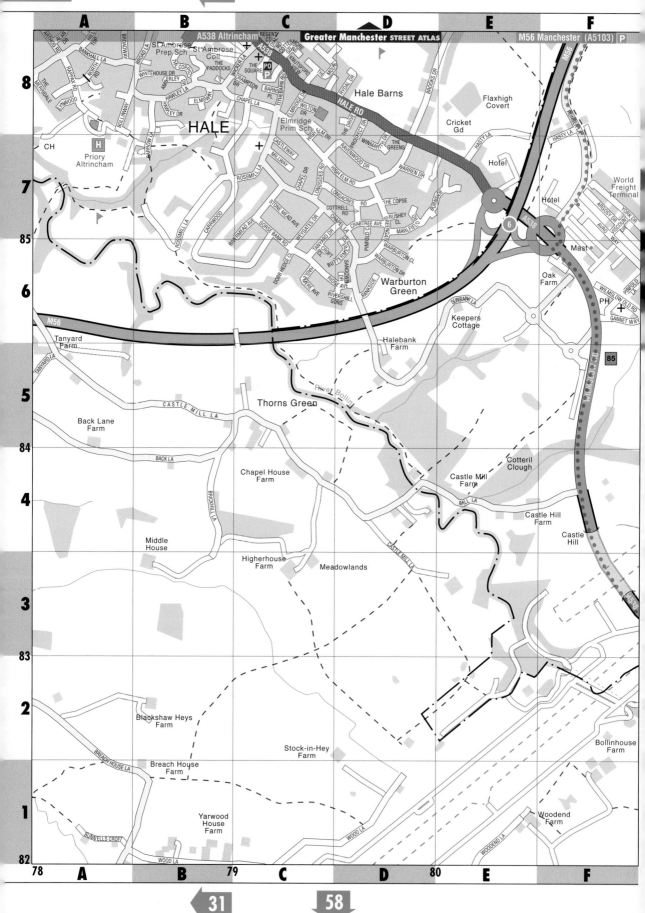

A B C D E F

8

HALE

Hale Barns

St Ambrose
Prep Sch

St Ambrose
Coll

THE
PADDOCKS

THE
SQUARE

Flaxhigh
Covert

Cricket
Gd

HALE RD

Elmridge
Prim Sch

CH

Priory
Altrincham

Hotel

7

Hotel

85

6

Warburton
Green

Oak
Farm

Mast

M56

Tanyard
Farm

Halebank
Farm

Keepers
Cottage

PH

85

5

Thorns Green

River Bollin

Back Lane
Farm

CASTLE MILL LA

84

Chapel House
Farm

Cotteril
Clough

4

BACK LA

Castle Mill
Farm

Castle Hill
Farm

Middle
House

Higherhouse
Farm

Meadowlands

MILL LA

Castle
Hill

3

83

2

Blackshaw Heys
Farm

Stock-in-Hey
Farm

Bollinhouse
Farm

BREACH HOUSE LA

Breach House
Farm

1

Yarwood
House
Farm

Woodend
Farm

BUNWELLS CROFT

WOOD LA

WOODEND LA

82

A B 79 C D 80 E F

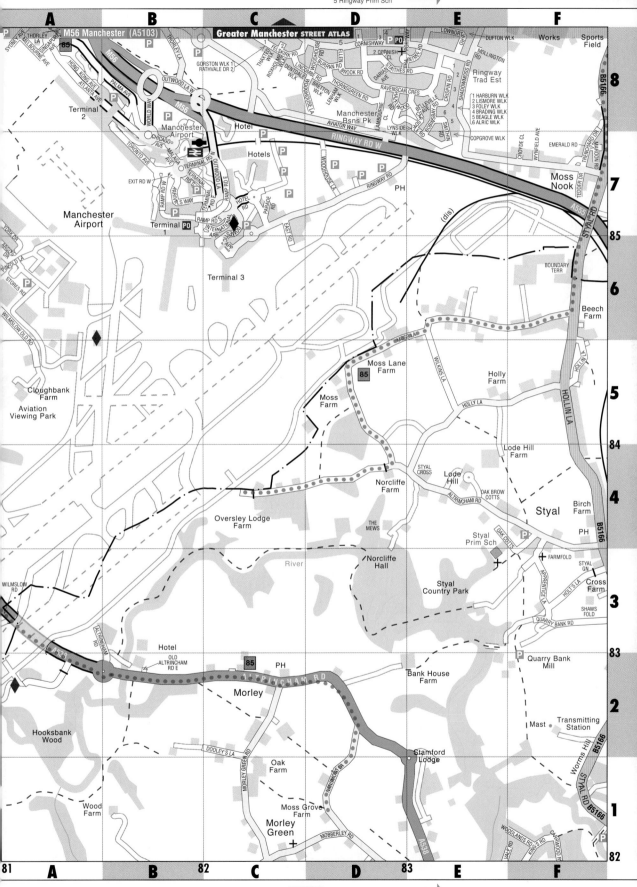

D8
1 ROSSETT AVE
2 WHITEFRIARS WLK
3 AUSTELL RD
4 Cornishway Ind Est
5 Ringway Prim Sch

Greater Manchester STREET ATLAS

M56 Manchester (A5103)

Terminal 2

Manchester Airport

Terminal 1

Terminal 3

Manchester Airport

Hotel

Hotels

Ringway Trad Est

1 HARBURN WLK
2 LISMORE WLK
3 FOLEY WLK
4 BRADING WLK
5 BEAGLE WLK
6 ALRIC WLK

COPGROVE WLK

Works

Sports Field

Manchester Bsns Pk

RINGWAY RD W

Moss Nook

(dis)

BOUNDARY TERR

Beech Farm

Cloughbank Farm

Aviation Viewing Park

Moss Lane Farm

85

Moss Farm

Holly Farm

Holly LA

Lode Hill Farm

Lode Hill

Styal Cross

Norcliffe Farm

OAK BROW COTTS

ALTRINCHAM RD

Styal

Birch Farm

PH

Oversley Lodge Farm

THE MEWS

Styal Prim Sch

FARMFOLD

STYAL GN

Cross Farm

River

Norcliffe Hall

Styal Country Park

SHAWS FOLD

QUARRY BANK RD

Quarry Bank Mill

Hotel

OLD ALTRINCHAM RD E

85

PH

ALTRINCHAM RD

Morley

Bank House Farm

Transmitting Station

Mast

Hooksbank Wood

DOOLEY'S LA

Oak Farm

MORLEY GREEN RD

Stamford Lodge

Wood Farm

Moss Grove Farm

Morley Green

MOBBERLEY RD

WOODLANDS RD

STYAL RD

B5166

Heald Green
Stanley Green
Gillbent
Handforth
Styal
Styal Green
Lacey Green
Finney Green
Beech Farm

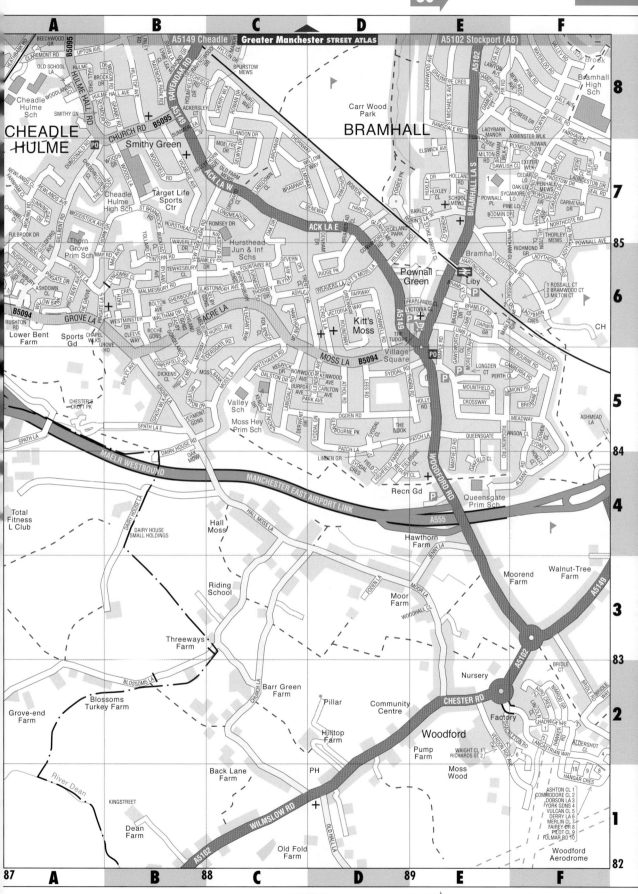

A B C D E F

8

7

85

6

5

84

4

3

83

2

1

82

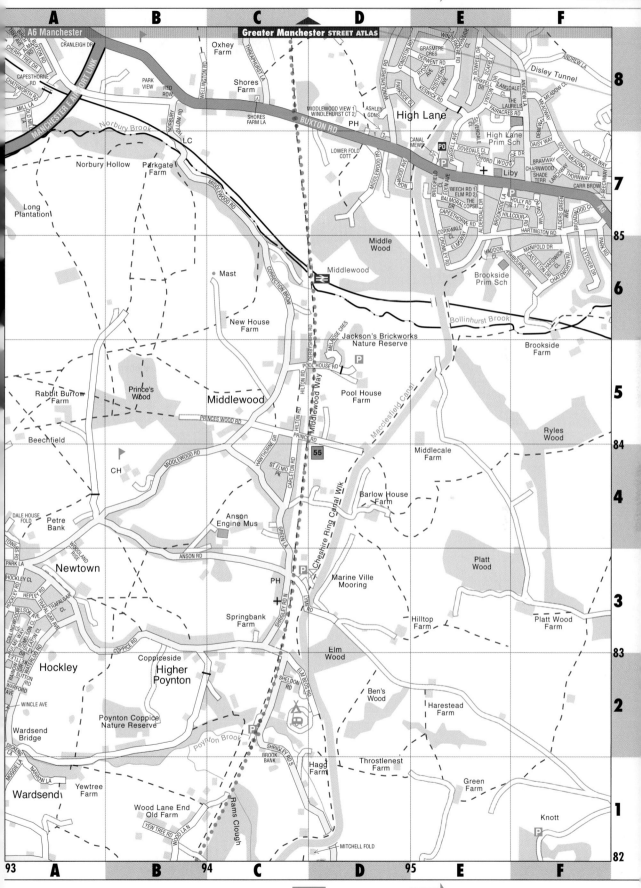

A6 Manchester

Greater Manchester STREET ATLAS

A   B   C   D   E   F

CRANLEIGH DR

Oxhey Farm

Disley Tunnel

ANDREW LA

8

CAPESTHORNE RD

PARK VIEW

RED ROW

Shores Farm

High Lane

High Lane Prim Sch

Middlewood View 1
WINDLEHURST CT 2

BUXTON RD

ASHLEY GDNS

PH

7

CHATSWORTH RD

Norbury Brook

LC

Norbury Hollow

Parkgate Farm

Middlewood Rd

LOWER FOLD COTT

Liby

85

Long Plantation

Middle Wood

Brookside Prim Sch

6

Mast

Middlewood

Bollinhurst Brook

Brookside Farm

Jackson's Brickworks Nature Reserve

5

Rabbit Burrow Farm

Prince's Wood

Middlewood

New House Farm

MELROSE CRES

P

Pool House Farm

Ryles Wood

Macclesfield Canal

Middlecale Farm

84

PRINCES WOOD RD

Beechfield

55

Barlow House Farm

4

CH

HAWTHORNE GR

ST ELMO PK

Anson Engine Mus

Platt Wood

Petre Bank

WOODLAND RISE

ANSON RD

PH

Marine Ville Mooring

Hilltop Farm

Platt Wood Farm

3

Newtown

Dale House Fold

Springbank Farm

Hockley

Coppiceside

Higher Poynton

Elm Wood

Ben's Wood

Harestead Farm

Throstlenest Farm

2

WINCLE AVE

Poynton Coppice Nature Reserve

SHELDON RD

Hagg Farm

Green Farm

Wardsend Bridge

Poynton Brook

BROOK BANK

Knott

P

1

Wardsend

Yewtree Farm

Wood Lane End Old Farm

Rams Clough

MITCHELL FOLD

82

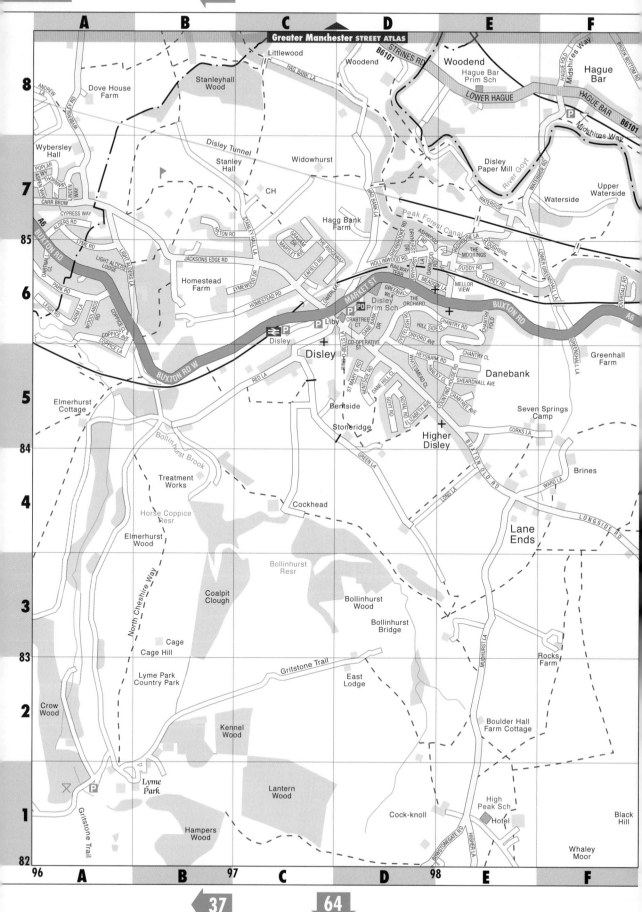

37

Greater Manchester **STREET ATLAS**

A **B** **C** **D** **E** **F**

8

Littlewood
Woodend
B6101 STRINES RD
Woodend
Hague Bar Prim Sch
Hague Bar
HAG BANK LA
LOWER HAGUE
HAGUE BAR
Midshires Way
B6101
BROOK BOTTOM RD
HAGUE FOLD

Dove House Farm
Stanleyhall Wood
WYBERSLEY RD
ANDREW LA

Disley Tunnel
Wybersley Hall
Stanley Hall
Widowhurst
Disley Paper Mill Govt
River Goyt
Upper Waterside
Waterside
Midshires Way
WATERSIDE RD

7

POPLAR WY
ASPEN WY
THORN WY
CARR BROW
CYPRESS WAY
CH
Hagg Bank Farm
Peak Forest Canal
Waterside
LOWER GREENSHALL LA

85

A6 BUXTON RD
ALDERS RD
LYME RD
HIXTON RD
STANLEY HALL LA
JACKSONS EDGE RD
GRAHAM DR
MARTLET AVE
THE RIDGEWAY
LEAFIELD RD
LOWERLEA
HOLLINWOOD RD
SHERBORNE RD
DRYHURST
ASHWOOD
OAKWOOD LA
REDHOUSE LA
The Moorings
DUDDY RD
STOREY RD
LOUGHSIDE

6
DARTINGTON CL
PARK RD
LEIGH RD
FARM LA
WOODLANDS RD
COPPICE CL
COPPICE AVE
COPPICE LA
Light Alders Lodge
LIGHT ALDERS LA
Homestead Farm
LYMEWOOD DR
HOMESTEAD RD
BUXTON RD W
RED LA
Liby
Disley
CO-OPERATIVE ST
CRABTREE CT
DANE BANK DR
HILL SIDE CL
ORFORD AVE
Disley Prim Sch
THE ORCHARD
MEADOW LA
MELLOR VIEW
CHANTRY RD
CHANTRY FOLD
CHANTRY CL
BUXTON RD
A6
GREENSHALL LA
OVERDALE RD
Greenhall Farm

Homestead Farm
MARKET ST
GREENWY WLY
Disley
PING-O-BELL'S LA
Danebank
HILL SIDE CL
HEYSBANK RD
WHITESMEAD CL
HANLEY CL
COUNTING HOUSE RD
SHEARDHALL AVE
CHANTRY CL
CRABTREE AVE
Seven Springs Camp

5
Elmerhurst Cottage
Bollinhurst Brook
ST MARY'S RD
BENTSIDE RD
DANE HILL CL
Bentside
GREEN LA
GOYT RD
ROYAL RD
ELIZABETH AVE
Stoneridge
Higher Disley
CORKS LA
BUXTON OLD RD
LONG LA
Lane Ends
WARD LA
Brines
LONGSIDE RD

84
Treatment Works
Horse Coppice Resr
Elmerhurst Wood
Cockhead
Bollinhurst Resr

4
North Cheshire Way
Coalpit Clough
Bollinhurst Wood
Bollinhurst Bridge
MUDHURST LA
Rocks Farm

3
Cage
Cage Hill
Gritstone Trail
East Lodge

83
Lyme Park Country Park
Crow Wood
Kennel Wood
Boulder Hall Farm Cottage
Black Hill

2

1
Gritstone Trail
Lyme Park
Hampers Wood
Lantern Wood
Cock-knoll
BRINKSWAYGATE RD
HIGHER LA
High Peak Sch
Hotel
Whaley Moor

82

96 **A** **B** 97 **C** **D** 98 **E** **F**

37

64

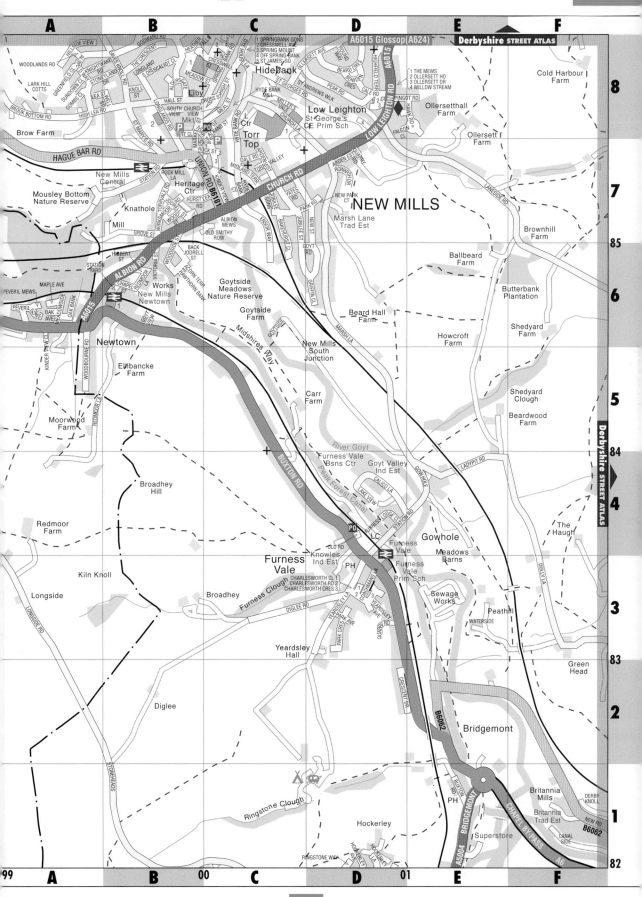

F8
1 STONEWAY CT
2 MAY RD
3 MOUNT CT
4 PYE RD
5 St Peter's CE
  Prim Sch

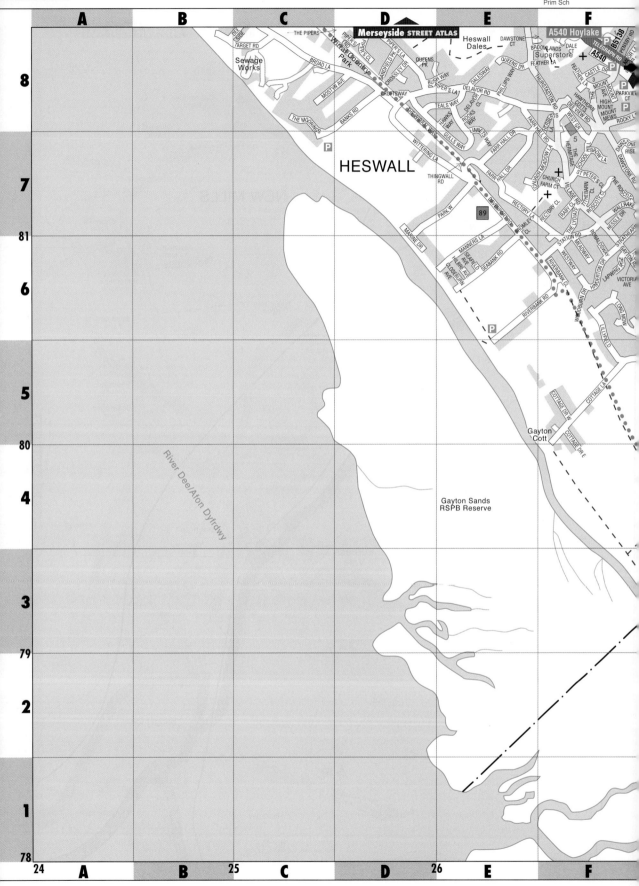

Merseyside STREET ATLAS

A540 Hoylake

HESWALL

Heswall Dales

River Dee/Afon Dyfrdwy

Gayton Cott

Gayton Sands
RSPB Reserve

Sewage
Works

A8
1 DOWNHAM CT
2 BIRCHES HO
3 CHERRY TREE MEWS
4 BEACON CT
5 THE CHASE
6 YEW TREE CT

7 HESWALL POINT

Merseyside STREET ATLAS

A551 Birkenhead (A552) | A5137 M53 Junc 4 | A5137

Heswall

Hilldene

Manor Wood

DOVESMEAD RD

Manor Wood

The Beacons
The Beacons

Motel

Barnston Prim Sch

New Hall Manor

New Hall Farm

Gayton
Gayton Prim Sch
CH

Gayton Wood

Widgeons Covert

Hotel

Westwood Farm

Leighton Cotts

The Grange Country Club

Backwood Hall Farm

Backwood Hall

Leighton Hall Farm

Ashfield Farm

Ashfield Hall Farm

Wirral Country Park

Cedar Court

Five Ways
Old Dairy Cl
Oakland Farm

Fiveways Pk

Parkgate HQ

Brook House

Factory

MILLENNIUM CT 1
WESTWOOD CT 2
WINDLE CT 3

Clayhill Light Ind Pk

The Looms

NESTON

Long Acres

The Birches

Parkgate Prim Sch

Neston Recreation Ctr

Neston High Sch

Parkgate

The Parade

Mealors Weint

Mostyn Sq

DEESIDE CT 1
MOSTYN GDNS 2
ALGERNON CL 3
PHOENIX CT 4
GEORGE DR 5
EDWARD PRICE CL6

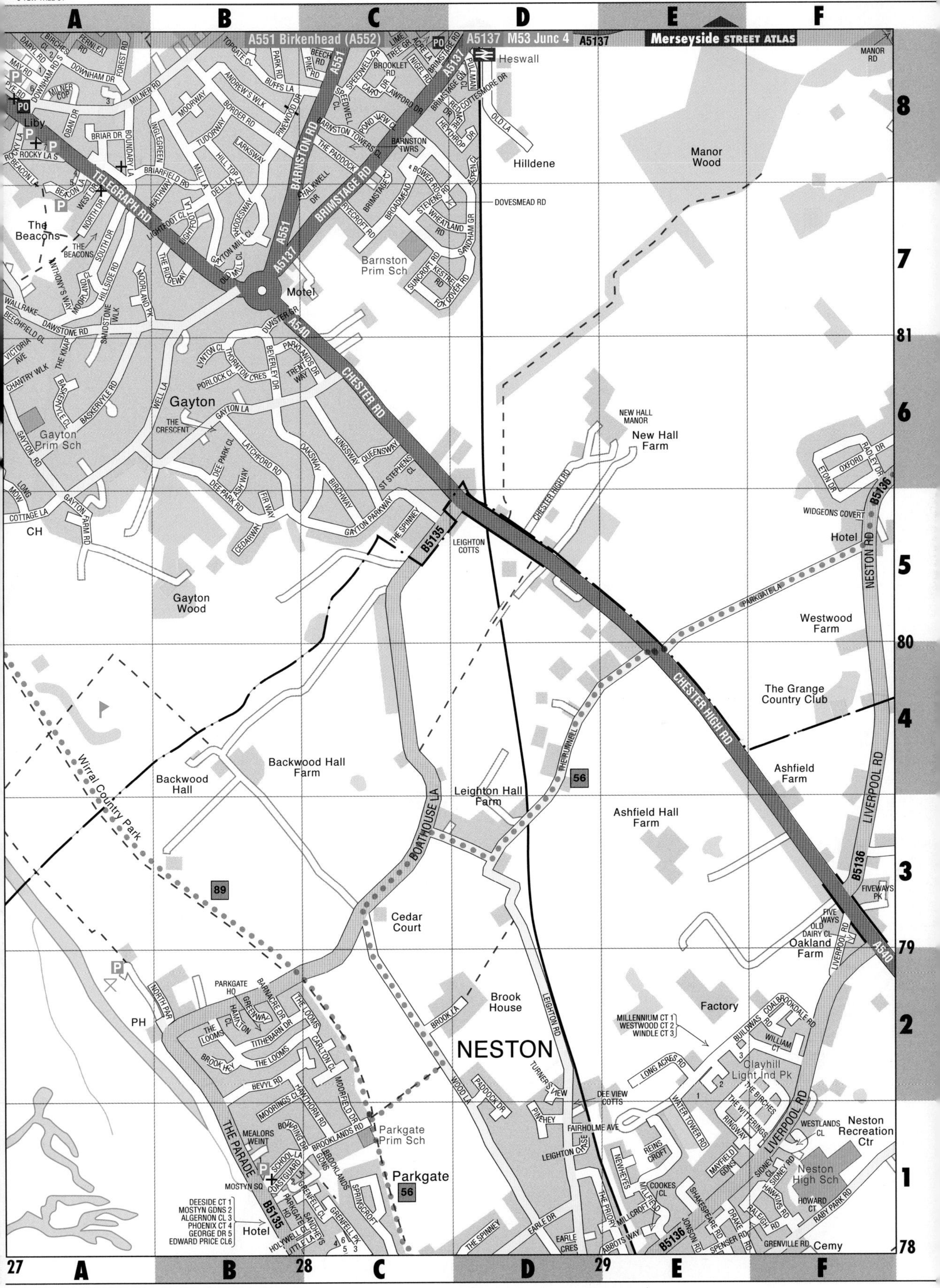

Hotel

Cemy

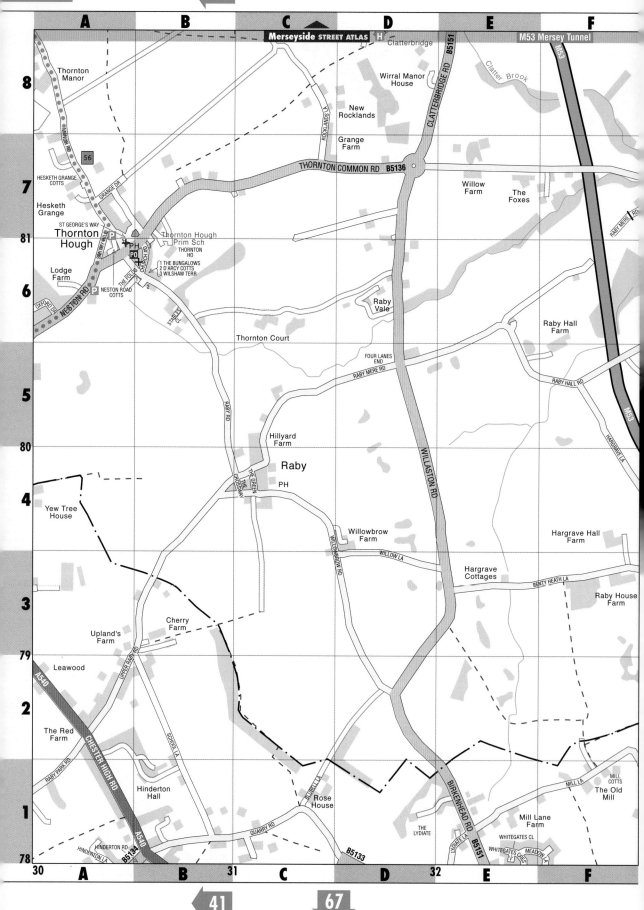

A B C D E F

8

7

81

6

5

80

4

3

79

2

1

78

Thornton Manor

Hesketh Grange Cotts

Hesketh Grange

St George's Way

Thornton Hough

Lodge Farm

Neston Road Cotts

Oxford Dr

Neston Rd

Grange Dr

Church Rd

The Folds

Swith My Hill

P

P

PH

PO

+

2

56

Thornton Hough Prim Sch

Thornton Ho

1 The Bungalows
2 D'Arcy Cotts
3 Wilshaw Terr

Stables Cl

Thornton Court

Clatterbridge

Wirral Manor House

New Rocklands

Grange Farm

Rocklands La

Clatterbridge Rd

B5151

Clatter Brook

THORNTON COMMON RD B5136

Willow Farm

The Foxes

Raby Mere Rd

Raby Vale

Four Lanes End

RABY MERE RD

Raby Hall Farm

RABY HALL RD

M53

Hillyard Farm

Raby

The Crossway

The Green

PH

Raby Rd

Yew Tree House

Willowbrow Farm

Willowbrow Rd

WILLOW LA

Willaston Rd

Hargrave Hall Farm

Hargrave Cottages

BENTY HEATH LA

Raby House Farm

Cherry Farm

Upland's Farm

Leawood

The Red Farm

A540

Raby Park Rd

Chester High Rd

Upper Raby Rd

School La

Hinderton Hall

A540

Hinderton Rd

Hinderton La

B5134

Rose House

Bubet La

Quarry Rd

B5133

Birkenhead Rd

Lydiate La

B5151

The Lydiate

Whitegates Cl

Whitegates Cres

Mill La

Mill Cotts

The Old Mill

Mill Lane Farm

Meadow La

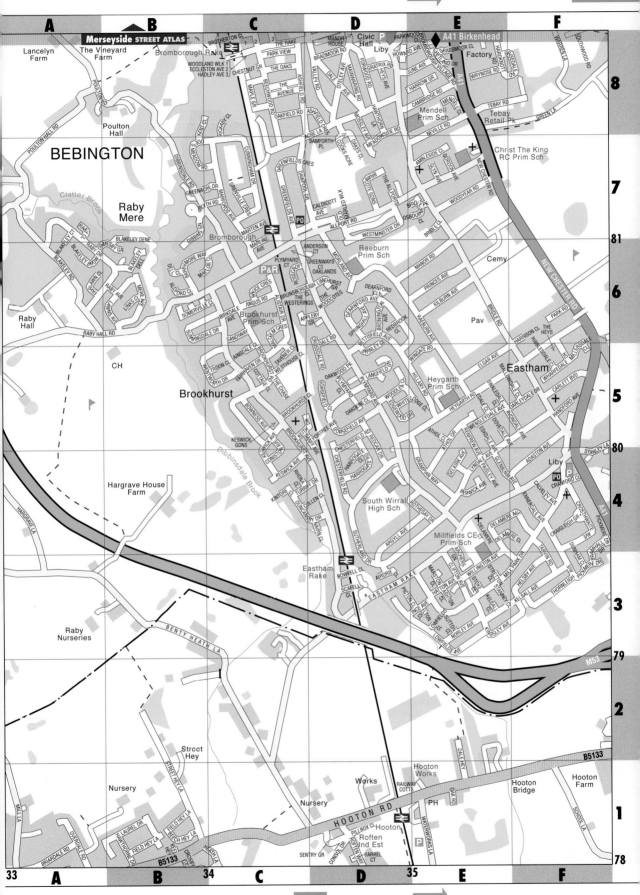

River Mersey

A B C D E F

8 Eastham Country Park
Visitor Ctr
Hotel
Eastham Ferry

The Warrens Farm

7 Wood Heath Way
Custom House
Eastham Locks

81 COLLEGE
CHAPEL VIEW
CH
FERRY RD

6 MAYFIELD DR
SEAVIEW AVE
Queen Elizabeth II Dock
CANAL RD

ST DAVID RD
ST JOHN'S RD
Tanks
POWER RD
Tanks

5 B5132
EASTHAM VILLAGE RD
VICARAGE ROW
Tanks
BANKFIELDS DR
Oil Storage Depot

80 STANLEY RD
B5132
CHURCH RD
HALL FARM
EASTHAM HO
EASTHAM MEWS
Tanks

Manchester Ship Canal

4 B5132
NORTH RD
Tanks
LC

WELSH RD
Hooton Park

3 David's Rough
MERTON RD
DUDLEY CRES
ERIC FOUNTAIN RD
NORTH RD
LC

79 ⑤
NEW CHESTER RD
RIVACRE RD
⑥
Booston Wood

2 REDVERS AVE
VERNON AVE
HOOTON WAY
PH
Kennel Wood
HOOTON PK LA
AIRFIELD WAY
Motor Vehicle Works

HOOTON RD
B5133
CHRISTON TQL
CONISTON CL
GRANGE CRES
DESWANT CTR
HOOTON GN
Park Farm
HOOTON LA

1 Hooton
WELSH RD
CHESTER RD A41
WOODCLOSE
NEW SCHOOL LA
RIVACRE VIEW
Rivacre Wood
B5132
⑦
M53
B5132

78 SCHOOL LA

36 A 37 B C 37 D 38 E F

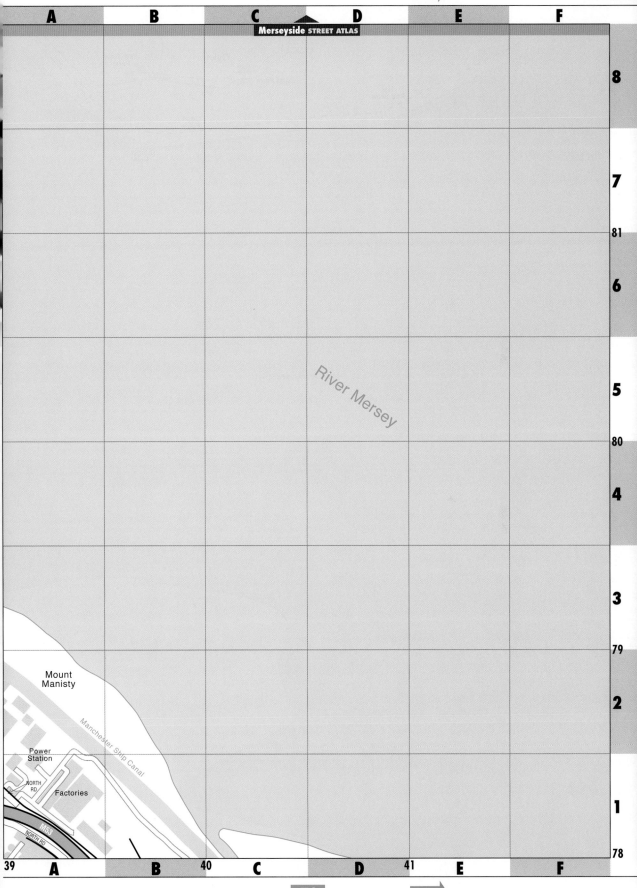

46

Merseyside STREET ATLAS

River Mersey

Mount
Manisty

Manchester Ship Canal

Power
Station

NORTH
RD

Factories

M53

NORTH RD

70

46

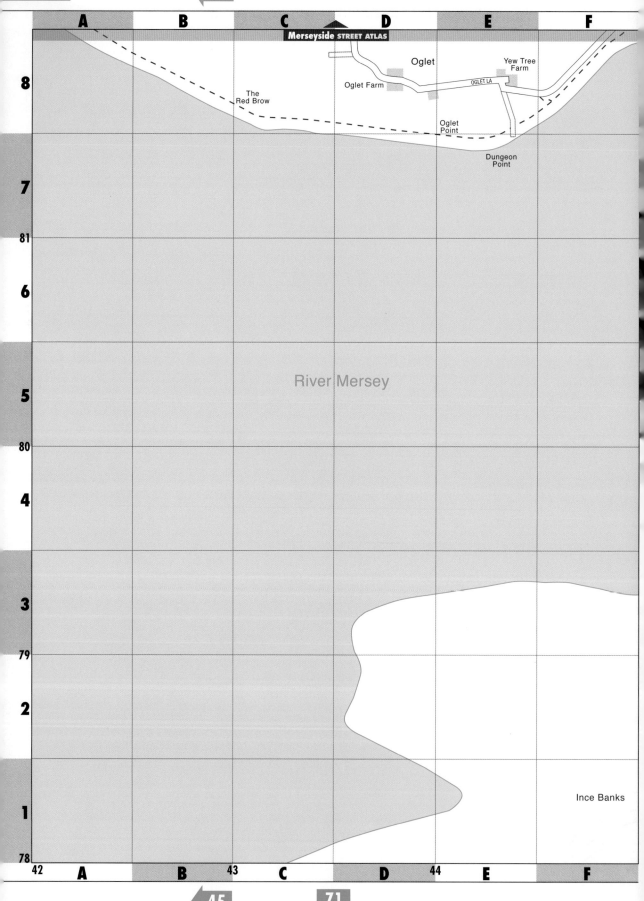

	A	B	C	D	E	F

Merseyside STREET ATLAS

Oglet

Yew Tree
Farm

Oglet Farm

OGLET LA

The
Red Brow

Oglet
Point

Dungeon
Point

8

7

81

6

River Mersey

5

80

4

3

79

2

Ince Banks

1

78

A

B

C

D

E

F

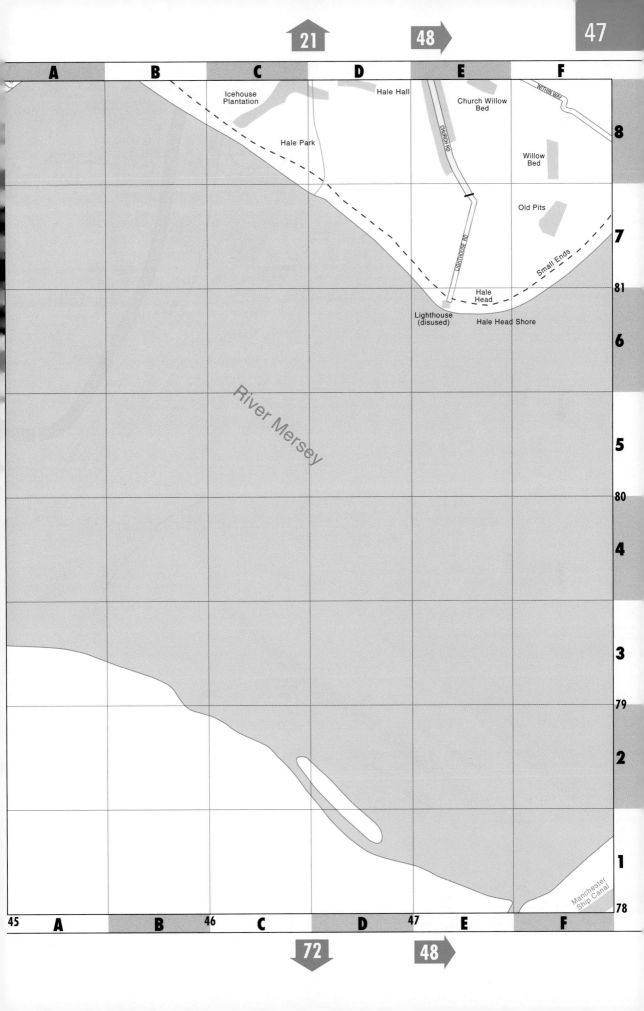

A   B   C   D   E   F

WITHIN WAY

Icehouse Plantation

Hale Hall

Church Willow Bed

Hale Park

CHURCH RD

Willow Bed

8

Old Pits

LIGHTHOUSE RD

7

Small Ends

81

Hale Head

Lighthouse (disused)

Hale Head Shore

6

River Mersey

5

80

4

3

79

2

1

Manchester Ship Canal

78

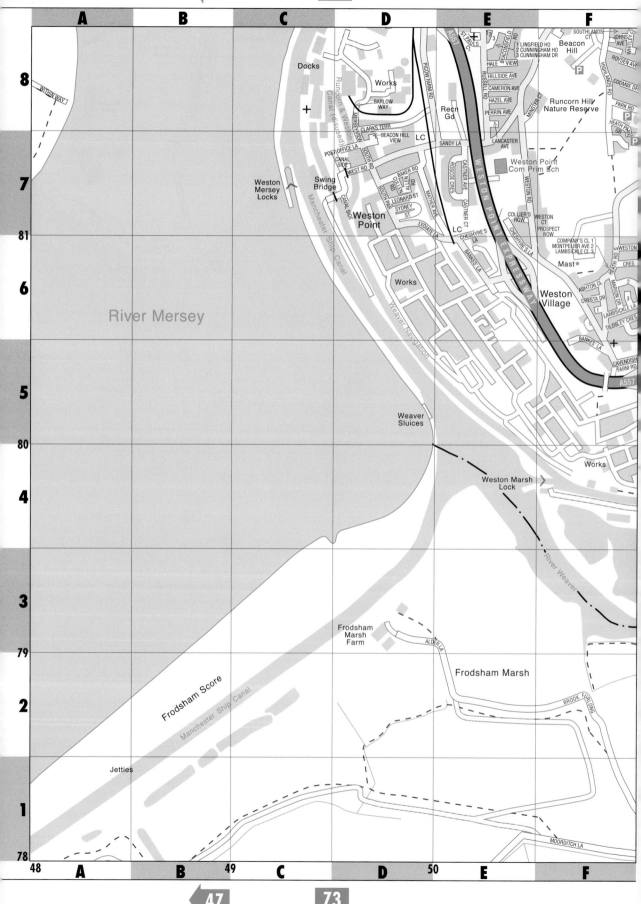

47
22

	A	B	C	D	E	F

8

WITTON WAY

Docks

Works

BARLOW WAY

PIGOT FARM RD

A557

ST PAUL'S CL

SOUTHLANDS CT

BEACONSFIELD RD

3
LINGFIELD HO
1
2 CUNNINGHAM HO
2 CUNNINGHAM DR

Beacon Hill

JOHNSEY AVE
WHITLEY AVE

ROYDEN AVE

COOMBE DR

HALE RD

HILLSIDE AVE

CAMERON AVE

Runcorn Hill
Nature Reserve

P

HIGHLANDS RD

PARK RD

HEATH PARK GR

P

Runcorn & Weston
Canal (disused)

MERSEY VIEW

RUSSELL RD

HAZEL AVE

PERRIN AVE

MINSTER CT

Recn Gd

CLARKS TERR

BEACON HILL VIEW

LC

SANDY LA

LANCASTER AVE

Weston Point
Com Prim Sch

WESTON RD

7

Weston Mersey Locks

Swing Bridge

POST OFFICE LA

CANAL SIDE

WEST RD

SOUTH RD

BAKER RD

CULLEN RD

ROSCOE CRES

CASTNER AVE

WESTON POINT EXPRESSWAY

WESTON RD

Manchester Ship Canal

CANAL SIDE

Weston Point

SOUTH PAR

KELLY RD

LEONARD ST

SYDNEY ST

MATHER AVE

CASTNER CT

COLLIER'S ROW

WESTON CT

PROSPECT ROW

81

LYDATE LA

CHESHYRE'S LA

LC

BANKS' LA

CHESHYRE'S LA

COMPANY'S CL 1
MONTPELIER AVE 2
LAMBSICKLE CL 3

HEATH RD

WESTON CRES

6

Works

Mast

Weston Village

ASHTON CL

CRESTA DR

MARION GR

2
3

LAMBSICKLE LA

River Mersey

Weaver Navigation

BANKS' LA

TILDSLEY CRES

5

CAVENDISH FARM RD

A557

Weaver Sluices

80

Works

4

Weston Marsh Lock

River Weaver

3

Frodsham Marsh Farm

ALDER LA

79

Frodsham Marsh

Frodsham Score

BROOK FURLONG

2

Manchester Ship Canal

1

Jetties

MOORDITCH LA

78

48	A	B	49	C	D	50	E	F

47
73

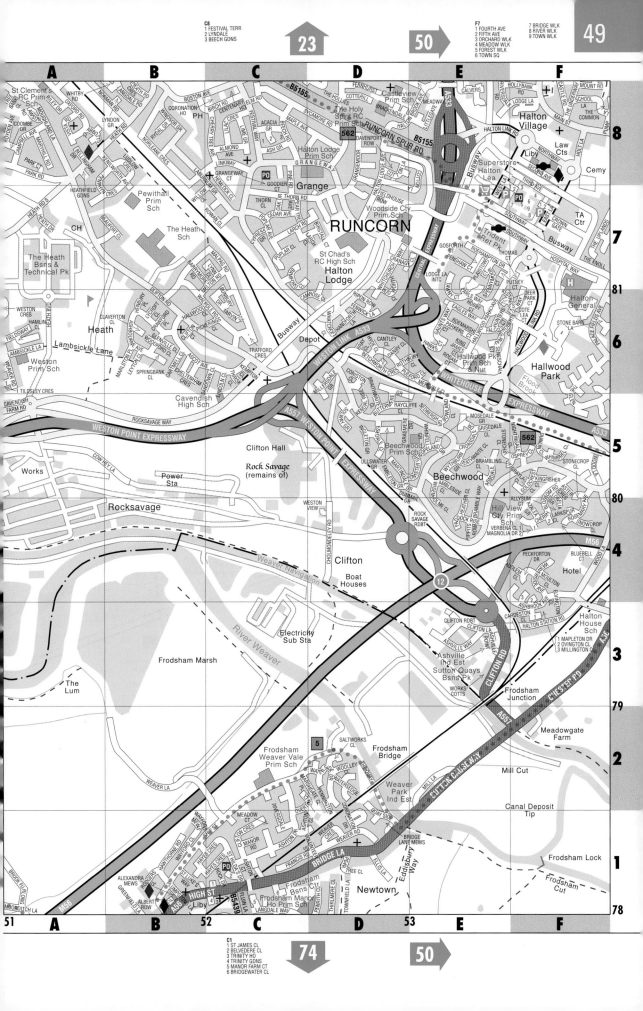

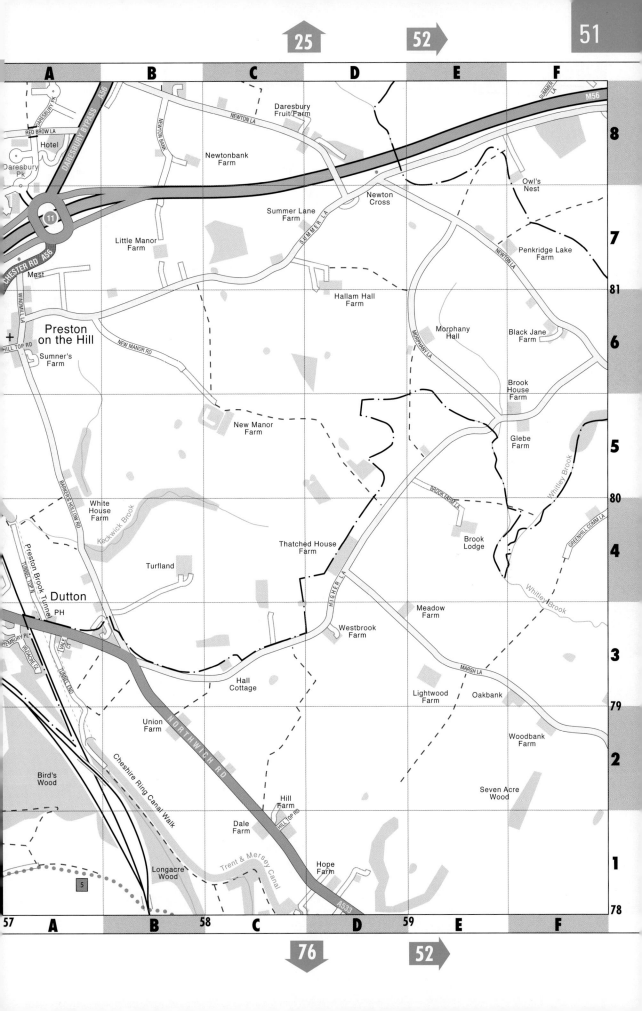

A B C D E F

8

NEWTON LA

Daresbury Fruit Farm

DARESBURY BYPASS A56

Red Brow La

Hotel

Daresbury Pk

NEWTON BANK

Newtonbank Farm

Owl's Nest

SUMMER LA

M56

11

Summer Lane Farm

Newton Cross

SUMMER LA

NEWTON LA

7

81

Little Manor Farm

Penkridge Lake Farm

CHESTER RD A56

Mast

Hallam Hall Farm

Morphany Hall

Black Jane Farm

6

WINDMILL LA

Preston on the Hill

HILL TOP RD

Sumner's Farm

NEW MANOR RD

MORPHANY LA

Brook House Farm

Whitley Brook

GREENHILL COMM LA

5

80

BARKERS HOLLOW RD

White House Farm

Keckwick Brook

New Manor Farm

BROOK FARM LA

Glebe Farm

4

Preston Brook Tunnel

TUNNEL TOP N

Dutton

PH

Turfland

Thatched House Farm

HIGHER LA

Brook Lodge

Whitley Brook

Meadow Farm

3

79

PREMBURY PL

RUNCAGE CL

VALE CT

TUNNEL END

Westbrook Farm

MARSH LA

Lightwood Farm

Oakbank

Hall Cottage

NORTHWICH RD

Union Farm

Cheshire Ring Canal Walk

Woodbank Farm

2

Bird's Wood

Hill Farm

HILL TOP RD

Seven Acre Wood

Dale Farm

Longacre Wood

5

Trent & Mersey Canal

Hope Farm

A533

1

78

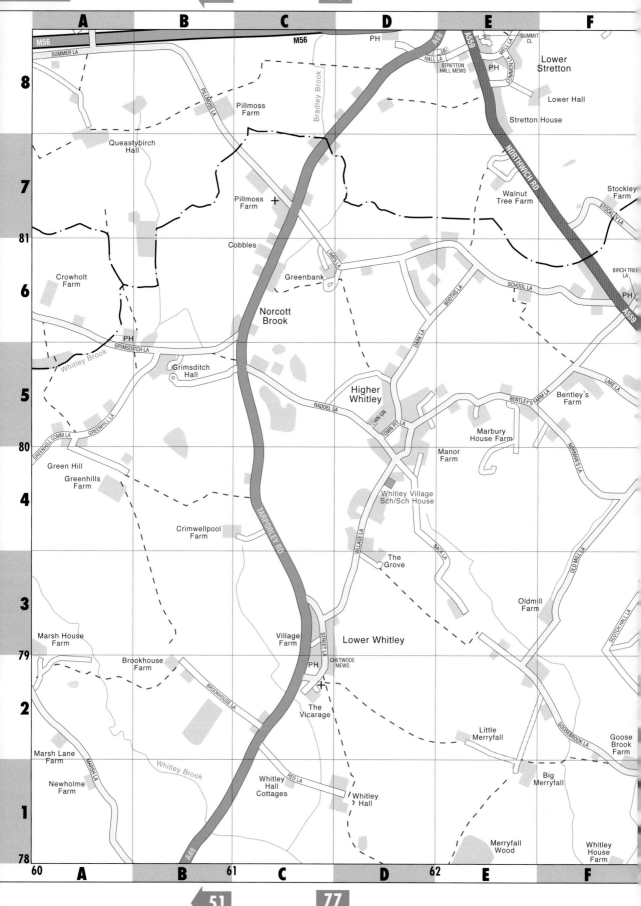

A B C D E F

8

7

81

6

81

5

80

4

3

79

2

1

78

Map labels:

M56
SUMMER LA
M56
PH
Lower Stretton
HALL LA
STRETTON HALL MEWS
PH
SUMMIT CL
WELL LA
ST COMMON
A49
A559
Lower Hall
Stretton House
Pillmoss Farm
PILLMOSS LA
Bradley Brook
Queastybirch Hall
NORTHWICH RD
Walnut Tree Farm
Stockley Farm
STOCKLEY LA
Pillmoss Farm
Cobbles
LIMES LA
Greenbank
Crowholt Farm
Norcott Brook
SCHOOL LA
BOOTHS LA
DARK LA
BIRCH TREE LA
PH
A559
PH
GRIMSDITCH LA
Grimsditch Hall
Whitley Brook
Higher Whitley
LAKE LA
Bentley's Farm
BENTLEY'S FARM LA
GREENHILL LA
RADDEL LA
TOWN GN
TOWN PIT LA
Marbury House Farm
NORMAN'S LA
GREENHILL COMM LA
Green Hill
Greenhills Farm
Manor Farm
Whitley Village Sch/Sch House
TARPORLEY RD
Crimwellpool Farm
VILLAGE LA
The Grove
BACK LA
Oldmill Farm
OLD MILL LA
SCOTCH HALL LA
Marsh House Farm
Brookhouse Farm
BROOKHOUSE LA
Village Farm
STREET LA
Lower Whitley
PH
CHETWODE MEWS
The Vicarage
Little Merryfall
GOOSEBROOK LA
Goose Brook Farm
Marsh Lane Farm
MARSH LA
Whitley Brook
Whitley Hall Cottages
RED LA
Big Merryfall
Newholme Farm
A49
Whitley Hall
Merryfall Wood
Whitley House Farm

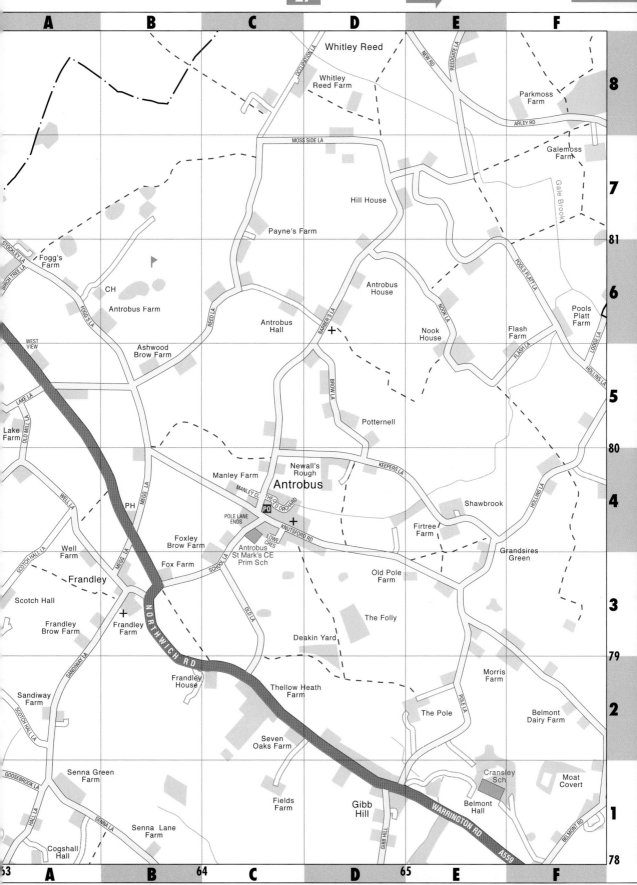

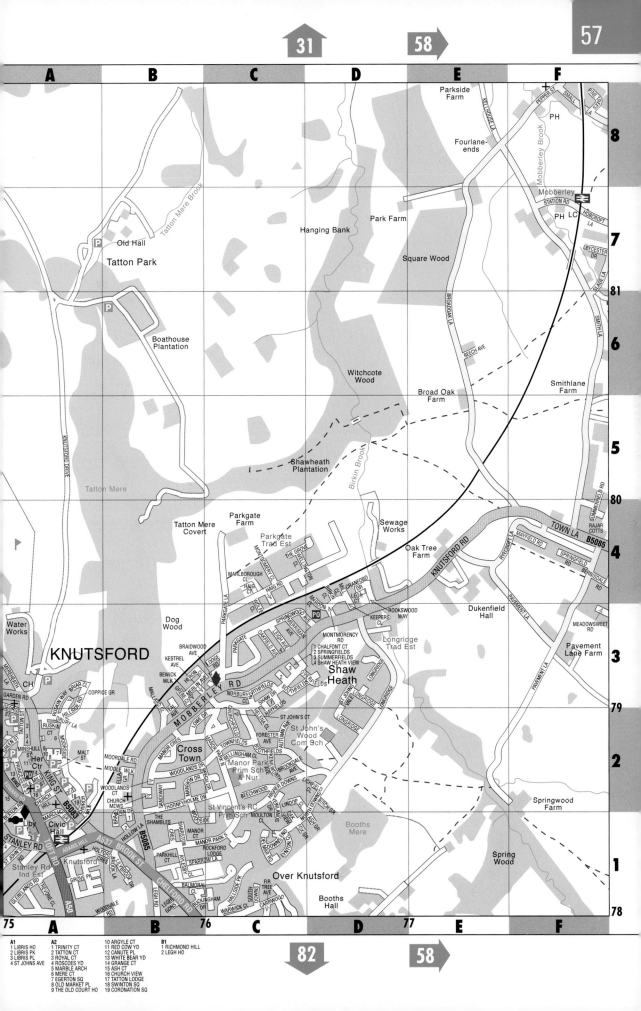

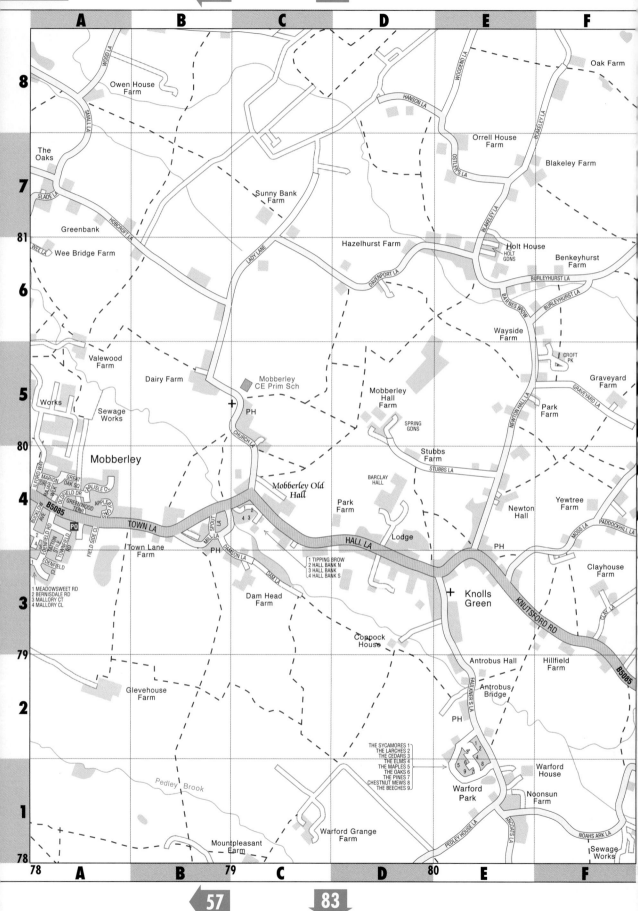

59   34

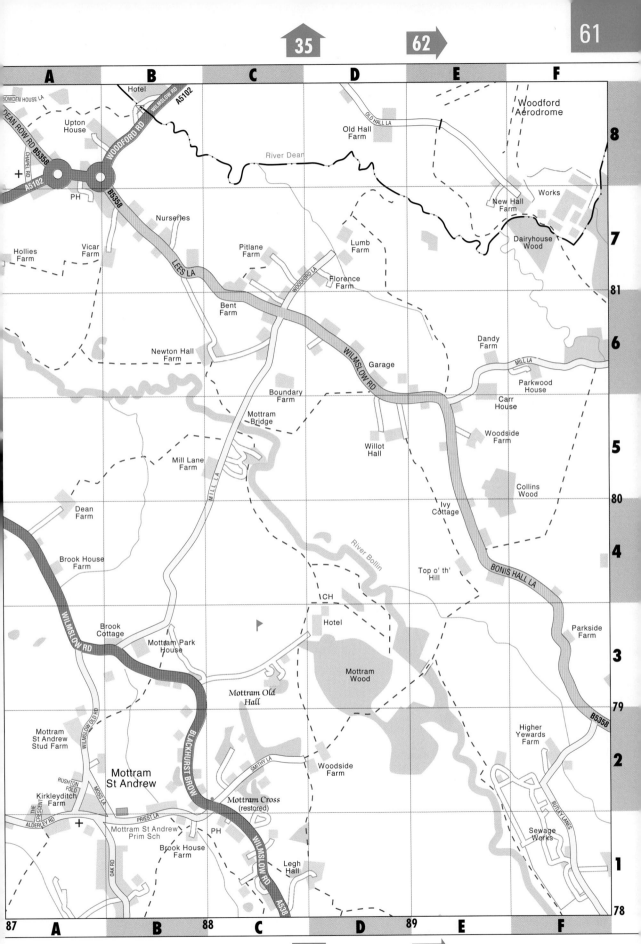

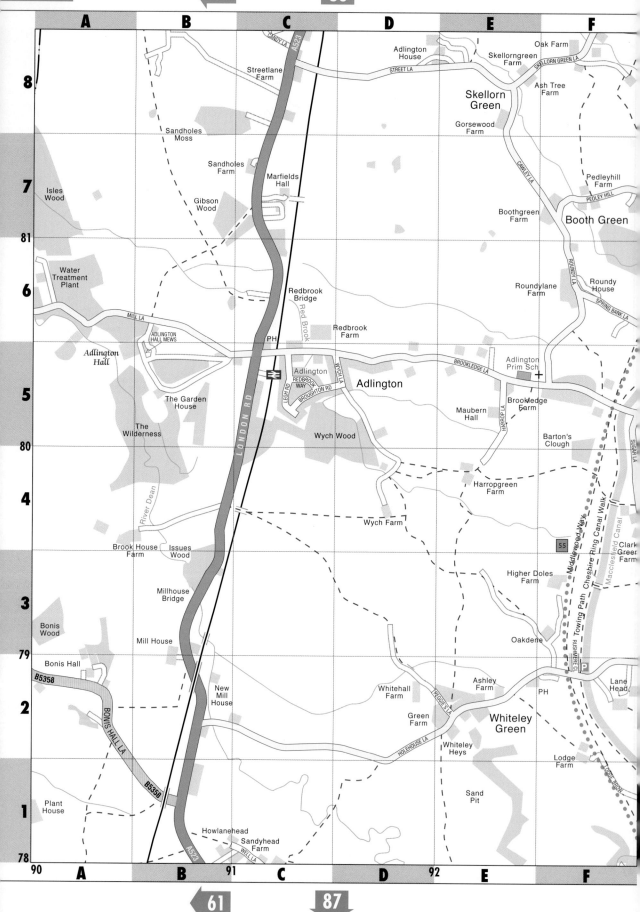

| | A | B | C | D | E | F |

8

Streetlane Farm

Adlington House

STREET LA

Oak Farm

Skellorngreen Farm

SKELLORN GREEN LA

Ash Tree Farm

Skellorn Green

Sandholes Moss

Sandholes Farm

Marfields Hall

Gorsewood Farm

7

Gibson Wood

CAWLEY LA

Pedleyhill Farm

PEDLEY HILL

81

Isles Wood

Boothgreen Farm

Booth Green

6

Water Treatment Plant

MILL LA

Redbrook Bridge

Red Brook

Redbrook Farm

ROUNDY LA

Roundylane Farm

Roundy House

SPRING BANK LA

ADLINGTON HALL MEWS

PH

Adlington Hall

Adlington

BROOKLEDGE LA

Adlington Prim Sch

5

The Garden House

REDBROOK WAY

LEGH RD

BROUGHTON RD

WYCH LA

Adlington

Maubern Hall

HARROP LA

Brookledge Farm

SUGAR LA

80

The Wilderness

Wych Wood

Barton's Clough

4

River Dean

Wych Farm

Harropgreen Farm

MIDDLEWOOD WAY

Clark Green Wood

Macclesfield Canal

55

Brook House Farm

Issues Wood

Higher Doles Farm

RUSHMERE CL

Cheshire Ring Canal Walk

Towing Path

3

Bonis Wood

Millhouse Bridge

Oakdene

79

Bonis Hall

Mill House

Whitehall Farm

DIGGERS LA

Ashley Farm

PH

Lane Head

B5358

BONIS HALL LA

2

New Mill House

Green Farm

Whiteley Green

LODGE BROW

B5358

Whiteley Heys

Lodge Farm

1

Plant House

Sand Pit

78

Howlanehead

Sandyhead Farm

WELL LA

A523

HOLEHOUSE LA

| 90 | A | B | 91 | C | D | 92 | E | F |

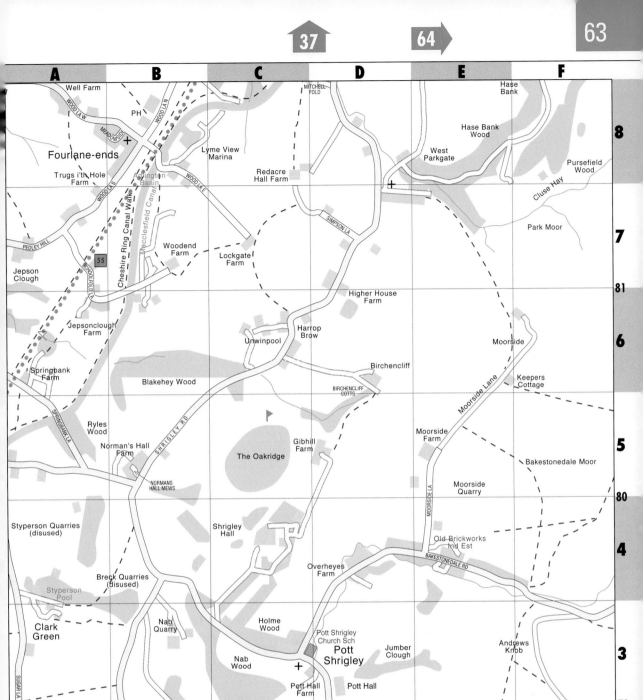

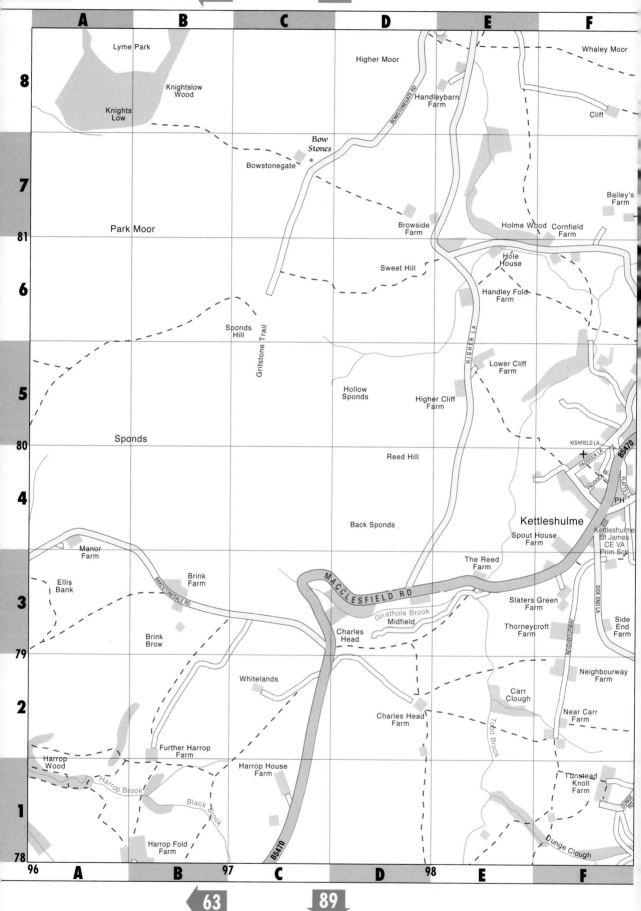

A B C D E F

8

Lyme Park

Higher Moor

Whaley Moor

Knightslow
Wood

Handleybarn
Farm

Cliff

Knights
Low

7

Bow
Stones

Bowstonegate

Bailey's
Farm

81

Park Moor

Browside
Farm

Holme Wood

Cornfield
Farm

Hole
House

6

Sweet Hill

Handley Fold
Farm

Sponds
Hill

Gritstone Trail

HIGHER LA

Lower Cliff
Farm

5

Hollow
Sponds

Higher Cliff
Farm

80

Sponds

KISHFIELD LA.

B5470

PADDOCK LA.

Reed Hill

FLATS LA.

4

PH

Kettleshulme

Back Sponds

Spout House
Farm

Kettleshulme
St James
CE VA
Prim Sch

Manor
Farm

The Reed
Farm

Ellis
Bank

Brink
Farm

BAKESTONEDALE RD

MACCLESFIELD RD

Slaters Green
Farm

SIDE END LA

3

Gnathole Brook

Thorneycroft
Farm

Side
End
Farm

Brink
Brow

Midfield

Charles
Head

NEIGHBOURWAY

79

Whitelands

Neighbourway
Farm

2

Carr
Clough

Near Carr
Farm

Charles Head
Farm

Todd Brook

Further Harrop
Farm

Harrop
Wood

Harrop House
Farm

Tunstead
Knoll
Farm

1

Harrop Brook

Black Brook

LODGE RD

B5470

Dunge Clough

78

Harrop Fold
Farm

96 A B **97** C D **98** E F

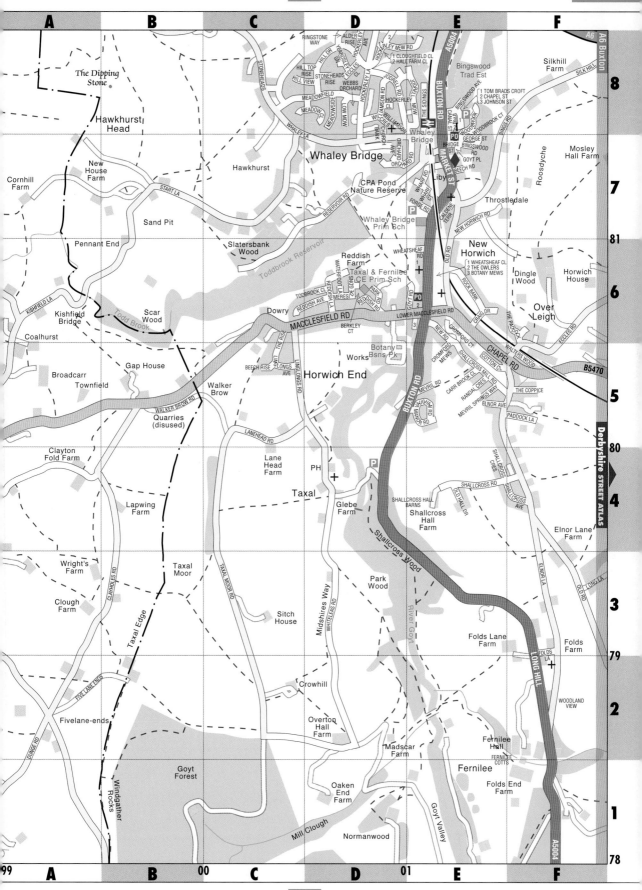

E8
1 MARLOWE RD
2 POPLAR WEINT
3 HADDON HO
4 DENWALL HO
5 ASHFIELD HO
6 HARGREAVE HO

7 THE CROSS
8 The Royal Sh Arc
9 ROKLIS GRANGE
10 SCHOLAR'S CT

F7
1 NORMANS COTTS

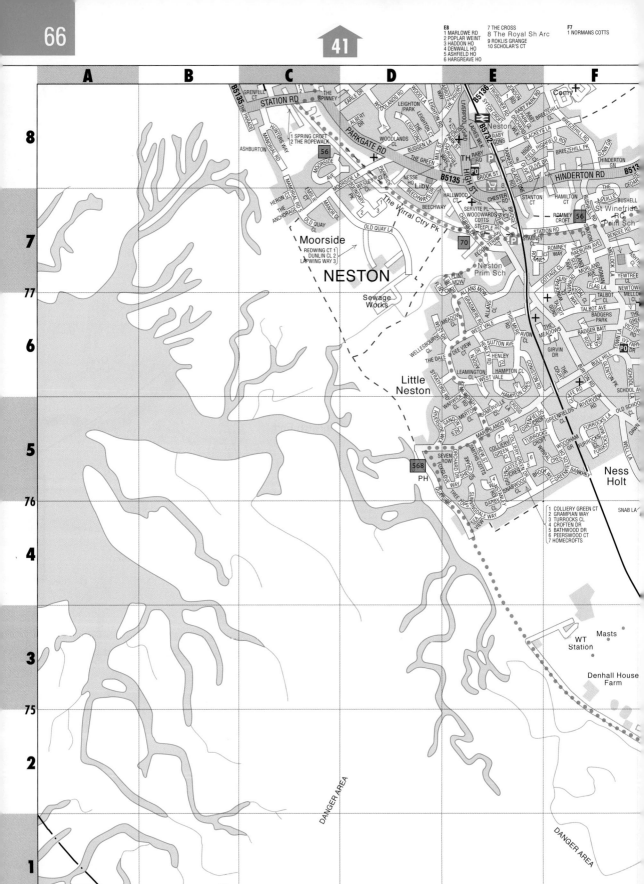

NESTON

Moorside
1 REDWING CT 1
DUNLIN CL 2
LAPWING WAY 3

Moorside

Sewage
Works

Little
Neston

Ness
Holt

1 COLLIERY GREEN CT
2 GRAMPIAN WAY
3 TURROCKS CL
4 CROFTEN DR
5 BATHWOOD DR
6 PEERSWOOD CT
7 HOMECROFTS

WT
Station

Masts

Denhall House
Farm

DANGER AREA

DANGER AREA

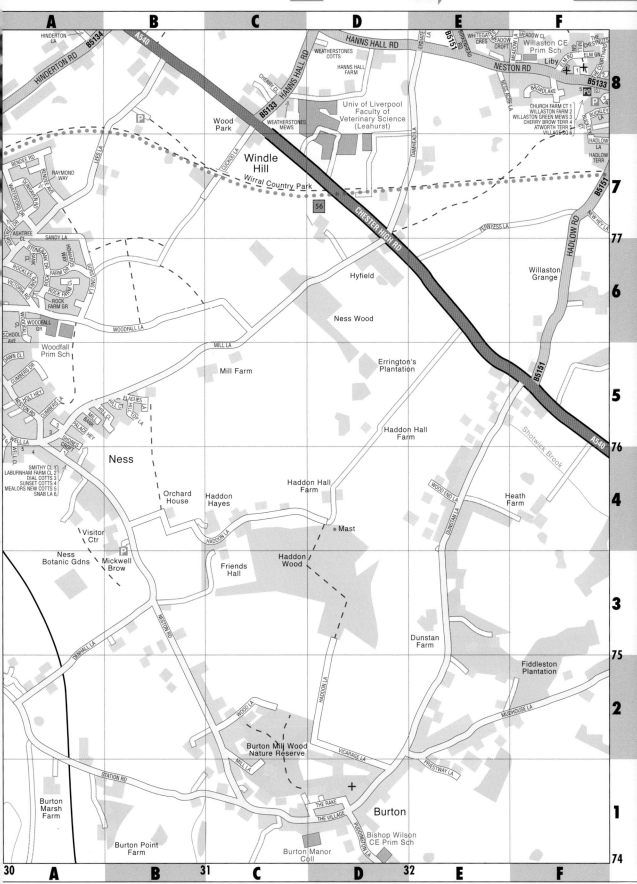

A · **B** · **C** · **D** · **E** · **F**

HINDERTON LA
B5134
A540
HANNS HALL RD
WEATHERSTONES COTTS
HANNS HALL FARM
B5133
LYDIATE LA
B5151
WHITEGATES CRES
MEADOW CROFT
MEADOW LA
Willaston CE Prim Sch
NESTON RD
Liby

HINDERTON RD
CHERRY CL
HANNS HALL RD
WEATHERSTONES MEWS
B5133
Univ of Liverpool Faculty of Veterinary Science (Leahurst)
NESS ACRE LA
DAMHEAD LA
THE CHESTNUTS
ELM GN
MILL RD
THE COURTYARD
B5133
8

BENDEE RD
RAYMOND WAY
LEES LA
P
Wood Park
CUCKOO LA
Windle Hill
Wirral Country Park
PO
P
BROADLAKE
CHURCH FARM CT 1
WILLASTON FARM 2
WILLASTON GREEN MEWS 3
CHERRY BROW TERR 4
ATWORTH TERR 5
VILLAGE SQ 6
BUCKLEY LA
HADLOW LA
HADLOW TERR

BENDEE AVE
WATERFORD DR
DUNCANSBY DR
ASHTREE CL
SANDY LA
56
CHESTER HIGH RD
FERNYESS LA
HADLOW RD
NEW HEY LA
B5151
7

ASHTREE DR
STONERANK SPARK
HOWARDS WAY
GORSTON LA
Hyfield
Willaston Grange
77

VICTORIA RD
ROCKLEE GDNS
ROCK DR
ROCK FARM
ROCK FARM GR
Ness Wood
6

SCHOOL AVE
WOODFALL GR
WOODFALL LA
MILL LA
Errington's Plantation
B5151
A540
5

DAWN CL
CUMBERS DR
Woodfall Prim Sch
Mill Farm
Haddon Hall Farm
Shotwick Brook
76

HOLT HEY
NESTON RD
CUMBERS LA
ELACHES
MILL BANK
PALACE HEY
HILL CL
HILLTOP LA
Haddon Hall Farm
WOOD END LA
Heath Farm
4

WELL LA
SHONES CROFT
Ness
SMITHY CL 1
LABURNHAM FARM CL 2
DIAL COTTS 3
SUNSET COTTS 4
MEALORS NEW COTTS 5
SNAB LA 6
Orchard House
Haddon Hayes
HADDON LA
Mast
DUNSTAN LA

Visitor Ctr
Ness Botanic Gdns
P
Mickwell Brow
Friends Hall
Haddon Wood
3

DENHALL LA
NESTON RD
Dunstan Farm
75

MUDHOUSE LA
Fiddleston Plantation
2

STATION RD
WOOD LA
MILL LA
HADDON LA
Burton Mill Wood Nature Reserve
VICARAGE LA
PRIESTWAY LA

Burton Marsh Farm
THE RAKE
THE VILLAGE
Burton
1

Burton Point Farm
Burton Manor Coll
Bishop Wilson CE Prim Sch
74

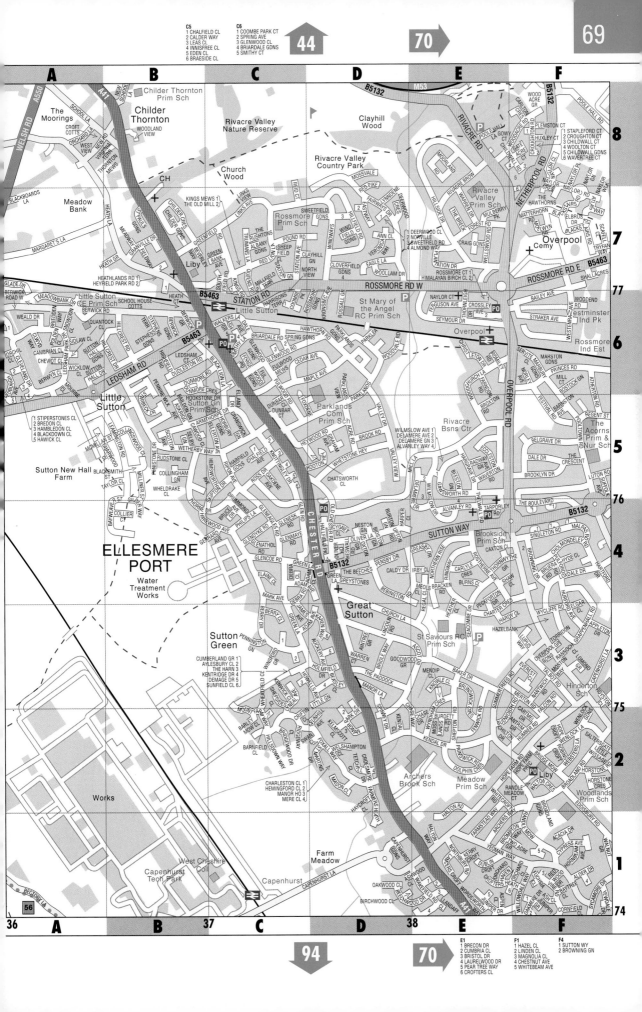

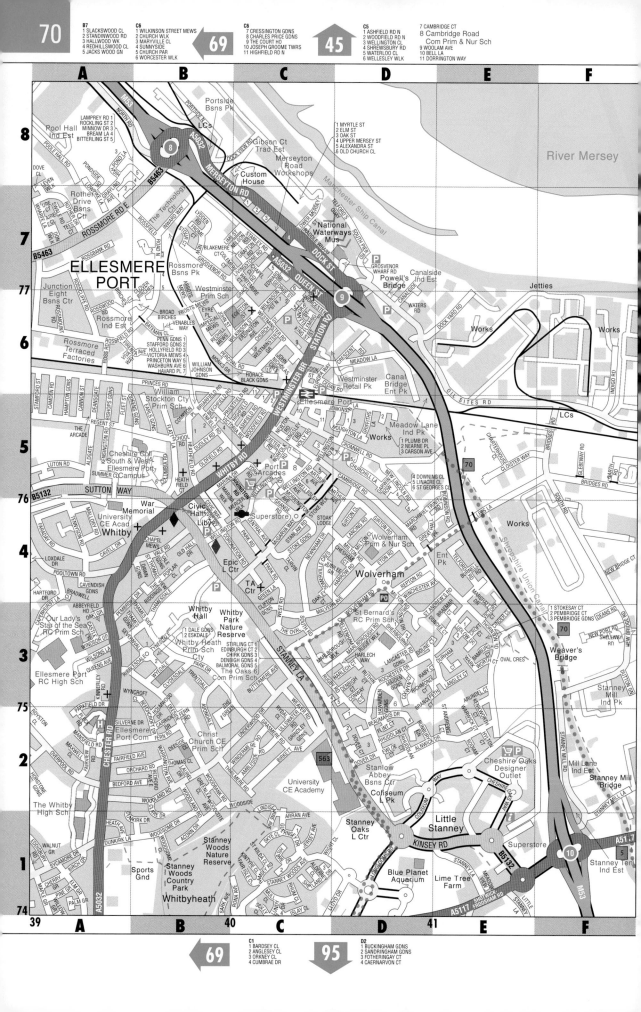

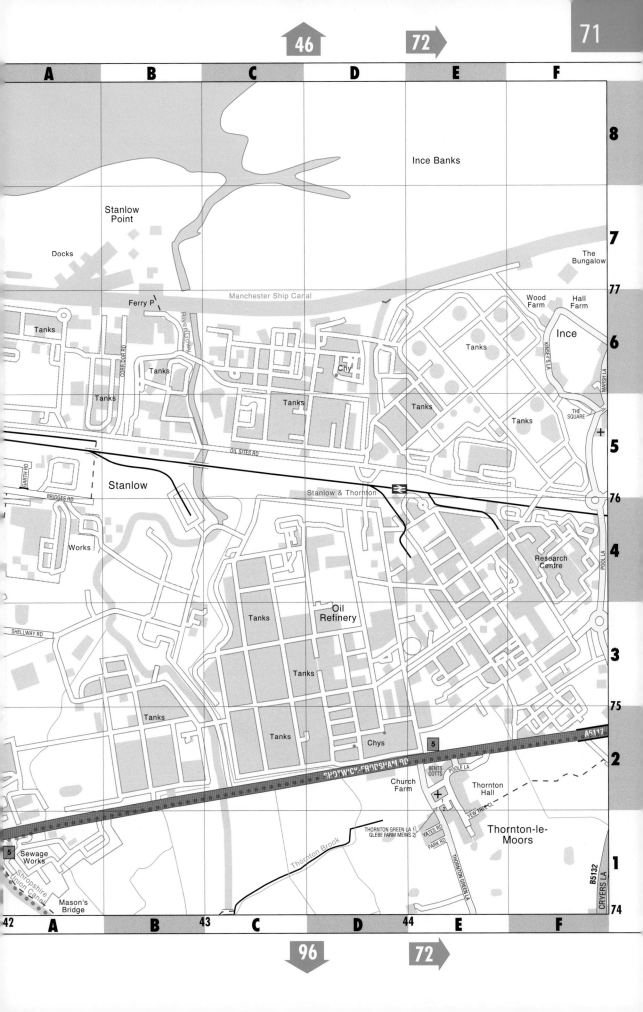

8

Ince Banks

Stanlow
Point

7

Docks

The
Bungalow

77

Ferry P

Wood
Farm

Hall
Farm

Manchester Ship Canal

Ince

6

Tanks

Tanks

Tanks

Tanks

THE
SQUARE

Tanks

Tanks

Tanks

OIL SITES RD

5

Stanlow

Stanlow & Thornton

76

Works

Research
Centre

4

SHELLWAY RD

Oil
Refinery

Tanks

Tanks

3

Tanks

75

Tanks

A5117

Tanks

Chys

5

2

SHOTWICK-FRODSHAM RD

BENTS
COTTS

POOLE LA

Church
Farm

Thornton
Hall

THORNTON GREEN LA 1
GLEBE FARM MEWS 2

Thornton-le-
Moors

5

Sewage
Works

Thornton Brook

B5132

CRYERS LA

1

Mason's
Bridge

74

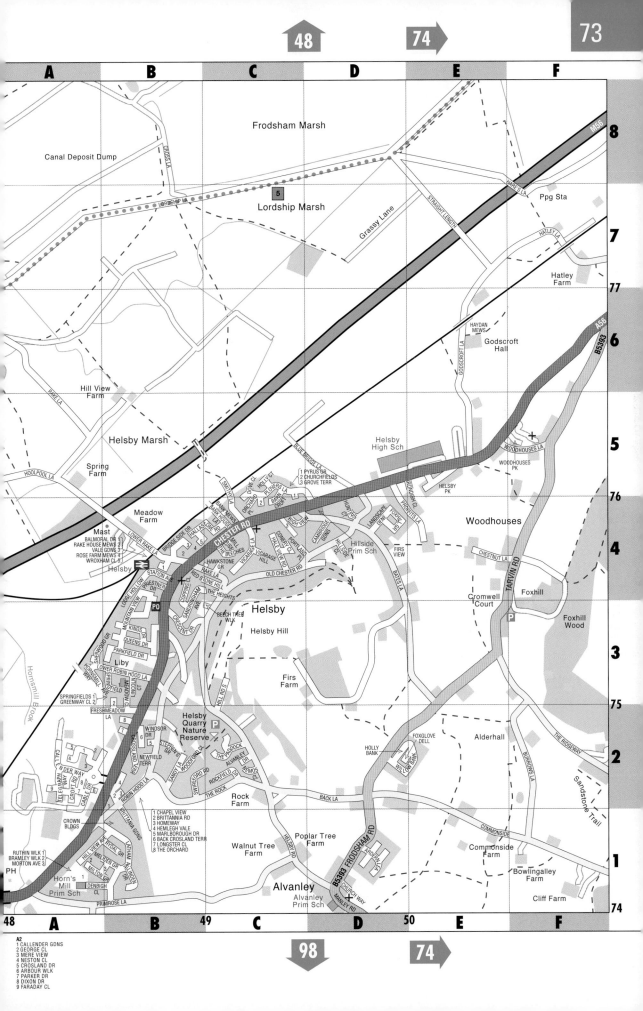

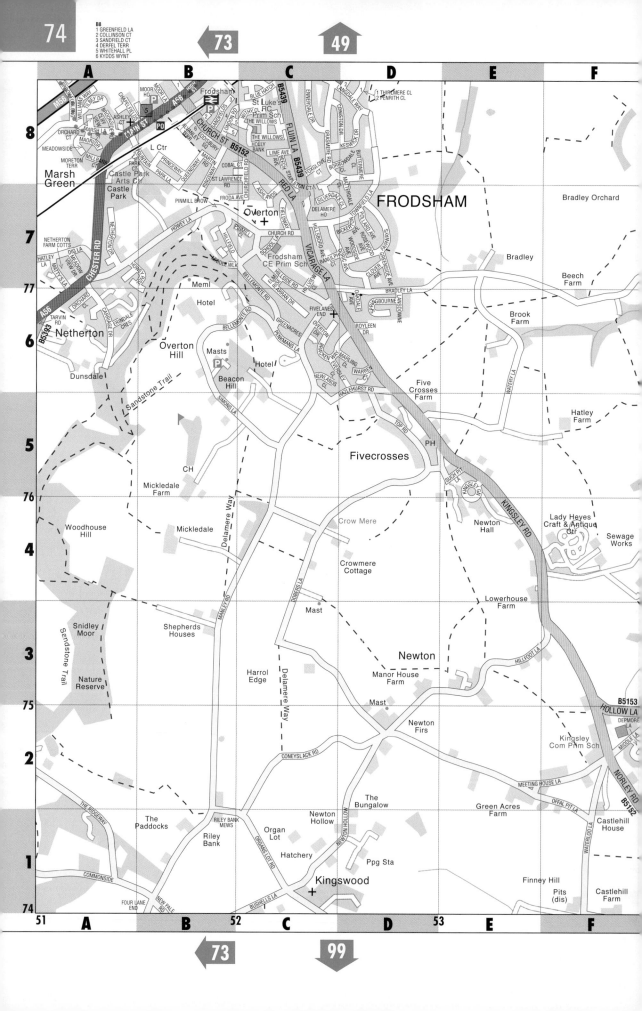

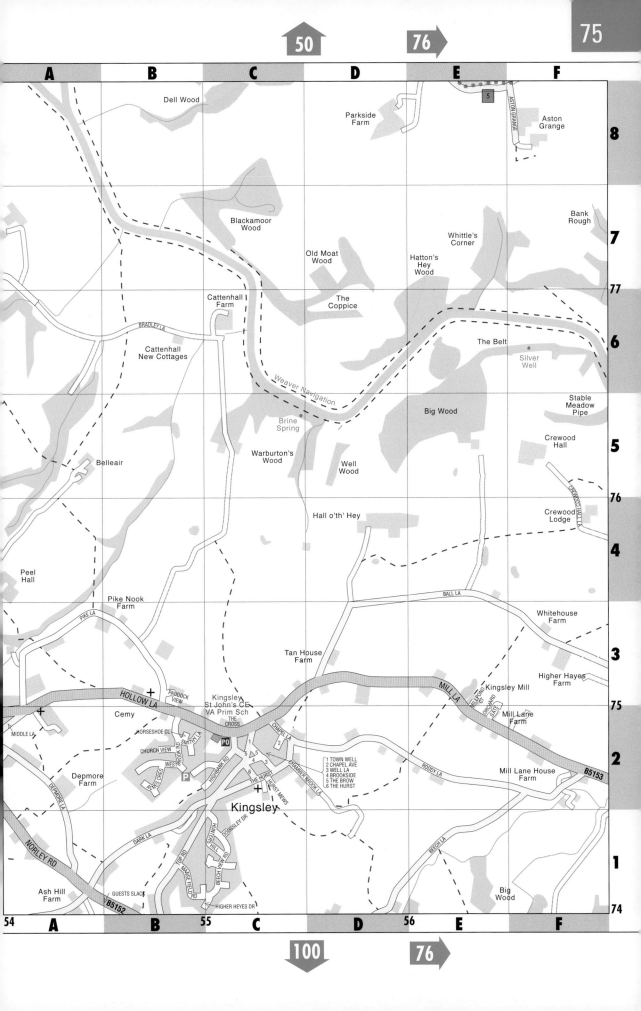

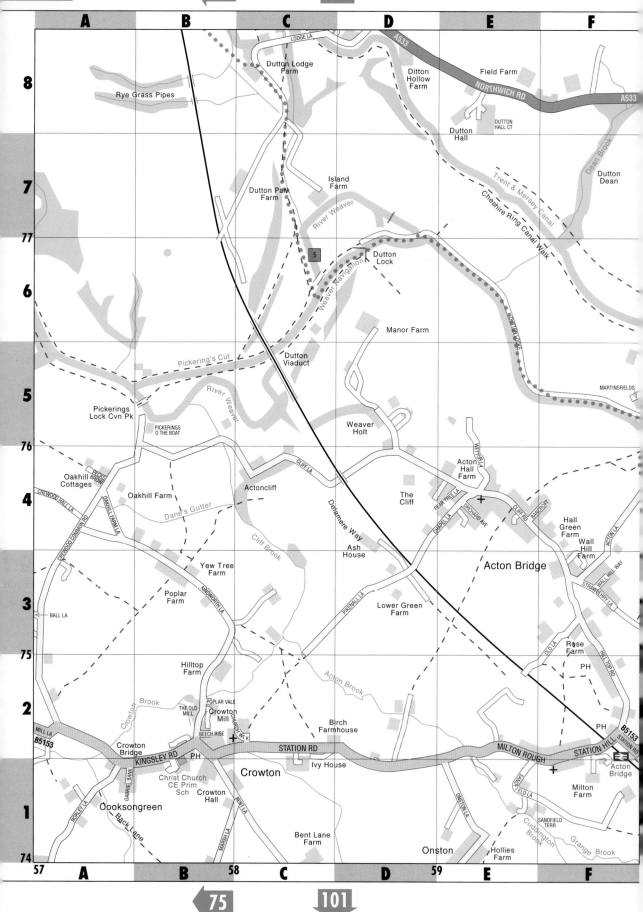

A B C D E F

8

Rye Grass Pipes

LODGE LA
Dutton Lodge
Farm

Ditton
Hollow
Farm

Field Farm

A533
NORTHWICH RD
A533

7

Dutton Park
Farm

Island
Farm

Dutton
Hall

DUTTON
HALL CT

Trent & Mersey Canal

Dean Brook

Dutton
Dean

Cheshire Ring Canal Walk

77

River Weaver

5

Dutton
Lock

Weaver Navigation

DUTTON LOCKS

6

Manor Farm

MARTINSFIELDS

Pickering's Cut

Dutton
Viaduct

River Weaver

5

Pickerings
Lock Cvn Pk

PICKERINGS
O THE BOAT

Weaver
Holt

Acton
Hall
Farm

WETTON LA

76

Oakhill
Cottages

PECK'S
BROW

Oakhill Farm

CLIFF LA

Actoncliff

The
Cliff

PEAR TREE LA

CHAPEL LA

ORCHARD AVE

CLIFF RD

BANCROFT

Hall
Green
Farm

Wall
Hill
Farm

ACTON LA

4

CREWOOD HALL LA

OAKHILL FARM LA

CREWOOD COMMON RD

Dane's Gutter

Cliff Brook

Delamere Way

Ash
House

WALL HILL WAY

STRAWBERRY LA

3

BALL LA

Yew Tree
Farm

Poplar
Farm

KINSWORTH LA

PIKENALL LA

Lower Green
Farm

Acton Bridge

Rose
Farm

OLD LA

HILL TOP RD

PH

75

Hilltop
Farm

Acton Brook

PH

2

Crowton
Brook

THE OLD
MILL

POPLAR VALE

Crowton
Mill

CONGUCH W.K

BEECH RISE

Birch
Farmhouse

STATION RD

MILTON ROUGH

STATION HILL

STATION RD

B5153

MILL LA

B5153

Crowton
Bridge

KINGSLEY RD

PH

Ivy House

Acton
Bridge

Milton
Farm

1

GABRIEL BANK

Christ Church
CE Prim
Sch

Crowton
Hall

BERTT LA

Crowton

SANDFIELD LA

ONSTON LA

SANDFIELD
TERR

Oooksongreen

NORLEY LA

Back Lane

MARSH LA

Bent Lane
Farm

Onston

Hollies
Farm

Cuddington
Brook

Grange Brook

74

57 A B 58 C D 59 E F

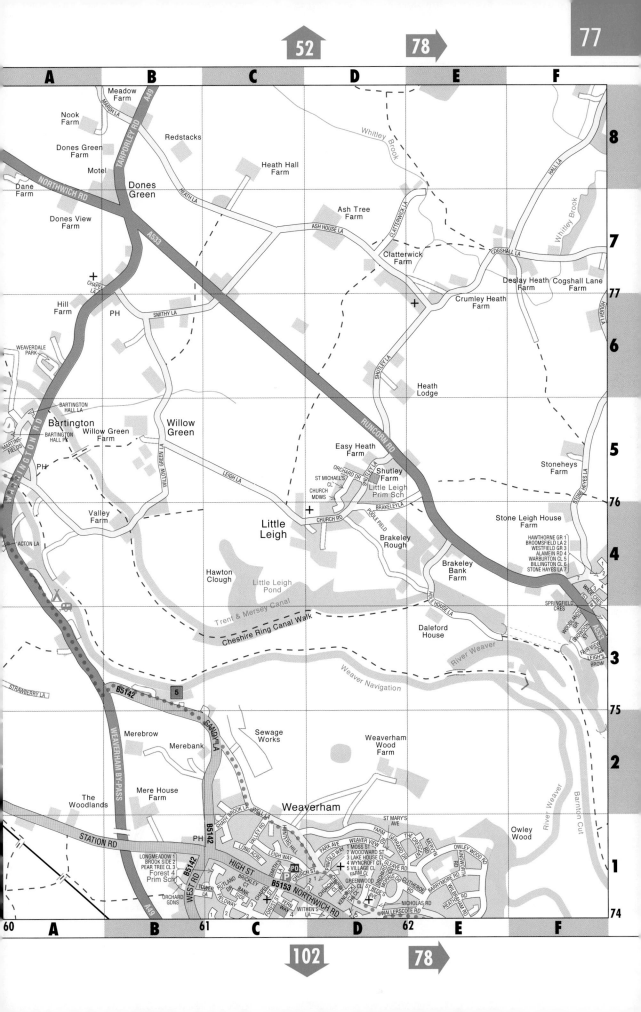

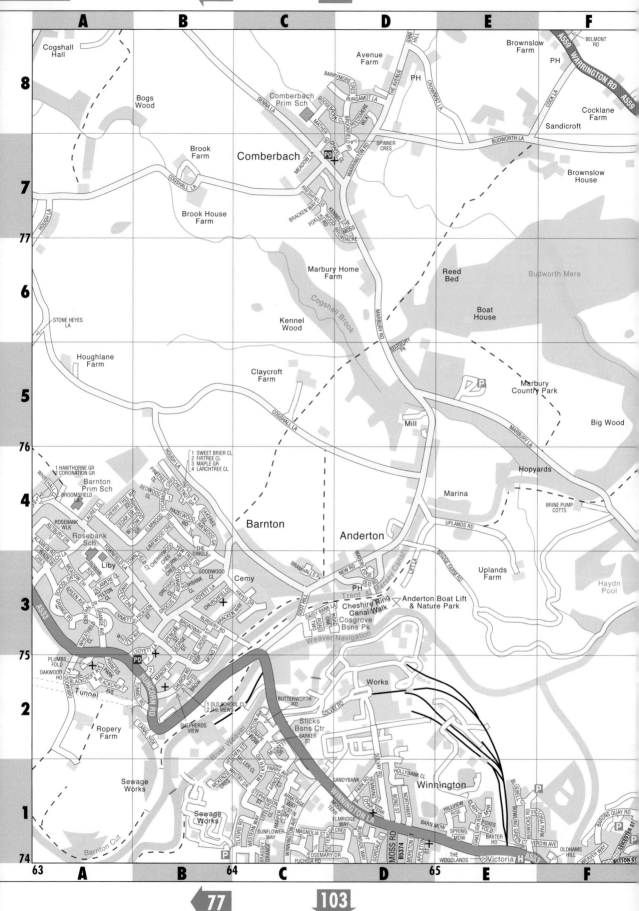

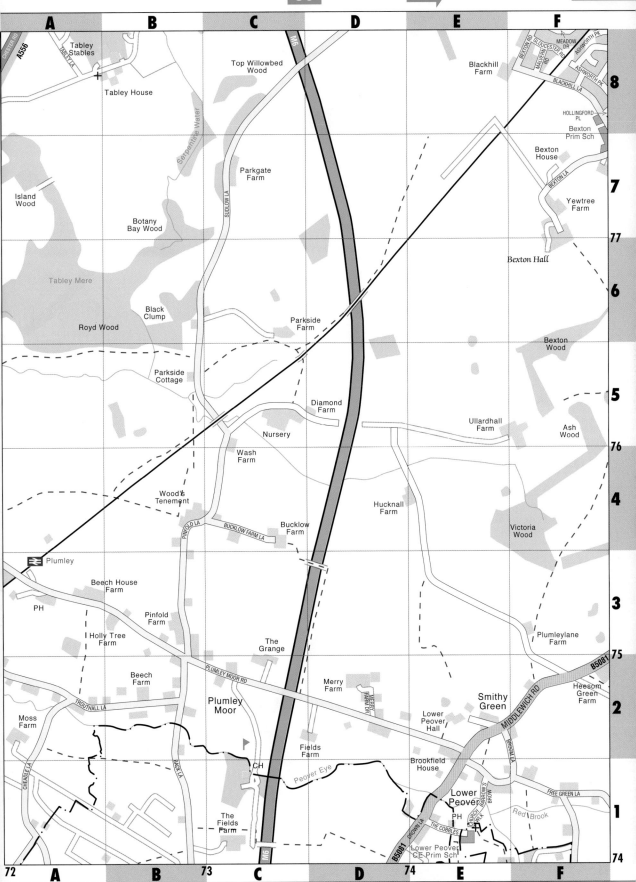

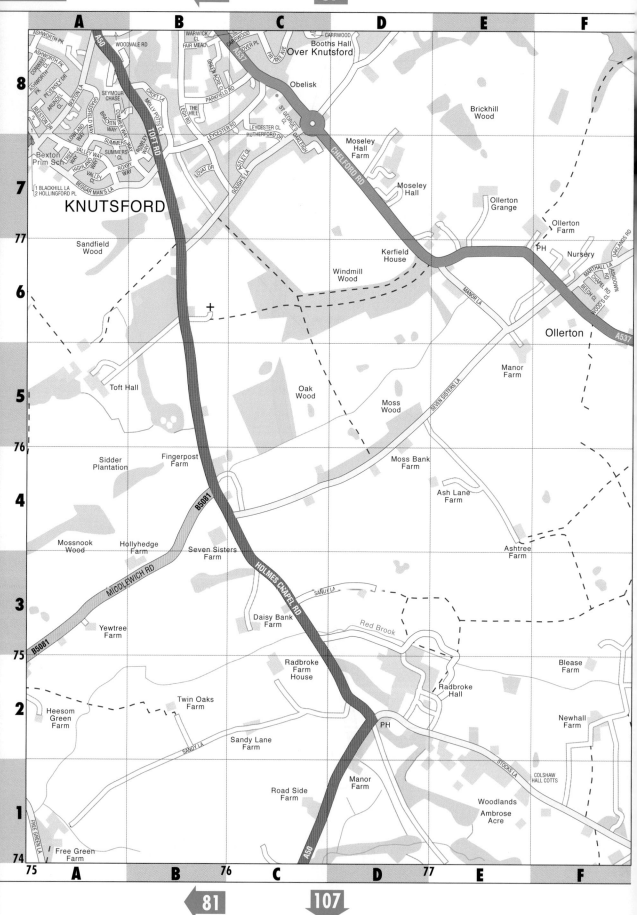

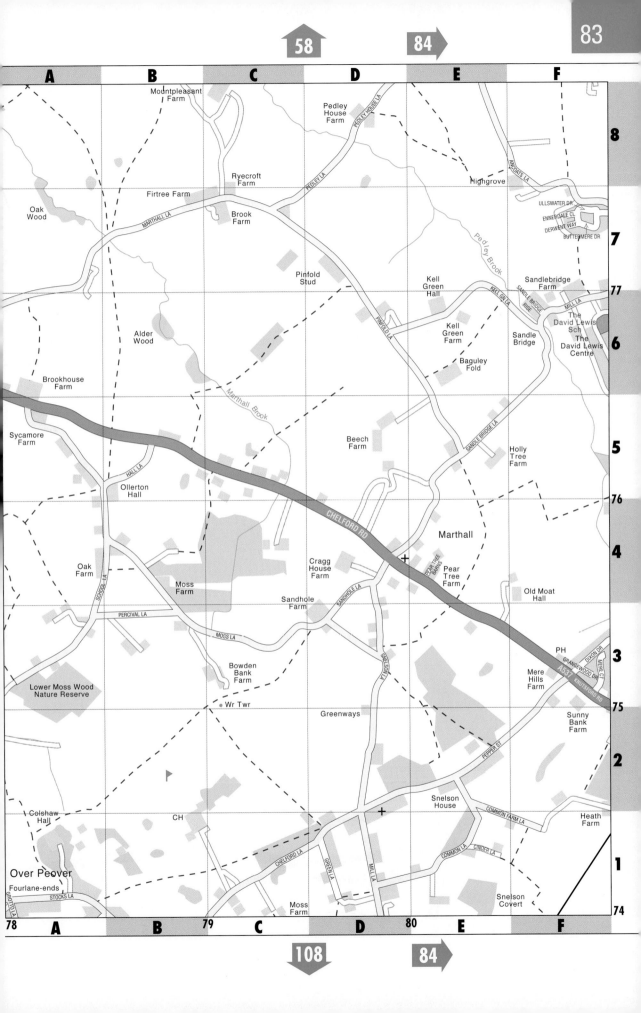

58
84

A **B** **C** **D** **E** **F**

8

Mountpleasant Farm

Pedley House Farm

Highgrove

7

Oak Wood

Firtree Farm

Ryecroft Farm

Brook Farm

MARTHALL LA

PEDLEY LA

PEDLEY HOUSE LA

Pedley Brook

ULLSWATER DR

ENNERDALE CL

DERWENT WAY

BUTTERMERE DR

77

Pinfold Stud

Alder Wood

Kell Green Hall

Kell Green Farm

SANDLE BRIDGE RISE

Sandlebridge Farm

MILL LA

The David Lewis Sch

The David Lewis Centre

6

PINFOLD LA

KELL GR LA

Sandle Bridge

Baguley Fold

5

Brookhouse Farm

Sycamore Farm

Marthall Brook

Beech Farm

SANDLE BRIDGE LA

Holly Tree Farm

76

Ollerton Hall

HALL LA

CHELFORD RD

Marthall

4

Oak Farm

SCHOOL LA

Moss Farm

Cragg House Farm

Sandhole Farm

SANDHOLE LA

PEAR TREE BARNS

Pear Tree Farm

Old Moat Hall

PERCIVAL LA

MOSS LA

SNEL SO LA

PH

Mere Hills Farm

GRANGEWOOD DR

DIXON DR

MERE CT

KNUTSFORD RD

A537

3

Lower Moss Wood Nature Reserve

Bowden Bank Farm

Wr Twr

Greenways

Sunny Bank Farm

75

PEPPER ST

2

Colshaw Hall

CH

Snelson House

Heath Farm

COMMON FARM LA

Over Peover

Fourlane-ends

STOCKS LA

GROTTO LA

CHELFORD LA

GREEN LA

MILL LA

Moss Farm

COMMON LA

CINDER LA

Snelson Covert

1

74

A **B** **C** **D** **E** **F**

108
84

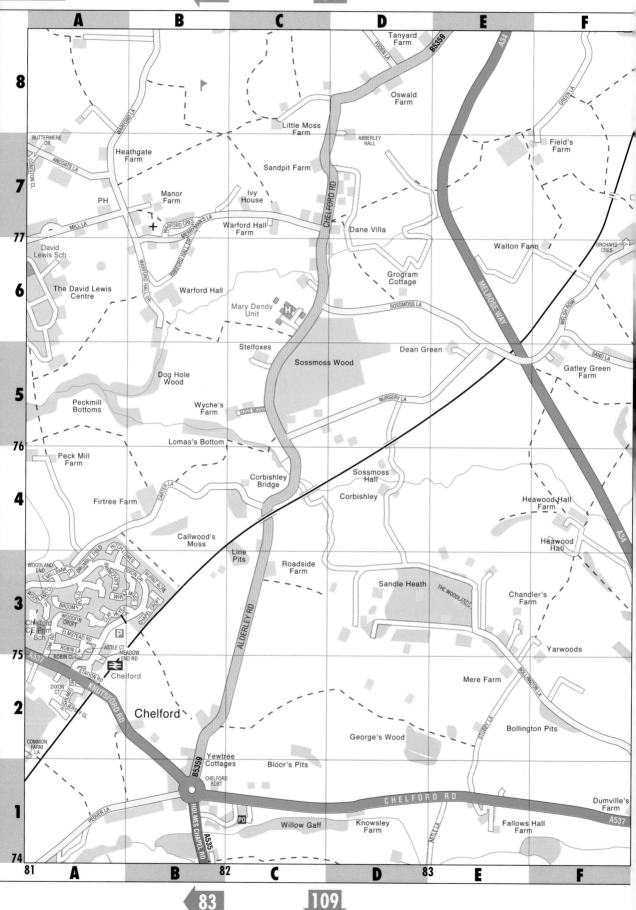

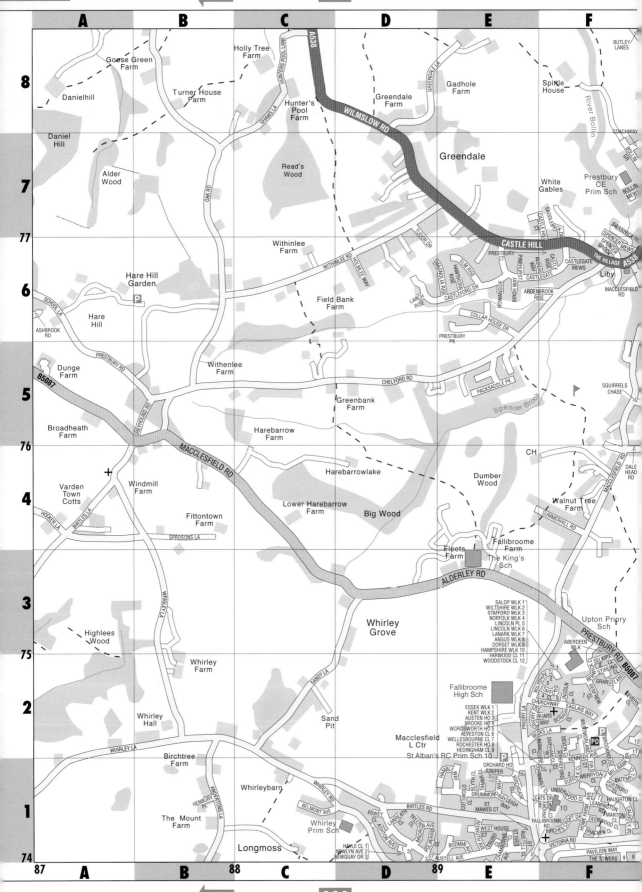

D3
1 Tytherington Sh Ctr
2 BROCKLEHURST CT
3 BROCKLEHURST MEWS
4 BLUEBELL MEWS
5 CAVENDISH CL

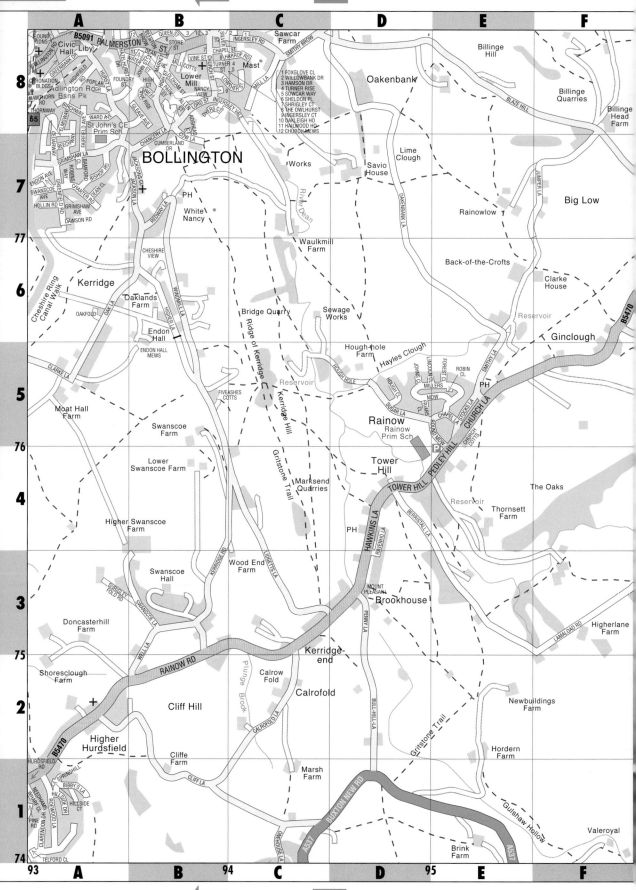

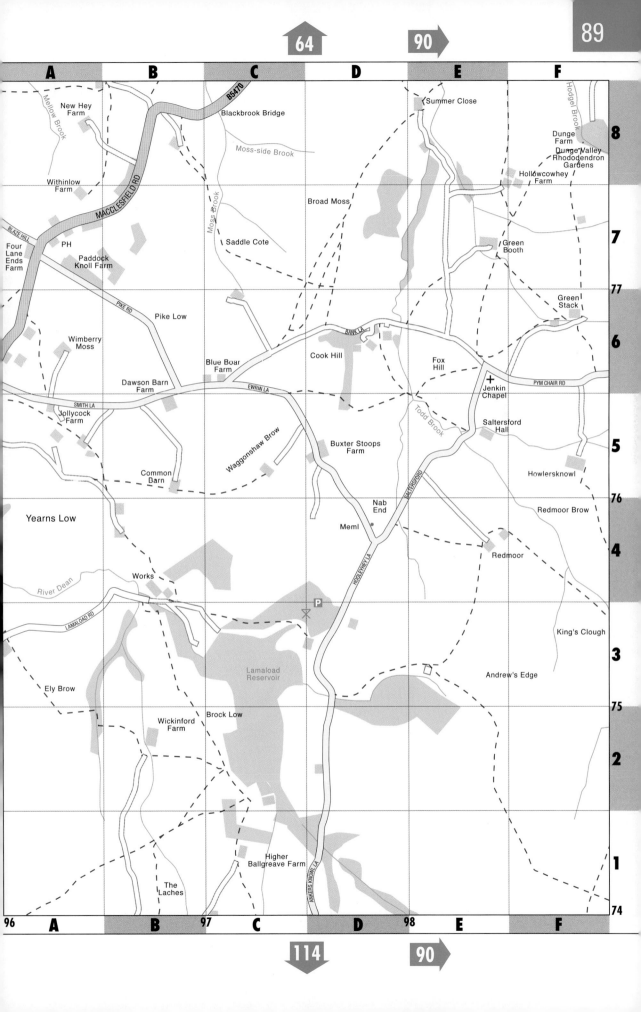

A B C D E F

8

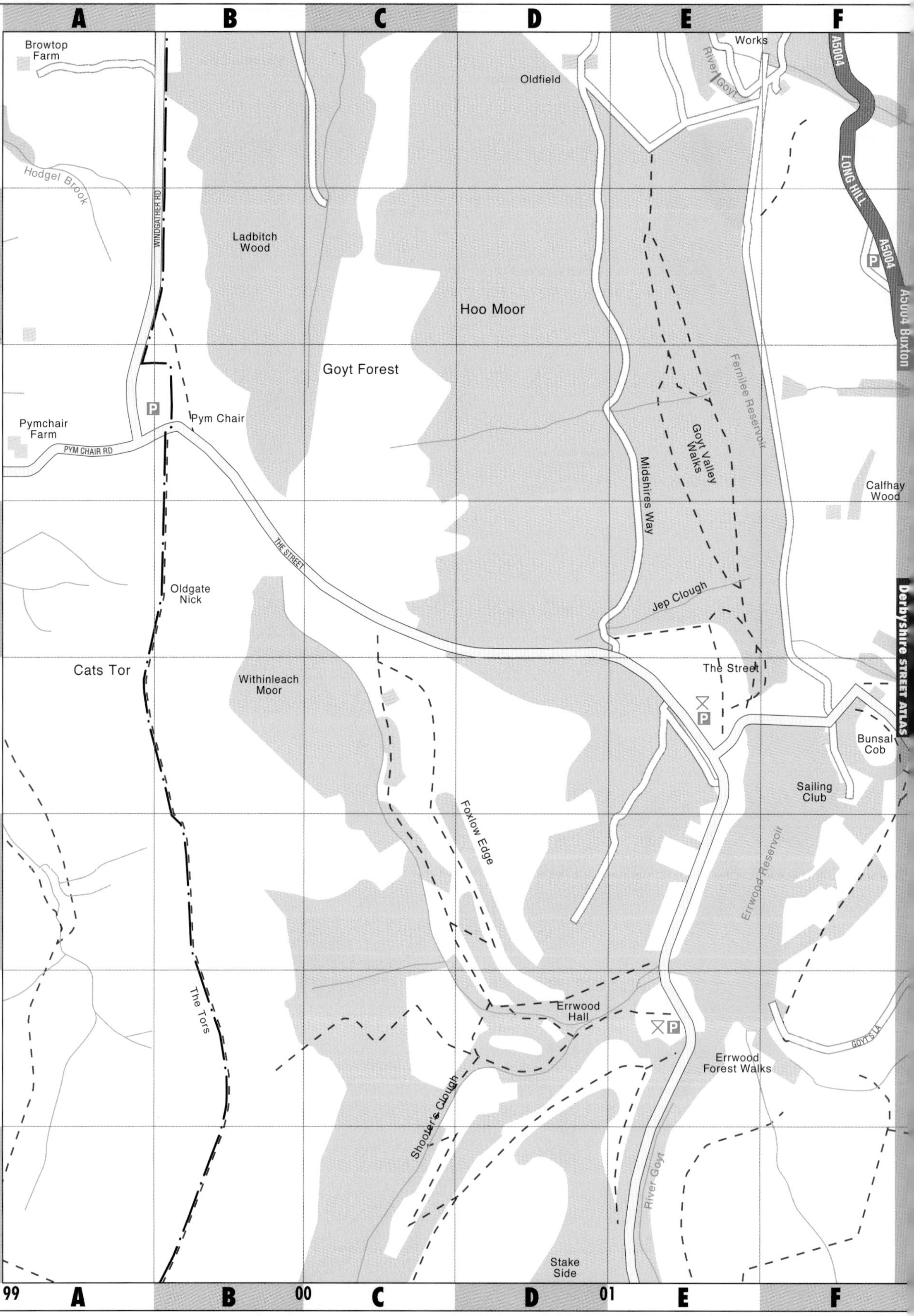

Browtop
Farm

Hodgel Brook

7

WINDGATHER RD

Ladbitch
Wood

Oldfield

Works

River Goyt

LONG HILL

A5004

A5004 Buxton

77

Goyt Forest

Hoo Moor

Fernilee Reservoir

6

Pymchair
Farm

P

Pym Chair

PYM CHAIR RD

Goyt Valley
Walks

Midshires Way

Calfhay
Wood

Derbyshire STREET ATLAS

5

Oldgate
Nick

THE STREET

Jep Clough

76

Cats Tor

Withinleach
Moor

The Street

P

Bunsal
Cob

4

Foxlow Edge

Sailing
Club

Errwood Reservoir

3

The Tors

Errwood
Hall

P

GOYT'S LA

75

Shooter's Clough

Errwood
Forest Walks

2

River Goyt

1

Stake
Side

74

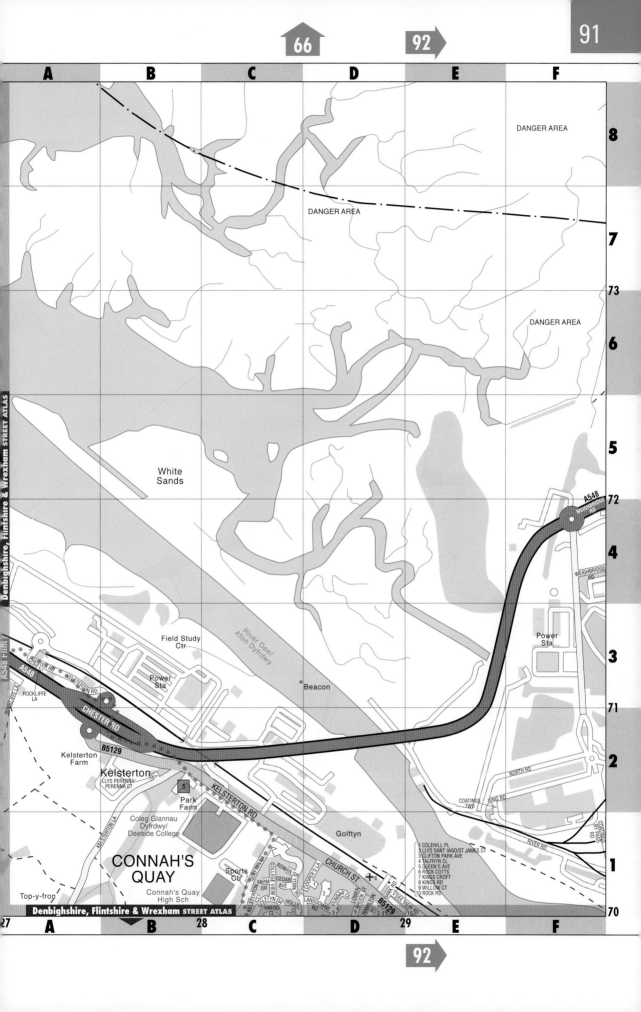

A B C D E F

8
7
73
6
5
72
4
71
2
1
70

DANGER AREA

DANGER AREA

DANGER AREA

A548

WEIGHBRIDGE RD

A548 FINT

A548

ROCKLIFFE LA

CHESTER RD

KELSTERTON RD

CHESTER RD

B5129

Kelsterton Farm

Kelsterton

LLYS PERENNA/ PERENNA CT

Park Farm

Coleg Glannau Dyfrdwy/ Deeside College

KELSTERTON LA

CONNAH'S QUAY

Top-y-fron

Connah's Quay High Sch

Sports Ctr

KELSTERTON RD

White Sands

Field Study Ctr

Power Sta

River Dee/ Afon Dyfrdwy

Beacon

Power Sta

NORTH RD

RING RD

COATINGS TWO

RIVER RD

COATINGS BYPASS RD

Golftyn

CHURCH ST

B5129

VICE VIEW RD

MAIN RD

HAMILTON

LOWER BROOK ST

DUNDAS CL

COOPER LA

LANSDOWNE RD

HAFOD CL

GOLFTYN DR

HOLLY CL

CEDAR AVE

ROWAN GR

COLLEGE VIEW

FARM DR

KELSTERTON RD

1 COLEHILL PL
2 LLYS SANT IAGO/ST JAMES CT
3 CLIFTON PARK AVE
4 TALFRYN CL
5 QUEEN'S AVE
6 ROCK COTTS
7 KINGS CROFT
8 KINGS RD
9 WILLOW CT
10 ROCK RD

27 A B 28 C D 29 E F

A   B   C   D   E   F

8

Puddington

The Mere

Marsh Covert

Burton Mere Fisheries RSPB Reserve

Barn Farm

PUDDINGTON LA

EARLES WAY

PIPERS LA

Burton Point

7

DANGER AREA

Old Hall

Puddington Hall

73

Rifle Range

Platts Covert

6

5

Reservoir

DANGER AREA

WEIGHBRIDGE RD

72

A548

LC

568

4

WEIGHBRIDGE RD

Works

SHOTWICK RD

A548

TENTH AVE

TENTH AVE

Mast

3

FOURTH AVE

SECOND AVE

SECOND AVE

71

Parc Ddiwydiannol Glannau Dyfrdwy/ Deeside Ind Pk

FOURTH AVE

FIRST AVE

2

Works

LC

PARKWAY

Newtech Sq

SIXTH AVE

Parkway Bsns Ctr

THIRD AVE

Birkenhead Junction

1

RIVER RD

5

70

30   A   B   31   C   D   32   E   F

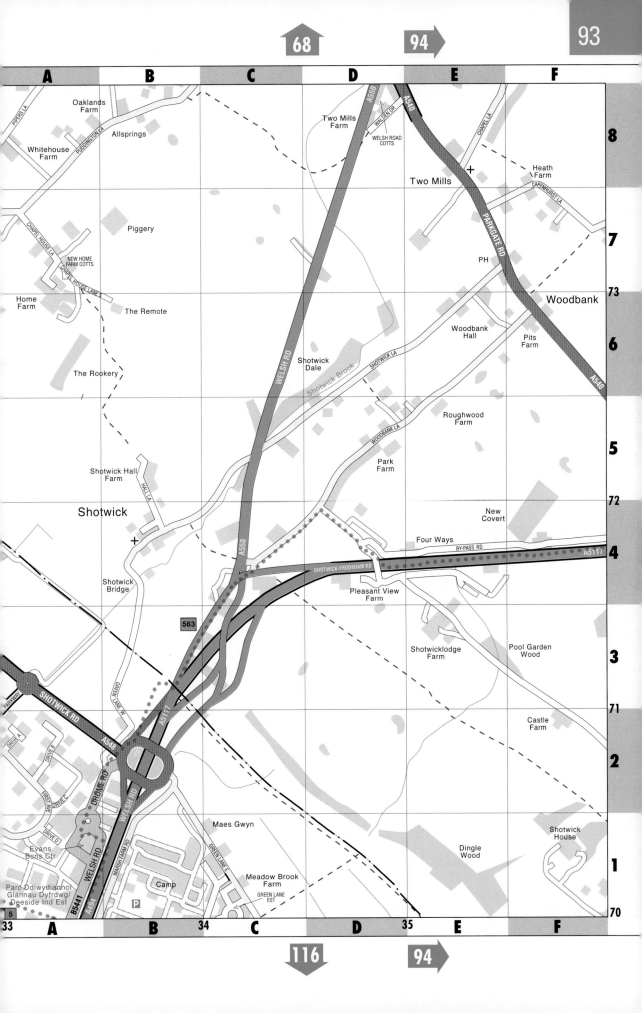

F8
1 BADGERS CL
2 BRAMLEY CL
3 HONEY SUCKLE CL
4 LAMBOURNE CL
5 SNOWBERRY WAY
6 SAXON WAY
7 WEST PARK DR
8 GREEN LAWNS DR
9 PARLIAMENT WAY
10 SALISBURY CL
11 BANGOR CL
12 ST DAVIDS DR
13 ST GEORGES AVE

Capenhurst

Capenhurst Tech Pk

MANOR FARM CRES

Capenhurst CE Prim Sch

Lower Brook Farm

LAURELWOOD DR

BAKEWELL CL
CANNOCK CL

PLOUGHMANS CL 1
THE FURROWS 2
PLOUGHMANS WAY 3
WELLS CL 4
CANTERBURY CL 5
GLOUCESTER CL 6

CHESTER RD

LINDEN CL
VINE CL

Backford Cross

56

Old Hall Farm

Dunkirk Farm

FALLOW ST

ROSEMERE DR 1
KINNINGTON WAY 2
BACKFORD GDNS 3
PETERBOROUGH CL 4

Acres Farm

Big Wood

North Cheshire Way

Manor Farm

Dunkirk

Depot Dunkirk Trad Est

Acres Wood

A540

M56

563

CHESTER BATES

THE PADDOCKS

Ashcroft Farm

Gibbet Mill

Rendova Farm

POWEY LA

M56

A5117

56

Lea Manor Farm

BY-PASS RD

A5117

Saughall Nurseries

Hill Farm

STRAWBERRY LA

Glebe Farm

Wood Farm

DEMAGE LA

Big Wood

Nursery

GROVE RD

TOWNFIELD LA

Grove Farm

Green Farm

Parkgate House

THE GREEN
LODGE LA

PARK AVE

LONG LA

St Oswald's CE Aided Prim Sch

GYPSY LA

STATION RD

Lea Farm

The Willows

Mollington

Warren Farm

HUMPHREY CL

THOMAS WEDGE RD

PARK WAY

FIELD WAY

NEWCROFT

KINGSTON CT

FIDDLERS LA

Astbury House

MOLLINGTON CL

WILLOW LEA

WELL LA

Saughall All Saints Prim CE Sch

MEADOWCROFT

GREENWAY

Parkside Farm

KINGSWOOD AVE

PH

FELLOWS CT

MEADOW CT

PO

CHURCH RD

SAUGHALL HEY

KINGSWOOD LA

OVERWOOD LA

HOME PK

ALDERSEY CL

DARLINGTON CRES

ANVIL

MAIN RD

RAKE WAY

THE CLOSE

Saughall

THE RIDINGS

A540

TARRANT CT

SMITHY CL

CHAPEL CL

FAIRHOLME CL

ROSEWOOD GR

OVERWOOD AVE

A B C D E F

WILLOW GR
ELM GR
LILAC GR
MAPLE GR
BLACKTHORNE AVE
CHESTER RD
A5032
FIRST AVE

THE GROVES
LABURNUM GR
STRAWBERRY GN
STRAWBERRY DR
STROMA AVE
LUNDY DR

Stanney Woods
Nature Reserve

P

STRAWBERRY WAYE

563

4 PUFFIN CL
5 BARRY CL
6 STANNEY WOODS AVE
7 FARNE CL
8 CUMBRIA DR
9 LEWIS CL

1 STAFFIN AVE
2 HANDA DR
3 SARK AVE

A5117

PH

Sunnydale

8

1 APPLEDALE DR
2 PINEDALE CL
3 CONIFER CL
4 LIME TREE CL
5 HEATHFIELD CT
6 STRAWBERRY PK

Strawberry
Farm

LITTLE STANNEY LA

M53

HEATH LA

HEATH LA

7

Heath
Farm

Heath
Wood

WHITBY LA

Rosscroft

Poplarhall

The Laurels

11

M56

M53

73

6

M56

Axes
Farm

A5032

Fairfield
House Farm

GORDON LA

POPLAR HALL LA

MOUNT
BARNS

Mount
Farm

RAKE LA

The Groves

LITTLE RAKE LA

The Dungeon

Croughton

Croughton
Cottage

Chorlton Lodge
Farm

Top
Farm

CROUGHTON RD

WERVIN RD

5

BLENCOWE CL
DENSON CL
ASHER CL

THE NOOK

THE CHANNEL

Backford
Hall

BRONTE
WLK

CHURCH LA

72

Backford

LIVERPOOL RD

Backford Brook

Greater
Grace
Christian
Sch

Chorlton
Hall

Rockbank

5

4

LEA HALL PK

DEMAGE LA

Lea Hall
Farm

Lea Hall

STATION RD

56

Friars
Park

Collinge Farm

Collinge
Wood

Croughall
Bridge

3

Shropshire Union Canal

71

56

Towing Path

CAUGHALL RD

BADGERS WLK

Caughall
Manor

Lea
Farm

Butter Hill

2

Viaduct
Wood

Moston
Hall

Moston Hill
Farm

MALTA RD

Moston

1 CROOKENDEN CL
2 SIMPSON CL
3 BRODIE CL

NORMANDY
RD

PROSSER RD

MOSTON RD

A41

P&R

5

Chester Zoo

WERVIN RD

SOMETHING
LAUREL BANK CL

GREENACRES
CT

GREEN

ACRES LA

1

The Dale

ALAMEIN RD

SALFERIO RD

CROOKENDEN RD

SIMPSON RD

CHARLES RD

A5116

4 DAUNCEY CL
5 HARINGTON CL
6 HARINGTON RD

FLAG LA N

70

39 A 40 B C 41 D E F

8 7 73 6 5 72 4 3 71 2 1 70

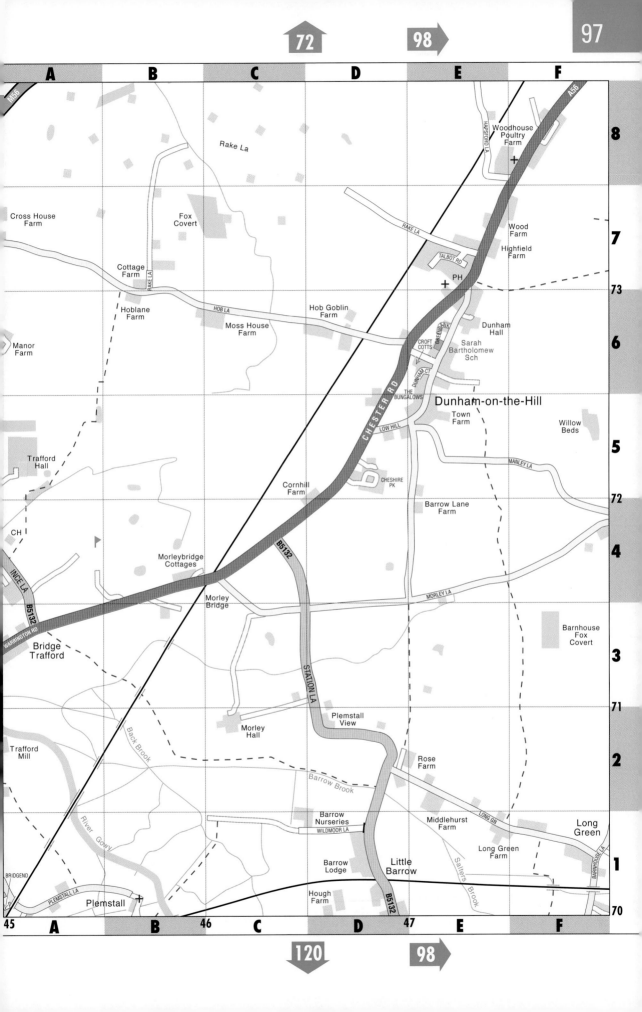

97
73

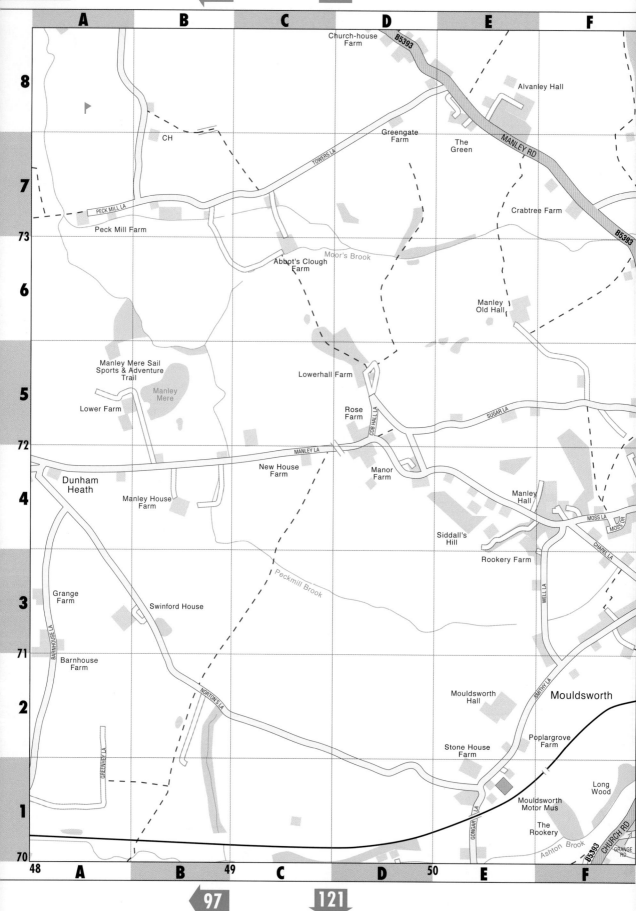

97
121

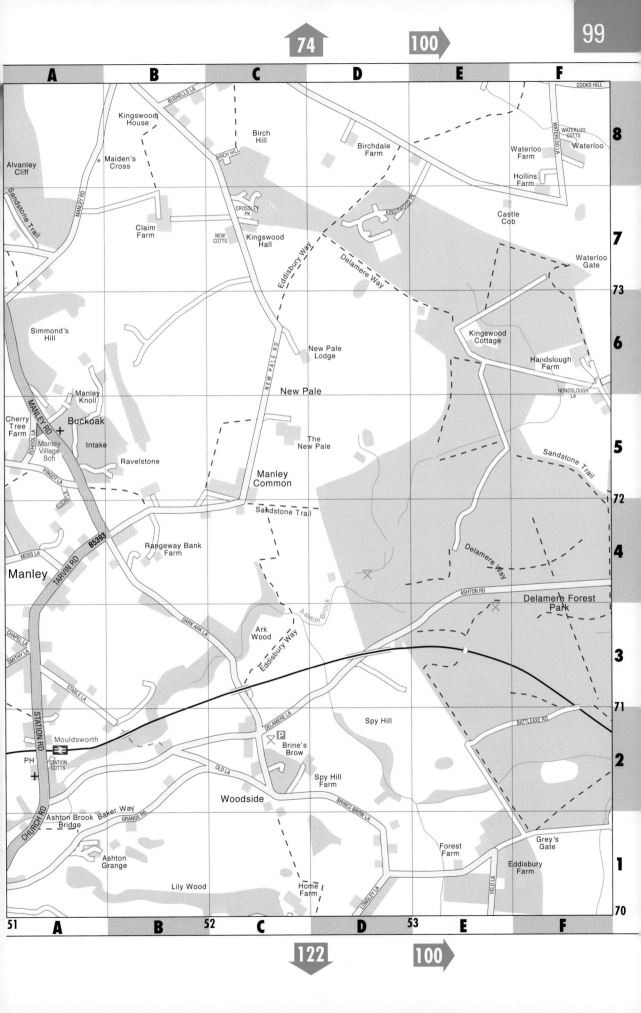

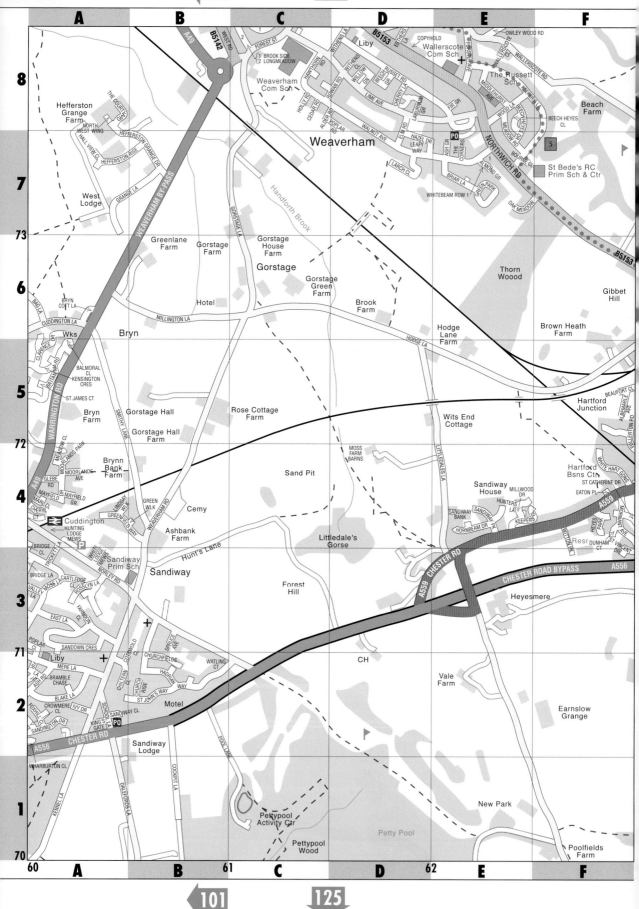

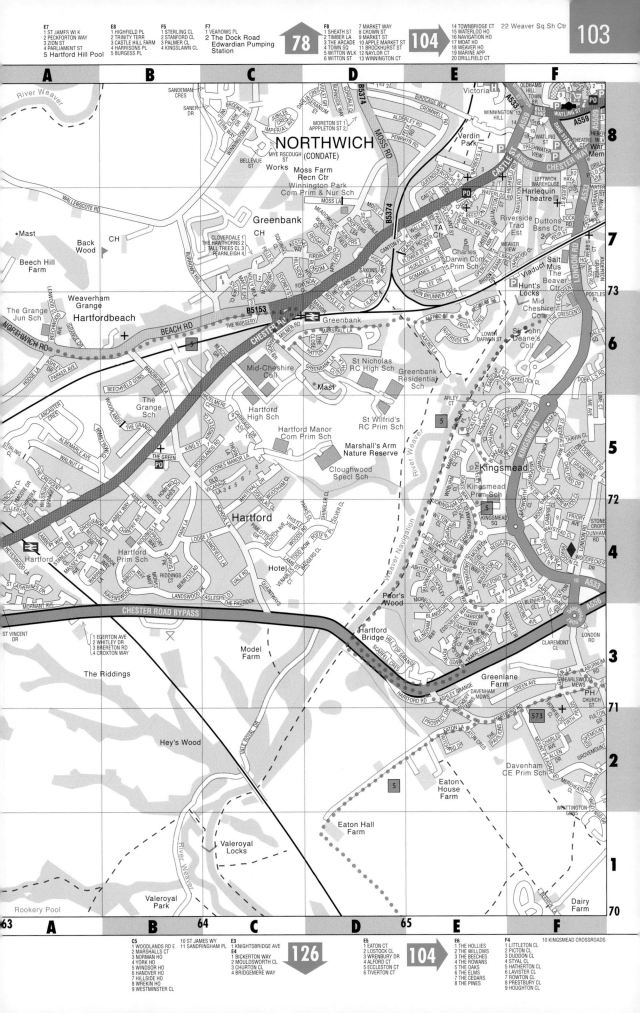

E7
1 ST JAMES WLK
2 PECKFORTON WAY
3 ZION ST
4 PARLIAMENT ST
5 HARTFORD HILL POOL

E8
1 HIGHFIELD PL
2 TRINITY TERR
3 CASTLE HILL FARM
4 HARRISONS PL
5 BURGESS PL

F5
1 STERLING CL
2 STANFORD CL
3 PALMER CL
4 KINGSLAWN CL

F7
1 VEAROWS PL
2 The Dock Road Edwardian Pumping Station

78

F8
1 SHEATH ST
2 TIMBER LA
3 THE ARCADE
4 TOWN SQ
5 WITTON WLK
6 WITTON ST

7 MARKET WAY
8 CROWN ST
9 MARKET ST
10 APPLE MARKET ST
11 BROCKHURST ST
12 NAYLOR ST
13 WINNINGTON CT

104

14 TOWNBRIDGE CT
15 WATERLOO HO
16 NAVIGATION HO
17 MOAT HO
18 WEAVER HO
19 MARINE APP
20 DRILLFIELD CT

22 Weaver Sq Sh Ctr

103

C5
1 WOODLANDS RD E
2 MARSHALLS CT
3 NORMAN HO
4 YORK HO
5 WINDSOR HO
6 HANOVER HO
7 HILLSIDE HO
8 WREKIN HO
9 WESTMINSTER CL

10 ST JAMES WY
11 SANDRINGHAM PL

E3
1 KNIGHTSBRIDGE AVE
E4
1 BICKERTON WAY
2 MOULDSWORTH CL
3 CHURTON CL
4 BRIDGEMERE WAY

126

E5
1 EATON CT
2 LOSTOCK CL
3 WRENBURY DR
4 ALFORD CT
5 ECCLESTON CT
6 TIVERTON CT

104

E6
1 THE HOLLIES
2 THE WILLOWS
3 THE BEECHES
4 THE ROWANS
5 THE OAKS
6 THE ELMS
7 THE CEDARS
8 THE PINES

F4
1 LITTLETON CL
2 PICTON CL
3 DUDDON CL
4 STYAL CL
5 HATHERTON CL
6 LAVISTER CL
7 ROWTON CL
8 PRESTBURY CL
9 HOUGHTON CL

10 KINGSMEAD CROSSROADS

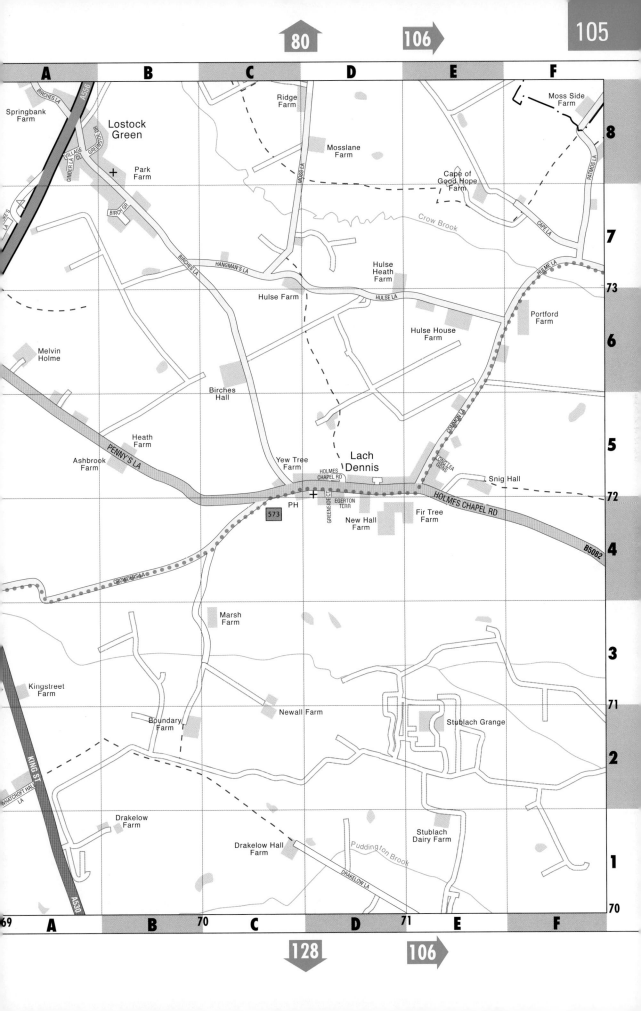

105
81

A **B** **C** **D** **E** **F**

Cheadle Farm

New Farm

CHEADLE LA

BACK LA

Back Lanes Farm

Backlane Farm

Millgate Farm

HULME LA

Hulme Covert

Bradshaw Brook

Hulme Hall

HULME HALL LA

Washlone Farm

OLD MIDDLEWICH RD

B5082

Highfield House

Allostock Hall

HOLMES CHAPEL RD

Sculshaw Green Farm

PH

BYLEY RD

B5081

Chestnut House Farm

The Croft

Stublach Farm

Earnshaw House Farm

B5081

Works

King's Lane Farm

KING'S LA

Shakerley Mere

P

M6

Crown Lane Farm

CROWN LA

B5081

Parkside Farm

PH

Swan Green

Yewtree Farm

SWAN GR

PO

BIRCHWOOD DR

CHERRY WLK

HOLLY TREE DR

ASH CL

OAK TREE LA

Birch Farm

Mast

573

BAKER'S LA

Springbank Farm

Graybrook Farm

Bradshawbrook Farm

Chapel Farm

MIDDLEWICH RD

DAMS LANE

Springfield

FOXCOVERT LA

Mill Bank Farm

Foxcover

Peover Eye

Heath Farm

HEATH LA

SANDY LA

Bradshaw House

TOWNFIELD LA

Old Mill Farm

Heath Farm

Townfield Farm

Axon's Smithy Farm

HOLE LA

Hole House

Hole House Wood

WASH LA

CHAPEL LA

Allostock

Chapel House Farm

Brookhouse Farm

BROOK VIEW

PRINCESS RD

LONDON RD

A50

Widow's Home Farm

Newplatt Wood

Sandhole Farm

Woodlands Farm

Rudheath Woods

NORTHWICH RD

SANDY LA

NEW PLATT LA

B5082

KNUTSFORD RD A50

Warrington Common

M6

A **B** **C** **D** **E** **F**

72 73 74

70 71 72 73

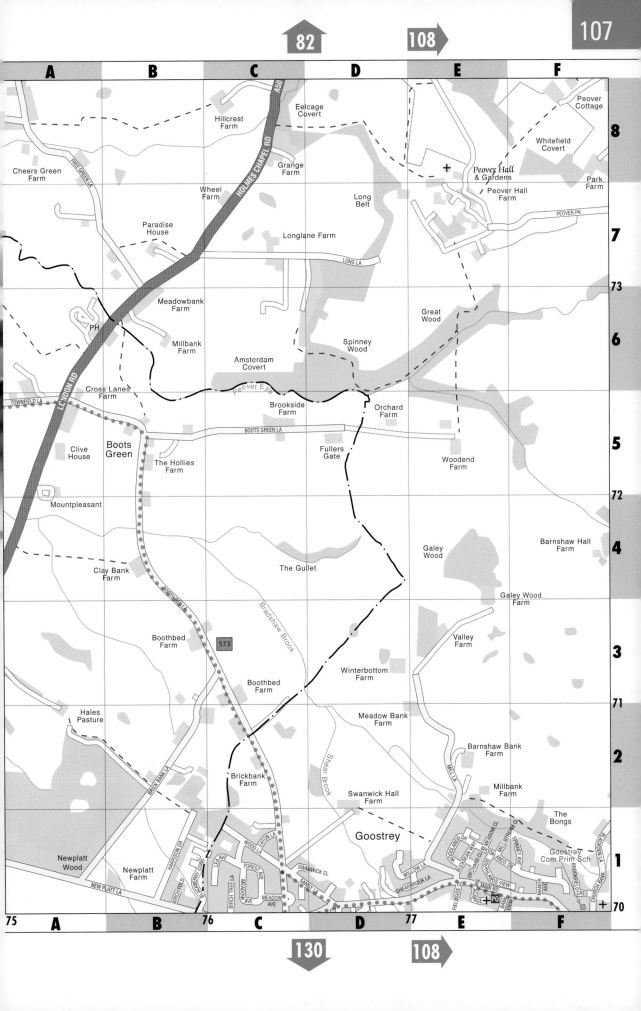

A B C D E F

8
7
73
6
5
72
4
3
71
2
1
70

Cheers Green Farm
Hillcrest Farm
Eelcage Covert
Peover Cottage
Whitefield Covert
Park Farm
FREE GREEN LA
HOLMES CHAPEL RD
A50
Grange Farm
Wheel Farm
Peover Hall & Gardens
Peover Hall Farm
PEOVER PK
Paradise House
Long Belt
Longlane Farm
LONG LA
PH
LONDON RD
Meadowbank Farm
Great Wood
Millbank Farm
Amsterdam Covert
Spinney Wood
TOWNFIELD LA
Cross Lanes Farm
Peover Eye
Brookside Farm
Orchard Farm
Boots Green
BOOTS GREEN LA
Clive House
The Hollies Farm
Fullers Gate
Woodend Farm
Mountpleasant
Barnshaw Hall Farm
Clay Bank Farm
The Gullet
Galey Wood
Galey Wood Farm
BOOTHBED LA
Bradshaw Brook
Boothbed Farm
573
Valley Farm
Boothbed Farm
Winterbottom Farm
Hales Pasture
Meadow Bank Farm
BRICK BANK LA
Shear Brook
Barnshaw Bank Farm
Millbank Farm
Brickbank Farm
Swanwick Hall Farm
The Bongs
Newplatt Wood
Newplatt Farm
Goostrey
WOODLANDS DR
BUCKBEAN CL
ORCHARD CL
MEADOW CL
BROOKLANDS CL
MILL STREAM CL
SPINNEY AVE
Goostrey Com Prim Sch
BLACKDEN LA
CHURCH BANK
HARRISON DR
BIRCH FOLD
HACKBERRY GLN
LEA AVE
WOOD LA
EATON LA
FOREST AVE
SWANWICK CL
SANDY LA
WILLOW LA
SHEARBROOK LA
SOUTHLANDS VIEW
FIELDSIDE CL
MAIN RD
BROOKLANDS DR
MANOR AVE
BROOKFIELDS CRES
NEW PLATT LA
BIRCH TREE LA
MEADOW AVE
MEADOW AVE
PO

A B C D E F

75 76 77

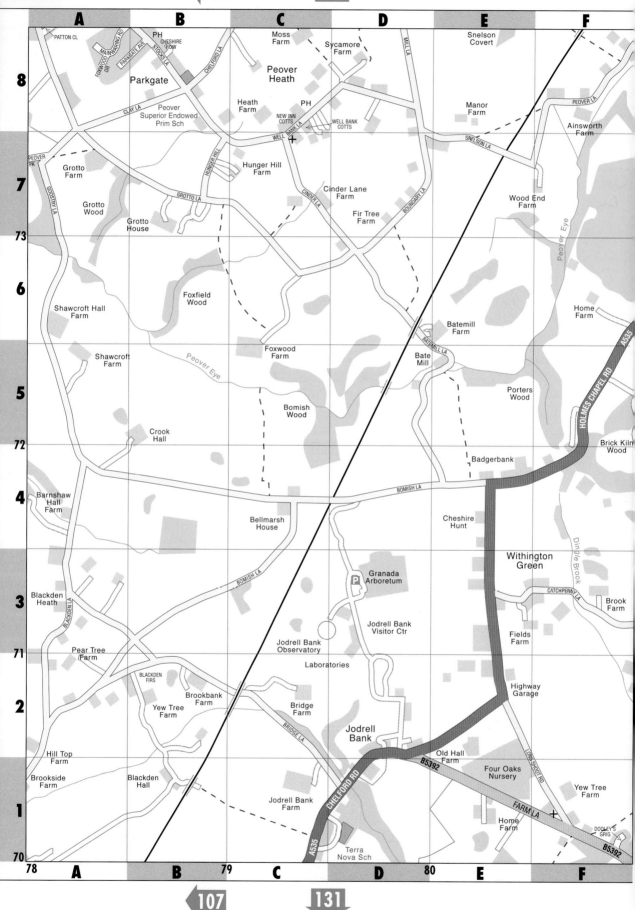

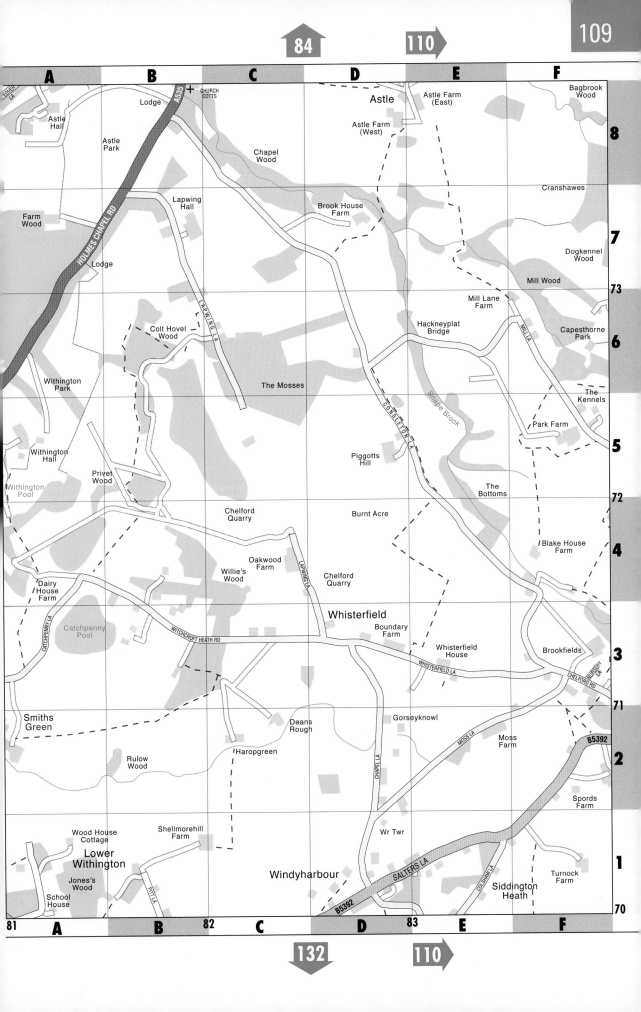

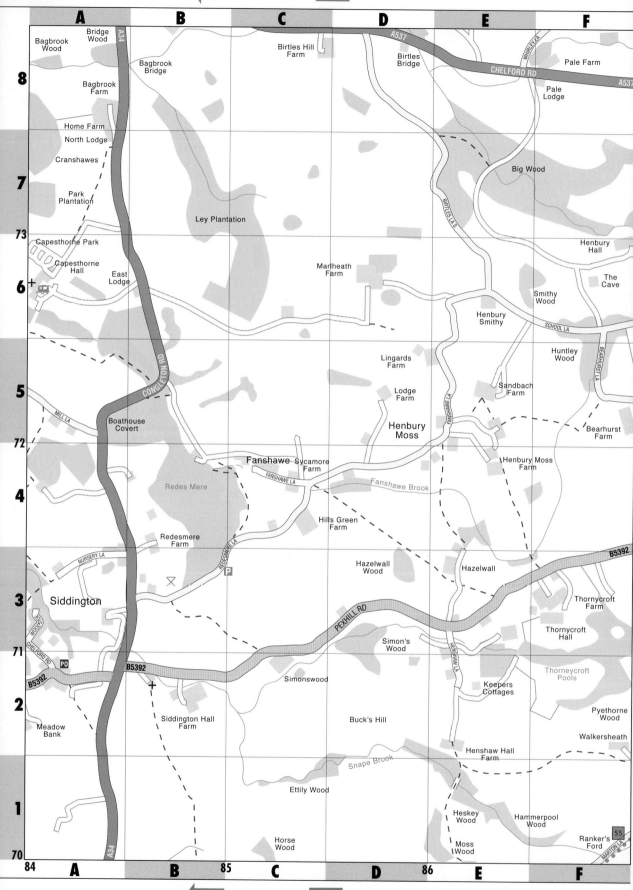

Bagbrook Wood
Bridge Wood
Bagbrook Bridge
Birtles Hill Farm
A537
Birtles Bridge
CHELFORD RD
Pale Farm
A537
WHIRLEY LA

Bagbrook Farm
Pale Lodge

Home Farm
North Lodge
Cranshawes
Big Wood

Park Plantation
Ley Plantation
BIRTLES LA S
Henbury Hall

Capesthorne Park
Marlheath Farm
The Cave

Capesthorne Hall
East Lodge
Henbury Smithy
Smithy Wood
SCHOOL LA
BEARHURST LA

CONGLETON RD
Lingards Farm
Huntley Wood

Lodge Farm
Sandbach Farm

MILL LA
Boathouse Covert
Henbury Moss
FANSHAWE LA
Bearhurst Farm

Redes Mere
Fanshawe
Sycamore Farm
Henbury Moss Farm

FANSHAWE LA
Fanshawe Brook

Redesmere Farm
Hills Green Farm

NURSERY LA
REDESMERE LA
P
Hazelwall Wood
Hazelwall
B5392

Siddington
Thornycroft Farm

PEXHILL RD
Thornycroft Hall

WOODS LA
CHELFORD RD
PO
Simon's Wood
HENSHAW LA
Thorneycroft Pools

B5392
B5392
Simonswood
Keepers Cottages
Pyethorne Wood

Meadow Bank
Siddington Hall Farm
Buck's Hill
Walkersheath

Snape Brook
Henshaw Hall Farm

Ettily Wood
Heskey Wood
Hammerpool Wood

A34
Horse Wood
Moss Wood
Ranker's Ford
MARTON LA
55

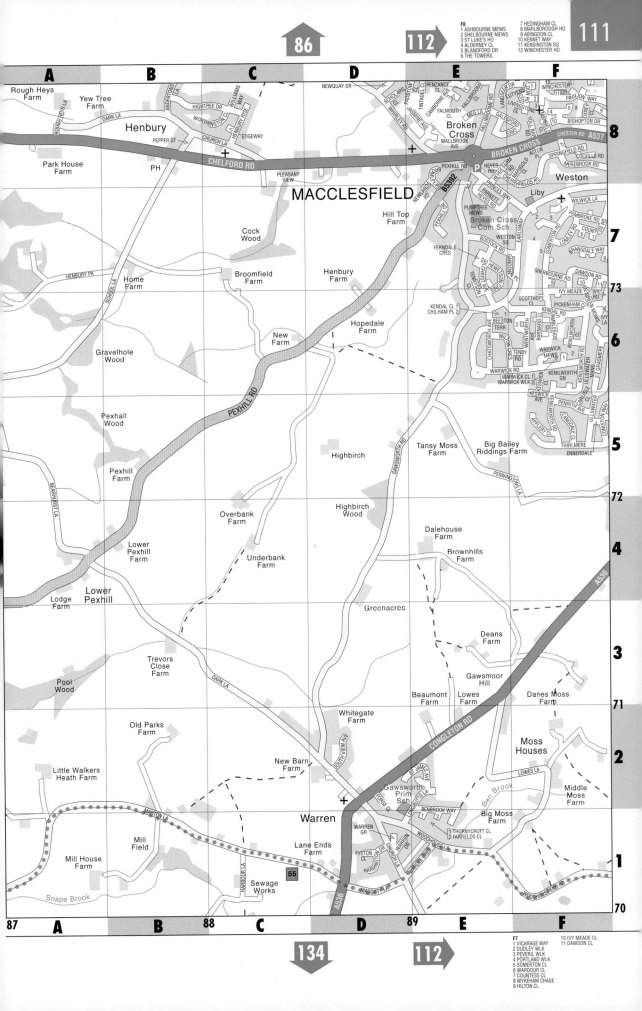

B6
1 ARMOURY TWRS
2 EVINGTON HO
3 BARRACKS SQ
4 ARMOURY COURT MEWS
5 QUEEN ANNES CT

C7
1 PETER ST W
2 ATHEY ST MILL
3 MARSDEN TERR
4 BACK PARADISE ST
5 HOLLAND ST
6 BLACKSHAW ST

D7
1 NEWGATE
2 DUKES CT
3 MARLBOROUGH CT

← 111

7 ST JOHN'S RD
8 BAKER ST
9 Parkroyal Com Sch

87

4 TOWNLEY ST
5 TOWNLEY PL
6 TOWNLEY MILL
7 WARDLE ST
8 TRAFALGAR CT
9 GRAPES ST
10 BROKEN BANKS

11 ST GEORGE'S PL
12 BRUNSWICK CT
13 LOWER EXCHANGE ST
14 Silk Mus & Her Ctr
15 Paradise Mill
Silk Mus

E7
1 BAILEY CT
2 ST PAUL'S CT
3 ST PAUL'S CT
4 HALLEFIELD DR
5 HALLEFIELD CRES
6 BROOKSIDE MILL

7 THORNYCROFT ST
8 CAWLEY ST
9 PEARSON ST
10 LOWER BANK ST
11 BUCKLOW WLK
12 KNUTSFORD ROAD WLK
13 WILMSLOW WLK

14 ALDERLEY WLK
15 ELIZABETH HO
16 PLUMLEY CL
17 STUBBS TERR
18 WINLOWE
19 BROOK STREET MILL

MACCLESFIELD

Danes Moss

Lyme Green

Sutton Lane Ends

C8
1 WILLERBY CL
2 WALKER ST
3 GROSVENOR ST
4 WESTMINSTER ST
5 STANLEY & BROCKLEHURST CT
6 COURT NO 4
7 MILLERS CT
8 MILLERS CROFT
9 BUCKDEN WAY

10 NEWBIGGIN WAY
11 SHARPLEY ST
12 BOOTHBY ST
13 GEORGES CT
14 WESTMINSTER ST
15 POYNTON ST
16 ANDERSON ST
17 SIMPSON'S CT
18 PINFOLD ST
19 REGENT & FOUNDRY CT

20 THE TOWER HO
21 LANGFORD ST
22 CHARLOTTE STREET W
23 CHARLTON ST
24 The Crown Ctr
25 EDGAR CT

D8
1 TUNNICLIFFE ST
2 CUMBERLAND ST
3 KING EDWARD RD

4 LITTLE ST
5 BRUNSWICK ST
6 CHURCH MEWS
7 STANLEY ST
8 UNICORN GATEWAY
9 CHATHAM ST
10 ST MICHAELS TERR.
11 SHORT ST
12 EXCHANGE CL
13 BACK WALLGATE

14 QUEEN VICTORIA ST
15 WELLINGTON ST
16 ALBERT PL
17 Grosvenor Sh Ctr

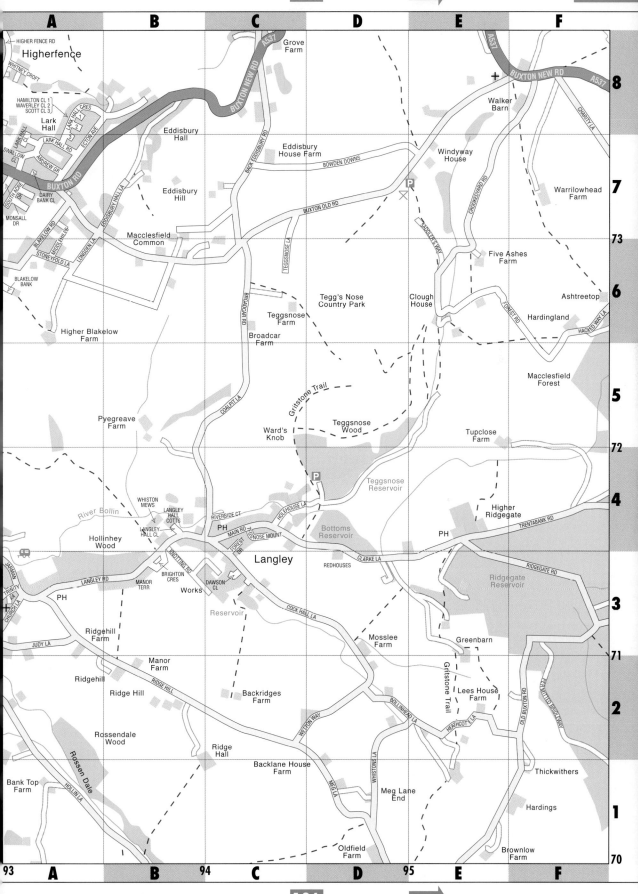

113
89

	A	B	C	D	E	F

8

Turnshawflat

A537

The Laches

Ankers Knowl Farm

ANKERS KNOWL LA

Fox Stake

Longclough Farm

A537

7

OLD BUXTON RD

BUXTON NEW RD

Hindsclough Farm

Fieldhead Farm

73

Greenways Farm

Brookhouse

HACKED WAY LA

OLD CHARITY LA

Whitehills

ANKERS LA

Long Clough

Tor Brook

6

OLD BUXTON RD

PH

Torgate Farm

Chapel House Farm

OVEN LA

Macclesfield Forest

Chambers Farm

5

Toot Hill

Bottom-of-the-Oven

72

FOREST SIDE

Torgate Hill

TRENTABANK RD

Broughs Place

4

Macclesfield Forest

Boltin Brook

Clough Brook

Dryknowle Farm

Trentabank Reservoir

STANDING STONE RD

P

3

High Ash Farm

71

Ferriser

Yarnshaw Hill

Nessit Hill

2

Buxtors Hill

Yarnshaw Brook

PERMITTED BRIDLEWAY

Dingers Hollow

P

The Vicarage

1

Highmoor Brook

Higher Barn

Vicarage Wood

High Moor

70

113
137

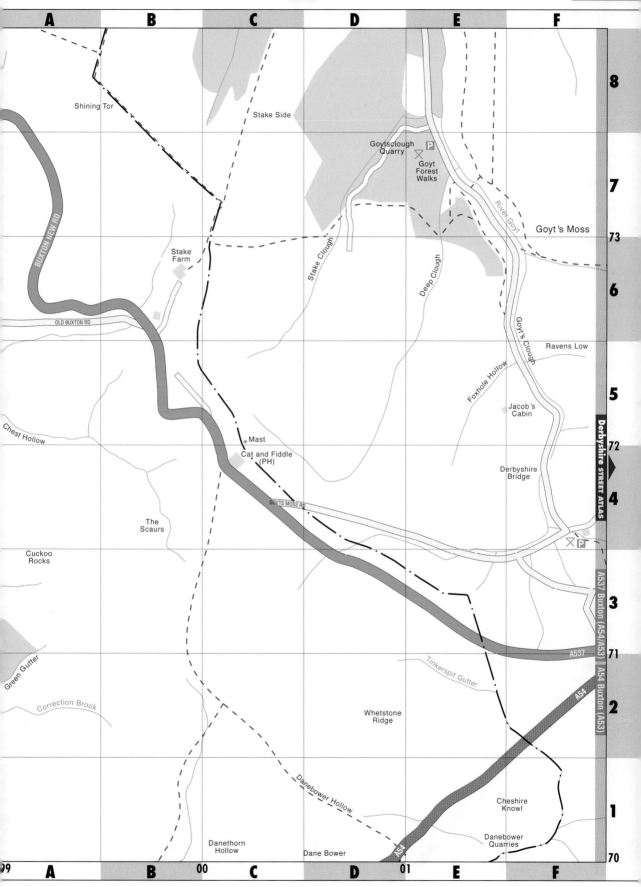

A B C D E F

8
7
73
6
5
72
4
71
3
2
1
70

A B C D E F

Shining Tor
Stake Side
Goytsclough Quarry
Goyt Forest Walks
Goyt's Moss
River Goyt
Stake Farm
Stake Clough
Deep Clough
Goyt's Clough
Ravens Low
BUXTON NEW RD
OLD BUXTON RD
Foxhole Hollow
Jacob's Cabin
Chest Hollow
Mast
Cat and Fiddle (PH)
Derbyshire Bridge
Derbyshire STREET ATLAS
The Scaurs
GOYTS MOSS RD
Cuckoo Rocks
A537 Buxton (A54/A53)
A54 Buxton (A53)
A537
Green Gutter
Tinkerspit Gutter
Correction Brook
Whetstone Ridge
A54
Cheshire Knowl
Danebower Hollow
Danebower Quarries
Danethorn Hollow
Dane Bower
A54

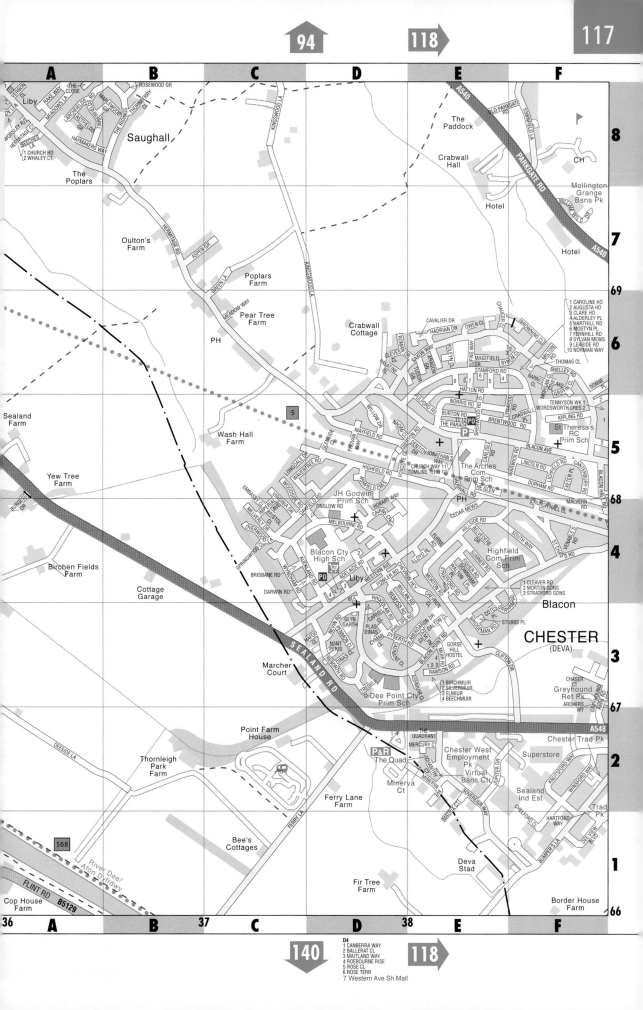

F2
1 St Werburgh's & St Columba's
RC Prim Sch

For full street detail of the highlighted area see page 237.

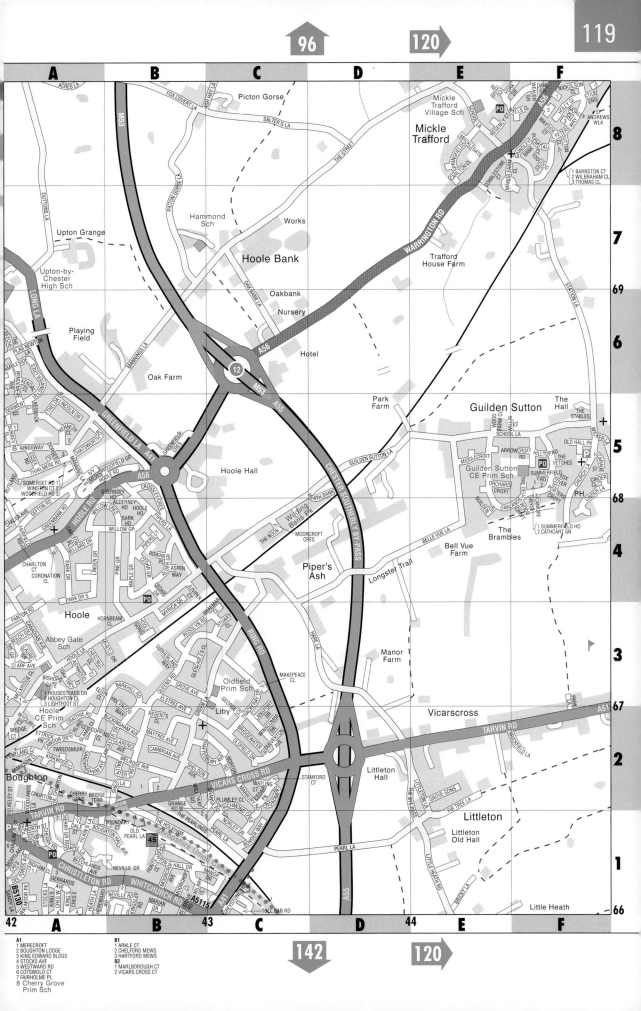

A1
1 MERECROFT
2 BOUGHTON LODGE
3 KING EDWARD BLDGS
4 STOCKS AVE
5 WESTWARD RD
6 COTSWOLD CT
7 FAIRHOLME PL
8 Cherry Grove
Prim Sch

B1
1 ARKLE CT
2 CHELFORD MEWS
3 HARTFORD MEWS
B2
1 MARLBOROUGH CT
2 VICARS CROSS CT

119
97

| | A | B | C | D | E | F |

8

LC

Holme Farm

B5132

PH

Broom Hill

BROOMHILL LA

Broomhill

Salters Brook

7

Ardmore

The Croft

THE AVENUE

BARROWMORE LA

Heath Farm

IRONS LA

Ferma La

Barrow Hill

Barrowmore Est

69

HAWKINS VIEW

HOLLOWMOOR HEATH

6

GREENFIELDS LODGE

LONG LOOMS

Great Barrow

GREYSFIELD FLATS

Barrow CE Prim Sch

LAMPITS LA

HEATH LA

MANOR PK

FERMA LA

Longster Trail

MAIN ST

VILLAGE RD

STACK YD

PO

NEW FARM CT

Barrow Hall

MILL LA

CHURCH RDS

Barrow Mill

MILL LANE COTTS

5

Oxen Bridge

Hill Farm House

CINDER LA

BARROW LA

68

THE STEADINGS

Milton Brook Lodge

Milton Brook

The Byatts

WICKER LA

4

Hillview Farm

River Gowy

Stamford Bridge

PH

LANSDOWNE RD

B5132

3

CH

TARVIN RD

Gowy Bank Farm

The Limes

Holme Bank

67

A51

Nursery

Stamford Heath

GREEN LA

Stamford Mill

MILL LANE

HOLME ST

Abbeyfield

2

COTTON LA

A51

Stamford Hollows Farm

Holme-street Hall

1

STAMFORD LA

Hollows Farm

Birch Bank Farm

Cotton Hall

66

| 45 | A | | 46 | B | C | | 47 | D | E | | F |

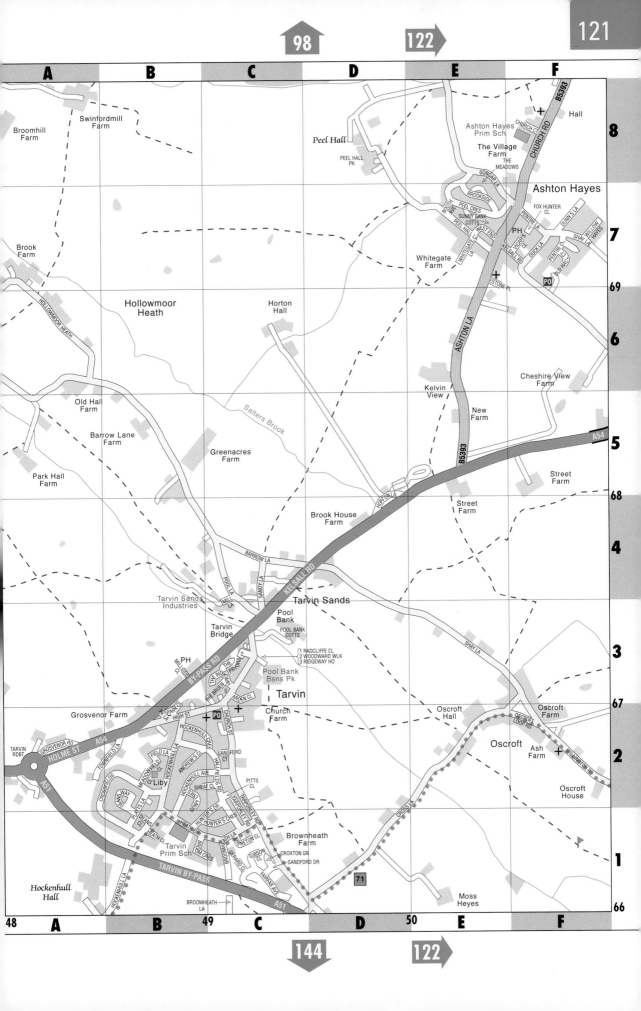

Park Farm

Ashton Hayes

Ash Wood

The Yeld Farm

Nettleford Wood

Longley Wood

The Top Lodge

Yeld Farm

Dale Covert

Mount Pleasant Gdns

Sandstone Trail

SHAY LA

Lower Longley Farm

Longley Farm

FOREST GATE LA

HOLLANDS LA

Nursery

King's Chair

SHAY LA

KELSALL BYPASS

CHESTER RD A54

MORREYS LA

NORTONS LA

YELD LA

LONGLEY LA

HALL LA

Kelsall Hall

Northwood Hall

HOLLANDS LA

BROOM'S LA

LONGLEY AVE

CLEMLEY CL

DINGLE

HILLCREST RD

PH

PRIMROSE HILL

Weldon Farm

Holly Farm

OLD COACH RD

DUTTONS LA

GRUB LA

EDALE DR

CHESTER RD

SWALLOW DR

WOODLAND RISE

A54

Childwall Farm

CHAPEL GN

EGERTON CT

DOG LA

REDHILL RD

EARLE'S LA

CHURCH BANK

BRAMLEY CT

ORCHARD WAY

QUARRY LA

Primrose Hill

PO

PH

KINGS WOOD WLK

THE DELL

ELIZABETH CL

Delamere Farm

CHURCH ST N

CHESTER RD

SIMS DR

BLACKBIRD

FIRECREST WAY

HALLOWS CL

THISTLE

CHURCH ST

BROOK DR

KELSBORROW WAY

FOX HILL

Kings Gate

Kelsall

Lower Grange Farm

PH

BRAMBLING CL

Kelsall Prim Sch

HALLOWSGATE CT

CARTER AVE

HILLSIDE RD

CASTLE CL

Castle Hill

ROOKERY CL

PASTURE CT

FLAT LA

THE WYND

BROOKSIDE

MEADOW BANK

THE PADDOCKS

WILLINGTON LA

GREEN LA

Kelsborrow Castle

Forest House

Hallowsgate

WASTE LA

THE COMMON

Boothsdale

Birch Hill

TIRLEY LA

Roughlow Farm

Common Farm

WILLINGTON RD

BOOTHSDALE

PH

ROUGH LOW

Pearl Hole

Beechs Farm

COMMON LA

GOOSEBERRY LA

Sandstone Trail

Manor Farm

WILLINGTON CNR

Weetwood Grange

Weetwood Common

WILLINGTON RD

MILL LA

71

OAK TREE CT

Willington Wood

MILL LANE A

CH

Pryors Hayes

Weetwood Farm

Willington-mill Farm

The Belt

Home Farm

Willington Hall

Rock Farm

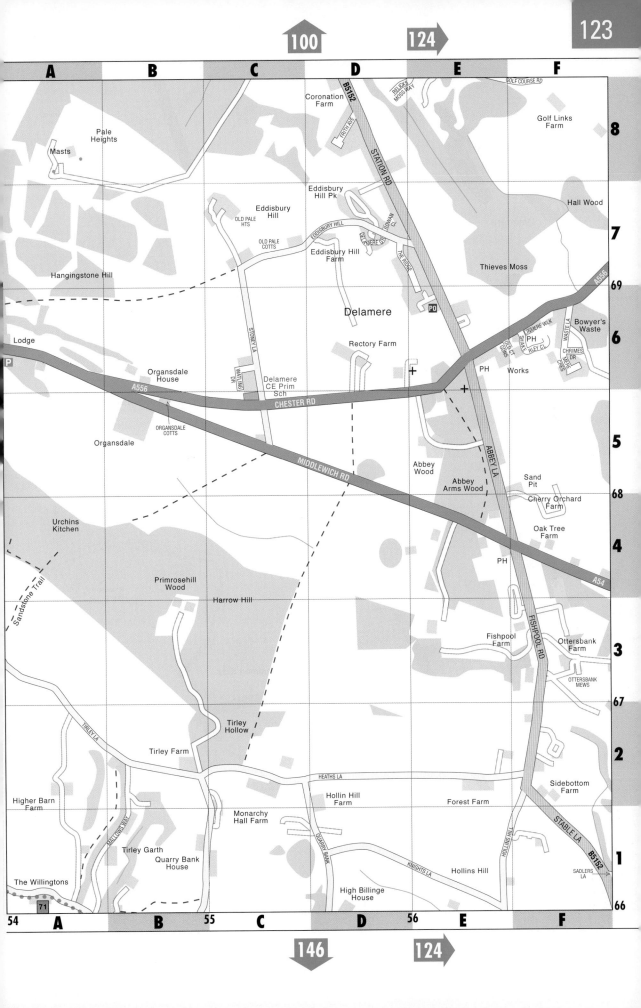

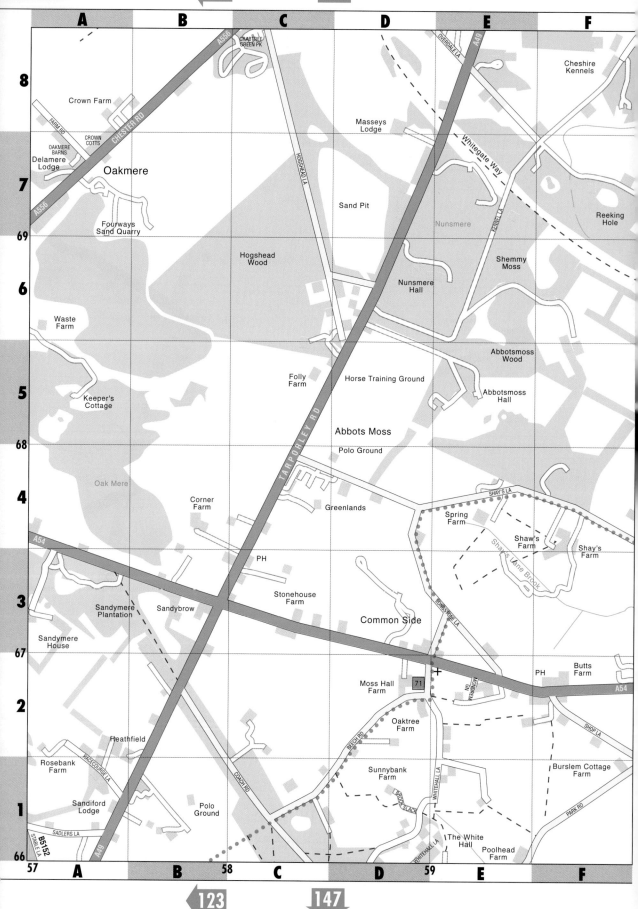

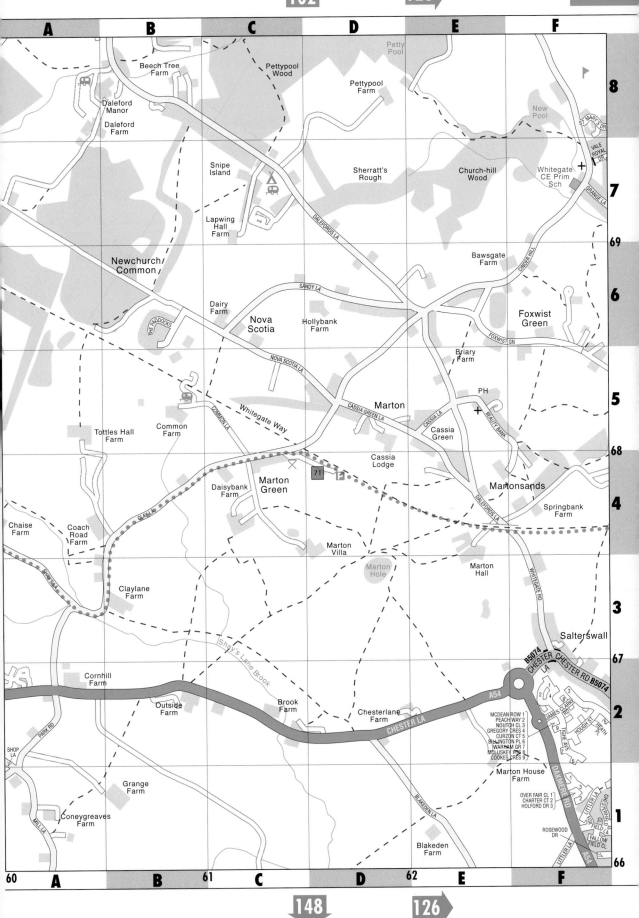

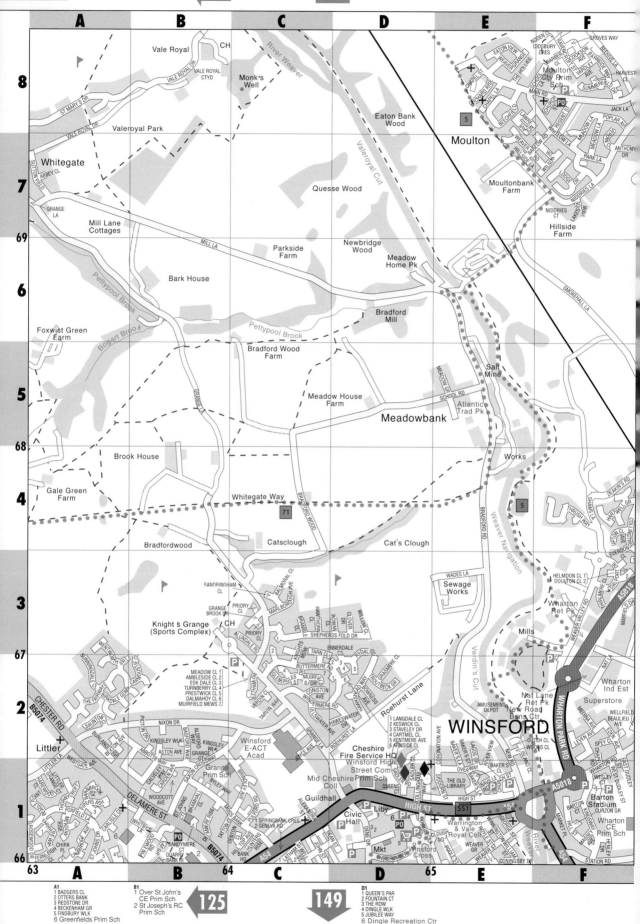

A1
1 BADGERS CL
2 OTTERS BANK
3 REDSTONE DR
4 BECKENHAM GR
5 FINSBURY WLK
6 Greenfields Prim Sch

B1
1 Over St John's
  CE Prim Sch
2 St Joseph's RC
  Prim Sch

D1
1 QUEEN'S PAR
2 FOUNTAIN CT
3 THE ROW
4 DINGLE WLK
5 JUBILEE WAY
6 Dingle Recreation Ctr

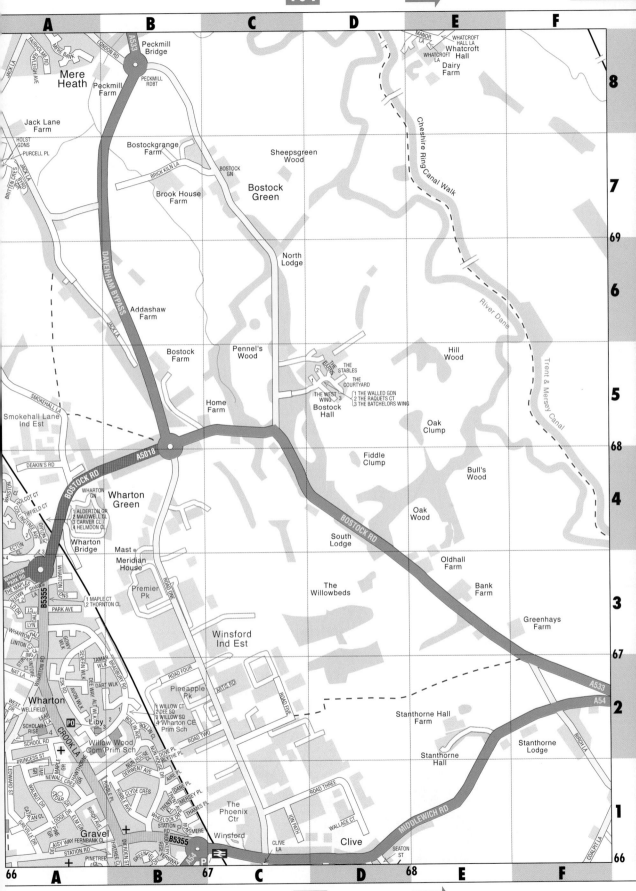

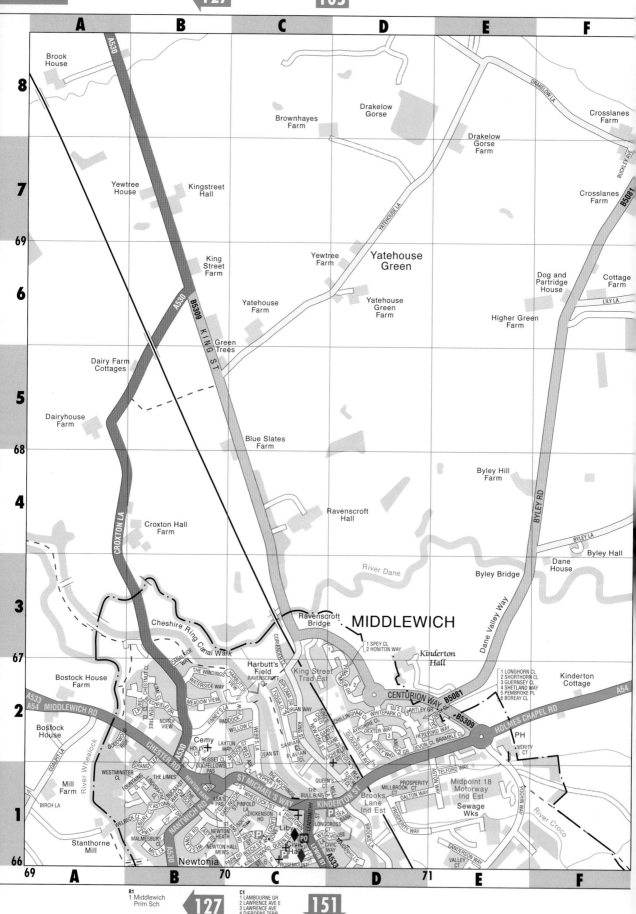

	A	B	C	D	E	F

8

Brook House

Drakelow Gorse

Brownhayes Farm

Crosslanes Farm

7

Yewtree House

Kingstreet Hall

Drakelow Gorse Farm

Crosslanes Farm

69

6

King Street Farm

Yewtree Farm

Yatehouse Green

Dog and Partridge House

Cottage Farm

Yatehouse Farm

Yatehouse Green Farm

Higher Green Farm

Green Trees

KING ST

5

Dairy Farm Cottages

Dairyhouse Farm

Blue Slates Farm

68

CROXTON LA

Byley Hill Farm

4

Croxton Hall Farm

Ravenscroft Hall

BYLEY RD

Byley LA

Byley Hall

Dane House

River Dane

Byley Bridge

3

Cheshire Ring Canal Walk

Ravenscroft Bridge

MIDDLEWICH

1 Spey Cl
2 Honiton Way

Kinderton Hall

Dane Valley Way

67

Bostock House Farm

Harbutt's Field

Ravenscroft CL

King Street Trad Est

CENTURION WAY   B5081

Kinderton Cottage

1 Longhorn Cl
2 Shorthorn Cl
3 Guernsey Cl
4 Shetland Way
5 Pembroke Pl
6 Boreay Cl

A54

2

A533
A54   MIDDLEWICH RD

CHESTER RD

Bostock House

HOLMES CHAPEL RD

B5309

PH

VERITY CT

Mill Farm

BIRCH LA

Midpoint 18 Motorway Ind Est

Brooks Lane Ind Est

1

ST MICHAEL'S WAY

NANTWICH RD

KINDERTON ST

Sewage Wks

River Croco

Stanthorne Mill

66

Newtonia

A533

69	A	**70**	B	C	**70**	D	**71**	E	F

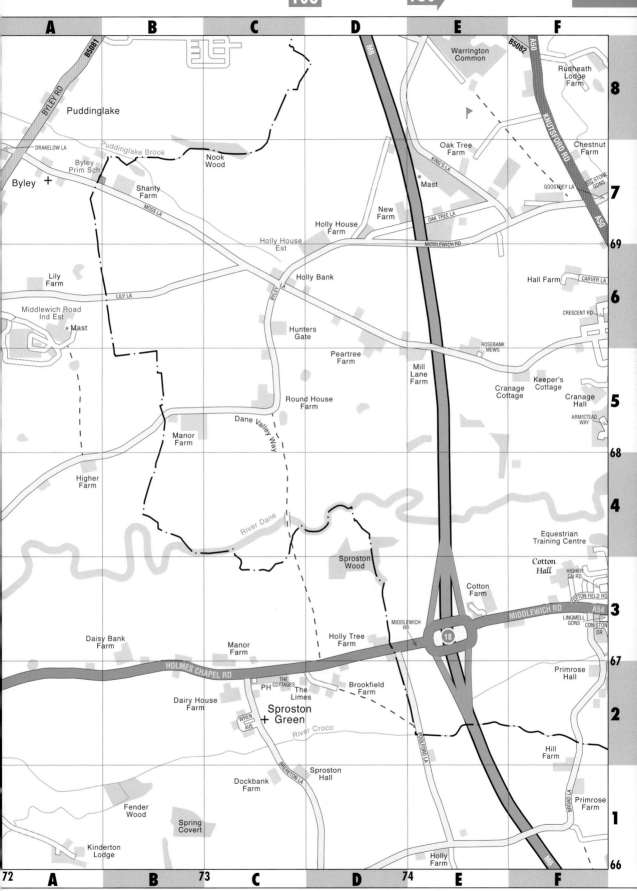

A　B　C　D　E　F

8
7
69
6
5
68
4
3
67
2
1
66

B5081
BYLEY RD
Puddinglake
DRAKELOW LA
Puddinglake Brook
Byley Prim Sch
Byley
Shanty Farm
Nook Wood
MOSS LA
Lily Farm
LILY LA
Middlewich Road Ind Est
Mast
Manor Farm
Higher Farm
BYLEY LA
Holly House Est
Holly House Farm
Holly Bank
Hunters Gate
Peartree Farm
Round House Farm
Dane Valley Way
River Dane
Daisy Bank Farm
Manor Farm
HOLMES CHAPEL RD
Dairy House Farm
PH
THE COTTAGES
The Limes
WREN AVE
Sproston Green
River Croco
BRERETON LA
Dockbank Farm
Sproston Hall
Fender Wood
Spring Covert
Kinderton Lodge

M6
New Farm
Mast
OAK TREE LA
MIDDLEWICH RD
Mill Lane Farm
Sproston Wood
Holly Tree Farm
MIDDLEWICH RD
18
Cotton Farm
Brookfield Farm
POLFORD LA
Holly Farm

Warrington Common
B5082
A50
KNUTSFORD RD
Rudheath Lodge Farm
Oak Tree Farm
KING'S LA
Chestnut Farm
GOOSTREY LA
BIG STONE GDNS
A50
Hall Farm
CARVER LA
CRESCENT RD
ROSEBANK MEWS
Cranage Cottage
Keeper's Cottage
Cranage Hall
ARMISTEAD WAY
Equestrian Training Centre
Cotton Hall
HIGHER GN RD
COTTON FIELD RD
MIDDLEWICH RD
A54
LINGMELL GDNS
CONISTON DR
Primrose Hall
Hill Farm
BROAD LA
Primrose Farm
M6

72　73　74
A　B　C　D　E　F

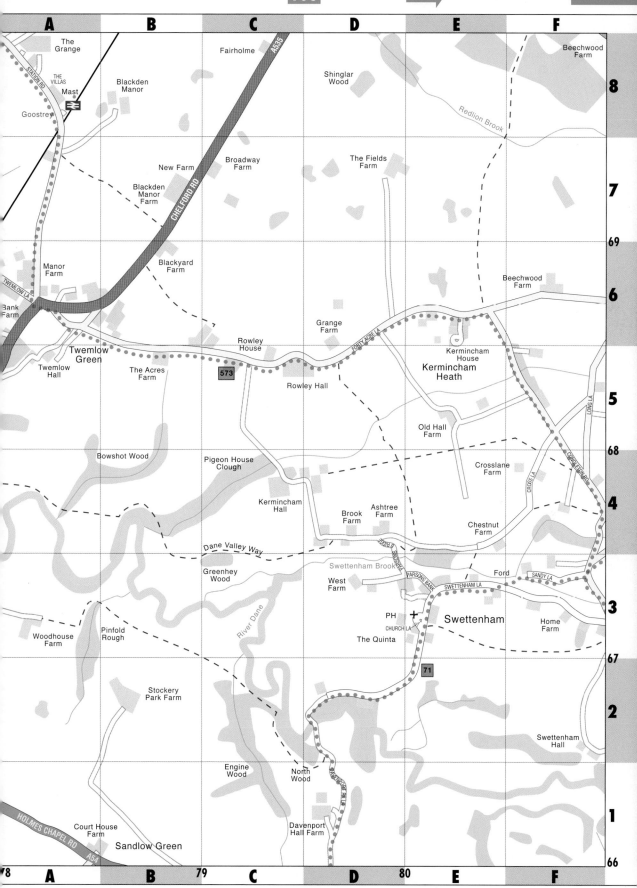

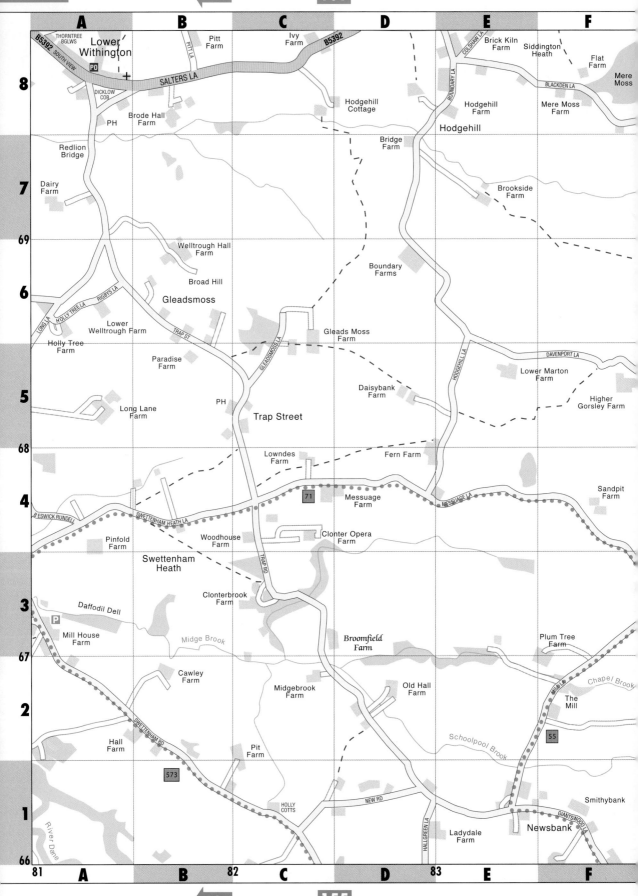

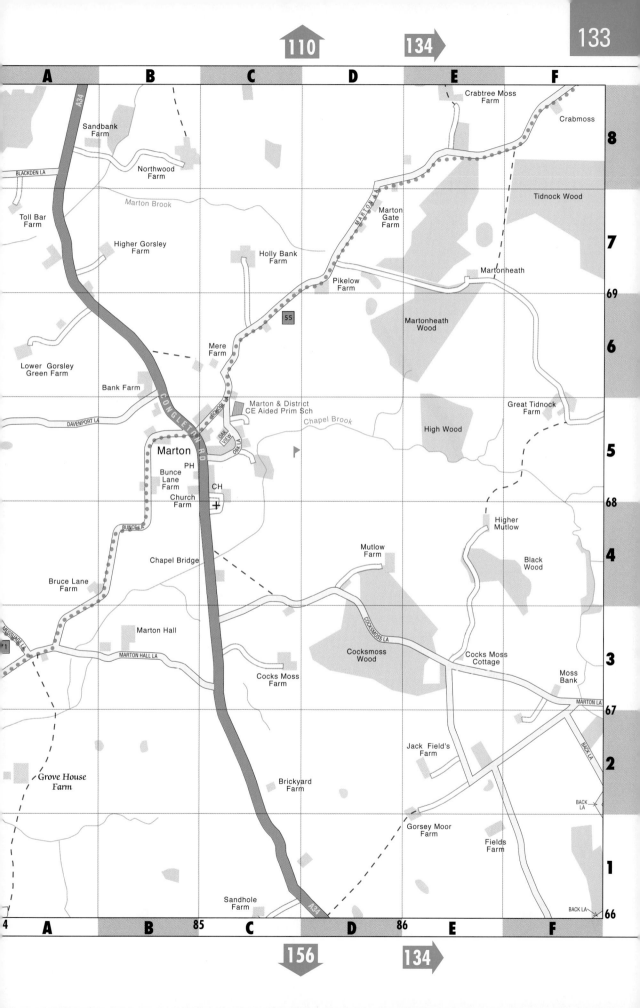

110
134

A **B** **C** **D** **E** **F**

8

Crabtree Moss Farm

Crabmoss

Sandbank Farm

Northwood Farm

BLACKDEN LA

Tidnock Wood

Marton Brook

Toll Bar Farm

MARTON LA

Marton Gate Farm

7

Higher Gorsley Farm

Holly Bank Farm

Martonheath

69

Pikelow Farm

55

Martonheath Wood

6

Lower Gorsley Green Farm

Mere Farm

Bank Farm

CONGLETON RD

Great Tidnock Farm

DAVENPORT LA

Marton & District CE Aided Prim Sch

Chapel Brook

High Wood

SCHOOL LA

OAK VIEW

OAK LA

Marton

5

PH

Bunce Lane Farm

Church Farm

CH

Higher Mutlow

68

BUNCE LR

Chapel Bridge

Mutlow Farm

Black Wood

4

Bruce Lane Farm

COCKSMOSS LA

Marton Hall

Cocksmoss Wood

Cocks Moss Cottage

Moss Bank

MESSUAGE LA

1

MARTON HALL LA

Cocks Moss Farm

MARTON LA

67

Jack Field's Farm

BACK LA

2

Grove House Farm

Brickyard Farm

BACK LA

Gorsey Moor Farm

Fields Farm

1

Sandhole Farm

A34

BACK LA

66

4 **A** **B** 85 **C** **D** 86 **E** **F**

156
134

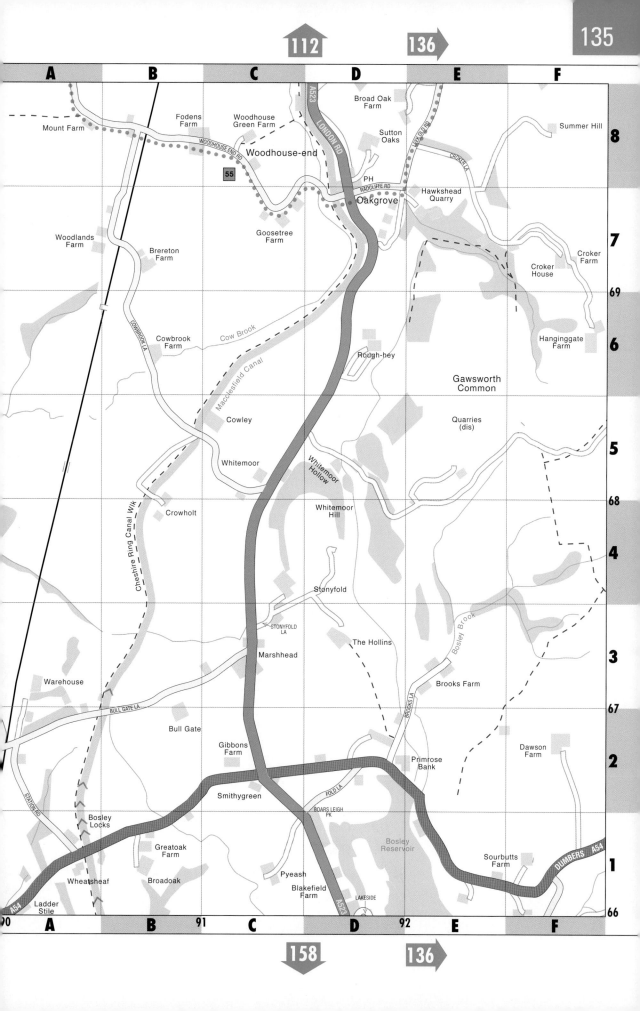

A B C D E F

8
Mount Farm
Fodens Farm
Woodhouse Green Farm
Broad Oak Farm
Sutton Oaks
Summer Hill
WOODHOUSE END RD
Woodhouse-end
55
LONDON RD
A523
LEEK OLD RD
CROKER LA
PH
RADCLIFFE RD
Oakgrove
Hawkshead Quarry

7
Woodlands Farm
Brereton Farm
Goosetree Farm
Croker House
Croker Farm
69
COWBROOK LA
Cowbrook Farm
Cow Brook
Hanginggate Farm
6
Rough-hey
Gawsworth Common
Macclesfield Canal
Cowley
Quarries (dis)
5
Whitemoor
Whitemoor Hollow
68
Cheshire Ring Canal Wlk
Crowholt
Whitemoor Hill
4
Stonyfold
Bosley Brook
3
STONYFOLD LA
Marshhead
The Hollins
Brooks Farm
Warehouse
BROOKS LA
67
BULL GATE LA
Bull Gate
Dawson Farm
2
STATION RD
Gibbons Farm
Primrose Bank
Smithygreen
FOLD LA
Bosley Locks
BOARS LEIGH PK
Bosley Reservoir
1
Greatoak Farm
Pyeash
Sourbutts Farm
DUMBERS A54
Wheatsheaf
Broadoak
Blakefield Farm
A523
A54
Ladder Stile
LAKESIDE
66

90   91   92
A B C D E F

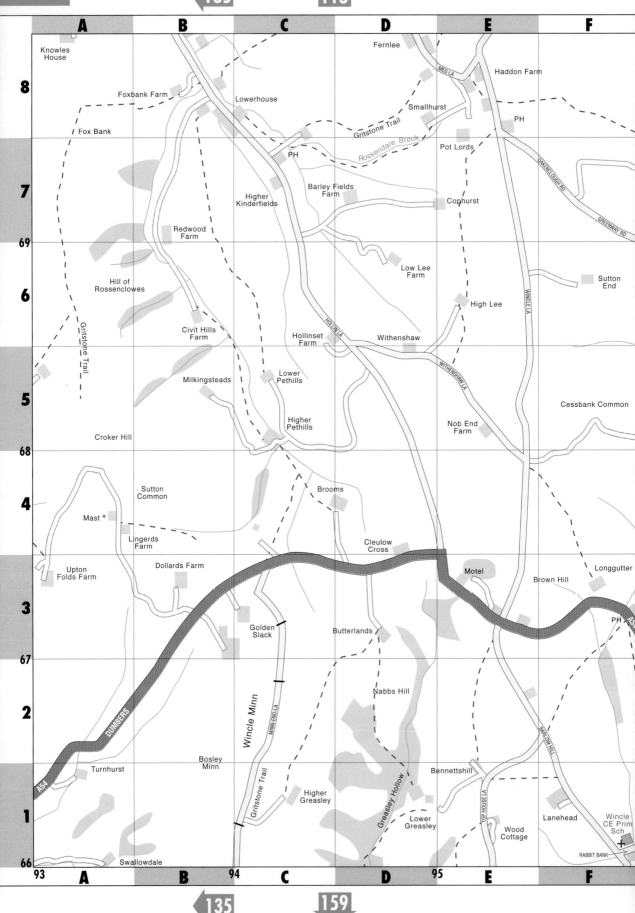

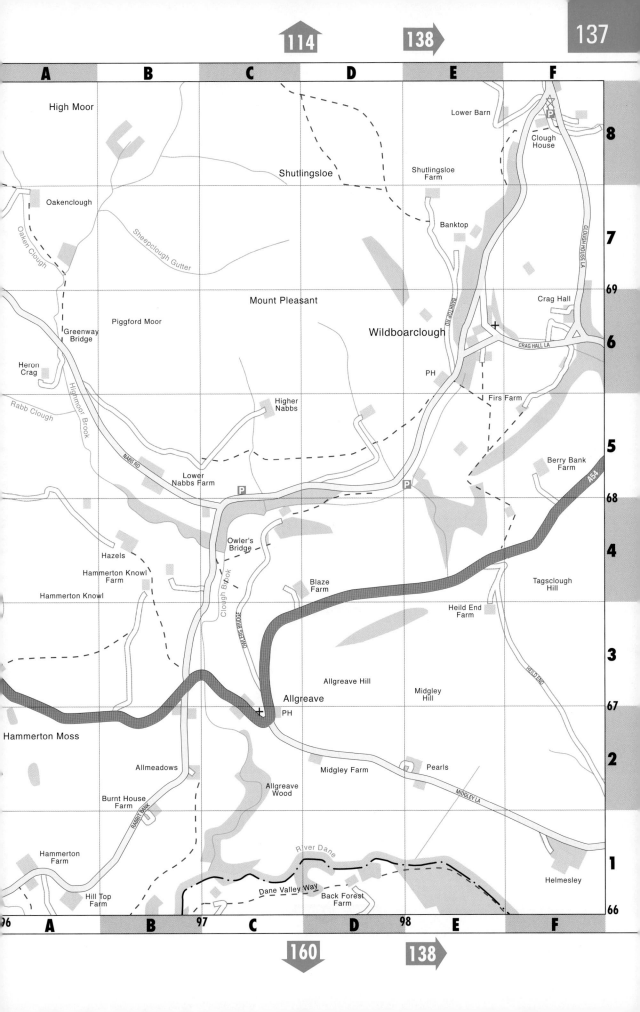

A   B   C   D   E   F

High Moor

Lower Barn

Clough House

8

Oakenclough

Shutlingsloe

Shutlingsloe Farm

Banktop

7

69

Mount Pleasant

Crag Hall

Greenway Bridge

Piggford Moor

Wildboarclough

Heron Crag

PH

Firs Farm

6

Rabb Clough

Higher Nabbs

Berry Bank Farm

Lower Nabbs Farm

5

68

Owler's Bridge

Hazels

Blaze Farm

Heild End Farm

Tagsclough Hill

4

Hammerton Knowl Farm

Hammerton Knowl

Allgreave Hill

Midgley Hill

3

67

Allgreave

PH

Hammerton Moss

Allmeadows

Midgley Farm

Pearls

2

Burnt House Farm

Allgreave Wood

Hammerton Farm

River Dane

Helmesley

1

Hill Top Farm

Dane Valley Way

Back Forest Farm

66

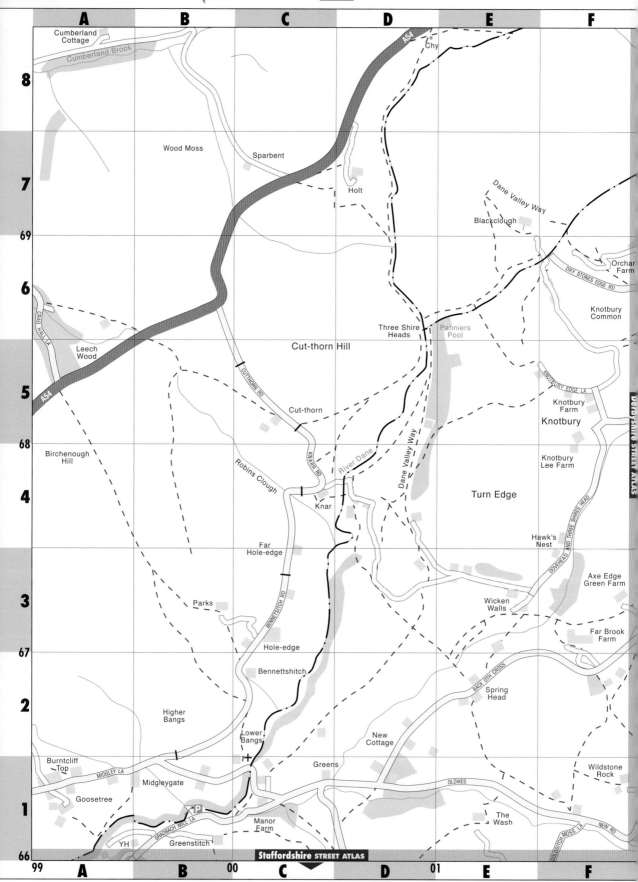

A | B | C | D | E | F

8

Cumberland
Cottage

Cumberland Brook

Wood Moss

Sparbent

A54

Chy

7

Holt

Dane Valley Way

Blackclough

Orchar
Farm

69

DRY STONES EDGE RD

6

CRAG HALL LA

Leech
Wood

Three Shire
Heads

Panniers
Pool

Knotbury
Common

Cut-thorn Hill

KNOTBURY EDGE LA

5

A54

CUTTHORN RD

Cut-thorn

Knotbury
Farm

Knotbury

68

Birchenough
Hill

Robins Clough

KNARR RD

River Dane

Dane Valley Way

Knotbury
Lee Farm

4

Knar

Turn Edge

Far
Hole-edge

BENNETTSTITCH RD

Hawk's
Nest

DOVEHEAD AND THREE SHIRES HEAD

Axe Edge
Green Farm

3

Parks

Hole-edge

Wicken
Walls

Far Brook
Farm

67

Bennettshitch

BACK O'TH CROSS

Spring
Head

2

Higher
Bangs

Lower
Bangs

New
Cottage

Burntcliff
Top

MIDGLEY LA

Greens

OLDIKES

Wildstone
Rock

1

Goosetree

Midgleygate

P

Manor
Farm

The
Wash

GOLDSITCH MOSS LA

NEW RD

66

YH

GRADBACH MILL LA

Greenstitch

99 | A | B | 00 | C | D | 01 | E | F

Derbyshire STREET ATLAS

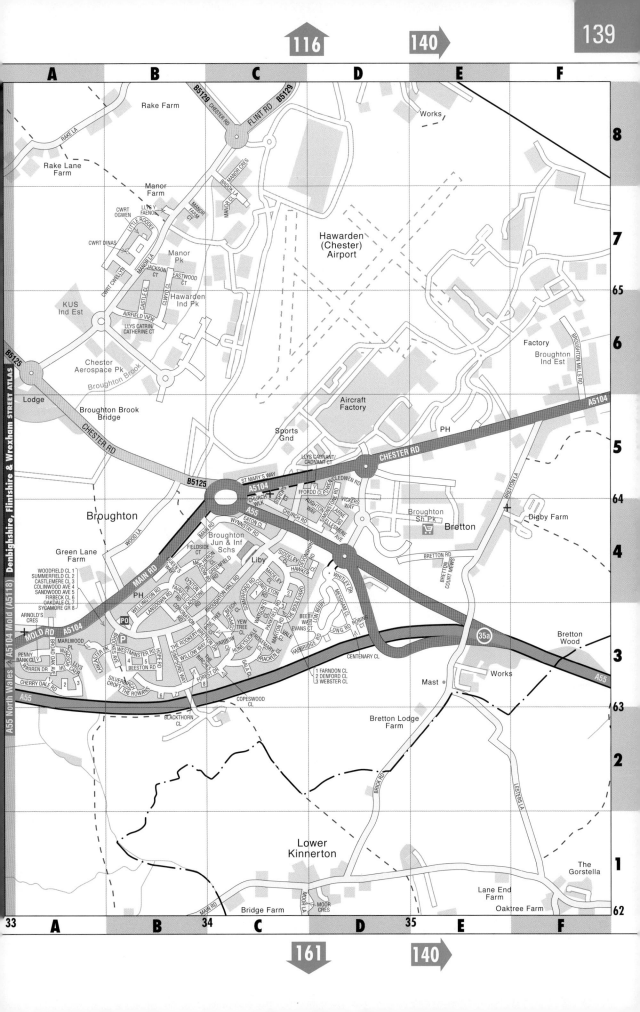

139 117

E6
1 HENRY WOOD CT
2 RHODFA LLYN
3 St Anthony's RC Prim Sch
4 Wood Memorial Prim Sch

F6
1 GUILDFORD CL
2 DOWNSFIELD RD
3 SUNBURY CRES
4 ABINGDON CRES
5 LLYS RHUDDLAN/RHUDDLAN CT
6 RHODFAR BONT

A B C D E F

8

Higher Ferry
Ferry House
B5129
FLINT RD
FERRY LA
Top Farm
BUMPER LA
Border House

NORTH ST
SALTNEY TERR
EWART ST

7

SALTNEY FERRY RD
B5129
River Dee/Afon Dyfrdwy
568
Riverside Trad Pk
Facit Glen Ind Est
MONTROSE CT 1
CHURCHSIDE WLK 2
DONNINGTON WAY 3
LEARNERS WAY 4

Parc Ddiwydiannol/Y Ffin/The Borders Ind Pk
Borders 2 Ind Pk
Chesterbank Bsns Pk
Brymau Four Trad Est
Brymau Three Trad Est
Brymau Two Trad Est
Brymau One Trad Est
Saltney Bsns Cre
CWAT
CERWAIN
RIVER LA
KELSALL CT
CHESTER ST
CURZON
CURZON CT
MT PLEASANT

65

BRADSHAW AVE
MAINWARING AVE
KYNASTON DR
BELMONT DR
MAYOR AVE
ST DAVID'S TERR
McCLELLAND
MILLERS PK
POPPY FIELD PK
St Davids Ret Pk
Central Trad Est
BRIDGE ST
St Davids
MARLEY WAY
MAKERS RDW
CHIUS CT
HIGH ST
A5104
SHREWSBURY WAY
CORONATION
TELFORD WAY
WENLOCK RD
ST MARKS RD
ASHTON DR
KINGSWINFORD RD
P
PO

6

DELTA CT
LEYLAND DR
PO
CHESTER RD
Saltney Ferry Cty Prim Sch
A5104
CARLTON AVE
HOWARD RD
NORTON AVE
ENGLEFIELD AVE
LINDEN GR
MOORCROFT MEWS
SALISBURY AVE
DEVA THE NOOK
AVE GR
BELGRAVE AVE
George Kenyon MEWS
THE ORCHARDS
STANLEY PK CT
ASHLEIGH CL
MAES-Y-COED
Liby
Wks
LINNELS RANDLESTOR
MERCER WAY
SHREWSM RAY
WESTBURY WAY
WENLOCK RD
CRAUFORD RD
HENLEY RD
OXFORD RD
REDHILL RD
LYNTON
Well House Farm

Saltney
SANDY LA
CELYN CRES
CONWAY CL
MARKY RD
PADRON
AYM QU
MAPLE GR
OAK GR
GELLI DDERW
BEECHWOOD RD
VICTORIA
BLOSSOM WAY
IFFORD Y BLODAU
IRVING'S CRES
REDWOOD
LABURNUM GR
EATON GR
BEAUMONT
BARWOODS DR
OAK AVE
ELM SQ
POPLAR RD
HOLLY
Lache Prim Sch

5

Hope's Place
CHESTER (DEVA)
Sandy Lane Farm
MOUNTAIN VIEW
BOUNDARY LA
MINKERTON
HALKYN CL
SHANNON CL
CLUEY PK
STANLEY PK
STANLEY PK CT
LOFT CL
BEAVER CL
WEYBOURNE
CAPELAND
TATTON
SHERINGHAM
AVONLEA CL
ELGER DR
SYCAMORE DR
WINCHESTER
BIRCH RD
CLOVER LA
CLOVER PL
LEYFIELD
DANEFELD RD
KINGS CL
LARKSPUR CL

Lache
COLCHESTER SQ

64

Bretton Hall
Greenlane Crossing
MEDLAR CL
CIRCULAR DR
ROWCLIFFE CT
LONSDALE CL

4

Balderton Brook
The Lache Eyes
LACHE LA
GREEN LA
BARONY WAY
FORGE WAY
LACHE HALL CRES
SMITHY PATHWAY
HAYMAKERS
RAMSDALE CT
GREENACRE RD
WHALDON CL

3

A55
BRETTON WOOD
LACHE LA

63

2

CHESTER SOUTHERLY BY-PASS
Decoy Farm
A55
Common Farm

1

Balderton
Balderton Lodge
LC
LACHE LA
BALDERTON GL
ROUGHLYN CRES
MARLSTON CT
Roughhill
Two Mile House
A483 WREXHAM RD

Gorstella

62

36 A B 37 C D 38 E F

For full street detail of the highlighted area see page 237.

118

142

141

A B C D E F

8

DEE HTS
RIVERSIDE
Dee Banks
Specl Sch

Queen's Park
Earl's Eye

Roodee
Chester Race Course
237
568

Chester Castle
Mus
Ct Co Hall

CHESTER
(DEVA)

Handbridge

7

B5130

River Dee
Curzon Park

Westminster Park

Liby
1 Compton Pl
2 Kensington Rd
3 Waltham Pl
4 Kensington Cl

Overleigh St Mary's CE Prim Sch
Cemy

West Cheshire Coll

The Roman Catholic High Sch

65

64

St Clare's RC Prim Sch
Lache Prim Sch

The Grosvenor (Private)

Ash Grove Farm

Belgrave Prim Sch

Chester Approach

Meadow Farm

Heronbridge

River Dee

Water Works

6

5

Marlston Heyes Farm

The King's Sch

Fir Tree Farm

63

Moat Farm

P&R PARK AND RIDE

Chester Bsns Pk
Hilliards Ct
Honeycomb

The Glebe

Half Moon Plantation

Eccleston CE Prim Sch

Eccleston

4

3

2

A55

Hotel

CHESTER SOUTHERLY BY-PASS

Mill Hill House

RAKE LA

Eccleston Hill
Lodge

Eccleston Ferry Farm

1

The Rake

Hill Farm

62

39 A B 40 C D 41 E F

142

A8
1 SANDY LA
2 WALMOOR PK
3 EDGEWOOD
4 STOCKS AVE
5 DRYERSFIELD

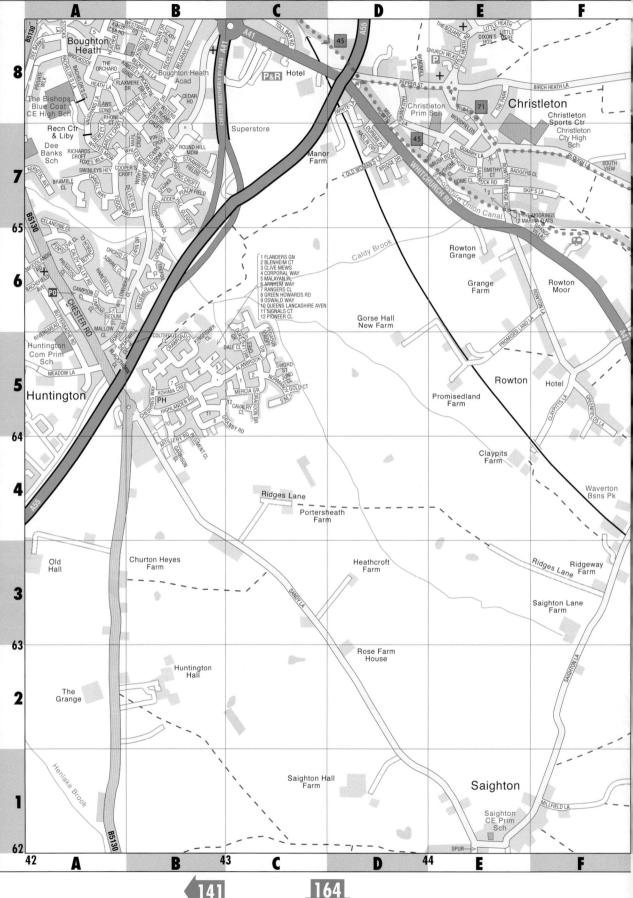

141
119
141
164

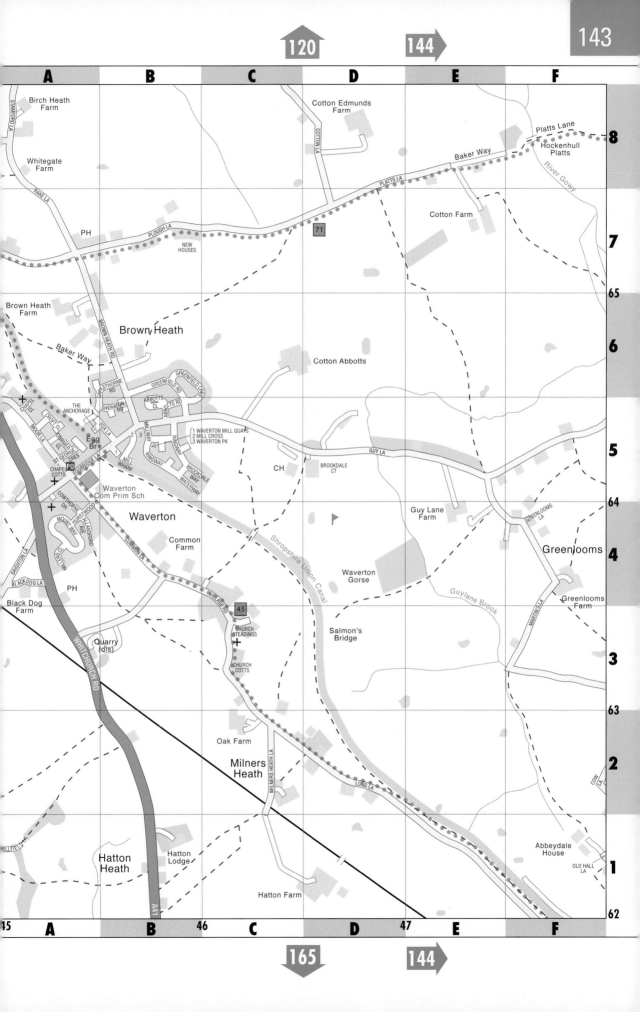

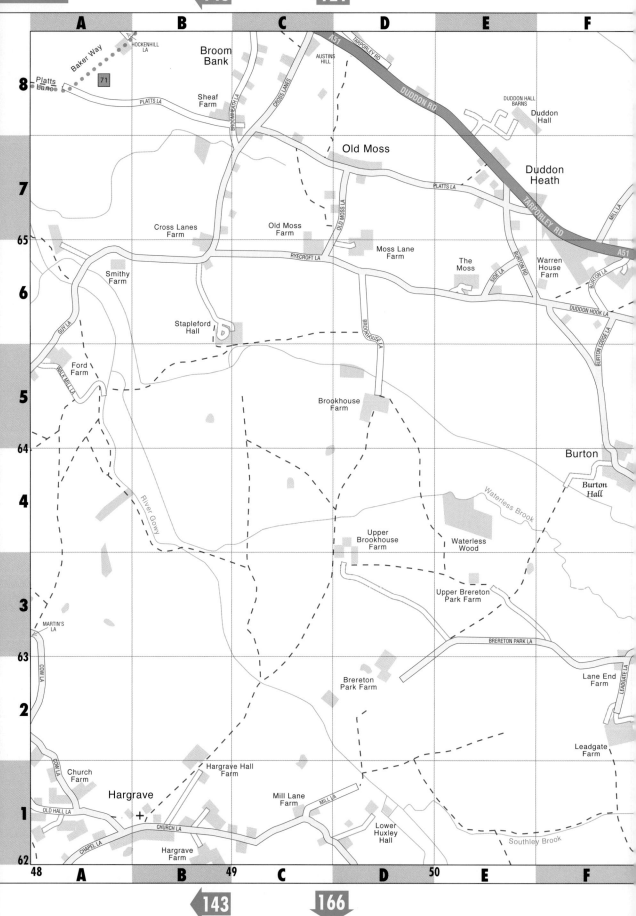

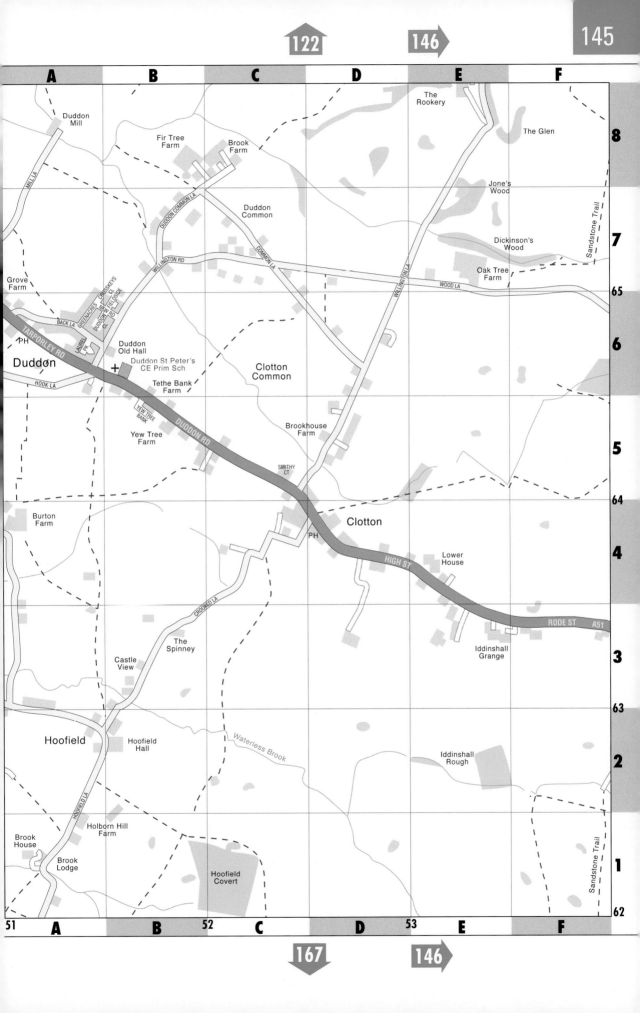

8

The Rookery

Duddon Mill

Fir Tree Farm

Brook Farm

The Glen

MILL LA

Jone's Wood

DUDDON COMMON LA

Duddon Common

7

Dickinson's Wood

WILLINGTON RD

COMMON LA

Oak Tree Farm

WILLINGTON LA

WOOD LA

65

Grove Farm

GREENACRES

CROSKEYS

DUDDON NEW RD

FIELDSIDE

BACK LA

6

TARPORLEY RD

PH

LAUREL PK

Duddon Old Hall

Duddon St Peter's CE Prim Sch

Duddon

Clotton Common

HOOK LA

Tethe Bank Farm

YEW TREE BANK

DUDDON RD

Yew Tree Farm

Brookhouse Farm

5

SMITHY CT

64

Burton Farm

Clotton

4

PH

HIGH ST

Lower House

CROOKED LA

RODE ST

A51

The Spinney

Iddinshall Grange

3

Castle View

63

Hoofield

Hoofield Hall

Waterless Brook

2

Iddinshall Rough

HOOFIELD LA

Brook House

Holborn Hill Farm

Sandstone Trail

Brook Lodge

Hoofield Covert

1

62

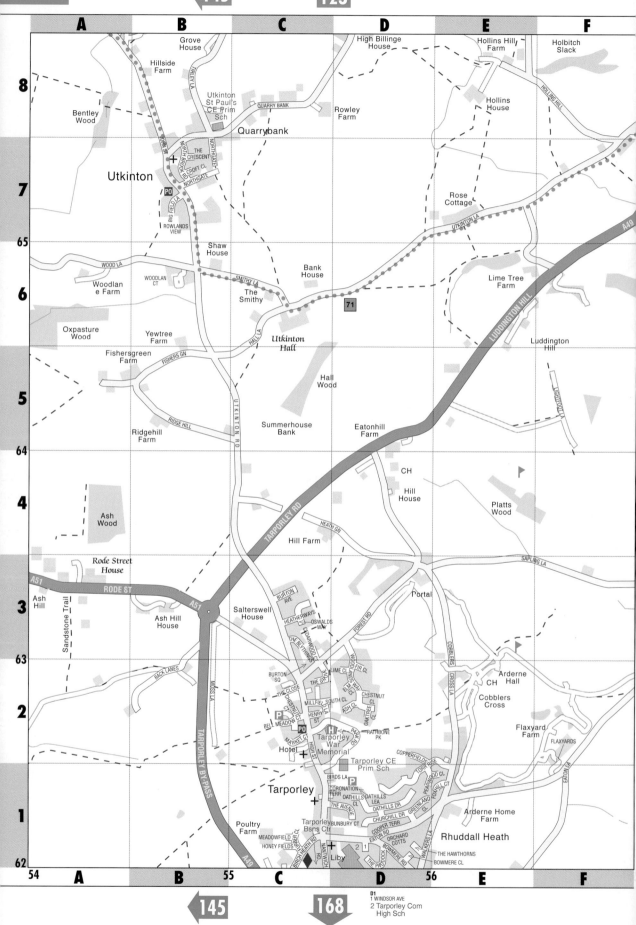

A   B   C   D   E   F

8

7

65

6

5

64

4

3

63

2

1

62

54   A   B   55   C   D   56   E   F

D1
1 WINDSOR AVE
2 Tarporley Com
High Sch

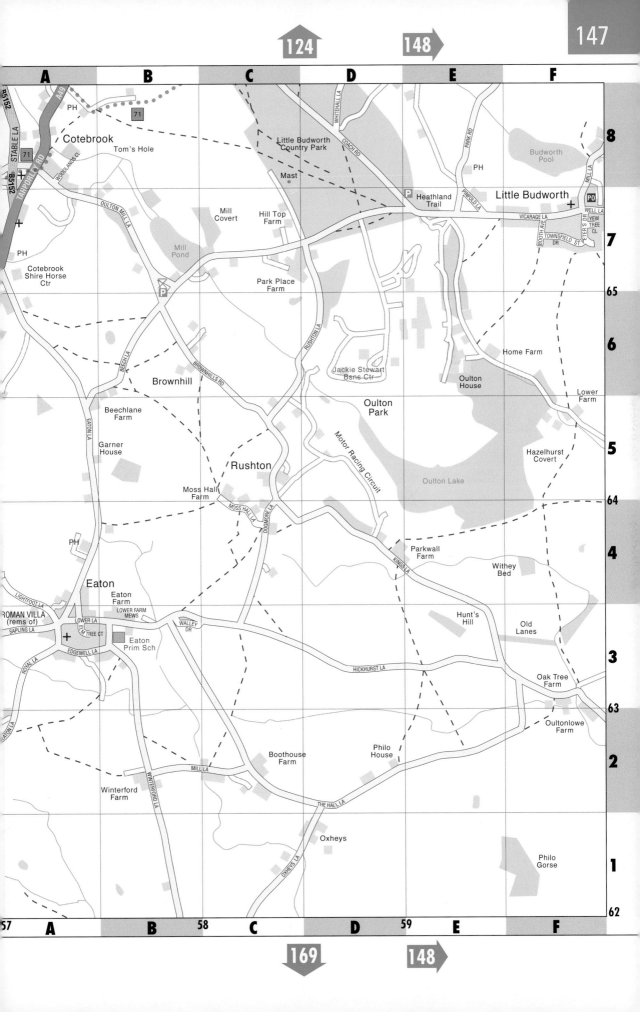

147
125

	A	B	C	D	E	F

MILLBROOK CL
LITTLER LA
A54
Cheshire Constabulary HQ
Lane End Farm
RANGERS WAY
BLAMEBERY LA
Woodford Par Ind Est
BROWNING

8

Brookhouse Farm

MILL LA

Old Hall

Chesterlane Brook

WELL LA

7

Lower Farm

WOODFORD LA W
Hebden Green

65

Poolstead Brook

Woodford Hall

6

Darley Brook

Fennywood Farm

Ash Brook

5

Darley Rough

Darley Hall

Darley Cottages

Adjuncts Covert

64

Darley Gorse

Pool Head Farm

4

Ash House

Cocked Hat Covert

Landing Strips (Private)

3

Bawk House

Ashcroft Farm

63

MILL LA

Stockerlane Farm

2

Oultonlowe Cottage

Oultonlowe Green

WETTES OF ROAD

Wettenhall Hall Cottages

WOODGATE FARM LA

Holmston Hall

Townfield Farm

551

1

Woodgate Farm

Oultonlowe Covert

Wettenhall Hall

62

60	A		B	61	C		D	62	E		F

147
170

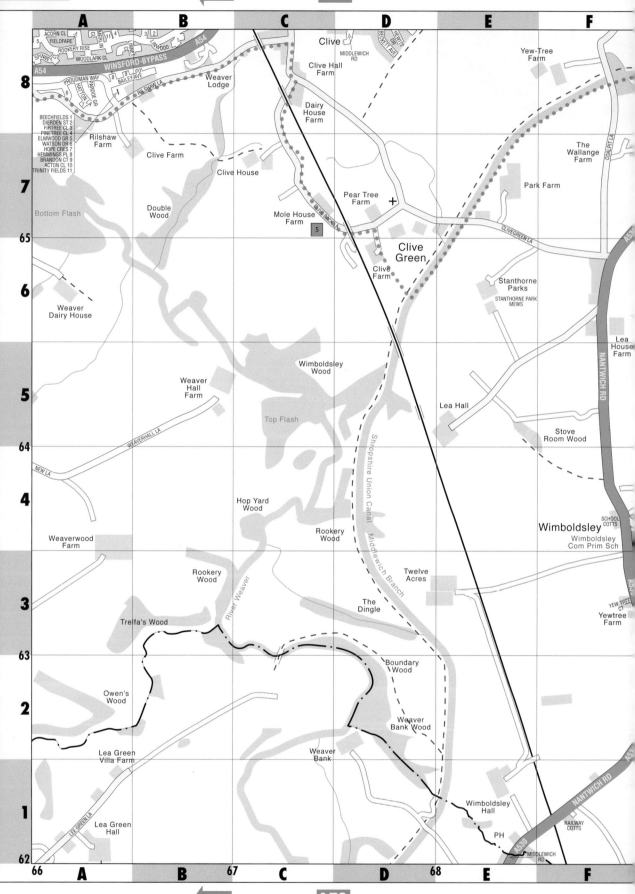

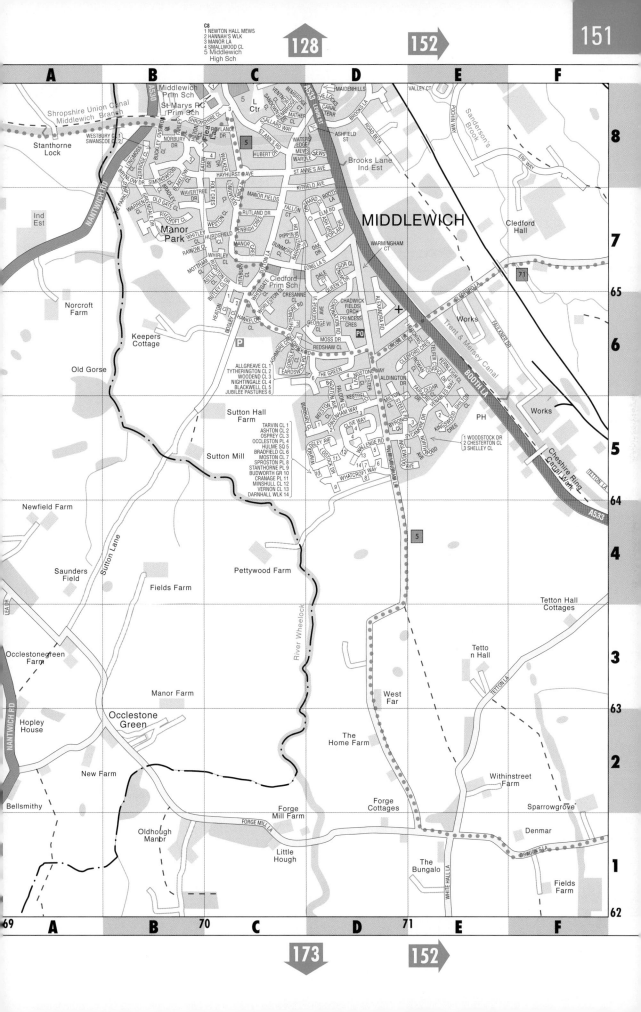

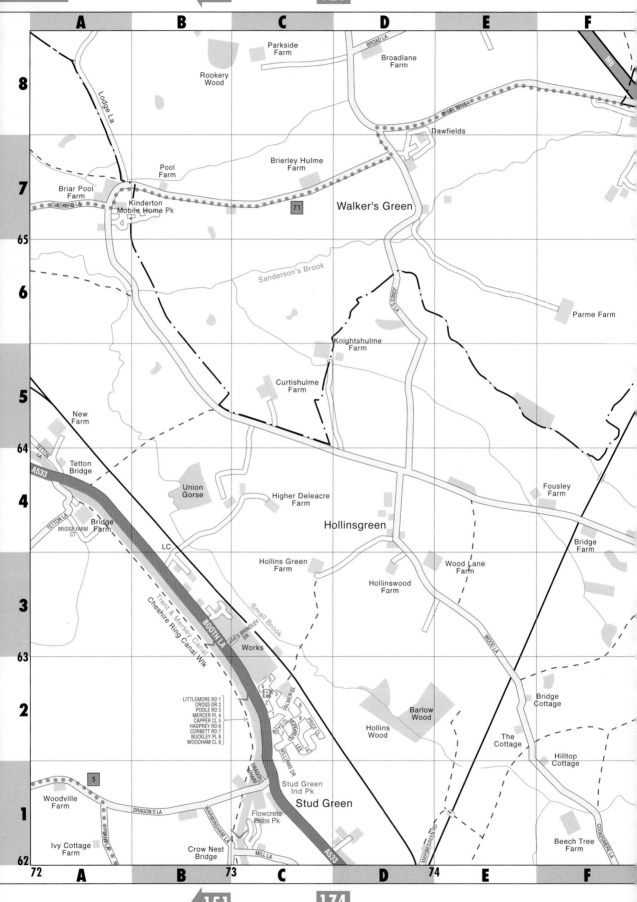

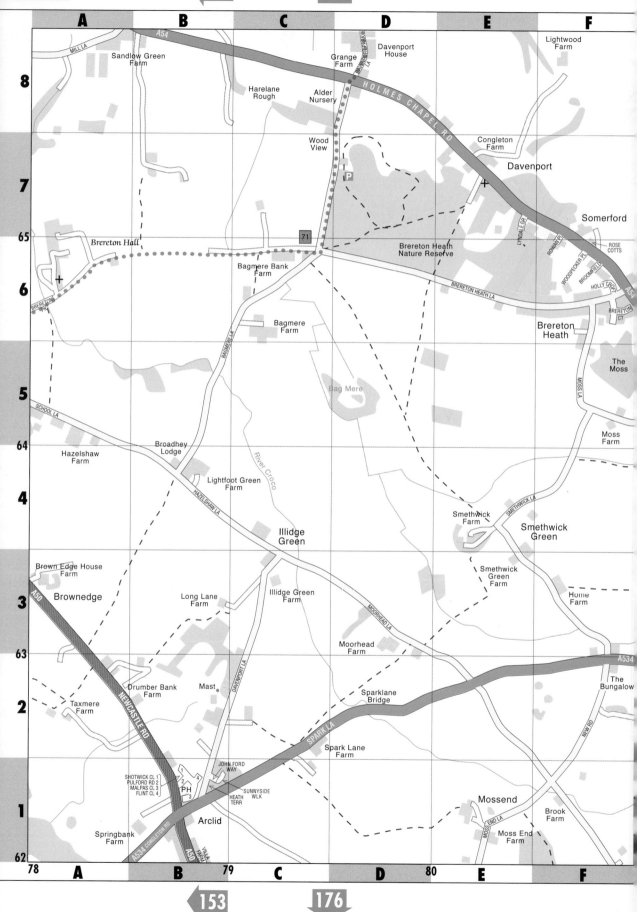

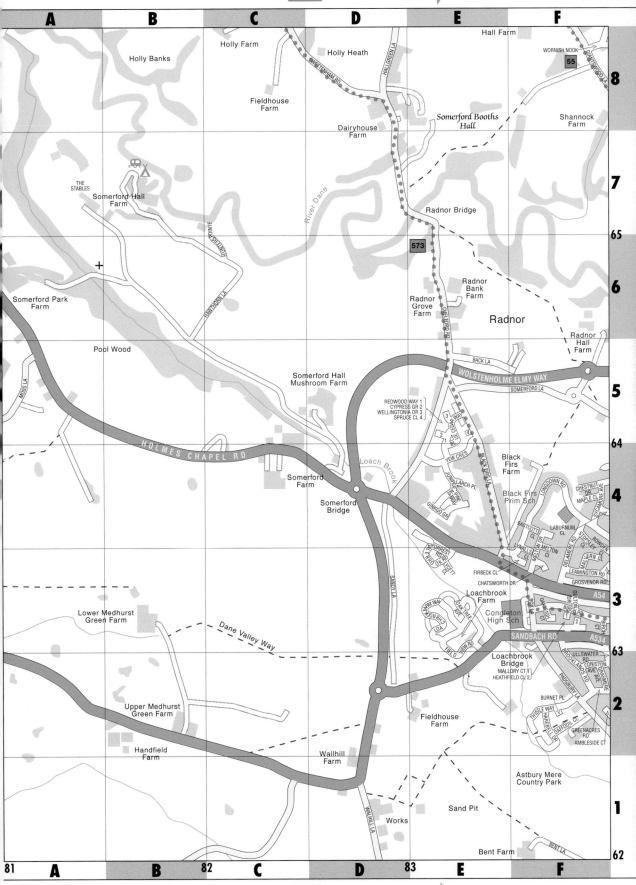

A   B   C   D   E   F

Holly Farm
Hall Farm
WORNISH NOOK
55

Holly Banks
Holly Heath
8

Fieldhouse
Farm
Somerford Booths
Hall
Shannock
Farm

THE
STABLES
Dairyhouse
Farm
7

Somerford Hall
Farm
Radnor Bridge
65

River Dane
573
6

Somerford Park
Farm
Radnor
Bank
Farm

Radnor
Grove
Farm
Radnor

Pool Wood
Radnor
Hall
Farm
BACK LA
WOLSTENHOLME ELMY WAY
5

Somerford Hall
Mushroom Farm
SOMERFORD LA

REDWOOD WAY 1
CYPRESS GR 2
WELLINGTONIA DR 3
SPRUCE CL 4
64

HOLMES CHAPEL RD
Loach Brook
Black
Firs
Farm

Somerford
Farm
YEW CRES
Black Firs
Prim Sch
4

Somerford
Bridge
CHESTNUT
DR
MAPLE CL

EASTCOTT
LABURNUM
CL
BOWDEN

Lower Medhurst
Green Farm
Dane Valley Way
FIRBECK CL
LEAMINGTON RD

CHATSWORTH DR
GROSVENOR RD

Loachbrook
Farm
A54
3

SANDY LA
Congleton
High Sch
SANDBACH RD   A534

Loachbrook
Bridge
63
MALLORY CT 1
HEATHFIELD CL 2

Upper Medhurst
Green Farm
BURNET PL

Fieldhouse
Farm
THISTLE WAY
GREENACRES
RD
AMBLESIDE CT
2

Handfield
Farm
Wallhill
Farm
Astbury Mere
Country Park

Sand Pit
1

WALHILL LA
Works

Bent Farm
BENT LA
62

81   A   82   B   C   D   83   E   F

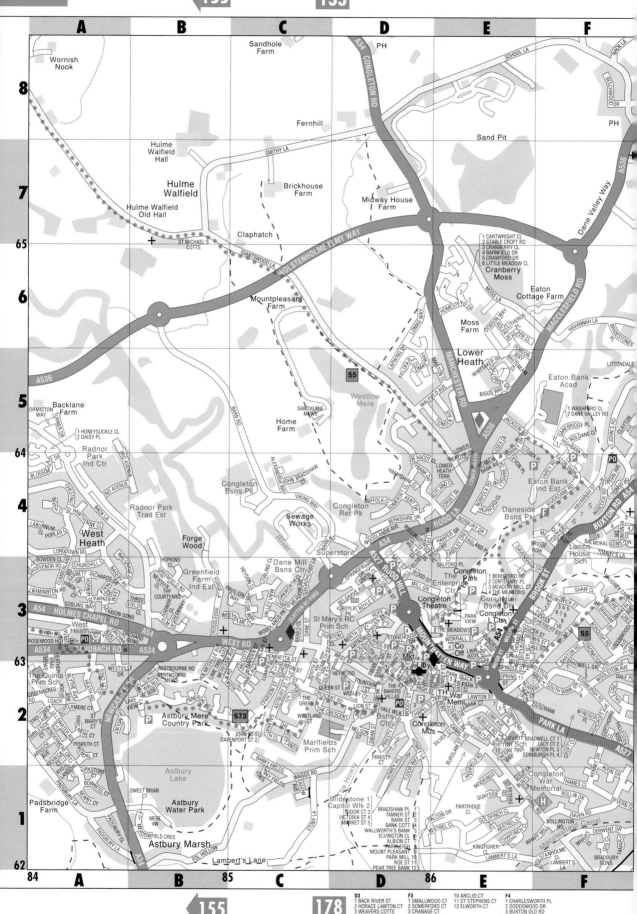

155   178

D3
1 BACK RIVER ST
2 HORACE LAWTON CT
3 WEAVERS COTTS
4 BROOKSIDE RD
5 MEADOW COTTS
6 STONEHOUSE GN

F3
1 SMALLWOOD CT
2 SOMERFORD CT
3 CRANAGE CT
4 GOOSTREY CT
5 MOSTON CT
6 BETCHTON CT
7 RODE CT
8 TETTON CT
9 NEWBOLD CT

10 ARCLID CT
11 ST STEPHENS CT
12 ELWORTH CT

F4
1 CHARLESWORTH PL
2 DODDSWOOD DR
3 BUXTON OLD RD
4 BUCKINGHAM CL
5 Buglawton Ind Est
6 Havannah Bsns Ctr
7 COUNCIL HOS
8 SANDRINGHAM RD
9 VICARAGE AVE

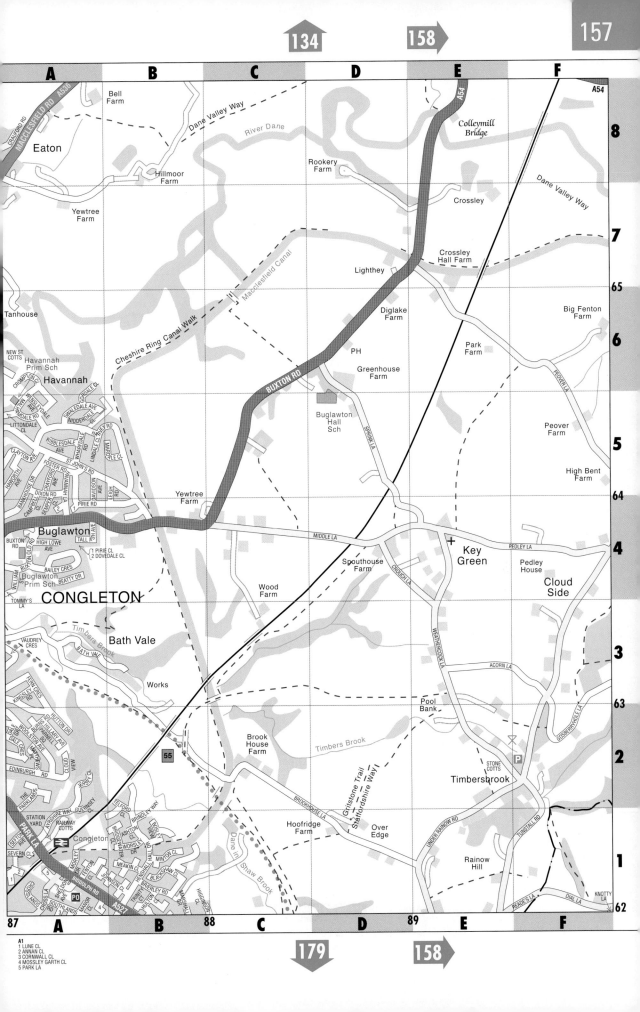

157
135

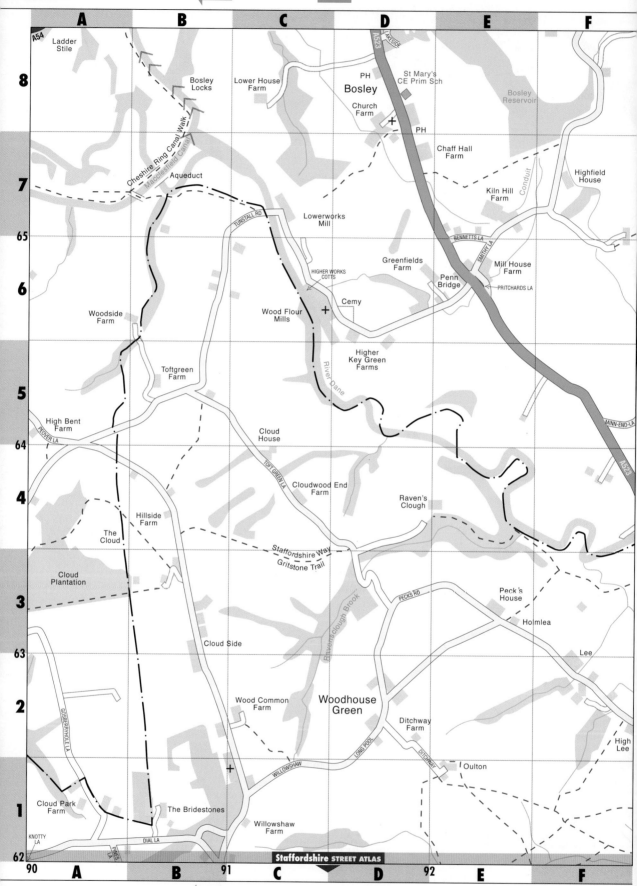

157

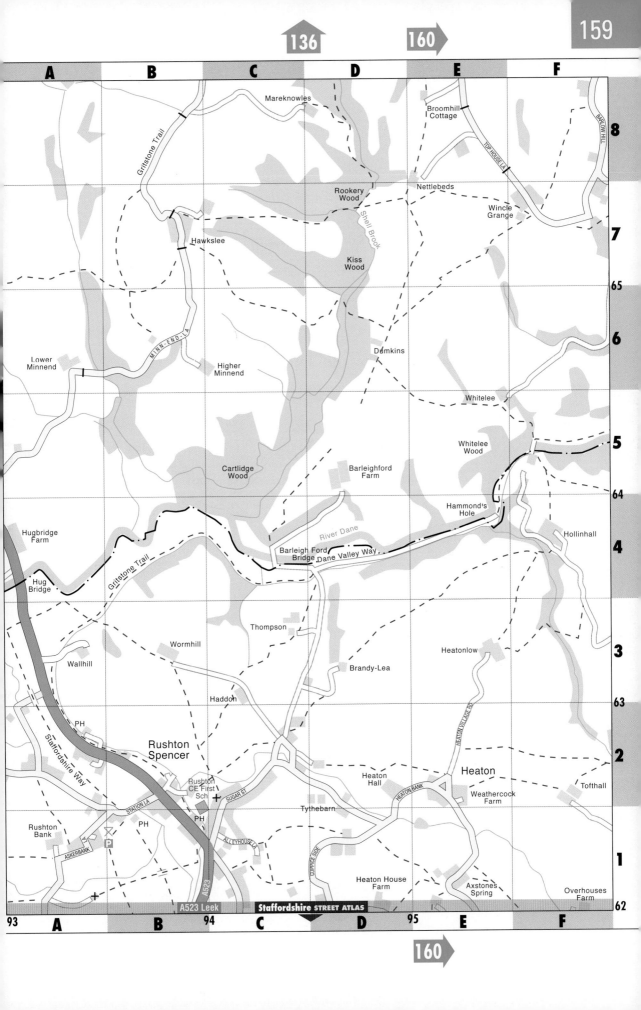

8

Mareknowles

Broomhill
Cottage

Gritstone Trail

Rookery
Wood

Nettlebeds

TOP HOUSE LA

BARLOW HILL

Wincle
Grange

7

Hawkslee

Shell Brook

Kiss
Wood

65

6

MINN-END-LA

Lower
Minnend

Higher
Minnend

Dumkins

Whitelee

Whitelee
Wood

5

Cartlidge
Wood

Barleighford
Farm

Hammond's
Hole

64

Hugbridge
Farm

River Dane

Hollinhall

4

Hug
Bridge

Gritstone Trail

Barleigh Ford
Bridge   Dane Valley Way

Thompson

Wormhill

Heatonlow

3

Wallhill

Brandy-Lea

Haddon

63

PH

Heaton Village Rd

Rushton
Spencer

Staffordshire Way

Heaton

2

STATION LA

Rushton
CE First
Sch

SUGAR ST

Heaton
Hall

HEATON BANK

Weathercock
Farm

Tofthall

Rushton
Bank

PH

PH

Tythebarn

ALLEYHOUSE LA

ASKERBANK

P

CUPPICE SIDE

1

A523

Heaton House
Farm

Axstones
Spring

Overhouses
Farm

62

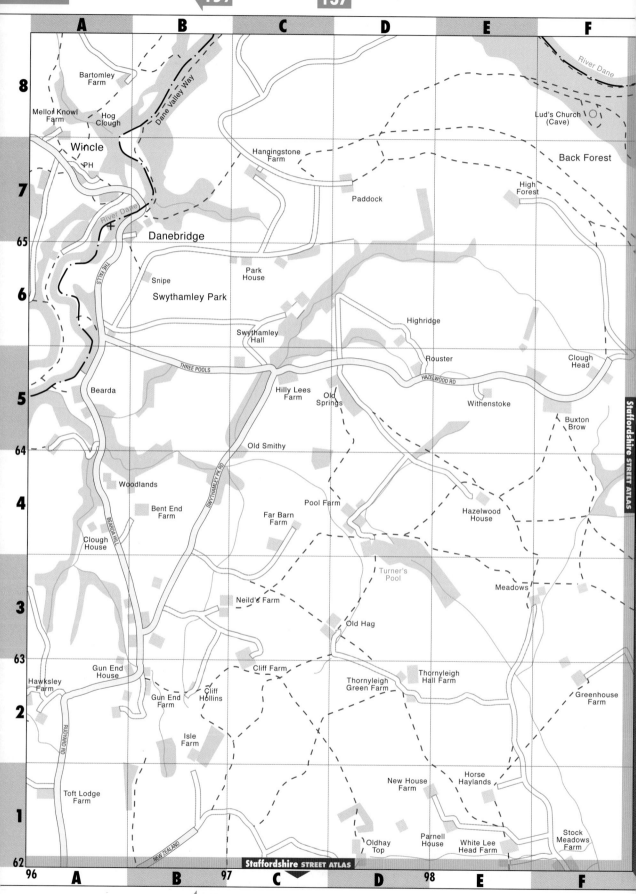

River Dane

A   B   C   D   E   F

8   Bartomley Farm

Lud's Church (Cave)

Mellor Knowl Farm   Hog Clough

Dane Valley Way

Back Forest

Wincle

PH

Hangingstone Farm

High Forest

7   Paddock

River Dane

Danebridge

65

Park House

Snipe   Swythamley Park

Highridge

6

Swythamley Hall

Rouster   Clough Head

THE FALLS

THREE POOLS   HAZELWOOD RD

5   Bearda   Hilly Lees Farm   Old Springs   Withenstoke   Buxton Brow

64   Old Smithy   Hazelwood House

SWYTHAMLEY PK RD

Woodlands   Pool Farm

4   Bent End Farm   Far Barn Farm

BEARDA HILL

Clough House   Turner's Pool   Meadows

3   Neild's Farm   Old Hag

63   Gun End House   Cliff Farm   Thornyleigh Hall Farm

Hawksley Farm   Thornyleigh Green Farm   Greenhouse Farm

2   Gun End Farm   Cliff Hollins

RUDYARD RD   Isle Farm   Horse Haylands

New House Farm

1   Toft Lodge Farm   Parnell House   Stock Meadows Farm

NEW ZEALAND   Oldhay Top   White Lee Head Farm

62

96   A   B   97   C   D   98   E   F

Staffordshire STREET ATLAS

A483

Belgrave Bridge

B5445

RAKE LA

Black Wood

Balderton Dr

Greenwalls

Dodleston Hall

CHURCH RD

Dodleston CE Prim Sch

ST MARY'S RD

Dodleston

MALLORY WLK

KINNERTON RD

PO

CROFT LA

EGERTON WLK

CHURCH

CROFT

PENFOLD BOYDELL WLK WLK

CASTLE WAY

BELGRAVE CL

Balderton Dr

Belgrave Cottages

Belgrave Farm

BELGRAVE AVE

Belgrave Lodge

Belgrave

Moat Farm

PULFORD LA

Dodleston Lane Farm

Oldfields Farm

OLDFIELD FARM RD

Cuckoo's Nest

WREXHAM RD

MAYFAIR CT

Bell Meadow Bsns Pk

BELGRAVIA CT

PARK LA

STRAIGHT MILE

Meadow House Farm

Moorfield Cottages

Elm Grange

The Elms

Lyndale Farm

BELGRAVE GDN MEWS

LC

DODLESTON LA

The Manor

Pulford

FARMMEADOW

BURGANEY CT

CASTLE CL

PULFORD CT

OLD LA

GRASS LA

Castlehill Hotel

Pulford Brook

PULFORD APP

Brookside Farm

Broadoak Farm

LC

Pulford Bridge

Cam-yr-Alyn Farm

LLYNDIR LA

Rossett Bsns Village

Collynie

CHESTER RD

DRIFT COTTS

THE MILLYARD

OAKLAND CT

ROSELANDS CT

Sewage Works

PH

BEECH HOLLOWS

Broadoak

Lavister

B5445

LAVISTER WLKS

ROSSETT PK

Llyndir Hall

DARLAND LA

A483

A **B** **C** **D** **E** **F**

RAKE LA
Rake Lane
Cottages

The
Gullet

Eaton
Lodge

River Dee

8

Eaton Estate
Office

Eaton
Stud

Johnson's
Rough

CHESTER APP

Lodge

7

61

BELGRAVE APP
Lodge

Mon

Eaton
Hall

6

Kennels Farm

Kennel
Wood

Matches Way

Belgrave Moat
Farm

Iron
Bridge

5

Lodge

60

Duck
Wood

River Dee

4

Blobb Hill

Poultonhall
Farm

PULFORD APP

Park
Plantation

Aldford

CHURCH LA

Wallet's
Farm

STRAIGHT MILE

Oxleisure
Pool

Abbey
Gate Coll

MIDDLE LA

The Old
School House

Far Acre

RUSHMERE
LA

3

OLD LA

Black and
White Cottages

GREEN LAKE
LA

MILL LA

59

Green
Farm

Poulton

SCHOOL LA

Townfield
Lands

2

Yew Tree
Farm

YEW TREE
CT

Jones
Wood

B5130

THE GN

CHAPEL LA

Old Pulford Brook

Speed's
Plantation

Alford
Hall

CHESTER RD

1

Chapelhouse
Farm

B5130

58

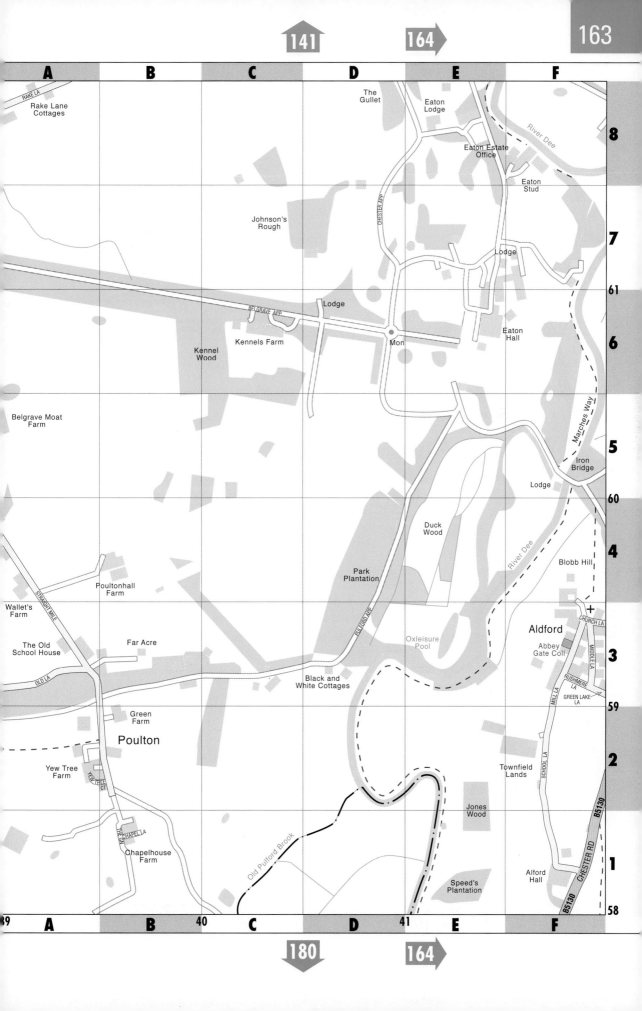

A　　B　　C　　D　　E　　F

8

Cheaveley
Bridge

Cheaveleyhall
Farm

Crook of
Dee

River Dee

7

Powsey Brook

Horse
Pasture

Smithy
Farm

Powseybrook
Bridge

61

Lodge

Sooty Fields
Plantation

BUERTON APP

Chapelhouse
Farm

WAVERTON APP

Platt's
Rough

6

Bruera

Buerton
Kennels

CHAPEL LA

PLATT'S LA

Coldharbour
Farm

Coldharbour

Churton Heath
Farm

5

60

Penlington's
Wood

Newbold

4

HILL
COTTS

Lea
Newbold
Farm

CHURCH LA

Brickyard
Farm

PH

Bank
Farm

Brickyard
Plantation

3

LEA LA

Lea
Cottages

GREEN LAKE
LA

59

CHESTER RD B5130

Leahall
Farm

2

Wim Bridge

LOWER LA

Aldford Brook

Bishop Bennet Way

Glebe
Farm

The
Ponderosa

1

Ford La

Ford Lane
Farm

58

42　　A　　B　43　C　　D　44　E　　F

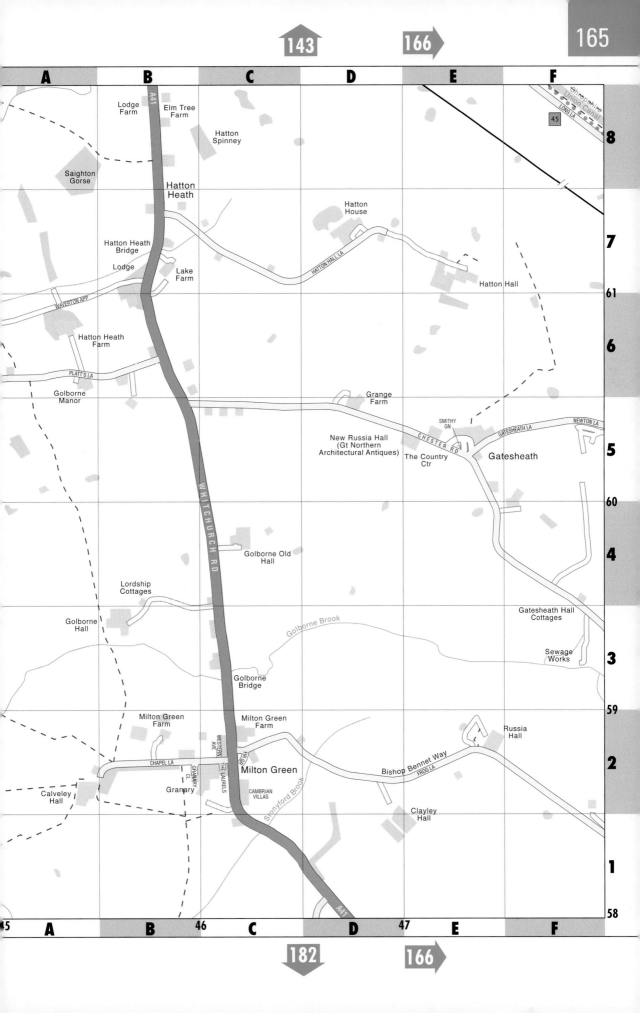

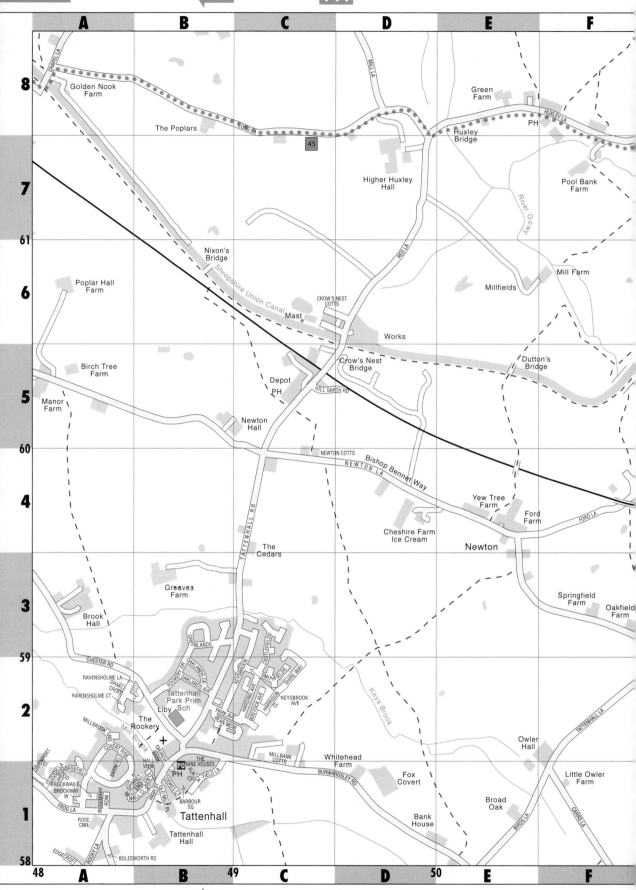

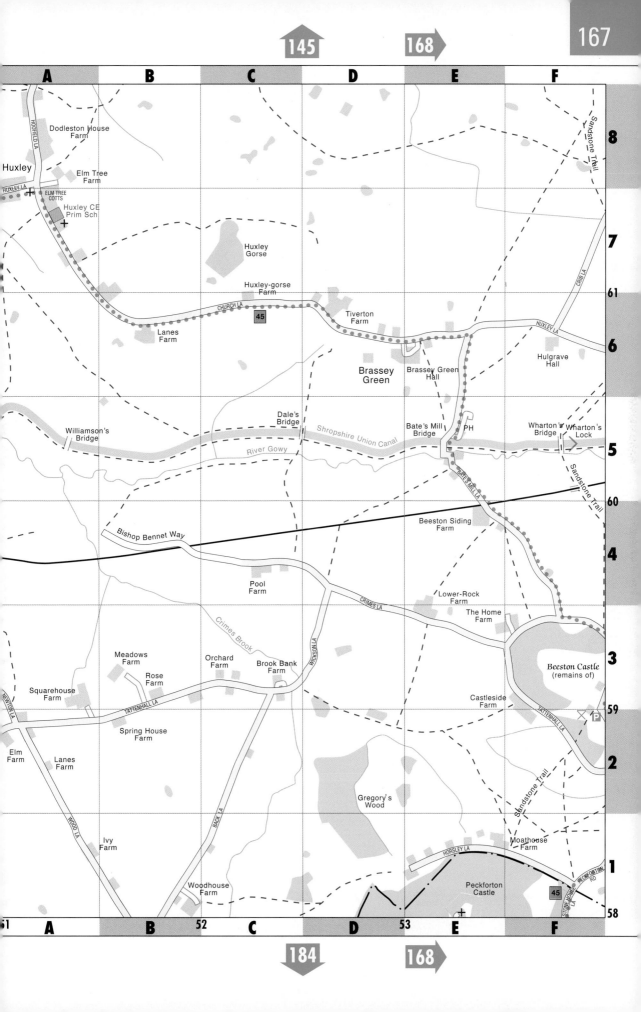

Sandstone Trail

8

HOOFIELD LA

Dodleston House
Farm

Huxley

Elm Tree
Farm

HUXLEY LA

ELM TREE
COTTS

Huxley CE
Prim Sch

7

Huxley
Gorse

CRIB LA

61

Huxley-gorse
Farm

CHURCH LA

45

Tiverton
Farm

HUXLEY LA

Lanes
Farm

Brassey Green
Hall

Hulgrave
Hall

6

Brassey
Green

PH

Wharton's
Bridge

Wharton's
Lock

Dale's
Bridge

Shropshire Union Canal

Bate's Mill
Bridge

Williamson's
Bridge

River Gowy

BATE'S MILL LA

Sandstone Trail

5

60

Beeston Siding
Farm

4

Bishop Bennet Way

Pool
Farm

CRIMES LA

Lower-Rock
Farm

The Home
Farm

Crimes Brook

Meadows
Farm

Orchard
Farm

Brook Bank
Farm

JACKSON LA

Beeston Castle
(remains of)

3

Rose
Farm

Squarehouse
Farm

TATTENHALL LA

Castleside
Farm

TATTENHALL LA

P

59

NEWTON LA

Spring House
Farm

2

Elm
Farm

Lanes
Farm

Sandstone Trail

WOOD LA

Ivy
Farm

BACK LA

Gregory's
Wood

Moathouse
Farm

1

Woodhouse
Farm

HORSLEY LA

Peckforton
Castle

STONE HOUSE LA

BECKFORTON RD

45

58

167 146

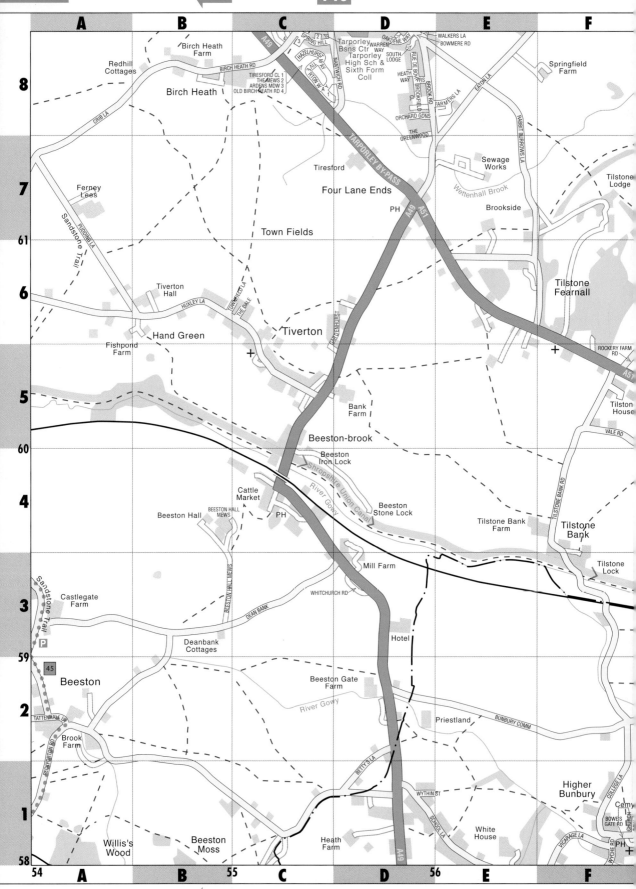

167 185

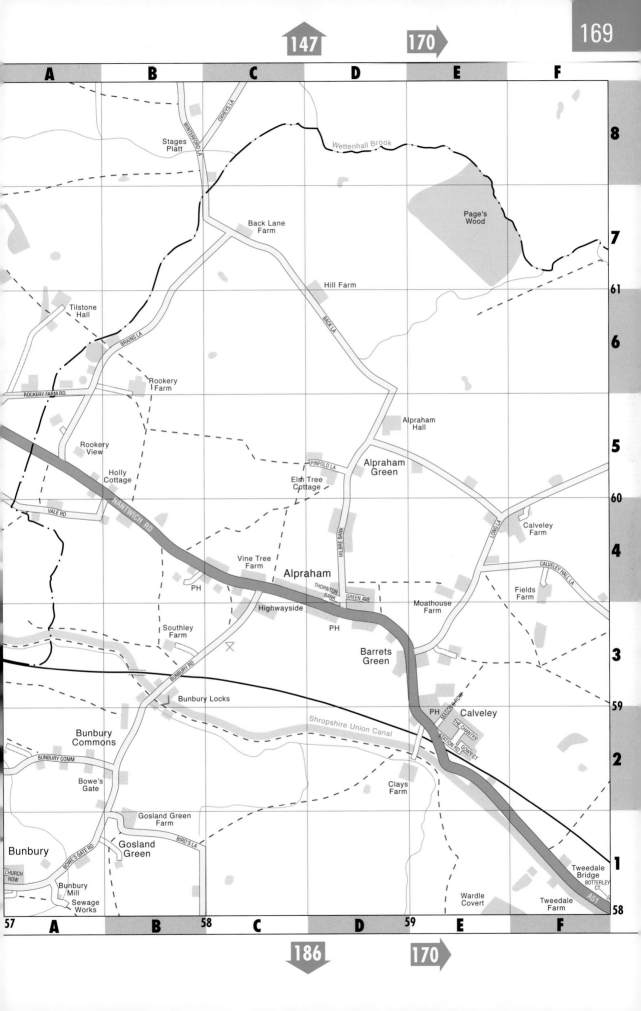

A B C D E F

8
Stages Platt
WINTERFORD LA
OXHEY'S LA
Wettenhall Brook

7
Back Lane Farm
Page's Wood

61
Hill Farm
Tilstone Hall
BRAINS LA
BACK LA

6
Rookery Farm
ROCKERY FARM RD
Alpraham Hall

5
Rookery View
Holly Cottage
PINFOLD LA
Elm Tree Cottage
Alpraham Green
NANTWICH RD
VALE RD

60
HILBRE BANK
LONG LA
Calveley Farm

4
Vine Tree Farm
Alpraham
PH
CALVELEY HALL LA
THORNTON BANK
GREEN AVE
Moathouse Farm
Fields Farm

Highwayside
Southley Farm
PH
BUNBURY RD

3
Barrets Green

Bunbury Locks
PH
MASON'S ROW
Calveley
59
THE CHANTRY
STATION RD
GOWY CT

Shropshire Union Canal

2
Bunbury Commons
BUNBURY COMM
Bowe's Gate
Clays Farm

Gosland Green Farm
BIRD'S LA

1
Bunbury
BOWE'S GATE RD
Gosland Green
CHURCH ROW
Tweedale Bridge
BOTTERLEY CT.
A51

Bunbury Mill
Sewage Works
Wardle Covert
Tweedale Farm
58

169
148

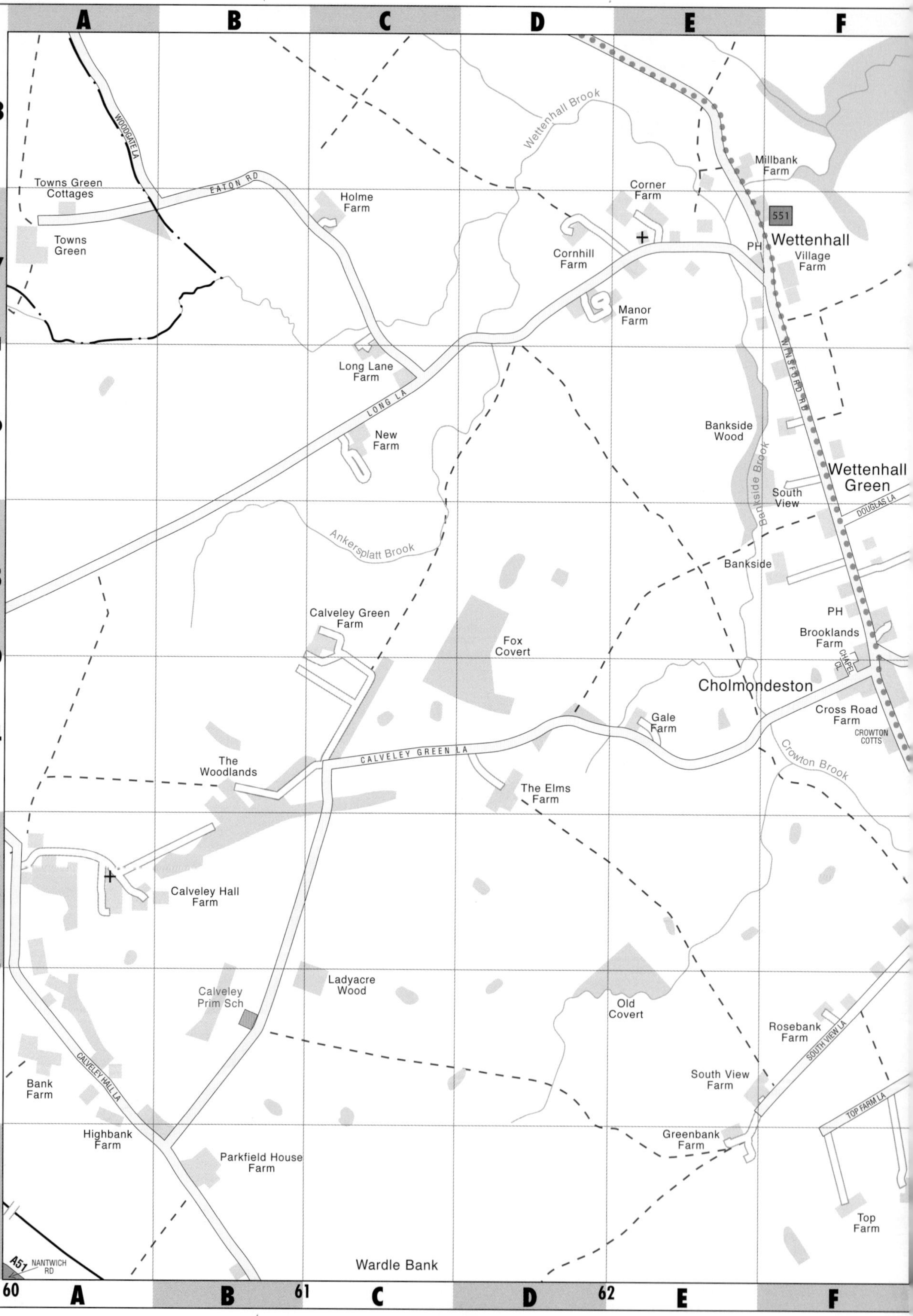

A **B** **C** **D** **E** **F**

8

Towns Green
Cottages

Wettenhall Brook

Corner
Farm

Millbank
Farm

Holme
Farm

7

Towns
Green

WOODGATE LA

EATON RD

Cornhill
Farm

PH

Wettenhall

551

Village
Farm

61

Long Lane
Farm

Manor
Farm

LONG LA

6

New
Farm

Bankside
Wood

Wettenhall
Green

South
View

DOUGLAS LA

Ankersplatt Brook

Bankside Brook

WINSFORD RD

5

Calveley Green
Farm

Fox
Covert

Bankside

PH

60

Brooklands
Farm

CHAPEL CL

Cholmondeston

Cross Road
Farm

4

The
Woodlands

CALVELEY GREEN LA

Gale
Farm

CROWTON
COTTS

Crowton Brook

The Elms
Farm

3

Calveley Hall
Farm

59

Calveley
Prim Sch

Ladyacre
Wood

Old
Covert

Rosebank
Farm

2

Bank
Farm

CALVELEY HALL LA

South View
Farm

SOUTH VIEW LA

Highbank
Farm

Greenbank
Farm

TOP FARM LA

Parkfield House
Farm

1

A51

NANTWICH
RD

Top
Farm

58

60

A 61 **B** **C** **D** 62 **E** **F**

Wardle Bank

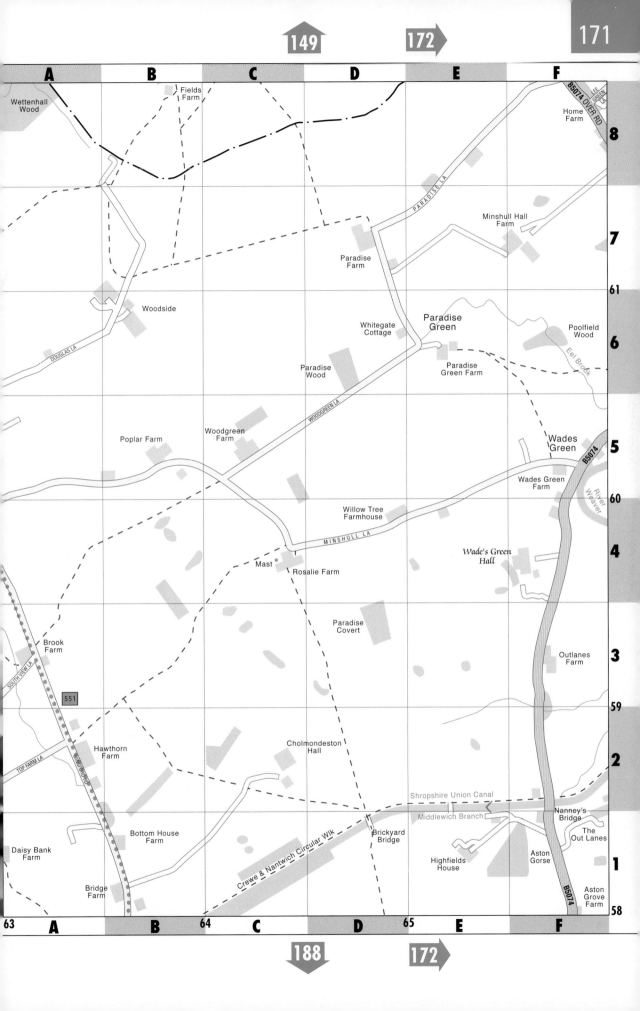

171
150

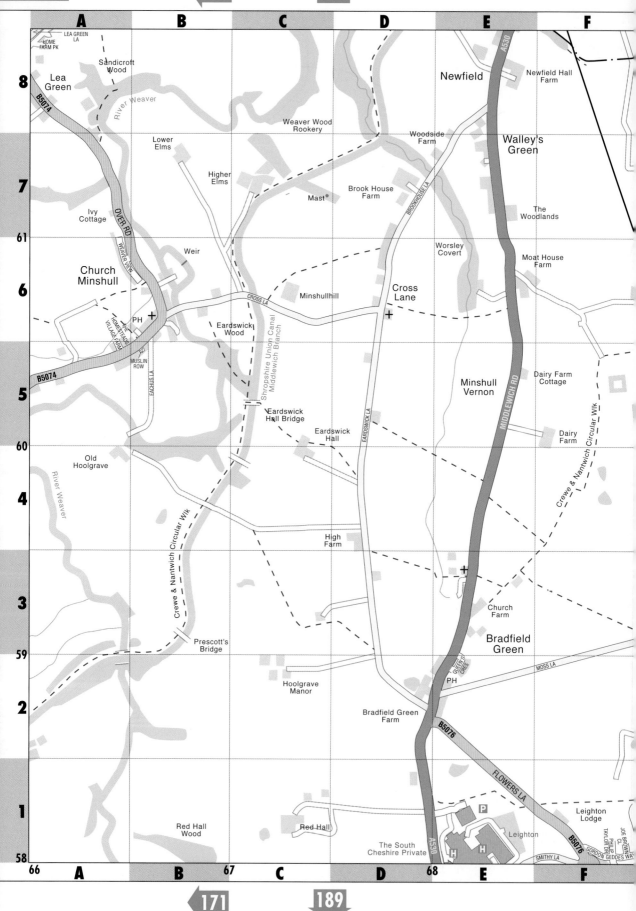

LEA GREEN LA

HOME
FARM PK

Lea
Green

Sandicroft
Wood

River Weaver

8

B5074

Lower
Elms

Higher
Elms

Weaver Wood
Rookery

Newfield

Newfield Hall
Farm

Woodside
Farm

Walley's
Green

7

Ivy
Cottage

OVER RD

WEAVER VIEW

Church
Minshull

Weir

Mast

Brook House
Farm

BROOKHOUSE LA

The
Woodlands

61

6

PH

Eardswick
Wood

CROSS LA

Minshullhill

Cross
Lane

Worsley
Covert

Moat House
Farm

THOMAS FARM
VILLAGE FARM

MUSLIN
ROW

EACHUS LA

Shropshire Union Canal
Middlewich Branch

Eardswick
Hall Bridge

Minshull
Vernon

MIDDLEWICH RD

A530

Dairy Farm
Cottage

B5074

Eardswick
Hall

EARDSWICK LA

Dairy
Farm

Crewe & Nantwich Circular Wlk

5

60

Old
Hoolgrave

Crewe & Nantwich Circular Wlk

River Weaver

4

High
Farm

Crewe & Nantwich Circular Wlk

Church
Farm

3

Prescott's
Bridge

59

Bradfield
Green

QUEEN'S CRES

MOSS LA

Hoolgrave
Manor

PH

2

Bradfield Green
Farm

B5076

FLOWERS LA

Red Hall
Wood

Red Hall

P

Leighton
Lodge

JOE BROWNS CL
PHILIP TAYLOR DR
GORDON ST GEDDES WAY

1

The South
Cheshire Private

A530

Leighton

B5076

H   H

SMITHY LA

58

171
189

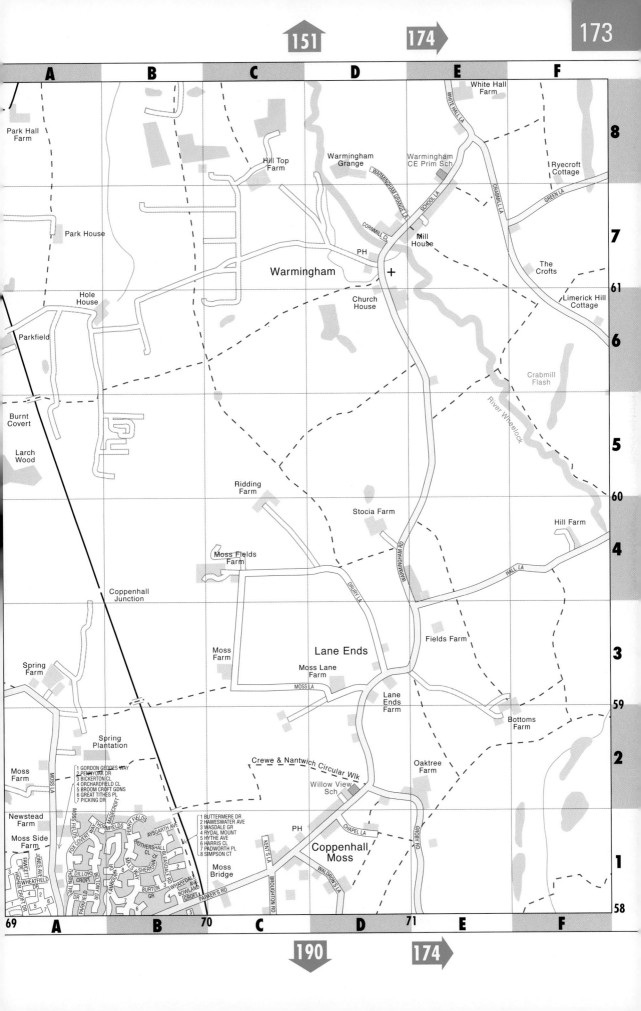

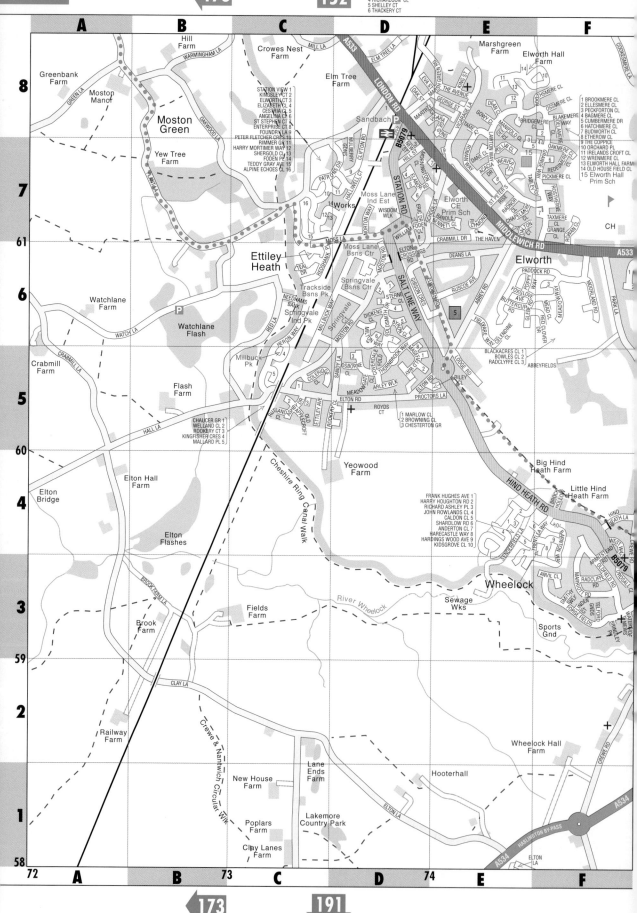

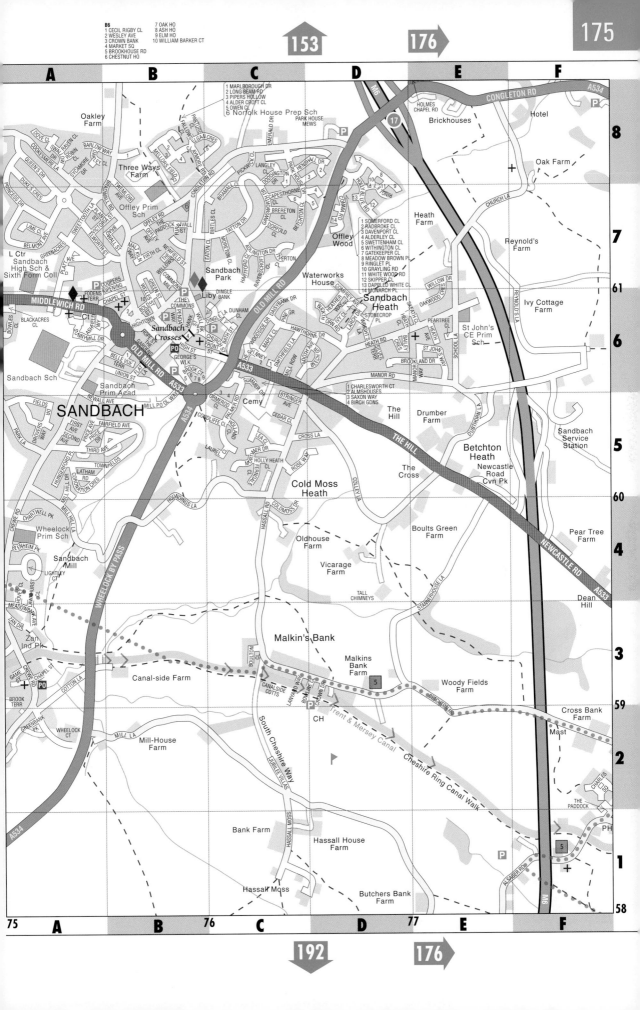

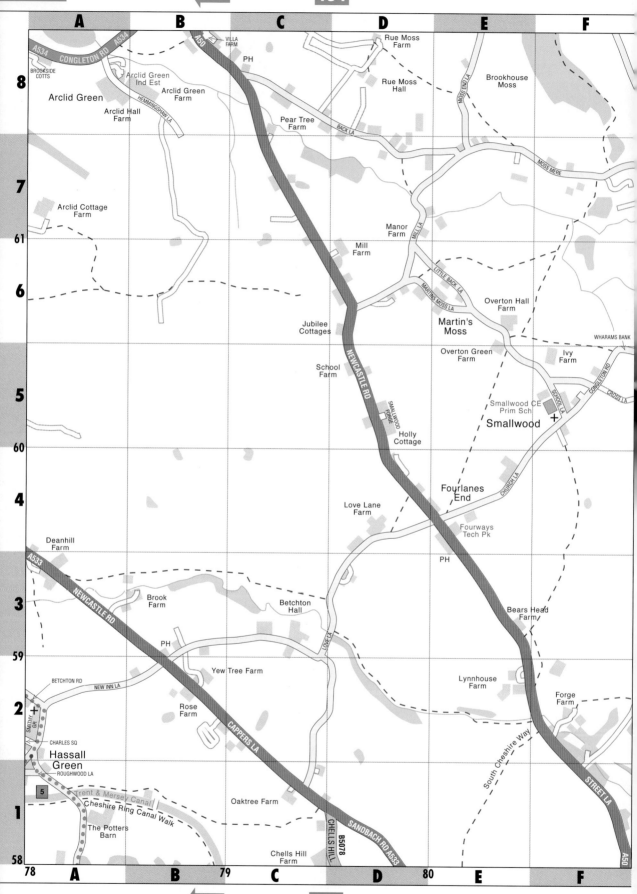

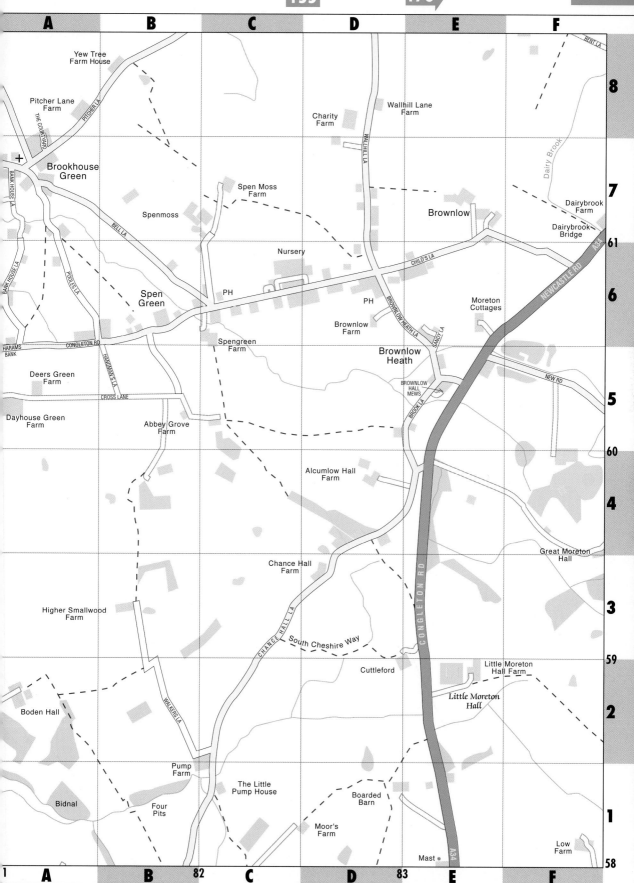

A B C D E F

8
7
61
6
5
60
4
3
59
2
1
58

Yew Tree Farm House
Pitcher Lane Farm
PITCHER LA
THE COURTYARD
BANK HOUSE LA
Brookhouse Green
BELL LA
POOLES LA
Spenmoss
Spen Moss Farm
Charity Farm
WALLHILL LA
Wallhill Lane Farm
BENT LA
Dairy Brook
Dairybrook Farm
Dairybrook Bridge
A34
NEWCASTLE RD
Brownlow
Nursery
CHILD'S LA
Spen Green
PH
PH
BROWNLOW HEATH LA
Brownlow Farm
SANDY LA
Moreton Cottages
HANGMAN'S LA
CONGLETON RD
HARAMS BANK
Deers Green Farm
CROSS LANE
Spengreen Farm
Brownlow Heath
BROWNLOW HALL MEWS
BROOK LA
NEW RD
Dayhouse Green Farm
Abbey Grove Farm
Alcumlow Hall Farm
Great Moreton Hall
Higher Smallwood Farm
Chance Hall Farm
CONGLETON RD
CHANCE HALL LA
South Cheshire Way
Cuttleford
Little Moreton Hall Farm
Little Moreton Hall
WALKERS LA
Boden Hall
Bidnal
Four Pits
Pump Farm
The Little Pump House
Moor's Farm
Boarded Barn
A34
Mast
Low Farm

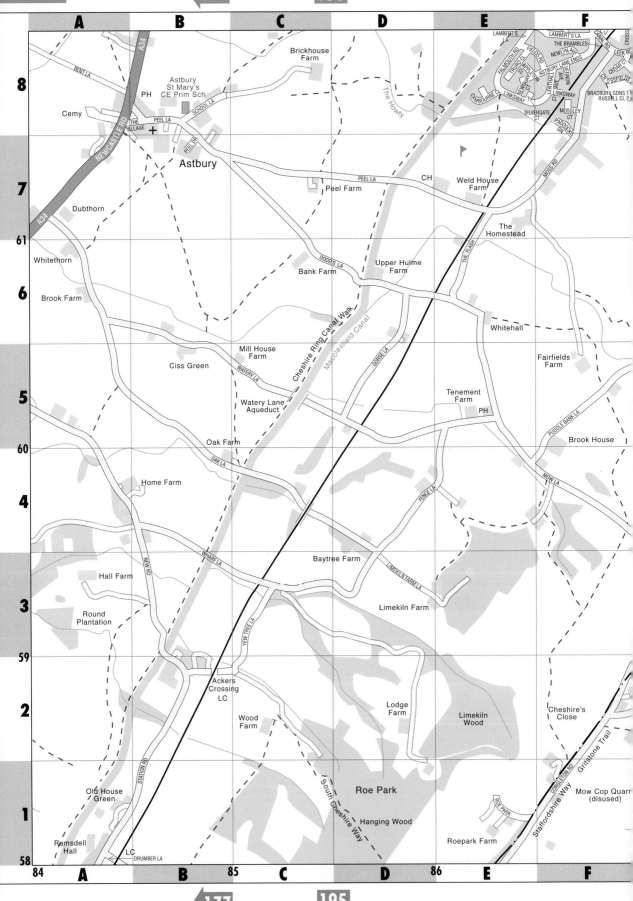

163

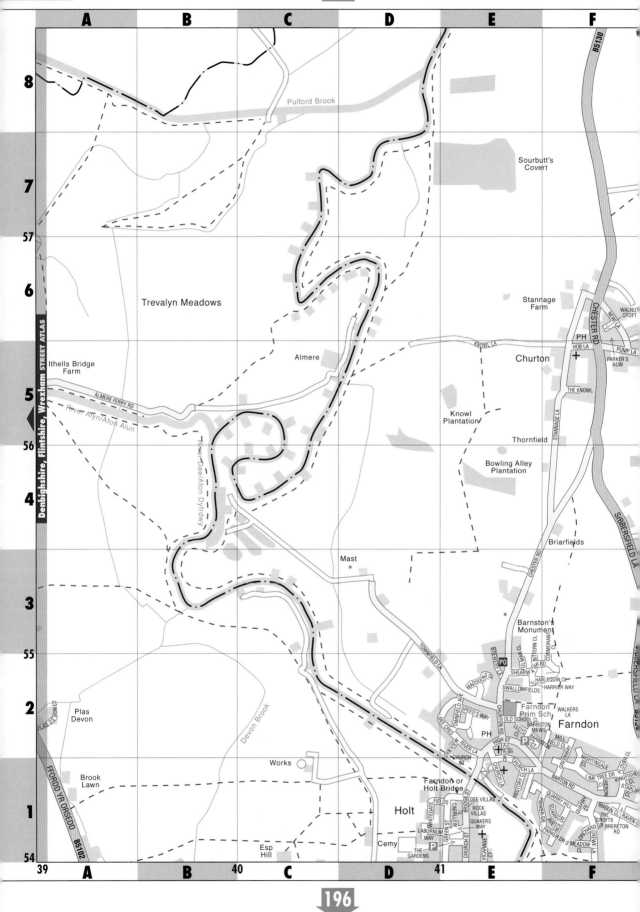

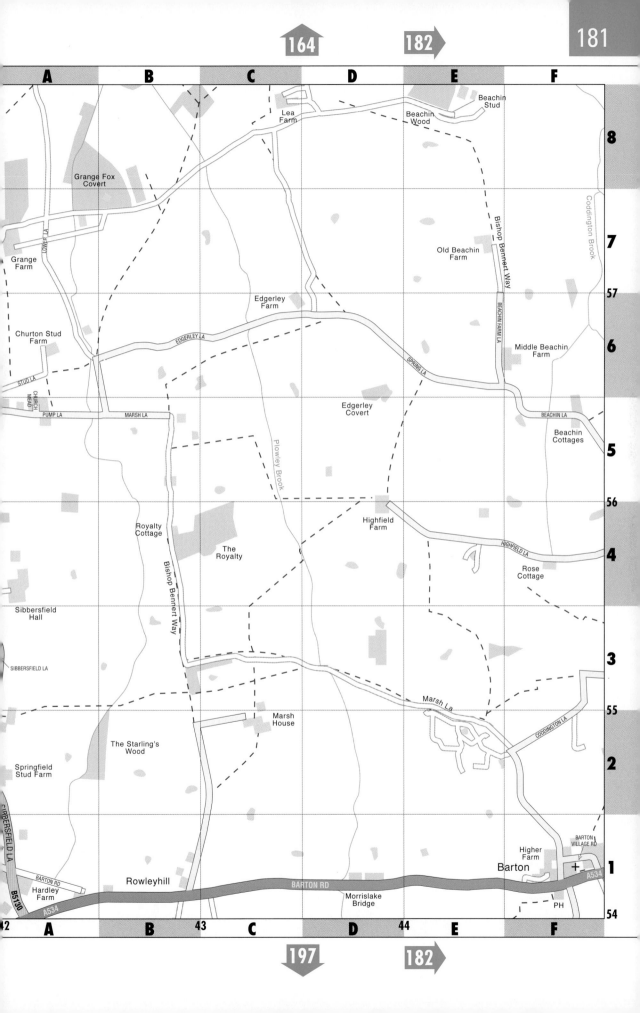

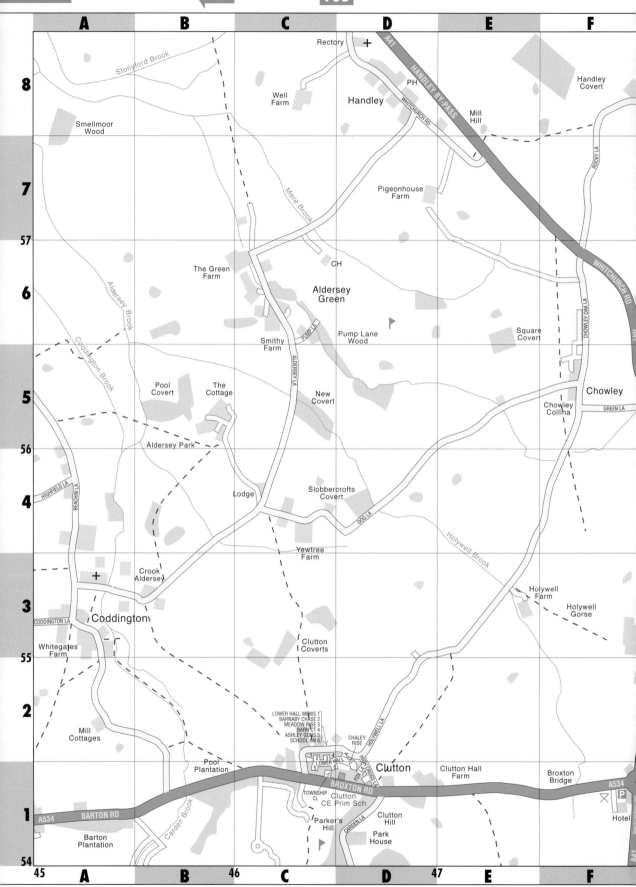

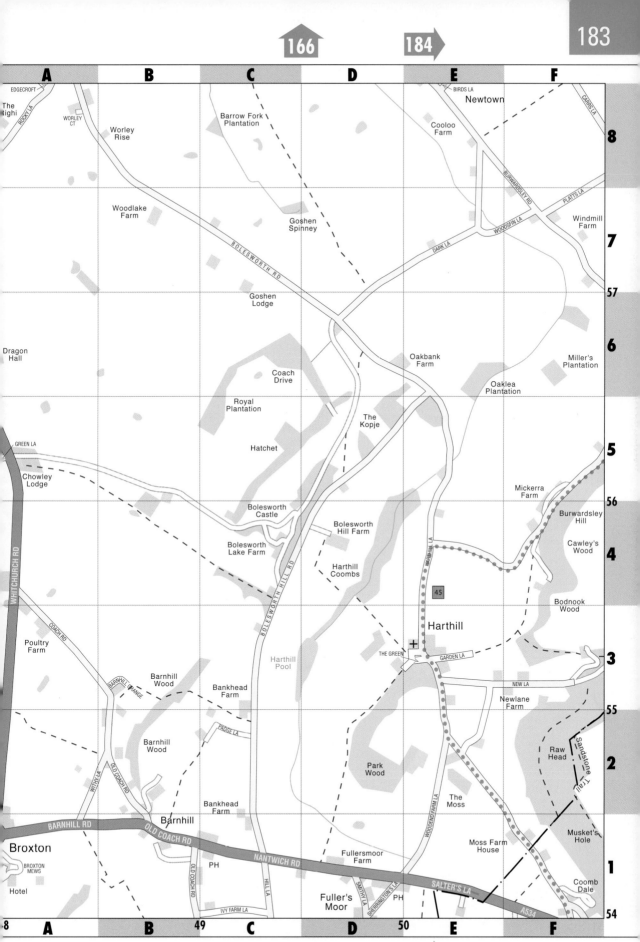

A   B   C   D   E   F

EDGECROFT

The
Right

ROCK LA

WORLEY
CT

Worley Rise

Barrow Fork
Plantation

BIRDS LA

Newtown

CARRS LA

Cooloo
Farm

8

Woodlake
Farm

Goshen
Spinney

BURWARDSLEY RD

WOODSFIN LA

DARK LA

Windmill
Farm

PLATTS LA

7

BOLESWORTH RD

Goshen
Lodge

57

Dragon
Hall

Coach
Drive

Oakbank
Farm

Oaklea
Plantation

Miller's
Plantation

6

GREEN LA

Royal
Plantation

Hatchet

The
Kopje

5

Chowley
Lodge

Mickerra
Farm

Burwardsley
Hill

56

WHITCHURCH RD

Bolesworth
Castle

Bolesworth
Lake Farm

BOLESWORTH HILL RD

Bolesworth
Hill Farm

Harthill
Coombs

MARHILL LA

Cawley's
Wood

4

45

Bodnook
Wood

Poultry
Farm

COACH RD

Harthill
Pool

Harthill

THE GREEN

GARDEN LA

3

BARNHILL GRANGE

Barnhill
Wood

Bankhead
Farm

NEW LA

Newlane
Farm

55

WITHY LA

OLD COACH RD

Barnhill
Wood

PADGE LA

Park
Wood

Raw
Head

Sandstone Trail

2

BARNHILL RD

Barnhill

OLD COACH RD

Bankhead
Farm

WOODEND FARM LA

The
Moss

Musket's
Hole

Broxton

BROXTON
MEWS

OLD COACH RD

NANTWICH RD

PH

HILL LA

Fullersmoor
Farm

SMITHY LA

SALTER'S LA

Moss Farm
House

Coomb
Dale

1

Hotel

IVY FARM LA

Fuller's
Moor

SHERRINGTON'S LA

PH

A534

54

8   A   B   49   C   D   50   E   F

183 167

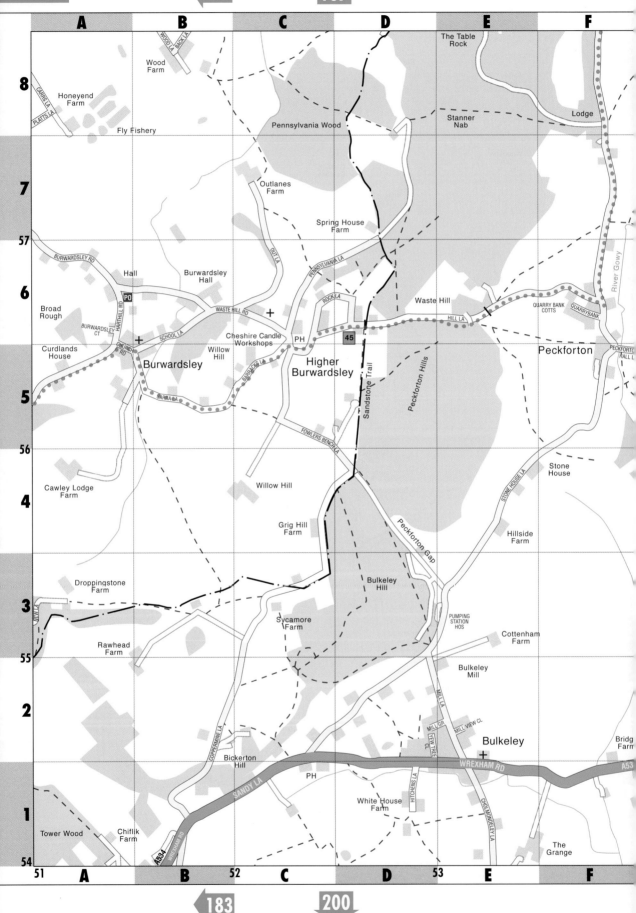

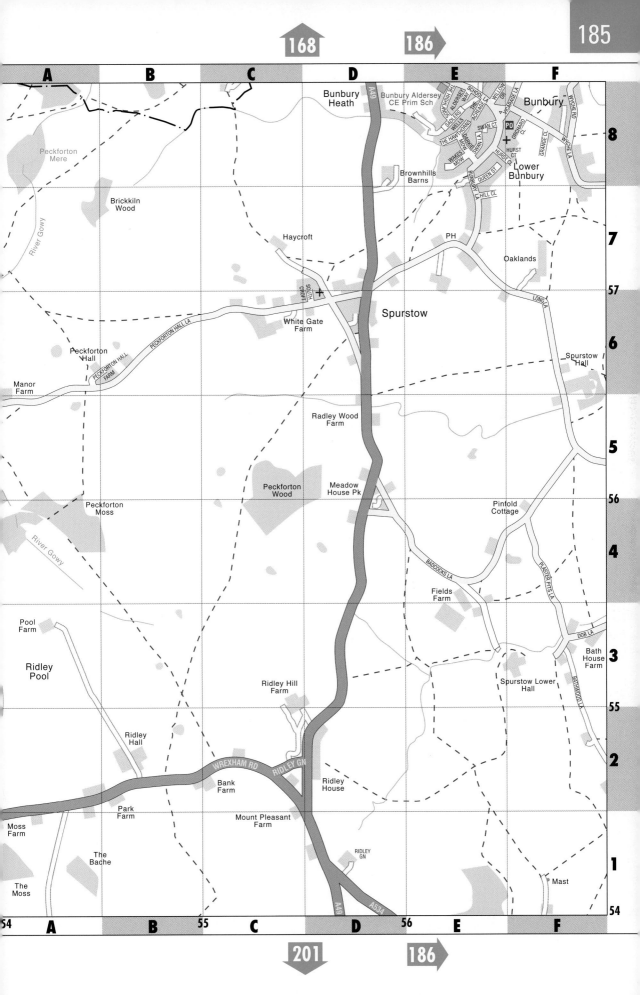

A B C D E F

8

7

57

6

5

56

4

3

55

2

1

54

Peckforton
Mere

Brickkiln
Wood

River Gowy

Bunbury
Heath

Bunbury Aldersey
CE Prim Sch

THE HAWTHORNS

HIGH ST

ALDERSEY CL

SCHOOL LA

ACREAGE LA

THE WELLS

SADLERS WAY

WILLOW DRI

VICARAGE LA

GRANGE CL

Bunbury

WYCHE RD

SWAN CT

PO

ORCHARD CL

HURST CT

BUNBURY LA

QUEEN ST

HILL CL

DANES WAY

WAKES MDW

SWAN LA

Lower
Bunbury

WYCHE LA

Brownhills
Barns

Haycroft

PH

Oaklands

LONG LA

Spurstow

Spurstow
Hall

Peckforton
Hall

PECKFORTON HALL LA

White Gate
Farm

SOUTH CROFT

Peckforton Hall
Farm

Manor
Farm

Radley Wood
Farm

Peckforton
Moss

Peckforton
Wood

Meadow
House Pk

Pinfold
Cottage

River Gowy

BADCOCKS LA

Fields
Farm

PLASTER PITS LA

DOB LA

Bath
House
Farm

Pool
Farm

Spurstow Lower
Hall

BATHWOOD LA

Ridley
Pool

Ridley Hill
Farm

Ridley
Hall

WREXHAM RD

RIDLEY GN

Bank
Farm

Ridley
House

Park
Farm

Mount Pleasant
Farm

Moss
Farm

RIDLEY
GN

Mast

The
Bache

The
Moss

A49

A49

A534

185
169

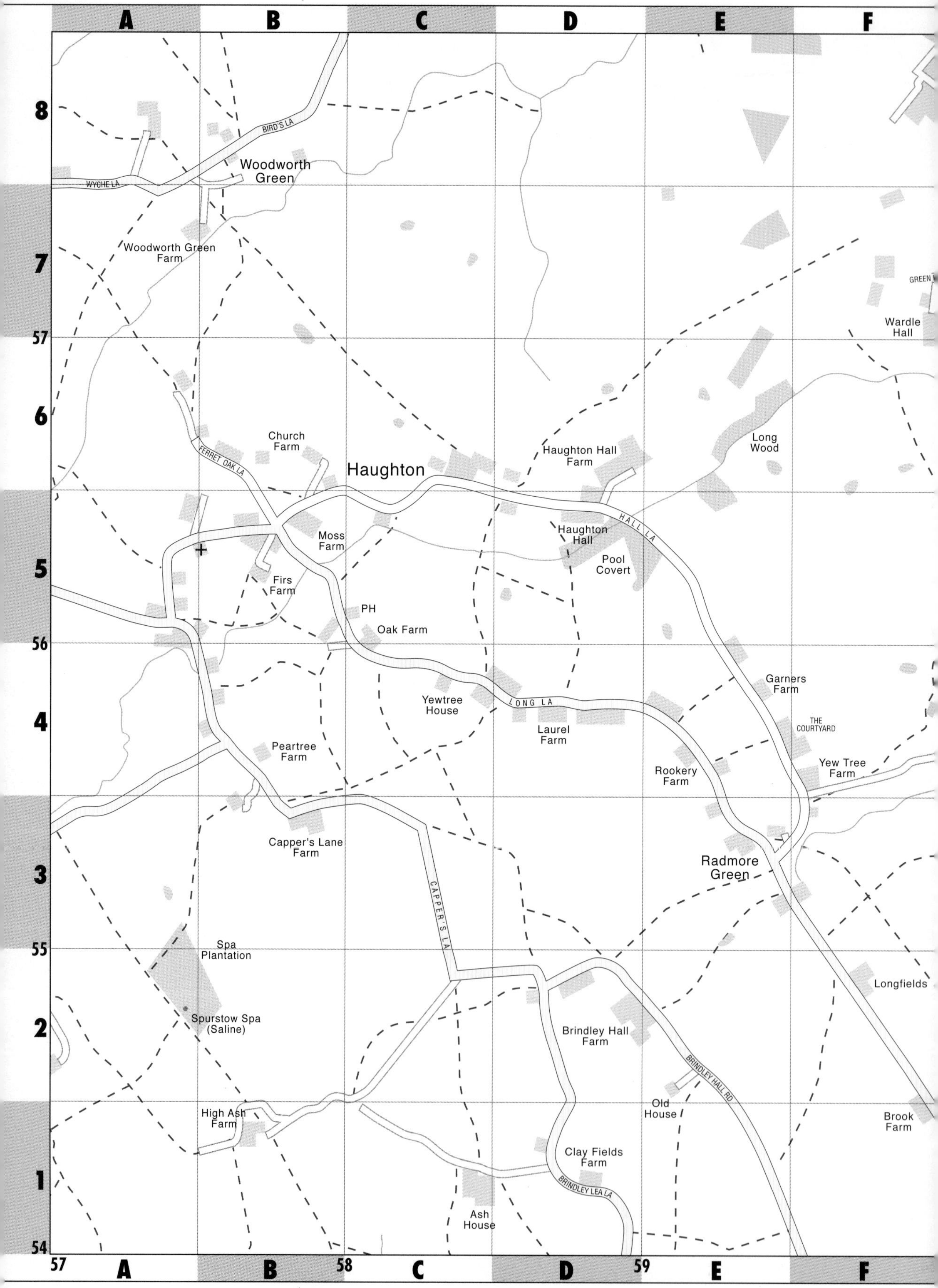

| A | B | C | D | E | F |

8

WYCHE LA

BIRD'S LA

Woodworth
Green

7

Woodworth Green
Farm

57

GREEN

Wardle
Hall

6

FERRET OAK LA

Church
Farm

Haughton

Haughton Hall
Farm

Long
Wood

5

Moss
Farm

Firs
Farm

Haughton
Hall

HALL LA

Pool
Covert

56

PH

Oak Farm

Garners
Farm

THE
COURTYARD

4

Yewtree
House

LONG LA

Laurel
Farm

Rookery
Farm

Yew Tree
Farm

Peartree
Farm

3

Capper's Lane
Farm

CAPPER'S LA

Radmore
Green

55

Spa
Plantation

Longfields

2

Spurstow Spa
(Saline)

Brindley Hall
Farm

BRINDLEY HALL RD

Old
House

Brook
Farm

High Ash
Farm

Clay Fields
Farm

1

BRINDLEY LEA LA

Ash
House

54

| 57 | A | B | 58 | C | D | 59 | E | F |

185
202

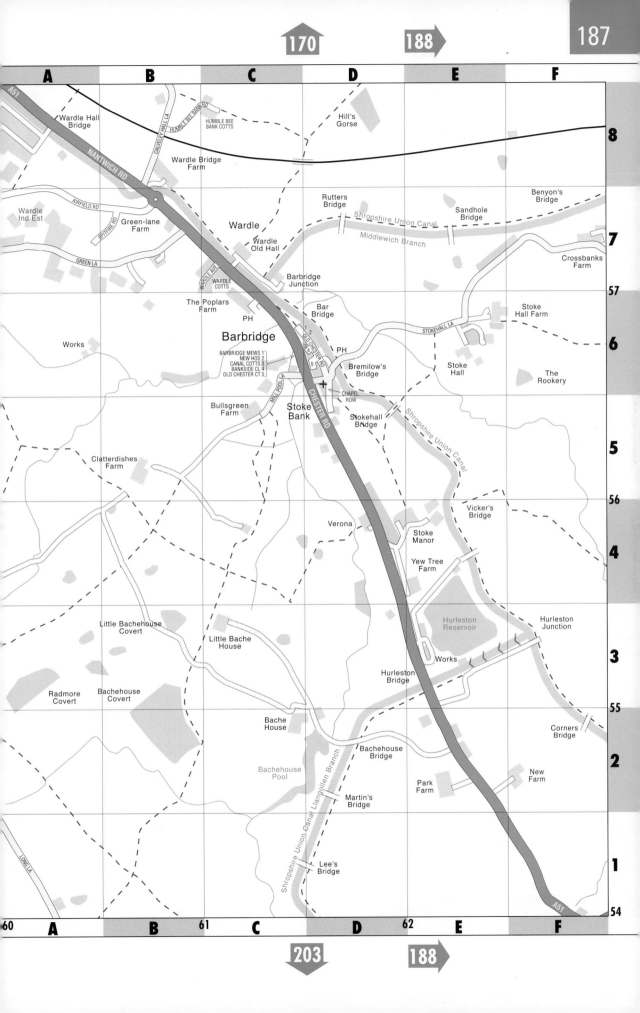

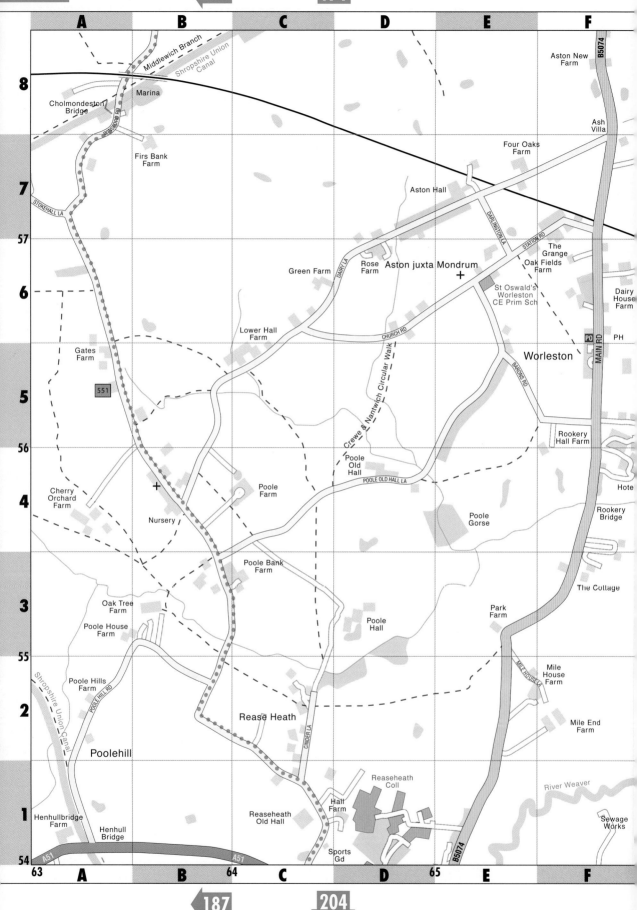

187
171

A   **B**   **C**   **D**   **E**   **F**

8

Middlewich Branch

Shropshire Union Canal

B5074

Aston New Farm

Marina

Cholmondeston Bridge

Ash Villa

7

WINSHIP RD

STOKEHALL LA

Firs Bank Farm

Four Oaks Farm

Aston Hall

DARLINGTON LA

STATION RD

57

Green Farm

DAIRY LA

Rose Farm

Aston juxta Mondrum

The Grange

Oak Fields Farm

6

St Oswald's Worleston CE Prim Sch

Dairy House Farm

Gates Farm

Lower Hall Farm

CHURCH RD

Worleston

MAIN RD

PO

PH

551

Crewe & Nantwich Circular Walk

BARONS RD

5

56

Cherry Orchard Farm

Poole Old Hall

POOLE OLD HALL LA

Rookery Hall Farm

Hote

4

Nursery

Poole Farm

Poole Gorse

Rookery Bridge

Poole Bank Farm

The Cottage

3

Oak Tree Farm

Poole Hall

Park Farm

Poole House Farm

MILE HOUSE LA

55

Shropshire Union Canal

Poole Hills Farm

POOLE HILL RD

Mile House Farm

2

Rease Heath

CINDER LA

Mile End Farm

Poolehill

River Weaver

Reaseheath Coll

1

Henhullbridge Farm

Reaseheath Old Hall

Hall Farm

B5074

Sewage Works

Henhull Bridge

A51

Sports Gd

54

63   A   A51   B   64   C   D   65   E   F

← 189   ↑ 173

← 189   206

5

A B C D E F

8

Whitehall Farm

Wheelockheath Farm

Fingerpost Farm

MILL LA

DAY GREEN RD

ROUGHWOOD HOLLOW

HASSALL RD

M6

Wheelock Heath

1 NURSERY FIELDS WAY
2 JOSEPH WOOD DR
3 SYDNEY NEWTON RD
4 JOHN SIMPSON CRES

School Farm

Daisy Bank House

Hassall Pool

Holly Tree Farm
Day Green

COPPICE RD

SANDY LA

ALSAGER RD

HASSALL HALL RD

Walnut Tree Farm

7

POOL LA

HASSALL RD

Hassall

Hassall Hall

57

Bridgehouse Farm

Bostock House

6

South Cheshire Way

Green Bank Farm

Dunnock's Fold Farm

Moss Cottage

5

Castle Farm

56

Moss End Farm

Homeshaw Farm

Oakhanger Hall

DUNNOCKS FOLD RD

Woodside Farm

4

JOHN CL DR
WAY

WILLIAM HIGGINS CL

WINDSOR DR

FRANK WILKINSON WAY

Heathfield Farm

Stockton Farm

SPENCER CL

DERWENT CL

DELAMERE CT

CRANBERRY CT

KENSINGTON CLOSE LA

BOLLIN CL

Oakhanger Farm

Ashfields

Masl

3

Hall o' the Heath

HOLMSHAW LA

HILLDITCHES LA

Gate Farm

NURSERY RD

HARRELL DR

BOWY CL

WEAZLY CL

Rose Tree Farm

TAYLORS LANE

55

Peartree Farm

Oakhanger Moss

White Moss Farm

Spartan Wood Farm

White Moss

HOMESTEAD CL

BARN FIELD WAY

Butterton Lane Farm

BUTTERTON LA

2

Moss Farm

CREWE RD

B5077

B5078

Oakhanger

Mast

Radway Green

B5017

BUTTERTON LA

DUNN'S COTTS

MILL LA

Mast

LC

RADWAY GREEN RD

B5078

NO 7 ROAD

CENTRAL AVE

NO 2 ROAD

NO 1 ROAD

1

Wks

Radway Green Bsns & Tech Ctr

54

F1
1 The King's Church of England (A) Sch
2 St John The Evangelist RC Prim Sch

Map labels

Close Farm
DRUMBER LA
Quarry Wood
South Cheshire Way
Mow Cop Trail
Mast
Old Man of Mow
Mainwairing Farm
Staffordshire Way
PH
CASTLE RD
Birch Tree Farm
STATION RD
WOOD ST
CORONATION MILL
TOP STATION RD
CLOSE LA
MANORS RD
LOWER HIGH ST
St THOMAS ST
TOWER HILL RD
Mow Cop Castle
WESTFIELD RD
PRIMITIVE ST
BOURNE ST
HIGH ST
WOODSIDE COTTS
HARDINGS ROW
HILLSIDE CL
MOORLAND RD
CHURCH LA
Perseverance Mill
AKESMOOR LA
The Bank
GRAY'S CL
THE BANK
MEADOWSIDE LA
MILL LA
SPRING BANK
MOUNT PLEASANT RD
BIRCH TREE LA
THE BRAKE
THE BRAKE VILLAGE
Gritstone Trail
Mow Cop
HALLS RD
STATION RD
WOODCOCK LA
Wesleyan Mus
CHAPEL BANK
Towerhill Farm
Lower Bank Farm
Woodcock's Well CE Prim Sch
PH
FERN CL
CENTRAL ST
CHAPEL ST
NORTH ST
CLARE ST
CHURCH ST
ROCKSIDE
MOW COP RD
FORDS LA
Castle Prim Sch
SANDS RD
RIDDULPH RD
MOORVIEW GDNS
57
Mount Pleasant
WEST ST
WILLMER CRES
SOUTH ST
PO
HEATHERSIDE
MELLORS BANK
DALE VW
DALES GREEN RD
6
Hall o' Lee
KNOWSLEY LA
MOW LA
THE HOLLOW
HIGH VIEW
THE MILL
Dales Green
ALDERHAY LA
Holly Farm
HIGH ST
HOLLY LA
Stone Trough
Staffordshire STREET ATLAS
Brieryhurst Farm
Hollin House Farm
BROWN LEES RD
5
Blue Pot Farm
PO
PH
Harriseahead
WAIN LEE
STRAMSHALL LA
56
COB MOOR RD
LAWTON ST
BANK ST
CHURCH ST
HARRISEAHEAD LA
CLARE ST
WILLOWCROFT WAY
LONG LA
Playing Field
THURSFIELD AVE 1
PRIORY PL 2
CASTLE HO
DOVE HO
The Rookery
Trubshaw Edge Farm
Thursfield Prim Sch
CHAPEL LA
LAUREL DR
ASPEN CL
COTTONWOOD GR
Bullocks House Farm
4
Maryhill High & Prim Schs
MARYHILL CL
St John the Evangelist Catholic Acad
RIGBY RD
BRIERYHURST RD
HILLARY RD
HAZEL CL
NEWCHAPEL RD
St ANDREWS DR
ACACIA CL
WOODHALL RD
WENTWORTH CL
BIRKDALE CH
ASTBURY
Trubshaw Farm
KITE GR
STARLING CL
LARK AVE
MERLIN WAY
BULLOCKS HOUSE RD
FREEDOM DR
FERNDALE GDNS
Thursfield Lodge
3
GLOUCESTER RD
DORCHESTER CL
PARK VIEW RD
MOSS CL
SALOP RD
TELFORD RD
HILARY RD
CASTLEVIEW
EVEREST RD
ROOKERY
EVEREST RD
OSPREY VIEW
LAPWING RD
WILD GOOSE AVE
IAN RD
ACORN GDNS
Newchapel Observatory & Natural Science Ctr
55
BEDFORD AVE
WARWICK CL
DORSET RD
WILLIAM RD
RUTLAND RD
WHITEHILL RD
TAWNEY CL
SPEY DR
DERWENT CRES
TRUBSHAW CT
PENNYFIELDS RD
GREEN CRES
HIGH ST
MEADOW GR
Newchapel
White Hill
Dove Bank
KING ST
LAMB ST
VICTORIA AVE
Dove Bank Prim Sch
LATTWOOD RISE
WELLINGTON ST
HARRISWOOD CL
TAMAR RD
HIGHFIELD AVE
WHITFIELD RD
WINDSOR RD
TERN AVE
OANE GDNS
PH
STATION RD
NEWTOWN
LORDSHIRE PL
JASMIN WAY 1
HAREBELL GR 2
WOODRUFF CL 3
2
1 SPARROWBUTTS GR
2 SANDPIPER CT
3 PHOENIX CL
QUEEN ST
BACK HEATHCOTE ST
HEATHCOTE ST
TH
WADE ST
MARKET ST
WATERLOO RD
POWY DR
ASH VIEW
WEIR GR
NABBS CL
VINE BANK RD
MELLOR RD
THOMAS ST
SAMUEL ST
CARR ST
LORRAINE GR
St Packmoor Prim Sch
KIDSGROVE
WOODSIDE AV
OLD SCHOOL
VALE PK
THE LOVATTS
LARKFIELD
SUMMERFIELD
KINGSWOOD
CHARNWOOD
BIRCHENWOOD WAY
5
CURLEW RD
BIRCHENWOOD RD
REDWING GR
1
MILL RISE
NELSON BLDGS
MOUNT PLEASANT
QUARRY TERR
LIVERPOOL RD
A50
STONE BANK RD
A50 Uttoxeter
CINDER ROCK WAY
REDROCK CRES
BIRCH
KING GEORGE WAY
LINNETT GR
WOODPECKER RD
SWALLOW RD
GOLDFINCH RD
TURNHURST RD
LAPWING RD
Packmoor
54

A1
1 St Thomas CE Prim Sch

A2
1 KINNERSLEY ST
2 GILBERT CL
3 NAPIER GDNS
4 PEEL CT
5 BANK CT
6 HIGHERLAND CT
7 WESLEY GDNS
8 VICTORIA CT

B2
1 SWALLOW CL
2 WHEELOCK WAY
3 DIAMOND AVE
4 MOSSFIELD CRES
5 LITTLE ROW
6 BRIGHTS AVE
7 BIRCHES WAY
8 SILVERMINE CL
9 MAGPIE CRES

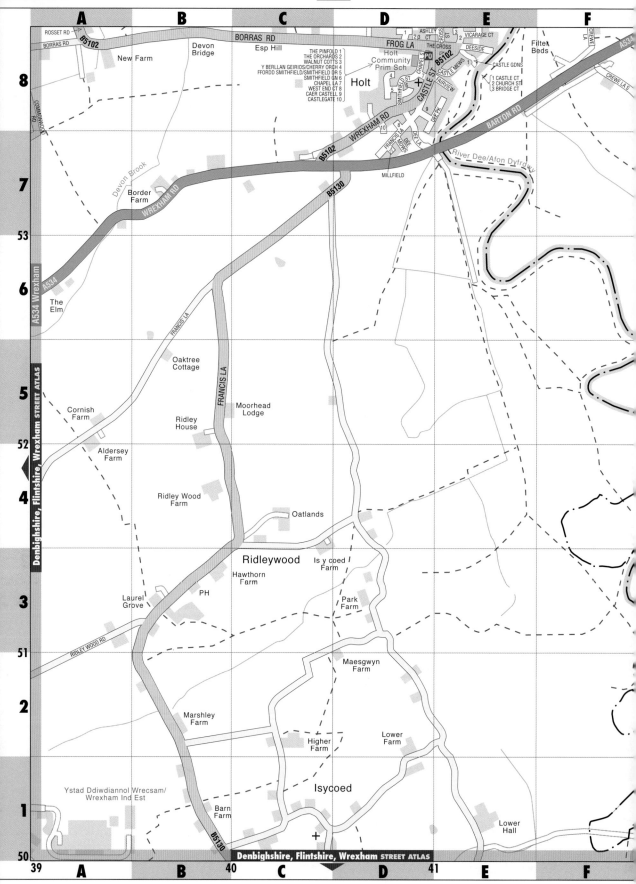

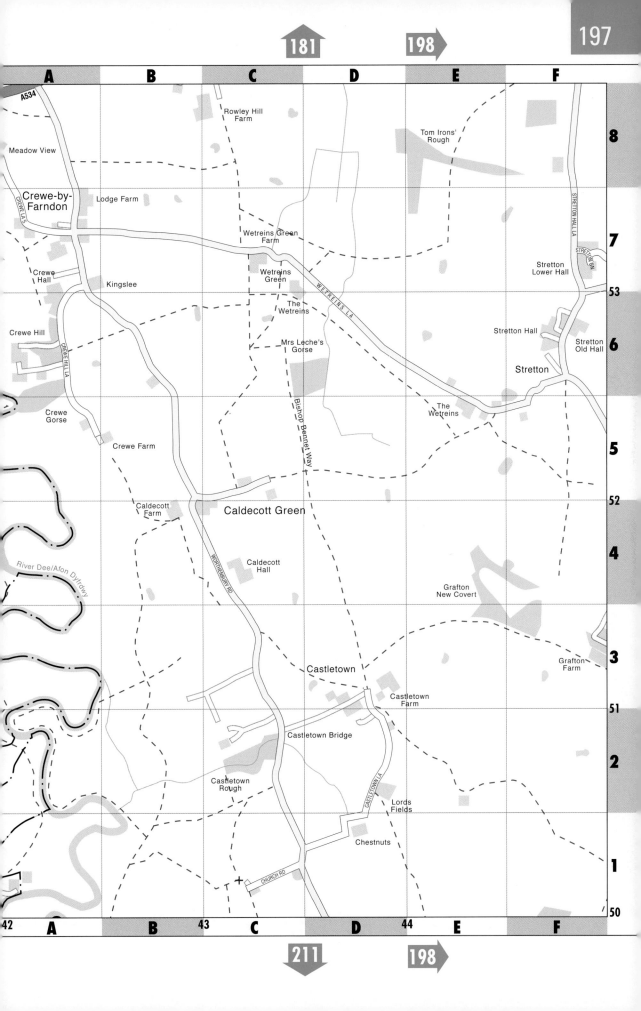

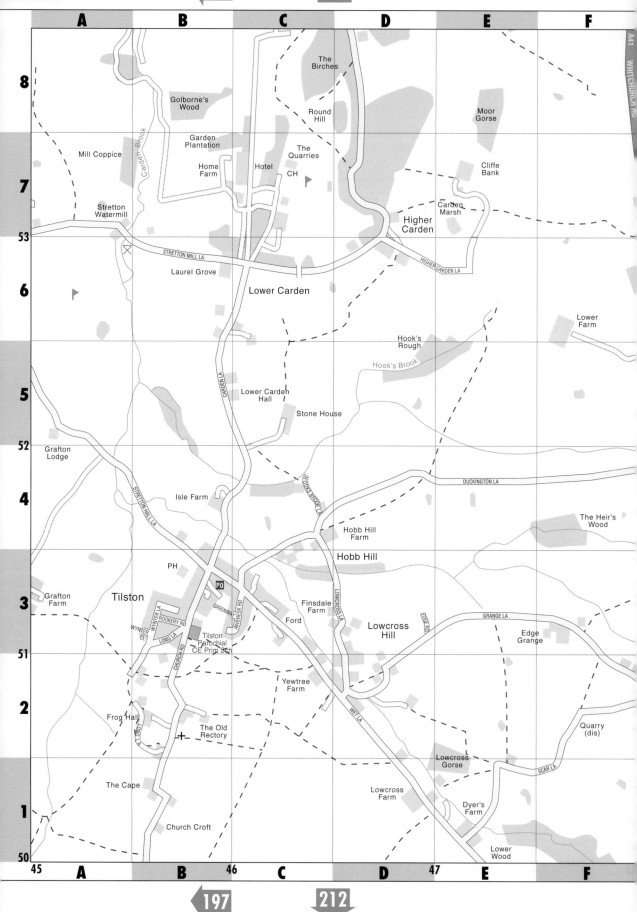

A41

WHITCHURCH Rd

A   B   C   D   E   F

8

The Birches

Golborne's Wood

Round Hill

Moor Gorse

Garden Plantation

7

Mill Coppice

Home Farm

Hotel

The Quarries

CH

Cliffe Bank

Stretton Watermill

Carden Marsh

Higher Carden

53

STRETTON MILL LA

Laurel Grove

HIGHER CARDEN LA

6

Lower Carden

CARDEN LA

Hook's Rough

Hook's Brook

Lower Farm

5

Lower Carden Hall

Stone House

52

Grafton Lodge

DUCKINGTON LA

4

Isle Farm

BROOK'S BROOK LA

Hobb Hill Farm

The Heir's Wood

Hobb Hill

PH

3

Grafton Farm

Tilston

PO

GREENWAY

INVERESK RD

Finsdale Farm

Ford

LOWCROSS LA

Lowcross Hill

GRANGE LA

EDGE RD

Edge Grange

WYNTER LA

ROOKERY RD

51

WYNTER CL

LONG LA

CHURCH RD

Tilston Parochial CE Prim Sch

2

Frog Hall

Yewtree Farm

The Old Rectory

WET LA

Quarry (dis)

Lowcross Gorse

SCAR LA

1

The Cape

Lowcross Farm

Dyer's Farm

Church Croft

Lower Wood

50

45 A   B 46 C   D 47 E   F

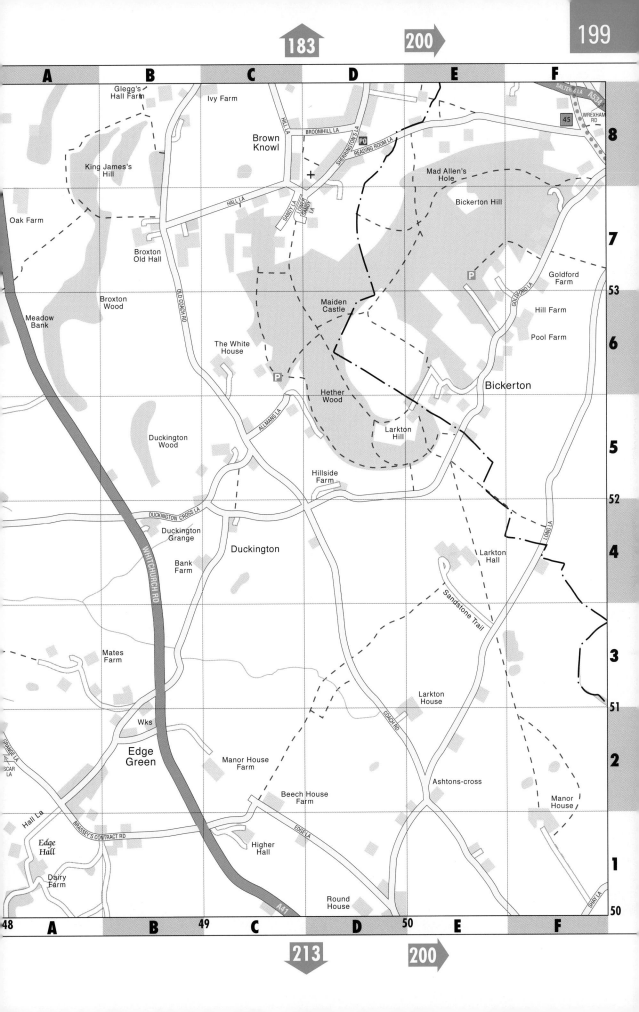

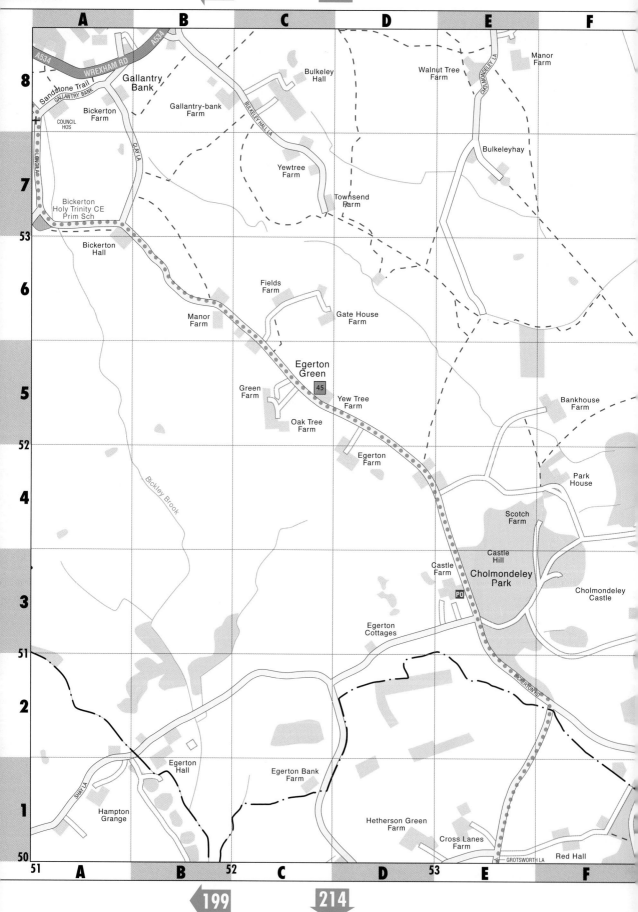

A   B   C   D   E   F

8

WREXHAM RD
Sandstone Trail
GALLANTRY BANK
Gallantry Bank
Bickerton Farm
COUNCIL HOS
Gallantry-bank Farm
Bulkeley Hall
Walnut Tree Farm
Manor Farm
CHOLMONDELEY LA

7

CLAY LA
BULKELEY HALL LA
Bickerton Holy Trinity CE Prim Sch
Yewtree Farm
Townsend Farm
Bulkeleyhay

53

Bickerton Hall

6

Manor Farm
Fields Farm
Gate House Farm

5

Green Farm
Egerton Green
45
Yew Tree Farm
Oak Tree Farm
Bankhouse Farm

52

Egerton Farm
Park House

4

Bickley Brook
Scotch Farm
Castle Hill
Cholmondeley Park
Cholmondeley Castle

3

Castle Farm
PO
Egerton Cottages

51

BICKERTON RD

2

SHAY LA
Egerton Hall
Egerton Bank Farm

1

Hampton Grange
Hetherson Green Farm
Cross Lanes Farm
Red Hall
GROTSWORTH LA

50

51   A   B   52   C   D   53   E   F

185

202

A B C D E F

Ridley
Farm

Oak
Farm

Meadow
Farm

A49

A534

Chesterton
Farm

Ridley
Wood

WREXHAM RD

Ridley Bank
Farm

Chesterton
Wood

8

A534

7

Croxton Green
Farm

53

CROXTON GN

Croxton
Green
Farm

Sicily Oak
Farm

Croxton
Green

6

Coronation
Wood

Croxton Green
Farm

Nevill's
Wood

Higginsfield
House

5

HIGGINSFIELD RD

CHORLEY GREEN LA

52

Chapel
Mere

CHOLMONDELEY PK

Garden
Covert

Beeston
Lodge

Rose-Ground
Farm

4

The Old
Hall

River Weaver

Dowse
Green

Cholmondeley
Castle
Gdns

The Long
Plantation

3

Weaver
Farm

Cholmondeley
Bridge

Wallstone

51

Deer Park
Mere

SAWMILL RD

NANTWICH RD

2

Marl Piece

Fields
Farm

Breeze
Hill

BICKERTON RD

PH

School
Farm

Chorley
Bank

Chorley
Stock

1

Moss
Wood

Ring Road

Moss Lane

WRENBURY RD

CHORLEY BANK
COUNCIL HOS

50

4

A B 55 C D 56 E F

215

202

201
186

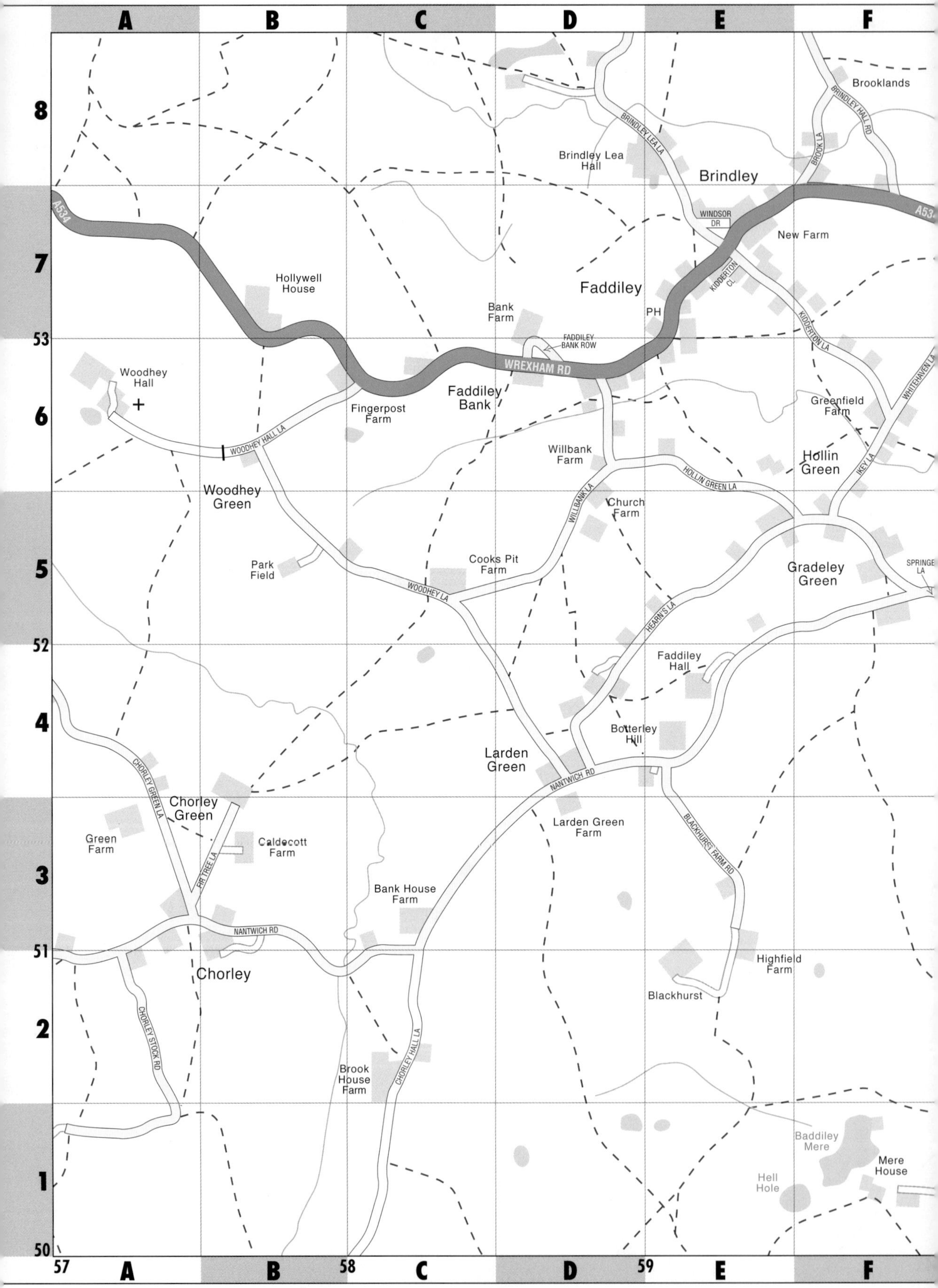

A **B** **C** **D** **E** **F**

8

Brooklands

BRINDLEY LEA LA

Brindley Lea Hall

Brindley

BROOK LA

BRINDLEY HALL RD

A534

WINDSOR DR

New Farm

7

Hollywell House

Faddiley

KIDDERTON CL

KIDDERTON LA

53

Bank Farm

PH

FADDILEY BANK ROW

WHITEHAVEN LA

Greenfield Farm

WREXHAM RD

Faddiley Bank

6

Woodhey Hall

Fingerpost Farm

Willbank Farm

Hollin Green

WOODHEY HALL LA

HOLLIN GREEN LA

HEY LA

Woodhey Green

WILLBANK LA

Church Farm

5

Park Field

WOODHEY LA

Cooks Pit Farm

Gradeley Green

SPRINGE LA

52

HEARN'S LA

Faddiley Hall

4

CHORLEY GREEN LA

Botterley Hill

Larden Green

BLACKHURST FARM RD

Chorley Green

Caldecott Farm

NANTWICH RD

Larden Green Farm

3

Green Farm

FIR TREE LA

Bank House Farm

51

NANTWICH RD

Highfield Farm

Chorley

Blackhurst

2

CHORLEY STOCK RD

CHORLEY HALL LA

Brook House Farm

Baddiley Mere

Mere House

1

Hell Hole

50

57 **A** 58 **B** **C** 59 **D** **E** **F**

201
216

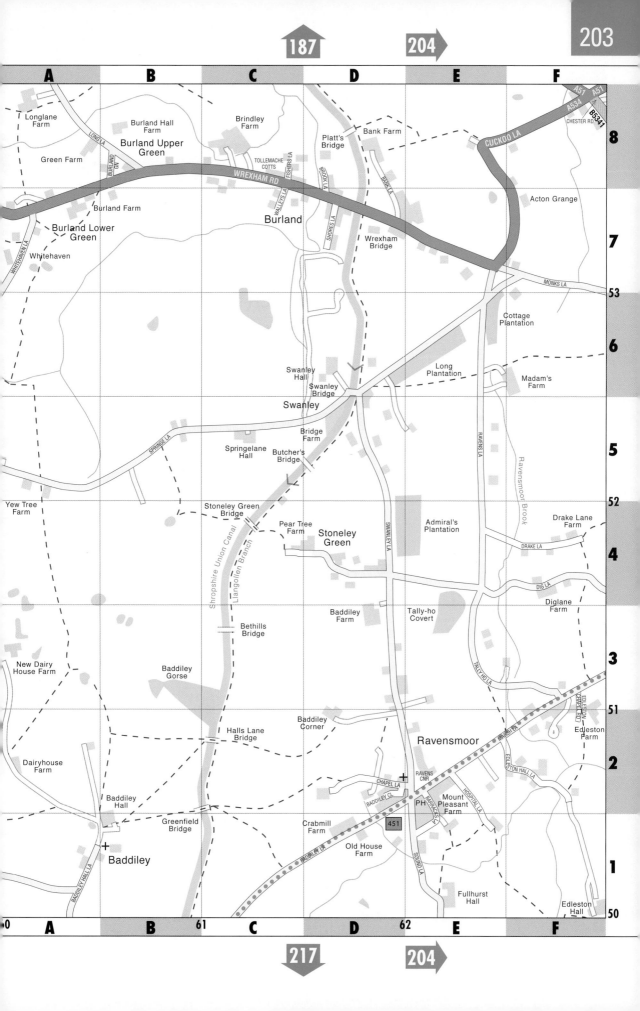

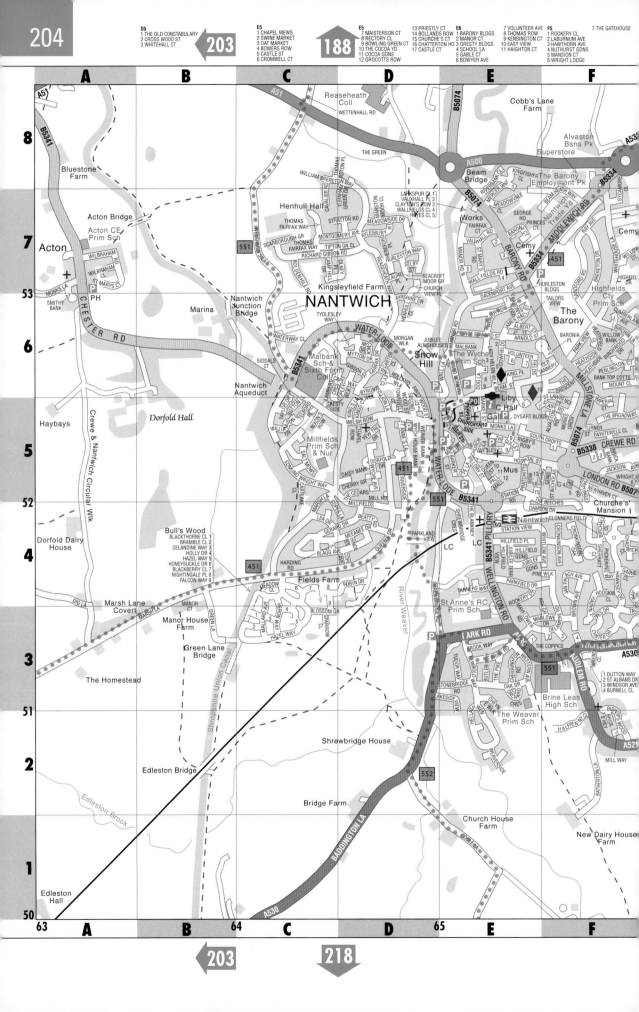

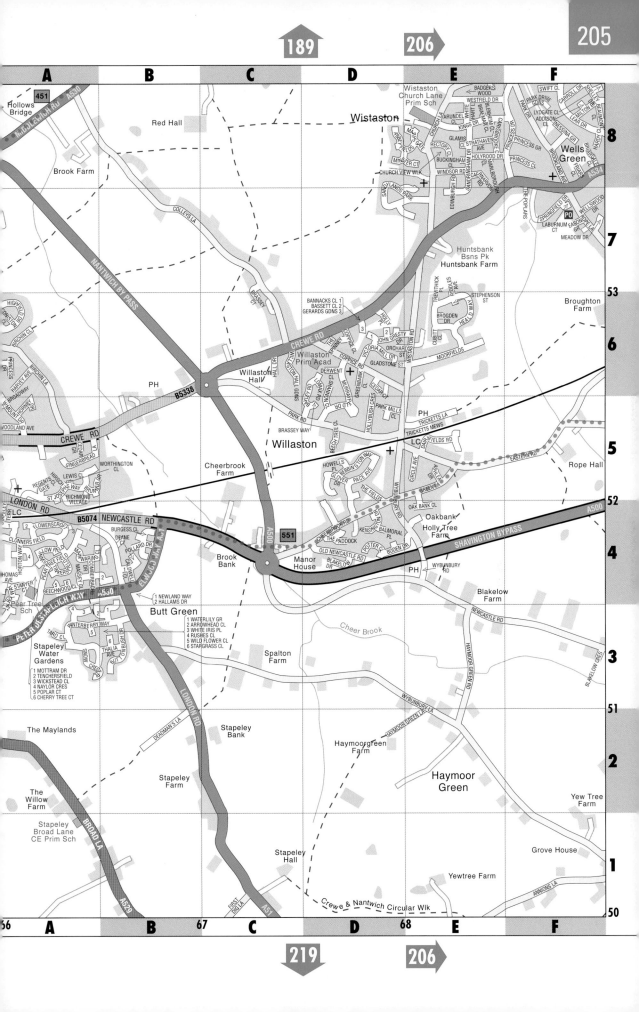

205
190
205
220

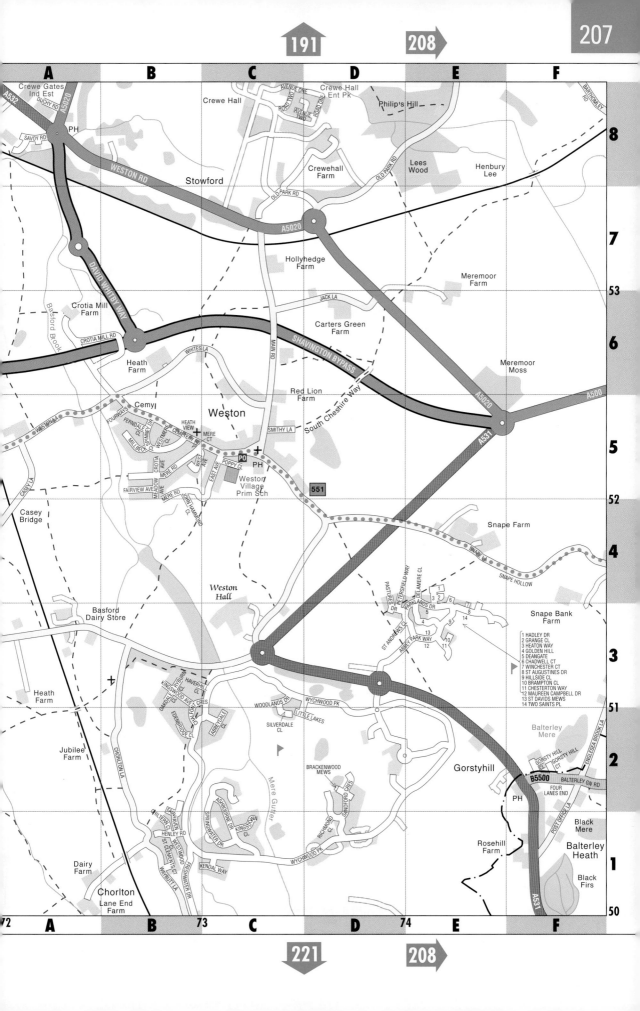

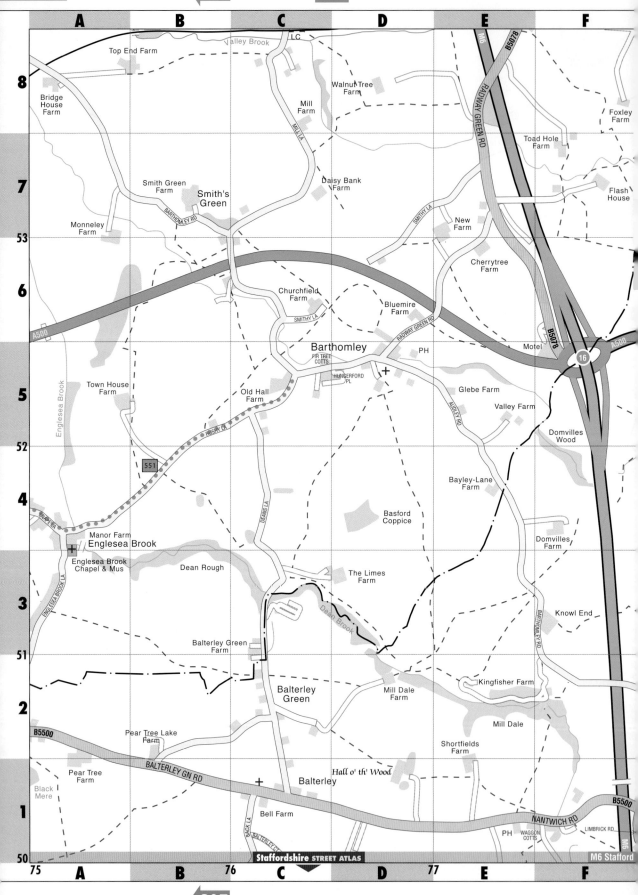

A | B | C | D | E | F

8

7

53

6

52

5

4

51

3

2

1

50

Valley Brook
LC
Top End Farm
Walnut Tree Farm
Bridge House Farm
Mill Farm
Foxley Farm
MILL LA
Toad Hole Farm
Smith Green Farm
Daisy Bank Farm
Flash House
Smith's Green
BARTHOMLEY RD
New Farm
SMITHY LA
Monneley Farm
Cherrytree Farm
Englesea Brook
A500
Churchfield Farm
Bluemire Farm
B5078
SMITHY LA
RADWAY GREEN RD
A500
Barthomley
PH
Motel
16
FIR TREE COTTS
Town House Farm
Old Hall Farm
HUNGERFORD PL
Glebe Farm
Valley Farm
Domvilles Wood
ROSERY LA
AUDLEY RD
52
551
Bayley-Lane Farm
Englesea Brook
DEANS LA
Basford Coppice
Domvilles Farm
SNAPE LA
Manor Farm
Englesea Brook
Englesea Brook Chapel & Mus
Dean Rough
The Limes Farm
BARTHOMLEY RD
Knowl End
ENGLESEA BROOK LA
Dean Brook
Balterley Green Farm
Kingfisher Farm
Balterley Green
Mill Dale Farm
Pear Tree Lake Farm
B5500
Mill Dale
BALTERLEY GN RD
Shortfields Farm
Pear Tree Farm
Hall o' th' Wood
B5500
Black Mere
Balterley
NANTWICH RD
BACK LA
Bell Farm
PH
WAGGON COTTS
LIMBRICK RD.
BALTERLEY COTTS
M6 Stafford

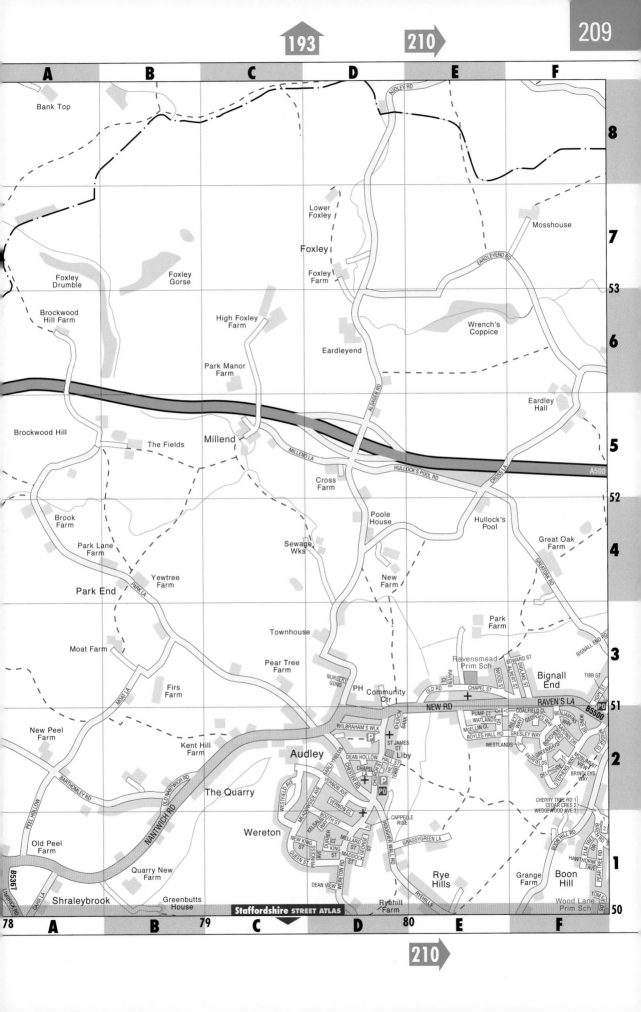

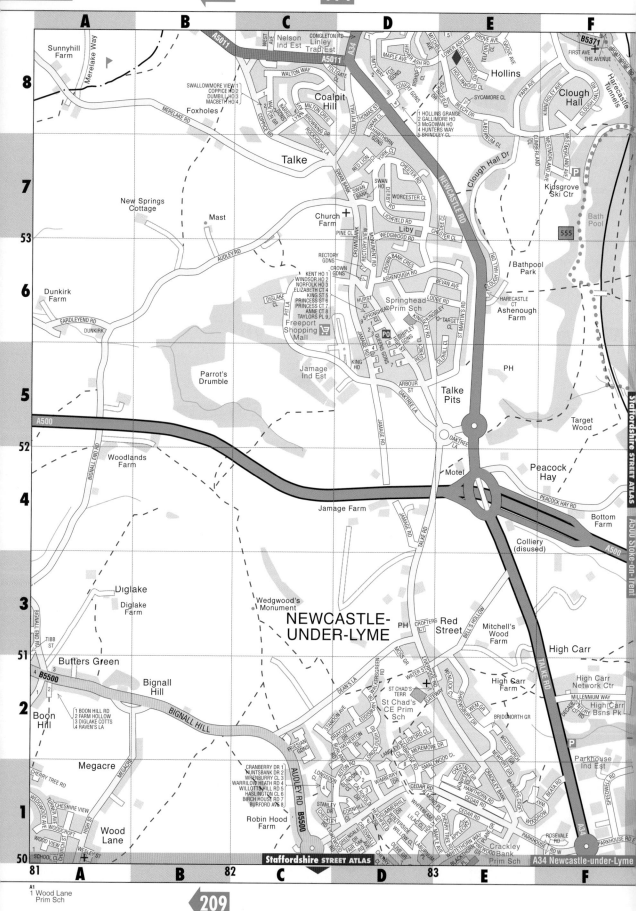

A1
1 Wood Lane
Prim Sch

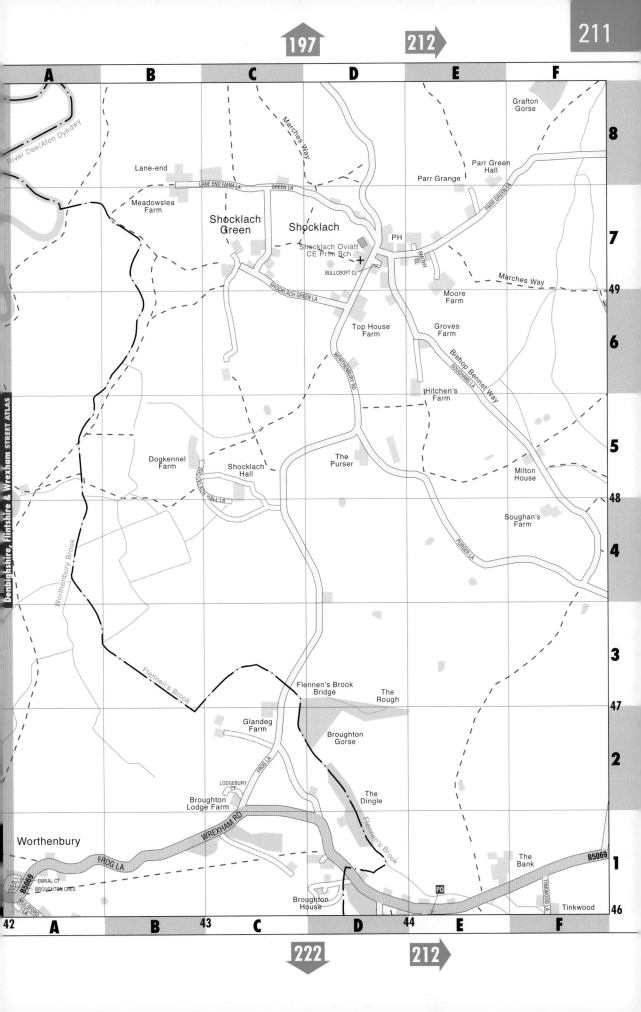

A   B   C   D   E   F

8

7

49

6

5

48

4

3

47

2

1

46

Grafton
Gorse

River Dee/Afon Dyfrdwy

Lane-end

Parr Green
Hall

Parr Grange

Meadowslea
Farm

LANE END FARM LA   GREEN LA

PARR GREEN LA

Shocklach
Green

Shocklach

Shocklach Oviatt
CE Prim Sch

PH

SMITHY CL

Marches Way

BULLCROFT CL

SHOCKLACH GREEN LA

Moore
Farm

Top House
Farm

Groves
Farm

Bishop Bennet Way

SOUGHANS LA

Hitchen's
Farm

WORTHENBURY RD

Dogkennel
Farm

Shocklach
Hall

The
Purser

Milton
House

SHOCKLACH HALL LA

Soughan's
Farm

Worthenbury Brook

PURSER LA

Flennen's Brook

Flennen's Brook
Bridge

The
Rough

Glandeg
Farm

Broughton
Gorse

FROG LA

LODGEBURY
CT

The
Dingle

Broughton
Lodge Farm

Flennen's Brook

Worthenbury

WREXHAM RD

The
Bank

B5069

FROG LA

EMRAL CT

BROUGHTON CRES

PO

TINKWOOD LA

B5069

MULSFORD
LA

Broughton
House

Tinkwood

42   A   B   43   C   D   44   E   F

211
198

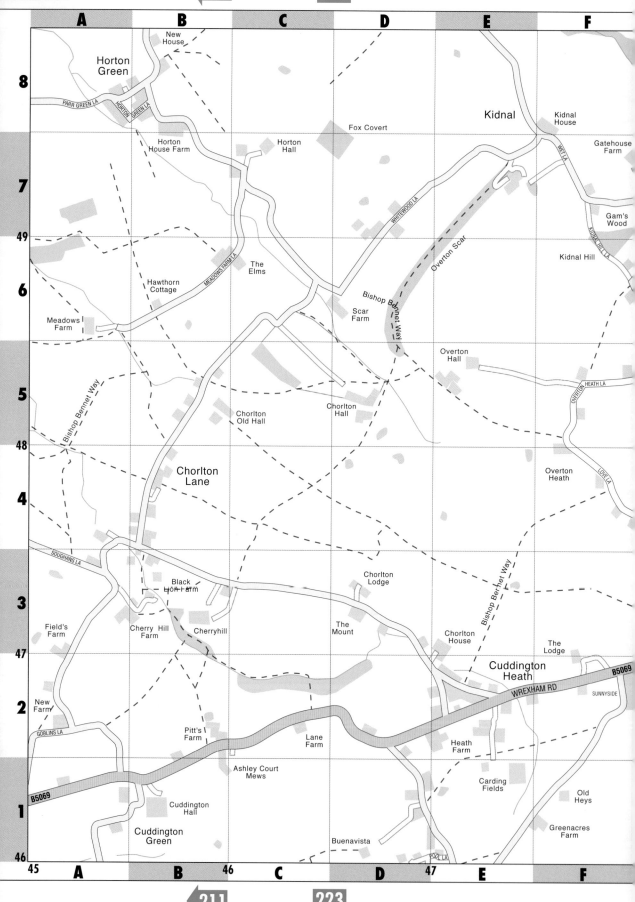

211
223

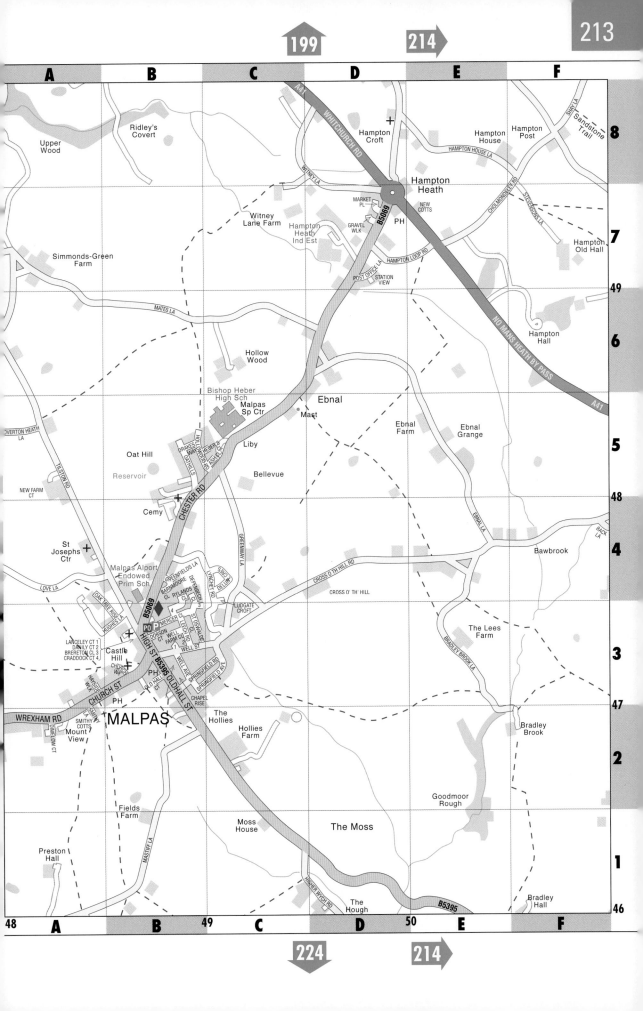

213
200

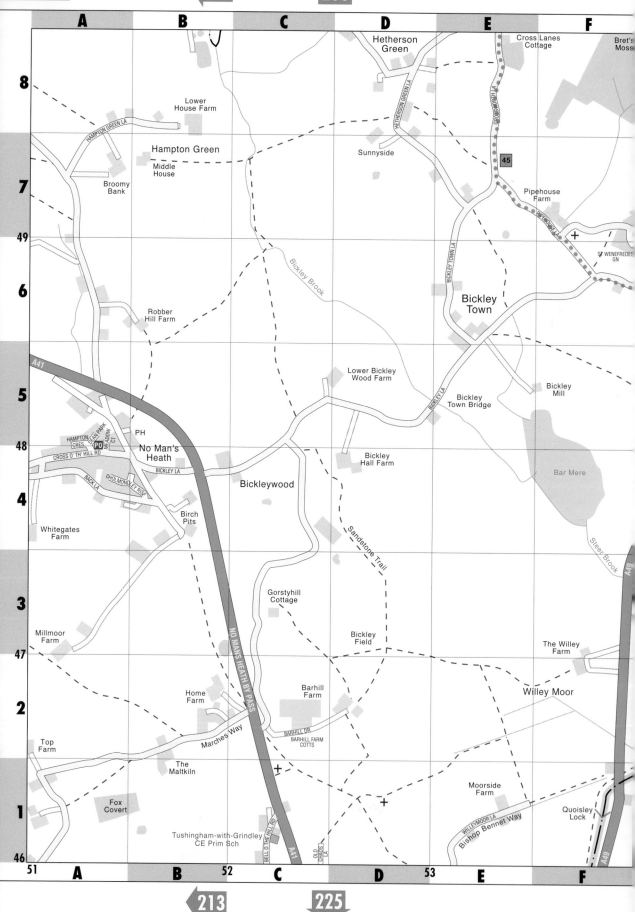

213
225

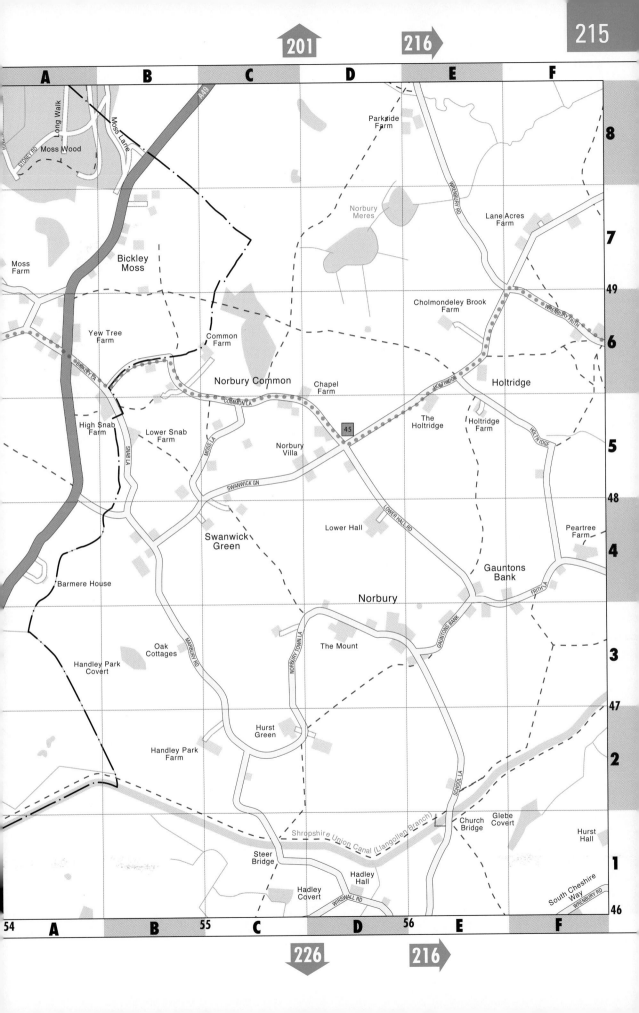

201
216

A B C D E F

8
7
49
6
5
48
4
3
47
2
1
46

A B C D E F

226
216

Long Walk
Moss Wood
STONEY RD
Moss Lane
Moss Farm
Bickley Moss
449
Yew Tree Farm
BICKLEY LA
Common Farm
Norbury Common
COMMON LA
Chapel Farm
45
The Holtridge
Holtridge
HOLT RIDGE
HOLT RIDGE
Holtridge Farm
Cholmondeley Brook Farm
WRENBURY RD
Lane Acres Farm
WRENBURY TRITH
Norbury Meres
Parkside Farm
High Snab Farm
SNAB LA
Lower Snab Farm
MOSS LA
Norbury Villa
SWANWICK GN
Lower Hall
LOWER HALL RD
Peartree Farm
FRITH LA
Gauntons Bank
Swanwick Green
Barmere House
Oak Cottages
Handley Park Covert
MARBURY RD
Norbury
NORBURY TOWN LA
The Mount
GAUNTONS BANK
Handley Park Farm
Hurst Green
SCHOLS LA
Church Bridge
Glebe Covert
Hurst Hall
Shropshire Union Canal (Llangollen Branch)
Steer Bridge
Hadley Hall
Hadley Covert
WIRSWALL RD
South Cheshire Way
WRENBURY RD

54 55 56

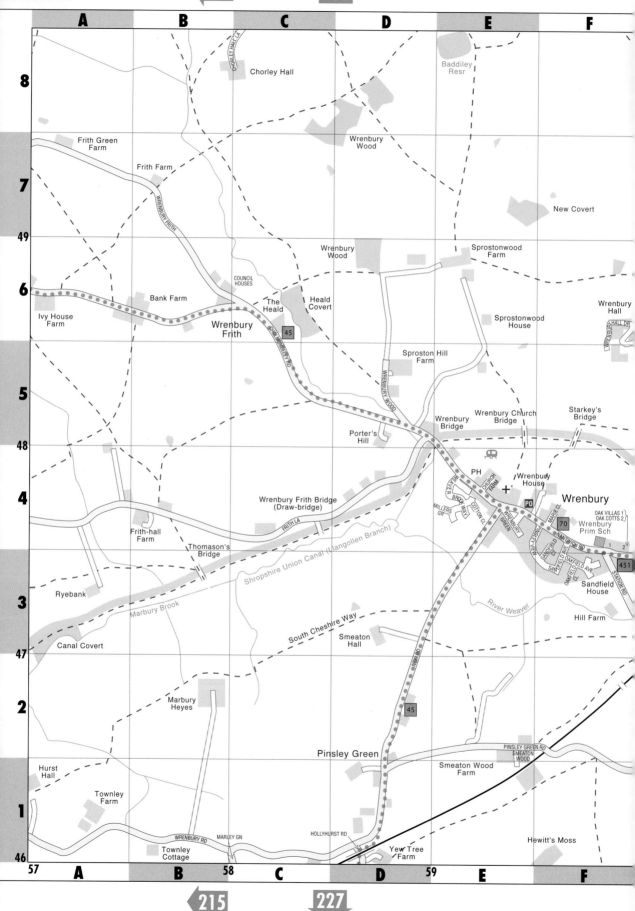

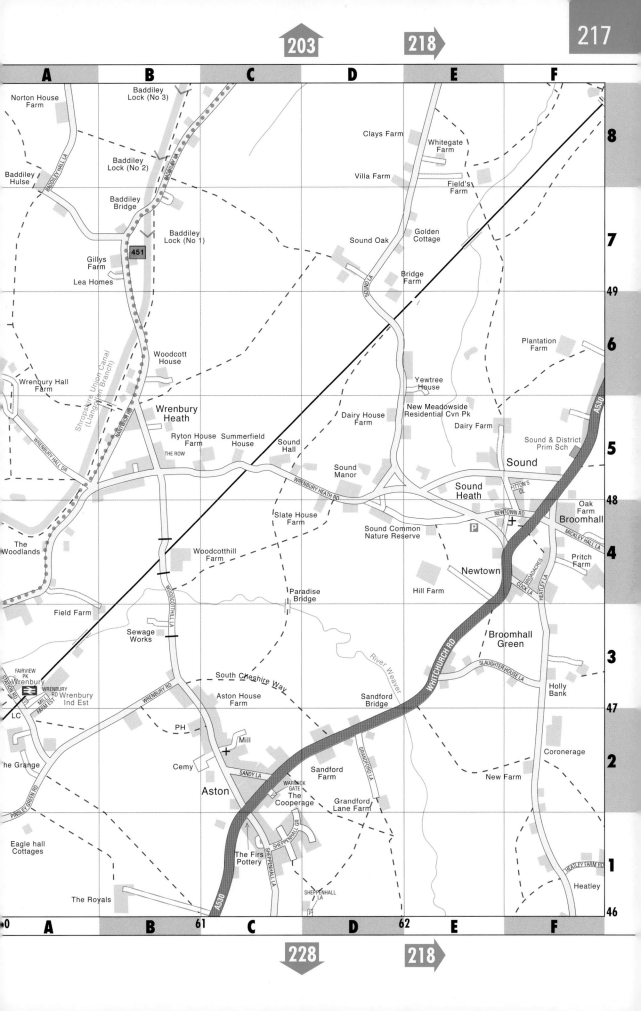

A **B** **C** **D** **E** **F**

8

Norton House Farm

Baddiley Lock (No 3)

Clays Farm

Whitegate Farm

Baddiley Hulse

Baddiley Lock (No 2)

Field's Farm

Villa Farm

Baddiley Bridge

7

Golden Cottage

Sound Oak

Baddiley Lock (No 1)

451

Gillys Farm

Bridge Farm

49

Lea Homes

6

Plantation Farm

Woodcott House

Shropshire Union Canal (Llangollen Branch)

Yewtree House

Wrenbury Hall Farm

New Meadowside Residential Cvn Pk

Dairy Farm

A530

Wrenbury Heath

THE ROW

Ryton House Farm

Summerfield House

Dairy House Farm

5

Sound & District Prim Sch

NANTWICH RD

Sound Hall

Sound

Sound Manor

Sound Heath

FITTON'S CL

48

The Woodlands

Slate House Farm

NEWTOWN RD

Oak Farm

Broomhall

P

Sound Common Nature Reserve

Woodcotthill Farm

4

Pritch Farm

Newtown

BROADACRES

HEATLEY LA

MICKLEY HALL LA

COCK LA

Field Farm

Hill Farm

Paradise Bridge

WOODCOTTHILL LA

Broomhall Green

3

River Weaver

WHITCHURCH RD

SLAUGHTER HOUSE LA

FAIRVIEW PK Wrenbury

South Cheshire Way

Holly Bank

STATION RD

Wrenbury RD Wrenbury Ind Est

WRENBURY RD

Aston House Farm

Sandford Bridge

47

MILL FARM EST

LC

PH

Coronerage

2

The Grange

Mill

Cemy

SANDY LA

Sandford Farm

New Farm

GRANDFORD LA

PINSLEY GREEN RD

Aston

WARWICK GATE

The Cooperage

Grandford Lane Farm

Eagle hall Cottages

SHEPPENHALL GR

HEATLEY FARM RD

1

The Firs Pottery

SHEPPENHALL LA

Heatley

The Royals

A530

SHEPPENHALL LA

46

A **B** **C** **D** **E** **F**

0 61 62

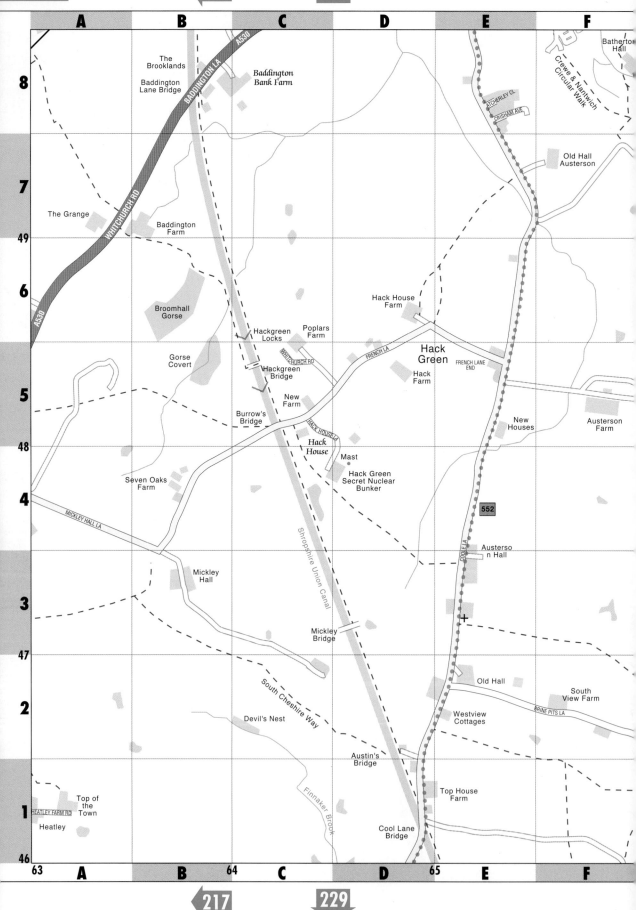

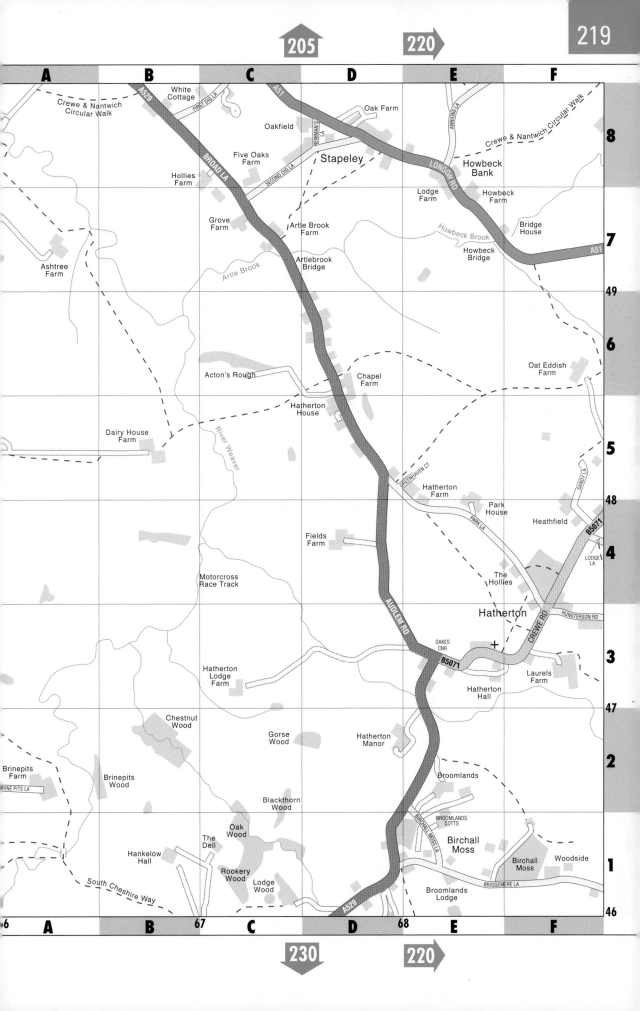

A B C D E F

8

Crewe & Nantwich Circular Walk

White Cottage

Oakfield

Oak Farm

Crewe & Nantwich Circular Walk

FIRST DIG LA

NEWMAN'S LA

ANNIONS LA

Five Oaks Farm

Stapeley

Howbeck Bank

SECOND DIG LA

Hollies Farm

BROAD LA

A529

A51

LONDON RD

Lodge Farm

Howbeck Farm

Howbeck Brook

Bridge House

7

Grove Farm

Artle Brook Farm

Artlebrook Bridge

Howbeck Bridge

A51

Ashtree Farm

Artle Brook

49

6

Acton's Rough

Chapel Farm

Oat Eddish Farm

Hatherton House

Dairy House Farm

River Weaver

5

GREENHAVEN CT

Hatherton Farm

SANDY LA

48

Park House

Heathfield

B5071

Fields Farm

PARK LA

4

LODGE LA

Motorcross Race Track

The Hollies

Hatherton

HUNSTERSON RD

CREWE RD

AUDLEM RD

Hatherton Lodge Farm

OAKES CNR

B5071

Hatherton Hall

Laurels Farm

3

47

Chestnut Wood

Gorse Wood

Hatherton Manor

2

Brinepits Farm

Brinepits Wood

Broomlands

BRINE PITS LA

Blackthorn Wood

BIRCHALL MOSS LA

BROOMLANDS COTTS

Oak Wood

Birchall Moss

Birchall Moss

Woodside

The Dell

Hankelow Hall

Rookery Wood

Lodge Wood

South Cheshire Way

A529

Broomlands Lodge

BRIDGEMERE LA

1

46

6 A B 67 C D 68 E F

219
206

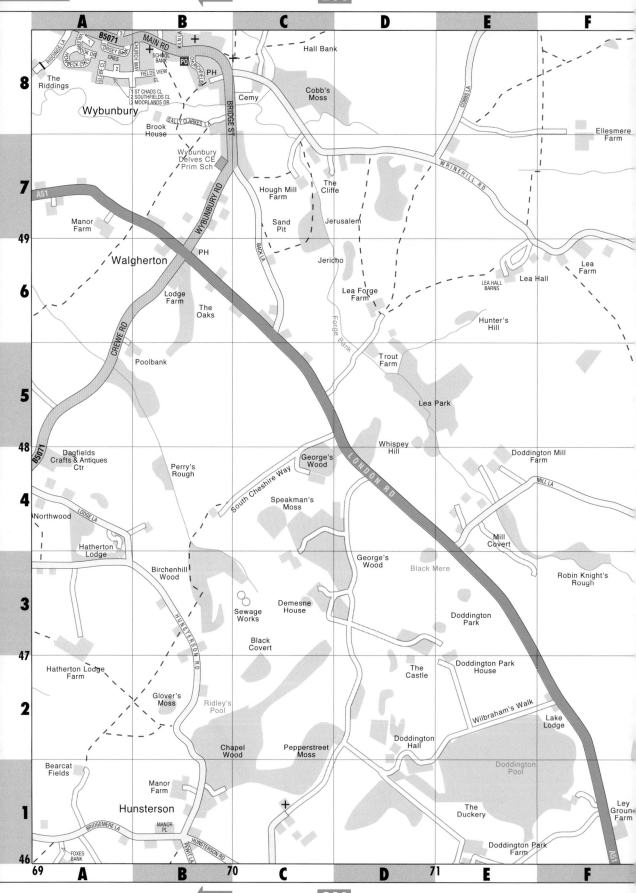

219
231

207

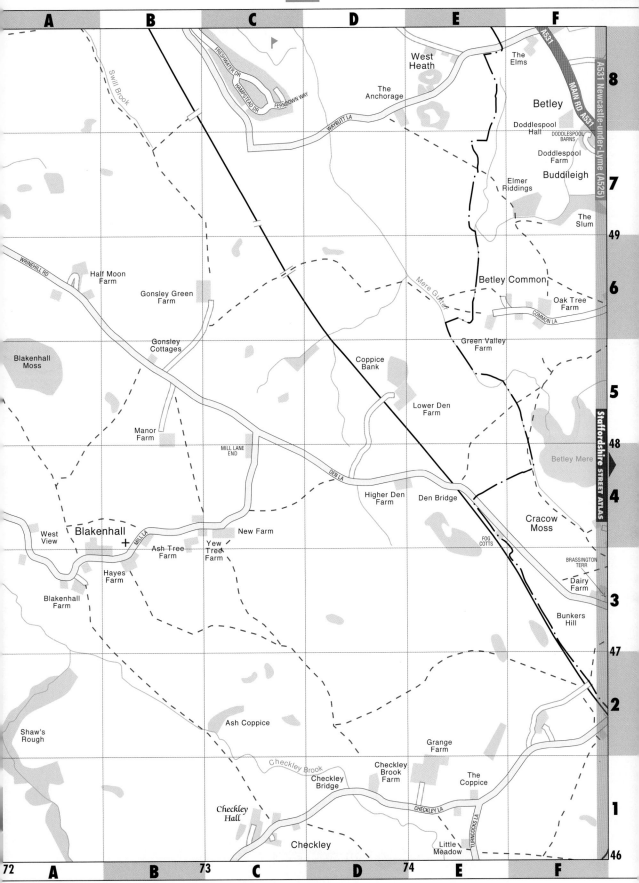

West Heath
The Anchorage
The Elms
Betley
Doddlespool Hall
DODDLESPOOL BARNS
Doddlespool Farm
Buddileigh
Elmer Riddings
The Slum

FRESHWATER DR
HAMPSTEAD DR
FERNDOWN WAY
WAYBUTT LA
Swill Brook

A531 Newcastle-under-Lyme (A525)
MAIN RD A531

Half Moon Farm
Gonsley Green Farm
Gonsley Cottages
Blakenhall Moss
Manor Farm
MILL LANE END
West View
Blakenhall
Ash Tree Farm
Yew Tree Farm
New Farm
Hayes Farm
Blakenhall Farm
MILL LA
WHINEHILL RD

Coppice Bank
Lower Den Farm
DEN LA
Higher Den Farm
Den Bridge
Mere Gutter

Betley Common
Oak Tree Farm
COMMON LA
Green Valley Farm

Betley Mere
Staffordshire STREET ATLAS

Cracow Moss
FOG COTTS
BRASSINGTON TERR
Dairy Farm
Bunkers Hill

Shaw's Rough
Ash Coppice
Checkley Brook
Checkley Bridge
Checkley Hall
Checkley
Grange Farm
Checkley Brook Farm
The Coppice
CHECKLEY LA
TURNCOCKS LA
Little Meadow

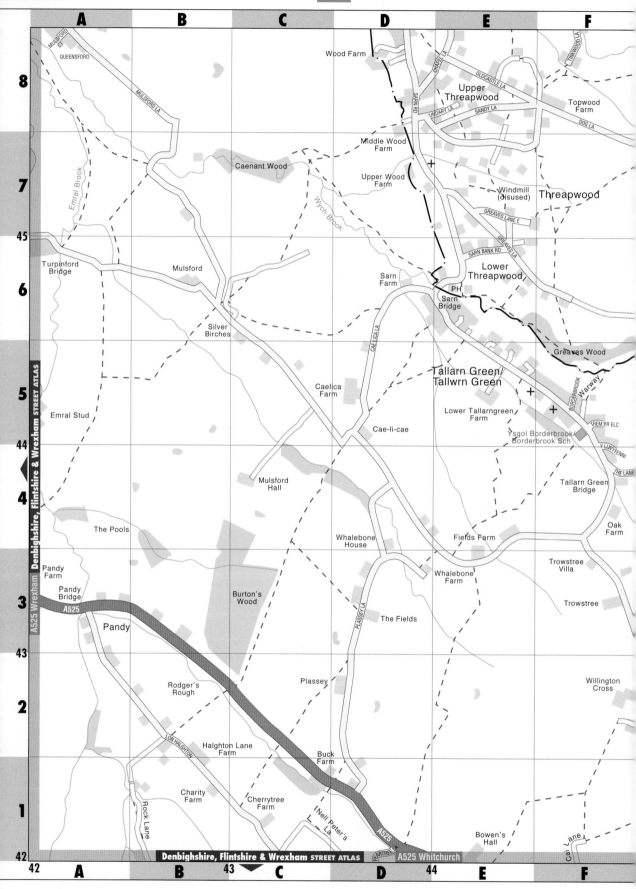

Wood Farm
Upper Threapwood
CHAPEL LA
OLDCASTLE LA
SARN RD
LINDARY LA
SANDY LA
Topwood Farm
DOG LA
TINKWOOD LA
Middle Wood Farm
Upper Wood Farm
Caenant Wood
Wych Brook
Windmill (disused)
Threapwood
GREAVES LANE E
GREAVES LA
Emral Brook
Turpinford Bridge
Mulsford
Sarn Farm
SARN BANK RD
PH
Lower Threapwood
Sarn Bridge
Greaves Wood
Silver Birches
CAELICA LA
Tallarn Green/ Tallwrn Green
BORDERBROOK
WARWAY
Emral Stud
Caelica Farm
Lower Tallarngreen Farm
Cae-li-cae
Ysgol Borderbrook/ Borderbrook Sch
TREM YR ELC
Y LLWYFENNI
THE LANE
Mulsford Hall
Whalebone House
Fields Farm
Tallarn Green Bridge
Oak Farm
The Pools
Whalebone Farm
Trowstree Villa
Pandy Farm
Burton's Wood
PLASSEY LA
The Fields
Trowstree
Pandy Bridge
A525
Pandy
Plassey
Willington Cross
Rodger's Rough
LON HALGHTON
Halghton Lane Farm
Buck Farm
Rock Lane
Charity Farm
Cherrytree Farm
I Nell Peter's La
A525
PEARTREE LA
Bowen's Hall
Cae Lane

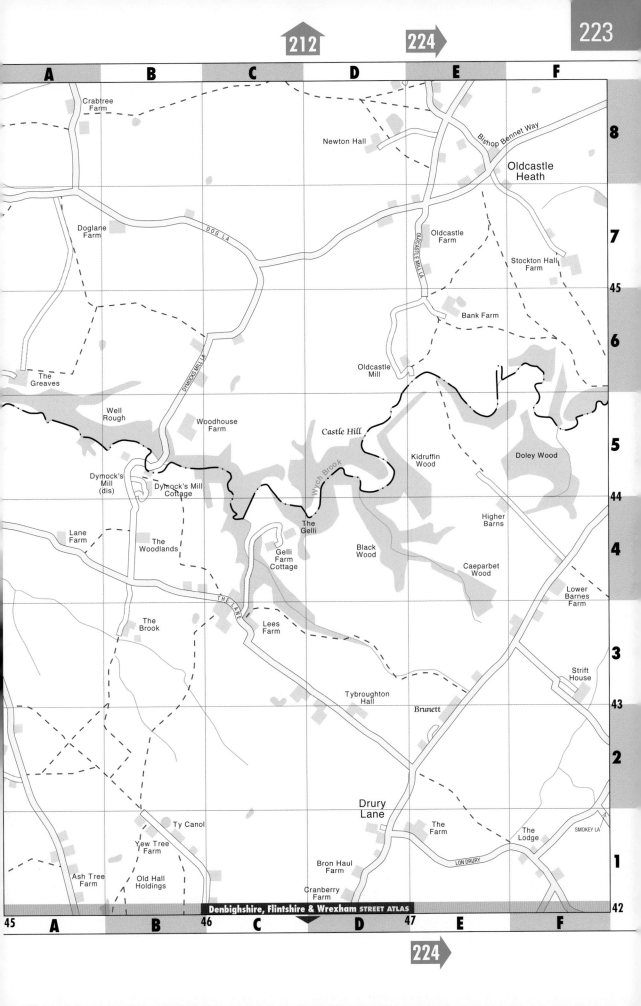

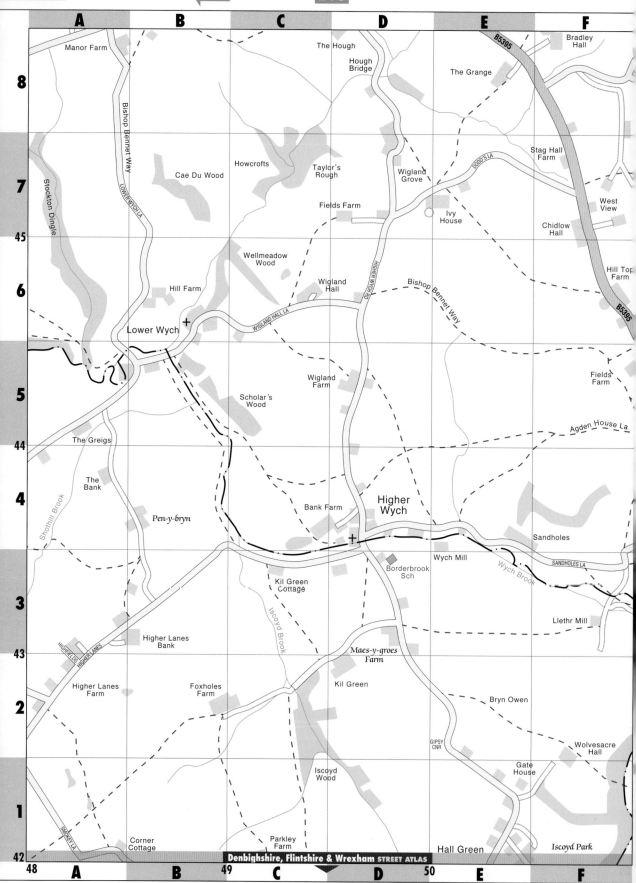

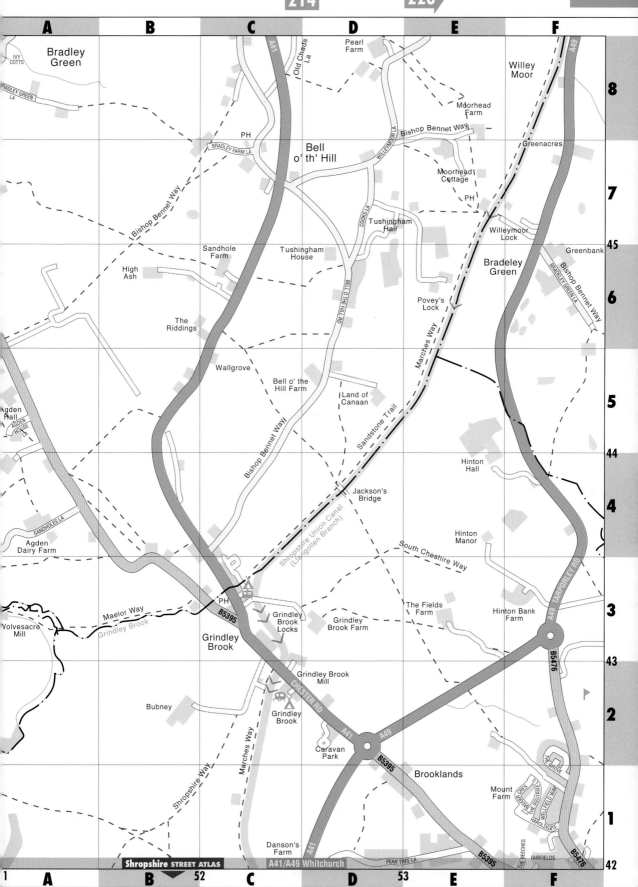

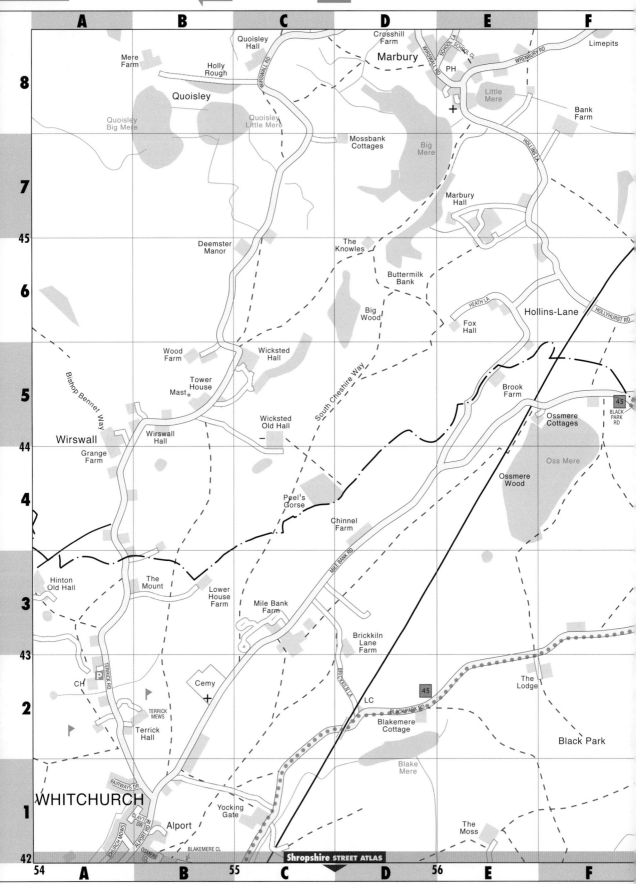

	A	B	C	D	E	F

8

Mere Farm

Holly Rough

Quoisley Hall

Quoisley

Quoisley Big Mere

Quoisley Little Mere

WIRSWALL RD

Crosshill Farm

Marbury

SCHOOL LA / SCHOOL CL

PH

WRENBURY RD

Limepits

Little Mere

Bank Farm

Mossbank Cottages

Big Mere

HOLLINS LA

7

Marbury Hall

45

Deemster Manor

The Knowles

Buttermilk Bank

6

Big Wood

Fox Hall

HEATH LA

Hollins-Lane

HOLLYHURST RD

Wood Farm

Wicksted Hall

South Cheshire Way

Tower House

Mast

Brook Farm

Ossmere Cottages

45

BLACK PARK RD

5

Wirswall

Bishop Bennet Way

Wirswall Hall

Wicksted Old Hall

Ossmere Wood

Oss Mere

44

Grange Farm

Peel's Gorse

Chinnel Farm

4

Hinton Old Hall

The Mount

Lower House Farm

Mile Bank Farm

MILE BANK RD

Brickkiln Lane Farm

BRICKKILN LA

The Lodge

43

CH

P

Cemy

LC

Black Park

2

TERRICK RD

TERRICK MEWS

Terrick Hall

BLACK PARK RD

Blakemere Cottage

Blake Mere

1

WHITCHURCH

FAIRWAYS DR

CLAYTON DR / ALPORT RD

Alport

Yocking Gate

The Moss

42

CHURCH MEWS / OSMERE CL

BLAKEMERE CL

54	A	B	55	C	D	56	E	F

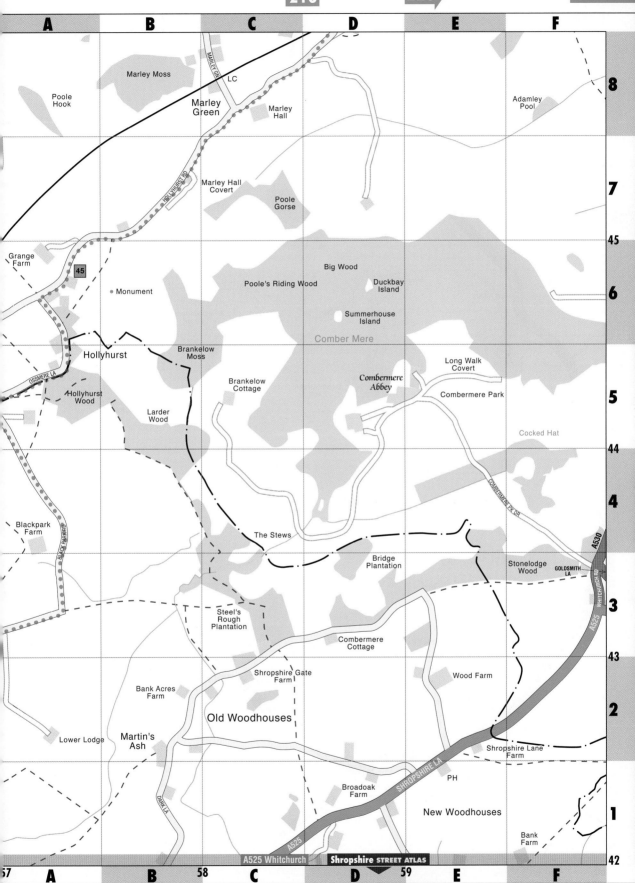

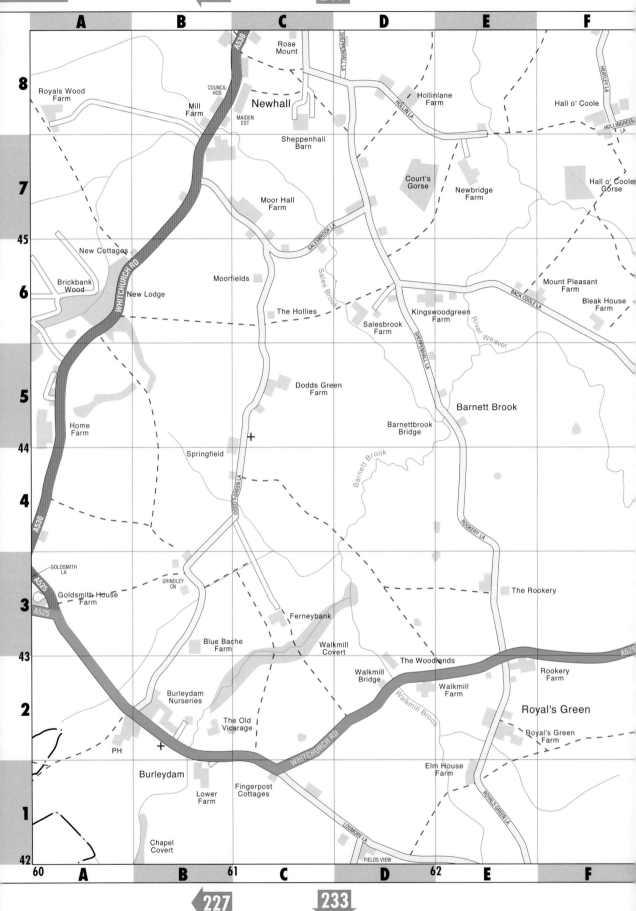

227
217
227
233

Royals Wood Farm

Mill Farm

COUNCIL HOS

MAIDEN EST

Rose Mount

Newhall

Sheppenhall Barn

Hollinlane Farm

Hall o' Coole

Court's Gorse

Newbridge Farm

Hall o' Coole Gorse

Moor Hall Farm

New Cottages

SALESBROOK LA

Mount Pleasant Farm

BACK COOLE LA

Bleak House Farm

Brickbank Wood

New Lodge

Moorfields

Sales Brook

The Hollies

Salesbrook Farm

Kingswoodgreen Farm

River Weaver

SHEPPENHALL LA

Home Farm

Dodds Green Farm

Barnettbrook Bridge

Barnett Brook

Springfield

DODD'S GREEN LA

Barnett Brook

ROOKERY LA

Goldsmith House Farm

GOLDSMITH LA

GRINDLEY CN

The Rookery

Ferneybank

Blue Bache Farm

Walkmill Covert

The Woodlands

A525

Rookery Farm

Burleydam Nurseries

Walkmill Bridge

Walkmill Farm

Royal's Green

The Old Vicarage

WHITCHURCH RD

Walkmill Brook

Royal's Green Farm

PH

Burleydam

Lower Farm

Fingerpost Cottages

Elm House Farm

ROYALS GREEN LA

Chapel Covert

LOOMORE LA

FIELDS VIEW

HEATLEY LA

HOLLIN LA

HOLLINGREEN LA

WHITCHURCH RD

A530

A525

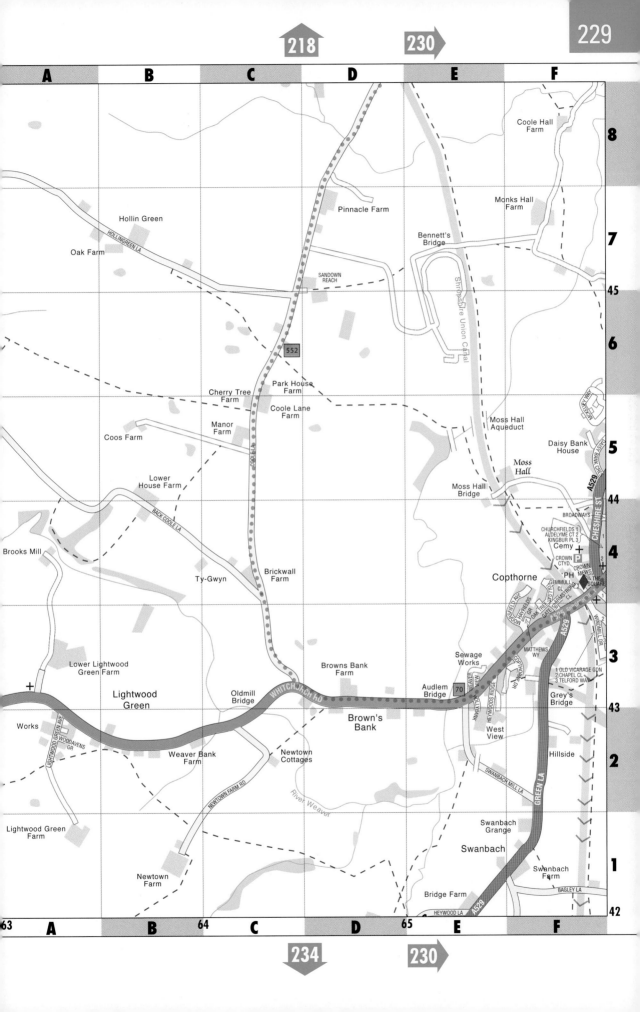

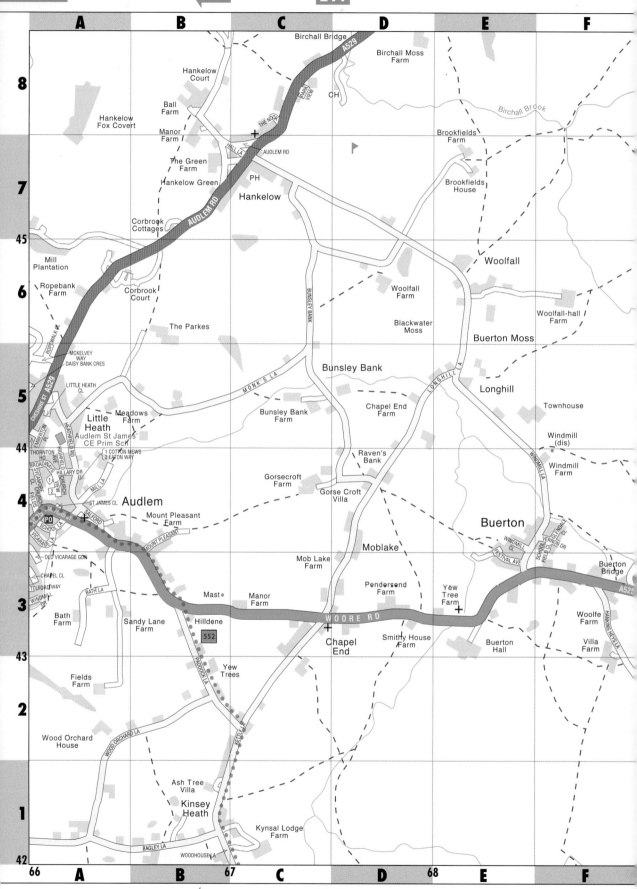

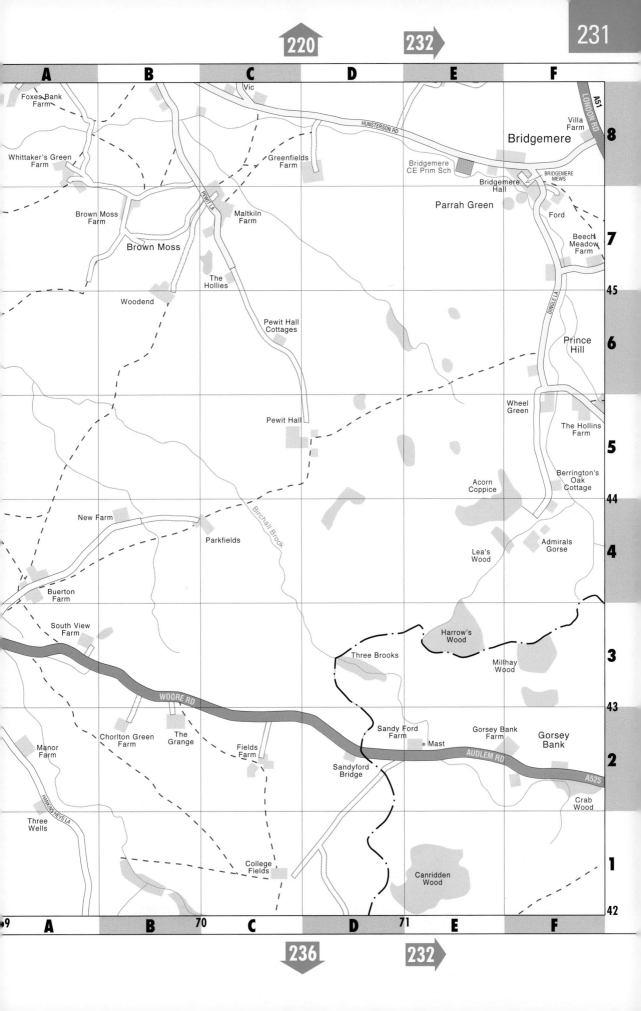

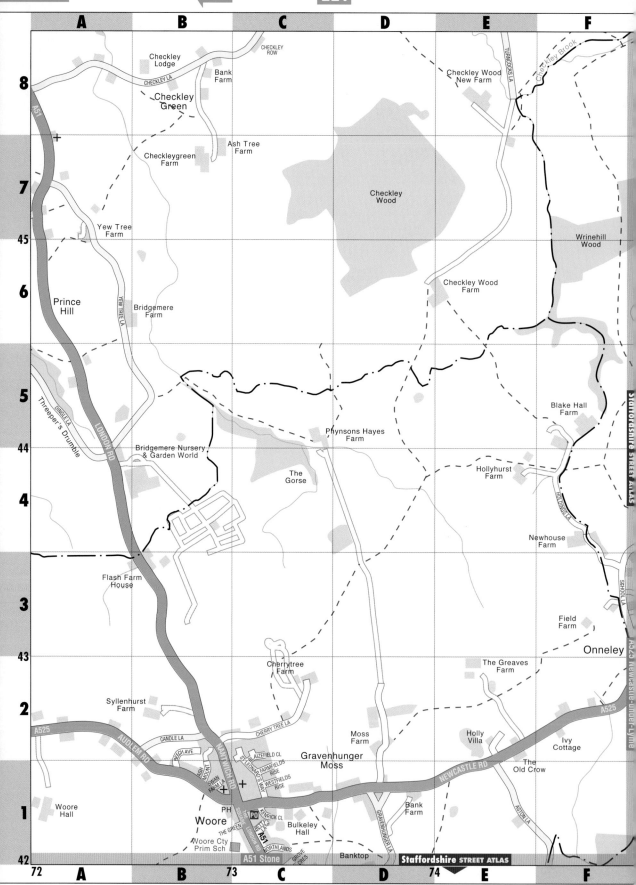

A B C D E F

8
Checkley Lodge
CHECKLEY LA
Bank Farm
CHECKLEY ROW
Checkley Wood New Farm
TURNDOCKS LA
Checkley Brook

Checkley Green

7
Checkleygreen Farm
Ash Tree Farm
Checkley Wood

45
Yew Tree Farm
Wrinehill Wood

6
Prince Hill
YEW TREE LA
Bridgemere Farm
Checkley Wood Farm

DINGLE LA
LONDON RD

5
Threeper's Drumble
Blake Hall Farm

44
Bridgemere Nursery & Garden World
Phynsons Hayes Farm
Hollyhurst Farm
HOLDINGS LA

4
The Gorse
Newhouse Farm

Flash Farm House
SCHOOL LA

3
Field Farm

43
Cherrytree Farm
Onneley

2
Syllenhurst Farm
The Greaves Farm
A525

A525
AUDLEM RD
CANDLE LA
CHERRY TREE LA
Moss Farm
Holly Villa
Ivy Cottage
NANTWICH RD
BEECH AVE
BLAIZEFIELD CL
FARMFIELDS RISE
Gravenhunger Moss
NEWCASTLE RD
The Old Crow
ASTON LA

ASH MOUNT
ST LEONARD'S WAY
WESTFIELDS RISE
SWAN FARM LA

1
Woore Hall
PH
PO
LENRICK CL
Bank Farm
BETLEY LA
THE GREEN
Bulkeley Hall
Woore
NORTHLANDS
A51
Woore Cty Prim Sch
GROVE CRES
Banktop

42
A51 Stone

72 A B 73 C D 74 E F

Butterley
Heys

Cox Bank

Butterley Heys
Cottages

Duckow
Wood

Lane
Farm

Heywood
Farm

Park Farm

Heyfields
Farm

Wilkesley
Farm

Heyfields
Cottages

Yewtree
Plantation

Kent's
Rough

Ferny Heys

Nethermost
Wood

Adderle
CE Prin
Sch

Adderley
Hall

Northwood's
Farm

Black
Covert

Yew Tree
Farm

Adderley Park

Adderley
Hall
Farm

THE
BUNGALOWS

Gas House

Bawhill
Wood

The
Spinneys

Gas House
Plantation

Shavington
Home Farm

Bankhouse
Farm

Shavington
Park

Shavington
Gardens

Big Pool

Big Wood

Tittenley
Pool

Adderley
Lodge

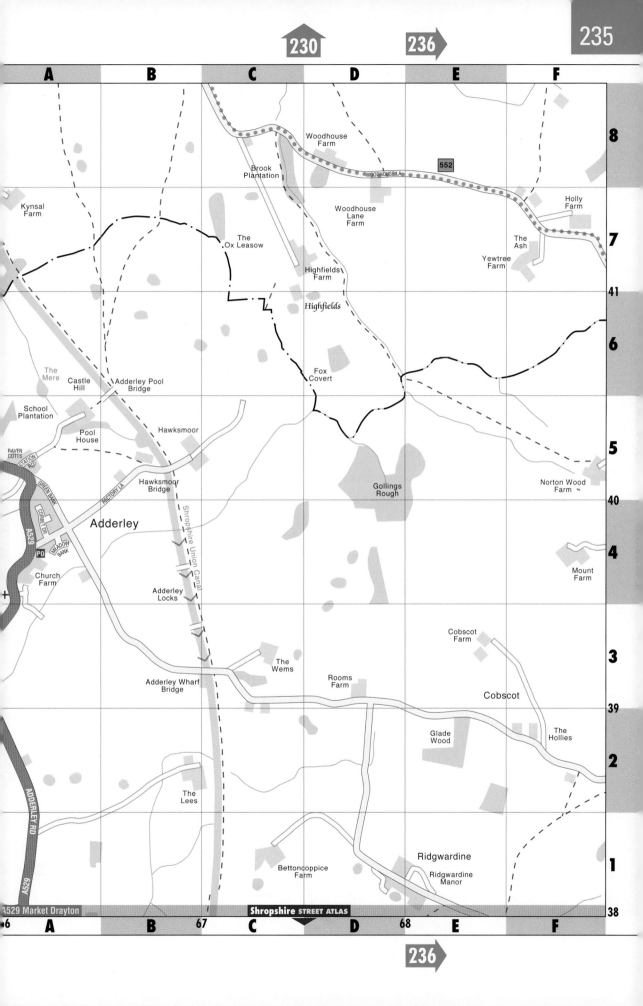

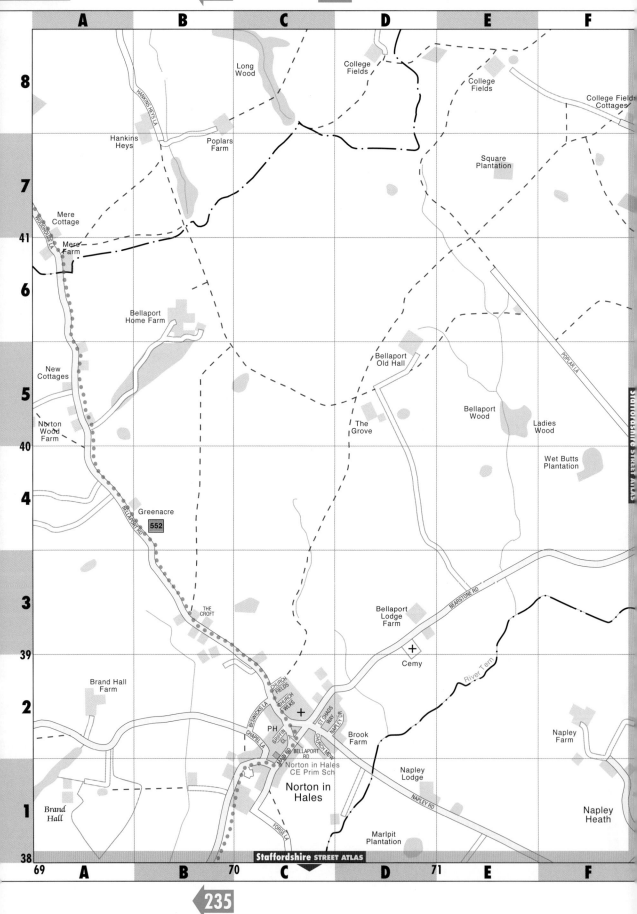

Long Wood

College Fields

College Fields

College Fields Cottages

HANKINS HEYS LA

Hankins Heys

Poplars Farm

Square Plantation

MOORFIELDS LA

Mere Cottage

Mere Farm

Bellaport Home Farm

Bellaport Old Hall

POPLAR LA

New Cottages

Bellaport Wood

Ladies Wood

Norton Wood Farm

The Grove

Wet Butts Plantation

BELLAPORT RD

Greenacre

552

Bearstone Rd

THE CROFT

Bellaport Lodge Farm

River Tern

Cemy

Brand Hall Farm

CHURCH FIELDS

CHURCH WLKS

BESWICKS LA

ST CHADS WAY

NAPLEY DR

Napley Farm

CHAPEL LA

PH

GRIFFIN CL

LAND CT

BELLAPORT RD

CHURCH LA/GROVE

Brook Farm

Napley Lodge

Napley Heath

Norton in Hales CE Prim Sch

Norton in Hales

NAPLEY RD

Brand Hall

FORGE LA

Marlpit Plantation

Staffordshire STREET ATLAS

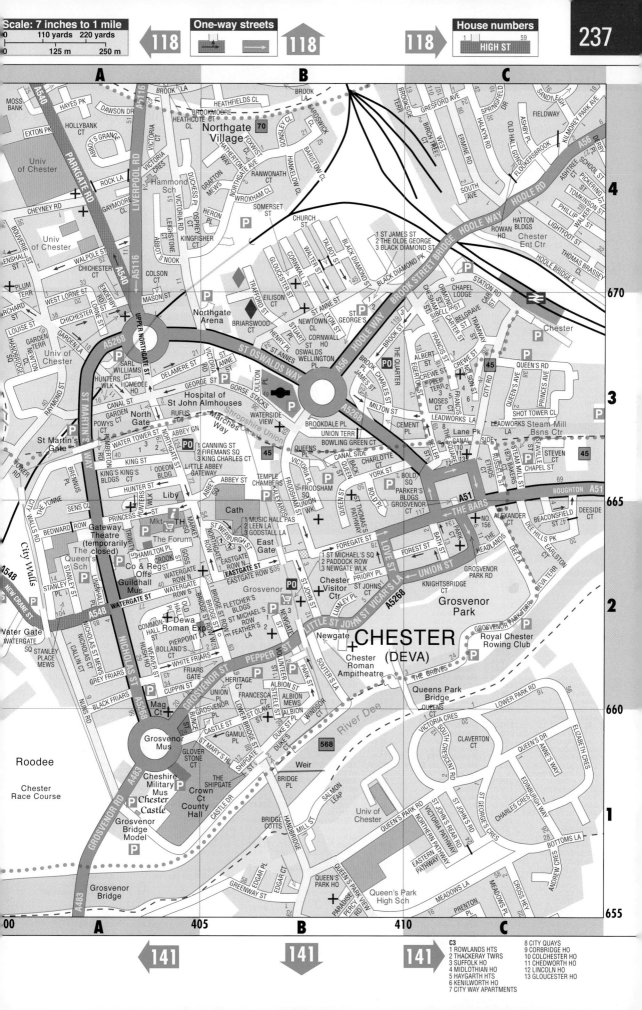

Index

Place name May be abbreviated on the map

Location number Present when a number indicates the place's position in a crowded area of mapping

Locality, town or village Shown when more than one place has the same name

Postcode district District for the indexed place

Page and grid square Page number and grid reference for the standard mapping

Church Rd 6 Beckenham BR2..........53 C6

Cities, towns and villages are listed in CAPITAL LETTERS

Public and commercial buildings are highlighted in magenta   **Places of interest** are highlighted in blue with a star ★

Abbreviations used in the index

Acad	Academy	Comm	Common	Gd	Ground	L	Leisure	Prom	Promenade
App	Approach	Cott	Cottage	Gdn	Garden	La	Lane	Rd	Road
Arc	Arcade	Cres	Crescent	Gn	Green	Liby	Library	Recn	Recreation
Ave	Avenue	Cswy	Causeway	Gr	Grove	Mdw	Meadow	Ret	Retail
Bglw	Bungalow	Ct	Court	H	Hall	Meml	Memorial	Sh	Shopping
Bldg	Building	Ctr	Centre	Ho	House	Mkt	Market	Sq	Square
Bsns, Bus	Business	Ctry	Country	Hospl	Hospital	Mus	Museum	St	Street
Bvd	Boulevard	Cty	County	HQ	Headquarters	Orch	Orchard	Sta	Station
Cath	Cathedral	Dr	Drive	Hts	Heights	Pal	Palace	Terr	Terrace
Cir	Circus	Dro	Drove	Ind	Industrial	Par	Parade	TH	Town Hall
Cl	Close	Ed	Education	Inst	Institute	Pas	Passage	Univ	University
Cnr	Corner	Emb	Embankment	Int	International	Pk	Park	Wk, Wlk	Walk
Coll	College	Est	Estate	Intc	Interchange	Pl	Place	Wr	Water
Com	Community	Ex	Exhibition	Junc	Junction	Prec	Precinct	Yd	Yard

Index of towns, villages, streets, hospitals, industrial estates, railway stations, schools, shopping centres, universities and places of interest

187–Alb

1875 Bakers Ct CH1, CH3 . **237** C3
1 Maureen Campbell Dr 12
CW2 . . . . **207** E3
2nd Ave CW12 . . . . **156** A4
3rd Ave CW12 . . . . **156** A4

A

Aarons Dr ST7 . . . . **209** F2
Abberley Hall SK9 . . . . . . **84** D7
Abbey Cl Croft WA3 . . . . . . .9 A8
  Whitegate CW8 . . . . . . **126** A7
  Widnes WA8 . . . . **22** C8
  Winsford CW7 . . . . **149** D5
Abbey Ct SK12 . . . . **36** D3
Abbeydale Cl Cheadle SK8 . **34** E7
  Chorlton CW2 . . . . **207** C2
Abbeyfield Ho
  2 Crewe CW2 . . . . **190** D2
  Ellesmere Port CH65 . . . . . **70** A3
  Knutsford WA16 . . . . **56** F1
Abbeyfields CW11 . . . . . . **174** F5
Abbey Fields CW2 . . . . . **205** E8
Abbey Gate Coll CH3 . . . **163** F3
Abbey Gate College Senior
  School CH3 . . . . **164** F8
Abbey Gate Sch CH2 . . . . **119** A3
Abbey Gn CH1 . . . . **237** A3
Abbey Hey WA7 . . . . **50** C8
Abbey La Delamere CW8 . . **123** E5
  Hartford WA8 . . . . **103** B4
Abbey Mill SK10 . . . . **87** A6
Abbey Park Way CW2 . . . **207** E3
Abbey Pl CW1 . . . . **190** D6
Abbey Rd Golborne WA3 . . . .4 C8
  Haydock WA11 . . . . .1 E7
  Macclesfield SK10 . . . . . . **87** B2
  Sandbach CW11 . . . . . . **174** E6
  Widnes WA8 . . . . **22** C8
Abbey Sq CH1 . . . . **237** B3
Abbey St CH1 . . . . **237** B3
Abbey Way CW8 . . . . **103** B4
Abbeyway N WA11 . . . . .2 A7
Abbeyway S WA11 . . . . .2 A7
Abbotsbury Cl
  Poynton SK12 . . . . **36** D5
  Wistaston CW2 . . . . . . **206** B8
Abbots Cl SK10 . . . . **87** B2
Abbots Ct CH2 . . . . **118** C4

Abbot's Dr CH2 . . . . **118** C4
Abbotsfield Cl WA4 . . . . . **26** E6
Abbot's Grange CH2 . . . . **237** A4
Abbots Knoll CH2 . . . . . . **118** C4
Abbotsley Rd WA4 . . . . . . **24** F3
ABBOT'S MEADS **118** A4
Abbotsmere Cl CW8 . . . . **101** F2
Abbots Mews CH65 . . . . . **70** B6
ABBOTS MOSS **124** D5
Abbot's Nook CH2 . . . . . . **237** A4
Abbots Pk Chester CH2 . . . **118** C4
  Runcorn WA7 . . . . **50** E5
Abbot's Terr CH1 . . . . . . **118** B5
Abbots Way
  Hartford CW8 . . . . **103** B4
  Neston CH64 . . . . **41** E1
Abbotts Cl Runcorn WA7 . . **49** A8
  Waverton CH3 . . . . **143** B5
Abbott's Cl CW12 . . . . . **179** B8
Abbotts Rd CH3 . . . . **143** B5
Abbotts Way CW7 . . . . . . **126** B2
Aberdare Cl WA5 . . . . .7 E1
Aberdaron Dr CH1 . . . . . **117** E3
Aberdeen Wlk SK10 . . . . . **86** F3
Aberfeldy Cl CW4 . . . . . **130** B2
Abingdon Ave WA1 . . . . . **17** E7
Abingdon Cl 9 SK11 . . . . **111** F8
Abingdon Cres 4 CH4 . . . **140** F6
Abington Cl CW1 . . . . . . **190** B6
Abington Wlk WA7 . . . . . . **50** C5
Abney Mews WA1 . . . . . . **16** E5
Abstone Cl WA1 . . . . **17** B7
Acacia Ave Knutsford WA16 . **56** E1
  Warrington WA1 . . . . **17** D7
  Widnes WA8 . . . . **13** B3
  Wilmslow SK9 . . . . **59** F5
Acacia Cl CH2 . . . . **72** C3
Acacia Cres CW1 . . . . . . **190** E6
Acacia Dr
  Ellesmere Port CH66 . . . . . **69** F1
  Sandbach CW11 . . . . . . **174** E7
Acacia Gdns ST7 . . . . . . **195** C3
Acacia Gr WA7 . . . . **49** C8
Acacia St WA12 . . . . .1 F4
Academy Pl 6 WA1 . . . . . **16** B5
Academy St WA1 . . . . **16** B5
Academy Way WA1 . . . . . . **16** B5
Acer Ave CW1 . . . . **190** E7
Achilles Ave WA2 . . . . .8 B2
Achilles St WA7 . . . . **24** A2
Ackerley Cl WA2 . . . . .8 F3
Ackers La WA4 . . . . **16** E1
Ackersley Ct SK8 . . . . **35** B8

Ackers Rd WA4 . . . . **16** E1
Ack Lane E SK7 . . . . **35** D7
Ack Lane W SK8 . . . . **35** C7
Acorn Bank Cl CW2 . . . . . **206** B7
Acorn Cl Cuddington CW8 . **101** F2
  Winsford CW7 . . . . **150** A8
Acorn Ct CH2 . . . . **118** E8
Acorn Dr CH65 . . . . **70** B1
Acorn La CW12 . . . . **157** E3
Acorns Prim Sch The
  CH65 . . . . **69** F5
Acorn St WA12 . . . . .2 D3
Acorns The CH2 . . . . **118** E8
Acorn Terr SK22 . . . . **39** B6
Acreage The
  Bunbury CW6 . . . . **185** E8
  Goostrey CW4 . . . . **107** L1
Acrefield Rd WA8 . . . . **12** B1
Acre Gn L26 . . . . **21** A6
Acre La Bebington CH62 . . . **43** D8
  Cheadle SK8 . . . . **35** C6
  Heswall CH60 . . . . **41** C8
Acre Rd CH66 . . . . **69** D5
Acres Cres WA6 . . . . **75** B2
Acres Dr CW2 . . . . **206** D7
Acresfield Prim Sch CH2 . **118** F8
Acres La CH2 . . . . **119** A8
Acreville Gr WA3 . . . . .5 C7
ACTON **204** A7
Acton Ave WA4 . . . . **26** D3
ACTON BRIDGE **76** E3
Acton Bridge Sta CW8 . . . . **76** F1
Acton CE Prim Sch CW5 . **204** A7
Acton Cl
  10 Clive Green CW7 . . . . **150** B8
  Haydock WA11 . . . . .1 C6
Acton La CW8 . . . . **76** F4
Acton Pl SK11 . . . . **111** F8
Acton Rd Burtonwood WA5 . . .6 E6
  Crewe CW2 . . . . **189** D4
Actons Wood La WA7 . . . . **24** E2
Acton Way ST7 . . . . **193** D6
Adam Ave
  Ellesmere Port CH66 . . . . . **69** D3
  Ellesmere Port, Great Sutton
  CH66 . . . . **69** C4
Adam Cl CH66 . . . . **69** D4
Adams Hill
  Newton-le-Willows WA12 . . .2 D2
  Poynton SK12 . . . . **36** E2
Adamson Ct WA4 . . . . **17** B2
Adamson Ho WA7 . . . . . . **22** E3

Adamson St WA4 . . . . **16** B3
Adam St WA2 . . . . **16** C7
Adaston Ave CH62 . . . . . . **43** F4
Adder Hill CH3 . . . . **142** B7
ADDERLEY **235** A4
Adderley CE Prim Sch
  TF9 . . . . **234** F5
Adderley Cl Crewe CW1 . **190** B7
  Runcorn WA7 . . . . **23** C1
Adderley Rd TF9 . . . . . . **235** A2
ADDER'S MOSS **85** F6
Addingham Ave WA8 . . . . **22** C7
Addison Cl CW2 . . . . **205** F8
Addison Sq WA8 . . . . **13** A1
Adelaide Ct 4 WA8 . . . . . **23** A7
Adelaide Rd Blacon CH1 . **117** D4
  Bramhall SK7 . . . . **35** F5
Adelaide Sch CW1 . . . . . **190** C5
Adelaide St Crewe CW1 . . **190** C5
  Macclesfield SK10 . . . . . . **87** E1
Adela Rd WA7 . . . . **22** F2
Adelphi Gr WA8 . . . . **23** C8
Adey Rd WA13 . . . . **19** A5
Adfalent La CH64 . . . . **68** A7
Adler Rd CW12 . . . . **156** E6
ADLINGTON **62** D5
Adlington Bsns Pk SK10 . . **36** C1
Adlington Cl SK12 . . . . **36** F2
Adlington Ct WA3 . . . . .9 F6
Adlington Dr
  Northwich CW9 . . . . **104** A5
  Sandbach CW11 . . . . . . **175** C7
Adlington Hall Mews
  SK10 . . . . **62** B5
Adlington Pk SK10 . . . . . . **36** C1
Adlington Prim Sch SK10 . **62** E5
Adlington Rd
  Bollington SK10 . . . . **63** A1
  Crewe CW2 . . . . **189** F3
  Runcorn WA7 . . . . **24** D2
  Wilmslow SK9 . . . . **60** E7
Adlington Road Bsns Pk
  SK10 . . . . **88** A8
Adlington St SK10 . . . . . . **112** C8
Adlington Sta SK10 . . . . . . **62** C5
Admiral Cl WA12 . . . . .1 E3
Admirals Rd WA3 . . . . .9 F3
Adshead Ct SK10 . . . . **88** B7
Adwell Cl WA3 . . . . .4 A8
Afton WA8 . . . . **12** A2
Agden Brow WA13 . . . . . . **19** E1
Agden Brow Pk WA13 . . . . **19** D1
Agden Hall Farm WA13 . . . **29** E7

Agden House La SY13 . . . **225** A5
Agden La Broomedge WA13 . **19** E1
  Little Bollington WA13 . . . . **29** E7
Agden Park La WA13 . . . . **29** D8
Agecroft Rd CW9 . . . . . . **104** C7
Agora Gdns ST7 . . . . **195** D2
Aidenswood Sch ST7 . . . . **194** E3
Ainley Cl WA7 . . . . **50** A5
Ainscough Rd WA3 . . . . . . .9 E3
Ainsdale Cl
  Bebington CH63 . . . . **43** C5
  Bramhall SK7 . . . . **36** A7
  Warrington WA5 . . . . **14** F4
Ainsworth La CW8 . . . . . . **76** B3
Ainsworth Rd CW8 . . . . . **77** E1
Aintree Gr CH66 . . . . **69** D3
Airdrie Cl CH62 . . . . **43** D3
Aire WA8 . . . . **12** B2
Aire Cl CH65 . . . . **70** A7
Airedale Cl WA5 . . . . **14** F7
Aire Dr CW9 . . . . **104** C5
Aire Pl CW7 . . . . **127** B1
Airfield Rd CW5 . . . . **187** A4
Airfield View CH5 . . . . . . **139** B6
Airfield Way CH65 . . . . . . **44** C2
Aitchison Rd CW9 . . . . . . **80** A2
Ajax Ave WA2 . . . . .8 B2
Ajmere Cl CW2 . . . . **189** E2
Akesmoor La
  Biddulph ST8 . . . . **179** B1
  Mow Cop ST7 . . . . **195** F7
Alamein Cres WA2 . . . . . . **16** C7
Alamein Dr CW7 . . . . **149** D8
Alamein Rd Barnton CW8 . . **78** A4
  Chester CH2 . . . . **95** B1
Alanbrooke Rd CH3 . . . . **142** C5
Alan Dr WA15 . . . . **32** A8
Alan St CW9 . . . . **104** B8
Alban Ret Pk WA2 . . . . .8 A1
Alban St CW1 . . . . **190** C5
Albany Cres WA13 . . . . . . **18** D4
Albany Gdns CH66 . . . . . . **69** C7
Albany Gr WA13 . . . . **18** C4
Albany Rd Bramhall SK7 . . . **35** F4
  Lymm WA13 . . . . **18** D4
  Wilmslow SK9 . . . . **59** F5
Albany Terr 14 WA7 . . . . . **23** A2
Albemarle Ave
  Northwich CW8 . . . . **103** A8
  Weaverham CW8 . . . . . . **102** F5
Albert Dr Neston CH64 . . . . **66** D8
  Warrington WA5 . . . . **14** D6
Albert Pl Congleton CW12 . **156** E2

Albert Pl *continued*
🔟 Macclesfield SK11 . . . . . 112 D8
Northwich CW9 . . . . 104 B8
Albert Rd Bollington SK10 . .87 E8
Warrington WA4 . . . . 17 A2
🔁 Widnes WA8 . . . . .13 B1
Wilmslow SK9 . . . . 60 A6
Albert Row WA4 . . . . .49 B1
Albert St Audley ST7 . . . . . 209 F3
Chester CH1. . . . . 237 C3
Crewe CW1 . . . . 190 C5
Irlam M44 . . . . .11 E6
Knutsford WA16 . . . . .56 F2
Macclesfield SK11 . . . . . . 112 C8
Nantwich CW5 . . . . 204 E6
🔟 Runcorn WA7 . . . . 23 A2
Albert Terr WA1 . . . . .1 E1
Albion Ct CW12 . . . . 156 E2
Albion Mews
Chester CH1. . . . . 237 B2
New Mills SK22 . . . . 39 C7
Albion Pk WA3 . . . . .5 C7
Albion Pl CH1. . . . . 237 B1
Albion Rd New Mills SK22 . . .39 B6
Northwich CW9 . . . . 79 A1
Albion St Chester CH1 . . . . 237 B2
Crewe CW2 . . . . 190 A3
Albion Wlk CW9. . . . . 79 A1
Albright Rd WA8 . . . . 22 A6
Albury Cl WA11 . . . . .1 D7
Alcock St 🔟 WA7 . . . . 23 A3
Alconbury Cl WA5 . . . . .15 B6
Alcott Pl WA2 . . . . .8 A6
Aldcliffe WA3 . . . . .3 F8
Aldelyme Ct CW3 . . . . 229 F4
Alder Ave Poynton SK12. . . .36 F3
Widnes WA8 . . . . .13 B3
Alderbank Rd WA5 . . . . . . 15 A6
Alder Cl SK8 . . . . 34 D8
Alder Cres WA2 . . . . 16 C8
Alder Croft Cl 🔟 CW11 . . 175 B8
Alder Ct SK10 . . . . .87 E5
Alderdale Dr SK6. . . . . .37 E7
Alderdale Gr SK9. . . . . .59 E5
Alder Dr Crewe CW1 . . . . . 189 F7
Ellesmere Port CH66 . . . . . .69 F1
Alderfield Dr L24. . . . . 21 A3
Alder Gr CH2 . . . . 119 B4
Alderhay La ST7 . . . . 195 C4
Alder La
Burtonwood WA2, WA5 . . . . .7 C7
Cronton WA8, L35. . . . . . . 12 A5
Frodsham WA6, WA7 . . . . . 48 D3
Warrington WA2 . . . . .16 B8
Alderley Ave WA3 . . . . .3 D7
Alderley Cl
Hazel Grove SK7. . . . . .36 F8
Poynton SK12. . . . . .36 F2
Sandbach CW11 . . . . 175 D7
ALDERLEY EDGE 60 C2
Alderley Edge★ SK9,SK10 . . 85 D8
Alderley Edge Com Prim Sch
SK9 . . . . 60 A2
Alderley Edge Sch for Girls
SK9 . . . . 60 A2
Alderley Edge Sta SK9. . . . . 60 A2
Alderley Lo SK9 . . . . 60 A5
Alderley Pl CH1 . . . . 117 E6
Alderley Rd
Alderley Edge SK10, SK9 . . . .60 F2
Chelford SK10 . . . . 84 C3
Northwich CW8 . . . . 103 E8
Prestbury SK10 . . . . .86 E3
Warrington WA4 . . . . 17 D4
Wilmslow SK9 . . . . 60 A6
Alderley Wlk 🔟 SK11 . . . . 112 E7
Alderman Bolton Com Sch
WA4 . . . . .16 F3
Alderney Cl
Ellesmere Port CH65 . . . . . 70 C1
🔟 Macclesfield SK11 . . . . 111 F6
Alderney Ho CH2 . . . . 119 B4
Alder Rd Golborne WA3 . . . .3 F6
Warrington WA1 . . . . 17 D7
Weaverham CW8 . . . . 102 D8
Alder Rise SK23 . . . . 65 D8
Alder Root La WA2 . . . . .7 D7
Alders SK9 . . . . .59 F6
Aldersey Cl Runcorn WA7 . . 24 D1
Saughall CH1 . . . . 94 A1
ALDERSEY GREEN 182 C6
Aldersey La CH3 . . . . 182 C5
Aldersey Rd CW2. . . . . 190 A2
Aldersey Way CW6 . . . . . . 185 E8
Aldersgate SK22 . . . . .39 B8
Aldersgate Ave WA7. . . . . . 50 D7
Aldersgate Dr L26. . . . . 21 A6
Aldersgate Rd SK8. . . . . . . 35 C5
Alders Green Ave SK6 . . . . .37 F7
Aldershot Cl WA8 . . . . 13 C3
Alders Rd SK12 . . . . 38 A7
Alder St WA12 . . . . .2 C3
Alders Way WA5. . . . . .86 F6
Alderton Cl L26 . . . . 21 A7
Alderton Gr CW7 . . . . 127 A4
Alder Way CW4 . . . . 130 E3
Alder Wood Ave L24. . . . . . 21 A3
Alderwood Ct WA8 . . . . . . .12 E4
Alderwood Lodge L24 . . . . . 21 A3
Alderwood Cl WA3. . . . . . . 10 A6
ALDFORD 163 F3
Aldford Cl Bebington CH63 . .43 B6
Hough CW2 . . . . 206 E2
Aldford Pl SK9 . . . . .59 F2
Aldford Rd CH2 . . . . 118 E6
Aldford Sch CH3 . . . . 163 F3
Aldford Way CW7 . . . . 126 B2
Aldgate CH65 . . . . 70 A5

Aldington Dr CW10 . . . . . . 151 D5
Aldridge Dr WA5 . . . . .6 F7
Aled Way CH4. . . . . 140 D5
Alexander Ct CH3 . . . . 237 C2
Alexander Dr WA8 . . . . 22 D8
Alexandra Ct 🔟 WA1 . . . . .11 F3
Alexandra Gr Irlam M44 . . .11 F8
Runcorn WA7 . . . . 23 C1
Alexandra Ind Est WA8 . . . .22 F7
Alexandra Mews WA6 . . . . .49 B1
Alexandra Pl CW1 . . . . 190 B5
Alexandra Rd
Middlewich CW10 . . . . 151 D6
Warrington WA4 . . . . .16 F2
Warrington, Stockton Heath
WA4 . . . . 16 D1
Alexandra Sq 🔟 CW7 . . . . 149 A8
Alexandra St
Ellesmere Port CH65 . . . . . 70 C7
Warrington WA1 . . . . .16 E7
Widnes WA8. . . . . 23 A7
Winsford CW7 . . . . 126 C1
Alexandra Stadium The
(Crewe Alexandra FC)
CW2 . . . . 190 D2
Alexandria Way CW12 . . . . 156 C4
Alford Ct 🔟 CW9 . . . . 103 E5
Alforde St WA8 . . . . 23 A7
Alfred Cl 🔟 WA8 . . . . .23 B8
Alfred Moseley Pl ST7 . . . . 193 F4
Alfred Rd Golborne WA3 . . . .4 A8
Haydock WA11. . . . . 1 F7
Alfred St Irlam M44 . . . . . . 11 E6
Newton-le-Willows WA12 . . .2 E3
Northwich CW9 . . . . 103 E6
Widnes WA8. . . . . 23 B8
Algernon Cl 🔟 CH64. . . . . 41 C1
Algernon St Runcorn WA7. . .22 F3
Warrington WA1 . . . . 16 D6
Warrington, Stockton Heath
WA4 . . . . 16 C1
Alice Ct WA8 . . . . 23 A4
Alison Dr Goostrey CW4 . . 130 D8
Macclesfield SK10 . . . . .87 F1
Alistair Dr CH63. . . . . 43 C6
Allans Cl CH64 . . . . .66 E6
Allansford Ave CH3. . . . . . 143 A4
Allans Mdw CH64 . . . . .66 E7
Allcard St WA5. . . . . .15 F7
Allen Ave WA3 . . . . .5 C4
Allenby Rd M44 . . . . 11 D4
Allendale WA7 . . . . .50 B6
Allen Dr CW9 . . . . 103 F2
Allen Pl CW1 . . . . 190 B5
Allen Rd WA7 . . . . 48 D7
Allen St Bollington SK10 . . . .88 B8
Macclesfield SK11 . . . . . . 112 E7
Warrington WA2 . . . . 16 A6
Allerby Way WA3. . . . . .3 E8
Allerton Rd WA8 . . . . .13 B1
Alleyhouse La SK11 . . . . . . 159 C1
ALLGREAVE 137 C3
Allgreave Cl CW10 . . . . . . 151 C6
All Hallows Catholic Coll
SK11. . . . . 112 B7
Allington Pl CH4 . . . . 141 E7
Allman Cl CW1 . . . . 189 F7
Allmans La
Duckington SY14 . . . . 199 C5
Duckington SY14 . . . . 199 C5
ALLOSTOCK 106 E3
Allotment Rd M44 . . . . 11 D6
Allport La CH62 . . . . .43 D7
Allport Rd CH62, CH63 . . . .43 D7
Alports The CH62. . . . . 43 D7
All Saints CE Prim Sch
WA7 . . . . 23 A3
All Saints Dr WA4 . . . . .17 E3
All Saints RC Prim Sch
WA3 . . . . .3 B8
All Saints Upton CE Prim Sch
WA8 . . . . .12 B3
Allysum Ct WA7 . . . . .49 F4
Alma Ave CW1 . . . . 190 C6
Alma Cl
Macclesfield SK11 . . . . . . 112 A7
Scholar Green ST7 . . . . . . 194 E7
Alma La SK9 . . . . 60 A7
Alma Rd SK7. . . . . 37 A8
Alma St Chester CH2 . . . . . 118 F2
Newton-le-Willows WA12 . . .2 B3
Almeda Rd L24. . . . . 21 A2
Almer Dr WA5 . . . . 15 C5
Almere Ferry Rd LL12. . . . . 180 A5
Almond Ave Crewe CW1 . . 190 D6
Almond Dr WA5. . . . . .6 F6
Almond Gr
Warrington WA1 . . . . .17 B7
Weaverham CW8 . . . . 102 E7
Widnes WA8. . . . . 22 D8
Almond Pl ST5 . . . . 210 E1
Almond Tree Cl L24 . . . . . . 21 E1
Almond Wlk M31. . . . . 11 D3
Almshouses CW11 . . . . . . 175 C6
Alnwick Dr CH65 . . . . 70 D2
Alpass Ave WA5. . . . . 16 A8
Alpine Echoes Cl 🔟
CW11. . . . . 174 C7
Alpine St WA12 . . . . .2 A3
ALPORT. 226 B1
Alport Rd SY13. . . . . 226 B1
ALPRAHAM. 169 D4
Alpraham Cres CH2 . . . . . . 118 E6
Alpraham Gn CW6. . . . . . . 169 E5
ALPRAHAM GREEN 169 D5
Alric Wlk M22. . . . . .33 E8
ALSAGER. 193 E5

Alsager Highfields
Foundation Prim Sch
ST7 . . . . 193 D4
Alsager L Ctr ST7 . . . . 193 E4
Alsager Rd Audley ST7. . . . 209 D5
Haslington CW11. . . . . 192 C7
Sandbach CW11 . . . . 175 E1
Alsager Sch ST7 . . . . 193 E4
Alsager Sta ST7. . . . . 193 E3
Alsfeld Way SK22 . . . . 39 A8
Alt WA8 . . . . .12 B2
Alton Dr SK10 . . . . .87 F1
Alton Rd SK9 . . . . .59 F7
Alton St CW2 . . . . 190 B3
ALTRINCHAM 31 C8
Altrincham Rd Styal SK9 . . 33 D4
Wilmslow SK9 . . . . 33 C2
Alt Wlk CW7 . . . . 127 A2
Alumbrook Ave CW4 . . . . . 130 C3
Alum Ct CW4 . . . . 130 C2
Alun Cres CH4 . . . . 141 A6
Alundale Rd CW7 . . . . 126 C3
ALVANLEY 73 C1
Alvanley Dr WA6 . . . . 73 C2
Alvanley Prim Sch WA6 . . . 73 D1
Alvanley Rd
Ellesmere Port CH66 . . . . . .69 E4
Helsby WA6 . . . . 73 C2
Alvanley Rise CW9 . . . . . . 104 A6
Alvanley Terr WA6 . . . . . . .74 B8
Alvanley View CW7. . . . . . .72 B3
Alvanley Way CH66. . . . . . .69 E4
Alvaston Bsns Pk CW5. . . . 204 F8
Alvaston Rd CW5. . . . . 204 F5
Alvaston Wlk CW2. . . . . . . 189 F2
Alverstone Cl WA5 . . . . 14 C7
Alverton Cl WA8 . . . . 22 D8
Alveston Cl SK10 . . . . .86 F1
Alveston Dr SK9 . . . . 60 C8
Alvingham Cl 🔟 CW9. . . . 104 B8
Alvis Rd CH5 . . . . 116 B3
Alwyn Gdns CH2 . . . . 118 F8
Alyndale Rd CH4 . . . . 140 D6
Alyn Rd CH2 . . . . .96 F1
Amberley Cl WA4 . . . . .27 B3
Amberley Dr WA15 . . . . . . .32 B8
Amberley Rd SK11 . . . . 112 A6
Ambleside CH2 . . . . 119 A6
Ambleside Cl
Bebington CH62. . . . . .43 E7
Crewe CW2 . . . . 189 E2
Macclesfield SK11 . . . . . . 111 F6
Runcorn WA7 . . . . .49 E5
Winsford CW7 . . . . 126 C3
Ambleside Cres WA2. . . . . . .8 C3
Ambleside Ct CW12 . . . . . 156 A2
Ambleside Rd CH65 . . . . . . 70 C2
Ambrose Ct WA1. . . . . 16 D6
Ambuscade Cl CW1 . . . . . 190 E5
Amelia Cl WA8 . . . . .13 B4
Amelia St WA2 . . . . 16 C7
Amersham Cl SK10 . . . . . . 87 C3
Amis Gr WA3 . . . . .3 E8
Ampleforth Ho 🔟 WA1 . . 16 C5
Amusement Depot CW7 . . 126 E2
Amy St CW2 . . . . 190 C3
Anchorage The
🔟 Lymm WA13 . . . . 18 D3
Neston CH64 . . . . .66 C7
Waverton CH3 . . . . 143 A5
Anchor Cl WA7. . . . . 50 D6
Anchor Ct WA1 . . . . 16 D6
Ancoats La WA4. . . . . .83 F8
Anderson Cl Crewe CW1. . . 191 A4
Warrington WA2 . . . . .9 B2
Anderson Ct CH62. . . . . . . 43 D6
Andersons Ind Est WA8 . . . .23 B6
Anderson St 🔟 SK10 . . . . 112 C8
ANDERTON 78 D4
Anderton Boat Lift & Nature
Park★ 78 D3
Anderton Cl 🔟 CW11. . . . 174 E4
Anderton Dr CW12 . . . . . . 156 D6
Anderton Grange CW9 . . . 103 F7
Andertons La SK10, SK11 . .86 B1
Anderton Way SK9 . . . . . . 34 D3
Andover Cl
Crow Wood WA8. . . . . 13 C4
Warrington WA2 . . . . .8 E1
Andover Rd WA11. . . . . .1 E8
Andrew Cl WA8 . . . . 22 C8
Andrew Cres CH4 . . . . 237 C1
Andrew Gr SK10. . . . . 113 A7
Andrew La SK6. . . . . .37 F8
Andrew's Cl CH3 . . . . 121 B2
Andrew's Wlk CH60 . . . . . .41 B8
Andromeda Way WA9 . . . . .6 B7
Anemone Way WA9 . . . . . . .6 A7
Angelina Cl CW11 . . . . 174 D7
Anglers Rest M44 . . . . .11 E5
Anglesey Cl 🔁 CH65. . . . . 70 C1
Anglesey Dr SK12 . . . . .36 F5
Anglesey Water SK12. . . . . .36 E6
Angus Ct CW7 . . . . 149 A7
Angus Gr CW10 . . . . 128 D2
Angus Rd CH63 . . . . 43 C6
Angus Wlk SK10. . . . . .86 F7
Ankers Knowl La SK11. . . . 114 D8
Ankers La SK11 . . . . 114 D6
Annable Rd M44 . . . . .11 F8
Annan Cl 🔁 CW12 . . . . . . 157 A1
Ann Cl CH66 . . . . 69 D7
Anne's Way CH4 . . . . 237 C1
Annette Ave WA12 . . . . . . .1 A7
Annie St WA2 . . . . 16 C6
Annions La CW5 . . . . 205 F1
Annis Cl SK9 . . . . .60 B2

Annis Rd SK9 . . . . .60 B2
Ann St Northwich CW9 . . . . 79 B1
Runcorn WA7 . . . . .23 B3
Ann Street W WA8 . . . . . . .23 B7
Ansdell Rd WA8 . . . . 13 C2
Anson Cl Bramhall SK7. . . . . 35 F5
🔁 Crow Wood WA8 . . . . . 13 C4
Anson Engine Mus★
SK12. . . . . 37 C4
Anson Rd Handforth SK9 . . .34 E1
Poynton SK12. . . . . .37 B3
Anthony Dr CW9 . . . . 126 F7
Anthony's Way CH60 . . . . .41 A7
Antons Ct L26. . . . . 21 A6
Antons Rd L26 . . . . 21 A6
Antony Rd WA4 . . . . .16 B1
Antrim Cl WA11 . . . . .1 C6
Antrim Dr CH66 . . . . .69 F2
Antrim Rd WA2 . . . . .8 A2
ANTROBUS 53 C4
Antrobus St Mark's CE Prim
Sch CW9 . . . . 53 C4
Antrobus St CW12 . . . . . . 156 D3
Anvil Cl Elton CH2 . . . . . . .72 B4
Haslington CW11 . . . . 174 F3
Saughall CH1 . . . . 94 A1
Anzac Dr CW1 . . . . 190 F6
Apollo Pk WA5 . . . . .7 B3
Apple Blossom Gr M44 . . . 11 D4
Appleby Cl
Macclesfield SK11 . . . . . . 111 F5
Widnes WA8. . . . . 22 C8
Appleby Cres WA16 . . . . . . 58 A4
Appleby Gr CH62 . . . . 43 D6
Appleby Rd WA2 . . . . .8 C3
Appleby Wlk 🔁 WA8 . . . . 22 C8
Applecroft ST5 . . . . 210 E1
Applecross Cl WA3 . . . . . . 10 A6
Appledale SK10 . . . . 87 C4
Appledale Dr CH66 . . . . . . 95 A8
Applefield CW8 . . . . 103 D7
Appleford Cl WA4 . . . . .26 E7
Apple Market St 🔟 CW9 . 103 F8
APPLETON 13 A2
Appleton Cl CW12 . . . . . . 178 E8
Appleton Dr CH65 . . . . .69 F2
Appleton Hall Gdns WA4. . .26 E5
Appleton Mews WA13 . . . . 18 C4
APPLETON PARK 26 D5
Appleton Rd Chester CH2 . . 118 E6
Widnes WA8. . . . . .13 B1
Appleton St Widnes WA8 . . .23 B7
Winnington CW8 . . . . 78 D1
APPLETON THORN. 27 B4
Appleton Thorn Prim Sch
WA4 . . . . 27 C4
Appleton Thorn Trad Est
. . . . 27 D5
Appleton Village WA8. . . . . .13 B1
Appleton Wlk 🔟 SK9 . . . . 34 E1
Apple Tree Cl L24 . . . . 21 E1
Appletree Gr WA2. . . . . .8 F2
Apple Tree Gr CH66 . . . . . .94 F8
Appleyards La CH4 . . . . . . 141 E2
Apprentice La SK9 . . . . 33 F3
April Rise SK10 . . . . 87 A1
Arabis Gdns WA9 . . . . .6 B7
Aragon Ct WA7 . . . . 24 C3
Aragon Gn CH1 . . . . 117 E6
Aran Cl L24 . . . . 21 D1
Arbour Cl
Macclesfield SK10 . . . . 87 D3
Northwich CW9 . . . . 104 C8
Arbour Cres SK10 . . . . 87 D3
Arbourhay St SK10 . . . . . . .87 E1
Arbour Mews SK10 . . . . . . 87 D3
Arbour St ST7. . . . . 210 D5
Arbour Wlk
🔟 Alvanley WA6 . . . . 73 A2
Frodsham WA6. . . . . 73 A2
Arbury La WA2. . . . . .8 C6
Arcade The
Ellesmere Port CH65 . . . . . 70 A5
🔁 Northwich CW9. . . . . . 103 F8
Archer Ave WA4 . . . . .16 E2
Archer Cl SK10. . . . . .87 E7
Archers Brook Sch CH66. . . .69 E2
Archers Gn CH62 . . . . .43 D5
Archers Green Rd WA5 . . . . .7 B3
Archers Way Blacon CH1. . . 118 A2
Ellesmere Port CH66 . . . . . .69 E1
Arches Com Prim Sch The
CH1. . . . . 117 E5
Archway Wlk WA12. . . . . . . .2 A3
ARCLID 154 B1
Arclid Ct 🔟 CW12 . . . . . . 156 F3
ARCLID GREEN 176 A8
Arclid Green Ind Est
CW11. . . . . 176 B8
Arden WA8 . . . . 12 A2
Ardenbrook Rise SK10. . . . .86 F6
Arden Cl Gatley SK8. . . . . . 34 C7
Tarvin CH3 . . . . 121 C3
Warrington WA3 . . . . .10 B6
Arden Ct CW12 . . . . 179 B7
Arden Dr CH64 . . . . .66 C6
Arden Est SK22 . . . . 39 D7
Ardens Mdw
🔟 Birch Heath CW6. . . . . 168 C8
Tarporley CW6 . . . . 168 C8
Arden Sq CW1 . . . . 191 A2
Arden St CW9 . . . . 79 C7
Arderne Ave CW2 . . . . 190 A4
Arderne Ho CH2 . . . . 118 F7
Arderne Pl 🔁 SK9. . . . . . . 60 A1
Arden Lea WA6 . . . . 73 D1
Ardleigh Cl CW1 . . . . 189 F8

Arena Gdns WA2 . . . . 16 D8
Argosy Dr M90. . . . . .32 F7
Argyle Ct 🔟 WA16. . . . . . . 57 A2
Argyll Ave Bebington CH62. .43 D4
Chester CH4. . . . . 141 A7
Argyll Cl SK10. . . . . 87 A1
Ariel Gdns WA3 . . . . .5 A2
Ariel Wlk 🔟 WA3. . . . . . . .3 E8
Arizona Cres WA5. . . . . . . .15 B7
Arkenshaw Rd WA3 . . . . . . .9 A7
Arkenstone Cl WA8 . . . . . . 12 C2
Arkle Ave SK8, SK9. . . . . . .34 E4
Arkle Ct 🔟 CH3 . . . . 119 B1
Arklow Dr L24 . . . . 21 D2
Arkwright Cl CW7 . . . . 149 A8
Arkwright Ct WA7. . . . . 23 F3
Arkwright Rd WA7 . . . . 23 F3
ARLEY 54 C7
Arley Ave WA4 . . . . 26 D8
Arley Cl Alsager ST7. . . . . . 193 C3
Chester CH2. . . . . 118 F6
Macclesfield SK11 . . . . . . 112 A7
Arley Dr WA8 . . . . .12 B2
Arley End WA16 . . . . 29 C4
ARLEY GREEN 54 E6
Arley Hall & Gardens★
CW9 . . . . 54 D6
Arley Mossend La CW9 . . . 54 D2
Arley Pk CW9 . . . . 54 C4
Arley Pl CW2 . . . . 206 A8
Arley Rd Antrobus CW9 . . . .54 B7
Appleton Thorn WA4. . . . . .27 C3
Northwich CW9 . . . . 104 C8
Arley Wlk CW11. . . . . 174 D5
Arlington Cl CW2 . . . . 206 C8
Arlington Cres SK9 . . . . . . .59 E5
Arlington Dr Golborne WN7 . .4 C8
Macclesfield SK11 . . . . . . 112 A7
Poynton SK12. . . . . .36 D3
Warrington WA5 . . . . .14 E4
Arlington Way SK9 . . . . . . .59 E5
Armistead Way CW4. . . . . . 130 A5
Armistice Dr 🔟 CW7 . . . . 149 E8
Armitage Way CW8. . . . . . . 78 C1
Armitstead Rd CW11 . . . . . 174 F4
Armitt St SK11 . . . . 112 C7
Armour Ave WA2. . . . . .8 B2
Armoury Court Mews 🔁
SK11 . . . . 112 B6
Armoury Twrs 🔟 SK11. . . . 112 B6
Armstrong Cl
Audlem CW3 . . . . 229 F4
Northwich CW8 . . . . 103 A5
Warrington WA3 . . . . .9 D4
Armthorpe Dr CH66 . . . . . . 69 C5
Arncliffe Dr WA5. . . . . .6 F6
Arndale WA7 . . . . .49 E5
Arnhem Cres WA2. . . . . 16 C7
Arnhem Way 🔟 CH3 . . . . 142 B5
Arnold Cl CW8 . . . . 78 C1
Arnold Pl WA8 . . . . 22 C7
Arnold's Cres CH4. . . . . . . 139 A3
Arnold St Nantwich CW5 . . 204 E6
Warrington WA1 . . . . 16 D6
Arnside Ave
Congleton CW12 . . . . 156 A2
Haydock WA11 . . . . .1 B6
Arnside Cl High Lane SK6. . . .37 E8
Winsford CW7 . . . . 126 D2
Arnside Gr WA4 . . . . .16 B2
Arpley Rd WA1 . . . . 16 B4
Arpley St WA1 . . . . 16 A4
Arradon Ct CH2 . . . . 118 E5
Arran Ave CH65 . . . . 70 C1
Arran Cl
Holmes Chapel CW4. . . . . . 130 C2
Warrington WA2 . . . . .9 A2
Arran Dr WA6. . . . . 74 C6
Arrivals Way M90. . . . . .33 B7
Arron Cl CW2 . . . . 189 D3
Arrowcroft Rd CH3 . . . . . . 119 F5
Arrowhead Cl 🔁 CW5 . . . 205 B3
Arrowsmith Dr ST7. . . . . . 193 B3
Arrowsmith Rd WA11. . . . . .1 F7
ARTHILL. 30 B8
Arthill La
Little Bollington WA14 . . . . 20 B1
Rostherne WA14 . . . . 30 B8
Arthog Dr WA15 . . . . .31 F8
Arthog Rd WA15 . . . . 32 A8
Arthur Ave CH65 . . . . 70 C5
Arthur Maddock Rd 🔟
ST7. . . . . 193 F4
Arthur St Chester CH1 . . . . 118 A2
🔟 Crewe CW2. . . . . 190 D2
Lostock Gralam CW9 . . . . . 80 A2
🔟 Runcorn WA7 . . . . 23 A2
Warrington WA1 . . . . 16 A6
Artillery Rd CH3. . . . . 142 B4
Artis Rd CW7 . . . . 127 C2
Artists La SK10. . . . . 85 C7
Artle Rd CW2 . . . . 206 C8
Arundel Ave SK7 . . . . 36 D8
Arundel Cl Knutsford WA16. 82 A8
Macclesfield SK10 . . . . .87 F2
Wistaston CW2 . . . . 205 E8
Arundel Ct CH65 . . . . .70 E3
Arundel Cl WA5 . . . . .6 F1
Arundel Rd SK8 . . . . 35 A6
Ascol Dr WA16. . . . . 80 C3
Ascot Ave WA5 . . . . 7 B3
Ascot Cl Congleton CW12. . 156 D4
Macclesfield SK10 . . . . 87 C3
Warrington WA4 . . . . 17 C2

Ascot Cl *continued*
Warrington, Martinscroft WA1 17 E7
Ascot Ct CW9 104 C8
Ascot Dr CH66 69 E3
Ascot Ho CH1 118 B2
Ash Acre Mdws WA4 17 A4
Ash Ave Irlam M44 11 D5
Newton-le-Willows WA12 2 C2
Ashbank CW9 104 D7
Ashbank Pl CW1 189 F6
Ashberry Cl **5** SK9 60 D8
Ashberry Dr WA4 27 B5
Ashberry Rd CH2 95 B4
Ashbourne Ave WA7 49 B6
Ashbourne Cl CH66 94 E8
Ashbourne Dr
Chorlton CW2 207 C1
High Lane SK6 37 F6
Ashbourne Mews **1** SK10 111 F8
Ashbourne Rd
Hazel Grove SK7 36 F8
Warrington WA5 15 B5
Ashbrook Ave WA7 49 F3
Ashbrook Cres WA2 16 D8
Ashbrook Dr SK10 87 A6
Ashbrook Rd
Bollington SK10 87 F7
Nether Alderley SK10 85 F6
Ashburton CH64 66 C8
Ashbury Cl WA7 24 D2
Ashbury Dr WA11 1 D7
Ashby Dr CW11 174 C5
Ashby Pl CH2 237 C4
Ash Cl Ellesmere Port CH66 69 F1
Holmes Chapel CW4 130 D4
Malpas SY14 213 C5
Swan Green WA16 106 D7
Tarporley CW6 146 D2
Ashcroft Ave CW2 206 B3
Ashcroft Cl SK9 59 F5
Ashcroft Ct M44 11 D5
Ashcroft Rd WA13 19 B4
Ash Ct **15** WA16 57 A2
Ashdale Cl ST7 193 C5
Ashdene Prim Sch SK9 59 F5
Ashdene Rd SK9 59 F5
Ashdown Cl SK8 35 A6
Ashdown La WA3 10 B5
Ashdown Rd WA16 82 F6
Ashenhurst Rd ST7 193 F3
Ashenough Rd ST7 210 D6
Asher Ct WA4 27 D4
Ashfield Cl WA13 19 B4
Ashfield Cres
Bebington CH62 43 D8
Blacon CH1 117 D5
Ashfield Dr SK10 87 A2
Ashfield Gdns WA4 16 F3
Ashfield Gr M44 11 E6
Ashfield Ho **5** CH64 66 E8
Ashfield Rd
Bebington CH62 43 C8
Ellesmere Port CH65 70 C5
Ashfield Road N **1** CH65 70 C5
Ashfield St CW10 151 D8
Ashfield Way CW11 175 A6
Ashford Cl SK9 34 C4
Ashford Dr WA4 26 E3
Ashford Rd SK9 60 A4
Ashford Way **1** WA8 13 D1
Ashgate La CW9 79 F6
Ash Gr Chester CH4 141 B5
Congleton CW12 156 A3
Ellesmere Port CH66 69 C6
Gatley SK8 34 B8
Golborne WA3 3 B8
Handforth SK9 34 C3
Knutsford WA16 57 D1
Macclesfield SK11 112 C4
Middlewich CW10 151 D7
Nantwich CW5 204 F3
Rode Heath ST7 193 F7
Runcorn WA7 49 C8
Warrington WA4 16 D3
Weaverham CW8 102 E7
Widnes WA8 22 D8
Ashgrove CW7 149 D8
Ash Grove Prim Sch SK11 112 C4
Ash Hay La
Hoole Bank CH2 119 C8
Picton CH2 96 C2
Ash Ho Chester CH2 118 C5
8 Sandbach CW11 175 B6
Ash House La CW8 77 D7
Ash La Warrington WA4 26 E8
Widnes WA8 22 A8
Ashlands WA6 74 C7
Ash Lawn Ct CH2 118 C4
Ashlea Dr CW5 205 E5
Ashleigh Cl CH4 140 E6
ASHLEY 31 E5
Ashley CE Prim Sch WA15 31 F5
Ashley Cl Warrington WA4 17 C3
Winterley CW11 191 F8
Ashley Ct Frodsham WA6 74 A8
Holt LL13 196 D8
Warrington WA4 26 C6
Ashley Dr Bramhall SK7 35 C5
Hartford CW8 103 A6
Ashley Gdns Clutton CH3 182 C1
High Lane SK6 37 D8
Ashley Gn WA8 22 D8
Ashley Grange CW9 103 E3
ASHLEY HEATH 31 E8
Ashley Mdw CW1 191 D5
Ashleymill La WA14 31 D7
Ashley Mill Lane N WA14 31 E8
Ashley Rd
Ashley WA14, WA15, WA16 31 C4
Ashley, Ashley Heath WA14, WA15 31 E7
Handforth SK9 34 B1
Mere WA16 56 D8
Runcorn WA7 23 D2
Ashley Ret Pk WA8 23 B7
Ashley Sch WA8 12 D1
Ashley Sta W14 31 E5
Ashley Way WA8 23 B7
Ashley Way W WA8 22 F7
Ash Lo SK12 36 D4
Ashmead Cl ST7 193 E3
Ashmead La Bramhall SK12 35 F5
Poynton SK12 36 A4
Ashmead Mews ST7 193 E3
Ashmore Cl
Middlewich CW10 151 C6
Warrington WA3 10 A3
Ashmore's La ST7 193 D3
Ash Mount CW3 232 B1
Ashmuir Cl Blacon CH1 117 E3
Crewe CW1 190 B6
Ashness Dr SK7 35 E8
Ash Priors WA8 12 D3
Ash Rd Crewe CW1 190 D6
Cuddington CW8 101 F2
Elton CH2 72 C3
Haydock WA11 1 E7
Hollinfare WA3 11 A2
Lymm WA13 18 C3
Partington M31 11 D3
Poynton SK12 36 F3
Warrington WA5 14 F4
Winwick WA2 8 B6
Ashridge St WA7 22 F3
Ash St CW9 79 A1
Ash Terr SK11 112 C4
Ashton Ave SK10 86 D1
Ashton Cl Bebington CH62 43 E3
Congleton CW12 157 B1
Frodsham WA6 49 C1
Middlewich CW10 151 D5
2 Middlewich CW10 151 D5
Northwich CW9 103 E4
Runcorn WA7 48 F6
Woodford SK7 35 F2
Ashton Ct WA6 49 C1
Ashton Dr WA6 49 C1
ASHTON HAYES 121 F7
Ashton Hayes Prim Sch CH3 121 F8
Ashton La CH3 121 E6
Ashton Rd Manley WA6 99 E4
Newton-le-Willows WA12 2 C5
Norley WA6 100 B4
ASHTON'S GREEN 1 B3
Ashton St WA2 16 B6
Ashtree Cl Neston CH64 67 A7
Prestbury SK10 87 C8
Ashtree Croft CH64 68 A7
Ashtree Ct CH2 237 C4
Ashtree Dr CH64 67 A7
Ashtree Farm Ct CH64 68 A7
Ash View ST7 195 B2
Ashville Ct CW2 206 B7
Ashville Ind Est WA7 49 E3
Ashville Point WA7 49 E3
Ashville Way WA7 49 E3
Ash Way CH60 41 B6
Ashwood WA14 31 B8
Ashwood Ave
Golborne WA3 3 D8
Warrington WA1 16 E7
Ashwood Cl Barnton CW8 78 B4
Ellesmere Port CH66 69 D1
Widnes WA8 22 A7
Ashwood Cres CW8 78 B3
Ashwood Ct CH2 119 A3
Ashwood Farm Ct CH2 96 B6
Ashwood La CH2 96 B5
Ashwood Rd SK12 38 D6
Ashworth Pk WA16 81 F8
Asiatic Cotts CH5 116 B3
Askerbank La SK11 159 A1
Askett Cl WA11 1 C7
Askrigg Ave CH66 69 B5
Aspen Cl
Ellesmere Port CH66 69 E1
Harriseahead ST7 195 E3
Heswall CH60 41 D8
Lower Heath CW12 156 E6
Aspen Gr Saughall CH1 117 B7
Warrington WA1 17 A7
Aspens The CW8 101 E5
Aspen Way Chester CH2 119 B4
High Lane SK6 38 A7
Aspinall Cl WA2 9 A3
Aspull Cl WA3 9 C4
Asquith Cl CW1 191 C5
Assheton Cl WA12 2 B4
Assheton Wlk L24 21 E2
ASTBURY 178 B7
Astbury Cl Crewe CW1 190 A7
Golborne WA3 4 B8
Kidsgrove ST7 195 C3
Astbury Dr CW8 78 A4
Astbury Lane Ends CW12 178 F8
ASTBURY MARSH 156 B1
Astbury Mere Ctry Pk* CW12 156 B2
Astbury St Mary's CE Prim Sch CW12 178 B8
Astbury St CW12 156 C2
Aster Cres WA7 49 F5
Aster Rd WA11 1 F7
Aster Wlk M31 11 F2
ASTLE 109 D8
Astle Cl CW10 151 C7
Astle Ct SK11 84 A3
Astle La SK10 84 E1
Astley Cl Knutsford WA16 82 C7
Warrington WA4 16 B3
Widnes WA8 12 C3
Astley Ct M44 11 E8
Astley Rd M44 11 E8
ASTMOOR 23 E3
Astmoor Bridge La WA7 23 F2
Astmoor East Intc WA7 24 A3
Astmoor Ind Est WA7 23 F3
Astmoor Prim Sch WA7 23 F2
Astmoor Rd WA7 23 E3
ASTON Nantwich 217 C2
Runcorn 50 D1
Aston Ave Warrington WA3 9 F4
Winsford CW7 126 B2
Aston by Sutton Prim Sch WA7 50 C2
Aston Ct WA1 9 C1
Aston Fields Rd WA7 50 E4
Aston Forge WA7 50 F5
Aston Gn WA7 50 E6
Aston Grange WA7 75 F8
ASTON HEATH 50 E2
ASTON JUXTA MONDRUM 188 D6
Aston La Aston WA7 50 C2
Runcorn WA7 50 F5
Woore CW3 232 E1
Aston Lane N WA7 50 E4
Aston Lane S WA7 50 E3
Aston Rd ST5 210 D1
Aston Way
13 Handforth SK9 34 D5
Middlewich CW10 128 E1
Astor Dr WA4 26 F8
Atcherley Cl CW5 218 E8
Athelbrae Cl CW8 103 F7
Atherton La M44 11 E5
Atherton Rd CH65 69 F6
Athertons Quay WA5 15 E4
Athey St Mill **2** SK11 112 C7
Athey St SK11 112 C8
Athlone Rd WA2 8 A1
Athol Cl Bebington CH62 43 E5
Newton-le-Willows WA12 1 F4
Athol Dr CH62 43 E5
Atholl Ave CW2 190 C1
Atholl Cl SK10 87 A1
Athol Rd SK7 35 D5
Atkin Cl CW12 156 A3
Atlanta Ave M90 33 A8
Atlanta Gdns WA5 15 B8
Atlantic Trad Pk CW7 126 E5
Atlas Way CH66 69 F7
Atterbury Cl WA8 12 C2
Attlebridge Gdns **4** WA5 14 E8
Attlee Ave WA3 5 C4
Attwood Cl CW1 191 C4
Attwood Rise ST7 195 A2
Attwood St ST7 195 A2
Atworth Terr CH64 67 F8
Aubourn Cl WA8 12 C3
Auckery Ave CH66 69 D3
Auckland Rd CH1 117 D4
AUDLEM 230 B4
Audlem Cl WA7 49 F4
Audlem Dr CW9 104 A6
Audlem Rd
Hankelow CW3 230 C7
Hatherton CW5 219 D3
Nantwich CW5 204 F3
Audlem St James' CE Prim Sch CW3 230 A5
AUDLEY 209 C2
Audley Cres CH4 141 E6
Audley Rd Alsager ST7 193 E1
Barthomley CW2 208 E5
Newcastle-under-Lyme ST7, ST5 210 B2
Talke ST7 210 B6
Audley St CW1 190 D5
Audley Street W CW1 190 D5
Audre Cl WA5 14 D6
Aughton Way CH4 139 D4
Augusta Dr SK10 87 B4
Augusta Gr **8** WA5 15 A7
Augusta Ho CH1 117 F6
Austell Rd **3** M22 33 D8
Austen Cl **1** CW11 174 D6
Austen Dr WA2 8 A6
Austen Ho SK10 86 F1
Austin Cl CW7 149 C6
Austin Dr CW8 78 C1
Austins Hill CH3 144 C8
Austin St CW9 79 D1
Austral Ave WA1 17 C7
Australia La WA4 17 C1
Autumn Ave WA16 57 C2
Ava Cl WA8 13 C3
Avebury Cl Golborne WA3 3 E8
Widnes WA8 13 F3
Aveley Cl WA1 17 B7
Avens Rd M31 11 F3
Avenue One CW1 207 C8
Avenue The
Alderley Edge SK9 60 A1
Alsager ST7 193 D4
Altrincham WA15 31 F8
Avenue The *continued*
Bebington CH62 43 C8
Comberbach CW9 78 D8
Great Barrow CH3 120 F7
High Legh WA16 29 C5
Kidsgrove ST7 194 F1
Lymm WA13 18 D1
Marston CW9 79 B3
Newton-le-Willows WA12 2 D4
Northwich CW9 79 B8
Sandbach CW11 174 E8
Tarporley CW6 146 D1
Avenue Two CW1 207 C8
Avery Cl WA2 8 E2
Avery Cres WA11 1 C7
Avery Rd WA11 1 C7
Avery Sq WA11 1 C7
Aviemore Dr WA2 9 A3
Avocet Cl
Newton-le-Willows WA12 2 C4
Warrington WA2 8 D3
Avocet Dr CW7 149 D6
Avon WA8 12 A2
Avon Ave WA5 14 F4
Avon Cl Kidsgrove ST7 195 B2
Macclesfield SK10 87 A2
Neston CH64 66 E6
Avon Ct ST7 193 C5
Avondale CH65 70 B2
Avondale Ave CH62 43 F5
Avondale Dr WA8 12 B1
Avondale Rd WA11 1 C7
Avondale Rise SK9 60 D6
Avon Dr Congleton CW12 156 F1
Crewe CW1 191 A5
Avonlea Cl CH4 140 E4
Avon Rd Altrincham WA15 31 E8
Culcheth WA3 5 A2
Gatley SK8 34 C7
Avonside Way SK11 112 C5
Avon Wlk CW7 127 A2
Avro Way M90 32 F7
Axminster Wlk SK7 35 E7
Aycliffe Wlk **6** WA8 22 C8
Aylesbury Cl
Ellesmere Port CH66 69 C3
Macclesfield SK10 87 D3
Aylesbury Rd CW5 204 D7
Aylesby Cl WA16 57 B1
Aylsham Cl WA8 12 C4
Ayrshire Cl CW10 128 D2
Ayrshire Dr CW5 204 D6
Ayrshire Way CW12 157 A1
Aysgarth Ave CW1 173 B1
Azalea Gdns WA9 6 A7
Azalea Gr WA7 49 F4

B

Babbacombe Rd WA5 14 E4
Babbage Rd CH5 116 A4
BACHE 118 B5
Bache Ave CH2 118 C5
Bache Dr CH2 118 D5
Bachefield Ave CH3 142 A6
Bache Hall Ct CH2 118 C5
Bache Hall Est CH2 118 C5
Bachelor's Ct CH3 142 A8
Bachelor's La CH3 142 A8
Bache Sta CH2 118 D5
Back Brook Pl WA4 16 E3
Back Coole La CW3 229 B4
Back Crosland Terr WA6 73 B2
Back Cross La
Congleton CW12 179 A8
Newton-le-Willows WA12 2 B4
Back Eastford Rd WA4 16 A1
Back Eddisbury Rd SK11 113 C7
BACKFORD 95 A4
Backford Cl WA7 50 C5
Backford Cross CH66 94 F7
Backford Gdns CH1 94 F7
Back Forshaw St WA2 16 C7
Back Heathcote St ST7 195 A2
Back High St **3** WA7 23 A2
Back Jodrell St SK22 39 B7
Back La Alpraham CW6 169 D6
Altrincham WA15 32 B4
Bate Heath CW9 54 D7
Betley CW2 208 C1
Brereton Green CW11 153 D6
Burtonwood WA5 6 D7
Congleton CW12 156 A4
Duddon CW6 145 A6
Helsby WA6 73 D2
Higher Whitley WA4 52 E4
High Legh WA14 29 F5
Marton CW12, SK11 133 F2
No Man's Heath SY14 214 A4
Partington WA14 20 C5
Plumley WA16 81 B1
Shavington CW2 206 E4
Smallwood CW11 176 D8
Swan Green WA16 106 B8
Tattenhall CH3 167 C2
Threapwood SY14 222 E7
Warrington WA5 14 A3
Wybunbury CW5 220 C6
Back La SY14 222 E7
Backlands CW1 190 C6
Back Lanes CW6 146 B2
Back Market St WA12 2 A3
Back Oth Cross SK17 138 E2
Back Paradise St **4** SK11 112 C7
Back Park St CW12 156 E2
Back Queen St CH1 237 B3
Back River St **1** CW12 156 D3
Back Union Rd **3** SK22 39 C7
Back Wallgate **13** SK11 112 D8
Badbury Cl WA11 1 D7
Badcock's La CW6 185 E4
BADDILEY 203 B1
Baddiley Cl CW5 203 D2
Baddiley Hall La CW5 217 A8
Baddiley La CW5 203 D1
Baddington La CW5 204 C1
Badens Croft Rd **3** CW2 206 D7
Badger Ave CW1 190 B5
Badger Bait CH64 66 F6
Badger Cl WA7 50 A6
Badger Cres SY13 225 F1
Badger Ho SK10 87 D2
Badger Rd
Macclesfield SK10 87 D2
Prestbury SK10 87 A7
Badgers Cl
Christleton CH3 142 E7
1 Ellesmere Port CH66 94 F8
Hartford CW8 103 D4
1 Winsford CW7 126 A1
Badgers Croft ST5 210 E1
Badgers Pk CH64 66 F6
Badgersrake La CH66 68 D3
Badgers Set CW8 101 D5
Badgers Wlk CH2 95 E2
Badgers Wood CW2 205 E8
Bag La
Cuddington CW8, WA6 101 E7
Norley WA6 101 A6
Bagley La CW3 230 B1
Bagmere Cl
Brereton Green CW11 153 F4
Sandbach CW11 174 F7
Bagmere La CW11 154 B5
Bagnall Cl WA5 15 C5
Bagot Ave WA5 15 F8
Bagstock Ave SK12 36 E2
Baguley Ave WA8 22 A5
Bahama Cl WA11 1 D8
Bahama Rd WA11 1 D8
Baildon Gn CH66 69 B5
Bailey Ave
Clive Green CW7 150 A8
Ellesmere Port CH65 69 F6
Bailey Bridge Cl CH2 118 D4
Bailey Bsns Pk SK10 87 F7
Bailey Cl CW1 190 C7
Bailey Cres
Congleton CW12 157 A4
Sandbach CW11 175 D6
Bailey Ct Alsager ST7 193 E3
1 Macclesfield SK10 112 E7
Bailey La M31 11 F3
Bailey Rd SK9 60 E8
Bailey's Bank ST8 179 D3
Baileys Cl WA8 13 A5
Baileys La L26 21 A7
Bailey's La L24 21 A1
Bailey Wlk WA14 31 C8
Bainbridge Ave WA3 3 F8
Bainbridge Cres WA5 14 E8
Baines Ave M44 11 F8
Bakehurst Cl SK22 39 C7
Baker Cl CW2 190 A2
Baker Dr CH66 69 E3
Baker Rd WA7 48 D7
Baker's Cl CW7 126 E1
Baker's Ct CW7 126 E1
Bakersfield Dr **3** WA5 15 A7
Baker's La
Swan Green WA16 106 D6
Winsford CW7 126 E1
Bakers Pl WA2 16 B7
Baker St **8** SK11 112 C7
Bakers Villas The CW12 156 D2
Bakestonedale Rd SK10 63 E4
Bakewell Cl CH66 94 E8
Bakewell Rd
Burtonwood WA5 7 A7
Hazel Grove SK7 36 E8
Bala Cl WA5 7 E2
BALDERTON 140 C1
Baldock Cl WA4 17 C3
Balfour Cl CW1 191 C4
Balfour St WA7 22 F1
Balham Cl WA8 13 B4
Balharry Ave WA11 1 E7
Ballantyne Pl WA2 8 A6
Ballantyne Way **5** WA3 3 E8
Ballater Cres CH3 119 B2
Ballater Dr WA2 8 E4
Ballerat Cl **2** CH1 117 D4
Balliol Cl SK11 112 F3
Ball La Bollington SK10 87 D5
Kingsley WA6 75 E4
BALL O' DITTON 12 E2
Ball Pathway WA8 12 E1
Balmoral Ave Crewe CW2 190 B1
Northwich CW9 104 A5
Balmoral Cl Bryn CW8 102 A5
Knutsford WA16 57 B1
Winsford CW7 126 C3
Balmoral Cres SK10 87 F2
Balmoral Dr Helsby WA6 73 B4
High Lane SK6 37 E7
Holmes Chapel CW4 130 B2
Poynton SK12 36 D3
Balmoral Gdns
Congleton CW12 156 F4
Ellesmere Port CH65 70 D3
Balmoral Pk CH1 118 B3
Balmoral Pl CW5 205 D4
Balmoral Rd
Warrington WA4 16 F2

Balmoral Rd continued
Widnes WA8 . . . . 13 A4
Balmoral Way SK9 . . . . 60 A6
BALTERLEY 208 C1
Balterley Ct CW2 . . . . 208 C1
Balterley Gn Rd
Balterley CW2 . . . . 208 B1
Gorstyhill CW2 . . . . 207 F2
BALTERLEY GREEN 208 C2
BALTERLEY HEATH 207 F1
Baltimore Gdns WA5 . . . . . 15 C7
Bamburgh Ct CH65 . . . . . . 70 E3
Bambury Dr ST7 . . . . 194 C1
Bamford Cl Bollington SK10 . 88 A7
Gatley SK8 . . . . 34 D8
Runcorn WA7 . . . . 49 C7
Bamford St SK10 . . . . 87 E1
Bamforth Pl CH62 . . . . 43 D7
Banastre Dr WA12 . . . . 2 F3
Banbury Cl SK10 . . . . 87 E2
Banbury Dr WA5 . . . . 15 C5
Banbury St ST7 . . . . 194 D1
Bancroft CW8 . . . . 76 F4
Bancroft Rd WA8 . . . . 13 D2
Bandon Cl L24 . . . . 21 D2
Banff Ave CH63 . . . . 43 D5
Bangor Cl 11 CH66 . . . . . . 94 F8
Bank Cl Chester CH2 . . . . . 118 C5
Macclesfield SK11 . . . . 112 E7
Neston CH64 . . . . 67 A6
Bank Cott CW12 . . . . 156 E2
Bank Ct 5 ST7 . . . . 195 A2
Bankes' La
Runcorn, Weston WA7 . . . . 48 F5
Runcorn, Weston Point WA7 . 48 E6
Wistaston CW2 . . . . 206 A7
Bankfield Ave Irlam M44 . . 11 D5
Wistaston CW2 . . . . 206 A7
Bankfield Rd WA8 . . . . 12 C1
Bankfield Sch The WA8 . . . 12 C1
Bankfields Dr CH62 . . . . . . 44 B5
Bank Gdns WA5 . . . . 14 E4
Bankhall La WA14, WA15 . . 31 F8
BANK HEATH 3 A8
Bankhey CH64 . . . . 66 F5
Bank Ho CW7 . . . . 126 C1
Bankhouse Dr CW12 . . . . . 157 A5
Bank House La
Helsby WA6 . . . . 73 C4
Smallwood CW11 . . . . 177 A6
Bank La Burland CW5 . . . . . 203 D8
Congleton CW12 . . . . 134 C1
Rainow SK10 . . . . 89 D6
Banklands Cl M44 . . . . 11 D5
Bank Mews WA6 . . . . 73 C4
Bank Pl SK9 . . . . 60 B7
BANK QUAY 15 F4
Bank Quay Trad Est WA1 . . 15 F4
Bank Rd CH5 . . . . 91 D1
Banks Cl CW12 . . . . 156 C3
Banks Cres WA4 . . . . 16 F4
Bankside Altrincham WA15 . 32 D6
Runcorn WA7 . . . . 50 E7
Warrington WA1 . . . . 16 A5
Bank Side CW8 . . . . 77 C1
Bankside Cl
Barbridge CW5 . . . . 187 D6
Handforth SK9 . . . . 34 D1
Bankside Ct ST7 . . . . 193 E5
Bank Sq SK9 . . . . 60 B7
Banks Rd CH60 . . . . 40 D8
Bank St Congleton CW12 . . 156 E2
Hollinfare WA3 . . . . 11 B5
Kidsgrove ST7 . . . . 195 C4
Macclesfield SK11 . . . . 112 E7
Newton-le-Willows WA12 . . . 1 F3
8 Warrington WA1 . . . . 16 B5
Widnes WA8 . . . . 23 A4
BANK THE 195 B7
Bank The ST7 . . . . 195 B7
Bank Top Cotts CW5 . . . . . 204 F6
Banktop Rd SK11 . . . . 137 E6
Bank View CW4 . . . . 107 E1
Banky Fields CW12 . . . . . . 156 E1
Banky Fields Cres CW12 . . 156 C1
Bannacks Cl CW5 . . . . 205 D6
Bannister Ct CW7 . . . . 149 B7
Bannister Gr CW7 . . . . 149 B6
Barbauld St WA1 . . . . 16 B5
Barber Cl CW9 . . . . 126 F8
Barber Dr ST7 . . . . 194 C1
Barberry Wlk M31 . . . . 11 F3
Barber's La Antrobus CW9 . 53 D6
Northwich CW8 . . . . 103 E8
Barber St SK11 . . . . 112 E6
Barbondale Cl WA5 . . . . . . 14 F7
Barbour Sq CH3 . . . . 166 B1
BARBRIDGE 187 C6
Barbridge Mews CW5 . . . . 187 D6
Barbridge Rd ST5 . . . . 210 D2
Barclay Hall WA16 . . . . 58 D4
Barclay Rd SK12 . . . . 36 E2
Bardell Cl SK12 . . . . 36 D2
Bardsey Cl 1 CH65 . . . . . . 70 C1
Barford Cl WA5 . . . . 7 B1
Barford Dr Golborne WA3 . . . 4 A8
Handforth SK9 . . . . 34 C1
Barford Grange CH64 . . . . . 68 B8
Barham Ct WA3 . . . . 9 D4
Bar Hill CW7 . . . . 24 F3
Barhill Dr SY13 . . . . 214 C2
Barhill Farm Cotts SY13 . . 214 C2
Barington Dr WA7 . . . . 50 E7
Baristow Cl CH2 . . . . 237 B4
Barker's Hollow Rd WA4 . . . 51 A5
Barker St Crewe CW2 . . . . 190 D1
Nantwich CW5 . . . . 204 E5
Winnington CW8 . . . . 78 C2

Barkhill Rd CH3 . . . . 119 B3
Bark St CW12 . . . . 156 E2
Barkston Heath Dr WA5 . . . 14 E8
Barley Castle Cl WA4 . . . . . 27 B3
Barleycastle La WA4 . . . . . . 27 D4
Barleycastle Trad Est
WA4 . . . . 27 D4
Barley Croft Alsager ST7 . . 193 E2
Chester CH3 . . . . 142 A7
Barleycroft Terr ST7 . . . . . 194 F7
Barley Dr SK7 . . . . 35 C7
Barleyfields ST7 . . . . 209 D2
Barley Mow Cl WA12 . . . . . . 69 C2
Barley Rd WA4 . . . . 17 C3
Barleywood Cl CW2 . . . . . . 206 B8
Barlow Dr CW7 . . . . 148 F8
Barlow Gr WA9 . . . . 1 A2
Barlow Hill Heaton SK11 . . 159 F8
Wincle SK11 . . . . 136 F2
Barlow Rd Handforth SK9 . . 34 B1
Moulton CW9 . . . . 126 F7
Barlow Way
Sandbach CW11 . . . . 175 A8
Weston Point WA7 . . . . 48 D8
Barmouth Cl WA7 . . . . 49 E2
Barnabas Ave CW1 . . . . . . 189 F5
Barnaby Chase CH3 . . . . . 182 C2
Barnaby Rd SK12 . . . . 36 D2
Barnack Cl WA1 . . . . 17 A8
Barnacre Dr CW4 . . . . 41 B2
Barnard Cl SK11 . . . . 111 F6
Barnard St WA5 . . . . 15 D3
Barnato Cl CW1 . . . . 189 F7
Barnbridge Cl ST7 . . . . . . 194 E7
Barnbrook Cl CW7 . . . . . . 126 A1
Barncroft WA7 . . . . 50 D7
Barn Croft WA6 . . . . 73 C4
Barncroft Cl SK11 . . . . 84 A3
Barn Croft Rd L26 . . . . 21 A7
Barn Ct CH3 . . . . 182 C2
Barnes Ave WA2 . . . . 9 B2
Barnes Brow WA16 . . . . 58 E6
Barnes Cl Blacon CH1 . . . . 117 F6
Haslington CW1 . . . . 191 C4
Warrington WA5 . . . . 15 A5
Widnes WA8 . . . . 13 D2
Barnes Rd WA8 . . . . 13 C2
Barneston Rd WA8 . . . . 13 E3
Barnett Ave WA12 . . . . 1 E3
BARNETT BROOK 228 E5
Barnett Gr CW12 . . . . 156 A3
Barnett St SK11 . . . . 112 B7
Barnett Wlk CW2 . . . . 206 C8
Barnfield CH3 . . . . 166 A2
Barnfield Ave WA7 . . . . 50 D7
Barnfield Cl CH66 . . . . 69 C2
Barn Field Cl 9 CW1 . . . . . 190 A8
Barnfield Dr CW12 . . . . . . 156 E6
Barnfield Rd
Bollington SK10 . . . . 87 F6
Warrington WA1 . . . . 17 C7
Barn Field Way ST7 . . . . . . 192 F2
Barnham Cl WA3 . . . . 3 A8
BARNHILL 183 B1
Barnhill Grange CH3 . . . . . 183 B3
Barnhill Rd CH3 . . . . 183 A1
Barnhouse La
Great Barrow CH3 . . . . 120 E7
Mouldsworth CH3 . . . . 98 A3
Barn La WA3 . . . . 2 F8
Barn Mdw CW8 . . . . 78 E1
Barn Meadow Way CW1 . . 190 C8
Barnmoore Cl SY14 . . . . . . 213 B4
Barn Rd Congleton CW12 . . 156 D4
West Heath CW12 . . . . 156 C5
Barnside Way
Macclesfield SK10 . . . . 87 C3
Moulton CW9 . . . . 126 F8
Barns La WA14 . . . . 20 A5
Barns Pl WA15 . . . . 32 C8
Barn St WA8 . . . . 23 A6
Barnstaple Way WA5 . . . . . 14 E4
Barns The CW10 . . . . 127 D5
Barnston Ave CH65 . . . . 69 F5
Barnston Ct Farndon CH3 . 180 E2
Mickle Trafford CH2 . . . . . 119 F8
Barnston Mews CH3 . . . . . 180 E2
Barnston Prim Sch CH60 . . 41 C7
Barnston Rd CH60 . . . . 41 C8
Barnston Towers Cl CH60 . 41 C8
Barnston Twrs CH60 . . . . . . 41 C8
Barnswood Cl WA4 . . . . 17 C1
BARNTON 78 C4
Barnton Cl 2 Golborne WA3 . 3 C7
Golborne WA3 . . . . 3 D7
Barnton Prim Sch CW8 . . . . 78 A4
Barnton Way CW11 . . . . . . 174 F4
Barn Way CW11 . . . . 2 B3
Barnwell Ave WA3 . . . . 4 D4
Barnwell Cl CW2 . . . . 206 B8
Barnwood CH66 . . . . 68 F7
Baron Cl WA1 . . . . 17 D7
Baronet Mews WA4 . . . . . . 16 A1
Baronet Rd WA4 . . . . 16 A1
Baron Gn SK8 . . . . 34 D7
Baronia Pl CW5 . . . . 204 E6
Barons Cl WA7 . . . . 23 F1
Baron's Cl WA8 . . . . 22 C8
Barons Ct CW2 . . . . 118 C4
Barons Quay Rd CW9 . . . . . 78 F1
Barons Rd
Shavington CW2 . . . . 206 B4
Worleston CW5 . . . . 188 E3
Barony Bldgs 1 CW5 . . . . . 204 E6
Barony Ct CW5 . . . . 204 E7
Barony Employment Pk The
CW5 . . . . 204 F8

Barony Rd CW5 . . . . 204 E7
Barony Terr CW5 . . . . 204 E6
BARONY THE 204 F6
Barony Way CH4 . . . . 140 E4
Barracks La
Burwardsley CH3 . . . . 184 C5
Macclesfield SK10 . . . . 112 F8
Ravensmoor CW5 . . . . 203 E2
Barracks Sq 3 SK11 . . . . . 112 B6
Barrastitch La CW8 . . . . . . 101 E6
Barratt Rd ST7 . . . . 193 F3
Barrel Cl CH66 . . . . 43 D1
Barrel Well Hill CH2 . . . . . 118 F1
BARRETS GREEN 169 D3
Barrie Gdns ST7 . . . . 210 C8
Barrie Gr CW1 . . . . 190 E4
Barrington Dr CW10 . . . . . 151 C7
Barrow Ave WA2 . . . . 8 E2
Barrow CE Prim Sch
CH3 . . . . 120 D3
Barrowdale Rd WA3 . . . . 3 B8
Barrow Hall Com Prim Sch
WA5 . . . . 14 E7
Barrow Hall Farm CH3 . . . . 120 E5
Barrow Hall La CW5 . . . . . 146 E7
Barrow La
Altrincham WA15 . . . . 32 B7
Golborne WA2 . . . . 3 C2
Great Barrow CH3 . . . . 120 C5
Tarvin CH3 . . . . 121 C4
Barrow Mdw SK8 . . . . 34 E8
Barrowmore Est CH3 . . . . . 120 F7
Barrow's Brow WA16 . . . . . . 81 E1
Barrows Cl CW1 . . . . 190 A8
BARROWS GREEN 189 F8
BARROW'S GREEN 13 E4
Barrow's Green La WA8 . . . 13 E3
Barrow's Row WA8 . . . . 13 B4
Barrule Cl WA4 . . . . 26 D7
Barry Cl CH65 . . . . 95 C8
Barrymore Ave WA4 . . . . . . 16 F4
Barrymore Cres CW9 . . . . . 78 D8
Barrymore Ct WA4 . . . . 17 A1
Barrymore Rd
Runcorn WA7 . . . . 49 B7
Warrington WA4 . . . . 17 A1
Weaverham WA6 . . . . 77 E1
Barrymore Way CH63 . . . . . 43 B6
Barry St WA4 . . . . 16 C4
Barsbank Cl WA13 . . . . 18 C3
Barsbank La WA13 . . . . 18 C3
Barshaw Gdns WA4 . . . . . . 26 E4
Bars The CH1, CH3 . . . . . . 237 C2
Bartholomew Ct WA4 . . . . . 17 B2
Bartholomew Way CH4 . . . 141 C6
BARTHOMLEY 208 C5
Barthomley Cres CW2 . . . . 189 D4
Barthomley Rd
Barthomley CW2 . . . . 208 B7
Betley ST7 . . . . 208 F3
BARTINGTON 77 A5
Bartington Hall La CW8 . . . 77 A5
Bartington Hall Pk CW8 . . . 77 A5
Bartlegate WA7 . . . . 50 B5
BARTON 181 F1
Barton Ave WA4 . . . . 17 A2
Barton Cl Handforth SK9 . . 34 D2
Runcorn WA7 . . . . 50 D7
Barton Ct Warrington WA2 . . 16 B6
Winsford CW7 . . . . 126 F1
Barton Rd
Congleton CW12 . . . . 156 F3
Farndon CH3 . . . . 180 F1
Holt LL13 . . . . 196 E8
Barton's Pl CW9 . . . . 79 B1
Barton St SK11 . . . . 112 C7
Barton Stadium (Winsford
United FC) CW7 . . . . 126 F1
Barton Village Rd
Barton CH3, SY14 . . . . 181 D1
Barton SY14 . . . . 181 F1
Barwood Ave ST7 . . . . 194 A5
Barwoods Dr CH4 . . . . 140 F6
BASFORD 206 E5
Basford Rd CW2 . . . . 206 D8
Basford Way CW7 . . . . 126 B2
Baskervyle Cl CH60 . . . . . . 41 A6
Baskervyle Rd CH60 . . . . . . 41 A6
Baslow Dr Gatley SK8 . . . . . 34 C8
Hazel Grove SK7 . . . . 36 F8
Bassett Cl CW5 . . . . 205 D6
Batchelors Wing The
CW10 . . . . 127 D5
BATE HEATH 54 F3
Bateman Almshouses
ST8 . . . . 179 E3
Bateman Cl Crewe CW1 . . . 190 A4
Ellesmere Port CH65 . . . . . . 70 B6
Bateman Rd CW7 . . . . 80 B2
Batemans Ct CW2 . . . . 206 B8
Batemill Cl SK11 . . . . 86 F1
Batemill La WA16, SK11 . . 108 E5
Bates La WA6 . . . . 73 D4
Bate's Mill La CW6 . . . . . . 167 E5
Bath Cres SK8 . . . . 35 B6
Batherton Cl WA8 . . . . 23 B7
Batherton La CW5 . . . . 204 F2
Bath La CW3 . . . . 230 A3
Bath St Chester CH1 . . . . . 237 C2
Sandbach CW11 . . . . 175 C6
Warrington WA1 . . . . 16 A5
BATH VALE 157 A3
Bath Vale Cotts CW12 . . . . 157 A3
Bathwood Dr CH64 . . . . 66 E5
Batley Ave CW6 . . . . 185 F3
Batterbee Ct CW1 . . . . 191 D5
Battersby La WA2 . . . . 16 C6
Battersea Ct WA8 . . . . 12 F3

Battery La Warrington WA1 . 17 F7
Wilmslow SK9 . . . . 59 D6
Bawtry Ct WA2 . . . . 8 E1
Baxter Cl Alsager ST7 . . . . 193 A4
Runcorn WA7 . . . . 50 D7
Baxter Ho CW8 . . . . 78 E1
Baxter St WA5 . . . . 15 E5
Baycliffe WA13 . . . . 18 D2
Bayley Rd CW5 . . . . 205 D6
Baynard Dr WA8 . . . . 22 C5
Bayswater Cl WA7 . . . . 24 F4
Baytree Cl CH66 . . . . 69 F1
Bayvil Cl WA7 . . . . 50 E7
Bayweaver St CH66 . . . . 69 B4
Beach Gr CW8 . . . . 103 C6
Beachin Farm La CH3 . . . . 181 E6
Beachin La CH3 . . . . 182 A4
Beach Rd CW8 . . . . 103 B6
Beacon Cl 4 CH66 . . . . 41 A8
Beacon Hill View WA7 . . . . 48 D7
Beacon La WA7 . . . . 41 A7
Beaconsfield Cres WA8 . . . 13 A4
Beaconsfield Gr WA8 . . . . . 13 B4
Beaconsfield Rd
Runcorn WA7 . . . . 22 E1
Widnes WA8 . . . . 13 B4
Beaconsfield St CH3 . . . . . 237 C2
Beacons The CH60 . . . . 41 A7
Beacons The WA3 . . . . 9 D5
Beadnell Dr WA5 . . . . 14 F3
Beagle Point CW7 . . . . 126 A1
Beagle Wlk M22 . . . . 33 E8
Beames Ho CW1 . . . . 190 B4
Beam Heath Way CW5 . . . . 204 F7
Beamish Cl WA4 . . . . 26 D3
Beamont Com Prim Sch
WA2 . . . . 16 C7
Beamont St WA5 . . . . 23 A4
Beam St CW5 . . . . 204 E6
Bearda Hill SK11 . . . . 160 A4
Beard Cres SK22 . . . . 39 D8
Beardsmore Dr WA3 . . . . . . 3 E8
Bearhurst La SK11 . . . . 111 A5
Bearstone Rd TF9 . . . . 236 E3
Beasley Cl CH66 . . . . 69 D3
Beata Rd ST5 . . . . 210 F1
Beatrice St WA4 . . . . 16 D3
Beatty Ave WA2 . . . . 8 C1
Beatty Dr CW12 . . . . 157 A4
Beatty Rd CW5 . . . . 204 D4
Beaufort Chase SK9 . . . . . . 34 F1
Beaufort Cl
Alderley Edge SK9 . . . . 60 B2
Runcorn WA7 . . . . 49 B7
Warrington WA5 . . . . 15 A5
Weaverham CW8 . . . . 102 F5
Widnes WA8 . . . . 22 A8
Beaufort St WA5 . . . . 15 E4
Beaulieu Ave CW7 . . . . 126 F2
Beaumaris Cres SK7 . . . . . . 36 C8
Beaumaris Dr CH65 . . . . . . 70 D2
Beaumaris Way WA7 . . . . . 23 F2
Beaumont Cl
Biddulph ST8 . . . . 179 D3
Chester CH4 . . . . 140 E6
Wistaston CW2 . . . . 205 F8
Beaumont Ct
Handforth SK9 . . . . 34 C5
Warrington WA4 . . . . 16 C2
Beaumont Prim Sch WA2 . . 16 C7
Beauty Bank
Whitegate CW7 . . . . 125 C5
Winsford CW7 . . . . 149 B3
Beauty Bank Cotts CW7 . . . 149 A3
Beaverbrook Ave WA3 . . . . . 5 B4
Beaver Cl Chester CH4 . . . . 140 E5
Pickmere WA16 . . . . 79 F7
Beaver Ctr The CW9 . . . . . 103 F7
Bebbington Way CW5 . . . . 205 D5
BEBINGTON 43 A7
Bebington Rd CH66 . . . . . . 69 C4
Becconsall Cl CW1 . . . . . . 190 A8
Becconsall Dr CW1 . . . . . . 190 A8
Bechers WA8 . . . . 12 B3
Beckenham Cl WA8 . . . . . . 13 D4
Beckenham Gr 4 CW7 . . . . 126 A1
Beckett Ave CW7 . . . . 150 D8
Beckett Dr Lymm WA13 . . . 19 B8
Winwick WA2 . . . . 8 A5
Beckett's La CH3 . . . . 142 B8
Beckford Cl CW1 . . . . 189 F8
Beck Pl 2 CW9 . . . . 104 C5
Becks La SK10 . . . . 86 F2
Bedale Cl WA12 . . . . 2 D1
Bedells La SK9 . . . . 60 A6
Bedford Ave CH65 . . . . 70 A2
Bedford Avenue E CH65 . . . 70 B2
Bedford Ct CW2 . . . . 190 D1
Bedford Gdns CW2 . . . . . . 190 C1
Bedford Gn M44 . . . . 11 B6
Bedford Gr CW7 . . . . 193 B5
Bedford Pl CW2 . . . . 190 C1
Bedford Rd
Kidsgrove ST7 . . . . 195 A3
Macclesfield SK11 . . . . 112 B7
Bedford Rise CW7 . . . . 149 C6
Bedford St Crewe CW2 . . . 190 C1
Moss Bank WA8 . . . . 23 C8
Warrington WA4 . . . . 26 C8
Bedward Row CH1 . . . . 237 A2
Beeby Way CH4 . . . . 139 D3
Beech Ave Culcheth WA3 . . . 5 A3
Frodsham WA6 . . . . 74 C8
Golborne WA3 . . . . 3 F7
Haydock WA11 . . . . 1 E7
Mobberley WA16 . . . . 57 C7
Rode Heath ST7 . . . . 193 F8
Warrington WA5 . . . . 14 C3

Beech Ave continued
Warrington, Thelwall WA4 . . 17 D3
Woore CW3 . . . . 232 B2
Beech Bank SK10 . . . . 87 D1
Beech Cl Alderley Edge SK9 . 60 B3
Congleton CW12 . . . . 156 A4
Cuddington CW8 . . . . 101 F2
Holmes Chapel CW4 . . . . . 130 D4
Newton-le-Willows WA12 . . . 2 C2
Ollerton WA16 . . . . 82 F6
4 Partington M31 . . . . 11 F3
Beech Cotts
Alderley Edge SK9 . . . . 85 A8
Stretton WA4 . . . . 26 E1
Beech Cres SK12 . . . . 36 E4
Beechcroft Ave CW2 . . . . . 206 B7
Beechcroft Dr CH65 . . . . . . 70 B2
Beech Ct WA8 . . . . 12 B3
Beech Dr Crewe CW2 . . . . . 189 E7
Knutsford WA16 . . . . 57 C2
Talke ST7 . . . . 210 E8
Beeches SK9 . . . . 59 F6
Beeches La CH1 . . . . 117 A8
Beeches The
Chester CH2 . . . . 119 A6
Ellesmere Port CH66 . . . . . 69 D4
Helsby WA6 . . . . 73 C4
Mobberley WA16 . . . . 58 E1
Nantwich CW5 . . . . 204 F5
3 Northwich CW9 . . . . 103 C6
Whitchurch SY13 . . . . 225 F1
Widnes WA8 . . . . 13 D4
Beech Farm Dr SK10 . . . . . 87 D2
Beechfield Moulton CW9 . . 126 E8
Wilmslow SK9 . . . . 60 A6
Beechfield Ave SK9 . . . . 59 E5
Beechfield Cl CH60 . . . . 41 A7
Beechfield Dr CW10 . . . . . 128 B2
Beechfield Gdns CW8 . . . . 103 B6
Beechfield Rd
Alderley Edge SK9 . . . . 85 B8
Cheadle SK8 . . . . 35 B8
Ellesmere Port CH65 . . . . . 70 B5
Warrington WA1 . . . . 17 A2
Beechfields CW7 . . . . 150 B8
Beech Gdns 3 WA7 . . . . . . 49 C8
Beech Gr Chester CH2 . . . . 119 A3
Crewe CW1 . . . . 190 E5
Ellesmere Port CH66 . . . . . 95 A8
Lymm WA13 . . . . 18 B2
Macclesfield SK11 . . . . 112 C5
Sandbach CW11 . . . . 175 D6
Warrington WA1 . . . . 17 A7
Warrington, Latchford WA4 . 16 D3
Weaverham CW8 . . . . 102 D8
Wilmslow SK9 . . . . 60 A6
Winsford CW7 . . . . 149 D8
Beech Hall Dr SK10 . . . . . . 87 C2
Beech Hall Sch SK10 . . . . . 87 C2
Beech Heyes Cl CW8 . . . . . 102 E8
Beech Heyes Dr CW8 . . . . . 102 E8
Beech Hey La CH64 . . . . . . 43 C7
Beech Hollows LL12 . . . . . 162 C1
Beech La Barnton CW8 . . . . 78 A3
Cotebrook CW6 . . . . 147 B6
Macclesfield SK10 . . . . 87 D1
Norley WA6 . . . . 75 E1
Wilmslow SK9 . . . . 60 A6
Beechlands Ave CH3 . . . . . 119 A1
Beechmill Dr WA3 . . . . 4 E3
Beechmoore WA4 . . . . 25 B5
Beechmuir CH1 . . . . 117 E3
Beech Rd
Alderley Edge SK9 . . . . 60 B3
Aston WA7 . . . . 50 B4
Heswall CH60 . . . . 41 C8
High Lane SK6 . . . . 37 F7
Little Budworth CW6 . . . . . 124 D2
Paddockhill WA16 . . . . 59 B5
Runcorn WA7 . . . . 49 C8
Warrington WA4 . . . . 26 C8
Whaley Bridge SK23 . . . . . . 65 E7
Beech Rise Crowton CW8 . . 76 B2
Horwich End SK23 . . . . 65 C5
Beech St CW10 . . . . 128 C1
Beech Street W CW1 . . . . . 190 C4
Beech Tree Cl CW5 . . . . . . 205 D5
Beechtree Farm Cl WA16 . . 29 C7
Beechtree La WA13 . . . . 29 B7
Beech Tree Wlk WA6 . . . . . 73 C3
Beech View Rd WA6 . . . . . . 75 C1
Beechway Bollington SK10 . 88 A7
Chester CH2 . . . . 118 C6
High Lane SK6 . . . . 37 F7
Neston CH64 . . . . 66 D7
Wilmslow SK9 . . . . 59 F5
Beechways WA4 . . . . 26 A3
Beechways Dr CH64 . . . . . . 66 D7
BEECHWOOD 49 E5
Beechwood
Knutsford WA16 . . . . 56 F3
Knutsford, Cross Town
WA16 . . . . 57 C2
Beechwood Ave
Hartford CW8 . . . . 103 A6
Newton-le-Willows WA12 . . . 2 D4
Runcorn WA7 . . . . 49 E5
Warrington WA5 . . . . 14 F5
Warrington, Padgate WA1 . . 16 E7
Beechwood CW5 . . . . 205 A4
Beechwood Dr
Alsager ST7 . . . . 193 B4
Eaton (nr Congleton)
CW12 . . . . 156 F8
Ellesmere Port CH66 . . . . . 69 D1

Beechwood Dr *continued*
Higher Wincham CW9 . . . . . .79 F6
Wilmslow SK9 . . . . .60 E8
Beechwood Gr SK8. . . . . . 35 A8
Beechwood La WA3 . . . . . . .4 D4
Beechwood Mews SK10 . . 87 C2
Beechwood Prim Sch
Crewe CW1 . . . . 190 C5
Runcorn WA7 . . . . .49 E5
Beechwood Rd
Bebington CH62 . . . . 43 C8
Saltney CH4 . . . . 140 E5
Beecroft Cl WA5 . . . . .7 D1
Beehive La CW9. . . . . 126 F8
BEESTON 168 A2
BEESTON-BROOK 168 C5
Beeston Brow SK10 . . . . . .88 B8
Beeston Castle ★ CW6 . . . 167 F3
Beeston Ct Bollington SK10 . 63 C1
Holmes Chapel CW4 . . . . . 130 A3
Middlewich CW10 . . . . . . 151 D5
Warrington WA3 . . . . .9 D4
Beeston Ct WA7 . . . . 24 C4
Beeston Dr Alsager ST7 . . 193 C3
Knutsford WA16 . . . . 82 A8
Winsford CW7 . . . . 149 C7
Beeston Gn CH66 . . . . .69 E5
Beeston Hall Mews
Beeston Hall CW6 . . . . . . 168 B3
Tiverton CW6 . . . . 168 B4
BEESTON MOSS 168 B1
Beeston Mount SK10 . . . . 63 C1
Beeston Pathway CH4 . . 141 E7
Beeston Rd
Broughton CH4 . . . . 139 B3
Handforth SK9 . . . . 34 D5
Higher Kinnerton CH4 . . . . 161 A7
Beeston St CW8. . . . . 103 E7
Beeston Terr SK11 . . . . . . 111 E6
Beeston View CH4 . . . . . . 141 E7
Beggar Man's La WA16 . . 82 A7
Begonia Gdns WA9. . . . . . .6 A7
Beilby Rd WA11 . . . . .1 E7
Belfry Cl SK9 . . . . 60 D8
Belfry Dr SK10 . . . . 87 C4
Belfry Gdns WA4 . . . . .26 E3
BELGRAVE. 162 E6
Belgrave App CH3. . . . . . 163 C6
Belgrave Ave Alsager ST7. 193 D5
Congleton CW12 . . . . 156 D3
Eccleston CH4 . . . . 162 F7
Saltney CH4 . . . . 140 E6
Warrington WA1 . . . . .16 F8
Belgrave Cl
Dodleston CH4 . . . . 162 A6
Golborne WN7 . . . . .4 C8
Widnes WA8. . . . . 13 E3
Belgrave Dr CH65 . . . . . . .69 F5
Belgrave Gdn Mews
CH4 . . . . 162 E6
Belgrave Prim Sch CH4 . . 141 B5
Belgrave Rd Chester CH3. 142 B8
Crewe CW2 . . . . 190 B2
Irlam M44 . . . . 11 D5
Macclesfield SK11 . . . . . . 112 C4
Northwich CW9 . . . . 104 A4
Belgrave St CH1 . . . . 237 C3
Belgravia Ct Pulford CH4. 162 E5
Widnes WA8. . . . . 12 F3
Belgravia Gdns WA15. . . . 31 E8
Bellaport Rd TF9 . . . . 236 A4
Bellard Dr CH2. . . . . 119 A4
Bell Ave SK11 . . . . 112 F3
Bellcast Cl WA4. . . . . 26 C5
Bellemonte Rd WA6. . . . . 74 C6
Bellerophon Way WA11. . . .1 E6
Belleville Ave M22 . . . . . . 33 E8
Bellevue La CH3 . . . . 119 C4
Bellevue St CW8 . . . . 103 C8
Belle Vue Terr CW11 . . . . 175 B6
Bell Farm Ct SK10. . . . . . . 87 C3
Bellflower Cl WA8. . . . . . .12 E4
Bellhouse La
Higher Walton WA4 . . . . . . 25 D7
Warrington WA4 . . . . 17 C1
Bell House Rd WA8. . . . . . 13 C1
Bellingham Cl WA16. . . . . 57 C2
Bellingham Dr WA7 . . . . . 49 A8
Bell La Ellesmere Port CH65 . 70 C5
Smallwood CW11. . . . . . . 177 B7
Warrington WA4 . . . . 17 C1
Bell Meadow Bsns Pk
CH4. . . . . 162 E5
Bell Meadow Ct CW6 . . . 146 C2
Bell O The Hill Rd SY13 . . 225 C5
BELL O' TH' HILL. 225 D7
Bell o' th' Hill Rd SY13 . . 214 C1
Bellsfield Ct WA13 . . . . . .18 F2
Bell's Hollow ST5 . . . . . . 210 E3
Bell View WA8 . . . . 13 C4
Belmont Ave
Macclesfield SK10 . . . . 86 C1
Sandbach CW11. . . . . 175 A7
Warrington WA4 . . . . .16 F3
Belmont Cres WA5 . . . . . . 15 A6
Belmont Dr CH4. . . . . 140 C6
Belmont Rd Bramhall SK7. . 35 F5
Great Budworth CW9. . . . . 53 F1
Northwich CW9 . . . . 104 C7
Widnes WA8. . . . . 13 E2
Belton Cl WA3 . . . . .3 A7
Beltony Dr CW1 . . . . 173 A1
Belvedere 9 WA7. . . . . . . 23 A3
Belvedere Cl 2 WA6 . . . . 49 C1
Belvedere Dr CH1 . . . . . . 117 E4

Belvedere Rd WA12 . . . . . . .2 B5
Belvedere Terr ST7 . . . . . 193 F7
Belvoir Ave SK7. . . . . 36 E8
Belvoir Rd Warrington WA4 .26 B8
Widnes WA8. . . . . .13 B1
Bembridge Cl
Warrington WA5 . . . . 14 C7
Widnes WA8. . . . . .12 F4
Bembridge Ct CW10 . . . . 151 C8
Bembridge Dr CW10 . . . . 151 C8
Benbrook Gr SK9. . . . . .34 E2
Benbrook Way SK11 . . . . . 111 E1
Bendee Ave CH64 . . . . 67 A7
Bendee Rd CH64. . . . . 67 A7
Benjafield Ct CW1. . . . . . 189 F7
Benjamins Way ST7. . . . . 209 F2
Bennet Cl CW8. . . . . .82 A8
Bennet Rd CW9 . . . . 104 D6
Bennetsitch Rd SK11 . . . . 138 C3
Bennett Ave WA1 . . . . .16 F6
Bennett Cl CW1. . . . . 190 E4
Bennett Ct CW7 . . . . 149 D5
Bennetts La SK11 . . . . 158 E7
Bennett's La
Higher Kinnerton CH4 . . . . 161 A7
Widnes WA8. . . . . .13 E1
Bennett St WA1. . . . . .16 B5
Ben Nevis Dr CH66 . . . . . . 68 F6
Benson Rd WA3. . . . . .9 D3
Benson Wlk 3 SK9. . . . . . 34 D2
Bentham Ave WA2 . . . . . . .8 C3
Bentham Rd WA3 . . . . .5 A2
Bentinck St WA7 . . . . .22 F3
Bent La Astbury CW12 . . . 178 A8
Culcheth WA3. . . . . .5 A2
Lymm WA13 . . . . 19 C6
Norley CW8 . . . . 101 C8
Bentley Dr CW1 . . . . 191 A5
Bentley Gr CW7 . . . . 149 C6
Bentleyhurst La
Mere WA16 . . . . 56 A7
Winterbottom WA16 . . . . . .55 F6
Bentley's Farm La WA4 . . .52 E5
Benton Dr CH2. . . . . 118 C4
Bents Cotts CH2. . . . . .71 E2
Bentside Rd SK12. . . . . . . 38 D5
Benty Heath La CH64,
CH66. . . . . .43 B3
Beresford Ct 4 SK9 . . . . . 60 A1
Beresford St WA1. . . . . . . .16 E7
Berisford Ho CW12 . . . . . 156 E3
Berkeley Ave ST7 . . . . . . 193 D5
Warrington WA5 . . . . .15 F6
Berkeley Cl Golborne WN7. . .4 C7
Warrington WA5 . . . . .15 F6
Berkeley Cres CW2 . . . . . 206 A8
Berkeley Ct
Newton-le-Willows WA12 . . . .1 F4
Runcorn WA7 . . . . 24 D4
Berkeley Prim Sch The
CW2 . . . . 206 B7
Berkeley Rise CW7 . . . . . 149 A8
Berkley Ct SK23 . . . . 65 D6
Berkley Dr CH4 . . . . 141 D6
Berkshire Cl SK10 . . . . . . .86 E2
Berkshire Dr
Congleton CW12 . . . . 156 D4
Irlam M44 . . . . 11 C5
Warrington WA1 . . . . .17 E7
Bermondsey Gr WA8 . . . . 13 D4
Bernard Ave WA4 . . . . 26 D8
Bernisdale Rd WA16. . . . . .57 F4
Bernsdale Cl CH5 . . . . 116 A3
Bernsdale Ct/Llys Bernsdale
CH5 . . . . 116 A3
Berrett La SK10. . . . . .88 D4
Berristall Rise SK10 . . . . . 63 C1
Berristal Rd SK10 . . . . . . .88 E3
Berry Cl
Ellesmere Port CH66 . . . . . 69 C3
Wilmslow SK9 . . . . 60 A5
Berry Dr CH66 . . . . 69 C3
Berry Rd WA8. . . . . 12 D1
Berrystead CW8 . . . . 103 B4
Bertram St WA12. . . . . .2 A4
Berwick Ave CH62. . . . . . . 43 E4
Berwick Cl
Macclesfield SK10 . . . . . . .86 F2
Warrington WA1 . . . . .17 E6
Berwick Ct CW4. . . . . 130 B2
Berwick Gdns CH66 . . . . . .69 B6
Berwick Gr CH66 . . . . .69 B6
Berwick Rd CH66 . . . . 69 A6
Berwick Rd W CH66. . . . . .68 F6
Berwick Road W CH66 . . . 69 A6
Berwyn Cl CH66 . . . . 69 A6
Bessancourt CW4 . . . . . . 130 C3
Bessemer Rd M44. . . . . . . .11 F6
Beswick Dr CW1 . . . . 191 A3
Beswick Rundell CW12 . . 132 A4
Beswicks La
Norton in Hales TF9 . . . . . . 236 C2
Row-of-Trees SK9. . . . . . . 59 C3
Beswicks Rd CW8 . . . . . . .78 E1
Beswick St SK11 . . . . 112 B7
Betchton Cl CW11. . . . . . . 175 C7
Betchton Ct 6 CW12 . . . . 156 F3
BETCHTON HEATH. 175 E5
Betchton Rd CW11 . . . . . . 175 E3
Bethany Cl WA11. . . . . .1 B7
Betjeman Cl WA4 . . . . .16 F1
Betjeman Way CW7 . . . . . 190 F5
BETLEY. 221 F8
Betley Cl CW9. . . . . 104 A5
Betley St CW1 . . . . 190 C4
Betsyfield Dr WA3. . . . . . . .9 A7
Bettisfield Ave CH62. . . . . 43 D6

Betty's La Beeston CW6. . . 168 D1
Woore CW3 . . . . 232 C1
Bevan Ave ST7 . . . . 210 E6
Bevan Cl WA5. . . . . 15 D6
Bevan Ct WA4. . . . . 16 B3
Bevan View WA5. . . . . . . .15 F7
Beverley Ave WA4 . . . . . . 26 D8
Beverley Dr CH60 . . . . . . .41 B6
Beverley Rd WA5. . . . . 15 C6
Beverley Way
Ellesmere Port CH66 . . . . . .69 B7
Macclesfield SK10 . . . . . . 87 C4
Bevin Ave WA3. . . . . .5 B4
Bevyl Rd CH64 . . . . .41 B2
Bewick Wlk WA16. . . . . . . .57 B3
Bewley Ct CH3 . . . . 142 A7
BEWSEY. 15 F8
Bewsey Bsns Ctr WA5. . . . .15 F6
Bewsey Farm Cl WA5 . . . . 15 B6
Bewsey Ind Est WA5 . . . . 16 A7
Bewsey Lodge Prim Sch
WA5 . . . . .15 F7
Bewsey New Hill Gdns
WA5. . . . . 15 D8
Bewsey Park Cl WA5. . . . . .15 F7
Bewsey Rd WA2, WA5 . . . . 16 A6
Bexhill Ave WA2 . . . . .8 B4
Bexington Dr CW1 . . . . . . 190 B8
Bexton Ave CW7 . . . . 126 A2
Bexton La WA16. . . . . 82 A8
Bexton Prim Sch
Knutsford WA16. . . . . .81 F7
Knutsford WA16. . . . . 82 A7
Bexton Rd WA16 . . . . .56 F1
Bibby Ave WA1. . . . . .16 E6
Bibby's La SK10. . . . . 88 A1
Bibby St ST7 . . . . 193 E7
BICKERTON. 199 E6
Bickerton Ave WA6. . . . . . 74 D7
Bickerton Cl
3 Coppenhall Moss
CW1 . . . . 173 A1
Warrington WA3 . . . . .9 D4
Bickerton Holy Trinity CE
Prim Sch SY14 . . . . 200 A7
Bickerton Rd SY14 . . . . . 201 B2
Bickerton Way 1 CW9 . . 103 E4
Bickley Cl Hough CW2 . . . 206 E2
Northwich CW9 . . . . 103 E5
Runcorn WA7 . . . . 23 C1
Warrington WA2 . . . . .8 F3
Bickley La
Bickleywood SY14 . . . . . . 214 B4
Norbury Common SY13 . . . 214 E5
BICKLEY MOSS. 215 B7
Bickley Town Cl SY14 . . . 214 E6
Bickley Town La SY14 . . . 214 E6
BICKLEYWOOD. 214 C4
Bicknell Cl WA5. . . . . .15 B8
Bida La CW12. . . . . 179 B8
Biddlestone Cross WA8. . . .12 E3
BIDDULPH. 179 B2
Biddulph Common Rd
ST8. . . . . 179 F7
Biddulph Grange ST8. . . . 179 E3
Biddulph Grange Ctry Pk ★
ST8 . . . . 179 F3
Biddulph Grange Gdn ★
ST8 . . . . 179 E3
Biddulph Park Rd ST8 . . . 179 F5
Biddulph Rd
Congleton CW12 . . . . 179 B8
Harriseahead ST7 . . . . . . 195 F6
Biddulph St CW12. . . . . . . 179 C7
Biddulph Valley L Ctr
ST8 . . . . 179 D1
Biddulph Valley Way Nature
Reserve ★ CW12. . . . . . . 179 D7
Bideford Rd WA5. . . . . . . .14 E4
Bidston Cl CH2. . . . . 118 D5
Bidston Dr SK9. . . . . .34 E2
Bidston Gn CH66. . . . . 69 D4
Bidvale Way CW1. . . . . . . 190 D7
Big Field Lc CW6. . . . . 146 B7
Biggin Ct WA2 . . . . .8 E1
Biggleswade Dr WA7. . . . .24 E3
Biggs Way CW12 . . . . 156 E5
BIGNALL END. 209 F3
Bignall End Rd
Audley ST7. . . . . 210 A3
Newcastle-under-Lyme
ST7. . . . . 210 A4
Bignall Hill ST7 . . . . 210 B2
Big Stone Gdns CW4 . . . . 129 F7
Billington Ave WA12. . . . . . .2 C5
Billington Cl Barnton CW8 . .77 F4
Crewe CW2 . . . . 190 A4
Warrington WA5 . . . . .14 E8
Billington Pl 6 CW7 . . . . 125 F2
Billington Rd WA8 . . . . . . .12 B3
Bilton Cl WA8. . . . . .13 E2
Bilton Way CW2 . . . . 189 E5
Bings Rd SK23 . . . . .65 F8
Bingswood Ave SK23. . . . . .65 E8
Bingswood Rd SK23 . . . . . .65 E8
Bingswood Trad Est SK23 . .65 E8
Binney Rd CW9 . . . . 104 B8
Binyon Way CW1 . . . . 191 A4
Birchall Ave WA3. . . . . .4 E4
BIRCHALL MOSS. 219 E1
Birchall Moss La CW5 . . . 219 E1
Birchall St WA3. . . . . .9 A7
Birchall Wlk CW2. . . . . . . 206 D8
Birch Ave Alsager ST7 . . . 193 E2
Crewe CW1 . . . . 190 F5
Irlam M44 . . . . 11 D5
Macclesfield SK10 . . . . . . .87 B1
Warrington WA4 . . . . .8 A4

Birch Ave *continued*
Wilmslow SK9 . . . . .59 F6
Winsford CW7 . . . . 127 A1
Birch Brook Rd WA13. . . . 19 C5
Birch Cl Crewe CW1. . . . . . 190 F5
Holmes Chapel CW4. . . . . 130 D3
Birch Cres WA12 . . . . .1 F4
Birch Ct CW12 . . . . 155 F3
Birchdale Cres WA4 . . . . . 26 C8
Birchdale St WA4 . . . . 26 C8
Birchdale Rd
Warrington WA4 . . . . 26 C8
Warrington, Paddington
WA1 . . . . 17 A7
Birchencliff Cotts SK10 . . . 63 D6
Birchen Rd L26 . . . . 21 A7
Birchenwood Rd ST6,
ST7. . . . . 195 E1
Birchenwood Way ST7 . . . 195 B1
Birches Cl CH60. . . . . .41 A8
Birches Croft Dr SK10 . . . .86 F1
Birches Ho 2 CH60 . . . . . 41 A8
Birches La CW9 . . . . 105 B7
Birches The
Broughton CH4. . . . . 139 B3
Crewe CW2 . . . . 206 C8
Neston CH64 . . . . .41 F7
Birches Way 7 ST7 . . . . . 195 B2
Birchfield Ave
Rode Heath ST7 . . . . 193 F7
Widnes WA8. . . . . 13 A5
Birchfield Rd Lymm WA13 . .19 B4
Warrington WA5 . . . . .15 B5
Widnes, Appleton WA8. . . . 13 A1
Birch Fold CW4 . . . . 107 B1
Birchgate Cl SK10 . . . . . . .86 E1
Birch Gdns CW11. . . . . . . 175 C5
Birch Gr
Ellesmere Port CH66 . . . . . 70 A1
Higher Wincham CW9 . . . . .79 F5
Knutsford WA16. . . . . 57 D2
Lostock Green CW9 . . . . . 105 B7
Warrington, Bruche WA1. . . .16 F7
Warrington, Latchford WA4 . 16 D3
Birchhall Cl CW5. . . . . 204 F4
Birch Heath La CH3 . . . . . 142 F8
Birch Heath Rd CW6. . . . . 168 C8
Birch Hill WA6 . . . . 99 C8
Birch Ho CH2 . . . . 118 C5
Birchinall Cl SK11 . . . . . . 112 A7
Birchin Cl CW5. . . . . 205 A6
Birchin La CW5 . . . . 205 A6
Birch La Hough CW2. . . . . 206 F2
Winsford CW10 . . . . 127 F2
Birchmuir CH1. . . . . 117 E3
Birchmuir Cl CW1. . . . . . . 190 B6
Birch Rd Audley ST7. . . . . 209 F1
Chester CH4. . . . . 140 F5
Congleton CW12 . . . . 155 F3
Haydock WA11. . . . . .1 C5
Hollinfare WA3. . . . . .11 B2
Partington M31 . . . . 11 D3
Poynton SK12. . . . . .36 F2
Runcorn WA7 . . . . 49 C8
Widnes WA8. . . . . .13 B3
Birch Rise CH2. . . . . 118 D6
Birch Tree Ave SK7. . . . . . 37 A8
Birch Tree Ct CH2 . . . . . . 237 C4
Birch Tree La
Antrobus WA4 . . . . 53 A6
Goostrey CW4 . . . . 107 C1
The Bank ST7 . . . . 195 B8
Birch Tree Rd 6 WA3 . . . . .3 F8
Birch Valley Rd ST7. . . . . 195 C1
Birchway Bollington SK10 . . 88 A8
Bramhall SK7. . . . . 35 D7
Heswall CH60 . . . . 41 C5
High Lane SK6. . . . . .37 F7
Birch Way SK10. . . . . .86 E6
Birchways WA4 . . . . 26 E5
BIRCHWOOD. 9 E5
Birchwood Bvd WA3 . . . . . .9 D2
Birchwood CE Prim Sch
WA3 . . . . .9 F3
Birchwood Cl
Ellesmere Port CH66 . . . . . 69 D1
Elton CH2. . . . . 72 C3
Birchwood Com High Sch
WA3 . . . . .9 D3
Birchwood Dr
Nantwich CW5 . . . . 204 F6
Swan Green WA16 . . . . . . 106 D7
Wilmslow SK9 . . . . 60 D8
BIRCHWOOD FOREST
PARK. 10 A5
Birchwood La Moore WA4 . 25 B8
Runcorn WA5. . . . . 24 D6
Birchwood L & Tennis Ctr
WA3 . . . . .9 D3
Birchwood Office Pk WA2. . .9 B3
Birchwood One Bsns Pk
WA3 . . . . .9 E2
Birchwood Park Ave WA3. . .9 D5
Birchwood Sh Ctr WA3 . . . .9 D2
Birchwood Sta WA3 . . . . . .9 A4
Birchwood Way WA2, WA3 . .9 D3
Birdcage Wlk CW8 . . . . . . 103 E8
Birds La Tarporley CW6 . . 146 C1
Tattenhall CH3 . . . . 166 E1
Bird's La CW6. . . . . 186 B8
Birdwell Dr WA5 . . . . 15 A4
Birkdale Ave CH63 . . . . . . 43 C6
Birkdale Cl Bramhall SK7. . . 36 A7
Macclesfield SK10 . . . . 87 C4
Birkdale Ct 3 CW9. . . . . . 104 B8

Birkdale Dr ST7 . . . . 195 C3
Birkdale Gdns CW7. . . . . . 126 A3
Birkdale Rd
Warrington WA5 . . . . .14 F4
Widnes WA8. . . . . .13 B5
Birkenhead Rd CH64 . . . . .42 E1
Birkenhead St CW9 . . . . . 104 C8
Birket Dr WA8 . . . . 13 A6
Birkin Cl WA16. . . . . .57 D4
Birkinheath La WA14. . . . . .31 B4
Birley St WA12. . . . . .2 D4
Birrell Way SK9 . . . . 60 C6
Birstall Ct WA7 . . . . 49 D7
Birtles Cl CW11 . . . . 175 C7
Birtles Hall SK10 . . . . .85 D2
Birtles La SK10. . . . . .85 E2
Birtles La S SK11 . . . . 110 C7
Birtles Rd
Macclesfield SK10 . . . . . . .86 D1
Warrington WA2 . . . . .8 D1
Birtles Way 4 SK9 . . . . . . 34 D5
Birtley Ct WA8 . . . . .12 B1
Birtwistle Rd CW9 . . . . . . 104 D6
Bisham Pk WA7 . . . . 24 D2
Bishopdale Cl
Warrington WA5 . . . . .14 F7
1 Warrington WA5 . . . . . 15 A7
Bishopgates Dr CW9 . . . . 103 E4
Bishop Heber High Sch
SY14 . . . . 213 C5
Bishop Rd SK10 . . . . .88 A7
Bishop Reeves Rd WA11 . . .1 E7
Bishops' Blue Coat CE High
Sch The CH3 . . . . 142 A8
Bishop's Cl ST7 . . . . 210 D8
Bishops Ct
Broughton CH4. . . . . 139 C4
Warrington WA2 . . . . .8 A4
Bishopsfield Ct CH2 . . . . . 118 F3
Bishops Gate CH2. . . . . . . 119 A3
Bishops Gdns CH65. . . . . . 70 A5
Bishop St CH2 . . . . 118 F3
Bishops Way WA8. . . . . . . 13 D3
Bishops Wood CW5 . . . . . 204 F2
Bishopton Dr SK11 . . . . . . 111 F8
Bishop Wilson CE Prim Sch
CH64. . . . . 67 D1
Bispham Rd WA5. . . . . . . .15 B4
Bitterling St CH65 . . . . . . .70 B8
Bittern Cl Farndon CH3 . . 180 E2
Poynton SK12. . . . . 36 A4
Runcorn WA7 . . . . 50 D8
Warrington WA3 . . . . .8 D3
Bittern Gr SK10 . . . . 87 A1
Bitteswell Ct WA7. . . . . . . 24 E2
Blackacres Cl CW11 . . . . . 174 F6
Blackberry Cl 7 CW5. . . . 204 C4
Blackbird Cl WA6 . . . . 122 C4
Blackbird Way ST7 . . . . . 195 F1
Blackboards La CH66. . . . . 69 A7
BLACKBROOK Haydock 1 A7
Warrington 8 E2
Blackbrook Ave WA2 . . . . . .8 F2
Blackbrook Cl WA8. . . . . . 12 C3
Blackburn Cl WA3. . . . . . . .3 E8
Blackburne Ave WA8 . . . . .22 B5
Blackburne Cl WA2. . . . . . .9 C2
Blackburne Dr WA12 . . . . . .2 A4
Blackcap Rd WA4 . . . . 27 A4
Blackcap Wlk WA3 . . . . . . .9 E3
Black Cat Ind Est WA8 . . . 23 A6
Blackcroft Ave CW8 . . . . . 78 A2
Black Croft Cl 5 CW2 . . . 206 D7
Blackden Firs CW4 . . . . . . 108 B2
Blackden La
Goostrey CW4 . . . . 108 A3
Siddington SK11. . . . . 132 F8
Black Denton's Pl WA8 . . . 13 C1
Blackden Wlk SK9. . . . . . . 34 D1
Black Diamond Pk CH1. . . 237 B6
Black Diamond St CH1. . . 237 B4
Black Dog La CH3. . . . . . . 143 A4
Blackdown Cl CH66 . . . . . 69 A5
Blackeys La CH64. . . . . . . .66 E8
Black Firs La CW12. . . . . . 155 E4
Black Firs Prim Sch
CW12 . . . . 155 F4
Black Friars CH1 . . . . 237 A2
Blackheath La WA7. . . . . . 24 F5
Blackhill La WA6 . . . . .81 F8
Black Horse La WA8. . . . . 13 A5
Blackhurst Brow SK10. . . . .61 B2
Blackhurst Farm Rd
CW5. . . . . 202 E3
Blackhurst St WA1 . . . . . .16 B5
Black La SK10. . . . . .87 E1
Blackledge Cl WA2. . . . . . .9 A3
Blackley Cl
Macclesfield SK10 . . . . . . .87 B4
Warrington WA3 . . . . 16 D3
Black Lion La CH66. . . . . . 69 C6
Black Moss Rd WA14 . . . . .20 F7
BLACK PARK. 226 F2
Black Park Rd SY13 . . . . . 226 D2
Black Rd SK11 . . . . 112 F7
Blackshaw Cl CW12 . . . . . 157 B1
Blackshaw Dr WA5. . . . . . .7 B1
Blackshaw La SK9. . . . . . .59 F1
Blackshaw St 6 SK11 . . . 112 C7
Blacksmith Cl CH66 . . . . . 69 B5
Blackstairs Rd
Overpool CH66. . . . . .69 F7
Overpool CH66. . . . . .69 F7
Blackthorn Cl
Broughton CH4. . . . . 139 B3
Huntington CH3 . . . . 142 A5
Wistaston CW2 . . . . 206 B8

Blackthorne Ave CH66.... 95 A8
Blackthorne Cl **1** CW5. 204 C3
Blackthorn Pl ST5.... 210 E1
Blackthorn Wlk **3** M31..11 E2
BLACON.............. 117 F3
Blacon Ave CH1....... 118 A5
Blacon Cty High Sch
CH1................. 117 D4
Blacon Hall Rd CH1.... 117 F5
Blacon Point Rd CH1... 117 F5
Bladon Cres ST7....... 193 C5
Blagg Ave CW5....... 204 C4
Blair Cl SK7......... 36 C8
Blair Dr WA8........ 12 C3
Blairgowrie Dr SK10.... 87 B4
Blaizefield Cl CW3..... 232 C2
Blakeacre Rd L26...... 21 A6
Blake Cl Blacon CH1.... 117 F6
Crewe CW2........ 189 F1
Blakeden La CW7...... 148 F8
Blakehill Dr WA5....... 15 B6
Blake La CW8....... 102 A2
Blakeley Brow CH63.... 43 A6
Blakeley Ct CH63...... 43 A7
Blakeley Dell CH63.... 43 B6
Blakeley Dene CH63... 43 B7
Blakeley La
Mobberley WA16....... 58 E7
Mobberley WA16....... 58 F8
Blakeley Rd CH63..... 43 A6
Blakelow Bank SK11.... 112 F6
Blakelow Cl CW10..... 151 B8
Blakelow Cres CW5.... 205 F3
Blakelow Dr CW5..... 205 D4
Blakelow Gdns SK10.... 112 F6
Blakelow Rd SK11..... 112 F6
Blakemere SY13...... 226 B1
Blakemere Ct CH65.... 70 C7
Blakemere Dr CW9.... 103 E5
Blakemere La WA6.... 100 C4
Blakemere Sh & Craft Ctr
CW8................ 101 F1
Blakemere Way CW11.. 174 F8
BLAKENHALL....... 221 A4
Blake St CW12....... 156 C3
Blandford Dr
5 Macclesfield SK11... 111 F8
Northwich CW9....... 103 E3
Blandford Rd WA5..... 15 B5
Blankney The CW5.... 204 E4
Blantern Rd CW5...... 161 A7
Blantyre St WA7....... 22 F3
Blaze Farm ★ SK11.... 137 D4
Blaze Hill SK10...... 88 E8
Bleadale Cl SK9....... 34 D1
Bleasdale Rd Crewe CW1. 173 B1
Newton-le-Willows WA12.. 2 C4
Bleeding Wolf La ST7... 194 E5
Blencowe Cl CH2....... 95 B4
Blenheim Cl
Macclesfield SK10...... 87 A1
Northwich CW9....... 103 F4
Poynton SK12........ 36 F4
Warrington WA2....... 8 F2
Wilmslow SK9........ 60 D7
Wistaston CW2....... 205 E8
Blenheim Ct Alsager ST7. 193 D5
2 Huntington CH3..... 142 C5
Blenheim Gdns **5** CW7. 149 C7
Blenheim Ho CH1..... 118 B3
Blenheim Pk CW11.... 175 A4
Bletchley Pk Way SK9... 60 E7
Bloomfield Cl SK8..... 34 E7
Bloomfield St CH66.... 69 A5
Bloomsbury Way WA8... 12 D3
Blossom Gr CW5...... 204 C3
Blossom Hts CW8..... 103 D7
Blossom Rd M31...... 11 E2
Blossoms La SK7....... 35 B2
Blossom Way/Ffordd Y
Blodau CH4......... 140 D5
Blount Cl CW1....... 190 B4
Blubell La CH64...... 42 C1
Bluebell Ave WA11..... 1 E7
Bluebell Cl
Huntington CH3..... 142 B6
Macclesfield SK10..... 87 D3
Winnington CW8....... 78 E1
Bluebell Ct WA7...... 49 F4
Bluebell La SK10...... 87 C3
Bluebell Mews **4** SK10.. 87 D3
Bluebell Rd
Holmes Chapel CW4.... 130 C1
Warrington WA5....... 15 E4
Bluebell Way Alsager ST7. 193 B3
Handforth SK9........ 34 C1
Blue Bridge La WA6.... 73 C5
Blue Cedar Way CW12.. 155 E5
Bluecoat St WA2...... 16 B7
Blue Hatch WA6....... 74 C8
Blue Lake Gdns WA5.... 15 B6
Blue Planet Aquarium ★
CH65................ 70 D1
Blue Ridge Cl WA5..... 14 E7
Blundell La WA8...... 22 D8
Blunstone Cl CW2..... 190 A2
Blyth Cl Macclesfield SK10.. 86 F1
Runcorn WA7........ 50 D5
Blythe Ave Bramhall SK7.. 35 C6
Congleton CW12...... 156 A2
Widnes WA8.......... 13 B5
Blythe Pl CW7....... 127 B2
Blythings The CW6.... 146 C3
Blyth Rd CH3........ 43 C7
Boardmans Pl CW9..... 104 A5
Boars Leigh Pk SK11... 135 D1
Boathorse Rd ST7...... 210 F8

Boathouse La CH64.... 41 C3
Boat Stage WA13...... 18 E3
Boat Wlk WA4....... 16 A1
Bob's La M44....... 11 D4
Boddington Dr WA4.... 27 A7
Boden Dr CW5....... 205 D4
Boden St SK11....... 112 D8
Bodiam Ct CH65...... 70 C2
Bodkin Gn WA5....... 7 B2
Bodmin Ave SK10..... 86 E1
Bodmin Cl WA7...... 50 B6
Bodmin Dr SK7....... 35 E7
Bodmin Ct CW1...... 190 A8

BOLD................ 6 B6
Bold Bsns Ctr WA9.... 6 B7
Bold Cross WA8...... 13 E7
Bolden Hill Rd CW5... 204 C7
Bold Ind Est WA8..... 13 C5
Bold Ind Park WA9.... 6 B6
Bold La WA5, WA9..... 6 C7
Bodiam Ct CH1...... 237 B3
Bold Sq CH1....... 237 C3
Bold St Haslington CW1. 191 C4
Runcorn WA7........ 23 B3
Sandbach CW11..... 175 B6
Warrington WA1..... 16 A5
Widnes WA8.......... 23 A7
Bolesworth Hill Rd CH3.. 183 C4
Bolesworth Rd
Chester CH2....... 118 F6
Tattenhall CH3....... 183 C7
Boleyn Cl CH1....... 117 E6
Boleyn Ct WA7....... 24 C3
Bolingbroke La **7** WA8.. 13 C4
Bolland's Ct CH1...... 237 A2
Bollands Row **14** CW5.. 204 E5
Bolleyn Wood Ct SK9... 34 B1
Bollin Ave
Altrincham WA14..... 31 B8
Winsford CW7....... 127 B2
Bollinbarn SK10...... 87 B2
Bollinbarn Dr SK10.... 87 A2
Bollinbrook CE Prim Sch
SK10................ 87 B2
Bollinbrook Rd SK10... 87 B2
Bollin Cl Alsager ST7... 192 F3
Culcheth WA3........ 5 A2
Lymm WA13....... 19 A4
Sandbach CW11...... 174 E7
Winsford CW7....... 127 B2
Bollin Ct Lunts Heath WA8.. 13 B6
Wilmslow SK9....... 60 C6
Bollin Dr Congleton CW12. 156 F1
Lymm WA13........ 19 A4
Prestbury SK10....... 87 A7
BOLLINGTON........ 88 B7
Bollington Ave CW9.... 104 A5
BOLLINGTON CROSS.. 87 F7
Bollington Cross CE Prim
Sch SK10.......... 87 E7
Bollington Ho CW12.... 156 F1
Bollington La SK10..... 84 E2
Bollington Old Rd SK10.. 87 D6
Bollington Rd SK10.... 87 E6
Bollinhead La SK11.... 113 D2
Bollin Hill Prestbury SK10.. 87 A5
Wilmslow SK9........ 60 B8
Bollin Mews SK10..... 86 F1
Bollinway WA15....... 32 A8
Bollin Way SK10...... 87 A6
Bollin Wlk SK9....... 60 C7
Bollinwood Chase SK9.. 60 D7
Bolshaw Cl WA1...... 190 A7
Bolshaw Farm La SK8... 34 C6
Bolshaw Prim Sch SK8.. 34 B7
Bolshaw Rd SK8....... 34 C6
Bolton Ave Cheadle SK8.. 35 B6
Warrington WA4...... 16 F4
Bolton Cl Golborne WA3... 4 B8
Poynton SK12........ 36 D4
Bolyn Cl SK9........ 60 E7
Bomish La CW4, SK11... 108 C3
Bond Cl WA5....... 15 D4
Bond St Macclesfield SK11. 112 C7
Winnington CW8..... 78 D1
Bonis Hall La SK10.... 61 F4
BOON HILL........ 210 A2
Boon Hill Rd ST7..... 209 F1
Booth Ave
Ashton Hayes CH3.... 121 E7
Little Budworth CW6... 147 F7
Sandbach CW11..... 175 C6
BOOTH BANK....... 30 B7
Boothbank La WA14.... 30 A6
Booth Bed La WA16, CW4.. 107 B4
Boothby St **12** SK10... 112 C8
Boothfields WA16..... 57 C2
BOOTH GREEN...... 62 F7
Booth La
Middlewich CW10..... 151 E6
Middlewich CW10, Stud Green CW10,
CW11............... 152 B3
Booth Rd Handforth SK9. 34 A1
Hartford CW8........ 103 A4
Booths Hill Cl WA13... 18 C2
Booths Hill Ho **3** WA13. 18 D3
Booth's Hill Rd WA13... 18 D3
Booths La WA4...... 52 E6
Boothsmere Cl **11** CW4.. 174 F8
Booth St Audley ST7.... 209 D1
Congleton CW12..... 156 C2
Warrington WA5..... 15 E4

BOOTS GREEN....... 107 B5
Boots Green La WA16... 107 C5
Borderbrook SY14..... 222 F5
Borderbrook Sch
Higher Wych SY14.... 224 D3
Tallarn Green/Tallwrn Green
SY14.............. 222 F5
Border Rd CH60..... 41 B8
Borders 2 Ind Pk CH4... 140 C7
Borders Ind Pk The/Parc
Ddiwydiannol Y Ffin
CH4................ 140 C7
Border Way CH3..... 119 C1
Boreay Cl **6** CW10.... 128 D2
Borough Rd CW12..... 156 F3
Borras Rd LL13....... 196 A8
Borron Ct WA12...... 2 A6
Borron Rd WA12..... 2 B5
Borron Road Ind Est WA12.. 2 C4
Borrowdale Ave WA2... 8 C3
Borrowdale Cl
Crewe CW2....... 189 E3
Frodsham WA6....... 74 D8
Borrowdale Rd WA8.... 22 C8
Bosden Cl SK9....... 34 D5
BOSLEY............ 158 D8
Bosley Brook CW12.... 179 D5
Bosley Cl Handforth SK9.. 34 D2
Middlewich CW10..... 151 C6
Bosley Dr SK12....... 37 A3
Bosley View CW12.... 157 B1
Bostock Ave CH3..... 166 C2
Bostock Gn
Bostock Green CW9.... 127 C7
Ellesmere Port CH65... 69 F6
BOSTOCK GREEN.... 127 C7
BOSTOCK HALL...... 127 D5
Bostock Rd
Macclesfield SK11.... 111 E7
Winsford CW7....... 127 A4
Bostock St WA5....... 15 E6
Boston Ave WA7...... 23 D1
Boston Bvd WA5...... 15 A7
Boston Cl Bramhall SK7.. 35 D7
Culcheth WA3........ 4 F4
Boswell Ave WA4..... 16 B2
Botany Bsns Pk SK23... 65 E6
Botany Mews SK23.... 65 E6
Boteler Ave WA5...... 15 F7
Botterley Ct CW6..... 169 F1
Bottoms La CH4....... 141 F8
Boughey Rd ST7...... 209 F2
BOUGHTON......... 119 A2
Boughton CH2, CH3.... 118 F2
Boughton Hall Ave CH3.. 119 A2
Boughton Hall Dr CH3.. 119 B1
BOUGHTON HEATH... 142 A8
Boughton Heath Acad
CH3................ 142 B8
Boughton Lodge **2** CH3. 119 A1
Boulevard The
Broughton CH4....... 139 C3
Ellesmere Port CH65... 69 F4
Boulting Ave WA5..... 7 F1
Boulton Cl CW11..... 175 C3
Boundary Ct CH3..... 119 B1
Boundary La Chester CH4.. 140 E5
Congleton CW12..... 179 B8
Heswall CH60...... 41 A8
Over Peover WA16, SK11.. 108 D7
Siddington SK11..... 132 E8
Threapwood SY14.... 222 E8
Boundary Lane N CW8... 101 F2
Boundary Lane S CW8... 101 F2
Boundary Pk CH64.... 66 D7
Boundary St
Northwich CW9..... 79 E2
Warrington WA1..... 16 E7
Boundary Stone La **1**
WA8................ 13 E4
Boundary Terr SK9.... 33 F6
Bourchier Way WA4.... 27 A8
Bourne Ave WA3..... 3 D8
Bourne Cl WA8...... 102 E7
Bournemouth Cl WA7... 50 D6
Bourne Rd ST7....... 194 F2
Bourne St Mow Cop ST7.. 195 C7
Wilmslow SK9....... 59 F6
Bouverie St CH1..... 237 A4
Boverton Rd WA5..... 7 E1
Bowden Cl
Congleton CW12..... 156 A3
Culcheth WA3........ 4 F4
Bowden Cres SK22.... 39 D8
Bowden Downs SK11... 113 D7
Bowden Dr CW9..... 104 C8
Bowden House La SK9... 61 A8
Bowden View La WA16.. 29 F2
Bowdon Cl WA1...... 16 F8
Bowen Cl Bramhall SK7.. 35 F5
Widnes WA8.......... 12 C1
Bowen Cooke Ave CW1.. 190 A5
Bower Cres WA4..... 26 D2
Bowerfield Ave SK7.... 36 D8
Bowerfield Cres SK7.... 36 E8
Bower Rd CH60...... 41 C8
Bowers Bsns Pk WA8... 23 B7
Bowers Row **4** CW5... 204 E5
Bower St WA8....... 13 C1
Bowery Ave SK8..... 34 F6
Bowery The CH1..... 116 D4
Bowe's Gate Rd CW6... 169 A1
Bowfell Cl CH62..... 43 D3
Bowfield La SK6..... 37 E8
Bow Green Rd WA14... 20 F1
Bowkers Croft CW11... 191 F8
Bow La WA14....... 31 B8

BOLD............... 6 B6

Bowland Cl Runcorn WA7..49 E5
Warrington WA3...... 10 B5
Bowland Croft CW1.... 173 B1
Bowles Cl CW11...... 175 A6
Bowline Cl CW11..... 175 D3
Bowling Alley St ST7... 194 C1
Bowling Green Ct
Chester CH1....... 237 B3
9 Nantwich CW5..... 204 E5
Winnington CW8...... 78 E1
Bowman Ave WA4..... 17 A5
Bowmans The SK10.... 87 B1
Bowmere Cl Biddulph ST8. 179 C1
Tarporley CW6....... 146 D1
Bowmere Dr CW7..... 149 C8
Bowmere Rd CW6..... 146 D1
Bowness Ave
Bebington CH63...... 43 C5
Irlam M44......... 11 D4
Warrington WA2...... 8 D2
Winsford CW7....... 126 D2
Bowness Cl CW4..... 130 A3
Bowness Ct CW4..... 156 A1
Bowness Rd CW2..... 189 E3
Bowood Ct WA2...... 8 A4
Bowring Dr CH64..... 41 B1
Bowstonegate Rd
Higher Moor SK12.... 64 D8
Lane Ends SK12...... 38 E1
Bowyer Ave **6** CW5.... 204 E6
Boxgrove Cl WA8..... 13 B3
Box La CW12........ 155 F3
Boxmoor Cl CH4...... 141 A5
Box Tree Mews SK11... 112 A8
Box Wlk M31....... 11 E3
Boyd Cl CW11....... 152 C2
Boydell Ave
Warrington WA4..... 17 B2
Warrington, Westy WA4... 16 F4
Boydell Way CH4..... 162 A6
Boyle Ave WA2....... 8 F1
Boyles Hall Rd ST7.... 209 E2
Bracken Cl
Broughton CH4....... 139 C3
Macclesfield SK10..... 86 F1
Rode Heath ST7...... 193 F8
Warrington WA3...... 9 C5
Brackendale Elton CH2... 72 B3
Runcorn WA7........ 49 D8
Brackenfield Way **11**
CW7................ 149 A8
Bracken Rd CH66..... 69 E4
Brackens The
Daresbury WA4...... 25 A1
Higher Kinnerton CH4... 161 A8
Bracken Way Barnton CW8. 78 B3
Comberbach CW9..... 78 C7
Frodsham WA6....... 74 C6
Knutsford WA16..... 82 A8
Wincham CW9....... 79 C3
Brackenwood Cl CW2... 206 B8
Brackenwood Dr WA8... 22 A8
Brackenwood Mews
Chorlton CW2....... 207 D2
1 Wilmslow SK9..... 60 E8
Brackley Ave M44.... 11 D6
Brackley St Runcorn WA7. 22 F3
Warrington WA4..... 16 C1
Bradburn Rd M44..... 11 E7
Bradburns La CW8.... 103 B6
Bradbury Gdns CW12... 156 F1
Bradbury Rd CW7..... 127 B2
Braddon Cl CW9..... 103 F4
BRADELEY GREEN... 225 A8
Bradeley Green La SY13. 225 C7
Bradeley Hall Rd CW1... 191 B5
Bradeley Rd CW1..... 191 C4
Bradfield Cl **6** CW10... 151 D5
BRADFIELD GREEN.. 172 E3
Bradfield Rd CW1..... 190 B7
Bradford La SK10..... 85 C6
Bradford Pl CH4...... 141 D7
Bradford Rd CW7..... 126 E4
Bradford St CW7..... 141 D7
Bradford Wood CW7... 126 C4
Bradgate St SK8...... 34 D8
Bradgate Cl WA5..... 15 F6
Brading Wlk M22.... 33 E8
Bradlegh Rd WA12..... 2 B1
Bradley Brook La SY14. 213 E3
Bradley Cl CW10..... 151 B7
Bradley Farm La SY13.. 225 C7
BRADLEY GREEN.... 225 A8
Bradley Green La SY13.. 225 A8
Bradley Hall Cotts WA4.. 27 F6
Bradley La Frodsham WA6.. 74 D7
Newton-le-Willows WA5,
WA12.............. 2 A1
BRADLEY MOUNT... 87 B2
Bradley St SK11..... 112 E6
Bradley Way WA8..... 13 B1
Bradmoor Rd CH62.... 43 D8
Bradshaw Ave CH4.... 140 B7
Bradshaw Cl SK9..... 60 E4
Bradshaw Com Prim Sch
WA4................ 17 B2
Bradshaw Hall La
Cheadle SK8......... 34 E8
Gatley SK8.......... 34 D8
Bradshaw La Lymm WA13. 19 D3
Warrington WA3..... 17 B3
Bradshaw Pl CW12.... 156 E2
Bradshaw St WA8..... 13 A4
BRADWALL GREEN.. 153 B3
Bradwall Rd CW11.... 175 B7
Bradwall St CW11.... 175 B7
Bradwell Cl CH65..... 70 A4

Bradwell Ct CW12.... 156 F2
Bradwell Dr SK8..... 34 C7
Bradwell Gr CW12.... 156 F2
Bradwell Rd Golborne WA3. 3 E7
Hazel Grove SK7..... 36 E8
Braemar Ave CW9.... 104 C7
Braemar Cl Chester CH3. 119 C3
Holmes Chapel CW4... 130 C2
Warrington WA2..... 9 A3
Wistaston CW2...... 205 E8
Braemar Ct CH65..... 70 E3
Braeside Cl
6 Ellesmere Port CH66... 69 C5
Macclesfield SK11..... 112 F6
Braidwood Ave WA16... 57 C3
Brains La CW6....... 169 B6
Braintree Rd M22.... 33 C8
Braithwaite Cl WA7.... 49 C5
Braithwaite Rd WA3.... 3 D8
Brakeley La CW8..... 77 D4
Brakenwood Mews WA4.. 17 C1
Brake The ST7....... 195 B8
Brake Village ST7..... 195 B7
Bramall Cl CW11..... 175 C7
Bramble Chase CW8.... 101 F2
Bramble Cl Chester CH3. 142 A7
Macclesfield SK10..... 87 B2
Middlewich CW10..... 128 E2
2 Nantwich CW5..... 204 C3
Warrington WA5..... 14 E3
Winsford CW7....... 126 C3
Brambles The
Burtonwood WA5..... 7 A7
Congleton CW12..... 178 F8
Haslington CW1..... 191 B4
Wincham CW9....... 79 C3
Bramble Way WA7.... 49 E4
Brambling Cl Kelsall CW6. 122 C4
Runcorn WA7....... 49 F5
Brambling Way WA3.... 3 E7
BRAMHALL........ 35 D8
Bramhall Cl CW7..... 126 B1
Bramhall Ct CW2.... 189 F2
Bramhall Dr
Bebington CH62...... 43 F4
Holmes Chapel CW4... 130 A3
Bramhall High Sch SK7.. 35 F8
Bramhall Hill CW12.... 134 C2
Bramhall Lane S SK7... 35 E7
Bramhall Moor La SK7.. 36 D7
Bramhall Pk SK7..... 35 E8
Bramhalls Pk CW9.... 78 C3
Bramhall St WA5..... 15 E5
Bramhall Sta SK7..... 35 E6
Bramhall Way SK10.... 112 A8
Bramley Cl Bramhall SK7. 35 E6
2 Ellesmere Port CH66... 94 F8
Wilmslow SK9....... 59 D4
Bramley Ct CW6..... 122 D5
Bramley Dr SK7...... 35 E6
Bramley Mews WA4.... 26 C8
Bramley Rd SK7..... 35 E6
Bramley Wlk WA6.... 73 A1
Brampton Ave SK10.... 87 A2
Brampton Ct CW2.... 207 E3
Brampton Ct WA3.... 1 B3
Bramshill Cl WA3.... 10 A6
Bramway Bramhall SK7.. 35 C7
High Lane SK6....... 37 F7
Bramwell Way SK9.... 60 E7
Bramwood Ct SK7.... 35 E6
Brancepeth Ct CH65.... 70 E3
Branch Way WA11.... 1 D6
Brancote Gdns CH62.... 43 D7
Branden Dr WA16..... 57 B1
Brandon WA8........ 12 B2
Brandon Cl SK9..... 34 D2
Brandon Ct **9** CW7.... 150 A8
Brandwood Ave WA2.... 8 B2
Brandwood Ho **2** WA1.. 16 C5
Bransdale Cl WA5..... 14 F7
Bransdale Way SK11... 111 F7
Brantfield Ct WA2.... 8 E2
Brassey Ct CW5...... 205 C6
Brassey Grange CW8... 78 C1
BRASSEY GREEN.... 167 D6
Brassey's Contract Rd
SY14.............. 199 A1
Brassey St CH3...... 118 F1
Brassey Way CW5..... 205 D5
Brassington Terr CW3... 221 F3
Brathay Cl WA2...... 8 C3
BRATT'S BANK...... 101 B5
Brattswood Dr ST7.... 194 A5
Bravo Way **1** WA5.... 14 F8
Bray Cl Crewe CW5.... 190 F3
Runcorn WA7........ 49 D6
Bray Rd CH4........ 140 F6
Breach House La WA16.. 32 A1
Bread St CH1....... 112 C7
Bream La CH65...... 70 B8
Brechvale Cl SK12..... 36 E3
Breck Rd WA8....... 13 B1
Breck The CH66..... 69 E7
Brecon Cl SK12...... 36 F4
Brecon Ct WA5...... 7 E2
Brecon Dr **1** CH66.... 69 E1
Breconway CW7..... 149 B8
Brecon Way CW2.... 206 A2
Bredon Cl CH66..... 69 A6
Breech Moss La WA6... 100 F5
Breen Cl CH3........ 166 B6
Breezehill Cl CH64.... 66 F8
Breezehill Pk CH64.... 66 F8
Breezehill Rd CH64.... 66 F8

Brendon Ave WA2 . . . . .8 A3
Brendon Gr WA9 . . . . .1 A4
Brennus Pl CH1 . . . . 237 A3
Brent Cl SK12 . . . . .36 B4
Brentfield WA8 . . . . 12 D2
Brentnall Cl WA5 . . . . 15 C5
Brentwood Ave M44 . . . . . 11 D6
Brentwood Rd CH1 . . . . . . 117 E5
Brereton CE Prim Sch
   CW11 . . . . 153 F5
Brereton Cl Chester CH3 . 121 C1
   Crewe CW2 . . . . 189 E2
   3 Malpas SY14 . . . . . . 213 B3
   Malpas SY14 . . . . 213 B3
   Runcorn WA7 . . . . .50 A8
   Sandbach CW11 . . . . 175 C7
Brereton Ct
   Brereton Green CW12 . . . 154 F6
   1 Cheadle SK8 . . . . . . .34 E8
Brereton Dr CW5 . . . . 204 F7
Brereton Gr M44 . . . . .11 C6
BRERETON GREEN 153 E5
BRERETON HEATH 154 F6
Brereton Heath La CW11,
   CW12 . . . . 154 E6
Brereton Heath Nature
   Reserve★ CW12 . . . . . . 154 D6
Brereton La CW4 . . . . 152 E8
Brereton Park La CH3 . . . 144 E3
Brereton Pk
   Brereton Green CW11 . . . 153 F5
   Brereton Hall CW5 . . . . . 154 A6
Brereton Rd Farndon CH3 . 180 F1
   Handforth SK9 . . . . .34 E3
   Hartford CW8 . . . . 103 A4
Bretland Dr WA4 . . . . 27 A7
Breton Cl CH2 . . . . 118 E5
BRETTON 139 E4
Bretton Ave WA1 . . . . .16 E5
Bretton Court Mews
   CH4 . . . . 139 E4
Bretton Dr CH4 . . . . 139 B3
Bretton La CH4 . . . . 139 F5
Bretton Rd CH4 . . . . 139 E4
Bretton Wlk M22 . . . . 33 D8
Breward Rd CW2 . . . . 206 D7
Brewery La CH3 . . . . 180 E3
Brian Ave Warrington WA2 . 16 D8
   Warrington, Stockton Heath
   WA4 . . . . .16 E1
Brian Bevan Island WA1 . .16 B4
Briar Ave WA16 . . . . .11 B2
Briar Cl WA16 . . . . .57 A3
Briardale Cl CW2 . . . . 205 F8
Briardale Gdns **4** CH66 . . 69 C6
Briardale Rd
   Ellesmere Port CH66 . . . . 69 C6
   Willaston CH64 . . . . 43 A1
Briar Dr CH60 . . . . 41 A8
Briarfield Ave WA8 . . . . . . 12 A1
Briarfield Rd
   Ellesmere Port CH65 . . . . .70 B5
   Heswall CH60 . . . . .41 B8
Briar La CW8 . . . . 102 E7
Briarlands Cl SK7 . . . . 35 D6
Briar Rd WA3 . . . . .3 B8
Briarstead Cl SK7 . . . . 35 D6
Briarswood Biddulph ST8 . 179 D1
   Kidsgrove ST7 . . . . 195 B1
Briarswood Ct CH1 . . . . . 237 B3
Briar Wlk WA3 . . . . .3 B8
Briarwood Runcorn WA7. . .50 B8
   Wilmslow SK9 . . . . 60 C7
Briarwood Ave
   Macclesfield SK11 . . . . . 112 D5
   Warrington WA1 . . . . .16 E7
Briarwood Ct CW7 . . . . . . 149 C8
Brick Bank CW5. . . . . 204 F5
Brick Bank La WA16,
   CW4 . . . . 107 B2
Brickfield Bsns Ctr CW9 . . 79 D1
Brickfield La CH3 . . . . 119 F2
Brickhill La WA15 . . . . .32 B4
Brickhurst Way WA1 . . . . . .17 B8
Brickiln Cl CW2 . . . . 206 D7
Brickkiln La
   Little Bollington WA14 . . . 20 C3
   Whitchurch SY13 . . . . . . 226 D2
Brick Kiln La CW10 . . . . . . 127 B7
Brickley Ct CW8. . . . . 77 C1
Brick Rd CH4 . . . . 139 D2
Brick St
   Newton-le-Willows WA12 . . .1 F3
   Warrington WA1 . . . . 16 C5
Bricky La CH3 . . . . 119 E1
Bridestone Sh Ctr CW12 . 156 D2
Bridestones Pl CW12 . . . . 156 F6
Bridewell Ct WA8 . . . . .13 B3
Bridge Ave WA4 . . . . .16 F4
Bridge Avenue E WA4 . . . .16 F5
Bridge Bank Cl WA3. . . . . . .3 B7
Bridge Cl Audley ST7 . . . . 209 F2
   Cuddington CW8 . . . . 102 A3
   Lymm WA13 . . . . .19 B4
   Wistaston CW2 . . . . 206 A7
Bridge Cotts CH4. . . . . 237 B1
Bridge Ct Chester CH2. . . . 119 A2
   Holt LL13 . . . . 196 E8
   Neston CH64 . . . . .66 E7
Bridge Dr Christleton CH3 . 142 D7
   Handforth SK9 . . . . .34 D3
Bridge End Dr SK10 . . . . . .87 A7
Bridge End La SK10 . . . . . .87 A7
Bridge Farm Ct CW10. . . . 152 A4
Bridge Farm Rd CW9 . . . . .78 E3

Bridgefield Ave SK9 . . . . . . 34 C1
Bridgefoot WA1. . . . . .16 B4
Bridgefoot Ind Est WA4 . . .16 B4
Bridge Foyer The CH1 . . . 118 B2
Bridge Gn SK10 . . . . 87 A7
Bridge La Cuddington CW8 101 F3
   Frodsham WA6. . . . . 49 D1
   Goostrey CW4 . . . . 108 C2
   Warrington WA4 . . . . .26 E7
   Warrington, Woolston WA1 . .9 F4
Bridge Lane Mews WA6 . . . 49 D1
Bridgeman Rd CH1 . . . . . . 117 E3
Bridgeman St WA5 . . . . . . 15 D4
Bridge Mdw CH66 . . . . .69 F2
BRIDGEMERE 231 F8
Bridgemere CE Prim Sch
   CW5 . . . . 231 E8
Bridgemere Cl CW11 . . . . 174 F8
Bridgemere La CW5 . . . . . 219 E1
Bridgemere Mews CW5. . . 231 F8
Bridgemere Nursery &
   Garden World★ CW5 . . . 232 B4
Bridgemere Way **4**
   CW9 . . . . 103 E4
BRIDGEMONT 39 E2
Bridgemont SK23 . . . . .39 E1
Bridgend CH2. . . . . .97 A1
Bridgend Cl WA8. . . . . 12 D3
Bridgend Dr WA8. . . . . 12 D3
Bridgeport Mews WA5 . . . 15 A7
Bridge Rd WA1 . . . . 17 C7
Bridge Ret Pk WA7 . . . . . . 23 A2
Bridge Row CW2 . . . . 156 F4
Bridge Sh Ctr The WA4. . . .16 F3
Bridge Side Dr WA6 . . . . . .73 B4
Bridges Rd CH65 . . . . .70 F5
Bridge St Chester CH1 . . . 237 B2
   Congleton CW12 . . . . 156 D2
   Golborne WA3 . . . . .3 A7
   Holt LL13 . . . . 180 E1
   Macclesfield SK11 . . . . . 112 C7
   Neston CH64 . . . . .66 E7
   Newton-le-Willows WA12 . . .2 B3
   Northwich CW9 . . . . .79 E2
   Runcorn WA7 . . . . .23 B2
   Saltney CH4 . . . . 140 D7
   Warrington WA1 . . . . .16 B5
   Whaley Bridge SK23. . . . . .65 E7
   Wybunbury CW5 . . . . 220 B8
Bridge Street Row E
   CH1 . . . . 237 B2
Bridge Street Row W
   CH1 . . . . 237 B2
Bridge Terr WA7 . . . . 119 B2
BRIDGE TRAFFORD 97 A3
Bridge View Cl WA8 . . . . . 23 A4
Bridgewater Ave WA4. . . . .16 F4
Bridgewater Cl
   Congleton CW12 . . . . 157 B1
   6 Frodsham WA6 . . . . 49 C1
   Gatley SK8 . . . . 34 D7
Bridgewater Ct
   1 Lymm WA13 . . . . . . 18 C3
   6 Runcorn WA7 . . . . . 23 B2
Bridgewater Dr CH3 . . . . . 119 C2
Bridgewater Expressway
   WA7 . . . . 23 C2
Bridgewater Grange WA7. .50 F5
Bridgewater High Sch
   Warrington WA4 . . . . 26 D6
   Warrington WA4 . . . . 26 D7
Bridgewater Intc WA7 . . . .23 E3
Bridgewater Mews WA4 . . 26 C8
Bridgewater Pl WA7 . . . . . .9 E4
Bridgewater St
   4 Lymm WA13 . . . . . . .18 E3
   6 Runcorn WA7 . . . . . 23 A3
Bridgeway E WA7 . . . . 24 C2
Bridgeway W WA7 . . . . . . 24 C2
Bridge Wlk **7** WA7. . . . . . .49 F7
Bridgewood Dr CH66 . . . . 69 C2
Bridgfield Cl SK6. . . . . .37 E7
Bridgnorth Gr ST5 . . . . . . 210 E2
Bridle Cl CH62 . . . . .43 E7
Bridle Ct Bramhall SK7. . . .35 F2
   Crewe CW2 . . . . 190 B4
Bridle Hey CW5 . . . . 204 F2
Bridle La CH1 . . . . .94 E6
Bridlemere Ct WA1. . . . . . .16 E8
Bridle Pk CH62. . . . . .43 E7
Bridle Rd Bebington CH62 . .43 E6
   Crewe CW2 . . . . 190 B4
   Woodford SK7. . . . . 35 F2
Bridle Way
   Ellesmere Port CH66 . . . . 69 D3
   Woodford SK7 . . . . 36 A2
Briedden Way CH66 . . . . . 69 A6
Brierley Bsns Ctr CW1 . . . 190 D4
Brierley Cl CW7. . . . . 149 F8
Brierley Prim Sch CW1 . . . 190 D4
Brierley Rd CW12 . . . . 157 B1
Brierley St CW1 . . . . 190 D4
Brierley Terr **6** WA8 . . . 13 C1
Briers CT WA2. . . . . .8 F3
Brieryhurst Rd ST7 . . . . . . 195 B3
Briggs Ave CW2 . . . . 190 D1
Brighton Cres SK11 . . . . . 113 B3
Brighton St WA5 . . . . .15 E6
Brights Ave **6** ST7 . . . . 195 B2
Bright St CW1. . . . . 190 B5
Brightwell Cl WA5 . . . . . . .14 E5
Brimelow Cres WA5 . . . . . .14 E3
Brimstage Cl CH60 . . . . . . 41 C8
Brimstage Gn CH60 . . . . . 41 D8
Brimstage Rd CH60. . . . . . 41 C7
Brimstone Dr WA12 . . . . . .1 E3
Brimstone Rd **6** CW7 . . 149 E8
BRINDLEY 186 E8

Brindley Ave
   Warrington WA4 . . . . .16 F4
   Winsford CW7 . . . . 126 C1
Brindley Cl Kidsgrove ST7 . 194 E1
   Talke ST7 . . . . 210 E8
Brindley Ct WA4 . . . . 26 D8
Brindley Gr SK9 . . . . .34 E2
BRINDLEY GREEN 153 E2
Brindley Hall Rd CW5. . . . 186 E2
Brindley La CW11 . . . . 153 C4
Brindley Lea La CW5 . . . . 186 D1
Brindley Pk CW11 . . . . 174 F3
Brindley Rd WA7 . . . . .23 F3
Brindley St WA7 . . . . .22 F3
Brindleys Way **2** WA7 . 209 F2
Brindley Way
   Congleton CW12 . . . . 157 B1
   Macclesfield SK11 . . . . . 112 C3
Brindley Wharf WA4. . . . . .50 F6
Brine Leas High Sch
   CW5 . . . . 204 F3
Brinell Dr M44 . . . . .11 F6
Brine Pits La CW5 . . . . . . 218 F2
Brine Pump Cotts CW9 . . .78 F4
Brine Rd CW5 . . . . 204 E3
Brines Brow La CH3 . . . . . 99 D2
Brinley Cl CH62 . . . . 43 D5
Brinton Cl WA8 . . . . .22 E8
Brisbane Cl SK7. . . . . 35 F5
Brisbane Rd CH1 . . . . 117 C4
Bristol Ave WA7 . . . . .50 E6
Bristol Cl Blacon CH1 . . . . 117 C4
   Gatley SK8 . . . . 34 C7
Bristol Dr **3** CH66 . . . . . 69 E1
Bristow Cl WA5 . . . . .15 B8
Britannia Dr CW9 . . . . 104 E7
Britannia Rd CW8 . . . . 102 A5
Britannia Trad Est SK23 . . .39 F1
Brittania Gdns WA6 . . . . . .73 B1
Brittannia Rd WA6 . . . . . . .73 B2
Britten Cres WA7 . . . . 127 A7
Brixham Ave SK8. . . . . .34 F7
Brixham Wlk SK7. . . . . 35 E7
Broadacre CW9 . . . . 78 D6
Broadacre Pl SK9 . . . . 59 D3
Broadacres CW5 . . . . 217 F4
Broadbent Ave WA4 . . . . . .16 F4
Broad Birches CH65. . . . . . 70 A6
Broadcar Rd SK11. . . . . . . 113 C6
Broad Ct SK9 . . . . .85 B8
Broadfields WA7 . . . . 50 C8
Broadheath Terr WA8 . . . . 12 D1
Broadheys La WA16 . . . . . 28 D6
Broadhurst Ave
   Culcheth WA3. . . . . .4 F2
   3 Warrington WA5 . . . . 15 D4
Broadhurst La CW12 . . . . . 156 C3
Broad La Altrincham WA15 . 32 B8
   Appleton Thorn WA4 . . . . . .27 A6
   Burtonwood WA5 . . . . .6 E8
   Haydock WA5, WA9 . . . . . . .1 C1
   Heswall CH60 . . . . .40 C8
   Holmes Chapel CW4. . . . . 129 F1
   Stapeley CW5 . . . . 205 A1
Broadlake CH64. . . . . .67 F8
Broadland Gdns CH66 . . . . 69 F2
Broadland Rd CH66 . . . . . . 69 F2
Broadleigh Way CW2 . . . . 206 C8
Broadley Ave Golborne WA3. .3 C7
   1 Golborne WA3. . . . . . .3 C7
Broadmead Chester CH3. . 119 C2
   Heswall CH60 . . . . .41 C7
BROADOAK 162 B1
Broad Oak Ave
   Broughton CH4. . . . . 139 A3
   Haydock WA11 . . . . .1 A6
   Warrington WA5 . . . . .14 E4
Broadoak La
   High Legh WA16 . . . . 29 D5
   Mobberley WA16 . . . . .57 C6
Broadoak Prim Sch WA9. . .1 A3
Broadoak Sch M31 . . . . . . .11 F2
Broadside Ave CH65. . . . . . 70 E3
Broad St Crewe CW1 . . . . 190 C6
   Crewe CW1 . . . . 190 D7
Broadstone Cl
   Alderley Park SK10. . . . . . .85 B3
   2 Lingley Green WA5 . . 14 D8
Broadwalk SK10 . . . . 87 A5
Broadway Altrincham WA15 32 A8
   Barnton CW8 . . . . .78 B3
   Widnes WA8 . . . . 12 A1
   Wilmslow SK9 . . . . .60 B6
Broadway E CH2 . . . . 118 E5
Broadways CW3 . . . . 230 A4
Broadway The CW5 . . . . . 204 F5
Broadway W CH2 . . . . 118 D5
Broad Wlk SK9. . . . . 59 F8
Broadwood Cl SK6 . . . . . . .37 F7
Brody Ct **5** CW2 . . . . . 190 D2
Brock Dr SK8 . . . . .35 B8
Brock Gdns L24 . . . . .21 E2
Brock Hollow CW11 . . . . . 174 F4
Brockhurst Mews CW9. . . 104 A6
Brockhurst St CW9. . . . . . 104 A8
Brockhurst Way CW9. . . . 104 A8
Brocklebank Dr CW8. . . . . 103 E7
Brocklehurst Ave SK10 . . . .87 F2
Brocklehurst Ct **2** SK10 . .87 D3
Brocklehurst Dr SK10 . . . . .87 A7
Brocklehurst Manor SK10. .87 E1
Brocklehurst Mews **3**
   SK10 . . . . 87 D3
Brocklehurst Way SK10. . . .87 D3
Brock Rd WA3 . . . . .9 D3
Brocks Croft Gdns ST8 . . 179 C1

Brock St SK10 . . . . 87 D1
Brockton Ct WA4. . . . . 26 C6
Brockway E CH3 . . . . 166 A1
Brockway W CH3 . . . . 166 A1
Brockwell Cl **2** CW7 . . . 149 A8
Brodie Cl CH2. . . . . 95 C1
Brogden Ave WA3. . . . . .4 E4
Brogden Dr CW5 . . . . 205 E6
Broken Banks **10** SK11 . 112 D7
BROKEN CROSS
   Macclesfield 111 E8
   Northwich 104 E7
Broken Cross SK11 . . . . . . 111 F8
Broken Cross Com Sch
   SK11 . . . . 111 E7
Brokencross Pl CW9 . . . . 104 E7
Bromborough Rake Sta
   CH62 . . . . 43 C8
Bromborough Sta CH63. . . 43 C7
Bromborough Village Rd
   CH62 . . . . .43 B8
Bromley Ave WA3 . . . . .3 D7
Bromley Cl Crewe CW1 . . . 189 F8
   Heswall CH60 . . . . .40 E7
   Warrington WA2 . . . . .8 F3
Bromley Dr CW4 . . . . 130 C2
Bromley Rd
   Congleton CW12 . . . . 156 F3
   Macclesfield SK10 . . . . . . 111 E8
Brompton Gdns WA5. . . . . .15 E7
Brompton Way
   Ellesmere Port CH66 . . . . .69 E1
   Handforth SK9 . . . . 34 C5
Bronington Ave CH62. . . . . 43 D6
Bronte Cl WA2 . . . . .8 A6
Bronte Wlk CH2 . . . . .8 A6
Brook Acre Prim Sch WA2 . .8 E1
Brookash Rd M22 . . . . 34 A8
Brook Ave Handforth SK9 . . 34 A8
   Shavington CW2. . . . . 206 C5
   Warrington, Stockton Heath
   WA4 . . . . .16 E1
   Warrington, Westy WA4. . . .16 F5
Brook Bank SK12. . . . . 37 C2
Brook Bottom Rd SK22 . . . 39 A8
Brook Cl Crewe CW1 . . . . 190 F4
   Cronton WA8 . . . . 12 C6
Brook Ct Chester CH1 . . . . 118 B3
   Sandbach CW11 . . . . 175 B6
Brookdale WA8 . . . . 12 A3
Brookdale Ave WA16 . . . . . 57 C2
Brookdale Ct CH3 . . . . 143 D5
Brookdale Pk CW2 . . . . . . 190 A3
Brookdale Pl CH1 . . . . 237 B3
Brookdale Way CH3 . . . . . 143 B5
Brook Dr Kelsall CW6 . . . . 122 D4
   Warrington WA5 . . . . 15 A5
Brooke Ave Chester CH2. . 118 F8
   Northwich CW8 . . . . 103 C8
Brooke Ct SK9 . . . . .34 A4
Brooke Dr SK9 . . . . 34 A4
Brooke Ho SK10. . . . . .86 F1
Brookes Ave CH4. . . . . 139 B3
Brooke Way SK9 . . . . 34 A4
Brook Farm Cl M31. . . . . . .11 E2
Brook Farm La
   Dutton WA4 . . . . 51 E5
   Ettiley Heath CW11 . . . . . 174 D3
Brookfield CW1. . . . . 191 D5
Brookfield Ave
   Poynton SK12. . . . . 36 C3
   Runcorn WA7 . . . . .23 E2
   Warrington WA1 . . . . .16 F7
Brookfield Cl Lymm WA13 . 18 D3
Brookfield Cotts **2** WA13. 18 D3
Brookfield Cres CW4 . . . . 107 F1
Brookfield Ct CW1 . . . . . . 190 B5
Brookfield Dr
   Alsager ST7 . . . . 193 C5
   Chester CH2. . . . . 118 C4
   Holmes Chapel CW4 . . . . 130 B3
Brookfield La SK11 . . . . . . 112 F7
Brookfield Pk WA4 . . . . . . 17 A2
Brookfield Rd
   Comberbach CW9 . . . . . . 78 D8
   Culcheth WA3. . . . . .4 D3
   Lymm WA13 . . . . 18 D3
Brookfields Sch WA8 . . . . 13 D2
Brookfield St WA12 . . . . . . .2 B3
Brook Furlong WA6 . . . . . . 48 F2
Brook Gdns ST8. . . . . 179 D1
Brook Hey CH64. . . . . .41 B2
Brook Ho WA4 . . . . .16 F3
BROOKHOUSE 88 D3
Brookhouse Cl SK10. . . . . .86 F1
Brookhouse La WA13 . . . . 18 D2
Brookhouse Dr CW2. . . . . 206 C8
BROOKHOUSE GREEN . . 177 A7
Brookhouse La
   Church Minshull CW1,
   CW10 . . . . 172 D7
   Congleton CW12 . . . . 157 C2
   Duddon CH3 . . . . 144 D6
   Lower Whitley WA4 . . . . . 52 B2
Brookhouse Rd
   Alsager ST7 . . . . 193 D3
   5 Sandbach CW11 . . . 175 B6
BROOKHURST 43 C5
Brookhurst Ave SK10. . . . . 43 C5
Brookhurst Cl CH63 . . . . . 43 C5
Brookhurst Prim Sch
   CH63. . . . . 43 C6
Brookhurst Rd CH63. . . . . . 43 C5
Brook La Alderley Edge SK9 . 59 F3
   Astbury CW12 . . . . 177 E5
   Broughton CH5. . . . . 139 C7
   Burland CW5 . . . . 203 D8

Brook La continued
   Chester CH2. . . . . 118 E4
   Faddiley CW5 . . . . 202 F8
   Knutsford WA16. . . . . .57 B1
   Neston CH64 . . . . 41 C2
   Northwich CW9 . . . . 104 D7
   Warrington WA3 . . . . .18 A3
Brookland Ave CW2 . . . . . 205 F8
Brookland Dr CW11 . . . . . 175 E6
Brookland La WA9 . . . . .1 A1
BROOKLANDS 225 E1
Brooklands Ave SK11 . . . . 112 B7
Brooklands Dr
   Goostrey CW4 . . . . 107 F1
   Northwich CW9 . . . . 104 A4
Brooklands Gdns CH64 . . . 41 C1
Brooklands Gr CW1 . . . . . 190 A6
Brooklands Pk **1** WA8 . . 13 C2
Brooklands Rd
   Congleton CW12 . . . . 155 F2
   Neston CH64 . . . . 41 C1
Brookland St WA1. . . . . . . .16 E7
Brooklands The CW2 . . . . 206 B3
Brooklea Mdws CH66. . . . . .68 F6
Brookledge La SK10 . . . . . .62 C5
Brooklet Rd CH60 . . . . 41 C8
Brooklyn Dr
   Ellesmere Port CH65 . . . . .69 F5
   Lymm WA13 . . . . .18 E4
Brooklyn St CW2 . . . . 190 C2
Brookmere Cl CW11 . . . . . 174 E8
Brookmills Cotts ST8 . . . . 179 C1
Brookmoore Ct CH2 . . . . . 237 A4
Brook Pl Chester CH1 . . . . 237 B3
   Warrington WA4 . . . . .16 E4
Brook Rd
   Ellesmere Port CH66 . . . . 69 D5
   Lymm WA13 . . . . .18 E4
   Tarporley CW6 . . . . 168 D8
Brooks Dr WA15 . . . . 32 D8
Brookside
   Ashton Hayes CH3 . . . . . . 121 E7
   Chester CH3. . . . . 142 A8
   Cuddington CW8 . . . . 101 F3
   Kelsall CW6 . . . . 122 C4
   Kingsley WA6 . . . . 75 C2
   Warrington WA3 . . . . .16 E3
Brook Side CW8 . . . . 102 C8
Brookside Ave
   Lymm WA13 . . . . 18 C4
   Poynton SK12. . . . . .36 E3
   Sutton Lane Ends SK11. . . 112 F2
   Warrington WA5 . . . . 15 A4
   Warrington, Stockton Heath
   WA4 . . . . 16 D3
Brookside Cotts WA11. . . . 176 A8
Brookside Ct SK10 . . . . . . 87 A1
Brookside Gn CW2 . . . . . . 206 C8
Brookside La SK6 . . . . .37 E7
Brookside Mill **6** SK11 . . 112 E7
Brookside Miniature Rly★
   SK12. . . . . .36 F7
Brookside Prim Sch
   Ellesmere Port CH66 . . . . .69 E4
   High Lane SK6 . . . . 37 E6
Brookside Rd
   4 Congleton CW12 . . . 156 D3
   Frodsham WA6. . . . . 74 A8
Brookside Terr
   Chester CH2. . . . . 237 C4
   Wilmslow SK9 . . . . .59 C3
Brookside View WA11 . . . . .1 B7
Brookside Way WA11. . . . . .1 B7
Brooks La Bosley SK11. . . . 135 E2
   Middlewich CW10 . . . . . . 128 D1
Brook Slack CW6 . . . . 124 D1
Brooks Lane Ind Est
   CW10 . . . . 128 D1
Brook St Chester CH1. . . . 237 B3
   Congleton CW12 . . . . 156 F3
   Crewe CW2 . . . . 190 D3
   Golborne, Bank Heath WA3 . .3 A8
   Knutsford WA16. . . . . .57 B1
   Macclesfield SK11 . . . . . 112 E7
   Neston CH64 . . . . .66 E8
   Northwich CW9 . . . . 79 A1
   Northwich, Lostock Gralam
   CW9 . . . . .79 E2
   2 Runcorn WA7 . . . . . 23 A2
   3 Widnes WA8 . . . . . . .13 B1
Brook Street Bridge CH1,
   CH2 . . . . 237 C4
Brook Street Mill **19**
   SK11 . . . . 112 E7
Brook Terr Runcorn WA7. . .23 E1
   Sandbach CW11 . . . . 175 A3
BROOKVALE 50 B5
Brookvale Avenue N WA7. .50 B6
Brookvale Avenue S WA7. .50 B6
Brookvale Cl WA5 . . . . .6 F6
Brookvale Prim Sch WA7 . .50 B5
Brook View
   Alderley Edge SK9 . . . . . . 60 A3
   Allostock WA16 . . . . 106 F3
Brookview Cl CW2 . . . . . . 206 C8
Brook Villas ST7 . . . . 193 E3
Brook Way
   Hartford CW8. . . . . 103 B4
   Nantwich CW5 . . . . 204 E3
   Warrington WA5 . . . . 15 A5
Brookway La **1** WA9. . . . .1 A1
Brook Well CH64. . . . . .66 F5
Brookwood Cl WA8 . . . . . . .13 A3
Brookwood Dr WA4 . . . . . .26 B8
Broom Ave WA4. . . . . 26 E6
BROOM BANK 144 B8
Broom Cres CH3 . . . . 121 B5

Broom Croft Gdns **5**
  CW1 . . . . .173 A1
Broome Ct WA7 . . . . .50 B5
BROOMEDGE 29 C8
Broomehouse Ave M44 . . . .11 E8
Broomfield CW12 . . . . .154 F6
Broomfield Cl
  Chelford SK11 . . . . 84 A3
  4 Wilmslow SK9 . . . . .60 E8
  13 Winsford CW7 . . . . . . .149 A8
Broomfield Jun Sch WA4 . .26 E7
Broomfields WA4 . . . . .26 E7
Broomfields La CW8 . . . . . . .77 F4
Broomfields Rd WA4 . . . . . 26 D7
BROOMHALL 217 F4
Broomhall Dr CW2 . . . . . .206 B5
BROOMHALL GREEN 217 F3
Broomheath La
  Tarvin CH3 . . . . .121 C1
  Tarvin, Broom Bank CH3 . . 144 C7
Broomhill La
  Brown Knowl CH3 . . . . . .199 D8
  Great Barrow CH3 . . . . . .120 E8
Broom La WA16 . . . . .81 F2
Broomlands Cotts CW5 . .219 E1
Broom Rd M31 . . . . .11 F2
Broomsfield La CW8 . . . . . 78 A4
Broom's La CW6 . . . . .122 D6
Broom St CW1 . . . . 190 A6
Broseley Ave WA3 . . . . .4 D4
Broseley La WA3 . . . . .4 D5
Broseley Pl WA3 . . . . 4 C5
Broseley Way **8** CW9 . . . . .80 B2
Brotherton Cl CH62 . . . . . . 43 C8
Brotherton Way WA12 . . . . .2 B4
Brough St W SK11 . . . . . . .112 C7
BROUGHTON 139 A4
Broughton Ave WA3 . . . . . . .3 D7
Broughton Cl WA4 . . . . .26 F8
Broughton Cres SY14 . . . . .211 A1
Broughton Hall Rd CH4 . . 139 C4
Broughton Ind Est CH4 . . . 139 F6
Broughton Inf Sch CH4 . . . 139 C4
Broughton Jun Sch CH4 . . 139 C4
Broughton La CW2 . . . . . . .189 F1
Broughton Mills Rd CH4 . . 139 F6
Broughton Rd
  Adlington SK10 . . . . 62 C5
  Crewe CW1 . . . . 190 C8
Broughton Sh Pk CH4 . . . . 139 E4
Broughton Way WA8 . . . . .22 B5
Brow Com Prim Sch The
  WA7 . . . . .23 F1
Brow La Antrobus CW9 . . . . 53 D5
  Heswall CH60 . . . . .40 F7
Browmere Dr WA3 . . . . .9 A7
Brown Ave
  Lawton-gate ST7 . . . . . . 194 A5
  Nantwich CW5 . . . . .204 F4
BROWNEDGE 154 A3
BROWN HEATH 143 B6
Brown Heath Rd CH3 . . . . .143 B6
BROWNHILL 147 B6
Brownhill Dr WA1 . . . . .16 F8
Brownhills Rd CW6 . . . . . . .147 C6
Browning Ave WA8 . . . . .22 F8
Browning Cl Blacon CH1 . . .117 F6
  Sandbach CW11 . . . . .174 D5
Browning Dr
  Ellesmere Port CH65 . . . . .69 F4
  Winwick WA2 . . . . .8 A6
Browning Gn **2** CH65 . . . .69 F4
Browning St CW1 . . . . .190 C4
Browning Way CW7 . . . . . .149 A7
BROWN KNOWL 199 C8
Brown Lees Cl **5** CW12 . .190 B1
Brown Lees Rd ST7 . . . . . . .195 F4
BROWNLOW 177 E2
Brownlow Cl SK12 . . . . .36 E2
Brownlow Hall Mews
  CW12 . . . . .177 D5
BROWNLOW HEATH 177 D5
Brownlow Heath CW12 . . .177 E5
Brownlow Heath La
  CW12 . . . . .177 D6
BROWN MOSS 231 B7
BROWN'S BANK 229 D2
Brown's La Chester CH4 . . .141 C7
  Wilmslow SK9 . . . . .60 E8
Brown St
  3 Alderley Edge SK9 . . . . .60 A1
  Congleton CW12 . . . . . . .156 E3
  Macclesfield SK11 . . . . . . .112 C7
  Widnes WA8 . . . . 23 D7
Brow The WA6 . . . . 75 C2
BROXTON 183 A1
Broxton CW10 . . . . .151 D6
Broxton Cl WA8 . . . . .12 C3
Broxton Mews CH3 . . . . . . .183 A1
Broxton Rd Clutton CH3 . . .182 D1
  Ellesmere Port CH66 . . . . .69 E5
Bruce Ave WA2 . . . . .8 D1
Bruce Cres CH63 . . . . 43 C6
Bruce Dr CH66 . . . . 69 C4
BRUCHE 16 F7
Bruche Ave WA1 . . . . .16 F8
Bruche Com Prim Sch
  WA1 . . . . .17 A7
Bruche Dr WA1 . . . . .16 F8
Bruche Heath Gdns WA1. . . 17 A8
Bruen The CH3 . . . . .121 C3
BRUERA 164 D6
Bruera Rd CH65 . . . . .69 F5
Brunel Ct CW9 . . . . .104 E5
Brunel Rd SK11 . . . . .112 C3
Brunner Gr CW5 . . . . .205 A5

Brunner Rd WA8 . . . . 23 A8
Brunsborough Cl CH62 . . . 43 C6
Brunswick **11** WA7 . . . . . . .23 A3
Brunswick Cl WA5 . . . . .15 B6
Brunswick Cres 69 E3
Brunswick Ct **12** SK11 . . . .112 D7
Brunswick Hill SK10 . . . . . .112 D8
Brunswick Rd WA12 . . . . . . .1 F4
Brunswick St
  Congleton CW12 . . . . . . .156 F3
  5 Macclesfield SK10 . . . . .112 D8
  St Helens WA9 . . . . .1 A3
Brunswick Terr SK10 . . . . . .112 D8
Bruntleigh Ave WA4 . . . . . .17 A3
Bryant Ave WA4 . . . . .16 F5
Brydson Cres CW2 . . . . . . .189 C3
Brymau Four Trad Est
  CH4 . . . . .140 D7
Brymau One Trad Est
  CH4 . . . . .140 E7
Brymau Three Trad Est
  CH4 . . . . .140 D7
Brymau Two Trad Est
  CH4 . . . . .140 D7
BRYN 102 A6
Bryn Cott La CW8 . . . . .102 A6
Brynlow Dr CW10 . . . . .151 B8
Brynmore Dr SK11 . . . . . . .112 F7
Brynn St WA8 . . . . 23 B8
Brynton Cl SK10 . . . . .87 C1
Brynton Rd SK10 . . . . .87 C1
Bryony Dr CW4 . . . . .130 C1
Buchanan Cl WA8 . . . . .12 F3
Buchan Cl WA5 . . . . .15 B8
Buchan Gr CW2 . . . . .190 B3
Buckbean Way CW4 . . . . . .107 E1
Buckden Way **9** SK10 . . . .112 C8
Buckfast Ave WA11 . . . . .2 A7
Buckfast Cl Cheadle SK8 . . . .35 B6
  Macclesfield SK10 . . . . . . .87 C2
  Poynton SK12 . . . . 36 D5
  Warrington WA5 . . . . .14 E3
Buckfast Ct WA7 . . . . .24 E3
Buckingham Ave
  Chester CH3 . . . . .119 B2
  Widnes WA8 . . . . 13 A4
Buckingham Cl
  4 Congleton CW12 . . . . .156 F4
  Wistaston CW2 . . . . .205 E8
Buckingham Dr
  Knutsford WA16 . . . . .57 B1
  Macclesfield SK11 . . . . . . .112 B5
  Northwich CW9 . . . . .103 E4
  Warrington WA5 . . . . .15 C4
  Winsford CW7 . . . . .149 C7
Buckingham Gdns **1**
  CH65 . . . . .70 D2
Buckingham Dr Irlam M44 . 11 C6
  Poynton SK12 . . . . 36 D3
  Wilmslow SK9 . . . . .59 F6
Buckingham Rise SK11 . . . .112 B4
Buck La CW2 . . . . .206 E3
Buckland Cl WA8 . . . . 22 D7
Buckley Ave
  Middlewich CW10 . . . . . .128 F7
  Wistaston Green CW2 . . . .189 D2
Buckley Cl CW10 . . . . .151 B8
Buckley Ct CH64 . . . . .67 F8
Buckley Pl **8** CW11 . . . . . .152 C2
Buckley St
  Macclesfield SK11 . . . . . . .112 D7
  Warrington WA2 . . . . .16 B6
Bucklow Ave
  Mobberley WA16 . . . . .58 A4
  Partington M31 . . . . .11 F3
Bucklow Farm La WA16. . . . 81 C4
Bucklow Gdns WA13 . . . . . .19 A4
BUCKLOW HILL 30 C3
Bucklowhill La WA16 . . . . . .30 B3
Bucklow Wlk **11** SK11 . . . . .112 E7
BUCKOAK 99 A5
Buckthorn Rd CW11 . . . . . .175 D6
Buckton St WA1 . . . . 16 D7
BUDDILEIGH 221 F7
Bude Cl Alsager ST7 . . . . . .193 B3
  Bramhall SK7 . . . . .35 F7
  Crewe CW1 . . . . 190 B8
Bude Rd WA8 . . . . .12 E2
Budworth Ave
  Warrington WA4 . . . . .16 F4
  Widnes WA8 . . . . 12 D2
Budworth Cl Runcorn WA7 . 49 D7
  Sandbach CW11 . . . . .174 F7
Budworth Gr **10** CW10 . . . .151 D5
BUDWORTH HEATH 54 A1
Budworth Heath La CW9 . . 54 C1
Budworth La CW9 . . . . .78 E7
Budworth Rd
  Bate Heath CW9. . . . . .54 E2
  Ellesmere Port CH66 . . . . .69 E2
  Over Tabley WA16 . . . . . . .55 C2
Budworth Wlk **1** SK9 . . . .34 E1
BUERTON 230 E4
Buerton App CH3 . . . . .164 B6
BUERTON MOSS 230 E6
Buffs La CH60 . . . . .41 B8
Buggen La CH64 . . . . 66 D8
BUGLAWTON 157 A4
Buglawton Hall Sch
  CW12 . . . . .157 D5
Buglawton Ind Est **5**
  CW12 . . . . .156 F4
Buglawton Prim Sch
  CW12 . . . . .157 A4
Buildwas Rd CH64 . . . . .41 F2
BULKELEY 184 E2
Bulkeley Hall La SY14. . . . .200 C8

Bulkeley Rd Handforth SK9 . 34 D3
  Poynton SK12 . . . . .36 E3
Bulkeley St Chester CH3 . . .119 A1
  Crewe CW1 . . . . 190 C5
Bullcroft Cl SY14 . . . . .211 D7
Bull Gate La CW12 . . . . . . .135 B2
Bull Hill 66 F6
Bull-Hill-La SK10, SK11 . . . 88 D2
Bullocks House Rd ST7 . . . .195 E3
Bullocks La SK11 . . . . .112 E3
Bull Ring CW9 . . . . .103 F8
Bull Ring The CW10 . . . . . .128 C1
Bumper's La CH1 . . . . .117 F1
BUNBURY 185 F8
Bunbury Aldersey CE Prim
  Sch CW6 . . . . .185 E8
Bunbury Cl
  Middlewich CW10 . . . . . .151 D5
  Northwich CW9 . . . . .104 A5
  Stoak CH2 . . . . .96 A7
Bunbury Comm CW6 . . . . .168 E2
BUNBURY COMMONS 169 A2
Bunbury Ct CW6 . . . . .146 D1
Bunbury Dr WA7 . . . . .49 C6
Bunbury Gn CH65 . . . . .70 D2
BUNBURY HEATH. 185 D8
Bunbury La CW6 . . . . .185 E8
Bunbury Mill★ CW6 . . . . . .169 A1
Bunbury Rd CW6 . . . . .169 B3
Bunce La SK11 . . . . .133 B4
Bunce St CH1 . . . . .237 A1
Bungalow Rd WA12 . . . . . . .2 E1
Bungalows The
  Adderley TF9 . . . . .234 B3
  Dunham-on-the-Hill WA6 . .97 E6
  Thornton Hough CH63 . . . .42 B6
Bunhill Fields WA8 . . . . . . .13 B3
Bunnells Croft WA16 . . . . . 32 A1
BUNSLEY BANK 230 D5
Bunsley Bank CW3 . . . . . . .230 C6
Bunting Cl **6** WA3 . . . . .3 E8
Buntingford Rd WA4 . . . . . 17 C3
Bunts La CW12 . . . . .156 E1
Burdett Rd CH66 . . . . .69 E2
Burfield Dr WA4 . . . . 26 D7
Burford Ave Bramhall SK7. . .35 D5
  Newcastle-under-Lyme
  ST5 . . . . .210 D1
Burford Cl SK9 . . . . .59 E5
Burford Cres SK9 . . . . .59 E5
Burford La WA13 . . . . .19 C2
Burgamot La CW9 . . . . .78 D8
Burganey Ct CH4 . . . . .162 D2
Burgess Ave WA4 . . . . .16 B2
Burgess Cl CW5 . . . . .205 B4
Burgess Dr CH1 . . . . .117 A5
Burgess Gr ST7 . . . . .193 B3
Burgess La WA6 . . . . .101 B6
Burgess Pl **5** CW8 . . . . . .103 E8
Burgess St SK10 . . . . .112 F8
Burges St CH2 . . . . .118 F3
Burjen Way CW1 . . . . .190 B6
Burkhardt Dr WA12 . . . . . . .2 E3
BURLAND 203 C7
Burland Cl WA7 . . . . .22 F1
Burland Gn CW5 . . . . .203 B1
Burland Gr CW7 . . . . .126 A2
BURLAND LOWER
  GREEN 203 A7
Burland Rd Halewood L26 . . 21 A6
  Newcastle-under-Lyme
  ST5 . . . . .210 D2
BURLAND UPPER
  GREEN 203 B8
Burlea Cl CW2 . . . . .189 E5
Burlea Dr CW2 . . . . .206 B5
BURLEYDAM 228 B1
Burleydam Rd SY13 . . . . . .233 A3
Burleyhurst La SK9, WA16 . .59 B7
Burley La WA4 . . . . .27 C4
Burlington Dr **4** WA5 . . . .15 A7
Burmarsh La WA8 . . . . .22 B5
Burnell Cl CW5 . . . . .204 F3
Burnell Rd CH65 . . . . .70 E4
Burnet Cl WA2 . . . . .9 C2
Burnet Pl CW12 . . . . .155 F2
Burnfell WA3 . . . . .3 E7
Burnham Cl Culcheth WA3 . .4 E4
  Warrington WA5 . . . . .14 F5
  Widnes WA8 . . . . 12 C5
Burnham Rd CH4 . . . . .140 F6
Burnsall Ave WA3 . . . . .3 F8
Burnsall Dr WA8 . . . . .12 C3
Burns Cl
  Ellesmere Port CH66 . . . . .69 E4
  Rode Heath ST7 . . . . .193 E8
Burns Cres WA8 . . . . .22 F8
Burns Dr CW1 . . . . .190 F4
Burns Gr WA2. . . . . .8 C2
Burnside WA15 . . . . .32 D7
Burnside Ave WA4 . . . . .16 D1
Burnside Cl SK9 . . . . .60 C6
Burnside Way
  Northwich CW8 . . . . .103 D8
  Winnington CW8 . . . . .78 D1
Burns Rd CW12 . . . . .157 A2
Burns Way CH1 . . . . .117 E6
Burnt Acre SK11 . . . . .84 B3
Burnt Mill La WA8 . . . . .21 D5
Burnwood Gr ST7 . . . . .195 B2
Burran Rd M22 . . . . 33 D8
Burrough Cl WA3 . . . . .9 F3
Burrows Hill CW8 . . . . .103 B7
Burrows La WA6 . . . . .73 F2
Burrows The CW8 . . . . .101 D5
Bursar Cl WA12 . . . . .2 D4
Burslam St CW12. . . . . .156 E2

BURTON Duddon 144 F4
  Neston 67 D1
Burton Ave CW6 . . . . .146 C3
  Widnes WA8 . . . . .12 F3
Burton Dr SK12 . . . . 36 D4
Burton Gn CH66 . . . . 69 D4
Burton Gr CW1 . . . . .173 B1
BURTON GREEN 161 C1
Burton Hall Rd LL12 . . . . . .161 E1
Burton La CW6 . . . . .144 A4
Burton Lodge La CW4 . . . . .144 F3
Burton Manor Coll CH64 . . 67 C3
Burton Mere Fisheries RSPB
  Reserve ★ CH64 . . . . .92 D8
Burton Mill Wood Nature
  Reserve ★ CH64 . . . . .67 C2
Burton Rd Blacon CH1 . . . . .117 E5
  Duddon CH3 . . . . .144 E6
  Neston CH64 . . . . .66 F6
  Warrington WA2 . . . . .8 D1
Burton Sq CW6 . . . . .146 C2
BURTONWOOD 6 E1
Burtonwood Com Prim Sch
  WA5 . . . . .6 E7
Burtonwood Ind Ctr WA5 . . .6 E7
Burtonwood Rd
  Warrington, Great Sankey
  WA5 . . . . 15 C6
  Warrington, Kingswood WA5 . .7 A2
BURWARDSLEY 184 B5
Burwardsley Ct CH3 . . . . . .184 A6
Burwardsley Rd CH3 . . . . . .166 D1
Burwardsley Way CW9 . . . .103 E4
Bushell Cl CH64 . . . . .66 F7
Bushell Rd CH64 . . . . .66 F7
Bushells La WA6 . . . . .99 B8
Bush Rd CH3 . . . . .142 E7
Bush Way CH60 . . . . .40 E8
Butler Way CW5 . . . . .204 E3
Butley Cl Macclesfield SK10 . 87 D3
  Middlewich CW10 . . . . . .151 C7
Butley Hall SK10 . . . . .87 A7
Butley Lanes SK10 . . . . .61 F1
BUTLEY TOWN 87 C8
Butterbache Rd CH3 . . . . . .142 A6
Butter Brook **7** WA5 . . . . .14 E8
Butterbur Cl CH3 . . . . .142 A6
Buttercup Cl WA5 . . . . .15 E3
Buttercup Cres CW5 . . . . . . 78 C1
Buttercup Rd CW11 . . . . . .174 E6
Buttercup Way WA16 . . . . . .79 F6
Buttermarket St WA1. . . . . .16 B5
Buttermere Ave
  Ellesmere Port CH65 . . . . .70 C3
  Warrington WA2 . . . . .8 C3
Buttermere Cl WA6 . . . . . . .74 D8
Buttermere Cres WA2 . . . . . .8 C3
Buttermere Ct CW12 . . . . . .156 A2
Buttermere Dr
  Alderley Edge SK9 . . . . . . .83 F7
  Altrincham WA15 . . . . .32 D6
  Crewe CW1 . . . . 173 B1
Buttermere Gr WA7 . . . . . . 49 D5
Buttermere Rd
  Partington M31 . . . . .11 E3
  Winsford CW7 . . . . .126 C2
BUTTERS GREEN 210 A2
Butterton La CW1 . . . . .192 B2
Butterworth Rd CW8 . . . . . .78 C2
BUTT GREEN 205 B3
Buttonbush Dr CW5 . . . . . .205 B3
Butts Gn WA5 . . . . .7 A3
Butts The ST7 . . . . .193 D4
Buxton Cl CW1 . . . . .190 E4
Buxton Cl WA5 . . . . 15 A8
Buxton New Rd
  Buxton SK11 . . . . .115 A6
  Macclesfield SK11 . . . . . . .88 E1
  Macclesfield Forest SK11 . .114 D7
Buxton Old Rd
  Congleton CW12 . . . . . . .157 A4
  Disley SK12 . . . . .38 C4
  Macclesfield SK11 . . . . . . .113 D7
Buxton Rd
  Congleton CW12 . . . . . . .157 C6
  High Lane SK6, SK7, SK12 . 37 D8
  Horwich End, New Horwich
  SK23 . . . . .65 E6
  Macclesfield SK10, SK11 . .113 A7
  New Mills SK22, SK23. . . . .39 C4
  Whaley Bridge SK23. . . . . .39 E1
Buxton Road W SK12 . . . . . 38 B5
Bye Pass The CH3 . . . . .119 E2
Byland Ave SK8 . . . . .35 B6
Byland Cl WA8 . . . . .13 C5
Bylands Cl SK12 . . . . 36 D4
BYLEY 129 A7
Byley La CW4, CW10 . . . . . .129 B3
Byley Prim Sch CW10 . . . . .129 B7
Byley Rd
  Middlewich CW10 . . . . . .128 E3
  Puddinglake CW10 . . . . . .129 A8
  Rudheath Woods CW10 . .106 B2
Byley Way CW7 . . . . .126 B1
Byng Ave M44 . . . . .11 D4
By-Pass Rd Chester CH1 . . . .93 E4
  Tarvin CH3 . . . . .121 B3
Byrd Gr CW7 . . . . .127 A7
Byron Cl Blacon CH1 . . . . . .117 F6
  Crewe CW1 . . . . 190 F4
  Middlewich CW10 . . . . . .151 D5
  Rode Heath ST7 . . . . .193 E8
  Sandbach CW11 . . . . .174 D6
Byron Ct WA2 . . . . .8 C2
Byron's La SK11 . . . . .112 E5
Byrons St SK11 . . . . .112 D6

Byron St WA7 . . . . 23 A1
Byron Way CW2 . . . . .190 A1
Byron Wlk CW5 . . . . .204 D6
Bythom Cl CH3 . . . . .142 E7

C

Cable Dr WA6 . . . . 73 A2
Cabot Cl WA5 . . . . .7 C1
Cabul Cl WA2 . . . . 16 D7
Cadet Cl WA8 . . . . 13 C4
CADISHEAD 11 E5
Cadishead Prim Sch M44 . .11 E6
Cadishead Way M44 . . . . . .11 F6
Cadnant Cl CH1 . . . . .117 D3
Cadnant Ct/Llys Cadnant
  CH4 . . . . .139 D5
Cadshaw Cl WA3 . . . . .9 C5
Cae Lica La SY14 . . . . .222 D5
Caer Castell LL13 . . . . .196 B8
Caerleon Cl CW7 . . . . .149 A8
Caerllew LL13 . . . . .180 E1
Caernarvon Ave CW7 . . . . .149 B7
Caernarvon Cl WA7 . . . . . . .23 F2
Caernarvon Ct **4** CH65 . . . 70 D2
Caernarvon Rd CW2 . . . . . .205 B3
Caesars Cl WA7 . . . . .23 E2
Cairn Brae WA12 . . . . .2 C4
Cairns Cres CH1 . . . . .117 D4
Cairo St WA1 . . . . 16 B5
Caister Way CW7 . . . . .149 C7
Caithness Ct **3** WA7 . . . . . .23 B2
Calamine St SK11 . . . . .112 E6
Calday Gr WA11 . . . . .1 A8
Caldbeck Ave WA2 . . . . .8 D2
Caldecott Cl CH2 . . . . .118 C6
Caldecott Cl CH1 . . . . .118 C6
CALDECOTT GREEN 197 C6
Caldene Terr SK23 . . . . .65 E7
Calder Cl Bollington SK10 . . .87 F8
  Poynton SK12 . . . . 36 D2
  Widnes WA8 . . . . 13 F3
Calderfield Cl WA4 . . . . .26 B8
Calder Way **2** CH66 . . . . . .69 C5
Caldicott Ave CH62 . . . . . . 43 D7
Caldicott Cl **2** CW7 . . . . . .149 C7
Caldon Cl **5** CW11 . . . . . .174 E4
Caldwell Ave WA5 . . . . .7 F2
Caldwell Cl CW5 . . . . .205 B4
Caldwell Rd WA8 . . . . .23 A7
Caldwell's Gate La CW9 . . . 54 B8
Caldy Cl CH2 . . . . .118 D5
Caldy Dr CH66 . . . . 69 D4
Caldy Rd Alsager ST7 . . . . .193 C4
  Handforth SK9 . . . . 34 D3
Caldy Valley Rd
  Chester CH3 . . . . .142 B7
  Huntington CH3 . . . . .142 A4
Cale Rd SK22 . . . . .39 D8
Calf Hey **8** WA5 . . . . .14 E8
Calico La SK23 . . . . .39 D4
California Cl WA5 . . . . .15 C8
Cal La SY14 . . . . .222 F1
Callands Cty Prim Sch
  WA5 . . . . .7 E2
Callands Rd WA5. . . . . .7 D2
Callender Gdns
  1 Alvanley WA6 . . . . .73 A2
  Helsby WA6 . . . . .73 A2
Callender Way WA6 . . . . . . .73 A2
Callin Ct CH1 . . . . .237 A2
Calmington La WA7 . . . . . . .24 F4
CALROFOLD 88 C2
Calrofold Dr ST5 . . . . .210 D1
Calrofold La SK10 . . . . .88 C2
Calstock Cl WA5 . . . . 14 E3
CALVELEY 169 E2
Calveley Ave CH62 . . . . .43 F4
Calveley Cl CW9 . . . . .103 E5
Calveley Green La CW6,
  CW7. . . . . .170 C4
Calveley Hall La CW5,
  CW6. . . . . .170 A2
Calveley Prim Sch CW6. . . .170 B2
Calveley Rd Halewood L26 . 21 A6
  Macclesfield SK10 . . . . . . .86 F1
Calveley Way **1** CW7 . . . . .126 B1
Calverley Cl **3** SK9 . . . . . .60 C8
Calverly Cl WA7 . . . . .50 C5
Calver Pk Rd WA2 . . . . .8 A3
Calver Rd WA2 . . . . .8 A3
Calvers WA7 . . . . .23 E1
Camberley Cl SK7 . . . . .36 A7
Camberwell Park Rd WA8 . 13 D4
Camborne Ave SK10 . . . . . .111 E8
Camborne Cl
  Congleton CW12 . . . . . . .178 E8
  Runcorn WA7 . . . . .50 C6
Cambourne Rd WA5. . . . . . .6 F6
Cambrai Ave WA4 . . . . .16 C2
Cambrian Ave CH3 . . . . . . .119 B2
Cambrian Cl CH66 . . . . .69 A6
Cambrian Ct CH1 . . . . .118 B2
Cambrian Rd CH1 . . . . .118 B2
Cambrian Villas CH3 . . . . . .165 C2
Cambrian Way CW7 . . . . . .149 B8
Cambridge Ave
  Macclesfield SK11 . . . . . . .112 B7
  Wilmslow SK9 . . . . .59 F7
  Winsford CW7 . . . . .126 A1
Cambridge Cl
  Biddulph ST8 . . . . .179 C1
  Warrington WA4 . . . . .26 B7
Cambridge Ct **7** CH65. . . . 70 C5

Cambridge Gdns
Helsby WA6 . . . . **73** D4
Warrington WA4 . . . . **26** C6
Cambridge Rd
Bebington CH62 . . . .**43** E8
Chester CH2. . . . . **118** F5
Ellesmere Port CH65 . . . . . **70** D5
Macclesfield SK11 . . . . . . **112** B7
Cambridge Road Com Prim Sch 🕮 CH65 . . . . **70** C5
Cambridge St
Runcorn WA7 . . . . **23** C2
Widnes WA8. . . . .**23** B7
Camden Ct WA7. . . . . . . **24** D1
Camden Rd CH65. . . . . . . **70** A5
Camden St CW1. . . . . . . **190** D4
Camellia Dr WA5. . . . .**15** E4
Camellia Gdns WA9 . . . .**6** B7
Camelot Cl WA12. . . . .**1** F4
Camelot Gr CW2 . . . . . . **206** C4
Camelot Way WA7 . . . . . . **50** A8
Cameron Ave
Runcorn WA7 . . . .**48** E8
Shavington CW2. . . . . . . **206** B3
Cameron Ct WA2. . . . .**8** A4
Cameron Rd WA8 . . . . **23** A8
Camm St CW2 . . . . **190** D2
Camomile Wlk 🟥 M31. . . .**11** F3
Campbell Ave WA7. . . . . . **49** A8
Campbell Cl
Congleton CW12 . . . . . . **157** A4
Haslington CW1 . . . . **191** C4
Macclesfield SK10 . . . . . . **87** A1
Northwich CW9 . . . . **103** F4
Campbell Cres WA5 . . . . . .**14** F6
Campbeltown Cl 🟥 WA7. . .**22** F2
Campden Way SK9 . . . . . . **34** D4
Camp Hill Dr CW5 . . . . . **204** C7
Campion Cl
Huntington CH3 . . . . **142** A6
Warrington WA3 . . . .**9** C4
Campsey Ash WA8 . . . .**12** F4
Campus Dr WA2 . . . . **22** E2
Camrose Cl WA7 . . . . **49** C6
Camsley La WA13. . . . . . . **18** B3
Canaan WA3. . . . .**4** C8
Canada Cl WA2 . . . .**9** A2
Canadian Ave CH2 . . . . . . **119** A3
Canal Bank WA13 . . . . **18** D3
Canal Bridge Ent Pk
CH65. . . . . **70** D6
Canal Cotts CW5 . . . . **187** D6
Canal Mews SK6 . . . . **37** E7
Canal Rd Congleton CW12 . **156** F1
Hooton CH62. . . . .**44** B6
Canal Reach WA7 . . . . **24** C2
Canalside CH65 . . . . **70** D6
Canal Side Barnton CW8. . . .**78** B2
Chester CH1. . . . . **237** C3
Macclesfield SK11 . . . . . . **112** F7
Moore WA4 . . . . **25** C5
Runcorn WA7 . . . .**48** D7
Warrington WA4 . . . . **17** C1
Whaley Bridge SK23. . . . . . **39** F1
Canalside Cotts CW11 . . . **175** C3
Canal Side Cotts WA7 . . . . .**50** F6
Canalside Ind Est CH65 . . . **70** D7
Canalside Way CW10 . . . . **128** B2
Canal St Chester CH1 . . . . . **237** A3
Congleton CW12 . . . . . . **156** E2
Macclesfield SK10 . . . . . . **112** E8
Newton-le-Willows WA12 . . . .**1** F4
Runcorn WA7 . . . .**23** B2
Whaley Bridge SK23. . . . . . **65** E8
Canal Terr CW10 . . . . **151** D8
Canberra Ave WA2 . . . .**8** D3
Canberra Rd SK7. . . . . **35** F5
Canberra Sq WA2 . . . .**8** D2
Canberra Way 🟥 WA1 . . . **117** D4
Candelan Way WA16 . . . . . **29** C4
Candle La CW3. . . . . **232** B2
Candleston Cl WA5. . . . .**7** E1
Candy La SK10 . . . . **62** C8
Canford Cl Crewe CW1 . . . **190** B8
Warrington WA5 . . . . **15** C6
Cannell Ct WA7. . . . . **50** A6
Cannell St 🟥 WA5. . . . . . . **15** D4
Canning St CH1. . . . . **237** A3
Canniswood Rd WA11. . . . . . .**1** A6
Cann La CW9 . . . . **55** A6
Cann Lane N WA4 . . . . **26** E5
Cann Lane S WA4 . . . . **26** F4
Cannock Cl CH66. . . . .**94** E8
Cannonbury Cl WA7. . . . . . **50** A8
Cannon St CH65. . . . . **70** A5
Cannon Way CH4. . . . . . . **161** A7
Canon Dr WA14. . . . . **31** B8
Canons Rd WA5 . . . . **15** D6
Canon St WA7 . . . .**22** F3
Canon Ward Way WA11. . . **191** E5
Canon Wilson Cl WA11 . . . . .**1** D6
Canterbury Cl CH66 . . . .**94** E8
Canterbury Rd
Blacon CH1 . . . . **117** F5
Widnes WA8. . . . . **22** C8
Canterbury St WA4. . . . . . **16** C4
Cantilever Bridge WA4 . . . .**16** E2
Cantilever Gdns WA4. . . . . .**16** E2
Cantilever South East Approach WA4 . . . . **16** C3
Cantley Cl WA7. . . . . **49** D6
Canton Pl WA8. . . . . **103** D7
Canton St CW11. . . . . **112** D6
Canton Wlks SK11. . . . . . . **112** D6
Canute Pl 🟥 WA16. . . . . . . **57** A2

Cape La WA16 . . . . **105** F7
Capeland Cl CH4 . . . . **140** E5
Capel Way CW5 . . . . **204** D6
CAPENHURST **94** A8
Capenhurst Ave
Crewe CW2 . . . . **190** A3
Warrington WA2 . . . .**9** A2
Capenhurst CE Prim Sch
CH1. . . . .**94** B8
Capenhurst Cl SK12 . . . . . . **36** F4
Capenhurst Gdns CH66 . . . **69** D1
Capenhurst La
Capenhurst CH1. . . . .**94** B8
Ellesmere Port CH65 . . . . . **70** A3
Woodbank CH1 . . . .**93** F7
Capenhurst Sta CH1. . . . . . **69** C1
Capenhurst Tech Pk CH1. . .**69** B1
Capesthorne Cl
Alsager ST7. . . . . **193** C3
Hazel Grove SK7. . . . . **36** F8
Holmes Chapel CW4. . . . . **130** B3
Northwich CW9 . . . . **103** F4
Sandbach CW11. . . . . . . **175** D4
Widnes WA8. . . . .**22** E8
Capesthorne Hall★
SK11 . . . . **110** A6
Capesthorne Rd
Crewe CW2 . . . . **189** F3
Hazel Grove SK7. . . . . **36** F8
High Lane SK6. . . . . **37** E7
Warrington WA2 . . . .**8** D2
Waverton CH3 . . . . **143** B6
Wilmslow SK9 . . . . **59** E5
Capesthorne Way SK11. . . **112** F7
Capitol Wlk CW12 . . . . . . **156** D2
Cappelle Rise ST7. . . . . . **209** D1
Capper Cl Kidsgrove ST7 . . **195** A2
🟥 Stud Green CW11 . . . . **152** C2
Cappers Cl CW11 . . . . **176** C2
Capper's La CW5, CW6 . . . **186** C3
Carden Ave CW7 . . . . **126** B1
Cardenbrook Gr 🟩 SK9. . . . **34** D2
Carden Cl WA3. . . . .**9** D4
Carden La Clutton CH3. . . . **182** D1
Hobb Hill SY14 . . . . **198** B5
Cardeston Cl WA7. . . . .**49** F3
Cardiff Cl CH66 . . . .**94** E8
Cardigan Cl
Macclesfield SK11 . . . . . . **112** A8
Warrington WA5 . . . .**7** D2
Cardinal Newman RC High Sch WA4 . . . .**16** F5
Cardway Bsns Pk ST7. . . . **193** F3
Carey St WA8 . . . . **13** B1
Carina Pk WA5. . . . .**7** B2
Carisbrook Ave SK10 . . . . . **87** E2
Carisbrook Dr CW7. . . . . . **149** C7
Carisbrooke Cl CW2 . . . . . **205** E8
Carleton Rd SK12 . . . . **37** C4
Carlett Bvd CH62. . . . .**43** F5
Carlingford Rd WA4. . . . . . .**26** B7
Carlisle Cl
Macclesfield SK11 . . . . . . **111** F5
Mobberley WA16 . . . . **58** A4
Winsford CW7 . . . . **126** A1
Carlisle Rd CH1 . . . . **117** E5
Carlisle St
🟥 Alderley Edge SK9 . . . . . **60** A1
Crewe CW2 . . . . **190** B2
Warrington WA8 . . . . **26** C8
Carlow Cl L24. . . . . **21** D2
Carlton Ave Bramhall SK7. . . **35** D5
Handforth SK9 . . . . **34** C2
Runcorn WA7 . . . .**23** D2
Saltney CH4 . . . . **140** D6
Carlton Cl
Mickle Trafford CH2 . . . . . **119** E8
Neston CH64 . . . . **41** C2
Carlton Cres CH66. . . . .**69** F8
Carlton Pl CH2 . . . . **119** A4
Carlton Rd Lymm WA13. . . . .**19** B5
Northwich CW9 . . . . **104** B7
Carlton St Warrington WA4. . .**26** C8
Widnes WA8. . . . .**23** A8
Carlton Way M44. . . . . **11** C5
Carlyle Cl ST7. . . . . **193** E8
Carlyle Cres CH66 . . . .**69** E4
Carmarthen Cl
Warrington WA5 . . . .**7** D2
🟥 Winsford CW7 . . . . . . **149** C7
Carmel Cl CH1. . . . . **117** D3
Carmel Ct WA8 . . . . **13** B4
Carmenna Dr SK7. . . . . **35** F7
Carmichael Cl 🟥 M31. . . . . **11** E3
Carnegie Cl SK10. . . . . **87** A1
Carnoustie Cl
Wilmslow SK9 . . . . **60** D8
Winsford CW7 . . . . **126** B2
Carnoustie Dr SK10 . . . . . . **87** D5
Carnoustie Gr WA11. . . . . . .**1** A5
Carol Dr CH60. . . . . **41** C8
Carolina Rd 🟥 WA5 . . . . . . **15** B7
Caroline Ho CH1 . . . . **117** F6
Caroline St Irlam M44. . . . . . **11** F4
Widnes WA8. . . . .**23** B7
Carol St WA4 . . . . **16** D4
Carpenter Gr WA2 . . . .**9** A1
Carpenters Ct SK9 . . . . **60** A1
Carr Brook Cl SK23. . . . . . . **65** E5
Carr Brow SK6 . . . . **38** A7
Carrgreen La WA13 . . . .**19** F6
Carriage Cl L24 . . . . **21** D1
Carriage Dr Biddulph ST8 . . **179** E1
Frodsham WA6. . . . . **74** A6
Northwich CW8 . . . . **103** C5
Carriage Ho 🟥 CW1 . . . . . **190** A5
Carrick Dr CH65. . . . .**70** B2
Carrick Rd CH4 . . . . **141** B7

Carrington Cl WA3. . . . .**9** C4
Carrington Way CW1 . . . . **190** B8
Carrington Wlk WA1 . . . . . . **16** C6
Carr La Alderley Edge SK9 . . **59** D2
Audley ST7. . . . . **209** A1
Golborne WA3 . . . .**4** A7
Golborne, Wash End WN7 . . .**4** E8
Hale L24, WA8 . . . . **21** E4
Carr Mill Mews SK9 . . . . . . **34** B1
Carroll Dr CW2. . . . . **205** F8
Carrs Ct SK9. . . . .**60** B7
Carrs La CH3. . . . . **166** F1
Carr St ST7 . . . . **195** F1
Carrwood Altrincham WA15 .**32** B7
Knutsford WA16. . . . . **57** C1
Carr Wood Ave SK7 . . . . . . **35** E8
Carrwood Cl WA11 . . . .**1** A6
Carrwood Rd SK9 . . . . **59** F8
Carsdale Rd M22. . . . . **33** E8
Carsington Water WA5 . . . . **14** C6
Carson Ave CH65 . . . . **70** D5
Car St CH1. . . . . **237** C3
Carter Ave CW6 . . . . **122** D4
Carter Bench Ho SK10 . . . . **63** A1
Carter Cl CW5 . . . . **204** D6
Carter La SK11. . . . . **84** B4
Carter St CH1 . . . . **237** C3
Cartier Cl WA5. . . . .**7** C1
Cartlake Cl CW5 . . . . **204** C5
Cartledge Cl CW8 . . . . **102** A3
Cartmel Ave WA2 . . . .**8** C3
Cartmel Cl
Holmes Chapel CW4. . . . . **130** A3
Macclesfield SK10 . . . . **87** B2
Warrington WA5 . . . .**7** E2
Winsford CW7 . . . . **126** D2
Cartmel Dr CH66 . . . .**69** F2
Cartmell Cl WA7 . . . .**49** B6
Cartridge La WA4 . . . . **27** C6
Cartwright Cl CW12 . . . . . **156** E6
Cartwright Rd CW1. . . . . . **191** D5
Cartwright St
Runcorn WA7 . . . .**23** C2
Warrington WA5 . . . . **15** E6
Carver Ave CW4. . . . . **130** A6
Carver Cl CW7 . . . . **127** A4
Carver La CW4 . . . . **129** F6
Case Rd WA11 . . . .**1** D6
Casey La CW2. . . . . **206** F4
Cash La WA6. . . . . **72** E2
Cassia Green La CW7 . . . . . **125** D5
Cassia La CW7, CW8 . . . . . **125** E5
Cassley Rd L24. . . . . **21** A3
Casson St CW1. . . . . **190** B5
Castle Bank CW8. . . . . **103** E7
Castle Cl Broughton CH5 . . . **139** B6
Kelsall CW6 . . . . **122** D4
Pulford CH4 . . . . **162** D2
Castle Croft Rd CH4 . . . . . **141** B5
Castle Ct Holt LL13. . . . . . . **196** E8
🟥 Nantwich CW5 . . . . . . **204** E5
Northwich CW8 . . . . **103** E7
Castle Dr Chester CH1 . . . . **237** B1
Ellesmere Port CH65 . . . . . **70** A3
Heswall CH60 . . . . **40** F8
Castle Farm SY14 . . . . **200** E3
CASTLEFIELDS. **23** F2
Castlefields CH3 . . . . **166** C3
Castlefields Avenue E
WA7. . . . . **24** A2
Castlefields Avenue N
WA7. . . . . **23** F2
Castlefields Avenue S
WA7. . . . . **24** A1
Castleford Dr SK10. . . . . . . **86** E6
Castlegate Prestbury SK10 . . **86** E6
Wrexham LL13 . . . . **196** D8
Castlegate Mews SK10 . . . . **86** F6
Castle Gn WA5. . . . .**7** B2
Castlehill CH4. . . . . **162** C2
Castle Hill
Newton-le-Willows WA12 . . . .**2** E4
Prestbury SK10 . . . . **86** E6
Castle Hill Ct SK10 . . . . **86** F7
Castle Hill Farm 🟩 CW8 . . **103** E8
Castle Ho ST7. . . . . **195** C3
Castle Inn Rd CW12 . . . . . **179** C7
Castlemead Wlk CW9. . . . . **103** E4
Castlemere Cl CH4 . . . . . . **139** A3
Castlemere Dr CW1 . . . . . **190** C7
Castle Mews LL13. . . . . . . **196** E8
Castlemilk Ct 🟩 CW7 . . . . **149** B7
Castle Mill La WA15 . . . . . . **32** B5
Castle Park Arts Ctr WA6 . . **74** A8
Castle Prim Sch ST7. . . . . **195** D6
Castle Rd Mow Cop ST7 . . . **195** D7
Runcorn WA7 . . . .**49** F8
Castle Rise Prestbury SK10 . .**86** F6
Runcorn WA7 . . . .**23** D2
Castleshaw Gr 🟥 WA5 . . . . **14** D8
Castle St Chester CH1 . . . . **237** B1
🟥 Crewe CW1. . . . . **190** C4
Holt LL13. . . . . **196** D8
Macclesfield SK11 . . . . . . **112** D8
🟥 Nantwich CW5 . . . . . . **204** E5
Northwich CW8 . . . . **103** F8
Sandbach CW11. . . . . **13** D1
Castleton Dr High Lane SK6 . .**37** F6
Warrington WA1 . . . . **16** E5
CASTLETOWN. **197** D3
Castletown Cl SK10 . . . . . . **87** D4
Castletown La CH3 . . . . . . **197** D2
Castleview Prim Sch
WA7. . . . . **49** D8
Castleview Rd ST7. . . . . . . **195** B3
Castleway WA15 . . . . **32** C7
Castle Way CH4 . . . . **162** A6

Castner Ave WA7. . . . .**48** E7
Catalan Cl CW7 . . . . **127** A1
Catalyst Ind Est WA8. . . . . . **23** A6
Catalyst – Science Discovery Ctr & Mus★ WA8 . . . . . . **23** A5
Catalyst Trade Pk WA8 . . . . **23** A6
Catchpenny La SK11. . . . . **108** F3
Catford CH14. . . . . **12** C2
Catfoss Cl WA2 . . . .**8** E1
Cathcart Gn CH3 . . . . **119** F5
Catherine Ct/Llys Catrin
CH5 . . . . **139** B6
Catherine St Chester CH1 . . **118** B2
Crewe CW2 . . . . **190** D2
Macclesfield SK11 . . . . . . **112** C8
Warrington WA5 . . . . **16** A7
Widnes WA8. . . . .**23** A7
Catherine Way WA12. . . . . . .**2** B2
Catholic High Sch The
CH4. . . . . **141** D6
Catterall Ave WA2. . . . .**8** D2
Cattle Way CW2 . . . . **206** D7
Caughall Rd CH2. . . . .**95** E2
Caunce Ave Golborne WA3 . . .**3** A7
Haydock WA11 . . . .**1** B6
Newton-le-Willows WA12 . . . .**2** C1
Causeway Ave WA4 . . . . . . **16** A7
Causeway Park WA4. . . . . . **16** C3
Cavalier Dr CH1. . . . . **117** E6
Cavalier Rd CW5 . . . . **204** C7
Cavalry Cl CH3 . . . . **142** C5
Cavan Dr WA11 . . . .**1** D7
Cavell Dr CH65. . . . . **70** A4
Cavendish Ave WA3 . . . .**9** F5
Cavendish Cl
🟥 Macclesfield SK10. . . . . **87** D3
Warrington WA5 . . . . **15** D7
Winsford CW7 . . . . **149** A8
Cavendish Cres ST7 . . . . . **193** D5
Cavendish Ct
Chester CH4. . . . . **141** A5
Widnes WA8. . . . .**12** F1
Cavendish Farm Rd WA7. . . **49** A5
Cavendish Gdns CH65 . . . . **70** A4
Cavendish High Sch WA7 . . **49** C5
Cavendish Mews SK9. . . . . **60** A6
Cavendish Pl WA3. . . . .**9** F5
Cavendish Rd
Chester CH4. . . . . **141** B6
Crewe CW2 . . . . **189** E5
Hazel Grove SK7. . . . . **36** E8
Cavendish St 🟨 WA7 . . . . . .**22** F2
Cavendish Way CW4. . . . . **130** A3
Caversham Cl WA4. . . . . . . **26** E6
Cawdor Dr CH3 . . . . **119** A2
Cawdor St Runcorn WA7. . . .**22** F3
Warrington WA4 . . . . **26** C8
Cawfield Ave WA8 . . . . **12** D1
Cawley Ave WA3 . . . .**4** E4
Cawley La SK10 . . . . **62** E7
Cawley St
🟦 Macclesfield SK11. . . . . **112** E7
Runcorn WA7 . . . .**23** A1
Cawood Cl CH66 . . . .**69** B5
Cawthorne Ave WA4 . . . . . . **17** A2
Caxton Cl
Ellesmere Port CH66 . . . . . **69** E4
Widnes WA8. . . . .**12** C3
Cecil Rd ST8 . . . . **179** C2
Cecil Rigby Cl 🟥 CW11 . . . **175** B6
Cecil St CH3 . . . . **119** A1
Cedab Rd CH65 . . . . **70** C6
Cedar Ave Alsager ST7 . . . . **193** D3
Aston WA7 . . . .**50** B4
Connah's Quay CH5 . . . . . . **91** C1
Ellesmere Port CH66 . . . . . **69** D6
Golborne WA3 . . . .**3** F7
Kidsgrove ST7 . . . . **194** D1
Runcorn WA7 . . . .**49** C7
Widnes WA8. . . . .**13** B4
Cedar Cl
Connah's Quay CH5 . . . . . **116** A7
Holmes Chapel CW4. . . . . **130** D4
Lostock Gralam CW9 . . . . . **80** A3
Middlewich CW10 . . . . . . **151** E6
Poynton SK12. . . . . **36** E3
Sandbach CW11. . . . . . . **175** C5
Cedar Cres Audley ST7 . . . . **209** F1
Newton-le-Willows WA12 . . . .**2** D2
Cedar Ct Alsager ST7 . . . . . **193** D3
Congleton CW12 . . . . . . **178** F8
Culcheth WA3. . . . .**4** F1
Willaston CW5 . . . . **205** D6
Cedardale Dr CH66 . . . .**94** F8
Cedardale Pk WA8. . . . .**13** E4
Cedar Dr Barnton CW8. . . . . .**78** A4
Chester CH2. . . . . **119** B4
Cedarfield Rd WA13. . . . . . .**19** B4
Cedar Gr Chester CH2 . . . . . **119** B4
Haydock WA11 . . . .**1** E7
Macclesfield SK11 . . . . . . **112** D5
Nantwich CW5 . . . . **205** A5
Neston CH64 . . . . **66** F8
Warrington WA1 . . . . **17** A7
Warrington, Latchford WA4 . . **16** D3
Winsford CW7 . . . . **127** A1
Cedar Ho CH3. . . . . **142** B8
Cedar Lo SK9 . . . . **35** F7
Cedar Mews CH1. . . . . **117** E4
Cedar Pk CH3 . . . . **119** C3
Cedar Rd
Newcastle-under-Lyme
ST5. . . . . **210** D1
Partington M31 . . . . **11** E3
Warrington WA5 . . . . **14** F6
Weaverham CW8 . . . . **102** C8

Cedars SK9 . . . .**59** F6
Cedars Cl CH2 . . . . **120** A8
Cedar Sq
Alderley Park SK10. . . . . . . **85** B2
Alderley Park SK10. . . . . . . **85** B2
Cedar St WA12. . . . .**2** C1
Cedars The Alsager ST7 . . **193** C3
Mobberley WA16 . . . . **58** E2
Nantwich CW5 . . . . **204** D5
🟨 Northwich CW9. . . . . . **103** E6
Cedarway Bollington SK10. . . **88** A7
Heswall CH60 . . . .**41** B5
Wilmslow SK9 . . . . **59** F5
Cedar Way CW2 . . . . **206** B3
Cedarways WA4 . . . . **26** D5
Cedarwood CW8 . . . . **101** C5
Cedarwood Ct CW6 . . . . . **146** C3
Cefny Cotts LL12 . . . . **161** B5
Celandine Cl CH3 . . . . **142** A7
Celandine Way
🟥 Nantwich CW5 . . . . . . **204** C3
St Helens WA9 . . . .**6** B7
Celendine Cl CW11. . . . . . **174** C6
Celyn Cres CH4 . . . . **140** D5
Cement Pl CH1. . . . . **237** B3
Cemetery Rd CW2. . . . . . . **207** B5
Cemlyn Cl CH1. . . . . **117** C3
Centenary Cl CH4 . . . . **139** D3
Centenary Ho WA7 . . . . . . **49** C8
Centenary Pl WA12. . . . . . **156** E5
Central Ave Alsager CW2 . . **192** F1
Ellesmere Port CH65 . . . . . **70** C4
Warrington WA2 . . . . **16** C8
Warrington, Latchford WA4 . .**16** B3
Central Dr Barnton CW8. . . . **78** A3
Gatley SK8 . . . . **34** D8
Haydock WA11 . . . .**1** B6
Central Expressway WA7 . . **49** E7
Central Gr CW9 . . . . **104** D6
Central Pl SK9 . . . .**60** B7
Central Rd
Northwich CW9 . . . . **104** D7
Partington M31 . . . . **11** F3
Warrington WA4 . . . . **16** C3
Central St ST7 . . . . **195** B6
Central Trad Pk CH4 . . . . . **140** E7
Central Way
Newton-le-Willows WA12 . . . .**2** E1
Warrington WA2 . . . . **16** B6
Centre Ct ST7 . . . . **193** E4
Centre Park WA1 . . . . **16** A4
Centre Park Sq WA1. . . . . . **16** A4
Centurion Cl WA3 . . . .**9** C4
Centurion Row WA7. . . . . . .**23** F2
Centurion Way CW10 . . . . **128** D2
Century Rd ST5 . . . . **210** F2
Century Way SK10. . . . .**87** F2
Cestria Cl CW11. . . . . **174** D7
Chads Gn CW5 . . . . **206** A1
Chadwell Ct CW2 . . . . **207** E4
Chadwick Ave Croft WA3 . . . .**9** B7
Warrington WA1 . . . . **16** E1
Chadwick Cl SK9 . . . . **34** C1
Chadwicke Cl CW5 . . . . . . **204** F4
Chadwick Fields Orch
CW10 . . . . **151** B6
Chadwick La WA8. . . . . **13** C3
Chadwick Pl WA3 . . . .**9** E5
Chadwick Rd
Middlewich CW10 . . . . . . **151** C6
Runcorn WA7 . . . .**23** F3
Chadwick Terr SK10. . . . . . .**87** C6
Chaffinch Cl
Congleton CW12 . . . . . . **156** E1
Warrington WA3 . . . .**9** E5
Chaffinch Way CW7 . . . . . **149** D6
Chaigeley Sch WA4. . . . .**17** F4
Chain Maker's Row CH4 . . **140** E7
Chaise Mdw WA13 . . . . . . **19** C5
Chaley Rise CH3 . . . . **182** D1
Chalfield Ave CH66. . . . . . . **69** C5
Chalfield Cl
🟥 Ellesmere Port CH66. . . . **69** C5
Wistaston CW2 . . . . **206** B7
Chalfont Cl WA4 . . . .**26** C4
Chalfont Cres CW2 . . . . . . **207** B2
Chalfont St WA16 . . . . **57** C3
Chalgrave Cl WA8. . . . . **13** F3
Chalkwell Dr CH60 . . . . **41** C7
Challinor St CH3 . . . . **119** A1
Chamber Brook La WA6 . . . **75** C2
Chamberlain Ct CW1 . . . . **191** C4
Chamberlain Dr SK9. . . . . . **34** D1
Chambers St CW2 . . . . . . **190** D2
Chance Hall La CW12,
ST7. . . . . **177** C3
Chancel La SK9 . . . .**60** D8
Chancellor Rd WA7 . . . . . . **24** D5
Chancery La Alsager ST7 . . **193** B3
Bollington SK10. . . . . **88** B7
Chandlers Ct WA7. . . . .**22** E1
Chandler Way WA3. . . . .**3** E8
Chandos Cl CH4. . . . . **141** E6
Change La CH64 . . . .**68** B8
Channel The CH1. . . . .**95** B4
Chantler Ave WA4. . . . .**16** E4
Chantry Cl SK12. . . . . **38** E5
Chantry Ct Chester CH1. . . . **117** E2
Crewe CW1 . . . . **190** D4
Macclesfield SK11 . . . . . . **112** D5
Chantry Fold SK12 . . . . **38** E6
Chantry Rd SK12. . . . . **38** E6
Chantry The CW6 . . . . **169** E2
Chantry Wlk CH60 . . . . **41** A6
Chapel Ave WA6. . . . . **75** C2
Chapel Bank ST7. . . . . **195** D6
Chapel By-Pass SK23. . . . . .**39** F1

Chapel Cl Audlem CW3 . . . 229 F3
Cholmondeston CW7 . . . . . 170 F4
Comberbach CW9 . . . . 78 D7
Ellesmere Port CH65 . . . . . . 70 C7
Mount Pleasant ST7 . . . . . . 195 B6
Saughall CH1 . . . . 94 A1
Waverton CH3 . . . . 143 A5
Chapel Cotts CH3 . . . . 143 A5
Chapel Croft SK11 . . . . 84 B3
Chapel Cross Rd WA2 . . . . . . 9 A2
Chapel Ct Northwich CW9 . 103 F7
Wilmslow SK9 . . . . 60 A6
Chapel Dr WA15 . . . . 32 C7
Chapelfields WA6 . . . . 74 A8
Chapel Gn CW6 . . . . 122 C5
Chapel House La CH64 . . . . 93 A7
Chapel House Lane S
CH64 . . . . 93 A7
Chapel House Mews 5
WA3 . . . . 3 D8
Chapel La
Acton Bridge CW8 . . . . 76 E4
Aldford CH3 . . . . 164 D5
Allostock WA16 . . . . 106 E3
Altrincham WA15 . . . . 32 C7
Appleton Thorn WA4 . . . . 27 B4
Audley ST7 . . . . 209 D2
Burtonwood WA5 . . . . 6 F6
Chester CH3 . . . . 119 A1
Crewe CW1 . . . . 173 D1
Dutton WA4 . . . . 77 B7
Hargrave CH3 . . . . 144 A1
Harriseahead ST7 . . . . 195 E4
Hollins Green WA3 . . . . 10 F1
Holt LL13 . . . . 196 D8
Kingsley WA6 . . . . 75 C2
Ledsham CH66 . . . . 68 F1
Manley WA6, CH3 . . . . 98 F3
Mere WA16 . . . . 30 B4
Milton Green CH3 . . . . 165 B2
Moulton CW9 . . . . 126 E8
Norton in Hales TF9 . . . . . . 236 C2
Partington M31 . . . . 11 F2
Poulton CH4 . . . . 163 B2
Rainow SK10 . . . . 88 E5
Ravensmoor CW5 . . . . 203 D2
Rode Heath ST7 . . . . 193 F7
Saighton CH3 . . . . 142 E1
Threapwood SY14 . . . . 222 E8
Warrington WA4 . . . . 26 C8
Widnes WA8 . . . . 12 C4
Wilmslow SK9 . . . . 60 A6
Windyharbour SK11 . . . . . . 109 D2
Woodbank CH1 . . . . 93 E8
Chapel Lodge CH1 . . . . . . 237 C3
Chapelmere Cl CW11 . . . . 174 E7
Chapelmere Ct CW1 . . . . . 190 C7
Chapel Mews
Alsager ST7 . . . . 193 C3
Ellesmere Port CH65 . . . . 70 B4
Elton CH2 . . . . 72 B3
1 Nantwich CW5 . . . . 204 E5
Chapel Rd
Alderley Edge SK9 . . . . 60 A1
Horwich End SK23 . . . . 65 E5
Ollerton WA16 . . . . 82 F6
Warrington WA5 . . . . 14 E3
Wilmslow SK9 . . . . 61 A8
Winsford CW7 . . . . 126 F1
Chapel Rise SY14 . . . . 213 B3
Chapel Row
Barbridge CW5 . . . . 187 D6
Nantwich CW5 . . . . 204 D5
Chapel St
7 Alderley Edge SK9 . . . . . . 60 A1
Audley ST7 . . . . 209 E3
Bollington SK10 . . . . 88 B8
Chester CH3 . . . . 237 C3
Congleton CW12 . . . . 156 D2
Crewe CW2 . . . . 190 D3
Haydock WA11 . . . . 1 E6
Holt LL13 . . . . 196 D8
Kidsgrove ST7 . . . . 194 D2
Macclesfield SK11 . . . . 112 D6
Moulton CW9 . . . . 126 E8
Mount Pleasant ST7 . . . . . . 195 B6
New Mills SK22 . . . . 39 B6
Newton-le-Willows WA12 . . . . 2 B3
Northwich CW8 . . . . 103 E7
Sandbach CW11 . . . . 175 B6
Sandbach, Wheelock
CW11 . . . . 175 A3
Weaverham CW8 . . . . 77 C1
Whaley Bridge SK23 . . . . 65 E8
Widnes WA8 . . . . 23 A7
Wincham CW9 . . . . 79 C3
Chapel Terr WA3 . . . . 4 B8
Chapel View
Bebington CH62 . . . . 44 A6
Helsby WA6 . . . . 73 B2
Chapel Wlk WA3 . . . . 4 B8
Chapel Wlks
Broomedge WA13 . . . . 19 D1
Cheadle SK8 . . . . 35 B6
Chapel Yd WA2 . . . . 16 A6
Chapman Cl WA8 . . . . 12 D4
Charcoal Rd WA14 . . . . 20 F3
Charity La SK11 . . . . 113 F8
Charlcote Cres CW2 . . . . . 206 C8
Charlecote Rd SK12 . . . . . . 36 F4
Charles Ave
Davenham CW9 . . . . 103 F2
Warrington WA5 . . . . 14 F6
Charles Barnett Rd
CW11 . . . . 191 F7
Charles Bennion Rd ST7 . 193 B5
Charles Bowden Pl CW1 . 191 D6
Charles Cres CH4 . . . . 237 C1
Charles Ct CW2 . . . . 190 C3
Charles Darwin Com Prim
Sch CW8 . . . . 103 E7
Charles Forbes Ct 7
WA1 . . . . 16 B5
Charles Price Gdns 8
CH65 . . . . 70 C6
Charles Rd CH2 . . . . 95 C1
Charles Sq CW11 . . . . 175 F2
Charles St Chester CH1 . . . 237 B3
Chester, Hoole Park CH2 . . 118 F3
4 Crewe CW1 . . . . 190 C4
Irlam M44 . . . . 11 E6
Widnes WA8 . . . . 23 A8
Charleston Cl CH66 . . . . . . 69 D2
Charleston Gr WA5 . . . . 15 B6
Charlesworth Cl SK23 . . . . 39 D3
Charlesworth Cres SK23 . . 39 D3
Charlesworth Ct CW11 . . 175 C6
Charlesworth Pl 1
CW12 . . . . 156 F4
Charlesworth Rd SK23 . . . . 39 D3
Charlesworth St CW1 . . . 190 D6
Charlock Wlk 6 M31 . . . . . . 11 F3
Charlotte Ct CH1 . . . . 237 B3
Charlotte Gr
7 Warrington WA5 . . . . 15 C7
6 Warrington WA5 . . . . 15 C7
Charlotte St Chester CH1 . 118 B2
Macclesfield SK11 . . . . 112 D7
Charlotte Street W 22
SK11 . . . . 112 C8
Charlotte Wlk 2 WA8 . . . . . 23 B7
Charlton Cl WA7 . . . . 50 A7
Charlton Ct CH2 . . . . 119 A4
Charlton St
23 Macclesfield SK11 . . . . 112 C8
Warrington WA4 . . . . 16 F3
Charminster Cl WA5 . . . . . . 15 B5
Charmouth Cl WA12 . . . . 2 B4
Charnock Ave WA12 . . . . 1 F3
Charnock Rd WA3 . . . . 4 F3
Charnwood High Lane SK6 . . 37 F7
Kidsgrove ST7 . . . . 195 B1
Charnwood Cl
Macclesfield SK10 . . . . 87 A1
Warrington WA3 . . . . 10 B5
Charnwood Cres SK7 . . . . . 36 D8
Charon Way WA5 . . . . 7 B3
Charter Ave WA5 . . . . 16 A8
Charter Cres CH66 . . . . 69 E3
Charter Ct 2 CW7 . . . . 125 F1
Charterhall Dr CH2 . . . . . . 118 F2
Charterhouse Cl CH65 . . . . . 70 E5
Charter Rd SK10 . . . . 88 A7
Charter Way SK10 . . . . 87 F3
Chartley Gr CW10 . . . . 128 D2
Chartwell Gdns WA4 . . . . . . 26 F5
Chartwell Gr CW7 . . . . 149 C5
Chartwell Pk CW11 . . . . . . 175 A4
Charwood Cl CH66 . . . . 69 B5
Chase Dr CH66 . . . . 69 E2
Chase Mdw WA13 . . . . 19 B5
Chaser Ct CH1 . . . . 117 F3
Chase The Bebington CH63 . 43 C5
5 Heswall CH60 . . . . 41 A8
Chasewater WA7 . . . . 24 F4
Chase Way CH66 . . . . 69 E2
Chassagne Sq CW1 . . . . . . 189 F7
Chatburn Ct WA3 . . . . 4 F2
Chater Dr CW5 . . . . 204 F3
Chatfield Dr WA3 . . . . 9 E3
Chatham St 9 SK11 . . . . . . 112 D8
Chatham Way CW1 . . . . . . 191 C5
Chatsworth Ave
Culcheth WA3 . . . . 4 F4
Macclesfield SK11 . . . . 111 E6
Chatsworth Cl
Ellesmere Port CH66 . . . . . . 69 C5
Northwich CW9 . . . . 104 A5
Wistaston CW2 . . . . 206 A7
Chatsworth Dr
Chester CH2 . . . . 119 A5
Congleton CW12 . . . . 155 F3
Widnes WA8 . . . . 12 C3
Chatsworth Ho CH1 . . . . . 118 B3
Chatsworth Rd
Hazel Grove SK7 . . . . 36 F8
High Lane SK6 . . . . 37 F6
Wilmslow SK9 . . . . 59 E4
Chatteris Pk WA7 . . . . 24 E2
Chatterton Dr WA7 . . . . 50 E8
Chatterton Ho 16 CW5 . . . 204 E5
Chaucer Cl CH1 . . . . 117 E6
Chaucer Gr CW11 . . . . 174 C5
Chaucer Pl WA4 . . . . 16 F4
Chaucer Rd CW1 . . . . 190 F6
Chaucer St WA7 . . . . 23 A1
CHEADLE HULME 35 A8
Cheadle Hulme High Sch
SK8 . . . . 35 B7
Cheadle Hulme Sch SK8 . . 35 A8
Cheadle La WA16 . . . . 81 A1
Cheadle Wood SK8 . . . . 34 E8
CHECKLEY 221 C1
Checkley Dr ST8 . . . . 179 D1
CHECKLEY GREEN 232 B8
Checkley La CW3, CW5 . . . 221 E1
Checkley Rd ST5 . . . . 210 C1
Checkley Row CW5 . . . . . . 232 C8
Cheddar Gr WA5 . . . . 6 F7
Cheddington Cl SK8 . . . . . . 35 A7
Cheddington Cres WA5 . . . 14 E8
Chedlee Dr SK8 . . . . 34 E8
Chedworth Dr WA8 . . . . 12 C4
Chedworth Ho 11 CH1 . . . 237 C3
Cheerbrook Rd CW5 . . . . . 205 D4
Cheese Hill La WA6, CW8 . 101 B4
CHELFORD 84 B2
Chelford Ave WA3 . . . . 3 D8
Chelford CE Prim Sch
SK11 . . . . 84 A3
Chelford Cl Chester CH1 . . 117 F1
Warrington WA4 . . . . 26 C8
Chelford Dr CW9 . . . . 103 F5
Chelford La WA16 . . . . 83 C1
Chelford Mews 2 CH3 . . 119 B1
Chelford Rd
Chelford SK10, SK11 . . . . . . 84 D1
Chelford, Marthall WA16,
SK11 . . . . 83 D4
Congleton CW12 . . . . 155 E6
Goostrey CW4 . . . . 131 B7
Handforth SK9 . . . . 34 D5
Macclesfield SK10, SK11 . . 111 C8
Monks Heath SK10 . . . . 85 B1
Nether Alderley SK9 . . . . 84 C7
Ollerton WA16 . . . . 82 D7
Prestbury SK10 . . . . 86 D5
Whisterfield SK11 . . . . 109 F3
Chelford Rdbt SK11 . . . . . . 84 B1
Chelford Sta SK11 . . . . 84 A2
Chells Hill CW11 . . . . 176 C1
Chell St CW1 . . . . 190 B5
Chelsea Cl ST8 . . . . 179 C1
Chelsea Gdns WA5 . . . . 15 C4
Chelston Dr SK8 . . . . 34 C6
Cheltenham Cl
2 Macclesfield SK10 . . . . . . 87 C4
Warrington WA5 . . . . 15 A8
Cheltenham Cres
Crewe CW1 . . . . 190 B7
Runcorn WA7 . . . . 49 B6
Cheltenham Dr WA12 . . . . . . 2 C5
Cheltenham Rd CH65 . . . . . 70 D3
Chemical St WA12 . . . . 2 B3
Cheney Wlk CW2 . . . . 206 D8
Chepstow Cl
Biddulph ST8 . . . . 179 C1
Macclesfield SK10 . . . . 87 C4
Warrington WA5 . . . . 7 E3
1 Winsford CW7 . . . . 149 C7
Cherington Cl SK9 . . . . 34 F3
Cherington Cres SK11 . . . 112 B7
Cherish Rd 3 CW9 . . . . 80 B2
Cheriton Way CW2 . . . . . . 206 A8
Cherrington Rd CW5 . . . . 204 E3
Cherry Blossom Rd WA7 . . . 49 F4
Cherry Brow Terr CH64 . . . . 67 F8
Cherry Cl
Newcastle-under-Lyme
ST5 . . . . 210 D1
Newton-le-Willows WA12 . . . . 1 F4
Willaston CH64 . . . . 67 C8
Cherry Cnr WA13 . . . . 28 A7
Cherry Cres CW7 . . . . 149 C8
Cherry Dale Rd CH4 . . . . . 139 A3
Cherryfields Rd SK11 . . . . 111 F8
Cherry Gdns CH3 . . . . 119 A1
Cherry Gr
Ellesmere Port CH66 . . . . . . 70 A1
Nantwich CW5 . . . . 204 D5
Cherry Grove Prim Sch 8
CH3 . . . . 119 A1
Cherry Grove Rd CH3 . . . . 119 A1
Cherry La
Congleton CW12 . . . . 179 E8
Cuddington CW8 . . . . 101 F2
Lawton Heath ST7 . . . . 193 E6
Lymm WA13 . . . . 18 C1
Weaverham CW8 . . . . 102 D8
Cherry La Farm ST7 . . . . . 193 F6
Cherry Mews 3 CW9 . . . . . 79 C3
Cherry Orch/Y Berllan
Geirios LL13 . . . . 196 D8
Cherry Rd CH3 . . . . 119 A1
Cherrysutton WA8 . . . . 12 B3
Cherrysutton Mews WA8 . . 12 B4
Cherry Tree Ave
Barnton CW8 . . . . 78 A4
Lawton-gate ST7 . . . . 194 A5
Lymm WA13 . . . . 18 D2
Poynton SK12 . . . . 36 F3
Runcorn WA7 . . . . 49 C8
Warrington WA5 . . . . 14 F4
Cherry Tree Cl Elton CH2 . . . 72 B4
Hale L24 . . . . 21 E1
Haydock WA11 . . . . 1 A5
2 Wilmslow SK9 . . . . 60 E8
Cherry Tree Ct CW5 . . . . . 205 A4
Cherry Tree Dr
Hazel Grove SK7 . . . . 37 A8
St Helens WA9 . . . . 1 A2
Cherry Tree Farm La
CH3 . . . . 184 A5
Cherry Tree Ho SK9 . . . . . . 85 C8
Cherry Tree La
Rostherne WA14 . . . . 30 E6
Woore CW3 . . . . 232 C2
Cherry Tree Mews 3
CH60 . . . . 41 A8
Cherry Tree Pl WA9 . . . . 1 A1
Cherry Tree Prim Sch
WA13 . . . . 18 C2
Cherry Tree Rd
Audley ST7 . . . . 209 F1
Crewe CW1 . . . . 190 E6
Golborne WA3 . . . . 3 F8
Newcastle-under-Lyme
ST5 . . . . 210 E1
Cherry Tree Way CW12 . . 156 E2
Cherry Wlk Cheadle SK8 . . . 35 C8
Partington M31 . . . . 11 D2
Swan Green WA16 . . . . 106 D7
Cherrywood Cres CW8 . . . . 78 B4
Cherwell Cl Cheadle SK8 . . . 35 A7
Cherwell Cl *continued*
Warrington WA2 . . . . 8 D2
Cheryl Ct CW8 . . . . 102 A4
Cheryl Dr WA8 . . . . 13 D1
Chesford Grange WA1 . . . . . 17 F7
Chesham Cl SK9 . . . . 59 F4
Chesham Ct CH65 . . . . 70 D4
Chesham Rd SK9 . . . . 59 F4
Chesham St CH1 . . . . 237 C3
Cheshire Acad CW1 . . . . . 190 E3
Cheshire Ave CW9 . . . . 80 B3
Cheshire Candle
Workshops★ CH3 . . . . . . 184 C5
Cheshire Cl WA12 . . . . 2 E3
Cheshire Coll South and
West - Ellesmere Port
Campus CH65 . . . . 70 B5
Cheshire Farm Ice Cream★
CH3 . . . . 166 D4
Cheshire Hospl (Private)
WA4 . . . . 26 D1
Cheshire Military Mus★
CH1 . . . . 237 A1
Cheshire Oaks Designer
Outlet (Sh Ctr) CH65 . . . . . 70 E2
Cheshire Oaks Way CH65 . . 70 E2
Cheshire Pk WA6 . . . . 97 D5
Cheshire Rd M31 . . . . 11 D2
Cheshire Row WA16 . . . . . 108 B8
Cheshire St CW3 . . . . 229 F4
Cheshires Way
Chester CH3 . . . . 142 B5
Huntington CH3 . . . . 142 B5
Cheshire View Audley ST7 210 A1
Bollington SK10 . . . . 88 B6
Chester CH4 . . . . 141 E7
Cheshyre Dr WA7 . . . . 23 F1
Cheshyre's La WA7 . . . . 48 E7
Chessington Cl WA4 . . . . . . 26 F6
CHESTER 237 B2
Chester Aerospace Pk
CH5 . . . . 139 B6
Chester App Aldford CH3 . 163 D7
Eccleston CH4 . . . . 141 D2
Chester Ave WA3 . . . . 3 D8
Chesterbank Bsns Pk
CH4 . . . . 140 D7
Chester Bsns Pk CH4 . . . . 141 B3
Chester Castle★ CH1 . . . . 237 A1
Chester Cathedral★ CH1 . 237 B2
Chester Catholic High Sch
The CH4 . . . . 41 D6
Chester Cl Handforth SK9 . . . 34 E2
Irlam M44 . . . . 11 D5
Runcorn WA7 . . . . 24 A2
Talke ST7 . . . . 210 E7
Chester Ent Ctr CH2 . . . . . 237 C4
Chesterfield Cl CW7 . . . . . 125 F1
Chesterfield Rd CH62 . . . . . 43 D4
Chestergate SK10, SK11 . . 112 D8
Chester Gates CH1 . . . . 94 D6
Chester High Rd
Neston CH64 . . . . 41 D5
Neston CH64 . . . . 41 E4
Willaston CH64 . . . . 67 D7
Chester History & Heritage
Ctr★ CH1 . . . . 237 B2
Chester La CW7 . . . . 125 D2
Chester New Rd WA4 . . . . . 25 F7
Chester Race Course★
CH1 . . . . 237 A1
Chester Rd Acton CW5 . . . . 204 A6
Aston WA7 . . . . 50 B4
Audley ST7 . . . . 209 D2
Barbridge CW5 . . . . 187 D5
Broughton CH4 . . . . 139 D5
Churton CH3 . . . . 180 F6
Connah's Quay CH6 . . . . 91 A3
Cuddington CW8 . . . . 101 D1
Daresbury WA4 . . . . 25 B1
Delamere CW6, CW8 . . . . . 123 C5
Dunham-on-the-Hill CH2,
WA6 . . . . 97 D5
Ellesmere Port, Great Sutton
CH66 . . . . 69 D4
Ellesmere Port, Whitby CH65,
CH66 . . . . 70 A2
Frodsham WA6 . . . . 74 A7
Gatesheath CH3 . . . . 165 E5
Grappenhall WA4 . . . . 17 B1
Hartford CW8 . . . . 102 E3
Hartford, Greenbank CW8 . 103 C6
Hazel Grove SK7 . . . . 36 D8
Helsby WA6 . . . . 73 C4
Heswall CH60, CH64 . . . . . . 41 C6
Higher Walton WA4 . . . . 25 D5
Holmes Chapel CW4 . . . . . . 130 B2
Huntington CH3 . . . . 142 A6
Kelsall CW6 . . . . 122 D5
Lavister LL12 . . . . 162 C1
Macclesfield SK11 . . . . 112 B8
Malpas SY14 . . . . 213 B4
Mere WA16 . . . . 56 B6
Middlewich CW10 . . . . 128 B2
Neston CH64 . . . . 66 E7
Over Tabley WA16 . . . . 56 A2
Plumley WA16 . . . . 80 E5
Poynton SK12 . . . . 36 B4
Rostherne WA14, WA16 . . . . 30 C5
Runcorn WA7 . . . . 50 E5
Saltney CH4 . . . . 140 C6
Sandycroft CH5 . . . . 116 A2
Talke ST7 . . . . 210 D7
Warrington WA4 . . . . 16 A2
Whitchurch SY13 . . . . 225 D2
Winsford CW7 . . . . 125 F2
Woodford SK7 . . . . 35 E2
Chester Ret Pk CH1 . . . . . . 118 A3
Chester Road Bypass
Hartford CW8 . . . . 103 B3
Sandiway CW8 . . . . 102 E3
Chester Roman
Ampitheatre★
CH1 . . . . 237 B2
Chester's Croft Pk SK8 . . . 35 A5
Chester Southerly By-Pass
Eccleston CH4 . . . . 141 A2
Guilden Sutton CH3 . . . . . . 119 D5
Roughhill CH4 . . . . 140 C2
Chester Sq CW1 . . . . 190 C4
Chester St Chester CH4 . . . 140 F7
Crewe CW1 . . . . 190 C4
Warrington WA2 . . . . 16 B6
Widnes WA8 . . . . 13 B1
Chester Sta CH1 . . . . 237 C3
Chesterton Cl CW10 . . . . . 151 E5
Chesterton Ct CH2 . . . . . . 118 D4
Chesterton Dr
Crewe CW2 . . . . 189 F1
Winwick WA2 . . . . 8 A5
Chesterton Gr CW11 . . . . . 174 D5
Chesterton Way CW2 . . . . . 207 E3
Chester Trad Pk CH1 . . . . . 117 F2
Chester Visitor Ctr★
CH1 . . . . 237 B2
Chester Way CW9 . . . . 104 A8
Chester West Employment
Pk CH1 . . . . 117 E2
Chester Zoo★ CH2 . . . . 95 E1
Chester Zoological Gdns★
CH2 . . . . 118 D8
Chestnut Ave
4 Ellesmere Port CH66 . . . . . 69 F1
Irlam M44 . . . . 11 D5
Macclesfield SK10 . . . . 87 E2
Rode Heath ST7 . . . . 193 F7
Shavington CW2 . . . . 206 C5
Warrington WA5 . . . . 14 F6
Widnes WA8 . . . . 13 B2
Chestnut Cl Chester CH2 . . 119 A3
Cuddington CW8 . . . . 101 F2
Middlewich CW10 . . . . 128 B2
Tarporley CW6 . . . . 146 D2
Wilmslow SK9 . . . . 60 E8
Chestnut Ct
Tarporley CW6 . . . . 146 C2
Widnes WA8 . . . . 12 D1
Chestnut Dr Alsager ST7 . . 193 E2
Congleton CW12 . . . . 156 A4
Holmes Chapel CW4 . . . . . . 130 D3
Poynton SK12 . . . . 36 F3
Chestnut Gr Barnton CW8 . . . 78 B4
Bebington CH62 . . . . 43 C8
Crewe CW1 . . . . 190 E5
Golborne WA3 . . . . 3 F8
Newcastle-under-Lyme
ST5 . . . . 210 E1
Winsford CW7 . . . . 149 C8
Chestnut Grange CH4 . . . 141 B7
Chestnut Ho 6 CW11 . . . . 175 B6
Chestnut La WA6 . . . . 73 E4
Chestnut Lodge Special
School WA8 . . . . 12 E1
Chestnut Mews WA16 . . . . . 58 E1
Chestnuts The CH64 . . . . . . 67 F8
Chestnut Wlk M31 . . . . 11 D2
Chetham Ct WA2 . . . . 8 A3
Chetton Dr WA7 . . . . 50 E7
Chetwode Mews WA4 . . . . . 52 C2
Chetwode St CW1 . . . . 190 C5
Chetwood Cl WA12 . . . . 2 B5
Chetwood Dr WA8 . . . . 12 F4
Cheveley Cl SK10 . . . . 87 C2
Chevin Gdns SK7 . . . . 36 A7
Cheviot Ave WA2 . . . . 8 A3
Cheviot Cl CH66 . . . . 69 A6
Cheviot Ct CW7 . . . . 149 B7
Cheviot Sq CW7 . . . . 149 B7
Chevron Cl CH1 . . . . 117 E4
Chevron Hey CH1 . . . . 117 E4
Cheyne Wlk CW5 . . . . 204 E3
Cheyney Rd CH1 . . . . 118 B3
Chicago Ave M90 . . . . 33 B7
Chicago Pl WA5 . . . . 15 B6
Chichester Cl
Grappenhall Heys WA4 . . . . . 27 A7
Runcorn WA7 . . . . 50 D6
Chichester Ct CH1 . . . . . . 237 A3
Chichester St CH1 . . . . . . 237 A3
Chidlow Cl Hough CW2 . . . 206 E2
Widnes WA8 . . . . 23 A5
Childer Cres CH66 . . . . 69 B7
Childer Gdns CH66 . . . . 69 B7
CHILDER THORNTON 69 B8
Childer Thornton Prim Sch
CH66 . . . . 69 B8
Child's La CW12 . . . . 177 E6
Childwall Ct CH66 . . . . 69 F8
Childwall Gdns CH66 . . . . . . 69 F8
Childwall Rd CH66 . . . . 69 F8
Chilham Cl CW7 . . . . 149 C7
Chilham Pl SK11 . . . . 111 F6
Chilington Ave WA8 . . . . . . 22 D8
Chillingham Cl CW10 . . . . 128 D2
Chillingham Rd CW7 . . . . 149 A7
Chiltern Ave SK11 . . . . . . 112 A7
Chiltern Cl Chester CH4 . . 141 B5
Chorlton CW2 . . . . 207 B1
Cuddington CW8 . . . . 102 A2
Chiltern Cres WA2 . . . . 8 A3
Chiltern Ct SK10 . . . . 87 D3
Chiltern Pl WA2 . . . . 8 A3
Chiltern Rd Culcheth WA3 . . . 4 E4

Chiltern Rd continued
St Helens WA9 . . . .**1** A3
Warrington WA2 . . . .**8** A3
Chiltern Way CW7 . . . . . .**149** B7
Chilton Dr CH66. . . . .**69** F2
Chilwell Cl WA8. . . . .**12** D4
Chilworth Cl CW2 . . . . . .**206** C8
China La WA4 . . . .**16** C2
Chines The CW8 . . . .**101** D5
Chipping Cl 2 WA3 . . . .**4** E5
Chippingdall Cl WA5 . . . . .**15** C5
Chipstead Cl CW8 . . . .**103** A4
Chirk Cl CH2 . . . .**118** F6
Chirk Gdns CH65 . . . .**70** D3
Chirk Pl CW7 . . . .**126** A1
Chirton Cl WA11 . . . .**1** D7
Chisledon Cl WA11 . . . .**1** D7
Chislet Ct WA8. . . . .**12** E4
Chiswick Cl WA7 . . . .**50** D7
Chiswick Gdns WA4 . . . . . .**26** F6
Chollerton Cl WA16 . . . . . .**29** C4
Cholmley Dr WA12 . . . .**2** E2
Cholmondeley Castle Gdns ★
SY14 . . . .**201** A4
Cholmondeley La SY14 . . .**200** E7
Cholmondeley Pk SY14 . . .**201** B4
Cholmondeley Rd
Ellesmere Port CH65 . . . . . .**69** F4
Hampton Heath SY14 . . . . .**213** E7
Runcorn WA7 . . . .**49** D4
Wrenbury CW5 . . . .**216** C5
Cholmondeley St
Macclesfield SK11 . . . .**112** D6
Widnes WA8. . . . .**23** A4
CHOLMONDESTON **170** E4
Cholmondley Rise SY14. . .**214** B4
Chorlegh Grange 8 SK9. . .**60** A1
CHORLEY. **202** B2
CHORLEY BANK **201** B1
Chorley Bank Council Hos
CW5. . . . .**201** E1
CHORLEY GREEN **202** A3
Chorley Green La CW5,
SY14. . . . .**201** C5
Chorley Hall La
Alderley Edge SK9 . . . .**60** A1
Faddiley CW5 . . . .**202** C2
Chorley's La WA8 . . . .**13** E3
Chorley St WA2 . . . .**16** B6
Chorley Stock Rd CW5. . . .**202** A2
Chorleywood Cl SK10. . . . . .**87** B4
CHORLTON **207** B1
Chorlton Cl WA7 . . . .**24** D1
Chorlton La CW2 . . . .**207** B2
CHORLTON LANE **212** B4
CHOWLEY **182** F5
Chowley Oak La CH3 . . . . .**182** F6
Chrimes Dr CW8 . . . .**123** F6
Christchurch Ave CW2. . . .**190** A1
Christ Church CE Prim Sch
Ellesmere Port CH65 . . . . . .**70** B2
Warrington WA2 . . . .**9** A1
Christie Cl CH66 . . . .**44** A2
Christie St WA8 . . . .**13** D1
CHRISTLETON **142** E8
Christleton Ave
Crewe CW2 . . . .**189** D5
Northwich CW9 . . . .**104** A4
Christleton Ct WA7. . . . .**24** C4
Christleton Dr CH66 . . . .**69** E6
Christleton High Sch
CH3. . . . .**142** F7
Christleton Prim Sch
CH3. . . . .**142** E8
Christleton Rd CH3. . . . . . .**119** A1
Christleton Sports Ctr
CH3. . . . .**142** F8
Christleton Way 15 SK9. . . .**34** D5
Christopher Dr CH62 . . . . . .**44** A5
Christopher Mitford Rd
ST7. . . . .**193** B2
Christ the King RC & CE Prim
Sch SK11 . . . .**112** D6
Christ The King RC Prim Sch
CH62. . . . .**43** E7
Church Ave SK9. . . . .**34** A2
Church Bank Audley ST7. . .**209** D2
Goostrey CW4 . . . .**107** F1
Kelsall CW6 . . . .**122** D5
Tattenhall CH3 . . . .**166** B2
Church Bk SK23 . . . .**65** D7
Church Cl Handforth SK9. . . .**34** D3
Weaverham CW8. . . . .**77** D1
Church College Cl CH1 . . . .**118** B3
Church Cotts Astle SK11. . . .**109** B8
Rainow SK10 . . . .**88** E5
Sealand CH1 . . . .**116** E6
Waverton CH3 . . . .**143** C3
Church Croft CH4 . . . .**162** A6
Church Ct
Ashton Hayes CH3 . . . .**121** F8
Farndon CH3 . . . .**180** E2
Church Dr WA3 . . . .**9** A1
Church End L24. . . . .**21** D1
Church End Mews L24. . . . . .**21** D1
Churche's Ct 15 CW5 . . . . .**204** E5
Churche's Mansion ★
CW5 . . . .**204** F5
Church Farm CW5. . . . .**216** E4
Church Farm Ct
Heswall CH60 . . . .**40** F7
Willaston CH64 . . . .**67** F8
Church Field Cl CW1 . . . . .**190** D8
Churchfield Rd WA6. . . . . . .**74** C8

Churchfields
Audlem CW3 . . . .**230** A4
Barnton CW8 . . . .**78** B3
Croft WA3. . . . .**9** B7
Cuddington CW8 . . . .**102** B2
Helsby WA6. . . . .**73** C4
Knutsford WA16. . . . .**57** C2
Widnes WA8. . . . .**13** B5
Wybunbury CW5 . . . .**220** B8
Church Fields TF9. . . . .**236** C2
Church Gn WA13. . . . .**19** B8
CHURCH GREEN **18** E2
Church Hall Cl CH1 . . . .**117** F4
CHURCH HILL **149** E7
Church Hill WA16 . . . .**57** A2
CHURCH HILL FARM **149** D7
Churchill Ave
Alderley Park SK10. . . . .**85** B2
Fowley Common WA3. . . . .**5** B4
Churchill Cl CW12. . . . .**156** A3
Churchill Dr CW6 . . . .**146** D1
Churchill Mans 10 WA7 . . . .**23** A3
Churchill Parkway CW7 . . .**149** D8
Churchill Way
Macclesfield SK11 . . . .**112** D8
Neston CH64 . . . .**66** E8
Church La
Alderley Edge SK9 . . . .**60** A2
Aldford CH3 . . . .**163** F3
Backford CH1. . . . .**95** B4
Bebington CH62. . . . .**44** A4
Bramhall SK7. . . . .**35** C2
Chester CH2. . . . .**118** D7
Congleton CW12 . . . .**134** E1
Culcheth WA3. . . . .**4** F3
Ellesmere Port CH66 . . . . . .**69** D3
Farndon CH3 . . . .**180** E1
Golborne WA3 . . . .**3** D7
Guilden Sutton CH3 . . . . . .**119** F5
Hargrave CH3 . . . .**144** B1
Henbury SK11 . . . .**111** C8
Huxley CH3, CW6 . . . .**167** C6
Lawton-gate ST7 . . . .**194** C4
Mobberley WA16 . . . .**58** C5
Mow Cop ST7 . . . .**195** E7
Nantwich CW5 . . . .**204** E5
Neston CH64 . . . .**66** E7
New Mills SK22 . . . .**39** C8
Rainow SK10 . . . .**88** E5
Sandbach CW11. . . . .**175** E7
Scholar Green ST7 . . . .**194** C7
Smallwood CW11. . . . .**176** E4
Stoak CH2 . . . .**96** A7
Sutton Lane Ends SK11. . . .**112** F3
Swettenham CW12. . . . . . .**131** E3
Warren SK11 . . . .**134** D8
Warrington WA4 . . . .**17** B1
Wistaston CW2 . . . .**205** E8
CHURCH LAWTON **194** C3
Church Lawton Sch ST7 . . .**194** A5
Church Mdw TF9. . . . .**236** C2
Church Mdws
Little Leigh CW8. . . . .**77** D5
Whitchurch SY13 . . . .**226** A1
Church Mead CH3 . . . .**181** A5
Church Meadow La CH60 . . .**40** F7
Church Meadow Wlk
WA8. . . . .**22** B5
Churchmere Cl CW1. . . . . .**190** C7
Church Mews
Bollington SK10 . . . .**88** B8
Higher Wincham CW9 . . . . . .**79** E5
Knutsford WA16. . . . .**57** B2
6 Macclesfield SK11. . . . . .**112** D8
CHURCH MINSHULL **172** A6
Church Par 5 CH65 . . . .**70** C6
Church Rd Alsager ST7. . . .**193** C4
Ashton Hayes CH3 . . . .**121** F8
Barnton CW8 . . . .**78** B2
Broughton CH4. . . . .**139** C4
Burwardsley CH3. . . . .**184** A5
Cheadle SK8. . . . .**35** B8
Dodleston CH4 . . . .**162** B8
Eccleston CH4 . . . .**141** E2
Frodsham WA6. . . . .**74** C7
Hale L24. . . . .**47** E8
Handforth SK9. . . . .**34** D3
Haydock WA11. . . . .**1** E7
Little Leigh CW8 . . . .**77** D4
Lymm WA13 . . . .**18** E2
Mouldsworth CH3 . . . .**98** F1
New Mills SK22 . . . .**39** C7
Northwich CW9 . . . .**104** A8
Saughall CH1. . . . .**94** A1
Shocklach CH3 . . . .**197** C1
Thornton Hough CH63 . . . . .**42** B6
Tilston SY14. . . . .**198** B2
Wilmslow SK9 . . . .**59** E4
Worleston CW5 . . . .**188** D6
Church Rds CH3 . . . .**120** D5
Church Rise CW8 . . . .**102** B2
Church Row CW6 . . . .**168** F1
Churchside SK10. . . . .**112** D8
Churchside CW1 . . . .**191** D5
Churchside Wlk CH4 . . . . .**140** F7
Church St Audley ST7 . . . . .**209** D2
Audlem, Wood Lane ST7. . . .**210** A1
Bollington SK10 . . . .**88** B8
Chester CH1. . . . .**237** B4
Connah's Quay CH5 . . . .**91** D1
Davenham CW9 . . . .**104** A3
Ellesmere Port CH65 . . . . . .**70** C6
Farndon LL13. . . . .**180** E2
Frodsham WA6. . . . .**74** B8
Great Budworth CW9 . . . . . .**79** A8
Higher Wincham CW9 . . . . . .**79** E5
Kelsall CW6 . . . .**122** D4

Church St continued
Kidsgrove, Butt Lane ST7 . . .**194** D1
Kidsgrove, The Rookery
ST7 . . . .**195** C4
Macclesfield SK10, SK11 . . .**112** D8
Malpas SY14 . . . .**213** B3
Moulton CW9 . . . .**126** F8
Mount Pleasant ST7 . . . . . .**195** C6
Newton-le-Willows WA12 . . . . .**2** E4
Runcorn WA7 . . . .**23** A3
Sandbach CW11. . . . .**175** C6
Tarvin CH3 . . . .**121** C2
Warrington WA1 . . . .**16** C5
Weaverham CW8 . . . .**77** D1
Widnes WA8. . . . .**23** A5
Wilmslow SK9 . . . .**60** B7
Winsford CW7 . . . .**126** E1
Church Steadings CH3 . . . .**143** C3
Church Street N CW6 . . . . .**122** C5
Church Street W SK11 . . . .**112** C8
Church Terr SK9 . . . .**34** D4
Church View
Audlem CW3 . . . .**230** A4
Handforth SK9 . . . .**34** A2
Haslington CW1 . . . .**191** D5
Kingsley WA6. . . . .**75** B2
16 Knutsford WA16. . . . .**57** A2
Lymm WA13 . . . .**19** E4
New Mills SK22 . . . .**39** C8
Church View Cl WA8 . . . .**13** B5
Church View Pl CW5 . . . . . .**204** D7
Church View Terr SK11 . . . .**112** F3
Church View Wlk CW2. . . . .**205** E8
Churchward Cl CH2 . . . . . .**118** D4
Churchway SK10. . . . .**86** F2
Church Way Alvanley WA6. . .**73** A1
Blacon CH1. . . . .**117** E5
Chester CH1. . . . .**94** A1
Wybunbury CW5 . . . .**220** B8
Churchway Rd L24 . . . .**21** A2
Church Wlk
Broughton CH4. . . . .**139** C5
Crowton CW8. . . . .**76** C2
2 Ellesmere Port CH65. . . . .**70** C6
Holmes Chapel CW4. . . . . .**130** C3
Knutsford WA16. . . . .**57** A2
Lower Peover WA16. . . . .**81** E1
Malpas SY14 . . . .**213** B3
Northwich CW9 . . . .**104** A8
Wilmslow SK9 . . . .**59** F6
Winwick WA2. . . . .**8** A6
Church Wlks
Christleton CH3 . . . .**142** E8
Norton in Hales TF9 . . . . . .**236** C2
Churchwood View WA13. . . .**18** F3
Churchyard Side CW5 . . . .**204** E5
CHURTON **180** E5
Churton Cl Hough CW2 . . . .**206** E3
3 Northwich CW9. . . . .**103** E4
Churton Rd Chester CH3. . . .**119** A2
Farndon CH3 . . . .**180** E2
Churton St CH3 . . . .**119** A2
Cicely Mill La WA16 . . . .**30** D3
Cinder Cl
Ellesmere Port CH65 . . . . . .**70** E3
Guilden Sutton CH3 . . . . . .**119** F5
Cinder Hill CW7. . . . .**125** F6
Cinder-Hill La ST7 . . . .**194** F7
Cinder La Chelford SK11 . . . .**83** E1
Guilden Sutton CH3 . . . . . .**119** F5
Lostock Green CW9 . . . . . .**105** A8
Nantwich CW5 . . . .**188** C2
Over Peover WA16 . . . .**108** C7
Warrington WA4 . . . .**17** F1
Cinder Rock Way ST7. . . . .**195** C1
CINNAMON BROW. **8** F4
Cinnamon Brow CE Prim Sch
WA2 . . . .**8** F3
Cinnamon La WA2 . . . .**8** F2
Cinnamon Lane N WA2 . . . . .**8** F3
Cinnamon Pk WA2 . . . .**9** B3
Circle Ave WA5 . . . .**205** E5
Circle The Crewe CW2 . . . . .**190** D1
Mere WA16 . . . .**30** C2
Circuit The
Alderley Edge SK9 . . . .**60** B3
Cheadle SK8. . . . .**35** A7
Wilmslow SK9 . . . .**59** D5
Circular Dr CH4 . . . .**140** F4
City Bank ST8. . . . .**179** C2
City Quays 8 CH1 . . . .**237** C3
City Rd CH1. . . . .**237** C3
City Walls Rd CH1 . . . .**237** A2
City Way Apartments 7
CH1 . . . .**237** C3
Civic Way
Ellesmere Port CH65 . . . . . .**70** B4
Middlewich CW10 . . . .**128** C1
Clair Ave CH5 . . . .**116** A3
Clamhunger La WA16 . . . . . .**56** D7
Clamley Gdns L24 . . . .**21** E2
Clanbrook Ave WA13 . . . . . .**19** A2
Clanfield Ave WA8 . . . .**12** C3
Clap Gate Cres WA8. . . . . . .**22** B5
Clap Gates Cres WA5 . . . . . .**15** E7
Clap Gates Rd WA5. . . . .**15** E7
Claphatch La ST7 . . . .**194** E7
Clare Ave Chester CH2. . . . .**119** A3
Handforth SK9 . . . .**34** C3
Clare Dr Crewe CW2 . . . . . .**189** F1
Ellesmere Port CH65 . . . . . .**70** B1
Macclesfield SK10 . . . .**87** C3
Clare Ho CH1 . . . .**117** F6
Claremont Ave WA8 . . . .**13** C4
Claremont Cl CW9 . . . .**103** F3
Claremont Dr WA8 . . . .**13** B4
Claremont Rd Cheadle SK8. .**35** A8
Crewe CW2 . . . .**190** B2

Claremont Rd continued
Culcheth WA3. . . . .**4** D4
Runcorn WA7 . . . .**23** B2
Clarence Ave
Chester CH3. . . . .**119** B2
Warrington WA5 . . . .**14** D6
Widnes WA8. . . . .**13** A4
Clarence Brow 4 SK10 . . . . .**63** A1
Clarence Ct
Newton-le-Willows WA12 . . . . .**2** A4
Wilmslow SK9 . . . .**60** A6
Clarence Dr CW8. . . . .**102** A5
Clarence Gr CW1. . . . .**190** B5
Clarence Mill Bsns Pk
SK10. . . . .**63** A1
Clarence Rd
Bollington SK10 . . . .**63** A1
Warrington WA4 . . . .**17** B2
Clarence St
Newton-le-Willows WA12 . . . . .**1** F4
Runcorn WA7 . . . .**22** F3
Warrington WA1 . . . .**16** E7
Clarence Terr
Bollington SK10 . . . .**63** A1
7 Runcorn WA7 . . . .**23** A3
Clarendon Cl
Chester CH4. . . . .**141** E6
Runcorn WA7 . . . .**50** D7
Clarendon Cotts SK9 . . . . . .**34** A3
Clarendon Ct WA2 . . . .**7** F4
Clarendon Dr SK10 . . . .**88** A1
Clarendon Rd M44 . . . .**11** F7
Clare Pl CW7 . . . .**149** C7
Clares Farm Cl WA1 . . . .**17** F7
Clare St Harriseahead ST7. .**195** C6
Mount Pleasant ST7 . . . . . .**195** C6
Clark Dr CW8 . . . .**103** C8
Clarke Ave Culcheth WA3 . . . .**5** A4
Warrington WA4 . . . .**16** D2
Clarke Gdns 3 WA8. . . . .**23** B7
Clarke La Bollington SK10 . . .**87** E5
Langley SK11 . . . .**113** D3
Clarke Terr SK11 . . . .**112** D6
CLARK GREEN **63** A3
Clarks Terr WA7 . . . .**48** D8
Clary Mdw CW8 . . . .**78** E1
Clatterbridge Hospl CH63. . .**42** D8
Clatterbridge Rd CH63. . . . .**42** D8
Clatterwick La CW8 . . . .**77** D7
Claude St WA1. . . . .**16** C6
Claud Godwin Dr ST7. . . . .**193** F4
Claughton Ave CW2 . . . . . .**190** C1
Claverton Cl WA7 . . . .**49** B6
Claverton Ct CH4. . . . .**237** C1
Claydon Gdns WA3 . . . .**10** F1
Clay Field Cl 6 CW2. . . . . .**206** D6
Clay Heyes SK11 . . . .**84** A3
Clayhill Gn CH66 . . . .**69** D7
Clayhill Gr WA3 . . . .**4** B8
Clayhill Light Ind Pk CH64 . .**41** F1
Clayholes Rd SK23 . . . .**65** B3
Clay La Bickerton SY14. . . . .**200** B3
Burtonwood WA5. . . . .**6** E5
Handforth SK9 . . . .**34** C5
Haslington CW1, CW11 . . . .**191** D7
Over Peover WA16 . . . .**108** B8
Sandbach CW11, CW1 . . . . .**174** B2
Wilmslow SK9 . . . .**59** C4
Winsford CW7 . . . .**125** B4
Claymore Rd CW11. . . . . . .**175** B8
Claypit Rd CH4 . . . .**141** B5
Claypits La CH3 . . . .**142** F5
Clayton Ave
Congleton CW12 . . . .**157** A5
Golborne WA3 . . . .**3** E8
Clayton-By-Pass CW12. . . .**156** C3
Clayton Cl CW1 . . . .**190** A7
Clayton Cres Runcorn WA7. . .**22** F1
Widnes WA8. . . . .**12** F1
Clayton Dr SY13. . . . .**226** B1
Clayton Rd WA3. . . . .**9** F6
Clayton's Row CW5 . . . .**204** E5
Cleadon Way WA8 . . . .**12** E4
Clearwater Quays WA4 . . . . .**17** A3
Cleaver Mews SK11 . . . . . .**112** C5
Cleaver Rd CH1 . . . .**117** E4
Cledford Cres CW10 . . . . . .**151** E6
Cledford La CW10 . . . .**151** E7
Cledford Prim Sch
CW10 . . . .**151** C7
Cledwen Rd/Ffordd Cledwen
CH4 . . . .**139** D5
Cleethorpes Rd WA7 . . . . . .**50** C7
Cleeves Cl WA1 . . . .**16** C5
Cleeve Way SK8. . . . .**35** B6
Clegge St WA2 . . . .**16** B7
Clelland St WA4. . . . .**16** C3
Clement Attlee Way WA8 . . . .**22** F5
Clement Dr CW1 . . . .**189** F7
Clemley Cl CW6 . . . .**122** D6
Clerewood Ave SK8. . . . .**34** F4
Clevedon Cl SK11 . . . .**112** A7
Cleveland Dr CH66 . . . .**69** A6
Cleveland Rd WA2 . . . .**8** B3
Cleveland Way CW7 . . . . . .**149** B8
Cleveleys Ave WA8 . . . .**13** D2
Cleveleys Rd WA5. . . . .**15** B4
Cleves Cl CH1 . . . .**117** D6
Cliffbrook Gr 2 SK9. . . . .**34** D2
Cliffe Rd Crewe CW1 . . . . . .**190** B7
Neston CH64 . . . .**66** F5
Warrington WA1 . . . .**26** C1
Cliffe St 3 WA8. . . . .**13** C1
Cliff La Acton Bridge CW8. . . .**76** C4
Lymm WA13 . . . .**28** A6
Macclesfield SK10, SK11 . . . .**88** B1
Primrose Hill WA13 . . . .**28** A6

Cliff La continued
Warrington WA4 . . . .**17** D1
Clifford Dr CH4 . . . .**140** F5
Clifford Gr CW1 . . . .**191** C6
Clifford Pl 4 CW7. . . . .**149** C7
Clifford Rd
Macclesfield SK11 . . . .**112** A8
Poynton SK12. . . . .**36** D3
Warrington WA5 . . . .**15** A4
Wilmslow SK9 . . . .**59** F6
Cliff Rd Acton Bridge CW8 . . .**76** E4
Wilmslow SK9 . . . .**60** B8
Cliff Side Wilmslow SK9. . . . .**60** B8
Wilmslow/Alderley Edge
SK9. . . . .**59** D5
Cliff View WA6. . . . .**74** A8
CLIFTON **49** E3
Clifton Ave Bebington CH62 . .**43** E4
Crewe CW2 . . . .**190** B3
Culcheth WA3. . . . .**4** D4
Clifton Cl WA1 . . . .**17** C7
Clifton Cres WA6. . . . .**49** C1
Clifton Ct WA7. . . . .**49** B6
Clifton Dr Blacon CH1 . . . . .**117** E3
Northwich CW9 . . . .**104** A5
Wilmslow SK9 . . . .**59** E4
Clifton Gdns CH65. . . . .**70** C3
Clifton La WA7 . . . .**49** E3
Cliftonmill Mdws WA3. . . . . . .**2** F8
Clifton Park Ave CH5 . . . . . .**91** E4
Clifton Rd
Runcorn, Clifton WA7 . . . . . .**49** E3
Runcorn, Heath WA7 . . . . . .**49** B6
Sandbach CW11. . . . .**174** D7
Clifton Rdbt WA7 . . . .**49** E3
Clifton St
Alderley Edge SK9 . . . .**60** A1
Crewe CW2 . . . .**190** B3
Warrington WA4 . . . .**16** C4
Cliftonville Rd WA1 . . . .**17** D6
Clincton Cl WA8 . . . .**22** A8
Clincton View WA8. . . . .**22** A8
Clincton Wood Nature
Reserve ★ WA8. . . . .**22** A7
Clipsley Cres WA11. . . . .**1** B7
Clipsley La WA11. . . . .**1** C6
Clitheroe Pl CW12. . . . .**156** E6
Clitheroe Rd CW8 . . . .**77** C1
CLIVE **127** D1
Clive Ave WA2 . . . .**8** C1
Clive Back La CW7 . . . .**150** D7
Cliveden Rd CH4 . . . .**140** F5
CLIVE GREEN **150** D6
Clivegreen La CW10 . . . . . .**150** E7
Clive La CW7. . . . .**150** C6
Clive Mews 3 CH3 . . . .**142** C6
Clive Rd CW1 . . . .**191** A6
Clive Way CW10. . . . .**151** D5
Clock Face Rd WA8 . . . .**13** E8
Clock La WA8. . . . .**13** F3
Clocktower The CW4 . . . . . .**130** D2
Clock Twr The WA4 . . . .**16** C2
Cloister Way CH65 . . . .**70** E5
Clonners Field CW5 . . . . . .**205** A4
Closeburn Ave CH60. . . . . . .**40** C4
Close La Alsager ST7 . . . . . .**192** F3
Mow Cop ST7 . . . .**195** D7
Close The Alsager ST7. . . . .**193** A3
Hartford CW8. . . . .**103** D6
Newton-le-Willows WA12 . . . . .**2** E1
Saughall CH1 . . . .**94** A1
Tarporley CW6 . . . .**146** C2
CLOTTON. **145** D4
Cloudberry Wlk M31 . . . .**11** F3
CLOUD SIDE **157** F4
Cloud The ★ CW12 . . . .**158** A4
Cloud View CW12 . . . .**157** A2
Clough Ave Handforth SK9 . . .**34** B2
Warrington WA2 . . . .**8** B2
Clough Bank SK10. . . . .**87** F7
Clough Field Cl SK23 . . . . . .**65** D8
CLOUGH HALL. **210** F8
Clough Hall Dr ST7. . . . .**210** E6
Clough Hall Rd ST7. . . . .**210** F8
Clough House La SK11. . . . .**137** F3
Clough La Hartford CW8 . . . .**103** D6
Tattenhall CH3 . . . .**166** A1
Clough Rd CW7 . . . .**126** C1
Cloughside SK12. . . . .**38** E6
Clough The WA7 . . . .**23** F1
Clough Wlk CW2 . . . .**206** D8
Cloughwalton Specl Sch
CW8 . . . .**103** D5
Clovelly Ave WA5 . . . .**14** E7
Clovelly Gr WA7. . . . .**50** C5
Clover Ave WA6. . . . .**74** D7
Clover Cl CW2 . . . .**190** C1
Clover Croft Pl CW1 . . . .**190** F8
Clover Ct WA7 . . . .**50** E5
Cloverdale CW8. . . . .**103** C7
Cloverdale Rd SK11 . . . .**112** B5
Clover Dr Pickmere WA16. . . .**79** F7
Winsford CW7 . . . .**126** D3
Cloverfield Lymm WA13 . . . . .**18** F4
Runcorn WA7 . . . .**50** C7
Cloverfield Gdns CH66. . . . .**69** D7
Cloverfields CW1 . . . .**191** B4
Clover La CH4. . . . .**140** F5
Clover Pl CH4. . . . .**140** F5
Clowes Ave ST7 . . . .**193** F2
Clowes St SK11 . . . .**112** B8
Clumber Cl SK12. . . . .**36** E3
Clumber Rd SK12. . . . .**36** E3
CLUTTON. **182** D1
Clutton CE Prim Sch
CH3. . . . .**182** D1
Clwyd Cl CH5 . . . .**139** B6
Clwyd Way CH66 . . . .**69** A6

Clyde Ave ST8 .... 179 E1
Clyde Cres CW7 .... 127 B1
Clyde Gr CW2 .... 190 A3
Clydesdale CH65 .... 70 B3
Clydesdale Ave CW2 .... 190 B3
Clydesdale Rd WA4 ..... 26 D8
Coach Ho The ST7 ...... 194 C4
Coachmans La SK23 .... 39 D3
Coach Rd Broxton CH3 .. 183 A3
 Edge Green SY14 ...... 199 D2
 Little Budworth CW6 .... 147 D8
Coachway SK10 ....86 F7
Coalbrookdale Rd CH64 ..41 F2
COALPIT HILL 210 C8
Coalpit Hill ST7 .... 210 D8
Coalpit La
 Clive Green CW10 ...... 150 F7
 Langley SK11 .... 113 C5
 Mollington CH1 .... 94 D4
Coalport Dr CW7 .... 126 F3
Coare St SK11 .... 87 D1
Coastguard La CH64 .....41 B1
Coates Pl CW1 .... 191 E5
Coatings By Pass Rd CH5 .91 F1
Coatings Two CH5 ......91 E2
Cobal Ct WA6 ....74 B8
Cobbett's Way SK9 ......59 F4
Cobblers Cross La CW6 .. 146 E2
Cobblers La/Lon Y Cryddion
 LL12 .... 161 B1
Cobbles The Chester CH4 . 141 D7
 Cuddington CW8 .... 101 D4
 Lower Peover WA16 .....81 E1
Cobblestone Ct CH2 .... 119 E8
COBBS 26 E8
Cobbs Inf Sch The WA4 ..26 E8
Cobbs La Hough CW2 ... 206 E2
 Warrington WA4 .... 26 E8
Cobden St
 Newton-le-Willows WA12 ..2 D4
 Warrington WA2 ....16 B6
Cob Hall La WA6 ....98 D5
Cob Moor Rd ST7 ...... 195 A4
Cob Rd CW2 .... 189 E1
COBSCOT 235 E3
Cockhall La SK11 .... 113 D3
Cockhedge La WA1 ..... 16 C5
Cockhedge Sh Pk WA1 ..16 B5
Cockhedge Way WA1 .....16 B5
Cockington Cl CW9 ..... 104 A4
Cock La
 Great Budworth CW9 .....78 F8
 Sound CW5 .... 217 F4
Cocklade La L24 .... 21 D1
Cock Lane Ends WA8 ....22 B4
Cockpit La CW8 .... 102 B1
Cockshades Farm CW5 . 206 C2
Cocksheadhey Rd SK10 ... 63 C1
Cocksmoss La
 Congleton SK11 .... 134 A3
 Marton SK11 .... 133 D3
Cocoa Gdns **11** CW5 .... 204 E5
Cocoa Yd The **10** CW5 .. 204 E5
CODDINGTON 182 A3
Coddington La
 Barton CH3 .... 181 F2
 Coddington CH3 .... 182 A3
Coe La WA14 .... 30 C7
Cogshall La Anderton CW9 . 78 C5
 Comberbach CW9 ....78 B7
Colchester Ho **10** CH1 .. 237 D4
Colchester Sq CH4 ..... 140 F5
COLDHARBOUR 164 F5
Coldmoss Dr CW11 .... 175 C4
COLD MOSS HEATH 175 C5
Coldstream Cl WA2 ......8 E3
Coldstream Dr CH66 .....68 F5
Cole Ave WA12 ....2 C4
Colebrook Cl WA3 ...... 10 A4
Coleclough Pl WA3 ......4 F4
Coleg Glannau Dyfrdwy/
 Deeside Coll CH5 ......91 B1
Colehill Bank CW12 .... 156 E2
Colehill Pl CH5 .... 91 D1
Colemere Cl WA1 ...... 17 A8
Colemere Ct CH65 ...... 70 C7
Coleport Cl WA4 .... 16 C3
Coleridge Cl Blacon CH1 . 118 A5
 Sandbach CW11 .... 174 C5
Coleridge Gr WA8 ...... 12 E1
Coleridge Way CW1 .... 190 F5
Colinwood Ave CH4 .... 139 B3
Coliseum L Pk CH65 .... 70 D2
Coliseum Way CH65 .... 70 D2
Collar House Dr SK10 ....86 E6
College Cl Warrington WA1 . 16 D5
 Warrington, Fearnhead WA2 ..9 B2
 Wilmslow SK9 .... 59 F8
College Ct SK11 .... 112 B5
College Fields
 Crewe CW1 .... 190 A1
 Widnes WA8 .... 12 F5
College Gn CH4 .... 141 D7
College La CW6 .... 168 F1
College Rd ST7 .... 193 B5
College View CH5 ...... 91 C1
College Way CH62 ..... 44 A7
Collegiate Rd WA2 ......8 B1
Collerick Cl ST7 ...... 193 A4
Colley La CW11 .... 175 D5
Colleys La CW5 .... 205 B3
Collier Ct CH66 ....69 B4
Colliers La CW9 ....54 E2
Collier St WA7 ....22 F3
Colliers' Row WA7 ......48 E7
Collier St WA7 ....22 F3
Colliery Green Cl CH64 ..66 E5
Colliery Green Ct CH64 ..66 E5
Colliery Green Dr CH64 ..66 E5

Collinbrook Ave CW2 ... 190 B1
Collingham Gn CH66 .....69 B5
Collingham Way CW7 ... 126 D1
Collingswood Cl CH66 ...69 B5
Collingtree Ave CW7 ... 127 A3
Collingwood Cl
 Macclesfield SK10 ......87 B2
 Poynton SK12 .... 37 A3
Collingwood Rd WA12 ....2 B3
COLLINS GREEN 1 E1
Collins Green La WA5 .....1 E1
Collinson Ct **2** WA6 .....74 B8
Collins St CW2 .... 190 A3
Collin St WA5 .... 15 F5
Colmere La M44 .... 11 E5
Colne Rd WA5 ....6 F6
Colorado Cl WA5 ...... 15 C7
Colshaw Dr SK9 .... 34 D2
Colshaw Hall Cotts WA16 ..82 F1
Colshaw La SK11 ...... 109 E1
Colson Ct CH2 .... 237 A4
Colstone Cl **2** SK9 .....60 E7
Coltsfoot Cl CH3 ...... 142 B5
Columbia Rd CH65 ..... 70 B5
Columbine Cl
 Huntington CH3 .... 142 A6
 Widnes WA8 .... 12 B4
Columbine Rd CW1 .... 190 F8
Columbine Way WA9 .....6 B7
Columbine Wlk **8** M31 ..11 F3
Columbus Pl **11** WA5 ... 15 B7
Colvend Way WA8 ...... 12 C1
Colville Ct WA2 ....8 A3
Colville Rd SK11 ...... 111 F8
Colwyn Cl
 Ellesmere Port CH65 .... 70 D3
 Warrington WA5 ....7 E2
Colwyn Rd SK7 .... 35 F8
Combermere Abbey★
 Sy1 .... 227 D5
COMBERBACH 78 C7
Comberbach Dr CW5 ... 205 A4
Comberbach Prim Sch
 CW9 .... 78 C8
Combermere Pk Dr
 SY13 .... 227 E4
Combermere Pl **8** CW1 . 190 D5
Comberton Cl WA7 ......24 F3
Comber Way WA16 ......82 A8
Comboy Dr CW9 .... 104 C6
Combs Cl SK22 .... 39 A8
Comfrey Ave CW11 .... 175 D6
Commander Drive **2**
 WA2 ....16 F7
Comma Rd CW11 ...... 175 D7
Commercial Ave SK8 ....34 F5
Commercial Rd SK10 ... 112 E8
Commissioner Sq
 Paddington WA1 .... 17 A7
 1 Warrington WA2 .....16 F7
Commodore Cl
 Crow Wood WA8 .... 13 C3
 Woodford SK7 .... 35 F8
Common Farm La SK11 ...83 E1
Commongate SK10 ..... 112 E8
Commonhall St CH1 ... 237 A2
Common La Betley CW3 . 221 F6
 Chelford SK11 ....83 E1
 Culcheth WA3 ....4 E4
 Duddon CW6 .... 145 C7
 Hapsford WA6 .... 72 D1
 Kelsall CW6 .... 122 C3
 Lach Dennis CW9 ..... 105 E5
 Norbury SY13 .... 215 C5
 Stretton WA4 .... 52 E8
 Warrington WA4 ....16 E2
 Waverton CH3 .... 143 B4
 Winsford CW7 .... 125 B5
Common Rd WA12, WA5 ....1 E3
COMMONSIDE 100 B8
Commonside WA6 ....73 E1
COMMON SIDE 124 D3
Commons Mill CW11 ... 175 B7
Common St WA12 ....1 E3
Commons The CW11 ... 175 B6
Common The Kelsall CW6 . 122 B3
 Runcorn WA7 .... 49 F8
Commonwealth Cl WA7 . 149 D6
Commonwood Rd LL13 . 196 A8
Company's Cl WA7 ......48 F5
Compass Cl WA7 .... 50 D5
Compton Cl WA11 ....1 C7
Compton Pl Chester CH4 . 141 A6
 Ellesmere Port CH65 ....70 B5
Concorde Pl WA2 ....8 D2
Concourse Way WA9 .....1 A2
Condliffe Cl CW11 ..... 175 C5
Conery Cl WA6 .... 73 C4
Coney Gr WA7 .... 50 B5
Coneyslack Rd WA6 .... 74 C2
CONGLETON 157 A4
Congleton Bsns Ctr
 CW12 .... 156 E3
Congleton Bsns Pk
 CW12 .... 156 C4
Congleton Cl SK9 ...... 85 A8
CONGLETON EDGE 179 B5
Congleton Edge Rd
 CW12 .... 179 B6
Congleton High Sch
 CW12 .... 155 F3
Congleton La SK11 .... 109 D5
Congleton L Ctr CW12 . 156 E3
Congleton Mus★ CW12 . 156 E2
Congleton Rd
 Alderley Edge SK9 ..... 60 A1
 Biddulph ST8 .... 179 D2
 Broughton CH4 .... 139 C4

Congleton Rd continued
 Kidsgrove ST7 .... 194 D1
 Macclesfield SK11 ..... 112 B5
 Marton SK11 .... 133 B5
 Mow Cop ST7 .... 178 F1
 North Rode SK11 ...... 134 C6
 Sandbach CW11 .... 175 B8
 Sandbach, Arclid Green
 CW11 .... 175 E8
 Scholar Green CW12, ST7 177 E3
 Siddington SK11 ...... 110 B5
 Smallwood CW11 ...... 177 A6
 Swettenham CW12 .... 131 F4
 Warren SK11 .... 111 E2
Congleton Ret Pk CW12 . 156 D4
Congleton Road N ST7 .. 194 E6
Congleton Road S ST7 .. 194 D3
Congleton Sta CW12 ... 157 A1
Congleton Theatre★
 CW12 .... 156 E3
Congleton War Memorial
 Hospl CW12 .... 156 F1
Conifer Cl CH66 ....95 A8
Conifer Gr Moore WA4 ...25 A7
 Warrington WA5 ....14 F7
Conifers The ST7 ...... 193 B3
Conifer Wlk M31 .... 11 E3
Coningsby Dr CW7 ..... 126 E1
Coningsby Gdns **13** WA3 ..3 E8
Coniston Ave
 Bebington CH63 ...... 43 C4
 Congleton CW12 ...... 155 F2
 Warrington WA3 ...... 14 D4
 Winsford CW7 .... 126 C2
Coniston Cl
 Alderley Edge SK9 ..... 84 C4
 Hooton CH66 .... 44 B2
 Nantwich CW5 .... 205 A6
 Runcorn WA7 .... 49 D6
Coniston Dr
 Frodsham WA6 .... 74 D8
 Handforth SK9 .... 34 C4
 Holmes Chapel CW4 ... 130 A3
Coniston Rd Chester CH2 . 118 F5
 High Lane SK6 .... 37 D8
 Neston CH64 .... 66 E6
 Partington M31 .... 11 E4
Coniston Way SK11 .... 111 F5
CONNAH'S QUAY 91 B1
Connah's Quay High Sch
 CH5 .... 91 C1
Connah's Quay Sports Ctr
 CH5 .... 91 C1
Connaught Ave WA1 ....16 E7
Connaught Cl SK9 ...... 60 C8
Connaught Cres **1** WA8 .12 F6
Connaught Dr WA12 ......2 C2
Conrad Cl CW1 .... 190 E4
Conroy Way WA12 ....7 C8
Consol Dr CH66 .... 43 D1
Consort Cl SK11 ....87 E7
Constable Dr SK9 ....60 E8
Constables Cl WA7 ..... 24 A1
Constable Sq
 Paddington WA1 .... 17 A8
 Warrington WA2 ....16 F8
Constance Ind Est WA8 . 23 A6
Constance Rd M31 ..... 11 F3
Constance Way WA8 .... 23 A5
Convamore Rd SK7 .....35 D7
Conway Ave Irlam M44 .. 11 E8
 Warrington WA5 ....7 F2
 Winsford CW7 .... 149 C7
Conway Cl Crewe CW1 .. 190 C8
 Knutsford WA16 ...... 82 A8
 Saltney CH4 .... 140 D5
 Warrington WA5 ....14 F6
Conway Cres SK10 ......87 F1
Conway Ct CH65 .... 70 D3
Conway Dr WA12 ....2 E3
Conwy Ct WA7 .... 24 A2
Coogee Ave WA5 ....14 E7
Cook Ave WA11 ....1 F7
Cookes Cl CH44 ....41 E1
Cookes Cres **9** CW7 ... 125 F2
Cookes Ct CH3 .... 166 B1
Cookes La CW9 .... 104 F6
Cooke's La CW9 .... 104 F6
Cookesmere La CW11 .. 175 A8
Cooks Acre CH62 ...... 43 D7
Cooks Hill WA6 .... 99 F8
Cooks La SY13 .... 225 D7
Cookson Ave CW9 ..... 126 F8
COOKSONGREEN 76 A1
Cook St CH65 .... 70 C6
Coole La Hack Green CW5 . 218 E3
 Newhall CW3 .... 229 C5
Coombe Dr WA7 .... 49 A8
Coombe Park Ct **1** CH6 . 69 C6
Coombe Pk CH66 ....69 C6
Co-operative St SK12 ... 38 D6
Cooper Ave
 Newton-le-Willows WA12 ...1 F3
 Warrington WA2 ....8 B2
Coope Rd SK10 ....87 E6
Cooper La WA11 ....1 C6
Cooper's Croft CH3 .... 142 A7
Cooper's Fold SK8 ..... 34 F6
Cooper's La CH5 ....91 D1
Coopers Opening CW11 . 175 B7
Coopers Pl WA4 .... 16 C1
Cooper St
 Congleton CW12 ...... 156 E3
 Runcorn WA7 .... 23 A4
 Widnes WA8 .... 13 B1
Cooper Terr CW6 ..... 146 D1
Cope Ave CW5 .... 204 D4
Copeland Ave WA7 .....49 E5

Copeland Rd WA4 ....16 C2
Copes La CW5 .... 204 C4
Copeswood Cl CH4 .... 139 C3
Copgrove Wlk M22 ......33 E7
Cop La CW5 .... 204 D5
Cop Mdw SK11 .... 112 F2
COPPENHALL 190 D7
Coppenhall Gr CW2 .... 190 A4
Coppenhall Heyes CW2 . 190 A4
Coppenhall La CW2 .... 189 D4
Coppenhall L Ctr CW1 . 190 E5
COPPENHALL MOSS ... 173 D1
Copper Beech CH4 .... 139 C3
Copperfield Cl WA3 ......9 C5
Copperfield Rd
 Cheadle SK8 ....35 B5
 Poynton SK12 .... 36 D2
Copperfields Poynton SK12 36 D2
 Tarporley CW6 .... 146 D2
 Wilmslow SK9 .... 60 C8
Copperhill Rd CW12 ... 179 B7
Coppermine La SY14 .. 184 B7
Copper St SK11 .... 112 E6
Copperwood WA7 ...... 24 A7
Copper Wood CW8 .... 101 C5
Coppice Ave SK12 ..... 38 A6
Coppice Cl High Legh SK12 . 38 A6
 Runcorn WA7 .... 24 A1
 Willaston CW5 .... 205 D6
Coppice Ct SK8 .... 34 B8
Coppice Dr CW10 ..... 151 E6
Coppice Gn Elton CH2 .. 72 C4
 Warrington WA5 ....7 A1
Coppice Gr WA16 ...... 57 A3
Coppice Ho Poynton SK12 . 36 D2
 Talke ST7 .... 210 C8
Coppice La SK12 ...... 38 A5
Coppicemere Dr CW1 .. 191 A2
Coppice Rd
 Haslington CW11 ..... 192 A8
 Poynton SK12 .... 37 B3
 Talke ST7 .... 210 C8
 Willaston CW5 .... 205 D6
Coppice Rise SK11 .... 112 D5
Coppice Side SK11 .... 159 D1
Coppice The
 Altrincham WA15 ..... 32 B8
 Cuddington CW8 ..... 101 D5
 Horwich End SK23 .... 65 F5
 Nantwich CW5 .... 204 F3
 Sandbach CW11 ...... 174 E7
 Wincham CW9 .... 79 C3
Coppice Way SK9 ...... 34 E3
Coppins Cl Chester CH3 . 119 A2
 Helsby WA6 .... 73 B4
Coppins The
 Warrington WA2 ....8 C2
 Wilmslow SK9 .... 59 E4
Copse The
 Altrincham WA15 ..... 32 D7
 High Lane SK6 .... 37 E7
 Newton-le-Willows WA12 ...2 B4
 Runcorn WA7 .... 50 A6
COPTHORNE 229 F4
Copthorne Cl CW12 ... 156 F2
Copthorne Dr CW3 .... 229 F3
Copyhold CW8 .... 102 D8
Corbet Ave WA2 .... 16 B8
Corbet Dr TF9 .... 235 A4
Corbet St WA2 .... 16 B8
Corbett Rd **7** CW11 .. 152 C2
Corbetts Cl CW2 ...... 189 D2
Corbridge Ho **9** CH1 .. 237 C3
Corfe Way CW7 .... 149 C7
Coriander Cl CW10 .... 128 C3
Corks La SK12 .... 38 E5
CORLTON 207 B1
Cormorant Cl Crewe CW1 . 190 F4
 Farndon CH3 .... 180 F2
Cormorant Dr WA7 .....22 E2
Corn Brook Ave WA7 ... 24 A2
Cornbrook Rd SK11 .... 112 C4
Corner Croft SK9 ...... 60 A4
Cornerhouse La WA8 ... 12 D3
Corners The CW8 ..... 102 E7
Cornerstones Sch WA4 . 17 A2
Cornfield Cl
 Ellesmere Port CH66 ....69 F1
 Macclesfield SK10 .....87 C3
Cornforth Way WA8 .... 12 F3
Cornhill Cl ST5 .... 210 D1
Cornish Cl M22 .... 33 D8
Cornishway M22 ...... 33 D8
Cornishway Ind Est **4**
 M22 .... 33 D8
Cornmill Cl WA3 ...... 173 D7
Cornmill Ct WA3 ....9 A8
Cornock Pl SK10 ....87 E5
Cornubia Rd WA8 ...... 23 D7
Cornwall Ave WA7 ..... 23 A2
Cornwall Cl
 3 Congleton CW12 ... 157 A1
 High Lane SK6 .... 37 E7
 Macclesfield SK10 .....86 E1
 Runcorn WA7 .... 23 F1
Cornwall Gr CW1 ..... 190 B5
Cornwall Ho CH1 ..... 237 B3
Cornwall Rd Chester CH2 . 118 F7
 Gatley SK8 .... 34 B8
 Irlam M44 .... 11 D5
 Widnes WA8 .... 13 B3
Cornwall St Chester CH1 . 237 B4
 Warrington WA1 ....16 E7
Cornwell Cl **3** SK9 .....60 D8
Coronation Ave
 Alsager ST7 .... 193 A3
 Glazebury WA3 ....5 C7
 Warrington WA4 ...... 17 C2

Coronation Ave continued
 Winsford CW7 .... 126 E1
Coronation Bldgs SK10 ..88 A8
Coronation Cl CH2 .... 119 A4
Coronation Cres
 Crewe CW1 .... 190 E6
 Kidsgrove ST7 .... 194 E1
 Sandbach CW11 ...... 175 A5
Coronation Dr
 Frodsham WA6 .... 49 D1
 Haydock WA11 ....2 A7
 Newton-le-Willows WA12 ..2 E1
 Warrington WA5 ....14 F4
 Widnes WA8 .... 22 C8
Coronation Gr CW8 .... 78 A4
Coronation Ho WA7 .... 49 C8
Coronation Mill ST7 ... 195 D7
Coronation Rd
 Broughton CH4 .... 139 B3
 Congleton CW12 ...... 156 F3
 Ellesmere Port CH65 ... 70 C4
 Middlewich CW10 .... 151 D6
 Runcorn, Higher Runcorn
 WA7 ....23 B1
 Runcorn, Preston Brook
 WA7 ....50 F6
Coronation Sq **19** WA16 . 57 A2
Coronation St
 Chester CH4 .... 140 F7
 Crewe CW1 .... 190 D5
 Macclesfield SK11 .... 112 D6
Coronation Terr CW6 .. 146 D1
Coroner's La WA8 ...... 13 A4
Coronet Ave CW9 ..... 103 F3
Coronet Way WA4 ......22 B8
Corporal Way **4** CH3 .. 142 B5
CORRA COMMON 233 C1
Correction Brow SK12 .. 37 C6
Corridor Rd CH65 ......71 B6
Corwen Cl WA5 ....7 E1
Cosgrove Bsns Pk CW9 . 78 D3
Cossack Ave WA2 ....8 C1
COTEBROOK 147 A8
Cotebrook Dr CH2 .... 118 E7
Cotebrook Rd WA7 .... 104 C8
Cotebrook Shire Horse Ctr★
 CW6 .... 147 A7
Cote Lea Ct WA7 ...... 49 F6
Cotes Pl CH1 .... 117 E3
Cotgreaves Cl CH4 .... 141 B5
Cotswold Ave WA3 ......3 D6
Cotswold Cl Chester CH2 . 118 F6
 Cuddington CW8 ..... 102 A2
 Macclesfield SK10 .....86 E1
Cotswold Ct **6** CH3 ... 119 A1
Cotswold Gdns WA3 .....3 E6
Cotswold Gr WA9 ....1 A3
Cotswold Pl WA2 ....8 B3
Cotswold Rd WA2 ....8 B3
Cotswold Way CW7 ... 149 B7
Cottage Cl Bebington CH63 . 43 C5
 Neston CH64 .... 66 F7
 Rudheath CW9 ...... 104 E8
Cottage Drive E CH60 ...40 F5
Cottage Drive W CH60 ..40 F5
Cottage Gr SK9 .... 59 F5
Cottage Hospital Ct **10**
 WA7 ....22 F1
Cottage La Heswall CH60 ..40 F5
 Macclesfield SK10 .... 112 F7
Cottage Lawns SK9 .....60 B2
Cottage Rd CH4 ...... 141 B5
Cottage St SK11 ...... 112 B8
Cottages The
 Lawton Heath ST7 .... 193 D6
 Sproston Green CW4 .. 129 C2
 Warrington WA4 ...... 17 F4
Cottam Dr WA2 ....9 A3
Cotterdale Cl WA5 ..... 14 F7
Cotterill WA7 .... 49 D8
Cotterill Dr WA1 ...... 17 C7
Cotterill St CW2 ...... 190 D6
Cottesmore Cl **4** WA5 ..14 F8
Cottesmore Dr CH60 ... 41 A8
Cottesmore Gdns WA15 . 32 C8
Cotton Cl High Peak SK23 . 65 E4
Cotton Cres SK10 ..... 87 D5
Cotton Field Rd CW4 .. 129 F3
Cotton La Christleton CH3 . 120 D2
 Runcorn WA7 .... 49 D8
 Sandbach CW11 ...... 175 A3
Cotton Mews CW3 .... 230 A4
Cottons Bridge WA4 ....50 F5
Cottonwood Gr ST7 ... 195 E4
Cottrell Rd WA15 ...... 32 D7
Coulton Rd WA8 .... 13 F3
Countess Ave SK8 ..... 34 E5
Countess Cl **7** SK11 .. 111 F7
Countess Ct CH1 ..... 118 B5
Countess of Chester Health
 Pk CH2 .... 118 B6
Countess of Chester Hospl
 CH2 .... 118 C5
Countess Rd SK11 .... 111 F7
Countess Way CH2 .... 118 C5
Counting House Rd SK12 . 38 E5
Country Ctr The★ CH3 . 165 E5
County High Sch Leftwich
 The CW9 .... 104 A4
County Terr WA16 ......56 F7
Courier Row SK11 ......87 F7
Court 2 SK10 ....87 F1
Court Ho The **9** CH65 .. 70 C6
Courtney Gn SK9 ...... 34 D2

Courtney Rd CH4........140 E5
Court No 4 **6** SK10.....112 C8
Court The CH64..........66 F6
Courtyard The
  Bostock Green CW10....127 D5
  Chester CH2............118 F6
  Congleton CW12........156 B3
  Cuddington CW8........101 E2
  Elton CH2..............72 B4
  Haughton CW6..........186 F4
  Newton-le-Willows WA12....2 E4
  Smallwood CW11........177 A7
  4 Warrington WA1.....16 B5
  Weaverham CW8........102 A8
  Willaston CH64.........67 F8
Cousens Cl CH1.........118 B4
Coventry Ave CH66......94 E8
Coverdale Cl WA5........14 F7
Coverdale Fold CW11....174 D5
Covert Cl CW7..........149 B8
Covert Gdns ST7........210 D8
Covert Rise CH3........166 A2
Covington Pl SK9........60 B6
Cowanway WA8..........12 F5
Cowbrook La SK11.......135 B6
Cowdell St WA2.........16 B7
Cowfields CW5..........204 E6
Cowhey Cl CH4.........141 B5
Cow Hey La WA6, WA7....49 A5
Cow La Ashley WA15.....31 F6
  Bollington SK10.........88 B7
  Hargrave CH3..........144 A2
  Macclesfield SK11......112 D6
  Norley WA6............101 A5
  Wilmslow SK9...........60 C7
  Winsford CW7..........149 E8
Cowley Way CW1........190 E1
Cowper Cl CW2.........206 A8
Cowthorne Dr CH3......143 A4
COX BANK..............234 F8
CPA Pond Nature Reserve★
  SK23..................65 D7
Crab La WA2.............9 B3
Crabmill Dr CW11.......174 E7
Crabmill La Norley WA6...100 E6
  Warmingham CW11....173 E7
Crabtree Ave
  Altrincham WA15........32 D7
  Disley SK12............38 E5
Crabtree Cl WA12........2 E3
Crab Tree Cl L24........21 E2
Crabtree Ct SK8.........38 D6
Crabtree Fold WA7......50 C8
Crabtree Gr CW1.......190 E6
CRABTREE GREEN........101 C1
Crabtree Green Ct CW8...101 C2
Crabtree Green Pk CW8..124 C8
Crabtree La WA13.......29 A7
Crabwall Pl CH1........117 F5
Crackley Bank ST5......210 E1
Crackley Bank Prim Sch
  ST5..................210 E1
Craddock Ct
  4 Malpas SY14.......213 B3
  Malpas SY14...........213 B3
Cradley WA8............12 C2
Crag Hall La
  Cut-thorn Hill SK11.....138 A6
  Wildboarclough SK11...137 F6
Cragside Way SK9........60 C6
Craig Cl SK11..........112 B5
Craig Dr SK23...........65 E6
Craig Gdns CH66........69 E7
Craigleigh Gr CH62......43 F4
Craig Rd Congleton CW12...156 F4
  Macclesfield SK11......112 B5
Craigside ST8..........179 C1
Craig Wlk ST7.........193 F2
Craithie Rd CH3........119 A2
Crampton Dr WA15......32 C8
CRANAGE..............130 A6
Cranage Cl
  3 Lingley Green WA5...14 E8
  Runcorn WA7...........49 D7
Cranage Ct **3** CW12....156 F3
Cranage La CW9.........79 D1
Cranage Pl **11** CW10...151 D5
Cranage Rd CW2.......190 A3
Cranage Way **16** SK9...34 D5
Cranberry Cl CW12.....156 E6
Cranberry Dr ST5......210 D1
Cranberry La ST7......193 A3
Cranberry Moss La ST7..193 A3
Cranberry Moss Nature
  Reserve★ ST7.........193 A3
Cranberry Prim Sch ST7..193 A3
Cranberry Rd M31.......11 F3
Cranbrook Cl CW1......190 A8
Crane Ho CH1..........118 B1
Cranfield Dr ST7.......193 A3
Cranford Ave
  Knutsford WA16........56 F1
  Macclesfield SK11......112 F7
Cranford Cl CH62.......43 F4
Cranford Ct Chester CH4..141 A5
  Warrington WA1........17 E8
Cranford Dr WA16.......57 D4
Cranford Mews ST7.....193 A3
Cranford Rd SK9........34 A1
Cranford Sq WA16.......56 F1
Cranham Ave WA3........3 E7
Cranleigh Cl WA4........26 B7

Cranleigh Cres CH1.....118 B4
Cranleigh Dr SK7.......37 A8
Cranmere Cl CW4.......104 A4
Cranshaw La WA8.......13 B6
Cransley Sch CW9.......53 E1
Cranswick Gn CH66.....69 C5
Crantock Dr SK8.........34 C8
Cranwell Ave WA3........4 F4
Cranwell Rd CW12.....157 A8
Craven Ave WA3.........3 E7
Craven Ct WA2...........7 F4
Crawford Ave WA8......12 B1
Crawford Cl CH3.......142 B5
Crawford Dr CW12.....156 E6
Crawford Pl WA7........49 B6
Crawfords Wlk CH3.....118 F3
Crawley Ave WA2........8 A3
Crayford Ave CW12.....157 A5
Cresanne Cl CW10......151 C7
Crescent Dr
  Furness Vale SK23......39 D2
  Helsby WA6.............73 B3
Crescent Rd
  Alderley Edge SK9.......60 B2
  Congleton CW12........156 C2
  Cranage CW4...........129 F6
  Ellesmere Port CH65....70 D6
  Rostherne WA16........30 B3
Crescent The
  Chester CH2............118 D4
  Congleton CW12........156 C2
  Ellesmere Port CH65....69 F5
  Hartford CW8..........103 A5
  Heswall, Gayton CH60...41 B6
  Lymm WA13.............18 F2
  Macclesfield SK10.......87 E1
  Middlewich CW10......128 B1
  Mottram St Andrew SK10...61 A1
  Nantwich CW5.........204 F6
  New Mills SK22.........39 B8
  Northwich CW9.........103 F6
  Rostherne WA16........30 B3
  Utkinton CW6..........146 B7
  Weaverham CW8........77 E1
Cressbrook Rd **2** WA4...16 C1
Cressington Gdns **7**
  CH65.................70 C6
Cresswell Ave
  Newcastle-under-Lyme
   ST5.................210 D1
  New Mills SK22.........39 C8
Cresswell Cl WA5........7 D2
Cresswellshawe Rd ST7...193 D4
Cresswell St SK22.......39 C8
Cresta Dr WA7..........48 F6
Crestwood Cl CW2......206 B7
Crew Ave SK10..........87 E1
CREWE.................190 E5
Crewe Bsns Pk CW1.....190 F2
CREWE-BY-FARNDON....197 A7
Crewe Gates Farm Ind Est
  CW1.................190 F2
Crewe Gates Ind Est
  CW1.................207 A8
CREWE GREEN..........191 B3
Crewe Green Ave CW1...191 B4
Crewe Green Rd CW1....191 A3
Crewe Her Ctr★ CW1....190 D3
Crewe Hill La CH3......197 A6
Crewe La CH3...........180 F1
Crewe Lane S CH3......197 A7
Crewe Rd Alsager ST7...193 B4
  Crewe CW1............190 F2
  Crewe, Crewe Green CW1...191 B3
  Haslington CW1, CW11...191 D5
  Hatherton CW5........219 F3
  Lawton-gate ST7.......193 F4
  Nantwich CW2, CW5....205 D6
  Sandbach CW11........175 A5
  Shavington CW2.......206 C6
Crewe St Chester CH1...237 C3
  Crewe CW1............190 D4
Crewe Sta CW1.........190 E2
Crewood Common Rd
  CW8..................76 A3
Crewood Hall La
  Crowton CW8...........76 A4
  Kingsley WA6...........75 F4
Crib La CW6...........168 A8
Cricketers Way CW4....130 C2
Criftin Cl CH66.........69 C2
Crimes La CH3, CW6....167 D4
Crisham Ave CW5......218 E8
Crispin Rd M22.........33 E8
Critchley Rd CH3.......21 A3
Croasdale Dr WA7.......49 E5
Crocus Gdns WA9........6 A7
Crocus St CW8..........78 B3
Croesmere Dr CH66.....69 D2
CROFT..................9 B8
Croft Cl Altrincham WA15...32 C6
  Congleton CW12........156 F2
  Utkinton CW6..........146 B7
  Waverton CH3.........143 A5
Croft Cotts
  Dunham-on-the-Hill WA6...97 C6
  Ellesmere Port CH66....69 A8
Croft Ct CH65...........70 E3
Croften Dr CH64.........66 E5
Crofters Cl
  6 Ellesmere Port CH66...69 E1
  Pickmere WA16........80 A7
  Wistaston CW2........206 B8
Crofters Ct
  Holmes Chapel CW4....130 C3
  Newcastle-under-Lyme
   ST5.................210 D3

Crofters Gn SK9.........59 F6
Crofters Heath CH66....69 E1
Crofters Lea CW8.......103 D7
Crofters Pk CH5........116 A3
Crofters Way CH1......116 F8
Croft Gdns WA4.........27 A7
Croft Gn Cl **7** WA3.....3 C7
Croft Heath Gdns WA3...9 A8
Croft Ho WA3............9 A7
Croft La Dodleston CH4..162 A7
  Knutsford WA16........82 B8
Crofton Cl WA4.........27 C5
Crofton Cotts WA6.....100 B8
Crofton Gdns WA3........4 E3
Crofton Rd WA7.........22 E1
Croft Pk WA16..........58 F5
Croft Primary School WA3...9 A8
Croft Rd Alvanley WA6...73 A2
  Wilmslow SK9...........59 E4
Croftside WA1...........17 F7
Croftside Way SK9.......60 C6
Croft St Golborne WA3....3 A8
  Widnes WA8............23 A6
Crofts The CH3.........180 F1
Croftsway CH60.........40 D8
Croft The Chester CH2...118 D5
  Norton in Hales TF9....236 B3
  Runcorn WA7...........23 F1
Croftwood Cl **10** CW7...149 A8
Croker La SK11........135 E8
Cromdale Way WA5......14 E6
Cromer Dr CW1.........190 B8
Cromford Ct SK23.......65 E6
Cromford Mews SK23....65 E5
Cromley Rd SK6.........37 E6
Crompton Cl CW12.....157 A6
Crompton Dr WA2........8 A6
Crompton Rd SK11.....112 C7
Crompton Way WA3......4 B8
Cromwell Ave WA5......15 D6
Cromwell Avenue S WA5...15 D4
Cromwell Cl **2** WA1.....2 A4
Cromwell Ct Irlam M44...11 E7
  6 Nantwich CW5.....204 E5
  Warrington WA1........16 A4
  2 Warrington WA1...16 A5
Cromwell Dr CW2.......206 C4
Cromwell Rd Bramhall SK7...35 D6
  Ellesmere Port CH65....70 D5
  Irlam M44..............11 E7
  Northwich CW8........103 E8
Cromwell St WA3........23 A6
Cronkinson Ave CW5....204 E5
Cronkinson Oak CW5....204 F4
CRONTON...............12 D5
Cronton CE Prim Sch
  WA8..................12 C6
Cronton Farm Ct WA8...12 E4
Cronton La Cronton WA8...12 B8
  Widnes WA8............12 C5
Cronton Park Ave WA8...12 C6
Cronton Park Cl WA8....12 C6
Cronton Rd L35, WA8....12 C5
Cronulla Dr WA5........14 E7
Crooked La CH3, CW6...145 C4
Crookedyard Rd SK11...113 E7
Crookenden Cl CH2......95 C1
Crookenden Rd CH2.....95 C1
Crook La CW7..........127 A2
Crook St CH1...........237 A2
Croppers Rd WA2........8 F3
Crosby Ave WA5.........16 A8
Crosby Gr CH64.........43 B8
Crosfield Ct WA5........15 A5
Crosfield St WA1........16 A5
Crosland Dr
  5 Alvanley WA6......73 A2
  Frodsham WA6.........73 A2
Crossall St SK11.......112 C7
Crossdale Rd CH62......43 D5
Cross Dr **2** CW11.....152 C2
Cross Farm WA2..........9 A2
Crossfield Ave
  Culcheth WA3............4 F2
  Lymm WA13.............18 E3
  Winsford CW7..........149 D7
Crossfield Rd
  Bollington SK10.........87 E6
  Handforth SK9..........34 D4
Crossfields CH3.........121 B2
Crossfields La CW12.....178 F8
Crossgates WA8..........13 F3
Cross Gn CH2...........118 E6
Cross Hey CH4..........237 C1
Crossings Ho **1** CW1...190 A5
Crossings The WA12......2 C3
Crosskeys Cl CW6......145 A6
Cross La Audley ST7....209 E5
  Church Minshull CW1,
   CW5................172 C6
  Congleton CW12.......157 A1
  Croft WA3..............9 D7
  Haslington CW1.......191 F8
  Lordship Marsh WA6....73 B8
  Middlewich CW10......151 D6
  Neston CH64...........66 E5
  Newton-le-Willows WA12...2 B4
  Sandbach CW11........175 D5
  Smallwood CW11......176 F5
  Swettenham CW12.....131 F4
  Tarvin CH3............121 E2
  Warrington WA4........17 A3
  Wilmslow SK9...........60 F8
Crossland Mews WA13...18 C4
Crosslands
  Congleton CW12.......157 A1
  Haslington CW1.......191 D4
Crossland Terr WA6......73 B2

CROSS LANE............172 D6
Cross Lane CW11.......177 B5
Cross Lane E M31........11 F3
Cross Lanes CH3.......144 C8
Cross Lane S WA3........9 E6
Cross Lane W M31.......11 F2
Crossledge CW12.......156 B3
Crossley Ave CH66.......69 E6
Crossley Cres CH2......119 B5
Crossley Dr CH60........40 D8
Crossley Pk WA6.........99 C7
Crossley St WA1........16 B5
Cross o' th' Hill SY14....213 D4
Cross o' th' Hill Rd
  Malpas SY14...........213 D4
  No Man's Heath SY14...214 A4
Cross Rd Gatley SK8.....34 B7
  Haslington CW1.......191 D4
Cross St Alsager ST7....193 C3
  Barnton CW8...........78 B3
  Chester CH2............118 F2
  Congleton CW12.......156 D3
  Crewe CW1............190 D3
  Golborne WA3...........3 A7
  Haslington CW1.......191 D4
  Holt LL13.............196 E8
  Macclesfield SK11......112 E6
  Marston CW9...........79 C3
  Neston CH64...........66 E8
  New Mills SK22.........39 C8
  20 Runcorn WA7.....23 A3
  Warrington WA2........16 B7
  Widnes WA8............13 C1
Cross The Holt LL13.....196 E8
  Kingsley WA6...........75 C2
  Lymm WA13.............18 E3
  7 Neston CH64.......66 E8
CROSS TOWN............57 B2
Crossway Bramhall SK7...35 E5
  Crewe CW1............190 D6
  Widnes WA8............22 D8
Crossways ST8..........179 E1
Crossways Rd ST7......194 A4
Crossway The CH63......42 C4
Cross Wood St **2** CW5...204 D5
Crosthwaite Ave CH62...43 F4
Croston Cl
  Alderley Edge SK9.......60 C1
  Widnes WA8............12 C3
Crotia Ave CW2........207 B5
Crotia Mill Rd CW2.....207 B6
Crouch La CW12........157 D4
Crouchley Hall Mews
  WA13.................18 F1
Crouchley La WA13......18 F1
CROUGHTON.............95 F5
Croughton Ct CH66......69 F8
Croughton Rd
  Ellesmere Port CH66....69 F8
  Stoak CH2..............96 A7
  Stoak, Croughton CH2...95 F6
Crowbrook Gr **7** SK9...34 D1
Crowder's La CW9......105 B4
Crowe Ave WA2..........8 B2
Crowland Gdns SK8......35 B6
Crow Lane E WA12.......2 C4
Crow Lane W WA12.......2 A4
Crowleygn Gdns **3** WA4...22 B1
Crowley La CW9, CW10...28 A3
Crowmere Cl CW8.......102 A2
Crown Ave WA8.........22 B8
Crown Bank
  3 Sandbach CW11...175 B6
  Talke ST7.............210 D6
Crown Bank Cres ST7...210 D6
Crown Bldgs WA6........73 B1
Crown Cotts CW8.......124 A7
Crown Ctr The **24** SK11...112 C8
Crown Ctyd CW3.......229 F4
Crown Dr CW11.........175 D3
Crownest La CW9.........78 E8
Crown Fields Cl WA12....2 B5
Crownford Cres WA4.....16 C3
Crown Gate WA7.........49 F7
Crown Gdns
  Newton-le-Willows WA12...2 B4
  Talke ST7.............210 D6
Crown Gn WA13..........19 B4
Crown La WA16.........106 D8
Crown Mews CW3......229 F4
Crown Park Dr WA12.....2 B5
Crown St W SK11.......112 C7
Crown St
  Newton-le-Willows WA12...2 A3
  8 Northwich CW8....103 F8
  2 Warrington WA1...16 B5
Crow's Nest Cotts CH3...166 C6
CROWTON...............76 B2
Crowton Christ Church CE
  Prim Sch CW8..........76 B1
Crowton Cotts CW7.....170 F4
Crowton Gn
  Croxton Green SY14....201 C6
  Tarvin CH3............121 C1
CROXTON GREEN........201 C6
Croxton La CW10.......128 A4
Croxton Way CW8.......103 A4
Croyde Cl M22..........33 F7
Croyde Rd L24..........21 A3
Crum Hill **2** CW9.....104 A8
Cryers La Elton CH2.....72 A2
  Thornton-le-Moors CH2...96 F8

Cuckooland★ WA16......80 F8
CUCKOO'S NEST.........162 F6
Cuckstoolpit Hill SK10...112 E8
CUDDINGTON...........101 F4
CUDDINGTON GREEN....212 B1
CUDDINGTON HEATH....212 C5
Cuddington La
  Cuddington CW8.......101 D4
  Sandiway CW8.........102 A6
Cuddington Prim Sch
  CW8.................101 F2
Cuddington Sta CW8....102 A4
Cuddington Way **7**
  SK9...................34 D5
CUERDLEY CROSS.......13 A2
Cuerdley Gn WA5........14 A2
Cuerdley Rd WA5........14 C3
Cuerdon Dr WA4.........17 D1
Culbin Cl WA3...........10 A6
CULCHETH...............4 E3
Culcheth Hall Dr WA3....4 F4
Culcheth Hall Farm Barns
  WA3...................4 F4
Culcheth High Sch WA3...5 A3
Culcheth Prim Sch WA3...5 A3
Culford Cl WA7.........24 D1
Culland St CW2.........190 C2
Cullen Cl CW2...........43 C4
Cullen Rd WA7..........48 D7
Culver Cl CW8.........103 E4
Cumber Cl SK9..........59 D4
Cumber Dr SK9.........59 D4
Cumber La SK9..........59 D4
Cumberland Arena
  CW1.................190 D5
Cumberland Ave
  Irlam M44.............11 C5
  Nantwich CW5.........204 F6
Cumberland Cl
  Crewe CW1............190 D5
  Talke ST7.............210 E2
Cumberland Cres WA11...1 A1
Cumberland Dr
  Altrincham WA14.......31 B8
  Bollington SK10.........88 B8
Cumberland Gr CH66....69 C3
Cumberland Rd
  Congleton CW12.......156 A3
  Partington M31.........11 E2
Cumberland St
  2 Macclesfield SK10...112 D8
  Warrington WA4........16 C3
Cumbermere Dr CW11...174 E7
Cumbers Dr CH64........67 A5
Cumbers La CH64........67 A5
Cumbrae Dr **4** CH65...70 C1
Cumbria Cl **2** CH66....69 E1
Cundiff Cl SK11........112 E6
Cunliffe Ave WA12.......2 B5
Cunliffe Cl WA7.........50 A7
Cunningham Cl WA5.....14 F5
Cunningham Dr
  Bebington CH63........43 C7
  Gatley M22.............34 B8
  Runcorn WA7...........22 D1
Cunningham Ho WA7.....48 E8
Cunningham Rd WA8.....22 D8
Cuppin St CH1.........237 A2
Curlender Way L24.......21 E2
Curlew Cl
  Golborne WA3...........3 D8
  Macclesfield SK10.......87 C5
  Winsford CW7.........149 C5
Curlew Gr WA3..........9 E3
Curlew Rd ST7.........195 E1
Currans Rd WA2.........8 B2
Curtis Cl **4** SK10.......87 E5
Curzon Ave
  Alsager ST7...........193 C5
  Winnington CW8........78 C2
Curzon Cl CH4.........141 B8
Curzon Ct
  Chester CH4...........140 F7
  5 Salterswall CW7....125 F2
Curzon Dr WA4..........27 A7
Curzon Gr CW7.........126 F1
Curzon Mews SK9.......60 A5
CURZON PARK..........141 B7
Curzon Park N CH4.....141 B7
Curzon Park S CH4.....141 B7
Curzon Rd
  Gatley SK8.............34 B7
  Poynton SK12..........36 E2
Curzon St
  Chester CH4...........140 F7
  5 Runcorn WA7......22 F1
Cutthorn Rd SK11......138 C5
Cwat Erwain CH4.......140 E7
Cwrt Cwellyn CH5......139 B7
Cwrt Dinas CH5........139 B7
Cwrt Ogwen CH5.......139 B7
Cwrt Y Terfyn CH4.....140 F6
Cygnet Cl CH66.........69 D4
Cygnet Ct WA1..........16 A3
Cygnet Dr **2** CW2....189 E1
Cyman Cl CH1..........117 D2
Cynthia Ave WA1........17 B7
Cynthia Rd WA7.........22 F1
Cypress Ave
  Ellesmere Port CH66....69 F1
  Widnes WA8............13 B2
Cypress Cl WA1.........17 E7
Cypress Gr
  2 Radnor CW12.....155 E5
  Runcorn WA7...........49 C7
Cypress Way SK6........38 C4
Cyril Bell Cl WA13......18 F3
Cyril St WA2............16 B7

D

Daffodil Cl Radnor CW12 . . 155 F2
Widnes WA8 . . . 13 E4
Daffodil Gdns WA9 . . . 6 A7
Dagfields Crafts & Antiques Ctr★ CW5 . . . 220 A4
Dagnall Ave WA5 . . . 7 F2
Dahlia Cl WA9 . . . 6 A7
Dahlia Cres CW8 . . . 103 D8
Daintry St SK11 . . . 112 E7
Daintry Terr SK10 . . . 112 E8
Dairy Bank CH2 . . . 72 B4
Dairy Bank Cl SK11 . . . 113 A7
Dairybrook Gr 7 SK9 . . . 34 E1
Dairy Farm Cl WA13 . . . 18 F4
Dairyfields Rd CW5 . . . 205 E5
Dairyground Rd SK7 . . . 35 F7
Dairy House La SK7 . . . 35 B4
Dairy House Rd SK7 . . . 35 B5
Dairy House Small Holdings SK7 . . . 35 B4
Dairy House Way CW2 . . . 189 F2
Dairy La CW5 . . . 188 D6
Dairylands Rd ST7 . . . 193 F4
Daisy Ave WA12 . . . 2 C2
Daisy Bank Alsager ST7 . . . 193 A4
Nantwich CW5 . . . 204 D5
Daisy Bank Cres CW3 . . . 229 F5
Daisybank Dr
Congleton CW12 . . . 156 D4
Sandbach CW11 . . . 175 C6
Daisy Bank La CW9 . . . 78 C3
Daisy Bank Mill Cl WA3 . . . 4 E3
Daisy Bank Rd
Lymm WA13 . . . 18 C3
Warrington WA5 . . . 14 F4
Daisy Cl WA16 . . . 79 F6
Daisy Dr CW8 . . . 101 F2
Daisy Pl CW12 . . . 156 A5
Daisy Way SK6 . . . 37 F7
Dakota Dr WA5 . . . 15 C7
Dalby Cl WA3 . . . 10 B5
Dalby Ct CW9 . . . 104 E5
Dale Ave Bebington CH62 . . . 43 D8
Bramhall SK7 . . . 35 F8
Ellesmere Port CH66 . . . 69 C6
Dalebrook Rd CW12 . . . 155 E3
Dale Cl Huntington CH3 . . . 142 C5
Warrington WA5 . . . 15 D4
Widnes WA8 . . . 22 A8
Dale Cres CW12 . . . 156 F2
Dalecroft WA6 . . . 72 E1
Dale Ct Heswall CH60 . . . 40 F8
Middlewich CW10 . . . 151 D7
Dale Dr Chester CH2 . . . 118 D8
Ellesmere Port CH65 . . . 69 F5
Daleford Manor CW8 . . . 125 B8
Dalefords La
Cuddington CW8 . . . 102 A1
Whitegate CW8 . . . 125 D7
Dale Gdns CH65 . . . 70 B3
Dale Gr Congleton CW12 . . 157 A2
Irlam M44 . . . 11 E6
Dale Head Rd SK10 . . . 86 F4
Dale Hey CH66 . . . 43 E2
Dale House Fold SK12 . . . 37 A4
Dale La WA4 . . . 26 E7
Dale Pl CW12 . . . 156 F2
Dale Rd Bebington CH62 . . . 43 D6
Golborne WA3 . . . 3 A7
New Mills SK22 . . . 39 C7
Dalesford Cl WN7 . . . 4 C8
Dalesford Cres SK10 . . . 111 E8
DALES GREEN . . . 195 C5
Dales Green Rd ST7 . . . 195 C5
Daleside CH2 . . . 118 D8
Dale's Sq CW9 . . . 103 F6
Dale St Chester CH3 . . . 119 A1
Macclesfield SK10 . . . 112 E8
Runcorn WA7 . . . 23 A1
Dalesway CH60 . . . 40 E8
Dale The Neston CH64 . . . 66 E6
Tiverton CW6 . . . 168 C6
Warrington WA5 . . . 14 F5
Dale View Kidsgrove ST7 . . 195 C5
Newton-le-Willows WA12 . . . 2 E4
Dale Way CW1 . . . 190 A5
Dalewood Cl WA2 . . . 16 A6
Dalewood Cres CH2 . . . 72 A3
DALLAM . . . 7 E2
Dallam Com Prim Sch WA5 . 7 F1
Dallam La WA2 . . . 16 A7
Dallas Dr WA5 . . . 15 A7
Dalmahoy Cl CW7 . . . 126 C2
Dalston Dr SK7 . . . 35 C5
Dalton Ave
Warrington WA5 . . . 15 F7
Warrington, Birchwood WA3 . . 9 E6
Dalton Bank WA1 . . . 16 C6
Dalton Cl CH1 . . . 117 E3
Dalton Ct Runcorn WA7 . . . 23 E3
Sandbach CW11 . . . 174 E7
Dalton St Runcorn WA7 . . . 23 D2
Warrington WA3 . . . 9 E5
Dalton Way CW10 . . . 128 D1
Dalwood Cl WA7 . . . 50 E7
Dame Hollow SK8 . . . 34 D7
Damery Ct SK7 . . . 35 E8
Damery Rd SK7 . . . 35 E8
Damhead La CH64 . . . 67 E7
Dam Head La WA3 . . . 11 A5
Damian Dr WA12 . . . 2 A5
Dam La Hollinfare WA3 . . . 11 A4
Mobberley WA16 . . . 58 C3
Warrington WA1 . . . 17 D7
Winwick WA3 . . . 8 F7
Dams La WA16 . . . 106 D5
Damson Dr CW5 . . . 204 E4
Damson La WA16 . . . 58 C3
Damson Wlk M31 . . . 11 D3
Danby Cl Runcorn WA7 . . . 49 D6
Warrington WA5 . . . 15 E7
Dane Ave M31 . . . 11 F4
DANEBANK . . . 38 E5
Dane Bank Ave
Congleton CW12 . . . 156 E4
Crewe CW2 . . . 190 A2
Dane Bank Dr SK12 . . . 38 D6
Dane Bank Rd
Lymm WA13 . . . 18 E4
Northwich CW9 . . . 104 B7
Dane Bank Road E WA13 . . . 18 E4
DANEBRIDGE . . . 160 B7
Dane Cl Alsager ST7 . . . 193 A3
Chester CH4 . . . 140 F5
Sandbach CW11 . . . 174 E7
Dane Dr Biddulph ST8 . . . 179 E1
Wilmslow SK9 . . . 60 D6
Danefield Ct SK8 . . . 34 D8
Danefield Rd
Holmes Chapel CW4 . . . 130 C4
Northwich CW9 . . . 104 B7
Dane Gdns ST7 . . . 195 C2
Dane Gr CH2 . . . 119 F8
Dane Hill Cl SK12 . . . 38 D5
DANE IN SHAW . . . 179 C8
Dane Mill Bsns Ctr CW12 . . . 156 C3
Dane Pl Crewe CW1 . . . 190 D6
Winsford CW7 . . . 127 B1
Dane Rd CW9 . . . 104 C6
Danescroft WA8 . . . 12 B3
Daneshill La M44 . . . 11 E5
Daneside Bsns Pk CW12 . 156 E4
Danes Sq SK11 . . . 112 D5
Dane St Congleton CW12 . . 156 C3
Middlewich CW10 . . . 128 D2
Northwich CW9 . . . 103 F8
Daneswell Rd L24 . . . 21 A2
Dane Valley Rd CW12 . . . 156 F5
Daniel Adamson Ave M31 . 11 D3
Daniel Cl WA3 . . . 10 A4
Daniel Ct M31 . . . 11 F4
Daniell Way CH3 . . . 142 A7
Danily Ct SY14 . . . 213 B3
Dan's Rd WA8 . . . 13 E2
Dappled White Cl 13 CW11 . . . 175 D7
Dappleheath Rd CW2 . . . 190 A1
Darby Cl CH64 . . . 66 E4
D'Arcy Cotts CH63 . . . 42 B6
Darent Rd WA11 . . . 1 B7
DARESBURY . . . 25 B2
Daresbury Bypass
Daresbury WA4 . . . 25 B1
Preston on the Hill WA4 . . . 51 A8
Daresbury Cl
Holmes Chapel CW4 . . . 130 A3
4 Wilmslow SK9 . . . 60 C8
Daresbury Ct WA8 . . . 13 E3
DARESBURY DELPH . . . 25 B1
Daresbury Firs Nature Reserve★ WA4 . . . 25 A2
Daresbury La WA4 . . . 25 D2
Daresbury Park WA7 . . . 50 F7
Daresbury Pk WA4 . . . 51 A8
Daresbury Pk WA4 . . . 51 A8
Daresbury Prim Sch WA4 . 25 B2
Darian Ave M22 . . . 33 D8
Dario Gradi Dr CW2 . . . 190 D1
Dark Ark La CH3, WA6 . . . 99 B3
Darkie Mdw CW6 . . . 185 E8
Dark La Henbury SK11 . . . 111 B8
Higher Whitley WA4 . . . 52 D6
Kingsley WA6 . . . 75 B1
Marston CW9 . . . 79 C6
Tattenhall CH3 . . . 183 E7
Warren SK11 . . . 111 C3
Whitchurch SY13 . . . 227 B1
Darland La LL12 . . . 162 C1
Darley Ave Crewe CW2 . . . 190 A3
Warrington WA2 . . . 8 E3
Darley Cl WA8 . . . 12 B3
Darleydale Dr CH62 . . . 43 F5
Darley Rd SK7 . . . 36 F7
Darlington Ave CW1 . . . 189 F5
Darlington Cres CH1 . . . 94 A1
Darlington Ct 3 WA8 . . . 23 A7
Darlington La CW5 . . . 188 E7
Darlington St CW10 . . . 128 C1
Darnaway Cl WA3 . . . 10 B6
DARNHALL . . . 149 A3
Darnhall Prim Sch CW7 . . 149 D6
Darnhall School La CW7 . 149 C6
Darnhall Wlk 14 CW10 . . . 151 D5
Dart Cl Alsager ST7 . . . 193 A4
Biddulph ST8 . . . 179 D1
Dartnall Cl SK12 . . . 38 A6
Dart Wlk CW7 . . . 127 B2
Darwen Gdns WA2 . . . 8 E1
Darwin Gr SK7 . . . 35 E6
Darwin Rd CH1 . . . 117 C4
Darwin St CW8 . . . 103 E7
Daryl Rd CH60 . . . 41 A8
Dashwood Cl WA4 . . . 27 A7
Daten Ave WA3 . . . 9 E6
Daten Pk WA3 . . . 9 F6
Dauncey Cl CH2 . . . 95 C1
Davehall Ave SK9 . . . 60 A7
DAVENHAM . . . 104 A2
Davenham Ave WA1 . . . 16 E8
Davenham Bypass
Bostock Green CW10 . . . 127 B6
Davenham CW9 . . . 104 B2
Davenham CE Prim Sch CW9 . . . 103 F2
Davenham Cres CW2 . . . 190 A3
Davenham Ct CW9 . . . 104 A3
Davenham Mdws CW9 . . . 103 E3
Davenham Rd
Davenham CW9 . . . 104 E3
Handforth SK9 . . . 34 D4
Davenham Rdbt CW9 . . . 103 F3
Davenham Way
Middlewich CW10 . . . 151 D5
Middlewich CW10 . . . 151 D5
DAVENPORT . . . 154 E7
Davenport Ave
Crewe CW2 . . . 206 D8
Nantwich CW5 . . . 204 E7
Warrington WA4 . . . 16 F5
Wilmslow SK9 . . . 59 E4
Davenport Cl
Sandbach CW11 . . . 175 D8
Tattenhall CH3 . . . 166 A1
DAVENPORT GREEN . . . 59 F3
Davenport La
Brereton Green CW11 . . . 154 C2
Marton SK11 . . . 132 F5
Mobberley WA16 . . . 58 D6
Davenport Park La CW12 . . . 131 D2
Davenport Rd CH60 . . . 40 E7
Davenport Row WA7 . . . 49 D8
Davenport St
Congleton CW12 . . . 156 C2
Crewe CW1 . . . 190 C6
Macclesfield SK10 . . . 112 E8
Daven Prim Sch CW12 . . . 156 E2
Daven Rd CW12 . . . 156 F1
Davenshaw Dr CW12 . . . 156 E4
Davey La SK9 . . . 60 B2
Daveylands SK9 . . . 60 D7
David Lewis Ctr The★ SK9 . . . 84 A6
David Lewis Sch SK9 . . . 83 F6
David Rd WA13 . . . 18 C3
David's Ave WA5 . . . 15 B5
Davidson Ave CW12 . . . 157 A5
David St CW8 . . . 103 E7
David Whitby Way CW2 . . 207 A7
Davies Ave Gatley SK8 . . . 34 B6
Newton-le-Willows WA12 . . . 2 C4
Warrington WA4 . . . 16 F4
Davies Cl WA8 . . . 23 A4
Davies St SK10 . . . 112 E8
Davies Way WA13 . . . 18 E3
Davis Cl ST7 . . . 193 E3
Davy Rd WA7 . . . 23 E3
Dawlish Ave SK8 . . . 34 F7
Dawlish Cl Bramhall SK7 . . . 35 E7
Hollinfare WA3 . . . 11 B3
Dawn Cl CH64 . . . 67 A5
Dawn Gdns CH65 . . . 70 B4
Dawpool Cl CH2 . . . 118 D5
Dawpool Ct CH2 . . . 118 D5
Dawpool Dr CH62 . . . 43 C7
Dawson Cl Langley SK11 . . 113 C3
11 Macclesfield SK11 . . . 111 F7
Dawson Dr CH2 . . . 237 A4
Dawson Rd Bollington SK10 . 88 A7
Gatley SK8 . . . 34 D8
Macclesfield SK11 . . . 111 F7
Dawson Way SK9 . . . 60 F8
Dawstone Ct CH60 . . . 40 E8
Dawstone Rd CH60 . . . 41 A7
Dawstone Rise CH60 . . . 40 F7
DAY GREEN . . . 192 F8
Day Green Rd CW11 . . . 192 E8
Deacon Rd WA8 . . . 13 B1
Deacons Cl WA3 . . . 9 A8
Deacon Trad Est WA12 . . . 2 A2
Deadman's La CW5 . . . 205 B2
Deakin's Rd CW7 . . . 126 F4
Deal Cl WA5 . . . 15 F6
Dean Bank CW6 . . . 168 C3
Dean Cl Bollington SK10 . . . 88 A7
Handforth SK9 . . . 34 C1
Partington M31 . . . 11 F4
Sandbach CW11 . . . 174 E8
7 Widnes WA8 . . . 23 B8
Dean Cres WA2 . . . 8 B2
Dean Ct Bollington SK10 . . . 88 B8
Golborne WA3 . . . 3 A7
Dean Dr SK9 . . . 34 D2
Deane Ct CW5 . . . 205 B4
Deanery Cl CH2 . . . 118 C4
Deangate CW2 . . . 207 E3
Dean Hollow ST7 . . . 209 D2
Dean La SK7 . . . 36 E8
Dean Mdw WA12 . . . 2 C4
Dean Pk SY14 . . . 214 A5
Dean Rd Golborne WA3 . . . 3 A7
Handforth SK9 . . . 34 E3
Irlam M44 . . . 11 E6
DEAN ROW . . . 60 F8
Dean Row Ct 9 SK9 . . . 34 D1
Dean Row Rd SK9 . . . 61 A8
Deans Cl Chester CH2 . . . 118 D6
Tarvin CH3 . . . 121 B1
Deansfield Way CH2 . . . 72 A3
Deansgate CH65 . . . 70 A5
DEANSGREEN . . . 29 A8
Deansgreen Ct WA13 . . . 29 A7
Deans La Sandbach CW11 . . 174 E6
Warrington WA4 . . . 17 F3
Dean's La
Barthomley CW2 . . . 208 C4
Newcastle-under-Lyme ST5 . . . 210 D2
Deans Rd CH65 . . . 70 F3
Dean St Middlewich CW10 . 128 C2
Dean St continued
Northwich CW9 . . . 104 C8
Widnes WA8 . . . 23 B8
Winsford CW7 . . . 126 D1
Deansway WA8 . . . 22 C8
Deans Way
Higher Kinnerton CH4 . . . 161 A7
Tarvin CH3 . . . 121 B2
Dean Valley Com Sch SK10 . . . 87 E8
Dean View ST7 . . . 209 D1
Deanwater Cl WA3 . . . 9 D4
Deanwater Ct SK8 . . . 34 D7
Deanway SK9 . . . 34 C1
Deanway Trad Est SK9 . . . 34 D3
Dearnford Ave CH62 . . . 43 D6
Dearnford Cl CH62 . . . 43 D6
Debra Cl CH66 . . . 69 C4
Debra Rd CH66 . . . 69 C4
Decade Cl ST5 . . . 210 F2
Dee Ave CW4 . . . 130 D2
Dee Banks Chester CH3 . . . 142 A8
Huntington CH3 . . . 141 F7
Dee Banks Sch CH3 . . . 142 A7
Dee Cl Biddulph ST8 . . . 179 E1
Sandbach CW11 . . . 174 E8
Talke ST7 . . . 210 E7
Dee Cres CH3 . . . 180 E2
Deefords CH3 . . . 118 F1
Dee Fords Ave CH3 . . . 119 A1
Dee Hills Pk CH3 . . . 237 C2
Dee La Chester CH1, CH3 . . 237 C2
Holt LL13 . . . 196 D7
Dee Mdws LL13 . . . 196 D7
Dee Park Cl CH60 . . . 41 B6
Dee Park Rd CH60 . . . 41 B5
Deepdale WA8 . . . 12 C3
Deep Dale WA5 . . . 14 F6
Dee Pk LL13 . . . 196 D8
Dee Point Cty Prim Sch CH1 . . . 117 D3
Dee Rd CH2 . . . 96 F1
Deer Park Ct WA7 . . . 49 F6
Deerwood Cl
Ellesmere Port CH66 . . . 69 D7
Macclesfield SK10 . . . 86 F1
Deerwood Cres CH66 . . . 69 D7
Deeside
Ellesmere Port CH65 . . . 70 B2
Holt LL13 . . . 196 E8
Dee Side CH60 . . . 40 C8
Deeside Cl CH65 . . . 70 B2
Deeside Coll/Coleg Glannau Dyfrdwy CH5 . . . 91 B1
Deeside Cres CH1 . . . 116 E5
Deeside Ct Chester CH3 . . 237 C2
Neston CH64 . . . 41 B1
Deeside Ind Pk/Parc Ddiwydiannol Glannau Dyfrdwy CH5 . . . 92 E2
Deeside La CH1 . . . 116 D4
Dee Sq CW7 . . . 127 B2
Dee View CH3 . . . 180 E2
Dee View Blvd CH1 . . . 117 F1
Dee View Cotts CH64 . . . 41 D1
Dee View Ct CH64 . . . 66 E6
Dee View Rd
Connah's Quay CH5 . . . 91 E1
Heswall CH60 . . . 40 F8
Dee Villas LL13 . . . 180 E1
Dee Way CW7 . . . 127 A2
Deirdre Ave WA8 . . . 13 A1
De Lacy Row WA7 . . . 24 A2
Delafield Cl WA2 . . . 8 F3
Delaisy Way CW7 . . . 127 A1
Delamare Pl 1 WA7 . . . 22 F1
DELAMERE . . . 123 D6
Delamere Ave
Bebington CH62 . . . 43 E4
Ellesmere Port CH66 . . . 69 E5
Golborne WA3 . . . 3 E6
Widnes WA8 . . . 12 C1
Delamere CE Prim Sch CW6 . . . 123 C5
Delamere Cl Barnton CW8 . 78 A3
Bebington CH62 . . . 43 E4
Chorlton CW2 . . . 207 E4
Sandbach CW11 . . . 174 F8
Delamere Ct Alsager ST7 . . 192 F4
Bebington CH62 . . . 43 E4
7 Crewe CW1 . . . 190 C4
Delamere Dr
Ellesmere Port CH66 . . . 69 E5
Macclesfield SK10 . . . 87 F2
Delamere Forest Pk★ CW8 . . . 100 B3
Delamere Gn CH66 . . . 69 E5
Delamere Gr CW8 . . . 123 D7
Delamere Ho WA6 . . . 74 C7
Delamere La CH3 . . . 99 C2
DELAMERE PARK . . . 101 C5
Delamere Park Way E CW8 . . . 101 D5
Delamere Park Way W CW8 . . . 101 D5
Delamere Rd
Congleton CW12 . . . 155 F3
Handforth SK9 . . . 34 E4
Macclesfield SK10 . . . 87 F1
Nantwich CW5 . . . 204 F3
Norley WA6 . . . 100 B6
Delamere Rise CW7 . . . 126 B1
Delamere St Chester CH1 . 237 A3
Crewe CW1 . . . 190 C4
Warrington WA5 . . . 15 E5
Winsford CW7 . . . 126 B1
Delamere Sta CW8 . . . 100 D1
Delamore's Acre CH64 . . . 68 A8
Delavor Cl CH60 . . . 40 E8
Delavor Rd CH60 . . . 40 E8
Delenty Dr WA3 . . . 9 E4
Delery Dr WA1 . . . 16 E8
Delfur Rd SK7 . . . 35 F7
Delhi Rd M44 . . . 11 F8
Dell Cl CH63 . . . 43 B6
Dell Dr WA2 . . . 9 A2
Dell La CH60 . . . 41 B7
Dell The Cuddington CW8 . . 101 D5
Guilden Sutton CH3 . . . 119 F5
Kelsall CW6 . . . 122 D5
Delmar Rd WA16 . . . 57 C1
Delphfields Rd WA4 . . . 26 C7
Delphield WA7 . . . 50 D8
Delph La Daresbury WA4 . . . 25 A2
Warrington, Houghton Gn WA2 . . . 8 E6
Winwick WA2 . . . 8 A5
Delphside ST7 . . . 209 F2
Delta Cres WA5 . . . 7 C2
Delta Ct CH4 . . . 140 B6
Deltic Cl WA12 . . . 2 D1
Delune Cres SY14 . . . 213 C4
Delves Ave WA5 . . . 15 F7
Delves Broughton Ct CW1 . . . 191 D5
Delves Cl CW2 . . . 206 B4
Delves Wlk CH3 . . . 142 B7
Delvine Dr CH2 . . . 118 D6
Demage Dr CH66 . . . 69 D3
Demage La Backford CH1 . . . 94 F4
Chester CH2 . . . 118 D8
Demage La S CH2 . . . 118 D7
Denbigh Cl
Hazel Grove SK7 . . . 36 C8
Helsby WA6 . . . 73 A1
Denbigh Cres CW10 . . . 151 C7
Denbigh Ct CH65 . . . 70 D3
Denbigh Dr CW7 . . . 149 B7
Denbigh Gdns CH65 . . . 70 C3
Denbigh St CH1 . . . 118 B3
Denbury Ave WA4 . . . 16 F2
Dene Ave WA12 . . . 1 F4
Dene Dr CW7 . . . 149 D8
Denehurst Cl WA5 . . . 14 F4
Denehurst Park Way CW8 . . . 101 D5
Denesgate 1 CW7 . . . 149 D8
Deneside Ave CW1 . . . 190 C6
Deneway Bramhall SK7 . . . 35 D7
High Lane SK6 . . . 37 F8
Denewood Ct 3 SK9 . . . 60 A6
Denford Cl CH4 . . . 139 C4
Denford Pl ST7 . . . 193 D6
Denhall Cl CH2 . . . 118 E5
Denhall La CH64 . . . 67 A3
Denham Ave WA5 . . . 15 B5
Denham Dr SK7 . . . 35 D7
Denise Ave WA5 . . . 14 E5
Denison Rd SK7 . . . 36 E8
Den La CW3, CW5 . . . 221 D4
Dennett Cl WA1 . . . 17 E6
Dennis Dr CH4 . . . 141 B6
Dennison Rd SK8 . . . 35 B8
Dennis Rd WA8 . . . 23 C7
Dennis Round Ct ST7 . . . 193 C3
Densham Ave WA2 . . . 8 B2
Denson Ct CH2 . . . 95 B4
Denston Cl CW2 . . . 190 B1
Denstone Dr CH4 . . . 141 A4
Dentdale Wlk M22 . . . 33 C8
Dentith Dr CH1 . . . 117 E5
Denton Cl CW7 . . . 126 C1
Denton Dr CW9 . . . 79 C1
Denton Drive Ind Est CW9 . . . 79 C2
Denton St WA8 . . . 13 C1
Denver Ave CW2 . . . 190 B3
Denver Dr WA5 . . . 15 B7
Denver Rd WA4 . . . 17 A3
Denwall Ho 4 CH64 . . . 66 E8
Depenbech Cl SY14 . . . 213 B4
Depmore La WA6 . . . 75 A2
Derby Cl Irlam M44 . . . 11 C5
Newton-le-Willows WA12 . . . 2 B3
Derby Dr WA1 . . . 16 F7
Derby Knoll SK23 . . . 39 F1
Derby Rd Golborne WA3 . . . 3 C8
Talke ST7 . . . 210 D7
4 Warrington WA4 . . . 16 C1
Widnes, Barrow's Green WA8 . . . 13 D4
Widnes, Lunts Heath WA8 . . . 13 B4
Derby Row WA12 . . . 7 D8
DERBYSHIRE HILL . . . 1 A2
Derbyshire Hill Rd WA9 . . . 1 A2
Derbyshire Rd
Partington M31 . . . 11 E2
Poynton SK12 . . . 37 D5
Derby St Congleton CW12 . . 156 D3
Crewe CW1 . . . 190 B5
Newton-le-Willows WA12 . . . 2 B3
Dereham Way WA7 . . . 24 D3
Derek Ave WA2 . . . 8 E1
Derfel Terr 4 WA6 . . . 74 B8
Derrington Ave CW2 . . . 190 C3
Derry La SK7 . . . 35 F2
Derwent Ave CW7 . . . 127 B1
Derwent Cl Alsager ST7 . . . 193 A4
Culcheth WA3 . . . 5 A2
Holmes Chapel CW4 . . . 130 A3
Macclesfield SK11 . . . 112 A6
Partington M31 . . . 11 F4
Willaston CW5 . . . 205 D6

Derwent Cres ST7...... 195 C2
Derwent Dr Biddulph ST8 . 179 E1
  Bramhall SK7...... 35 C5
  Congleton CW12..... 156 F1
  Handforth SK9..... 34 C5
  Hooton CH66......44 B2
Derwent Rd Chester CH2. 119 A5
  High Lane SK6......37 E8
  Warrington WA4..... 16 B2
  Widnes WA8...... 12 C1
Derwent Way
  Alderley Edge SK9........ 83 F7
  Neston CH64......66 F7
Desoto Rd WA8........ 22 E5
Desoto Road E WA8.....22 F6
Desoto Road W WA8....22 F6
De Trafford Mews [9] SK9. 34 D2
Detroit Cl WA5......15 B6
Deva Ave CH4...... 140 D6
Deva Bsns Pk CH5.. 116 A8
Deva Cl SK12......36 B4
Deva Ct CH2...... 118 F2
Deva Hts CH3...... 141 F7
Deva La CH2...... 118 C6
Deva Link CH1...... 118 B3
Devana Gdns CH4..... 141 B4
Deva Rd CW2...... 189 D4
Deva Ret Pk CH1..... 118 A3
Deva Terr CH3...... 237 C2
Devon Cl Macclesfield SK10..86 F2
  Middlewich CW10...... 128 D2
Devon Gr ST8...... 179 C1
Devon Pl Congleton CW12. 156 E4
  Widnes WA8...... 13 B3
Devon Rd Chester CH2.. 118 F5
  Irlam M44...... 11 D5
  Partington M31...... 11 E2
Devonshire Dr SK9......60 B2
Devonshire Gdns WA12....2 C2
Devonshire Pl CH4..... 141 E7
Devonshire Rd
  Broughton CH4...... 139 C4
  Hazel Grove SK7...... 36 F8
  Warrington WA1...... 16 F8
Dewar Ct WA7......23 E3
Dewa Roman Experience★
  CH1...... 237 B2
Dewar St WA3......9 E5
Dewes La WA4......17 F3
Dewes St CW1...... 190 B5
Dewhurst Rd WA3......9 D2
Dexter Way CW10..... 128 D2
Dial Cotts CH64...... 67 A5
Dial La CW12, SK11..... 158 B1
Dial Rd WA15...... 32 C8
Dial St WA1...... 16 C5
Diamond Ave [3] ST7..... 195 B2
Diamond Cl CW2...... 206 C3
Dibbinsdale Rd CH63.....43 B7
Dibbins Gn CH63.....43 B7
Dickens Cl Cheadle SK8....35 B5
  Sandbach CW11...... 174 D6
Dickens La SK12......36 E2
Dickenson Ho CW10..... 128 C1
Dickenson St WA2...... 16 C7
Dickinson Cl WA11...... 1 A6
Dickinson Way ST7..... 193 A3
Dicklow Cob SK11..... 132 A8
Dickson Cl WA8......23 B8
Dicksons Dr CH2...... 118 D4
Dickson St [2] Widnes WA8..23 B8
  Widnes, Kingsway WA8..... 23 A8
Didsbury Cres CW9..... 126 F8
Dierden St CW7...... 127 B1
Dierdens Terr [4] CW10. 128 C1
Dig La Acton CW5...... 203 F4
  Frodsham WA6......74 A7
  Shavington CW5...... 206 B2
  Warrington WA2......9 B3
Diglake Cl ST7...... 210 C6
Diglake Cotts ST7..... 210 A2
Diglake St ST7...... 209 F3
Diglee Rd SK23...... 39 C3
Dillors Croft CW1...... 173 A1
Dimelow Ct SY14..... 213 A2
Dinas Cl CH1...... 117 D3
Dingle Ave
  Newton-le-Willows WA12....1 F2
  Row-of-Trees SK9...... 59 D3
Dingle Bank Chester CH4. 141 C7
  Sandbach CW11...... 175 C6
Dingle Bank Cl WA13.....18 E3
Dinglebrook Gr [5] SK9..34 D1
Dingle Cl SK10......87 B3
Dingle La
  Bridgemere CW5...... 231 F6
  Kelsall CW6...... 122 E6
  Sandbach CW11...... 175 C6
  Warrington WA4......26 F6
  Winsford CW7...... 126 E1
Dingle Prim Sch The
  CW1...... 191 D6
Dingle Recn Ctr [6] CW7. 126 D1
Dingle The Barnton CW8....78 B4
  Haslington CW1...... 191 D5
  Lymm WA13......18 E3
Dingleway WA4...... 26 D8
Dingle Way CW8...... 101 E6
Dingle Wlk [4] CW7...... 126 D1
Dinnington Cy WA4......12 E3
Diploma Dr CW10...... 128 C2
Dipping Brook Ave WA4 ..26 F4
DISLEY...... 38 C5
Disley Prim Sch SK12..... 38 D6
Disley Sta SK12...... 38 C6

Distaff Rd SK12......36 B4
District CE Prim Sch The
  WA12...... 2 A4
Ditchfield La WA16...... 29 D3
Ditchfield Pl WA8......22 B8
Ditchfield Rd
  Warrington WA5...... 14 E3
  Widnes WA8......22 B8
Ditchway CW12...... 158 D2
DITTON...... 22 C8
Ditton Rd WA8...... 22 D6
Dixon Ave WA12......2 C5
Dixon Cl WA11......2 A8
Dixon Ct SK11......84 A2
Dixon Dr [8] Alvanley WA6.. 73 A2
  Chelford SK11......84 B3
Dixon Rd CW12...... 157 A5
Dixon's Hos CH3...... 142 E8
Dixon St Irlam M44...... 11 F8
  Warrington WA1...... 16 A5
Dobb Hedge Cl WA15.... 32 C6
Dobb La WA16......29 E2
Dobell's Rd CW9...... 103 F5
Dobers La WA6......74 C4
Dob La CW6...... 185 F3
Dobson Ct SY14...... 213 B3
Dobson La SK7......35 F2
Dobson Way CW12..... 156 E5
Dock Rd Northwich CW9.. 103 F7
  Widnes WA8...... 23 A5
Dock Road Edwardian
  Pumping Station The★ [2]
  CW9...... 103 F7
Dock St
  Ellesmere Port CH65...... 70 C7
  Widnes WA8...... 23 A5
Dock View Rd CH65...... 70 C8
Dock Yard Rd CH65...... 70 E6
Dodd Dr [3] WA4......17 B3
Doddington Dr CW11..... 175 C8
Doddington Rd CW2...... 190 A3
Doddlespool Barns CW3,
  SY13...... 228 C4
Dodd's Green La CW5,
  CW11...... 228 C4
Dodd's La CW12...... 178 C6
  Higher Wych SY13, SY14... 224 E7
Doddswood Dr [2] CW12. 156 F4
Dodgsley Dr WA6...... 75 C1
DODLESTON...... 162 B7
Dodleston CE Prim Sch
  CH4...... 162 A7
Dodleston La CH4...... 162 C3
Doeford Cl WA3......4 E5
Doe's Meadow Rd CH63..43 B7
Dog La
  Brereton Green CW4,
  CW11...... 153 E7
  Kelsall CW6...... 122 B5
  Nantwich CW5...... 204 E6
  Tattenhall CH3...... 182 D4
  Threapwood SY14...... 223 C7
Dogmore La CW6...... 147 C4
Dolly La SK23......39 F3
Dolmans La [9] WA1......16 B5
Dolphin Cres CH66...... 69 E2
Dolphin Ct CH4...... 141 A7
Dombey Rd SK12......36 D2
Domestic App M90...... 33 C6
Domville Ct WA13...... 18 E3
Donagh Cl SK10......86 F2
DONES GREEN...... 77 B8
Donkey La SK9......60 A5
Donne Pl CH1...... 117 F6
Donnington Way CH4.... 140 F7
Don Wlk CH65......70 A7
Dood's La WA4......27 A5
Dooley's Grig SK11..... 108 F1
Dooley's La SK9......33 C2
Dorac Ave SK8......34 C7
Dorchester Cl
  Kidsgrove ST7...... 195 A3
  Wilmslow SK9......60 D8
Dorchester Pk WA7......24 E3
Dorchester Pk Nature
  Reserve★ WA7...... 24 D3
Dorchester Rd
  Chester CH4...... 140 F5
  Warrington WA5...... 15 C5
Dorchester Way
  Burtonwood WA5......6 F6
  Macclesfield SK10...... 87 C4
Doreen Ave CW12...... 179 B8
Dorfold Cl CW11...... 175 C7
Dorfold Dr CW5...... 204 D5
Dorfold Hall★ CW5...... 204 B5
Dorfold St CW1...... 190 C4
Dorfold Way CH2...... 118 E6
Doric Ave WA6......74 D7
Dorin Park Specl Sch
  CH2...... 118 D6
Dormer Cl CH3...... 143 A5
Dorney Cl WA4......26 E6
Dornoch Ct CW4...... 130 B2
Dorothea Cres [3] WA8....13 E4
Dorothea St WA2......16 C7
Dorric Way CW1...... 190 C7
Dorrington Cl WA7......50 E8
Dorrington Way CH65.... 70 C5
Dorrit Cl SK12......36 E2
Dorset Cl CW12...... 156 E4
Dorset Dr ST8...... 179 C1
Dorset Gdns WA7......50 A6
Dorset Pl Chester CH2.... 119 A5
  Kidsgrove ST7...... 195 A2
Dorset Rd Chester CH2 .. 118 F7
  Irlam M44...... 11 D5
Dorset Way WA1......87 B8
Dorset Wlk SK10......86 F2

Douglas Ave WA9......6 B6
Douglas Cl
  Northwich CW8...... 103 C5
  Widnes WA8......13 F3
Douglas La CW7...... 171 A6
Douglas Pl CH4...... 140 E6
Doulton Cl
  Wilderspool WA4...... 16 C3
  Winsford CW7...... 126 F3
Doune Ct CH65...... 70 D3
Dounrey Cl WA2......9 A2
DOVE BANK...... 195 A2
Dove Bank Prim Sch
  ST7...... 195 A2
Dove Cl
  Ellesmere Port CH66...... 70 A8
  Elton CH2......72 C4
  Helsby WA6......73 C5
  Sandbach CW11...... 175 A8
  Warrington WA3......9 F4
Dovecote Cl CW2...... 206 B8
Dovecote Dr WA11......1 C7
Dovecote Gn WA5......7 A1
Dovedale Ave CH62......43 E5
Dovedale Cl
  Congleton CW12...... 157 A4
  High Lane SK6......37 E7
  Warrington WA2......8 E3
Dovedale Ct WA8......12 B3
Dove Gr ST8...... 179 D1
Dovehead And Three Shires
  Head...... 138 F4
Dove Ho ST7...... 195 C3
Dove Pl CW7...... 127 B2
Dover Cl WA7......50 E6
Dover Ct CH65...... 70 D2
Dover Ct WA4......16 F3
Dover Dr
  Ellesmere Port CH65...... 70 D2
  Winsford CW7...... 149 B6
Dover Rd Chester CH4.... 141 A6
  Macclesfield SK10......87 F2
  Warrington WA4...... 17 A3
Dover St WA7......23 B3
Dovesmead Rd CH60..... 41 C7
Dovestones WA5...... 14 C7
Doward St WA8......13 C2
Downes Cl SK10......87 A1
Downesway SK9......59 F1
Downham Ave WA3......4 F2
Downham Ct [1] CH60..... 41 A8
Downham Dr CH60...... 41 A8
Downham Pl CH1...... 117 E4
Downham Road S CH60.. 41 A8
Downing Cl
  Ellesmere Port CH65...... 70 D5
  Sutton Lane Ends SK11... 112 F3
Downs End WA16...... 57 C1
Downsfield Rd CH4..... 141 A6
Downside WA8......12 B3
Downs Rd WA7......23 A1
Downs The CW8...... 101 D5
Downswood Ct CH2...... 118 C4
Downswood Dr CH2..... 118 C4
Downway La WA9......1 A1
Dragon's La
  Middlewich CW11...... 151 F1
  Sandbach CW11...... 152 B1
Dragons Wharf CW11.... 152 C1
Dragon Yd WA8......13 B4
Dragoon Dr CH3...... 142 C5
Drake Ave M44...... 11 E6
Drake Cl WA5......7 D1
Drake La CW5...... 203 F4
Drakelow La CW10...... 128 F8
Drake Rd CH64......41 E1
Drakes Way SY14...... 213 B5
Drapers Ct WA3......3 F7
Draycote Water [4] WA5 .. 14 D8
Draycott Dr ST5...... 210 D2
Drayton Cl
  [12] Handforth SK9...... 34 D1
  Runcorn WA7......22 F1
  [5] Warrington WA5......15 B6
Drayton Cres CW1...... 190 F5
Drayton Dr SK8......34 B7
Drenfell Rd ST7...... 194 F7
Drift Cotts LL12...... 162 C1
Drillfield Ct [20] CW9..... 103 F8
Drillfield Rd CW9...... 104 A8
Drill Field Rd CW9...... 103 F8
Drive A CH5......93 A2
Drive B CH5......93 A2
Drive C CH5......93 A2
Drive D CH5......93 A1
Drive The Altrincham WA15. 32 D8
  Bollington SK10......87 F7
  Broomedge WA13...... 19 D1
  Holmes Chapel CW4...... 130 C2
Drome Rd CH5......93 A2
Drovers Way CW11...... 175 A5
Droxford Ct SK9......60 B6
Druitt Ct CW1...... 191 D4
Drumber La ST7...... 195 B8
Drumber The CW7...... 126 D1
Drumble Field SK11......84 A3
Drummond Ave CH66..... 69 C4
Drummond Ct WA8...... 13 D2
Drummond Way SK10......86 E1
Druridge Dr WA5......14 F4
Drury Cl WA7...... 190 F5
Drury La Knutsford WA16... 57 A2
  Tallarn Green/Tallwrn Green
  SY13...... 223 E1
  Warmingham CW1...... 173 D4
DRURY LANE...... 223 D1
Dryden Cl CW2...... 190 A1
Dryden Pl WA4......8 C2

Dryersfield [5] CH3...... 142 A8
Dryhurst Dr SK12......38 D6
Dryhurst La SK12......38 D6
Dry Stones Edge Rd
  SK17...... 138 F6
Dublin Croft CH66......69 E1
Dubthorn La CW11...... 175 E5
Duchess Pl CH2...... 237 A4
Duchy Rd CW1...... 207 A8
DUCKINGTON...... 199 C4
Duckington Cross La
  Duckington SY14...... 199 B4
  Duckington SY14...... 199 C4
Duckington La SY14..... 198 C3
Duck La CH3...... 121 F7
Duckworth Gr WA2......9 A1
DUDDON...... 145 A6
Duddon Cl Duddon CW6... 145 B6
  [3] Northwich CW9...... 103 F4
Duddon Common La
  CW6...... 145 B7
Duddon Hall Barns CW6.. 144 E8
Duddon Heath...... 144 E8
Duddon Hook La CW6.... 144 F6
Duddon Rd Duddon CW6... 145 B5
  Old Moss CH3...... 144 D8
Duddon St Peter's CE Prim
  Sch CW6...... 145 B6
Duddy Rd SK12......38 E6
Duddleston Rd CH66......69 B6
Dudley Ave WA7......23 D2
Dudley Cres CH65......44 B3
Dudley Rd
  Ellesmere Port CH65...... 70 B5
  Irlam M44...... 11 D4
Dudley St WA2......16 B7
Dudley Wlk [2] SK11..... 111 F7
Dudlow Green Rd WA4....26 E5
DUDLOW'S GREEN......26 E5
Dufton Wlk M22......33 E8
Duke Ave Cheadle SK8......34 F6
  Glazebury WA3......5 C7
Duke Cl WA7......22 F2
Duke Gr CH3...... 142 C5
Dukesbridge Ct [7] WA13..18 E3
Duke's Cres CW11...... 175 A7
Dukes Ct [2] SK11...... 112 D7
Duke's Ct CH1...... 237 B1
DUKESFIELD......22 E3
Duke St Alderley Edge SK9...60 D8
  Chester CH1...... 237 B1
  Congleton CW12...... 156 D2
  Crewe CW2...... 190 C3
  Macclesfield SK11...... 112 D7
  Newton-le-Willows WA12...2 B3
Dukesway CH2...... 118 E7
Dukes Way CW9...... 103 E5
Dukes Wharf WA7......50 E6
Dulas Ct CW2...... 118 E8
Dulverton Ave CH3...... 119 C2
Dumbah La SK10......87 D6
Dumbers SK11...... 136 A3
Dumbill Ho ST7...... 210 C8
Dunbar Cl
  Connah's Quay CH5...... 91 D1
  Ellesmere Port CH65...... 69 C5
  Holmes Chapel CW4...... 130 C2
Dunbar Ct CH66...... 69 C5
Duncan Ave
  Newton-le-Willows WA12....2 C5
  Runcorn WA7...... 23 C1
Duncansby Cres WA5......14 E6
Duncansby Dr CH63...... 43 C4
Duncan St WA2......16 C7
Dundalk La WA8......22 D8
Dundalk Rd WA8......22 E8
Dundee Cl WA2......16 C1
Dundee Ct CH65...... 70 E3
Dundonald Ave [5] WA4.. 16 C1
Dundonald Rd SK8......35 A7
Dundrennan Cl SK12......36 D5
Dunge Rd
  Horwich End SK23...... 65 A2
  Kettleshulme SK23...... 64 F1
Dunge Valley Rhododendron
  Gdns★ SK23......89 F8
Dunham Cl Alsager ST7... 193 C3
  Bebington CH62......43 F3
  Sandbach CW11...... 175 C6
Dunham Cres CW2...... 206 B8
Dunham Ct
  Dunham-on-the-Hill WA6..97 E6
  Hartford CW8...... 102 F4
DUNHAM HEATH......98 A4
Dunham Massey Hall★
  WA14...... 20 D3
DUNHAM-ON-THE-HILL...97 E5
Dunham Pk (Deer Pk)★
  WA14...... 20 D3
Dunham Rd
  Altrincham, Bowgreen
  WA14...... 20 F1
  Handforth SK9...... 34 D5
  Mossbrow WA13...... 19 E7
  Northwich CW9...... 104 A4
DUNHAM TOWN......20 E4
Dunham Way CH2...... 118 F6
DUNHAM WOODHOUSES...20 B4
DUNKIRK......94 E6
Dunkirk ST7...... 210 A6
Dunkirk Ave CW7...... 149 D8
Dunkirk Dr CH65......70 B1
Dunkirk La Capenhurst CH1 94 C7
  Ellesmere Port CH65...... 70 A1
Dunkirk Trad Est CH1..... 94 E6
Dunkirk Way Dunkirk CH66..94 E6
  Holmes Chapel CW4...... 130 C1
Dunley Cl WA3......10 A5

Dunlin Ave WA12......2 C4
Dunlin Cl [2] Neston CH64.. 66 D7
  Poynton SK12......36 A4
  Runcorn WA7......49 F5
  Warrington WA2......8 E3
Dunlin Rise SK10......87 B5
Dunlop St WA4......16 B3
Dunmail Gr WA7......49 E5
Dunmore Cl CW10...... 151 C2
Dunmore Cres CH66......69 B6
Dunmore Rd CH66......69 B6
Dunmow Rd WA4...... 17 C3
Dunnillow Field CW5.... 205 A4
Dunnock Cl WA2......8 E3
Dunnock Gr WA3......9 E4
Dunnocksfold Rd ST7.... 193 A4
Dunnockswood ST7...... 193 A4
Dunn's Cotts CW1...... 192 C1
Dunn's La CH3...... 121 F7
Dunoon Cl CW4...... 130 B2
Dunraven Rd CH64......67 A7
Dunscar Cl WA3......9 D5
Dunsford WA8......12 B3
Dunsmore Cl WA11......1 C7
Dunstan La CH64......67 E3
Dunster Cl CW9...... 104 A4
Dunster Gr CH60......41 B7
Dunster Rd SK10......87 F1
Dunwood Dr ST7...... 193 D6
Dunwoody Way CW1,
  CW2...... 190 B4
Durban Ave CH3...... 142 D7
Durber Ct ST7...... 209 D1
Durham Cl
  Macclesfield SK10......86 F2
  Warrington WA1...... 17 E7
Durham Ct CH65...... 70 E3
Durham Dr CW7...... 149 C6
Durham Gr M44...... 11 C6
Durham Rd Blacon CH1... 117 F5
  Widnes WA8...... 13 B3
Durlston Cl WA8...... 12 C2
Durrell Way WA3......3 E8
Dutch Cl CW7...... 126 E2
DUTTON...... 51 A4
Dutton Ct WA1...... 16 C5
Dutton Gn CH2......70 F3
Dutton Hall Ct WA4......76 E8
Dutton La CW8, WA6..... 101 B6
Dutton Locks CW8......76 E6
Duttons Bsns Ctr CW9... 103 F7
Duttons La CH2...... 119 A7
Dutton's La CW6...... 122 C5
Dutton Way Crewe CW1.. 190 B6
  Nantwich CW5...... 204 E3
Duxford Cl WA4......24 F2
Duxford Ct WA2......8 E1
Dyar Terr CW8......78 D1
Dye House La SK22......39 C8
Dyers Cl WA13...... 19 A4
Dyers Ct SK10......88 B8
Dyers La WA13...... 19 A4
Dykin Cl WA8...... 13 E3
Dykin Rd WA8...... 13 E3
Dymocks Mill La SY14... 223 B6
Dysart Bldgs CW5...... 204 E5
Dyserth Rd CH1...... 117 D3
Dystelegh Rd SK12......38 D6

E

Eachus La CW5...... 172 B5
Eadie Gr CW1...... 190 A7
Eaglais Way SK10......86 F2
Eagland Pl CW12...... 156 E4
Eagle Brow WA13...... 18 D3
Eagle La CH66...... 69 D7
Eagle Mount WA4...... 16 C2
Eagle Park Dr WA2......8 A1
Eaglesfield CW8...... 103 C4
Eagles Rd SK10......85 A2
Eagles Way WA7......49 E6
Ealing Cl WA7......24 D1
Ealing Rd WA5......15 B5
Eanleywood Farm Cl WA7. 50 C7
Eanleywood La WA7...... 50 C7
Eardley Cres CW12...... 156 E4
Eardley Ct [6] CW1...... 190 B5
Eardleyend Rd ST7...... 209 E7
Eardswick Cl CH2...... 237 B4
Eardswick La CW1...... 172 C5
Eardswick Rd CW10...... 151 C6
Earle Cl WA12......1 F3
Earle Cres CH64...... 41 D1
Earle Dr CH64...... 41 D1
Earle Rd WA8...... 23 C7
Earles La CW9......79 E6
Earle's Rd CW2...... 122 C5
Earle St Crewe CW1...... 190 D4
  Newton-le-Willows WA12 ... 2 A3
EARLESTOWN...... 2 B2
Earlestown Sta WA12......2 B3
Earles Way CH64......92 F7
Earl Rd SK8, SK9......34 E5
Earls Gdns CH65......70 B5
Earls Oak CH2...... 118 B2
Earl's Port CH1...... 118 B2
Earls Rd CW2...... 206 B4
Earl St WA2......16 B7
Earlston Ct CH3...... 237 C2
Earlsway Chester CH4.... 141 A8
  Macclesfield SK11...... 111 F7
Earls Way Northwich CW9. 103 E4
  Runcorn WA7......49 E6
Earlswood Mews CW9.... 103 F3
Easby Cl Cheadle SK8......35 B6
  Poynton SK12......36 D4

Easby Cl *continued*
Runcorn WA7 . . . 23 C2
Easenhall Cl WA8 . . . 13 C5
East Ave Bollington SK10 . . . 87 F7
Gatley SK8 . . . 34 D8
Northwich CW9 . . . 104 D6
Warrington WA2 . . . 16 C8
Warrington, Great Sankey WA5 . . . 15 A4
Warrington, Stockton Heath WA4 . . . 16 D1
Weston CW2 . . . 207 C5
Eastbury Cl WA8 . . . 13 C5
Eastcott Cl CW12 . . . 155 F4
East Ct ST7 . . . 193 E4
Eastdale WA15 . . . 31 F8
Eastdale Rd WA1 . . . 17 A7
East Dam Wood Rd L24 . . . 21 A2
East Dudley St CW7 . . . 126 F1
Easter Ct WA5 . . . 7 B2
Eastern Expressway WA4 . 25 A3
Eastern Pathway CH4 . . . 237 C1
Eastern Rd CW5 . . . 205 F5
Eastfields Gr CH1 . . . 117 A8
Eastford Rd WA4 . . . 16 A1
Eastgate SK10 . . . 112 E8
Eastgate Rd
Holmes Chapel CW4 . . . 130 D3
Runcorn WA7 . . . 24 E5
Eastgate Row N CH1 . . . 237 B2
Eastgate Row S CH1 . . . 237 B2
Eastgate St CH1 . . . 237 B2
Eastgate Way WA7 . . . 24 D4
East Gn CH5 . . . 116 A6
EASTHAM . . . 43 F5
Eastham Ctry Pk★ CH62 . . 44 A8
EASTHAM FERRY . . . 44 B8
Eastham Ho CH62 . . . 44 A4
Eastham Mews CH62 . . . 44 A4
Eastham Rake CH62, CH64 . 43 D3
Eastham Rake Sta CH63 . . 43 D3
Eastham Village Rd CH62 . 44 A5
Eastham Way 11 SK9 . . . 34 D5
East La Cuddington CW8 . . . 102 A3
Runcorn WA7 . . . 49 F7
East Lancashire Rd WA11, WA12, WA3 . . . 2 C7
East Mains L24 . . . 21 A3
East Millwood Rd L24 . . . 21 A4
East Park Rd SK11 . . . 112 B5
East Rd Halewood L24, L26 . . 21 A5
Middlewich CW10 . . . 128 B1
Wythenshawe M90 . . . 33 C7
East St WA8 . . . 13 D1
East Terr WA16 . . . 56 F1
East View
10 Nantwich CW5 . . . 204 E6
Warrington WA4 . . . 17 B2
Eastward Ave SK9 . . . 59 F6
Eastway
Ellesmere Port CH66 . . . 69 D7
Widnes WA8 . . . 12 D1
Eastwood WA7 . . . 24 C2
Eastwood Ave WA12 . . . 2 F3
Eastwood Ct CH5 . . . 139 B7
Eastwood Rd WA5 . . . 6 F7
EATON Congleton . . . 157 A8
Tarporley . . . 147 A4
Eaton Ave CH4 . . . 141 D7
Eaton Bank CW12 . . . 156 F4
Eaton Bank Acad CW12 . . 156 F5
Eaton Bank Ind Est CW12 . . . 156 F4
Eaton Cl Broughton CH4 . . . 139 C4
Poynton SK12 . . . 37 A3
Sandbach CW11 . . . 175 C7
Eaton Cres CW9 . . . 103 E2
Eaton Ct
1 Northwich CW9 . . . 103 E5
Wilmslow SK9 . . . 60 A6
Eaton Dr Alderley Edge SK9 . . 59 F2
Middlewich CW10 . . . 151 B8
Eaton Gr CH4 . . . 140 E6
Eaton La Davenham CW9 . . 103 E2
Eaton CW6 . . . 147 A5
Goostrey CW4 . . . 107 C1
Macclesfield SK11 . . . 112 D5
Tarporley CW6 . . . 168 E8
Eaton Mews CH4 . . . 141 D7
Eaton Pl CW8 . . . 102 F4
Eaton Prim Sch CW6 . . . 147 B3
Eaton Rd Alsager ST7 . . . 193 D4
Chester CH4 . . . 141 E4
Tarporley CW6 . . . 146 D1
Wettenhall CW7 . . . 170 B8
Eaton St Crewe CW2 . . . 190 C4
12 Runcorn WA7 . . . 23 A2
Eaton View CW9 . . . 126 E8
Eaton Way CW3 . . . 230 A4
Eaves Brow Rd WA3 . . . 9 B7
Eaves Knoll Rd SK22 . . . 39 B8
EBNAL . . . 213 D5
Ebnal La SY14 . . . 213 E4
Ebury Pl CH4 . . . 141 D7
Eccles Cl SK23 . . . 65 D8
Eccles Rd SK23 . . . 65 F6
ECCLESTON . . . 141 E1
Eccleston Ave
Bebington CH62 . . . 43 C8
Chester CH4 . . . 141 D6
Ellesmere Port CH66 . . . 69 E5
Eccleston CE Prim Sch CH4 . . . 141 E2
Eccleston Cl WA3 . . . 9 C5
Eccleston Ct 5 CW9 . . . 103 E5
Eccleston Dr WA7 . . . 23 C1
Eccleston Rd CH4 . . . 161 A7
Eccleston Way 3 SK9 . . . 34 D4
Eccups La SK9 . . . 59 C8
Echo Cl CH4 . . . 140 E5
Echo Gr 2 WA5 . . . 14 F8
Ecton Ave SK10 . . . 113 A7
Ecton Cl CW7 . . . 127 A4
Edale Cl Bebington CH62 . . . 43 E5
Gatley SK8 . . . 34 D7
Warrington WA1 . . . 16 E5
Edale Dr CW6 . . . 122 D5
Edburton Ct WA3 . . . 3 A8
Eddington Way WA3 . . . 9 F5
Eddisbury Cl SK11 . . . 112 F7
Eddisbury Dr ST5 . . . 210 D2
Eddisbury Hall La SK11 . . 113 B7
Eddisbury Hill CW6, CW8 . 123 D7
Eddisbury Hill Pk CW8 . . . 123 D7
Eddisbury Rd CH66 . . . 69 F1
Eddisbury Sq WA6 . . . 74 B8
Eddisbury Terr SK11 . . . 112 F7
Eddisbury Way CW9 . . . 103 E3
Eddisford Dr WA3 . . . 4 D4
Edelsten St WA5 . . . 15 F5
Eden Ave
Fowley Common WA3 . . . 5 C4
High Lane SK6 . . . 37 E7
Winsford CW7 . . . 126 F2
Edenbridge Cl CW2 . . . 207 B2
Edenbridge Gdns WA4 . . . 26 E3
Eden Cl Biddulph ST8 . . . 179 E1
5 Ellesmere Port CH66 . . . 69 C5
Kidsgrove ST7 . . . 195 B2
Wilmslow SK9 . . . 59 E5
Edendale WA8 . . . 12 B2
Eden Dr SK10 . . . 87 F1
Edenfield Cl WA16 . . . 58 A3
Edenfield Rd WA16 . . . 58 A4
Eden Gr CW4 . . . 130 D2
Edenhall Cl CW4 . . . 130 A3
Eden Park Rd SK8 . . . 34 E8
Edgar Ct Chester CH4 . . . 237 B1
25 Macclesfield SK11 . . . 112 C8
Edgar Pl CH4 . . . 237 B1
Edgars Dr WA2 . . . 9 A1
Edgecroft CH3 . . . 166 A1
Edge Gr CH2 . . . 118 F2
EDGE GREEN . . . 199 B2
Edgehill Chase SK9 . . . 60 E7
Edge La SY14 . . . 199 C1
Edge Rd SY14 . . . 198 D3
Edgerley La CH3 . . . 181 B6
Edgerton Rd WA3 . . . 3 F8
Edge View La SK9 . . . 59 B2
Edgeview Rd CW12 . . . 179 B7
Edgewater Pl
2 Grappenhall WA4 . . . 17 B3
Grappenhall WA4 . . . 17 B4
Edgeway Henbury SK11 . . . 111 C8
Wilmslow SK9 . . . 60 B5
Edgewell La CW6 . . . 147 A3
Edgewood 3 CH3 . . . 142 A8
Edgewood Cl WA8 . . . 22 B7
Edgewood Dr
Bebington CH62 . . . 43 D5
Wistaston CW2 . . . 206 A7
Edgworth St WA2 . . . 16 A6
Edinburgh Ct CH65 . . . 70 D3
Edinburgh Dr SK10 . . . 87 A1
Edinburgh Pl CW12 . . . 156 F2
Edinburgh Rd
Congleton CW12 . . . 156 F2
Widnes WA8 . . . 22 A8
Wistaston CW2 . . . 205 E8
Edinburgh Way CH4 . . . 237 C1
Edison Rd WA7 . . . 23 D3
Edith St WA7 . . . 22 F3
Edleston Chapel Rd CW5 . 203 F3
Edlestone Gr 2 SK9 . . . 34 E1
Edleston Hall La CW5 . . . 203 F2
Edleston Prim Sch CW2 . 190 C3
Edleston Rd CW2 . . . 190 D3
Edmund Wright Way CW5 . . . 204 C5
Edna St CH2 . . . 118 F3
Edward Gdns WA1 . . . 17 F6
Edward Kemp Cl CW2 . . . 189 F3
Edward Price Cl 6 CH64 . . 41 B1
Edward Rd WA5 . . . 14 D6
Edwards Ave CW2 . . . 206 C5
Edwards Cl CW2 . . . 206 C5
Edwards Rd CH4 . . . 141 A6
Edward St Audley ST7 . . . 209 F3
Crewe CW2 . . . 190 D2
Ellesmere Port CH65 . . . 70 C7
Haydock WA11 . . . 1 A6
Macclesfield SK11 . . . 112 B7
Northwich CW9 . . . 104 C8
Widnes WA8 . . . 13 D1
Edwards Way
Alsager ST7 . . . 193 E4
Widnes WA8 . . . 22 C8
Edward Woolf Cl CW1 . . . 191 D6
Edwin St WA8 . . . 13 C1
Egdon Cl WA8 . . . 13 E2
Egerton WA16 . . . 29 C5
Egerton Ave
Hartford CW8 . . . 103 A4
Partington WA13 . . . 19 C8
Warrington WA1 . . . 16 F7
Egerton Ct CW6 . . . 122 B5
Egerton Dr CH2 . . . 118 D5
EGERTON GREEN . . . 200 C5
Egerton Mews 1 WA4 . . . 16 C1
Egerton Moss WA15 . . . 31 E5
Egerton Prim Sch WA16 . . 56 F2
Egerton Rd Blacon CH1 . . . 117 E5
Handforth SK9 . . . 34 B1
Lymm WA13 . . . 18 C2
Egerton Sq 7 WA16 . . . 57 A2
Egerton St Chester CH1 . . . 237 C3
Congleton CW12 . . . 156 C2
Ellesmere Port CH65 . . . 70 C6
Runcorn WA7 . . . 22 F3
Warrington, Howley WA1 . . . 16 D5
Warrington, Stockton Heath WA4 . . . 16 C1
Egerton Terr CW9 . . . 105 D4
Egerton Wlk CH4 . . . 162 A7
Eggbridge La CH3 . . . 143 A5
Egremont Ct WA4 . . . 16 C3
Egypt St
3 Warrington WA1 . . . 16 A5
Widnes WA8 . . . 22 F7
Eiger Cl ST8 . . . 179 E1
Eilison Ct CH1 . . . 237 B3
Elaine Cl
Ellesmere Port CH66 . . . 69 C4
Widnes WA8 . . . 13 C1
Elaine Price Ct 3 WA7 . . . 22 F1
Elaine St WA1 . . . 16 D7
Elanor Rd CW11 . . . 174 D7
Elbrus Dr CH66 . . . 69 F7
Elcombe Ave WA3 . . . 3 E7
Elderberry Way
Wilmslow SK9 . . . 60 E8
11 Wilmslow Park SK9 . . . 60 E8
Elderberry Wlk M31 . . . 11 E3
Elder Dr CH4 . . . 140 E5
Eldon Rd SK10 . . . 111 F8
Eldon St WA1 . . . 16 C5
Eldon Terr CH64 . . . 66 E7
Eleanor Cl CW1 . . . 189 F5
Eleanor St
Ellesmere Port CH65 . . . 70 C6
5 Widnes WA8 . . . 23 A7
Electra Way CW1 . . . 191 A2
Electricity St CW2 . . . 190 C3
Elgan Cres
Sandbach CW11 . . . 175 B8
Sandbach CW11 . . . 175 B8
Elgar Ave CH62 . . . 43 E5
Elgar Cl CH65 . . . 69 F3
Elgin Ave
Holmes Chapel CW4 . . . 130 B2
Macclesfield SK10 . . . 87 A2
Warrington WA4 . . . 16 A2
Elgin Cl CH3 . . . 119 B3
Eliot Cl CW1 . . . 191 A4
Elizabethan Way CW9 . . . 104 E6
Elizabeth Ave SK12 . . . 38 D5
Elizabeth Cl Kelsall CW6 . . 122 D5
Sandbach CW11 . . . 174 D7
Elizabeth Cres CH4 . . . 237 C1
Elizabeth Ct Talke ST7 . . . 210 D5
Widnes WA8 . . . 23 B7
Elizabeth Dr WA1 . . . 17 A8
Elizabeth Gaskell Ct WA16 . . . 56 F2
Elizabeth Ho 15 SK11 . . . 112 E7
Elizabeth Rd Haydock WA11 . . 1 E7
Partington M31 . . . 11 F4
Elizabeth St
Congleton CW12 . . . 156 C2
Crewe CW1 . . . 190 B5
Macclesfield SK11 . . . 112 D7
Elizabeth Terr WA8 . . . 12 D1
Elkan Cl WA8 . . . 13 E2
Elkan Rd WA8 . . . 13 E2
Elkington Way SK9 . . . 60 A3
Ella Gr WA16 . . . 57 B2
Elland Dr CH66 . . . 69 C5
Ellen Brook Rd M22 . . . 33 D8
Ellen St WA5 . . . 15 F7
Ellerby Cl WA7 . . . 50 E7
Ellerton Ave CH66 . . . 69 C5
Ellerton Cl WA8 . . . 12 D3
Ellesmere Ave
Broughton CH4 . . . 139 D4
Chester CH2 . . . 118 D5
Ellesmere Cl CW11 . . . 174 F8
Ellesmere Pl 10 CW1 . . . 190 B5
ELLESMERE PORT . . . 70 A7
Ellesmere Port Com Hospl CH65 . . . 70 A2
Ellesmere Port Greyhound Stad CH65 . . . 70 E3
Ellesmere Port RC High Sch CH65 . . . 70 A3
Ellesmere Port Sta CH65 . . 70 C5
Ellesmere Rd Culcheth WA3 . . 4 E3
Northwich CW9 . . . 104 A4
Warrington WA4 . . . 16 B1
Ellesmere St Runcorn WA7 . . 23 B2
Warrington WA1 . . . 16 C5
5 Warrington WA1 . . . 16 C5
Ellesworth Cl WA5 . . . 15 C8
Ellingham Way CW9 . . . 103 E3
Ellington Dr WA5 . . . 15 B5
Elliot Ho CH1 . . . 118 A5
Elliot St 9 WA8 . . . 23 B8
Elliott Ave WA1 . . . 16 E7
Ellis Cl CW2 . . . 206 B5
Ellis La WA6 . . . 49 D1
Ellison St Moss Bank WA8 . . 23 C8
Warrington, Howley WA1 . . . 16 C5
Warrington, Stockton Heath WA4 . . . 16 D1
Ellis St Crewe CW1 . . . 190 B6
Widnes WA8 . . . 22 F7
Elloway Rd L24 . . . 21 A3
Ellwood Cl L24 . . . 21 E2
Ellwood Gn CW2 . . . 206 E3
Elm Ave
Newton-le-Willows WA12 . . . 2 C2
Widnes WA8 . . . 13 B2
Elm Beds Rd SK12 . . . 37 C2
Elm Cl Crewe CW2 . . . 189 E2
Elm Cl *continued*
2 Partington M31 . . . 11 F3
Poynton SK12 . . . 36 F3
Tarporley CW6 . . . 146 D2
Elm Cres SK9 . . . 60 B3
Elm Ct CW1 . . . 190 D6
Elm Dr Crewe CW1 . . . 190 E6
Holmes Chapel CW4 . . . 130 D4
Macclesfield SK10 . . . 87 E2
Elmfield Cl SK9 . . . 60 B2
Elmfield Rd SK9 . . . 60 B2
Elm Gn CH64 . . . 67 F8
Elm Gr Alderley Edge SK9 . . . 60 B2
Alsager ST7 . . . 193 E4
Ellesmere Port CH66 . . . 70 A1
Handforth SK9 . . . 34 C3
Saltney CH4 . . . 140 E5
Warrington WA1 . . . 16 F7
Widnes WA8 . . . 13 B1
Winsford CW7 . . . 127 A1
Elmgrove Cl CW7 . . . 149 D6
Elm Ho Chester CH2 . . . 118 C5
9 Sandbach CW11 . . . 175 B6
Elmore Cl
Holmes Chapel CW4 . . . 130 B3
Runcorn WA7 . . . 24 D1
Elm Rd Congleton CW12 . . . 156 B3
Haydock WA11 . . . 1 E7
High Lane SK6 . . . 37 F7
Hollinfare WA3 . . . 11 A2
Middlewich CW10 . . . 151 D7
Runcorn WA7 . . . 49 C8
Warrington WA5 . . . 14 F4
Warrington, Winwick Quay WA2 . . . 8 B4
Weaverham CW8 . . . 102 D7
Willaston CH64 . . . 67 F8
Elmridge Ct WA3 . . . 3 F8
Elmridge Dr WA15 . . . 32 C8
Elmridge Prim Sch WA15 . 32 C8
Elmridge Way CW8 . . . 78 D1
Elm Rise Frodsham WA6 . . . 74 C7
Prestbury SK10 . . . 86 E6
Elms SK9 . . . 59 F6
Elmsett Cl WA5 . . . 14 E5
Elm Sq CH4 . . . 140 F6
Elm St
Ellesmere Port CH65 . . . 70 C7
Northwich CW9 . . . 79 B1
Elmstead Cres CW1 . . . 189 F8
Elmstead Rd SK11 . . . 84 A3
Elms The Golborne WA3 . . . 3 F7
Mobberley WA16 . . . 58 E2
6 Northwich CW9 . . . 103 E6
Runcorn WA7 . . . 22 F1
Tallarn Green/Tallwrn Green SY14 . . . 222 F5
Elmsway Altrincham WA15 . . 32 B8
Bollington SK10 . . . 88 A8
Bramhall SK7 . . . 35 C7
High Lane SK6 . . . 37 E6
Elm Terr CW1 . . . 190 E6
Elm Tree Ave Lymm WA13 . 18 D2
Warrington WA1 . . . 16 F8
Elm Tree Cotts CH3 . . . 167 A7
Elm Tree Ct CW6 . . . 147 A3
Elm Tree Dr ST7 . . . 209 F1
Elm Tree La CW11 . . . 174 D8
Elm Tree Rd Golborne WA3 . . 3 F8
Lymm WA13 . . . 18 D2
Sealand CH1 . . . 116 F7
Elmuir CH1 . . . 117 E3
Elmwood WA7 . . . 24 C1
Elmwood Ave
Chester CH2 . . . 118 F4
Warrington WA1 . . . 16 E7
Elmwood Cl ST7 . . . 194 A4
Elmwood Gr CW7 . . . 149 F8
Elmwood Rd CW8 . . . 78 B4
Elnor Ave SK23 . . . 65 E5
Elnor La SK23 . . . 65 F4
Elphins Dr WA4 . . . 16 C2
Elsby Rd ST7 . . . 193 F2
Elston Ave WA12 . . . 2 C5
Elstree Ave CH3 . . . 119 B3
Elstree Ct WA8 . . . 13 D4
Elswick Ave SK7 . . . 35 E7
Eltham Cl WA8 . . . 13 E3
Eltham Wlk WA8 . . . 13 E3
ELTON . . . 72 C3
Elton Cl Bebington CH62 . . . 43 E3
Golborne WA3 . . . 3 E7
Handforth SK9 . . . 34 E1
Warrington WA3 . . . 9 C4
Elton Crossings Rd CW11 . . . 174 D6
Elton Dr SK7 . . . 36 D8
ELTON GREEN . . . 72 A3
Elton La Elton CH2 . . . 72 E4
Haslington CW11, CW1 . . . 174 D1
Winterley CW11 . . . 191 F8
Elton Prim Sch CH2 . . . 72 B4
Elton Rd CW11 . . . 174 D5
Elton Shopping Precinct CH2 . . . 72 B3
Elvington Cl
Congleton CW12 . . . 156 E2
Runcorn WA7 . . . 49 F4
Elwood Way CW5 . . . 205 B4
ELWORTH . . . 174 E6
Elworth Ave WA8 . . . 13 A5
Elworth CE Prim Sch CW11 . . . 174 E7
Elworth Ct
12 Congleton CW12 . . . 156 F3
Sandbach CW11 . . . 174 D7
Elworth Hall Farm Rd 13 CW11 . . . 174 E8
Elworth Hall Prim Sch 15 CW11 . . . 174 E7
Elworth Hall Prim Sch CW11 . . . 174 E7
Elworth Rd CW11 . . . 174 E6
Elworth St CW11 . . . 175 A7
Elworth Way 6 SK9 . . . 34 D4
Elwyn Dr L26 . . . 21 A8
Ely Cl CH66 . . . 94 E8
Ely Pk WA7 . . . 24 E2
Embassy Cl CH1 . . . 117 C4
Emberton Pl CW3 . . . 230 A5
Emberton Rd ST7 . . . 193 A4
Embleton Ct WA7 . . . 49 D5
Embleton Gr WA7 . . . 49 D5
Embridge Cswy SK10 . . . 90 B5
Emerald Dr CW11 . . . 175 C8
Emerald Rd M22 . . . 33 F7
Emes Cl CW2 . . . 206 D5
Emily St 7 WA8 . . . 23 A7
Emmett St CW8 . . . 78 A3
Emperor Ave CH4 . . . 141 B4
Empress Dr CW2 . . . 190 B3
Emral Ct SY14 . . . 211 A1
Emslie Ct CH64 . . . 66 C7
Enderby Rd CH1 . . . 237 A3
Endon Ave SK10 . . . 88 A7
Endon Hall Mews SK10 . . . 88 B5
Endsleigh Cl CH2 . . . 118 E8
Endsleigh Gdns CH2 . . . 118 E8
Enfield Cl CW2 . . . 206 B3
Enfield Park Rd WA2 . . . 9 A3
Enfield Rd CH65 . . . 70 B5
Engineer Pk CH5 . . . 116 A4
Englefield Ave CH4 . . . 140 D6
Englefield Cl CW1 . . . 190 A8
ENGLESEA BROOK . . . 208 A4
Englesea Brook Chapel & Mus★ CW2 . . . 208 A3
Englesea Brook La CW2 . 208 A3
Englesea Gr CW2 . . . 190 B1
Englesea Way ST7 . . . 193 A4
Ennerdale Chester CH2 . . . 118 F5
Macclesfield SK11 . . . 111 F5
Ennerdale Ave
Bebington CH62 . . . 43 F4
Warrington WA2 . . . 8 B3
Ennerdale Cl
Alderley Edge SK9 . . . 83 F7
Winsford CW7 . . . 126 D3
Ennerdale Dr
Congleton CW12 . . . 156 B2
Frodsham WA6 . . . 74 C8
Ennerdale Rd
Crewe CW2 . . . 189 D3
Partington M31 . . . 11 E3
Ennis Cl L24 . . . 21 D2
Ensor Way SK22 . . . 39 C7
Enterprise Ct CW11 . . . 174 D7
Enterprise Ctr The CW12 . 156 E3
Enterprise Way WA3 . . . 4 A7
Enticott Rd M44 . . . 11 C5
Enville St WA4 . . . 16 C4
Epic L Ctr CH65 . . . 70 C4
Epping Dr WA1 . . . 17 D8
Epsom Ave SK8, SK9 . . . 34 E4
Epsom Ct CH1 . . . 118 B2
Epsom Gdns WA4 . . . 26 E7
Epworth Cl WA5 . . . 6 F7
ERF Way CW10 . . . 151 E8
Eric Ave WA1 . . . 16 E8
Eric Dr CW11 . . . 174 D7
Eric Fountain Rd CH65 . . . 44 D3
Eric St WA8 . . . 13 C2
Erindale Cres WA6 . . . 74 A6
Ermine Rd CH2 . . . 237 C4
Ernest Cope Rd 6 CW1 . . 190 A8
Ernest St CW2 . . . 190 C1
Ernley Cl CW5 . . . 204 D6
Errington Ave CH65 . . . 70 C6
Errwood Forest Walks★ SK17 . . . 90 E2
Erskine Rd M31 . . . 11 F3
Erwood St WA2 . . . 16 B6
Eskdale CH65 . . . 70 B3
Eskdale Ave
Bebington CH62 . . . 43 E5
Bramhall SK7 . . . 35 C5
Warrington WA2 . . . 8 C3
Eskdale Cl WA7 . . . 49 D5
Esk Dale Cl CW7 . . . 126 C2
Esk Rd CW7 . . . 127 A2
Essex Cl CW12 . . . 156 E5
Essex Dr Biddulph ST8 . . . 179 D2
Kidsgrove ST7 . . . 194 F2
Essex Gdns M44 . . . 11 C4
Essex Rd CH2 . . . 119 A5
Essex Wlk SK10 . . . 86 F1
Esthers La CW8 . . . 102 D8
Estone Pl CH3 . . . 121 E7
Etchells Prim Sch SK8 . . . 34 C8
Ethelda Dr CH2 . . . 119 A5
Etherley Dr WA12 . . . 2 D1
Etherow Cl CW11 . . . 174 E7
Ethos Ct CH1 . . . 237 C3
Eton Dr CH63 . . . 41 F6
Eton Rd CH65 . . . 70 D4
Ettiley Ave CW11 . . . 174 C5
ETTILEY HEATH . . . 174 C6
Ettrick Pk CH3 . . . 119 A2
Euclid Ave WA4 . . . 17 B2
Europa Bvd WA5 . . . 7 D3
Europa Way CH65 . . . 70 C6
Eustace St WA2 . . . 16 A6
Evans Bsns Ctr CH5 . . . 93 A1

Evans CI WA11 ....1 F7
Evans Ct CH4 ......139 D3
Evansleigh Dr CH5 ...116 A3
Evans PI WA4 ......16 D3
Evans St CW1 ......190 C6
Eva St CW11 ......174 D8
Evelyn St WA5 ......15 D4
Evelyn Street Prim Sch
  WA5 ......15 E4
Evenwood CI WA7 ....24 E4
Everdon CI CW7 .....126 F4
Everest CI CH66 .....69 F3
Everest Rd ST7 ......195 C3
Everglade CI SK11 ....112 B5
Evergreens The CW9 ...80 A3
Evergreen Way WA9 ...6 A7
Everite Rd WA8 ......22 B7
Everite Road Ind Est WA8 ..22 B7
Eversley CI Frodsham WA6 ..74 C6
  Warrington WA4 ......26 F5
Eversley Ct CH2 ......118 C4
Eversley Pk CH2 ......118 C4
Evesham CI
  Macclesfield SK10 ....87 E4
  Warrington WA4 ......26 C8
Evesham Dr SK9 ......34 C2
Evington Ho **2** SK11 ...112 B6
Ewart St CW3 ......140 B7
Ewloe Ct CH65 ......70 D2
Ewrin La SK10 ......89 D5
Excalibur Ind Est ST7 ..193 E3
Excalibur Prim Sch ST7 ..193 E2
Excalibur Way M44 ....11 F7
Exchange CI **12** SK11 ...112 D8
Exchange St SK11 ....112 D8
Exeter CI ST8 ......34 F8
Exeter PI CH1 ......117 F5
Exeter Rd CH65 ......70 C5
Exeter Wlk SK7 ......35 F7
Exit Rd L24 ......21 A5
Exit Rd W M90 ......33 B7
Exmouth Cres WA7 ...50 E6
Exmouth Way WA5 ....6 F6
Express Ind Est WA8 ...22 A7
Exton Pk CH1 ......237 A4
Eyam Rd SK7 ......36 E8
Eyebrook Rd WA14 ....20 F2
Eyre PI CH65 ......70 B6
Eyston CI CW9 ......103 E5

F

Facit Glen Ind Est CH4 ..140 F7
Factory La
  Warrington WA1, WA5 ..15 F4
  Widnes WA8 ......13 B3
Factory Rd CH5 ......116 A3
FADDILEY 202 D7
FADDILEY BANK 202 C6
Faddiley Bank Row CW5 ..202 D6
Fairacre Dr CW10 .....151 E6
Fairacres Rd SK6 ......37 E8
Fairbourne Ave
  Alderley Edge SK9 ....60 B3
  Wilmslow SK9 ......59 F4
Fairbourne CI
  Warrington WA5 ......7 E3
  Wilmslow SK9 ......59 F4
Fairbourne Dr SK9 ....59 F4
Fairbrook CW2 ......189 E2
Fairbrother Cres WA2 ..8 D2
Fairburn Ave CW2 ....189 F4
Fairburn CI WA8 ......13 E3
Fairclough Ave WA1 ...16 C4
Fairclough Cres WA11 ..1 A6
Fairclough St
  Burtonwood WA5 ......6 E6
  Newton-le-Willows WA12 ..2 B3
Fairey Dr SK7 ......35 F1
Fairfax Ave CH3 ......121 C1
Fairfax CI ST8 ......179 C1
Fairfax Ct CW5 ......204 E7
Fairfax Dr Nantwich CW5 ..204 D6
  Runcorn WA7 ......23 D2
  Wilmslow SK9 ......59 F4
Fairfield Ave
  Bollington SK10 ......88 A8
  Ellesmere Port CH65 ...70 A2
  Sandbach CW11 ......175 B5
Fairfield Gdns WA4 ...16 E2
Fairfield Jun Sch WA8 ..13 B2
Fairfield Rd
  Broughton CH4 ......139 B4
  Chester CH2 ......119 A4
  Irlam M44 ......11 C5
  Lymm WA13 ......18 F3
  Northwich CW9 ......104 A4
  Warrington WA4 ......16 E2
  Widnes WA8 ......13 B2
Fairfields Audley ST7 ..209 F2
  Whitchurch SY13 .....225 F1
Fairfield St WA1 ......16 D6
Fairford CI **2** WA5 ....15 B6
Fairford Rd CH4 ......140 F6
Fairford Way SK9 .....60 D7
Fairhaven CW2 ......207 B1
Fairhaven CI Bramhall SK7 ..35 F8
  Macclesfield SK10 ....87 B8
  Warrington WA5 ......15 B4
Fairhaven Dr CH63 ....43 C5
Fairhaven Rd WA8 ....13 C2
Fair Haven's Ct WA8 ..23 B8
Fairhills Ind Est M44 ..11 F8

Fairhills Rd M44 ......11 F8
Fairholme Ave CH64 ...41 D1
Fairholme CI CH1 .....94 B1
Fairholme PI **7** CH3. ..119 A1
Fairholme Rd CW9 ....127 A8
Fair Isle CI CH65 ......70 C1
Fairlawn CI CH63 .....43 A6
Fair Mead WA16 ......82 B8
Fairmeadow CH4 .....162 D2
Fairmont Dr **7** WA5. ..15 A7
Fairoak CI **12** CW7 ....149 A8
Fairoak Ct WA7 ......50 F3
Fairoak La WA7 ......50 F3
Fair Oak Rd ST5 ......210 D1
Fairview LL13 ......196 E8
Fairview Ave Alsager ST7 ..193 D4
  Weston CW2 ......207 B5
Fair View CI CW8. .....77 F3
Fairview Rd
  Ellesmere Port CH65 ...70 A2
  Macclesfield SK11 ....112 A6
Fairway Bramhall SK7 ..35 D6
  Sandycroft CH5 ......116 A2
Fairways Frodsham WA6 ..74 D7
  Warrington WA4 ......26 D5
Fairways Dr
  Ellesmere Port CH66 ...69 D7
  Whitchurch SY13 .....226 A1
Fairways The
  Macclesfield SK10 ....87 B4
  Winsford CW7 ......126 A2
Fairway The ST7 ......193 C4
Fairway Trad Est WA8. ..22 E6
Fairywell CI SK9 ......34 D1
Falcon CI
  Middlewich CW10 ....151 D5
  New Mills SK22 ......39 D8
  Winsford CW7 ......149 D6
Falcondale Rd WA2 ...8 B6
Falcon Dr
  Congleton Park CW12 ..156 E1
  Crewe CW1 ......190 B8
Falconers Gn WA5 ....7 B2
Falcon Rd CH66 ......69 F3
Falcons Way WA7 ....49 E6
Falcon Way **9** CW5 ...204 C4
Falkirk Ave WA8 ......12 F3
Fallibroome CI SK10. ..111 E8
Fallibroome High Sch
  SK10 ......86 E2
Fallibroome Rd SK10. ..111 E8
Fallon Ct CW10 ......151 C7
Fallowfield WA7 ......23 D1
Fallowfield CI CW7. ...125 F1
Fallowfield Ct CW1. ...190 A6
Fallowfield Gr WA2 ...9 B1
Fallows CI CW11 .....175 B8
Fallow St CH1. ......94 F7
Falls The SK11 ......160 A6
Falmouth CI SK10 ....111 E8
Falmouth Dr WA5 ....14 E3
Falmouth PI WA7 .....50 E6
Falmouth Rd
  Congleton CW12 .....178 E8
  Crewe CW1 ......190 A6
Falstone CI WA3 ......10 B6
Falstone Dr WA7 .....50 E7
Fanner's La WA16 ....28 D5
Fanny's Croft ST7 ....193 D2
FANSHAWE 110 C4
Fanshawe La SK11 ....110 E5
Fanshawe Wlk CW2 ..206 C8
Faraday CI **9** WA6. ...73 A2
Faraday Rd
  Ellesmere Port CH65 ...70 A4
  Runcorn WA7 ......23 D3
Faraday St WA3 ......9 E5
Farams Rd ST7 ......193 E7
Farbailey CI CH4 .....141 B5
Farcroft CI WA13 .....19 C5
Farfields CI SK11 .....111 E1
Farley CI CW10 ......151 B8
Farm CI
  2 Shavington CW2 ...206 D7
  Weaverham WA8 .....77 D1
Farmdale Dr CH2. .....72 A3
Farm Dr CH5. ......91 C1
Farmer CI CW2. ......190 A4
Farmers Heath CH66 ..69 D2
Farmers La CW6 ......168 E8
Farmer's La WA5. .....7 A6
Farmfield Dr SK10. ...87 C3
Farmfields Rise CW3 ..232 C1
Farmfold SK9. ......33 F3
Farm Hollow ST7. ....210 A2
Farm La High Lane SK12. ..38 A6
  Warrington WA4 ......26 E8
  Withington Green SK11 ..108 E1
Farmleigh Dr CW1 ....189 F8
Farmleigh Gdns WA5. ..15 C6
Farm Rd Northwich CW9 ..104 F7
  Weaverham CW8 .....77 D1
Farmside CI WA5. .....15 F7
Farmstead Way CH66. ..69 E1
Farm Way WA12 ......2 E1
Farm Wlk WA14 ......20 E1
Farndale WA8 ......13 A5
Farndale CI
  Warrington WA5 ......14 F7
  Wistaston CW2 ......206 A6
Farndale Wlk SK11 ...112 D6
FARNDON 180 E2
Farndon CI
  Broughton CH4. .....139 C4
  Cuddington SK8 ......102 A3
Farndon Prim Sch CH3 ..180 E2
Farndon Rd CH66 ....69 E6
Farne CI CH65 ......95 C8

Farnham Ave SK11 ....112 A6
Farnham CI Cheadle SK8. ..35 A7
  Warrington WA4 ......26 E7
Farnhill CI WA7 ......50 D8
Farnley CI WA7 ......24 D1
FARNWORTH 13 A3
Farnworth CE Prim Sch
  WA8 ......13 A4
Farnworth CI WA8 ....13 B3
Farnworth Ct WA8 ....13 B3
Farnworth Rd WA5 ...14 C4
Farnworth St WA8 ....13 B4
Farrant St WA8 ......23 B8
Farrell Dr ST7. ......192 F2
Farrell Rd WA4 ......26 C8
Farrell St WA1 ......16 D5
Farr Hall Dr CH60 ....40 E7
Farr Hall Rd CH60 ....40 F8
Farrier Ct CW1. ......190 D7
Farriers Way CW7. ...126 A1
Farringdon Rd WA2 ...8 B6
Farthing La CW9 ......79 B8
Farthings The WA13. ..18 D4
Farwood CI SK10. ....86 F2
Faulkner Dr CW10. ...151 E6
Faulkners CI CH4. ....161 A7
Faulkners La CH3 .....142 D8
Faulkner's La WA16. ..58 E2
Faulkner St CH2 ......118 F3
Fawcett PI CW1. .....173 A1
Fawns Keep SK9. .....60 D7
Fawns Leap CW8. ....101 E5
Fearndown Way SK10 ..87 C4
FEARNHEAD 9 B2
Fearnhead Cross WA2. ..8 F2
Fearnhead La WA2. ...9 A2
Fearnleigh CW8. .....103 C7
Fearnley Way WA12 ..2 C1
Feather La CH60 ......40 F8
Feather's La CH1. ....237 B2
Feilden Ct CH1. ......94 F1
Felix Rd CW8 ......103 E8
Fence Ave SK10. .....112 E8
Fence Ave Ind Est SK10 ..112 E8
Fence Ct SK10 ......112 E8
Fence La CW12 ......178 D4
Fenham Dr WA5 ......14 F1
Fennel St WA1 ......16 C5
Fenton CI
  Congleton CW12 .....157 A1
  Widnes WA8. ......12 C3
Fenwick La WA7 ......49 D6
Fenwick Rd CH66 .....69 E2
Ferguson Ave CH66 ...69 E6
Ferguson Dr WA2 .....8 D1
Ferma La CH3. ......120 D6
Fernbank CI Crewe CW1. ..190 F3
  Warrington WA3 ......9 E4
  Winsford CW7 ......127 B1
Fernbank Rise SK10. ..88 B8
Fern CI
  Mount Pleasant ST7. ..195 C6
  Warrington WA3 ......9 D4
Fern Cres CW12. .....157 A3
Fern Ct CW1 ......190 E3
Ferndale Ave CH2 ....72 A3
Ferndale CI
  Bold Heath WA8. .....13 E7
  Sandbach CW11 ......175 C5
  Warrington WA1 ......17 C7
  Weston CW2 ......207 B5
Ferndale Cres SK11 ...111 E7
Ferndale Gdns ST7. ..195 E3
Ferndown Way CW2 ..221 C8
Fernhill Rd CH1 ......117 E6
Fernhurst WA7 ......49 D8
FERNILEE 65 E1
Fernilee Cotts SK23. ..65 E1
Fernlea Ct CH1. ......116 F8
Fern Lea Dr SK11. ....112 A8
Fernleaf CI ST7 ......193 F8
Fernlea Rd Heswall CH60 ..41 A8
  Marston CW9. ......79 B6
Fernleigh CI
  Middlewich CW10 ....151 E6
  Winsford CW7 ......126 A1
Fern Rd CH65 ......70 B2
Fernway CW7. ......127 B1
Fern Way CW7. ......77 C1
Fernwood WA7 ......24 B1
Fernwood Gr SK9 ....60 C8
Fernworthy WA5 .....14 C6
Fernyess La CH64 ....67 E7
Ferret Oak La CW6 ...186 B6
Ferrous Way M44 .....11 F6
Ferry CI CH5 ......116 A6
Ferry La Sealand CH1 ..117 C1
  Warrington WA4 ......17 E4
Ferry Rd CH62 ......44 A6
Festival Ave Buerton CW3 ..230 E3
  Warrington WA2 ......8 D2
Festival Cres WA2. ....8 D2
Festival Dr SK10 ......85 F6
Festival Hill CW12. ...156 F2
Festival Terr **1** WA7. ..49 C8
Festival Way WA7 ....49 C8
Ffordd Cledwen/Cledwen Rd
  CH4 ......139 D5
Ffordd Maes Y Awyr
  CH5 ......116 A8
Ffordd Smithfield/Smithfield
  Dr LL13 ......196 B8
Ffordd Y Blodau/Blossom
  Way CH4 ......140 D5
Ffordd Yr Orsedd LL13. ..180 A1
Fiddlers Ferry WA4. ..14 E1

Fiddlers Ferry Rd WA8. ..23 C8
Fiddler's Ferry Rd WA8 ..13 D1
Fieldacre CI **3** WA3. ...3 C7
Field Ave CW2 ......189 F1
Fieldbank Rd SK11 ...112 B8
Field CI Bollington SK10. ..87 F7
  Bramhall SK7. ......35 D4
  Northwich CW8 ......103 C7
  Tarvin CH3 ......121 B2
Fieldfare CW7 ......150 A8
Fieldfare CI Golborne WA3. ..3 D8
  Lower Heath CW12 ...156 D5
  Warrington WA3 ......9 F4
Fieldfare Way CW11. ..174 E6
Fieldgate WA8 ......22 B6
Fieldhead Mews SK9. ..60 E8
Fieldhead Rd SK9. ....60 E8
Field Hey La CH64. ...43 B1
Fieldhouse Row WA7. ..49 D7
Fielding Ave SK12. ....36 E2
Fields CI Crewe CW2 ...189 E2
  Tarvin CH3 ......121 B2
  Tattenhall CH3 ......166 B1
  Warrington WA4 ......26 C6
Field Mdw CI **5** WA3. ..3 C7
Fields Dr CW11 ......175 A5
Fieldsend Dr WN7. ....4 C8
Fieldside CW6 ......145 B6
Fieldside CI Bramhall SK7. ..35 D4
  Goostrey CW4 ......107 E1
Field Side CI WA16 ...58 A4
Fieldside Ct CH4 .....139 B4
Fields Rd Alsager ST7 ..193 E3
  Congleton CW12 .....178 F8
  Haslington CW1 ......191 D4
Fields The CW5 ......205 D5
Fields View SY13 .....228 D1
Fields View CI CW5. ..220 B8
Fieldsway WA7 ......49 A6
Field View ST8 ......179 D1
Fieldview Dr WA2. ....8 E1
Field View Dr SK11 ...112 E5
Field View Rd CW12. ..155 E3
Fieldway Chester CH2. ..118 E4
  Ellesmere Port CH66 ..69 B7
  Frodsham WA6. ......74 C7
  Saughall CH1. ......94 A2
  Weaverham WA8 .....77 C1
  Widnes WA8. ......13 E2
Field Way ST7 ......193 E4
Fieldways WA13 ......18 C4
Field Wlk **7** M31. .....11 E3
Fife Rd WA1 ......16 E7
Fifth Ave Kidsgrove ST7. ..194 F1
  2 Runcorn WA7. ....49 F7
Fildes CI WA5. ......15 C5
Filkin's La CH3. ......119 A1
Fillmore Gr WA8 ......12 F3
Finchdale Gdns WA3 ..4 B8
Finchett Ct CH1. .....118 B3
Finchett Dr CH1. .....118 B3
Finch La L26 ......21 A7
Finch Woods Acad L26 ..21 A7
Findlay CI WA3. ......2 C2
Finger Post La WA6 ..101 A4
Finlan Rd WA8 ......22 F7
Finlay Ave WA5 ......14 E3
Finlow Hill La SK10. ..85 E6
Finney CI SK9 ......34 C2
Finney Dr SK9 ......34 C2
Finney Gr WA11. .....1 E6
FINNEY GREEN 34 E2
Finney La SK8. ......34 B8
Finney's La CW10 ....128 B2
Finningley Ct WA2. ...8 E1
Finsbury CI WA5 ......15 C4
Finsbury Pk WA8. ....13 C5
Finsbury Way SK9 ....34 E2
Finsbury Wlk CW7 ...149 A8
Fir Ave Bramhall SK7. ..35 E8
  Halewood L26 ......21 A8
Firbank CH2 ......72 C3
Firbank CI WA7 ......72 C3
Firbeck CI Broughton CH4. ..139 B3
  Congleton CW12 .....155 F3
Firbeck Gdns WA5. ...189 D4
Fir CI Halewood L26 ...21 A8
  Poynton SK12. ......36 F3
  Tarporley CW6 ......146 D2
Fir St SK10 ......86 F1
Firdale Rd CW8 ......103 D7
Firdor CH64 ......66 E6
Fir Gr M44 ......11 C6
Firecrest Ct WA1. ....16 A3
Firecrest Way CW6. ..122 C4
Firemans Sq CH1. ...237 A3
Fir View Bramhall SK7. ..35 E8
  Halewood L26 ......21 A8
Firbank CH2 ......72 C3
Firbank CI WA7 ......72 C3
Firbeck CI Broughton CH4. ..139 B3
  Congleton CW12 .....155 F3
Firbeck Gdns WA5. ...189 D4
Fir CI Halewood L26 ...21 A8
  Poynton SK12. ......36 F3
  Tarporley CW6 ......146 D2
Fir St SK10 ......86 F1
Firdale Rd CW8 ......103 D7
Firdor CH64 ......66 E6
Fir Gr M44 ......11 C6
Firmstone Way M44. ..66 E7
Firnza Ave CH65 .....70 A6
Fir Gr Macclesfield SK11. ..112 D5
  Warrington WA1 ......16 F7
  Weaverham WA8 .....102 E8
Fir Grove CH3. ......165 C2
Fir La CW8. ......102 A2
Firman CI WA5. ......15 B8
Fir Rd SK7. ......35 E8
Firrview Pk CW5. .....217 A3
Firs La WA4. ......26 B6
Firs Pottery The* CW5. ..217 C1
Firs Sch The CH2 .....118 E5
Fir St Irlam M44. .....11 D6
  Widnes WA8. ......13 C2
First Ave
  Connah's Quay CH5. ..93 A2
  Crewe CW2 ......190 F2
  Kidsgrove ST7 ......194 E1
  Poynton SK12. ......36 D1
  Sandbach CW11. ....175 A5
First Dig La CW5 ......219 C8
Firs The SK9 ......60 A5

First Wood St CW5 ...204 D5
Firs View WA6 ......73 D4
Firth Bvd WA2 ......16 C7
Firth CI CW11 ......175 B7
Firth Fields CW9 .....103 F2
Firthfields CI CW9. ...103 F2
Firtree Ave WA1 ......17 A8
Fir Tree Ave Chester CH4 ..141 B5
  Golborne WA3 ......3 F8
  Knutsford WA16. ....82 C8
Firtree Rd Barnton CW8 ..78 B4
  Winsford CW7 ......127 B1
Fir Tree CI WA4 ......26 D1
Fir Tree Cotts CW2 ...208 C5
Firtree Gr CH66 ......95 A8
Fir Tree La Burtonwood WA5. ..7 A7
  Chester CH3. ......119 E2
  Faddiley CW5. ......202 B3
Fir Tree Wlk WA3 .....3 F8
Fir Way CH60 ......41 B5
Firwood Rd ST8. .....179 E1
Firwood Wlk CW2 ....190 C1
Fisher Ave WA1. .....8 B2
Fisherfield Dr WA3. ..10 A6
Fishermans CI CW11 ..191 F7
Fisher PI WA8 ......23 C8
Fisher Rd CH1 ......117 E4
Fishers Gn CW6 ......146 B5
Fishers La CW5 ......203 C8
Fisher St WA7 ......23 B3
Fishpool Rd CW8. ....123 F3
Fishwicks Ind Est WA11. ..1 F8
Fistral Ave SK8. ......34 C8
Fit City Sports Ctr M44 ..11 D5
Fitton CI **3** SK9 ......60 E7
Fitton's CI CW5 ......217 F5
Fitton St CW9. ......80 A2
Fitz CI SK10. ......87 D3
Fitz Cres SK10. ......87 D3
Fitzherbert St WA2. ..16 C7
Fitzwalter Rd WA1 ...17 D7
Fitzwilliam Ave SK11. ..112 F3
Fiveashes Cotts SK10. ..88 B5
FIVECROSSES 74 D5
Five Ashes Rd CH4 ...141 B5
FIVECROSSES 74 D5
Five Lane Ends SK23. ..65 A2
Fivelanes End WA6. ..74 C6
Five Ways CH64 ......41 F3
Fiveways Par SK7. ...36 A8
Fiveways Pk CH64. ...41 F3
Flacca Ct CH3. ......166 B1
Flag La Crewe CW1, CW2. ..190 C4
  Neston CH64 ......66 F7
Flag Lane N CH2 ......118 E8
Flag Lane S CH2. .....118 E8
Flander CI WA8 ......12 C2
Flanders Cres **8** CW7 ..149 E8
Flanders Gn **1** CH3 ..142 C5
Flashes La CH4 ......67 B5
Flash La Antrobus CW9 ..53 F5
  Bollington SK10 ......87 D7
Flash The CW12 ......178 E6
Flat La Kelsall CW6. ...122 C4
  Sandbach CW11. ....175 B6
Flatt La CH65 ......70 B5
Flatts La SK23. ......64 F4
Flavian CI CW10. .....128 C2
Flavian CI WA7 ......23 E2
Flaxley CI WA3. ......10 A3
Flaxmere Dr CH3. ....142 B8
Flaxyards CW6. ......146 F2
Fleet La WA9 ......1 A2
Fleet St CH65 ......70 A5
Fleetwood CI WA5 ....15 B4
Fleetwood Dr WA12 ..2 B4
Fleetwood Wlk WA7. ..50 C6
Fleming Dr WA2 ......8 A6
Fleming St WA5 ......70 C6
Flers Ave WA4 ......16 C3
Fletcher Ct WA16 .....56 F1
Fletcher Dr SK12. ....37 F6
Fletcher Gr CW9 ......104 C6
Fletcher's Bldgs
  Chester CH1. ......237 B2
  6 Runcorn WA7. ....23 F1
Fletchers La WA13. ..18 F4
Fletcher's Row **5** WA7. ..23 F1
Fletcher St Crewe CW1. ..190 B5
  Warrington WA4 ......16 B3
Fletsand Rd SK9. ....60 D6
Flint CI **4** Arclid CW11. ..154 B1
  Neston CH64 ......66 E6
Flint Ct CH65. ......70 D2
Flint Dr CH64 ......66 E6
Flint Gr M44 ......11 C6
Flint Mdw CH64. .....66 E7
Flint Rd Broughton CH5. ..139 C8
  Chester CH1. ......140 B8
  Sandycroft CH4 ......116 E1
  Sandycroft CH4 ......117 A1
Flint St SK10. ......112 E8
Flittogate La WA16. ..80 E8
Flixton Dr CW2. ......190 A2
FLOOKERSBROOK 118 E4
Flookersbrook CH1. ..237 C4
Florence St WA4 ......16 D3
Florida CI WA5. ......15 C7
Flour Mill Way CW1. ..191 A3
Flowcrete Bsns Pk
  CW11 ......152 C1
Flowerscroft CW5. ...205 A4
Flowers La CW1. .....172 E1
Flower St CW8. ......103 E7
Floyd Dr WA2. ......8 B1
Fluin La WA6 ......74 C8
Flying Fields Dr SK11. ..112 A5
Foden Ave ST7. ......194 A3
Foden La Alderley Edge SK9. ..59 C1

Foden La *continued*
 Bramhall SK7 . . . . 35 D3
Foden Pl **14** CW11 . . . . . 174 C7
Foden St SK10 . . . . 87 D1
Fodens Terr CW11 . . . . . 175 A6
Foden Wlk **7** SK9 . . . . . . 34 D2
Fog Cotts CW3 . . . . 221 E4
Fogg's La CW9, WA4 . . . . . 53 A6
Fold La Biddulph ST8 . . . 179 E4
 Bosley SK11 . . . . 135 D2
Folds La SK23 . . . . .65 F3
Folds The CH63 . . . . 42 A6
Fold The SK10 . . . . 87 A8
Foley Wlk M22 . . . . .33 E8
Fol Hollow CW12 . . . . . . 156 B1
Folkestone Cl SK10 . . . . . .87 B2
Folkstone Way WA2 . . . . . 50 C7
Folly Farm Cl WA5 . . . . . . 16 A8
Folly La WA5 . . . . .15 F7
Forbes Cl WA3 . . . . .9 E3
Forbes Pk SK7 . . . . 35 D7
Ford Cl CW1 . . . . 190 B5
Ford Ct CW7 . . . . 149 C6
Ford Farm Cl WA4 . . . . . . 16 A1
Fordington Rd WA5 . . . . . .15 B5
Ford La Crewe CW1 . . . . . 190 B6
 Tattenhall CH3 . . . . 166 F4
Fords La ST7 . . . . 195 D6
Ford's La SK7 . . . . 35 D6
Ford St WA1 . . . . 16 D6
Fordton L Ctr WA2 . . . . .8 A3
Foregate St CH1 . . . . 237 B2
Foreland Cl WA5 . . . . 14 C7
Forest Ave CW4 . . . . 107 C1
Forest Cl Cuddington CW8 . 101 F3
 Rainow SK10 . . . . 88 A8
Forest Dr Broughton CH4 . . 139 C3
 Langley SK11 . . . . 113 C4
Forest Gate Com Prim Sch
 M31 . . . . 11 D3
Forest Gate La CW6 . . . . 122 E7
Forest Gdns M31 . . . . 11 D3
Forest Ho SK10 . . . . .87 F2
Forest La WA6 . . . . 100 C6
Forest Pl **3** CW9 . . . . . . 79 A1
Forest Prim Sch CW8 . . . . 77 C5
Forest Rd
 Cuddington CW8 . . . . . . 101 F2
 Delamere CW6 . . . . 124 B1
 Ellesmere Port CH66 . . . . 69 E7
 Heswall CH60 . . . . 41 A8
 Macclesfield SK11 . . . . . 113 E6
 Tarporley CW6 . . . . 146 D3
 Winsford CW7 . . . . 149 B8
Forest Road Pk CW8 . . . . 101 E2
Forest Side SK11 . . . . . . 114 D4
Forest St Chester CH1 . . . 237 C2
 Weaverham CW8 . . . . . . 102 C8
Forest Wlk **5** WA7 . . . . . .49 F7
Forge Cl Cronton WA8 . . . . 12 C5
 Warren SK11 . . . . 111 D2
Forge Fields CW11 . . . . . 174 F3
Forge La Congleton CW12 . 156 B3
 Norton in Hales TF9 . . . . 236 C1
Forge Mill La CW10 . . . . . 151 C1
Forge Rd
 Ellesmere Port CH66 . . . . 69 C6
 Warrington WA5 . . . . . . .14 F5
 Whaley Bridge SK23 . . . . .65 E7
Forge Sh Ctr The WA4 . . . . 16 C1
Forge St CW1 . . . . 190 D4
Forge Way CH4 . . . . 140 F4
Formby Cl WA5 . . . . 14 F4
Formby Dr SK8 . . . . .34 B8
Forrest Rd CW12 . . . . 155 E3
Forrest Way WA5 . . . . 15 D3
Forshaw's La WA5 . . . . .6 E8
Forshaw St WA2 . . . . 16 C7
Forster Ave CW8 . . . . 102 E8
Forster St WA2 . . . . .16 B7
Forsythia Wlk **2** M31 . . . .11 E2
Fortis Way CH4 . . . . 141 B4
Forty Acre La CW4,
 CW12 . . . . 131 D6
Forum Sh Ctr The CH1 . . . 237 A2
Forwood Rd CH62 . . . . 43 D8
Fossa Cl CW10 . . . . 128 C2
Foster Rd CW12 . . . . 157 A5
Foster St WA8 . . . . .13 B1
Fothergill St WA1 . . . . . . 16 D7
Fotheringay Ct **3** CH65 . . . 70 D2
Foulkes Ave CW1 . . . . . . 189 F6
Foundry Bank CW12 . . . . 156 E3
Foundry Ct **1** SK12 . . . . . 39 C7
Foundry Ind Est WA8 . . . . .23 B7
Foundry La
 9 Moston Green CW11 . . . 174 D7
 Sandbach CW11 . . . . . . 174 D7
 Scholar Green ST7 . . . . . 194 F7
 Widnes WA8 . . . . 22 C5
Foundry St Bollington SK10 . .88 B8
 Newton-le-Willows WA12 . . . .2 B3
 Warrington WA2 . . . . . . .16 B6
Fountain Cl SK10 . . . . 88 B8
Fountain Ct Biddulph ST8 . . 179 D1
 2 Winsford CW7 . . . . . 126 D1
Fountain Ho SK10 . . . . . . 112 E8
Fountain La
 Davenham CW9 . . . . . . 103 F2
 Frodsham WA6 . . . . .74 B8
Fountain Pl SK12 . . . . 36 D4
Fountains Ave WA11 . . . . . .1 F7
Fountains Cl
 Middlewich CW10 . . . . . 128 B1
 Runcorn WA7 . . . . 50 C5
Fountain Sq SK12 . . . . . . 38 D6

Fountains Rd SK8 . . . . . . 35 C6
Fountain St
 Congleton CW12 . . . . . . 156 D2
 Macclesfield SK10 . . . . . 112 E8
Fountains Wlk WA3 . . . . . . .4 B8
FOURLANE-ENDS 63 A8
FOUR LANE ENDS 168 D7
Four Lane Ends
 Alvanley WA6 . . . . .74 B1
 Warrington WA3 . . . . .9 D3
Four Lanes Ct **3** CW7 . . 149 B8
FOURLANES END 176 E4
Four Lanes End
 Betley CW3 . . . . 207 F2
 Thornton Hough CH63 . . . 42 D5
Fourseasons Cl CW2 . . . . 206 B8
Fourth Ave
 Connah's Quay CH5 . . . . . .92 E2
 Crewe CW1 . . . . 190 F1
 Kidsgrove ST7 . . . . 194 F1
 1 Runcorn WA7 . . . . . . .49 C7
Fourways CW2 . . . . 207 B5
Fourways Tech Pk CW11 . . 176 E4
Fowey Cl SK10 . . . . 86 D1
Fowler Cl CW2 . . . . 190 D1
Fowler Rd CH1 . . . . 117 D4
Fowlers Bench La CH3 . . . . 184 C5
Fowler St SK10 . . . . 87 D1
FOWLEY COMMON 5 B5
Fowley Common La WA3 . . . .5 C5
Foxall Way CH66 . . . . 69 D2
Fox Bank Cl WA8 . . . . .12 F4
Fox Bench Cl SK7 . . . . . . 35 C6
Foxcote WA8 . . . . .12 B2
Foxcote Cl CH1 . . . . 117 D5
Foxcote Gdns **10** WA5 . . . .14 E8
Fox Cover CH3 . . . . 119 F5
Fox Cover Rd CH60 . . . . . . 41 D7
Fox Covert WA7 . . . . 50 C7
Foxcovert La WA16 . . . . . 106 E7
Fox Covert La
 Hoole Bank CH2 . . . . . . 119 B8
 Picton CH2 . . . . 96 A1
Fox Covert Way CW1 . . . . 173 A7
Foxdale Cl WA4 . . . . 26 C7
Foxdene CH66 . . . . 69 D5
Foxendale Cl WA8 . . . . . . 103 D7
Foxes Bank CW5 . . . . . . 220 A1
Foxes Fold CW8 . . . . .78 E1
Foxes Hey CW8 . . . . 101 D5
Foxes Hollow CW1 . . . . . 190 E7
Foxes Wlk CH3 . . . . 142 A7
Foxfield Cl WA2 . . . . .8 C3
Foxfield La CW7 . . . . 126 A1
Fox Gdns Lymm WA13 . . . . 18 C4
 Talke ST7 . . . . 210 D8
Foxglove Ave CW11 . . . . . 174 E6
Foxglove Cl
 Bollington SK10 . . . . 88 C8
 2 Golborne WA3 . . . . . . .3 D8
 Huntington CH3 . . . . . . 142 A6
 Wistaston CW2 . . . . . . 206 B7
Foxglove Ct WA6 . . . . 74 C8
Foxglove Dell WA6 . . . . . . 73 D2
Foxglove Way CH64 . . . . . .66 E5
Foxglove Wlk M31 . . . . . . .11 F2
Fox Gr WA16 . . . . 57 C1
Fox Hill CW6 . . . . 122 D4
Foxhill Cl CW8 . . . . 102 A2
Foxhill Cl CW6 . . . . 146 E1
Foxhill Gr WA6 . . . . 73 D4
Foxhills Cl WA4 . . . . 26 D3
Foxholme Cl WA8 . . . . . . 191 A6
Fox Hunter Cl CH3 . . . . . 121 F7
Fox La Clutton CH3 . . . . . 182 D1
 Waverton CH3 . . . . 143 B5
Foxlea CW9 . . . . 78 C7
Fox Lea CH1 . . . . 117 A8
FOXLEY 209 D7
Foxley Cl WA13 . . . . 19 A2
Foxley Hall Mews WA13 . . 19 A1
Foxley Heath WA8 . . . . . . .22 E8
Fox's Dr CH5 . . . . 116 A6
Fox St Congleton CW12 . . . 156 F3
 Runcorn WA7 . . . . 23 A1
 Warrington WA5 . . . . . . .15 E5
Foxwist Cl CH2 . . . . 237 B4
Foxwist Gn WA4 . . . . 125 E6
FOXWIST GREEN 125 F6
Foxwood Dr WA16 . . . . . . 108 A8
Fox Wood Sch WA3 . . . . . . .9 E3
Francesca Cl CH1 . . . . . . 237 B2
Frances St Crewe CW2 . . . 190 D2
 Irlam M44 . . . . .11 E5
 Macclesfield SK11 . . . . . 112 B8
Francis Cl WA8 . . . . 22 C8
Francis Ct CH1 . . . . 237 C1
Francis La Holt LL13 . . . . . 196 D7
 Ridleywood LL13 . . . . . 196 B5
Francis' La LL13 . . . . 196 B6
Francis Rd Frodsham WA6 . . 49 C1
 Irlam M44 . . . . .11 E5
 Warrington WA4 . . . . . . .16 B1
Francis St CH1 . . . . 237 C3
FRANDLEY 53 A3
Frank Bott Ave CW1 . . . . 190 A7
Frank Hughes Ave **1**
 CW11 . . . . 174 E4
Franklin Cl
 Macclesfield SK11 . . . . . 112 B5
 Warrington WA5 . . . . . . 15 C5
Franklin Mews CW9 . . . . . 79 C1
Franklyn Ave CW2 . . . . . 190 B3
Franklyn Dr **4** WA12 . . . . .2 D1
Frank Mayer Rd **4** ST7 . . 193 F3
Frank Perkins Way M44 . . . 11 F7
Frank St WA8 . . . . 13 C1
Frank Webb Ave CW1 . . . 190 A6

Frank Wilkinson Way
 ST7 . . . . 192 F4
Frappel Ct WA2 . . . . 16 B6
Fraser Ct CH4 . . . . 141 D7
Fraser Rd WA5 . . . . 14 D6
Frawley Ave WA12 . . . . . . .2 C5
Freckleton Cl WA5 . . . . . . .15 B4
Frederick Howarth Dr **5**
 CW11 . . . . 191 F8
Frederick St
 Warrington WA4 . . . . . . .16 E3
 Widnes WA8 . . . . 23 B8
Frederick Terr WA8 . . . . . 22 A4
Fredric Pl WA7 . . . . .23 B3
Freedom Dr ST7 . . . . 195 E3
Free Green La WA16 . . . . 107 A8
Freeport Shopping Mall
 ST7 . . . . 210 C6
Fremont Pl **12** WA5 . . . . . .15 B7
French Ave CW5 . . . . . . 218 C5
French Lane End CW5 . . . 218 E5
French St WA8 . . . . 13 D1
Freshfield SK8 . . . . .34 B8
Freshfield Dr SK10 . . . . . . 87 C3
Freshfields
 Comberbach CW9 . . . . . . 78 C7
 Knutsford WA16 . . . . . . .56 E3
 Wistaston CW2 . . . . . . 206 A7
Freshfields Dr WA2 . . . . . . .9 C1
Freshmeadow La WA6 . . . .73 B2
Freshwater Cl WA5 . . . . . 14 D7
Freshwater Dr CW2 . . . . . 221 C8
Freshwater View CW8 . . . 103 F8
Friars Ave WA5 . . . . .14 E5
Friars Cl Rainow SK10 . . . . 88 D5
 Wistaston CW2 . . . . . . 205 F8
Friar's Cl SK9 . . . . .59 E8
Friars Ct **11** WA1 . . . . . . .16 B5
Friars Gate Chester CH1 . . 237 B2
 Warrington WA1 . . . . . . .16 B4
Friars La WA1 . . . . .16 B4
Friars Way SK10 . . . . .86 F2
Frida Cres CW9 . . . . 103 E6
Friends La WA5 . . . . 14 D6
Friesian Gdns ST5 . . . . . 210 C2
Frith Ave CW8 . . . . 123 D8
Frith La CW5 . . . . 216 C4
Frith Terr SK11 . . . . 112 C4
Frobisher Ct WA5 . . . . . . 15 D8
Frobisher Rd CH64 . . . . . .66 E8
Froda Ave WA6 . . . . .74 B7
FRODSHAM 49 C1
Frodsham Bsns Ctr WA6 . . 49 C1
Frodsham CE Prim Sch
 WA6 . . . . .74 C7
Frodsham L Ctr WA6 . . . . .74 B8
Frodsham Manor House Prim
 Sch WA6 . . . . 49 C1
FRODSHAM MARSH 48 E2
Frodsham Rd WA6 . . . . . . 73 D1
FRODSHAM SCORE 48 B2
Frodsham Sq CH1 . . . . . . 237 B3
Frodsham St CH1 . . . . . . 237 B3
Frodsham Sta WA6 . . . . . .74 B8
Frodsham Way SK9 . . . . . .34 E4
Frodsham Weaver Vale Prim
 Sch WA6 . . . . 49 C2
Froghall La WA16 . . . . 29 D7
Frog La Holt LL13 . . . . . . 196 D8
 Milton Green CH3 . . . . . 165 E2
 Pickmere WA16 . . . . 30 E3
 Worthenbury LL13, SY14 . . 211 B1
Frome Cl CH65 . . . . .70 B7
Front St CW11 . . . . 175 C6
Frosts Mews CH65 . . . . . .70 B6
Fryer Rd CW9 . . . . 80 A3
Fryer St **16** WA7 . . . . 23 A3
Fuchsia Cl WA8 . . . . 12 C2
Fuchsia Rd CW8 . . . . 78 C1
Fulbeck WA8 . . . . 12 C2
Fulbeck Cl CW2 . . . . 206 B8
Fulbrook Dr SK8 . . . . 35 A6
Fulford Cl WA4 . . . . .26 E2
Fuller Dr CW2 . . . . 206 B7
FULLER'S MOOR 183 D1
Fullerton Rd CW8 . . . . . . 103 A4
Fulmar Cl Farndon CH3 . . . 180 E2
 Poynton SK12 . . . . 36 A4
Fulmards Cl SK9 . . . . 60 C7
Fulmar Rd SK7 . . . . .35 F1
Fulshaw Ave SK9 . . . . . . 60 A6
Fulshaw Cross SK9 . . . . . 60 A5
Fulshaw Ct SK9 . . . . 60 A5
FULSHAW PK 60 B5
Fulshaw Pk SK9 . . . . 60 A5
Fulshaw Pk S SK9 . . . . . . 60 A4
Fulton Cl WA4 . . . . .17 B4
Fulton Gr CW9 . . . . 103 F2
Fulwood Gdns CH66 . . . . . 69 C6
Fulwood Mews CH66 . . . . 69 C6
Fulwood Rd
 Ellesmere Port CH66 . . . . 69 C5
 Golborne WA3 . . . . .3 E7
Furber Cl CW6 . . . . 146 C1
Furber St CW1 . . . . 190 C5
Furne Rd CH1 . . . . 117 E4
Furness Cl
 Holmes Chapel CW4 . . . . 130 A3
 Poynton SK12 . . . . 36 D4
 Winsford CW7 . . . . 149 B8
Furness Ct WA7 . . . . .24 F4
Furness Lodge Cl SK23 . . . 39 D4
Furness Rd SK8 . . . . 35 C6
FURNESS VALE 39 C3
Furness Vale Bsns Ctr
 SK23 . . . . 39 D4
Furness Vale Prim Sch
 SK23 . . . . 39 D3

Frank Wilkinson Way
Furness Vale Sta SK23 . . . 39 D4
Furnival St CW11 . . . . . . 175 B7
Furnival St CW2 . . . . 190 C2
Furrocks Cl CH64 . . . . .66 F5
Furrocks La CH64 . . . . .66 F5
Furrocks Way CH64 . . . . . .66 F5
Furrows The CH66 . . . . . . .94 E8
Fusilier Rd **9** CW7 . . . . . 149 E8
Fylde Ave SK8 . . . . 34 C8
Fytton Cl SK11 . . . . 111 D1

G

Gable Ave SK9 . . . . 60 A7
Gable Ct **5** CW5 . . . . . . 204 E6
Gables Cl WA2 . . . . .8 F3
Gable St WA12 . . . . .2 B3
Gables The ST7 . . . . 193 C3
Gabriel Bank CW8 . . . . . . 76 A1
Gadbrook Bsns Ctr CW9 . . 104 D5
Gadbrook Pk CW9 . . . . . . 104 D5
Gadbrook Rd CW9 . . . . . . 104 D6
Gail Cl SK9 . . . . .60 B2
Gainford Cl WA8 . . . . 12 C3
Gainsborough Cl **4** SK9 . . 60 D8
Gainsborough Rd **4** WA16 . . .56 E3
Gainsborough Prim Sch
 CW2 . . . . 190 B2
Gainsborough Rd
 Crewe CW2 . . . . 190 B3
 Warrington WA4 . . . . . . .16 B2
Gairloch Cl WA2 . . . . .8 F4
Gaisgill Ct WA8 . . . . 12 C1
Gala Cl CH4 . . . . 139 C3
Galbraith Cl WA12 . . . . . 156 C2
Gale Ave WA5 . . . . .7 F1
Galebrook Way **4** WA4 . . .27 B4
Galion Way WA4 . . . . .12 B3
GALLANTRY BANK 200 B8
Gallantry Bank SY14 . . . . 200 A8
Galleys Bank ST7 . . . . . . 195 B3
Gallimore Ho ST7 . . . . . . 210 D8
Galloway Cl
 Holmes Chapel CW4 . . . . 130 C2
 Middlewich CW10 . . . . . 128 C2
Galloway Gn CW12 . . . . . 156 E5
Gallowsclough La WA6 . . . 100 F4
Galway Ave WA8 . . . . .12 E3
Galway Cres WA11 . . . . . . .1 D7
Galway Gr CW2 . . . . 206 B4
Game St CW11 . . . . 175 A3
Gamul Pl CH1 . . . . 237 B1
Gannet Way WA15 . . . . . . .32 F6
Ganton Cl WA8 . . . . .13 B4
Garden Cl SK10 . . . . .87 E1
Garden Ct CH1 . . . . 237 A3
Gardenhurst CW6 . . . . . . 168 C6
Garden La Chester CH1 . . . 237 A3
 Harthill CH3 . . . . 183 E3
Garden Rd WA16 . . . . .56 F3
Gardens The
 Lawton-gate ST7 . . . . . . 194 C4
 Sandbach CW11 . . . . . . 175 B6
Garden Terr Chester CH1 . . 237 A3
 Chester, Boughton CH2 . . 118 F2
Garden Wlk **8** M31 . . . . . .11 E2
Gardiner Ave WA11 . . . . . . .1 C6
Garfit St CW10 . . . . 128 C2
Garner St WA2 . . . . 16 C7
Garnett Ave WA4 . . . . 17 A4
Garnett Cl CW5 . . . . 204 F4
Garnetts La WA8 . . . . 22 A3
Garrett Field WA3 . . . . .9 D5
Garrigill Cl WA8 . . . . 13 C5
Garrison Cl CH3 . . . . 142 B4
Garsdale Cl WA5 . . . . .14 F7
Garside Ave WA3 . . . . .3 D7
Garston Cres WA12 . . . . . .2 D1
Garth Dr CH2 . . . . 118 C5
Garth Hts SK9 . . . . 60 C7
Garth Rd CH65 . . . . 71 A5
Garton Dr WA3 . . . . .3 E8
Garven Pl WA1 . . . . 16 A5
Garwood Cl WA5 . . . . 15 C8
Gaskell Ave
 Knutsford WA16 . . . . . . .56 F2
 Warrington WA4 . . . . . . 17 A3
Gaskell Pl SK10 . . . . 87 D4
Gaskell St WA4 . . . . 16 C1
Gas Rd SK11 . . . . 112 D8
Gas Works Ind Est ST7 . . 194 E2
Gatcombe Mews **1** SK9 . . 60 A6
Gateacre Ct CH66 . . . . . . .69 F8
Gatefield St CW1 . . . . . . 190 C4
Gatehouse The **7** CW5 . . 204 F5
Gatekeeper Ct **7** CW11 . . 175 D8
Gateley Cl WA4 . . . . .17 E3
GATESHEATH 165 C5
Gatesheath Dr CH2 . . . . . 118 E7
Gatesheath La CH3 . . . . . 165 F5
Gatewarth Ind Est WA5 . . 15 C3
Gate Warth St WA5 . . . . . 15 D4
Gateway Crewe CW1 . . . . . 190 F2
 Newcastle-under-Lyme
 ST5 . . . . 210 D2
Gateway Theatre★ CH1 . . 237 A2
Gateway Trad Pk WA5 . . . 16 A7
Gathurst Ct WA8 . . . . 12 C2
Gauntlet Birds of Prey, Eagle
 & Vulture Park★ WA16 . . 56 D5
GAUNTONS BANK 215 E4
Gauntons Bank SY13 . . . . 215 E3
Gaunts Way WA7 . . . . . . .49 E6
Gavin Rd WA8 . . . . .22 B7

Gaw End La SK11 . . . . . . 112 C2
Gawer Pk CH2 . . . . 118 C4
GAWSWORTH 135 E8
Gawsworth Ave CW2 . . . . 189 F3
Gawsworth Cl
 Alsager ST7 . . . . 193 C3
 Bramhall SK7 . . . . .35 E6
 Holmes Chapel CW4 . . . . 130 B3
 Northwich CW9 . . . . . . 104 A4
 Poynton SK12 . . . . .36 F2
Gawsworth Ct WA3 . . . . . . .9 E5
Gawsworth Dr CW11 . . . . 175 C7
Gawsworth Hall★ SK11 . . 134 E8
Gawsworth Prim Sch
 SK11 . . . . 111 D2
Gawsworth Rd
 Ellesmere Port CH66 . . . . 69 E5
 Macclesfield SK11 . . . . . 111 D2
Gawsworth Way SK9 . . . . .34 E4
Gayhurst Ave WA2 . . . . . . .8 F2
Gaymoore Cl CW2 . . . . . . 237 A4
Gaynor Ave WA11 . . . . . . .1 F7
GAYTON 41 B6
Gayton Cl CH2 . . . . 118 C5
Gayton Farm Rd CH60 . . . 41 A5
Gayton La CH60 . . . . .41 B6
Gayton Mill Cl CH60 . . . . .41 C5
Gayton Parkway CH60 . . . 41 C5
Gayton Prim Sch CH60 . . . 41 A6
Gayton Rd CH60 . . . . 41 A6
Gayton Sands RSPB
 Reserve★ CH60 . . . . . . .40 E4
Gazebank WA6 . . . . 100 F5
Gelli Dderw/Oak Gr
 CH4 . . . . 140 D5
GEMINI 7 D3
Gemini Bsns Pk WA5 . . . . . .7 E3
Gemmull Cl CW3 . . . . . . 229 F4
General St WA1 . . . . 16 C5
Genesis Ctr The WA3 . . . . .9 E5
Geneva Rd CW7 . . . . 126 C1
Geneva Way WA8 . . . . . . 179 E1
Geo. Hampson's Bldgs
 WA3 . . . . .5 C8
George Bates Cl ST7 . . . . 193 C3
George Cl **2** Alvanley WA6 . . 73 A2
 Helsby WA6 . . . . 73 A2
 Hoole CH3 . . . . 119 A2
George Crawford Rd
 CW1 . . . . 190 D7
George Dr **5** CH64 . . . . . 41 C1
George Edward Rd CW2 . . 206 C4
George Gallimore Dr
 CW11 . . . . 191 F6
George Ho CW5 . . . . 204 E7
George Kenyon Mews
 CH4 . . . . 140 E6
George Rd WA5 . . . . 15 C4
George St W SK11 . . . . . 112 C8
George's Cl SK12 . . . . . . .36 E3
Georges Cres WA4 . . . . . .17 B2
Georges Ct **18** SK10 . . . . . 112 C8
George's La CW9 . . . . 54 D1
George's Prec WA5 . . . . . 14 D6
George's Road E SK12 . . . .36 E3
George's Road W SK12 . . . .36 E3
George St
 Alderley Edge SK9 . . . . . . 60 A1
 Audley ST7 . . . . 209 D1
 Barnton CW8 . . . . .78 B3
 Chester CH1 . . . . 237 A3
 Ellesmere Port CH65 . . . . 70 C7
 Knutsford WA16 . . . . . . 57 A2
 Macclesfield SK11 . . . . . 112 D7
 Newton-le-Willows WA12 . . 2 A4
 Sandbach CW11 . . . . . . 174 E8
 Whaley Bridge SK23 . . . . .65 E7
 Winsford CW7 . . . . 126 E1
Georges Way **2** ST7 . . . . 209 F2
George's Wlk CW11 . . . . 175 B6
George VI Ave CW10 . . . . 151 D6
George VI Cl CW10 . . . . . 151 D6
Georgia Pl WA5 . . . . 15 C7
Geranium St CW8 . . . . . . 103 D8
Gerard Cl CH3 . . . . 121 C1
Gerard Dr CW5 . . . . 204 C4
Gerards Gdns CW5 . . . . . 205 D6
Gerosa Ave WA2 . . . . .8 B8
Gerrard Ave
 Ellesmere Port CH66 . . . . 69 C4
 Warrington WA5 . . . . . . .15 F7
Gerrard Dr CW8 . . . . 77 D1
Gerrard Rd WA3 . . . . .9 A7
Gerrards Ave CH3 . . . . . . 119 A1
Gerrard St WA8 . . . . .23 B8
Giantswood La
 Congleton CW12 . . . . . . 156 C6
 Marton CW12 . . . . 132 F1
GIBB HILL 53 D1
Gibb Hill CW9 . . . . 53 D1
Gibbon Dr CW9 . . . . .80 B3
Gibson Cl Nantwich CW5 . . 204 D6
 Tarvin CH3 . . . . 121 C1
Gibson Cres CW11 . . . . . 174 D6
Gibson Ct Trad Est CH65 . . 70 C8
Gibson St
 Warrington, Howley WA1 . . 16 C5
 Warrington, Stockton Heath
 WA4 . . . . 16 D1
Gigg La Moore WA4 . . . . . .25 B5
 Warrington WA4 . . . . . . .17 E3
Gig La WA11 . . . . .2 A8
Gilbert Cl **2** ST7 . . . . . . 195 A2
Gilbert Ct WA3 . . . . .4 F3
Gilbert Dr WA4 . . . . .17 B3

Gilbert Ho WA7 . . . .**22** E3
Gilchrist Ave SK11 . . . . . . **111** E7
Gilchrist Rd M44 . . . .**11** F6
Gilderdale Cl WA3 . . . .**10** B5
Gilder Way CH66 . . . .**69** B4
Giles Dr WA4 . . . .**17** B3
Gillan Cl WA7 . . . .**50** C5
GILLBENT **34** F6
Gillbent Rd SK8 . . . .**35** A7
Gillow Cl CW1 . . . .**190** A8
GILLOW HEATH **179** C2
Giltbrook Cl WA8 . . . .**12** F3
Gilwell Cl WA4 . . . .**17** C2
Gilwern Cl CH2 . . . .**118** C4
GINCLOUGH **88** F6
Gingerbread La CW5 . . . . .**205** A5
Ginkgo Gr CW12 . . . .**155** C4
Gipsy Cnr SY13 . . . .**224** E2
Girton Cl CH65 . . . .**70** D4
Girton Rd CH65 . . . .**70** D4
Girvin Dr CH65 . . . .**66** F6
Glade Dr CH66 . . . .**68** F6
Gladewood Cl SK9 . . . .**60** C8
Gladstone Ave CH1 . . . . . .**118** B2
Gladstone Mews WA2 . . .**16** A6
Gladstone Rd
 Broughton CH4 . . . .**139** B3
 Chester CH1 . . . .**118** B3
 Neston CH64 . . . .**66** E8
Gladstone St
 Northwich CW8 . . . .**103** E7
 Warrington WA2 . . . .**16** A6
 8 Widnes WA8 . . . .**23** B8
 Willaston CW5 . . . .**205** D6
 Winsford CW7 . . . .**149** D8
Gladstone Way WA12 . . . . . .**2** B4
Glaisdale Cl CW2 . . . .**206** A6
Glamis Cl Chester CH3 . . . .**119** A2
 Wistaston CW2 . . . .**205** E8
Glanaber Ct CH4 . . . .**141** A7
Glan Aber Pk CH4 . . . .**141** A7
Glandon Dr SK8 . . . .**35** C8
Glastonbury Ave
 Cheadle SK8 . . . .**35** C6
 Chester CH2 . . . .**118** F7
 Golborne WA3 . . . .**4** C8
Glastonbury Cl WA7 . . . . . .**24** F3
Glastonbury Dr
 Middlewich CW10 . . . .**128** B1
 Poynton SK12 . . . .**36** D5
Glastonbury Mews WA4 . .**16** E2
GLAZEBROOK **11** B6
Glazebrook La
 Hollinfare WA3 . . . .**11** B5
 Lunts Heath WA8 . . . .**13** A6
Glazebrook St WA1 . . . .**16** D6
Glazebrook Sta WA3 . . . . . .**11** A5
GLAZEBURY **5** B7
Glazebury CE Prim Sch
 WA3 . . . .**5** C7
Glazebury Mill Cl WA3 . . . . .**5** C7
Glaziers La WA3 . . . .**4** D2
Gleadmere WA8 . . . .**12** C2
GLEADSMOSS **132** B6
Gleaner Cl WA7 . . . .**22** F3
Gleave Ave SK10 . . . .**88** B8
Gleave Rd Burtonwood WA5 . .**6** F6
 Weaverham CW8 . . . .**77** D1
Glebe Ave WA4 . . . .**17** C1
Glebe Cl CW5 . . . .**220** A8
Glebecroft Ave CH2 . . . . . .**72** A3
Glebe Ct ST7 . . . .**194** D2
Glebe Farm Mews WA4 . .**71** E2
Glebe Green Dr CW7 . . . .**149** C6
Glebe La WA8 . . . .**13** B5
Glebeland WA3 . . . .**4** E2
Glebelands Rd WA16 . . . . . .**57** A1
Glebe Mdws CH2 . . . .**96** F1
Glebe Rd CW8 . . . .**102** A4
Glebe St ST7 . . . .**194** D2
Glebe The WA7 . . . .**23** E1
Glebeway Rd CH65 . . . .**70** F5
Gleggs Cl CH3 . . . .**142** B7
Glegg St SK11 . . . .**112** E7
Glenathol Rd CH66 . . . .**69** C4
Glenbourne Pk SK7 . . . . . .**35** D5
Glenburn Ave CH62 . . . .**43** E4
Glen Cl WA3 . . . .**11** B2
Glencoe Cl WA4 . . . .**130** C2
Glencoe Rd CH66 . . . .**69** C4
Glencourse Rd WA8 . . . . . .**13** A5
Glendale Ave Elton CH2 . . .**72** A3
 Sandycroft CH5 . . . .**116** A3
Glendale Bsns Pk CH5 . .**116** A3
Glendale Cl Buerton CW3 . .**230** F4
 Crewe CW2 . . . .**189** D3
Glendale Pk CH5 . . . .**116** A3
Glendale Rd WA7 . . . .**24** A2
Glendene Ave SK7 . . . .**35** D5
Glendyke Rd CH66 . . . .**69** C4
Gleneagles Cl
 Bramhall SK7 . . . .**36** A7
 Chester CH3 . . . .**119** B3
 Golborne WA3 . . . .**3** F7
 Wilmslow SK9 . . . .**60** D8
Gleneagles Dr
 Haydock WA11 . . . .**1** A5
 Holmes Chapel CW4 . . . . .**130** B2
 Macclesfield SK10 . . . .**87** C4
 Widnes WA8 . . . .**13** B5
 Winsford CW7 . . . .**126** C2
Gleneagles Rd CH66 . . . . . .**69** C4
Glenesk Rd CH66 . . . .**69** C4
Glenfield Dr SK12 . . . .**36** D3
Glenholme Rd SK7 . . . .**35** D7

Glenmaye Rd CH66 . . . .**69** C4
Glenn Pl WA8 . . . .**12** E1
Glenorchy Cl CW4 . . . .**130** C2
Glen Rd CH66 . . . .**69** C4
Glenside Cl CH1 . . . .**117** D5
Glenside Dr SK9 . . . .**60** C6
Glen The Blacon CH1 . . . . .**117** E5
 Runcorn WA7 . . . .**49** F5
Glenton Pk CH64 . . . .**66** F6
Glenville Cl Cheadle SK8 . . .**34** F7
 Runcorn WA7 . . . .**49** B6
Glenwood WA7 . . . .**24** C1
Glenwood Cl **8** CH66 . . . . .**69** C6
Glenwood Gdns CH66 . . . .**69** C6
Glenwood Rd CH66 . . . .**69** C6
Gleyve WA16 . . . .**29** C5
Gloucester Ave
 Golborne WA3 . . . .**3** B8
 Middlewich CW10 . . . .**128** D2
Gloucester Cl
 Ellesmere Port CH66 . . . . . .**94** E8
 Macclesfield SK10 . . . .**87** E4
 Warrington WA1 . . . .**17** D7
Gloucester Ho **13** CH1 . . .**237** C3
Gloucester Rd Gatley SK8. . **34** C7
 Kidsgrove ST7 . . . .**195** A3
 Knutsford WA16 . . . .**81** F8
 Poynton SK12 . . . .**36** D4
 Widnes WA8 . . . .**13** B3
Gloucester St CH1 . . . .**237** B4
Glover Dr CW5 . . . .**205** D5
Glover Rd WA3 . . . .**9** C4
Glovers Loom CH3 . . . .**142** B7
Glover St Crewe CW1 . . . . .**190** A5
 Newton-le-Willows WA12 . . . .**2** C3
Gloverstone Ct CH1 . . . . . .**237** B1
Glyn Ave CH62 . . . .**43** E7
Glyn Garth CH1 . . . .**117** D3
Go Ape! Delamere ★
 CW8 . . . .**100** B2
Goathland Way SK11 . . . . .**112** D6
Goblins La SY14 . . . .**212** A2
Goddard Ct **13** CW1. . . . . .**190** B5
Goddard Rd WA7 . . . .**23** E3
Goddard St CW1 . . . .**190** B5
Godfrey St WA2 . . . .**16** D7
Godscroft La WA6 . . . .**73** E6
Godshill Cl WA5 . . . .**14** D7
Godstall La CH1 . . . .**237** B2
Godstow WA7 . . . .**24** E4
Godward Rd SK22 . . . .**39** B8
GOLBORNE **3** B7
Golborne Cty Prim Sch
 WA3 . . . .**3** A8
Golborne Dale Rd WA3,
 WA12. . . . .**3** A5
Golborne La WA16 . . . .**28** F3
Golborne Rd Golborne WA3 . .**3** C8
 Winwick WA12,WA2 . . . .**8** A7
Golborne St WA12 . . . .**2** E4
Goldcliff Cl WA5 . . . .**7** D3
Goldcrest Cl Runcorn WA7 . .**49** F5
 Winsford CW7 . . . .**149** C5
Gold Ct CH3 . . . .**142** C5
Golden Hill CW2 . . . .**207** E3
Golden Nook Rd CW8. . . . .**101** F2
Golden Sq (Sh Ctr) WA1 . .**16** B5
Goldfinch Cl CW12 . . . .**156** E1
Goldfinch Dr ST7 . . . .**193** B3
Goldfinch La WA3 . . . .**9** E4
Goldfinch Rd ST7 . . . .**195** F1
Goldford La SY14 . . . .**199** F6
Golding Dr CW1 . . . .**190** 5C
Goldsitch Moss La SK17 . .**138** F1
Goldsmith Dr CW11 . . . . . .**174** D6
Goldsmith La SY13 . . . . . .**228** A3
Gold Triangle Ind Est
 WA8 . . . .**22** C5
Golf Course Rd CW8. . . . .**100** D1
Golftyn Dr CH5 . . . .**91** C1
Golftyn La CH5 . . . .**91** C1
GOLLY **161** B1
Gongar La
 Ashton Hayes CH3 . . . .**121** E8
 Mouldsworth CH3 . . . .**98** E1
Gonsley Cl CH2 . . . .**237** B4
Gonville Ave SK11 . . . .**112** F3
Gooch Dr WA12 . . . .**2** D2
Goodall's Cnr CW2 . . . . . .**206** C3
Goodall St SK11 . . . .**112** E7
Goode Way CW2 . . . .**190** D1
Goodier Ct WA7 . . . .**49** C7
Goodrington Rd SK9 . . . . . .**34** E3
Good St CH3 . . . .**166** A1
Goodwin Cl **3** SK10 . . . . . .**87** E5
Goodwin Cres CW2 . . . . . .**206** C4
Goodwood Cl Barnton CW8 . **78** B3
 Chester CH1 . . . .**118** B2
Goodwood Gr CH66 . . . .**69** D3
Goodwood Rise CW10 . . .**128** A2
Gooseberry La
 Kelsall CW6 . . . .**122** C3
 Runcorn WA7 . . . .**24** D1
Goosebrook Cl CW9 . . . . . .**78** D8
Goosebrook La WA4, CW9 . **52** F2
Goose La WA4 . . . .**26** A2
Goosetrey Cl SK9 . . . .**34** E1
GOOSTREY **107** D1
Goostrey Com Prim Sch
 Goostrey CW4 . . . .**107** F1
 Goostrey CW4 . . . .**130** F8
Goostrey Ct **4** CW12 . . . .**156** F3
Goostrey La CW4 . . . .**130** B8
Goostrey Sta CW4 . . . .**131** A8
Goostry La WA16 . . . .**108** A7
Gordale Cl
 Congleton CW12 . . . .**157** A5
 Northwich CW8 . . . .**103** D8

Gordale Cl continued
 Warrington WA5 . . . .**14** F7
 Winnington CW8 . . . .**78** D1
Gordon Ave
 Bebington CH62 . . . .**43** E7
 Haydock WA11 . . . .**1** F7
 Warrington WA1 . . . .**17** B7
Gordon Geddes Way
 Bradfield Green CW1 . . . . .**172** F1
 1 Coppenhall Moss CW1 .**173** A1
Gordon La CH1 . . . .**95** B5
Gore La SK9 . . . .**59** C3
Gorran Haven WA7 . . . .**50** C5
Gorse Cl WA6 . . . .**101** A6
GORSE COVERT **10** B5
Gorse Covert CW9 . . . .**79** C3
Gorse Covert Prim Sch
 WA3 . . . .**10** B5
Gorse Covert Rd WA3 . . . . .**10** B6
Gorsefield CH3 . . . .**166** A1
Gorsefield Ave CH62 . . . . . .**43** D5
Gorsefield Cl CH62 . . . .**43** D5
Gorsefield Hey SK9 . . . .**60** E8
Gorse La CW12 . . . .**178** D5
Gorselands SK8 . . . .**35** B5
Gorse Sq M31 . . . .**11** D3
Gorse Stacks CH1 . . . .**237** B3
Gorse The WA14 . . . .**31** B8
Gorse Way CH3 . . . .**142** A5
Gorsewood Prim Sch
 WA7 . . . .**50** D7
Gorsewood Rd WA7 . . . . . .**50** D6
GORSEY BANK **231** F2
Gorsey Bank Cres CW5 . . .**220** A8
Gorsey Bank Prim Sch
 SK9 . . . .**59** F7
Gorsey La Partington WA13. .**20** B7
 St Helens WA5,WA9. . . . .**6** C5
 Warrington WA1,WA2 . . . . . .**16** D7
 Widnes WA8 . . . .**13** E1
Gorsey Rd SK9 . . . .**59** F8
Gorseywell La WA7. . . . .**50** F6
Gorsley Cl CW10 . . . .**151** C6
GORSTAGE **102** C6
Gorstage La CW8. . . . .**102** C7
GORSTELLA **140** A1
Gorstons La CH64 . . . .**67** A6
Gorston Wlk M22 . . . .**33** C8
GORSTYHILL **207** E2
Gorsty Hill Cl CW2 . . . .**207** F2
Gorsty Hill Ct CW2 . . . .**207** F2
Gosberryhole La CW12 . . .**158** A2
Gosforth Cl WA7 . . . .**49** E7
Gosforth Pl CH2 . . . .**118** F3
GOSLAND GREEN **169** B1
Gosling Cl WA4 . . . .**26** A1
Gosling Rd WA3. . . . .**9** B7
Gosling Way CW12 . . . . . .**156** A3
Gosport Cl WA2 . . . .**8** F1
Goss Pl ST7 . . . .**193** B3
Goss St CH1 . . . .**237** A2
Gough Ave WA2. . . . .**8** B2
Gough's La WA16 . . . .**82** C7
Goulden Cl **10** SK10 . . . . . .**87** C5
Goulden St Crewe CW1 . . .**190** A5
 Warrington WA5 . . . .**15** E6
Goulders Ct WA7. . . . .**50** B5
GOWHOLE **39** E4
Gow Hole SK23 . . . .**39** E4
Gowy Cl Alsager ST7 . . . . .**192** F3
 Handforth SK9 . . . .**34** E1
 Sandbach CW11 . . . .**174** E8
Gowy Cres CH3 . . . .**121** B2
Gowy Ct Calveley CW6 . . . .**169** E2
 Ellesmere Port CH66 . . . . . .**69** E8
Gowy Rd CH2 . . . .**96** F1
Gowy Wlk CW7. . . . .**127** A3
Goyt Forest Walks ★
 SK11 . . . .**115** E7
Goyt Pl SK23 . . . .**65** E7
Goyt Rd Disley SK12 . . . . . .**38** D5
 Horwich End SK23 . . . .**65** E6
 New Mills SK22 . . . .**39** D6
Goytside SK22 . . . .**39** C6
Goytside Mdws Nature
 Reserve ★ SK22 . . . .**39** C6
Goyt's La SK17. . . . .**90** F7
Goyt Valley Ind Est SK23. .**39** D4
Goyt Valley Walks ★ SK23. .**90** E6
Goyt View SK22. . . . .**39** B6
Grace Ave WA2 . . . .**16** B8
Grace Cl CW1 . . . .**191** C4
Grace Rd CH65 . . . .**70** C7
Gradbach Mill La SK17. . . .**138** B1
GRADELEY GREEN **202** F5
Grafton Mews CH2 . . . . . .**237** B4
Grafton Rd CH65 . . . .**70** C7
Grafton St
 Newton-le-Willows WA12 . . . .**2** B3
 Warrington WA5 . . . .**15** E6
Graham Ave CH66 . . . .**69** D5
Graham Cl WA8 . . . .**12** C1
Graham Cres M44. . . . .**11** C3
Graham Dr Disley SK12 . . . .**38** C6
 Halewood L26 . . . .**21** A8
Graham Rd Blacon CH1 . . .**117** F3
 Widnes WA8. . . . .**22** C8
Grainger's Rd CW9. . . . . . .**103** F5
Grakle Croft CH3 . . . .**166** A2
Gralam Gr **7** CW9. . . . .**80** B2
Grammar School Ct WA4 . .**16** F3
Grammar School Rd
 Lymm WA13 . . . .**18** F2
 Warrington WA4 . . . .**16** F3
Grampian Way
 Bebington CH62. . . . .**43** E4
 Neston CH64 . . . .**66** E5

Grampian Way continued
 Winsford CW7 . . . .**149** A7
Granary Cl CH3 . . . .**165** B2
Granary Mews SK12 . . . . . .**36** E3
Granary Mill WA7 . . . .**50** F6
Granby Cl WA7. . . . .**50** C5
Granby Rd Cheadle SK8. . . .**35** B8
 Huntington CH3 . . . .**142** B5
 Warrington WA4 . . . .**26** B8
Grandford La CW5 . . . .**217** D2
Grand Junction Ret Pk
 CW1 . . . .**190** D3
GRANGE Runcorn **49** D7
 Warrington **17** E8
Grange Academy The
 WA7 . . . .**23** C1
Grange Ave Barnton CW8 . . .**78** B3
 Warrington WA4 . . . .**16** E4
Grangebrook Dr CW7. . . . .**126** C3
Grange Brook Dr CW7 . . . .**126** C3
Grange Cl Bunbury CW6 . .**185** F8
 Chorlton CW2. . . . .**207** E4
 Crewe CW1 . . . .**190** E3
 Golborne WA3 . . . .**3** C6
 Sandbach CW11 . . . .**174** F7
Grange Cres CH66. . . . .**44** A1
Grange Ct Biddulph ST8 . .**179** D2
 14 Knutsford WA16 . . . .**57** A2
 Winsford CW7 . . . .**126** B5
Grange Dr Hartford CW8 . .**103** A6
 Thornton Hough CH63 . . . . .**42** A7
 Warrington WA5 . . . .**15** A4
 Widnes WA8. . . . .**12** D1
Grange Farm Cl WA5 . . . . .**15** D6
Grangefields ST8 . . . .**179** E4
Grange Green Manor
 WA4. . . . .**25** E7
Grange Jun Sch The
 CW8 . . . .**103** A6
Grange La Tilston SY14 . . .**198** E3
 Weaverham CW8 . . . .**102** A7
 Whitegate CW8 . . . .**125** F7
 Winsford CW7 . . . .**126** B5
Grangelands SK10 . . . .**86** F2
Grange Lea CW10 . . . .**128** B1
Grangemoor WA7 . . . .**49** D8
Grange Park Ave
 Runcorn WA7 . . . .**23** C2
 Wilmslow SK9 . . . .**60** A8
Grange Park Dr ST8 . . . . .**179** E3
Grange Pl M44. . . . .**11** E5
Grange Prim Sch CW7. . . .**126** B5
Grange Rd Barnton CW8 . . .**78** A3
 Biddulph ST8 . . . .**179** E3
 Chester CH2 . . . .**118** D4
 Chester, Vicarscross CH3. . .**119** C2
 Cuddington CW8 . . . .**101** F3
 Ellesmere Port CH65 . . . . . .**70** C4
 Haydock WA11,WA12 . . . .**1** B5
 Macclesfield SK11 . . . .**112** C6
 Mouldsworth CH3 . . . .**99** B1
 Northwich, Rudheath CW9 . .**104** D6
 Runcorn WA7 . . . .**23** C2
Grange Road N WA7. . . . . .**23** C2
Grange Road W CH3. . . . .**119** C2
Grange Sch The CW8 . . . .**103** B6
Grangeside CH2 . . . .**118** D7
Grange The
 Congleton CW12 . . . .**179** B8
 Hartford CW8. . . . .**103** B5
 Macclesfield SK11 . . . .**112** A6
Grange Valley WA11. . . . . . .**1** D6
Grange Valley Prim Sch
 WA11 . . . .**1** D5
Grange Villas CW8 . . . .**78** A3
Grangeway Handforth SK9 . **34** D4
 Runcorn WA7 . . . .**49** C8
Grange Way CW1 . . . .**174** F7
Grangeway Ct WA7. . . . .**49** C8
Grangewood Dr SK11. . . . .**83** F3
Granston Cl WA5. . . . .**7** E2
Grant Cl WA5 . . . .**7** D1
Grantham Ave
 Warrington WA4 . . . .**26** B8
 Warrington, Bruche WA1 . . . .**16** E7
Grantham Cl CW9 . . . .**104** C3
Granthams La WA13 . . . . . .**28** F7
Granville Dr CH66 . . . .**69** B7
Granville Rd Chester CH1 . .**118** B3
 Northwich CW9 . . . .**104** A5
 Wilmslow SK9 . . . .**59** F5
Granville Sq CW7 . . . .**149** E8
Granville St
 15 Runcorn WA7 . . . .**23** A3
 Warrington WA1 . . . .**16** D6
 Winsford CW7 . . . .**149** E8
Grapes St **9** SK11 . . . .**112** D7
GRAPPENHALL **17** A1
Grappenhall Hall Sch
 WA4 . . . .**17** B1
GRAPPENHALL HEYS **27** A8
Grappenhall Heys Com Prim
 Sch WA4 . . . .**27** A7
Grappenhall La WA4 . . . . . .**27** E6
Grappenhall Rd
 Ellesmere Port CH65 . . . . . .**69** F3
 Warrington WA4 . . . .**16** D1
Grasmere SK11 . . . .**112** A6
Grasmere Ave
 Congleton CW12 . . . .**155** F2
 Crewe CW2 . . . .**189** F5
 Warrington WA2 . . . .**8** E3
Grasmere Cl CW7 . . . .**126** D2
Grasmere Cres
 Bramhall SK7 . . . .**35** E8
 High Lane SK12 . . . .**37** E8
Grasmere Dr
 Holmes Chapel CW4 . . . . .**130** A3

Grasmere Dr continued
 Runcorn WA7 . . . .**49** D5
Grasmere Rd
 Alderley Edge SK9 . . . .**60** A1
 Chester CH2 . . . .**118** F5
 Ellesmere Port CH65 . . . . . .**70** C2
 Frodsham WA6. . . . .**74** C8
 Lymm WA13. . . . .**18** F4
 Neston CH64 . . . .**66** E6
 Partington M31 . . . .**11** B3
Grason Ave SK9. . . . .**34** C1
Grassfield Way WA16 . . . . .**82** A8
Grassmoor Cl CH62. . . . . . .**43** E8
Grassygreen La ST7 . . . . .**209** E1
Gratrix Rd CH62 . . . .**43** D8
GRAVEL **127** A1
Gravel La SK9 . . . .**59** E5
Gravel Wlk SY14. . . . .**213** D7
Gravenhurst La CW3. . . . . .**232** D1
GRAVENHUNGER MOSS . . .**232** B2
Graveyard La WA16 . . . .**58** F5
Gray Ave WA11. . . . .**1** D6
Graylag Cl WA7 . . . .**49** F5
Grayling Ave CH65 . . . .**70** A7
Grayling Cl WA12 . . . .**1** E4
Grayling Dr **10** CW11 . . . . .**175** D8
Graymarsh Dr SK12 . . . .**36** E2
Gray's Cl ST7 . . . .**195** B7
Greasby Dr CH66 . . . .**69** E4
Great Ashfield WA8 . . . .**12** D3
GREAT BARROW **120** E6
GREAT BUDWORTH **79** A7
Great Budworth CE Prim Sch
 CW9 . . . .**79** B8
Great Delph WA11 . . . .**1** D7
Greater Grace Christian
 School CH1 . . . .**95** B4
Great Hall Pk CH65 . . . .**70** D4
Great King St SK11 . . . . . .**112** C8
Greatoak Rd ST7 . . . .**209** F4
Great Oak Sq WA16. . . . . . .**58** A4
Great Queen St SK11 . . . . .**112** C8
Great Riding WA7 . . . .**50** C7
GREAT SANKEY **15** A6
Great Sankey High Sch
 WA5 . . . .**14** E7
Great Sankey L Ctr WA5. . .**14** E7
Great Sankey Prim Sch
 WA5 . . . .**15** A5
GREAT SUTTON **69** D3
Great Tithes Pl **6** CW1 . . .**173** A1
Greaves La SY14 . . . .**222** E6
Greaves Lane E SY14 . . . .**222** E7
Greaves Rd SK9 . . . .**59** E7
Grebe Cl Knutsford WA16 . . .**57** B3
 Poynton SK12. . . . .**36** B4
Greeba Ave WA4 . . . .**16** B3
Greek St WA7. . . . .**22** F3
Greenacre SK8. . . . .**34** C7
Greenacre Dr CH63. . . . . . .**43** C7
Greenacre Rd CH4 . . . .**140** F4
Greenacres Crewe CW1 . . .**190** D6
 Duddon CW6 . . . .**145** A6
 Frodsham WA6. . . . .**74** C6
 Sandbach CW11. . . . .**175** A7
Greenacres Cl WA3 . . . .**4** B8
Greenacres Ct CH2 . . . .**95** F1
Greenacres Rd CW12. . . . .**155** F2
Greenacres The WA13. . . . .**19** A4
Greenall Ave WA5. . . . .**14** D4
Greenall Rd CW9. . . . .**104** B8
Greenall's Ave WA4 . . . . . .**16** C2
Green Ave Alpraham CW6 . .**169** D4
 Barnton CW8 . . . .**78** A3
 Davenham CW9 . . . .**103** F3
GREENBANK **103** C7
Greenbank Chester CH4 . . .**141** E6
 Dunham-on-the-Hill WA6 . . . .**97** C4
Green Bank Adderley TF9 . .**235** A5
 Chester CH4 . . . .**141** E6
Greenbank Ave CH66 . . . . .**69** C7
Greenbank Cl CW5 . . . .**205** D6
Greenbank Dr SK10 . . . .**88** A4
Greenbank Gdns WA4 . . . .**16** F2
Greenbank La CW8 . . . . . .**103** D6
Greenbank Pk CW11. . . . . .**175** A2
Greenbank Rd
 Chester CH2. . . . .**119** A4
 Warrington WA4 . . . .**16** F2
Greenbank Residential Sch
 CW8 . . . .**103** D6
Greenbank St WA4 . . . .**16** C2
Greenbank Sta CW8 . . . . .**103** D6
Green Bridge Cl WA7. . . . . .**24** C2
Greenbridge Rd WA7. . . . . .**24** B2
Green Coppice WA7. . . . . . .**50** C8
GREENDALE **86** E7
Greendale Dr
 Middlewich CW10 . . . .**151** B7
 Newcastle-under-Lyme
 ST5 . . . .**210** D1
Greendale Gdns CW1. . . . .**190** E5
Greendale La SK10 . . . .**86** D8
Green Dr Alsager ST7. . . . .**193** D4
 Handforth SK9 . . . .**34** D2
Green Farm Rd CW6 . . . . .**163** B2
Greenfield Ave CH4 . . . . . .**161** A7
Greenfield Cl SK22 . . . .**39** A8
Greenfield Cres
 Chester CH2. . . . .**119** C5
 Waverton CH3. . . . .**143** B6
Greenfield Farm Ind Est
 CW12 . . . .**156** B3
Greenfield Gdns CH2 . . . . .**72** B3
Greenfield La
 Chester CH2. . . . .**119** B5

Greenfield La continued
Frodsham WA6. . . . .**49** B1
Greenfield Rd
Bollington SK10 . . . . **88** A7
Broughton CH4. . . . . **139** C4
Congleton CW12 . . . . **156** B3
Ellesmere Port CH66. . . . . .**69** B7
Waverton CH3 . . . . **143** B6
Greenfields Chester CH2. . . **95** F1
Winsford CW7 . . . . **127** B1
Greenfields Ave
Bebington CH62. . . . . **43** C7
Shavington CW2. . . . . . . **206** B4
Warrington WA4 . . . . **26** D8
Greenfields Cl
Neston CH64 . . . .**66** F5
Newton-le-Willows WA12 . . . .**2** C4
Warrington WA1 . . . . **17** C7
Greenfields Cres CH62 . . . **43** C7
Greenfields Croft CH64 . . .**66** E5
Greenfields Dr
Alsager ST7 . . . . **193** E3
Neston CH64. . . . .**66** F5
Greenfields La
Malpas SY14 . . . . **213** B4
Rowton CH3. . . . . **142** F5
Greenfields Lodge CH3 . . **120** D6
Greenfields Prim Sch 6
CW7 . . . . **126** A1
Greenfield Way CW8 . . . . **102** A4
Green Field Way CW1 . . . **190** F7
Greenfinch Gr WA3 . . . .**9** E3
Greengate WA15 . . . . **32** D7
Greengate Rd ST7. . . . . . **193** F5
Greengates Cres CH64. . . . .**66** E5
Greengate Way 3 WA8. . . **13** C4
Green Hall Mews SK9. . . . . **60** B6
Greenhaven Ct CW5 . . . . . **219** E5
Greenhey La CH3. . . . . **98** A1
Greenhill Comm La
Green Hill WA4. . . . . **52** A4
Higher Whitley WA4. . . . . . **51** F4
Higher Whitley WA4. . . . . . **52** A5
Greenhill La WA4. . . . . **52** A5
Greenhills Cl SK11 . . . . . . **112** E7
Greenhill Wlk SK12. . . . . . . **38** D6
Greenhouse Farm Rd
WA7. . . . .**50** B6
Green Howards Rd 8
CH3 . . . . **142** B5
Greenhythe Rd SK8. . . . . . . **34** C6
Greenings Ct WA2. . . . . **16** C6
Green Jones Brow WA5 . . . . .**6** F6
Green La Acton CW5 . . . . . **204** B3
Alderley Edge SK9 . . . . **59** F1
Audlem CW3 . . . . **229** F2
Barbridge CW5 . . . . **187** A7
Bebington CH62. . . . .**43** F8
Bollington SK10 . . . .**63** B1
Burtonwood WA5. . . . .**6** E7
Chester CH4. . . . . **140** E4
Chester, Vicarscross CH3. . **119** B3
Christleton CH3 . . . . **120** C2
Davenham CW9 . . . . **103** F3
Disley SK12. . . . . **38** D4
Ellesmere Port, Great Sutton
CH66. . . . . **69** C4
Ellesmere Port, Wolverham
CH65. . . . . **70** C4
Higher Kinnerton CH4 . . . . **161** B6
Higher Wincham CW9 . . . . . **79** F4
Irlam M44 . . . . **11** E5
Kelsall CW6 . . . . **122** D4
Knutsford WA16. . . . . **56** D4
Lindow End SK9 . . . . **84** F8
Over Peover WA16. . . . . . . **83** D1
Picton CH2. . . . .**96** C3
Poynton SK12. . . . . **37** C4
Sandbach CW11. . . . . **173** F7
Saughall CH1. . . . . **117** C2
Shocklach SY14 . . . . **211** C7
Tattenhall CH3 . . . . **182** F5
Warrington, Dudlow's Green
WA4 . . . .**26** F5
Warrington, Paddington
WA1 . . . . **17** A8
Widnes WA8. . . . . **12** E1
Willaston CW5 . . . . **205** A6
Wilmslow SK9 . . . . **60** B7
Winwick WA2. . . . .**8** A7
Green Lake La CH3 . . . . . . **163** F3
Greenland Cl CW6. . . . . . **146** D1
Greenlands CH3 . . . . **166** B3
Greenlands Cl 3 SK8. . . . . **34** E8
Green Lane Cl WA2. . . . .**8** A7
Green Lane E
Connah's Quay CH5 . . . . . . **93** C1
Sealand CH5 . . . . **116** D7
Green Lane Est
Connah's Quay CH5 . . . . . . **93** C1
Sealand CH5 . . . . **116** C4
Green Lane Specl Sch
WA1 . . . .**17** B8
Green Lane W CH5 . . . .**93** B3
Greenlaw Cl CW9 . . . . **104** A5
Green Lawns Dr 8 CH66. . . **70** B2
Greenlea Cl CH65 . . . .**70** B2
GREENLOOMS **143** F4
Greenlooms La CH3 . . . . . **143** F4
Green Mdw Ind Prim Sch 7
WA3 . . . .**3** F8
Green Mdws Golborne WA3 . .**3** E5
Macclesfield SK11 . . . . . . **111** F6
Greenoaks Farm Ind Est
WA8 . . . .**23** C8
Green Oaks Path WA8 . . . . . **23** C8
Green Oaks (Sh Ctr) WA8 . **23** B8
Green Oaks Way WA8 . . . . **23** C8

Greenock Mews WA8. . . . . . **12** E3
Greenore Dr L24. . . . . **21** D2
Green Pk SK8 . . . . **102** E7
Green Rd M31. . . . . **11** E3
Greensbridge La L26. . . . . . **21** A8
Greenshall La SK12. . . . . . . **38** F5
Greenshank Cl WA12. . . . .**2** C4
Greenside Ave WA6 . . . . . . **74** D7
Greenside Ct CW9. . . . . . . **105** D5
Greenside Dr CW9. . . . . . . **105** A8
Green St
5 Alderley Edge SK9. . . . . **60** A1
Holt LL13 . . . . **180** E1
Knutsford WA16. . . . . **57** A2
Macclesfield SK10 . . . . . . **112** E7
Sandbach CW11. . . . . **175** B6
Warrington WA5 . . . . **15** E5
Greens The WA15 . . . . **32** D7
Greensway CH4 . . . . **141** A7
Green The Cheadle SK8. . . . **34** F8
Congleton CW12 . . . . **156** C2
Ellesmere Port CH65 . . . . . . **70** B2
Hale L24. . . . . **21** D1
Handforth SK9 . . . . **34** E3
Hartford CW8. . . . . **103** B5
Harthill CH3 . . . . **183** E3
Higher Kinnerton CH4 . . . . **161** B7
Lawton-gate ST7 . . . . **194** A4
Middlewich CW10 . . . . . . **151** D6
Nantwich CW5. . . . . **204** D8
Neston CH64 . . . .**66** D8
Neston, Little Neston CH64 . .**66** F6
Partington M31 . . . . **11** F4
Poulton CH4. . . . . **163** B2
Saughall CH1. . . . . **94** A2
Thornton Hough CH63 . . . . . **42** C4
Woore CW3 . . . . **232** C1
Green View WA13. . . . . **19** B5
Green Villa Pk SK9. . . . . **59** E4
Greenway Alsager ST7. . . . . **193** B5
Bramhall SK7 . . . . **35** D6
Congleton CW12 . . . . **156** B3
Crewe CW1 . . . . **190** D7
Farndon CH3 . . . . **180** F1
Neston CH64 . . . . **41** B2
Saughall CH1. . . . . **94** A1
Tilston SY14. . . . . **198** C3
Warrington WA4 . . . . **26** D7
Warrington, Great Sankey
WA5 . . . .**14** E7
Wilmslow SK9 . . . . **60** B6
Greenway Cl Helsby WA6. . . .**73** B3
Rode Heath ST7. . . . . **193** F8
Greenway Dr CW7. . . . . . . **104** C7
Greenway La SY14 . . . . . . **213** D4
Greenway Rd
Biddulph ST8 . . . . **179** E2
Cophurst SK11 . . . . **136** F7
Gatley SK8 . . . . **34** C6
Runcorn WA7 . . . . **23** A1
Speke L24. . . . . **21** A3
Widnes WA8. . . . . **13** B1
Greenways ST7 . . . . **209** F2
Greenway St ST7. . . . . **237** B1
Greenway Wlk CW9 . . . . . . **104** C7
Greenwich Ave WA8. . . . . . **13** D4
Green Wlk
Cuddington SK8 . . . . **102** B4
Partington M31 . . . . **11** E3
Greenwood Ave
Chester CH4. . . . . **141** D7
Congleton CW12 . . . . **156** F3
Greenwood Cl CW8 . . . . **77** D1
Greenwood Cres WA2 . . . .**8** E2
Greenwood Ct WA3 . . . .**4** F1
Greenwood Dr
Newton-le-Willows WA12 . . . .**2** D2
Runcorn WA7 . . . . **24** F4
Wilmslow SK9 . . . . **60** D8
Greenwood Rd WA13 . . . .**18** F2
Greenwood Terr WA16 . . . . . **58** A4
Greenwood The CW6. . . . . . **168** D8
Greg Ave SK10. . . . . **87** E8
Greg Mews SK8 . . . . **34** B2
Gregory Cl WA5. . . . . **15** C7
Gregory Cres 4 CW7. . . **125** F2
Gregorys Row WA3. . . . .**4** A8
Gregson Rd WA8. . . . . **13** C1
Grenfell Cl CH64 . . . . **41** C1
Grenfell Ct CH64. . . . . **66** C8
Grenfell Pk CH64. . . . . **41** C1
Grenfell St 11 WA8 . . . . **23** B8
Grenville Cl CW1. . . . . **191** C5
Grenville Cres CH63 . . . . **43** C7
Grenville Rd CH64. . . . . **41** F1
Gresford Ave CH2 . . . . **237** C4
Gresford Cl WA5 . . . .**7** E1
Gresley Way ST7 . . . . **209** F2
Gresty Bldgs 3 CW5 . . . . **204** E6
Gresty Green Rd CW2 . . . . **206** D7
Gresty La CW2 . . . . **206** B7
Gresty Rd CW2 . . . . **190** D1
Gresty Side CW5 . . . . **204** C5
Gresty Terr CW1 . . . . **190** E4
Greta Ave SK8 . . . . **34** C6
Greville Dr CW7 . . . . **127** A1
Grey Friars CH1 . . . . **237** A2
Greyfriars Cl WA2 . . . .**9** A3
Greyhound Park Rd CH1. . **118** A3
Greyhound Pk CH1. . . . . . **118** A3
Greyhound Rd SK10. . . . . . . **86** B5
Greymist Ave WA1 . . . . **17** C7
Greys Ct WA1. . . . .**9** C1

Greysfield Flats CH3. . . . . **120** D6
Grey St WA1. . . . . **16** C6
Greystoke Dr SK9. . . . . **60** A2
Greystoke Rd SK10. . . . .**87** F2
Greystone Pk CW1 . . . . . . **190** D4
Greystone Rd WA5. . . . . **14** F4
Greystones CH66. . . . . **69** D4
Greystones Rd CH3. . . . . . **119** C1
Greywillow Dr CW5 . . . . . . **206** B3
Grice St WA4 . . . . **16** C1
Griffin Cl Blacon CH1. . . . . **117** F6
New Mills SK22 . . . . **39** D6
Norton in Hales TF9 . . . . . **236** C2
Griffin La SK8. . . . . **34** D7
Griffin Mews SK8. . . . . **13** B3
Griffith Ave WA3. . . . .**9** E5
Griffiths Dr CW9 . . . . **104** D6
Griffiths Rd
Lostock Gralam CW9 . . . . . . **79** F1
Northwich CW9 . . . . **104** E8
Griffiths St WA4. . . . . **16** F4
Grig Pl ST7 . . . . **193** C5
Grimsditch La WA4 . . . . **52** B5
Grimshaw Ave SK10 . . . . **88** A7
Grimshaw Cl SK9. . . . . **60** E8
Grimshaw La SK10 . . . . **88** A7
Grindley Bank CH2 . . . . . . **119** F8
GRINDLEY BROOK **225** C3
Grindley Gdns CH65 . . . . . . **70** C2
Grindley Gn SY13 . . . . **228** B3
Grinsome Rd CH2 . . . . **72** A5
Grisedale Ave WA3. . . . .**8** B3
Grisedale Cl WA7. . . . . **49** E5
Grisedale Rd CH62 . . . . **43** F8
Grisedale Way SK11. . . . . . **112** A5
Gritstone Dr SK10 . . . . **112** A8
Grizedale WA8. . . . . **12** B2
Grizedale Cl CW2 . . . . **189** D2
Groarke Dr WA5. . . . . **14** D5
Groby Rd CW1 . . . . **190** E8
Grocotts Row 12 CW5 . . . **204** E5
Grosmont Way 5 WA8 . . . **13** C4
Grosvenor Ave
Alsager ST7 . . . . **193** D5
3 Golborne WA3. . . . .**3** D8
Hartford CW8. . . . . **103** A4
Warrington WA1 . . . . **16** F7
Grosvenor Cl
Warrington WA5 . . . . **15** C5
Wilmslow SK9 . . . . **60** A4
Grosvenor Cotts CH4 . . . . **141** D7
Grosvenor Ct
Chester CH1. . . . . **237** C2
12 Crewe CW1. . . . . **190** B5
7 Winsford CW7 . . . . . . **149** C7
Grosvenor Dr SK12. . . . . . . **36** D3
Grosvenor Gdns WA12. . . . . .**2** C2
Grosvenor Grange WA1 . . . . .**9** B1
Grosvenor Mus ★ CH1. . . . **237** A1
Grosvenor Nuffield Hospl
The CH4 . . . . **141** C6
Grosvenor Pk Rd CH1. . . . **237** C2
Grosvenor Pk Terr CH1,
CH3 . . . . **237** C2
Grosvenor Pl CH1 . . . . **237** B1
Grosvenor Rd
Chester CH4. . . . . **141** C7
Congleton CW12 . . . . **156** A3
Haydock WA11. . . . .**1** B7
Tarvin CH3 . . . . **121** A2
Widnes WA8. . . . . **13** B5
Grosvenor Sh Ctr
Chester CH1. . . . . **237** B2
17 Macclesfield SK11. . . . **112** D8
Grosvenor St
Chester CH1. . . . . **237** A2
Crewe CW1 . . . . **190** B5
3 Macclesfield SK10. . . . . **112** C8
Runcorn WA7 . . . . **23** B3
Winsford CW7 . . . . **149** E8
Grosvenor Wharf Rd
CH65 . . . . **70** D7
Grotsworth La SY14. . . . . . **214** E8
Grotto La WA16 . . . . **108** B7
Grounds St WA2 . . . . **16** B7
Grove Arc SK9. . . . . **60** A2
Grove Ave Chester CH3 . . . **119** B3
Kidsgrove ST7 . . . . **194** E1
Lawton-gate ST7 . . . . **194** A4
Lostock Gralam CW9 . . . . . . **80** A3
Lymm WA13 . . . . **18** C3
Wilmslow SK9 . . . . **60** B7
Winsford CW7 . . . . **149** D6
Grove Cl 11 CW5 . . . . **204** E6
Grove Cres CW3 . . . . **232** C1
Grove Ct Alsager ST7 . . . . **193** E4
Lymm WA13 . . . . **18** C3
Grove Gdns CH3 . . . . **119** E2
Grove Ho SK8 . . . . **35** B6
Grove La SK8 . . . . **35** A6
Grovemount CW9 . . . . **103** F2
Grove Park Ave ST7 . . . . . . **194** A4
Grove Pk WA16 . . . . **57** A1
Grove Rd CH1. . . . . **94** E4
Grove Rise WA13. . . . . **18** E3
Grove St Moss Bank WA8 . . . . **23** C8
New Mills SK22 . . . . **39** B7
Runcorn WA7 . . . . **22** F3
Warrington WA4 . . . . **16** C4
Wilmslow SK9 . . . . **60** B7
Groves The Chester CH1. . . . **237** B3
Ellesmere Port CH66 . . . . . . **95** A8
Groves Way CW9 . . . . **126** F8
Grove Terr WA6. . . . . **73** C4
Grove The Cheadle SK8 . . . . **35** A6
Knutsford WA16. . . . . **57** C4
Lawton-gate ST7 . . . . **194** A4
Lymm WA13 . . . . **18** E3

Grove The continued
Tarporley CW6 . . . . **146** C2
Warrington WA5 . . . . **14** F4
Whitchurch SY13 . . . . **225** F1
Grove Way SK9. . . . . **60** B7
Grovewood Mews SK11 . . . **112** C6
Grub La CW6. . . . . **122** C5
Grundy Cl WA8. . . . . **12** F3
Grundy St WA3. . . . .**3** A7
Guardian St WA5. . . . . **15** F6
Guardian Street Ind Est
WA5. . . . . **15** F6
Guernsey Cl
Congleton CW12 . . . . **157** A2
3 Middlewich CW10 . . . . **128** D2
Middlewich CW10 . . . . . . **128** D2
Warrington WA4 . . . . **26** D8
Guernsey Dr CH65. . . . . **70** C1
Guernsey Ho CH2 . . . . **119** B5
Guernsey Rd WA8. . . . . **13** E3
Guests Slack WA6. . . . . . . **100** B8
Guest St WA8 . . . . **23** A7
Guilden Gn CH3. . . . . **119** E4
GUILDEN SUTTON **119** E4
Guilden Sutton CE Prim Sch
CH3. . . . . **119** F5
Guilden Sutton La CH3 . . . **119** D5
Guildford Ave SK8. . . . . **35** A6
Guildford Cl
1 Chester CH4 . . . . **140** F6
Warrington WA2 . . . .**9** A1
Guildhall Mus ★ CH1. . . . . **237** A2
Guillemot Cl CW1 . . . . **190** F5
Gullane Cl SK10. . . . . **87** B4
Gull Cl SK12 . . . . **36** B3
Gullet The CW5 . . . . **204** E5
Gulliver's World ★ WA5 . . . . .**7** E1
Gulls Way CH60 . . . . **40** E7
Gunco La
Macclesfield SK11 . . . . . . **112** E6
Prestbury SK10 . . . . **87** C8
Gunn Gr CH64. . . . .**66** F8
GURNETT **112** F4
Gutterscroft CW1 . . . . **191** D5
Gutticar Rd WA8 . . . . **12** B1
Guy La CH3 . . . . **143** D5
Gypsy La CH1. . . . . **94** F2

H

Hacked Way La SK11 . . . . **113** F6
HACK GREEN **218** D5
Hack Green Secret Nuclear
Bunker ★ CW5 . . . . **218** D4
Hack House La CW5 . . . . . **218** C5
Haddon Cl
Alderley Edge SK9. . . . . . . **59** F2
High Lane SK6 . . . . **37** E6
Holmes Chapel CW4. . . . . **130** B3
Macclesfield SK11 . . . . . . **112** B5
Wistaston CW2 . . . . **206** B7
Haddon Dr WA8. . . . . **12** C3
Haddon Ho 3 CH64 . . . . . . **66** E8
Haddon La CH64 . . . . **67** C4
Haddon Rd Burton CH64 . . . .**67** D2
Gatley SK8 . . . . **34** C2
Hadfield Cl WA8 . . . . **13** E2
Hadfield St CW9 . . . . **79** B1
Hadleigh Cl WA5 . . . . **14** E5
Hadleigh Gr 1 WA7 . . . . . . **23** F2
Hadley Ave CH62. . . . . **43** C8
Hadley Dr CW2. . . . . **207** E4
Hadlow La CH64. . . . . **67** F7
Hadlow Rd CH64 . . . . **67** F7
Hadlow Terr CH64. . . . . **67** F7
Hadrian Dr CH1 . . . . **117** E6
Hadrian Way
Cuddington CW8 . . . . **102** B2
Middlewich CW10 . . . . . . **128** C2
Hadyn Jones Dr CW5 . . . . **204** F4
Hafod Cl Blacon CH1 . . . . . **117** D3
Connah's Quay CH5 . . . . . . **91** C1
HAGUE BAR **38** F8
Hague Bar Prim Sch SK22. . **38** E8
Hague Fold SK22. . . . . **38** F8
Haig Ave Irlam M44 . . . . **11** C4
Warrington WA5 . . . . **15** A5
Haig Ct WA16 . . . . **57** C4
Haighton Ct 11 CW5 . . . . **204** E6
Haig Rd Knutsford WA16 . . . . **57** C4
Widnes WA8. . . . . **13** A1
Hailwood Ho SK10. . . . .**88** B8
Haldene Rd SK11. . . . . **112** B8
HALE Altrincham **32** B8
Liverpool **21** D1
Hale Ave SK12 . . . . **36** D2
HALE BANK **22** A4
Halebank CE VA Prim Sch
WA8 . . . . **22** A5
Halebank Rd WA8. . . . . **21** F5
Hale Bank Terr WA8. . . . . . . **22** A4
HALE BARNS **32** D8
Hale CE VA Prim Sch L24. . . **21** A1
Hale Ct WA8 . . . . **22** A4
Hale Gate Rd Hale WA8. . . . . **21** F3
Widnes WA8. . . . . **22** A3
Hale Gr WA5 . . . . **15** A6
HALE HEATH **21** A1
Hale Rd Hale L24. . . . . **21** B2
Hale Rd Woodland Nature
Reserve ★ WA8 . . . . **22** B4
Hale Road Ind Est WA8 . . . . **22** B4
Hale St WA2 . . . . **16** B7
Halesworth Gdns 6 WA5 . **14** E8

Gre–Hal 257

Hale View WA7. . . . . **48** E8
Hale View Rd WA6 . . . . **73** C4
HALEWOOD **21** B7
Halewood Animal Ctr
(RSPCA) ★ L26 . . . . **21** B6
Halewood Lane Ends L26 . . . **21** A8
Halewood L Ctr L26 . . . . **21** A7
HALEWOOD VILLAGE **21** A8
Haley Road N WA5. . . . .**6** E6
Haley Road S WA5 . . . .**6** E6
Halfacre La WA4 . . . . **17** F2
Halfpenny Cl CW5 . . . . **204** F2
Half St SK11. . . . . **112** D6
Halifax Cl WA2. . . . .**8** D2
Halkett Cl CH4 . . . . **140** E5
Halkyn Rd CH2. . . . . **237** C4
Hall Acres La SK8 . . . . **34** E8
Hallams Dr CW5 . . . . **205** B4
Hallastone Rd WA6. . . . . **73** C4
Hall Ave WA8 . . . . **12** A1
Halla–Way WA4 . . . . **16** E3
Hall Bank WA16. . . . . **58** C4
Hall Bank N WA16 . . . . **58** C4
Hall Bank S WA16. . . . . **58** C4
Hall Cl SK11. . . . . **87** D4
Hallcroft M31. . . . . **11** F4
Hallcroft Pl WA4 . . . . **17** A2
Hall Dr Alsager ST7. . . . . . . **193** C3
Alsager ST7 . . . . **193** C3
Marston CW9. . . . . **79** B6
Warrington WA4 . . . . **26** D6
Willaston CW5 . . . . **205** C6
Hallefields Cres 5 SK11 . . **112** E7
Hallefields Dr 4 SK11 . . . **112** E7
Hallefields Rd SK10, SK11 . . **112** E7
Hall Farm CH62 . . . . **44** A4
Hall Farm Cl SK23. . . . . **65** D8
Hallfield Dr CH2 . . . . **72** B3
Hallfield Pk CH66 . . . . **69** D4
Hallfields Rd Tarvin CH3. . . **121** C2
Warrington WA5. . . . .**8** D1
Hall Gr SK10 . . . . **87** D3
HALL GREEN
Scholar Green **194** E5
Whitchurch **224** E1
Hall Green Dr ST7. . . . . **194** E5
Hallgreen La CW12 . . . . . . **155** D8
Hall Hill SK10. . . . .**87** E7
Halliday Cl WA3 . . . .**9** F3
Hallington Cl WA5. . . . . **14** C7
Halliwel Jones Stad The
(Warrington Wolves RLFC)
WA2 . . . . **16** A6
Halliwell Ct CW11 . . . . **174** D7
Halliwell's Brow WA16 . . . . . **29** B3
Hall La Appleton Thorn WA4. . **27** B8
Brown Knowl CH3 . . . . . . **199** C7
Cronton L35 . . . . **12** C7
Cronton WA8 . . . . **12** C8
Daresbury WA4 . . . . **25** D2
Haughton CW6 . . . . **186** D5
Kelsall CW6 . . . . **122** D6
Little Leigh CW9. . . . . **77** F8
Lostock Gralam CW9 . . . . . . **79** F3
Mobberley SK9. . . . . **58** D4
Newton-le-Willows WA5 . . . . .**7** B8
Ollerton WA16. . . . . **83** B5
Partington M31 . . . . **11** F4
Pickmere WA16. . . . . **55** B1
St Helens WA9 . . . .**6** A4
Sandbach CW11. . . . . **174** B5
Shotwick CH1. . . . . **93** B5
Stretton WA4 . . . . **52** D8
Sutton Lane Ends SK11. . . **112** F3
Utkinton CW6. . . . . **146** C6
Winsford CW7 . . . . **149** B3
Hall La The CW6 . . . . **147** D2
Hall Moss La SK7 . . . . **35** C4
Hall Nook WA5. . . . . **14** F3
Hall O'shaw St CW1 . . . . . **190** E4
Hallows Ave WA2 . . . . **16** D8
Hallows Cl CW6 . . . . **122** C4
Hallows Dr CW6. . . . . **122** C4
HALLOWSGATE **122** C4
Hallowsgate Ct CW6. . . . . . **122** C4
Hall Rd Handforth SK9. . . . . . **34** E3
Haydock WA11. . . . .**1** E7
Warrington WA1 . . . . **17** C7
Wilmslow SK9 . . . . **60** A7
Halls Farm La WA14 . . . . . . **20** C1
Hallsgreen La CH2 . . . . **96** F7
Hallshaw Ave CW1 . . . . **190** E5
Hallside Pk WA16 . . . . **57** C1
Halls Rd Biddulph ST8. . . . . **179** C1
Mow Cop ST7 . . . . **195** C7
Hall St Audley ST7. . . . . **209** D2
Macclesfield SK10 . . . . . . **112** C8
New Mills SK22 . . . . **39** B8
Warrington WA1 . . . . **16** C5
Hall Terr WA5. . . . . **14** E7
Hall View CH3 . . . . **166** B1
Hall View Cl WA4 . . . . **102** A7
Hall Wood Ave WA11. . . . .**1** E8
Hallwood Cl WA7 . . . . **49** B6
Hallwood Ct CH64. . . . . **66** E7
Hallwood Dr CH66 . . . . **68** D4
HALLWOOD PARK **49** F6
Hallwood Park Ave WA7 . . . **49** E6
Hallwood Pk Prim Sch & Nur
WA7 . . . . **49** E6
Hallwood Rd SK9. . . . . **34** D2
Hallwood Wlk 3 CH65. . . . . **70** B7
Halsall Ave WA2 . . . . **16** D8

Halsall Cl WA7 50 C5
Halsall's Cotts WA8 21 E5
Halstone Ave SK9 59 E4
HALTON BROOK 23 D1
Halton Brook Ave WA7 23 D1
Halton Brow WA7 23 E1
Halton Castle* WA7 23 F1
Halton Cres CH66 69 F2
Halton Ct WA7 23 D2
Halton Dr CW2 189 D5
Halton General Hospl WA7 49 F7
Halton House Sch WA7 49 F3
Halton Lea (Sh Ctr) WA7 49 E8
Halton Link Rd WA7 49 E8
HALTON LODGE 49 D7
Halton Lodge Ave WA7 49 D7
Halton Lodge Prim Sch WA7 49 D8
Halton Miniature Railway* WA7 50 B7
Halton Rd Chester CH2 118 F6
Ellesmere Port CH66 69 E2
Runcorn WA7 23 D2
Warrington WA5 14 F6
Halton Sch WA7 23 F1
Halton St WA11 1 E6
Halton Station Rd WA7 49 F3
HALTON VIEW 13 C1
Halton View Rd WA8 13 C1
HALTON VILLAGE 49 F8
Halton Way CH66 69 E1
Hambledon Cl CH66 69 A6
Hamble Dr WA5 14 F3
Hambleton Cl WA8 12 C3
Hambleton Rd SK8 34 C8
Hambleton Way CW7 149 A7
Hambletts Hollow WA6 100 F6
Hamble Way SK10 86 E1
Hamilton Ave Irlam M44 11 D4
Sandycroft CH5 116 A3
Hamilton Cl
Grappenhall WA4 17 B4
Haslington CW1 191 C4
Macclesfield SK10 113 A8
Neston CH64 41 B2
Hamilton Ct CH64 66 F8
Hamilton Pl CH1 237 A2
Hamilton Rd CH5 91 D1
Hamilton St CH2 118 F3
Hamlet The CH4 141 A7
Hamlin Cl WA7 49 A6
Hammersmith Way WA8 13 D4
Hammond Sch
Chester CH1 237 A4
Hoole Bank CH2 119 B7
Hammond St CW2 190 C3
Hamnett Ct WA3 9 E3
Hampshire Cl CW12 156 D4
Hampshire Gdns ST7 194 F2
Hampshire Rd M31 11 D2
Hampshire Wlk SK10 86 F2
Hampson Ave WA3 4 F3
Hampson Cres SK9 34 C4
Hampstead Ct 7 CW7 149 A8
Hampstead Dr CW2 221 C8
Hampton Cl Neston CH64 66 E6
Widnes WA8 13 E3
Hampton Court Way WA8 13 D4
Hampton Cres
Neston CH64 66 E6
No Man's Heath SY14 214 A5
Hampton Ct Gatley SK9 34 D5
Runcorn WA7 24 C4
Hampton Dr Cronton WA8 12 C5
Warrington WA5 15 C4
Hampton Gdns CH65 70 A5
HAMPTON GREEN 214 B7
Hampton Green La SY14 214 A8
HAMPTON HEATH 213 E7
Hampton Heath Ind Est SY14 213 D7
Hampton House La SY14 213 E8
Hampton Loop Rd SY14 213 D7
Hampton Rd Chester CH4 140 F6
Irlam M44 11 D4
Hamson Dr SK10 63 B1
Hamsterley Cl WA3 10 B6
Hanbury Cl CW2 206 B7
Hancock Ct WA4 16 C4
Hancock Rd CW12 156 F4
Handa Dr CH65 95 B8
HANDBRIDGE 141 E7
Handbridge CH4 237 B1
Handbridge Sq CH2 237 A3
Handford Ave CH62 43 F5
Handford Rd CH2 118 F6
HANDFORTH 34 C4
Handforth Bypass SK8 34 E8
Handforth Cl WA4 17 C3
Handforth Dean Ret Pk SK9 34 E4
Handforth La WA7 49 D6
Handforth Rd
Crewe CW2 189 E3
Handforth SK9 34 E1
Handforth Sta SK9 34 D3
HAND GREEN 168 B6
HANDLEY 182 D8
Handley By-Pass CH3 182 D8
Handley Dr WA2 8 E1
Handley Hill CW7 149 C8
Handley St WA7 22 F3
Hand St SK11 112 B8
Hanging Birches WA8 12 F5
Hangman's La
Lostock Green CW9 105 C7
Smallwood CW11 177 B5
HANKELOW 230 C7
Hankelow Cl Chester CH2 237 B4
Middlewich CW10 151 C6
Hankey St 2 WA7 22 F2
Hankins Heys La CW3 231 A1
Hankinson Cl M31 11 E2
Hanley Cl Disley SK12 38 D5
Widnes WA8 12 C1
Hanley Rd WA8 12 C1
Hannah's Wlk 2 CW10 151 C8
Hanns Hall Farm CH64 67 D8
Hanns Hall Rd CH64 67 D8
Hanover Ct WA7 50 A6
Hanover Dr 2 CW7 149 D6
Hanover Ho 6 CW8 103 C5
Hanover St WA1 16 A4
Hanson La WA16 58 D8
Hapsdale View WA6 72 E1
HAPSFORD 72 F1
Hapsford Cl WA3 9 C4
Hapsford La
Dunham-on-the-Hill WA6 97 E8
Elton CH2 72 D4
Hapsford Mews WA6 72 E2
Harbord St WA1 16 C4
Harbour Cl Chester CH2 118 E7
Runcorn WA7 50 D6
Harbour La SK11 111 C1
Harbridge Rd CH4 139 D3
Harburn Wlk M22 33 E8
Harbutt's View CW10 128 C2
Harcourt Cl WA3 9 E3
HARDEN PARK 60 A3
Harden Pk SK9 60 A3
Harding Ave
Tattenhall CH3 166 C2
Warrington WA2 8 E1
Harding Rd Chester CH2 118 B8
Nantwich CW5 204 C4
Hardings Mdw ST7 194 F2
Hardings Row ST7 195 D7
Hardings Wood ST7 194 E2
HARDING'S WOOD 194 E2
Hardings Wood Ave 9 CW11 174 F4
Hardingswood Rd ST7 194 E2
Hardknott Rd CH62 43 E8
Hardwick Cl SK6 37 F6
Hardwick Dr SK11 112 B5
Hardwicke Ct CW1 190 E4
Hardwicke Rd SK12 36 F4
Hardwick Grange WA1 17 E8
Hardwick Rd WA7 23 D3
Hardy Cl
Ellesmere Port CH66 69 F3
Wistaston CW2 205 F8
Hardy Dr SK7 35 D7
Hardy Rd WA13 18 C2
Hardy St WA2 16 B6
Harebell Cl
Huntington CH3 142 A6
Widnes WA8 12 E4
Harebell Dr CW12 155 F2
Harebell Gr ST7 195 F1
Harecastle Ave ST7 194 E1
Harecastle Ct ST7 210 E6
Harecastle Villas ST7 194 E2
Harecastle Way 8 CW11 174 F4
Harefield Dr SK9 60 B5
Harefield Rd SK9 34 E4
Hare Hill Gdn* SK10 86 B6
Hare La CH3 119 D3
Hare's La WA6 73 F7
Harewood Ave CH66 69 C4
Harewood Cl
Northwich CW9 103 F4
Winsford CW7 126 A1
Harewood Way SK11 112 B5
Harfield Gdns CH66 69 C5
Harford Cl WA5 14 F4
HARGRAVE 144 A1
Hargrave Ave CW2 189 F3
Hargrave Dr CH66 69 E5
Hargrave La
Bebington CH64 43 A4
Thornton Hough CH63, CH64 42 F5
Hargreave Ho 6 CH64 66 E8
Hargreaves Ct WA8 13 D1
Hargreaves Ho 5 WA8 13 D1
Hargreaves Rd CW9 104 C8
Harington Cl CH2 118 C8
Harland Gn L24 21 A3
Harlech Cl WA5 7 E2
Harlech Ct CH65 70 D3
Harlech Gr 3 WA7 23 F1
Harlech Way CH65 70 D3
Harlequin Cl CH3 180 E2
Harlow Cl WA4 17 C3
Harlyn Ave SK7 35 F7
Harlyn Gdns WA5 14 D3
Harn The CH66 69 C3
Haroldgate SY13 225 F1
Harold Rd WA11 1 F7
Harper Cl
Ellesmere Port CH66 69 D4
Winnington CW8 78 C1
Harper Gr CW12 156 E4
Harpers Rd WA2 9 B2
Harpur Cl SK11 112 D6
Harpur Cres ST7 193 B5
Harrier Rd WA2 8 F2
Harrier Way CH3 180 E2
Harriet St M44 11 E5
Harrington Dr SK11 111 D1
Harris Cl CW1 173 B1
HARRISEAHEAD 195 E4
Harriseahead La ST7 195 D4
Harrison Cl Eastham CH62 43 F6
Tattenhall CH3 166 C2
Warrington WA1 16 C6
Harrison Dr Crewe CW1 190 B4
Goostrey CW4 107 B1
Haydock WA11 1 A6
Harrison Gr CH5 116 A3
Harrisons Pl 4 CW8 103 E8
Harrison Sq WA5 7 F1
Harrison St WA8 22 B6
Harrisons Terr CH66 69 C6
Harrison Way WA12 2 C4
Harris Rd CW9 80 A2
Harris St WA8 13 C1
Harrogate Cl
Bebington CH62 43 D4
Warrington WA5 7 A1
Harrogate Rd CH62 43 D4
Harrop La SK10 62 E5
Harrop Rd Bollington SK10 88 C8
Runcorn WA7 23 B1
Harrow Cl Crewe CW2 190 A1
Warrington WA4 26 E6
Wilmslow SK9 60 D8
Harrow Dr WA7 23 E2
Harrow Gr CH62 43 E8
Harrow Rd CH65 70 D4
Harrow Way CW9 103 E3
Harry Houghton Rd 2 CW11 174 E4
Harry Mortimer Way 12 CW11 174 C7
HARTFORD 103 C4
Hartford Ave SK9 59 F5
HARTFORDBEACH 103 A6
Hartford Bsns Ctr CW8 102 F4
Hartford Cl CW11 175 C7
Hartford Dr CH65 69 F4
Hartford High Sch CW8 103 C5
Hartford Hill Pool 5 CW8 103 E7
Hartford Manor Com Prim Sch CW8 103 C5
Hartford Mews 3 CH3 119 B1
Hartford Prim Sch CW8 103 B4
Hartford Rd CW9 103 E3
Hartford Sta CW8 103 A4
Hartford Way CH1 118 A2
HARTHILL 183 E3
Harthill Cl CW9 103 E5
Harthill La CH3 183 E4
Harthill Rd Blacon CH1 117 E6
Burwardsley CH3 184 A6
Hartington Dr SK7 36 E8
Hartington Rd
Bramhall SK7 35 E6
Gatley SK8 34 D8
High Lane SK12, SK6 37 F7
Hartington St CH4 141 E7
Hartland Cl Poynton SK12 36 D5
Widnes WA8 13 A5
Hartley Cl WA13 18 F3
Hartley Gdns CW12 179 B8
Hartley Gn SK10 87 F8
Harton Cl WA8 12 E3
Hartswood Cl WA4 26 E3
Hartwell Gr CW7 126 F4
Harty Rd WA11 1 A5
Harvard Cl WA7 24 D2
Harvard Ct WA2 8 A3
Harvest Cl CW9 126 F8
Harvest Rd SK10 87 C3
Harvey Ave
Nantwich CW5 205 A6
Newton-le-Willows WA12 1 F3
Harvey Ct WA2 8 B3
Harvey La WA3 3 A8
Harvey Rd CW12 157 A5
Harwood Gdns WA4 17 A2
Haryngton Ave WA5 15 F7
Haseley Cl SK12 36 E5
Haslemere Ave WA15 32 C6
Haslemere Dr WA5 14 D4
Haslemere Way CW1 190 D6
Haslin Cres CH3 142 D7
HASLINGTON 191 D4
Haslington By-Pass
Ettiley Heath CW11 174 E1
Haslington CW1 191 C6
Haslington Cl ST5 210 D1
Haslington Gr L26 21 A6
Haslington Prim Sch CW1 191 D4
Hasprey Rd 6 CW11 152 C2
HASSAL 192 C7
HASSALL GREEN 176 A2
Hassall Hall Rd CW11 192 E8
Hassall Moss CW11 175 C1
Hassall Rd Alsager ST7 193 B5
Haslington CW11 192 B7
Sandbach CW11 175 C4
Wheelock CW11 191 F8
Hassall Way 7 SK9 34 E5
Hassals La CH2 96 F3
Hastings Ave WA2 8 B4
Hastings Rd CW5 204 F5
Hasty La Altrincham WA15 32 E8
Hale WA15 32 E8
Wythenshawe WA15 32 F8
Hatchery Cl WA4 27 B4
Hatchings The WA13 18 E2
HATCHMERE 100 D4
Hatch Mere* WA6 100 C4
Hatchmere Cl
Sandbach CW11 174 F7
Hatchmere Cl *continued*
Warrington WA5 15 E5
Hatchmere Dr CH3 142 B8
Hatchmere Pk WA6 100 C5
Hatfield Ct CW4 130 B3
Hatfield Gdns WA4 26 E4
Hathaway Cl SK8 34 B7
Hathaway Dr SK11 112 C5
HATHERTON 219 E3
Hatherton Cl
Newcastle-under-Lyme ST5 210 D2
5 Northwich CW9 103 F4
Hatherton Gr L26 21 A6
Hatherton Way CH2 237 B4
Hatlequin Theatre* CW9 103 F7
Hatley La WA6 73 F7
Hatters Cl WA4 25 B2
Hatter St CW12 156 E3
HATTON 26 A2
Hatton Ave CH62 43 E3
Hatton Bldgs CH2 237 C4
Hatton Brow Terr SK11 112 F4
Hatton Hall La CH3 165 D7
HATTON HEATH 143 B1
Hatton La
Clive Green CW7 150 A8
Hartford CW8 103 D6
Stretton WA4 26 B1
Hatton Rd CH1 117 E6
Hatton St SK11 112 C7
HAUGHTON 186 C6
Haughton Cl SK10 86 F1
HAVANNAH 157 A6
Havannah Bsns Ctr 6 CW12 156 F4
Havannah La
Congleton CW12 156 F6
St Helens WA9 1 B3
Havannah Prim Sch CW12 157 A5
Havannah St CW12 156 F4
Havard Pl CH65 70 B5
Haven The Crewe CW1 190 D7
Sandbach CW11 174 E7
Havergal St 4 WA7 22 F1
Haverhill Cl CW2 207 C3
Haverty Prec WA12 2 B1
Havisham Cl WA3 9 D5
Hawarde Cl WA12 2 A4
Hawarden (Chester) Airport CH4, CH5 139 D7
Hawarden Gdns CH65 70 D2
Hawarden Ind Pk CH5 139 B6
Haweswater Ave
Crewe CW1 173 B1
Haydock WA11 1 A6
Haweswater Cl WA7 50 A5
Haweswater Dr CW7 126 D2
Hawick Cl CH66 69 A5
Hawker Cl CH4 139 C4
Hawkins La SK10 88 D4
Hawkins Rd CH64 41 F1
Hawkins View CH3 120 E6
Hawksey Dr CW5 204 F4
Hawk Rd SK22 39 E8
Hawks Ct WA7 49 E6
Hawkshaw Cl WA3 9 C4
Hawkshead Cl WA7 50 A4
Hawkshead Rd WA5 6 E6
Hawkshead Way CW7 126 D2
Hawk St CW11 175 B6
Hawkstone Gr WA6 73 C4
Hawks Way CH60 40 E8
Hawley Dr WA15 32 B8
Hawley La WA15 32 B8
Hawley's Cl WA5 7 F1
Hawley's La WA2, WA5 8 A1
Hawley's Lane Trad Pk WA2 8 A1
Haworth Ave CW12 157 A5
Haworth Cl SK11 112 B5
Hawthorn Ave
3 Nantwich CW5 204 F5
Newton-le-Willows WA12 2 D3
Runcorn WA7 23 A1
1 Widnes WA8 13 B2
Wilmslow SK9 60 A7
Hawthorn Bank SK22 39 B6
Hawthorn Cl
Holmes Chapel CW4 130 D3
Winsford CW7 126 C3
Hawthorn Cotts CH60 40 F8
Hawthorn Dr M44 11 D5
Hawthorne Ave
Audley ST7 209 F1
Fowley Common WA3 5 C4
Warrington WA5 15 A6
Warrington, Woolston WA1 17 B7
Hawthorne Bsns Pk WA5 16 A8
Hawthorne Cl
Congleton CW12 156 A4
Haydock WA11 1 A5
Hawthorne Ct ST7 193 E4
Hawthorne Dr
Sandbach CW11 175 D6
Willaston CH64 43 B1
Hawthorne Gr
Barnton CW8 77 F4
Poynton SK12 37 C4
Warrington WA4 16 D3
Warrington, Bruche WA1 16 F7
Winsford CW7 127 A1
Hawthorne Rd
Frodsham WA6 49 B1
Warrington WA4 26 C8
Hawthorne St WA5 16 A8
Hawthorn Gdns ST7 210 D8
Hawthorn Gn SK9 60 A7
Hawthorn Gr Bramhall SK7 35 C6
Crewe CW1 190 D7
Warrington WA4 16 D1
Wilmslow SK9 60 B7
Hawthorn La
Bebington CH62 43 D8
Congleton CW12 155 C6
Crewe CW2 189 F2
Wilmslow SK9 60 A7
Hawthorn Pk SK9 60 A7
Hawthorn Rd
Bollington SK10 87 F8
Chester CH4 141 A6
Christleton CH3 142 E7
Ellesmere Port CH66 69 D6
Lymm WA13 18 D3
Neston CH64 41 C1
Newcastle-under-Lyme ST5 210 E1
Plumley WA16 80 F3
Weaverham CW8 102 C8
Hawthorn Rise SK10 86 E6
Hawthorn St SK9 60 A6
Hawthorns The
Bunbury CW6 185 E8
Ellesmere Port CH66 69 F7
Haslington CW1 191 D5
Northwich CW8 103 C7
Tarporley CW6 146 D1
Hawthorn Terr SK9 60 A6
Hawthorn View
Connah's Quay CH5 116 A7
Lindow End WA16 59 B2
Wilmslow SK9 60 A7
Hawthorn Villas CW4 130 C3
Hawthorn Way SK10 87 E2
Hawthorn Wlk
3 Partington M31 11 E3
Wilmslow SK9 60 A7
Wincham CW9 79 C3
Haycroft SK8 34 E8
Haycroft Cl CH66 69 D2
Haydan Ct CH2 118 D4
Haydan Mews WA6 73 E6
Haydn Jones Dr CW5 204 F3
HAYDOCK 1 D6
Haydock Cl Chester CH1 118 B2
Macclesfield SK10 87 C3
Haydock English Martyrs' RC Prim Sch WA11 1 E7
Haydock High Sch WA11 1 C6
Haydock La WA11 1 C7
Haydock Lane Ind Est WA11 1 E8
Haydock L Ctr WA11 1 B6
Haydock Park Racecourse WA3 2 E8
Haydock St
Newton-le-Willows WA12 2 A3
Warrington WA2 16 B6
Hayes Cl CW5 204 E7
Hayes Cres WA6 49 C1
Hayes Dr CW8 78 C3
Hayes Pk CH1 237 A4
Haye's Rd M44 11 E5
Hayfield Cl SK10 87 B3
Hayfield Rd
New Mills SK22 39 D8
Warrington WA1 17 C7
Hayfields WA16 57 C3
Hayfields Gr CW3 229 F3
Haygarth Hts 5 CH1 237 C3
Hayhead Cl ST7 195 B2
Hayhurst Ave CW10 151 C8
Hayhurst Cl CW9 103 F8
Hayle Cl SK10 86 D1
Hayling Cl Crewe CW1 190 B8
Stretton WA4 26 E2
Haymakers Cl CH4 140 F4
Haymakers Way CH1 117 A8
HAYMOOR GREEN 205 E2
Haymoor Green La CW5 205 D2
Haymoor Green Rd CW5 205 E3
Hayscastle Cl WA5 7 E1
Hayside Wlk SY14 213 A3
Hayton St WA16 56 F1
Haywood Cres WA7 24 D2
Hazel Ave
Macclesfield SK11 112 A5
Runcorn WA7 48 E8
Hazelbadge Cl SK12 36 C4
Hazelbadge Rd SK12 36 C4
Hazelbank CH65 69 F3
Hazelborough Cl WA3 10 B5
Hazel Cl
1 Ellesmere Port CH66 69 F1
Kidsgrove ST7 195 B3
Hazelcroft SK9 85 A8
Hazelcroft Gdns SK9 85 A8
Hazeldean Ct 17 SK9 34 E1
Hazel Dr Gatley M22 34 A8
Lymm WA13 18 F2
Poynton SK12 36 F3
Weaverham CW8 102 D7
Winsford CW7 149 C8
Hazel Gr Alsager ST7 194 A3
Crewe CW1 190 C7
Golborne WA3 3 B8
Runcorn WA7 24 D4
Warrington WA1 17 A8
Hazel Grove High Sch SK7 36 C8
Hazelhurst Dr SK10 88 A8
Hazelhurst Way CW6 168 C8
Hazelmere Cl CW8 103 C5
Hazel Rd CH4 140 F6

Hazelshaw La CW11 . . . . . . 154 B4
Hazel St WA1 . . . . 16 D7
Hazel Way Nantwich CW5 . 204 C3
⬛5 Nantwich CW5 . . . . 204 C3
Hazelwood Cl WA8 . . . . 22 A8
Hazelwood Mews WA4 . . . 17 C1
Hazelwood Rd
 Barnton CW8 . . . . .78 B4
 Danebridge SK11 . . . . 160 D5
 Wilmslow SK9 . . . . 60 D8
 Wythenshawe M22 . . . . 33 D8
Hazlehurst Rd WA6 . . . . 74 D6
Hazlemere Ave SK11 . . . . . 112 A6
Headland Cl WA3 . . . . 9 E4
Headlands The CH1, CH3 . 237 C2
Headworth Cl CW9 . . . . 103 F4
HEALD GREEN 34 B8
Heald Green Sta SK8 . . . . . 34 A8
Heald St WA12 . . . . 1 F3
Heald Way CW5 . . . . 205 E6
Healey Cl CW1 . . . . 190 A8
Hean Castle Cl WA7 . . . . . . .22 E3
Heapy St SK11 . . . . 112 E6
Hearn's La CW5 . . . . 202 E5
HEATH 49 A6
Heath Ave
 Ellesmere Port CH65 . . . . . . 70 A1
 Rode Heath ST7 . . . . 193 F7
 Sandbach CW11 . . . . 175 E6
Heath Bank CH3 . . . . 119 D5
Heathbank Rd SK8 . . . . .34 F8
Heathbrook Cotts CW9 . . . 104 E7
Heath Bsns & Technical Pk
 The WA7 . . . . 49 A7
Heath Bvd WA7 . . . . 49 A6
Heath Cl Chester CH3 . . . . 142 B8
 Sandbach CW11 . . . . 175 D6
 Tarvin CH3 . . . . 121 B1
Heathcote Cl CH2 . . . . 118 C4
Heathcote Gdns CW9 . . . . 104 D7
Heathcote La SK11 . . . . . . 113 E2
Heathcote St ST7 . . . . 195 A2
 Ellesmere Port CH66 . . . . . . 69 B6
Heath Dr Knutsford WA16 . .56 F2
 Runcorn WA7 . . . . 49 A7
 Tarvin CH3 . . . . 121 B1
Heath End Rd ST7 . . . . 193 B5
Heather Ave M44 . . . . 11 D6
Heather Brae WA12 . . . . . . .2 A4
Heather Brae Mews
 CW12 . . . . 156 A3
Heather Cl
 Ellesmere Port CH66 . . . . . . 69 E3
 Macclesfield SK11 . . . . 112 C3
 Runcorn WA7 . . . . 49 E4
 Warrington WA3 . . . . .9 D5
Heather Ct CW3 . . . . 142 A8
Heather Dr Handforth SK9 . . . 34
Heather Falls SK22 . . . . 39 B8
Heatherfield Ct SK9 . . . . . . .60 E8
Heathergate Pl CW2 . . . . . 206 B8
Heatherside ST7 . . . . 195 C6
Heather Way CW11 . . . . . . 175 D6
Heatherways WA6 . . . . 146 C3
Heather Wlk M31 . . . . 11 E3
Heathfield SK9 . . . . .60 A5
Heathfield Ave CW1 . . . . . 190 C4
Heath Field Cl ⬛10 WA3 . . . . .3 C7
Heathfield Ct
 Ellesmere Port, Whitby
  CH65 . . . . .70 B5
 Ellesmere Port, Whitbyheath
  CH66 . . . . 95 A8
Heathfield Dr ST5 . . . . 210 D1
Heathfield Gdns WA7 . . . . . 49 A8
Heathfield Pk
 Warrington WA4 . . . . 17 A2
 Widnes WA8 . . . . 12 D3
Heathfield Rd
 Audlem CW3 . . . . 230 A5
 Ellesmere Port CH65 . . . . . . 70 B5
Heathfields Cl CH2 . . . . . . 237 B4
Heathfields Sq WA16 . . . . . .56 F2
Heathgate Ave L24 . . . . 21 A2
Heath Gn CW6 . . . . 146 C4
Heath Gr CH66 . . . . .69 B7
Heath La Chester CH3 . . . . 142 A8
 Culcheth WA3 . . . . .4 A1
 Ellesmere Port, Little Sutton
  CH66 . . . . .69 B7
 Golborne WA3 . . . . .3 D6
 Golborne, Kenyon WA3 . . . . .3 F2
 Great Barrow CH3 . . . . 120 E6
 Great Budworth CW9 . . . . . 54 A1
 High Legh WA16 . . . . 28 D5
 Little Leigh WA4, CW8 . . . . .77 B7
 Marbury SY13 . . . . 226 E6
 Stoak CH2 . . . . .95 E7
 Swan Green WA16 . . . . 106 F6
 Willaston CH64, CH66 . . . . . 68 D7
 Wincham CW9 . . . . 79 C3
Heathlands Ho WA16 . . . . . .56 F2
Heathlands Rd CH66 . . . . . .69 B7
Heathmoor Ave WA3 . . . . . 3 D6
Heath Park Gr WA7 . . . . . . .48 F8
Heath Pl CW7 . . . . 125 F2
Heath Rd Bollington SK10 . .87 E6
 Chester CH2 . . . . 118 E7
 Congleton CW12 . . . . 156 A2
 Runcorn WA7 . . . . .23 B2
 Sandbach CW11 . . . . 175 D6
 Warrington WA5 . . . . .14 F5
 Weaverham CW8 . . . . .77 E1

Heath Rd continued
 Widnes WA8 . . . . 12 D2
Heath Road Cres WA7 . . . .49 B8
Heath Road S WA7 . . . . .48 F6
Heath Sch WA7 . . . . 49 B7
Heathside CW5 . . . . 204 F6
Heaths La CW6 . . . . 123 D2
Heath St Crewe CW1 . . . . . 190 D4
 Golborne WA3 . . . . .3 A8
 Warrington WA4 . . . . 26 C8
Heath Terr Chester CH2 . . . 118 E8
 Smallwood CW11 . . . . 154 B1
Heathview CW1 . . . . 191 D3
Heath View Alsager ST7 . . . 193 E5
 Weston CW2 . . . . 207 B5
Heathview Cl WA8 . . . . 22 A5
Heathview Rd WA8 . . . . 22 A5
Heathway CH60 . . . . .41 B7
Heath Way CW6 . . . . 168 D8
Heathwood ST7 . . . . 193 F7
Heathwood Dr ST7 . . . . . . 193 B5
Heathwood Gr WA1 . . . . . . .17 B7
HEATLEY 19 C5
Heatley Cl WA13 . . . . 19 A4
Heatley Farm Rd CW5 . . . . 217 F1
Heatley La CW5 . . . . 217 F3
Heatley Way ⬛5 SK9 . . . . . 34 D4
HEATON 159 E2
Heaton Bank SK11 . . . . 159 D2
Heaton Cl CW10 . . . . 151 C6
Heaton Ct WA3 . . . . .9 F6
Heaton Sq WA7 . . . . 149 C8
Heaton Village Rd SK11 . . 159 E2
Heaton Way CW2 . . . . 207 E4
Hebden Ave WA3 . . . . 5 B5
HEBDEN GREEN 148 F7
Hebden Green Com Sch
 CW7 . . . . 149 A7
Hebden Green Com Sch ⬛1
 CW7 . . . . 149 A7
Heber's Cl SY14 . . . . 213 C5
Heber Wlk CW9 . . . . 104 A8
Hedge Hey WA7 . . . . 24 A1
Hedge Row SK10 . . . . .63 E1
Hedgerow Dr CW9 . . . . 79 C3
Hedgerows Rd WA11 . . . . . .1 F7
Hedingham Cl ⬛7 SK10 . . 111 F8
Hefferston Grange Dr
 CW8 . . . . 102 A7
Hefferston Rise CW8 . . . . . 102 A7
Heights The WA6 . . . . 73 C4
Heild End SK11 . . . . 137 F3
Helena Cl WA16 . . . . 57 C2
Hellath Wen CW5 . . . . 204 E2
Hellyar-Brook Rd ST7 . . . . 193 B4
Helmdon Cl CW1 . . . . 127 A3
Helmsdale Cl CW1 . . . . 190 B6
Helmsdale La WA5 . . . . 15 C6
Helmsley Cl WA5 . . . . .15 E7
HELSBY 73 C3
Helsby Ave CH62 . . . . .43 F3
Helsby High Sch WA6 . . . . . 73 D5
HELSBY MARSH 73 B5
Helsby Pk 73 B5
Helsby Quarry Nature
 Reserve ★ WA6 . . . . .73 B2
Helsby Rd WA6 . . . . 73 C1
Helsby St WA1 . . . . 16 D6
Helsby Sta WA6 . . . . .73 B4
Helsby Way ⬛4 SK9 . . . . . 34 D4
Helston Cl Bramhall SK7 . . .35 F7
 Runcorn WA7 . . . . 50 B5
 Warrington WA5 . . . . .14 E5
Helston Gr SK8 . . . . 34 C8
Helton Cl CW4 . . . . 130 A3
Hemingford Cl CH66 . . . . . 69 D2
Hemlegh Vale WA6 . . . . 73 B2
Hemlock WA7 . . . . .49 C8
Hemmingshaw La CW11 . . 176 B8
Hemmings Pl ⬛8 CW7 . . . . 150 A8
Hemming St CW8 . . . . 78 D1
Hemswell Cl CW7 . . . . 149 E8
Hemsworth Ave CH66 . . . . 69 C5
HENBURY 111 B8
Henbury Cl CW10 . . . . 151 C7
Henbury Gdns WA4 . . . . . . 26 E3
Henbury La SK8 . . . . .34 F6
HENBURY MOSS 110 D5
Henbury Pk SK11 . . . . 111 A7
Henbury Pl Longmoss SK10 .86 B1
 Runcorn WA7 . . . . .49 B6
Henbury Rd SK9 . . . . 34 C4
Henbury Rise SK11 . . . . . . 111 C8
Henderson Cl WA5 . . . . 14 D6
Henderson Rd
 ⬛2 Widnes WA8 . . . . 13 A1
 Widnes, Lower House WA8 . .22 F8
Henderson St WA1 . . . . 112 C7
Hendon Cl Crewe CW1 . . . 190 F5
 ⬛2 Wilmslow/Alderley Edge
  SK9 . . . . 60 D8
Henhull Cl CW5 . . . . 204 D6
Henley Ave M44 . . . . .11 E6
Henley Cl
 Macclesfield SK10 . . . . .87 B4
 Neston CH64 . . . . .66 E6
 Warrington WA4 . . . . 26 E6
Henley Ct WA7 . . . . 23 D2
Henley Dr CW7 . . . . 126 F1
Henley Rd Chester CH4 . . . 140 F6
 Chorlton CW2 . . . . 207 B1
 Neston CH64 . . . . .66 E6
Henrietta St CW12 . . . . 156 C2
Henry Hughes Dr CW2 . . . 206 C4
Henry Pl CH1 . . . . 237 B3
Henry St Crewe CW1 . . . . . 190 D5
 Haslington CW1 . . . . 191 D4

Henry St continued
 ⬛2 Lymm WA13 . . . . .18 E3
 Tarporley CW6 . . . . 146 C2
 Warrington WA1 . . . . 16 A5
 ⬛4 Widnes WA8 . . . . 13 C1
Henry Wood Ct ⬛1 CH4 . . 140 E6
Henshall Ave WA4 . . . . .16 F4
Henshall Cl ⬛2 CW2 . . . . . 206 D5
Henshall Dr CW11 . . . . 175 D8
Henshall Hall Dr CW12 . . . 157 B1
Henshall La WA14 . . . . 20 C6
Henshall Rd SK10 . . . . .87 F7
Henshall St CH1 . . . . 237 A4
Henshaw La SK11 . . . . 110 E2
Hepherd St WA5 . . . . 15 D4
Hepley Rd SK12 . . . . 37 A3
Herald Dr CW1 . . . . 190 E3
Herald Pk CW1 . . . . 190 E3
Herald Pk CW1 . . . . 190 E3
Heralds Cl WA8 . . . . 22 C8
Heralds Gn WA5 . . . . .7 A2
Herberts La CH60 . . . . .40 F8
Herbert St Burtonwood WA5 .6 E4
 Congleton CW12 . . . . 156 F3
 Crewe CW1 . . . . 191 A5
 Lostock Gralam CW9 . . . . . . 80 A2
Herbert Swindells Cl
 CW2 . . . . 190 D1
Herdman St CW2 . . . . 190 D2
Hereford Ave
 Ellesmere Port CH66 . . . . . . 94 E8
 Golborne WA3 . . . . .3 B8
Hereford Cl
 Macclesfield SK10 . . . . .86 F7
 Warrington WA1 . . . . 17 D7
Hereford Dr SK9 . . . . .34 E3
Hereford Pl Blacon CH1 . . . 118 A5
 Nantwich CW5 . . . . 204 D7
Hereford Way CW10 . . . . . 128 E2
Hereward Rd CH3 . . . . 119 B1
Heritage Ct CH1 . . . . 237 B2
Hermitage Ct
 Holmes Chapel CW4 . . . . . . 130 D3
 Saughall CH1 . . . . 117 A8
Hermitage Dr CW4 . . . . 130 D3
Hermitage Green La WA2,
 WA12 . . . . .8 A3
Hermitage La CW4 . . . . 130 C7
Hermitage Prim Sch
 CW4 . . . . 130 D4
Hermitage Rd CH1 . . . . 117 B7
Hermitage The CH60 . . . . . .40 F7
Heron Bsns Pk WA8 . . . . . . 23 D8
Heron Cl Broughton CH4 . . 139 C4
 Farndon CH3 . . . . 180 F1
 Knutsford WA16 . . . . 57 B3
 Runcorn WA7 . . . . 50 D8
 Winsford CW7 . . . . 149 D5
Heron Cres CW1 . . . . 190 F5
Heron Ct Neston CH64 . . . . 66 C7
 Northwich CW9 . . . . 79 C2
Heron Dr SK12 . . . . 36 A3
Heron Pl CH2 . . . . 237 B4
Herons Reach WA3 . . . . .5 C6
Herons Way Chester CH4 . . 141 B2
 Runcorn WA7 . . . . .24 F4
Heron Way
 Ettiley Heath CW11 . . . . . . 174 C5
 Nantwich CW5 . . . . 204 C3
Herrick Cl CW2 . . . . 206 A8
Hertford Apartments WA2 . .9 A3
Hertford Cl
 Congleton CW12 . . . . 156 E4
 Warrington WA1 . . . . 17 E7
Hertford Gr M44 . . . . 11 C6
Hesketh Cl WA5 . . . . .14 F4
Hesketh Croft CW1 . . . . 190 A8
Hesketh Dr CW9 . . . . 80 A3
Hesketh Grange Cotts
 CH63 . . . . 42 A7
Hesketh Meadow La WA3 . . 3 F8
Hesketh Rd L24 . . . . 21 E2
Hesketh St ⬛5 WA5 . . . . . . 15 D4
Hesketh Street N WA5 . . . . 15 D4
Hesnall Cl WA3 . . . . .5 C8
Hessle Dr CH60 . . . . 40 F7
HESWALL 40 D7
Heswall Ave WA3 . . . . .4 E4
Heswall Point ⬛7 CH60 . . . . 41 A8
Heswall Rd CH66 . . . . 69 D4
Heswall St SK10 . . . . 41 D8
Hetheington Sq ⬛8 SK10 . . .87 E5
Hetherson Ave WA5 . . . . . . .7 F2
HETHERSON GREEN 214 D8
Hetherson Green La
 SY14 . . . . 214 D8
Hewell Grange WA7 . . . . . . .22 E3
Hewetson Cres SK11 . . . . . 111 E7
Hewitt Dr CW7 . . . . 150 D8
Hewitt St CW7 . . . . .79 F5
Hewitt St Chester CH2 . . . . 118 F3
 Crewe CW2 . . . . 190 D2
 Northwich CW9 . . . . 79 D2
 Warrington WA4 . . . . 16 C3
Hexham St CH1 . . . . 118 B2
Hexham Way ⬛4 SK10 . . . . 87 C4
Heybridge La SK10 . . . . .87 B6
Heydon Cl
 Congleton CW12 . . . . 156 C3
 Halewood L26 . . . . 21 A7
Heyes Ave WA11 . . . . .1 D5
Heyes Farm Rd SK11 . . . . . 111 E8
Heyes Ho SK11 . . . . 111 E8
Heyes La Alderley Edge SK9 . .60 B3
 Warrington WA4 . . . . .26 E8
Heyes Pk CW8 . . . . 102 F4

Heyes Rd WA8 . . . . 22 C8
Heyeswood La CW8 . . . . . . 103 A4
Heyfield Park Rd CH66 . . . .69 B7
Heygarth Prim Sch CH62 . .43 E5
Heygarth Rd CH62 . . . . .43 E5
Hey Lock Cl WA12 . . . . .7 C8
Heyrose La WA16 . . . . .55 E3
Heys Ave CH62 . . . . 43 E5
Heysbank Rd SK12 . . . . 38 D5
Heysham CW1 . . . . 50 D6
Hey Shoot La WA3 . . . . .5 C5
Heysoms Ave CW8 . . . . 103 D7
Heysoms Cl CW8 . . . . 103 D7
Heys The Bebington CH62 . .43 F5
 Runcorn WA7 . . . . .23 E1
Heythrop Dr CH60 . . . . 41 D8
Heywood Cl SK9 . . . . .60 B2
Heywood Gn CW2 . . . . 206 C8
Heywood La CW3, SY13 . . . 234 C7
Heywood Rd
 Alderley Edge SK9 . . . . .60 B2
 Ellesmere Port CH66 . . . . . . 69 D5
Heywoods Ridge CW3 . . . . 229 E3
Heywood St CW12 . . . . 156 C2
Heywoods The CH2 . . . . . . 118 C4
Hibbert St New Mills SK22 . .39 B6
 ⬛6 Widnes WA8 . . . . .23 B8
Hibel Rd SK10 . . . . .87 D1
Hickhurst La CW6 . . . . 147 D3
Hickmore Heys CH3 . . . . . . 119 F5
Hickory Cl WA1 . . . . .17 E7
Hickson St CW8 . . . . .78 B3
Hidcote Cl CW2 . . . . 206 B8
HIDEBANK 39 C8
Hield Brow CW9 . . . . 79 C7
Hield Gr CW9 . . . . 79 C7
Hield La CW9 . . . . 79 C8
Higginbotham Gn SK11 . . . 112 E6
Higginsfield Rd SY14 . . . . . 201 E5
Higginson Ct CW12 . . . . . . 179 C8
Higham Ave WA5 . . . . .7 F1
Highbank Cl CW8 . . . . .78 B3
Highbank Cl M44 . . . . 11 D6
Highbank Rd Kingsley WA6 . .75 C2
 Northwich CW8 . . . . 103 D7
High Bent Ave SK8 . . . . 35 A6
HIGH CARR 210 F3
High Carr Bsns Pk ST5 . . . 210 F2
High Carr Network Ctr
 ST5 . . . . 210 F2
Highcliffe Ave CH1 . . . . 118 B4
Highcroft Ave CW12 . . . . . 156 F2
High Cross La CH3 . . . . 182 D1
High Ct SK10 . . . . .88 B8
High Elm Dr WA15 . . . . 32 C8
High Elm Rd WA15 . . . . 32 D7
High Elms SK8 . . . . 35 B5
Higher Ash Rd ST7 . . . . 210 D8
Higher Ashton WA8 . . . . . . .12 F3
HIGHER BUNBURY 168 F1
HIGHER
 BURWARDSLEY 184 C5
HIGHER CARDEN 198 D7
Higher Carden La SY14 . . . 198 D6
Higher Croft Dr
 Coppenhall Moss CW1 . . . . 173 A1
 ⬛7 Crewe CW1 . . . . 190 A8
HIGHER DISLEY 38 E4
Higher Downs WA16 . . . . . . 57 C2
HIGHERFENCE 88 A2
Higher Fence Rd SK10 . . . . .87 F1
HIGHER FERRY 140 C8
Higher Gn Rd CW4 . . . . 129 F3
Higher Heyes Dr WA6 . . . . 75 C1
HIGHER HURDSFIELD 88 A2
HIGHER KINNERTON 161 B8
Higher Knutsford Rd WA4 . .16 F2
Higher La Bollington SK10 . .88 B6
 Disley SK12 . . . . .38 E1
 Dutton WA4 . . . . 51 D4
 Kettleshulme SK23 . . . . .64 E6
 Lymm WA13 . . . . .19 B1
Higherland Ct ⬛6 ST7 . . . . 195 A2
Higher Lanes SY13 . . . . 224 A2
HIGHER MARSTON 79 C6
HIGHER POYNTON 37 B2
Higher Rd L26, WA8 . . . . . . 21 C5
HIGHER RUNCORN 23 A1
HIGHER SHURLACH 104 E6
HIGHER WALTON 25 F7
HIGHER WHITLEY 52 D5
HIGHER WINCHAM 79 F4
Higher Works Cotts
 SK11 . . . . 158 C6
HIGHER WYCH 224 D7
Higher Wych Rd
 Lower Wych SY14 . . . . 224 D6
 Malpas SY14 . . . . 213 C1
Highfield Elton CH2 . . . . . . .72 B4
 Prestbury SK10 . . . . 87 A5
High Field WA14 . . . . .20 B2
Highfield Ave
 Audlem CW3 . . . . 230 A4
 Golborne WA3 . . . . .2 F8
 Kidsgrove ST7 . . . . 195 B2
 Lostock Gralam CW9 . . . . . . 80 A3
 Warrington WA5 . . . . 15 A5
 Warrington, Dudlow's Green
  WA4 . . . . 26 D4
Highfield Cl CH64 . . . . .66 E8
Highfield Com Prim Sch
 CH1 . . . . 117 F4
Highfield Cres
 Handforth SK9 . . . . 34 C1
 Widnes WA8 . . . . 13 A2
Highfield Dr Lymm WA13 . . 18 C2
 Macclesfield SK10 . . . . .87 A1

Haz–Hil 259

Highfield Dr continued
 Nantwich CW5 . . . . 205 A6
Highfield Est SK9 . . . . 34 C1
Highfield La
 Coddington CH3 . . . . 181 E4
 Golborne WA3 . . . . .3 C5
 Winwick WA2 . . . . .8 C7
Highfield Parkway SK7 . . . . 35 D4
Highfield Pl ⬛1 CW8 . . . . . 103 E8
Highfield Rd Blacon CH1 . . . 117 D5
 Bollington SK10 . . . . 88 A8
 Cheadle SK8 . . . . .34 F8
 Congleton CW12 . . . . 156 E2
 Ellesmere Port CH65 . . . . . . 70 C5
 Ellesmere Port, Little Sutton
  CH66 . . . . .69 B6
 Lymm WA13 . . . . 18 C2
 Macclesfield SK11 . . . . 112 C7
 Neston CH64 . . . . .66 F8
 Northwich CW8 . . . . 103 F7
 Poynton SK12 . . . . 36 A4
 Widnes WA8 . . . . 13 A2
Highfield Road N ⬛11 CH65 .70 C6
Highfields SY13 . . . . 224 A2
Highfields Com Prim Sch
 CW5 . . . . 204 F6
Highfield Terr SK22 . . . . 39 D8
Highgate Cl Crewe CW1 . . . 190 A8
 Runcorn WA7 . . . . 24 D1
High Gates Cl WA5 . . . . .15 E7
High Gates Lodge WA5 . . . .15 E7
Highgrove Mews ⬛2 SK9 . . 60 A6
High Hill Rd SK22 . . . . 39 D8
Highlander Rd CH3 . . . . 142 B5
Highland Dr SK11 . . . . 84 A2
Highlands Rd WA7 . . . . .48 F8
Highlands The CW6 . . . . . . 185 E8
Highland Way WA16 . . . . . . 82 A7
HIGHLANE 134 C6
HIGH LANE 37 E8
High Lane Prim Sch SK6 . . .37 F8
High Lea Rd SK22 . . . . 39 A8
HIGH LEGH 29 B5
High Legh Prim Sch
 WA16 . . . . 29 C5
High Legh Rd WA13 . . . . . . 29 C8
High Lowe Ave CW12 . . . . . 157 A4
Highmarsh Cres WA12 . . . . . 2 B4
High Mdw ⬛2 SK8 . . . . 34 E8
High Mount CH60 . . . . 40 F8
High Peak Sch SK12 . . . . . . 38 E1
High Pond La CH65 . . . . 70 A8
High St Audley ST7 . . . . 210 A1
 Bollington SK10 . . . . .88 B8
 Clotton CW6 . . . . 145 D4
 Congleton CW12 . . . . 156 D2
 Crewe CW2 . . . . 190 D3
 Farndon CH3 . . . . 180 E2
 Frodsham WA6 . . . . .49 B1
 Golborne WA3 . . . . .3 A8
 Great Budworth CW9 . . . . . 79 A7
 Hale L24 . . . . 21 D1
 Harriseahead ST7 . . . . 195 E5
 Kidsgrove, The Rookery
  ST7 . . . . 195 C4
 Macclesfield SK11 . . . . 112 C8
 Malpas SY14 . . . . 213 B3
 Mow Cop ST7 . . . . 195 D7
 Nantwich CW5 . . . . 204 E5
 Neston CH64 . . . . .66 E7
 Newchapel ST7 . . . . 195 E2
 New Mills SK22 . . . . 39 C8
 Newton-le-Willows WA12 . . . .2 D4
 Norley WA6 . . . . 100 F5
 Northwich CW9 . . . . 103 F8
 Runcorn WA7 . . . . 23 A2
 Saltney CH4 . . . . 140 E7
 Sandbach CW11 . . . . 175 B6
 Talke ST7 . . . . 210 D6
 Tarporley CW6 . . . . 146 C2
 Tarvin CH3 . . . . 121 B2
 Tattenhall CH3 . . . . 166 B1
 Warrington WA1 . . . . 16 C5
 Weaverham CW8 . . . . 77 C1
 Winsford CW7 . . . . 126 D1
Hightown Crewe CW1 . . . . 190 C4
 Middlewich CW10 . . . . 128 C1
 Sandbach CW11 . . . . 175 B6
Hightown Appts ⬛6 CW1 . 190 C4
Hightree Dr SK11 . . . . 111 C8
High View Helsby WA6 . . . . 73 C4
 Mount Pleasant ST7 . . . . . . 195 B5
HIGH WARREN 26 C6
High Warren Cl WA4 . . . . . . 26 C5
Highwood Rd WA4 . . . . 26 C7
Hignett Ave WA9 . . . . .1 B2
Hilary Ave SK8 . . . . 34 B8
Hilary Cl Chester CH3 . . . . . 119 B1
 Warrington WA5 . . . . 14 D6
 Widnes WA8 . . . . 13 E3
Hilbre Ave CH60 . . . . .40 E6
Hilbre Bank CW6 . . . . 169 D4
Hilbre Dr CH65 . . . . 70 C1
Hilden Pl WA2 . . . . 16 D8
Hilden Rd WA2 . . . . .8 E1
Hilditch Ave CW8 . . . . 103 D4
Hillary Ave CW12 . . . . 157 A2
Hillary Dr CW3 . . . . 230 A4
Hillary Rd Bebington CH62 . .43 E5
 Kidsgrove ST7 . . . . 195 B3
Hillberry Cres WA4 . . . . .16 B3
Hillbre Way ⬛1 SK9 . . . . . . 34 D4
Hillbrook Rd SK7 . . . . 35 D6
Hill Cl Bunbury CW6 . . . . . . 185 E7
 Neston CH64 . . . . .67 B5

HILLCLIFFE 26 C8
Hill Cliffe Rd WA4 . . . . . .26 B8
Hill Cotts CH3. . . . . 164 A4
Hillcourt Rd SK6 . . . . .37 F7
Hillcrest WA7. . . . . 23 D1
Hillcrest Ave CW4 . . . . . . 130 B3
Hillcrest Dr CH66. . . . . . . 69 A6
Hillcrest Rd
  Bollington SK10 . . . . .87 F7
  Ellesmere Port CH66 . . . .69 B6
  Kelsall CW6 . . . . 122 E6
  Warren SK11 . . . . 112 A4
Hill Ct CH64. . . . . .67 B5
Hillditches La CW1 . . . . . 192 C3
Hill Dr Handforth SK9. . . . . .34 E3
  Whaley Bridge SK23. . . . 65 D8
Hillesden Rise CW2 . . . . 156 F2
Hillfield Frodsham WA6 . . .74 B7
  Runcorn WA7. . . . . 50 D8
Hillfield Gdns CW5 . . . . . 204 E4
Hillfield Pl CW5. . . . . 204 E4
Hillfield Rd CH66. . . . . 69 D7
Hillfields CW12 . . . . 156 D4
Hill Fields CW12 . . . . 156 D3
Hill Fields Cl CW12 . . . . . 156 D4
Hillfield View CW5 . . . . . 204 E4
Hillfoot Cres WA4 . . . . .26 B7
Hillfoot La WA4. . . . . .74 E3
Hill Garth Rd CH3 . . . . . . 166 C5
Hilliards Ct CH4. . . . . 141 B3
Hillingden Ave L26 . . . . . . 21 A7
Hill La Brown Knowl CH3. . 199 C8
  Peckforton CW6. . . . . . . 184 E6
Hillock La WA1 . . . . 17 C8
Hill Rd CH4. . . . . 141 E2
Hill Road N WA6. . . . . 73 D3
Hill Road S WA6. . . . . 73 C3
Hillsboro Ave WA4 . . . . . . 74 C7
Hillsdown Way CH66 . . . . 69 C2
Hillside Broomedge WA13 . .19 E1
  Northwich CW8 . . . . 103 C7
Hillside Ave
  Newton-le-Willows WA12 . . .1 F2
  Runcorn WA7. . . . . .48 E8
Hillside Cl Bramhall SK7 . . 36 A7
  Chorlton CW2. . . . . 207 E3
  Helsby WA6 . . . . 73 D4
  Mow Cop ST7 . . . . 195 D7
Hill Side Cl SK12. . . . . .38 E6
Hillside Ct
  Macclesfield SK10 . . . . . . 88 A1
  Warrington WA4 . . . . 26 D3
Hillside Dr Crewe CW1 . . 190 E5
  Ellesmere Port CH66 . . . .69 E7
  Macclesfield SK10 . . . . . . 88 A1
Hillside Gr WA5 . . . . .14 F4
Hillside Ho 7 CW8 . . . . . 103 C5
Hillside La CW7 . . . . 126 E7
Hillside Prim Sch WA6. . . 73 D4
Hillside Rd Blacon CH1 . . 117 E4
  Frodsham WA6. . . . . 74 C7
  Heswall CH60 . . . . 41 A7
  Kelsall CW6 . . . . 122 D4
  Knutsford WA16. . . . . 57 A2
  Warrington WA4 . . . . 26 D3
Hillside View SK22 . . . . . . 39 A8
Hill St Crewe CW1. . . . . . 190 D4
  Macclesfield SK11 . . . . . 112 D6
  Runcorn WA7. . . . . 23 A2
  Sandbach CW11. . . . . . . 174 D7
  Warrington WA1 . . . . .16 B5
  Winsford CW7 . . . . 126 F1
Hill Terr ST7 . . . . 209 D2
Hill The Knutsford WA16 . . .82 B8
  Sandbach CW11. . . . . . . 175 D5
HILLTOP. 60 B8
Hilltop WA7. . . . . 50 C7
Hill Top Altrincham WA15 . . 32 A8
  Barnton CW8. . . . . .78 B2
Hill Top Ave Cheadle SK8 . .35 B8
  Wilmslow SK9 . . . . .60 B8
  Winsford CW7 . . . . 126 C1
Hill Top Grange CW9 . . . 103 D3
Hill Top La Heswall CH60. . .41 B8
  Neston CH64. . . . . .67 B5
Hilltop Pk WA16. . . . . .79 D7
Hilltop Rd
  Guilden Sutton CH3 . . . . 119 F5
  Lymm WA13 . . . . 18 C2
Hill Top Rd
  Acton Bridge CW8 . . . . . . 76 F2
  Dutton WA4 . . . . 51 C1
  Runcorn WA7. . . . . .50 F6
  Warrington, Stockton Heath
    WA4 . . . . .16 F2
  Warrington, Woolston WA1 . .17 C7
Hill Top Rise SK23. . . . . . . 65 D8
Hill View Bollington SK10. . .87 F7
  Whaley Bridge SK23. . . . 65 C8
  Widnes WA8. . . . . 12 F5
Hill View Ave WA6 . . . . . . 73 A1
Hillview Cl WA6. . . . . 74 C7
Hill View Cty Prim Sch
  WA7. . . . . .49 E4
Hillview Rise CW8. . . . . . .78 E1
Hilton Ave WA5 . . . . .15 B5
Hilton Cl
  9 Macclesfield SK11. . . . 111 F7
  Middlewich CW10 . . . . . . 151 B8
Hilton Dr M44. . . . . 11 C5
Hilton Gr SK12 . . . . 36 D4
Hilton Rd Disley SK12 . . . . .38 B7
  Poynton SK12. . . . . .37 C5
Himalayan Birch Cl CH66 . .69 E6
Hinchley Cl CW8 . . . . 103 A5

Hinckley Ct CW12 . . . . . . 156 A3
Hinderton Dr CH60. . . . . . .40 F6
Hinderton Gn CH64. . . . . . .66 F8
Hinderton La CH64. . . . . . . 67 A8
Hinderton Rd CH64. . . . . . .66 F8
Hinderton Sch CH65. . . . . .69 F3
Hinde St CW5 . . . . 204 D4
Hind Heath La CW11 . . . . 174 F4
Hind Heath Rd CW11 . . . . 174 E4
Hindle Ave WA5. . . . . .7 F1
Hindley Cres CW8 . . . . 78 A3
Hinton Cres WA4. . . . . .26 E8
Hinton Rd Crewe CW2. . . 206 D8
  Runcorn WA7. . . . . 23 A1
Hirsch Cl CW5 . . . . 205 A4
Hitchen's Cl WA7 . . . . 50 D7
Hitchens La SY14. . . . . . . 184 D1
Hitchen St CW8 . . . . .78 B1
Hitch Lowes SK11. . . . . . . 84 A3
Hobart Cl SK7. . . . . .35 F4
Hobart Way CH1 . . . . 117 D4
Hobb La WA4 . . . . 25 C5
Hobbs Cl CW1 . . . . 191 D4
Hobbs Hill La WA16 . . . . . .28 E1
Hobby Ct WA7 . . . . .49 E6
Hobcroft La WA16. . . . . . . 58 A7
Hob Hey La WA3 . . . . .4 D3
Hob La Churton CH3 . . . . 180 F5
  Dunham-on-the-Hill WA6 . .97 C6
Hobson St SK11. . . . . 112 D6
Hockenhull Ave CH3 . . . . 121 B2
Hockenhull Cres CH3. . . . 121 B2
Hockenhull La
  Tarvin CH3. . . . . 121 B1
  Tarvin, Broom Bank CH3. . 121 B1
Hocker La
  Adder's Moss SK10 . . . . . .85 F3
  Nether Alderley SK10. . . . 85 C4
Hockerley Ave SK23. . . . . 65 D8
Hockerley La SK23. . . . . . 65 D8
Hockerley La SK23. . . . . . 65 D8
Hockerley New Rd SK23. . 65 D8
HOCKLEY. 37 A2
Hockley Cl SK12. . . . . 37 A3
Hockley Paddock SK12 . . .36 F3
Hockley Rd SK12. . . . . 37 A3
HODGEHILL. 132 E8
Hodgehill La SK11. . . . . . 132 E5
Hodge La Hartford CW8. . 103 A6
  Weaverham CW8 . . . . . . 102 D5
Hodgkin Cl CW5 . . . . 204 F4
Hodgkinson Ave WA5. . . . . .7 F1
Hoghton Rd L24. . . . . .21 E2
Hogshead La CW8. . . . . . 124 C7
Holbeck WA7. . . . . 50 C7
Holbein Cl CH4 . . . . 141 E6
Holborn Ct WA8. . . . . 12 F3
Holbrook Cl WA5. . . . . 14 E5
Holbury Cl CW1 . . . . 190 B8
Holcombe Ave WA3 . . . . . . .3 C8
Holcombe Dr SK10 . . . . . . 87 B3
Holcot Ct CW7 . . . . 127 A4
Holcroft Dr CW8 . . . . 101 F2
Holcroft La WA3 . . . . .5 D2
Holdings La CW3. . . . . . . 232 F4
Holehouse La
  Langley SK11. . . . . 113 C4
  Scholar Green ST7 . . . . . 194 D8
  Whiteley Green SK10. . . . 62 D2
Holford Ave
  Lostock Gralam CW9 . . . . 80 A3
  Warrington WA5 . . . . .15 F8
Holford Cres WA16. . . . . . .57 B1
Holford Dr
  3 Saltersswall CW7 . . . . 125 F1
  Wilmslow/Alderley Edge
    SK9 . . . . 59 C7
Holford Moss WA7 . . . . . . 24 D3
Holford St CW12 . . . . 156 D3
Holford Way WA12 . . . . . . .2 F1
Holgrave Cl WA16. . . . . . . 29 C4
Holkam Cl CW9 . . . . 103 F5
Holker Cl SK12. . . . . .36 F4
Holkham Cl WA8 . . . . .12 F1
Holkham The CH3 . . . . . . 119 B1
Holland Cl CW11 . . . . 175 C5
Holland Ct SK12. . . . . .36 E3
Holland Park SK7. . . . . . . 35 D7
Holland Rd SK7 . . . . 35 E7
Hollands La CW6. . . . . . . 122 C5
Hollands Pl SK11. . . . . . . 112 F7
Hollands Rd CW9 . . . . . . 103 F7
Holland St Crewe CW1 . . 190 B6
  5 Macclesfield SK11. . . . 112 C7
Holland Wlk CW5 . . . . . . 204 D6
Hollies La SK9 . . . . .60 F7
Hollies The Moulton CW9 . 126 E8
  1 Northwich CW9. . . . . . 103 E6
  Runcorn WA7. . . . . 49 D8
  Shavington CW2. . . . . . . 206 B4
HOLLINFARE. 11 A3
Hollingford Pl WA16. . . . . 82 A8
HOLLIN GREEN 202 F6
Hollingreen La CW5 . . . . 229 B2
Hollin Green La CW5 . . . . 202 E6
Hollinhey Prim Sch SK11 112 F3
Hollin La Langley SK11. . . 113 A1
  Newhall CW5 . . . . 228 D1
  Styal SK9. . . . . 33 F5
  Sutton Lane Ends SK11. . 136 C6
Hollin Rd SK10. . . . . 88 A7
HOLLINS. 210 E8
Hollins Cres ST7 . . . . 194 E1
Hollins Dr WA2 . . . . .8 A6
Hollins Grange ST7. . . . . 210 D8

HOLLINSGREEN 152 D4
HOLLINS GREEN. 11 B2
Hollinshead Cl ST7. . . . . 194 F7
Hollins Hill CW6 . . . . 146 F8
Hollins La Antrobus CW9. . .53 F4
  Marbury SY13 . . . . 226 E2
  Winwick WA2. . . . . .7 E6
HOLLINS-LANE. 226 E6
Hollins Park Hospl WA2 . . . .7 F6
Hollins Rd SK11 . . . . 112 F6
Hollins Terr SK11 . . . . 112 F6
Hollins Way WA8. . . . . .22 B5
Hollinwood Cl ST7 . . . . . 210 E8
Hollinwood Rd
  Disley SK12. . . . . 38 D6
  Talke ST7. . . . . 210 E8
Holloway WA7. . . . . .22 F1
Hollow Dr WA4 . . . . .16 E1
Hollow La Kingsley WA6 . . .75 B3
  Knutsford WA16. . . . . 57 B1
Hollowmoor Heath CH3 . . 121 A6
Hollow Oak La CW8 . . . . 101 D4
Hollowood La WA16. . . . . . 55 E4
Hollowood Rd SY14 . . . . 213 B5
Hollow The ST7. . . . . 195 B5
Holly Ave WA12. . . . . .2 D3
Hollybank Audlem CW3. . 229 E3
  Moore WA4. . . . . .25 B5
Holly Bank Chester CH1. . 237 A4
  Frodsham WA6. . . . . 74 C8
  Helsby WA6 . . . . 73 D2
  Lymm WA13 . . . . 18 D2
Hollybank Cl CW8 . . . . . . .78 D1
Hollybank Ct
  Chester CH1. . . . . 237 A4
  Widnes WA8. . . . . 12 F1
Hollybank Rd WA7 . . . . . . .49 F8
Holly Bank Rd SK9 . . . . . . 34 B1
Holly Blue Rd CW11 . . . . 175 D7
Hollybush Cres CW5. . . . 205 D5
Holly Bush La WA3 . . . . . . 10 C2
Holly Cl Connah's Quay CH5 . 91 C1
  Hale L24. . . . . 21 D2
Holmes Chapel CW4. . . . 130 D3
  Mickle Trafford CH2 . . . . 119 F8
Holly Cotts CW12. . . . . . . 132 C1
Holly Croft CW12. . . . . . . 154 F6
Holly Ct Helsby WA6 . . . . . 73 C5
  Middlewich CW10 . . . . . . 128 B2
Holly Dr
  4 Nantwich CW5 . . . . . . 204 C3
  Winsford CW7 . . . . 149 D8
Holly Farm Ct WA8 . . . . . . 12 E4
Hollyfield Rd CH65. . . . . . .70 B5
Hollyfields CW11. . . . . . . 191 F8
Holly Gr Over Tabley WA16 . 56 A3
  Warrington WA1 . . . . 17 A7
Holly Heath Cl CW11 . . . 175 C5
Holly Hedge La WA4. . . . . 25 D6
Holly House Est CW10 . . 129 C6
HOLLYHURST. 227 A5
Hollyhurst Rd SY13. . . . . 227 B7
Holly La Alsager ST7. . . . 193 E3
  Harriseahead ST7 . . . . . 195 F5
  Wythenshawe SK9. . . . . . 33 E5
Holly Mount CW2 . . . . . . 206 E5
Holly Pl CW5. . . . . 205 D6
Holly Rd Bramhall SK7. . . . 35 E5
  Chester CH4. . . . . 140 F5
  Ellesmere Port CH65 . . . . 70 C5
  Golborne WA3 . . . . .3 C8
  Haydock WA11. . . . . .1 A6
  High Lane SK6 . . . . 37 F7
  Lymm WA13 . . . . 19 B5
  Macclesfield SK11 . . . . . 112 B7
  Newcastle-under-Lyme
    ST5 . . . . 210 D1
  Poynton SK12. . . . . .36 E3
  Warrington WA5. . . . . .14 E5
  Weaverham CW8 . . . . . . 102 C8
Holly Road N SK9. . . . . . . .60 B6
Holly Road S SK9. . . . . . . .60 B5
Holly Terr WA5 . . . . 14 F5
Hollythorn Ave SK8 . . . . . 35 C7
Holly Tree Dr
  Biddulph ST8 . . . . 179 C2
  Swan Green ST7. . . . . . . 106 D7
Holly Tree La CW12. . . . . 132 A6
Hollytree Rd WA16 . . . . . . 80 F3
Holly Wlk Northwich CW8 . 103 C7
  Partington M31 . . . . 11 D3
Holm Dr Elton CH2 . . . . . . .72 B4
  Elton CH2. . . . . 72 C3
HOLMES CHAPEL 130 C4
Holmes Chapel Bsns Ctr
  CW4 . . . . 130 D3
Holmes Chapel Comp Sch
  CW4 . . . . 130 A2
Holmes Chapel L Ctr
  CW4 . . . . 130 A2
Holmes Chapel Prim Sch
  CW4 . . . . 130 B3
Holmes Chapel Rd
  Allostock WA16 . . . . 106 B3
  Brereton Green CW4,
    CW12 . . . . 154 D8
  Congleton CW12 . . . . . . 155 C4
  Knutsford WA16. . . . . 82 C3
  Lach Dennis CW9. . . . . . 105 D5
  Lach Dennis CW9. . . . . . 105 E4
  Middlewich CW10 . . . . . . 128 E2
  Sandbach CW11. . . . . . . 153 E1
  Sproston Green CW4,
    CW10 . . . . 129 B2
  Withington Green SK11. . 130 D2
Holmes Chapel Sta CW4 . 130 D2
Holmes Ct WA3 . . . . .9 C4
Holme St CH3. . . . . 120 F2

Holmesville Ave CW12. . . 156 B3
Holmeswood Cl SK9. . . . . 60 C8
Holmfield CH9 . . . . 85 A8
Holmfield Ave WA7 . . . . . . 23 C2
Holmfield Dr Cheadle SK8. . .35 B8
  Ellesmere Port CH66 . . . . 69 D3
Holmlea Dr CW1 . . . . 190 F3
Holmlee Way SK10. . . . . . 86 D6
Holm Oak Way CH66. . . . . 94 F8
Holmsfield Rd WA1 . . . . . . 16 D5
Holmshaw La CW1 . . . . . 192 B3
Holmwood Dr CH65 . . . . . .70 B2
Holst Gdns CW9. . . . . 127 A7
HOLT 196 D8
Holt Community Primary
  School LL13 . . . . 196 D8
Holt Gdns M16. . . . . .58 C6
Holt Hey CH64 . . . . 67 A5
Holt La WA7 . . . . .49 F8
HOLTRIDGE. 215 E6
Holtridge Norbury SY13. . 215 E6
  Norbury SY13. . . . . 215 F5
Holt's La SK9 . . . . 33 F3
Holt St CW1 . . . . 190 B4
Holy Family RC Prim Sch
  WA8 . . . . 12 D5
Holyhead Cl WA5 . . . . .7 D3
Holyrood Ave WA8 . . . . . . 13 A4
Holyrood Dr CW2 . . . . . . 205 E8
Holyrood Way CH3 . . . . . 119 B2
Holy Spirit Prim Sch WA9 . .1 A3
Holy Spirit RC Prim Sch The
  WA7 . . . . 49 D8
Holywell Cl CH64. . . . . . . .41 B1
Holywell Dr WA1 . . . . 16 C5
Holywell La CH3 . . . . 182 D2
Home Cl CH3 . . . . 142 E7
Homecrofts CH64 . . . . . . .66 E5
Homedee Ho CH1 . . . . . . 237 A3
Home Farm WA16. . . . . . . 56 B8
Home Farm Ave SK10. . . . .86 F1
Home Farm La CW8 . . . . . 101 C5
Home Farm Pk CW5 . . . . 172 A8
Home Pk CH1. . . . . .94 F1
Homeshire Ho ST7 . . . . . 193 D3
Homestead Ave WA11. . . . . .1 E6
Homestead Cl ST7 . . . . . 192 F2
Homestead Ct CW9 . . . . . 104 D7
Homestead Rd SK12. . . . . 38 C6
Homesteads The CW5 . . . 172 A6
Homeway WA6. . . . . .73 B2
Homewood Cres CW8 . . . 103 B5
Hondslough La
  Forestgate WA6 . . . . 100 A6
  New Pale WA6 . . . . .99 F6
Honeycomb CH4 . . . . 141 B3
Honey Fields CW6. . . . . . 146 C1
Honey Spot Cres 6 WA8. .13 C4
Honeysuckle Ave WA5. . . .15 E4
Honeysuckle Cl
  Broughton CH4. . . . . 139 C3
  West Heath CW12 . . . . . 156 A4
  Widnes WA8. . . . . 13 E4
Honeysuckle Cl 3 CH66 . .94 F8
Honeysuckle Dr 6 CW5 . 204 C4
Hong Kong Ave M90. . . . . 33 A8
Honister Ave WA2. . . . . . . .8 C2
Honister Gr WA7 . . . . .49 E5
Honiton Way
  Middlewich CW10 . . . . . . 128 D2
  Warrington WA5 . . . . .14 E4
HONKLEY 161 C3
Hood Gr CW1 . . . . 190 F6
Hood La WA5 . . . . 15 C4
Hood Lane N WA5. . . . . . . 15 C6
HOOD MANOR 15 D5
Hood Manor Centre WA5 . 15 C6
Hood Rd WA8. . . . . 12 F1
HOOFIELD 145 A2
Hoofield La CH3 . . . . 145 A1
HOO GREEN. 29 F2
Hoo Green La WA16. . . . . . 29 E1
Hooker St CW8. . . . . 103 E7
Hook La CW6 . . . . 145 A6
Hooks Brook La SY14. . . . 198 C4
Hookstone Dr CH66. . . . . . 69 C6
HOOLE. 119 A3
HOOLE BANK. 119 C7
Hoole Bridge E CH2 . . . . 237 C4
Hoole CE Prim Sch CH2. . 119 A3
Hoole Gdns CH2 . . . . 119 B3
Hoole Ho CH2. . . . . 119 B4
Hoole La CH2 . . . . 119 A3
HOOLE PARK. 118 F3
Hoole Pk CH2. . . . . 118 F2
Hoole Rd CH2. . . . . 118 F2
Hoole Way CH1 . . . . 237 B3
Hooleyhey La SK10, SK11. . 89 D4
Hoolpool La Elton CH2 . . . .72 F5
  Helsby WA6 . . . . 73 A5
HOOTON 44 A1
Hooton Gn CH66. . . . . .44 B2
Hooton Hey CH66. . . . . . . 69 D5
Hooton La CH66. . . . . .44 B1
Hooton Pk La CH65. . . . . . 44 C4
Hooton Rd CH64, CH66 . . 43 D1
Hooton Sta CH66. . . . . . . 43 D1
Hooton Works CH66. . . . . .43 E1
Hope Ave SK9. . . . . 34 C3
Hope Cres 7 CW7. . . . . . 150 A8
Hope Croft CH66. . . . . .69 F2
Hope Farm Prec CH66. . . . 69 F2
Hope Farm Rd CH66. . . . . .69 F2
Hopefield Rd WA13. . . . . . .19 B4
Hope Green Way SK10. . . 36 D2

Hope La Midway SK10 . . . . 36 D3
  Wardsend SK10 . . . . .36 E1
Hope Rd CH4. . . . . 139 B3
Hope St Audley ST7 . . . . 209 F3
  Chester CH4. . . . . 140 F7
  Crewe CW2 . . . . 190 D2
  Macclesfield SK10 . . . . . 112 C8
  Newton-le-Willows WA12 . . . .2 B3
  Northwich CW8 . . . . 103 F7
  Sandbach CW11. . . . . . . 175 B6
Hope Street W SK10. . . . . 112 C8
Hopkins Cl CW12. . . . . . . 156 B3
Hopkinson Ct CH1. . . . . . 118 B1
Hopsedge Cl CW2. . . . . . 206 B3
Hopwood Cl 5 WA3. . . . . . .3 F8
Hopwood St WA1 . . . . 16 C6
Horace Black Gdns CH65 . 70 C6
Horace Lawton Ct 2
  CW12. . . . . 156 D3
Horbury Gdns CH66. . . . . 69 C5
Hornbeam Ave CH66 . . . . .69 F1
Hornbeam Cl
  Chester CH2. . . . . 119 B3
  Runcorn WA7. . . . . 24 C1
Hornbeam Dr CW8 . . . . . 102 E4
Hornbeam Rd L26. . . . . . . 21 A7
Hornbeam Way 4 CW9. . . 79 C3
Hornby Dr
  Congleton CW12 . . . . . . 156 A3
  Nantwich CW5 . . . . 205 A5
Hornby La WA4 . . . . .8 A6
Horncastle Cl 4 WA3 . . . . .3 F8
Hornsmill Ave WA8. . . . . . 13 A6
Horn's Mill Prim Sch WA6. 73 A1
Hornsmill Way WA6 . . . . . 73 A3
Horridge Ave WA12 . . . . . . .2 C5
Horrocks La WA1 . . . . .16 F5
Horrocks Rd CH2. . . . . . . 118 C5
Horsemarket St WA1 . . . . .16 B5
Horseshoe Cl WA6 . . . . . . .75 B2
Horseshoe Cres WA2 . . . . .8 E3
Horseshoe Dr SK11. . . . . 112 B7
Horseshoe La SK9. . . . . . . 60 A2
Horsley La CW6 . . . . 167 E1
Horstone Cres CH66. . . . . .69 F2
Horstone Gdns CH66. . . . . 70 A2
Horstone Rd CH66. . . . . . . .69 F2
HORTON GREEN 212 A8
Horton Green La SY14. . . 212 B8
Horton La CH3 . . . . 121 D4
Horton Way CW5. . . . . . . 205 A4
HORWICH END 65 D5
Hoscar Ct WA8. . . . . 22 D7
Hospital La CW5. . . . . . . 203 E2
Hospital of St John
  Almhouses CH1. . . . . . . 237 A3
Hospital St Crewe CW1. . 190 D6
  Nantwich CW5 . . . . 204 E6
Hospital Way WA7 . . . . . . .49 F7
Hotel Rd M90. . . . . 33 C7
Hotel St WA12 . . . . .2 B3
Hothershall Cl CW1 . . . . . 173 B1
Hotspur Rd CW1 . . . . 190 F6
HOUGH Alderley Edge 60 D1
  Crewe 206 F3
Hough Cl SK10. . . . . 88 D5
HOUGH COMMON 206 F2
Hough Cotts CW2 . . . . . . 206 E3
Hougher Wall Rd ST7. . . . 209 D1
  Chester CH4. . . . . 141 B7
HOUGH GREEN 12 B2
Hough Green Rd WA8 . . . . 12 B3
Hough Green Sta WA8. . . . 12 B2
Hough Hole SK10 . . . . 88 D5
Hough La
  Alderley Edge SK9 . . . . . . 60 D3
  Barnton CW8, CW9 . . . . . .78 B4
  Comberbach CW9 . . . . . . 78 A4
  Norley WA6 . . . . 100 F5
Houghley Cl SK10. . . . . . . 87 C2
Hough's La WA4 . . . . 26 A6
Hough St CW7 . . . . 125 F2
Houghton Cl Chester CH2. 118 F3
  Newton-le-Willows WA12 . . . .2 B3
  9 Northwich CW9. . . . . . 103 F4
  Widnes WA8. . . . . 13 D2
Houghton Croft WA8 . . . . 12 C5
HOUGHTON GREEN 8 E4
Houghton St
  Newton-le-Willows WA12 . . . .2 B3
  Warrington WA2 . . . . .16 B6
  Widnes WA8. . . . . 13 D2
Houndings La CW11 . . . . 175 B4
Hourd Way CH66. . . . . .94 E8
Housesteads Dr CH2 . . . . 118 F3
House Yard Cl 11 CW1 . . 190 A8
Housman Cl CH1 . . . . 118 A5
Houston Gdns WA5. . . . . . 15 A8
Hove Cl CW1. . . . . 190 B8
Hove The WA7 . . . . 50 D6
Hovey Cl CW11 . . . . 175 A4
Hovis Mill SK11 . . . . 112 E7
Howard Ave
  Bebington CH62. . . . . 43 D8
  Lymm WA13 . . . . .19 B4
Howard Ct Neston CH64 . . .41 F1
  Runcorn WA7. . . . . 24 C4
Howard Rd Culcheth WA3. . .5 A2
  Saltney CH4. . . . . 140 D6
Howard St CW1 . . . . 191 A5
Howards Way CH64. . . . . . 67 A6
Howarth Ct 4 WA7. . . . . . 23 B2
HOWBECK BANK 219 E8
Howbeck Cres CW5 . . . . . 220 A8
Howbeck Wlk CW2 . . . . . 206 D8
Howells Ave CH66 . . . . . . 69 D3
Howells Pl CW5 . . . . 205 D5

Howe Rd CH4 141 B7
Howe St SK10 87 F1
Howey Hill CW12 156 D1
Howey La
Congleton CW12 156 D2
Frodsham WA6 74 B7
Howey Rise WA6 74 B7
Howgill Cl CH66 68 F6
HOWLEY 16 D5
Howley La WA1 16 E5
Howley Quay Ind Est WA1 16 D5
Howson Rd WA2 8 C3
Howty Cl SK9 34 D1
Hoy Dr WA12 2 A2
Hoylake Cl WA7 50 C6
Hoyle St WA5 15 F7
Hubert Dr CW10 151 C8
Hubert Worthington Ho 9 SK9 60 A1
Hucklow Dr WA1 16 E5
Hudson Cl WA5 15 D8
Hudson Gr 9 WA3 3 E8
Hudson Rd WA2 8 E2
Hughes Ave WA2 8 D2
Hughes Dr CW2 189 F4
Hughes La SY14 213 B3
Hughes Pl WA2 8 D2
Hughes St WA4 16 C3
Hugh St CH4 141 D7
Hulley Pl SK10 87 F1
Hulley Rd SK10 87 F2
Hullock's Pool Rd ST7 209 E5
HULME 8 B3
Hulme Hall Ave SK8 35 B8
Hulme Hall Cres SK8 35 A8
Hulme Hall La WA16 106 B4
Hulme Hall Rd SK8 35 A8
Hulme La WA16 106 C7
Hulme Sq
Macclesfield SK11 112 D5
5 Middlewich CW10 151 D5
Hulme St CW1 189 F5
HULME WALFIELD 156 B7
HULSEHEATH 30 A4
Hulseheath La WA16 30 A3
Hulse La CW9 105 D6
Hulton Cl CW12 157 B1
Humber Cl WA8 13 F3
Humber Dr Biddulph ST8 179 E1
Holmes Chapel CW4 130 D2
Humber Rd
Ellesmere Port CH66 69 F2
Warrington WA2 8 E2
Humble Bee Bank Cotts CW5 187 C8
Humble Bee Bank Rd CW5 187 B8
Hume St WA1 16 D6
Humphrey Cl CH1 94 A2
Humphrey's Cl WA7 50 D7
Humphry Pl CW2 206 D5
Hungerford Ave CW1 190 E4
Hungerford Pl
Barthomley CW2 208 D5
Sandbach CW11 175 A5
Hungerford Prim Sch CW1 190 E4
Hungerford Rd CW1 190 F4
Hungerford Terr CW1 190 F4
Hungerford Villas CW1 190 F4
Hunger Hill WA16 108 B7
HUNSTERSON 220 B1
Hunsterson Rd
Bridgemere CW5 231 D8
Hatherton CW5 220 B3
Hunt Cl WA5 15 B8
Hunter Ave
Shavington CW2 206 D7
Warrington WA2 8 B3
Hunters Cl SK9 34 F1
Hunter's Cres CH3 121 C1
Hunters Ct Helsby WA6 73 D4
Runcorn WA7 49 E6
Hunter's Dr CH3 121 C1
Huntersfield CW2 206 B3
Hunters Field CW8 103 D7
Hunters Hill Kingsley WA6 75 C1
Weaverham CW8 77 C1
Hunters La CW8 102 E4
Hunters Lodge SK9 34 F1
Hunters Mews SK9 60 C7
Hunters Pointe CW12 155 C6
Hunters Pool La SK10 86 C8
Hunters Rise CW7 126 C1
Hunter St CH1 237 A3
Hunter's View SK9 34 C3
Hunters Way Neston CH64 66 C8
Talke ST7 210 D8
Hunters Wlk CH1 237 A2
Hunting Lodge Mews CW8 102 A4
HUNTINGTON 142 A5
Huntington Com Prim Sch CH3 142 A5
Huntley St WA5 15 C4
Huntly Chase SK9 60 C7
Hunt Rd WA11 1 E6
Huntsbank Bsns Pk CW2 205 E7
Huntsbank Dr ST5 210 D1
Hunts Cl CH3 119 B1
Hunts Field Cl WA13 18 D2
Hunts La WA4 16 F2
Huntsman Dr M44 11 F7
Hurcomb Way CW1 190 F6
HURDSFIELD 87 E2
Hurdsfield Cl CW10 151 C7
Hurdsfield Com Prim Sch SK10 87 F2
Hurdsfield Gn SK10 87 E2
Hurdsfield Ind Est SK10 87 E3
Hurdsfield Rd SK10 87 E1
Hurford Ave CH65 69 F3
Hurlbote Cl SK9 34 D5
Hurleston Bldgs CW5 204 E6
Hurlestone Cl CH2 96 F1
Hurleston Way CW5 204 D7
Hurley Cl WA5 15 C5
Hurn Cl CW1 190 B8
HURST 179 F3
Hurst Ave SK8 35 C6
Hurst Cl Bunbury CW6 185 E8
Talke ST7 210 D6
Hurst Ct CW6 185 F8
Hurst Gn Gdns 1 WA3 4 E5
Hursthead Inf Sch SK8 35 C6
Hursthead Jun Sch SK8 35 C7
Hursthead Rd SK8 35 B7
Hurst La Bollington SK10 88 A8
Glazebury WA3 5 C7
Hurst Lea Ct SK9 60 A2
Hurst Lea Rd SK22 39 C7
Hurst Mews WA6 75 C2
Hurst Mill La WA3 5 C8
Hurst Rd ST8 179 F4
Hurst St WA8 23 A4
Hurst The WA6 75 C2
Hurstwood CH3 143 A4
Hush Ho CH1 237 A2
Huskisson Way WA12 2 B4
Hutchins' Cl CW10 151 E6
Hutchinson St WA8 22 F6
Huttfield Rd L24 21 A4
Hutton Cl WA3 4 E5
Hutton Dr CW12 157 A2
HUXLEY 167 A8
Huxley CE Prim Sch CH3 167 A7
Huxley Cl Bramhall SK7 35 E7
Macclesfield SK10 87 B2
Huxley Ct CH66 69 F8
Huxley Dr SK7 35 E7
Huxley La Millfields CH3 166 F8
Tiverton CW6 168 B6
Huxley St CW8 103 E7
Hyacinth Cl WA11 1 F6
Hyde Bank Ct SK22 39 C7
Hyde Bank Mill SK22 39 C8
Hyde Bank Rd SK22 39 C8
Hyde Cl
Ellesmere Port CH65 69 F4
Runcorn WA7 49 D6
Hydra Cl WA5 7 C2
Hydrangea Way WA9 6 A7
Hylton Ct CH65 70 E2
Hylton Dr SK8 35 C8
Hythe Ave CW1 190 B8

I

Ian Rd ST7 195 D3
Iberis Gdns WA9 6 A7
Ibis Ct WA1 16 A3
Ikey La CW5 202 F6
Ikins Dr ST7 209 F2
Ilex Ave WA2 8 B7
Ilford Way WA16 58 A4
ILLIDGE GREEN 154 C4
Imperial Ave Blacon CH1 117 C4
Northwich CW8 103 C8
Imperial Ct CW5 204 F5
Imperial Mews
Crewe CW2 190 D3
Ellesmere Port CH65 70 B6
INCE 71 F6
Ince Ave CH62 43 E3
Ince Dr CH3 180 F1
Ince & Elton Sta CH2 72 B4
Ince La Elton CH2 72 B3
Wimbolds Trafford CH2 96 F5
Ince Orchards CH2 72 B4
Incline Way WA8 13 C2
Indigo Rd CH65 70 F6
Ingersley Ct SK10 88 B8
Ingersley Rd SK10 88 C8
Ingersley Vale SK10 88 B8
Ingham Ave WA12 2 C1
Ingham Cl CH3 119 A1
Ingham Rd WA8 12 F4
Inghams Rd WA3 4 A1
Inglegreen CH60 41 B8
Inglenook Rd WA5 14 F4
Ingleton Cl
Holmes Chapel CW4 130 A3
Newton-le-Willows WA12 2 B4
Ingleton Gr WA7 49 D5
Inglewood Ave CW10 151 D5
Inglewood Cl
Partington M31 11 F4
Warrington WA3 10 B6
Inman Ave WA9 1 B2
Inner Gosling Cl WA4 25 F1
Innisfree Cl 4 CH66 69 C5
Innovation Ho CW7 149 A7
Innovation Way WA4 25 B3
Insall Rd WA2 8 F2
Intack La WA16 28 B3
Intake Cl CH64 68 A8
International App M90 33 C7
Inveresk Rd SY14 198 C3
Inward Way CH65 70 B7
Ionacres 5 WA8 12 F6
Iona Cres WA8 12 F6
Ion Path CW7 127 C1
Irby Cl CH66 69 E4
Ireland Blackburne Ho WA1 16 E7
Ireland Rd Hale L24 21 E1
Haydock WA11 1 C6
Irelands Croft Cl 11 CW11 174 E8
Ireland St Warrington WA2 16 B8
Widnes WA8 13 D2
Iris Cl WA8 12 C2
Iris Rise 7 CW8 101 F2
Iris Wlk 7 M31 11 E2
Irlam and Cadishead Coll M44 11 E7
Irlam Ind Est M44 11 E7
Irlam Sta M44 11 E7
Ironbridge Dr CW4 130 C2
Irondish Cl WA6 73 D5
Irons La CH3 120 F7
Irvin Dr M22, SK8 34 A8
Irving's Cres CH4 140 E6
Irwell La WA7 23 B3
Irwell Rd WA4 16 B2
Irwell Rise SK10 87 F7
Irwell St WA8 23 A4
Irwin Dr SK9 34 C5
Isabella Ct CH4 140 E6
Isherwood Cl WA2 8 F3
Isis Cl CW12 156 F1
Islay Cl CH65 70 C1
Islington Gn WA8 13 D4
ISYCOED 196 C1
Ivatt Dr CW2 190 E1
Iveagh Cl WA7 50 A7
Iver Cl Chester CH2 118 E7
Cronton WA8 12 C6
Iver Rd CH2 118 E7
Ivy Ave WA12 2 C2
Ivy Bank Prim Sch SK11 112 A5
Ivychurch Mews WA7 23 D2
Ivy Cl CW11 175 D6
Ivy Cotts SY13 225 A8
Ivy Ct CH4 162 D2
Ivy Dr CW8 102 A2
Ivy Farm Ct L24 21 D1
Ivy Farm Dr CH64 66 F6
Ivy Farm Gdns WA3 4 D4
Ivy Farm La CH3 183 C1
Ivy Gdns CW12 156 C2
Ivy Ho Macclesfield SK11 112 A7
Nether Alderley SK9 84 C7
Ivyho Gdns 2 WA4 27 B4
Ivy House Rd ST8 179 C2
Ivy La Alsager ST7 193 E2
Macclesfield SK11 112 A6
Ivy Meade Cl 10 SK11 111 F7
Ivy Meade Rd SK11 111 F6
Ivy Mews CH2 119 A5
Ivy Rd Golborne WA3 3 B8
Macclesfield SK11 112 A7
Poynton SK12 36 E3
Warrington WA1 17 E7
Ivy St WA7 23 A1
Ivy Wlk M31 11 D3

J

Jackie Stewart Bsns Ctr CW6 147 D6
Jack La
Moulton CW9, CW10 127 A7
Weston CW2 207 D6
Jackman Cl 6 WA12 2 D1
Jack Mills Way CW2 206 D7
Jack Search Way WA7 50 C5
Jackson Ave Culcheth WA3 4 E3
Nantwich CW5 204 F5
Warrington WA1 16 F6
Jackson Ct CH5 139 B7
Jackson Dr 10 SK9 60 E8
Jackson La SK10 88 B7
Jackson Rd CW12 156 E5
Jackson's Brickworks Nature Reserve* SK12 37 D6
Jacksons Cl SK10 88 B7
Jacksons Edge Rd SK12 38 B6
Jackson's La SK7 36 C8
Jackson St Burtonwood WA5 6 E6
Haydock WA11 1 A7
Macclesfield SK11 112 D6
Jacks Wood Gn CH65 70 B7
Jacobs Way WA16 79 F7
Jamage Ind Est ST7 210 C5
Jamage Rd ST7 210 D5
James Atkinson Way CW1 189 F7
James Ave CH66 69 C3
James Brindley Dr CW11 152 C3
James Cl WA8 23 A4
James Clarke Rd CW7 125 F2
James Gibbons Rd CW1 190 F7
James Hall St CW5 204 E6
James Pl CH2 118 F2
James Rd WA11 1 F7
James St Chester CH1 237 B3
Macclesfield SK11 112 D6
Northwich CW9 104 C8
5 Warrington WA1 16 B5
Jamestown Ave WA5 15 A7
Jamieson Cl Alsager ST7 193 E4
Chester CH3 119 A2
Jamie Webb Dr SK9 34 F3
Jane Maddock Homes ST7 193 B3
Jan Palach Ave CW5 204 F4
Japonica Gdns WA9 6 A7
Jarman SK11 112 F4
Jasmine Ave SK10 111 E8
Jasmine Cres ST7 195 D2
Jasmine Gdns
St Helens WA9 6 A7
Warrington WA5 15 E4
Jasmine Gr WA8 22 D8
Jasmine Wlk M31 11 F2
Jasmin Way ST7 195 F2
Jay Cl WA3 10 A4
Jays Cl WA7 50 E7
Jedburgh Ave CH66 69 A6
Jefferson Dr WA5 15 B7
Jefferson Gdns WA8 12 F3
Jellicoe Ave M44 11 E6
Jennets La WA3 5 D8
Jennet's La WA3 5 C8
Jenny La SK7 35 E4
Jensen Ct WA7 23 C3
Jersey Ave CH65 70 C1
Jersey Cl Chelford SK11 84 A2
Congleton CW12 157 A2
Jersey Way CW10 128 D2
Jervis Cl WA2 9 A3
Jesmond Cres CW2 190 B2
Jesmond Gr SK8 35 B8
Jesmond Rd CH1 118 B2
Jessop Ho WA7 22 E3
Jessop Way CW1 191 C4
JH Godwin Prim Sch CH1 117 D4
Jibcroft Brook La 3 WA3 4 E5
Jockey St WA2 16 B7
JODRELL BANK 108 D2
Jodrell Bank (Granada) Arboretum* SK11 108 D3
Jodrell Bank Obsy & Visitor Ctr* CW4 108 C3
Jodrell Cl
Holmes Chapel CW4 130 A3
Macclesfield SK11 112 E7
Jodrell Dr WA4 27 A7
Jodrell Mdw SK23 65 E8
Jodrell Rd SK23 65 D8
Jodrell St
Macclesfield SK11 112 E7
New Mills SK22 39 B7
Joe Brown Cl CW1 172 F1
John Bradshaw Ct CW12 156 C4
John Brunner Cres CW9 103 E6
John Cliff Way ST7 192 F4
John Ford Way CW11 154 B1
John Fryer Ave CW9 80 A5
John Gresty Dr CW5 205 D6
John Hammond Cl CW2 207 B5
John Jobson Rd CW2 206 C4
John Lloyd Ct M44 11 F8
John Maddock Dr CW1 190 F7
John May Ct SK10 87 B2
John Middleton Cl L24 21 E2
John Nicholas Cres CH65 70 C6
John Rd WA13 18 C3
John Rowlands Cl 4 CW11 174 E4
Johns Ave Haydock WA11 1 E7
Runcorn WA7 48 F8
Johns Cl SK10 88 D5
John Simpson Cres 4 CW11 192 A7
Johnson Ave WA12 2 B5
Johnson Cl CW12 157 B1
Johnsons Cl CH4 141 B5
Johnsons La WA8 23 E8
Johnson's La WA8 13 E1
Johnson St SK23 65 E8
John St Bollington SK10 88 B8
Congleton CW12 156 C2
Crewe CW1 190 C5
Ellesmere Port CH65 70 B6
Golborne WA3 3 A8
Irlam M44 11 E5
Macclesfield SK11 112 D6
1 Northwich CW9 104 A8
Utkinton CW6 146 B7
Warrington WA2 16 B6
Winsford CW7 126 C1
Jonathan's Way CH1 117 E5
Jones Ave CW1 173 A1
Jones's La CW10 152 D6
Jonson Rd CH64 66 E8
Jordangate SK10 112 D8
Joseph Cres ST7 193 F2
Joseph Groome Twrs 10 CH65 70 C6
Joseph Locke Dr 7 CW2 206 D6
Joseph St WA8 13 C2
Joseph Wood Dr 2 CW11 192 A7
Joyce Ave CW7 126 C2
Joy La WA5 6 E4
Jubilee Almshouses CW5 204 E6
Jubilee Ave Crewe CW2 190 B3
Warrington WA5 14 E4
Warrington, Padgate WA1 16 F8
Jubilee Cres Haydock WA11 1 F7
Northwich CW8 103 C8
Jubilee Ct
2 Handforth SK9 34 E5
Holmes Chapel CW4 130 A3
Jubilee Gdns
Nantwich CW5 204 E4
New Mills SK22 39 C7
Jubilee Gn CH65 70 C4
Jubilee Gr WA13 18 C4
Jubilee Pastures 6 CW10 151 C6
Jubilee Rd CW12 156 E2
Jubilee St SK22 39 C7
Jubilee Terr CW5 204 E4
Jubilee Villas CW11 175 C2
Jubilee Way
Warrington WA2 16 B8
Widnes WA8 12 E1
5 Winsford CW7 126 D1
Jubits La WA8 13 A8
Juddfield St WA11 1 A7
Judy La SK11 113 A3
Julian Way WA8 12 F4
July Bglws CH4 141 E2
Jumper La SK10 88 F7
Junction Eight Bsns Ctr CH65 70 A7
Junction Ho 4 CW1 190 A5
Junction La WA12 2 B3
June Ave CH62 43 E8
Juniper Ave CW12 155 E4
Juniper Cl
Holmes Chapel CW4 130 D3
Newcastle-under-Lyme ST5 210 E1
Juniper Ct CH2 119 B4
Juniper Dr CH66 69 E1
Juniper Gr CH66 69 F1
Juniper La WA3 18 A7
Juniper Rise SK10 86 E1
Juno Cl CH3 142 C5
Jupiter Dr CH1 117 E2
Jurby Ct WA2 8 F1
Justice St SK10 87 D1

K

Kaleyards CH1 237 B2
Kansas Pl WA5 15 B7
Karen Cl WA5 7 A6
Karen Way CH66 69 D3
Kaye Ave WA3 4 F3
Kay La WA13 29 B8
Kays Croft Dr CW1 190 C8
Keats Cl
Ellesmere Port CH66 94 E8
Widnes WA8 22 F8
Keats Dr Macclesfield SK10 86 F1
Rode Heath ST7 193 E8
Wistaston CW2 206 A8
Keats Gr WA2 8 C2
Keats La CW9 80 A5
Keats Terr CH1 118 A5
Keble St WA8 23 B7
KECKWICK 25 A3
Keckwick La WA4 25 A3
Keele Cres SK11 112 B6
Keel Hey CH64 43 B1
Keepers Cl
Knutsford WA16 57 D3
Northwich CW8 102 E4
Keepers La CW9 53 D4
Keeper's La CW8 102 E8
Keeper's Rd WA4 27 A7
Keepers Wlk WA7 23 F2
Keith Ave WA5 14 E6
Keith Dr CH63 43 D5
Kelburn Ct WA3 9 F6
Kellet Way ST7 193 A4
Kell Gn La WA16 83 E6
Kellhouse La
Altrincham WA16 31 E1
Tatton Park WA16 57 E8
Kelmscott Cl CH66 69 D2
KELSALL 122 C4
Kelsall Ave CH62 43 F3
Kelsall Bypass CW6 122 C6
Kelsall Cl Bebington CH62 43 E3
Warrington WA3 9 C3
Widnes WA8 12 D1
Kelsall Prim Sch CW6 122 C4
Kelsall Rd CH3 121 C4
Kelsall St CW12 156 E3
Kelsall Way Audley ST7 209 D1
6 Handforth SK9 34 D5
Kelsborrow Cl CW9 103 E3
Kelsborrow Way CW6 122 D4
Kelso Way SK10 87 C4
Kelstern Cl 2 CW9 104 B8
KELSTERTON 91 B2
Kelsterton Ct CH5 91 C1
Kelsterton La CH6 91 B1
Kelsterton Rd
Connah's Quay CH5, CH6 91 C2
Kelsterton CH6 91 A3
Kelvin Cl WA3 9 D6
Kelvin Gr CH2 118 E4
Kelvin St WA3 9 F5
Kemberton Dr WA8 13 A5
Kemble Cl CW2 206 B8
Kemmel Ave WA4 16 C3
Kempsell Way L26 21 A7
Kempsell Wlk L26 21 A7
Kempton Ave CW1 190 C7
Kempton Cl Chester CH1 118 B2
Newton-le-Willows WA12 2 D5
Runcorn WA7 49 C6
Kempton Way SK10 87 C4
Kendal Ave WA2 8 C2
Kendal Cl Chester CH2 119 A6
Ellesmere Port CH66 69 D2
Macclesfield SK11 111 E6
Kendal Ct CW12 156 A2
Kendal Dr Bramhall SK7 35 C5
Ellesmere Port CH66 69 E2
Kendal Rd
Macclesfield SK11 111 F6
Widnes WA8 12 C1

Kendal Rise WA7........ 49 D5
Kendal Way CW2...... 207 C1
Kendrick Cl CW8........ 77 D1
Kendrick St WA1...... 16 A5
Kenilworth Ave
 Handforth SK9........... 34 D3
 Knutsford WA16........ 57 C2
 Runcorn WA7...........49 B8
Kenilworth Cl
 Macclesfield SK11...... 111 F6
 Wistaston CW2........ 206 A7
Kenilworth Ct CH65.....70 E2
Kenilworth Dr
 Hazel Grove SK7........ 36 D8
 Warrington WA1.......16 F8
Kenilworth Gdns WA12.....2 C1
Kenilworth Gn SK11..... 111 F6
Kenilworth Ho 6 CH1 . 237 C3
Kenilworth Rd
 Golborne WA3............3 E7
 Macclesfield SK11...... 111 F6
 Neston CH64............66 E5
Kenley Ave WA8 .... 12 D5
Kenmare Bank CW9..... 104 A5
Kenmore Gr M41....... 11 D6
Kennedy Ave SK10.......86 F2
Kennedy Cl CH2........ 119 A5
Kennedy Ct 4 WA5......15 B7
Kennel La
 Cuddington CW8....... 102 A1
 Little Budworth CW8... 124 E7
Kennels Gn CW9........ 54 C4
Kennelwood Rd CW9..... 78 C7
Kennerley's Ct SK9....... 60 A7
Kennerley's La SK9....... 60 A7
Kennet Cl SK9........... 34 D2
Kennet Dr CW12...... 156 F1
Kenneth Rd WA8........ 22 C8
Kennet Rd WA11..........1 C6
Kennet Way 10 SK11..... 111 F8
Kennington Pk WA8......12 E4
Kenrick Cl CW3........ 232 C1
Kensal Gn WA8 .... 13 C3
Kensington Ave WA4.... 17 C2
Kensington Cl
 Chester CH4........... 141 A6
 Widnes WA8............ 13 D4
Kensington Cres CW8... 102 A5
Kensington Ct
 Alsager ST7........... 192 F3
 9 Nantwich CW5..... 204 E6
 Wilmslow SK9.......... 60 A4
 Winsford CW7........ 149 C7
Kensington Dr
 Congleton CW12...... 156 F4
 Willaston CW5........ 205 D4
Kensington Gn CH4.... 140 F6
Kensington Rd
 Chester CH4........... 141 A6
 Ellesmere Port CH65.... 70 A5
Kensington Sq 11 SK10 . 111 F8
Kensington Way CW9... 103 E3
Kent Ave SK10...........87 E6
Kent Cl CH63............43 B8
Kent Dr CW12........ 156 D4
Kent Gdns CH2........ 118 F5
Kent Gr WA7............ 23 B1
Kent Ho ST7........... 210 D6
Kent Rd Chester CH2 ... 118 F5
 Irlam M44............. 11 C5
 Partington M31.........11 E2
 Warrington WA5........ 15 C4
Kentridge Dr CH66...... 69 D3
Kent's Green La CW1,
 CW11............... 191 E7
Kent's La CW11........ 173 C1
Kent St Warrington WA4 .. 16 C4
 Widnes WA8............13 B1
Kentucky Cl 10 WA5.....15 B7
Kent Way WA12...........2 C1
Kentwell Dr SK10...... 87 C3
Kenview Cl WA8 .... 22 A4
Kenwick Cl CH66....... 69 C3
Kenwood Ave SK7....... 35 D5
Ken Woolley Rd CW1 . 189 F5
KENYON................3 F3
Kenyon Ave WA5........14 E5
Kenyon Ct WA8 .... 23 A6
Kenyon La Culcheth WA3....4 A4
 Golborne WA3............3 F5
 Golborne, Heath WA3....3 F3
Kenyons Lane N WA11....1 F8
Kenyon's Lane S WA11 ....1 F7
Kerfoot Bsns Pk WA2... 16 A8
Kerfoot St WA2........ 16 A7
Keristal Ave CH3...... 142 A7
KERRIDGE............. 88 A6
Kerridge Cl CW10..... 151 B8
Kerridge Dr WA1.......16 E5
KERRIDGE-END.......... 88 D3
Kerridge Rd SK10...... 88 B3
Kerry Croft CH66........69 E1
Kershaw Gr SK11...... 112 B8
Kershaw St WA8........ 12 D1
Kershaw Way WA12.......2 C5
Kestrel Ave WA16.......57 B3
Kestrel Cl
 Congleton CW12...... 156 E1
 Middlewich CW10..... 151 D6
 Winsford CW7........ 149 D5
Kestrel Dr CW1........ 190 B8

Kestrel La WA3 ....9 E4
Kestrel Rd Heswall CH60... 41 C7
 Northwich CW8........ 103 C7
Kestrels Way WA7........49 F6
Keswick Ave
 Bebington CH63........ 43 C4
 Macclesfield SK11..... 111 F5
 Warrington WA2..........8 C2
Keswick Cl Chester CH2 . 119 A5
 Crewe CW2........... 189 E3
 Irlam M44............. 11 D4
 Macclesfield SK11...... 111 F6
 Widnes WA8............ 12 C1
 Winsford CW7........ 126 D2
Keswick Cres WA7........8 C2
Keswick Ct CW12...... 156 A2
Keswick Dr Bramhall SK7 .. 35 C5
 Frodsham WA6......... 74 D8
Keswick Gdns CH63..... 43 C5
Keswick Rd SK6.........37 E8
Ketlan Ct CH4......... 140 E7
Kettell Ave CW1...... 190 A6
Ketteringham Dr WA5....14 F8
Kettle La CW3......... 230 C2
Kettleshulme St James CE
 VA Prim Sch SK23.......64 F4
Kettleshulme Way SK12 .. 37 A3
Kettleshulme Wlk 4 SK9.. 34 E1
Kew Cl 5 SK10..........87 E5
Kew Gardens Cl WA8.... 13 D4
Keyes Cl WA3............9 F4
Keyes Gdn WA3..........9 F4
KEY GREEN............ 157 E4
Keysbrook CH3........ 166 C2
Keysbrook Ave CH3.... 166 C2
Kidderton Cl CW5...... 202 E7
Kidderton La CW5...... 202 F7
KIDNAL............... 212 E8
Kidnal Hill La SY14..... 212 F6
KIDSGROVE............ 195 B1
Kidsgrove Cl 12 CW11 . 174 F4
Kidsgrove Ski Ctr ST7 . 210 F7
Kidsgrove Sta ST7..... 194 F1
Kidston Dr CW1....... 189 F7
Kilbuck La WA11..........2 A8
Kilburn Ave CH62.......43 E6
Kilburn Cl SK8..........34 B7
Kildare Cl L24.......... 21 D2
Kildonan Rd WA4....... 17 A2
Kilford Cl WA5...........7 E2
Killingworth La WA3.....10 B5
Kilmorey Park Ave CH2 . 237 C4
Kilmorey Park Rd CH2 . 118 F3
Kilmorey Pk CH2....... 118 F4
Kilncroft WA7..........50 B5
Kiln Croft La SK9.......34 E4
Kiln La CW5........... 220 B8
Kilsby Dr WA8.......... 13 E2
Kilshaw Rd WA5..........6 F6
Kilsyth Cl WA2..........8 F4
Kimberley Dr WA4...... 16 C1
Kimberley St WA5.......15 E5
Kimberley Terr CH2.... 118 F2
Kinder Dr CW2........ 189 D3
Kinderton Cl WA16..... 29 C4
Kinderton Mobile Home Pk
 CW10................ 152 A7
Kinderton St CW10.... 128 D1
Kinder View SK22....... 39 C7
Kinder View Cl SK22.... 39 A5
King Arthur's Wlk WA7.. 24 A1
Kingbur Pl CW3....... 229 F4
King Charles Ct CH1.... 237 A3
King Edward Bldgs 3
 CH3................ 119 A1
King Edward Cl CW9 . 103 F5
King Edward Rd
 Knutsford WA16....... 57 A2
 3 Macclesfield SK10.. 112 D8
King Edward St
 Macclesfield SK10..... 112 D8
 Middlewich CW10..... 128 C1
 Warrington WA1.......16 E7
Kingfisher Cl
 Congleton CW12...... 156 E1
 Farndon CH3......... 180 F1
 Huntington CH3...... 142 B5
 Nantwich CW5........ 204 E8
 Runcorn WA7...........49 F6
 Warrington WA3..........9 F4
Kingfisher Cres 4
 CW11................ 174 C5
Kingfisher Ct
 Chester CH2.......... 237 A4
 Northwich CW9........ 79 C2
Kingfisher Dr 5 CW7 . 149 D6
Kingfisher Gr CW9......79 F5
King George Ave CW9 . 104 B8
King George Cres WA1 .. 16 E7
King George Rd WA11.....2 A7
King George Way ST7 . 195 C1
Kingham Cl 3 WA8 ... 13 D1
King Ho ST7........... 210 D5
King James Ct WA7......49 E6
King Oswald Cres 2 WA8..12 F6
King Pl CW5........... 204 E6
King Pool Pl SK12.......36 F5
King's Ave WA3...........3 F7
King's Bldgs CH1...... 237 A3
Kingsbury Cl WA4...... 26 D3
Kingsbury Dr 14 SK9... 34 D1
Kingsbury Rd WA1..... 13 D4
King's Church of England (A)
 Sch The 1 ST7...... 194 F1
Kings Cl Chester CH4 ... 140 F5
 Wilmslow SK9.......... 60 A6
King's Cres CW10..... 128 C2

King's Crescent E CH3... 119 A1
King's Crescent W CH3.. 119 A1
Kings Croft CH5...........5 F6
Kings Ct Nantwich CW5 . 204 D5
 Runcorn WA7.......... 24 D4
King's Ct CH1......... 237 A3
Kingsdale Rd
 Warrington WA5.........14 F7
 2 Warrington WA5.... 15 A7
Kingsdown Cl CW2.... 207 C1
Kings Dr Helsby WA6.....73 B3
 Wistaston CW2....... 205 E8
Kingsfield Ct CH4...... 141 C3
King's Gate CW1...... 102 A2
Kings Grove Sch CW2 . 190 A3
Kingshead Cl WA7...... 24 A2
Kings La CW6......... 147 D4
King's La
 Allostock CW10, WA16 . 106 C1
 Nantwich CW5........ 204 D5
Kingsland Grange WA1....9 D1
Kingslawn Cl 4 CW9 . 103 F5
Kings Lea Ho CH3..... 142 A8
Kingsleigh Cl WA6..... 101 A5
KINGSLEY............. 75 C2
Kingsley Ave
 Bebington CH62.........43 E3
 Handforth SK9......... 34 C2
Kingsley Cl
 Northwich CW8....... 103 C5
 Talke ST7............ 210 D6
Kingsley Com Prim Sch
 WA6.................74 F2
Kingsley Cres WA7..... 23 A1
Kingsley Ct CW11..... 174 D8
Kingsley Dr
 Northwich CW9....... 104 A6
 Warrington WA4....... 26 C7
Kingsley Gdns CH3.... 142 B8
Kingsley Gn WA6.......74 E5
Kingsley Rd Chester CH3.. 142 B8
 Congleton CW12...... 157 A3
 Crowton CW8...........76 B1
 Ellesmere Port CH65.... 70 C5
 Frodsham WA6.........74 E4
 Haslington CW1...... 191 C4
 Runcorn WA7.......... 23 A1
 Talke ST7............ 210 D6
Kingsley St John's CE VA
 Prim Sch WA6......... 75 C2
Kingsley Wlk CW7..... 126 B2
Kings Mdw Hough CW2 . 206 E2
 Runcorn WA7.......... 50 C8
KINGSMEAD............ 103 E5
Kingsmead Chester CH2 . 118 C8
 Northwich CW9....... 103 F5
Kingsmead Crossroads 10
 CW9................ 103 F4
Kingsmead Prim Sch
 CW9................ 103 E5
Kingsmead Sq CW9 .. 103 E4
Kings Mews CH66...... 69 C7
Kings Rd
 Connah's Quay CH5 ... 91 D1
 Ellesmere Port CH66.... 69 C7
 Golborne WA3...........3 A7
 Irlam M44............. 11 E6
 Warrington WA2..........9 A2
King's Rd 5 WA3.......59 E8
King's Sch The
 Chester CH4.......... 141 B4
 Macclesfield SK10...... 87 C1
King's Sch The SK10.... 86 E3
King St Audlem ST7 ... 209 D1
 Chester CH1.......... 237 A3
 Congleton CW12...... 156 F4
 Ellesmere Port CH65.... 70 C6
 Hartford CW8........ 103 B5
 Kidsgrove ST7........ 195 A2
 Knutsford WA16....... 57 A2
 Macclesfield SK10..... 112 E8
 Middlewich CW10..... 128 B5
 Newton-le-Willows WA12 ...2 B3
 Northwich CW9....... 104 F6
 Runcorn WA7.......... 23 A3
 Sandbach CW11....... 174 E8
 Talke ST7............ 210 D5
King Street Trad Est
 CW10................ 128 C2
KINGSWAY............. 23 A8
Kingsway Bollington SK10..87 E7
 Chester CH2.......... 118 F5
 Crewe CW2........... 190 B2
 Frodsham WA6.........74 B8
 Heswall CH60......... 41 C6
 Newton-le-Willows WA12 ...2 C2
 Northwich CW9....... 104 B8
 Widnes WA8........... 13 A1
 Winsford CW7........ 126 F1
Kingsway Ho WA4.......16 F4
Kingsway La WA16.......16 F4
Kingsway N WA1........16 F6
Kingsway W CH1...... 118 E4
Kingswood 5 WA1, WA4 . 16 F4
Kingswood W CH1..... 118 E4
KINGSWOOD Frodsham . 74 C1
 Warrington..........7 B2
Kingswood Kidsgrove ST7. 195 B1

Kingswood continued
 Warrington WA5...........7 B2
Kingswood Dr
 Chorlton CW2......... 207 B3
 Saughall CH1.......... 94 C1
Kingswood Cres CW10.. 151 E5
Kingswood La CH1...... 94 C1
Kingswood Pk WA6..... 99 D7
Kingswood Rd WA5.......7 A2
Kings Wood Wlk CW6 . 122 D5
Kinloch Cl Crewe CW1.. 190 B6
 Halewood L26......... 21 A7
Kinnerley Rd CH65...... 70 A3
Kinnersley Ave ST7.... 210 F8
Kinnersley St 1 ST7... 195 A3
Kinnerton Cl CH4...... 140 E5
KINNERTON GREEN..... 161 B7
Kinnerton Hts CH4.... 161 A7
Kinnerton La CH4..... 161 A8
Kinnerton Rd CH4..... 162 A7
Kinnington Way CW1....94 F7
Kinnock Pk WA5..........6 E6
Kinross Cl WA2..........8 F4
Kinsale Dr WA3..........9 C4
KINSEY HEATH......... 230 B1
Kinsey Rd CH65........ 70 D1
Kinsey's La CH2........71 F6
Kinsey St ST7......... 156 E2
Kintore Cl Bebington CH63 . 43 C4
 Winsford CW7........ 127 A3
Kintore Dr WA5....... 14 D6
Kintyre Cl CH65........ 70 C1
Kipling Ave WA2.........8 C1
Kipling Cres WA8.......22 F8
Kipling Rd CH1........ 117 F5
Kipling Way CW1...... 190 F4
Kirby Cl CH2.......... 118 D5
Kirkacre Ave WA12......7 C8
Kirkby Rd WA3..........4 F3
Kirkcaldy Ave WA5..... 14 D6
Kirkfell Dr SK6.........37 E8
Kirkham Ave WA3........3 E6
Kirkham Cl WA5........15 B4
Kirkham Rd Gatley SK8.. 34 C8
 Widnes WA8........... 13 C2
Kirkstall Cl
 Macclesfield SK10......87 B2
 Poynton SK12.......... 36 D4
Kirkstead Rd SK8....... 35 C6
Kirkstead Way WA3.......3 A8
Kirkstone Ave WA2.......8 C2
Kirkstone Cres WA7..... 50 A4
Kirkstone Ct CW12.... 156 A1
Kirkwall Dr WA5....... 15 A3
Kirkwood Cl CH3..... 119 A2
Kirtley Dr 5 WA12.......2 D1
Kishfield La SK23....... 65 A6
Kitchener Ave M44..... 11 C4
Kitchener Rd CW1..... 190 F6
Kitchen St CH1........ 118 B1
Kite Gr ST7........... 195 D3
Kitfield Ave CW10..... 151 D7
KITT'S MOSS........... 35 D6
Kitt's Moss La SK7...... 35 D6
Knap The CH60........ 41 A6
Knarr Rd SK11........ 138 C4
Knebworth Ct CW12... 179 B8
Knight Rd WA5...........6 F6
Knightsbridge Ave
 1 Northwich CW9.... 103 E3
 Warrington WA4....... 17 C2
Knightsbridge Cl
 13 Handforth SK9..... 34 D1
 Widnes WA8........... 13 D4
Knightsbridge Ct
 Chester CH4.......... 237 C2
 Warrington WA1....... 16 A5
Knights Cl 2 WA8.......13 C4
Knight's Cl SK11...... 112 E7
Knight's Grange (Sports
 Complex) CW7........ 126 B3
Knights La CW6....... 123 E1
Knights Mdw CW7..... 126 C3
Knight St SK11........ 112 E7
Knights Way CW2..... 206 B3
Knightwake Rd SK22.... 39 A8
Knole Ave SK12........36 F4
Knolls Green WA16......58 E3
Knoll Cl SK22..........39 B8
Knoll The WA7..........49 F7
KNOTBURY............ 138 F5
Knotbury Edge La SK17.. 138 F5
Knottingley Dr CH66.... 69 C5
Knotting Rd SK11..... 113 B3
Knott Mill Way WA7.... 24 A2
Knott's Hos WN7..........4 B8
Knotty La CW12....... 179 F8
Knowe The CH64....... 68 A8
Knowle Cl CH66.........69 E3
Knowle Gn SK9........ 34 C3
Knowle Pk SK9......... 34 C3
Knowles Ind Est SK23... 39 D3
Knowles St 2 WA8..... 13 C2
Knowl Hey Rd L26..... 21 A6
Knowl La CH3......... 180 E5
Knowl The CH3....... 180 F5
Knowsley Ave WA3.......3 B8
Knowsley Ct CH2...... 118 F2
Knowsley Expressway L35,
 WA8.................21 E8
Knowsley La ST7...... 194 F4
Knowsley Rd Chester CH2. 118 F4
 Hazel Grove SK7.......36 F8
 Macclesfield SK11..... 112 C5
KNUTSFORD........... 57 A3
Knutsford Acad WA16 . 56 E1
Knutsford District Com Hospl
 WA16.................56 F1

Knutsford Heritage Ctr★
 WA16................. 57 A2
Knutsford High Sch WA16.. 56 F1
Knutsford L Ctr WA16.... 56 A1
Knutsford Old Rd WA4.... 17 A2
Knutsford Rd Alsager ST7. 193 F6
 Antrobus CW9......... 53 D4
 Chelford SK11......... 84 A2
 Grappenhall WA4...... 17 C1
 Great Budworth CW9... 54 A2
 Holmes Chapel CW4... 130 B5
 Mobberley WA16.......57 F4
 Row-of-Trees SK9, WA16 . 59 D3
 Warrington WA4....... 16 E3
Knutsford Road Wlk 12
 SK11................ 112 E7
Knutsford Sta WA16.... 57 A1
Knutsford View WA15... 32 C8
Knutsford Way CH1.... 117 F2
Kohima Cres CH3..... 142 B5
Kronsbec Ave CH66..... 69 D6
KUS Ind Est CH5..... 139 A6
Kydds Wynt 6 WA6.....74 B8
Kynaston Dr CH4...... 140 C7

L

Laburnum Ave
 Crewe CW2........... 189 F2
 2 Nantwich CW5..... 204 F5
 Warrington WA1....... 17 C7
Laburnum Cl
 Congleton CW12...... 156 A4
 Talke ST7............ 210 E8
Laburnum Cres CW8.....78 B3
Laburnum Ct Lymm WA13... 19 B4
 Wistaston CW2........ 205 F7
Laburnum Farm Cl CH64.. 67 A5
Laburnum Gr Crewe CW1. 190 D6
 Ellesmere Port CH66.... 95 A8
 Runcorn WA7......... 49 C7
 Saltney CH4.......... 140 E6
 Weaverham CW8...... 102 D8
Laburnum La
 Altrincham WA15........31 E8
 Warrington WA5...... 14 C5
Laburnum Pl ST5...... 210 E1
Laburnum Rd
 Davenham CW9....... 103 F2
 Golborne WA3..........3 F7
 Irlam M44............. 11 D5
 Macclesfield SK11..... 112 E5
 Northwich CW9....... 104 C6
Laburnum Way LL13.... 180 D1
Lacey Av SK9.......... 34 B1
Lacey Ct Handforth SK9... 34 B1
 Widnes WA8........... 23 B7
Lacey Gn SK9.......... 34 B1
Lacey Gr SK9.......... 34 C1
LACEY GREEN.......... 34 B1
Lacey Green Prim Sch
 SK9..................34 B1
Lacey St WA8......... 23 A7
LACH DENNIS......... 105 D5
LACHE............... 140 F5
Lache Hall Cres CH4... 140 F4
Lache La
 Chester, Westminster Park
 CH4................ 141 B5
 Roughhill CH4........ 140 E3
Lache Park Ave CH4.... 141 A6
Lache Prim Sch CH4.... 141 A5
Lacy Ct CW12......... 156 F2
Ladies Mile WA16.......56 F2
Ladies Wlk CH64........66 E8
Ladies' Wlk WA9.........6 A3
Lady Acre Cl WA13..... 18 D2
Ladybarn Ave WA3.......2 F7
Ladybarn Cres SK7...... 35 F6
Ladybarn Manor SK7.... 35 F8
Ladybrook Gr 6 SK9... 34 D2
Ladybrook Prim Sch 1
 SK7..................35 F7
Ladycroft Cl WA1...... 17 C7
Ladyfield St SK9........60 B7
Ladyfield Terr SK9..... 60 C7
Lady Helen Wlk CW5 . 204 E6
Lady Heyes Crafts & Antiques
 Ctr★ WA6............74 F4
Lady La Croft WA3.......9 C8
 Culcheth WA3...........4 C1
 Mobberley WA16...... 58 C6
Lady Mary's Sq WA16... 30 E3
Ladypit Rd SK23....... 39 E4
Ladypool L24.......... 21 C2
Lady Richeld Cl WA7.... 24 D3
Ladys Cl SK12......... 36 E4
Ladythorn Cres SK7.... 35 F6
Ladythorn Gr SK7...... 35 F6
Ladythorn Rd SK7...... 35 F6
Ladywood Rd WA5.......7 D1
Lagos Gr CW2......... 126 E2
Laidon Ave CW2...... 206 A7
Laira Ct WA2.......... 16 C7
Laira St WA2.......... 16 C7
Lake House Cl CW8..... 77 D1
Lake La WA4...........52 F5
Lakelands Cl SK10..... 112 F7
Lakemore Ctry Pk★
 CW1................ 174 C1
Lakenheath Cres WA5... 14 F8
Lakeside Bosley SK11... 158 D8
 Chester CH4.......... 141 D4
 Wilmslow/Alderley Edge
 SK9................. 59 C7
Lakeside Cl Chester CH2.. 118 F7
 Widnes WA8........... 22 A8

Lakeside Dr Poynton SK12 . .36 E5
 Warrington WA1 . . . . 16 A3
Lakeside Rd WA13 . . . . . . 18 D2
Lakeside View
 Moulton CW7 . . . . 126 F7
 Nantwich CW5 . . . . 204 E3
Lake View Alsager ST7 . . 193 C2
 Congleton CW12 . . . . 156 B2
 Furness Vale SK23 . . . . 39 D4
Lakewood CH4 . . . . 141 B2
Laleston Cl WA8 . . . . .22 E8
Lamaload Rd
 Brookhouse SK10 . . . . .88 F3
 Yearns Low SK10 . . . . .89 A3
Lambert Cres CW5 . . . . . 204 C6
Lambert's La CW12 . . . . . 156 E1
Lambert Way CW8 . . . . . 103 A4
Lamb La WA14 . . . . 31 D4
Lambourn Ave WA8 . . . . . 12 C5
Lambourn Cl SK12 . . . . 36 C5
Lambourn Dr CW1 . . . . . 173 B1
Lambourne Cl
 4 Ellesmere Port CH66 . . . .94 F8
 Wythenshawe M22. . . . . . 33 D8
Lambourne Gr
 1 Middlewich CW10 . . 128 C1
 St Helens WA9 . . . . .1 A4
Lambs House Sch CW12 . 156 F4
Lambsickle Cl WA7. . . . . . .48 F6
Lambsickle La WA7 . . . . . . 49 A6
Lambs La WA1 . . . . 17 A7
Lamb St Hartford CW8 . . 103 D4
 Kidsgrove ST7 . . . . 195 A2
Lamerton Cl WA5 . . . . 14 D4
Lamerton Way SK9 . . . . . . 34 E2
Lampeter Cl WA5 . . . . .7 E2
Lampits La CH3 . . . . 120 E6
Lamport Cl WA8 . . . . 13 E3
Lamprey Rd CH65 . . . . 70 A7
Lanark Gdns WA8 . . . . 12 E3
Lanark Wlk SK10 . . . . .86 F2
Lancashire Rd M31 . . . . . . .11 E2
Lancaster Ave
 Golborne WA3 . . . . .3 C8
 Runcorn WA7 . . . . .48 E8
 Widnes WA8. . . . . 12 A2
Lancaster Cl
 Hazel Grove SK7. . . . . 36 D8
 Newton-le-Willows WA12 . . .1 F4
 Warrington WA2 . . . . .8 F2
 Winsford CW7 . . . . 149 D6
Lancaster Cres CH65 . . . 103 A5
Lancaster Ct 3 WA4 . . . .16 E1
Lancaster Dr CH3 . . . . . . 119 B2
Lancaster Fields CW1 . . 191 A2
Lancaster Gdns CH65. . . . 70 D3
Lancaster Pk CH4 . . . . . . 139 A3
Lancaster Rd
 Handforth SK9. . . . . .34 E1
 Irlam M44 . . . . 11 D5
 Widnes WA8. . . . . 13 B3
Lancaster St WA5 . . . . 15 E5
Lanceley Ct SY14 . . . . . . 213 B3
Lancelyn Dr SK9 . . . . 60 D8
Lancers Croft CH66. . . . . .69 E1
Lancing Ave WA2 . . . . .8 A4
Lancing Rd CH65 . . . . 70 C4
Land Cut La WA3 . . . . .9 D3
Lander Cl WA5 . . . . 15 D7
Land La SK9 . . . . 60 C6
Landor Cl WA3 . . . . .3 E8
Landscape Dene WA6 . . . 73 D4
Landseer Ave Neston CH64. .66 F7
 Warrington WA4 . . . . .16 B2
Landseer Dr SK10 . . . . . . 111 E8
Landsend Farm La CW9. . . .54 F3
Landswood Pk CW8 . . . . 103 B4
Lane End Farm La SY14 . . 211 E3
LANE ENDS 173 D3
Lane Ends WA8 . . . . 21 D5
LANE HEAD 3 E6
Lane Head Ave WA3 . . . . . .3 F8
Lanehead Rd SK23 . . . . . . 65 C5
Laneside Rd SK22 . . . . . . .39 E7
Lane The SY13, SY14 . . . . 223 C3
Langcliffe Cl WA3 . . . . .4 E3
Langdale Ave WA3 . . . . . . .18 F4
Langdale Cl High Lane SK6 . .37 E8
 Macclesfield SK11 . . . . . . 111 F5
 Warrington WA2 . . . . .8 A2
 Widnes WA8. . . . . 22 C8
 Winsford CW7 . . . . 126 D2
Langdale Rd Bramhall SK7 . 35 C5
 Crewe CW2 . . . . 189 D2
 Partington M31 . . . . .11 E3
 Runcorn WA7 . . . . .23 B1
Langdale Way WA6. . . . . . 49 C1
Langden Cl WA3 . . . . .4 D4
Langdon Ho CH4 . . . . 141 B7
Langfield WA3 . . . . .3 E7
Langfield Gr CH62. . . . . . . 43 D5
Langford L24 . . . . 21 C2
Langford Ct CH3 . . . . 121 C2
Langford Gr CW9 . . . . 80 A3
Langford St 21 SK11 . . . 112 C8
Langford Way WA4 . . . . . . 27 D4
Langland Cl WA5. . . . . .7 E2
LANGLEY 113 C3
Langley Ave WA12. . . . . . . .2 C1
Langley Beck WA8 . . . . . . 13 C4
Langley Cl
 Newcastle-under-Lyme
 ST5 . . . . 210 D1
 Sandbach CW11. . . . . 175 C8
Langley Ct CH65 . . . . .70 E3
Langley Dr Crewe CW2 . . 190 A2
 Handforth SK9 . . . . .34 E3

Langley Dr continued
 Macclesfield SK11 . . . . 112 B4
Langley Hall Cl SK11. . . . 113 B4
Langley Hall Cotts SK11 . 113 B4
Langley Rd Langley SK11. . 113 A3
 Northwich CW9 . . . . 104 A6
Langport Dr CH3 . . . . 119 C2
Langton Cl
 Newton-le-Willows WA12 . . .2 A4
 Widnes WA8. . . . . 12 B3
Langton Gn WA1 . . . . 17 D7
Langwell Cl WA3 . . . . 10 A5
Lanreath Cl SK10. . . . . 86 D1
Lansbrook Ct SK8. . . . . . . 35 C7
Lansdown Culcheth WA3. . . . .4 E2
 Frodsham WA6. . . . . 74 D6
Lansdowne Gr CH4 . . . . . 141 A7
Lansdowne Rd
 Connah's Quay CH5 . . . . . . 91 D1
 Crewe CW1 . . . . 190 F5
 Great Barrow CH3 . . . . . . 120 D3
Lansdowne St SK10 . . . . . .87 E1
Lansdown Rd CH4. . . . . . . 139 B4
Lanyard Way CW11 . . . . . 175 C3
Lapwing Cl Golborne WA3. . .3 D8
 Newton-le-Willows WA12 . . .2 C3
 Packmoor ST7 . . . . 195 E1
 Winsford CW7 . . . . 149 C5
Lapwing Dr CW12 . . . . . . 156 D5
Lapwing Gr WA7 . . . . 50 A6
Lapwing La Moore WA4. . . 25 A8
 Whisterfield SK11 . . . . . . 109 C4
Lapwing Rd ST7. . . . . 195 D3
Lapwing Rise CH60 . . . . . .40 F6
Lapwing Way 3 CH64 . . . 66 D7
Larch Ave Hough CW2 . . . 206 F5
 Macclesfield SK11 . . . . . . 112 A5
 Newton-le-Willows WA12 . . .2 C2
 Warrington WA5 . . . . .14 E5
 Widnes WA8. . . . . 13 B2
Larch Cl Golborne WA3 . . . .3 F6
 Poynton SK12. . . . . .36 F3
 Runcorn WA7 . . . . .49 C7
 Weaverham CW8 . . . . . . 102 D7
Larchdale Cl CH66. . . . . . . .94 F8
Larch Dr CW11 . . . . 175 D6
Larches The WA16 . . . . .58 E2
Larchfields CH1. . . . . 117 A8
Larch Pl CW12 . . . . 155 E4
Larch Rd Crewe CW2 . . . . 189 E2
 Haydock WA11 . . . . .1 E7
 Partington M31 . . . . .11 E3
 Runcorn WA7 . . . . .49 C7
Larch Rise SK10 . . . . 86 D6
Larchtree Cl WA8 . . . . .78 B4
Larchway Bramhall SK7 . . . 35 C7
 High Lane SK6 . . . . .37 F7
Larch Way CH4 . . . . 140 E6
Larchways WA4. . . . . 26 D5
Larchwood Dr SK9 . . . . . . .60 E8
LARDEN GREEN 202 D4
Lark Ave ST7. . . . . 195 D3
Larkfield ST7. . . . . 195 B1
Larkfield Ave WA1 . . . . . . 17 A7
Lark Hall Cl SK11. . . . . . . 113 A7
Lark Hall Cres SK10 . . . . . 113 A8
Lark Hall Rd SK10 . . . . . . 113 A7
Lark Hill Cotts SK22 . . . . 39 A8
Larkspur Cl Chester CH4. . 140 F4
 Nantwich CW5 . . . . 204 E8
 Runcorn WA7 . . . . .49 F4
Larkspur Dr SK10 . . . . .15 E3
Larkstoke Cl WA4 . . . . .26 E6
Larksway CH60 . . . . .41 B8
Larkwood Way SK10. . . . . .87 E5
Larne Cl WA8 . . . . 12 E2
Larne Dr CH4 . . . . 139 D4
Laskey La WA4. . . . . .17 F4
LATCHFORD 16 C3
Latchford Rd CH60 . . . . . . .41 B6
Latchford St James CE Sch
 WA4. . . . . .16 B4
Latchford St WA4 . . . . 17 A3
Lately Comm WA3. . . . . . . .5 B8
Latham Ave Helsby WA6. . . .73 B1
 Newton-le-Willows WA12 . . .2 C4
Latham Ho WA12. . . . . .2 B4
Latham Rd CW11. . . . . 175 A5
Latham St CW7 . . . . 126 C1
Lathom Ave WA2. . . . . . . .16 B8
Lathom Rd M44 . . . . .11 F8
Lathom Way SK10. . . . . . . .87 F2
Latimer Dr CW2. . . . . 190 A4
Latimer Rd WA8 . . . . 13 C4
Launceston Cl
 Runcorn WA7 . . . . 50 C6
 Winsford CW7 . . . . 149 B7
Launceston Dr
 Bramhall SK7. . . . . .35 F7
 Warrington WA5 . . . . .14 E3
Laura St CW2 . . . . 190 D1
Laurel Ave
 Newton-le-Willows WA12 . . .2 D3
 Warrington WA1 . . . . 17 D7
Laurel Bank
 Warrington WA4 . . . . 17 C1
 Widnes WA8. . . . . 13 A3
 Winsford CW7 . . . . 149 D8
Laurel Bank Cl CH2. . . . . . .95 F1
Laurel Ct Barnton CW8. . . . .78 A4
 Middlewich CW10 . . . . . . 128 B2
 Sandbach CW11. . . . . 175 C5
Laurel Dr Crewe CW2. . . . 189 F2
 Ellesmere Port CH65 . . . . . .70 B2
 Harriseahead ST7 . . . . . . 195 E4
 Willaston CH64 . . . . .43 B1

Laurel Gr Chester CH2 . . . . 119 A3
 Golborne WA3 . . . . .3 D8
Laurel Pk CW6 . . . . 145 A6
Laurel Pl CW5 . . . . 204 D7
Laurels Farm Ct CH2 . . . . .72 B3
Laurels The High Lane SK6 . .37 E8
 Milton Green CH3. . . . . . . 165 C2
 5 Wincham CW9 . . . . . . 79 C3
Laurel Way SK8 . . . . 35 C8
Laurel Wlk M31 . . . . 11 E2
Laurelwood Dr 4 CH66. . . .69 E1
Laureston Ave CW1 . . . . . 190 F4
Lavender Cl WA7. . . . . 23 C1
Lavender Dr CW9 . . . . 104 E7
Lavender Gdns
 St Helens WA9 . . . . .6 A7
 Warrington WA5 . . . . .15 E4
Lavender Wlk M31 . . . . 11 E2
Lavenham Cl
 Hazel Grove SK7. . . . . .36 E8
 Macclesfield SK10 . . . . . . 87 C2
Laverne Dr WA5. . . . . .15 B6
LAVISTER 162 C1
Lavister Cl 6 CW9 . . . . . 103 F4
Lavister Wlks LL12 . . . . . . 162 C1
Lawford Cl WA1. . . . . 189 F8
Lawford Dr CH60 . . . . 41 C8
Lawn Ave WA1. . . . . .16 F8
Lawn Dr CH2. . . . . 118 D7
Lawnhurst Cl
 Sandbach CW11. . . . . 175 A3
 Stanley Green SK8 . . . . .34 F7
Lawns Ave CH63 . . . . .43 B6
Lawnsdale CW8. . . . . 101 D5
Lawns Rd SK7. . . . . 35 A8
Lawns The WA5 . . . . .59 E4
Lawnswood Gr CH2 . . . . . .72 B3
Lawrence Ave
 3 Middlewich CW10 . . . 128 C1
 Moulton CW9 . . . . 126 E8
Lawrence Avenue E 2
 CW10. . . . . 128 C1
Lawrence Cl
 Cranage CW4. . . . . 130 A5
 3 Sandbach CW11. . . . . 174 D6
Lawrence Pl SK12. . . . . 36 D2
 Sandycroft CH5 . . . . 116 A3
Lawrence St Crewe CW1. . 190 C4
 Warrington WA5 . . . . .15 F5
Law St CH2 . . . . 118 F3
 Lawton Ave Bramhall SK7. . .35 E8
 Lawton-gate ST7 . . . . 194 D3
Lawton Cl WA3 . . . . .4 E3
Lawton Coppice ST7 . . . . 194 E4
LAWTON-GATE 194 A4
Lawtongate Est ST7 . . . . . 194 A5
Lawton Hall ST7 . . . . 194 E4
Lawton Hall Dr ST7 . . . . . 194 C4
LAWTON HEATH 193 E6
LAWTON HEATH END . . . 193 C6
Lawton Heath Rd ST7. . . . 193 F5
Lawton Rd ST7. . . . . 193 E4
Lawton St
 Congleton CW12 . . . . 156 E2
 Crewe CW2 . . . . 190 C3
 Kidsgrove ST7 . . . . 195 C4
Lawton Way CW11 . . . . . . 174 E7
Laxey Ave WA1. . . . . 17 D6
Laxton Cl CH66. . . . . .94 F8
Laxton Way CW10 . . . . . . 128 C2
Layland Ave WA3 . . . . .4 E4
Layton Cl WA3 . . . . .9 E3
Lea Ave Crewe CW1 . . . . . 190 F4
 Goostrey CW4 . . . . 107 C1
Lea Bank Cl SK11. . . . . 112 A8
Lea Cl CW11 . . . . 175 C5
Leacroft Rd WA3 . . . . 10 A7
Lea Cross Gr WA8. . . . . . . 12 C3
Leadbeaters Cl SK11 . . . . 112 F7
Leadbeaters Rd SK11. . . . . 112 F7
Leadgate La CH3. . . . . 144 F2
Lea Dr Nantwich CW5. . . . 204 C6
 Wimboldsley CW10 . . . . . 151 A4
Leadsmithy St CW10. . . . . 128 C1
Leadworks La CH1 . . . . . . 237 C3
Leaf Gr CW7 . . . . 126 B1
Leafield Dr SK8 . . . . 38 C6
Leafield Rd SK12 . . . . 38 C6
Leaf La CW7 . . . . 127 A2
Leafy Way CW8 . . . . 102 D7
Lea Gn Cl 8 WA3 . . . . .3 C7
LEA GREEN 172 A8
Lea Hall Barns CW5 . . . . . 220 E6
Lea Hall Pk CH1 . . . . 95 A3
Lea Homes CW5 . . . . 217 B7
Leahurst Cl CH2. . . . . 118 F4
Lea La CH3 . . . . 164 C3
Leaman Rd CW1 . . . . 191 E5
Leamington Ave WA12. . . . .2 C1
Leamington Rd
 Neston CH64 . . . . .66 E6
 Warrington WA5 . . . . 15 A8
Lear Dr CW2 . . . . 205 F8
Learners Way 4 CH4. . . . 140 F7
Leas Cl 3 CH66 . . . . 69 C5
Leaside WA7. . . . . 23 D1
Leaside Rd CH1 . . . . 117 E6
Leaside Way SK9. . . . . 60 C6
Lea's Pas CW10 . . . . 128 B1
Lea St Moss Bank WA8 . . . . 23 C8
 New Mills SK22 . . . . 39 A8
Leatham Cl WA3. . . . . .9 E3
Leathers La L26 . . . . 21 A7

Lea Way ST7. . . . . 193 D3
Leawood Cl CW8 . . . . 103 A6
Ledbury Dr CW2 . . . . 206 A7
Ledge Ley SK8 . . . . .34 E8
Ledger Rd WA11 . . . . .1 A5
Ledley St SK10 . . . . .87 F7
LEDSHAM 68 F2
Ledsham Cl WA3 . . . . .9 C3
Ledsham Ct CH66. . . . . . . .69 B6
Ledsham Hall La CH66 . . . .68 E4
Ledsham La CH66 . . . . .68 F3
Ledsham Park Dr CH66 . . . 69 A6
Ledsham Rd CH66. . . . . . . .69 B6
Ledsham Village CH66. . . . .68 F2
Ledston Cl WA7. . . . . 24 D1
Ledward St CW7 . . . . 127 A1
Ledyard St WA5 . . . . 15 D7
Leech Rd SY14 . . . . 213 B3
Lee Cl WA16. . . . . .56 F1
Lee Ct Runcorn WA7 . . . . . 23 D2
 Warrington WA2 . . . . .8 C2
Lee Dr CW8. . . . . 103 E7
Lee Green La CW5 . . . . . . 150 A1
Leek Old Rd SK11 . . . . 112 E2
Leek Rd CW12 . . . . 179 A8
Leen La CH1 . . . . 237 B2
Lee Pl CW11 . . . . 152 C2
Lee Rd WA5 . . . . .15 B6
Lees La
 Ellesmere Port CH65 . . . . . .70 E4
 Mottram St Andrew SK10. . .61 B7
 Neston CH64 . . . . 67 A7
Lees Mill 4 SK22. . . . . 39 C7
Lees Rd SK7. . . . . 35 C5
Lees The WA5 . . . . 15 A8
LEFTWICH 104 B5
Leftwich Com Prim Sch
 CW9 . . . . 104 A4
Leftwich Warehouse
 CW9. . . . . 103 F7
Legend St CH4 . . . . 141 B4
Legh Cl SK12 . . . . .36 E4
Legh Ct Golborne WA3 . . . . .3 A8
 Knutsford WA16 . . . . 57 D4
Legh Gdns WA16 . . . . .57 B1
Legh Ho 2 WA16 . . . . .57 B1
Legh Rd Adlington SK10 . . . 62 C5
 Haydock WA11 . . . . 1 B6
 High Lane SK12 . . . . 38 A6
 Knutsford WA16 . . . . .82 B8
 Prestbury SK10 . . . . 87 A8
Legh St Golborne WA3 . . . . .3 A8
 3 Lymm WA13 . . . . .18 E3
 Newton-le-Willows WA12 . . .2 A3
 Warrington WA1 . . . . 16 A3
Legh Vale Prim Sch WA11 . .1 B6
Leicester Ave ST7 . . . . . . 193 D5
Leicester St
 Northwich CW9 . . . . 79 A1
 Warrington WA5 . . . . .15 F5
Leigh Ave Knutsford WA16 . 57 C2
 Widnes WA8. . . . . 13 A1
Leigh Green Cl 4 WA8 . . . 22 C8
Leigh La CW8 . . . . 77 C5
Leigh Rd Congleton CW12 . 157 B5
 Wilmslow SK9 . . . . 59 D5
Leigh's Brow CW8. . . . . . . .77 F3
Leigh St SK11 . . . . 112 E7
Leighstone Ct CH2 . . . . . . 237 A4
Leighton Chase CH64. . . . . 41 D1
Leighton Cotts CH64 . . . . . 41 D5
Leighton Ct CH64 . . . . 66 D8
Leighton Dr WN7. . . . . .4 B8
Leighton Hospl CW1 . . . . 172 E1
Leighton Prim Sch CW1 . 189 F8
Leighton Rd CH64 . . . . 41 D2
Leighton St 11 CW1 . . . . 190 B5
Leightons The CH64. . . . . . 66 D8
Leighton View CW1 . . . . . 190 A8
Leigh Way CW8 . . . . 77 C1
Leinster Gdns WA7. . . . . . 22 F3
Leinster St WA7. . . . . 22 F3
Leira Way WA7. . . . . 23 A2
Leiria Way WA7. . . . . 23 B2
Lenham Wlk M22 . . . . 33 D8
Lenthall Ave CW12 . . . . . . 178 F8
Leonard St Chester CH1 . . 118 B3
 Runcorn WA7 . . . . 48 D7
 Warrington WA2 . . . . 16 C7
 Warrington, Stockton Heath
 WA4 . . . . 16 C1
Leon Cl WA5. . . . . 14 D7
Leslie Rd CW7 . . . . 149 A7
Leslie Weston Cl 1
 CW2. . . . . 206 D7
Lessingham Rd WA8 . . . . . 12 F3
Lester Cl ST7 . . . . 193 D4
Lesters La CH4. . . . . 139 F2
Leven Ave CW7 . . . . 126 F2
Levens Cl WA5. . . . . .15 F6
Levens Way 1 WA8 . . . . . 22 C8
Leven Wlk CH66. . . . . 70 A7
Leveret Rd L24. . . . . 21 A3
Levisham Gdns WA5. . . . . . 15 E7
Lewin St CW10 . . . . 128 C1
Lewis Ave WA5 . . . . .7 F2
Lewis Cl
 Ellesmere Port CH65 . . . . . 95 C8
 Nantwich CW5 . . . . 205 A5
Lewis Cres WA8. . . . . 23 A7
Lewis Gr WA8 . . . . 12 D1
Lewis St CW1 . . . . 190 C3
Lexden St WA5. . . . . .15 E6
Lexington Wlk 2 WA5. . . . 15 C7
Leycester Cl WA16 . . . . . . .82 C8
Leycester Dr WA16 . . . . . . .57 F7

Leycester Rd WA16. . . . . . .82 B8
Leyfield Ct CH4 . . . . 140 F5
Leyland Dr CH4 . . . . 140 C6
Leyland Gr
 Haslington CW1 . . . . 191 C4
 Haydock WA11 . . . . .1 B6
Leyland Wlk CW7 . . . . 149 C6
Leyton Cl WA7. . . . . .49 B6
Liberation Rd 3 WA12 . . . .2 D1
Liberty Cl WA5 . . . . 15 C7
Libris Ho 1 WA16. . . . . . . .57 A1
Libris Pk 2 WA16 . . . . .57 A1
Libris Pl 3 WA16. . . . . .57 A1
Libson Cl WA2 . . . . .9 A3
Lichfield Ave Golborne WA3. .3 D8
 Grappenhall Heys WA4. . . . 27 A7
Lichfield Cl WA16 . . . . 57 D2
Lichfield Ct 7 CW7 . . . . . 149 D7
Lichfield Dr CH66 . . . . .94 E8
Lichfield Rd Blacon CH1 . . 117 F5
 Talke ST7 . . . . 210 D7
Lichfield St CW10 . . . . 128 D2
Lidgetts La SK10 . . . . 88 C3
Lift La CW9 . . . . 78 D3
Light Alders La SK12 . . . . . 38 A6
Light Alders Lodge SK12. . 38 A6
Lightburn St 6 WA7. . . . . . 22 F1
Lightfoot Cl CH60. . . . . .41 B7
Lightfoot La Eaton CW6 . . 147 A4
 Heswall CH60 . . . . .41 B7
 Quarrybank CW6 . . . . 146 F5
Lightfoot St CH2 . . . . 118 F2
Lighthouse Rd L24. . . . . . . .47 E7
Lightley Cl CW11 . . . . 175 A4
Lightley Ct CW11 . . . . 175 A4
Light Oaks Rd WA3 . . . . . . .5 C6
LIGHTWOOD GREEN 229 B3
Lightwood Green Ave
 CW3. . . . . 229 A2
Lightwood Rd ST5. . . . . . . 210 D1
Lilac Ave Knutsford WA16 . .56 E1
 Warrington WA5 . . . . 15 A5
 Widnes WA8. . . . . 13 B2
Lilac Cl Kelsall CW6 . . . . . . 122 C2
 Newcastle-under-Lyme
 ST5. . . . . 210 D1
Lilac Cres WA7 . . . . .49 C8
Lilac Ct CW12 . . . . 156 E2
Lilac Dr CW8. . . . . 103 D6
Lilac Gr
 Ellesmere Port CH66 . . . . . 95 A8
 Warrington WA4 . . . . .16 E1
Lilac Wlk M31. . . . . .11 E3
Lilbourne Cl WA7 . . . . 24 C1
Lilford Ave WA5. . . . . .15 F8
Lilford Dr WA5. . . . . 14 F6
Lilford Sq SK11 . . . . 112 D5
Lilford St WA5 . . . . .15 F7
Lillyfield CH60 . . . . .40 F6
Lilybrook Dr WA16 . . . . . . .57 B1
Lily La CW10 . . . . 129 B6
Limbrick Rd ST7 . . . . 209 A1
Lime Ave Frodsham WA6. . . 74 C8
 Northwich CW9 . . . . 103 F5
 Weaverham CW8 . . . . . . 102 D8
 3 Widnes WA8 . . . . 13 B2
Lime Cl Hollinfare WA3. . . . 11 A2
 Middlewich CW10 . . . . . . 128 B2
 Sandbach CW11 . . . . 175 A7
 Tarporley CW6 . . . . 146 D2
Lime Ct Leftwich CW9. . . . 104 A4
 Northwich CW9 . . . . 103 F5
Lime Field SK10 . . . . 63 A1
Limefield Ave WA13 . . . . . .18 F2
Lime Gr Alsager ST7. . . . . . 193 C2
 Chester CH2. . . . . 119 A3
 Elton CH2 . . . . 72 A3
 Golborne WA3 . . . . .3 E6
 Macclesfield SK10 . . . . . . 112 E8
 Runcorn WA7 . . . . 49 C8
 Saltney CH4 . . . . 140 D6
 Shavington CW2 . . . . 206 C4
 Winsford CW7 . . . . 127 A1
Limehurst Gr CH62 . . . . . . 43 D6
Limekiln Farm La CW12. . 178 D3
Limekiln La WA5 . . . . .6 E3
Lime Kiln La ST7 . . . . 194 E2
Limekiln Row WA7 . . . . . . 50 A8
Limerick Cl WA8 . . . . 12 E3
Limes Cl CW1 . . . . 191 C4
Limes La WA4. . . . . 52 C6
Lime St Congleton CW12 . . 156 D2
 Crewe CW1 . . . . 190 C6
 Ellesmere Port CH65 . . . . . 70 C6
Limes The Culcheth WA3. . . .4 D4
 Golborne WA3 . . . . .3 D6
 Middlewich CW10 . . . . . . 128 B1
Lime Tree Ave
 Congleton CW12 . . . . 156 B3
 Crewe CW1 . . . . 190 E6
Lime Tree Cl
 Ellesmere Port CH66 . . . . . 95 A8
 Winsford CW7 . . . . 149 C8
Lime Tree Dr CH3 . . . . 180 F1
Lime Tree Gr CH60 . . . . 41 C8
Lime Tree La WA16. . . . . . . 29 D6
Limeways WA4 . . . . 25 D8
Lime Wlk 6 Handforth SK9. . 34 D1
 Partington M31 . . . . 11 D3
Lime Wood Cl CH2 . . . . . . 118 F4
Limewood Cres CW8 . . . . . .78 B4

Limewood Gr CW8 . . . . . . .78 B4
Linacre Cl CH65 . . . . . . 70 D5
Linacre La WA8 . . . . .12 E5
Lincoln Ave Gatley SK8 . . . .34 B7
  Irlam M44 . . . . 11 C4
Lincoln Cl Golborne WN7. . . . .4 C8
  Macclesfield SK10 . . . . . . .86 F2
  Rainow SK10 . . . . .88 E5
  Runcorn WA7 . . . . 49 C6
  Warrington WA1 . . . . .17 E6
Lincoln Ct Helsby WA6 . . . .73 B3
 5 Warrington WA5 . . . . . .15 B7
Lincoln Dr CH2. . . . . . . 119 A5
Lincoln Ho **12** CH1. . . . . 237 C3
Lincoln Pl SK10. . . . . .86 F2
Lincoln Rd Blacon CH1. . . 117 F5
  Ellesmere Port CH66 . . . . . 69 D3
  Handforth SK9. . . . . .34 E1
  Kidsgrove ST7 . . . . 194 F2
Lincoln Sq WA8 . . . . .13 B2
Lincoln St **3** CW1 . . . . . 190 B5
Lincoln Wlk SK10 . . . . . . .86 F2
Lincombe Hey WA6 . . . . 87 C8
Lincombe Rd M22 . . . . . . 33 D8
Lindale CW12 . . . . 157 A5
Linden Cl
  Congleton CW12 . . . . . . 179 A8
  Ellesmere Port CH66 . . . . . .94 F8
  Lymm WA13 . . . . 19 A4
  Warrington WA1 . . . . 17 D7
Linden Ct
  Macclesfield SK10 . . . . . . .87 B2
  Sandbach CW11. . . . . . . 174 F3
  Widnes WA8. . . . . .12 F4
Linden Dr Biddulph ST8 . . 179 C1
  Crewe CW1 . . . . 190 F4
  Helsby WA6 . . . . .73 B1
  Mickle Trafford CH2 . . . . . .96 F1
Linden Gr Biddulph ST8 . . 179 C1
  Bramhall SK7 . . . . 35 D4
  Chester CH2. . . . . 119 A4
  Saltney CH4 . . . . 140 D6
Linden Way High Lane SK6 . 38 A7
  Widnes WA8. . . . . .12 F4
Lindfield Cl WA4 . . . . 25 A5
Lindfield Estate N SK9. . . 60 A6
Lindfield Estate S SK9 . . . .59 F6
Lindfields CH4 . . . . 140 F6
Lindi Ave WA4 . . . . 17 C2
Lindisfarne Ave
  Ellesmere Port CH65 . . . . . 70 C2
  Golborne WA3. . . . . .4 C8
Lindisfarne Cl CW10. . . . 128 B1
Lindisfarne Ct
 4 Cronton WA8. . . . . . . .12 F6
  Widnes WA8. . . . . .12 F6
Lindisfarne Dr SK12 . . . . 36 D4
Lindley Ave WA4 . . . . . . .16 F4
Lindop Cl WA16 . . . . 57 C2
Lindow Comm Nature
  Reserve★ SK9. . . . . .59 E7
Lindow Com Prim Sch
  SK9. . . . . 59 D3
Lindow Court Pk WA16 . . .59 B5
Lindow Ct SK9. . . . . .59 E8
LINDOW END 59 E2
Lindow Fold Dr SK9 . . . . .59 D5
Lindow La SK9 . . . . 59 E6
Lindow Par SK9 . . . . .59 F6
Lindrick Cl SK10 . . . . . . 87 C4
Lindrum Ave SK11 . . . . . 112 D2
Lindsay Way ST7 . . . . . . 193 A4
Lindsay Wlk CW8. . . . . . 102 A4
Lindsworth Cl WA5 . . . . . 15 C6
Linear View WA12. . . . . . .2 C1
Linenhall Pl CH1 . . . . . . 237 A2
Lines Rd M44 . . . . .11 F8
Lingdale Wlk SK11 . . . . . 112 D5
Lingfield Cl SK10. . . . . . 87 C4
Lingfield Dr CW1. . . . . . 190 C7
Lingfield Ho WA7 . . . . . . .48 E8
Lingfield Rd WA7 . . . . . . .22 E1
LINGLEY GREEN 14 C7
Lingley Green Ave WA5 . . 14 D8
Lingley Mere Bsns Pk
  WA5 . . . . 14 D8
Lingley Rd WA5 . . . . 14 D6
Linglongs Ave SK23 . . . . 65 C5
Linglongs Rd SK23 . . . . . 65 C5
Lingmell Gdns CW4 . . . . 129 F3
Lingwell Ave WA8. . . . . . .12 E2
Lingwell Pk WA8. . . . . . . .12 E2
Lingwood Rd WA5 . . . . . .14 F6
Links Ave CH66 . . . . 69 C7
Links Cl CH63 . . . . .43 B6
Linkside Ave WA2. . . . . . . .8 B6
Linkside Way CH66 . . . . . .94 F8
Links Rd SK9. . . . . .59 E4
Links View CH66 . . . . . . 69 C7
Linksway Chester CH2 . . . 118 C7
  Congleton CW12 . . . . . . 178 E8
Linksway Cl CW12. . . . . . 178 F8
Link The SK9. . . . . .34 D3
Linkway WA7 . . . . 49 C8
Link Wlk M31 . . . . .11 D2
Linley Gr ST7 . . . . 193 F3
Linley La ST7 . . . . 194 A2
Linley Rd Alsager ST7 . . . 193 F2
  Cheadle SK8. . . . . .35 B8
  Talke ST7 . . . . 210 C8
Linley Trad Est ST7 . . . . 194 C1
Linmere Visitor Ctr★
  CW8 . . . . 100 B2
Linmere Wlk CW8. . . . . . 123 F6
Linnards La CW9, WA16 . . . .80 B5

Linnet Cl
  Newton-le-Willows WA12 . . . .2 C3
  Warrington WA3 . . . . .8 D3
  Winsford CW7 . . . . 150 B8
Linnet Gr
  Macclesfield SK10 . . . . . . 87 A1
  Warrington WA3 . . . . .9 E4
Linnets Pk WA7 . . . . 23 C3
Linnets Way CH60 . . . . . .40 E8
Linnett Cl CW1. . . . . . . 190 A7
Linnett Gr ST7 . . . . 195 E1
Linton Cl CW7 . . . . 127 A3
Lintott Gdns **6** WA1. . . . 16 C5
Linum Gdns WA9. . . . . . . .6 B7
Linwood CW7. . . . . 150 B8
Linwood Cl WA7 . . . . 50 C5
Lion Salt Works★ CW9. . . .79 C3
Lion St CW12. . . . . 156 D2
Liskeard Cl WA7 . . . . . . .50 B6
Liskeard Dr SK7. . . . . . . .35 F7
Lismore Wlk M22 . . . . . . 33 E8
Lister Cl CW10 . . . . 151 D6
Lister Rd WA7 . . . . 23 C3
Little Abbey Gateway
  CH1 . . . . 237 A3
Little Aston Cl SK10 . . . . 87 C4
Little Back La CW11 . . . . 176 E6
Little Birches CH65. . . . . 70 A6
LITTLE BOLLINGTON. . . .20 B2
Little Bollington CE Prim Sch
  WA14. . . . . .20 B2
Littlebourne WA7. . . . . . .50 E7
LITTLE BUDWORTH 147 F8
  Little Budworth Ctry Pk★
  CW6 . . . . 147 C8
Little Clover WA13 . . . . . 19 A4
Littlecote Gdns WA4 . . . . 26 D4
Little Cross Cl CW1. . . . . 190 D7
Littledale Rd WA5 . . . . . .14 F7
Littledales La CW8 . . . . . 102 E4
Little Delph WA11. . . . . . .1 C7
Littlegate WA7. . . . . .49 E8
Little Gn CH66 . . . . 69 D3
LITTLE HEATH. 230 A5
Little Heath Cl CW3 . . . . 230 A5
Little Heath La WA14 . . . . 20 D5
Little Heath Rd
  Chester CH3. . . . . 119 E1
  Christleton CH3 . . . . 142 E8
Little Hey **5** WA13 . . . . . .18 F4
Little La CH64 . . . . 41 C1
Little Lakes CW2 . . . . . . 207 D2
LITTLE LEIGH 77 C4
Little Leigh Prim Sch
  CW8 . . . . 77 D5
Little Lowes Mdw WA3 . . . .3 C7
Little Mdw **6** WA13 . . . . .18 F4
Little Meadow Cl
  Lower Heath CW12 . . . . . 156 E6
  Prestbury SK10 . . . . .87 B7
Little Meadow Pl **4**
  CW2. . . . . 206 D7
Little Mere CH3 . . . . 142 E8
Littlemore Rd **1** CW11 . . 152 C2
Little Moreton Hall★
  CW12 . . . . 177 E2
LITTLE-MOSS 194 E6
Little Moss Cl ST7 . . . . . 194 E5
Little Moss La ST7 . . . . . 194 E5
LITTLE NESTON 66 D6
LITTLER 126 A2
Little Rake La CH2. . . . . . 95 D5
Littler Cl CW8. . . . . .78 C1
Littler Grange Ct CW7 . . . 126 A1
Littler La CW7 . . . . 125 F1
Little Roodee CH5. . . . . . 139 B7
Little Row **5** ST7. . . . . . 195 B2
Little Rowley La WA16 . . . 29 D1
Littler Rd WA11 . . . . .1 A5
Little St John St CH1 . . . 237 B2
Little St Congleton CW12 . . 156 D2
 4 Macclesfield SK10. . . . 112 D8
LITTLE STANNEY 70 E1
Little Stanney La CH2. . . . .95 F8
Littlestone Cl WA8 . . . . . 13 A4
LITTLE SUTTON 69 B5
Little Sutton CE Prim Sch
  CH66. . . . . 69 A6
Little Sutton Sta CH66 . . . 69 C6
LITTLETON 119 E1
Littleton Cl
 1 Northwich CW9. . . . . . 103 F4
  Warrington WA5 . . . . 15 D4
Littleton La CH3. . . . . . . 119 E2
LITTLE TOWN 4 C1
Little Wissage CH66. . . . . .69 F2
Littondale Cl CW12. . . . . 157 A5
Liverpool Pl WA8 . . . . . . 12 C1
Liverpool Rd
  Backford CH1, CH2. . . . . . .95 B4
  Chester CH2. . . . . 118 C6
  Haydock WA11. . . . . .1 B8
  Haydock, Stanley Bank WA11. .1 A7
  Irlam, Cadishead M44 . . . . 11 D4
  Kidsgrove ST7 . . . . 195 A1
  Neston CH64 . . . . .41 F1
  Newcastle-under-Lyme
    ST5 . . . . 210 D2
  Warrington WA5, WA1. . . . . 15 F5
  Warrington, Great Sankey
    WA5 . . . . .14 E6
  Warrington, Penketh WA5 . . 15 B4
  Widnes WA8. . . . . .12 C1
Liverpool Road E ST7 . . . 194 E2
Liverpool Road W ST7 . . . 194 B4
Liverpool Row WA12 . . . . .7 D8
Liverpool St CW9 . . . . . . 104 C8
Livesley Rd SK10 . . . . . . .87 E5

Livingstone Cl
  Macclesfield SK10 . . . . . . 111 F8
Livingstone Rd CH65 . . . . 70 C7
Livingstone Way CW10 . . 151 D6
Liz Kaye Ho SK11 . . . . . . 112 E7
Llandaff Cl CH66 . . . . . . .69 E1
Llandovery Cl CW7 . . . . . 149 B7
Lloyd Cl CH3 . . . . 180 E2
Lloyd Cres WA12. . . . . . . .1 F3
Lloyd Dr CH65. . . . . 70 D1
Lloyd Jones Rd CW1. . . . 191 E5
Lloyd Pl CH1 . . . . 117 E4
Llyndir La
  Burton Green LL12. . . . . . 161 E2
  Lavister LL12 . . . . 162 B1
Llys Bernsdale/Bernsdale Ct
  CH5 . . . . 116 A3
Llys Cadnant/Cadnant Ct
  CH4 . . . . 139 D5
Llys Caer/Chester Ct
  CH5 . . . . 139 A3
Llys Catrin/Catherine Ct
  CH5 . . . . 139 B6
Llys Derwen CH4. . . . . . 161 A8
Llys Maes Y Ffynnon/
  Springfield Ct CH4. . . . . 161 A8
Llys Perenna/Perenna Ct
  CH6 . . . . .91 B2
Llys Rhuddlan/Rhuddlan Ct
 5 CH4. . . . . 140 F6
Llys Sant Iago/St James Ct
  CH5 . . . . .91 D1
Llys Y Faenol CH5 . . . . . 139 B7
Loachbrook Ave CW12. . . 156 A2
Loachbrook Farm Way
  CW12 . . . . 155 E3
Lobelia Gr WA7 . . . . .49 F4
Lobelia Wlk **6** M11 . . . . . .11 C2
Lochinvar Ave CH66 . . . . .68 F6
Lochleven Rd CW2 . . . . . 206 A7
Lochmaben Cl CW4 . . . . 130 E3
Loch St **4** Runcorn WA7 . . 23 A2
 14 Runcorn WA7 . . . . . . 23 A3
Locke Ho CW1 . . . . 190 B4
Locker Ave WA2 . . . . .8 B2
Lockerbie Cl
  Holmes Chapel CW4. . . . . 130 C2
  Warrington WA2 . . . . .8 E3
Lockett Rd WA8. . . . . . . .13 B3
Lockett St WA4 . . . . .16 F3
Lockgate E WA7 . . . . 24 C2
Lockgate W WA7. . . . . . . 24 C2
Lockheed Rd
  Burtonwood WA5. . . . . . . .6 E3
  Warrington WA5 . . . . .7 A3
LOCKING STUMPS 9 C3
Locking Stumps Com Prim
  Sch WA3 . . . . .9 D4
Locking Stumps La WA3 . . .9 B4
Lockitt St CW2. . . . . 190 D3
Lock La WA11. . . . . .11 E3
Lock Rd Bebington CH62 . . 44 A8
  Warrington WA1 . . . . 16 F6
Locks The
  Grappenhall WA4 . . . . .17 B3
  Middlewich CW10 . . . . . . 151 D8
Lockton La WA5. . . . . . . .15 E7
Lockwood View WA7 . . . . .50 F5
Lodge Brow SK10 . . . . . . 63 A1
Lodgebury Ct SY14 . . . . . 211 C2
Lodge Cl WA13. . . . . .19 B4
  Moulton CW9 . . . . 126 F7
  Winsford CW7 . . . . 127 A1
Lodgefields Dr CW2 . . . . 189 E4
Lodge Gdns CH2 . . . . . . 118 D6
Lodge Hollow WA6. . . . . . 73 B4
Lodge La Antrobus CW9. . . 54 A6
  Dutton WA4 . . . . 76 C8
  Hartford CW8 . . . . 103 B4
  Hatherton CW5 . . . . 220 A4
  Haydock WA11, WA12, WN4. . 2 B8
  Lostock Gralam CW9 . . . . . 80 A2
  Runcorn WA7 . . . . .49 F8
  Saughall CH1 . . . . 94 A2
  Warrington WA5 . . . . 15 F7
  Widnes WA8. . . . . .12 B4
Lodge Lane Intc WA7. . . . .49 E7
Lodge Rd Alsager ST7 . . . 193 C4
  Knutsford WA16. . . . . 57 C3
  Sandbach CW11. . . . . . . 174 E5
  Talke ST7 . . . . 210 D6
  Widnes WA8. . . . . .22 B8
Lodmore La SY13 . . . . . . 233 C6
Lofthouse Gate WA8 . . . . .12 F4
Lomas Sq SK11 . . . . 112 D5
Lomas Way CW12 . . . . . 156 D6
Lomax Rd CW5. . . . . 205 D6
Lomond Gr CH66 . . . . . . .69 F3
Lon Beeby CH4 . . . . 139 D3
London Rd Adlington SK10 . 62 C5
  Alderley Edge SK9 . . . . . . 60 A1
  Allostock WA16 . . . . 106 F3
  Bridgemere CW5, CW3 . . . 232 A5
  Davenham CW9 . . . . 104 A1
  Frodsham WA6. . . . . .74 B8
  Hatherton CW5 . . . . 220 D4
  Holmes Chapel CW4. . . . . 130 C2
  Macclesfield SK11 . . . . . . 112 D3
  Nantwich CW5. . . . . 204 F5
  Northwich CW9 . . . . 103 F7
  Northwich, Leftwich CW9. . 103 F4
  Pewterspear WA4 . . . . 26 D4
  Sandbach CW11. . . . . . . 174 D8
  Stapeley CW5. . . . . 205 B3
  Warrington WA4 . . . . 26 D5
  Woore CW3 . . . . 232 C1
London Road N SK12 . . . . 36 E1

London Road S SK12 . . . . 36 D3
London Road Terr SK11. . . 112 D5
Lon Drury SY13 . . . . 223 E1
Loney St SK11. . . . . 112 C7
Long Acre
  Cuddington CW8 . . . . . . 101 D4
  Weaverham CW8 . . . . 77 C1
Longacres Rd WA15 . . . . . 32 D7
Long Acres Rd CH64. . . . .41 E2
Longacre St SK10 . . . . . . 112 C8
LONGBARN. 9 B1
Longbarn Bvd WA2. . . . . . .9 C2
Long Barn La
  Warrington WA2 . . . . .9 B1
  Warrington, Woolston WA1 . . 17 D8
Long Beam Rd **2** CW11. . 175 B8
Longbenton Way WA7. . . . 24 B4
Longburgh Cl CH2. . . . . . 118 F3
Longbutt La WA13. . . . . . 19 A2
Longbutts La SK11 . . . . . 111 E2
Longclough Rd ST5 . . . . 210 D2
Long Croft La SK8. . . . . . .34 E8
Longcross Ct CW10 . . . . 128 C1
Longdale Dr CH1. . . . . . . 117 C5
Longden Ct SK7. . . . . 35 E5
Longden La SK11. . . . . . 113 A6
Longdin St WA4. . . . . . . .16 F3
Longdown Rd CW12 . . . . 155 F4
Longfield Ave
  Chester CH2. . . . . 118 E7
  Gatley SK8 . . . . .34 C7
Longfield Gdns WA2 . . . . . .8 C1
Longfield Rd WA2. . . . . . . .8 C1
LONGFORD 8 B1
Longford Dr WA8 . . . . . . .12 E2
Longford St
 4 Crewe CW2. . . . . 190 D2
  Warrington WA2 . . . . .16 B7
Long Gn CH3. . . . . .97 E1
LONG GREEN. 97 F1
Longhill CW8. . . . . 230 E5
Long Hill SK23 . . . . 65 F2
Longhill La CW3 . . . . . . 230 E5
Longhorn Cl CW10 . . . . . 128 D2
Long La Alpraham CW6 . . 169 E4
  Bickerton SK10 . . . . 199 F4
  Bollington SK10 . . . . .63 B2
  Burland CW5 . . . . 203 A8
  Chester CH2. . . . . 118 F7
  Hargrave CH3 . . . . 143 D2
  Harriseahead ST7 . . . . . . 195 E4
  Haughton CW6 . . . . 186 D4
  Horwich End SK23 . . . . . . 64 F3
  Huxley CH3 . . . . 166 C8
  Lane Ends SK12 . . . . .38 E4
  Middlewich CW10 . . . . . . 151 C7
  Saughall CH1 . . . . 94 B2
  Swan Green SK16 . . . . . . 107 D7
  Swettenham CW12. . . . . . 131 F5
  Tilston SY14 . . . . 198 B2
  Tilston SY14. . . . . 198 B3
  Warrington WA3 . . . . .8 B1
  Wettenhall CW6, CW7 . . . . 170 C6
Long Lane S CW10 . . . . . 151 D7
Long Lea Gdns CW9 . . . . 105 E5
Longley Ave CW6 . . . . . . 122 D6
Longley La CW6. . . . . . . .99 D1
Long Looms CH3 . . . . . . 120 D6
Longlooms Rd CH65 . . . . 70 D1
Long Marl Dr SK9 . . . . . . 34 F4
Longmeade Gdns SK9 . . . 60 C6
Longmeadow Cheadle SK8. 35 C7
  Weaverham WA8 . . . . 102 C8
LONGMOSS 86 C1
Longmoss Cl CW10 . . . . 151 B8
Longmynd Rise CW7 . . . . 149 B8
Longnor Rd Gatley SK8 . . . 34 D8
  Hazel Grove SK7. . . . . . . .36 E7
Long Pool CW12 . . . . . . 158 D2
Long Rd CH4. . . . . 139 D3
Longridge WA16 . . . . 57 D3
Longridge Trad Est WA16 . . 57 D2
Long Row ST7 . . . . 195 A1
Longsdon Cl ST5 . . . . . . 210 C1
Longshaw St WA5. . . . . . . .7 F1
Long Shoot CW4 . . . . . . 130 D8
Long Shoot Rd SK11. . . . 108 E1
Longside Rd
  Broughton CH4 . . . . 139 A3
  Lane Ends SK12 . . . . .38 E4
Longsides Rd WA15 . . . . . 32 C7
Longsight La SK8 . . . . . . .34 F6
Long Spinney WA7 . . . . . . 50 C8
Longster Cl WA4 . . . . .73 B2
Longstone La CW6 . . . . . 124 E3
Longstone Rd M22 . . . . . 34 A8
Longton Ave WA3 . . . . . . .3 C7
Long Valley Rd ST8. . . . . 179 C2
Longview Ave ST7. . . . . . 193 E4
Long Wlk Marl Piece SY14 . 201 A1
  Partington M31 . . . . 11 D3
Longwood Rd WA4 . . . . . .26 E5
Lon Halghton LL13 . . . . . 222 B2
Lonsdale Cl
  Warrington WA7 . . . . 14 F8
 3 Widnes WA8 . . . . 22 C8
Lonsdale Ct CH4 . . . . . . 140 F6
Lon Y Cryddion/Cobblers La
  LL12. . . . . 161 B1
Lon yr Orsaf/Station App
  CH1 . . . . 116 F7
Lon yr Ywen/Yew Tree Ave
  CH1 . . . . 116 F7

Looe Cl WA8. . . . . .12 E2
Looms The CH64. . . . . . . .41 B2
Loont The CW7 . . . . 149 C7
Lord Nelson St WA1 . . . . 16 C5
Lordship La WA6. . . . . . . .73 B7
Lordshire Pl ST7 . . . . . . 195 F2
Lords La WA3 . . . . .9 C4
Lords Mill Rd CW2 . . . . . 206 B4
Lord's St M44 . . . . 11 C5
Lord St Bollington SK10 . . .88 B8
  Chester CH3. . . . . 118 F2
  Crewe CW2 . . . . 190 D3
  Croft WA3. . . . . .9 A8
  Macclesfield SK11 . . . . . . 112 D6
  Newton-le-Willows WA12 . . . .2 A3
  Runcorn WA7 . . . . .22 F3
  Warrington WA4 . . . . .16 B4
Lorne St CH1 . . . . 237 A3
Lorraine St ST7 . . . . 195 F1
Lostock Ave Poynton SK12 . 36 B4
  Warrington WA5 . . . . 15 F8
Lostock Cl **2** CW9 . . . . . 103 E5
Lostock Dr CW10. . . . . . 151 D5
Lostock Gn CW9 . . . . 80 A1
LOSTOCK GRALAM. 80 A3
Lostock Gralam CE Prim Sch
  CW9. . . . . 80 A2
Lostock Gralam Sta CW9 . . 80 A2
LOSTOCK GREEN. 105 B8
Lostock Hall Prim Sch
  SK12. . . . . 36 B3
Lostock Hall Rd SK12. . . . .36 B3
Lostock Hollow CW9 . . . . 80 A2
Lostock Rd SK12 . . . . . . 36 D2
Lostock Way SK9. . . . . . . 34 D4
Lotus Gdns WA9. . . . . . . .6 A4
Louise St CH1. . . . . 237 A3
Louisiana Dr WA5 . . . . . . .15 B6
Loushers La WA4 . . . . . . 16 D2
Lovage Cl WA2. . . . . .9 C1
Lovat Dr WA16 . . . . .82 B7
Lovatt Cl WA13 . . . . 19 B4
Lovatts The ST7. . . . . . . 195 A1
Love La
  Hassall Green CW11 . . . . . 176 C3
  Nantwich CW5 . . . . 204 F5
Love Lane SY14 . . . . 213 A4
Lovell Ct CW5 . . . . 130 C3
Lovell Rise SK10 . . . . 87 D4
Lovels Way WA8 . . . . .21 F6
Lovel Terr WA8 . . . . .22 B5
Lovely La WA5 . . . . .15 E6
Love St CH1 . . . . 237 B2
Lowcross La SY14 . . . . . 198 D3
Lowe Ave
  Congleton CW12 . . . . . . 156 E2
  Warrington WA4 . . . . .16 F4
Lowe Cres CW9 . . . . 53 C4
Lowe St WA16 . . . . .57 B2
Lower Appleton Rd WA8. . . 13 B1
Lower Ash Rd ST7 . . . . . 194 E1
Lower Bank St **10** SK11 . . 112 E7
Lower Beech Cotts SK10 . . 87 D2
Lower Bridge St CH1 . . . . 237 B1
Lower Brook St CH5. . . . . 91 D1
LOWER BUNBURY 185 F8
LOWER CARDEN. 198 C6
Lower Church St WA8 . . . 23 A5
Lower Cl L26. . . . . 21 A8
Lower Darwin St CW9 . . . 103 E6
Lower Exchange St **13**
  SK11 . . . . 112 D7
Lower Farm Mews CW6. . . 147 B3
Lowerfield Rd SK10 . . . . . 87 E1
Lower Field Rd CH4 . . . . 141 A5
Lower Fold Cott SK6. . . . . 37 D7
Lower Greenshall La SK12 . 38 F6
Lower Haigue SK22 . . . . . 38 B8
Lower Haigh St **3** CW7 . . 149 C8
Lower Hall La CH3. . . . . . 182 D2
Lower Hall Mews CH3 . . . 182 C2
Lower Hall Rd SY13 . . . . 215 D4
LOWER HEATH 156 E5
Lower Heath CW12 . . . . . 156 E4
Lower Heath Ave CW12. . . 156 E4
Lower Heath Terr CW12 . . 156 E4
Lower High St ST7 . . . . . 195 D7
Lower Hill Top Rd WA1 . . . 16 A4
LOWERHOUSE 87 E8
Lowerhouse SK10. . . . . . .87 E8
LOWER HOUSE 22 E8
Lowerhouse La WA16. . . . .31 F4
Lower House La WA8. . . . .22 F8
LOWER KINNERTON. . . . 139 D1
Lower La Aldford CH3. . . . 164 A2
  Churton CH3 . . . . 181 A7
  Eaton CW6 . . . . 147 A2
Lowerlea SK12. . . . . 38 C6
Lower Macclesfield Rd
  SK23 . . . . .65 C6
Lower Meadow Dr CW12. 156 C3
Lower Meadow Rd SK9 . . . 34 E4
Lower Mersey St CH65. . . 70 C7
Lower Nook Mdw WA3 . . . .4 B8
Lower Park Cres SK12 . . . 36 C6
Lower Park Prim Sch
  SK12. . . . . 36 C4
Lower Park Rd
  Chester CH4. . . . . 237 C2
  Poynton SK12. . . . . .36 B5
Lower Park St SK12. . . . . 156 E3
LOWER PEOVER. 81 E1
Lower Peover CE Prim Sch
  WA16 . . . . .81 E1
Lower Rake La WA6 . . . . . .73 B4
Lower Rd L26, WA8 . . . . . 21 C7
Lower Robin Hood La
  WA6. . . . . .73 B3

Lower Rock St 2 SK22 39 C7
Lower Sandy La CH3 199 C7
LOWER STRETTON 52 F8
LOWER THREAPWOOD 222 E6
LOWER WALTON 26 A8
Lower Wash La WA4 16 E3
LOWER WHITLEY 52 D3
LOWER WITHINGTON 132 A8
LOWER WYCH 224 B6
Lower Wych La SY14 224 A7
Lowes Fold WA3 3 C7
Lowes La SK11 111 F2
Lowe St Golborne WA3 3 A8
Macclesfield SK11 112 D7
Loweswater Cl WA2 8 B3
Loweswater Cres WA11 1 A6
Lowfield Gdns WA3 5 C7
Lowfields Ave CH62 43 E3
Lowfields Cl CH62 43 E3
Low Hill WA6 97 D5
Lowlands Rd 6 WA7 22 F2
Lowland Way WA16 82 A8
LOW LEIGHTON 39 D8
Low Leighton Rd SK22 39 D8
Low Mdw SK23 65 D8
Lownorth Rd M22 33 E8
Lowpike La CH65 70 A7
Lowry Cl WA5 15 D6
Low St ST7 193 E8
Lowther Ave WA3 4 F4
Lowther St SK10 88 C8
LOWTON 3 E8
Lowton Bsns Pk WA3 4 A7
LOWTON COMMON 4 A8
Lowton Gdns WA3 3 B5
LOWTON HEATH 3 C6
Lowton High Sch WA3 4 B8
Lowton Jun & Inf Sch WA3 4 A7
Lowton Rd WA3 3 C8
LOWTON ST MARY'S 3 F8
Lowton St Mary's CE Prim Sch WA3 4 A8
Lowton West Prim Sch WA3 3 D8
Loxdale Dr CH65 69 F4
Loxley Cl
Macclesfield SK11 112 B7
Warrington WA5 15 A8
Loyola Hey L35 12 E8
Lucerne Cl CH3 142 B6
Lucerne Rd ST8 179 E1
Luddington Hill CW6 146 E6
Ludford Cl ST5 210 D2
Ludford St CW1 190 C5
Ludgate Croft SY14 213 C4
Ludlow Ave CW1 190 F3
Ludlow Cl
Macclesfield SK10 87 E2
Warrington, Paddington WA1 17 B8
Winsford CW7 149 B7
Ludlow Cres WA7 49 B8
Ludlow Dr CH65 70 E3
Ludlow Rd CH1 118 A5
Ludwell Cl CH4 141 B6
LUGSDALE 23 C7
Lugsdale Rd WA8 23 B7
Lulworth Cl CW7 149 B7
Lumb Brook Mews 5 WA4 16 E1
Lumb Brook Rd
Appleton Thorn WA4 27 A5
Cobbs WA4 26 F7
Warrington WA4 26 F8
Lumb Cl SK7 35 E6
Lumber La WA5 6 F8
Lumb La SK7 35 E6
Lumley Pl CH1 237 B2
Lumley Rd Chester CH2 118 C4
Macclesfield SK11 111 F7
Lumley Wlk L24 21 E1
Lumpy St CW12 156 C3
Lundy Dr CH65 95 C8
Lune Cl 1 CW12 157 A1
Lune Cres 1 CW9 104 C5
Lunehurst 12 WA3 3 E8
Lune Way WA8 12 C1
Lunt Ave CW2 190 C2
LUNTS HEATH 13 A5
Lunts Heath Prim Sch WA8 13 B5
Lunt's Heath Rd WA8 13 B5
Lunts Moss ST7 194 C6
Luntswood Gr WA12 2 A4
Lupin Dr Haydock WA11 1 F6
Huntington CH3 142 B6
Lupus Way CH66 69 F3
Luscombe Cl L26 21 A8
Luther Gr WA9 1 B2
Luton Rd CH65 70 A5
Luton St WA8 23 A7
Lutterworth Ave WA7 24 E2
Lutyens Cl SK10 111 F8
Lycett Cl CW12 155 E3
Lyceum Cl CW1 190 A8
Lyceum Theatre★ 1 CW1 190 D4
Lyceum Way CW1 190 A8
Lychgate WA4 25 F7
Lycroft Cl WA7 49 B6
Lydbury Cl WA5 7 D2
Lydden Rd CH65 70 B7
Lydgate Cl CW2 205 F8
Lydiate La Runcorn WA7 48 D7
Willaston CH64 42 E1
Lydiate The Heswall CH60 40 F7
Willaston CH64 42 D1
Lydiat La SK9 60 A1
Lydney Ave SK8 34 C7
Lydstep Ct WA5 7 E2
Lydyett La CW8 78 B3
Lymcote Dr CW8 103 A4
Lyme Ave Handforth SK9 34 B1
Macclesfield SK11 112 D5
Lyme Com Prim Sch WA12 1 F4
Lyme Gr WA13 18 C2
LYME GREEN 112 D2
Lyme Green Bsns Pk SK11 112 C3
Lyme Green Settlement SK11 112 D2
Lyme Lea Cl SK8 35 B8
Lyme Park★ SK12 38 B1
Lyme Park Ctry Pk★ SK12 38 B2
Lyme Rd High Lane SK12 38 A6
Poynton SK12 37 C3
Lyme St Haydock WA11 1 E6
Newton-le-Willows WA12 1 F4
Lyme View SK11 112 D2
Lymewood Dr Disley SK12 38 C6
6 Wilmslow SK9 60 E8
LYMM 18 E4
Lymm Brook 1 WA13 18 E3
Lymm Hall WA13 18 E3
Lymmhay La WA13 18 E4
Lymm High Sch WA13 19 B3
Lymmington Ave WA13 18 C3
Lymm Quay 8 WA13 18 E3
Lymm Rd
Little Bollington WA14 20 B1
Warrington WA4 17 F3
Lynalls Cl CW12 155 F3
Lynbrook Rd CW1 190 F4
Lyncastle Rd WA4 27 D4
Lyncastle Way WA4 27 D4
Lynchet Rd SY14 213 C4
Lyncombe Cl SK8 35 B6
Lyncroft Cl CW1 190 F3
Lyndale 2 WA7 49 C8
Lyndale Ave
Bebington CH62 43 E4
Warrington WA2 16 D8
Warrington, Fearnhead WA2 8 F2
Lyndale Ct CW7 127 A3
Lyndale Gr CW12 154 E7
Lyndhurst Cl SK9 59 D5
Lyndon Gr WA7 49 B8
Lyneal Ave CH66 69 C3
Lyngard Cl SK9 34 E1
Lynham Ave WA5 15 B5
Lynn Ave ST7 210 C8
Lynn Cl WA7 49 C7
Lynndene CH66 69 D7
Lynn Gr SK11 112 C6
Lynside Wlk M22 33 E8
Lynthorpe Ave M44 11 D6
Lynton Ave M44 11 E6
Lynton Cl Chester CH4 140 F6
Heswall CH60 41 B6
Knutsford WA16 57 C1
Warrington WA5 14 E4
Lynton Cres WA8 12 E2
Lynton Dr SK6 37 E8
Lynton Gdns WA4 26 D4
Lynton Gr CW1 191 D5
Lynton La SK9 60 A2
Lynton Mews SK9 60 A2
Lynton Park Rd SK8 34 F8
Lynton Pl Alsager ST7 193 D4
Broughton CH4 139 B4
Lynton Way CW2 206 A8
Lynwood Altrincham WA15 32 A8
Wilmslow SK9 60 A6
Lynwood Ave Golborne WA3 3 A6
Warrington WA4 26 C7
Lynwood Rd CH1 117 F5
Lyon Ct WA4 16 F3
Lyon's La WA4 26 E6
Lyons Rd WA5 15 A4
Lyon St Chester CH1 237 B3
Crewe CW1 190 D4
Macclesfield SK11 112 C7
Warrington WA4 16 F3
Lysander Com High Sch WA2 8 F2
Lysander Dr WA2 8 E2
Lyster Cl WA3 9 F3
Lytham Cl WA5 15 B3
Lytham Dr Bramhall SK7 36 A7
Winsford CW7 126 C2
Lytham Rd WA8 13 C2
Lytherton Ave M44 11 D4
Lythgoes La WA2 16 B6

M

Mableden Cl SK8 34 D8
Mablins La CW1 190 B8
Mablins Lane Com Prim Sch CW1 190 B8
Macbeth Ho ST7 210 C8
MACCLESFIELD 112 B4
Macclesfield Academy SK11 112 B6
Macclesfield Coll SK11 112 B6
Macclesfield District General Hospl SK10 112 B8
MACCLESFIELD FOREST 114 D5
Macclesfield Forest Walks★ SK11 114 A3
Macclesfield L Ctr SK10 86 D2
Macclesfield Rd
Alderley Edge SK9 85 D7
Congleton CW12 156 F6
Macclesfield Rd *continued*
Eaton CW12 134 B2
Hazel Grove SK7 36 F8
Holmes Chapel CW4 130 E4
Kettleshulme SK23, SK10 64 D3
Prestbury SK10 86 F4
Rainow SK10 89 B7
Wilmslow SK9 60 D6
Macclesfield Sta SK11 112 D8
Macdermott Rd WA8 22 F5
Macdonald Rd M44 11 E8
Maclean Way SK9 60 C8
Macon Ct CW1 190 E3
Macon Ind Pk CW1 190 E3
Macon Way CW1 190 E3
Maddocks Cl CH3 180 E2
Maddocks Hill WA6 100 F5
Maddock St ST7 209 D1
Madeley Cl
Altrincham WA14 31 E8
Broughton CH4 139 C4
Madeley St CW2 190 C1
Madeline McKenna Ct WA8 12 C3
Madison Cl WA9 1 A2
Madron Ave SK10 86 D1
Maelor Cl CH63 43 C6
Maelr Westbound SK9 35 B4
Maes-y-Coed CH4 140 E6
Magdala Pl CW9 104 C8
Magdalen Ct CW2 190 A1
Magecroft CW1 173 B1
Magenta Ave M44 11 E6
Maggoty La SK11 111 D1
Mag La WA13, WA16 28 F6
Magna Park WA7 24 E2
Magnolia Cl
3 Ellesmere Port CH66 69 F1
5 Partington M31 11 E2
Warrington WA1 17 E7
Magnolia Dr WA7 49 F4
Magnolia Rise SK10 86 E6
Magnolia St CW8 78 C1
Magpie Cres 9 ST7 195 B2
Maiden Est CW5 228 C8
Maiden Gdns CH65 70 D3
Maidenhills CW10 128 D1
Maidstone Cl SK10 87 B2
Maidwell Cl CW7 127 A4
Main Cl WA11 1 A6
Main Dr WA14 20 E3
Maine Gdns 6 WA5 15 A7
Main La WA3 3 F3
Main Rd Betley CW2, CW3 221 F8
Broughton CH4 139 B4
Goostrey CW4 107 E1
Higher Kinnerton CH4 161 A8
Langley SK11 113 C4
Moulton CW9 126 F8
Norton in Hales TF9 236 C1
Shavington CW2 206 B4
Weston CW2 207 C6
Worleston CW5 188 F5
Wybunbury CW5 220 B8
Main St Frodsham WA6 74 B8
Great Barrow CH3 120 E5
Runcorn WA7 49 F8
Maintree Cres L24 21 A4
Mainwaring Cl CW5 205 A4
Mainwaring Dr
Saltney CH4 140 C7
Wilmslow SK9 60 D8
Mainwaring Rd
Bebington CH62 43 D8
Over Peover WA16 108 A8
Mairesfield Ave WA4 17 B2
Maisemore Fields WA8 12 E3
Maisterson Ct 7 CW5 204 E5
Maisterson Dr SK10 85 B2
Maitland Way 3 CH1 117 D4
Maitland-Wood Cl CW9 104 D7
Major Cross St 6 WA8 23 A7
Makepeace Cl CH3 119 C3
Makerfield Dr WA12 2 A5
Malaga Ave M90 33 B7
Malahide Ct WA8 12 E2
Malam Dr CW9 104 D6
Malayan Pl 5 CH3 142 B5
Malbank CW5 204 E6
Malbank Rd CW2 189 E4
Malbank Sch & Sixth Form Coll CW5 204 C6
Malcolm Ave WA2 8 D1
Malcolm Cres CH63 43 C6
Malcolm St WA7 23 B2
Malden Rd 1 WA12 2 D1
Malham Cl WA5 14 E8
Malhamdale Rd CW12 157 A5
Malin Cl L24 21 D2
Maliston Rd WA5 15 B5
MALKINS BANK 175 C3
Mallaig Cl CW4 130 C2
Mallard Ave CW5 204 C3
Mallard Cl Knutsford WA16 57 B3
Warrington WA2 8 D3
Mallard Cres SK12 36 A4
Mallard Ct Chester CH2 118 F7
Crewe CW1 191 A2
Gatley SK8 34 B8
Mallard La WA3 9 F3
Mallard Pl 5 CW11 174 C5
Mallard Way Crewe CW1 191 A2
Winsford CW7 149 D6
Mallory Cl WA16 58 A4
Mallory Ct
Congleton CW12 155 F3
Mobberley WA16 58 A4
Mallory Rd CH65 70 A4
Mallory Wlk CH4 162 A7
Mallow Cl CH3 142 A6
Mallowdale Cl CH62 43 F5
Mallows Way CW6 123 B1
Mallow Wlk M31 11 F2
Malmesbury Cl
Middlewich CW10 128 B1
Poynton SK12 36 D4
Malmesbury Pk WA7 24 E2
Malmesbury Rd SK8 35 B6
Malory Cl CW1 190 F5
MALPAS 213 B2
Malpas Alport Endowed Prim Sch SY14 213 B4
Malpas Cl 3 Arclid CW11 154 B1
Handforth SK9 34 E1
Northwich CW9 104 B7
Malpas Dr WA5 15 C4
Malpas Rd
Ellesmere Port CH65 69 F4
Northwich CW9 104 C7
Runcorn WA7 49 C7
Malpas Sports Ctr SY14 213 C5
Malpas Way WA5 15 C4
Malta Rd CH2 95 B1
Malt Kiln Rd WA16 80 F4
Malt Kiln Way CW11 175 B7
Maltmans Rd WA13 18 D3
Malton Ave WA3 3 E7
Malton Cl WA8 12 C5
Malton Dr SK7 36 D7
Malt St WA16 57 A2
Malvern Ave CH65 70 D3
Malvern Cl
Congleton CW12 155 F3
Shavington CW2 206 B4
Warrington WA5 15 A8
Malvern Dr SK10 87 E4
Malvern Rd Blacon CH1 118 A5
Haydock WA9 1 A4
Knutsford WA16 81 F8
Malvern Way CW7 149 B7
Manchester Airport M90 33 A7
Manchester Airport Sta M90 33 B7
Manchester Bridge CW1 190 E4
Manchester Bsns Pk M22 33 D8
Manchester E Airport Link SK7 37 A8
Manchester East Airport Link SK7 35 C4
Manchester New Rd M31 11 F4
Manchester Rd
Congleton CW12 156 E5
Handforth SK9 34 C2
Hollinfare WA3 11 A2
Hollins Green WA3 11 B3
Knutsford WA16 56 E4
Macclesfield SK10 87 D4
Warrington WA3 18 D7
Warrington, Bruche WA1 16 F7
Warrington, Woolston WA1 17 C7
Wincham CW9 79 D1
Manchester Row WA12 7 D8
Mancroft Cl WA1 17 E7
Mandarin Ct WA1 16 A3
Manhattan Gdns 1 WA5 15 B7
Manifold Cl CW11 174 E8
Manifold Dr SK6 37 F6
MANLEY 99 A4
Manley Cl Antrobus CW9 53 C4
Holmes Chapel CW4 130 A3
Northwich CW9 104 A5
MANLEY COMMON 99 C5
Manley Cty Prim Sch WA6 99 A5
Manley Gdns WA5 15 F5
Manley Gr SK7 35 E6
Manley La
Dunham-on-the-Hill WA6 97 F5
Manley WA6 98 C4
Manley Mere Sail Sports & Adventure Trail★ WA6 98 B5
Manley Rd Frodsham WA6 74 B3
Manley WA6 98 E7
Warren SK11 112 A5
Manley View CH2 72 C3
Manley Village Sch WA6 99 A5
Manna Dr CH2 72 C3
Manners La CH60 40 E6
Mannings La CH2 119 B6
Mannings Lane S CH2 119 A5
Manning St CW2 190 D1
Manora Rd CW9 104 A8
Manor Ave Crewe CW2 190 A1
Golborne WA3 3 C8
Goostrey CW4 107 F1
Marston CW9 79 B6
Newton-le-Willows WA12 1 F4
Manor Bsns Pk CW4 130 D3
Manor Cl Broughton CH5 139 C7
Cheadle SK8 35 C8
Congleton CW12 157 A1
Great Barrow CH3 120 E6
Lymm WA13 18 E2
Neston CH64 66 C7
Warrington WA1 17 D7
Wilmslow SK9 59 F8
Manor Cres
Broughton CH4 139 C8
Knutsford WA16 57 B2
Macclesfield SK10 87 D3
Middlewich CW10 151 C7
Manor Ct Acton CW5 204 B4
Crewe CW2 190 B1
Golborne WA3 3 C8
Knutsford WA16 57 B1
2 Nantwich CW5 204 E6
Manor Dr Barnton CW8 78 B2
Chester CH3 119 C1
Northwich, Rudheath CW9 104 C7
Manor Farm Cl CH2 119 F8
Manor Farm Cres CH1 94 B8
Manor Farm Ct
Broughton CH5 139 B7
5 Frodsham WA6 49 C1
Manor Farm Mews WA7 24 D4
Manor Farm Rd WA7 24 D4
Manor Fell WA7 50 B7
Manorfield Cl CH1 69 A1
Manor Fields CW10 151 C7
Manor Gdns
Nantwich CW5 204 E6
Wilmslow SK9 60 D7
Manor Gr CW8 103 C6
Manor Ho Bebington CH62 43 D8
Ellesmere Port CH66 69 D2
Row-of-Trees SK9 59 D3
Manorial Rd CH64 66 C8
Manorial Road S CH64 66 C7
Manor Ind Est WA4 16 E4
Manor La Broughton CH5 139 B7
Davenham CW9 104 D2
Ellesmere Port CH66 69 D3
Holmes Chapel CW4 130 D3
3 Middlewich CW10 151 C8
Ollerton WA16 82 E6
MANOR PARK Middlewich 151 B7
Runcorn 24 B3
Manor Park Ave WA7 24 C4
Manor Park Dr CH66 69 D2
Manor Park N WA16 57 C2
Manor Park Prim Sch and Nur WA16 57 C2
Manor Park Rd CW12 134 D2
Manor Park S WA16 57 C1
Manor Pk CH5 139 B7
Manor Pk CH3 120 E6
Manor Pl Hatherton CW5 220 B1
Widnes WA8 12 B1
Manor Rd Bebington CH62 43 E6
Chester CH4 141 B5
Cuddington CW8 101 F2
Frodsham WA6 49 C1
Haydock WA11 1 F7
Horwich End SK23 65 E5
Lymm WA13 18 E2
Mow Cop ST7 195 D7
Nantwich CW5 204 E6
Runcorn WA7 23 D2
Sandbach CW11 175 D6
Sealand CH5 116 A6
Thornton Hough CH63 42 A7
Widnes WA8 12 B1
Wilmslow SK9 59 E8
Manor Road N CW5 204 E7
Manor Sq CW7 149 A8
Manor St CW8 103 D6
Manor Terr SK11 113 B3
Manor The WA1 17 F7
Manor Way Crewe CW2 190 C1
Sandbach CW11 175 E6
Manse Field Rd WA6 75 B1
Manse Gdns WA12 2 D4
Mansell Cl WA8 13 C5
Mansfield Apartments WA2 9 A3
Mansfield Cl WA3 10 A4
Mansfield Rd CH65 70 A2
Mansion Ct 5 CW5 204 F5
Mansion Dr WA16 57 B2
Manston Rd WA5 14 F3
Manuel Perez Rd 1 WA5 15 B6
Manx Rd WA4 16 B3
Maori Dr WA6 74 A8
Maple Ave Alsager ST7 193 E2
Aston WA7 50 A4
Disley SK12 39 A6
Ellesmere Port CH66 69 D6
Golborne WA3 3 F7
Haydock WA11 1 B7
Macclesfield SK11 112 D5
Newcastle-under-Lyme ST5 210 E1
Newton-le-Willows WA12 2 D2
Poynton SK12 36 F3
Runcorn WA7 49 C8
Talke ST7 210 D8
5 Widnes WA8 13 B2
Maple Cl
Brereton Green CW11 153 F5
Congleton CW12 155 F4
Holmes Chapel CW4 130 D4
Sandbach CW11 175 C6
Maple Cres WA5 14 F3
Maple Ct CW7 127 A3
Maple Gr Barnton CW8 78 B4
Bebington CH62 43 C8
Chester CH2 119 B4
Crewe CW1 190 E6
Ellesmere Port CH66 95 A8
Northwich, Greenbank CW8 103 C7
Saltney CH4 140 D5
Warrington WA4 16 D3
Winsford CW7 127 A1
Maple La CW8 101 F2
Maple Pl ST7 193 F7
Maple Rd
Alderley Edge SK9 60 B3
Bramhall SK7 35 E6
Partington M31 11 E3
Warrington WA1 17 E7

Maple Rd *continued*
Winwick WA2 . . . .**8** B6
Maples SK9 . . . .**59** F6
Maples The
Mobberley WA16 . . . .**58** E1
Winsford CW7 . . . .**127** A3
Mapleton Dr WA7 . . . .**49** F3
Maplewood SK11 . . . .**112** D5
Maplewood Cl WA8 . . . .**22** A7
Maplewood Gr CH1 . . . .**117** B8
Maplewood Rd SK9 . . . .**60** E8
Maplins Moss Pl CW1 . . . . .**190** C8
Mapplewell Cres WA5 . . . . . .**15** A6
Mara Dr CW8 . . . .**100** D1
Marble Arch **5** WA16 . . . . . .**57** A2
MARBURY **226** E8
Marbury Ctry Pk★ CW9 . . . .**78** E5
Marbury Gdns CH65 . . . .**69** F6
Marbury House Farm
WA4 . . . .**52** E5
Marbury La CW9 . . . .**78** E5
Marbury Pk CW9 . . . .**78** D5
Marbury Rd Chester CH3 . . . .**118** E7
Comberbach CW9 . . . .**78** D6
Handforth SK9 . . . .**34** B1
Norbury SY13 . . . .**215** B3
Marbury St WA4 . . . .**16** C3
March St CW1 . . . .**190** E4
Marchwiel Rd CH65 . . . .**70** D4
Marcien Way WA8 . . . .**12** F3
Marcliff Gr WA16 . . . .**57** A1
Marcross Cl WA5 . . . .**7** E1
Mardale Ave WA2 . . . .**8** C3
Mardale Cl CW12 . . . .**157** B5
Mardale Cres WA13 . . . .**18** F3
Mardale Ct CW4 . . . .**130** A2
Mardon Cl WA16 . . . .**57** D3
Marford Cl CW9 . . . .**103** E5
Marfords Ave CH63 . . . .**43** C7
Margaret Ave WA1 . . . .**17** B2
Margaret Ct WA8 . . . .**23** B7
Margaret's La CH66 . . . .**69** A7
Margery Ave ST7 . . . .**194** E7
Marian Ave WA12 . . . .**1** F3
Marian Dr CH3 . . . .**142** B8
Marian Rd WA11 . . . .**1** E7
Maricopa Cl WA7 . . . .**24** E2
Marie Cl CW5 . . . .**216** F4
Marie Dr WA4 . . . .**17** D2
Marigold Cl SK11 . . . .**111** F8
Marigold Pl WA5 . . . .**15** D3
Marigold Way WA9 . . . .**6** A7
Marina Ave WA5 . . . .**15** C4
Marina Cl SK9 . . . .**34** D5
Marina Dr Chester CH2 . . . . .**118** E2
Ellesmere Port CH65 . . . . . .**70** B5
Warrington WA2 . . . .**8** C1
Marina Flats CH3 . . . .**142** E7
Marina Gr WA7 . . . .**23** B1
Marina La WA7 . . . .**50** E7
Marina Village WA7 . . . .**50** E7
Marina Wlk CH65 . . . .**70** B5
Marine App **19** CW9 . . . .**103** F8
Marine Ave M31 . . . .**11** D3
Marine Dr CH60 . . . .**40** D6
Mariner Cl WA7 . . . .**50** D6
Mariners Way M44 . . . .**11** F8
Marion Dr
Mobberley WA16 . . . .**58** A4
Runcorn WA7 . . . .**48** F6
Maritime Cl WA12 . . . .**2** C5
Mark Ave CH66 . . . .**69** C4
Mark Cl CH2 . . . .**118** F2
Market Cl CW1 . . . .**190** D5
Market Ct CW6 . . . .**146** C2
Market Ctr The CW1 . . . . . .**190** D4
Market Gate WA1 . . . .**16** B5
Market Pl Bollington SK10 . . .**88** B8
Hampton Heath SY14 . . . . .**213** D7
Macclesfield SK10, SK11 . .**112** D8
Winsford CW7 . . . .**126** F1
Market Sq Chester CH1 . . . .**237** A2
Congleton CW12 . . . .**156** D2
Crewe CW1 . . . .**190** D4
4 Sandbach CW11 . . . . . .**175** B6
Market St
Congleton CW12 . . . .**156** D3
Crewe CW1 . . . .**190** D4
Disley SK12 . . . .**38** D6
Kidsgrove ST7 . . . .**195** A1
Nantwich CW5 . . . .**204** E5
New Mills SK22 . . . .**39** B7
Newton-le-Willows WA12 . . . .**2** A4
9 Northwich CW9 . . . . . .**103** F8
Whaley Bridge SK23 . . . . . .**65** E7
Widnes WA8 . . . .**23** A7
Market Way **7** CW9 . . . . . .**103** F8
Marlborough Ave
Alderley Edge SK9 . . . .**60** B2
Winsford CW7 . . . .**126** C3
Marlborough Cl
Knutsford WA16 . . . .**57** C4
Macclesfield SK10 . . . .**87** D4
Wistaston CW2 . . . .**205** E8
Marlborough Cres
Warrington WA4 . . . .**16** F2
Widnes WA8 . . . .**13** A5
Marlborough Ct
1 Chester CH3 . . . .**119** B2
3 Macclesfield SK11 . . . .**112** D7
Marlborough Dr
Helsby WA6 . . . .**73** B2
Macclesfield SK10 . . . .**87** D4
1 Sandbach CW11 . . . . .**175** B8
Sandbach CW11 . . . .**175** B8

Marlborough Ho **8**
SK11 . . . .**111** F8
Marlborough Prim Sch The
SK10 . . . .**87** D4
Marlborough Rd CH65 . . . . . .**70** D3
Marlborough Way WA11 . . . . . .**1** E8
Marlborough Wlk CH65 . . . . .**70** C3
Marl Cl CW8 . . . .**102** A4
Marl Croft CH3 . . . .**142** B7
Marl Edge SK10 . . . .**87** A5
Marley Ave CW1 . . . .**190** B7
Marley Gn SY13 . . . .**227** C8
MARLEY GREEN **227** C8
Marley Rd SK12 . . . .**36** E2
Marley Way CH4 . . . .**140** E2
Marlfield Ave WA13 . . . .**19** A2
Marlfield Rd
Altrincham WA15 . . . .**32** D7
Warrington WA4 . . . .**17** A2
Marlfields Prim Sch
CW12 . . . .**156** C2
Marl Heys CH2 . . . .**118** E7
Marline Ave CH63 . . . .**43** C6
Marling Cl WA6 . . . .**74** D6
Marling Pk WA8 . . . .**12** B1
Marlow Ave CH2 . . . .**118** F7
Marlow Cl
Sandbach CW11 . . . .**174** D5
Warrington WA3 . . . .**9** C5
Marlow Dr
Altrincham WA14 . . . .**20** F2
Handforth SK9 . . . .**34** C5
Marlowe Cl Blacon CH1 . . . .**118** A5
Widnes WA8 . . . .**12** F1
Wistaston CW2 . . . .**206** A8
Marlowe Ct SK11 . . . .**112** C5
Marlowe Dr CW5 . . . .**204** F3
Marlowe Rd
1 Neston CH64 . . . .**66** E8
Northwich CW9 . . . .**104** C6
Marlston Ave CH4 . . . .**141** A6
Marlston Ct CH4 . . . .**140** E1
Marlston Pl WA7 . . . .**49** B6
Marlwood Pl CH4 . . . .**139** A3
Maroon Rd M22 . . . .**33** F7
Marquis Dr SK8 . . . .**34** D7
Marrabone Rd WA8 . . . .**23** C8
Marriott Rd CW11 . . . .**174** F3
Marron Ave CW2 . . . .**8** B2
Marryat Cl WA2 . . . .**8** A6
Marsden Ave WA4 . . . .**17** A4
Marsden Ct WA8 . . . .**12** E4
Marsden Terr **3** SK11 . . . . .**112** C7
Marshall Ave WA5 . . . .**7** F2
Marshall Dr CH65 . . . .**70** E3
Marshall Gr CW12 . . . .**179** B8
Marshall La CW8 . . . .**103** D6
Marshall Rd WA1 . . . .**17** D7
Marshall's Arm Nature
Reserve★ CW8 . . . .**103** D5
Marshalls Ct **2** CW8 . . . . . .**103** C5
Marsh Ave ST7 . . . .**195** E2
Marsh Brook Cl WA3 . . . .**11** A2
Marsh Brook Rd WA8 . . . . . .**13** B6
Marsh Cl ST7 . . . .**193** A3
Marsh Farm Rd
Maes Gwyn CH5 . . . .**93** B1
Sealand CH5 . . . .**116** A8
Marshfern Pl CW2 . . . .**206** B3
Marshfield Ave CW2 . . . .**189** D4
MARSHFIELD BANK **189** C4
Marshfield Bank CW2 . . . . . .**189** D4
Marshfield La ST8 . . . .**179** C2
Marshgate WA8 . . . .**22** B4
Marshgate Pl WA6 . . . .**49** D2
Marsh Gr ST8 . . . .**179** C2
MARSH GREEN Biddulph . . .**179** D3
Frodsham **74** B8
Marsh Green Cl ST8 . . . .**179** D2
Marshgreen Rd ST8 . . . .**179** D3
Marsh Green Rd CW11 . . . . .**174** E8
Marsh Hall Pad WA8 . . . .**13** B4
Marsh House La WA1,
WA2 . . . .**16** C7
Marsh La Alsager ST7 . . . . .**193** A3
Churton CH3 . . . .**181** B5
Dutton WA4 . . . .**51** E3
Frodsham WA6 . . . .**74** A8
Holmes Chapel CW4 . . . . .**130** E2
Ince CH2 . . . .**72** D6
Mere WA16 . . . .**30** F3
Nantwich CW5 . . . .**204** C5
New Mills SK22, SK23 . . . . .**39** D6
Norley CW8, WA6 . . . .**101** B7
Ravensmoor CW5 . . . .**203** F2
Runcorn WA7 . . . .**23** F3
Warrington, Penketh WA5 . . .**14** C2
Marshlands Rd CH64 . . . .**66** E5
Marsh Lane Trad Est
SK22 . . . .**39** D7
Marsh Rd WA4 . . . .**27** B4
Marsh St Warrington WA1 . . . .**16** D7
Widnes WA8 . . . .**23** A6
Marshway Dr WA12 . . . .**2** B5
Marson St WA2 . . . .**16** A6
MARSTON **79** B4
Marston Cl CH62 . . . .**43** E3
Marston Gdns CH65 . . . .**69** F6
Marston La CW9 . . . .**79** C6
Marston Moor Cl CW5 . . . . .**204** D7
Marten Ave CH63 . . . .**43** C7
Martens Rd M44 . . . .**11** E5
MARTHALL **83** E4
Marthall La WA16 . . . .**83** B7
Marthall Way **8** SK9 . . . . . .**34** E5
Martham Cl WA4 . . . .**17** A3

Martin Ave
Newton-le-Willows WA12 . . . .**2** C5
Warrington WA2 . . . .**8** E1
Martin Cl Chester CH2 . . . . .**118** C8
Runcorn WA7 . . . .**50** A7
Martindale Gr WA7 . . . .**49** D5
Martin Ray Dr CW2 . . . .**206** C4
Martin Rd Chester CH2 . . . . .**118** C8
Frodsham WA6 . . . .**74** B8
MARTIN'S ASH **227** B2
MARTINSCROFT **17** F7
Martinscroft Gn WA1 . . . . . .**17** F7
Martinsfields CW8 . . . .**77** A5
Martin's La CH3 . . . .**143** F3
Martins Mill CW12 . . . .**179** C8
MARTIN'S MOSS **176** E6
Martins Moss La CW11 . . . . .**176** E5
Martland Ave WA3 . . . .**3** E7
Martlet Ave SK12 . . . .**38** C6
MARTON **133** B5
Marton Cl
Congleton CW12 . . . .**156** E5
Culcheth WA3 . . . .**4** E4
Hough CW2 . . . .**206** E3
Macclesfield SK10 . . . .**86** F1
Marton & District CE Aided
Prim Sch SK11 . . . .**133** C5
MARTON GREEN **125** C4
Marton Hall La SK11 . . . . . .**133** B3
Marton La Marton SK11 . . . .**133** D7
Warren SK11 . . . .**111** B1
Marton Rd CH4 . . . .**139** C3
MARTONSANDS **125** F4
Marton Way **5** SK9 . . . .**34** E5
Martree Ct CW11 . . . .**174** D8
Mary Dendy Unit (Hospl)
SK10 . . . .**84** C6
Maryfield Cl WA3 . . . .**3** A7
Maryhill Cl ST7 . . . .**195** A3
Maryhill High Sch ST7 . . . . .**195** A3
Maryhill Prim Sch ST7 . . . . .**195** A3
Maryhill Rd WA7 . . . .**49** A8
Maryland Cl WA5 . . . .**15** C7
Mary Stage CW2 . . . .**205** E8
Mary St Crewe CW1 . . . . . .**190** E5
Widnes WA8 . . . .**23** D7
Maryville Cl **3** CH65 . . . . . .**70** C6
Marzahn Way WA8 . . . .**13** C3
Masefield Ave WA8 . . . .**22** F8
Masefield Dr Blacon CH1 . . . .**117** E6
Crewe CW1 . . . .**190** F4
Winwick WA2 . . . .**8** A5
Masefield Way CW11 . . . . . .**174** D5
Maskery Pl CW12 . . . .**156** E4
Mason Ave
Warrington WA1 . . . .**16** E8
Widnes WA8 . . . .**13** B4
Mason Cl
Ellesmere Port CH66 . . . . . .**69** D2
Farndon CH3 . . . .**180** F1
Masons Cl SK10 . . . .**87** F1
Mason's Row CW6 . . . .**169** E2
Mason St Chester CH2 . . . . .**237** A3
Runcorn WA7 . . . .**23** C3
Warrington WA1 . . . .**16** C5
Massey Ave Hartford CW8 . . .**103** A4
Lymm WA13 . . . .**18** B2
Warrington WA5 . . . .**7** F2
Massey Brook La WA13 . . . . .**18** B2
Massey Cl CW5 . . . .**205** A4
Masseyfield Rd WA7 . . . .**50** B5
Massey St **6** SK9 . . . .**60** A1
Masters Ct WA16 . . . .**56** F1
Mastiff La SY14 . . . .**213** B1
Mates La SY14 . . . .**213** B6
Mather Ave Golborne WA3 . . . .**3** A6
Runcorn WA7 . . . .**48** D7
Mather Cl CW10 . . . .**151** C8
Mather Dr
Comberbach CW9 . . . .**78** C8
Northwich CW9 . . . .**104** D7
Mathers Cl WA2 . . . .**9** A4
Mathieson Rd WA8 . . . .**22** E5
Matilda Ct CH66 . . . .**68** D8
Matlock Cl WA5 . . . .**15** A8
Matlock Dr SK7 . . . .**36** E8
Matlock Rd SK8 . . . .**34** C7
Matrix Ct CH1 . . . .**117** E1
Matterdale Cl WA6 . . . .**74** D7
Matterhorn Rd CH66 . . . .**69** F7
Matthew Cl CH2 . . . .**118** F2
Matthews Pl CW12 . . . .**157** A2
Matthews St WA1 . . . .**16** D7
Matthews Way CW3 . . . .**229** F3
Matty's La WA6 . . . .**74** A7
Mavor Ct CW1 . . . .**190** B4
Mawdsley Ave WA1 . . . .**17** E7
Mawdsley Cl ST7 . . . .**193** A3
MAW GREEN **190** E7
Maw Green Cl CW1 . . . .**190** E7
Maw Green Rd CW1 . . . .**190** F7
Maw La CW1 . . . .**191** C7
Mawson Cl WA5 . . . .**15** D8
Maxfield Cl SK11 . . . .**111** F8
Maxwell Rd CH65 . . . .**70** A2
Maxwell Rd CW12 . . . .**179** A8
Maxwell St Crewe CW2 . . . . .**190** C3
Warrington WA3 . . . .**9** E6
May Ave SK8 . . . .**35** B6
Mayberry Gr WA2 . . . .**9** A1
Maybrook Pl WA4 . . . .**16** F3
Maydor Ave CH4 . . . .**140** C7
Mayfair Cl Poynton SK12 . . . .**36** E4
Warrington WA5 . . . .**14** D7
Mayfair Ct CH4 . . . .**162** E5
Mayfair Dr Crewe CW1 . . . . .**190** F6
Northwich CW9 . . . .**103** F3

Mayfair Gr WA8 . . . .**12** D1
Mayfield Ave
Macclesfield SK11 . . . .**112** C5
Widnes WA8 . . . .**12** B1
Mayfield Cl CW4 . . . .**130** D3
Mayfield Ct WA4 . . . .**13** A2
Mayfield Dr
Bebington CH62 . . . .**44** B6
Cuddington CW8 . . . .**102** A4
Golborne WN7 . . . .**4** C8
Winsford CW7 . . . .**127** A3
Mayfield Gdns CH64 . . . .**41** E1
Mayfield Gr
Cuddington CW8 . . . .**102** A4
Wilmslow SK9 . . . .**59** E5
Mayfield Mews CW1 . . . .**189** F6
Mayfield Pk CH4 . . . .**140** D6
Mayfield Rd Blacon CH1 . . . .**117** D5
Bramhall SK7 . . . .**35** E4
Mobberley WA16 . . . .**57** F4
Northwich CW9 . . . .**104** C8
Warrington WA4 . . . .**17** A2
Mayfield Terr SK11 . . . .**112** C5
Mayfield View WA3 . . . .**18** F2
Mayflower Rd CW5 . . . .**204** E3
May Pd Cheadle SK8 . . . .**35** B6
Heswall CH60 . . . .**41** A8
Maysville Cl WA5 . . . .**15** B6
Maythorn Ave WA3 . . . .**9** A7
Maytree Ave CH3 . . . .**119** B2
May Wlk **2** M31 . . . .**11** E3
McCarthy Cl WA3 . . . .**10** A3
McClellan Pl WA8 . . . .**13** B1
Mccorquodale Gdns 6
WA12 . . . .**2** E3
Mcdean Row **1** CW7 . . . . .**125** D2
McEllin Cl ST7 . . . .**209** E2
McGarva Way CH65 . . . .**70** C4
McGowan Ho ST7 . . . .**210** D8
McKeagney Gdns WA8 . . . . .**22** C7
McKee Ave WA2 . . . .**8** B2
Mckelvey Way
Audlem CW3 . . . .**230** A5
Copthorne CW3 . . . .**229** F5
Mckenzie Cres CW8 . . . .**78** B1
McKinley St WA5 . . . .**15** A7
McKinley Way WA8 . . . .**12** F3
McLaren St CW1 . . . .**190** C7
McCluskey Hts **8** CW7 . . . .**125** F2
Mcmillan St CW1 . . . .**69** A5
Mcmillen Rd CW1 . . . .**191** E5
McMinnis Ave WA9 . . . .**1** B2
McNeill Ave CW1 . . . .**190** A5
Mead Ave ST7 . . . .**194** E7
Mead Cl Elworth CW11 . . . . .**174** F6
Knutsford WA16 . . . .**56** F1
Meade The SK9 . . . .**60** C8
Meadow Ave
Congleton CW12 . . . .**156** C1
Goostrey CW4 . . . .**107** C1
Warrington WA4 . . . .**16** B2
Weston CW2 . . . .**207** B5
MEADOWBANK **126** D5
Meadow Bank
Adderley TF9 . . . .**235** A4
Kelsall CW6 . . . .**122** C4
Meadowbank Ave CW11 . . . .**175** A3
Meadowbank Dr CH66 . . . . . .**69** A6
Meadowbank Gdns WA3 . . . . .**5** C7
Meadow Brow SK9 . . . .**60** A2
Meadow Brown Pl **8**
CW11 . . . .**175** D8
Meadow Cl
Cuddington CW8 . . . .**102** A4
Farndon CH3 . . . .**180** F1
Goostrey CW4 . . . .**107** E1
Helsby WA6 . . . .**73** B3
High Lane SK6 . . . .**37** F8
Nantwich CW5 . . . .**204** C4
Neston CH64 . . . .**66** E6
Newton-le-Willows WA12 . . . .**1** F3
Shavington CW2 . . . .**206** D5
Tarvin CH3 . . . .**121** B2
Whaley Bridge SK23 . . . . . .**65** C8
Widnes WA8 . . . .**12** D3
Willaston CH64 . . . .**67** F8
Wilmslow SK9 . . . .**59** E4
Winsford CW7 . . . .**126** C3
Meadow Cotts **5** CW12 . . .**156** D3
Meadowcroft
Higher Kinnerton CH4 . . . . .**161** A7
Saughall CH1 . . . .**94** B1
Meadow Croft
Alsager ST7 . . . .**193** E2
Willaston CH64 . . . .**67** E8
Meadowcroft Ct WA7 . . . .**50** A8
Meadow Ct
Frodsham WA6 . . . .**49** C1
Mollington CH1 . . . .**94** F1
Newchapel ST7 . . . .**195** E2
No Man's Heath SY14 . . . . .**214** A5
Meadow Dr Barnton CW8 . . .**78** A3
Knutsford WA16 . . . .**81** F8
Prestbury SK10 . . . .**87** B7
Wistaston CW2 . . . .**205** F7
Meadow End Rd SK11 . . . . . .**84** A2
Meadowfield
Tarporley CW6 . . . .**146** C1
Whaley Bridge SK23 . . . . . .**65** D8
Meadow Field Rd CH4 . . . . .**141** A5
Meadow Gate CW9 . . . .**79** F5
Meadowgate Cl CW11 . . . . .**174** D5
Meadowgate Farm WA7 . . . . .**49** F2
Meadow Gr
Northwich CW9 . . . .**104** B5
Winsford CW7 . . . .**126** F1
Meadow Home Pk CW7 . . . .**126** D6
Meadow House Pk CW6 . . . .**185** D5

Meadow La
Comberbach CW9 . . . .**78** C7
Disley SK12 . . . .**38** D6
Ellesmere Port CH65 . . . . . .**70** D6
Huntington CH3 . . . .**142** A5
Moulton CW9 . . . .**126** F8
Warrington WA2 . . . .**9** A2
Willaston CH64 . . . .**67** F8
Meadow Lane Ind Pk
CH65 . . . .**70** D5
Meadow Mill Ct CW12 . . . . .**156** E3
Meadow Prim Sch CH66 . . .**69** D2
Meadow Rd
Broughton CH4 . . . .**139** B4
Weaverham CW8 . . . .**102** E7
Meadow Rise
Clutton CH3 . . . .**182** D2
Winsford CW7 . . . .**126** A1
Meadow Row WA7 . . . .**24** A1
Meadows Farm La SY14 . . . .**212** B6
Meadowside Disley SK12 . . . .**39** A6
Fourlane-ends SK10 . . . .**63** B8
Frodsham WA6 . . . .**74** A8
Northwich CW8 . . . .**103** D7
Whaley Bridge SK23 . . . . . .**65** D8
Meadowside Ave ST7 . . . . . .**209** D2
Meadowside Com Prim Sch
WA2 . . . .**8** B1
Meadowside Dr CW5 . . . . . .**204** D5
Meadowside La ST7 . . . .**195** B7
Meadowside Mews CH1 . . . .**118** B4
Meadowside Rd CH62 . . . . . .**43** D8
Meadows La Chester CH4 . . .**237** C1
Saughall CH1 . . . .**117** A8
Meadows Pl CH4 . . . .**141** E7
Meadows Rd Cheadle SK8 . .**34** F8
Kidsgrove ST7 . . . .**194** F1
Meadow St New Mills SK22 . .**39** C8
3 Northwich CW9 . . . . . .**104** A8
Meadows The
Ashton Hayes CH3 . . . .**121** E8
Congleton CW12 . . . .**156** E3
Irlam M44 . . . .**11** E6
Neston CH64 . . . .**66** F6
Meadowsway CW2 . . . .**118** D8
Meadowsweet Rd WA16 . . . . .**57** F3
Meadow The CW4 . . . .**130** D8
Meadowvale Cl CW5 . . . .**204** E7
Meadow View
Chester CH3 . . . .**118** F1
Ellesmere Port CH2 . . . .**70** E1
Elton CH2 . . . .**72** A3
Lymm WA13 . . . .**18** D4
Middlewich CW10 . . . .**128** B2
Sealand CH5 . . . .**116** A6
Meadow View Dr WA6 . . . . . .**74** A7
Meadow Way
Elworth CW11 . . . .**174** F6
Lawton-gate ST7 . . . .**194** A5
Macclesfield SK10 . . . .**87** E2
Saughall CH1 . . . .**117** C6
Wilmslow SK9 . . . .**59** E4
Meadow Wlk
Partington M31 . . . .**11** D1
4 Runcorn WA7 . . . .**49** F7
Mead Rd WA1 . . . .**17** A8
Meadscroft Dr SK9 . . . .**59** F1
Meads Rd ST7 . . . .**193** D4
Meadway Bramhall SK7 . . . .**35** E5
Ellesmere Port CH66 . . . . . .**69** B7
Golborne WA3 . . . .**3** D1
Heswall CH60 . . . .**40** F6
High Lane SK6 . . . .**37** F8
Poynton SK12 . . . .**36** B4
Prestbury SK10 . . . .**87** A5
Runcorn WA7 . . . .**49** E8
Widnes WA8 . . . .**12** A1
Meakin Cl CW12 . . . .**157** D1
Mealors New Cotts CH64 . . . .**67** A4
Mealors Weint CH64 . . . .**41** B1
Meal St SK22 . . . .**39** C8
Meddings Cl SK9 . . . .**85** A8
Medina Ave CW7 . . . .**126** F2
Medina Way ST7 . . . .**195** B2
Medlar Cl CH4 . . . .**140** F5
Medlock Cl WA7 . . . .**24** A2
Medlock St CW9 . . . .**104** C6
Medway Cl Golborne WN7 . . . .**4** C3
Handforth SK9 . . . .**34** D2
Warrington WA2 . . . .**8** E2
Medway Dr ST8 . . . .**179** D1
Medway Rd WA3 . . . .**5** A2
Meeanee Dr CW5 . . . .**204** D4
Mee St SK11 . . . .**112** E5
Meeting House La WA6 . . . . .**74** E2
Meeting La WA5 . . . .**14** E5
MEGACRE **210** A1
Megacre ST7 . . . .**210** A1
Megg La CW9 . . . .**53** B4
Meg La Langley SK11 . . . . . .**113** D1
Macclesfield SK10 . . . .**111** E8
Melbourne Ave M90 . . . .**33** A8
Melbourne Gr CW1 . . . .**191** C5
Melbourne Rd
Blacon CH1 . . . .**117** D4
Bramhall SK7 . . . .**35** F5
Melbury Ct WA3 . . . .**9** F6
Melbury Rd SK8 . . . .**35** B6
Melchett Cres CW9 . . . .**104** D7
Melford Cl CW2 . . . .**206** C8
Melford Ct WA1 . . . .**17** D8
Melford Dr
Macclesfield SK10 . . . .**87** C2
Runcorn WA7 . . . .**23** C1
Meliden Gr WA6 . . . .**73** B1
Melksham Cl SK11 . . . .**112** A7
Mellard St ST7 . . . .**209** D1

Mellock Cl CH64 . . . . .66 F6
Mellock La CH64 . . . . .66 F7
Mellor Cl WA7 . . . . .24 D1
Mellor Cres WA16 . . . . .56 E1
Mellors Bank ST7 . . . . .195 D6
Mellors Field Cl CW11 . . . . .175 B8
Mellor St Crewe CW1 . . . . . .190 D5
  Packmoor ST7 . . . . .195 F2
Mellor View SK12 . . . . .38 E6
Melrose Ave
  Burtonwood WA5 . . . . .6 F7
  Chester CH3 . . . . .119 B2
  Warrington WA4 . . . . .26 D8
Melrose Cres SK12 . . . . .37 D5
Melrose Ct 15 SK9 . . . . .34 E1
Melrose Dr Crewe CW1 . . . . .190 B8
  Ellesmere Port CH66 . . . . . . .94 F8
Melrose Way
  Chelford SK10 . . . . .84 E6
  Row-of-Trees SK9 . . . . .59 F2
  Wilmslow SK9 . . . . .60 A3
Melton Ave WA4 . . . . .26 B8
Melton Cl CW12 . . . . .155 F3
Melton Dr CW12 . . . . .155 F3
Melton Rd WA7 . . . . .49 C7
Melverly Dr CH1 . . . . .117 C6
Melville Cl Warrington WA2 . .16 B7
  2 Widnes WA8 . . . . .13 D1
Melville Rd M44 . . . . .11 C5
Membury Dr WA5 . . . . .14 E8
Mendell Cl CH62 . . . . .43 E8
Mendell Prim Sch CH62 . . . . .43 E8
Mendip Ave WA2 . . . . .8 B3
Mendip Cl
  Ellesmere Port CH66 . . . . . . .69 E3
  Gatley SK8 . . . . .34 B7
  Winsford CW7 . . . . .149 B8
Menin Ave WA4 . . . . .16 C3
Menlow Cl WA4 . . . . .17 C1
Mentmore Gdns WA4 . . . . . .26 F5
Meols Cl
  Ellesmere Port CH66 . . . . . . .69 E4
  Hale L24 . . . . .21 E2
Mercer Cl SY14 . . . . .213 B3
Mercer Pl 4 CW11 . . . . . . .152 C2
Mercer Rd WA11 . . . . .1 D6
Mercer St Burtonwood WA5 . . .6 E6
  Newton-le-Willows WA12 . . . .2 D4
Mercer Way Chester CH4 . .140 F6
  Nantwich CW5 . . . . .204 E7
Mercer Wlk CH65 . . . . .70 C4
Merchants Ct CW1 . . . . .190 C7
Mercia Gr CH3 . . . . .142 C5
Mercian Cl CW2 . . . . .206 B4
Mercury Ct CH1 . . . . .117 E2
MERE 56 B8
Mere Ave CH63 . . . . .43 B6
Mere Bank CW9 . . . . .127 A8
Merebank Rd CW2 . . . . .190 B1
Merebrook Cl SK11 . . . . . . .112 A8
Merebrook Rd SK11 . . . . . . .111 F8
Mere Brook Wlk CW2 . . . . . .190 C1
Mere Cl
  Ellesmere Port CH66 . . . . . . .69 D2
  Haslington CW1 . . . . .191 D4
  Pickmere WA16 . . . . .80 A7
Mere Cres CW8 . . . . .123 F6
Merecroft 1 CH3 . . . . .119 A1
Mere Ct Alsager ST7 . . . . . .193 D4
  Chelford SK11 . . . . .83 F3
  6 Knutsford WA16 . . . . . . .57 A2
  Weston CW2 . . . . .207 B5
  Winsford CW7 . . . . .149 E8
Meredith Ave WA4 . . . . .17 B2
Meredith St CW1 . . . . .190 C5
Mere Hall WA16 . . . . .56 A8
Mere Hall Est WA16 . . . . .56 A7
Merehaven Cl WA16 . . . . .80 A7
MERE HEATH 127 A8
Mereheath Cl CW9 . . . . .103 F2
Mereheath Dr WA16 . . . . .56 E7
Mereheath La WA16 . . . . .56 E8
Mereheath Pk WA16 . . . . .56 F3
Mere Heyes La
  High Legh WA16 . . . . .29 C1
  Northwood Hall WA16 . . . . . .55 C8
Mere Ho ST7 . . . . .194 B8
Mere La Cuddington CW8 . . .102 A2
  Pickmere WA16 . . . . .79 F7
Merelake Rd ST7 . . . . .210 B8
Merelake Way
  Alsager ST7 . . . . .193 F2
  Lawton-gate ST7 . . . . .194 A1
Mere Mill La WA3 . . . . .30 D1
Meremore Dr ST5 . . . . .210 D2
Mere Rd Marston CW9 . . . . . .79 B6
  Newton-le-Willows WA12 . . . .2 F4
  Warrington WA2 . . . . .9 A2
  Weston CW2 . . . . .207 B5
  Weston CW2 . . . . .207 B5
Mereside Ave CW12 . . . . . . .156 B3
Mereside Cl SK10 . . . . .87 A1
Mereside Gdns SK23 . . . . . . .65 D6
Mereside Rd WA16 . . . . .30 C2
Mere St CW1 . . . . .191 D4
Merevale Cl WA7 . . . . .49 E6
Mere View
  3 Alvanley WA6 . . . . .73 A2
  Astbury Marsh CW12 . . . . . .156 B1
  Helsby WA6 . . . . .73 A2
Mere View Gdns WA4 . . . . . .26 E5
Merewood Cl WA2 . . . . .8 D3
Mereworth Dr CW9 . . . . .103 F5
Meridian Ho CW7 . . . . .127 B3
Meriton Rd SK9 . . . . .34 D4
Merlin Ave WA16 . . . . .57 B3
Merlin Cl Macclesfield SK10 . .87 D5
  Runcorn WA7 . . . . .24 A1

Merlin Cl continued
  Winsford CW7 . . . . .150 A8
  Woodford SK7 . . . . .35 F2
Merlin Ct 4 CW1 . . . . .190 A8
Merlin Way Crewe CW1 . . . . .190 A8
  Kidsgrove ST7 . . . . .195 D3
Merrick Cl WA2 . . . . .8 E3
Merridale The WA15 . . . . . . .32 A8
Merrill's Ave CW2 . . . . .189 E5
Merriman Ave WA16 . . . . . . .57 C3
Merrivale Rd CW2 . . . . .206 B8
Merrydale Cl SK10 . . . . .86 F1
Merry Farm Dr WA16 . . . . . . .81 D2
Merryman's La SK9 . . . . .84 B7
Mersey Pl CW7 . . . . .127 B1
Mersey Rd Runcorn WA7 . . . .23 A3
  Widnes WA8 . . . . .23 A4
Mersey St St Helens WA9 . . . .1 A3
  Warrington WA1 . . . . .16 B5
Merseyton Rd CH65 . . . . .70 B8
Merseyton Road Workshops
  CH65 . . . . .70 C7
Mersey View WA7 . . . . .48 D7
Mersey View Rd WA8 . . . . . . .22 B4
Mersey Wlk WA4 . . . . .16 F5
Mersham Ct WA8 . . . . .12 F4
Merton Ave SK7 . . . . .36 F8
Merton Cl CH64 . . . . .66 E5
Merton Dr CH4 . . . . .141 A4
Merton House Sch CH2 . . . .118 C4
Merton Rd Bebington CH65 . .44 B3
  Ellesmere Port CH66 . . . . . . .69 F3
  Poynton SK12 . . . . .36 B4
Mertoun Rd WA8 . . . . .16 B1
Mervyn Rd WA8 . . . . .77 E1
Merwood Ave SK8 . . . . .34 D8
Messham Ct CW4 . . . . .139 D4
Messuage La CW12 . . . . . . .132 E4
Meteor Cres WA2 . . . . .8 D2
Metfield Gdns 6 WA5 . . . . . .14 F8
Mevagissey Rd WA7 . . . . . . .50 C5
Mevril Rd SK23 . . . . .65 E5
Mevril Springs Way SK23 . . .65 E5
Mews The Barnton CW8 . . . . .78 B2
  2 Birch Heath CH3 . . . . . . .168 C8
  Burtonwood WA5 . . . . .6 E6
  Holmes Chapel CW4 . . . . . .130 C3
  New Mills SK22 . . . . .39 D8
  Tarporley CW6 . . . . .168 C8
  Willaston CH64 . . . . .68 A8
  Wilmslow SK9 . . . . .33 D4
Meynell Cl CW2 . . . . .190 A1
Meynell Pl CH1 . . . . .118 A5
Meyrick Cl WA12 . . . . .2 A3
Miami Cl 9 WA5 . . . . .15 B7
Micawber Rd SK12 . . . . .36 E2
Michigan Pl WA5 . . . . .15 C7
Micklegate
  Mickle Trafford CH2 . . . . . .119 E8
  Runcorn WA7 . . . . .50 D7
MICKLE TRAFFORD 119 E8
Mickle Trafford Village Sch
  CH2 . . . . .119 E8
Micklewright Ave CW1 . . . . .190 D5
Mickley Hall La CW5 . . . . . . .218 A4
Mid-Cheshire Coll (Hartford
  Campus) CW8 . . . . .103 C6
Mid Cheshire Coll (London
  Road Site) CW9 . . . . .103 F6
Mid Cheshire Coll (Verdin
  Ctr) CW7 . . . . .126 D1
Middlecroft CH3 . . . . .119 E5
Middlefield Cl ST7 . . . . .193 A4
Middlehills SK11 . . . . .113 A6
Middlehurst Ave CW8 . . . . . .102 E8
Middlehurst Rd WA4 . . . . . . .17 A2
Middle La Aldford CH3 . . . . .163 F3
  Congleton CW12 . . . . .157 D4
  Kingsley WA6 . . . . .74 F2
MIDDLEWICH 128 D3
Middlewich High Sch
  6 Middlewich CW10 . . . . . .128 C1
  5 Middlewich CW10 . . . . . .151 C8
Middlewich L Ctr CW10 . . . .151 C8
Middlewich Prim Sch
  CW10 . . . . .151 B8
Middlewich Rd
  Allostock WA16 . . . . .106 D5
  Church Minshull CW1,
    CW10 . . . . .172 E5
  Cranage CW4, CW10 . . . . . .129 E6
  Crewe CW1 . . . . .189 D6
  Delamere CW6, CW8 . . . . . .123 D5
  Holmes Chapel CW4 . . . . . .130 B3
  Knutsford WA16 . . . . .82 A3
  Lower Peover WA16 . . . . .81 F2
  Nantwich CW5 . . . . .189 B1
  Nantwich CW5 . . . . .204 F7
  Northwich CW9 . . . . .104 D7
  Sandbach CW11 . . . . .174 E7
  Winsford CW7, CW10 . . . . . .127 E1
Middlewich Road Ind Est
  CW10 . . . . .129 A6
Middlewich St CW1 . . . . . . .190 D6
Middle Wlk Frodsham WA6 . .74 B7
  Knutsford WA16 . . . . .57 D7
MIDDLEWOOD 37 C5
Middlewood WA3 . . . . .3 E8
Middlewood Rd
  Hazel Grove SK7, SK12 . . . . .37 C7
  High Lane SK6 . . . . .37 D7
  Poynton SK12 . . . . .37 B4
Middlewood Sta SK12 . . . . . .37 D6
Middlewood View SK6 . . . . . .37 D7
Midfield Cl ST8 . . . . .179 C2
Midgley La
  Turn Edge SK11 . . . . .138 A1

Midgley La continued
  Wildboarclough SK11 . . . . . .137 E2
Midhurst Cl SK8 . . . . .34 F8
Midland St WA8 . . . . .13 B1
Midland Terr SK22 . . . . .39 C7
Midland Way WA1, WA5 . . . . .16 B5
Midlothian Ho 4 CH1 . . . . . .237 C3
Midpoint 18 Motorway Ind
  Est CW10 . . . . .128 E1
MIDWAY 36 D2
Midway SK8 . . . . .35 B5
Midway Dr SK12 . . . . .36 D2
Midwood St 14 WA8 . . . . . . .23 B8
Milborne Cl CW2 . . . . .118 E5
Mildenhall Cl WA5 . . . . .15 B6
Milford Gdns WA4 . . . . .26 D4
Milk St CW12 . . . . .156 D3
Millar Cres WA8 . . . . .23 A7
Mill Ave WA5 . . . . .14 E7
Millbank WA13 . . . . .18 E3
Mill Bank CH3 . . . . .67 A5
Millbank Cl SK11 . . . . .84 A3
Millbank Cotts CH3 . . . . .166 C2
Millbank WA6 . . . . .74 A8
Millbank Dr SK10 . . . . .86 F1
Millbeck Cl CW2 . . . . .207 B5
Mill Bridge Cl CW1 . . . . .190 F3
Millbridge Gdns WA12 . . . . . . .2 E3
Millbrook Cl
  Fowley Common WA3 . . . . . . .5 C5
  Winsford CW7 . . . . .148 F8
Millbrook Ct
  Middlewich CW10 . . . . .128 D1
  Warrington WA2 . . . . .8 B2
Millbrook End CH3 . . . . .166 A2
Millbrook Fold SK7 . . . . .36 F8
Mill Brow WA8 . . . . .13 C1
Millbuck Pk CW1 . . . . .174 C5
Millbuck Way CW11 . . . . .174 C6
Mill Cl Chester CH2 . . . . .118 D6
  Knutsford WA16 . . . . .57 D4
  Warrington WA2 . . . . .8 E4
Mill Cotts Bollington SK10 . . .88 B8
  Christleton CH3 . . . . .142 D8
  Willaston CH64 . . . . .42 F1
Millcroft Neston CH64 . . . . . .41 E1
  Sandbach, Wheelock
    CW11 . . . . .191 F8
Mill Cross CH3 . . . . .143 B5
Mill Ct CH65 . . . . .69 F6
Milldale Rd WN7 . . . . .4 B8
MILLEND 209 C5
Millend La ST7 . . . . .209 C5
Millenium Way 8 WA5 . . . . . .15 B7
Millennium Ct CW4 . . . . .41 E2
Millennium Way ST5 . . . . . . .210 F2
Miller Cl CW8 . . . . .78 C1
Millers Cl CH3 . . . . .143 A4
Millers Croft 8 SK10 . . . . . .112 C8
Millers Ct 7 SK10 . . . . .112 C8
Millersdale Cl CH62 . . . . .43 F5
Millersdale Gr WA7 . . . . .49 D6
Millers Gr CW5 . . . . .216 E4
Millers La WA13 . . . . .19 B5
Millers Mdw SK10 . . . . .88 E5
Millers Pk CH4 . . . . .140 D6
Miller St WA4 . . . . .16 C4
Miller's Vale SK22 . . . . .39 C8
Millers View CW7 . . . . .195 A1
Millers Wharf ST7 . . . . .193 E7
Milley La WA16 . . . . .80 C7
Mill Farm Cl WA2 . . . . .8 E4
Mill Farm Cotts CW7 . . . . . .149 B3
Mill Farm Est CW5 . . . . .217 A3
Millfield Holt LL13 . . . . .196 D7
  Neston CH64 . . . . .41 E1
Millfield Bsns Ctr WA11 . . . . . .1 E8
Mill Field Cl CH3 . . . . .180 F2
Millfield La Haydock WA11 . . . .1 E8
  Milners Heath CH3 . . . . .143 A1
  Saighton CH3 . . . . .142 F1
  Tarporley CW6 . . . . .146 C2
Millfield Pk 4 WA3 . . . . .3 B8
Millfield Rd WA8 . . . . .13 C2
Millfields CW5 . . . . .204 D4
Millfields CE Prim Sch
  CH62 . . . . .43 E4
Millfields Prim Sch & Nur
  CW5 . . . . .204 C5
Millfield Terr CH66 . . . . .69 C7
Millgate CW8 . . . . .101 A4
Mill Gn Congleton CW12 . . . .156 D3
  Willaston CH64 . . . . .67 F8
Mill Gr Bulkeley SY14 . . . . . .184 E2
  Kidsgrove ST7 . . . . .194 D1
Mill Green La WA8 . . . . .13 C5
Mill Green Sch WA12 . . . . . . .2 E3
Mill Hill Ave SK12 . . . . .36 D2
Mill Hill Dr CW11 . . . . .175 A5
Mill Hill Hollow SK12 . . . . . . .36 D7
Mill Hill La CW11 . . . . .175 A4
Mill Ho CW5 . . . . .204 D5
Millhouse Ave WA4 . . . . .16 D1
Millhouse La WA3 . . . . .9 A6
Milliner St CH66 . . . . .69 B5
Milling Field The CW4 . . . . .130 C2
Millingford Ind Est WA3 . . . . . .3 A8
Millington Cl Runcorn WA7 . . .49 F3
  Widnes WA8 . . . . .22 F8
Millington Gdns WA13 . . . . . .19 C4
Millington Hall La WA14 . . . . .30 B5
Millington La
  Rostherne WA14 . . . . .30 B6
  Weaverham CW8 . . . . .102 B6

Mill La Adlington SK10 . . . . . .62 B6
  Aldford CH3 . . . . .163 F3
  Alsager CW11 . . . . .192 E8
  Altrincham WA15 . . . . .32 E4
  Audlem, Little Heath CW3 . . .230 A4
  Audlem, Swanbach CW3 . . . .229 E2
  Barthomley CW2 . . . . .208 C7
  Blakenhall CW5 . . . . .221 B4
  Bold Heath WA8 . . . . .13 D6
  Bollington SK10 . . . . .88 C8
  Brereton Green CW4 . . . . . .153 E8
  Bulkeley SY14 . . . . .184 E2
  Burton CH64 . . . . .67 C1
  Chester CH2 . . . . .118 D6
  Christleton CH3 . . . . .120 D2
  Congleton CW12 . . . . .179 C8
  Cronton WA8 . . . . .12 D6
  Cuddington CW8 . . . . .101 F4
  Duddon CW6 . . . . .145 A7
  Eaton CW6 . . . . .147 B2
  Ellesmere Port CH66 . . . . . . .69 E5
  Frodsham WA6 . . . . .49 C2
  Goostrey CW4 . . . . .107 E2
  Great Barrow CH3 . . . . .120 E5
  Hazel Grove SK7 . . . . .36 F8
  Heswall CH60 . . . . .41 B8
  Higher Walton WA4 . . . . .25 E7
  Holmes Chapel CW4 . . . . . .154 A8
  Huxley CH3 . . . . .144 C1
  Kelsall CW6 . . . . .122 C1
  Kingsley WA6 . . . . .75 E3
  Lindow End SK9 . . . . .84 A7
  Little Budworth CW6 . . . . . .148 A8
  Lymm WA13 . . . . .19 C4
  Macclesfield SK11 . . . . .112 D7
  Marton CW12 . . . . .132 F2
  Middlewich CW10 . . . . .128 D1
  Middlewich, Stud Green
    CW11 . . . . .152 C1
  Mobberley WA16 . . . . .58 B4
  Mottram St Andrew SK10 . . . .61 C5
  Neston CH64 . . . . .67 C5
  Newton-le-Willows WA12 . . . .2 E3
  Over Peover WA16, SK11 . . .108 D8
  Prestbury SK10 . . . . .61 F6
  Sandbach CW11 . . . . .174 C8
  Sandbach, Wheelock
    CW11 . . . . .175 B2
  Siddington SK11 . . . . .109 F6
  Smallwood CW11 . . . . .176 D7
  Tarvin CH3 . . . . .121 C4
  The Bank ST7 . . . . .195 A7
  Warrington WA2 . . . . .7 F4
  Warrington, Houghton Gn
    WA2 . . . . .8 E4
  Warrington, Stockton Heath
    WA4 . . . . .16 E1
  Whitegate CW7, CW8 . . . . . .126 B6
  Willaston CH64 . . . . .42 F1
Mill Lane Cotts CH3 . . . . . . .120 E5
Mill Lane End CW5 . . . . .221 C4
Mill Lane Ind Est CH2 . . . . . . .70 F2
Mill Mdw WA12 . . . . .2 E3
Millmead ST7 . . . . .193 F7
Mill Park Dr CH62 . . . . .43 E3
Millpond Ct WA6 . . . . .75 E2
Mill Pool La CW5 . . . . .187 C6
Mill Pool Way CW11 . . . . . . .175 B5
Millport Cl WA2 . . . . .9 A2
Millrace Dr CW2 . . . . .206 B8
Mill Rd Macclesfield SK11 . . .112 D6
  Wilmslow SK9 . . . . .60 B7
Mill Rise Helsby WA6 . . . . . . .73 C4
  Kidsgrove ST7 . . . . .195 A1
Mill Row CW11 . . . . .175 C6
Millside Cl CH3 . . . . .121 B3
Mill St Chester CH4 . . . . . . .237 B1
  Congleton CW12 . . . . .156 D3
  Congleton, Buglawton
    CW12 . . . . .156 F4
  Crewe CW2 . . . . .190 D3
  Golborne WA3 . . . . .3 A8
  Macclesfield SK11 . . . . .112 D7
  Nantwich CW5 . . . . .204 E5
  Neston CH64 . . . . .66 D8
  Wilmslow SK9 . . . . .60 B7
Millstone Ave ST7 . . . . .194 E1
Millstone Cl SK12 . . . . .36 F5
Millstone La CW5 . . . . .204 F5
Millstone Pas SK11 . . . . . . .112 E6
Mill Stream Cl CW4 . . . . .107 E1
Mills Way CW1 . . . . .173 B1
Mill The ST7 . . . . .195 C5
Mill View Cl SY14 . . . . .184 E2
Mill View Prim Sch CH2 . . . .118 E6
Millway Altrincham WA15 . . . .32 C7
  Waverton CH3 . . . . .143 B5
Mill Way CW5 . . . . .204 F2
Millway Rd L24 . . . . .21 A4
Mill Wharf CH3 . . . . .143 B5
Millwood WA7 . . . . .24 C1
Mill Wood & Alder Wood
  Nature Reserve * L24 . . . . . .21 B4
Millwood Cl 4 SK8 . . . . .34 E8
Millwood Ct L24 . . . . .21 A4
Millwood Dr CW8 . . . . .102 E4
Millyard The CH4 . . . . .162 C1
Milne Cl CW2 . . . . .189 F1
Milner Cop CH60 . . . . .41 A8
Milner Rd Heswall CH60 . . . . .41 A8
  Northwich CW8 . . . . .103 C6
MILNERS GREEN 143 C2
Milners Heath La CH3 . . . . . .143 C2
Milner St WA5 . . . . .15 F5
Milnthorpe Rd WA5 . . . . .6 E5
Milton Ave Irlam M44 . . . . . . .11 E6
  Newton-le-Willows WA12 . . . .2 B3
  Widnes WA8 . . . . .22 F8

Milton Cl
  Ellesmere Port CH65 . . . . . . .70 D4
  Higher Wincham CW9 . . . . . .80 A5
  Middlewich CW10 . . . . .151 D5
Milton Cres ST7 . . . . .210 C8
Milton Ct SK7 . . . . .35 F6
Milton Dr Poynton SK12 . . . . .36 D4
  Wistaston CW2 . . . . .206 A8
Milton Gr Helsby WA6 . . . . . . .73 A1
  Warrington WA4 . . . . .16 D3
MILTON GREEN 165 C2
Milton Rd Blacon CH1 . . . . . .117 F6
  Bramhall SK7 . . . . .35 E7
  Ellesmere Port CH65 . . . . . . .70 D4
  Golborne WA3 . . . . .3 D7
  Widnes WA8 . . . . .23 A8
Milton Rough CW8 . . . . .76 E2
Milton St Chester CH1 . . . . . .237 B3
  Widnes WA8 . . . . .23 A5
Milton Way CW11 . . . . .174 D6
Milvain Dr WA2 . . . . .8 C1
Milverton Dr SK7 . . . . .35 B5
Mimosa Cl CW2 . . . . .72 C4
Miners Way Speke L24 . . . . . .21 A3
  Widnes WA8 . . . . .23 A7
Minerva Ave CH1 . . . . .117 E2
Minerva Cl WA4 . . . . .16 D2
Minerva Ct CH1 . . . . .117 E2
Mine Way WA11 . . . . .1 F7
Minn-End-La SK11 . . . . .159 B6
Minnow Dr CH65 . . . . .70 A8
Minor Ave WA5 . . . . .112 D3
Minshull Cl 12 CW10 . . . . . .151 D5
Minshull La CW5, CW7 . . . . .171 D4
Minshull New Rd CW1 . . . . .189 F7
Minshull St WA16 . . . . .57 A2
MINSHULL VERNON 172 E5
Minster Cl CW7 . . . . .149 D5
Minster Ct Runcorn WA7 . . . . .48 E8
  Wistaston CW2 . . . . .205 E8
Minster Dr WA14 . . . . .31 A8
Minton Cl CW12 . . . . .157 B1
Minton Way WA8 . . . . .13 B5
Mirfield Cl WA3 . . . . .3 D7
Mirion St CW1 . . . . .190 D4
Mission Mews CH2 . . . . .118 F2
Missouri Dr WA5 . . . . .15 A7
Misty Cl WA8 . . . . .12 C2
Mitchell Ave
  Burtonwood WA5 . . . . .6 E5
  Kidsgrove ST7 . . . . .194 D1
Mitchell Dr ST7 . . . . .194 D1
Mitchell Fold
  Fourlane-ends SK10 . . . . .63 D8
  High Lane SK6 . . . . .37 D1
Mitchell St Golborne WA3 . . . .3 A8
  Warrington WA4 . . . . .26 C8
Mithril Cl WA8 . . . . .13 E3
Mitton Cl WA3 . . . . .4 E5
MMU Institute of Education
  (Alsager) ST7 . . . . .193 A5
MMU Institute of Education
  (Crewe) CW1 . . . . .190 F3
Moat Ho 17 CW8 . . . . .103 F8
Moat House Dr CW2 . . . . . . .190 A2
Moat La Audley ST7 . . . . . . .209 B3
  Hollins Green WA3 . . . . .10 E2
MOBBERLEY 58 A4
Mobberley CE Prim Sch
  WA16 . . . . .58 C5
Mobberley Cl WA4 . . . . .17 D4
Mobberley Rd
  Ashley WA14, WA15,
    WA16 . . . . .31 E3
  Knutsford WA16 . . . . .57 B3
  Wilmslow SK9 . . . . .33 D1
Mobberley Sta WA16 . . . . . . .57 F7
MOBLAKE 230 D4
Modyn CH2 . . . . .118 C4
Moelfre Dr SK8 . . . . .35 C7
Moelwyn Dr CH66 . . . . .69 F7
Moggie La SK10 . . . . .36 F1
Mold Rd CH4 . . . . .139 A3
Molesworth Cl 2 WA5 . . . . . .14 E8
MOLLINGTON 94 E2
Mollington Ct CH1 . . . . .94 E2
Mollington Grange Bsns Pk
  CH1 . . . . .117 F8
Mollington Rd M22 . . . . .33 C8
Molly Potts Cl WA16 . . . . .82 B8
Molyneux Ave WA5 . . . . .15 F8
Monarch Cl Crewe CW2 . . . .189 F4
  Irlam M44 . . . . .11 C6
Monarch Dr CW9 . . . . .103 E5
Monarch Pl 14 CW11 . . . . . .175 D7
Monck Dr CW5 . . . . .204 D6
Mond Rd M44 . . . . .23 A8
Mondrem Gn CW6 . . . . .124 E2
Mond St WA8 . . . . .78 B3
Monica Dr WA8 . . . . .13 A5
Monk Cl 7 SK10 . . . . .87 E7
Monks Coppenhall Prim Sch
  CW1 . . . . .190 E7
Monks Gr CH65 . . . . .70 B6
MONKS HEATH 85 A1
Monk's Heath Crossroads
  SK10 . . . . .85 A1
Monks Heath Hall Wrkshps
  SK10 . . . . .85 B1
Monks La Acton CW5 . . . . . .203 F7
  Crewe CW1 . . . . .189 F5
  Nantwich CW5 . . . . .204 E5
Monk's La CW3 . . . . .230 C5
Monks Orch CW5 . . . . .204 F5
Monks Pl WA2 . . . . .16 C7

Monks St WA5 . . . . .15 E6
Monk St CW1 . . . . 190 A5
Monks Way CW8 . . . . 103 B4
Monkswood Cl WA5 . . . . .7 E2
Monmouth Cl WA1 . . . . .17 E7
Monroe Cl WA1 . . . . .17 B8
Monsall Cl SK11 . . . . 112 F7
Monsall Dr SK11 . . . . 112 F7
Montague Rd WA8 . . . . 22 A6
Montana Cl 3 WA5 . . . . 15 C7
Montclare Cres WA4 . . . . . . .16 F2
Montcliffe Cl WA3. . . . . .9 C5
Monterey Cl 3 WA8 . . . . 15 B6
Montgomery Ave CW5. . . 204 C7
Montgomery Cl
  Knutsford WA16 . . . . 57 C4
  Warrington WA5 . . . . 15 A8
Montgomery Rd WA8 . . . . . 22 D8
Montgomery Way CW7 . . 149 B7
Montmorency Rd WA16. . . 57 D3
Montpelier Ave WA7 . . . . . .48 F6
Montrose Cl
  Macclesfield SK10 . . . . . . 87 A1
  Shavington CW2 . . . . 206 B3
  Warrington WA3 . . . . .8 F4
Montrose Ct Chester CH4 . 140 F7
  Holmes Chapel CW4. . . . . 130 B2
Monument Rd ST7 . . . . 210 D6
Monument View ST7 . . . . 209 F2
Moody St CW12 . . . . 156 D2
Moor Cl ST8 . . . . 179 E1
Moor Cres WA4 . . . . 139 D1
Moorcroft WA16 . . . . .80 F3
Moorcroft Ave CH3 . . . . . . 119 B1
Moorcroft Cres CH3 . . . . . 119 C4
Moorcroft Ct CH3 . . . . 119 B1
Moorcroft Mews WA4 . . . 140 D6
Moordale Rd WA16 . . . . . . .57 B2
Moorditch La WA6 . . . . . . .48 F1
MOORE 25 B6
Moore Ave St Helens WA9. . . .1 B3
  Warrington WA4 . . . . 17 D3
Moore Cl WA8 . . . . 13 D2
Moore Dr WA11 . . . . .1 F6
Moore Gr WA13 . . . . .19 B5
Moore La WA4 . . . . 25 C7
Moore Pk Way WA11 . . . . . . .1 D8
Moore Prim Sch WA4 . . . . . 25 A5
Moore Reserve * WA4 . . . . 25 C8
Moorfield Cres WA3. . . . . . . .4 A7
Moorfield Cty Prim Sch
  WA8 . . . . 13 D3
Moorfield Dr Neston CH64. . 41 C1
  Wilmslow SK9 . . . . .59 E5
Moorfield Rd WA8 . . . . 13 D3
Moorfields CW5 . . . . 205 E6
Moorhead La CW11 . . . . . 154 D3
Moorhill Rd SK11 . . . . 112 C4
Moor Ho WA6. . . . . .74 B8
Moorhouse Ave ST7 . . . . . 193 E4
Moorhouse Cl CH2 . . . . . . 118 D5
Mooring Cl WA7 . . . . 50 D6
Moorings CW12 . . . . 156 E1
Moorings Cl
  Barbridge CW5 . . . . 187 C6
  Neston CH64 . . . . .41 B1
Moorings The
  Christleton CH3 . . . . 142 E7
  Disley SK12 . . . . 38 E6
  Heswall CH60 . . . . 40 C8
  Middlewich CW10 . . . . 128 C1
Moor La Bramhall SK7 . . . . . 35 E3
  Elton WA6 . . . . .72 E1
  Frodsham WA6 . . . . .74 B8
  Heswall CH60 . . . . 40 F8
  Higher Kinnerton CH4 . . . 161 D8
  Lower Kinnerton CH4 . . . . 161 C6
  Sandycroft CH5 . . . . 116 A3
  Waverton CH3 . . . . 143 A5
  Widnes WA8 . . . . .22 F7
  Wilmslow SK9 . . . . .59 E5
Moorland Cl CH60 . . . . 41 A7
Moorland Dr Cheadle SK8. . .34 F8
  Runcorn WA7 . . . . 50 E7
Moorland Pk CH60 . . . . 41 A7
Moorland Rd
  Biddulph ST8 . . . . 179 D1
  Ellesmere Port CH66 . . . . . 69 E8
  Elworth CW11 . . . . 174 F6
  Mow Cop ST7 . . . . 195 D7
Moorlands Ave CW8. . . . . 102 A4
Moorlands Cl SK10 . . . . . . 87 C3
Moorlands Dr CW5 . . . . . . 206 A1
Moorlands Pk CW8. . . . . . 102 A4
Moor Lane Bsns Ctr 9
  WA8 . . . . 23 A7
Moor Lane S WA8 . . . . .22 F7
Moor-Park Way CW9 . . . . 103 F4
Moorsbrook Gr 9 SK9. . . . .34 E1
Moorsfield Ave WA3. . . . . 229 F3
MOORSIDE 66 C7
Moorside Knutsford WA16. . 57 A2
  Warrington WA4 . . . . .16 E4
Moorside Ave CH64 . . . . . . 66 C8
Moorside Ct WA8 . . . . .22 F7
Moorside La Neston CH64. . 66 D8
  Pott Shrigley SK10 . . . . 63 E4
Moors La CW7 . . . . 149 D5
Moorson Ave ST7 . . . . 194 F8
Moor St CW12 . . . . 156 E2
Moorview Gdns ST7 . . . . 195 E6
Moorway CH60. . . . . .41 B8
Moran Cl SK9 . . . . .34 E2
Moran Cres SK11 . . . . 112 B7
Moran Dr WA5 . . . . 15 A6

Moran Rd SK11 . . . . 112 B7
Morcott La Hale L24 . . . . . . 21 D2
  Hale L24 . . . . 21 D2
Moresby Cl WA7 . . . . .50 E7
Moreton Ave SK7 . . . . .35 E5
Moreton Cl CW11 . . . . 175 C7
Moreton Dr Alsager ST7 . . 193 C3
  Handforth SK9 . . . . .34 E3
  Holmes Chapel CW4. . . . . 130 B3
  Poynton SK12 . . . . .36 F4
Moreton Pl ST7 . . . . 194 E6
Moreton Rd CW2. . . . . 189 F3
Moreton St CW8 . . . . 78 D1
Moreton Terr WA6 . . . . 74 A8
Moreville Cl CW9 . . . . 103 E3
Morgan Ave WA2 . . . . .8 C2
Morgan Cl Blacon CH1. . . . 117 F6
  Crewe CW2 . . . . 190 A4
Morgan Rd CW1 . . . . 152 C2
Morgans Way WA3 . . . . .4 A3
Morgan Wlk CW5 . . . . 204 D6
Morland Ave
  Bebington CH62 . . . . 43 D6
  Neston CH64 . . . . .66 F7
MORLEY 33 C2
Morley Cl CH2 . . . . 119 F8
MORLEY COMMON. 15 F1
Morley Dr WA12 . . . . 157 A1
MORLEY GREEN 33 C1
Morley Green Rd SK9. . . . . 33 C1
Morley La WA6 . . . . .97 E4
Morley Rd Runcorn WA7 . . 23 C1
  Warrington WA4 . . . . 16 A1
Morley St WA1 . . . . 16 D6
Mornant Ave CW8. . . . . . . 103 A3
Mornington Ave CH65 . . . . 70 C5
Mornington Cl CW11 . . . . 174 D7
Morphany La WA4. . . . . . . .51 E6
Morreys La CW6 . . . . 122 F6
Morris Ave WA4. . . . . .16 F4
Morris Cl WA11 . . . . .1 A5
Morris Dr
  Alderley Park SK10 . . . . . . .85 B3
  Weaverham WA8 . . . . 77 D1
Morris Oak CH4 . . . . 141 E1
Morrison Cl WA5 . . . . 15 A5
Morris Pk CW8. . . . . 103 B4
Morston Rd WA7 . . . . .24 E1
Mort Ave WA4 . . . . 17 A5
Mortimer Ave WA2 . . . . . . .16 B8
Mortimer Dr CW11 . . . . . . 175 C5
Mortlake Cl WA8 . . . . 12 C3
Mortlake Cres CH3 . . . . . . 119 A1
Morton Ave WA6 . . . . .73 B1
Morton Cl WA5 . . . . 15 C8
Morton Dr SK11 . . . . 112 F3
Morton Gdns CH1 . . . . 117 E4
Morton Rd Blacon CH1. . . . 117 E4
  Runcorn WA7 . . . . 50 D8
Morval Cres WA7 . . . . 23 D1
Morven Cl WA2 . . . . .8 E3
Moscardini Cl 3 WA7 . . . . .23 F2
Mosedale Gr WA7 . . . . .49 E5
Moseley Ave WA4 . . . . 17 A3
Moses Ct CH1 . . . . 237 C3
MOSS BANK 23 D8
Moss Bank Bramhall SK7. . . 35 C5
  Chester CH2. . . . . 118 C4
  Winsford CW7 . . . . 126 C1
Moss Bank Rd WA8 . . . . . . 23 D7
Moss Bower Rd SK11 . . . . 112 C4
MOSSBROW 19 E7
Moss Brow SK10 . . . . .87 E7
Moss Brow La WA16 . . . . . 28 D4
Moss Cl Warrington WA4 . . .16 E2
  Willaston CH64 . . . . 68 A8
Moss Croft CW1. . . . . 190 A8
Mossdale Cl Crewe CW2. . 189 E4
  Warrington WA5 . . . . 15 A7
Moss Dr Manley WA6 . . . . . .98 F4
  Middlewich CW10 . . . . 151 D6
MOSSEND 154 E1
Moss End La CW11 . . . . . . 176 E8
Moss Farm Barns CW8. . . 102 D4
Moss Farm Recn Ctr
  CW8 . . . . 103 D8
Mossfield Cres 4 ST7 . . . . 195 B2
Moss Fields Alsager ST7 . . 193 A3
  Crewe CW1 . . . . 173 A1
Mossford Ave CW1 . . . . . . 190 B7
Moss Gate WA3 . . . . 10 A5
Moss Gr Lymm WA13 . . . . . .19 B4
  Newcastle-under-Lyme
  ST5 . . . . 210 D3
  Saltney CH4 . . . . 140 D6
Moss Green Way WA9 . . . . .1 A1
Mosshall La WA4 . . . . .26 F1
Moss Hall La CW6 . . . . 147 C4
Moss Hey Prim Sch SK7. . . 35 C5
MOSS HOUSES 111 F2
Moss La Alderley Edge SK9. . 60 B1
  Bollington SK10 . . . . .87 E8
  Bramhall SK7 . . . . 35 D5
  Brereton Green CW12 . . . 154 F5
  Byley CW10 . . . . 129 B7
  Congleton CW12 . . . . 156 E6
  Crewe CW1 . . . . 173 A2
  Cuddington CW8 . . . . 102 A3
  Dunham Woodhouses WA13. . 20 B8
  Fowley Common WA3. . . . . . .5 D5
  Golborne WA3 . . . . .3 B5
  Higher Wincham CW9 . . . . .79 E6
  High Legh WA16 . . . . .29 E6
  High Legh, Sink Moss WA16. . 28 D4
  Hollins Green WA3. . . . . . . 10 E5
  Irlam M44 . . . . 11 D5
  Lawton-gate ST7 . . . . 194 F4

Moss La continued
  Lostock Green CW9 . . . . . 105 D8
  Macclesfield SK11 . . . . . . 112 C4
  Manley WA6. . . . . 99 A4
  Mere WA16 . . . . 56 C5
  Mobberley WA16 . . . . .58 F4
  Moore WA4 . . . . 25 A6
  Mottram St Andrew SK10. . 61 A2
  Norbury SY13. . . . . 215 C5
  Norley WA6 . . . . 101 B5
  Northwich CW8 . . . . 103 D7
  Over Peover WA16. . . . . . . 83 C3
  Partington M31 . . . . .11 F3
  Partington, Mossbrow
  WA13 . . . . .11 F1
  St Helens, Moss Nook WA9. . .1 A1
  Sandbach CW11. . . . . 174 C7
  Siddington SK11. . . . . 109 E2
  Tarporley CW6 . . . . 146 B2
  Warmingham CW1. . . . . . 173 C3
  Warrington WA3 . . . . .9 E1
  Wythenshawe SK9 . . . . . . .33 E6
Mosslands Cl CH66. . . . . . 69 E2
Moss Lane Bsns Ctr
  CW11 . . . . 174 D6
Moss Lane Ind Est CW11 . 174 D7
MOSSLEY 179 A8
Mossley Ave CH62. . . . . . . 43 D8
Mossley CE Prim Sch
  CW12 . . . . 179 B8
Mossley Ct CW12. . . . . . . 178 F8
Mossley Garth Cl 4
  CW12. . . . . 157 A1
Moss Mere CW11. . . . . . . 176 F7
MOSS NOOK 33 F7
Moss Pl ST7 . . . . 195 B3
Moss Rd Alderley Edge SK9 . 60 C2
  Congleton CW12 . . . . 178 F2
  Irlam M44 . . . . 11 C7
  Northwich CW8 . . . . 103 D8
  Warrington WA4 . . . . 17 A3
Moss Rose SK9. . . . . .60 B2
Moss Rose (Macclesfield
  Town FC) SK11. . . . . 112 D4
Moss Side La
  Antrobus CW9 . . . . 53 D7
  Hollins Green WA3. . . . . . . 10 F3
  Moore WA4 . . . . .24 F7
Moss Side Rd M44. . . . . . . .11 E6
Moss Sq Crewe CW1 . . . . . 190 D4
  Macclesfield SK11 . . . . . . 112 D4
Moss St Weaverham CW8 . . 77 D1
  Widnes WA8. . . . . 23 D1
Moss Terr Warren SK11. . . 112 A5
  Wilmslow SK9 . . . . .60 F8
  Winnington CW8 . . . . 78 D1
Moss The CW9 . . . . 78 D7
Mossvale CH66. . . . . 69 D8
Moss View Rd SK11. . . . . . 112 A4
Moss Way ST7 . . . . 193 A3
Mossways Gn SK9. . . . . . . 59 C7
Mossways Pk SK9 . . . . 59 C7
Mosswood Rd SK9 . . . . . . .34 E1
MOSTON 95 C1
Moston Cl 7 CW10. . . . . . . 151 D5
Moston Ct 5 CW12. . . . . . . 156 F3
Moston Gr WA13 . . . . 18 D3
MOSTON GREEN. 174 B8
Moston Rd Chester CH2. . . 118 D8
  Sandbach CW11. . . . . 174 D6
Mostyn Ave CH60. . . . . 40 C8
Mostyn Gdns CH64 . . . . . . .41 B1
Mostyn House Sch 7
  CH64 . . . . 41 C1
Mostyn Pl CH1 . . . . 117 E6
Mostyn Sq CH64. . . . . .41 B1
Mote Hill Ct WA1. . . . . 16 D6
Motherwell Cl WA8 . . . . . . 12 E3
Mottershead Cl 1 WA8. . . 23 A8
Mottershead Rd WA8. . . . . 23 A8
Mottershead Way 1
  CW2. . . . . 206 D5
Mottram Ave SK9 . . . . 34 C4
Mottram Cl
  Middlewich CW10 . . . . 151 B7
  Warrington WA4 . . . . .17 B3
Mottram Dr CW5 . . . . 205 A4
Mottram Rd SK9 . . . . 60 D1
MOTTRAM ST ANDREW. . .61 B2
Mottram St Andrew Prim Sch
  SK10 . . . . .61 B1
Mottram St Andrew Stud
  Farm * SK10. . . . . 61 A2
Mottram Way SK10. . . . . . .87 E2
Moughland La WA7 . . . . . . 49 A8
Moulders La WA1 . . . . .16 B4
MOULDSWORTH. 98 F2
Mouldsworth Cl 2 CW9 . 103 E4
Mouldsworth Motor Mus *
  CH3. . . . . .98 E1
Mouldsworth Sta CH3 . . . 99 A2
MOULTON 126 E7
Moulton Cl
  Knutsford WA16. . . . . 57 C1
  Northwich CW9 . . . . 103 E4
  Runcorn WA7 . . . . .49 F4
Moulton Cty Prim Sch
  CW9 . . . . 126 F8
Mountain View
  Helsby WA6 . . . . .73 B3
  Saltney CH4 . . . . 140 E6
Mount Ave CH60. . . . . 40 F8
Mount Barns CH2 . . . . 95 C6
Mountbatten Ct CW2. . . . 190 A3
Mountbatten Way CW12. . 156 E3
Mount Cl CW5 . . . . 204 F6

Mount Ct 3 CH60. . . . . .40 F8
Mount Dr CW5 . . . . 204 F6
Mount Farm Way CH66 . . 69 C2
Mountfield Rd SK7 . . . . . . .35 E5
Mount Mews CH60. . . . . . . 40 F8
Mount Pl CH2 . . . . 118 F2
MOUNT PLEASANT
  Mow Cop 195 B6
  Winsford 149 A7
Mount Pleasant
  Audlem CW3 . . . . 230 B4
  Chester CH4. . . . . 140 F7
  Congleton CW12 . . . . 156 E2
  Crewe CW1 . . . . 190 B6
  Elton CH2. . . . . 72 A4
  Haslington CW1 . . . . 191 D4
  Kidsgrove ST7 . . . . 195 A1
  Macclesfield SK10 . . . . . . .87 B1
  Rainow SK10 . . . . 88 D3
  Widnes WA8. . . . . 13 B2
  Wilmslow SK9 . . . . .60 B8
Mount Pleasant Ave WA9. . 1 B3
Mount Pleasant Dr CW7 . 149 A7
Mount Pleasant Gdns *
  CW6 . . . . 122 E7
Mount Pleasant Rd
  Davenham CW9 . . . . 103 F2
  The Bank ST7 . . . . 195 B7
Mount Pleasant Residential
  Pk CW4 . . . . 130 D8
Mount Rd Kidsgrove ST7 . . 195 B2
  Runcorn WA7 . . . . .49 F8
Mount St WA8 . . . . .13 B1
Mount Terr SK11 . . . . 112 F7
Mount The Chester CH3 . . 118 F1
  Congleton CW12 . . . . 156 E2
  Great Budworth CW9 . . . . . 79 A7
  Hale CH63 . . . . 32 C8
  Heswall CH60 . . . . 40 F8
  Kidsgrove ST7 . . . . 195 A1
  Scholar Green ST7 . . . . . . 194 E7
Mount Way CH3 . . . . 143 A4
Mourne Cl CH66. . . . . 69 A6
Mousley Bottom Nature
  Reserve * SK22 . . . . 39 A7
MOW COP 195 C7
Mow Cop Rd ST7 . . . . 195 D6
Mowcroft La WA5 . . . . .14 B3
Mow La
  Mount Pleasant ST7 . . . . . 195 A5
  Mow Cop ST7 . . . . 179 B2
Mowpen Brow WA16 . . . . .29 B6
Moxon Ave WA4 . . . . .16 F5
Moyles Cl WA8 . . . . 12 D2
Mudhouse La CH64. . . . . . .67 F2
Mudhurst La SK12. . . . . 38 E3
Muirfield Cl
  Northwich CW9 . . . . 104 A5
  Warrington WA2 . . . . .9 A3
  Wilmslow SK9 . . . . .60 D8
Muirfield Dr
  Macclesfield SK10 . . . . . . 87 D4
  Winsford CW7 . . . . 126 C2
Muirfield Mews CW7 . . . . 126 C2
Muir Rd CH1 . . . . 117 E3
Mulberry Ave Golborne WA3. . 3 F7
  Windess WA8. . . . . 23 C7
Mulberry Cl Elton CH2. . . . 72 C3
  Gatley SK8 . . . . 34 C7
  Warrington WA1 . . . . .17 E7
Mulberry Ct
  Macclesfield SK11 . . . . . . 112 D4
  Warrington WA4 . . . . 16 D1
Mulberry Dr SK10 . . . . 87 E1
Mulberry Gdns CW11 . . . 174 D7
Mulberry Pk CH65. . . . . . . .69 E7
Mulberry Rd CW2 . . . . 189 E2
Mulberry Rise CW8. . . . . . 103 C7
Mulcaster Ct CW1. . . . . . . 191 D5
Mull Cl CH65. . . . . 70 C1
Mullein Cl WA3 . . . . .3 D8
Mullen Cl WA5 . . . . .7 F1
Mullins Ave WA12. . . . . 2 C5
Mullion Cl WA7 . . . . .50 B6
Mullion Gr WA2. . . . . .9 A1
Mulsford Cl LL13. . . . . 222 A8
Mulsford La LL13, SY14. . . 222 B8
Muncaster Ct 2 WA7. . . . .23 F2
MURDISHAW 50 D7
Murdishaw Ave WA7 . . . . . 50 D6
Murdishaw West CP Sch
  WA7 . . . . 50 D6
Murdishaw Wood & Valley
  Nature Reserve * WA7. . . . 50 E6
Muriel Cl WA5 . . . . 14 D6
Murray Cl SK10 . . . . 87 A1
Murrayfield SK10 . . . . 87 A5
Murrayfield Dr CW5 . . . . . 205 D5
Museum St WA1 . . . . 16 A4
Music Hall Pass CH1. . . . . 237 B2
Muskett Dr CW8 . . . . 78 C2
Muslin Row CW5 . . . . 172 A5
Mustard La WA3 . . . . .4 B1
Myddleton La WA2 . . . . .8 C6
Mye Rscough St CW8. . . . 103 C8
Myrica Gr CH2 . . . . 119 B3
Myrtle Ave
  Haydock WA11. . . . . .1 B7
  Higher Kinnerton CH4 . . . 161 A8
  Newton-le-Willows WA12 . . . 2 C2
Myrtle Gr Warrington WA4 . 16 C3
  Widnes WA8. . . . . 22 D8
Myrtle Rd M31 . . . . 11 D3
Myrtle St Crewe CW2 . . . . 190 C3
  Ellesmere Port CH65 . . . . . 70 C7
Myrtle Wood Rd 1 ST7. . . 193 F4
Mytholme Ave M44. . . . . . 11 C3
Mytton Dr CW5 . . . . 204 D6

N

Nabbs Cl ST7 . . . . 195 B2
Nabbswood Rd ST7 . . . . . 195 B2
Nab Cl SK10 . . . . 63 C1
Nab Headey SK10 . . . . 63 C1
Nab La SK10 . . . . 63 C1
Nabs Rd SK11 . . . . 137 B5
Nairn Ave CW4. . . . . 130 B2
Nairn Cl Bebington CH63 . . 43 D4
  Warrington WA2 . . . . .9 B3
Nancy View SK10. . . . . .88 B8
Nansen Cl WA5 . . . . 15 D7
Nansmoss La SK9 . . . . 33 D1
Nant Peris CH1 . . . . 117 D3
NANTWICH 204 D6
Nantwich By Pass CW5 . . 205 A7
Nantwich Mus * CW5 . . . . 204 E5
Nantwich Rd Audley ST7. . 209 B1
  Barbridge CW5 . . . . 187 B8
  Betley ST7 . . . . 208 E1
  Broxton CH3. . . . . 183 C1
  Chorley Bank CW5 . . . . . . 201 E2
  Crewe CW2 . . . . 190 C2
  Ellesmere Port CH66 . . . . . 69 F3
  Middlewich CW10 . . . . 151 A4
  Sound CW5 . . . . 217 B5
  Wimboldsley CW10 . . . . . 150 F5
  Wistaston CW2, CW5. . . . 189 C2
  Woore SK3 . . . . 232 B1
Nantwich Sta CW5 . . . . . . 204 E4
Nantwich Trade Yd CW5. . 204 F7
Nantwich Way 6 SK9. . . . .34 E5
Naomi Cl CH1 . . . . 117 D5
Napier Gdns 3 ST7 . . . . . 195 A2
Napier Rd CH2 . . . . 118 C8
Napier St WA1 . . . . 16 C5
Napley Dr TF9 . . . . 236 C2
NAPLEY HEATH 236 F1
Napley Rd TF9 . . . . 236 D1
Nares Cl WA5 . . . . .7 C1
Narrow La
  Crewe, Crewe Green
  CW1 . . . . 191 C3
  Wardsend SK10 . . . . 37 A1
Naseby Rd WA2 . . . . 156 A3
Nashville Dr WA5 . . . . .15 B7
Nathan Dr WA11 . . . . .1 E6
Nathans Mdw CW12 . . . . 179 C7
National Waterways Mus *
  CH65. . . . . 70 C7
Nat La CW7 . . . . 126 F2
Nat Lane Ret Pk CW7 . . . . 126 F2
Naughton Lea WA8 . . . . . . 12 D3
Naughton Rd 3 WA8 . . . . 23 A8
Navan Ct CW1 . . . . 190 B5
Navigation Cl WA7 . . . . . . 50 D6
Navigation Ho 16 CW9 . . 103 F8
Navigation Rd CW8 . . . . . 103 F7
Navigation St WA1 . . . . 16 D5
Naylor Ave WA3 . . . . .3 B8
Naylor Cl CH66. . . . . .69 F8
Naylor Cres
  Ellesmere Port CH66 . . . . . 69 F8
  Nantwich CW5 . . . . 205 A4
Naylor Ct
  Ellesmere Port CH66 . . . . . 69 E6
  12 Northwich CW9. . . . . . 103 F8
Naylor Gn CH66 . . . . .69 F8
Naylor Pl CH66. . . . . .69 F8
Naylor Rd Overpool CH66 . . 69 F7
  Widnes WA8. . . . . 13 D1
Naylor St WA1 . . . . .16 B5
Naylor Wlk CH66. . . . . .69 F7
Nazareth House La WA8 . . 22 C7
Neal Ave SK8 . . . . 34 A8
Nearnc Pl CH65 . . . . 70 D5
Neath Cl SK12. . . . . 36 D5
Needham Cl WA7 . . . . 23 D2
Needham Dr
  Cranage CW4. . . . . 130 A5
  Hartford CW8. . . . . 103 A4
Needhams Bank CW11. . . 174 C6
Needhams Wharf Cl SK10. . 88 A1
Neighbourway SK23. . . . . . .64 F3
Neills Rd WA5 . . . . .6 B6
Neil St WA8 . . . . 13 C2
Nelson Ave SK12 . . . . 37 A3
Nelson Cl SK12. . . . . 37 A3
Nelson Dr M44. . . . . .11 E6
Nelson Gr ST7 . . . . 193 F2
Nelson Ind Est ST7 . . . . . . 194 C1
Nelson Rd CH65. . . . . 70 C7
Nelson St Chester CH1. . . 237 C3
  Congleton CW12 . . . . 156 D2
  Crewe CW2 . . . . 190 C2
  Macclesfield SK11 . . . . . . 112 D7
  Newton-le-Willows WA12 . . . 2 A3
  Widnes WA8. . . . . 23 A6
Nemos Cl WA6 . . . . 73 C2
Neptune Cl WA7 . . . . 50 D7
Nesfield Cl CW11 . . . . 191 F7
Nesfield Dr CW11 . . . . 191 F7
NESS 67 B4
Ness Acre La CH64 . . . . . . .67 E8
Ness Botanic Gdns *
  CH64. . . . . 67 A3
Nesse Ho CH64. . . . . 66 D8
NESS HOLT 66 F5
Nessina Gr CW2. . . . . 205 F8
NESTON 66 D7
Neston Cl 4 Alvanley WA6 . 73 A2
  Frodsham WA6. . . . . 73 A2
Neston Dr CH2. . . . . 118 E5
Neston Gn CH66. . . . . 69 D4
Neston High Sch CH64. . . .41 F1

Neston Prim Sch CH64. . . . .66 E7
Neston Rd
Heswall CH63, CH64 . . . . . . .41 F5
Neston CH64 . . . . .67 B3
Willaston CH64 . . . . .67 F8
Neston Recn Ctr CH64 . . . . .41 F1
Neston Road Cotts CH63 . . 42 A6
Neston Sta CH64 . . . . .66 E8
Neston Way SK9 . . . . 34 D3
NETHER ALDERLEY 85 A6
Nether Alderley Mill★
SK10. . . . . 85 A5
Nether Alderley Prim Sch
SK10. . . . . 85 A6
Netherfield WA8. . . . . .22 E8
Netherfields SK9. . . . . 85 A8
Nether Fold SK10 . . . . 87 A8
Nether Lea CW4. . . . . 130 C8
Netherley Rd WA8. . . . . 12 A2
Netherpool Rd CH66. . . . . . .69 F8
NETHER TABLEY 80 F8
NETHERTON 74 A6
Netherton Dr WA6 . . . . 74 A7
Netherton Farm Cotts
WA6. . . . . 74 A7
Neumann St CW9 . . . . 104 B8
Nevada Cl WA5 . . . . 15 C8
Neville Ave St Helens WA9 . . .1 B2
Warrington WA2 . . . . .8 D1
Neville Cres WA5 . . . . 15 A3
Neville Dr CH3 . . . . 119 B1
Neville Rd Bebington CH62 . .43 E8
Chester CH3. . . . . 119 B1
Neville St Crewe CW2 . . . . 190 D1
Newton-le-Willows WA12 . . . .2 A3
Nevin Cl SK7. . . . . 36 A7
Nevin Rd CH1. . . . . 117 D3
Nevis Dr CW2. . . . . 189 D3
New Albert Terr WA7. . . . . .23 B3
Newall Ave CW11 . . . . 175 A5
Newall Cl CH3 . . . . 166 B1
Newall Cres CW7. . . . . 127 A1
Newark Dr WA5. . . . . 15 A6
Newarth Dr WA13 . . . . 19 A2
New Bank Pl WA8. . . . . .12 B1
New Bank Rd WA8 . . . . .12 B1
New Barnet WA8. . . . . .12 F4
Newbiggin Way 10 SK10 . 112 C8
Newbold Ct 9 CW12 . . . . . 156 F3
New Bold Ct WA9 . . . . .6 A7
Newbold Way CW5. . . . . . 204 E3
Newborough Cl WA5 . . . . . . .7 E2
NEW BOSTON. 1 E7
Newbridge Cl
Runcorn WA7. . . . . 50 C6
Warrington WA5 . . . . .7 D2
New Bridge Ct CH65. . . . . . .70 F4
Newbridge Rd CH65. . . . . . .70 F4
New Bridge Rd CH65, CH2 . .70 F3
Newburgh Cl WA7. . . . . 24 D1
Newbury Ave Crewe CW1. 190 C7
5 Winsford CW7. . . . . 149 A8
Newbury Cl Cheadle SK8. . . 35 A6
Widnes WA8. . . . . 13 A3
Newbury Ct SK9. . . . . 60 A6
Newbury Rd Chester CH4 . 140 F6
Gatley SK8 . . . . 34 C7
Newby Ct CW12 . . . . 156 A1
Newcastle Rd
Astbury CW12 . . . . 178 A7
Brereton Green CW11 . . . . 153 F4
Congleton CW12 . . . . 156 A2
Hassall Green CW11 . . . . . 176 A3
Nantwich CW5 . . . . 205 B4
Shavington CW2, CW5 . . . . 206 C3
Smallwood CW11. . . . . 176 D6
Talke ST7 . . . . 210 E7
Willaston CW5 . . . . 205 E4
Woore CW3 . . . . 232 E1
Newcastle Road N CW11. 153 E5
Newcastle Road S CW11. 153 F5
Newcastle St CW1. . . . . . . 190 A5
NEWCASTLE-UNDER-LYME. 210 D3
NEWCHAPEL. 195 E2
Newchapel Obsy & Natural Science Ctr★ ST7 . . . . . . 195 E2
Newchapel Rd ST7 . . . . . . 195 C3
New Chester Rd CH62 . . . . .43 E7
Newchurch Com Prim Sch
WA3 .4 E2
Newchurch La WA3 . . . . .4 F2
Newcombe Ave WA2 . . . . . .16 E8
New Cotts
Hampton Heath SY14. . . . . 213 E7
Manley WA6. . . . . 99 C7
New Crane Bank CH1. . . . 118 B1
New Crane St CH1. . . . . . . 118 B1
Newcroft CH1. . . . . .94 B2
New Cut Ind Est WA1 . . . . . 17 C7
New Cut La WA1 . . . . .17 B7
Newdigate St CW1 . . . . . . 190 C4
New Farm Cotts WA3. . . . . 11 A7
New Farm Ct
Great Barrow CH3 . . . . 120 E5
Malpas SY14 . . . . 213 A5
NEWFIELD. 172 E8
Newfield Ct WA13. . . . . 19 A5
Newfield Dr CW1. . . . . 190 E5
Newfield Rd WA13 . . . . 18 D3
Newfield St CW11 . . . . 175 B7
Newfield Terr WA6. . . . . . . .73 B2
Newgate
1 Macclesfield SK11. . . . . 112 D7
Wilmslow SK9 . . . . .59 E7
Newgate Rd SK9 . . . . 59 D7
Newgate St CH1. . . . . 237 B2
Newgate Wlk CH1. . . . . . . 237 B2
New Grosvenor Rd CH65. . .70 B7
NEWHALL 228 C8
New Hall Ave SK8 . . . . .34 B7
Newhall Ct CH2. . . . . 118 E6
New Hall La Culcheth WA3 . . .5 A2
Culcheth, Wigshaw WA3. . . . . .4 E1
New Hall Manor CH64 . . . . .41 E6
Newhall Rd CH2. . . . . 118 F6
New Hall St SK10. . . . . 87 D1
Newham Cl SK11. . . . . 112 F3
New Hampshire Cl 7
WA5. . . . . .15 B7
Newhaven Ct CW5 . . . . . . 204 F5
Newhaven Rd WA2. . . . . .8 B4
Newheyes CH64. . . . . .41 E1
New Hey La CH64 . . . . 68 A6
New Home Farm Cotts
CH64 . . . . 93 A7
NEW HORWICH. 65 E6
New Horwich Rd SK23 . . . . .65 E7
New Hos CW5. . . . . 187 D6
New Houses CH3. . . . . 143 B7
New Inn Cotts WA16. . . . . 108 C8
New Inn La CW11. . . . . 176 A2
New King St Audley ST7 . . 209 C1
Middlewich CW10 . . . . 128 C2
New La Appleton Thorn WA4 .27 B5
Churton CH3 . . . . 180 F6
Croft WA3. . . . . .9 B7
Harthill CH3 . . . . 183 F3
Winsford CW7 . . . . 149 F4
Newland Cl WA8 . . . . 12 C3
Newland Mews WA3 . . . . . . .4 E5
Newlands SK9 . . . . 59 C7
Newlands Ave
Bramhall SK7 . . . . .35 F8
Cheadle SK8. . . . . 35 A7
Newlands Cl Cheadle SK8 . . 35 A7
Frodsham WA6. . . . . 74 C6
Newlands Dr Golborne WA3 . .3 D8
Wilmslow SK9 . . . . .59 E5
Newlands Rd
Macclesfield SK10 . . . . 111 E7
Warrington WA4 . . . . .16 F2
Newland Way CW5 . . . . . . 205 B4
NEW LANE END. 4 A2
New Lane End WA3. . . . . .4 A2
Newlyn Ave
Congleton CW12 . . . . 178 F8
Macclesfield SK10 . . . . 86 D1
Newlyn Cl WA7 . . . . .50 B6
Newlyn Gdns WA5. . . . . 14 D3
New Manchester Rd WA1. 17 A7
Newman Cl CW12 . . . . 156 B3
New Manor Rd WA4 . . . . . .51 B6
Newman's La CW5 . . . . . . 219 D8
Newman St WA4 . . . . .16 F3
Newmarket Cl 1 SK10. . . . 87 C4
New Market Wlk 10 WA1. . .16 B5
New Meadowside Residential Cvn Pk CW5. . . . . 217 E5
NEW MILLS 39 D7
New Mills Central Sta
SK22. . . . . .39 B7
New Mills Heritage Ctr★
SK22. . . . . .39 B7
New Mills L Ctr SK22 . . . . . 39 C8
New Mills Newtown Sta
SK22. . . . . .39 B6
New Mills Prim Sch 1
SK22. . . . . .39 B8
New Mills Sch and Sixth From Centre 1 SK22. . . . 39 C8
Newmoore La WA7. . . . . . . .24 F4
New Moss Rd M44. . . . . 11 D6
Newnham Dr CH65 . . . . 70 C4
New Pale Rd WA6 . . . . 99 C6
New Park Ct SK22 . . . . 39 D7
New Platt La CW4 . . . . 107 B1
Newport Gr ST5. . . . . 210 E2
New Port Rd CH65. . . . . . . .70 F3
Newquay Cl WA7. . . . . .50 B6
Newquay Ct CW12. . . . . . . 178 E8
Newquay Dr Bramhall SK7 . .35 F7
Macclesfield SK10 . . . . 111 D8
New Rd Anderton CW9. . . . . 78 D4
Antrobus CW9 . . . . 27 D1
Astbury CW12 . . . . 178 B4
Audley ST7. . . . . 209 E3
Buxton SK17. . . . . 138 F1
Duddon CW6 . . . . 145 B6
Ellesmere Port CH66 . . . . . . 69 A8
Horwich End SK23 . . . . .65 E6
Lymm WA13 . . . . .18 E3
Marton CW12. . . . . 132 D1
Mossend CW11 . . . . 154 F2
Prestbury SK10 . . . . 87 A7
Rostherne WA16 . . . . .30 E3
Warrington WA4 . . . . 16 C4
Whaley Bridge, Bridgemont
SK23. . . . . .39 F1
Winsford CW7. . . . . 126 E2
Wrenbury CW5 . . . . 216 D3
New Road Bsns Ctr CW7 . 126 E2
New Russia Hall (Gt Northern Architectural Antiques)★ CH3 . . . . 165 E5
Newry Ct CH2. . . . . 118 D4
Newry Park E CH2. . . . . . . 118 D4
Newry Pk CH2 . . . . 118 D4
New St La SY13 . . . . 233 C1
NEWSBANK. 132 F1
New School La CH66 . . . . . .44 B1
Newsham Cl WA8 . . . . .12 B4
Newsholme Cl WA3 . . . . .4 F3
Newspaper House WA5. . . 14 D3
New St Congleton CW12. . . 156 E2
Haslington CW1. . . . . 191 C5
New St *continued*
Neston CH64 . . . . .66 E5
New Mills SK22 . . . . 39 D7
8 Runcorn WA7 . . . . 23 A2
Sandbach CW11. . . . . 174 D7
Widnes WA8. . . . . .23 B8
Wilmslow SK9 . . . . .59 E5
Newstead Cl SK12. . . . . 36 D5
Newstead Rd WA8 . . . . .21 F6
New Street Cotts CW12. . 157 A6
Newtech Sq CH5 . . . . .92 F2
NEWTON Chester 118 F5
Frodsham. 74 D3
Tattenhall. 166 E4
Newton Ave WA3. . . . . .9 E5
Newton Bank
Middlewich CW10 . . . . 128 B1
Preston on the Hill WA4 . . . . .51 B8
Newton Bank Prep Sch
WA12 . . . . .2 E4
Newton Cl CH2. . . . . 237 A3
Newton Com Hospl WA12 . . .2 B2
Newton Cotts CH3. . . . . . . 166 C4
Newton Gdns WA3 . . . . .4 A8
Newton Gr WA2. . . . . .8 F3
Newton Hall CH2. . . . . 118 F5
Newton Hall Ct CH2 . . . . . 118 F5
Newton Hall Dr CH2 . . . . . 118 F5
Newton Hall La WA16. . . . . .58 E5
Newton Hall Mews 1
CW10. . . . . 151 C8
Newton Heath CW10 . . . . 128 B1
Newton Ho CH2. . . . . 118 F5
Newton Hollow WA6 . . . . . 74 D1
NEWTONIA 128 B1
Newton La Chester CH2. . . 118 F4
Daresbury WA4 . . . . 51 C8
Golborne WA12 . . . . .2 E6
Tattenhall CH3 . . . . 166 D4
NEWTON-LE-WILLOWS 2 B2
Newton-le-Willows Com High Sch WA12 . . . . .2 D5
Newton-le-Willows Prim Sch
WA12 . . . . .2 C3
Newton-le-Willows Sta
WA12 . . . . .2 E3
Newton Park Dr WA12. . . . . .2 F3
Newton Park View CH2 . . 118 D4
Newton Pl CW12 . . . . 156 F2
Newton Prim Sch CH2. . . . 118 E4
Newton Rd
Ellesmere Port CH65 . . . . . . 70 C5
Golborne, Lowton Common WA3, WN7 . . . . .4 A8
Golborne, Town of Lowton WA12, WA3 . . . . .3 D5
Handforth SK9 . . . . 34 A1
St Helens WA9 . . . . .1 A3
Winwick WA2 . . . . .8 A5
Newtons Cres CW11. . . . . 191 F7
Newtons Gr CW11. . . . . . . 191 E7
Newtons La CW11. . . . . . . 191 E7
Newton St Crewe CW1. . . . 190 D5
Macclesfield SK11 . . . . 112 C7
NEWTOWN Burwardsley. . . 183 E8
Frodsham. 49 D1
New Mills. 39 B6
Poynton 37 A3
Sound. 217 E4
Widnes. 23 B6
Newtown Neston CH64 . . . . .66 F7
Newchapel ST7 . . . . 195 F2
Newtown Cl CH1. . . . . 237 B3
Newtown Farm Rd CW3 . 229 C2
Newtown Prim Sch 1
SK22. . . . . .39 B6
Newtown Rd CW5. . . . . . . 217 F5
New Warrington Rd CW9 . 79 C2
New William Cl M31. . . . . . .11 F4
NEW WOODHOUSES 227 E1
New York Cotts WA16 . . . . .29 F2
New Zealand SK11 . . . . . . 160 B1
Nicholas Ave CW9. . . . . . . 104 C6
Nicholas Ct CH1. . . . . 237 A2
Nicholas Rd
Weaverham CW8. . . . . 77 D1
Widnes WA8. . . . . 22 C8
Nicholas St Mews CH1. . . 237 A2
Nicholas St CH1. . . . . 237 A2
Nicholls St WA4. . . . . .17 B2
Nicholson Ave SK10. . . . . . .87 E1
Nicholson Cl SK10. . . . . .87 E1
Nicholson St WA1. . . . . .15 F5
NICK I' TH' HILL 179 B4
Nickleby Rd SK12 . . . . .36 E3
Nickleford Hall Dr WA8. . . .12 F6
Nickolson Cl CH2 . . . . 119 F8
Nicol Ave WA1. . . . . .17 F8
Nidderdale Cl CW12. . . . . 157 A5
Niddries Ct CW9 . . . . 126 F7
Niddries La CW9 . . . . 126 F7
Nield Ct CH2. . . . . 118 D7
Nigel Gresley Cl CW1. . . . 191 A4
Nigel Rd CH60 . . . . 41 C8
Nightingale Cl
Farndon CH3 . . . . 180 F1
Handforth SK9 . . . . .34 B1
Middlewich CW10 . . . . 151 D6
Runcorn WA7. . . . . .49 F5
Warrington WA3 . . . . .9 F4
Nightingale Ct 4 CW7. . . 149 D6
Nightingale Pl 8 CW5. . . 204 C4
Nightingale Way ST7 . . . . 193 B3
Nightshade Pl CW4. . . . . . 130 C1
Nile St CW2. . . . . 190 C2
Nine Hos The CH3. . . . . . . 166 B1
Nixon Dr CW7. . . . . 126 B2
Nixon Rd CW8 . . . . 101 F3
Nixon's Row CW5 . . . . 204 C5
Nixon St Crewe CW1 . . . . . 189 F5
Macclesfield SK11 . . . . 112 B8
No. 156 CH1 . . . . 237 C2
No 1 Road N CW2 . . . . 192 F1
No 1 Road S CW2. . . . . 192 F1
No 2 Road N CW2 . . . . 192 F1
No 2 Road S CW2. . . . . 192 F1
Noahs Ark La WA16 . . . . . . .58 F1
Noble Cl WA3. . . . . .9 E3
Noden Cl CW9 . . . . 126 F8
NO MAN'S HEATH 214 B4
No Mans Heath By Pass
Ebnal SY14. . . . . 213 E6
The Maltkiln SY14. . . . . 214 C3
Nook La Antrobus CW9. . . . . .53 E6
Golborne WA3 . . . . .3 B8
Warrington WA4 . . . . 17 A3
Warrington, Fearnhead WA2 . . 9 B2
Nook The Backford CH1. . . . .95 B4
Bramhall SK7 . . . . 35 D5
Chester CH2. . . . . 118 E4
Guilden Sutton CH3 . . . . . . 119 C4
Hankelow CW3. . . . . 230 C8
Saltney CH4 . . . . 140 E6
Noon Ct WA12 . . . . .2 B1
Noonsun Farm WA16. . . . . .58 E1
Nora St WA1. . . . . 16 C5
Norbreck Ave CW2. . . . . . 190 B2
Norbreck Cl WA5 . . . . 15 A4
NORBURY 215 D4
Norbury Ave WA2 . . . . 16 D8
Norbury Cl Hough CW2 . . . 206 E3
Knutsford WA16. . . . . 57 C3
Widnes WA8. . . . . .13 E1
NORBURY COMMON 215 C6
Norbury Dr
Congleton CW12 . . . . 156 E4
Middlewich CW10 . . . . 151 B8
Norbury Hollow Rd SK7. . . .37 B8
Norbury St
Macclesfield SK11 . . . . 112 C7
Northwich CW9 . . . . 104 B8
Norbury Town La SY13 . . 215 C3
Norbury Way 9 SK9. . . . . . 34 D5
Norcop Rd CW1. . . . . 190 D7
Norcott Ave WA4. . . . . 16 D2
NORCOTT BROOK. 52 C6
Norcott Dr WA5. . . . . .6 F6
Norden Cl WA3 . . . . .9 C5
Norfolk Cl M44. . . . . 11 C5
Norfolk Dr WA5. . . . . .14 E6
Norfolk Gr ST8. . . . . 179 C1
Norfolk Ho ST7 . . . . 210 D6
Norfolk House Prep Sch
CW11 . . . . 175 B7
Norfolk House Prep Sch 6
CW11. . . . . 175 B8
Norfolk Pl WA8 . . . . 22 C8
Norfolk Rd Chester CH2 . . 118 F4
Congleton CW12 . . . . 156 E4
Ellesmere Port CH65 . . . . . . 70 C5
Kidsgrove ST7 . . . . 194 F2
Norfolk St WA7 . . . . .23 B3
Norfolk Wlk SK10 . . . . .86 F2
Norgrove Cl WA7 . . . . .50 E8
Norland's La L35, WA8 . . . . .12 F7
Norlands Pk WA8 . . . . .12 F6
Norland St WA8. . . . . 13 D1
Norleane Cres WA7 . . . . . . .49 B8
NORLEY. 100 F6
Norley Ave Bebington CH62. .43 E3
Ellesmere Port CH65 . . . . . . .69 F6
Norley CE Prim Sch
WA6 . . . . 100 F5
Norley Cl WA5 . . . . .15 E6
Norley Dr CH3 . . . . 119 C1
Norley La CW8. . . . . 101 A8
Norley Pl CW9 . . . . 103 E5
Norley Rd
Cuddington CW8, WA6. . . . 101 E4
Kingsley WA6. . . . . 75 A1
Norley WA6 . . . . 100 D7
Sandiway CW8. . . . . 102 A3
Norman Ave Haydock WA11 . .2 A7
Newton-le-Willows WA12 . . . .2 E3
Normanby Cl WA5. . . . . .15 E7
Norman Cl CH66 . . . . .94 F8
Norman Dr CW7 . . . . 149 C6
Normandy Ave 2 CW7 . . . 149 D8
Normandy Cres CH3. . . . . 142 C5
Normandy Rd CH2 . . . . 95 C1
Norman Ho 3 CW8. . . . . . 103 C5
Norman Pidduck Cl 2
ST7. . . . . 193 F4
Norman Rd WA7 . . . . 23 A1
Normans Cotts 1 CH64. . . .66 F7
Norman's Hall Farm SK10. .63 B5
Normans Hall Mews SK10. .63 B5
Norman's La WA4 . . . . .52 F4
Norman St WA2. . . . . .16 B6
Norman Way CH1 . . . . 117 E5
Norreys Ave WA5 . . . . .15 F8
Norris Gr WA8 . . . . 22 C5
Norris Rd CH1 . . . . 117 E5
Norris St WA2 . . . . 16 D8
Northacre Cl 4 WA3 . . . . . . .3 C7
North Ave WA2 . . . . .16 B8
Northbank Ind Pk M44. . . . . .11 F6
Northbank Wlk CW2. . . . . 206 C8
North Brook Rd CW6 . . . . . 146 B7
Northbury Rd CH66. . . . . . . .69 E1
Northcote Rd SK7 . . . . .35 F7
Northdale Rd WA1 . . . . 17 A8
North Downs WA16. . . . . . . .57 B1
North Dr Heswall CH60 . . . . 41 A7
High Legh WA16. . . . . 29 C4
Northwich CW9 . . . . 104 E7
Northern La WA8 . . . . 12 A3
Northern Pathway CH4 . . 237 C1
Northern Rise CH66 . . . . . . .69 E4
Northfield Dr
Biddulph ST8 . . . . 179 E2
Wilmslow SK9 . . . . 60 D8
Northfield Pl CW2. . . . . . . 206 C5
Northfields WA16 . . . . 57 C3
NORTH FLORIDA 1 D8
North Florida Rd WA11 . . . . .1 D8
Northgate CW6 . . . . 146 B7
Northgate Arena CH2. . . . 237 B3
Northgate Ave
Chester CH2. . . . . 237 B4
Macclesfield SK10 . . . . 87 C1
Northgate Row CH1 . . . . . 237 B2
Northgate St CH1 . . . . 237 A3
NORTHGATE VILLAGE 237 B4
North Gn CH5. . . . . 116 A6
Northlands CW3 . . . . 232 C1
Northmead SK10. . . . . 87 A5
Northolt Ct WA2 . . . . .8 E1
North Par CH64 . . . . .41 B2
North Park Brook Rd WA5 . .7 F2
North Rd Altrincham WA15 . 32 A8
Bebington CH65. . . . . .44 E3
Connah's Quay CH5 . . . . .91 F2
Ellesmere Port CH65 . . . . . . .70 B8
Halewood L26 . . . . 21 A5
NORTH RODE 134 E2
North St Chester CH3. . . . . . 119 A1
Congleton CW12 . . . . 156 D3
Crewe CW1 . . . . 190 C7
Haydock WA11. . . . . .1 E6
Mount Pleasant ST7. . . . . . 195 B6
Newton-le-Willows WA12 . . . . .1 F4
Saltney CH4 . . . . 140 B7
Sandycroft CH5 . . . . 116 A3
North Stafford St CW1. . . 190 D4
Northumberland Rd
3 Cronton WA8. . . . . .12 F6
Partington M31 . . . . .11 E2
North View Crewe CW1. . . . 190 A6
Ellesmere Port CH66 . . . . . 69 C7
Middlewich CW10 . . . . 128 B2
Warrington WA5 . . . . .14 E7
Northward Rd SK9 . . . . .59 F6
Northway Chester CH4 . . . 141 A7
Lymm WA13 . . . . 18 D4
Runcorn WA7. . . . . .49 F8
Warrington WA2 . . . . .8 B2
Widnes WA8. . . . . 12 D1
Winnington CW8 . . . . 78 D1
North Way
Holmes Chapel CW4. . . . . . 130 C3
Shavington CW2. . . . . 206 D5
North West Wing CW8. . . 102 A8
NORTHWICH. 103 D8
Northwich Rd
Allostock CW4, WA16. . . . . 106 E1
Antrobus CW9 . . . . .53 B2
Dutton WA4 . . . . .51 B2
Great Budworth CW9. . . . . . .78 F8
Knutsford WA16. . . . . 56 D1
Runcorn, Brookvale WA7 . . . 50 C5
Weaverham CW8. . . . . 102 E7
Northwich Ret Pk CW9 . . . 79 C1
Northwich Sta CW9 . . . . . 104 B8
Northwood Ave
Middlewich CW10 . . . . 151 E5
Newton-le-Willows WA12 . . . .2 F3
Northwood La WA16 . . . . . .28 F1
Northwood Rd WA7 . . . . . . .23 E2
NORTON 24 C1
Norton Ave Saltney CH4 . . 140 D6
Warrington WA5 . . . . .14 E5
Norton Cotts WA7. . . . . .50 E7
Norton Gate WA7 . . . . 50 C8
Norton Hill WA7 . . . . 24 C2
NORTON IN HALES. 236 C1
Norton in Hales CE Prim Sch
TF9 . . . . 236 C2
Norton La
Runcorn, Norton WA7. . . . . . 24 D1
Runcorn, Town Park WA7 . . . 50 A8
Norton Priory Mus & Gdns★
WA7 . . . . .24 B3
Norton Priory Walled Gdns★
WA7 . . . . .24 B3
Norton Rd CH3. . . . . 119 C2
Nortons La CW6. . . . . 122 F7
Norton's La CH3 . . . . .98 B2
Norton St SK10 . . . . 112 E8
Norton Station Rd WA7. . . . 50 D8
Norton View WA7 . . . . 50 A8
Norton Village WA7 . . . . . . 24 D1
Norton Way CW11. . . . . . . 174 D7
Nortonwood La WA7 . . . . . 24 C1
Norville CH66. . . . . 69 D7
Norwich Ave WA3. . . . . .3 D8
Norwich Dr CH66. . . . . .94 E8
Norwood Ave
Bramhall SK7 . . . . 35 D5
Golborne WA3 . . . . .3 F7
High Lane SK6 . . . . 37 D7
Norwood Dr CH4. . . . . 141 B6
Nottingham Cl WA1 . . . . . . .17 E6
Noutch Cl 3 CW7 . . . . 125 F2
Nova Ct 14 CW1 . . . . 190 B5
NOVA SCOTIA 125 C6
Nova Scotia La CW7 . . . . . . 125 C5
Nun House Cl CW7 . . . . 127 B2
Nun House Dr CW7. . . . . . . 127 B2
Nunsmere Cl CW7. . . . . 127 B1
Nuns Rd CH1. . . . . 237 A1

Nursery Ave WA15 . . . . . . .31 E8
Nursery Cl Crewe CW2 . . . 190 A2
  Kidsgrove ST7 . . . . 194 D1
  Shavington CW2. . . . . 206 C3
  Widnes WA8 . . . . 13 D3
Nursery Dr Biddulph ST8 . 179 C2
  Poynton SK12 . . . . 36 D4
Nursery Fields Way **1**
  CW11 . . . . 192 A7
Nursery Gdns ST7 . . . . . . 209 D3
Nursery Gr M31 . . . . .11 F4
Nursery La
  Congleton CW12 . . . . 156 E2
  Nether Alderley SK10. . . . . 84 D5
  Siddington SK11 . . . . 110 A3
  Wilmslow SK9 . . . . .59 F5
Nursery Pk WA6 . . . . 100 B7
Nursery Rd Barnton CW8 . .78 B3
  Bollington SK10 . . . . .87 E7
  Oakhanger CW1, ST7 . . . . 192 D3
  Scholar Green ST7 . . . . . . 194 E5
Nursery The CW8 . . . . 103 C6
Nutfield Ave CW1 . . . . 190 B7
Nuthatch Cl **2** CW7 . . . . 149 D7
Nuthurst Gdns **4** CW5 . . 204 F5
Nuttall Ct WA3 . . . . .9 C4
Nuttall St M44 . . . . .11 E6

O

Oak Ave Alsager ST7 . . . . 193 E2
  Disley SK12 . . . . 39 A6
  Golborne WA3 . . . . .3 B8
  Haydock WA11 . . . . .1 E7
  Irlam M44 . . . . 11 D5
  Macclesfield SK11 . . . . . . 112 A5
  Newton-le-Willows WA12 . . .2 D3
  Wilmslow SK9 . . . . .59 F5
  Winsford CW7 . . . . 149 D7
Oak Bank
  Alderley Edge SK9 . . . . 60 A2
  Disley SK12 . . . . 39 A6
Oak Bank St CW5. . . . . . . 205 E4
Oak Bank Dr SK10. . . . . . . .63 B1
Oak Bank La CW2. . . . . . . 119 C6
Oak Brow Cotts SK9 . . . . . .33 E4
Oak Cl SK9. . . . . .59 F6
Oak Cotts Styal SK9 . . . . . .33 E4
  Wrenbury CW5 . . . . 216 F4
Oakdale Ave
  Frodsham WA6. . . . . 74 D6
  Warrington WA4 . . . . 16 D1
Oakdale Cl
  Broughton CH4. . . . . 139 B3
  Chorlton CW2. . . . . 207 B3
Oakdene Ave
  Ellesmere Port CH66 . . . . . 69 C5
  Gatley SK8. . . . . 34 C7
  Warrington WA1 . . . . 17 C7
Oakdene Cl CH62. . . . . 43 D5
Oakdene Ct SK9. . . . . .34 B1
Oakdene Way CW6 . . . . . . 168 D8
Oak Dr Cheadle SK7 . . . . . . 35 C7
  Higher Kinnerton CH4 . . . 161 A7
  Middlewich CW10 . . . . . . 151 D7
  Runcorn WA7 . . . . 49 C7
  Scholar Green ST7 . . . . . . 194 E6
Oakefield Prim Sch CW1. 190 B6
Oakenbank La SK10 . . . . . . 88 D7
Oakenclough Cl SK9. . . . . . 34 D2
Oakenclough Rd SK11 . . 136 F7
Oakes Cl CH62. . . . . 43 D7
Oakes Cnr CW5 . . . . 219 E3
Oak Farm CW6 . . . . 186 C5
Oakfield Ave Chester CH2. 118 E8
  Knutsford WA16. . . . . 57 C3
  Wrenbury CW5 . . . . 216 F3
Oakfield Cl
  Alderley Edge SK9 . . . . . . .60 B3
  Bramhall SK7 . . . . .35 E4
  Wrenbury CW5 . . . . 216 F3
Oakfield Com Prim Sch
  WA8 . . . . .22 B8
Oakfield Dr Chester CH2 . . 118 E8
  Widnes WA8 . . . . 22 A8
Oakfield Rd
  Alderley Edge SK9 . . . . . . .60 B2
  Bebington CH62. . . . . 43 C8
  Blacon CH1. . . . . 117 D4
  Ellesmere Port CH66 . . . . . .68 E8
  Plumley WA16 . . . . .80 F3
  Poynton SK12. . . . . .36 F4
Oakfield Rise CW4 . . . . . . 130 B3
Oakfield Terr CH66 . . . . . . .68 E8
Oakfold SK10 . . . . 88 A6
Oak Gr Ellesmere Port CH65. 70 A3
  Nantwich CW5. . . . . 204 E3
  Poynton SK12. . . . . 36 D4
Oak Green SK8. . . . . .34 E5
Oak Green Rd WA3 . . . . . . .3 C7
Oak Gr/Gelli Dderw
  CH4 . . . . 140 D5
OAKGROVE 135 D7
Oakgrove Sch SK8 . . . . 34 C7
OAKHANGER 192 C2
Oakhill Cl SK10 . . . . .87 B4
Oakhill Farm La CW8 . . . . . 76 A4
Oak Ho Chester CH2 . . . . . 118 C5
  7 Sandbach CW11. . . . . 175 B6
Oak House La CW7 . . . . . . 149 B8
Oakhurst Chase SK9. . . . . . 60 A2
Oakhurst Dr CW2 . . . . 206 B7
Oak La Astbury CW12 . . . . 178 B4
  Cuddington CW8 . . . . 101 F2

Oak La continued
  Kerridge SK10 . . . . 88 A6
  Marton SK11 . . . . 133 C5
  Wilmslow SK9 . . . . .59 F6
Oakland Ave CW1 . . . . . . 191 C4
Oakland Ct Lavister LL12. . 162 C1
  Poynton SK12. . . . . 36 D4
Oakland Gdns WA1. . . . . . .16 E7
Oaklands Bebington CH62 . . 43 D6
  Guilden Sutton CH3 . . . . . 119 F4
Oaklands Ave CH3. . . . . . 166 B2
Oaklands Cl SK9 . . . . .34 E1
Oaklands Cres CH3. . . . . . 166 B2
Oaklands Dr WA13 . . . . . . 18 D2
Oaklands Rd Golborne WA3 . .3 F7
  Ollerton WA16 . . . . .82 F6
Oaklands SpecI Sch
  CW7 . . . . 149 B7
Oakland St
  Warrington WA1 . . . . .16 E7
  Widnes WA8. . . . . 23 A4
Oaklea Ave CH2. . . . . 118 F4
Oak Lea Ave SK9 . . . . 60 A5
Oakleaf Lodge SK11 . . . . . 112 D5
Oakleigh WA16 . . . . 82 C7
Oakleigh Ct CW12. . . . . . 155 F3
Oakleigh Ho SK10 . . . . . . .88 B8
Oakleigh Rd SK8 . . . . .34 E8
Oakleigh Rise CW8 . . . . . .78 E1
Oakley Cl CW11 . . . . 175 A8
Oakley Ct CH65. . . . . 70 C4
Oakley Dr ST7 . . . . 193 B5
Oakley St CW1 . . . . 190 C5
Oak Lo SK7 . . . . .35 F7
Oak Mdw Bramhall SK7 . . . .35 B4
  Weaverham CW8 . . . . 102 F2
OAKMERE 124 A7
Oakmere Barns CW8 . . . 124 A7
Oakmere Cl CW11 . . . . . . 174 F7
Oakmere Dr Chester CH3 . 142 B8
  Ellesmere Port CH66 . . . . .69 C1
  Warrington WA5 . . . . .14 F3
Oakmere Hall CW8 . . . . . 101 E1
Oakmere La WA6. . . . . 72 D1
Oakmere Pl **9** CW1 . . . . 190 B5
Oakmere Rd
  Handforth SK9. . . . . 34 D5
  Winsford CW7 . . . . 149 B8
Oakmere St **6** WA7 . . . . . 23 A2
Oak Mews SK9. . . . . 34 C1
Oakmoore WA7 . . . . .24 F4
Oak Pk SK9 . . . . .60 B2
Oak Rd Chelford SK11. . . . . 84 A3
  Chester CH4. . . . . 140 F6
  Hooton CH66 . . . . .43 E1
  Lymm WA13 . . . . 18 C3
  Mottram St Andrew SK10. . .86 B7
  Paddockhill WA16 . . . . . . .59 B5
  Partington M31 . . . . 11 D2
  Warrington WA5 . . . . .14 F3
Oaks Com Prim Sch The
  CH65. . . . . 70 D3
Oaks Dr The CH2 . . . . 118 D7
Oaks Gdns WA5 . . . . .14 E4
Oaks Pl WA8. . . . . 23 A7
Oak St Crewe CW2 . . . . . . 190 D3
  Croft WA3. . . . . .9 A7
  Ellesmere Port CH65 . . . . . 70 C7
  Northwich CW9 . . . . .79 A1
  Rode Heath ST7 . . . . 193 E8
  Sandbach CW11. . . . . 174 D8
Oaks The Bebington CH62 . . 43 C8
  Goostrey CW4 . . . . 130 D8
  Mobberley WA16 . . . . .58 E1
  5 Romiley SK9 . . . . 103 E6
  Stoke-on-Trent ST7 . . . . . 194 E7
  Widnes WA8. . . . . 13 D4
Oaksway CH60. . . . . 41 C6
Oakthorn Gr WA12 . . . . . . .1 C6
Oak Tree Ave CW12 . . . . . 155 E3
Oaktree Cl Barnton CW8 . . .78 B4
  Tarporley CW6. . . . . 146 D2
Oak Tree Cl CW1 . . . . 190 F5
Oaktree Ct CH2 . . . . 119 A3
Oak Tree Ct CW6 . . . . 122 E2
Oak Tree Dr CW1 . . . . 190 F5
Oak Tree Gate CW3 . . . . . 229 F3
Oaktree La ST7 . . . . 210 D5
Oak Tree La
  Cranage CW10. . . . . 129 E7
  Swan Green WA16 . . . . . . 106 D7
Oak Tree Rise SY14. . . . . . 213 A6
Oak View Knutsford WA16. . 57 C1
  Marton SK11 . . . . 133 C5
  Speke L24. . . . . 21 A3
Oak Villas CW5 . . . . 216 F4
Oakways WA4 . . . . 26 D5
OAKWOOD 9 F4
Oakwood WA16. . . . . .56 F3
Oakwood Ave
  Warrington WA1 . . . . .16 E7
  Wilmslow SK9 . . . . .59 E6
Oakwood Avenue Com Prim
  Sch WA1 . . . . 16 D7
Oakwood Cl CH66. . . . . . . 69 D1
Oakwood Cres
  Crewe CW2 . . . . 189 E4
  Sandbach CW11. . . . . 175 E6
Oakwood Ct WA14 . . . . . . .31 B8
Oakwood Dr SK10 . . . . 87 C6
Oakwood Gate WA3 . . . . . .9 D4
Oakwood Ho
  Alderley Edge SK9 . . . . . . .85 B8
  Barnton CW8 . . . . 78 A2
Oakwood La
  Altrincham WA14 . . . . .31 B8
  Barnton CW8 . . . . 78 A2
  Sandbach CW11. . . . . 174 B8

Oakwood Pk CH62. . . . . . . 43 D5
Oakwood Rd Disley SK12 . . 38 D6
  Rode Heath ST7 . . . . 193 F8
Oak Wood Rd WA16 . . . . . . .29 F2
Oakworth Cl CW12 . . . . . . 156 C3
Oathills SY14 . . . . 213 B5
Oathills Cl CW6 . . . . 146 D1
Oathills Dr CW6. . . . . 146 D1
Oathills Lea CW6. . . . . . . 146 D1
Oatlands SK9. . . . . .85 B8
Oat Market **3** CW5. . . . . 204 E5
Oban Dr CH60. . . . . 41 A8
Oban Gr WA2. . . . . .9 A3
Obelisk Way CW12 . . . . . . 156 C3
OCCLESTONE GREEN. . . . 151 B2
Occleston Pl **4** CW10 . . . 151 D5
Occupation La
  Whitley Reed CW9 . . . . 27 D1
  Whitley Reed CW9 . . . . 53 C8
O'Connell Cl WA11. . . . . . .1 C6
Octans Rd **2** WA5. . . . . . . .7 B2
Oddfellows Pas CW10 . . 128 B1
Odeon Bldg CH1. . . . . 237 A3
Offal Pit La WA6 . . . . .74 F2
Offley Ave CW11 . . . . 175 B7
Offley Prim Sch CW11 . . . 175 B7
Offley Rd CW11. . . . . 175 B7
Off Spring Bank SK22. . . . . 39 C8
Ogden Rd SK7 . . . . 35 D5
Oglet La L24. . . . . 45 C6
Ohio Gr WA5. . . . . 15 C6
Oil Sites Rd CH65. . . . . . . 71 C5
Okell St WA7 . . . . 23 A2
Oklahoma Blvd WA5. . . . . . 15 A6
Old Albert Terr WA7. . . . . . .23 B3
Old Alder La WA2, WA5. . . . .7 D5
Old Altrincham Road East
  SK9 . . . . .33 B2
Old Applecroft CW11. . . . . 174 C5
Old Birch Heath Rd **4**
  CW6 . . . . 168 C8
OLD BOSTON. 2 A8
Old Boston WA11 . . . . 2 A7
Old Boston Trad Est WA11 . . .2 B8
Old Brickworks Ind Est
  SK10 . . . . .63 E4
Old Butt La ST7 . . . . 194 D2
Old Buxton Rd
  Goyt s Moss SK11. . . . . . . 115 A6
  Langley SK11. . . . . 113 F2
  Macclesfield Forest SK11. . 114 F6
Old Castle La SY14 . . . . . . 222 E8
Oldcastle La SY14 . . . . . . 222 E8
Old Castle Mill La SY14 . . 223 E7
Old Charity La SK11 . . . . . 114 B6
Old Cherry La WA13 . . . . . 28 A7
Old Chester Ct CW5 . . . . . 187 D6
Old Chester Rd
  Barbridge CW5 . . . . 187 D6
  Ellesmere Port CH66 . . . . . 69 D4
  Helsby WA6 . . . . 73 C4
  Higher Walton WA4 . . . . . . .25 F7
Old Church Cl CH65. . . . . . 70 C7
Old Coach Rd
  Brown Knowl SY14, CH3. . 199 B6
  Kelsall CW6 . . . . 122 D5
  Runcorn WA7 . . . . .22 F3
Old Constabulary The **1**
  CW5 . . . . 204 D5
Old Court Ho The **9**
  WA16. . . . . 57 A2
Old Ct Gdns CW8 . . . . 123 E6
Old Dairy Cl CH64 . . . . . . .41 F3
Olde George The CH1 . . . 237 B3
Old Farm Cl
  Macclesfield SK10 . . . . 87 A2
  Willaston CH64 . . . . 68 A8
Old Farm Cotts CH1 . . . . . 116 E3
Old Farm Mews SK8. . . . . . 35 C7
Oldfield Cres CH4. . . . . . . 140 F5
Oldfield Ct Chester CH3 . . 119 C2
Oldfield La WA14. . . . . .20 F4
Oldfield Pl CH4 . . . . 141 A5
Oldfield Prim Sch CH3. . . 119 C3
Oldfield Rd
  Ellesmere Port CH65 . . . . . .70 B5
  Lymm WA13 . . . . 18 C4
  Sandbach CW11. . . . . 174 F3
Oldgate WA8 . . . . 22 C7
Old Gate Cl CW10 . . . . . . 151 B7
Old Gorse Cl CW2 . . . . . . 189 E3
OLD HALL 15 C8
Old Hall Cl WA4 . . . . 26 A8
Oldhall Cres SK9 . . . . .34 E3
Old Hall Ct
  Ashton Hayes CH3 . . . . . . 121 F7
  Malpas SY14 . . . . 213 B3
Old Hall Dr
  Ellesmere Port CH65 . . . . . .70 B4
  Horwich End SK23 . . . . . . .65 E4
Old Hall Gdns CH2. . . . . . 237 C4
Old Hall La Elton CH2. . . . . .72 B3
  Hargrave CH3 . . . . 144 A1
  Over Tabley WA16. . . . . . . .55 E4
  Woodford SK7 . . . . 35 D1
Old Hall Pk CH3 . . . . 119 F5
Old Hall Pl CH1 . . . . 237 A2
Old Hall Rd
  Northwich CW9 . . . . 104 A5
  Warrington WA5 . . . . 15 D7
Oldhall St SY14 . . . . 213 B3
Old Hall St SK10. . . . . 87 D1
Oldhams Hill
  Kingsmead CW8 . . . . 103 F8
  Winnington CW8 . . . . .78 F1
Oldham's Rise SK10 . . . . . 87 D3

Oldham St Bollington SK10 . .88 B8
  Warrington WA4 . . . . 16 D3
Old Hey Wlk WA12 . . . . . . .2 C1
Old Higher Rd WA8. . . . . . 21 D5
Oldhill Cl ST7 . . . . 210 E5
Old House Field Cl **14**
  CW11. . . . . 174 E8
Old Hutte La L26 . . . . 21 A6
Oldikes SK17 . . . . 138 E1
Old Knutsford Rd ST7 . . . 194 A6
Old La Acton Bridge CW8 . . .76 F3
  Antrobus CW9 . . . . 53 C3
  Davenham CW9 . . . . 104 D2
  Heswall CH60 . . . . 41 D8
  Mouldsworth CH3 . . . . 99 C2
  Pulford CH4 . . . . 162 E2
Old Library The CW7 . . . . 126 E1
Old Liverpool Rd WA5 . . . . 15 E4
Old Man of Mow* ST7. . . 195 D8
Old Market Pl
  8 Knutsford WA16. . . . . 57 A2
  12 Warrington WA1 . . . . .16 B5
Old Marled Wlk CH62. . . . . 43 D7
Old Marsh Farm Ho CH5 . 116 A8
Old Meadow Dr CH1. . . . . .94 E7
Old Mill Cl Heswall CH60. . .41 B7
  Lymm WA13 . . . . 19 C6
Old Mill Ct CH2 . . . . 118 D6
Old Mill La
  Hazel Grove SK7. . . . . 37 A8
  Higher Whitley WA4 . . . . . . .52 F3
  Macclesfield SK11 . . . . . . 112 E6
Old Mill Pl CH3. . . . . 166 B1
Old Mill Rd CW11. . . . . . . 175 C6
Old Mill The Crowton CW8 . . 76 B2
  Ellesmere Port CH66 . . . . . 69 C7
OLD MOSS. 144 D7
Old Moss La
  Fowley Common WA3. . . . . . .5 E6
  Tarvin CH3 . . . . 144 D7
Old Nantwich Rd ST7 . . . . 209 B2
Old Newcastle Rd CW5 . . 205 D4
Old Orchard SK9. . . . . 60 A7
Old Orchard The
  Antrobus CW9 . . . . 53 C4
  Cuddington CW8 . . . . 101 F4
Old Paddock The CW4. . . 130 F8
Old Pale Cotts CW8 . . . . . 123 C7
Old Pale Hts CW8 . . . . 123 C7
Old Parkgate Rd CH1. . . . 117 E8
Old Park Rd CW1. . . . . . . 207 D8
Old Pearl La CH3 . . . . 119 B2
Old Pewterspear La WA4 . .26 E4
Old Port Sq CH1. . . . . 118 B2
Old Pump Ho The CH66. . .68 E8
Old Quay Cl CH64 . . . . 66 C7
Old Quay La CH64 . . . . 66 D7
Old Quay St WA7 . . . . .23 B3
Old Quays The WA4 . . . . . .16 E3
Old Rd Anderton CW9 . . . . 78 D3
  Audley ST7 . . . . 209 E3
  Furness Vale SK23 . . . . . . 39 D4
  Handforth SK9 . . . . 34 D3
  Horwich End SK23 . . . . . . .65 F3
  Horwich End, New Horwich
    SK23 . . . . .65 E6
  Warrington WA4 . . . . .16 B4
  Wilmslow SK9 . . . . .60 B8
Old Ribbon Mill The
  SK11 . . . . 112 D6
Old School Cl
  Barnton CW8 . . . . .78 B2
  Farndon CH3 . . . . 180 E2
  Kidsgrove ST7 . . . . 195 A1
  Neston CH64 . . . . .66 F5
Old School House La WA2 . . .8 A7
Old School La SK8. . . . . . . 35 A8
Old Seals Way CH1. . . . . . 118 A3
Old Smithy La WA13 . . . . . 18 C2
Old Smithy Row SK22. . . . 39 C7
Old Spot Way CW7 . . . . . . 149 A7
Old Stack Yd CH3 . . . . . . 120 E6
Old Tannery CW5 . . . . 204 F6
Old Upton La WA8 . . . . . . .12 E4
Old Vicarage Gdn CW3. . . 230 A3
Old Vicarage La CW8 . . . . 103 C5
Old Vicarage Rd CH64. . . . .68 A8
Old Wargrave Rd WA12. . . .2 C3
Old Warrington Rd CW9 . . 79 A2
Old Whint Rd WA11 . . . . . . .1 A6
Old Woman's La CH3 . . . . 142 D7
OLD WOODHOUSES 227 C2
Old Wrexham Rd CH4. . . . 141 C7
O'leary St WA1. . . . . 16 C7
Olive Dr CH64 . . . . .66 F8
Olive Gr ST5 . . . . 210 D1
Oliver Cl SK10. . . . . .87 F7
Olive Rd CH64 . . . . .66 E8
Oliver Ho CH66. . . . . 69 D4
Oliver La CH66 . . . . 69 D4
Oliver St WA2. . . . . .16 B6
Ollersett Ave SK22 . . . . . . 39 D8
Ollersett Dr SK22. . . . . 39 D8
Ollersett Ho SK22 . . . . 39 D8
Ollershaw La CW9. . . . . . . 79 C4
OLLERTON. 82 F6
Ollerton Cl WA4. . . . . .17 B3
Ollerton Pk WA5 . . . . .6 E7
Ollerton Rd SK9. . . . . 34 E5
Ollier St **1** WA8. . . . . 23 A7
Olney Pl CW5. . . . . 204 C7
Olympia Pl WA5. . . . . .15 B7
Omega Bvd WA5. . . . . .6 D1
Onehouse La SK11 . . . . . . 88 C1
One Oak La SK9 . . . . .60 F7
ONNELEY. 232 F3
Onslow Rd CH1 . . . . 117 D4
ONSTON 76 C1

Onston La CW8 . . . . 101 E8
Openshaw La M44. . . . . . . .11 E6
Orange Gr WA2 . . . . .8 E2
Orchard Ave
  Acton Bridge CW8 . . . . . . .76 E4
  Lymm WA13 . . . . .18 F3
  Partington M31 . . . . .11 F4
  Whaley Bridge SK23. . . . . . 65 D7
Orchard Brow WA3. . . . . . 11 A3
Orchard Cl Barnton CW8. . .78 B3
  Bunbury CW6. . . . . 185 F8
  Cheadle SK8. . . . . 35 C7
  Chester CH2. . . . . 118 D5
  Ellesmere Port CH66 . . . . . 69 F1
  Frodsham WA6. . . . . 74 A6
  Frodsham WA6. . . . . .75 E2
  Goostrey CW4 . . . . 107 E1
  Higher Wincham CW9 . . . . 80 A6
  Macclesfield SK11 . . . . . . 112 B6
  Middlewich CW10 . . . . . . 151 D7
  Poynton SK12. . . . . 36 E3
  Weaverham CW8 . . . . .77 D1
  Wilmslow SK9 . . . . .59 F5
  Winsford CW7 . . . . 149 D7
Orchard Cotts CW6. . . . . . 146 D1
Orchard Cres
  Kidsgrove ST7 . . . . 194 D1
  Nantwich CW5 . . . . 204 E3
  Nether Alderley SK10. . . . . .84 F6
Orchard Croft CH3 . . . . . . 119 E5
Orchard Ct Alsager ST7. . . 193 E4
  Croft WA3. . . . . .9 A8
  Frodsham WA6. . . . . 74 A8
  Haslington CW1. . . . . 191 D4
Orchard Dene CW8. . . . . . 101 D5
Orchard Dr Handforth SK9. . .34 E2
  Little Leigh WA6. . . . . 77 D5
Orchardfield Cl **4** CW1. . 173 A1
Orchard Gate WA6 . . . . . . .75 E2
Orchard Gdns
  Congleton CW12 . . . . 156 A3
  Tarporley CW6. . . . . 168 D8
  Weaverham CW8 . . . . .77 B1
Orchard Gn SK9. . . . . .60 B1
Orchard Gr CH3 . . . . 180 F1
Orchard Haven CH66 . . . . . 69 E1
Orchard Ho SK10. . . . . . . .86 F5
Orchard La CH66 . . . . 69 A8
Orchard Park La CH2 . . . . .72 B4
Orchard Pk CH2. . . . . .72 B4
Orchard Pl
  10 Elworth CW11. . . . . . 174 F8
  Helsby WA6 . . . . 73 C4
  Poynton SK12. . . . . 36 D4
Orchard Rd
  Ellesmere Port CH65 . . . . . .70 B2
  Lymm WA13 . . . . .19 B5
  Whaley Bridge SK23. . . . . . 65 D7
Orchard Rise CW9. . . . . . . 126 E8
Orchard St Chester CH1 . . 237 A3
  Crewe CW1 . . . . 190 C5
  Northwich CW9 . . . . 104 B8
  Warrington WA1 . . . . 16 C5
  Warrington, Fearnhead WA2 . .9 A2
  Warrington, Stockton Heath
    WA4 . . . . 26 C6
  Willaston CW5 . . . . 205 D6
Orchards The Holt LL13 . . 196 B6
  Pickmere WA16 . . . . .79 F7
  Saltney CH4 . . . . 140 D6
  Shavington CW2. . . . . 206 C4
Orchard The
  Alderley Edge SK9 . . . . . . .85 B8
  Chester CH3. . . . . 142 A8
  Disley SK12 . . . . 38 D6
  Helsby WA6 . . . . 73 B2
Orchard Way
  Congleton CW12 . . . . 156 A3
  Kelsall CW6 . . . . 122 D5
  Widnes WA8. . . . . 12 A3
Orchard Wlk Neston CH64 . .66 E8
  3 Runcorn WA7 . . . . .49 F7
Orchid Cl Handforth SK9 . . . 34
  Huntington CH3 . . . . 142 A6
  Irlam M44 . . . . .11 E8
Orchid Way WA9 . . . . .6 B7
Orchil Cl CH66 . . . . 69 A6
Ordnance Ave
  Warrington WA3 . . . . .9 F4
  Warrington, Birchwood
    WA3 . . . . 10 A5
Ordsall Cl CW11. . . . . 174 F3
ORFORD 8 D2
Orford Ave Disley SK12 . . . 38 D6
  Warrington WA1, WA2 . . . . 16 C7
Orford Cl Golborne WA3 . . . .3 A7
  Hale L24. . . . . 21 E2
  High Lane SK6 . . . . .37 E7
Orford Gn WA2 . . . . .8 D1
Orford La WA2 . . . . .16 B7
Orford Rd WA2. . . . . .16 B8
Orford St WA1. . . . . 16 B5
Organsdale Cotts CW6 . . 123 B5
Organs Lot Rd WA6. . . . . . 74 C1
Oriel Ho CH2. . . . . 118 C4
Orion Bvd WA5. . . . . .6 E1
Orion Way CW1 . . . . 191 B1
Orkney Cl
  3 Ellesmere Port CH65. . . 70 C1
  Widnes WA8. . . . . .13 E3
Orlando Dr WA5 . . . . 15 C7
Orme Cl Macclesfield SK10 . 87 D3
  Prestbury SK10 . . . . 87 A8
Orme Cres SK10. . . . . 87 D3
Ormerod Cl CW11 . . . . . . 175 C5
Ormesby Gr CH63 . . . . . . .43 B6
Orme St SK9 . . . . 60 A1

Ormiston Bolingbroke Acad
WA7 . . . . .50 C6
Ormiston Way CW12 . . 156 A5
Ormond Cl WA8 . . . . .12 C2
Ormonde Rd CH2 . . . . . 118 C4
Ormonde St CH1 . . . . . 237 C3
Orrell Cl WA5 . . . . .15 A6
Orton Cl CW7 . . . . 127 A4
Orwell Cl SK9 . . . . .34 D2
Orwell Rd WA7. . . . . .24 F3
Osborne Ave WA2 . . . . . . .8 D1
Osborne Cl CW11 . . . . . 174 D5
Osborne Gr CW2 . . . . . 206 C5
Osborne Rd Golborne WA3 . . .3 E7
  Warrington WA4 . . . . . . .16 B1
Osbourne Cl
  Bebington CH62 . . . . . . .43 E7
  Wilmslow SK9 . . . . .60 D6
OSCROFT. 121 E2
Oscroft Loop Rd CH3 . . 121 F2
Osier Cl CH2 . . . . .72 C3
Osmere Cl SY13 . . . . . . 226 B1
Osnath Wks WA2 . . . . . . .16 B6
Osprey Ave CW7 . . . . . 149 D5
Osprey Cl
  Middlewich CW10 . . . . . 151 D5
  ⬛ Middlewich CW10 . . . 151 D5
  Runcorn WA7 . . . . .49 F5
  Warrington WA2 . . . . .8 E3
Osprey Ct CH2 . . . . 237 A4
Osprey Dr SK9 . . . . .60 C8
Osprey View ST7 . . . . . 195 D3
Ossett Cl WA7 . . . . .50 D8
Ossmere Cl CW11 . . . . . 174 F8
Ossmere La SY13 . . . . . 227 A5
Ostler's La WA16 . . . . . . .58 E7
Oswalds Way CW6 . . . . 146 C3
Oswald Way ⬛ CH3 . . . 142 B5
Oteley Ave CH62 . . . . . . .43 D8
Otley Cl ⬛ WA12 . . . . . . .1 F2
Otterburn St WA7 . . . . . .24 E3
Otters Bank ⬛ CW7 . . . 126 A1
Ottersbank Mews CW8 . . 123 F3
OUGHTRINGTON 19 C4
Oughtrington Cres WA13 . .19 B4
Oughtrington La WA13 . . .19 A4
Oughtrington Prim Sch
  WA13. . . . . .19 B4
Oughtrington View WA13. . .19 B4
Oulton Ave CH2 . . . . . . 118 E7
Oulton Cl WA4 . . . . .17 B2
Oulton Dr CW12 . . . . . . 155 F3
Oulton Mill La CW6. . . . 147 B7
Oulton Pl CH1. . . . . 237 B3
Our Lady Mother of the
  Saviour RC Prim Sch
  WA7 . . . . .50 A6
Our Lady of Lourdes RC Prim
  Sch M31. . . . . .11 E3
Our Lady of Perpetual
  Succour RC Prim Sch
  WA8 . . . . .22 A8
Our Lady's RC Prim Sch
  WA4 . . . . .16 E3
Our Lady's Star of the Sea RC
  Prim Sch CH65 . . . . .70 A3
Ousel Nest CW8. . . . . . 101 D4
Out La CH3 . . . . 184 C6
Outwood Dr SK8 . . . . . . .34 A8
Outwood La M90. . . . . . .33 C7
Outwood Lane W M90 . . . .33 B8
Outwood Prim Sch SK8 . . .34 D7
Outwood Rd SK8. . . . . . .34 B7
Oval Cres CH65 . . . . .70 E3
Oval The
  Ellesmere Port CH65 . . . .70 C3
  Gatley SK8 . . . . .34 B8
Ovenhouse La SK10 . . . . .87 E7
Oven La SK11 . . . . 114 D5
OVER 149 B8
Overdale La CW8. . . . . . 101 D1
Overdale Rd
  New Mills SK12 . . . . .38 F6
  Willaston CH64 . . . . .43 A1
Overdene Rd CW7 . . . . 149 D8
Over Fair Cl ⬛ CW7 . . . 125 F1
Overfields WA16 . . . . . . .57 D3
Over Hall Com Sch CW7 . 149 B7
Over Hall Dr CW7 . . . . . 149 C7
Overhill Dr SK9 . . . . .60 E7
Overhill La SK9 . . . . .60 E7
Overhill Rd SK9 . . . . .60 D7
OVER KNUTSFORD. 57 C1
OVER LEIGH 65 F6
Overleigh Ct CH4. . . . . . 141 D7
Overleigh Rd CH4 . . . . . 141 C7
Overleigh St Mary's CE Prim
  Sch CH4. . . . . 141 D6
Overleigh Terr CH4 . . . . 141 C7
OVER PEOVER. 83 A1
Over Pl WA16 . . . . .82 C8
OVERPOOL. 69 F7
Overpool Gdns CH66 . . . . .69 F3
Overpool Rd
  Ellesmere Port CH66 . . . .70 A2
  Ellesmere Port, Great Sutton
  CH65, CH66. . . . . .69 F5
Overpool Sta CH66 . . . . . .69 E6
Over Rd
  Church Minshull CW5. . . 172 A7
  Winsford CW7 . . . . 149 D6
Over St John's CE Prim Sch
  ⬛ CW7. . . . . 126 B1
OVER TABLEY. 56 A5
OVERTON 74 C7
Overton Cl
  Congleton CW12 . . . . . . 156 C3
  Middlewich CW10 . . . . . 151 B8

Overton Cl continued
  Newtown WA6. . . . . .49 C2
Overton Dr WA6 . . . . .74 C6
Overton Heath La SY14 . 212 F5
Overton Rd ST8 . . . . 179 F6
Overton Way ⬛ SK9 . . . .34 D5
Overway CW7 . . . . 126 E1
Overwood Ave CH1. . . . . .94 E1
Overwood La Blacon CH1 . 117 C4
  Mollington CH1 . . . . .94 E1
Ovington Cl WA7. . . . . . . .49 F3
Owen Cl Blacon CH1. . . . 117 E6
  ⬛ Sandbach CW11 . . . . 175 B7
Owens Cnr WA4 . . . . .26 D3
Owen St Crewe CW2 . . . 190 C2
  Northwich CW9 . . . . 104 B8
  Warrington WA2 . . . . . . .16 A7
Owlers Bridge SK11. . . . 137 C3
Owlers The SK23 . . . . . . .65 E6
Owley Wood Rd CW8. . . . .77 E1
Owlhurst Cl SK10 . . . . . . .88 B8
Owl Ind Est The CH5 . . . 116 B6
Owlsfield WA12 . . . . .2 E3
Oxborough Cl WA8 . . . . . .12 F4
Oxenham Rd WA2 . . . . . . .8 A3
Oxford Cl CH66 . . . . .94 E8
Oxford St WA1 . . . . .16 D6
Oxford Dr Halewood L26 . . 21 A8
  Heswall CH63 . . . . .41 F6
Oxford Gr M44 . . . . .11 C6
Oxford Rd Chester CH4 . . 140 F6
  Macclesfield SK11 . . . . . 112 B7
  Runcorn WA7 . . . . .49 A8
Oxford St Crewe CW1 . . 190 B5
  Newton-le-Willows WA12 . . .2 B3
  Warrington WA4 . . . . . . .16 C4
  Widnes WA8. . . . . .23 B7
Ox-Hey Cres ST8. . . . . . 179 D1
Ox-Hey Dr ST8. . . . . 179 D1
Oxhey Fst Sch ST8. . . . . 179 E1
Oxheys WA7 . . . . .50 C8
Oxheys La CW6 . . . . 169 C8
Oxmead Cl WA2 . . . . .9 B1
Oxmoor Cl WA7 . . . . .50 A5
Oxmoor Wood Nature
  Reserve★ WA7. . . . . .24 D3
Oxney Cl SK11 . . . . 111 E8
Oxton Cl WA8 . . . . .12 C4
Oxton Gn CH66 . . . . .69 D4

P

Pace Ave CW5 . . . . 205 D5
Pack Horse Cl CW9. . . . . .80 B2
PACKMOOR. 195 F1
Packmoor Prim Sch ST7 . 195 F1
Padarn Cl CH4 . . . . 140 D5
PADDINGTON 17 A8
Paddington Bank WA1 . . . .16 F6
Paddington Mdws Nature
  Reserve★ WA1. . . . . .17 A6
Paddock Brow SK10. . . . . .87 A5
Paddock Chase SK12 . . . .36 F6
Paddock Cl SK23 . . . . . . .64 F4
Paddock Dr CH64 . . . . . . .41 D2
PADDOCKHILL 59 A4
Paddockhill WA16 . . . . . . .59 A3
Paddock La Audlem CW3. . 230 B2
  Horwich End SK23 . . . . . .65 F5
  Kettleshulme SK23 . . . . . .64 F4
  Lymm WA13 . . . . .19 C7
  Partington WA13, WA14. . . .20 B5
Paddock Rd
  Eccleston CH4 . . . . 141 E1
  Elworth CW11 . . . . 174 E6
Paddock Rise WA7 . . . . . .49 E4
Paddock Row CH1 . . . . . 237 B2
Paddocks Gn CW12. . . . . 178 F8
Paddocks The Chester CH1 . .94 B5
  Hale WA15 . . . . .32 B8
  Hallowgate CW6 . . . . . . 122 D4
  Prestbury SK10 . . . . .87 A5
  Whitegate CW8 . . . . 125 B6
Paddock The
  Chester CH4. . . . . 141 B7
  Ellesmere Port CH66 . . . .69 D3
  Elton CH2. . . . . .72 A3
  Handforth SK9 . . . . .34 D4
  Hartford WA6. . . . . 103 C3
  Helsby WA6 . . . . .73 C2
  Heswall CH60 . . . . .41 C8
  Hassall Green CW11 . . . . 175 F2
  Horwich End SK23 . . . . . .65 F6
  Lymm WA13 . . . . .19 C4
  Sandbach CW11 . . . . 175 B7
  Tarporley CW6 . . . . 146 D1
  Willaston CW5. . . . . 205 D4
Paddock View
  Kingsley WA6. . . . . .75 B3
  Middlewich CW10 . . . . . 128 C3
Paddock Way CW8 . . . . . 161 A7
Paddock Wlk CW8 . . . . . 101 D5
PADGATE. 8 F1
Padgate Bsns Ctr WA1. . . .17 B8
Padgate La
  Warrington WA1 . . . . . . .16 D7
  Warrington, Padgate WA1 . . .16 F8
Padgate Sta WA1. . . . . . . .9 A1
Padgbury Cl CW12 . . . . . 156 A1
Padgbury La CW12 . . . . . 156 A1
Padge La CH3. . . . . 183 C2
Padley Mews WA1 . . . . . . .16 E5
Padmore Cl CW1 . . . . . . 190 A7
Padston Dr ST7 . . . . 193 B3
Padstow Cl Crewe CW1. . 190 C8
  Macclesfield SK10 . . . . . 111 E8

Padstow Cl continued
  Warrington WA5 . . . . . . .14 E3
Padstow Dr SK7. . . . . . . .35 F7
Padstow Sq WA7. . . . . . . .50 B5
Padworth Pl CW1 . . . . . 173 B1
Page Gr CW2 . . . . 206 B3
Page La WA8 . . . . .13 C1
Paignton Cl WA5 . . . . . . .14 E4
Painswick Rd CH66. . . . . .69 E2
Paisley Ave CH62 . . . . . . .43 E4
PALACE FIELDS 50 A6
Palace Fields Ave WA7 . . . .50 A6
Palace Fields Local Ctr
  WA7 . . . . .50 A6
Palacefields Prim Sch
  WA7. . . . . .50 A6
Palace Hey CH64 . . . . . . .67 A5
Palatine Cl CH1 . . . . 117 D6
Palatine Ind Est WA4 . . . . .16 C3
Palgrave Cl CH1. . . . . . . 118 A5
Palin Dr WA5 . . . . .14 F6
Palliser Cl WA3 . . . . .10 A3
Pall Mall CW5. . . . . 204 E5
Palma Ave M90 . . . . .33 B8
Palmarsh Rd WA8. . . . . . .22 B5
Palmdale Gdns ⬛ WA5 . . .15 B6
Palmer Cl
  ⬛ Northwich CW9. . . . . 103 F5
  Stud Green CW11. . . . . . 152 C2
Palmer Cres WA5 . . . . . . .15 D8
Palmer Rd CW11 . . . . . . 175 C5
Palmerston Cl CW1 . . . . 191 C5
Palmerston Cl CH11 . . . . 118 B4
Palmerston Rd SK11. . . . 112 A7
Palmerston St SK10 . . . . . .88 B8
Palmerston Way ST8 . . . 179 D1
Palm Gr CH66 . . . . .70 A1
Palmyra Square N WA1. . .16 A5
Palmyra Square S WA1. . .16 A5
PANDY. 222 A3
Pangbourne Cl WA4. . . . . .26 E6
Panton Pl CH2 . . . . 118 F3
Panton Rd CH2. . . . . 118 F3
Parade Rd M90 . . . . .33 C7
Parade The
  ⬛ Alderley Edge SK9. . . .60 A1
  Blacon CH1 . . . . 117 E5
  Culcheth WA3. . . . . .4 E3
  Neston CH64 . . . . .41 B1
Paradise CH4 . . . . 237 B1
PARADISE GREEN 171 E6
Paradise La ⬛ CW5 . . . . 171 E7
Paradise Mill Silk Mus★ ⬛
  SK11. . . . . 112 D7
Paradise St SK11 . . . . . . 112 C7
Paragon Cl WA8 . . . . .13 B5
Parbold Ct WA8. . . . . . . .22 D8
Parc Ddiwydiannol Glannau
  Dyfrdwy/Deeside Ind Pk
  CH5. . . . . .92 C2
Parc Ddiwydiannol Y Ffin/
  Borders Ind PkThe
  CH4. . . . . 140 C7
Parchments The WA12 . . . .2 D4
Pardoe Gr CW7 . . . . 150 A8
Parish Cl ST7 . . . . 193 B4
Park And Ride CH4 . . . . . 141 A3
Park Ave Bramhall SK7. . . .35 D5
  Furness Vale SK23 . . . . . .39 D3
  Haydock WA11. . . . . .1 A6
  Poynton SK12 . . . . .36 E4
  Saltney CH4 . . . . 140 E6
  Saughall CH1 . . . . .94 A2
  Talke ST7 . . . . 210 E8
  Tattenhall CH3 . . . . 166 B2
  Warrington WA4 . . . . . . .16 D3
  Weaverham CW8. . . . . . . .77 D1
  Widnes WA8. . . . . .13 B1
  Wilmslow SK9 . . . . .60 C8
  Winsford CW7. . . . . 127 A3
Park Avenue N WA12 . . . . .2 C2
Park Avenue S WA12 . . . . .2 C2
Park Bank CW12 . . . . . . 156 F2
Park Brook Rd SK11 . . . . 112 A8
Park Bvd 16 B4
Park Cl CH3. . . . . 121 B2
Park Cres
  Cuddington CW8 . . . . . . 101 F4
  Furness Vale SK23 . . . . . .39 D3
  Handforth SK9 . . . . .34 B1
  Warrington WA4 . . . . . . .26 D6
Park Ct Chester CH1. . . . 237 C2
  Frodsham WA6. . . . . .74 A8
  ⬛ Runcorn WA7 . . . . . . .49 A8
Parkdale Ind EstWA1. . . . .16 C4
Parkdale Rd WA1 . . . . . . .17 A7
Park Dr Chester CH2 . . . 119 A4
  Ellesmere Port CH65 . . . .70 B3
  Handforth SK9 . . . . .34 B1
  Wistaston CW2 . . . . 205 F8
Park Drive S CH2. . . . . . 119 A4
PARK END 209 A4
Parker Ave CH66 . . . . . . 103 A6
Parker Dr ⬛ Alvanley WA6 . . 73 A2
  Farndon CH3 . . . . 180 E1
Parker Drive S CH3. . . . . 180 F1
Parker's Bldgs CH1. . . . . 237 C3
Parkers Ct WA7 . . . . .49 E6
Parker's Rd CW1. . . . . . 190 A8
Parker's Row CH3. . . . . . 180 F6
Parker St
  Macclesfield SK11 . . . . . 112 E7
  Runcorn WA7 . . . . .23 B3
  Warrington WA1 . . . . . . .16 A5
Park Road Com Prim Sch
  WA5 . . . . .14 E6
Park Road N WA12 . . . . . . .2 E4
Park Road S WA12 . . . . . . .2 D2
Park Road W CH4 . . . . . . 141 A7

Orm–Pax 271

Parkroyal Com Sch ⬛
  SK11 . . . . 112 C7
Parks Cl CW8 . . . . 103 E4
Parkside Bsns Pk WA3 . . . . .3 A8
Parkside Cl High Lane SK6. . .37 D8
  Neston CH64 . . . . .66 D8
Parkside Ct WA8 . . . . .13 A2
Parkside Pl CW12 . . . . . 156 E3
Parkside Rd WA12, WA2. . . .3 B2
Park St Bollington SK10. . . .88 B8
  Chester CH1. . . . . 237 B2
  Congleton CW12 . . . . . . 156 E2
  Haydock WA11. . . . . .1 A6
  Macclesfield SK11 . . . . . 112 D7
  Neston CH64 . . . . .66 E8
  Northwich CW8 . . . . 103 E7
Parkstone Dr Crewe CW1. 190 B8
  Stretton WA4 . . . . .26 E3
Parksway WA1 . . . . .17 D7
Park The Christleton CH3. . 142 E8
  Warrington WA5 . . . . . . .14 D3
Park Vale Rd SK11. . . . . 112 C6
Park View Audlem CW3. . 230 C8
  Bebington CH62 . . . . . . .43 C8
  Congleton CW12 . . . . . . 156 E3
  Hazel Grove SK7. . . . . . . .37 B8
  Little Bollington WA14 . . . .20 B2
  Nantwich CW5 . . . . 204 F6
  Newton-le-Willows WA12 . . .2 E3
  Warrington WA2 . . . . .8 E3
Parkview Ct CH60 . . . . . . .40 F8
Park View Ct SK12. . . . . . .36 E4
Parkview Pk WA13 . . . . . .29 D8
Park View Rd ST7 . . . . . 195 D3
Park W CH60. . . . . .40 E7
Parkway
  Connah's Quay CH5 . . . . . .92 E1
  Holmes Chapel CW4. . . . 130 C3
  Wilmslow SK9 . . . . .60 B6
Park Way CW1 . . . . .94 A2
Parkway Bsns Ctr CH5 . . . .92 C1
Park Wlk CH2 . . . . 118 E4
Parkwood Cl
  Bebington CH62 . . . . . . .43 E8
  Lymm WA13 . . . . .18 D2
Parliament St ⬛ CW8 . . . 103 E7
Parliament Way ⬛ CH66. . .94 F8
Parlington Ct WA4. . . . . . .22 C7
Parn Cl CW1 . . . . 190 F6
Parnell Sq CW12 . . . . . . 157 A2
PARRAH GREEN 231 E7
Parr Gr WA11 . . . . .1 A6
Parr Green La
  Horton Green SY14 . . . . . 212 A8
  Shocklach SY14 . . . . 211 E7
Parr St Macclesfield SK11. . 112 C8
  ⬛ Warrington WA1 . . . . .16 C4
Parrs Wood View WA4. . . . .17 B1
Parry Ave CW8 . . . . .78 C1
Parry Dr WA4 . . . . .17 E3
Parsonage Gn Hale L24 . . . .21 C3
  Wilmslow SK9 . . . . .60 B7
Parsonage Rd WA8 . . . . . .23 A4
Parsonage St SK11 . . . . . 112 D7
Parsonage Way WA5 . . . . .15 A5
Parsons Bank CW12 . . . . 131 E3
Parsons Bridge CW1 . . . . 131 D3
Parsons La CH2 . . . . 118 E2
Parson St CW12 . . . . . . 156 C2
PARTINGTON 11 F4
Partington L Ctr M31 . . . . .11 F3
Partington Prim Sch M31. . .11 F3
Partington Sh Ctr M31. . . . .11 F3
Partington Sq WA7. . . . . . .24 F4
Partisan Gn WA5. . . . . . . .7 B2
Partridge Cl
  Congleton CW12 . . . . . . 156 E1
  Warrington WA3 . . . . .9 E4
  Winsford CW7 . . . . 149 D5
Partridge Way CW9 . . . . . .79 F5
Parvey La SK11 . . . . 112 E2
Pasadena Ave WA5. . . . . .15 A7
Pasture Cl Kelsall CW6 . . 122 C4
  Macclesfield SK10 . . . . . . .87 C3
  Sandbach CW11 . . . . 175 B8
Pasture Dr WA3. . . . . .9 B7
Pasture La WA2 . . . . .9 B1
Pastures Dr CW2. . . . . . 207 D3
Pastures The WA9 . . . . . . .6 A7
Patch La SK7 . . . . .35 D5
Patmos La WA16 . . . . . . 105 F8
Patrivale Cl WA1 . . . . .16 F6
Patrons Dr CW11. . . . . . 174 C7
Patten La WA1 . . . . .16 B5
Patterdale Ave WA2. . . . . .8 C7
Patterdale Cl CW2 . . . . . 189 D3
Patterdale Rd M31 . . . . . .11 E3
Patterson Cl
  ⬛ Macclesfield SK10. . . . .87 E5
  Warrington WA3 . . . . .9 E3
Patterson St WA12 . . . . . . .2 B3
Patton Cl WA16 . . . . 108 A8
Patton Dr WA5 . . . . .15 B6
Paul Cl WA5 . . . . .14 D6
Paulden Rd CW9 . . . . . . .80 A2
Paul St WA2 . . . . .16 A6
Pavement La WA16. . . . . . .57 F3
Pavilion Ct WA1 . . . . .2 A3
Pavilions The CW9 . . . . . 103 E2
Pavilion Way
  Congleton CW12 . . . . . . 156 C2
  Macclesfield SK10 . . . . . . .86 F1
Pavillion Way ⬛ CW9 . . . .80 B2
Paxford Pl SK9. . . . . .60 A5

Paxman Cl WA12 . . . . .2 D1
Payne Cl WA5. . . . . 15 D6
Paythorne Cl WA3. . . . . .4 F3
Peace Ctr WA5 . . . . 15 D5
Peace Dr WA5 . . . . 15 D5
Peach Field CH3 . . . . 142 B7
Peach Gr WA11 . . . . .1 E7
Peach La CW5 . . . . 189 A1
Peach Tree Cl L24. . . . . . .21 E2
Peach Way **2** CW7 . . . . 125 F2
Peacock Ave
  Warrington WA1 . . . . .16 E6
  Winsford CW7 . . . . 149 C5
Peacock Cl WA12 . . . . .1 E3
Peacock Dr SK8. . . . . .34 B6
Peacock Hay Rd ST7. . . . 210 F4
Peacock La WA5 . . . . 34 D5
Peacock Way **5** SK9 . . . . 34 D5
Peak Rd SK22 . . . . 39 D8
Pearle St SK10 . . . . 87 D1
Pearlings The CH3 . . . . . . 119 B1
Pearl La Chester CH3 . . . . 119 C1
  Littleton CH3 . . . . 119 D1
Pearl St SK10 . . . . 87 A7
Pearson Ave WA4 . . . . 16 D2
Pearson St **9** SK11 . . . . 112 E7
Pear Tree Ave
  Crewe CW1 . . . . 190 B7
  Runcorn WA7 . . . . 49 C7
Pear Tree Bank CW12 . . 156 E2
Pear Tree Barns WA16. . . .83 E4
Peartree Cl CW11 . . . . . . 175 E6
Pear Tree Cl
  Frodsham WA6. . . . . 49 D1
  Hale L24. . . . . 21 E1
  Weaverham CW8. . . . . . . 77 C1
  Winsford CW7 . . . . 149 D7
Peartree Cres WA12. . . . . . .2 C2
Pear Tree Dr CW9. . . . . . . 80 A6
Pear Tree Farm Cotts
  CW9. . . . . 104 F4
Pear Tree Field CW5 . . . . 205 A4
Peartree La SY14. . . . . . . 222 D1
Pear Tree La
  Acton Bridge CW8 . . . . . . .76 E4
  Whitchurch SY13 . . . . . . 225 D1
Peartree Pl WA4 . . . . 16 C4
Pear Tree Rd ST7. . . . . . 209 F1
Pear Tree Sch CW5 . . . . . 205 A4
Pear Tree Way
  Chester CH2. . . . . 118 F6
  5 Ellesmere Port CH66. . .69 E1
Pearwood Cl CW6. . . . . . 146 D1
Peasley Cl WA2 . . . . .9 B1
Pebble Brook Prim Sch
  CW2 . . . . 190 C1
Peckfield Cl WA7 . . . . 50 A5
PECKFORTON 184 F5
Peckforton Castle★
  CW6 . . . . 167 E1
Peckforton Cl CW11 . . . . 174 E7
Peckforton Dr
  Ellesmere Port CH66 . . . . . .69 E3
  Runcorn WA7. . . . . 49 F4
Peckforton Hall Farm
  CW6 . . . . 185 A6
Peckforton Hall La CW6 . 185 B6
Peckforton Rd CW6 . . . . 168 A2
Peckforton Way
  Chester CH2. . . . . 118 F6
  2 Northwich CW8. . . . . 103 E7
Peckforton Wlk **11** SK9 . .34 E2
Peck Mill La WA6 . . . . 98 A7
Peckmill Rdbt CW9. . . . . 127 B8
Pecks Brow CW8. . . . . 76 A4
Pecks Rd CW12 . . . . 158 D3
Pedley Hill
  Booth Green SK10 . . . . . . .62 F7
  Rainow SK10 . . . . 88 E4
Pedley House La WA16 . . . .58 E1
Pedley La Chelford WA16. . . 83 D8
  Congleton CW12 . . . . . . 157 F4
Pedley St **2** CW2 . . . . . 190 D2
Peebles Cl
  Ellesmere Port CH66 . . . . . .68 F6
  Holmes Chapel CW4. . . . 130 B2
Peel Cl WA1 . . . . 17 D6
Peel Cres CH3 . . . . 121 E7
Peel Ct **4** ST7 . . . . 195 A2
Peel Dr CW12 . . . . 178 B7
Peel Hall La CH3 . . . . 121 E7
Peel Hall Pk CH3 . . . . 121 D8
Peel Hollow ST7 . . . . 209 A2
Peel House La WA8 . . . . . .13 B2
Peel La CW12 . . . . 178 D7
Peel Sq **1** CW1 . . . . . . 190 B5
Peel St Crewe CW1 . . . . . 190 B5
  Macclesfield SK11 . . . . . 112 D6
  Newton-le-Willows WA12 . . .2 A3
  Runcorn WA7. . . . . 22 F3
Peel Terr CH1 . . . . 237 C3
Peerswood Ct CH64 . . . . . .66 E5
Peewit Cl
  Lower Heath CW12 . . . . . 156 D5
  Winsford CW7 . . . . 149 D5
Pegasus Croft CH3 . . . . . 142 C5
Pegasus Dr **3** WA5. . . . . .7 B2
Peggie's La SK10. . . . . . . .62 E2
Peggy Walsh CW1 . . . . . . 17 C8
Pelham Rd WA4 . . . . 16 D2
Pelham Rd WA4 . . . . 17 C3
Pelican Cl CW1 . . . . 191 A5
Pelton Cl CW8 . . . . 78 A3
Pemberton Cl CH64 . . . . . 68 A8

Pemberton Rd CH1. . . . . . 237 A3
Pembridge Ct CH65 . . . . . .70 E3
Pembridge Gdns CH65. . . .70 E3
Pembroke Apartments
  WA2. . . . . .9 A3
Pembroke Cl CH4 . . . . . . 141 E6
Pembroke Cl WA7 . . . . . . 24 D5
Pembroke Dr CH65. . . . . . 70 A3
Pembroke Gdns WA4 . . . . 26 D4
Pembroke Gr WA4. . . . . . . 11 C6
Pembroke Pl **5** CW10 . . 128 D2
Pembroke Rd SK11 . . . . . 111 F7
Pembroke Way CW7 . . . . 149 B7
Penare WA4 . . . . 50 C6
Penbrook Cl CW2 . . . . . . 189 D3
Penda Way CW11 . . . . . . 175 B6
Pendennis Ct WA7 . . . . . .23 F2
Pendine Cl WA5. . . . . .7 C2
Pendlebury Gdns SK11 . . 112 D2
Pendlebury St WA4 . . . . . 17 A3
Pendle Cl Crewe CW1 . . . 191 A5
  Ellesmere Port CH66 . . . . . .68 F6
Pendle Gdns WA3 . . . . . . .4 E2
Pendleton Way SK9 . . . . . 60 C5
Penfold Cl CH1 . . . . .94 B8
Penfold Hey CH2 . . . . . . 118 D7
Penfolds WA7 . . . . 23 D1
Penfold Way CW4 . . . . . . 162 A7
Penhale Mews SK7. . . . . . 35 F7
Peninsula Dr WA12. . . . . . .2 D1
Peninsula Ho WA2 . . . . . . 16 C7
Penistone Dr CH66 . . . . . .69 B5
PENKETH. 14 D4
Penketh Ave WA5. . . . . . . 15 F8
Penketh Bsns Pk WA5 . . . .15 B4
Penketh Com Prim Sch
  WA5 . . . . 14 D4
Penketh Ct
  1 Runcorn WA7 . . . . . . .23 B2
  Warrington WA5 . . . . 14 D4
Penketh Cty High Sch
  WA5 . . . . 15 A5
Penketh Rd WA5 . . . . 15 A4
Penketh's La **19** WA7 . . . 23 A3
Penketh South Com Prim
  Sch WA5 . . . . .14 E3
Penkford La WA5 . . . . .1 D2
Penkford Sch WA12. . . . . . .1 E2
Penkford St WA12. . . . . . . .1 E3
Penkmans La WA6. . . . . . . 74 C6
Penlington Ct CW5 . . . . . 204 F6
Penmann Cres L26 . . . . . . 21 A7
Penmark Cl WA5. . . . . .7 C2
Penmon Cl CH1 . . . . 117 D3
Pennant Cl WA3 . . . . 10 A3
Penn Bridge SK11 . . . . . . 158 E6
Penn Gdns CH65 . . . . 70 B5
Penn House Cl SK7. . . . . . 35 E8
Pennine Ct SK10 . . . . .87 E2
Pennine Rd WA2 . . . . .8 E2
Pennine Way
  Biddulph ST8 . . . . 179 E1
  Winsford CW7 . . . . 149 B8
Pennine Wlk CH66 . . . . . . .69 B6
Pennington Cl WA6 . . . . . 49 D2
Pennington Dr WA12. . . . . .2 E3
Pennington Gn CH66 . . . . 69 C3
Pennington La WA5, WA9 . .1 D2
Penningtons La SK11. . . . 111 F5
Penn La WA7 . . . . 22 F1
Pennsylvania La CH3 . . . . 184 C6
Penny Bank Cl CH4 . . . . . 139 A3
Pennyfields Rd ST7 . . . . . 195 D2
Penny La Collins Green WA5 . .1 D1
  Cronton L35, WA8. . . . . . .12 B6
  Haydock WA11. . . . . .2 B7
  Rainow SK10 . . . . 88 D3
Pennymoor Dr CW10 . . . . 128 D2
Pennyoak Dr **2** CW1 . . . 173 A1
Pennypleck Dr **1** WA4 . . .27 B4
Pennypleck La CW11 . . . . 28 A2
Penny's La
  Northwich CW9 . . . . 104 F7
  Rudheath CW9. . . . . 105 B5
Pen Rd CW2 . . . . 189 E1
Penrhyn Cres
  Hazel Grove SK7. . . . . . . 36 C8
  Runcorn WA7. . . . . 49 B7
Penrhyn Rd CW8 . . . . . . 103 E8
Penrith Ave
  Macclesfield SK11 . . . . . 111 F5
  Warrington WA2 . . . . .8 C2
Penrith Cl Frodsham WA6. . 49 D1
  Partington M31 . . . . .11 E4
Penrith Ct CW12 . . . . 156 A2
Penrose Gdns WA5. . . . . . 14 D3
Penry Ave M44. . . . . .11 E6
Penryn Cl WA5. . . . . 14 E3
Pensarn Gdns WA5. . . . . . .7 D2
Pensby Ave CH2. . . . . 118 D5
Pensby Dr CH66. . . . . 69 D4
Pensby Rd CH60. . . . . 40 F8
Penshaw Ct WA7. . . . . . . .49 E7
Pentland Ave WA3. . . . . . . .8 B3
Pentland Cl Chester CH3. . 119 A2
  Winsford CW7 . . . . 149 B8
Pentland Pl WA2 . . . . .8 B3
Pentre Cl CH3 . . . . 121 F7
Pentre La CH3 . . . . 121 F7
Penzance Cl SK10 . . . . . . 111 E8
Peony Gdns WA9. . . . . .6 B7
Peover Hall & Gardens★
  WA16 . . . . 107 E8
PEOVER HEATH 108 C8
Peover La Chelford SK11 . . 108 F8
  Congleton CW12 . . . . . . 157 F6
Peover Pk Goostrey WA16. 107 F7
  Parkgate WA16 . . . . 108 A7

Peover Rd SK9 . . . . .34 E5
Peover Superior Endowed
  Prim Sch WA16 . . . . . . 108 B8
Pepper Ct SK9 . . . . 60 A6
Pepper St
  Appleton Thorn WA4. . . . . .27 B3
  Ashley WA16. . . . . .31 F1
  Chelford SK11 . . . . .83 E2
  Chester CH1. . . . . 237 B2
  Christleton CH3 . . . . 142 D8
  Hale L24. . . . . 21 D1
  Henbury SK11 . . . . 111 B8
  Lymm WA13 . . . . .18 F3
  Middlewich CW10 . . . . . . 128 C1
  Nantwich CW5. . . . . 204 E5
Peppers The WA13 . . . . . . 18 F3
Percival Cl CH2 . . . . 118 C8
Percival Dr WA7. . . . . 22 D1
Percival La Ollerton WA16. . 83 B3
  Runcorn WA7. . . . . 22 E2
Percival Rd Chester CH2. . 118 C8
  Ellesmere Port CH65 . . . . . .70 B6
Percival St WA1. . . . . 16 C5
Percy James Cl ST7 . . . . 193 E4
Percy Rd CH4 . . . . 141 D7
Percy St Northwich CW9 . 104 A8
  Warrington WA5 . . . . 15 E5
Percyvale St SK10 . . . . . . 112 E8
Peregrine Cl CW7 . . . . . . 149 D5
Perenna Ct/Llys Perenna
  CH1. . . . . .91 B2
Perimeter Rd CH2. . . . . . . 72 D5
Permitted Bridleway
  High Moor SK11 . . . . 114 C1
  Langley SK11 . . . . 113 F2
Perranporth Cl WA4 . . . . . 26 C2
Perrin Ave WA7. . . . . .48 E8
Perrins Rd WA5. . . . . .6 F6
Perry Fields CW1 . . . . . . 173 B1
Perry St WA7 . . . . .23 B2
Perth Cl Bramhall SK7. . . . 35 F5
  Holmes Chapel CW4. . . . 130 B2
  Warrington WA2 . . . . .8 F3
Peterborough Cl
  Ellesmere Port CH66 . . . . . .94 F7
  Macclesfield SK10 . . . . . . 87 A2
Peter Destapleigh Way
  CW5. . . . . 205 A3
Peter Ellson Cl CW2 . . . . 190 D1
Peterfield Way SK12. . . . . 36 A4
Peter Fletcher Cres **10**
  CW11. . . . . 174 C7
Peter House Rd SK11 . . . . 112 F3
Peter Pl **7** CW1. . . . . . 190 B5
Peters Cl SK10. . . . . 87 A7
Petersfield Gdns WA3 . . . . .4 E4
Petersfield Way CW2. . . . 207 D3
Petersgate WA7 . . . . 50 D7
Petersham Dr WA4 . . . . . . 26 E5
Peter St Golborne WA3 . . . .3 A8
  Macclesfield SK11 . . . . . 112 C7
  Northwich CW9 . . . . .79 B1
Peter Street W **1** SK11 . 112 C7
Petham Ct WA8. . . . . .12 E4
Petrel Ave SK12. . . . . 36 B4
Petrel Cl CW7. . . . . 149 D5
Petunia Cl WA9. . . . . .6 A7
Petunia Gr SK11 . . . . 112 B5
Petworth Ave WA2 . . . . . . .8 B3
Petworth Cl CW2. . . . . . . 206 B8
Pevensey Dr WA16 . . . . . . 82 A8
Peveril Cl WA4. . . . . 26 D8
Peveril Dr SK7. . . . . 36 F8
Peveril Gdns SK12. . . . . . . 39 A6
Peveril Mews SK12. . . . . . 39 A6
Peveril Wlk **3** SK11 . . . 111 F7
Pewithall Prim Sch WA7 . . .49 B7
Pewit La CW5. . . . . 231 C7
PEWTERSPEAR. 26 E4
Pewterspear Green Rd
  WA4. . . . . 26 E3
Pewterspear La WA4 . . . . . 26 E4
Pexall Rd SK11 . . . . 134 C3
Pex Hill Ct WA8 . . . . 12 E5
Pexhill Dr SK10 . . . . 111 E7
Pexhill Rd SK11 . . . . 111 C5
Pheasant Cl WA3. . . . . .9 F4
Pheasant Dr CW9 . . . . . . .79 F5
Pheasant Field L24. . . . . . 21 C2
Pheasant Way CW7. . . . . 149 D5
Pheasant Wlk WA16 . . . . . 29 C4
Philip Rd WA8 . . . . 22 B8
Philips Dr WA5. . . . . 14 E4
Philips La CH66. . . . . 69 C4
Philip St CH5 . . . . 116 A2
Philip Taylor Dr
  Bradfield Green CW1 . . . . 172 F1
  5 Crewe CW1. . . . . . 190 A8
Phillips Rd CH1 . . . . 117 D3
Phillip St CH2. . . . . 118 F3
Phillips Way CH60. . . . . . .40 E8
Phipps' La WA5. . . . . .6 E7
Phoenix Ave WA5. . . . . . . .7 F2
Phoenix Cl ST7. . . . . 195 C2
Phoenix Cl **4** CH64. . . . 41 C1
Phoenix Ctr The CW7 . . . 127 C1
Phoenix L Pk CW1. . . . . . 190 C3
Phoenix Pl WA5 . . . . 15 A7
Phoenix St CH5 . . . . 116 A3
Phythian Cres WA5. . . . . . 14 F4
Pichael Nook WA4. . . . . . 17 A4
Pickenham Cl SK11. . . . . . 111 F6
Pickering Cres WA4. . . . . . 17 D3
Pickering Croft Pl CW1 . . 190 D7
Pickerings Cl WA7 . . . . . . 49 C6

Pickerings O The Boat
  CW8. . . . . .76 B5
Pickering's Pasture Nature
  Reserve★ WA8. . . . . .22 B3
Pickerings Rd WA8. . . . . . .22 B3
Pickering St CH2. . . . . . . 237 C4
Pickering Way CW5 . . . . . 204 F4
Pickford St SK11 . . . . 112 D7
Picking Dr **7** CW1 . . . . 173 A1
PICKMERE. 80 A7
Pickmere Cl CW11 . . . . . . 174 E7
Pickmere Ct Crewe CW1. . 190 C5
  10 Handforth SK9 . . . . . 34 D5
Pickmere Dr
  Bebington CH62. . . . . . . .43 F3
  Bebington CH62. . . . . . . .43 F4
  Chester CH3. . . . . 142 B8
  Runcorn WA7. . . . . 50 C5
Pickmere La
  Higher Wincham CW9 . . . . .79 F6
  Pickmere WA16 . . . . 55 D2
Pickmere Rd SK9 . . . . 34 D5
Pickmere St WA5 . . . . 15 E5
Pickwick Cl CW11 . . . . . . 175 C8
Pickwick Pl ST7. . . . . 194 D2
Pickwick Rd SK12 . . . . . . 36 D3
Picow Farm Rd WA7. . . . . 22 E1
Picow St **2** WA7 . . . . . . 22 F1
PICTON 96 C3
Picton Ave
  Ellesmere Port CH65 . . . . . .70 C5
  Runcorn WA7. . . . . 23 B2
Picton Cl Bebington CH62 . . 43 E3
  2 Northwich CW9. . . . . 103 F4
  Warrington WA3 . . . . .9 C4
Picton Dr Handforth SK9 . . .34 E2
  Winsford CW7 . . . . 126 B2
Picton Gorse La CH2 . . . . 119 B7
Picton La CH2 . . . . 96 C4
Picton Sq CW4 . . . . 130 C3
Picton Valley CH2. . . . . . . 96 C3
Piele Rd WA11 . . . . .1 E8
Pierce St SK11 . . . . 112 C8
Pierpoint La CH1. . . . . . . 237 B2
Pierpoint St WA5 . . . . 15 F7
Pigginshaw SK9 . . . . 59 E8
Pigot Pl WA4 . . . . 16 F5
Pike La WA6. . . . . 75 A3
Pikemere Prim Sch ST7. . 193 B5
Pikemere Rd ST7. . . . . . . 193 B5
Pikenall La CW8 . . . . 76 D3
Pike Rd SK10 . . . . .89 B6
Pike St WA4 . . . . 16 D1
Pike The CW5. . . . . 204 E3
Pilgrim Cl WA2 . . . . .8 A6
Pilgrims Way WA7 . . . . . . 24 D2
Pillar Box La CW11 . . . . . 153 B3
Pillbox Cl CH66 . . . . 43 D1
Pillmoss La WA4 . . . . .52 B8
Pillory St CW5 . . . . 204 E5
Pilot Cl SK7. . . . . 35 F1
Pimblett Rd WA11 . . . . . . .1 E7
Pimblett St WA3 . . . . .3 A7
Pimlico Rd WA7. . . . . 22 C2
Pimlotts Gr CW8 . . . . 103 D4
Pinders Farm Dr WA1 . . . . 16 C5
Pineapple Pk CW7 . . . . . . 127 B2
Pine Ave
  Newton-le-Willows WA12 . . .2 D2
  4 Widnes WA8. . . . . . . 13 B2
Pine Cl Haydock WA11. . . . . .1 C6
  Macclesfield SK10 . . . . . . 87 F1
  Talke ST7. . . . . 210 D7
Pine Ct ST7. . . . . 193 E4
Pinedale Cl CH66. . . . . . . 95 A8
Pine Gdns CH2. . . . . 118 C6
Pine Gr Chester CH2. . . . . 119 B4
  Ellesmere Port CH66 . . . . . .70 A1
  Golborne WA3 . . . . .3 C8
  Sandbach CW11. . . . . . . 175 C6
  Warrington WA1 . . . . 17 A7
  Winsford CW7 . . . . 127 A1
Pinehey CH64. . . . . 41 D1
Pine Ho CH2 . . . . 118 C5
Pinehurst SK10 . . . . .86 E6
Pinellas WA7 . . . . 23 B3
Pine Lo SK7. . . . . 35 F7
Pine Rd Bramhall SK7. . . . 35 F8
  Heswall CH60. . . . . 41 C8
  Macclesfield SK10 . . . . . . 87 F1
  Poynton SK12. . . . . 36 F3
  Runcorn WA7. . . . . 49 C8
Pines La CW12 . . . . 158 A1
Pines The Mobberley WA16. .58 E1
  8 Northwich CW9. . . . . 103 E6
  Widnes WA8. . . . . 13 D4
Pinetree Cl Barnton CW8 . . .78 B4
  Winsford CW7 . . . . 127 A1
Pine Tree Cl CH4. . . . . . . 139 C3
Pine Trees WA16 . . . . .57 F8
Pine Way CW12 . . . . 155 E4
Pineways WA4 . . . . 26 C3
Pine Wlk Nantwich CW5. . . 204 F4
  1 Partington M31. . . . . .11 E3
Pinewood Ave WA1 . . . . . .16 E7
Pinewood Cl CH2 . . . . 72 C3
Pinewood Ct CW2. . . . . . . 206 B7
Pinewood Dr CH60 . . . . . .41 B8
Pinewood Gr ST5 . . . . 210 E1
Pinewood Rd
  Burtonwood WA5. . . . . . . .6 F7
  Wilmslow SK9 . . . . .60 E8
  Winsford CW7 . . . . 126 B1
Pinfold Cl WA15. . . . . 32 D7
Pinfold Ct CH4. . . . . 141 C7
Pinfold La Alpraham CW6 . 169 D5
  Chelford WA16. . . . . .83 D6
  Chester CH4. . . . . 141 D6

Pinfold La continued
  Little Budworth CW6 . . . . 147 E7
  Middlewich CW10 . . . . . . 128 E1
  Plumley WA16 . . . . .81 B4
  Wythenshawe M90, WA15 . .32 F6
Pinfold St **18** SK11. . . . . 112 C8
Pinfold The LL13 . . . . 196 D8
Pinfold Way CW8 . . . . 77 C1
Pingard's La CW8. . . . . . . 101 C6
Pingate Dr SK8. . . . . 35 A6
Pingate La SK8. . . . . 35 A6
Pingate Lane S SK8 . . . . . 35 A6
Pingot Croft CH3. . . . . . . 142 B7
Pingot La WA6. . . . . 99 A5
Pingot Rd SK22 . . . . 39 D8
Pinmill Brow WA6. . . . . . . .74 B7
Pinmill Cl WA6. . . . . 74 C7
Pinners Brow WA2 . . . . . . .16 B6
Pinners Brow Ret Pk WA2. .16 B6
Pinners Fold WA7. . . . . . . .24 B1
PINSLEY GREEN 216 D2
Pinsley Green Rd CW5. . . 216 E2
Pinsley View CW5 . . . . . . 216 E4
Pintail Pl CW7 . . . . 149 D6
Pinwood Ct
  13 Handforth SK9 . . . . . .34 E1
  8 Wilmslow Park SK9 . . .60 E8
Pioneer Cl **12** CH3 . . . . 142 C5
Pipehouse La SY13 . . . . . 214 F7
Pipers Ash CW7. . . . . 126 A1
PIPER'S ASH 119 D4
Piper's Cl CH60 . . . . 40 D8
Pipers Ct CH2. . . . . 119 B4
Piper's End CH60. . . . . . . 40 D8
Pipers Hollow **3** CW11 . 175 B8
Pipers La Chester CH2. . . . 119 B4
  Puddington CH64 . . . . . . 93 A8
Piper's La CH60. . . . . 40 D8
Pipers The Golborne WA3 . . .3 F8
  Heswall CH60 . . . . 40 D8
Pipit Ave WA12 . . . . .2 C3
Pipit La WA3. . . . . .9 E3
Pippin Cl CW10 . . . . 151 C7
Pippits Row WA7. . . . . . . .49 E4
Pirie Cl CW12 . . . . 157 A4
Pirie Rd CW12 . . . . 157 A4
Pitcher La CW11 . . . . 177 A8
Pitfield Way SK10 . . . . . . .85 B3
Pit La Hough CW2 . . . . . . 206 E2
  Talke ST7. . . . . 210 C6
  Widnes WA8. . . . . 13 A4
Pitt La SK11. . . . . 132 B8
Pitts Cl CH3. . . . . 121 C2
Pitts Heath La WA7. . . . . . .24 E3
Pitt St Macclesfield SK11 . . 112 D6
  Warrington WA5 . . . . .15 F7
  Widnes WA8. . . . . 23 A5
Pitville Terr WA8. . . . . 22 C7
Pk La CH3 . . . . 121 B2
Plaistow Ct WA7 . . . . .49 E7
Plane Gr ST5. . . . . 210 E1
Plane Tree Dr CW1 . . . . . 190 E6
Plane Tree Gr WA11. . . . . . .2 A7
Plane Tree Rd M31 . . . . . . 11 D3
Planewood Gdns WA3. . . . .3 F7
Plantagenet Cl **3** CW7 . 149 D6
Plantation Cl WA7. . . . . . . 24 A1
Plantation Dr CH66. . . . . . .69 E7
Plant La CW11 . . . . 174 B7
Plant St CW11 . . . . 175 A7
Plas Devon Cl LL13 . . . . . 180 A2
Plas Dinas CH1. . . . . 117 D3
Plas Newton La CH2. . . . . 118 F5
Plas Newydd CH4 . . . . . . 161 B6
Plassey La SY14. . . . . 222 D3
Plaster Pits La CW6 . . . . . 185 F4
Platt Ave CW11 . . . . 175 A7
Platts La Christleton CH3. . 143 D8
  Duddon CH3, CW6. . . . . . 144 E7
  Tarvin CH3 . . . . 121 B2
  Tarvin, Broom Bank CH3. . 144 B8
  Tattenhall CH3 . . . . 183 F7
Platt's La CH3. . . . . 164 E5
Platts St WA11 . . . . .1 A6
Pleasance Way WA12. . . . . .2 D4
Pleasant St
  Macclesfield SK10 . . . . . . 87 F1
  Moss Bank WA8 . . . . 23 C8
  Northwich CW9 . . . . 103 E7
Pleasant View SK10 . . . . . 111 C8
Pleasant Way SK8. . . . . . . 35 C6
Pleck Rd CH65 . . . . 70 A2
PLEMSTALL. 97 B1
Plemstall Cl CH2 . . . . 119 F8
Plemstall La CH2. . . . . 97 A1
Plemstall Way CH2. . . . . . . 96 F1
Plemston Ct CH66. . . . . . . .69 F8
Plex The ST7. . . . . 193 D4
Plinston Ave WA4 . . . . .16 F4
Plough Croft ST7. . . . . . . 193 A3
Plough La CH3 . . . . 143 B7
Ploughmans Cl CH66 . . . . .94 E8
Ploughmans Way
  Ellesmere Port CH66 . . . . . .94 E8
  Macclesfield SK10 . . . . . . 87 B3
Plover Ave CW7 . . . . 149 D5
Plover Cl Farndon CH3 . . . 180 C1
  Macclesfield SK10 . . . . . . 87 B4
  Newton-le-Willows WA12 . . .2 C3
Plover Dr WA7 . . . . 50 D8
Plovers La WA6. . . . . 73 C5
Plover Way WA3 . . . . .3 E8
Plumb Dr CH65 . . . . 70 D5
Plumbs Fold CW8 . . . . 78 A2
PLUMLEY. 80 F3
Plumley Cl Chester CH3. . . 119 C1
  16 Macclesfield SK11. . . 112 E7
Plumley Gdns WA8. . . . . . 12 A1

PLUMLEY MOOR. 81 C2
Plumley Moor Rd WA16. . . . 81 C2
Plumley Rd SK9. . . . . 34 D5
Plumley Sta WA16. . . . . 81 A3
Plumpstons La WA6. . . . . . .49 B1
Plumpton Cross ▣ WA8. . .13 B2
Plumpton Mews ▤ WA8. . . 13 C1
Plum Terr CH1. . . . . 237 A3
Plymouth Cl WA7. . . . . .50 E6
Plymouth Dr SK7. . . . . .35 F7
Plymyard Ave CH62. . . . . . 43 D5
Plymyard Cl CH62. . . . . 43 D5
Plymyard Ct CH62. . . . . . . 43 C6
Poachers' La WA4. . . . . . . .16 F3
Pochard Ave CW7. . . . . . . 149 D6
Pochard Cl CW2. . . . . 189 E1
Pochard Dr SK12. . . . . 36 A4
Pochard Rise WA7. . . . . . . 50 D8
Pochin Way CW10. . . . . . . 128 E1
Pocket Nook La WA3. . . . . .4 B7
Pocklington Ct WA2. . . . . . .8 F1
Points Ho ▤ CW1. . . . . . . 190 A5
Polden Cl CH66. . . . . 69 A6
Poleacre Dr WA8. . . . . 12 D2
Pole La CW9. . . . . .53 E2
Pole Lane Ends CW9. . . . . 53 C4
Pollard Ave WA6. . . . . 74 D7
Pollard Dr CW5. . . . . 205 B4
Polperro Cl
  Macclesfield SK10. . . . . . . 86 D1
  Warrington WA5. . . . . .14 E3
Pond Cotts CH2. . . . . 72 A3
Pondside Dr CH65. . . . . . . 70 A8
Pond St WA3. . . . . .4 A8
Pond View Cl CH60. . . . . . 41 C8
Pond Wlk WA9. . . . . .1 A1
Pool Bank Bsns Pk CH3. . 121 C3
Pool Bank Cotts CH3. . . . 121 C3
Poole Ave WA2. . . . . .8 B2
Poole Cres WA2. . . . . .8 B2
Poole Field CW8. . . . . 77 D4
Poole Hall La CH66. . . . . . .69 F8
Poole Hall Rd CH66. . . . . . .69 F8
POOLEHILL. 188 A2
Poole Hill Rd CW5. . . . . . 188 A2
Poole La CH2. . . . . .71 E2
Pool End Cl SK10. . . . . 87 D4
Pool End Rd SK10. . . . . . . 87 D4
Poole Old Hall La CW5. . 188 D4
Poole Rd ▣ CW11. . . . . . . 152 C2
Pooles La CW11. . . . . 177 A6
POOLFOLD. 179 F4
Poolford La CW4. . . . . 129 E2
Pool Hall Ind Est CH65,
  CH66. . . . . 70 A8
Pool House Rd SK12. . . . . 37 D5
Pool La Cuddington CW8. . 102 B2
  Haslington CW11. . . . . 192 A7
  Ince CH2. . . . . .71 F4
  Lymm WA13. . . . . .18 B4
  Malpas SY14. . . . . 212 D1
  Runcorn WA7. . . . . .23 B3
  Tarvin CH3. . . . . 121 C4
  Warrington WA4. . . . . 16 A1
Pool Meadows Rd CW1. . 191 B4
Pool Rd WA3. . . . . 11 A3
Pool Side WA3. . . . . 194 A8
Poolside Ct ST7. . . . . 193 E4
Poolside Rd WA7. . . . . .23 B1
Pools Platt La CW9. . . . . . .53 E6
  Widnes WA8. . . . . .23 B7
Pool St Macclesfield SK11. .112 E6
  Widnes WA8. . . . . .23 B7
Pooltown Rd CH65. . . . . . .69 F5
Pool View CW11. . . . . 177 A6
Poplar Ave Culcheth WA3. . . .4 F3
  Moulton CW9. . . . . 126 F8
  Newton-le-Willows WA12. . . .2 D3
  Runcorn WA7. . . . . 49 C7
  Warrington WA3. . . . . .14 E3
  Wilmslow SK9. . . . . .59 F5
Poplar Cl Congleton CW12. 156 A4
  Cuddington CW8. . . . . 102 A3
  Ellesmere Port CH65. . . . . .70 B4
  Runcorn WA7. . . . . 49 C7
  Winsford CW7. . . . . 149 B8
Poplar Ct CW5. . . . . 205 A4
Poplar Dr Alsager ST7. . . 193 E2
  Kidsgrove ST7. . . . . 195 A1
  Middlewich CW10. . . . . . . 151 D7
Poplar Gr Bollington SK10. . 88 A8
  Crewe CW1. . . . . 190 E5
  Elton CH2. . . . . 72 A3
  Haydock WA11. . . . . .1 C6
  Irlam M44. . . . . 11 D6
Poplar Hall La CH2. . . . . . 95 C6
Poplar La TF9. . . . . 236 F5
Poplar Rd Chester CH4. . . 140 F5
  Haydock WA11. . . . . .1 C6
  Macclesfield SK11. . . . . . . 112 D6
  Weaverham CW8. . . . . 102 D8
Poplars Ave
  Warrington, Hulme WA2. . . .8 C3
  Warrington, Winwick Quay
    WA2. . . . . .8 D2
Poplars Pl WA2. . . . . .8 D2
Poplars The
  Golborne, Wash End WN7. . . .4 C8
  Lymm WA13. . . . . .18 D4
  Wistaston CW2. . . . . 205 F7
Poplar Vale CW8. . . . . .76 B2
Poplar View WA4. . . . . 25 A7
Poplar Way SK6. . . . . 38 A7
Poplar Weint ▤ CH64. . . . .66 E8
Poplar Wlk M31. . . . . 11 D3
Poppy Ave CW11. . . . . 174 E6
Poppy Cl
  ▣ Ravensclough CW8. . . . 101 F1

Poppy Cl continued
  Weston CW2. . . . . 207 C5
Poppy Field Pk CH4. . . . . 140 D6
Poppyfields Alsager ST7. . 193 B3
  Warrington WA5. . . . . 15 D3
Porlock Cl Heswall CH60. . .41 B6
  Warrington WA5. . . . . .14 E4
Port Arcades Sh Ctr CH65. 70 C5
Porter Ave WA12. . . . . .2 C5
Porter Dr CW9. . . . . 104 C6
Porters Croft CH3. . . . . . 119 F5
Porter St WA7. . . . . 23 C2
Porter Way CW9. . . . . 104 C6
Portford Cl SK10. . . . . .86 F1
Porthcawl Cl WA8. . . . . . . 12 C3
Porthleven Rd WA7. . . . . . .50 B5
Portland Dr
  Biddulph ST8. . . . . 179 D2
  Scholar Green ST7. . . . . . . 194 E6
  Winsford CW7. . . . . 149 B8
Portland Gr CW1. . . . . 191 D5
Portland Pl WA6. . . . . 73 C4
Portland Rd WA5. . . . . 15 A8
Portland St
  Newton-le-Willows WA12. . . .1 F4
  Runcorn WA7. . . . . .22 F3
Portland Trad Pk WA2. . . . 16 A6
Portland Wlk ▤ SK11. . . . 111 F7
Portloe Rd SK8. . . . . 34 B7
Portman Pl ▤ CW7. . . . . . 149 A8
Portmarnock Cl SK10. . . . . .87 B3
Portola Cl WA4. . . . . 17 C2
Portree Ave CH63. . . . . . . 43 D5
Portree Dr CH63. . . . . 130 B2
Portrush Cl
  Macclesfield SK10. . . . . . . 87 C4
  Widnes WA8. . . . . .12 E3
Portside WA7. . . . . .50 E7
Portside Bsns Pk CH65. . . .70 B8
Portside N CH65. . . . . .70 B8
Portsmouth Pl WA7. . . . . . .50 E6
Portway M22. . . . . 33 E8
Postles Pl CW9. . . . . 103 F6
Post Office La
  Betley CW2. . . . . 207 F1
  Hampton Heath SY14. . . . . 213 D7
  Norley WA6. . . . . 100 E5
  Runcorn WA7. . . . . 48 D7
Post Office Pl ▣ CW9. . . . . 79 A1
Potter Cl CW5. . . . . 205 D4
Potter Pl CW8. . . . . 103 E4
Potters Barn The★
  CW11. . . . . 176 A1
Potters End ST8. . . . . 179 C1
Potters La WA8. . . . . .21 F5
Pott Hall SK10. . . . . 63 D3
Potton Cl WA7. . . . . .24 E3
POTT SHRIGLEY. 63 D3
Pott Shrigley Church Sch
  SK10. . . . . 63 C3
POULTON. 163 B2
Poulton Cres WA1. . . . . 17 D8
Poulton Dr WA8. . . . . 22 D8
Poulton Hall Rd CH63. . . . 43 A7
Poulton Rd CH63. . . . . 43 A8
Pound Rd CH66. . . . . 69 C7
Povey Rd WA2. . . . . .8 D1
Powder Mill Rd
  Grappenhall WA4. . . . . .17 B4
  Warrington WA4. . . . . 17 A3
Powell's Orch CH4. . . . . . 141 C7
Powell St WA4. . . . . 16 F3
Power Ho Rd CH62. . . . . . .44 B5
Powey La CH1. . . . . .94 B5
Pownall Ave SK7. . . . . .35 F7
Pownall Ct SK9. . . . . 59 E8
POWNALL GREEN. 35 E6
Pownall Green Prim Sch ▣
  SK7. . . . . 35 E7
Pownall Hall Sch SK9. . . . 59 E8
POWNALL PARK. 59 F7
Pownall Pl SK7. . . . . .35 E7
Pownall Rd SK9. . . . . 59 E8
Pownall Sq SK11. . . . . 112 C8
Pownall St SK10. . . . . 87 D1
Powy Dr ST7. . . . . 195 B2
Powys Ct CH1. . . . . 237 A3
Powys St WA5. . . . . .15 F5
POYNTON. 36 E4
Poynton Cl WA4. . . . . .17 B3
Poynton Coppice Nature
  Reserve★ SK12. . . . . .37 B2
Poynton High Sch SK12. . . 36 F3
Poynton Ind Est SK12. . . . 36 D1
Poynton L Ctr SK12. . . . . . .36 F2
Poynton ▣ SK10. . . . . 112 C8
Poynton Sta SK12. . . . . . . 36 C4
Pratchitts Row CW5. . . . . 204 E5
Precinct The CW2. . . . . . . 189 F2
Preece Cl WA8. . . . . 12 D4
Preece Ct CW1. . . . . 190 B5
Preesall Ave SK8. . . . . .34 B8
Premier Pk CW7. . . . . 127 B3
Prenton Pl CH4. . . . . 141 E7
Prescot Rd WA8. . . . . 12 D2
Prescot St CH2. . . . . 118 F3
Prescott Rd SK9. . . . . 34 B1
Prescott St WA4. . . . . 16 E3
PRESTBURY. 87 B7
Prestbury CE Prim Sch
  SK10. . . . . .86 F7
Prestbury Cl
  ▤ Northwich CW9. . . . . . . 103 F4
  Widnes WA8. . . . . .22 E8
Prestbury Ct SK10. . . . . . . .86 F6
Prestbury Dr WA4. . . . . . . 17 D4
Prestbury La SK10. . . . . .87 B7
Prestbury Pk SK10. . . . . . . .86 E6

Prestbury Rd
  Adder's Moss SK10. . . . . . . .85 F6
  Macclesfield SK10. . . . . . . .87 B1
  Nether Alderley SK10. . . . . 86 A5
  Wilmslow SK9. . . . . .60 E5
Prestbury Sta SK10. . . . . . 87 A7
Preston Ave M44. . . . . .11 F7
PRESTON BROOK. 50 F5
Preston Brook Marina
  WA7. . . . . .50 E7
PRESTON ON THE HILL. . . 51 A6
Preston Street W SK11. . . 112 B6
Prestwich Ave WA3. . . . . . .4 E3
Prestwick Cl
  Macclesfield SK10. . . . . . . 87 C5
  Widnes WA8. . . . . .12 F3
  Winsford CW7. . . . . 126 C2
Prestwood Ct WA3. . . . . . . 10 A7
Pretoria St CH4. . . . . 141 D7
Price Ave CW11. . . . . 175 A5
Price Cl CW11. . . . . 152 C2
Price Dr CW11. . . . . 175 A5
Pride CW12. . . . . .2 E2
Priestfield Rd CH65. . . . . . 70 C5
Priest La SK10. . . . . .61 B1
Priestfield Rd SK11. . . . . . 158 E6
Priestley Bsns Ctr WA5. . . 15 F5
Priestley Coll WA4. . . . . . . 16 C3
Priestley St WA4. . . . . 16 C2
Priestley St WA5. . . . . 15 F5
Priestly Ct ▣ CW5. . . . . . 204 E5
Priestner Dr WA6. . . . . . . .73 B4
Priestway La CH64. . . . . . . .67 E1
Priesty Ct CW12. . . . . 156 D2
Priesty Fields CW12. . . . . 156 D2
Primary Cl M44. . . . . 11 D5
Primitive St ST7. . . . . 195 C7
Primrose Ave
  Haslington CW1. . . . . 191 C5
  Macclesfield SK11. . . . . . . 112 B5
Primrose Chase CW4. . . . 130 D8
Primrose Cl Alsager ST7. . 193 C3
  Huntington CH3. . . . . 142 A6
  Runcorn WA7. . . . . 50 A8
  Warrington WA2. . . . . .8 D2
  Widnes WA8. . . . . .12 E1
Primrose Gr WA11. . . . . .1 F7
PRIMROSE HILL. 28 C6
Primrose Hill Crewe CW2. 189 F3
  Cuddington CW8. . . . . 101 F4
  Kelsall CW6. . . . . 122 E6
Primrose La WA6. . . . . .73 B1
Primrose Way Handforth SK9. . 34
Primula Cl WA9. . . . . .6 A7
Primula Dr WA3. . . . . .3 D8
Prince Albert St CW1. . . . 190 B3
Prince Edward St CW5. . . 204 E6
Prince Henry Sq ▤ WA1. .16 B5
PRINCE HILL. 231 F6
Prince Rd SK12. . . . . 37 C5
Princes Ave
  Bebington CH62. . . . . .43 E6
  Chester CH1. . . . . 237 C3
  Northwich CW9. . . . . 104 B8
Princes Cl WA7. . . . . .23 F1
Princes Ct CW5. . . . . 204 E7
Princes Pk CW8. . . . . 78 A2
Princes Pl WA8. . . . . 12 E1
Princes Rd CH65. . . . . .70 B6
Princess Ave Audley ST7. . 209 D1
  Haydock WA11. . . . . .2 A7
  Warrington, Bruche WA1. . .16 F6
  Warrington, Great Sankey
    WA5. . . . . .14 E7
  Warrington, Padgate WA1. . 17 A8
Princess Cl CW2. . . . . 205 F8
Princess Cres
  Middlewich CW10. . . . . . . 151 D6
  Warrington WA1. . . . . .16 F6
Princess Ct ST7. . . . . 210 D5
Princess Dr
  Bollington SK10. . . . . .87 E7
  Nantwich CW5. . . . . 205 A6
  Sandbach CW11. . . . . 175 A7
  Wistaston CW2. . . . . 205 F8
Princess Gr CW2. . . . . 205 F8
Princess Rd
  Allostock WA16. . . . . 106 E3
  Lymm WA13. . . . . 18 C3
  Wilmslow SK9. . . . . .59 F5
Princess St
  Bollington SK10. . . . . .87 F7
  Chester CH1. . . . . 237 A2
  Congleton CW12. . . . . 156 D3
  Crewe CW1. . . . . 190 C6
  Knutsford WA16. . . . . 57 A2
  Northwich CW9. . . . . .79 E2
  ▤ Runcorn WA7. . . . . 23 A3
  Talke ST7. . . . . 210 D5
  ▤ Warrington WA5. . . . . . 15 D4
Princes St WA12. . . . . .2 B3
Prince's St WA8. . . . . 23 A8
Princes Wlk SK7. . . . . 36 A7
Princes Way WA11. . . . . . 111 E7
Princes Wood Rd SK12. . . . 37 B5
Princeton Way CH65. . . . . .70 B5
Princeway WA6. . . . . .74 B8
Prince William Ave CH5. . 116 B3
Prior Cl CW2. . . . . 189 F1
Priory Ave CW9. . . . . 103 F4
Priory Cl Chester CH2. . . . 118 C4
  Congleton CW12. . . . . 179 B7
  Crewe CW1. . . . . 190 A8
  Winsford CW7. . . . . 126 C2
Priory Ct SK10. . . . . .86 F1
Priory Dr SK10. . . . . .86 E2

Priory Hospl Altrincham The
  WA15. . . . . 32 A7
Priory La SK10. . . . . .86 E2
Priory Pl Chester CH1. . . . 237 B3
  Kidsgrove ST7. . . . . 195 B3
Priory Rd Altrincham WA14. .31 B8
  Runcorn WA7. . . . . 24 C2
  Wilmslow SK9. . . . . .59 E8
Priory St Northwich CW9. . 104 A8
  Warrington WA8. . . . . .16 B3
Priory The Neston CH64. . . .41 E1
  Winwick WA2. . . . . .8 A7
Priory Way CW8. . . . . 103 B4
Pritchard Dr CW9. . . . . . . 103 E2
Pritchards La SK11. . . . . . 158 C6
Private Wlk CH3. . . . . 142 A8
Probert Cl CW2. . . . . 190 A4
Proctors Cl WA8. . . . . 13 D2
Proctors La CW11. . . . . . . 174 E5
Proffits La WA6. . . . . .73 E4
Promised Land La CH3. . . 142 E5
Prospect Ave M44. . . . . . . .11 E6
Prospect Dr
  Altrincham WA15. . . . . 32 D8
  Davenham CW9. . . . . 103 E2
Prospect La WA3. . . . . 10 D3
Prospect Rd M44. . . . . .11 E6
Prospect Row WA7. . . . . . .48 F7
Prospect St CW12. . . . . . . 156 C2
Prosperity Ct CW10. . . . . 128 D1
Prosperity Way CW10. . . . 128 D1
Prosser Rd CH2. . . . . 95 C1
Protector Way M44. . . . . . .11 F8
Proudman Way CW7. . . . . 150 A4
Provan Way CH1. . . . . 117 D5
Provident St WA9. . . . . .1 A3
Prunus Rd CW1. . . . . 190 E6
Pryors The CH3. . . . . 121 C3
Ptarmigan Pl CW7. . . . . . . 149 D5
Public Hall St ▤ WA7. . . . 23 A3
Pudding La CW6. . . . . 168 A7
PUDDINGLAKE. 129 A8
PUDDINGTON. 92 F8
Puddington La CH64. . . . . . .92 F8
Puddle Bank La CW12. . . . 178 F5
Puffin Ave SK12. . . . . .36 B4
Puffin Cl CH65. . . . . 95 C8
PULFORD. 162 D3
Pulford App Aldford CH3. . 163 D3
  Northwich CW9. . . . . 103 E4
  Runcorn WA7. . . . . 49 E6
Pulford Ct CH4. . . . . 162 D2
Pulford La CH4. . . . . 162 A6
Pulford Rd
  ▤ Arclid CW11. . . . . 154 B1
  Blacon CH1. . . . . 117 C5
  Ellesmere Port CH65. . . . . .69 F4
  Winsford CW7. . . . . 126 C1
Pullman Cl CH60. . . . . 41 D8
Pullman Dr CW9. . . . . 104 C8
Pump St ST7. . . . . 209 E2
Pumping Station Hos
  CW6. . . . . 184 E3
Pump La Churton CH3. . . . 181 A5
  Tattenhall CH3. . . . . 182 C6
Pumptree Mews SK11. . . . 111 E7
Purcell Pl CW9. . . . . 127 A7
Purdy Cl WA5. . . . . .7 D1
Puritan Bldgs WA7. . . . . . . 23 C2
Purley Dr M44. . . . . 11 C5
Purser La SY14. . . . . 211 E4
Puss Bank Sch SK10. . . . . 112 F8
Putney St WA7. . . . . .49 F7
Pye Cl WA11. . . . . .2 B8
Pyecroft St WA5. . . . . 14 E6
Pyecroft Rd WA5. . . . . 14 D6
Pyecroft St CH4. . . . . 141 D7
Pye Rd CH60. . . . . 41 A8
Pym Chair Rd
  Goyt Forest SK23. . . . . 90 A6
  Yearns Low SK10. . . . . .89 F6
Pym's La CW1. . . . . 189 E6
Pyramid Theatre★ WA1. . .16 A4
Pyrus Ave CW1. . . . . 190 E6
Pyrus Gr WA6. . . . . 73 C4
Pytcheley Hollow WA6. . . 100 F6

Q

Quadrant Cl WA7. . . . . 50 D6
Quadrant The CH1. . . . . . . 117 C3
QuadrantThe WA3. . . . . . . .9 F5
Quad The CH1. . . . . 117 E2
Quail Cl WA2. . . . . .8 D3
Quaintways CW8. . . . . 103 C4
Quakers Coppice CW1. . . 191 A2
Quakers Way LL13. . . . . . . 180 C1
Quantock Cl
  Ellesmere Port CH66. . . . . . 69 A6
  Winsford CW7. . . . . 149 A7
QUARRYBANK. 146 C8
Quarrybank CW6. . . . . 184 F6
Quarry Bank CW6. . . . . . . 146 C8
Quarry Bank Cotts CW6. . 184 F6
Quarry Bank Mill★ SK9. . . .33 F2
Quarry Bank Rd SK9. . . . . . 33 F3
Quarry Bank Rise CW7. . . 149 B8
Quarry Cl Chester CH4. . . . 141 C2
  Runcorn WA7. . . . . 23 D1
Quarry Ct Farndon CH3. . . 180 F1
  Widnes WA8. . . . . 12 C1
Quarry Hill CH3. . . . . 180 F1
Quarry La Christleton CH3. 142 E7
  Kelsall CW6. . . . . 122 D5

Quarry La continued
  Warrington WA4. . . . . 26 C6
Quarry Rd
  Bridgemont SK23. . . . . 39 D3
  Neston CH64. . . . . 42 C1
  New Mills SK22. . . . . 39 D7
Quarry Terr ST7. . . . . 195 A1
QUARRY THE. 209 B1
Quarter The CH1. . . . . 237 B3
Quay Fold WA5. . . . . .15 F4
Quayle Cl WA11. . . . . .1 C6
Quay Pl WA7. . . . . .50 E7
Quayside Congleton CW12. 156 E1
  Neston CH64. . . . . 66 E5
Quay Side WA6. . . . . 49 D1
Quayside Mews WA13. . . . .18 F3
Quayside Way SK11. . . . . . 112 E7
Quay The WA6. . . . . 49 D2
Queastybirch La
  Hatton WA4. . . . . 25 F1
  Norley WA4. . . . . 26 A1
Quebec Rd WA2. . . . . 16 D7
Queen Anne Ct SK9. . . . . . 60 C6
Queen Annes Ct ▤ SK11. . 112 B6
Queen Elizabeth Ho CW9. . 79 A1
Queens Ave
  Ellesmere Port CH65. . . . . . 70 A3
  Warrington WA1. . . . . .16 E7
Queen's Ave Chester CH1. . 237 C3
  Connah's Quay CH5. . . . . . 91 D1
  Glazebury WA3. . . . . .5 C7
  Macclesfield SK10. . . . . . . .87 E2
  Sandycroft CH5. . . . . 116 A3
  Widnes WA8. . . . . .22 B8
Queensbury Cl
  ▥ Handforth SK9. . . . . 34 D1
  ▣ Wilmslow SK9. . . . . 60 D8
Queensbury Way WA8. . . . .12 E3
Queens Cl SK10. . . . . 87 E6
Queen's Cl
  Macclesfield SK10. . . . . . . .87 E2
  Runcorn WA7. . . . . .22 F1
Queens Cres Chester CH2. . 118 E7
  Warrington WA3. . . . . 17 A8
Queen's Cres CW1. . . . . . . 172 E2
Queens Ct Chester CH4. . . 237 C1
  Winsford CW7. . . . . 126 D1
Queen's Ct CW10. . . . . 128 D1
Queens Dr Golborne WA3. . . .3 C8
  Helsby WA6. . . . . .73 B3
  Heswall CH60. . . . . 40 E8
  Newton-le-Willows WA12. . . .2 C5
  Warrington WA4. . . . . 17 A2
Queen's Dr Chester CH4. . . 237 C1
  Middlewich CW10. . . . . . . 151 D7
  Nantwich CW5. . . . . 204 D4
  Sandbach CW11. . . . . 175 A8
Queensford LL13. . . . . 222 A8
Queensgate Bramhall SK7. . .35 E5
  Chester CH1. . . . . 118 C4
  Northwich CW8. . . . . 103 E8
Queensgate Prim Sch
  SK7. . . . . 35 E4
Queens Gdns
  Ellesmere Port CH65. . . . . .70 B5
  Talke ST7. . . . . 210 B5
Queens Lancashire Aven ▮
  CH3. . . . . 142 B5
Queen's Par ▣ CW7. . . . . 126 D1
QUEEN'S PARK. 141 F8
Queen's Park Dr CW1. . . . 189 F3
Queen's Park Gdns CW2. . 189 E4
Queen's Park High Sch
  CH4. . . . . 237 B1
Queen's Park Ho CH4. . . . 237 B1
Queen's Park Rd CH4. . . . . 237 B1
Queen's Park View CH4. . . 237 B1
Queens Pk CH60. . . . . 40 D8
Queens Pl CH1. . . . . 237 B3
Queens Rd Chester CH3. . . 119 B3
  Ellesmere Port CH66. . . . . . 69 C7
  Haydock WA11. . . . . .2 A7
Queen's Rd Chester CH1. . . 237 C3
  Runcorn WA7. . . . . .22 F1
  Wilmslow SK9. . . . . 60 A6
Queen's Sch (Lower) The
  CH2. . . . . 118 C4
Queen's Sch The CH1. . . . 237 A2
Queen St Audley ST7. . . . . 209 C1
  Bollington SK10. . . . . .88 B8
  Bunbury CW6. . . . . 185 E8
  Chester CH1. . . . . 237 B2
  Congleton CW12. . . . . 156 C2
  Congleton, Buglawton
    CW12. . . . . 156 F4
  Crewe CW1. . . . . 190 E5
  Ellesmere Port CH65. . . . . . 70 C7
  Golborne WA3. . . . . .3 B8
  Kidsgrove ST7. . . . . 195 A2
  Knutsford WA16. . . . . 56 F7
  Macclesfield SK10. . . . . . . 112 D8
  Middlewich CW10. . . . . . . 128 C1
  Nantwich CW5. . . . . 204 D5
  Newton-le-Willows WA12. . .2 B3
  Northwich CW9. . . . . 103 F7
  ▤ Runcorn WA7. . . . . 23 A3
  Shavington CW2. . . . . 206 C4
Queens Terr SK9. . . . . 34 D1
Queensway Alsager ST7. . . 193 B5
  Chester CH2. . . . . 118 F5
  Crewe CW1. . . . . 190 C4
  Frodsham WA6. . . . . .74 B8
  Gatley SK8. . . . . 34 C8
  Heswall CH60. . . . . 41 C6
  Knutsford WA16. . . . . .56 E3

Queensway continued
Partington M31 . . . .**11** F4
Poynton SK12. . . . . **36** D3
Runcorn WA7. . . . .**22** F3
Widnes WA8. . . . .**22** F6
Winsford CW7 . . . . **149** D8
Queen's Way CH4 . . . . **139** B4
Queensway Trad Est WA8 . . **23** A5
Queen Victoria St 14
SK11 . . . . **112** D8
Quill Ct M44 . . . .**11** E6
Quillet The CH64 . . . .**66** F7
Quinn St 13 WA8 . . . .**23** B8
Quinta Prim Sch The
CW12 . . . . **156** A2
Quinta Rd CW12. . . . . **156** A3
QUOISLEY **226** B8

R

Rabbit Bank
Lanehead SK11 . . . . **136** F1
Wildboarclough SK11. . . . . . **137** B1
Rabbit Burrows La CW6 . . **168** E8
RABY **42** C4
Raby Ave CH63. . . . .**43** B6
Raby Cl Bebington CH63 . . . .**43** A7
Heswall CH60 . . . .**40** F7
Widnes WA8. . . . .**13** E2
Raby Ct CH65 . . . .**70** D3
Raby Dr CH63 . . . .**43** A6
Raby Gdns CH64. . . . .**66** E8
Raby Hall Rd CH63 . . . .**43** A6
RABY MERE **43** B7
Raby Mere Rd CH63 . . . .**42** D5
Raby Park Cl CH64 . . . .**66** E8
Raby Park Rd CH64. . . . .**41** F1
Raby Rd Neston CH64. . . . . . .**66** E8
Thornton Hough CH63. . . . . .**42** B5
Racecourse La CW6 . . . . . . **124** A1
Racecourse Pk SK9 . . . .**59** F6
Racecourse Rd SK9. . . . .**59** E6
Racefield Cl WA13 . . . .**18** F3
Racefield Rd WA16. . . . .**56** F2
Race The SK9 . . . .**34** D2
Rackheath Cres 5 WA5 . . . .**14** E8
Radbroke Cl CW11 . . . . **175** D8
Radcliffe Ave WA3 . . . .**4** E3
Radcliffe Cl CH3 . . . . **121** C3
Radcliffe Rd
Sandbach CW11. . . . . **174** F3
Sutton Lane Ends SK11. . . . **135** D7
Winsford CW7 . . . . **149** B6
Radclyffe Cl 3 CW11 . . . . . **174** F6
Raddel La WA4 . . . .**52** C5
Raddle Wharf CH65 . . . .**70** C7
Raddon Pl WA4 . . . .**16** E3
Radford Cl WA8 . . . .**22** C7
Radlett Cl WA5. . . . .**14** E3
Radley Dr CH63 . . . .**41** F6
Radley La WA2 . . . .**8** E4
RADMORE GREEN **186** E3
RADNOR **155** E6
Radnor Cl
Congleton CW12 . . . . **156** B3
Sandbach CW11. . . . . **174** E7
Radnor Dr Chester CH4. . . . **141** A4
Widnes WA8. . . . .**12** D2
Radnor Park Ind Ctr
CW12 . . . . **156** A4
Radnor Park Trad Est
CW12 . . . . **156** B4
Radnor St WA5 . . . .**15** E6
RADWAY GREEN. **192** F1
Radway Green Bsns & Tech
Ctr CW2 . . . . **192** F1
Radway Green Rd
Alsager CW2 . . . . **208** E8
Barthomley CW2 . . . . **208** D6
Raeburn Ave
Bebington CH62. . . . .**43** E6
Neston CH64 . . . .**66** F7
Raeburn Prim Sch CH62 . . .**43** D6
Raglan Cl WA3. . . . .**9** F6
Raglan Rd SK10. . . . .**87** F2
Ragley Cl SK12. . . . .**36** F4
Raikes Cl WA5 . . . .**15** C6
Railton Ave CW1 . . . . **190** A7
Railway Cotts
Congleton CW12 . . . . **157** A1
Hollinfare WA3. . . . .**11** B5
Hooton CH66 . . . .**43** E1
Wimboldsley SK10 . . . . **150** F1
Railway St Crewe CW2 . . . . **190** D2
Newton-le-Willows WA12 . . . .**2** B3
Railway Terr Disley SK12 . . .**38** D6
Sandycroft CH5 . . . . **116** B3
Railway View WA5 . . . .**1** D1
Rainbow Cl WA8 . . . .**12** C3
Rainbow St CW1 . . . . **190** D4
Rainford Cl ST7 . . . . **195** F1
RAINOW. **88** D5
Rainow Cl CW10 . . . . **151** B7
Rainow Dr SK12. . . . .**37** A2
Rainow Prim Sch SK10 . . . . .**88** D4
Rainow Rd SK10. . . . .**88** B2
Rainow View SK10 . . . .**63** C1
Rainow Way 10 SK9 . . . .**34** E1
Rajar Cotts WA16 . . . .**57** C7
Rajar Wlk WA16. . . . .**58** A4
Rake House Mews WA6. . . . .**73** B4
Rake La Backford CH2 . . . . . .**95** D6
Broughton CH5. . . . . **139** A8

Rake La continued
Christleton CH3 . . . . **143** A7
Dunham-on-the-Hill WA6 . . . .**97** B7
Dunham-on-the-Hill WA6 . . . .**97** B7
Eccleston CH4 . . . . **141** C1
Helsby WA6. . . . .**73** C4
Helsby, Helsby Marsh WA6. . .**73** A5
Rake The Bebington CH62 . . .**43** C8
Burton CH64. . . . .**67** D1
Rake Way CH1 . . . .**94** A1
Raleigh Cl
Newton-le-Willows WA12 . . . .**2** D1
Warrington WA5 . . . .**7** D1
Raleigh Rd CH64 . . . .**41** F1
Ramany's Caravan ✱ SK9. . .**60** B6
Rampit Cl WA11. . . . .**1** F7
Ramp Road E M90. . . . . **33** C7
Ramp Road S M90. . . . . **33** C7
Ramp Road W M90 . . . .**33** B7
Ramsay Cl WA3. . . . .**9** E3
Ramsbottom St 2 CW1. . . . **190** B5
Ramsbrook La L24, WA8. . . . . **21** C3
Ramsbury Ct 5 WA5 . . . .**14** F8
Ramsdale Rd SK7 . . . .**35** E8
Ramsden Ct CH4 . . . . **140** F4
Ramsey Cl WA8 . . . .**13** E3
Ramsey Rd CH65 . . . .**70** C1
Ramsfield Rd L24 . . . .**21** A4
Randal Cres SK23 . . . .**65** E5
Randall Cl WA12 . . . .**2** B4
Randalls Dr CW1 . . . . **190** D8
Randle Bennett Cl CW11. . **174** E7
Randle Mdw CH66. . . . .**69** F1
Randle Meadow Ct CH66. . .**69** F2
Randles Dr CH4 . . . . **140** F6
Randle's View CW12. . . . . . **179** C8
Range Ct SK10 . . . .**87** E1
Rangemoor Cl WA3 . . . .**10** A6
Rangers St 7 CH3. . . . . **142** B5
Rannoch Cl CH66. . . . .**69** F3
Ranulph Ct WA6 . . . .**74** C7
Ranwonath Ct CH2 . . . . **237** B4
Ranworth Dr WA3. . . . .**3** E7
Ranworth Rd WA5. . . . .**14** E6
Rappax Rd WA15 . . . .**32** A8
Raquets Ct The CW10. . . . . **127** D5
Rathbone Pk CW6. . . . . **146** D2
Rathlin Cl WA8 . . . .**13** E3
Rathmell Cl WA3. . . . .**4** E3
Rathvale Dr M22. . . . . **33** C8
Ravenbank Com Prim Sch
WA13 . . . .**18** F3
Sandbach CW11. . . . . **175** A8
Raven Cl Farndon CH3 . . . . **180** F1
Sandbach CW11. . . . . **175** A8
Raven Cotts TF9 . . . . **235** A5
Ravencroft St CW9 . . . . **126** F8
Ravendale Cl CW7. . . . . **149** E8
Ravenfield Cl WA3 . . . .**5** C4
Ravenfield Dr WA8. . . . .**12** C3
Ravenho La SK10. . . . .**88** D4
Ravenhurst Ct WA3 . . . .**9** F5
Ravenoak Park Rd SK8 . . . . .**35** B8
Ravenoak Rd SK8 . . . .**35** B8
Ravenscar Cres M22. . . . . . . **33** D8
Ravens Cl ST7 . . . . **209** E3
Ravenscliffe Rd ST7. . . . . . **195** A1
RAVENSCLOUGH **101** E3
Ravens Cnr CW5 . . . . **203** E2
Ravenscroft CW4 . . . . **130** A3
Ravenscroft Cl
Middlewich CW10 . . . . **128** C2
Sandbach CW11. . . . . **175** C7
Ravenscroft Rd CW2 . . . . . **189** E3
Ravensdale Cl WA2. . . . .**8** D3
Ravensfield CW8 . . . . **101** D4
Ravensholme Ct CH3. . . . . . **166** A2
Ravensholme La CH3. . . . . . **166** A2
Ravens La CW5 . . . . **203** E5
Raven's La ST7. . . . . **209** E3
Ravensmead Prim Sch
ST7. . . . . **209** E3
RAVENSMOOR **203** E2
Ravensthorpe WA5. . . . .**14** C6
Ravenswood WA8. . . . . **103** B4
Ravenswood Dr SK8. . . . .**35** B8
Ravenswood Rd SK9. . . . .**59** E4
Ravenwood Dr WA15 . . . .**32** D7
Rawcliffe Cl WA8 . . . .**12** F4
Rawdon Cl WA7. . . . .**50** A7
Rawlings Cl WA3. . . . .**9** F3
Rawlinson Cres L26 . . . .**21** B8
Rawson Rd CH1 . . . . **117** E3
Ray Ave CW5. . . . . **204** F7
Raycliffe Cl WA7 . . . .**49** D5
Rayleigh Ave CW9 . . . . **127** A8
Rayleigh Way SK10 . . . .**86** E1
Raymond Ave WA4 . . . .**16** D2
Raymond St CH1 . . . . **237** A3
Raymond Way CH64 . . . .**67** A7
Rays Brow CW8 . . . .**78** B2
Readesdale Ave CW2 . . . . . **189** F2
Reade's La CW12. . . . . **179** D8
Reading Room La SY14,
CH3 . . . . **199** D8
Rean Mdw CH3 . . . . **166** B2
Reaper Cl WA5. . . . .**15** D6
REASE HEATH. **188** C2
Reaseheath Coll CW5 . . . . . **188** D1
Reaseheath Way CW5 . . . . **204** D7
Reay St WA8 . . . .**13** C2
Recn Gd WA2 . . . .**16** F8
Rectory Ave WA3 . . . .**3** C8
Rectory Cl Farndon CH3. . . . **180** E1
Heswall CH60 . . . .**40** F7
8 Nantwich CW5 . . . . **204** E5
Winwick WA2. . . . .**8** A6
Wistaston CW2 . . . . **205** E8
Rectory Gdns Lymm WA13 . .**18** E3

Rectory Gdns continued
Talke ST7 . . . . **210** D6
Rectory La Adderley TF9 . . **235** B5
Capenhurst CH1. . . . .**94** A8
Heswall CH60 . . . .**40** E7
Lymm WA13 . . . .**18** E3
Winwick WA2. . . . .**8** A6
Rectory View ST7 . . . . **210** D6
Redacre SK12. . . . .**36** F6
Redacre Cl WA4. . . . .**51** A3
Red Bank Ave WA12 . . . .**2** F1
Redbourne Dr
Chorlton CW2. . . . . **207** D1
Widnes WA8. . . . .**12** B4
Redbrook Cl CH62. . . . .**43** D6
Redbrook Gr 2 SK9 . . . . **34** D1
Redbrook Rd M31. . . . .**11** E2
Redbrook Way SK10 . . . .**62** C5
Red Brow La WA7, WA4 . . . . .**50** F8
Red Clover Dr CW11. . . . . . . **174** F6
Red Cow Yd 11 WA16 . . . .**57** A2
Reddish Ave SK23. . . . .**65** D6
Reddish Cres WA13 . . . .**18** F4
Reddish La
Horwich End, SK23 . . . .**65** D6
Lymm WA13 . . . .**19** A5
Reddish Rd SK23. . . . .**65** D6
Reddy La WA14 . . . .**30** B8
Redesdale Cl WA2. . . . .**8** E2
Redesmere Cl
Macclesfield SK10 . . . .**87** A1
Northwich CW9 . . . . **104** A5
Sandbach CW11. . . . . **174** F7
Redesmere Dr SK9. . . . .**60** A1
Redesmere La SK11 . . . . . . **110** B3
Redesmere Rd SK9. . . . .**34** D5
Redfern Ave CW12 . . . . **156** F4
Red Gables WA4. . . . .**27** B3
Redgate CW8 . . . . **103** D7
Redhill Cl 4 WA5 . . . .**15** B6
Redhill Mews CH65. . . . .**70** B6
Redhill Rd Chester CH4 . . . . **140** F6
Kelsall CH3. . . . . **122** C5
Redhillswood Cl CH65 . . . . . .**70** B7
Red Ho SK10. . . . .**87** E1
Redhouse La SK12 . . . .**38** E7
Red House La WA14 . . . .**20** C8
Redhouses SK11 . . . . **113** D3
Red La Disley SK12 . . . .**38** C5
Frodsham WA6. . . . .**74** C7
Huxley WA4 . . . . **166** D6
Lower Whitley WA4 . . . .**52** C1
Sandbach CW11. . . . . **174** C6
Warrington WA4 . . . .**26** C7
Redland Cl CH4 . . . . **141** A7
Redland Ho CH4 . . . . **141** B7
Red Lion Cl ST7 . . . . **210** D7
Red Lion La
Ellesmere Port CH66 . . . .**69** C7
Nantwich CW5 . . . . **204** D5
Red Lodge SK12. . . . .**38** A6
Redmain Gr WA3. . . . .**3** E8
Redmayne Cl WA12 . . . .**2** B4
Redmere Dr CH60. . . . .**41** D8
Redmires Cl WA5. . . . .**14** C6
Redmoor La Disley SK12. . . . .**39** A4
New Mills SK22 . . . .**39** B6
Red Pier Cres WA7. . . . .**22** F2
Red Pike CH66 . . . .**69** D8
Redpoll La WA3. . . . .**9** E4
Redruth Ave SK10 . . . .**86** E1
Redruth Cl WA7 . . . .**50** C6
Redshank Ave CW7. . . . . . . **149** C5
Redshank Cl WA12 . . . .**2** C4
Redshank Dr SK10 . . . .**87** C5
Redshank La WA3. . . . .**9** F4
Redshank Pl CW11. . . . . **174** C6
Redshaw Cl CW10 . . . . **151** C6
Redstart Cl 7 WA3. . . . .**3** E8
Redstone Dr 3 CW7. . . . . . **126** A1
Red Stone Hill WA6 . . . .**73** C4
RED STREET **210** B3
Redtail Cl WA7. . . . .**22** F3
Redvales Ct WA3. . . . .**9** C4
Redvers Ave CH66. . . . .**44** A2
Redway La SK10. . . . .**88** B7
Redwing Ct 1 CH64. . . . .**66** D7
Redwing Gr ST7. . . . . **195** F1
Redwood Cl Barnton CW8. . .**78** B4
Holt LL13 . . . . **196** D8
Saltney CH4 . . . . **140** E6
Warrington WA1 . . . .**17** E7
Redwood Ct
1 Macclesfield SK10. . . . . . .**87** E5
Macclesfield SK10 . . . .**87** E5
Redwood Dr Crewe CW1. . . **189** F7
Ellesmere Port CH66 . . . .**69** F1
Elton CH2 . . . .**72** C4
Redwood Way 1 CW12. . . . **155** E5
Reece Cl CH2 . . . . **119** E8
Reedgate La CW9 . . . .**27** F1
Reed La CW9 . . . .**53** C6
Reedsmere Cl WA4. . . . .**16** E2
Reedsmere Wlk CW9 . . . .**78** D3
Reeman St SK9 . . . .**34** B2
Rees Cres CW4. . . . . **130** C3
Reeves Rd CH3. . . . . **142** B8
Reeve St WA3. . . . .**4** B8
Regal Cl
Ellesmere Port CH66 . . . .**69** E3
Northwich CW9 . . . . **103** E4
Regal Cres WA8. . . . .**22** B8
Regency Cl ST7 . . . . **210** D5

Regency Ct Chester CH2. . . **119** E8
Winsford CW7 . . . . **149** C7
Regency Gdns SK8 . . . .**34** E8
Regency Hospl (Private)
SK11 . . . . **112** B8
Regency Pk Wilmslow SK9 . . .**59** F5
Windes WA8. . . . .**12** E3
Regency Sq WA5. . . . .**15** F6
Regency Way CW9 . . . . **103** E4
Regent Ave Haydock WA11 . .**1** B7
Macclesfield SK11 . . . . **112** B6
Warrington WA1 . . . .**17** A8
Regent Cl Bramhall SK7. . . . . .**35** D4
Shavington CW2. . . . . **206** B3
Wilmslow SK9 . . . .**59** F5
Regent St WA15 . . . .**32** C8
Regent & Foundry Ct 19
SK11 . . . . **112** C8
Regent Rd WA8 . . . .**13** B1
Regents Cl CH3 . . . . **119** B2
Regents Gate CW5 . . . . **205** A5
Regent St
Ellesmere Port CH65 . . . .**70** A5
Moulton CW9 . . . . **126** F8
Newton-le-Willows WA12 . . . .**2** A3
12 Runcorn WA7 . . . .**23** A3
Warrington WA1 . . . .**16** A5
Regents The SK9 . . . .**60** C8
Regents Way 4 CW7 . . . . . **149** A8
Regiment Cl WA3 . . . . **142** B4
Reginald Mitchell Prim Sch
The ST7. . . . . **194** D1
Reginald Settle Rd ST7 . . **193** B2
Registry Cl CW9 . . . . **103** E4
Reid Ave WA5. . . . .**15** F8
Reid Ct CH66. . . . .**69** C7
Reid St CW1 . . . . **190** C6
Reins Croft CH64. . . . .**66** F7
Relicks Moss Way CW8 . . **123** D8
Rembury Pl WA4 . . . .**51** A3
Remer St CW1 . . . . **190** D7
Renaissance Way CW1 . . . **191** A3
Rendel Cl WA12 . . . .**2** D2
Rendlesham Cl WA3. . . . .**10** B6
Renfrew Ave CH62 . . . .**43** E5
Renfrew Cl SK10 . . . .**86** F2
Rennie Dr 4 WA4 . . . .**26** C8
Renown Cl WA3. . . . .**9** D4
Renshaw St CW9. . . . .**79** D2
Rensherds Pl WA16 . . . .**29** C5
Renton Ave WA7 . . . .**23** D2
Repton Ave WA16. . . . .**29** C4
Repton Dr CW1 . . . . **191** D5
Repton Rd CH65. . . . .**70** D4
Reservoir Rd SK23 . . . .**65** D7
Reservoir Terr CH2. . . . . . . **118** F2
Retreat The CW1 . . . . **190** C6
Revesby Cl WA8. . . . .**12** D2
Rex Bldgs SK9 . . . .**60** B6
Reynolds Ave St Helens WA9 .**1** B2
Warrington WA3 . . . .**9** E5
Reynold's La CW11 . . . . **175** F6
Reynolds Mews 5 SK9 . . . . .**60** E8
Reynolds St WA4. . . . .**16** F3
Rhoden St CW1 . . . . **191** A6
Rhodes Cl CW1 . . . . **191** D4
Rhodes St WA2 . . . .**16** C7
Rhodesway CH60. . . . .**41** B7
Rhodfa Llyn 2 CH4 . . . . **140** E6
Rhodfar Bont 6 CH4 . . . . . . **140** F6
Rhona Cl CH63 . . . .**43** C4
Rhona Dr WA5 . . . .**14** E6
Rhone Ct CH3. . . . . **142** A8
RHUDDALL HEATH. **146** E1
Rhuddlan Ct CH65 . . . .**70** D2
Rhuddlan Ct/Llys Rhuddlan
5 CH4. . . . . **140** F6
Rhuddlan Rd CH1 . . . . **117** D3
Rhum Cl CH65 . . . .**70** C1
Rhyl St WA8 . . . .**22** F7
Ribble Ave Leftwich CW9. . . **104** C6
Winsford CW7 . . . . **127** B1
Ribble Cl Culcheth WA3 . . . . . .**4** F2
Holmes Chapel CW4. . . . . . **130** D2
Widnes WA8. . . . .**13** F3
Ribble Dr ST8. . . . . **179** E1
Ribble Pl CW7 . . . . **127** B1
Ribblesdale CH65. . . . .**70** B3
Ribblesdale Ave CW7 . . . . . **157** A5
Ribblesdale Cl CH62. . . . .**43** F5
Ribchester Gdns WA3 . . . .**5** A3
Richard Ashley Pl 3
CW11. . . . . **174** E4
Richard Cl WA7 . . . .**24** E4
Richard Gibson Rd CW5 . . **204** C7
Richard Moon St CW1 . . . . **190** B5
Richard Reynolds Ct M44. .**11** E6
Richards Croft CH3. . . . . . . **142** A7
Richards Gr CW12. . . . . **156** A3
Richardson Cl
4 Sandbach CW11 . . . . . . **174** D6
Shavington CW2. . . . . **206** D5
Richardson St WA2. . . . .**16** C8
Richards St SK7. . . . .**35** E2
Richard St Crewe CW1 . . . . **190** B5
Northwich CW9 . . . . **104** C4
Richard Woodcock Way
5 Alsager ST7. . . . . **193** F3
Alsager ST7. . . . . **193** F4
Richbell Cl M44 . . . .**11** F7
Richmond Ave
Grappenhall WA4 . . . .**17** C3
Handforth SK9 . . . .**34** D4
Haydock WA11 . . . .**1** B7
Runcorn WA7 . . . .**23** E2
Warrington WA4 . . . .**17** A4

Richmond Cl
Chorlton CW2. . . . . **207** D1
Culcheth WA3. . . . .**4** D4
Lymm WA13 . . . .**19** B4
Sandbach CH5. . . . . **174** E7
Richmond Cres CH3 . . . . . . **119** C2
Richmond Ct Chester CH3 . **118** F2
Ellesmere Port CH65 . . . .**70** D3
Warrington WA4 . . . .**17** A3
Widnes WA8. . . . .**13** C1
Richmond Dr Lymm WA13 . . .**19** B4
Northwich CW9 . . . . **104** A4
Richmond Gdns WA12. . . . . . .**2** C2
Richmond Gr SK7 . . . .**35** F6
Richmond Hill
1 Knutsford WA16 . . . .**57** B1
Macclesfield SK11 . . . . **112** E6
Richmond Mews CH2. . . . . **118** F2
Richmond Pl SK11 . . . . **112** E6
Richmond Rd CW1 . . . . **190** E5
Richmond St
Warrington WA4 . . . .**17** A3
Widnes WA8. . . . .**13** C1
Richmond Village CW5 . . . . **205** A5
Rickaby Cl CH63 . . . .**43** C8
Ridding Dr CW1. . . . . **190** F7
Ridding La WA7. . . . .**50** B5
Riddings Ct CW8 . . . . **103** B4
Riddings La Hartford CW8. . **103** B4
Wybunbury CW5 . . . . **220** A8
Riddings The CH65 . . . .**70** B4
Riddles Ave CW5. . . . . **205** E6
Ridge Ave WA15 . . . .**32** D6
Ridgeborne Cl WA5 . . . .**7** D2
Ridgegate Rd SK11. . . . . **113** F3
Ridge Hill Langley SK11. . . . **113** B2
Utkinton CW6. . . . . **146** C3
Ridge Pk SK7 . . . .**35** D6
Ridge The CW8 . . . . **123** D7
Ridge View SK11 . . . . **112** C5
Ridgeway Golborne WA3. . . . . .**3** E7
Wilmslow SK9 . . . .**60** F7
Ridgeway Cl CH66. . . . .**69** C2
Ridgeway Ho CH3. . . . . **121** C3
Ridgeway The
Alvanley WA6. . . . .**74** A1
Cronton WA8 . . . .**12** C6
Disley SK12 . . . .**38** C6
Heswall CH60 . . . .**41** B7
Runcorn WA7 . . . .**50** D6
Tarvin CH3. . . . . **121** C3
Ridgewell Ave 4 WA3. . . . . . .**3** D8
Ridgmont Rd SK7 . . . .**35** E5
RIDGWARDINE **235** E1
Ridgway Gdns WA13 . . . .**18** D3
Ridgway St Crewe CW1. . . . **190** D5
Warrington WA2 . . . .**16** D8
Ridings The Haydock WA11 . .**1** D6
Saughall CH1. . . . . **117** B8
Wilmslow SK9 . . . .**59** D4
Ridley Cl CW2. . . . . **206** E2
Ridley Dr WA5 . . . .**15** C4
Ridley Gn Spurstow CW6 . . . **185** C2
Spurstow CW6. . . . . **185** D1
Ridley Hill Farm CW6. . . . . . **185** C3
Ridley Rd SK10. . . . .**87** E8
RIDLEYWOOD **196** C3
Ridley Wood Rd LL13 . . . . . **196** A3
Ridsdale 2 WA8 . . . .**22** C8
Riflemans Cl WA5. . . . .**59** E5
Rigby Ave CW1. . . . . **190** A7
Rigby Rd ST7 . . . . **195** B3
Rigbys La SK11. . . . . **132** A6
Rigby's Row CW5 . . . . **204** E5
Rigby St WA3 . . . .**3** A8
Rigg St 5 CW1. . . . . **190** B5
Riley Bank Mews WA6. . . . . .**74** B1
Riley Cl CW11 . . . . **174** E5
Riley Dr WA7 . . . .**49** A8
Rileys Way ST7 . . . . **209** F2
Rilshaw La CW7. . . . . **150** B8
Rilston Ave WA3 . . . .**4** D3
Rimington Cl WA3. . . . .**4** E3
Rimmer Gr 11 CW11 . . . . . . **174** D7
Rimsdale Cl CW2. . . . . **206** A7
Ringlet Pl
Sandbach CW11. . . . . **175** D7
9 Sandbach CW11 . . . . . . **175** D7
Ring-o-Bells La SK12 . . . .**38** D6
Ring Rd
Bickley Moss SY14 . . . . **215** A8
Chester CH2, CH3 . . . . **119** C3
Connah's Quay CH5 . . . .**91** E2
Ringsfield Rd L24 . . . .**21** A2
Ringstead Cl SK9. . . . .**34** D1
Ringstead Dr SK9 . . . .**34** D1
Ringstone Way SK23 . . . .**65** D8
Ringway
Ellesmere Port CH66 . . . .**69** E4
Neston CH64 . . . .**41** E1
Waverton CH3 . . . . **143** B5
Ringway Cl SK10. . . . .**87** B4
Ringway Prim Sch 5
M22. . . . .**33** D8
Ringway Rd Runcorn WA7 . . .**22** F1
Wythenshawe M22, M90. . . .**33** D7
Ringway Road W M22,
M90. . . . .**33** D8
Ringway Trad Est M22 . . . . .**33** E8
Ringwood Cl WA3 . . . .**10** B5
Ripley Ave SK8. . . . .**35** B5
Ripley Cl SK7 . . . .**36** E8
Ripley St WA5. . . . .**15** C4
Ripon Ave
Ellesmere Port CH66 . . . .**69** C5
Golborne WA3 . . . .**3** D8
Ripon Cl Macclesfield SK10 . .**87** C3
Newton-le-Willows WA12 . . . .**2** C5

Ripon Dr CW2 206 A7
Ripon Row WA7 49 D6
Riseley St SK10 112 C8
Rise The SK23 65 C6
Rising Sun Cl SK11 112 A5
Rising Sun Rd SK11 112 A4
RISLEY 9 E6
Risley Moss Nature Reserve* WA3 10 B5
Risley Rd WA3 9 F6
Rivacre Brow CH66 69 E8
Rivacre Bsns Ctr CH66 69 E5
Rivacre Rd CH62, CH65, CH66 44 C2
Rivacre Valley Ctry Pk* CH66 69 D8
Rivacre Valley Nature Reserve* CH66 69 C8
Rivacre Valley Prim Sch CH66 69 E7
Rivacre View CH66 44 C1
Rivenhall Cl WA5 14 F8
Rivenmill Cl WA8 13 C5
Riverbank Cl
Bollington SK10 87 F8
Heswall CH60 40 F6
Nantwich CW5 204 E8
Riverbank Rd CH60 40 E6
Riverdane Rd CW12 156 F4
River La Chester CH4 141 C7
Farndon CH3 180 E2
Partington M31 11 F4
Saltney CH4 140 E7
Rivermead Ave WA15 32 C7
River Rd Connah's Quay CH5 91 F1
Warrington, Latchford WA4 16 B3
Warrington, Wilderspool WA4 16 C2
Riversdale Frodsham WA6 49 C1
Warrington WA1 17 F7
Riversdale Rd WA7 49 E8
Rivershill Gdns WA15 32 D6
Riverside Nantwich CW5 204 D5
Northwich CW9 104 B5
Riverside Bsns Pk SK9 60 B7
Riverside Cl WA1 16 D4
Riverside Coll (Cronton Campus) WA8 12 E5
Riverside Coll (Kingsway Campus) WA8 23 A8
Riverside Coll (Runcorn Campus) WA7 22 E3
Riverside Cres CW4 130 C4
Riverside Ct
Huntington CH3 141 F7
Langley SK11 113 C4
Riverside Ct & Bollin House Bsns Pk SK9 60 C8
Riverside Dr SK10 87 A5
Riverside Gr CW2 189 D3
Riverside Pk CW9 103 E6
Riverside Pk Nature Reserve* SK10 87 A4
Riverside Ret Pk WA1 16 C4
Riverside Trad Est
Northwich CW8 103 F7
Warrington WA5 14 D1
Riverside Trad Pk CH4 140 E7
Riverside Wlk CH64 66 D5
Riversmead CH3 142 A6
River St Congleton CW12 156 D3
Macclesfield SK11 112 E6
Wilmslow SK9 60 B8
River View CW7 126 E1
Riverview Rd CH64 66 F5
River Wlk 8 WA7 49 F7
Rivington Ct WA1 17 E8
Rivington Gr M44 11 D6
Rivington Rd
Ellesmere Port CH65 70 C5
Runcorn WA7 50 F3
Rixton Ave WA5 15 F8
Rixton Clay Pits Nature Reserve* WA3 10 E2
Rixton Park Homes WA3 10 F2
Roaches The SK11 112 B5
Road Beta CW10 151 D8
Road Five CW7 127 C2
Road Four CW7 127 B2
Road One Weston CW1 207 D8
Winsford CW7 127 B3
Roadside Ct WA3 3 C8
Road Three CW7 127 D1
Road Two Anderton CW9 78 C3
Weston CW1 207 C8
Winsford CW7 127 B2
Roan Ct SK11 112 F7
Roan House Way SK11 112 F7
Roan Mews SK11 112 F7
Roan Way SK9 85 B8
Robert Moffat WA16 29 C5
Roberts Ave WA11 1 A5
Roberts Ct WA7 49 F6
Roberts Dr CW9 104 D6
Roberts Fold WA3 9 D4
Roberts Rd CW9 80 A2
Robert St Northwich CW9 103 E6
Runcorn WA7 23 C2
Warrington WA5 15 F6
Widnes WA8 13 B1
Robert's Terr CH1 118 B1
Robin Cl Chelford SK11 84 A2
Rainow SK10 88 E5
Runcorn WA7 50 D7
Sandbach CW11 175 A8
Robin Cres SK11 112 D2
Robin Dr CW5 204 D4
Robin Hood Ave SK11 112 D5
Robin Hood La WA6 73 B2
Robin La Chelford SK11 84 A3
Sutton Lane Ends SK11 112 D2
Robinsbay Rd M22 33 E8
Robins Cl SK7 35 E7
Robins Croft CH66 69 F2
Robins Ct CH4 139 D3
Robins La WA3 4 D2
Robin's La SK7 35 E7
Robinson Cl SK9 60 E7
Robinson Rd CH65 70 E4
Robinsons Croft CH3 142 B7
Robins Way SK10 88 A7
Rob La WA12 2 E5
Robson St WA1 16 D6
Robson Way 3 WA3 3 F8
Roby Gr WA5 15 A6
Roche Gdns SK8 35 B6
Rochester Cl Golborne WA3 3 A8
Warrington WA5 15 C5
Rochester Cres CW1 190 F6
Rochester Dr CH65 70 D3
Rochester Ho SK10 86 F1
Rock Bank SK23 65 E6
Rock Bank Rise SK10 63 A1
Rock Cotts CH5 91 D1
Rock Dr WA6 49 C1
Rock Farm Cl CH64 67 A6
Rock Farm Dr CH64 67 A6
Rock Farm Gr CH64 67 A6
Rockfield Cl WA8 12 D2
Rockfield Dr WA6 73 C2
Rockfield Mews WA4 16 F2
Rockford Gdns WA5 15 A8
Rockford Lodge WA16 57 C1
Rockhouse La ST7 210 C7
Rockingham Cl WA3 10 C6
Rock La Burwardsley CH3 184 C6
Chester CH2 237 A4
Widnes WA8 12 F4
Rocklands La CH63 42 C8
Rocklee Gdns CH64 67 A6
Rockliffe La CH6 91 A3
Rockling St CH65 70 A7
Rock Mill La SK22 39 B7
Rock Rd Connah's Quay CH5 91 E1
Warrington WA4 16 E4
ROCKSAVAGE 49 B4
Rock Savage Rdbt WA7 49 E4
Rockside ST7 195 C6
Rock St SK22 39 C7
Rock The WA6 73 C2
Rock Villas LL13 180 E1
Rockwood Ave CW2 190 A3
Rockwood Cl CW2 190 A3
Rocky La Heswall CH60 40 F8
Tattenhall CH3 182 F7
Rocky Lane S CH60 41 A8
Roddy La WA6 75 E2
Rode Ct 7 CW12 156 F3
Rode Hall & Gdns* ST7 194 B7
RODEHEATH 134 B3
RODE HEATH 193 E7
Rodeheath Cl SK9 60 D7
Rode Heath Prim Sch ST7 193 F7
Rodehouse Cl ST7 193 F7
Rode Mill Ct ST7 193 F6
Rodepool Cl SK9 34 D2
Rode St CW6 146 A3
Rode The ST7 193 D4
Rodgers Cl WA6 49 B1
Rodney St SK11 112 D7
Roebourne Rise 4 CH1 117 D4
Roebuck St CW1 190 C5
Roeburn Way WA5 14 D3
Roedean Wlk CW1 190 D6
Roehampton Dr WA7 49 E7
Roehurst La CW7 126 D2
Roemarsh Ct WA7 49 E6
Roe Pk CW12 178 E1
Roe St Congleton CW12 156 E2
Macclesfield SK11 112 D7
Roewood La SK10 88 A1
Roften Ind Est CH66 43 D1
Roften Way
Brookhurst CH66 43 D1
Willaston CH66 68 D8
Rokeby Ct WA7 24 D5
Rokeden WA12 2 D4
Roklis Grange 9 CH64 66 E8
Roland Ave WA7 22 F1
Rolands Wlk WA7 23 F2
Rolleston St WA2 16 A6
Rolls Ave CW1 190 A6
Rolt Cres CW10 151 C7
Roman Cl
Newton-le-Willows WA12 2 C2
Runcorn WA7 23 E2
Roman Cres CH4 141 B4
Roman Ct CH64 66 F7
Roman Dr CH1 117 D6
Romanes St CW8 103 E7
Roman Rd WA4 16 C1
Roman Way CW11 174 E7
Romiley Rd CH66 69 E6
Romney Cl Neston CH64 66 E7
Widnes WA8 13 E2
Romney Croft CH64 66 F7
Romney Way CH64 66 F7
Romsey Dr SK8 35 C6
Rona Ave CH65 70 C1
Ronald Dr WA2 9 B2
Ronaldshay WA8 13 E2
Ronaldsway Halewood L26 21 A8
Heswall CH60 40 F6
Ronan Rd WA8 22 E5
ROODEE 237 A1
Rood Hill CW12 156 D3
Rood La CW12 156 E4
Rookery Cl
1 Nantwich CW5 204 F5
Sandbach CW11 174 C5
Tarporley CW6 122 C4
Rookery Ct CW11 174 C5
Rookery Dr
Nantwich CW5 204 E4
Tattenhall CH3 166 B2
Rookery Farm Rd CW6 169 A6
Rookery Gdns CW9 103 E3
Rookery La SY13 228 E4
Rookerypool Cl SK9 34 D2
Rookery Rd
Kidsgrove ST7 195 C3
Tilston SY14 198 B3
Rookery Rise CW7 150 A8
ROOKERY THE 195 C3
Rookery The
Broughton CH4 139 B3
Newton-le-Willows WA12 2 D4
Rook St CW2 190 C2
Rooks Way CH60 40 E8
Rookswood Way WA16 57 D3
Roome St WA2 16 C7
Rope Bank Ave CW2 206 A7
Rope Hall La
Shavington CW2 206 A5
Willaston CW5 205 F5
Rope La Shavington CW2 206 A5
Wistaston CW2 205 F7
Ropewalk Cl CW3 230 A5
Ropewalk The CH64 66 C8
Rope Wlk CW12 156 D3
Ropeworks The CH1 118 B2
Rosam Ct WA7 49 E6
Roscoe Ave
Newton-le-Willows WA12 2 E3
Warrington WA2 16 D8
Roscoe Cres WA7 48 E7
Roscoe Rd WA8 11 F8
Roscoes Yd 4 WA16 57 A2
Roscommon Way WA8 12 E3
Roscote Cl CH60 40 F7
Roscote The CH60 40 F7
Rose Ave WA11 1 E6
Rose Bank Bollington SK10 87 F7
Lymm WA13 18 E3
Rosebank Cl CW7 149 F8
Rosebank Mews CW10 129 E5
Rosebank Rd M44 11 C4
Rosebank Sch CW8 78 A3
Rosebank Wlk CW8 78 A4
Rosebery Way CW1 191 C4
Rose Cl 5 Blacon CH1 117 D4
Halewood L26 21 A7
Ravensclough CW8 101 F2
Runcorn WA7 50 D5
Rose Cnr CH3 166 A1
Rose Cotts CW12 154 F6
Rose Creek Gdns WA5 15 B6
Rose Cres WA8 22 F7
Rosecroft CH62 43 C6
Rosedale Ave Golborne WA3 3 C7
Warrington WA1 17 C7
Rosedene Cl CH2 118 E8
Rose Farm Ct CW9 79 E4
Rose Farm Mews WA6 73 B4
Rose Gdns CH64 66 F6
Roseheath Dr L26 21 A6
Rosehill Ave WA9 6 B5
Rosehill Rd CW2 190 B1
Roselands Ct LL12 162 C1
Rose Lea Cl WA8 13 A4
Rosemary Ave
Runcorn WA7 49 F4
Warrington WA4 16 E2
Rosemary Cl
Broughton CH4 139 C3
Warrington WA5 15 C6
Rosemary Cres 5 CW7 149 E8
Rosemary Dr
Newton-le-Willows WA12 2 F3
Shavington CW2 206 B3
Winnington CW8 78 C1
Rosemary La LL12 161 D1
Rosemary Row CH3 166 A1
Rosemary Wlk M31 11 F2
Rosemere Dr CH1 94 F7
Rosemoor Gdns WA4 26 F5
Rosemount CW10 128 C1
Rosemount Cotts WA2 8 B8
Rose St WA8 22 F7
Rose Terr 6 Blacon CH1 117 D4
Crewe CW1 190 C5
Rosetree Mdw CW9 80 A2
Rosevale Rd ST5 210 F1
Rose View Ave WA8 13 A2
Roseville Dr CW12 179 B8
Roseway SK11 112 D5
Rose Way CW11 175 C5
Roseway Ave M44 11 E5
Rose Wharf SK11 112 E7
Rose Wlk 5 M31 11 E3
Rosewood Ave
Chester CH2 118 D5
Frodsham WA6 74 D7
Warrington WA1 16 E7
Rosewood Cl Crewe CW1 190 E6
Ellesmere Port CH66 69 A5
Rosewood Dr CW7 126 A1
Rosewood Farm Ct WA8 12 E4
Rosewood Gr
Saughall CH1 117 B8
Widnes WA8 22 B8
Rosewood Ho CW12 156 A3
Rossall Cl L24 21 E2
Rossall Ct SK7 35 E6
Rossall Dr SK7 35 E6
Rossall Gr CH66 69 D6
Rossall Rd Warrington WA5 15 B4
Widnes WA8 13 D2
Rossbank Rd CH65 70 A7
Ross Cl WA5 15 D7
Rosscliffe Rd CH65 70 A6
Ross Dr CH66 69 C5
Rossenclough Rd SK9 34 D1
Rossendale Dr WA3 10 A6
Rossendale Rd SK8 34 C8
Rossett Ave 1 M22 33 D8
Rossett Bsns Village LL12 162 B1
Rossett Cl Northwich CW9 103 E4
Warrington WA5 7 E2
Rossett Pk LL12 162 C1
Rossfield Rd CH65 70 A6
Rossfield Road N CH65 70 B7
Rosslyn Cl CH5 116 A2
Rosslyn La CW8 102 A3
Rosslyn Rd CH3 119 B3
Rossmill La WA15 32 B7
Rossmore Bsns Pk CH65 70 B7
Rossmore Ct CH66 69 E6
Rossmore Gdns CH66 69 D6
Rossmore Ind Est CH65 70 A6
Rossmore Prim Sch CH66 69 C7
Rossmore Road E CH65 69 F7
Rossmore Road W CH66 69 D7
Rossmore Terraced Factories CH65 70 A6
Rossmount Rd CH65 70 A6
Ross Rd CH65 70 A6
Ross St WA8 13 B1
Rosswood Rd CH65 70 A6
ROSTHERNE 30 E4
Rostherne Ave
Ellesmere Port CH66 69 E4
Golborne WA3 3 D8
High Lane SK6 37 E8
Rostherne Cl 1 WA5 15 D4
Rostherne Cres WA8 12 D2
Rostherne Dr WA16 30 F1
Rostherne La WA16 30 E4
Rostherne Mere National Nature Reserve* WA14 30 E5
Rostherne Rd SK9 59 F4
Rostherne Way CW11 174 F7
Rosyth Cl WA2 8 F3
Rotary Dr ST7 193 A4
Rotary Way CW2 206 D7
Rothay Dr WA5 14 D3
Rothbury Cl WA7 49 D6
Rother Dr CH65 70 A7
Rother Dr Bsns Ctr CH65 70 A7
Rotherhead Dr SK11 112 B5
Rotherwood Rd SK9 59 D6
Rothesay Cl WA7 23 F2
Rothesay Dr CH62 43 E4
Rothesay Rd CH4 141 A7
Rough Bank CW12 179 E8
Rough Heys La SK11 111 A8
ROUGHHILL 140 E1
Roughlea Ave WA3 4 D4
Roughley Ave WA5 15 D4
Rough Low CW6 122 E2
Roughlyn Cres CH4 140 E1
Roughwood Hollow
Alsager ST7 193 A8
Day Green CW11 192 F8
Roughwood La
Alsager CW11, ST7 193 B7
Hassall Green CW11 176 A1
Roundabout The WA8 12 D6
Round Gdns SK10 88 A8
Roundhey SK8 34 C8
Round Hill Mdw CH3 142 B7
Round Mdw SK10 88 E5
Round Thorn WA3 9 A8
Roundway SK7 35 D6
Round Way SK22 39 D8
Roundy La SK10 62 F6
Routledge St WA8 13 B1
Rowallan Pl CW1 190 F6
Rowan Ave WA3 3 F7
Rowan Cl Alsager ST7 193 D3
Delamere CW8 123 D7
Lawton Heath ST7 193 D6
Middlewich CW10 151 E6
Runcorn WA7 49 C7
Sandbach CW11 174 F7
Warrington WA5 14 F6
Winsford CW7 126 D3
Rowan Ct SK9 60 B7
Rowan Dr SK8 35 C8
Rowan Gr CH5 91 C1
Rowan Ho CH2 237 C4
Rowan Lo SK7 35 F7
Rowan Pk CH3 142 E7
Rowan Pl Chester CH2 119 B4
Somerford CW12 154 F6
Rowan Rd CW8 102 D8
Rowan Rise CW8 78 A3
Rowans Cl CW1 189 F7
Rowanside SK10 86 E6
Rowanside Dr SK9 60 E8
Rowans The
Broughton CH4 139 B3
4 Northwich CW9 103 E6
Widnes WA8 13 D4
Rowan Tree Rd WA16 59 B5
Rowan Way SK10 87 E1
Rowan Wlk M31 11 E2
Rowarth Dr SK22 39 D7
Rowcliffe Ave CH4 141 A4
Rowena Ct CH2 118 F3
Rowhurst Cres ST7 194 C1
Rowland Cl WA2 9 A3
Rowlands Hts 1 CH1 237 C3
Rowlands View CW6 146 B7
Rowley Bank La WA16 29 B1
ROWLEYHILL 181 B1
Rowley Rd SK7 36 E8
Rowley Way WA16 82 B7
ROWLINSON'S GREEN 28 C5
ROW-OF-TREES 59 D3
Rowson Dr M44 11 D6
Rowswood Ctyd WA4 25 E5
Rowswood Farm WA4 25 E5
Row The
3 Winsford CW7 126 D1
Wrenbury CW5 217 B5
Rowthorn Cl WA8 22 E8
ROWTON 142 E5
Rowton Bridge Rd CH3 142 E7
Rowton Cl 7 CW9 103 F4
Rowton La CH3 142 F6
Rowton Rd CW2 189 D4
Roxborough Cl WA5 7 A6
Roxburgh Cl SK10 87 A1
Roxburgh Rd CH66 68 F6
Roxby Way WA16 82 A7
Roxholme Wlk M22 33 C8
Royal Arc 5 CW1 190 C4
Royal Ave WA8 12 A1
Royal Ct 3 WA16 57 A2
Royal Gdns
Altrincham WA14 20 F2
Northwich CW9 103 E3
Royal La CW6 147 A3
Royal Mdws SK10 87 A1
Royal Mews CW9 104 D5
Royal Pl WA8 22 B8
Royal Rd SK12 38 D5
ROYAL'S GREEN 228 E1
Royals Green La SY13 228 E1
Royal Sh Arc The 8 CH64 66 E8
Royce Cl CW1 190 A7
Royce Ct WA16 56 F2
Royden Ave Irlam M44 11 F8
Runcorn WA7 49 A8
Royds Cl CW8 103 B4
Royds Ct CW11 174 D5
Roylance Dr CW10 151 C8
Royleen Dr WA6 74 D6
Royle Pk CW12 156 D3
Royle's Pl CW8 103 D6
Royles Sq 2 SK9 60 A1
Royle St Congleton CW12 156 D3
Northwich CW9 104 B8
Winsford CW7 126 E1
Royston Ave
Warrington WA1 17 A7
4 Warrington WA2 16 F7
Royston Cl
Ellesmere Port CH66 69 F3
2 Golborne WA3 3 E8
Rozel Cres WA5 15 B5
Rubin Dr CW1 189 F7
Ruby Springs WA5 15 C6
Rudd Ave WA9 1 B2
RUDHEATH 104 D6
Rudheath Cl CW2 189 D5
Rudheath Com Prim Sch CW9 104 D6
Rudheath La WA7 24 D3
Rudheath L Ctr CW9 104 D7
Rudheath Way CW9 104 E5
Rudloe Ct WA2 8 F1
Rudstone Cl CH66 69 B5
Rudyard Cl SK11 112 B6
Rudyard Lake 3 WA5 14 D8
Rudyard Rd SK11 160 A2
Rue De Bohars CW6 168 D8
Rufford Cl Widnes WA8 12 C2
Wistaston CW2 206 B8
Rufford Ct WA1 17 E8
Rufus Ct CH1 237 A3
Rugby Cl SK10 87 E4
Rugby Dr SK10 87 E4
Rugby Ho SK10 87 D3
Rugby Rd CH65 70 D3
Rugby Wlk CH65 70 D3
Ruislip Ct WA2 8 F1
RULOE 101 D7
RUNCORN 23 C1
Runcorn Docks Rd WA7 22 E2
Runcorn East Sta WA7 50 D7
Runcorn Hill Nature Resetve* WA7 48 F8
Runcorn Mkt WA7 23 A3
Runcorn Rd Barnton CW8 78 B2
Higher Walton WA4 25 D6
Little Leigh CW8 77 D5
Runcorn Spur Rd WA7 23 B1
Runcorn Sta WA7 22 F2
Runcorn Swim Pool WA7 23 A3
Runger La M90, WA15 32 F8
Runnell The CH64 41 D4
Runnymede WA1 17 D7
Runnymede Ct 2 WA8 13 C1
Runnymede Dr WA11 1 A6
Runnymede Gdns 5 WA8 13 C1
Runnymede Wlk 3 WA8 13 C2
Rupert Row WA7 50 A8
Ruscoe Ave CW11 174 E6
Ruscolm Cl WA5 14 D7
Rushes Cl 4 CW5 205 A3
Rushes Mdw WA13 19 B5
Rushey Cl WA15 32 D7
Rushfield Cres WA7 50 B5

Rushfield Rd Cheadle SK8. . 35 A6
Chester CH4. . . . . 141 B5
Rush Gdns WA13. . . . . 19 A4
RUSHGREEN. 19 A4
Rushgreen Rd WA13. . . . . . . 19 A4
Rushmere Cl SK10 . . . . 62 F2
Rushmere La CH3 . . . . 163 F3
Rushmore Gr WA1 . . . . 17 A7
Rusholme Cl L26 . . . . 21 A6
Rushside Rd SK8. . . . . 35 A6
RUSHTON 147 C5
Rushton Ave WA4 . . . . 2 B4
Rushton CE First Sch
  SK11 . . . . 159 B2
Rushton Cl Burtonwood WA5 . 6 F7
  Northwich CW9 . . . . 104 C7
  Widnes WA8. . . . . 12 F3
Rushton Dr Chester CH2 . . . 118 E7
  Hough CW2 . . . . 206 E2
  Middlewich CW10 . . . . . . 151 C7
Rushton Fold SK10 . . . . 61 A2
Rushton La CW6 . . . . 147 D6
Rushton Rd SK8. . . . . 35 A6
RUSHTON SPENCER 159 B2
Rushy La CW2 . . . . 208 B5
Rushy View WA12. . . . . 2 A4
Ruskin Ave
  Newton-le-Willows WA12 . . 2 C4
  Warrington WA2 . . . . 8 C2
Ruskin Com High Sch
  CW2 . . . . 190 C2
Ruskin Ct WA16 . . . . 57 A2
Ruskin Dr CH65 . . . . 70 D3
Ruskin Rd
  Congleton CW12 . . . . 156 C2
  Crewe CW2 . . . . 190 C2
Ruskin Way WA16 . . . . 57 A3
Russel Ct WA8 . . . . 13 B4
Russell Ave Alsager ST7 . . . 193 D5
  High Lane SK6 . . . . 37 E7
Russell Cl CW12. . . . . 179 A8
Russell Dr CW1 . . . . 191 C5
Russell Rd Runcorn WA7 . . . 48 E8
  Winsford CW7 . . . . 149 C8
Russell St CH1, CH3 . . . . . 237 C3
Russet Cl CW10 . . . . 128 B2
Russet Rd CW8. . . . . 102 D8
Russett Sch The CW8 . . . . . 102 E8
Russet Way SK9. . . . . 59 E3
Rutherford Dr WA16. . . . . . 82 C7
Ruthin Cl WA5 . . . . 7 F3
Ruthin Ct CH65. . . . . 70 D3
Ruthin Wlk WA6 . . . . 73 A1
Rutland Ave Golborne WA3. . 3 D7
  Halewood L26 . . . . 21 A8
  Warrington WA4 . . . . 26 B8
Rutland Cl
  Congleton CW12 . . . . 156 E4
  Sandbach CW11. . . . . . . 174 C5
Rutland Dr
  Middlewich CW10 . . . . . . 151 C7
  Weaverham CW8. . . . . . . 77 C1
Rutland Pl CH2. . . . . 119 A5
Rutland Rd
  Hazel Grove SK7. . . . . . . 36 E8
  Irlam M44 . . . . 11 D5
  Kidsgrove ST7 . . . . 195 A2
  Macclesfield SK11 . . . . . . 112 D4
  Partington M31 . . . . 11 E2
Rutland St 🗍 WA7 . . . . 22 F2
Rutter Ave WA5. . . . . 7 F2
Rutter Cl CW2 . . . . 206 B5
Ryburn Cl CW2. . . . . 207 B3
Ryhurn Rd SK11. . . . . 112 A5
Rydal Ave High Lane SK6 . . . 37 E8
  Warrington WA2 . . . . 16 A2
Rydal Cl
  Ellesmere Port CH65 . . . . . 70 C2
  Holmes Chapel CW4. . . . . 130 B2
  Neston CH64 . . . . 66 F6
  Winsford CW7 . . . . 126 D3
Rydal Cl CW12 . . . . 156 A2
Rydal Dr WA15. . . . . 32 D8
Rydal Gr Chester CH4. . . . . 141 A6
  Helsby WA6 . . . . 73 B1
  Runcorn WA7 . . . . 49 B8
Rydal Mount CW1 . . . . 173 B1
Rydal Pl SK11 . . . . 112 A6
Rydal St WA12 . . . . 2 C3
Rydal Way Alsager ST7 . . . . 193 C5
  Widnes WA8. . . . . 12 C1
Ryde Cl CW1. . . . . 190 B8
Ryder Gr ST7 . . . . 194 C1
Ryder Rd Warrington WA1. . . 17 C7
  Widnes WA8. . . . . 13 B4
Ryders St WA8 . . . . 103 E8
Ryebank Ave CW1. . . . . . . 190 B7
Ryebank Way SK10 . . . . 87 C3
Rye Cl ST7. . . . . 193 B3
Ryecroft CH2 . . . . 72 B3
Ryecroft Cl CW10 . . . . 151 B7
Ryecroft La
  Duddon CH3, CW6 . . . . . . 144 C6
  Mobberley WA16. . . . . . . 57 E4
Ryecroft Rd CH60 . . . . 41 C7
Ryedale Way CW12. . . . . . 179 C8
Ryehills ST7 . . . . 209 E1
RYE HILLS 209 E1
Rylands Cl SY14. . . . . 213 B4
Rylands Dr WA2. . . . . 16 C7
Rylands St Warrington WA1 . 16 B5
  🗍 Widnes WA8. . . . . 23 B8
Ryles Cl SK11. . . . . 112 C5
Ryles Cres SK11. . . . . 112 C5
Ryles Ho SK11 . . . . 112 C5

Ryle's Park Rd SK11 . . . . . 112 C6
Ryle St SK11. . . . . 112 D6
Ryleys Farm SK9 . . . . 59 F1
Ryleys La SK9 . . . . 59 F1
Ryleys Sch The SK9. . . . . . . 59 F1

S

Sable Rd CW2. . . . . 206 B3
Sabre Cl WA7 . . . . 50 D7
Sack La CW9. . . . . 54 F6
Sacred Heart RC Prim Sch
  WA5 . . . . 15 E5
Saddleback Dr SK10. . . . . . . 86 F7
Saddlers Rise WA7. . . . . 50 C8
Saddler's Way SK11 . . . . . . 113 E7
Saddlery Way CH1 . . . . 118 B3
Sade Ct 🗍 CW1 . . . . 190 B5
Sadler Cl CW7 . . . . 126 D1
Sadler Rd CW7. . . . . 126 D1
Sadler's Cl CW4. . . . . 130 B3
Sadlers La CW6 . . . . 124 A1
Sadler St WA8 . . . . 13 C1
Sadlers Wells CW6 . . . . . . 185 E8
Saffron Cl Golborne WA3. . . . 3 E8
  Warrington WA2 . . . . 9 B1
Saffron Wlk M31. . . . . 11 F2
Sagars Rd Handforth SK9 . . . 34 C3
  Styal SK9 . . . . 34 B4
Sage Cl WA2. . . . . 9 C2
SAIGHTON 142 E1
Saighton CE Prim Sch
  CH3. . . . . 142 E1
Saighton La CH3. . . . . 142 F2
St Aelred's RC Tech Coll
  WA12 . . . . 2 D4
St Alban Rd WA5. . . . . 14 E5
St Albans Cl WA11. . . . . 2 A7
St Albans Dr CW5. . . . . . . 204 F3
St Alban's RC Prim Sch
  Macclesfield SK10. . . . . . . 86 F1
  Warrington WA5 . . . . 15 F6
St Albans St SK22. . . . . 39 C8
St Ambrose Coll WA15. . . . . 32 B8
St Ambrose Ct WA4 . . . . . . 16 B2
St Ambrose RC Prim Sch
  L24. . . . . 21 A2
St Ambrose Rd WA8. . . . . . 13 C1
St Andrew's Ave CW2. . . . . 190 C1
St Andrew's CE Prim Sch
  WA2 . . . . 8 C3
St Andrews Cl
  Gorstyhill CW2. . . . . 207 D3
  Gorstyhill CW2. . . . . 207 D3
  Northwich CW9 . . . . 104 E7
  Warrington WA2 . . . . 9 A4
St Andrews Ct
  Crewe CW2 . . . . 190 C1
  Ellesmere Port CH65. . . . . 70 E2
  Macclesfield SK11 . . . . . . 112 B7
St Andrews Dr
  Holmes Chapel CW4. . . . . 130 B2
  Kidsgrove ST7 . . . . 195 C3
St Andrew's Gdns ST7 . . . . 193 E2
St Andrew's Rd
  Ellesmere Port CH65 . . . . . 70 E3
  Macclesfield SK11 . . . . . . 112 B7
St Andrews Wlk
  Mickle Trafford CH2 . . . . . . 96 F1
  New Mills SK22 . . . . 39 D8
St Annes CH1 . . . . 237 B3
St Annes Ave WA4. . . . . 17 B2
St Anne's Ave CW10 . . . . . . 151 D8
St Annes Avenue E WA4 . . . 17 B2
St Anne's Fulshaw CE Prim
  Sch SK9 . . . . 59 F6
St Anne's La CW5 . . . . 204 D5
St Anne's RC Prim Sch
  CW5 . . . . 204 E3
St Anne's Rd WA8. . . . . 13 C2
St Anne St CH1. . . . . 237 B3
St Ann's CE Prim Sch
  WA2 . . . . 16 C8
St Ann's Rd CW10. . . . . . . 151 C8
St Ann's Rd S SK8. . . . . . . 34 C8
St Ann's Sq SK8. . . . . 34 C8
St Anns Wlk 🗍 CW10 . . . . . 128 C1
St Anthony Pl WA2 . . . . 8 B6
St Anthony's RC Prim Sch 🗍
  CH4. . . . . 140 E6
St Asaph Dr WA5. . . . . 7 E3
St Asaph Rd CH66 . . . . 94 E8
St Augustine's Ave WA4 . . . 16 F4
St Augustines Dr CW2 . . . . 207 E3
St Augustine's RC Prim Sch
  Runcorn WA7 . . . . 24 A2
  Warrington WA4 . . . . 16 F4
St Austell Cl WA5 . . . . 14 E3
St Austell Cl
  Macclesfield SK10 . . . . 86 E1
  Runcorn WA7 . . . . 50 B6
St Austell Dr SK8. . . . . 34 B8
St Austins La WA1. . . . . . . 16 B4
St Barnabas CE Prim Sch
  WA5 . . . . 15 F5
St Barnabas Cl SK11. . . . . . 112 D6
St Barnabas Pl WA5 . . . . . . 15 E6
St Bartholomews Ct CH5. 116 E6
St Basil's RC Prim Sch
  WA8 . . . . 12 A2
St Bede's Ave CW8 . . . . 77 D1
St Bede's RC Inf Sch WA8 . . 13 A1
St Bede's RC Jun Sch
  WA8 . . . . 13 A1
  CW8 . . . . 102 F7

St Benedicts Cl WA2. . . . . . 16 B7
St Benedict's RC Prim Sch
  Handforth SK9. . . . . 34 E3
  Warrington WA2 . . . . 16 D7
St Bernard's RC Prim Sch
  CH65. . . . . 70 D3
St Berteline's CE Prim Sch
  WA7 . . . . 50 C8
St Brannocks Rd SK8. . . . . . 35 B7
St Brides Cl WA5. . . . . 14 E3
St Bridgets Cl
  Warrington WA2 . . . . 8 F3
  Widnes WA8. . . . . 23 A5
St Bridgets Ct CH4 . . . . . . 141 B6
St Bridget's RC Prim Sch
  WA2 . . . . 8 E3
St Catherine Dr CW8 . . . . . 103 A4
St Catherine's RC Prim Sch
  WA3 . . . . 3 E7
St Chad's CE Prim Sch
  Newcastle-under-Lyme
  ST5 . . . . 210 D2
  Winsford CW7 . . . . 149 E8
St Chads Cl CW5 . . . . 220 A8
St Chad's Fields CW7. . . . . 149 C5
St Chad's RC High Sch
  WA7 . . . . 49 D7
St Chad's Rd CH1 . . . . 117 F4
St Chad's Terr ST5 . . . . . . 210 D2
St Chads Way TF9 . . . . 236 C2
St Christophers Cl CH2 . . . 118 D8
St Clair St CW2. . . . . 190 D1
St Clare's RC Prim Sch
  CH4. . . . . 141 A5
St Clements Ct CW2. . . . . . 207 B1
St Clement's RC Prim Sch
  WA7 . . . . 49 A8
St David Rd CH62. . . . . 44 A6
St Davids Dr
  🗍 Ellesmere Port CH66. . . . 94 F8
  Warrington WA5 . . . . 7 E2
St David's High Sch CH4 . . . 140 C6
St Davids Mews 🗍 CW2 . . . 207 E3
St David's Ret Pk CW4 . . . . 140 D7
St David's Terr CW4. . . . . . 140 C6
St Edwards Cl SK11. . . . . . 112 D6
St Edward's RC Prim Sch
  WA7 . . . . 23 B3
St Elmo Pk SK12 . . . . 37 C4
St Elphin (Fairfield) CE (VA)
  Prim Sch WA1 . . . . 16 D6
St Elphins Cl WA1. . . . . . . 16 C5
St Elphin's View WA4. . . . . 25 F2
SS Peter & Paul RC High Sch
  WA8 . . . . 12 F2
St Gabriels Ct ST7. . . . . . . 193 C3
St Gabriel's Ct CW9 . . . . . . 193 C3
  ST7 . . . . 193 C3
St George's Cl CH1 . . . . . . 237 B3
St Georges Ave 🗍🗍 CH66 . . . 94 F8
St George's CE Prim Sch
  SK22 . . . . 39 C8
St Georges Cl
  Ellesmere Port CH65 . . . . . 70 D4
  Warrington WA4 . . . . 26 E3
St George's Cl WA16 . . . . . . 82 C8
St George's Cres
  Chester CH4. . . . . 237 C1
  Waverton CH3 . . . . 143 A5
St George's Pl 🗍🗍 SK11. . . . 112 D7
St Georges Rd SK22 . . . . . . 39 C8
St George's Rd CW7 . . . . . . 149 C8
St George's St SK11 . . . . . . 112 D6
St Georges Way SK9. . . . . . 34 C4
St George's Way
  Northwich CW9 . . . . 103 F5
  Thornton Hough CH63 . . . . 42 A7
St Gerard's RC Prim Sch
  WA8 . . . . 23 B7
St Gregory's RC High Sch
  WA5 . . . . 15 D5
St Gregory's RC Prim Sch
  SK10 . . . . 87 F8
ST HELENS 1 A1
St Helens CE Prim Sch
  WA3 . . . . 11 B2
St Helens Cl WA3 . . . . 11 B3
St Helens Coll Newton
  Campus WA12 . . . . 2 B4
St Helens Rd Golborne WN7 . . 4 B8
  🗍 Northwich CW9. . . . . . . 104 A8
St Hilarys Pk SK9. . . . . 85 A8
St Hilda's Dr WA6. . . . . 49 C1
St Ives Cl SK10 . . . . 86 E1
St Ives Pk CH5 . . . . 116 A3
St Ives Pk CH5 . . . . 116 A3
St Ives Way CH5. . . . . 116 A3
St James Ave
  Chester CH2. . . . . 118 F7
  Congleton CW12 . . . . 156 C2
  Warren SK11 . . . . 111 E2
St James Cl Audlem CW3 . . 230 A4
  🗍 Frodsham WA6 . . . . 49 C1
St James Ct Audley ST7. . . . 209 D2
  Bryn CW8. . . . . 102 A5
  Cheadle SK8. . . . . 34 F6
  Chester CH2. . . . . 118 F3
St James' Ct
  Biddulph ST8 . . . . 179 E3
  Warrington WA8 . . . . 16 B3
St James Ct/Llys Sant Iago
  CH5 . . . . 91 D1
St James' Dr SK9. . . . . 60 A6
St James' Prim Sch WA11. . . 1 E6
St James' RC High Sch
  SK8. . . . . 34 F6
St James' Sq SK22. . . . . 39 C8

St James St CH1 . . . . 237 B3
St James Terr 🗍 CW7 . . . . 149 A8
St James' Way CW8 . . . . . . 103 E7
St James' Way SK8. . . . . 34 F6
St James Wlk 🗍 CW8. . . . . 103 E7
St John Ave WA4. . . . . 16 B2
St John Fisher RC Prim Sch
  WA8 . . . . 13 D1
St Johns Ave 🗍 WA16 . . . . 57 A1
St John's Ave
  Knutsford WA16. . . . . 56 F1
  Lostock Gralam CW9 . . . . 79 F3
St John's Brow WA7. . . . . . 23 B3
St John's CE Prim Sch
  Bollington SK10 . . . . 88 A7
  Sandbach CW11. . . . . . . 175 E6
St John's Cl CW9 . . . . 103 E7
St Johns Ct Chester CH1 . . . 237 B2
  Winsford CW7 . . . . 126 B1
St John's Ct
  Knutsford WA16. . . . . 57 C2
  Warrington WA1 . . . . 16 F7
St Johns Dr CW7 . . . . 149 A8
St John's Rd
  Bebington CH62. . . . . 44 A5
  Chester CH4. . . . . 237 C1
  Congleton CW12 . . . . 157 A5
  Knutsford WA16. . . . . 57 A1
  🗍 Macclesfield SK11. . . . . 112 C7
  Wilmslow SK9 . . . . 59 E3
St John's Rear Rd CH4. . . . 237 C1
St John's St WA7. . . . . 23 B3
St John St Chester CH1 . . . 237 B2
  Newton-le-Willows WA12 . . 2 A3
Saint Johns Vale WA16 . . . . 57 D3
St John's Way
  Cuddington CW8 . . . . 102 B2
  Sandbach CW11. . . . . . . 175 E6
St John's Wood ST7 . . . . . . 194 F1
St John's Wood Com Sch
  WA16 . . . . 57 D2
St John the Evangelist
  Catholic Acad ST7 . . . . . 195 A3
St John the Evangelist CE
  Prim Sch SK11 . . . . 112 A7
St John the Evangelist RC
  Prim Sch 🗍 ST7 . . . . 194 F1
St Joseph's Cl WA5. . . . . . . 14 E5
St Joseph's RC Prim Sch
  Warrington WA5 . . . . 14 E5
  Winsford CW7 . . . . 149 B8
St Josephs Way CW5 . . . . . 205 A5
St Katherines Way WA1. . . . 16 D5
St Kilda Cl CH65 . . . . 70 C1
St Lawrence Cl CW5. . . . . . 204 F6
St Lawrence Rd WA6 . . . . . 74 B8
St Leonard's Way CW3 . . . . 232 C1
St Lewis RC Prim Sch WA3 . . 4 B1
St Luke's Ave WA3 . . . . 3 D8
St Luke's CE Prim Sch
  WA3 . . . . 3 E1
St Lukes Cl CW4. . . . . 130 D3
St Luke's Cres WA8 . . . . . . 13 B4
St Luke's Ho 🗍 SK10 . . . . . 111 F8
St Luke's RC Prim Sch
  WA6 . . . . 74 C8
St Luke's Way WA6. . . . . . . 49 B1
St Margaret's Ave WA2 . . . . 8 D1
St Margaret's CE Prim Sch
  WA2 . . . . 8 D1
St Marks Cres CH66 . . . . . . 94 F8
St Mark's Prim Sch CW9 . . 53 C4
St Mark's St WA11. . . . . . . 1 A6
St Martins Dr CH66 . . . . . . 69 D2
St Martins La WA7 . . . . 50 D7
St Martins RC Prim Sch
  WA7 . . . . 50 D7
St Martin's Rd ST7 . . . . . . 210 E6
St Martin's Way CH1 . . . . . 237 A3
St Mary of the Angels RC
  Prim Sch CH66 . . . . 69 D6
St Mary's Ave CW8 . . . . . . 77 D1
St Mary's CE Prim Sch
  Bosley SK11 . . . . 158 D8
  Irlam M44 . . . . 11 C5
  Runcorn WA7 . . . . 50 A8
St Mary's Cl Alsager ST7. . . 193 C5
  Hale L24. . . . . 21 E2
  Warrington WA4 . . . . 26 C6
St Marys Ct CW5 . . . . 204 A7
St Mary's Ct
  Congleton CW12 . . . . 156 A2
  Golborne WA3 . . . . 4 B8
  Partington M31 . . . . 11 F4
St Mary's Dr CW8 . . . . 126 A8
St Mary's Hill CH1. . . . . . . 237 B1
St Mary's Hospl WA2 . . . . . 8 B1
St Mary's RC Jun Sch
  WA12 . . . . 2 B3
St Mary's RC Prim Sch
  Congleton CW12 . . . . 156 D3
  Crewe CW2 . . . . 190 A1
  Middlewich CW10 . . . . . . 151 C8
  🗍 New Mills SK22 . . . . . . 39 B8
St Mary's RC School WA12 . . 2 A4
St Mary's Rd Disley SK12. . . 38 D5
  Dodleston CH4. . . . . 162 A7
  New Mills SK22 . . . . 39 B8
  Runcorn WA8 . . . . 23 F1
  Warrington WA5 . . . . 14 F5
  Widnes WA8. . . . . 23 F1
St Mary's St Crewe CW1 . . . 190 C4
  Warrington WA4 . . . . 16 D3
St Mary's Way CH4 . . . . . . 139 C5

St Matthews CE Prim Sch
  WA4 . . . . 26 E2
St Matthews Cl
  Haslington CW1. . . . . 191 B3
  Warrington WA4 . . . . 26 D7
St Mawes Cl WA8 . . . . 12 E2
St Mawes Ct SK10. . . . . . . 86 E1
St Mawgan Ct WA2. . . . . . . 8 F2
St Michael's Ave SK7 . . . . . 35 E8
St Michael's Catholic Prim
  Sch WA8 . . . . 22 C7
St Michael's Cl
  Little Leigh CW8. . . . . 77 D5
  Widnes WA8. . . . . 22 C7
St Michael's Cotts CW12 . . 158 E7
St Michael's Ind Est WA8 . 22 C7
St Michael's Rd WA8 . . . . . 22 C7
St Michael's Row CH1 . . . . 237 B2
St Michael's Sq CH1 . . . . . 237 B2
St Michaels Terr 🗍🗍
  SK11 . . . . 112 C8
St Michael's View CW1 . . . . 190 B5
St Michaels Vw WA8 . . . . . 22 D7
St Michael's Way CW10. . . 128 C1
St Monicas Cl WA4 . . . . . . 26 D7
St Monica's RC Prim Sch
  WA4 . . . . 26 D7
St Nicholas Ct CW5. . . . . . 204 F5
St Nicholas RC High Sch
  CW8 . . . . 103 D6
St Nicholas Rd WA3 . . . . . . 4 A8
St Olave St CH1 . . . . 237 B1
St Oswalds CH1 . . . . 237 B3
St Oswald's CE Aided Prim
  Sch CH1 . . . . 94 C7
St Oswalds Cl
  Malpas SY14 . . . . 213 B3
  Winwick WA2 . . . . 8 B6
St Oswald's Cres CW11 . . . 153 F5
St Oswald's RC Prim Sch
  WA1 . . . . 16 F7
St Oswalds Way CH1,
  CH2 . . . . 237 B3
St Oswald's Worleston CE
  Prim Sch CW5 . . . . 188 E6
St Patricks Cl WA8 . . . . . . 23 A5
St Paul of the Cross RC Prim
  Sch WA5 . . . . 6 C1
St Pauls Cl WA7 . . . . 48 E8
St Paul's Cl CW1 . . . . 190 C4
St Paul's Ct
  🗍 Macclesfield SK11. . . . . 112 C7
  Warrington WA2 . . . . 16 A4
St Pauls Gdns CH66 . . . . . . 69 B7
St Paul's Pl 🗍 CW9. . . . . . . 79 A1
St Paul's RC Prim Sch
  SK12. . . . . 36 E2
St Paul's Rd
  🗍 Macclesfield SK11. . . . . 112 C7
  Widnes WA8. . . . . 23 A7
St Paul's St CW1 . . . . 190 C4
St Peter's Ave WA16. . . . . . 56 F1
St Peter's CE Prim Sch
  🗍 Heswall CH60. . . . . 40 F8
  Newton-le-Willows WA12 . . 2 E4
St Peter's Cl
  Heswall CH60. . . . . 40 F8
  Lymm WA13. . . . . 19 A4
St Peter's Dr WA2 . . . . 16 C6
St Peter's Dr CW6 . . . . 147 F7
St Peter's Ho SK11 . . . . . . 112 E6
St Peter's RC Prim Sch
  WA1 . . . . 17 C7
St Peters Rd CW12 . . . . . . 156 E1
St Peter's Rise CW11 . . . . . 174 E7
St Peter's Way CH2 . . . . . . 119 F8
St Peter's Way WA2 . . . . . . 16 B6
St Peters Wk WA8. . . . . . . 13 D3
St Philip (Westbrook) CE
  Prim Sch WA5 . . . . 7 B1
St Saviour's CE Prim Sch
  ST7 . . . . 194 D1
St Saviour's RC Prim Sch
  CH66. . . . . 69 E3
St Saviour's St ST7 . . . . . . 194 D1
Saints Peter and Paul
  Catholic Coll WA8 . . . . . . 12 F2
St Stephen Rd WA5. . . . . . 14 F5
St Stephen's Ave WA2 . . . . . 8 B3
St Stephens Cl CH60. . . . . 41 C6
St Stephens Ct
  🗍🗍 Congleton CW12 . . . . . 156 F3
  Sandbach CW11. . . . . . . 174 D7
St Stephen's RC Prim Sch
  WA2 . . . . 8 B2
St Teresa's RC Prim Sch
  M44. . . . . 11 B4
St Theresa's RC Prim Sch
  CH1. . . . . 117 F5
St Thomas CE Prim Sch
  🗍 Kidsgrove ST7. . . . . 195 A1
  Warrington WA4 . . . . 16 D1
St Thomas Ct WA8 . . . . . . 12 E1
St Thomas More RC High Sch
  CW2 . . . . 206 B8
St Thomas of Canterbury CE
  Jun Sch CH1. . . . . 237 A4
St Thomas's Pathway
  CH1 . . . . 237 B2
St Thomas St ST7 . . . . 195 E7
St Thomas Terr WA8 . . . . . 12 E1
St Thomas' View CH65. . . . 70 B4
St Vincent Dr CW8 . . . . . . 102 F3
St Vincent Rd WA5 . . . . . . 14 F5
St Vincent's RC Prim Sch
  Knutsford WA16. . . . . 57 C1
  Warrington WA5 . . . . 14 F3
St Wenefredes Gn SY13. . . 214 F6

St Werburgh's & St Columba's RC Prim Sch 1 CH2 118 F2
St Werburgh St CH1 237 B2
St Wilfreds Rd WA8 13 E4
St Wilfrid's CE Aided Prim Sch WA4 17 B1
St Wilfrids Cl CW9 104 A3
St Wilfrid's Dr WA4 17 C1
St Wilfrid's RC Prim Sch CW8 103 D5
St Winefride's RC Prim Sch CH64 66 F7
Salander Cres CW2 206 A7
Salary Row 9 CW9 80 B2
Salerno Rd CH2 95 B1
Salesbrook La CW5 228 C7
Salford CW3 230 A4
Salford Pl CW12 156 E3
Salisbury Ave
Crewe CW2 190 C1
Saltney CH4 140 E6
Salisbury Cl Crewe CW2 190 C1
10 Ellesmere Port CH66 94 F8
Salisbury Pl SK10 87 E4
Salisbury Rd WA11 1 E8
Salisbury St Chester CH1 118 B3
Golborne WA3 3 A8
Runcorn WA7 23 A1
Warrington WA1 16 D6
4 Widnes WA8 23 B8
Salkeld St 8 CW9 104 B8
Sally Clarkes La CW5 220 B8
Salmon Leap CH4 237 B1
Salop Pl ST7 195 A3
Salop Wlk SK10 86 F2
Saltash Cl WA7 50 B6
Saltersbrook Gr 12 SK9 34 E1
Saltersford SK10 89 E5
Saltersford Cnr CW4 130 E3
Saltersgate CH66 69 F2
Salters La
Lower Withington SK11 132 B8
Windyharbour SK11 109 D1
Salter's La Bickerton SY14 199 F8
Broxton CH3, SY14 183 E1
Hoole Bank CH2 119 C8
Saltersley La SK9 59 B7
SALTERSWALL 125 F3
Salt Line Way CW11 174 D6
Salt Mdws CW5 204 C5
Salt Mus The* CW9 103 F7
SALTNEY 140 D6
Saltney Bsns Ctr CH4 140 F7
Saltney Ferry Cty Prim Sch CH4 140 B6
Saltney Ferry Rd CH4 140 B7
Saltney Terr CH4 140 B7
Salton Gdns WA5 15 E7
Saltwood Dr WA7 50 C5
Saltworks Cl WA6 49 D2
Samian Cl CW10 128 C2
Samphire Gdns WA9 6 B7
Samson Cl CW1 190 F8
Samuel Armstrong Way CW1 190 D7
Samuel Broadhurst Pl CW2 206 D4
Samuel Jones Way ST7 193 A3
Samuel St Crewe CW1 190 B5
Macclesfield SK11 112 D7
Packmoor ST7 195 F1
Warrington WA5 15 E4
Samuel Twemlow Ave CW11 191 F7
Sanbec Gdns WA8 12 D5
Sanctuary Mews SK9 34 F3
Sandalwood WA7 24 C1
Sandalwood Cl WA2 8 D2
SANDBACH 175 B5
Sandbach Crosses* CW11 175 B6
Sandbach Dr CW9 103 E6
SANDBACH HEATH 175 D6
Sandbach High Sch & Sixth Form Coll CW11 175 A7
Sandbach L Ctr CW11 175 A7
Sandbach Prim Acad CW11 175 A6
Sandbach Rd
Congleton CW12 156 A3
Rode Heath ST7 193 E7
Sandbach Road N ST7 193 C4
Sandbach Road S ST7 193 D3
Sandbach Sch CW11 175 A6
Sandbach Sta CW11 174 D8
Sandeman Cres CW8 103 C8
Sanderling Rd WA12 2 C4
Sanders Hey Cl WA7 50 B5
Sanderson Cl Crewe CW2 206 C8
Warrington WA5 14 D6
Sanderson Way CW10 128 E1
Sanders Sq SK11 112 D5
Sandfield Ave CW5 216 F3
Sandfield Cl 3 WA3 3 E8
Sandfield Cres WA3 5 C7
Sandfield Ct
3 Frodsham WA6 74 B8
Wrenbury CW5 216 F4
Sandfield Hall WA3 3 A4
Sandfield La
Acton Bridge CW8 76 E1
Hartford CW8 103 C4
Sandfield Pk CH60 40 D8
Sandfields WA6 74 B8
Sandfield Terr CW8 76 F1
Sandford Cres CW2 207 D2
Sandford Dr CH3 121 C1
Sandford Rd CW5 204 F7
Sandgate Rd SK10 87 F2
Sandham Gr CH60 41 D7
Sandham Rd L24 21 A4
Sandheys CH64 41 C1
Sandhill Terr WA4 16 E3
Sandhole Cotts 2 CW7 149 B8
Sandhole La
Chelford WA16 83 D4
Crowton CW8 101 B7
Sandholes La
Agden Dairy Farm SY13 225 A4
Sandholes SY13 224 F3
Sandhurst Ave CW2 190 A1
Sandhurst Dr 2 SK9 60 C8
Sandhurst Rd L26 21 A6
Sandhurst St WA4 16 F3
Sandicroft Cl WA3 9 C5
San Diego Dr WA5 15 B6
Sandiford Rd CW4 130 C3
Sandiford Sq CW9 104 A8
Sandileigh Ave WA16 56 F2
Sandington Dr CW8 101 F2
SANDIWAY 102 B3
Sandiway Bebington CH63 43 C6
Knutsford WA16 57 B2
Sandiway Ave WA8 12 A1
Sandiway Bank CW8 102 E4
Sandiway Cl CW8 102 A2
Sandiway La CW9 53 A2
Sandiway Pk CW8 102 E4
Sandiway Prim Sch CW8 102 B3
Sandiway Rd Crewe CW1 190 A7
Handforth SK9 34 D5
Sand La SK10 84 F5
Sandlebridge Farm SK9 83 F6
Sandle Bridge La WA16, SK9 83 E5
Sandle Bridge Rise WA16 83 F6
SANDLOW GREEN 131 B1
Sandmoor Pl WA13 19 A2
Sandon Cres CH64 66 E5
Sandon Park Gdns CW2 189 D4
Sandon Pl WA8 13 D1
Sandon Rd CH2 118 E4
Sandon St CW1 190 D4
Sandown Cl Culcheth WA3 4 F4
Middlewich CW10 151 C8
Runcorn WA7 49 C6
Wilmslow SK9 60 D8
Sandown Cres CW8 102 A3
Sandown Dr WA15 32 D6
Sandown Pl SK11 111 F7
Sandown Rd CW1 190 C7
Sandown Reach CW5 229 D7
Sandown Terr CH3 118 F1
Sandpiper Cl
Macclesfield SK10 87 B4
Newton-le-Willows WA12 2 C4
Sandpiper Ct
Chester CH4 141 B2
Kidsgrove ST7 195 C2
Sandpiper Way CH4 141 B3
Sandra Dr WA12 2 E3
Sandringham Ave
Chester CH3 119 A2
Helsby WA6 73 B4
Sandringham Cl
Altrincham WA14 20 F1
Northwich CW9 103 E4
Winsford CW7 126 C3
Sandringham Ct
Golborne WA3 3 E7
5 Wilmslow SK9 60 A6
Sandringham Dr
Poynton SK12 36 D3
Warrington WA5 15 C4
Wistaston CW2 205 E8
Sandringham Gdns 2 CH65 70 D2
Sandringham Pl 11 CW8 103 C5
Sandringham Rd
8 Congleton CW12 156 F4
Macclesfield SK10 87 F1
Widnes WA8 13 A4
Sandringham Way 4 SK9 60 A6
Sandrock Rd CH3 142 E7
Sandsdown Cl ST8 179 C1
Sandside Rd ST7 193 B3
Sands Rd ST7 195 E6
Sandstone Mews WA8 12 E4
Sandstone Wlk CH60 41 A7
Sandwich Dr SK10 87 C4
Sandwood Ave CH4 139 B3
Sandybank CW8 78 D1
Sandy Brow La WA3 3 E2
Sandy Cl SK10 87 F7
SANDYCROFT 116 B2
Sandycroft Ind Est CH5 116 A3
Sandyfield Ct ST8 179 C1
Sandyhill Pl 1 CW7 149 D6
Sandyhill Rd CW7 149 D6
Sandy La Allostock CW4 106 E1
Astbury CW12 177 E6
Aston CW5 217 C2
Bold Heath WA8 14 B6
Brown Knowl CH3 199 C7
Bulkeley SY14 184 C1
Chester CH3 119 A1
Congleton CW12 155 D3
Congleton, Astbury Marsh CW12 156 B2
Croft WA3 9 A8
Cronton WA8 12 D5
Golborne WA3 2 F8
Golborne, Lowton Common WA3 4 A8
Goostrey CW4 107 D1
Sandy La *continued*
Haslington CW11 192 B7
Hatherton CW5 219 F5
Helsby WA6 73 B2
Higher Kinnerton CH4 161 A6
Huntington CH3 141 F8
Knutsford WA16 82 D3
Lymm WA13 19 B4
Macclesfield SK10 86 C2
Neston CH64 67 A7
Runcorn WA7 48 E7
Runcorn, Preston Brook WA7 50 F6
Saighton CH3 142 C3
Saltney CH4 140 D6
Sandbach CW11 174 D5
Swan Green WA16 106 E6
Swettenham CW12 131 F3
Tarvin CH3 121 C4
Threapwood SY14 222 E8
Warrington, Longford WA2 8 C2
Warrington, Penketh WA5 15 A4
Warrington, Stockton Heath WA4 26 D8
Weaverham CW8 77 C2
Whitegate CW8 125 D6
Wilmslow SK9 59 E8
Sandylands Cres ST7 193 F5
Sandylands Pk CW2 205 D7
Sandylane Mews CW12 156 C5
Sandy Lane W WA2 8 B3
Sandymere Ct CW7 126 B1
Sandymoor La WA7 24 D3
Sandymoor Sch WA7 24 F3
Sandy Rd ST8 179 C2
Sandy Way CW7 149 B8
Saner Dr CW8 103 C8
SANKEY BRIDGES 15 C4
Sankey Bridges Ind Est WA5 15 C4
Sankey for Penketh Sta WA5 14 F6
Sankey La WA4 25 F1
Sankey St Golborne WA3 3 A8
Newton-le-Willows WA12 2 A3
Warrington WA1 16 A5
Widnes WA8 23 A6
Sankey Valley Ind Est WA12 2 A2
Sankey Valley Pk*
Newton-le-Willows WA5 1 D3
Warrington WA5 15 D5
Sankey Valley St James Prim Sch WA5 15 C6
Sankey Way WA5 15 D5
Santa Rosa Bvd WA5 15 A7
Santon Dr WA3 3 E8
Sapling La CW6 146 F3
Sarah Bartholomew Sch WA6 97 E6
Sark Ave CH65 95 B8
Sark Ho CH2 119 B4
Sarl Williams Ct CH1 237 A3
Sarn Bank Rd SY14 222 E6
Sarn Rd SY14 222 D8
Sarra La CH3 184 B5
Sarsfield Ave 1 WA3 3 D8
Sarus Ct WA7 24 B4
SAUGHALL 117 B8
Saughall All Saints Prim CE Sch CH1 94 A1
Saughall Cl CW9 103 E4
Saughall Hey CH1 94 A1
Saughall Rd Blacon CH1 117 E5
Blacon, Abbot's Meads CH1 118 A4
Saundersfoot Cl WA5 7 E2
Saunders St CW1 190 B4
Saunderton Cl WA11 1 C7
Saunton Cl CW7 126 A2
Savannah Pl 5 WA5 15 C7
Saville Ave WA5 15 F7
Saville Rise CW7 126 E1
Saville St SK11 112 E7
Savoy Rd CW1 207 A8
Sawley Cl Culcheth WA3 5 A2
Runcorn WA7 50 E7
Sawley Dr SK8 35 C6
Sawmill Rd SY14 201 B2
Sawpit St WA13, WA14 20 A6
Sawyer Dr ST8 179 C1
Saxon Cl WA4 26 B5
Saxon Crossway CW7 126 B1
Saxon Rd WA7 23 C2
Saxons La CW8 103 D7
Saxon Terr 4 WA8 13 B1
Saxon Way Blacon CH1 117 E6
6 Ellesmere Port CH66 94 F8
Sandbach CW11 175 C6
Sayce St WA8 13 B1
Scafell Ave WA2 8 C3
Scafell Cl Bebington CH62 43 D3
High Lane SK6 37 E8
Overpool CH66 69 F7
Scaife Rd CW5 204 F5
Scaliot Cl SK22 39 B8
Scampton Cl 1 WA8 13 C4
Scarborough Dr WA12 2 A2
Scarborough Gr CW5 204 C7
Scarfell Cres CW9 103 D3
Scar La SY14 198 F1
Sceptre Cl WA12 2 A3
SCHOLAR GREEN 194 E8
Scholar Green Prim Sch ST7 194 E6
Scholar Rise CW7 127 A2
Scholars Cl SK10 111 D8
Scholar's Ct 10 CH64 66 E8
Scholars Green La WA13 18 F2
School Ave CH64 66 F6
School Bank Norley WA6 101 A6
Wybunbury CW5 220 B8
School Brow WA1 16 C6
School Cl Audley ST7 210 A1
Knutsford WA16 56 E1
Marbury SY13 226 E8
Poynton SK12 36 F3
School Cotts
Bradwall Green CW11 153 B4
Wimboldsley CW10 150 F4
School Cres CW1 190 E4
School Dr Barnton CW8 78 A3
Lymm WA13 19 C5
School Field Cl CW3 230 F4
Schoolfold La SK10 63 A7
School Gn CH3 182 C1
SCHOOL GREEN 149 C5
School Hill CH60 40 F7
School Hos SK11 109 A1
School House Cotts CH66 69 B6
School La Aldford CH3 163 F2
Antrobus CW9 53 C3
Astbury CW12 178 B8
Audlem CW3 230 A4
Bold Heath WA8 13 E7
Brereton Green CW11 153 F5
Bunbury CW6 168 E1
Burwardsley CH3 184 B6
Cuddington CW8 102 A2
Eaton (nr Congleton) CW12 156 E8
Ellesmere Port CH66 69 A8
Elton CH2 72 B3
Frodsham WA6 74 C7
Great Budworth CW9 79 B8
Guilden Sutton CH3 119 E5
Hartford CW8 103 C4
Henbury SK11 111 B6
Higher Whitley WA4 52 E6
Hollinfare WA3 11 A2
Hooton CH66 43 F1
Irlam, Cadishead M44 11 D5
Lostock Gralam CW9 80 A2
Manley WA6 99 A5
Marton SK11 133 C5
Mickle Trafford CH2 119 E8
Moulton CW9 126 F8
4 Nantwich CW5 204 E6
Neston CH64 42 B2
Neston, Little Neston CH64 66 F6
Neston, Parkgate CH64 41 B1
Nether Alderley SK10 86 A6
Norbury SY13 215 E2
Norley WA6 100 D5
Ollerton WA16 83 B4
Onneley CW3 232 F3
Partington WA14 20 D5
Poynton SK12 36 F4
Runcorn WA7 49 F8
Sandbach CW11 174 D7
Sandbach Heath CW11 175 E6
Smallwood CW11 176 F5
Warmingham CW11 173 E7
Warrington WA3 10 D5
School Mews SK7 35 E7
School Rd
Ellesmere Port CH65 70 B5
Handforth SK9 34 D4
Higher Shurlach CW9 104 D5
Warrington WA2 8 C1
Winsford, Meadowbank CW7 126 E5
Winsford, Wharton CW7 127 A2
School Road N CW9 104 E6
School Road S CW9 104 E6
School St Chester CH2 118 F3
Golborne WA3 3 A8
Haslington CW1 191 D5
Newton-le-Willows WA12 2 B3
Warrington WA4 16 B4
School Terr WA3 3 A8
School Way
Northwich CW9 104 A8
Widnes WA8 13 D3
Schooner Cl WA7 50 D6
Scilly Cl CH65 70 C1
Scope Ho CW1 190 E1
Scotch Hall La CW9 53 A3
Scotia Wlk 1 WA3 3 F8
Scotland Rd WA1 16 B5
Scott Ave Crewe CW1 190 F4
Widnes WA8 22 F8
Scott Cl Macclesfield SK10 113 A7
Rode Heath ST7 193 E8
2 Sandbach CW11 174 D6
Scott Ct WA2 16 B6
Scotthope Cl SK11 111 F6
Scotton Ave CH66 69 B5
Scott Pl SK9 60 E7
Scott Rd SK10 87 A7
Scottsdale Rd WA7 24 B2
Scotts Ind Est WA5 16 A7
Scott St WA2 16 C6
Scott Wlk WA12 2 C1
Scout Hut La CH2 72 A4
Scroggins La M31 11 F4
Sea Bank CW10 128 D1
Seabank Rd CH60 40 E6
Seabury St WA4 17 A3
Seacombe Dr CH66 69 E3
Seacroft Ave WA4 26 E2
Seacroft Moor Gr CW5 204 D7
Seafield Ave CH60 40 E6
Seaford Cl WA7 24 D1
Seaford Pl WA2 8 A4
Seagrave Cl CW9 103 F5
Seagull Cl CW1 190 F5
Seahill Rd CH1 116 F8
Sea La WA7 23 D2
SEALAND 116 E6
Sealand Cl WA2 8 E1
Sealand Ind Est CH1 117 F2
Sealand Rd Blacon CH1 117 C3
Chester CH1 118 A2
Sealand CH1, CH5 116 D6
Sealand Trad Pk CH1 117 F2
Sealand Way 2 SK9 34 D4
Seal Rd SK7 36 A7
Seashell Trust SK8 34 D6
Seasons The 11 WA7 22 F1
Seathwaite Cl WA7 49 E5
Seaton Cl CW1 190 B8
Seaton Pk WA7 24 E3
Seaton St CW7 127 D1
Seattle Cl 3 WA5 15 B7
Sea View CH64 66 E4
Seaview Ave CH62 44 B6
Seaville St CH3 237 C3
Secker Ave WA4 16 D2
Secker Cl WA4 16 D2
Second Ave
Connah's Quay CH5 92 F3
Crewe CW1 190 F2
Kidsgrove ST7 194 E1
Poynton SK12 36 D1
Runcorn WA7 49 F8
Sandbach CW11 175 A5
Second Dig La CW5 219 C8
Second Wood St CW5 204 D5
Sedbergh Cl CW4 130 A3
Sedbergh Gr WA7 49 E5
Seddon St CW10 128 C2
Sedgefield Cl 3 SK10 87 C4
Sedgefield Rd CH1 118 B2
Sedgeford Cl SK9 34 D1
Sedgewick Cres WA5 6 E6
Sedgmere Ave CW1 190 A8
Sedum Cl CH3 142 A6
Sefton Ave
Congleton CW12 157 A1
Widnes WA8 13 A3
Sefton Dr SK9 34 C2
Sefton Rd CH2 119 A4
Sefton St WA12 1 F3
Selbourne Cl ST7 193 B5
Selby Cl Poynton SK12 36 D5
Runcorn WA7 24 F4
Selby Gdns SK8 35 C6
Selby Gn CH66 69 B5
Selby St Nantwich CW5 204 D7
Warrington WA5 15 E5
Selkirk Ave
Bebington CH62 43 E4
Warrington WA4 17 A3
Selkirk Cl
Ellesmere Port CH66 68 F5
Macclesfield SK10 86 F2
Selkirk Dr Chester CH4 141 A7
Holmes Chapel CW4 130 B2
Selkirk Rd CH4 141 A7
Seller St CH1 237 C3
Selsdon Ct CH4 141 C7
Selsey Cl CW1 190 B8
Selworthy Dr Crewe CW1 190 B7
Warrington WA4 17 D3
Selwyn Cl
Newton-le-Willows WA12 2 B5
Widnes WA8 13 E3
Selwyn Dr Cheadle SK8 35 C7
Sutton Lane Ends SK11 112 F3
Selwyn Jones Sport Ctr WA12 2 D5
Semper Cl CW12 157 A4
Senderfield La CW11 174 E4
Seneschal Ct WA7 49 E6
Senna La CW9 78 C8
Sennen Cl WA7 50 C5
Sens Cl CH1 237 A2
Sentry Gr CH66 43 D1
Sephton Ave WA3 4 E3
Serin Cl WA12 2 C3
Serpentine The CH4 141 B7
Servite Cl CH65 69 F6
Servite Pl CH64 66 E7
Sett Cl SK22 39 B8
Sevenoaks Cl SK10 87 B2
Seven Row CH64 66 E5
Seven Sisters La WA16 82 E5
Severn Cl Biddulph ST8 179 E1
Congleton CW12 156 F1
Macclesfield SK10 86 F2
Warrington WA2 8 E2
Widnes WA8 13 F3
Severn Dr SK7 35 C6
Severn Rd WA3 4 F2
Severnvale CH65 70 B3
Severn Way CW4 130 D2
Severn Wlk CW7 127 A2
Sewell St 7 WA7 23 B2
Sextant Cl WA7 50 D6
Sexton Ave WA9 1 B2
Seymour Chase WA16 82 A8
Seymour Ct WA7 24 C4
Seymour Dr
Ellesmere Port CH66 69 E6
Warrington WA1 17 A8
Seymour Ho 16 SK9 34 E1
Seymour Rd SK8 35 A8
Shackleton Ave WA8 13 C4
Shackleton Cl WA5 15 D8
Shade Terr SK6 37 F7

Shadewood Cres WA4 . . . . . .17 B2
Shadewood Rd SK11 . . . . . 112 A6
Shadowmoss Rd M22 . . . . . .33 E8
Shady Brook La CW8 . . . . . 77 C1
Shady Gr ST7 . . . . 193 D4
Shaftesbury Ave
  Chester CH3 . . . . 119 C2
  Warrington WA5 . . . . .14 E2
Shaftesbury Way WA5 . . . . . .6 F7
Shaftway Cl WA11 . . . . .1 F7
Shakerley Ave CW12 . . . . . 156 F3
Shakerley Cl CW8 . . . . 123 F6
Shakespeare Cl CW9 . . . . . 104 C7
Shakespeare Dr CW1 . . . . . 191 A4
Shakespeare Gr WA2 . . . . . . .8 C2
Shakespeare Rd
  Neston CH64 . . . . .41 E1
  Widnes WA8 . . . . 13 A1
Shalcombe Cl L26 . . . . 21 A7
Shallacres CH65 . . . . .69 F7
Shallcross Ave SK23 . . . . . .65 E4
Shallcross Cres SK23 . . . . . .65 E4
Shallcross Hall Barns
  SK23 . . . . .65 E5
Shallcross Mill Rd SK23 . . . .65 E5
Shallcross Rd SK23 . . . . . . .65 E4
Shambles The WA16 . . . . . . .57 B1
Shanklin Cl WA14 . . . . 14 C6
Shannon Cl Chester CH4 . . 140 E5
  Willaston CW5 . . . . 205 D6
Shannon Gr WA8 . . . . .12 E2
Shardlow Rd CW11 . . . . . . 174 E4
Shargate Cl WA5 . . . . 34 C1
Sharnbrook Dr CW2 . . . . . 189 D4
Sharon Park Cl WA4 . . . . . . 17 C1
Sharpley St SK10 . . . . 112 C8
Sharp St Warrington WA2 . . 14 C6
  Widnes WA8 . . . . 23 A8
Sharston Cres WA16 . . . . . . .57 B1
SHAVINGTON 206 C5
Shavington Ave CH2 . . . . . 118 F4
Shavington Bypass
  Butt Green CW5 . . . . 205 E4
  Shavington CW2 . . . . 206 C6
  Weston CW2 . . . . 207 C6
Shavington High Sch
  CW2 . . . . 206 A5
Shavington L Ctr CW2 . . . . 206 A5
Shavington Pk TF9 . . . . . . 234 B4
Shavington Prim Sch
  CW2 . . . . 206 C4
Shavington Way CW9 . . . . 103 F2
Shawbury Gr WA1 . . . . 17 A8
Shaw Cl
  Congleton Park CW12 . . . . 156 F3
  Ellesmere Port CH66 . . . . . 69 E4
Shaw Dr Knutsford WA16 . . 57 C3
  Winsford CW7 . . . . 149 D6
Shawell Ct WA8 . . . . .13 E2
Shaw Entry L35, WA8 . . . . . 12 A7
SHAW HEATH 57 D3
Shaw Heath View WA16 . . . 57 C3
Shaw's Ave WA2 . . . . 16 C8
Shaws Fold SK9 . . . . .33 F3
Shaws La
  Macclesfield SK10 . . . . . . 86 C8
  Winsford CW7 . . . . 126 F4
  Winsford, Wharton CW7 . . . 127 A3
Shaw St Culcheth WA3 . . . . .5 A3
  Haydock WA11 . . . . .1 E6
  Macclesfield SK11 . . . . . . 112 C8
  Runcorn WA7 . . . . .22 F2
Shay La Ashton Hayes CH3 . 121 F7
  Hampton Heath SY14 . . . . 200 A1
  Tarvin CH3 . . . . 121 E3
Shay's La CW6 . . . . 124 E4
Sheaf Cl CH3 . . . . 121 C2
Shearbrook La CW4 . . . . . . 107 E1
Sheardhall Ave SK12 . . . . . .38 E5
Shearwater Rd CH3 . . . . . . 180 E2
Sheath St CW9 . . . . 104 A8
Shed La CH3 . . . . 119 B2
Sheen Gdns M22 . . . . 34 A8
Sheepfield Cl CH66 . . . . . . 69 C7
Sheerwater Cl WA1 . . . . . . .16 F7
Sheffield Cl WA5 . . . . 15 C5
Sheffield Row WA12 . . . . . . .7 D8
Sheilings The WA3 . . . . .3 F8
Shelagh Ave WA8 . . . . 13 A1
SHELL GREEN 23 E8
Shell Green Est WA8 . . . . . .23 E8
Shellow La CW12, SK11 . . . 134 C5
Shellway Rd CH2 . . . . 71 A3

Shelton Cl WA8 . . . . .13 F3
Shenhurst Cl SK9 . . . . .59 E4
Shepcroft La WA4 . . . . 26 C3
Shepherds Fold Dr CW7 . . 126 C3
Shepherds Gr 3 WA5 . . . . .14 F8
Shepherd's La CH2 . . . . . . 118 D5
Shepherds Row WA7 . . . . . .23 F2
Shepherds View CW8 . . . . . .78 B2
Shepley Cl SK7 . . . . 36 D8
Sheppard Cl CW1 . . . . 190 D5
Sheppenhall Gr CW5 . . . . . 217 C1
Sheppenhall La CW5,
  SY13 . . . . 228 D5
Shepperton Cl WA4 . . . . . . .26 E6
Shepsides Cl CH66 . . . . . . 69 C3
Shepton Rd CH66 . . . . .69 E2
Sheraton Rd CH3 . . . . 143 B5
Sherborne Cl WA7 . . . . . . .24 F3
Sherborne Rd CW1 . . . . . . 190 D6
Sherbourne Ave CH4 . . . . . 141 B5
Sherbourne Cl SK8 . . . . . . .35 B6
Sherbourne Rd
  Ellesmere Port CH65 . . . . . 70 D3
  Macclesfield SK11 . . . . . . 111 F7
Sherbourne Way WA5 . . . . . .6 F6
Sherbrooke Rd SK12 . . . . . 38 D6
Sherbrook Rise SK9 . . . . . . 60 C6
Shergold Cl 13 CW11 . . . . 174 C7
Sheridan Ave WA3 . . . . .3 D7
Sheridan Cl CW1 . . . . 173 B1
Sheridan Pl WA2 . . . . .8 A5
Sheridan Way WA7 . . . . . . 24 D2
Sheri Dr WA12 . . . . .2 E2
Sheringham Cl CH4 . . . . . . 140 E5
Sheringham Dr CW1 . . . . . 190 B8
Sheringham Rd WA5 . . . . . .14 E6
Sherlock Ave WA11 . . . . .1 E7
Sherratt Cl
  Congleton CW12 . . . . 156 E2
  Nantwich CW5 . . . . 204 F4
Sherrington's La CH3 . . . . . 199 D8
Sherwin St CW2 . . . . 190 C1
Sherwood Cl WA8 . . . . 12 C1
Sherwood Cres WA5 . . . . . . .6 E6
Sherwood Gr WA6 . . . . 73 A3
Sherwood Rd Blacon CH1 . 117 C5
  Macclesfield SK11 . . . . . . 112 A6
Shetland Cl Warrington WA2 . .8 E4
  Widnes WA8 . . . . 13 E3
Shetland Dr
  Bebington CH62 . . . . .43 D8
  Ellesmere Port CH65 . . . . . 70 C1
Shetland Way 4 CW10 . . . 128 D2
Shevington Cl WA8 . . . . . . .13 E3
Shevington Wlk WA8 . . . . . .13 E3
Shiggins Cl WA5 . . . . 15 D6
Shillingford Cl WA4 . . . . . . .26 E5
Shilton Cl CW10 . . . . 151 B8
Shingler Cl CW8 . . . . 103 E4
Shipbrook Rd
  Chester CH2 . . . . 118 F6
  Davenham CW9 . . . . 104 C3
  Northwich CW9 . . . . 104 C6
Shipgate St CH1 . . . . 237 B1
Shipgate The CH1 . . . . 237 B1
Shipley Gdns ST7 . . . . 210 D6
Ship St WA6 . . . . 49 C1
Shipton Cl Warrington WA5 . .15 B8
  Widnes WA8 . . . . 12 D3
Shire Way CH3 . . . . 166 C2
Shirley Ave SK8 . . . . 34 C6
Shirley Dr WA4 . . . . 17 A2
Shirleys Cl SK10 . . . . 87 A6
Shirleys Dr SK10 . . . . 87 A6
SHOCKLACH 211 D7
Shocklach Green La
  SY14 . . . . 211 D7
Shocklach Hall La SY14 . . . 211 B5
Shocklach Oviatt CE Prim
  Sch SY14 . . . . 211 C7
Shocklach Rd CH2 . . . . . . 118 F6
Shones Croft CH64 . . . . . . 67 A5
Shop La Congleton CW12 . . 156 E1
  Little Budworth CW6 . . . . . 124 F2
Shoreham Dr WA5 . . . . 15 A3
Shores Farm La SK7 . . . . . . 37 C1
Shores Green Dr CW9 . . . . .79 F5
Shores La CH5 . . . . 203 D7
Short Cl WA12 . . . . .1 E3
Shorthorn Cl CW10 . . . . . . 128 D2
Short St Haydock WA11 . . . .1 E6
  11 Macclesfield SK11 . . . . 112 D8
  Newton-le-Willows WA12 . . .1 E3
  Widnes WA8 . . . . 23 A5
Shorwell Cl WA5 . . . . 14 C7
Shot Tower Cl CH1 . . . . . . 237 C3
SHOTWICK 93 B4
Shotwick Cl 1 CW11 . . . . 154 B1
Shotwick-Frodsham Rd
  Little Stanney CH65 . . . . . .70 E1
  Shotwick CH1 . . . . 93 D4
  Thornton-le-Moors CH2 . . . 71 D2
Shotwick La CH1 . . . . 93 D6
Shotwick Rd CH5 . . . . .92 F3
Shoveler Cl CW2 . . . . 189 E1
SHRALEYBROOK 209 A1
Shrewbridge Cres CW5 . . . 204 E4
Shrewbridge Rd CW5 . . . . 204 D4
Shrewsbury Dr
  Newcastle-under-Lyme
  ST5 . . . . 210 E2
  Shavington CW2 . . . . 206 D5
Shrewsbury Gdns SK8 . . . . 35 C6
Shrewsbury Rd 4 CH65 . . . 70 C5
Shrewsbury St WA4 . . . . . . 16 D3
Shrewsbury Way CH4 . . . . 140 F6
Shrigley Cl SK9 . . . . 34 D1

Shrigley Ct SK10 . . . . .88 B8
Shrigley Fold Rd SK10 . . . 88 A3
Shrigley Rd SK10 . . . . .63 B5
Shrigley Rise SK10 . . . . . . 63 C1
Shrigley Road N SK12 . . . . 37 C3
Shrigley Road S SK10,
  SK12 . . . . 37 C2
Shropshire Cl
  Middlewich CW10 . . . . . . 151 C8
  Warrington WA1 . . . . .17 E6
Shropshire La SY13 . . . . . 227 E2
Shropshire St CW3 . . . . . . 229 F4
Shuldham Cl WA16 . . . . . . 29 C4
Shurlach La CW9 . . . . 104 C4
Shurlach Rd CW9 . . . . 104 D6
Shutley La CW8 . . . . 77 D6
Shutlingsloe Way SK10 . . . 112 A8
Sibbersfield La CH3 . . . . . 180 F4
Sibell St CH1 . . . . 237 C3
Siddall St 7 CW9 . . . . 104 B8
Siddals Ct CW5 . . . . 204 C5
Siddeley Cl CH4 . . . . 139 C4
Siddeley Dr WA12 . . . . .1 F4
SIDDINGTON 110 A3
Siddington Ave CW9 . . . . . 104 A4
SIDDINGTON HEATH 109 E1
Siddington Rd
  Handforth SK9 . . . . 34 D5
  Poynton SK12 . . . . .36 F2
Siddorn St CW7 . . . . 126 E1
Side End La SK23 . . . . .64 F3
Side La CW6 . . . . 146 E6
Sidings Cl WA1 . . . . 16 C6
Sidings The SK23 . . . . .65 E8
Sidlaw Cl CH66 . . . . 69 A6
Sidmouth Cl WA5 . . . . .14 E4
Sidmouth Gr SK8 . . . . .34 F7
Sidney Cl CH64 . . . . .41 F1
Sidney Rd CH64 . . . . 41 F1
Siemens Rd M44 . . . . 11 E5
Sienna Cl M44 . . . . 11 E6
Signal Ct CH2 . . . . 118 F2
Signals Ct 11 CH3 . . . . . . 142 B5
Silk Heritage Mus ★
  SK11 . . . . 112 D7
Silk Hill SK23 . . . . .65 F8
Silk Mill
  Macclesfield SK11 . . . . . . 112 D6
  Poynton SK12 . . . . 36 C4
Silk Mill St WA16 . . . . 57 A2
Silk Mus & Her Ctr ★ 14
  SK11 . . . . 112 D7
Silk Rd SK10 . . . . 87 B6
Silk Rd The Bollington SK10 . .87 E4
  Hurdsfield SK10 . . . . 87 D2
  Macclesfield SK10 . . . . . . 112 E7
Silk St CW12 . . . . 156 C2
Silkstone Cres WA7 . . . . . . .50 B7
Silsden Ave WA3 . . . . 4 B8
Silvan Cl SK10 . . . . .87 B1
Silver Ave WA11 . . . . .1 A5
Silverbirch Croft CH4 . . . . 139 B3
Silverbirch Way CH66 . . . . .94 C8
Silverdale Cl WA8 . . . . 103 D7
Silverdale Cl
  Chorlton CW2 . . . . 207 C2
  Frodsham WA6 . . . . 74 C7
  High Lane SK6 . . . . .37 E8
Silverdale Rd
  Newton-le-Willows WA12 . . .2 B4
  Warrington WA4 . . . . .16 B2
Silvergate Ct CW12 . . . . . 178 E8
Silver La Croft WA3 . . . . . . .9 F7
  Warrington WA3 . . . . .10 C6
Silverlea Rd CW9 . . . . .80 B2
Silvermine Cl 8 ST7 . . . . . 195 B2
Silvermuir CH1 . . . . 117 E3
Silverne Dr CH65 . . . . 70 A2
Silver St Bollington SK10 . . .88 B8
  Congleton CW12 . . . . 156 E2
  Warrington WA2 . . . . .16 B6
Silver Terr CW11 . . . . 175 C6
Silverwood ST7 . . . . 195 B1
Simkin Ave WA4 . . . . .16 F4
Simmonds Cl CW9 . . . . . . 103 E3
SIMM'S CROSS 23 B8
Simms Cross Prim Sch
  WA8 . . . . 23 A8
Simonside WA8 . . . . 12 C2
Simons La WA6 . . . . .74 B5
Simonstone Rd CH4 . . . . . 139 D4
Simonswood Cl CW10 . . . . 151 B8
Simpson Cl CH2 . . . . 95 C1
Simpson Ct CW1 . . . . 173 B1
Simpson La SK10 . . . . 63 D7
Simpson Rd CH2 . . . . 95 C1
Simpson's Ct 17 SK11 . . . . 112 C8
Simpson St SK9 . . . . .59 F6
Simpsons Way CH4 . . . . . . 139 B3
Sinclair Ave Alsager ST7 . . 193 B3
  Warrington WA2 . . . . .8 B2
  Widnes WA8 . . . . 23 A8
Sinderland La
  Partington WA13 . . . . .20 B8
  Partington WA13 . . . . .20 E8
Singapore Ave M90 . . . . . . 33 A8
Singleton Ave CW1 . . . . . . 190 C6
Singleton Rd CH65 . . . . . . .69 F4
SINK MOSS 28 D3
Sir John Deane's Coll
  CW9 . . . . 103 F6
Sir Thomas Boteler CE High
  Sch WA4 . . . . .16 E3
Sir William Stanier Com Sch
  CW1 . . . . 190 E6
Siskin Cl WA12 . . . . .2 C3
Six Acre Gdns WA4 . . . . . . 25 A5

Six Acre La WA4 . . . . 25 A5
Sixth Ave CH5 . . . . .92 E1
Skeath Cl CW11 . . . . 175 E6
Skellern St ST7 . . . . 194 D2
SKELLORN GREEN 62 E8
Skellorn Green La SK10 . . . 62 E8
Skiddaw Cl WA7 . . . . 50 A4
Skipper Cl CW11 . . . . 175 D7
Skip's La CH3 . . . . 142 F7
Skipton Cl Hazel Grove SK7 . 36 C8
  3 Newton-le-Willows WA12 . .1 F2
  2 Runcorn WA7 . . . . .23 F1
Skipton Dr CH66 . . . . 69 C5
Skye Cl
  Ellesmere Port CH65 . . . . . 70 C1
  Widnes WA8 . . . . 13 E3
Skylark Cl CW1 . . . . 189 F7
Sky Lark Rise WA9 . . . . .1 A3
Skyline Dr WA5 . . . . .6 E2
Slacken La ST7 . . . . 194 D2
Slack St SK11 . . . . 112 E6
Slackwood Cl 1 CH65 . . . . .70 B7
Slade La Mobberley WA16 . . 58 A7
  Nether Alderley SK10 . . . . .85 E5
Slade St 5 CW9 . . . . 104 B8
Slag La Golborne WA3 . . . . .3 D8
  Haydock WA11 . . . . .1 B7
Slater St
  Macclesfield SK11 . . . . . . 112 C6
  Warrington WA4 . . . . .16 D3
Slaters Way CW7 . . . . 148 F8
Slaughter Hill CW1 . . . . . . 191 D2
Slaughter House La
  CW5 . . . . 217 E3
Slicks Bsns Ctr CW8 . . . . . 78 C2
Slindon Cl ST5 . . . . 210 D1
Slutchers La
  Hood Manor WA1 . . . . . . .15 F3
  Warrington WA1 . . . . 16 A3
Small Ave WA2 . . . . .8 C2
Smallbrook Wlk CW2 . . . . 206 C8
Small Cres WA2 . . . . .8 C2
Small La WA16 . . . . 58 A8
Smallman Rd CW2 . . . . . . 190 C1
SMALLWOOD 176 F5
Smallwood CE Prim Sch
  CW11 . . . . 176 F5
Smallwood Cl
  4 Middlewich CW10 . . . . 151 C8
  Newcastle-under-Lyme
  ST5 . . . . 210 D1
Smallwood Ct 1 CW12 . . . 156 F3
Smallwood Forge CW11 . . 176 D5
Smeaton Wood CW5 . . . . . 216 E2
SMETHWICK GREEN 154 F4
Smethwick La CW11,
  CW12 . . . . 154 E4
Smith Cl ST7 . . . . 193 B4
Smith Cres WA2 . . . . 16 D8
Smith Dr WA2 . . . . 16 D8
Smithers Cl WA5 . . . . 204 F4
Smithfield Dr/Ffordd
  Smithfield LL13 . . . . 196 D8
Smithfield Gn LL13 . . . . . . 196 D8
Smithfield La CW11 . . . . . 175 C6
Smithfields CH3 . . . . 166 C2
Smithfield St LL13 . . . . . . 196 D8
Smith Gr CW1 . . . . 190 A6
Smith La Mobberley WA16 . . .57 F6
  Rainow SK10 . . . . 89 A5
Smith Rd WA8 . . . . .22 F7
Smiths Cotts CH64 . . . . . . .66 E5
SMITHS GREEN 109 A2
SMITH'S GREEN 208 B7
Smith's La CW8 . . . . 77 C1
Smiths Lawn SK9 . . . . 60 A5
Smith St
  Macclesfield SK11 . . . . . . 112 D6
  Warrington WA1 . . . . .16 B5
Smithy Bank Acton CW5 . . 204 A6
  Winsford CW7 . . . . 149 A3
Smithy Brow
  Bollington SK10 . . . . 88 C8
  Winwick WA3 . . . . .8 F7
Smithy Cl Cronton WA8 . . . 12 C5
  Neston CH64 . . . . 67 A4
  Saughall CH1 . . . . 94 A1
  Shocklach SY14 . . . . 211 E7
Smithy Cotts SY14 . . . . . . 213 A2
Smithy Ct Christleton CH3 . 142 E7
  Duddon CW6 . . . . 145 C5
  5 Ellesmere Port CH66 . . . 69 C6
Smithy Dr WA14 . . . . 20 D3
Smithy Gn Cheadle SK8 . . . 35 A8
  Gatesheath CH3 . . . . 165 C5
Smithy Gr CW11 . . . . 176 A2
SMITHY GREEN
  Cheadle Hulme 35 B7
  Lower Peover 81 E2
Smithy Hill CH63 . . . . 42 A6
Smithy La Alsager CW2 . . . 208 D7
  Altrincham WA14 . . . . 20 D3
  Barthomley CW2 . . . . 208 C6
  Biddulph ST8 . . . . 179 D2
  Bosley SK11 . . . . 158 E6
  Broxton CH3 . . . . 183 D1
  Congleton CW12 . . . . 156 C7
  Crewe CW1 . . . . 189 E8
  Croft WA3 . . . . .9 A7
  Cronton WA8 . . . . 12 C5
  Cuddington CH3 . . . . 102 A5
  Ellesmere Port CH66 . . . . . 69 C6
  Great Budworth CW9 . . . . .79 A8
  Helsby WA6 . . . . 73 C5
  Kingsley WA6 . . . . .75 B2
  Little Leigh CW8 . . . . .77 B6

Smithy La continued
  Lostock Gralam CW9 . . . . . 80 A2
  Malpas SY14 . . . . 213 A2
  Mottram St Andrew SK10 . . 61 C2
  Mouldsworth CH3 . . . . . . .98 F2
  Partington M31 . . . . .11 F3
  Rainow SK10 . . . . .88 E5
  Utkinton CW6 . . . . 146 C6
  Weston CW2 . . . . 207 C5
  Willaston CH64 . . . . 68 A7
Smithy Pathway CH4 . . . . . 140 F4
Smithy The CH2 . . . . 118 E8
Smithy Wlk CW11 . . . . 174 F3
Smokehall La CW7, CW9 . . 126 F6
Smokehall Lane Ind Est
  CW7 . . . . 127 A5
Smokey La SY13 . . . . 224 A1
Smokies Way ST8 . . . . 179 C1
Smyth Rd WA8 . . . . 13 D2
Snab La Neston CH64 . . . . 66 F4
  Norbury SY13 . . . . 215 B5
Snabwood Cl CH64 . . . . . . 66 E5
Snaefell Rise WA4 . . . . 26 C4
Snapebrook Gr 6 SK9 . . . . 34 E1
Snape Hollow CW2 . . . . . . 207 E4
Snape La CW2 . . . . 207 E4
Snape Rd Crewe CW2 . . . . 206 D8
  Macclesfield SK10 . . . . . . .87 E2
Snape Row CW8 . . . . 78 C2
Snelson La Chelford SK11 . 108 E7
  Chelford, Marthall WA16,
  SK9 . . . . 83 D3
Snipe Cl SK12 . . . . 36 A4
Snowberry Cl WA8 . . . . . . .13 E4
Snowberry Cres WA5 . . . . .15 C3
Snowberry Way 5 CH66 . . .94 E8
Snowberry Wlk M31 . . . . . 11 E3
Snow Crest Pl CW5 . . . . . 205 A3
Snowdon Cl
  Ellesmere Port CH66 . . . . . 69 A6
  Warrington WA5 . . . . .14 E6
Snowdon Cres CH4 . . . . . . 141 A5
Snowdon Dr CW2 . . . . 189 D3
Snowdonia Way CW7 . . . . 149 B8
Snowdon St CW8 . . . . .77 F3
Snowdrop Cl WA7 . . . . . . .49 F4
SNOW HILL 204 D6
Snow Hill SK11 . . . . 112 E6
Soay Cres CW7 . . . . 149 A7
Solly Cres CW12 . . . . 156 A2
Solvay Rd CW8 . . . . .78 D1
Solway Cl WA2 . . . . .8 F4
Solway Cl CW1 . . . . 191 A2
Solway Ct CW1 . . . . 191 A2
Solway Gr WA7 . . . . 49 D5
SOMERFORD 154 F7
Somerford Ave CW2 . . . . . 190 A3
Somerford Cl CW11 . . . . . 175 C8
Somerford Ct 2 CW12 . . . 156 F3
Somerford Ho SK12 . . . . . .36 E4
Somerford La CW12 . . . . . 155 F5
Somerford Rd CH4 . . . . . . 139 C4
Somerford Way 3 SK9 . . . 34 E5
Somerford Wlk WA8 . . . . . .13 E3
Somerley Cl CW1 . . . . 190 B8
Somerset Ave ST7 . . . . . . 194 F2
Somerset Cl
  Congleton CW12 . . . . 156 D4
  Irlam M44 . . . . 11 D6
Somerset Rd CH2 . . . . 118 F5
Somerset St CH1 . . . . 237 B4
Somerset Way WA1 . . . . . . .17 B8
Somerton Cl 5 SK11 . . . . . 111 F7
Somerton Rd SK11 . . . . . . 111 F7
Somerville Cl
  Bebington CH63 . . . . .43 B6
  High Legh WA16 . . . . 29 C4
  Neston CH64 . . . . .66 E5
Somerville Cres CH65 . . . . 70 C4
Somerville St CW2 . . . . . . 190 B2
Sonoran Cl WA7 . . . . 24 B1
Soot Hill CW8, CW9 . . . . . 78 C3
Sophia Dr WA5 . . . . .14 F8
Sorbus Cl CH2 . . . . 72 C3
Sorbus Dr CW1 . . . . 190 E6
Sorby Rd M44 . . . . .11 F7
Sorrel Cl Huntington CH3 . . 142 A6
  Warrington WA2 . . . . .9 C2
Soss Moss La SK10 . . . . . . 84 C5
Sossmoss La SK10 . . . . . . 84 D6
Soughans La
  Chorlton Lane SY14 . . . . . 212 A3
  Shocklach SY14 . . . . 211 E6
SOUND 217 F5
Sound Commom Nature
  Reserve ★ CW5 . . . . 217 D4
Sound & District Prim Sch
  CW5 . . . . 217 F5
SOUND HEATH 217 E5
Sound La
  Ravensmoor CW5 . . . . . . 203 E1
  Sound CW5 . . . . 217 D2
Souter's La CH1 . . . . 237 B2
South Acre Dr
  Handforth SK9 . . . . 34 D3
  Macclesfield SK11 . . . . . . 113 A7
Southampton Way WA7 . . . .50 C4
South Ave Chester CH2 . . . 237 C4
  Haslington CW1 . . . . 191 D4
  Warrington WA2 . . . . .16 B8
  Warrington, Stockton Heath
  WA4 . . . . 16 C1
Southbank CW9 . . . . .79 A7
South Bank CH2 . . . . 118 C4
Southbank Ave CW2 . . . . . 206 C5
South Bank Cl SK9 . . . . . . .60 B2
South Bank Gr CW12 . . . . 156 F2
South Bank Terr WA7 . . . . .22 F3

South Cheshire Coll
  CW2 . . . . 190 B2
South Cheshire Private Hospl
  The CW1 . . . . 172 E1
South Cl Tarporley CW6 . . 146 C2
  Wilmslow SK9 . . . . 59 F6
South Crescent Rd CH4 . . 237 C1
South Croft CW6 . . . . 185 D6
South Crofts CW5 . . . . . . 204 F5
South Dale WA5 . . . . 14 F5
Southdale Rd WA1 . . . . 17 A7
Southdown Cl SK10 . . . . . . 87 D4
Southdown Cres SK8 . . . . . 34 F8
South Downs WA16 . . . . . . 57 C1
South Downs Dr WA14. . . 31 D8
South Downs Rd WA14 . . . 31 E8
South Dr Heswall CH60 . . . 41 A7
  Northwich CW9 . . . . 104 D6
  Plumley WA16 . . . . 80 F3
  Wilmslow SK9 . . . . 60 B6
Southern St WA4 . . . . 16 C1
Southey Cl
  8 Sandbach CW11 . . . . . 174 D6
  Widnes WA8 . . . . 22 F8
Southfield SK10 . . . . 87 A4
Southfield Cl WA5 . . . . 34 C3
Southfield Rd CH66 . . . . . . 69 C7
Southfields WA16 . . . . 57 C3
Southfields Ave WA5 . . . . . 14 F6
Southfields Cl CW5 . . . . . 220 A8
South Gn CH5. . . . . 116 A6
South Gr 10 SK9. . . . . 60 A1
South La
  Warrington WA5, WA8 . . . . 14 E5
  Widnes WA8 . . . . 13 F4
Southlands CW4 . . . . 130 C2
Southlands Ave WA5 . . . . . 14 F5
Southlands Ct WA7. . . . . . . 48 F8
Southlands Mews 8 WA7 . 22 F1
Southlands Rd CW7 . . . . . 157 A1
Southlands View CW4 . . . 107 E1
South Lane Entry WA8 . . . . 13 F5
Southlawn SK9 . . . . 60 A5
South Lodge CW6 . . . . . . 168 D8
South Mdw Cl 9 WA3 . . . . . 3 C7
Southmead WA3 . . . . 3 C7
South Mead SK12 . . . . 36 B5
South Meadway SK6 . . . . . . 37 F7
South Oak La SK9 . . . . 59 F5
South Par WA7 . . . . 48 D7
South Park Ct Bsns Ctr
  SK11 . . . . 112 D6
South Park Dr SK12 . . . . . . 36 F5
South Park Rd SK11 . . . . . 112 C7
South Pier Rd CH65 . . . . . . 70 D7
Southport St WA9 . . . . 1 A3
South Rd
  Altrincham, Ashley Heath
    WA14 . . . . 31 B8
  Ellesmere Port CH65 . . . . . 70 C3
  Halewood L24 . . . . 21 A4
  Runcorn WA7 . . . . 48 D7
  Stanlow CH65 . . . . 70 F4
South St Alderley Edge SK9 . 60 A1
  Chester CH3 . . . . 119 A1
  Congleton CW12 . . . . 156 D3
  Crewe CW2 . . . . 190 D2
  Mount Pleasant ST7 . . . . . 195 B6
  3 Widnes WA8 . . . . 23 B8
South Terr 14 SK9. . . . . 60 A1
South View Chester CH4 . . 141 D7
  Christleton CH3 . . . . 142 F7
  Lower Withington SK11 . . . 132 A8
  New Mills SK22 . . . . 39 B8
South View Ave SK11 . . . . 111 D2
South View La CW7 . . . . . 170 F2
South View Rd CH1. . . . . . 118 B2
Southward Rd WA11 . . . . 2 A7
Southwark Pl CW7 . . . . . . 149 A8
Southway
  Middlewich CW10 . . . . . . 128 C1
  Runcorn WA7 . . . . 49 F7
  Widnes WA8 . . . . 22 D8
South Way CW1 . . . . 117 F4
Southway Ave WA4 . . . . 26 D7
Southwell Cl WA3 . . . . 3 C8
South West Ave SK10 . . . . . 87 F6
South Wirral High Sch
  CH62 . . . . 43 D4
Southwold Cres WA5 . . . . . 14 E5
Southwood Ave WA7 . . . . . 24 C2
Southwood Rd CH62. . . . . . 43 F8
Southworth Ave WA5 . . . . . 15 F8
Southworth La WA2, WA3 . . 8 E7
Southworth Rd WA12 . . . . . . 2 F4
Sovereign Cl
  Golborne WA3 . . . . 3 E7
  Northwich CW9 . . . . 104 F6
  Runcorn WA7 . . . . 50 D7
Sovereign St WA3 . . . . 9 C4
Sovereign Way CH1 . . . . . 117 E2
Sowcar Way SK10 . . . . 88 C8
Spark Hall Cl WA4 . . . . 26 E1
Spark La Runcorn WA7 . . . . 23 F1
  Smallwood CW11 . . . . 154 C2
Sparks Cl CH3 . . . . 142 B7
Sparrowbutts Gr ST7 . . . . 195 C2
Sparrow Cl CW5 . . . . 204 C3
Sparrowhawk Cl WA7 . . . . . 50 A7
Sparrow La WA16 . . . . 57 B1
Spath La SK8 . . . . 34 F5
Spath Lane Cl SK8 . . . . 35 A5
Spath Wlk SK8 . . . . 35 B5
Spawell Cl WA3 . . . . 3 E7
Speakman Ave WA12 . . . . . . 2 C5
Speakman St WA7 . . . . 22 F3
Speed's Way CH3 . . . . 180 E2

Speedwell Cl
  11 Golborne WA3 . . . . 3 E8
  Heswall CH60 . . . . 41 C8
  Huntington CH3 . . . . 142 A5
Speedwell Dr CH60 . . . . . . 41 C8
Speedwell Rd ST5 . . . . . . 210 F1
SPEKE 21 A3
Speke Bvd L24, L26, WA8 . . 21 B5
Speke Ho L24 . . . . 21 A2
Speke Rd WA8 . . . . 22 C6
Spencer Brook SK10 . . . . . 86 F6
Spencer Cl Alsager ST7 . . 192 F4
  Wistaston CW2 . . . . 206 A8
Spencer Mews SK10. . . . . . 86 F6
Spencer St Barnton CW8 . . . 78 B3
  Northwich CW8 . . . . 103 E7
Spenders La WA7 . . . . 50 D1
Spenlow Cl SK12 . . . . 36 E1
Spennymoor Ct WA7 . . . . . 49 E7
Spenser Cl WA8 . . . . 12 F1
Spenser Rd CH64 . . . . 41 E1
Spey Cl Middlewich CW10 . 128 D3
  Winsford CW7 . . . . 126 F2
Spey Dr ST7 . . . . 195 C2
Spike Island ★ WA8 . . . . . . 23 A5
Spindle St SK22 . . . . 156 E2
Spink La WA16 . . . . 80 A6
Spinnaker Cl WA7 . . . . 50 D5
Spinner Cres CW9 . . . . 78 D7
Spinners La SK12 . . . . 36 C4
Spinners Pl WA1 . . . . 16 C6
Spinners Way SK10 . . . . . . 87 F7
Spinney Ave
  Goostrey CW4 . . . . 107 F1
  Widnes WA8 . . . . 12 A1
Spinney Avenue Church of
  England Primary School
    WA8 . . . . 12 E1
Spinney Cl Handforth SK9 . . 34 C3
  Winsford CW7 . . . . 150 A8
Spinney Dr
  Ellesmere Port CH66 . . . . . 69 D2
  Weston CW2 . . . . 207 B5
Spinney End CH3 . . . . 166 A1
Spinney Gdns WA4 . . . . 27 B4
Spinney La WA16 . . . . 56 E3
Spinney Mead SK10 . . . . . . 87 E2
Spinney The
  Cuddington CW8 . . . . 101 D5
  Heswall CH60 . . . . 41 C5
  Lawton-gate ST7 . . . . 194 E4
  Neston CH64 . . . . 41 D1
  Norley WA6 . . . . 100 E5
  Sandbach CW11 . . . . 175 C6
  Willaston CW5 . . . . 205 D6
Spinney Wlk WA7 . . . . 24 A1
Spires Gdns WA2. . . . . 8 A7
Spital Wlk CH2 . . . . 118 F2
Spitfire Rd CW5 . . . . 187 B7
Spodegreen La WA14 . . . . . 30 C8
Spout La WA16 . . . . 58 B4
Spragg St CW12 . . . . 156 E3
Spring Ave 2 CH66 . . . . . . 69 C6
Springbank SK10 . . . . 87 F7
Spring Bank ST7 . . . . 195 A7
Springbank Cl WA7 . . . . . . 49 B6
Springbank Cres CW7 . . . 149 C8
Springbank Gdns
  Lymm WA13 . . . . 19 B5
  New Mills SK22 . . . . 39 B8
Springbank La SK10 . . . . . 63 A5
Springbank Rd WA7 . . . . . 206 D7
Spring Bank Rd SK22 . . . . 39 C8
Springbourne WA6 . . . . 74 D6
Springbrook WA4 . . . . 26 A8
Springburn Gdns WA1 . . . . . 17 F7
Spring Cl ST7 . . . . 193 E8
Springcroft CH64 . . . . 41 C1
Spring Ct 2 WA7 . . . . 23 B2
Springe Cl CW5 . . . . 203 B5
Springfield Ave
  Golborne WA3 . . . . 2 F8
  Grappenhall WA4 . . . . 17 B3
  Helsby WA6 . . . . 73 B3
  Lymm WA13 . . . . 19 B5
  Malpas SY14 . . . . 213 C3
  Warrington, Padgate WA1 . . 17 A8
Springfield Cl CH4 . . . . . . 161 A7
Springfield Cres CW8 . . . . . 77 F3
Springfield Ct/Llys Maes Y
  Ffynnon CH4 . . . . 161 A8
Springfield Dr Talke ST7 . 210 E8
  Wilmslow SK9 . . . . 59 D5
  Wistaston CW2 . . . . 205 F7
Springfield Pk WA11 . . . . . . 1 C7
Springfield Rd
  Macclesfield SK11 . . . . . . 111 F8
  Malpas SY14 . . . . 213 B3
  Mobberley WA16 . . . . 57 F4
  Widnes WA8 . . . . 22 A8
Springfields
  Cuddington CW8 . . . . 101 D4
  Helsby WA6 . . . . 73 B3
  Knutsford WA16 . . . . 57 C3
  Mickle Trafford CH2 . . . . . 119 E8
  Prestbury SK10 . . . . 87 A7
Springfield Sch CW11 . . . 191 A3
Springfields Dr CW12 . . . 156 D3
Springfield St WA1 . . . . . . 16 A5
Spring Gdns Crewe CW1 . . 190 E5
  Ellesmere Port CH66 . . . . . 69 C6
  Macclesfield SK10 . . . . 87 D1
  Mobberley WA16 . . . . 58 D1
  Nantwich CW5 . . . . 204 F5
Springhead Cl ST7 . . . . . . 210 D6
Springhead Prim Sch
  ST7 . . . . 210 D6

Springhill SK10 . . . . 88 A1
Spring Hill CW6 . . . . 168 C8
Springhill Ave CW6 . . . . . . 168 C8
Springholm Dr WA4 . . . . . . 26 D3
Spring La Coddington CH3 . 181 E6
  Croft WA3. . . . . 9 B6
  Lymm WA13 . . . . 19 F3
Spring Mdw CW8 . . . . 78 E1
Springmount WA3 . . . . 3 E7
Spring Mount SK22. . . . . . . 39 C8
Spring Rd SK12 . . . . 36 F2
Spring St Congleton CW12 . 156 E2
  Widnes WA8 . . . . 23 A6
  Wilmslow SK9 . . . . 60 A7
Springvale Bsns Ctr
  CW11 . . . . 174 D6
Springvale Ct CW11 . . . . . 174 D6
Springvale Ind Pk CW11 . . 174 C6
Springwater Dr CW2 . . . . . 207 C1
Springwell Cl CW2 . . . . . . 206 C8
Springwood Ave WA16 . . . . 57 C3
Springwood Cl
  Blacon CH1 . . . . 117 C4
  Macclesfield SK10 . . . . 87 D5
Springwood Way
  Macclesfield SK10 . . . . 87 D5
  Macclesfield SK10 . . . . 87 D5
Sprink La CW12 . . . . 157 D5
Sprosons La SK10 . . . . 86 B4
SPROSTON GREEN 129 C2
Sproston Pl 8 SK10 . . . . . 151 D5
Sproston Way CW9 . . . . . . 103 E4
Spruce Ave WA8 . . . . 102 B3
Spruce Cl Golborne WA3 . . . 3 F7
  4 Radnor CW12 . . . . 155 E5
  Warrington WA1 . . . . 17 E7
Spruce Gr ST7 . . . . 193 E7
Spuley La SK10 . . . . 63 D2
Spunhill Ave CH66 . . . . 69 D2
Spurling Rd WA5 . . . . 6 F6
Spurston Ave WA16 . . . . . . 29 C4
SPURSTOW 185 D6
Spurstow Mews SK8 . . . . . . 35 C8
Square St SK11 . . . . 112 E6
Square The
  Altrincham WA15 . . . . 32 C8
  Audlem CW3 . . . . 229 F4
  Chester CH1 . . . . 237 C3
  Christleton CH3 . . . . 142 E8
  Holmes Chapel CW4 . . . . . 130 C3
  Ince CH2 . . . . 71 F5
  6 Lymm WA13 . . . . 18 E3
  Woore CW3 . . . . 232 C1
Squires Ave WA8 . . . . 23 A8
Squires Cl WA11 . . . . 1 B6
Squirrels Chase SK10. . . . . 86 F5
Squirrel's Jump SK9 . . . . . . 60 C1
Squirrels The SY13 . . . . . . 225 F1
Stable Croft Cl CW1 . . . . . 190 D8
Stable Croft Rd CW1 . . . . . 190 D8
Stable La Mouldsworth CH3 . 99 A3
  Utkinton CW6 . . . . 123 F1
Stables Cl CH63 . . . . 42 B6
Stables The
  Bostock Green CW10 . . . . 127 D5
  Brereton Heath CW12 . . . 155 A7
  Guilden Sutton CH3 . . . . . 119 F5
  Lawton-gate ST7 . . . . 194 C4
Stablings The SK9. . . . . 60 A5
Stadium Way WA1 . . . . 118 B3
Stadmorslow La ST7 . . . . . 195 F4
Staffin Ave CH65 . . . . 95 B8
Stafford Cl SK10 . . . . 86 F2
Stafford Gdns CH65 . . . . . . 70 B5
Stafford Rd WA4 . . . . 16 C2
Stafford St Audlem CW3 . . 230 A4
  Crewe CW1 . . . . 190 C5
Stafford Wlk SK10 . . . . 86 F2
Stage La WA13 . . . . 19 C4
Stainer Cl WA12. . . . . 2 B5
Staines Cl WA4 . . . . 26 E5
Stainforth Cl WA3 . . . . 4 D4
Stainmore Cl WA3 . . . . 10 B6
Staithes Rd M22 . . . . 33 D8
Stalbridge Dr WA7 . . . . 24 F4
Stalbridge Rd CW2 . . . . . . 190 C2
Stallard Way CW10 . . . . . . 151 C8
Stalmine Ave SK8 . . . . 34 B8
Stamford Ave CW2 . . . . . . 190 A3
STAMFORD BRIDGE 120 D4
Stamford Cl SK11 . . . . 112 C4
Stamford Ct Chester CH3 . 119 C2
  Lymm WA13 . . . . 18 F3
  Macclesfield SK11 . . . . . . 112 C5
Stamford La CH3 . . . . 120 A1
Stamford Rd
  Alderley Edge SK9 . . . . 60 B1
  Blacon CH1 . . . . 117 E6
  Handforth SK9 . . . . 34 A1
  Little Bollington WA14 . . . . 20 B2
  Macclesfield SK11 . . . . . . 112 C4
Stamford St CH65 . . . . 70 A5
Stamp Ave CW1. . . . . 190 D6
Stamp Cl CW1 . . . . 190 D6
Stanbridge Cl WA5 . . . . 15 B6
Standford Dr CW9 . . . . 104 A5
Standing Stone Rd SK11 . . 114 B3
Standinwood Rd 2 CH65 . . 70 B7
Standon Ave CW2 . . . . 190 A3
Stanford Cl 2 CW9. . . . . . 103 F5
Stanhoe Dr
  Lingley Green WA5 . . . . 14 F8
  Lingley Green WA5 . . . . 14 F8
Stanhope Ave WA5 . . . . . . 190 E3
Stanhope Cl SK9 . . . . 60 D8
Stanier Cl Crewe CW1 . . . 191 A4
  Sutton Lane Ends SK11 . . . 112 D2

Stanlaw Rd CH65 . . . . 70 C4
Stanley Ave
  Warrington WA5 . . . . 14 D7
  Warrington, Stockton Heath
    WA4 . . . . 16 F2
STANLEY BANK 1 A7
Stanley Bank Rd WA11. . . . . 1 A7
Stanley Bank Way WA11 . . . 1 A7
Stanley & Brocklehurst Ct 5
  SK10 . . . . 112 C8
Stanley Cl Hartford CW8 . . 103 A4
  Widnes WA8 . . . . 13 C2
Stanley Ct ST7 . . . . 193 C1
Stanley Dr ST5 . . . . 210 C1
Stanley Gr CW7 . . . . 79 E2
STANLEY GREEN 34 E6
Stanley Green Ind Est
  SK8 . . . . 34 E5
Stanley Green Ret Pk SK8 . 34 F6
Stanley Hall La SK12 . . . . . 38 C6
Stanley La CH62 . . . . 43 F4
Stanley Park La CH4 . . . . . 140 E5
Stanley Park Dr CH4 . . . . . 140 E5
Stanley Pl Chester CH1 . . . 237 A2
  Warrington WA4 . . . . 16 F2
Stanley Place Mews
  CH1 . . . . 237 A2
Stanley Rd Biddulph ST8 . . 179 C2
  Ellesmere Port CH65 . . . . . 70 C7
  Handforth SK8, SK9 . . . . . . 34 E6
  Knutsford WA16 . . . . 56 F2
Stanley Road Ind Est
  WA16 . . . . 57 A1
Stanley St Chester CH1 . . . 237 A2
  2 Crewe CW1 . . . . 190 C4
  7 Macclesfield SK11 . . . . 112 D8
  Newton-le-Willows WA12 . . . 2 A3
  Northwich CW9 . . . . 104 C8
  Runcorn WA7 . . . . 23 B3
  Warrington WA1 . . . . 16 B4
Stanley Villas 7 WA7 . . . . . 22 F1
STANLOW 71 B5
Stanlow Abbey Bsns Ctr
  CH65. . . . . 70 D2
Stanlow & Thornton Sta
  CH2 . . . . 71 D5
Stanmore Rd WA7 . . . . 23 D2
Stannage La CH3 . . . . 180 F5
Stanner Cl WA5 . . . . 7 D2
Stannerhouse La WA11 . . . 175 E4
Stanney Cl Bebington CH62 . .43 E3
  Neston CH64 . . . . 66 E7
Stanney La
  Ellesmere Port CH65 . . . . . 70 C3
  Stoak CH2 . . . . 70 E1
Stanneylands Cl SK9 . . . . . 34 C2
Stanneylands Dr SK9 . . . . . 34 B2
Stanneylands Rd SK9 . . . . . 34 B2
Stanney Mill Ind Est CH2 . . 70 F2
Stanney Mill La CH2 . . . . . . 70 F2
Stanney Mill Rd CH2. . . . . . 70 F2
Stanney Oaks L Ctr CH65 . . 70 D1
Stanney Ten Ind Est CH2 . . 70 F2
Stanney Woods Ave CH65 . 70 C1
Stanney Woods Nature
  Reserve ★ CH65 . . . . 70 B1
Stannybrook La
  Norley WA6 . . . . 100 F7
  Norley Bank CW8 . . . . 101 A7
Stansfield Ave WA1 . . . . . . 16 F6
Stansfield Dr WA4 . . . . 27 A4
Stanstead Ave WA5 . . . . . . 14 F3
Stanthorne Ave CW2 . . . . . 190 A3
Stanthorne Dr CW7 . . . . . . 149 D6
Stanthorne Park Mews
  CW10 . . . . 150 E6
Stanthorne Pl 9 CW10 . . . 151 D5
Stanton Cl SK9 . . . . 1 C6
Stanton Ct CH64 . . . . 66 E8
Stanton Dr CH2 . . . . 118 C3
Stanton Rd WA4 . . . . 17 D3
Stanyer Ct CW5 . . . . 205 A4
STAPELEY 219 D8
Stapeley Broad Lane CE Prim
  Sch CW5 . . . . 205 A1
Stapeley Cl CW9 . . . . 103 E4
Stapeley Ct CW1 . . . . 190 B5
Stapeley Gdns L26 . . . . 21 A6
Stapeley Terr CW5 . . . . . . 205 A4
Stapeley Water Gdns ★
  CW5 . . . . 205 A3
Stapleford Ct CH66 . . . . . . 69 F8
Stapleton Ave WA2. . . . . . . 16 D8
Stapleton Cl WA6 . . . . 74 C8
Stapleton Rd SK10 . . . . 87 B2
Stapleton Way WA8 . . . . . . 22 B5
Stapley Cl WA7 . . . . 22 F1
Starbeck Dr CH66 . . . . 69 B5
Stargrass Cl 6 CW5 . . . . . 205 B3
Starkey Gr WA4 . . . . 16 F4
Star La Lymm WA13 . . . . . . 18 C4
  Macclesfield SK11 . . . . . . 112 D4
Starling Cl
  Farndon CH3 . . . . 180 F1
  Kidsgrove ST7 . . . . 195 D3
  Runcorn WA7 . . . . 50 D7
Start La SK23 . . . . 65 B7
STATHAM 18 C4
Statham Ave Lymm WA13. . 18 D3
  Warrington WA2 . . . . 8 C1
Statham Cl WA13. . . . . 18 D3
Statham Dr WA13 . . . . 18 D3
Statham La WA13 . . . . 18 D3
Statham Prim Sch WA13 . . 18 C4
Statham St SK11 . . . . 112 D4
Station App/Lon yr Orsaf
  CH1 . . . . 116 F7

Sou−Ste 279

Station Ave
  Ellesmere Port CH66 . . . . . 69 C7
  Helsby WA6 . . . . 73 B4
Station Cl CH64 . . . . 66 F7
Station Cotts
  Mouldsworth CH3 . . . . 99 A2
  Saughall CH1 . . . . 116 F7
Station Gn CH66 . . . . 69 C7
Station Hill CW8 . . . . 76 F2
Station La
  Dunham-on-the-Hill CH3 . . . 97 D3
  Guilden Sutton CH2, CH3 . 119 F7
  Rushton Spencer SK11 . . . 159 B2
Station Rd Adderley TF9 . . 235 A5
  Alsager ST7 . . . . 193 D3
  Astbury ST7, CW12 . . . . . 178 B1
  Aston WA7 . . . . 50 B4
  Backford CH1 . . . . 95 A3
  Biddulph ST8 . . . . 179 C1
  Bosley CW12 . . . . 135 A2
  Burton CH64 . . . . 67 B1
  Calveley CW6 . . . . 169 E2
  Chelford SK11 . . . . 84 A2
  Chester CH1. . . . . 237 A3
  Crowton CW8. . . . . 76 D2
  Delamere CW8. . . . . 123 D8
  Ellesmere Port CH65 . . . . . 70 C6
  Ellesmere Port, Little Sutton
    CH66. . . . . 69 C6
  Elton CH2 . . . . 72 A5
  Furness Vale SK23 . . . . 39 D4
  Goostrey CW4 . . . . 131 A8
  Handforth SK9 . . . . 34 D3
  Haydock WA11 . . . . 1 C6
  Heswall CH60 . . . . 40 F6
  Holmes Chapel CW4. . . . . 130 C3
  Irlam WA3 . . . . 11 E7
  Kidsgrove ST7 . . . . 194 F1
  Lostock Gralam CW9 . . . . . 80 A2
  Mobberley WA16 . . . . 57 F7
  Mouldsworth CH3 . . . . 99 A2
  Mow Cop ST7 . . . . 195 C8
  Nantwich CW5 . . . . 204 E5
  Neston CH64 . . . . 66 F7
  Neston, Parkgate CH64 . . . 66 C8
  Newchapel ST7 . . . . 195 E2
  New Mills SK22 . . . . 39 B7
  Northwich CW9 . . . . 79 B1
  Partington WA14 . . . . 20 B5
  Runcorn WA7 . . . . 22 F2
  Sandbach CW11 . . . . 174 D7
  Sandycroft CH5 . . . . 116 A2
  Scholar Green ST7 . . . . . . 194 F7
  Styal SK9 . . . . 34 A4
  Warrington WA4 . . . . 16 E2
  Warrington, Fearnhead WA2 . . 9 A2
  Warrington, Great Sankey
    WA5 . . . . 14 F6
  Warrington, Penketh WA5 . . 14 A5
  Weaverham CW8 . . . . 77 A1
  Wilmslow SK9 . . . . 60 B7
  Winsford CW7 . . . . 127 A1
  Worleston CW5 . . . . 188 E6
  Wrenbury CW5 . . . . 216 F3
Station Road Ind Est WA4 . . 16 F2
Station Road N WA2 . . . . 9 A1
Station Road S WA2 . . . . 9 A1
Station St SK10 . . . . 87 D1
Station Terr WA7 . . . . 50 B4
Station View Chester CH2 . 118 F2
  Hampton Heath SY14 . . . . 213 D7
  Nantwich CW5 . . . . 204 E4
  Sandbach CW11 . . . . 174 D8
Station Yard
  Congleton CW12 . . . . 157 A1
  New Mills SK22 . . . . 39 B6
Station Yard Trad Est
  CW4 . . . . 130 D3
Staveley Dr CW7 . . . . 126 D2
Steadings Rise WA16 . . . . . 56 D6
Steadings The CH3 . . . . . . 120 A4
Steam Mill Bsns Ctr CH1 . 237 C3
Steam Mill St CH1, CH3. . . 237 C3
Stearns Cl CH1 . . . . 118 A5
Stearns Ho CH1 . . . . 118 A5
Steele Rd CW10 . . . . 151 D5
Steele St CH1 . . . . 237 B2
Steel St WA1 . . . . 16 D7
Steeple Cl CH64 . . . . 66 E7
Steeple St SK10 . . . . 87 E1
Steers Cl WA4 . . . . 17 B4
Stein Ave WA3 . . . . 3 E8
Stendall Rd CH1 . . . . 118 A3
Stenhills Cres WA7. . . . . . . 23 C2
Stephens Gdns CH66 . . . . . 69 B6
Stephen's Gr WA6. . . . . 73 B2
Stephenson Dr CW1. . . . . . 191 A4
Stephenson Rd WA12 . . . . . . 2 D2
Stephenson St
  Willaston CW5 . . . . 205 E6
  Winnington CW8 . . . . 78 D1
Stephenson Wlk CW7 . . . . 149 A8
Stephen St WA1 . . . . 16 D6
Stephens Terr CH66 . . . . . . 69 B6
Stephens Way ST7 . . . . . . 209 F2
Stepping Stone Mews
  WA8 . . . . 13 D4
Sterling Cl 1 CW9 . . . . . . 103 F5
Sterne St CW1 . . . . 174 D6
Stetchworth Rd WA4 . . . . . 16 B1
Steuber Dr M44 . . . . 11 F5
Stevenage Cl SK11 . . . . . . 112 B7
Stevenage Dr SK11 . . . . . . 112 B7
Steven Ct CH3 . . . . 237 C3
Stevensons La SY14 . . . . . 213 F7

Stevens Rd CH60 . . . . 41 C7
Stevens St SK9. . . . . 60 A1
Steventon WA7 . . . . 24 E4
Steward's Ave WA8 . . . . . .22 F8
Stewart St CW2 . . . . 190 A3
Stile End CH2 . . . . 119 F8
Stiles The CW8. . . . . 101 D5
Stiperstones Cl CH66. . . . . 69 A6
Stirling Cl Chester CH3 . . 119 A2
 Congleton CW12 . . . . 156 C3
 Macclesfield SK10 . . . . . . .86 F2
 Northwich CW8 . . . . 103 A5
 Warrington WA1 . . . . .17 E7
 Winsford CW7 . . . . 127 A3
Stirling Ct
 Ellesmere Port CH65 . . . . 70 D3
 Holmes Chapel CW4 . . . . 130 B2
Stirrup Cl WA2 . . . . .9 A3
Stirrup Field WA3 . . . . .3 A8
Stirrups Farm Rd WA3 . . . .3 C7
Stirrups Mdw WA3 . . . . . . .3 A7
STOAK 96 A2
Stoak Lodge CH65. . . . . . . 70 C4
Stobart Stad Halton (Widnes
 Vikingsfc) WA8 . . . . .22 F8
Stockdale Cres WA5. . . . . .14 E7
Stockdale Ct WA5. . . . . . . .14 E7
Stockdale Dr WA5. . . . . . . .14 E7
Stockham Cl WA7 . . . . 50 A8
Stockham La WA7 . . . . 50 C6
Stock La Shavington CW2 . 206 B3
 Shavington CW2, CW5 . . . 206 B2
Stockley Farm ★ CW9. . . . .54 E7
Stockley La WA4 . . . . .52 F7
Stockport Rd WA4 . . . . . . .17 E3
Stocks Ave 🏠 CH3 . . . . . 119 A1
Stocks Ct The WA3 . . . . . . .3 D8
Stocks Hill CW7. . . . . 149 F7
Stocks La Chester CH3. . . 119 A1
 Ollerton WA16 . . . . .82 E1
 Rainow SK10 . . . . .88 E5
 Warrington WA5 . . . . 14 D5
STOCKTON HEATH. 16 D1
Stockton Heath Prim Sch 🟧
 WA4 . . . . 16 C1
Stockton La WA4 . . . . .16 F1
Stockton Rd SK9 . . . . .59 E4
Stockton View WA4 . . . . . .16 B2
Stockwell Farm Ct WA8. . .12 E4
Stoke Abbott Cl SK7. . . . . .35 E7
Stoke Cl CH62. . . . . .43 E3
Stoke Gdns CH65. . . . . 70 C4
Stokehall La CW5 . . . . 187 E6
Stokesay Ct CH65 . . . . .70 E3
Stokes St WA3 . . . . .9 E5
Stoke Wlk CH65. . . . . 70 C4
Stoneacre Cl WA3. . . . . .3 C7
Stoneacre Gdns WA4. . . . .26 E4
Stonebank Dr CH64 . . . . . . 67 A6
Stone Bank Rd ST7 . . . . . 195 B1
Stone Barn La WA7 . . . . . . .49 F6
Stonebridge Rd CW5 . . . . 204 E3
Stone Chair La ST7. . . . . . 194 E7
Stonechat Cl
 🔟 Golborne WA3. . . . . .3 E8
 Runcorn WA7 . . . . .49 E5
Stone Cotts CW12 . . . . . . 157 E2
Stone Croft Chester CH3 . . 142 E7
 Kingsmead CW9. . . . . 103 F5
Stonecrop Cl Runcorn WA7 .49 F4
 Warrington WA3 . . . . .9 C4
Stonecrop Pl CW11. . . . . . 175 D6
Stone Cross Dr WA8. . . . . .12 E5
Stone Cross Lane N WA3. . .3 C7
Stone Cross Lane S WA3. . .3 C6
Stone Cross Pk WA3. . . . . . .3 B7
Stonegate La CW9 . . . . 54 D3
Stonehaven Dr WA2 . . . . . . .9 A3
Stone Hayes Lane Lane
 CW8. . . . . .77 F4
Stoneheads
 Whaley Bridge SK23. . . . . .39 B1
 Whaley Bridge SK23. . . . . 65 C8
 Whaley Bridge SK23. . . . . 65 C8
Stoneheads Rise SK23. . . . 65 B8
Stone Heyes La CW8, CW9 .77 F5
Stonehill Cl WA4 . . . . 26 D4
Stonehills La WA7 . . . . 23 C2
Stonehills La WA7 . . . . 23 C2
Stonehouse Gn 🟧 CW12. 156 D3
Stone House La CW6 . . . . 184 E4
Stonelea WA7 . . . . .24 B2
Stoneleigh Cl SK10 . . . . . . 87 C2
Stoneleigh Gn WA4 . . . . . . 17 D1
Stoneleigh Gdns WA4 . . . . 17 D1
Stoneley Ave CW1. . . . . . . 190 D7
STONELEY GREEN 203 D4
Stoneley Rd CW1. . . . . 190 D8
Stone Mead Ave WA15. . . 32 C7
Stone Pit La WA3. . . . . .3 F2
Stone Pl CH2 . . . . 118 F3
Stones Manor La CW8 . . . 103 C5
Stoneway Ct 🟧 CH60 . . . . .40 F8
Stoneyfold La SK11. . . . . . 113 A6
Stoneyford La CW8. . . . . . 101 C2
Stoney Holt WA7 . . . . 50 C8
Stoney La Delamere CW6 . 123 C6
 Wilmslow SK9 . . . . .59 F5
Stoneyland Dr SK22 . . . . . .39 B8
Stoney Rd SY13 . . . . 215 A8
Stonyfold La SK11 . . . . . . 135 C3
Stonyhurst Cres WA3. . . . . .4 D5
Stony La CW12 . . . . 156 C1
Stopsley Cl CW12 . . . . 155 F4

Stores Rd M90 . . . . 33 A6
Store St SK10 . . . . .88 B8
Storey St SK12 . . . . .38 E6
Stour Ct CH65. . . . . .70 B7
STOWFORD 207 C8
Stradbroke Cl WA3. . . . . . . .4 A7
Straight Length WA6 . . . . .73 E7
Straight Mile CH4 . . . . . . 162 F5
Straker Ave CH65. . . . . . . .69 F6
Stratford Gdns CH1 . . . . . 117 E4
Stratford Rd Blacon CH1 . . 117 E4
 Neston CH64 . . . . 66 D6
Stratford Sq SK8. . . . . 34 C7
Stratford Way SK11 . . . . . 112 C5
Strathaven Cl CW2. . . . . . 205 E8
Strathearn Rd CH60. . . . . .40 F7
Strathmore Cl CW4. . . . . . 130 B2
Stratton Cl WA7. . . . . .50 B6
Stratton Pk WA8 . . . . .12 F5
Stratton Rd
 Nantwich CW5 . . . . 204 C7
 Warrington WA5 . . . . .15 B5
Strawberry Cl WA3. . . . . . . .9 C4
Strawberry Dr CH66. . . . . . 95 A8
Strawberry Fields CH3 . . 142 B7
Strawberry Gn CH66. . . . . 95 A8
Strawberry La
 Acton Bridge CW8 . . . . . . .76 F3
 Mollington CH1 . . . . 94 D4
 Wilmslow SK9 . . . . .59 E6
Strawberry Pk CH66. . . . . . 95 A8
Strawberry Way E CH1. . . . .95 B8
Street Hey La CH64 . . . . . .43 B1
Street La
 Lower Whitley WA4 . . . . . 52 C3
 Rode Heath ST7 . . . . 176 F2
 Skellorn Green SK10 . . . . . 62 D8
Street The
 Mickle Trafford CH2 . . . . . 119 D8
 Whaley Bridge SK10, SK17. . 90 C5
STRETTON Farndon. 197 F6
 Warrington 26 C2
Stretton Ave WA3 . . . . .3 F1
Stretton Cl CH62. . . . . .43 E3
Stretton Gn WA3 . . . . 197 F7
Stretton Hall La SY14. . . . 198 B4
Stretton Hall Mews WA4. . .52 E8
Stretton Mill La SY14. . . . 198 B6
Stretton Rd WA4 . . . . .26 E2
Stretton Watermill ★
 SY14 . . . . 198 A7
Stretton Way 🟧 SK9. . . . . 34 D5
Stretton Wlk CW9 . . . . 103 F4
Strickland Cl WA4. . . . . . . 27 A7
Strines Rd SK6. . . . . 38 D8
Stringer Ave CW11 . . . . . . 175 C5
Stringer Cres WA4 . . . . . . .16 E4
Stringer's La LL12, CH4. . . 161 B4
Stroma Ave CH65 . . . . .95 B8
Stromford Cl WA8. . . . . 13 A6
Stromness Cl WA2 . . . . .9 B3
Stuart Cl Chester CH3 . . . 119 C3
 Winsford CW7 . . . . 149 C5
Stuart Ct SK10 . . . . .87 B2
Stuart Dr WA4 . . . . .16 F2
Stuart Pl CH1 . . . . 237 B3
Stuart Rd WA7 . . . . 24 C4
Stubbs La
 Lostock Gralam CW9. . . . . 80 A2
 Mobberley WA16 . . . . .58 E4
Stubbs Pl CH1 . . . . 117 E3
Stubbs Terr 🔷 SK11 . . . . . 112 E7
Stubby La SK10 . . . . .84 E2
STUD GREEN. 152 C1
Stud Green Ind Pk CW11. 152 C1
Stud La Churton CH3. . . . . 180 F6
 Rowlevhill CH3. . . . . 181 A6
Sturgess St WA12 . . . . .1 F3
STYAL 33 F4
Styal Cl 🟧 CW9 . . . . 103 F4
Styal Cross SK9. . . . . 33 E3
Styal Ctry Pk ★ SK9 . . . . . 33 E3
Styal Gn SK9 . . . . 33 F3
STYAL GREEN 34 A3
Styal Prim Sch SK9. . . . . . 33 E4
Styal Rd Wilmslow SK9. . . .60 B8
 Wythenshawe M22. . . . . . . 34 A5
Styal Sta SK9. . . . . 34 A4
Styal View SK9. . . . . .34 B2
Styperson Way SK12 . . . . .36 E3
Such Pit La WA6 . . . . .74 E5
Sudbrook Cl WA3 . . . . .3 E8
Sudbury Dr SK8 . . . . 34 C8
Sudbury Rd SK7. . . . . 36 E8
Sudlow La
 Knutsford WA16. . . . . 56 D1
 Plumley WA16 . . . . 81 C7
Suez St
 Newton-le-Willows WA12. . .2 B3
 Warrington WA1 . . . . .16 B5
Suffolk Ave CH65. . . . . . . .69 F5
Suffolk Cl
 Congleton CW12 . . . . 156 D4
 Macclesfield SK10 . . . . . . .86 F1
 Warrington WA1 . . . . .17 E6
Suffolk Dr SK9 . . . . 34 C1
Suffolk Ho 🟧 CH1. . . . . . 237 C3
Suffolk Pl WA8. . . . . 22 C7
Suffolk St WA7. . . . . 22 F3
Sugar La Bollington SK10. . . 63 A3
 Frodsham WA6. . . . . 99 A5
 Manley WA6. . . . . .98 E5
 Rainow SK10 . . . . .88 D5
Sugar Pit La WA16 . . . . . . .56 E3
Sugar St SK11. . . . . 159 C2
Sulby Ave WA4. . . . . .16 B3
Sulgrave Ave SK12 . . . . . . .36 F4
Sullivan Rd WA7. . . . . 23 D7

Summer Cl
 Ellesmere Port CH65 . . . . . 70 A5
 🟧 Runcorn WA7 . . . . .23 F1
Summercroft WA3. . . . . .3 A7
Summer Dr CW11 . . . . 175 C6
Summerfield ST7 . . . . 195 B1
Summerfield Ave WA5 . . . . .7 F2
Summerfield Cl CH4. . . . . 139 A3
Summerfield Dr CW9. . . . . 126 F8
Summerfield Ho CH3. . . . . 119 F5
Summerfield Pl SK9. . . . . . 60 A5
Summerfield Rd
 Guilden Sutton CH3 . . . . . 119 F5
 Mobberley WA16. . . . . .57 F4
Summerlea WA16 . . . . 57 C3
Summerlea Cl SK10 . . . . . . 87 D1
Summers Cl WA16 . . . . 82 A7
Summers Way WA16 . . . . . 82 A7
Summertrees Rd CH66. . . .69 E3
Summerville Gdns WA4 . . . .16 F1
Summerville Wlk 🟧 WA5 . 15 C7
Summit Cl WA4 . . . . 26 E1
Sumner Rd CH1. . . . . 117 E4
Sumner St WA11 . . . . .1 A6
Sumpter Pathway CH2. . . 118 F3
Sunart Cl CW2 . . . . 206 B6
Sunbank La WA15. . . . . . . .32 E6
Sunbeam Cl WA7 . . . . .22 F3
Sunbeam St WA12 . . . . .2 C3
Sunbury Cl SK9 . . . . 34 E2
Sunbury Cres 🟧 CH4 . . . . 140 F6
Sunbury Gdns WA4. . . . . . .26 E7
Suncroft Cl WA1 . . . . .17 E7
Suncroft Rd CH60 . . . . 41 C7
Sundale Dr CW2 . . . . 189 D4
Sunderland St SK11 . . . . . 112 D7
Sundew Rd CW5 . . . . 206 B3
Sundial Ho WA3. . . . . .4 F3
Sundown Cl SK22 . . . . 39 A8
Sunfield Cl CH66 . . . . 69 D3
Sunflower Cl WA9. . . . . .6 A7
Sunningdale Ave WA8 . . . . 12 B1
Sunningdale Cl
 Burtonwood WA5 . . . . .6 F6
 Northwich CW9 . . . . 104 E7
 Winsford CW7 . . . . 126 A2
Sunningdale Dr
 Bebington CH63 . . . . .43 B6
 Bramhall SK7 . . . . 36 A7
Sunningdale Rd
 Cheadle SK8. . . . . 35 A7
 Macclesfield SK11 . . . . . . 112 A6
Sunningdale Way CH64 . . .66 E4
Sunninghey Ct SK9. . . . . . .59 F2
Sunnybank WA5 . . . . .60 B6
Sunny Bank SK11 . . . . 112 D5
Sunnybank Cl WA12 . . . . . .2 C4
Sunny Bank Cl SK11 . . . . . 112 D5
Sunny Bank Cotts
 Ashton Hayes CH3 . . . . . . 121 E7
 Warrington WA8 . . . . 14 A4
Sunnybank Dr SK9. . . . . . . 60 A6
Sunnybank Rd CW1, CW2. 189 E5
Sunny Bank Rd WA14. . . . 31 C8
Sunny Lea Mews SK9. . . . . 60 A6
Sunnymill Dr CW11. . . . . . 175 A6
Sunnyside Alsager ST7 . . . 193 A4
 🟧 Ellesmere Port CH65. . . 70 C6
 Malpas SY14 . . . . 212 F2
 Warrington WA5 . . . . .14 E6
Sunnyside La WA7 . . . . .24 E4
Sunnyside Wlk CW11 . . . . 154 B1
Sunset Bsns Ctr WA8 . . . . 23 A5
Sunset Bvd WA5 . . . . .15 B6
Sunset Cotts CH64 . . . . . . 67 A4
Surrey Dr CW7. . . . . 156 C5
Surrey St Crewe CW1. . . . 190 E4
 🟧 Runcorn WA7 . . . . 23 A2
 Warrington WA4 . . . . 16 D3
Surridge WA16. . . . . 29 C5
Susan Dr WA5. . . . . 14 D5
Susan St WA8. . . . . 13 C2
Sussex Ave SK11 . . . . 112 A5
Sussex Dr ST7 . . . . 194 F2
Sussex Pl CW12 . . . . 156 E5
Sussex Rd Chester CH2 . . 118 F4
 Irlam M44 . . . . 11 C6
 Partington M31 . . . . .11 E2
Sussex St WA8. . . . . 13 D1
Sussex Way CH2 . . . . 118 F4
Sutch La WA13. . . . . 19 A3
Sutherland Ct 🟧 WA7. . . .23 B2
Sutherland Dr
 Bebington CH62 . . . . 43 D4
 Macclesfield SK10 . . . . . . .87 A1
Sutherland Way CH3 . . . . 119 B3
Sutton Ave Culcheth WA3 . . .4 F4
 Neston CH64 . . . . 66 E6
Sutton Cl Bebington CH62 . .43 E3
 Higher Wincham CW9 . . . . . 79 F6
 Macclesfield SK11 . . . . . . 112 D5
 Mickle Trafford CH2 . . . . . 119 F8
 Nantwich CW5 . . . . 204 C5
Sutton Cswy WA6, WA7. . . .49 C2
Sutton Field CW8 . . . . 126 A1
SUTTON GREEN 69 C3

Sutton Green Prim Sch
 CH66. . . . . 69 C5
Sutton Hall Dr CH66. . . . . 69 A6
Sutton Hall Gdns CH66 . . 69 A6
SUTTON LANE ENDS 112 E2
Sutton Quays Bsns Pk
 WA7. . . . . .49 E3
Sutton Rd
 Alderley Edge SK9 . . . . .59 F2
 Poynton SK12. . . . . 37 A2
Sutton's La 🟧 WA4. . . . . . .23 B7
Sutton St Runcorn WA7 . . .23 B2
 Warrington WA1 . . . . 16 C4
Sutton Way
 🔷 Ellesmere Port CH65. . .69 F4
 🔷 Handforth SK9. . . . . . . .34 E5
SUTTON WEAVER 50 B3
Swain Cl WA7. . . . . 49 C8
Swain Dr 🟧 CW11 . . . . . . 191 F8
Swale Cl SK9 . . . . .34 E2
Swaledale Ave CW12 . . . . 157 A5
Swaledale Cl
 Bebington CH62 . . . . .43 E5
 Warrington WA5 . . . . .14 F7
Swale Rd CH65 . . . . 70 A7
Swallow Cl
 🔷 Kelsall WA6 . . . . 122 D5
 Sandbach CW11. . . . . 175 A8
 Warrington WA3 . . . . .9 F4
Swallow Ct Handforth SK9. . .34 B1
 Winsford CW7 . . . . 149 D5
Swallow Dr Alsager ST7 . . 193 B3
 Kelsall CW6 . . . . 122 D5
 Sandbach CW11. . . . . 175 A8
Swallowfield Cl CW2 . . . . 206 A8
Swallowfield Gdns WA4 . . .26 F5
Swallowfields CH3 . . . . . . 188 D2
Swallowmoor View ST7 . . 210 C8
Swallow Rd ST7 . . . . 195 F1
Swanage Cl WA4 . . . . .16 C7
Swanage Ct
 Winsford CW7 . . . . 149 D5
 🟧 Winsford CW7 . . . . 149 D6
Swan Ave WA9. . . . . .1 A2
SWANBACH 229 C1
Swanbach Mill La CW3 . . 229 E2
Swan Bank
 Congleton CW12 . . . . 156 D2
 Talke ST7 . . . . 210 D8
Swan Cl
 Ellesmere Port, Great Sutton
 CH66. . . . . 69 D2
 Poynton SK12. . . . . .36 B4
 Talke ST7 . . . . 210 D8
Swan Ct Bunbury CW6 . . . 185 E8
 Crowton CW8. . . . . 101 E7
Swan Farm La CW3. . . . . . 232 B1
Swan Gr WA16 . . . . 106 D7
Swan Ho ST7 . . . . 210 D7
Swan La Bunbury CW6 . . . 185 E8
 Cheadle SK8. . . . . .35 B8
SWANLEY 203 C5
Swanley La CW5 . . . . 203 D4
Swanlow Ave CW7 . . . . . . 149 D5
Swanlow Dr CW7. . . . . 149 D6
Swanlow La CW7 . . . . 149 E5
Swan Rd WA12. . . . . .1 E4
Swanscoe Ave SK10 . . . . . 88 A7
Swanscoe Cl CW10 . . . . . . 151 B8
Swanscoe La SK10 . . . . . . .88 B3
Swan St Congleton CW12 . 156 D2
 Wilmslow SK9 . . . . .60 B7
Swanwick Cl WA4 . . . . 107 C1
Swanwick Gn SY13 . . . . . . 215 C5
SWANWICK GREEN 215 C4
Swanwick Ho SK11 . . . . . . .86 F6
Sweet Briar Cres CW2 . . . 189 F3
Sweet Briar Ct CW2 . . . . . 156 B1
Sweet Brier Cl CW8 . . . . . .78 B4
Sweet Field Cl CW2 . . . . . 190 B2
Sweetfield Gdns CH66. . . . 69 D7
Sweetfield Rd CH66 . . . . . . 69 D7
Sweettooth La CW11 . . . . . 175 A7
Sweet Water Ct 🟧 CW9. . . 80 A2
SWETTENHAM 131 E3
Swettenham Cl
 Alsager ST7 . . . . 193 C3
 Sandbach CW11. . . . . 175 D7
SWETTENHAM HEATH. . . 132 B3
Swettenham Heath La
 CW12. . . . . 132 B4
Swettenham La CW12 . . . 131 E3
Swettenham Rd
 🔷 Handforth SK9 . . . . 34 D5
 Swettenham CW12. . . . . . 132 B2
Swettenham St SK11 . . . . 112 E7
Swift Cl Kidsgrove ST7 . . . 195 B2
 Warrington WA2 . . . . .8 E3
 Wistaston CW2 . . . . 205 F8
Swinburne Dr CW1 . . . . . . 190 F4
Swindale Ave WA2 . . . . .8 B3
Swinden Cl WA7 . . . . 24 D2
Swine Market 🔷 CW5 . . . 204 E5
Swineyard La WA16 . . . . . 28 C4
Swinfen Lake WA5 . . . . . . .14 E8
Swinford Ave WA8 . . . . . . .13 C2
Swinhoe Pl WA3 . . . . .4 D3
Swinley Chase SK9 . . . . . . 34 F1
Swinley Forest Dr WA4 . . .26 E2
Swinleys Hey CH3 . . . . . . 142 A7
Swinnerton St CW2 . . . . . 190 C2
Swinton Sq 🔷 WA16. . . . . 57 A2
Swireford Rd WA6 . . . . 73 D2
Swiss Cott
 Alderley Edge SK9 . . . . . . 60 C1
 Macclesfield SK10 . . . . . . .87 B2

Swiss Hill SK9. . . . . .60 B1
Swithin Rd M22. . . . . .33 D8
Sword St CH3. . . . . 142 C5
SWORTON HEATH 28 E5
Swynnerton Way WA3. . . . 4 B5
Swythamley Pk SK11 . . . . 160 B4
Sycamore Ave
 Alsager ST7 . . . . 193 E2
 Congleton CW12 . . . . 155 F4
 Crewe CW1 . . . . 190 D6
 Haydock WA11. . . . . .1 A5
 Newton-le-Willows WA12 . . .2 C3
 Rode Heath ST7 . . . . 193 F7
 Widnes WA8. . . . . .13 B2
 Winsford CW7 . . . . 149 D8
Sycamore Cl
 Audlem CW3 . . . . 230 A4
 Biddulph ST8 . . . . 179 E2
 Handforth SK9. . . . . .34 B2
 Holmes Chapel CW4 . . . . 130 C3
 Nantwich CW5 . . . . 204 F7
 Talke ST7 . . . . 210 E8
Sycamore Cres
 Barnton CW8 . . . . .78 B4
 Hollinfare WA3. . . . . .11 B2
 Macclesfield SK11 . . . . . . 112 A7
Sycamore Ct WA7. . . . . . . 24 D5
Sycamore Dr Aston WA7. . .50 B4
 Chester CH4. . . . . 140 F5
 Ellesmere Port CH66 . . . . . 70 A1
 Lymm WA13 . . . . .18 D4
 Middlewich CW10 . . . . . . 151 C6
Sycamore Gr
 Broughton CH4. . . . . 139 C3
 Sandbach CW11. . . . . 175 A8
Sycamore La WA5. . . . . . . .15 B6
Sycamore Lane Com Prim
 Sch WA5 . . . . 15 B5
Sycamore Lo SK7. . . . . . . .35 F7
Sycamore Rd
 Paddockhill WA16 . . . . . . .59 B5
 Partington M31 . . . . .11 E3
 Runcorn WA7 . . . . 49 D8
Sycamore Rise SK11. . . . . 112 B6
Sycamores The WA16 . . . . 58 E2
Syddal Cl SK7. . . . . 35 D5
Syddal Cres SK7 . . . . 35 D4
Syddal Gn SK7. . . . . 35 D5
Syddall Ave SK8. . . . . 34 D8
Syddall Rd SK7 . . . . 35 D5
SYDNEY 191 A5
Sydney Ave M90 . . . . 33 A8
Sydney Newton Rd 🔷
 CW11. . . . . 192 A7
Sydney Rd Bramhall SK7. . .35 F5
 Chester CH1. . . . . 118 B3
 Crewe CW1 . . . . 190 F6
Sydney St Northwich CW8 . 103 C7
 Runcorn WA7 . . . . 48 D7
Syers Ct WA1 . . . . .16 E8
Sylvan Ave SK9 . . . . 59 F5
Sylvan Cl CW8 . . . . 103 C7
Sylvan Mews CH1 . . . . 117 E6
Sylvia Cres WA2 . . . . .8 D1
Symmonds Cl 🔷 SK9 . . . . .60 E7
Symondley Rd SK11 . . . . . 112 F2
Synge St WA2. . . . . 16 C7
Sytch Croft CH64 . . . . .66 E8

T

Tabley Ave WA8. . . . . 12 D4
Tabley Cl Knutsford WA16 . . 56 E3
 Macclesfield SK10 . . . . . . 112 A8
 Sandbach CW11. . . . . 174 E7
Tabley Ct WA16 . . . . 56 B4
Tabley Gr WA16. . . . . 56 E1
Tabley Hill La WA16. . . . . . 56 B2
Tabley House ★ WA16 . . . .81 B8
Tabley La
 Botany Bay Wood WA16 . . .81 A8
 Tabley Hill WA16. . . . . 56 A1
Tabley Rd Crewe CW2 . . . 189 E3
 Handforth SK9. . . . . 34 D5
 Knutsford WA16. . . . . 56 D5
Tabley St WA9 . . . . 79 A1
Tabley Stables WA16. . . . . 81 A8
Tabor St SK11. . . . . 112 E6
Tailors View CW5 . . . . 204 E6
Talbot Ave CH64 . . . . 66 F6
Talbot Cl Neston CH64. . . . 66 F6
 Shavington CW2. . . . . 206 B4
 Warrington WA3 . . . . .9 E3
Talbot Gdns CH64 . . . . 66 F6
Talbot Rd
 Alderley Edge SK9 . . . . . . .60 B1
 Dunham-on-the-Hill WA6. . .97 E2
 Ellesmere Port CH66 . . . . .69 F3
Talbot St Chester CH1 . . . 237 B4
 Golborne WA3 . . . . .3 A8
Talbot Way CW5 . . . . 205 A3
Talfryn Cl CH5 . . . . 91 D1
Talisman Cl WA7. . . . . 50 D7
TALKE 210 C7
Talke Rd Alsager ST7 . . . . 193 E3
 High Carr ST5. . . . . 210 F2
 Newcastle-under-Lyme ST7,
 ST5 . . . . 210 D4
TALLARN GREEN/TALLWRN
 GREEN 222 E5
Tall Ash Ave CW12 . . . . . . 157 A4
Tall Chimneys CW11. . . . . 175 D4
Tall Trees Cl CW8 . . . . 103 C6
Tally Ho La CW5 . . . . 203 E3
Tamar Cl Congleton CW12 . 156 F1
 Macclesfield SK10 . . . . . . .86 E1
Tamar Rd Haydock WA11. . . .1 C6

Tamar Rd continued
Kidsgrove ST7 . . . . 195 B2
Tamar Wlk CW7 . . . . 127 A2
Tame Cl Biddulph ST8 . . 179 D1
Sandbach CW11 . . . . . . 174 E8
Tame Ct WA8 . . . . 13 A6
Tame Wlk 8 SK9 . . . . . . 34 D2
Tamworth Cl SK7 . . . . . . 36 D8
Tamworth St WA12 . . . . . .2 A3
Tanhouse WA7 . . . . 23 E1
Tanhouse Ind Est WA8 . . 23 C7
Tanhouse La WA8 . . . . . 23 D7
Tan House La
Burtonwood WA5 . . . . .7 A5
Widnes WA8 . . . . 23 D8
Tankersley Gr WA5 . . . . . 15 B6
Tanners La WA2 . . . . 16 A6
Tanner's La WA3 . . . . .3 B8
Tanner St CW12 . . . . . . 156 E2
Tanners Way CW5 . . . . . 204 E4
Tannery La Neston CH64 . .66 E8
Warrington WA5 . . . . 14 D3
Tanning Court Ind Est
WA1 . . . . 16 C4
Tanning Ct 3 WA1 . . . . . 16 C5
Tanyard Cl SK9 . . . . 60 E7
Tanyard Dr WA15 . . . . . . 32 C6
Tanyard La WA15 . . . . . . 32 A5
Tapley Ave SK12 . . . . . . 36 E2
Taplow Cl WA4 . . . . 26 E6
Target Cl ST7 . . . . 210 E6
Target Life Sports Ctr
SK8 . . . . 35 B7
Target Rd CH60 . . . . 40 C8
Tarmalane Rd CW1 . . . . 190 D7
Tarnbeck WA7 . . . . 50 D8
Tarn Cl CW7 . . . . 126 C3
Tarn Ct WA1 . . . . 17 F7
Tarn Mount SK11 . . . . . 112 A5
Tarnway WA3 . . . . .3 F7
Taro Cl CW5 . . . . 205 A3
TARPORLEY 146 C1
Tarporley Bsns Ctr CW6 . 168 C8
Tarporley By-Pass
Tarporley CW6 . . . . 146 B2
Tarporley CW6 . . . . 168 D7
Tarporley CE Prim Sch
CW6 . . . . 146 D2
Tarporley Com High Sch 2
CW6 . . . . 146 D1
Tarporley Rd Duddon CH3 . 144 E7
Ellesmere Port CH66 . . . . .69 E4
Little Budworth CW6, CW8 . 124 C5
Lower Whitley WA4 . . . . . 52 C4
Tarvin CW6 . . . . 121 C1
Utkinton CW6 . . . . 146 E6
Whitchurch SY13 . . . . . 225 F3
Tarporley War Memorial
Hospl CW6 . . . . 146 D2
Tarrant Ct CH1 . . . . 94 F1
TARVIN 121 C3
Tarvin Ave CW2 . . . . . . 189 D4
Tarvin Bridge CH3 . . . . . 119 A2
Tarvin By-Pass CH3 . . . . 121 B1
Tarvin Cl
Ellesmere Port CH65 . . . . 70 C4
Golborne WA3 . . . . .3 E7
Macclesfield SK11 . . . . . 112 E5
1 Middlewich CW10 . . . 151 D5
Middlewich CW10 . . . . . 151 D5
Northwich CW9 . . . . 103 F5
Runcorn WA7 . . . . 49 C6
Tarvin Prim Sch CH3 . . . 121 B1
Tarvin Rd Alvanley WA6 . .73 F4
Bebington CH62 . . . . 43 F3
Chester, Boughton CH3 . . 119 A2
Chester, Vicarscross CH3 . 119 C2
Christleton CH3 . . . . 120 C3
Manley WA6 . . . . 99 A4
Tarvin Rdbt CH3 . . . . . . 121 A2
TARVIN SANDS 121 C4
Tarvin Sands Industries
CH3 . . . . 121 B4
Tarvin Way
1 Handforth SK9 . . . . . . 34 D5
Winsford CW7 . . . . 126 C2
Tasman Cl WA5 . . . . 15 C8
Tate Cl WA8 . . . . 12 D2
Tate Dr CW1 . . . . 191 C4
TATTENHALL 166 B1
Tattenhall La
Beeston CW6 . . . . 167 F2
Tattenhall CH3 . . . . 167 B3
Tattenhall Park Prim Sch
CH3 . . . . 166 B2
Tattenhall Rd CH3 . . . . . 166 C4
Tatton Cl Alsager ST7 . . 193 C4
Chester CH4 . . . . 140 E5
Northwich CW9 . . . . 103 F4
Winsford CW7 . . . . 126 C1
Tatton Ct 4 Handforth SK9 . 34 E5
2 Knutsford WA16 . . . . . 57 A2
Warrington WA1 . . . . .9 D1
TATTON DALE 30 E1
Tatton Dr CW11 . . . . . . 175 C7
Tatton Lodge 17 WA16 . . 57 A2
Tatton Park ✳ WA16 . . . 56 F7
Tatton Rd Crewe CW2 . . 189 D2
Handforth SK9 . . . . 34 E5
Tatton St WA16 . . . . 57 A2
Tatton Stile WA16 . . . . . 58 A4
Taurus Pk WA5 . . . . .7 D3
Tavener Cl CH63 . . . . . . 43 C5
Tavistock Rd WA5 . . . . . .14 E4
Tavlin Ave WA5 . . . . .7 F1
Tawney Cl ST7 . . . . 195 B2
Tawny Ct WA7 . . . . 49 E7

TAXAL 65 D4
Taxal and Fernilee CE Prim
Sch SK23 . . . . 65 D6
Taxal Moor Rd SK23 . . . . 65 C3
Taxi Rd M90 . . . . 33 B7
Taxmere Cl CW11 . . . . . 174 F7
Tay Cl ST8 . . . . 179 E1
Taylor Bsns Pk WA3 . . . . .4 F1
Taylor Cl CW66 . . . . 69 B5
Taylor Dr CW5 . . . . 204 C5
Taylor Ind Est WA3 . . . . . .4 F1
Taylor Rd Altrincham WA14 . 20 F5
Haydock WA11 . . . . .1 F7
Wistaston Green CW2 . . 189 D2
Taylor's La
Oakhanger CW1 . . . . . . 192 C3
Warrington WA5 . . . . 14 A2
Taylors Row WA7 . . . . . . 23 C2
Taylor St Warrington WA4 . 16 A1
Widnes WA8 . . . . 13 C1
Taylor Way 9 SK9 . . . . . 60 E8
Teal Ave Knutsford WA16 . .57 B2
Poynton SK12 . . . . 36 A4
Tealby Cl CW9 . . . . 104 B8
Teal Cl Warrington WA2 . . .8 E3
Winsford CW7 . . . . 149 D5
Teal Dr CW11 . . . . 174 C6
Teal Gr WA3 . . . . .9 F3
Teals Way CH60 . . . . 40 E8
Teal Way CW2 . . . . 189 E1
Tebay Rd CH62 . . . . 43 E8
Tebay Ret Pk CH62 . . . . . 43 E8
Technology Ctr The CH65 . 70 B7
Tedder Dr M22 . . . . 33 F7
Tedder Sq WA8 . . . . 22 D8
Teddington Cl WA4 . . . . . 26 E5
Teddy Gray Ave 15
CW11 . . . . 174 C7
Tees Ct CH65 . . . . 70 A7
Teesdale Cl WA8 . . . . . . 14 F7
Teesdale Rd WA11 . . . . . .1 C7
Tegg's Nose Ctry Pk✳
SK11 . . . . 113 D6
Teggsnose La SK11 . . . . 113 C6
Tegid Way CH4 . . . . 140 D5
Tegsnose Mount SK11 . . 113 C4
Telegraph Rd CH60 . . . . . 41 A7
Telegraph Way WA6 . . . . 73 A2
Telfer Ct CW10 . . . . 151 E6
Telford Cl
Congleton CW12 . . . . . . 157 B2
Macclesfield SK10 . . . . . 88 A1
Talke ST7 . . . . 210 E8
Warrington WA4 . . . . 17 A3
Widnes WA8 . . . . 12 D4
Telford Gdns CW11 . . . . 174 F7
Telford Ho ST7 . . . . 195 B3
Telford Pl CW5 . . . . 204 C5
Telford Rd
Ellesmere Port CH65 . . . . 70 E4
Winnington CW8 . . . . . . 78 C1
Telford's Quay CH65 . . . . 70 D7
Telford Way Audlem CW3 . 230 A3
Chester CH4 . . . . 140 F6
Middlewich CW10 . . . . . 128 E1
Tempest Rd SK9 . . . . 60 C1
Templar Ct SK10 . . . . . . 87 A1
Temple Chambers CH1 . . 237 B3
Temple Ct WA3 . . . . .9 E6
Templeton Dr WA2 . . . . . .9 A3
Tempsford Cl WA7 . . . . . .24 E3
Tenbury Cl WA5 . . . . 15 A8
Tenby Cl WA5 . . . . .7 F2
Tenby Dr WA7 . . . . 23 D2
Tenby Rd SK11 . . . . 111 F6
Tenchersfield CW5 . . . . . 205 A4
Tennyson Ave CW1 . . . . 190 F4
Tennyson Cl Crewe CW2 . 190 A1
Macclesfield SK11 . . . . . 111 E6
Northwich CW9 . . . . 104 C6
Rode Heath ST7 . . . . . . 193 E8
Tennyson Dr WA2 . . . . . .8 C2
Tennyson Rd
Ellesmere Port CH65 . . . . 70 A4
Widnes WA8 . . . . 13 A1
Tennyson Wlk CH1 . . . . 118 A5
Tensing Cl WA5 . . . . .15 B8
Tenth Ave CH5 . . . . 92 D3
Terence Ave WA3 . . . . . . .16 F6
Terminal Road E M90 . . . 33 C7
Terminal Road N M90 . . . 33 B7
Terminal Road S M90 . . . 33 B7
Tern Ave ST7 . . . . 195 C2
Tern Cl WA8 . . . . 13 B4
Tern Dr SK12 . . . . 36 B4
Terrace Rd WA8 . . . . 23 A5
Terra Nova Sch CW4 . . . 108 D1
Terrick Mews SY13 . . . . 226 B2
Terrick Rd SY13 . . . . . . 226 A2
Tetchill Cl
Ellesmere Port CH66 . . . . 69 D2
Runcorn WA7 . . . . 50 D8
Tetton Cl 8 CW12 . . . . . 156 F3
Tetton La CW10 . . . . . . 151 E3
Tewkesbury Cl
Cheadle SK8 . . . . 35 B6
Chester CH2 . . . . 118 F7
Ellesmere Port CH66 . . . . 94 E8
Middlewich CW10 . . . . . 128 B1
Poynton SK12 . . . . 36 D4
Tewkesbury Dr SK10 . . . .87 E4
Tewkesbury Rd WA3 . . . . .3 B8
Thackeray Dr CH3 . . . . . 119 C3
Thackeray Twrs 2 CH1 . . 237 C3
Thackery Ct 6 CW11 . . . 174 D6
Thalia Ave CW5 . . . . 205 B3
Thames Cl
Congleton CW12 . . . . . . 156 F1

Thames Cl continued
Warrington WA2 . . . . .8 D2
Thamesdale CH65 . . . . . .70 B4
Thames Dr ST8 . . . . 179 D1
Thames Gdns CH65 . . . . .70 B3
Thames Pl CW7 . . . . 127 B1
Thames Rd WA3 . . . . .5 A2
Thames Side CH65 . . . . . 70 B3
Thames Trad Ctr M44 . . . 11 F7
Thatchers Mount WA5 . . . .1 D1
Thaxted Wlk M22 . . . . . . 33 C8
Theatre Ct CW9 . . . . . . 103 F8
THELWALL 17 E3
Thelwall Com Jun Sch
WA4 . . . . 17 D3
Thelwall Inf Sch WA4 . . . 17 C3
Thelwall La WA4 . . . . . . .17 B3
Thelwall New Rd WA4 . . . 17 C3
Thelwall New Rd Ind Est
WA4 . . . . 17 C3
Thelwall Rd CH66 . . . . . .69 E4
Thetford Cl SK10 . . . . . . 87 C3
Thetford Rd WA5 . . . . . . .14 E6
Thewlis St WA5 . . . . 15 E5
Thingwall Rd CH60 . . . . . 40 E7
Third Ave
Connah's Quay CH5 . . . . .92 F1
Crewe CW1 . . . . 190 F1
Kidsgrove ST7 . . . . 194 F1
Poynton SK12 . . . . 36 D1
Runcorn WA7 . . . . 49 F8
Sandbach CW11 . . . . . . 175 A5
Thirlmere St5 . . . . 111 F5
Thirlmere Ave WA2 . . . . . .8 C2
Thirlmere Cl
Alderley Edge SK9 . . . . . .59 F1
Frodsham WA6 . . . . 49 D1
Holmes Chapel CW4 . . . 130 A3
Winsford CW7 . . . . 126 F3
Thirlmere Ct CW12 . . . . 156 A2
Thirlmere Dr WA13 . . . . .18 F3
Thirlmere Lodge 5 WA13 .18 E3
Thirlmere Rd
Chester CH2 . . . . 119 A5
Crewe CW2 . . . . 190 A2
Ellesmere Port CH65 . . . . 70 C2
Neston CH64 . . . . 66 E6
Partington M31 . . . . 11 E4
Thirlmere Way WA8 . . . . 22 C8
Thirsk Cl WA7 . . . . 49 C6
Thirsk Way SK10 . . . . . . 87 C3
Thistle Cl Kelsall CW6 . . 122 C4
Pickmere WA16 . . . . .79 F7
Thistle Sq M31 . . . . 11 E2
Thistleton Cl SK11 . . . . . 112 D6
Thistle Way CW12 . . . . . 155 F2
Thistle Wlk 4 M31 . . . . . 11 E2
Thistlewood Dr SK9 . . . . .60 D8
Thomas Ave CW5 . . . . . 205 A3
Thomas Brassey Cl CH2 . 237 C4
Thomas Cl Alsager ST7 . . 193 E4
Blacon CH1 . . . . 117 F6
Ellesmere Port CH65 . . . . 70 B2
Mickle Trafford CH2 . . . . 119 F8
Thomas Ct WA7 . . . . .49 F7
Thomas Fairfax Way
Nantwich CW5 . . . . 204 C7
Nantwich CW5 . . . . 204 C7
Thomas Ho CH1 . . . . . . 118 A5
Thomas Hodges Ct CW4 . 130 D3
Thomas Jones Way WA7 . 23 A2
Thomasons Bridge La
WA4 . . . . 25 E6
Thomas Row 8 CW5 . . . 204 E6
Thomas St Biddulph ST8 . 179 D1
Congleton CW12 . . . . . . 156 E3
Crewe CW1 . . . . 190 D4
Golborne WA3 . . . . .3 A8
Packmoor ST7 . . . . 195 F1
Runcorn WA7 . . . . 23 B3
Talke ST7 . . . . 210 D8
2 Widnes WA8 . . . . 23 A7
Thomas Wedge Rd CH1 . .94 A2
Thompson Ave WA3 . . . . .4 E3
Thompson Cl WA12 . . . . .2 C1
Thompson Farm Mdw 6
WA3 . . . . .3 C7
Thompson Gn 9 CW8 . . . 101 F4
Thomson Gdns CW12 . . . 156 A3
Thomson St WA3 . . . . . . .9 E5
Thoresway Rd SK9 . . . . . .59 F5
Thorlby Rd WA3 . . . . .9 F3
Thorley Gr CW2 . . . . . . 190 A1
Thorley La M90 . . . . .33 A8
Thorley Mews SK7 . . . . . .35 F7
Thornberry Cl CW1 . . . . 117 B8
Thornbrook Way CW11 . . 174 D5
Thornbury Ave WA3 . . . . .3 E7
Thorn Cl Runcorn WA7 . . . 49 C7
Warrington WA5 . . . . 14 F3
Thorn Dr M22 . . . . 34 A8
Thorne Cl SK10 . . . . 87 A5
Thorne Dr CH66 . . . . .69 B4
Thorneycroft Dr WA1 . . . . 16 C6
Thorneycroft Way CW1 . . 190 F6
Thorney Dr SK8 . . . . 35 C6
Thorneyholme Dr WA16 . .57 B2
Thornfield SK9 . . . . 60 A4
Thornfield Cl WA3 . . . . . .3 C8
Thornfield Hey SK9 . . . . .60 E8
Thornfields CW1 . . . . . . 173 B1
Thorn Gr SK8 . . . . 35 A7
Thorngrove Dr SK9 . . . . . 60 C6
Thorngrove Hill SK9 . . . . 60 C6
Thorn Grove Prim Sch
SK8 . . . . 35 A7
Thorngrove Rd SK9 . . . . . 60 C6
Thornhills WA8 . . . . .12 A3

Thorn Ho CH4. . . . . 141 A5
Thorn La CH8. . . . . 103 C5
Thornleigh Ave CH62 . . . .43 F3
Thornleigh Dr CH66 . . . . .69 E6
Thornley Cl 1 WA13 . . . . 18 C3
Thornley Rd WA13 . . . . . 18 C3
Thorn Rd Bramhall SK7 . . 35 E5
Runcorn WA7 . . . . 49 C7
Warrington WA1 . . . . 17 A8
THORNS GREEN 32 C5
Thornsgreen Rd M22 . . . . 33 D8
Thornton WA8 . . . . 22 E8
Thornton Ave SK11 . . . . 112 A5
Thornton Bank CW6 . . . . 169 D4
Thornton Cl CW7 . . . . . . 127 A3
Thornton Common Rd
CH63 . . . . 42 D7
Thornton Cres CH60 . . . . .41 B6
Thorntondale Dr WA5 . . . 14 F7
Thornton Dr Chester CH2 . 118 D5
Handforth SK9 . . . . 34 D3
1 Newton-le-Willows WA12 . .1 F2
Wistaston CW2 . . . . 206 A7
Thornton Green La CH2. . .71 E1
Thornton Ho
Audlem CW3 . . . . 230 A5
Thornton Hough CH63 . . . 42 B6
THORNTON HOUGH 42 A7
Thornton Hough Prim Sch
CH63. . . . . .42 B7
THORNTON-LE-MOORS . . 71 F1
Thornton Mews CH66. . . . 69 B8
Thornton Rd
Ellesmere Port CH65 . . . . 70 E3
Gatley SK8 . . . . 34 C8
Warrington WA5 . . . . .15 B4
Thornton Sq SK11 . . . . . 112 A5
Thorntree Bglws SK11 . . 132 A8
Thorn Tree Cl L24 . . . . . . 21 E2
Thorn Tree Dr CW1 . . . . 173 A1
Thorntree Gn WA4 . . . . . 27 B5
Thornway Bollington SK10 . 88 A7
Bramhall SK8 . . . . 35 C7
High Lane SK6 . . . . 37 F7
Thorn Wlk M31 . . . . .11 E2
Thornwythe Gr CH66 . . . .69 E4
Thornycroft CW1 . . . . . . 126 A1
Thornycroft Cl SK11 . . . . 111 E1
Thornycroft St 7 SK11 . . 112 E7
Thorpe Cl CW1 . . . . 189 F8
Thorp St SK10 . . . . 112 D8
Thorton Rd CW1 . . . . . . 191 E5
Thowler La WA14 . . . . . . 30 A5
Threaphurst La SK12 . . . .37 C8
Three Acres La SK8 . . . . . 34 E7
Three Fields Cl CW12 . . . 156 B3
Three Pools SK11 . . . . . . 160 B5
Threeways CW8 . . . . 101 D4
Thrush Way CW7 . . . . . . 126 F4
Thurlow WA3 . . . . .3 E7
THURLWOOD 193 E7
Thursfield Ave ST7 . . . . . 195 C3
Thursfield Cl CH1 . . . . . . 118 B1
Thursfield Prim Sch ST7 . 195 E3
Thurstaston Rd CH60 . . . . 40 F8
Thurston Cl WA5 . . . . 15 D6
Thurston Gn SK9 . . . . . . 60 A1
Thurston Rd CH4 . . . . . . 140 E5
Thynne St WA1 . . . . 16 A4
Tibbs Cross La WA8 . . . . 13 D8
Tibb St ST7 . . . . 209 F2
Tiberius Way CH4 . . . . . . 141 B4
Tickford Bank WA8 . . . . . .12 E2
Tidal La WA1 . . . . .16 F7
Tideswell Cl SK8 . . . . . . 34 D8
Tideswell Rd SK7 . . . . . . 36 E8
Tidnock Ave CW12 . . . . . 156 E5
Tidnock La SK11 . . . . . . 134 B6
Tiffield Ct CW7 . . . . 127 A4
Tighe Ave CW7 . . . . 125 F2
Tilbey Dr WA6 . . . . 74 A8
Tilbury Pl WA7 . . . . 50 E6
Tildsley Cres WA7 . . . . . .48 F6
Tilewright Cl ST7 . . . . . . 195 B2
Tilley St WA1 . . . . 16 C6
Tilman Cl WA5 . . . . .15 B8
TILSTON 198 B3
Tilston Ave WA4 . . . . 17 A4
TILSTONE BANK 168 F4
Tilstone Bank Rd CW6 . . 168 F4
Tilstone Cl Hough CW2 . . 206 E2
Northwich CW9 . . . . 104 A5
TILSTONE FEARNALL . . . 168 E4
Tilston Parochial CE Prim
Sch SY14 . . . . 198 B3
Tilston Rd SY14 . . . . 213 A5
Tilston Wlk 5 SK9 . . . . . 34 E1
Timbercroft Rd CH1 . . . . 117 A8
Timber La 2 CW9 . . . . . . 103 F8
TIMBERSBROOK 157 E2
Timbersbrook Gr 5 SK9. . 34 D2
Timbersombe Gdns WA1 . 17 E6
Timber St SK10 . . . . .87 F1
Timbrell Ave CW1 . . . . . 190 A6
Timmis Cl WA2 . . . . 16 A4
Timmis Cres WA8 . . . . . . 13 A1
Timperley Ave WA4 . . . . . 17 A4
Tinkersfield CW5 . . . . . . 205 A4
Tinkwood La SY14. . . . . . 211 F1
Tinsley St WA4 . . . . 16 F3
Tintagel Cl
Macclesfield SK10 . . . . . 111 E8
Runcorn WA7 . . . . 50 B6
Tintern Ave CH2 . . . . . . 118 F8
Tintern Cl Poynton SK12 . .36 D5
Warrington WA5 . . . . .7 E2
Tintern Rd SK8. . . . . 35 B6

Tipping Brow WA16 . . . . . 58 C4
Tipton Gn Cl CW5 . . . . . 204 C7
Tiresford Cl 1 CW6 . . . . 168 C8
Tirley La CW6 . . . . 123 A2
Tithebarn Cl CH66 . . . . . .40 F7
Tithebarn Dr CH64 . . . . . .41 B2
Tithebarn Rd WA15 . . . . . 32 C8
Tithings The WA7 . . . . . . .23 E1
TIVERTON 168 C6
Tiverton Cl Chester CH2 . 118 F5
Sandbach CW11 . . . . . . 175 C7
Widnes WA8 . . . . 12 C3
Tiverton Ct 6 CW9 . . . . . 103 E5
Tiverton Dr SK9 . . . . 34 D1
Tiverton Sq WA5 . . . . . . .14 E4
Tiverton Way CW6 . . . . . 168 C8
Tiveton Ct CW9 . . . . 103 F5
Tobermory Cl WA11 . . . . .1 A5
Todbrook Cl SK23 . . . . . . 65 D6
Todd Row CW8 . . . . 103 D4
Todds Bldgs WA8 . . . . . . 23 A6
Toft Cl Chester CH4 . . . . 140 E5
Widnes WA8. . . . . 12 F1
Toft Green La CW12 . . . . 158 C4
Toft Rd WA16 . . . . .82 B7
Toft Way SK9 . . . . 34 E4
Tolland La WA15 . . . . .31 F8
Tollard Cl SK8 . . . . 35 B6
Toll Bar Ave SK11 . . . . . 112 F7
Toll Bar Pl WA2 . . . . .8 A4
Toll Bar Rd Chester CH3 . 142 C8
Macclesfield SK11 . . . . . 111 F8
Warrington WA3 . . . . .8 A3
Tollemache Cotts CW5 . . 203 B3
Tollemache Dr CW1 . . . . 190 A8
Tollemache Terr CH2. . . . 118 F2
Tolleson Rd WA7 . . . . . . .24 B1
Tollgate Cl ST7 . . . . 210 C8
Tollgate Dr CW3 . . . . . . 229 F1
Tollitt St CW1 . . . . 190 C4
Tom Brads Croft SK23 . . . .65 E8
Tom Fields ST7 . . . . 209 F1
Tomkinson Cl CW1 . . . . . 189 F7
Tomkinson St CH2 . . . . . 237 C4
Tom La WA14 . . . . 30 E6
Tomlinson Ave WA2 . . . . . 16 D8
Tomlins Terr CH1 . . . . . . 117 E5
Tommy's La
Congleton CW12 . . . . . . 156 F4
Crewe CW1 . . . . 190 F2
Tonbridge Cl SK10 . . . . . .87 B2
Toogood Cl CH2 . . . . 119 F8
Topgate Cl CH60 . . . . . . .41 B8
Top House La
Heaton SK11 . . . . 159 E8
Lanehead SK11 . . . . 136 E1
Top Park Cl WA13 . . . . . . 11 E1
Topping Ct WA3 . . . . .9 B4
Top Rd Frodsham WA6 . . . 74 D5
Kingsley WA6 . . . . 75 B1
Top Station Rd ST7 . . . . 195 C7
Torbrook Gr 1 SK9 . . . . . 34 D2
Torkington Rd SK9 . . . . . 60 D6
Toronto Ave M90 . . . . . . .33 B7
Torr Dr CH62. . . . . 44 A7
Torridon Gr CH66 . . . . . . .69 F3
Torr Rd SK11 . . . . 112 C4
Torr Rise CW6 . . . . 146 D1
Torrs Valley SK22 . . . . . . 39 C7
Torr Top St SK22 . . . . 39 C7
TORR TOP 39 C8
Torr Top St SK22 . . . . 39 C7
Torvale Rd SK22. . . . . . . 39 B7
Total Fitness Wilmslow L
Club SK9 . . . . 35 A4
Totland Cl WA5 . . . . 14 C7
Totland Gr CH2 . . . . 118 E4
Tourney Gn WA5 . . . . . . .7 A2
Towergate CH1 . . . . 118 B1
TOWER HILL 88 D4
Tower Hill SK10 . . . . 88 D4
Tower Hill Rd ST7 . . . . . 195 F7
Tower Ho The 20 SK11 . . 112 C8
Tower La Lymm WA13 . . . .18 F2
Runcorn WA7 . . . . 50 D7
Weaverham CW8 . . . . . . .77 B1
Tower Rd CH1 . . . . 118 B2
Towers Cl Poynton SK12 . .36 F5
Wistaston CW2 . . . . 206 A7
Towers Ct WA5 . . . . 15 E7
Towers La WA6 . . . . 98 C7
Towers Rd SK12. . . . . . . 36 F5
Towers The 6 SK10 . . . . 111 F8
Towers Yard Barns SK12. . 36 F5
Tower Way CW1 . . . . 190 C4
Townbridge Ct 14 CW8 . . 103 F8
Towneley Ct WA8 . . . . . . 13 A1
TOWN END 12 C6
Town Farm La WA6. . . . . 100 E7
Townfield Ave CH3 . . . . . 180 E2
Townfield Cl ST7 . . . . . . 194 D2
Townfield Ct CW8 . . . . . . 78 A3
Townfield La Barnton CW8 . 78 A3
Blacon CH1 . . . . 117 F8
Farndon CH3 . . . . 180 D2
Frodsham WA6. . . . . 74 D7
Lymm WA13 . . . . .19 B7
Mollington CH1 . . . . 94 D2
Swan Green WA16 . . . . . 106 C5
Tarvin CH3 . . . . 121 B2
Tiverton CW6 . . . . 168 C6
Townfield Rd
Mobberley WA16 . . . . 58 A4
Runcorn WA7 . . . . 24 C2
Townfields WA16 . . . . . . 57 C2

TOWN FIELDS 149 D7
Town Fields CW11 . . . . 175 B5
Townfields Cotts **6**
CW7. . . . . .149 C7
Townfields Cres CW7. . . . 149 D7
Townfields Dr CW7. . . . . 149 C7
Townfields Gdns
Winsford CW7 . . . . 149 D7
3 Winsford CW7 . . . . . . 149 D7
Townfields Rd CW7. . . . . 149 D7
Townfield View WA7. . . . . 24 C2
Townfield Villas CH2. . . . .72 B3
Towngate Bsns Ctr WA8 . .22 B7
Town Green WA4 . . . . 52 D5
Town Hill WA1. . . . . .16 B5
Town La Hale L24, WA8. . . .21 E2
Mobberley WA16. . . . . .58 B4
Neston CH64. . . . . .66 F6
Townley Mill **6** SK11 . . . .112 D7
Townley Pl **5** SK11. . . . . 112 D7
Townley St **4** SK11. . . . . 112 D7
TOWN OF LOWTON 3 B5
TOWN PARK 50 B8
Town Pit La WA4. . . . . 52 D5
Townsend Farm ST7 . . . . 193 E2
Townsend La ST7 . . . . . . 194 A8
Townsend Rd CW12 . . . . 156 E2
Townsfield Dr CW6. . . . . . 147 F7
Townsfield La WA2. . . . . . . .8 A5
Townshend Rd CW9 . . . . . .80 A3
Township Cl CH3. . . . . . . 182 C1
Town Sq
4 Northwich CW9. . . . . 103 F8
6 Runcorn WA7. . . . . . .49 F7
Town Well WA6. . . . . 75 C2
Townwell Ct CW5 . . . . . . 204 D5
Town Wlk **9** WA7. . . . . . .49 F7
Trackside Bsns Pk CW11. 174 C6
Tracy Dr WA12. . . . . .2 E3
Trafalgar Ave SK12. . . . . . 37 C5
Trafalgar Cl
Northwich CW9 . . . . 103 E3
Poynton SK12. . . . . .37 A3
Trafalgar Ct
8 Macclesfield SK11. . .112 D7
Widnes WA8. . . . . 23 A6
Trafford Ave WA5. . . . . . . .15 F7
Trafford Cres WA7. . . . . . . 49 C6
Trafford Pl SK9. . . . . 60 D6
Trafford Rd
Alderley Edge SK9. . . . . . . .60 B1
Handforth SK9. . . . . .34 B1
Trafford St CH1. . . . . 237 B3
Tragan Dr WA5. . . . . 14 D3
Tramway Rd M44. . . . . .11 F7
Tramway St CH1. . . . . 237 C3
Tranmere Dr SK9. . . . . .34 E2
Tranquility Sq WA5 . . . . .7 C2
Trap Rd CW12. . . . . 132 C3
Trap St SK11. . . . . 132 B6
TRAP STREET 132 C5
Travers' Entry WA9. . . . . . . .6 A7
Travis St **10** WA8 . . . . . . .23 B8
Treborth Rd CH1. . . . . . . 117 D3
Tree Bank Cl WA7. . . . . . . 49 A8
Treen Cl SK10. . . . . 86 D1
Tree Tops CH64. . . . . .66 E4
Treetops Cl WA1. . . . . .16 F7
Tree Way WA16. . . . . 82 A7
Trefoil Cl Huntington CH3 . 142 B6
Warrington WA3. . . . . .9 C5
Tregele Cl CH1. . . . . 117 D3
Trem Yr Elc SY14. . . . . . . 222 F5
Trenance Cl WA7 . . . . 50 C5
Trenchard Dr M22. . . . . . . .33 F7
Trentabank Rd
Langley SK11. . . . . 113 F4
Macclesfield Forest SK11. . 114 B4
Trent Ave CW7. . . . . 127 B1
Trent Cl Bramhall SK7. . . . .35 C6
Culcheth WA3. . . . . .5 A2
Widnes WA8. . . . . .13 B4
Winsford CW7 . . . . 127 B1
Trentdale CH65. . . . . 70 B3
Trentham Cl WA8 . . . . .13 B4
Trentham Gdns **9** WA5. . .14 E8
Trentham St WA7. . . . . . . .22 F3
Trentlea Way CW11 . . . . 174 F4
Trent Way CH60. . . . . 41 C6
Tresham Dr WA4. . . . . 27 A8
Trevithick Cl CW1. . . . . . . 191 A4
Trevithick Pl CW5. . . . . . . 205 E6
Trevone Cl WA16. . . . . 57 A1
Trickett La CW8. . . . . 102 A3
Tricketts La CW5. . . . . . . 205 E5
Tricketts Mews CW5 . . . . 205 E5
Trident Bsns Pk WA3 . . . . . .9 E6
Trident Ind Est WA3 . . . . . . .9 F6
Trident Ret Pk WA7. . . . . . . 49 E7
Trident Way SK11. . . . . . . 112 A5
Trinity Cl CW2 . . . . 190 A1
Trinity Ct Congleton CW12. 157 B1
1 Knutsford WA16. . . . . 57 A2
Warrington WA3. . . . . .9 F5
Trinity Fields **11** CW7. . . 150 A8
Trinity Gdns **4** WA6. . . . . 49 C1
Trinity Ho **3** WA6 . . . . . . 49 C1
Trinity La SK11. . . . . 112 F3
Trinity Pl Congleton CW12. 179 B8
1 Widnes WA8. . . . . . . .23 B7
Trinity Rd CH65. . . . . 70 E4
Trinity Sq SK10 . . . . 87 F1
Trinity St Chester CH1 . . . 237 A2
Runcorn WA7. . . . . .23 B3
Trinity Terr **2** CW8. . . . . 103 E8

Troon Cl Bebington CH63. . . 43 C5
Bramhall SK7. . . . . 36 A7
Haydock WA11. . . . . .1 A5
Holmes Chapel CW4. . . . . 130 C2
Trossach Cl WA2. . . . . .8 E2
Troutbeck Ave
Congleton CW12 . . . . 156 A2
Newton-le-Willows WA12 . . .1 E4
Warrington WA5 . . . . .15 F8
Warrington WA5 . . . . .16 A8
Troutbeck Cl WA7. . . . . . . 50 A5
Troutbeck Gr CW7 . . . . . . 126 D2
Trouthall La WA16. . . . . . . 81 A2
Trubshaw Ct ST7. . . . . . . 195 C3
Trubshaw Pl ST7. . . . . . . 195 B3
Truman Cl WA8. . . . . .12 F3
Truman Ct **6** WA5 . . . . . .15 B7
Trumans La CH66. . . . . . . 69 C7
Truro Cl Bramhall SK7. . . . .35 C6
Congleton CW12 . . . . 178 E8
Ellesmere Port CH66 . . . . .94 F8
Macclesfield SK10 . . . . . . .86 E1
Runcorn WA7. . . . . 50 C6
Warrington WA1 . . . . .17 B8
Tryfan Way CH65. . . . . 69 F7
Tucana Cl **4** WA5 . . . . . . .7 B2
Tudor Cl
Ellesmere Port CH66 . . . . .94 F8
Middlewich CW10 . . . . . . 128 D1
Northwich CW9 . . . . 104 E6
Warrington WA4 . . . . .17 A2
Winsford CW7 . . . . 149 D6
Tudor Ct Congleton CW12. 156 D2
4 Warrington WA4. . . . . 16 E1
Tudor Dr SK10. . . . . 86 D7
Tudor Gn Blacon CH1. . . . . 117 E6
Handforth SK9. . . . . .34 E1
Tudor Rd Handforth SK9. . . 34 E1
Runcorn WA7. . . . . 24 C3
Tudorway CH60. . . . . 41 B8
Tudor Way Chester CH3. . . 142 B7
Congleton CW12 . . . . 156 D1
Nantwich CW5 . . . . 204 E3
Tue La WA8. . . . . .12 B6
Tulip Gr WA5. . . . . 15 E3
Tulip Rd Haydock WA11. . . . .1 F6
Partington M31 . . . . .11 E2
Tully Ave WA12. . . . . 1 F3
Tulsa Gdns **5** WA5. . . . . 15 A7
Tulworth Rd SK12. . . . . . . 36 D4
Tunnel End WA4. . . . . 51 A3
Tunnel Rd CW8. . . . . .78 B2
Tunnel Top N WA4. . . . . . . 51 A4
Tunnicliffe Rd SK11. . . . . 112 F3
Tunnicliffe St **1** SK10. . . 112 D8
Tunstall Rd
Biddulph CW12, SK11. . . . 158 C7
Congleton CW12 . . . . 157 F2
Turf La SK11. . . . . 112 C3
Turnall Rd WA8. . . . . .22 B7
Turnberry Cl Lymm WA13. . 18 C4
Macclesfield SK10. . . . . . . 87 C4
Northwich CW9 . . . . 104 E7
Winsford CW7 . . . . 126 C2
Turnberry Dr SK9. . . . . . . 60 D8
Turncocks La
Checkley CW3 . . . . 221 F1
Checkley Wood CW5. . . . . 232 E8
Turner Ave ST7 . . . . 210 A1
Turner Cl Crewe CW1 . . . . 190 A8
Widnes WA8. . . . . .12 D3
Turner Dr CW12. . . . . 156 A5
Turner Rise SK10. . . . . 88 C8
Turner St Bollington SK10. . .88 B8
Nantwich CW5 . . . . 204 F5
Turner's View CH64. . . . . . 41 D2
Turnham Green Dr CW5. 204 D7
Turnhurst Rd ST7. . . . . . . 195 F1
Turnock St SK11. . . . . . . 112 E7
Turnstone Ave WA12. . . . . .2 C4
Turnstone Bsns Pk WA8. . .23 C7
Turret Hall Dr **1** WA3. . . .3 E8
Turrocks Cl CH64 . . . . . . .66 E5
Turrocks Croft CH64. . . . . 66 E5
Turton Cl Hale L24. . . . . . . 21 E1
Warrington WA3. . . . . .9 C5
Turton St WA3 . . . . .3 A8
Turville Ho SK9. . . . . 34 D2
Tuscan Cl WA8. . . . . .13 B5
Tushingham Cl CH3 . . . . . 142 B7
Tushingham-with-Grindley
CE Prim Sch SY13. . . . . . 214 C1
Tuson Dr WA8 . . . . .12 F4
Tutor Bank Dr WA12. . . . . .2 D3
Tweedsmuir CH3. . . . . . . 119 A2
Tweedsmuir Cl WA2. . . . . . .9 A4
Twemlow Ave CW11 . . . . 175 B7
Twemlow La CW4 . . . . . . 130 D6
Twenty Acre Rd WA5 . . . . 15 C8
Twinnies Rd SK9. . . . . 34 B1
TWISS GREEN 4 E4
Twiss Green Dr WA3 . . . . . 4 E4
Twiss Green La WA3. . . . . . .4 E4
Twiss Green Prim Sch
WA3 . . . . 4 E4
Twist Ave WA3 . . . . .3 C8
Two Acre Gr CH66. . . . . . . 69 F1
TWO MILLS. 93 E8
Two Saints Pl **14** CW2. . 207 E3
Twyford Cl WA8. . . . . .13 B5
Twyford La WA8 . . . . 13 D6
Tyldesley Way CW5 . . . . 204 D6
Tyler St SK9. . . . . 60 A1

Tyne Cl WA2 . . . . .8 E2
Tynedale Ave CW2 . . . . . 190 C2
Tynedale Cl SK11. . . . . . . 112 C8
Tynemouth Rd WA7 . . . . . 50 C6
Tynesdale CH65. . . . . 70 B3
Tynwald Cres WA8 . . . . . . .12 F5
Tynwald Dr WA4 . . . . 26 C7
Tyrer Rd WA12. . . . . 2 C2
Tyrer Wlk **2** WA3 . . . . 3 F8
TYTHERINGTON 87 C3
Tytherington Bsns Pk
SK10 . . . . 87 D5
Tytherington Cl CW10 . . . 151 C6
Tytherington Ct SK10. . . . . 87 D3
Tytherington Dr SK10 . . . . .87 E4
Tytherington Gn SK10 . . . . 87 C4
Tytherington La SK10. . . . . 87 D5
Tytherington Park Rd
SK10 . . . . 87 D2
Tytherington Sch SK10. . . . 87 D2
Tytherington Sh Ctr **1**
SK10 . . . . 87 D3

U

Ullapool Cl CH66. . . . . 68 F6
Ullswater SK11 . . . . 111 F5
Ullswater Ave
Crewe CW2 . . . . 189 E3
Warrington WA2 . . . . .8 D3
Winsford CW7 . . . . 126 C2
Ullswater Cres CH2 . . . . . 119 A6
Ullswater Dr SK9. . . . . .83 F7
Ullswater Gr WA7 . . . . 49 D5
Ullswater Mans SK11. . . . 111 F6
Ullswater Rd
Congleton CW12 . . . . 156 A2
Ellesmere Port CH65 . . . . . 70 C2
Handforth SK9. . . . . 34 C4
Ulverston Ave WA2. . . . . . . .8 B4
Ulverston Cl WA11. . . . . . . .1 A6
Ulviet Gate WA16. . . . . . . 29 C4
Underbridge La WA4. . . . . .25 E6
Undercliffe Ho WA4 . . . . . .25 E6
Under Rainow Rd CW12 . 157 E1
Underway The WA7 . . . . . .49 F8
Underwood Bsns Pk
CW1 . . . . 190 A6
Underwood Cl SK10 . . . . . .86 F1
Underwood Ct CW1 . . . . . 190 B6
Underwood Dr CH65. . . . . 70 C2
Underwood La CW1 . . . . . 190 B6
Underwood Rd SK9 . . . . . . 60 C1
Underwood West Acad
CW1 . . . . 190 A5
Unicorn Gateway **8**
SK10 . . . . 112 D8
Union Cl CW12 . . . . 156 D3
Union Ind Est SK11. . . . . . 112 E7
Union Pl CH1 . . . . 237 B2
Union Rd
Macclesfield SK11 . . . . . . 112 E7
New Mills SK22 . . . . 39 C7
Union Sq WA5 . . . . .15 A8
Union St Chester CH1. . . . 237 C2
Congleton CW12 . . . . 156 D3
Crewe CW2 . . . . 190 D3
Macclesfield SK11 . . . . . . 112 D7
Runcorn WA7. . . . . .23 B2
Union Terr CH1. . . . . 237 B3
Union Wlk CH1. . . . . 237 B2
Unity Way ST7 . . . . 210 D2
University CE Acad
Ellesmere Port CH65 . . . . . 70 A4
Ellesmere Port CH65 . . . . . 70 C2
University of Liverpool,
Faculty of Veterinary
Science (Leahurst)
CH64. . . . . 67 D8
University Way
Crewe CW1 . . . . 191 B2
Sydney CW1. . . . . 191 B2
Univ of Chester Acad
Northwich CW9. . . . . 104 D7
Univ of Chester (Chichester
House) CH1 . . . . 237 A3
Univ of Chester/Kingsway
campus CH2 . . . . 118 F5
Univ of Chester (Warrington
Campus) WA2 . . . . .9 B3
Unsworth Ct WA2. . . . . 8 F1
Upcast La SK9. . . . . .59 E3
Uplands CH8 . . . . 101 D4
Uplands Rd CW9 . . . . .78 E4
Uplands The
Biddulph ST8 . . . . 179 E2
Macclesfield SK11 . . . . . . 112 A8
Runcorn WA7. . . . . .23 B2
Upper Cambrian Rd CH1. 118 B2
Upper Haigh St CW7 . . . . 149 C8
Upper Mersey Rd WA8. . . . 23 A5
Upper Mersey St CH65 . . . .70 C2
Upper Northgate St CH1. 237 A3
Upper Raby Rd CH64 . . . . 42 A2
UPPER THREAPWOOD . . . 222 E7
UPTON Chester 118 D6
Widnes. 12 C4
Upton Ave SK8. . . . . 35 A8
Upton Bridle Path WA8 . . .12 F4
Upton-by-Chester High Sch
CH2. . . . . 118 F6
Upton Cl Golborne WA3 . . . .3 D8
Winsford CW7 . . . . 126 F4
Upton Dr Chester CH2 . . . 118 C6
Warrington WA5 . . . . .14 F5

Upton Grange
Chester CH2. . . . . 118 C6
Widnes WA8. . . . . .12 D4
UPTON HEATH 118 F8
Upton Heath CE Prim Sch
CH2. . . . . 118 E8
Upton La Chester CH2 . . . 118 D7
Widnes WA8. . . . . .12 F4
Upton Mount SK10. . . . . . 87 A1
Upton Pk CH2. . . . . 118 D6
Upton Priory Sch SK10. . . .86 F2
Upton Rd CH66. . . . . 69 D4
UPTON ROCKS. 12 E4
Upton Rocks Ave WA8. . . . 12 E4
Upton Rocks Mews WA8. . .12 E4
Upton Way **12** SK9. . . . . 34 D5
Upwood Rd WA3. . . . . .3 D7
Ure Cl CH65 . . . . 70 A7
Urmston Ave WA12. . . . . . .2 B5
Ursuline Way CW2 . . . . . . 190 B1
UTKINTON 146 B7
Utkinton La CW6. . . . . . . 146 E7
Utkinton Rd CW6. . . . . . . 146 C5
Utkinton St Paul's CE Prim
Sch CW6 . . . . 146 B8

V

Vahler Terr WA7 . . . . 23 C2
Vale Ave WA2. . . . . .16 B8
Valebrook Dr CW5 . . . . . 220 A8
Vale Bsns Ctr CW12. . . . . 156 D2
Vale Cl CH4. . . . . 139 C3
Vale Ct WA4. . . . . 51 A3
Vale Gdns Alsager ST7. . . 193 E4
Ellesmere Port CH65 . . . . . 70 B4
Helsby WA6. . . . . .73 B4
Vale Head SK9. . . . . 34 D2
Valentine Rd
Kidsgrove ST7. . . . . 195 A1
Newton-le-Willows WA12 . . .1 F3
Vale Owen Rd WA2. . . . . . .8 D1
Vale Rd Alpraham CW6. . . 169 A4
Ellesmere Port CH65 . . . . . 70 B4
Hartford CW8. . . . . 103 C4
Marston CW9 . . . . .79 B6
Wilmslow SK9. . . . . .59 E8
Vale Royal Cl **5** CW9. . . .80 B3
Vale Royal Ctyd CW8 . . . 126 B8
Vale Royal Dr
Northwich CW8 . . . . 103 C2
Whitegate CW8 . . . . 126 A8
Vale Royal River Park Cvn
Site CW9. . . . . 126 E6
Vale View CW9. . . . . 79 D1
Vale Wlk CW12. . . . . 156 D2
Valiant Cl WA2. . . . . .8 F2
Valley Brook Bsns Ctr
CW2 . . . . 190 D3
Valley Cl Alsager ST7 . . . . 192 F3
Knutsford WA16. . . . . 82 A7
Valley Ct Crewe CW2 . . . . 190 B3
Middlewich CW10 . . . . . . 128 E1
Warrington WA2 . . . . .8 F1
Valley Dr Chester CH2 . . . 118 C5
Ellesmere Port CH66 . . . . . 69 D5
Handforth SK9. . . . . 34 C3
Valley La Cuddington CW8. 101 F3
Sandiway CW8. . . . . 102 A3
Valley Rd Bebington CH62 . . 43 D8
Bramhall SK7. . . . . 35 F8
Crewe CW2 . . . . 189 F1
Macclesfield SK11 . . . . . . 112 A6
Weaverham WA6. . . . . 77 C1
Wilmslow/Alderley Edge
SK9. . . . . .59 C7
Valley Sch SK7. . . . . 35 C5
VALLEY THE 190 A4
Valley View
Congleton CW12 . . . . 156 C3
Ellesmere Port CH66 . . . . . 69 D5
Newton-le-Willows WA12 . . .2 B1
Northwich CW9 . . . . 104 C7
Valley Way WA16. . . . . 82 A7
Vanguard Ct WA3. . . . . .9 D4
Varden Rd SK12. . . . . 36 E3
Varden Town Cotts SK10. . 86 A4
Vardon Dr SK9. . . . . 60 D6
Varey Rd CW12. . . . . 156 F4
Vaudrey Cres CW12 . . . . 156 F3
Vaudrey Dr WA1 . . . . 17 D7
Vaughan Rd SK23. . . . . . . .65 E5
Vaughans La CH3 . . . . . . 142 A8
Vauxhall Cl WA5 . . . . 14 F4
Vauxhall Rd WA5. . . . . . . 204 E7
Vauxhall Way CW7 . . . . . . 149 C6
Vearows Pl **1** WA7. . . . . . 49 F7
Vela Cl **1** WA5. . . . . .7 B2
Venables Ct CW8. . . . . . . 103 D4
Venables Rd CW9 . . . . 79 A1
Venable's Rd CH1 . . . . . . 117 F4
Venables Way
Ellesmere Port CH65 . . . . . 70 B6
High Legh WA16. . . . . 29 C4
Middlewich CW10 . . . . . . 151 E6
Venns Rd WA2. . . . . .16 D7
Ventnor Cl
Middlewich CW10 . . . . . . 151 C8
Warrington WA5. . . . . .14 D7
Ventura Dr WA5. . . . . .15 B7
Venture Fields WA8 . . . . . .23 B7
Venture Way SK12. . . . . . . 36 F7
Verbena Cl Partington M31. .11 F3
Runcorn WA7. . . . . .49 F7
Verdin Ave CW8. . . . . 78 F1
Verdin Cl Moulton CW9 . . 126 F7

Verdin Cl continued
Winsford CW7 . . . . 126 C5
Verdin Ct CW1 . . . . 190 A8
Verdin St CW9 . . . . 104 C8
Vere St CW1 . . . . 190 C5
Verity Cl CW1 . . . . 191 C4
Verity Ct CW10 . . . . 128 C2
Vermont Cl WA5 . . . . 15 C7
Vermont Gdns SK7. . . . . . .35 B5
Vernay Gn CW4. . . . . 141 B5
Vernon Ave Audley ST7. . . 209 D2
Congleton CW12 . . . . 178 F8
Hooton CH66 . . . . 44 A2
Vernon Cl Audley ST7. . . . 209 D2
13 Middlewich CW10 . . 151 D5
Poynton SK12. . . . . .36 D2
Saughall CH1 . . . . 117 A8
Vernon Dr CW3 . . . . 230 F4
Vernon Prim Sch SK12. . . . 36 E3
Vernon Rd Chester CH1. . . 118 B2
Poynton SK12. . . . . .36 E2
Vernon St Crewe CW1 . . . 190 B5
Macclesfield SK10 . . . . . . 112 F8
Warrington WA1 . . . . .16 B4
Vernon Way CW1 . . . . 190 C4
Veronica Mews WA8 . . . . . 12 D1
Veronica Way CH66. . . . . . 69 D7
Vetch Cl WA3 . . . . .11 B5
Vetches The CH5. . . . . . . 119 F5
Viaduct St WA12 . . . . .2 A3
Vicarage Ave Cheadle SK8. . 35 B7
9 Congleton Park CW5. 156 F4
Vicarage Cl
Guilden Sutton CH3 . . . . . 119 F5
Hale L24. . . . . .21 E1
Vicarage Ct LL13 . . . . 196 E8
Vicarage Dr WA11. . . . . . . .1 B7
Vicarage Gdns CW11 . . . . 174 E8
Vicarage Gr CW7. . . . . . . 149 D5
Vicarage Hill WA6. . . . . . . 73 C4
Vicarage La Audlem CW3 . 230 A4
Bunbury CW6. . . . . 168 F1
Burton CH64 . . . . 67 D2
Frodsham WA6. . . . . 74 C7
Helsby WA6. . . . . 73 C4
Little Budworth CW6 . . . . 147 F7
Poynton SK12. . . . . .36 E5
Sandbach CW11. . . . . 174 E8
Vicarage Rd Chester CH2. . 118 F3
Haslington CW1. . . . . 191 D6
Haydock WA11. . . . . .1 A7
Northwich CW9 . . . . 104 B8
Widnes WA8. . . . . 23 A7
Vicarage Row CH62 . . . . . 44 A5
Vicarage Way **1** SK11. . . 111 F7
Vicarage Wlk
Northwich CW9 . . . . 104 B7
Warrington WA4 . . . . 26 C8
Vicar's Cl CH3 . . . . 121 F7
VICARSCROSS 119 E2
Vicars Cross Ct **2** CH3 . . 119 B2
Vicars Cross Rd CH3. . . . . 119 C2
Vicar's La CH1. . . . . 237 B2
Vickers Way
Broughton CH4. . . . . 139 D4
Northwich CW9 . . . . 104 A7
Victoria Ave Crewe CW2. . 190 A4
Grappenhall WA4 . . . . 17 A2
Haslington CW1. . . . . 191 C4
Heswall CH60 . . . . 41 A6
Holmes Chapel CW4. . . . . 130 C2
Kidsgrove ST7 . . . . 194 F2
Warrington WA5 . . . . 13 A3
Widnes WA8. . . . . 13 A3
Victoria Cl SK7. . . . . 35 D6
Victoria Cres
Chester CH2. . . . . 237 A4
Chester, Queen's Park
CH4. . . . . 237 C1
Victoria Ct Chester CH2. . 237 A4
3 Crewe CW1. . . . . . . 190 C4
Haslington CW1. . . . . 191 C4
8 Kidsgrove ST7. . . . . 195 A2
Knutsford WA16. . . . . .56 F1
2 Widnes WA8. . . . . . . 23 A8
Victoria Gr WA8. . . . . 13 A3
Victoria Infirmary CW8 . . 103 E8
Victoria Inf Sch CH1 . . . . 237 A4
Victoria Mews CH65 . . . . .70 B5
Victoria Mill Dr CW5 . . . . 205 D6
Victoria Pathway CH4 . . . 237 C1
Victoria Pk CW8 . . . . .78 F1
Victoria Pl Chester CH1. . 237 B3
Warrington WA4 . . . . 16 C1
Victoria Promenade WA8. 23 A4
Victoria Rd
Chester CH1, CH2 . . . . . . 237 B3
Ellesmere Port CH65 . . . . . 70 C5
Macclesfield SK10 . . . . . . .87 A1
Neston CH64 . . . . 67 A6
Newton-le-Willows WA12 . . .2 C3
Northwich CW9 . . . . 104 B8
Runcorn WA7. . . . . .23 A2
Saltney CH4 . . . . 140 D5
Warrington WA4 . . . . .16 F2
Warrington, Great Sankey
WA5. . . . . .15 B4
Warrington, Penketh WA5. 14 D4
Warrington, Stockton Heath
WA4 . . . . 16 D1
Widnes WA8. . . . . 23 A6
Wilmslow SK9. . . . . 60 A6
Victoria Road Prim Sch
10 Northwich CW9. . . . 104 B8
Runcorn WA7. . . . . .23 A2
Victoria Sq
Warrington WA4 . . . . 16 C1
8 Widnes WA8. . . . . . . 23 A4

Victoria Sq *continued*
Winsford CW7 . . . . 149 A8
Victoria St
Congleton CW12 . . . . . . 156 D2
Crewe CW1 . . . . 190 C4
Knutsford WA16 . . . . .56 F2
New Mills SK22 . . . . .39 B6
Northwich CW9 . . . . .79 E2
Sandbach CW11 . . . . . . 175 B7
Warrington WA1 . . . . . . 16 C5
Widnes WA8 . . . . .23 B7
Victoria Stad (Northwich
Victoria FC) CW9 . . . . . . .79 D3
Victoria Trad Ctr WA8 . . 23 A6
Victoria Way SK7 . . . . . . 35 D6
Victoria Wlk SK10 . . . . 112 E8
Victory Ct CH65 . . . . .70 E3
Victory Rd M44 . . . . 11 C4
Viewlands Dr SK9 . . . . . . 34 D2
Viking Way CW12 . . . . . 156 C4
Villa Farm CW11 . . . . . . 176 B8
Village Cl
Lostock Green CW9 . . . . . 105 A8
Northwich CW8 . . . . .77 D1
Runcorn WA7 . . . . 50 A8
Warrington WA4 . . . . .17 E4
Village Ct 8 SK9 . . . . 34 D1
Village Farm CW5 . . . . 172 A5
Village La WA4 . . . . 52 D4
Village Mews SK10 . . . . . 87 A6
Village Rd Christleton CH3 142 E8
Great Barrow CH3 . . . . . . 120 E6
Heswall CH60 . . . . .40 F7
Waverton CH3 . . . . 143 C4
Village Sq 6 CH64 . . . . . .67 F8
Village Square Sh Ctr,
Bramhall SK7 . . . . .35 E6
Village St WA7 . . . . 24 C2
Village Terr The 6 WA4 . 16 C1
Village The
Astbury CW12 . . . . 178 B8
Burton CH64 . . . . 67 D1
Prestbury SK10 . . . . .86 F6
Village Way 11 SK9 . . . . . 34 D1
Villa Rd CH5 . . . . 116 B7
Villars St WA1 . . . . 16 C5
Villas The CW4 . . . . 131 A8
Villiers Russell Cl CW1 . 190 D5
Vincent Cl WA5 . . . . 15 C8
Vincent Dr CH4 . . . . 141 C6
Vincent St Crewe CW1 . . 190 E4
Macclesfield SK11 . . . . . . 112 D7
Vine Bank Rd ST7 . . . . . 195 A1
Vine Cl SK11 . . . . 112 A6
Vine Cres WA5 . . . . .14 F6
Vine Rd CH66 . . . . .69 F1
Vine St Bollington SK10 . . .88 B8
10 Runcorn WA7 . . . . 23 A2
Widnes WA8 . . . . 23 A7
Vine Terr WA8 . . . . 12 A2
Vine Tree Ave
Crewe CW2 . . . . 190 B1
Shavington CW2 . . . . 206 B5
Vine Tree Prim Sch
CW2 . . . . 190 A1
Vineyard The CW2 . . . . . 206 B4
Vineyard Way WA8 . . . . . 23 C8
Violet Cl WA3 . . . . .9 C5
Violet Gr CW8 . . . . 103 D8
Violet St WA8 . . . . 23 A7
Violet Way CW4 . . . . 130 C1
Virginia Chase SK8 . . . . . .34 F8
Virginia Dr CH1 . . . . 117 C4
Virginia Gdns WA5 . . . . . 15 B8
Virginia Terr CH66 . . . . . .69 B8
Virtual Bsns Ctr CH1 . . . 117 E2
Viscount Dr Gatley SK8 . . 34 D7
Wythenshawe M90 . . . . . . .32 F7
Viscount Rd WA2 . . . . . . .8 E2
Vista Ave WA12 . . . . .2 A4
Vista Rd
Newton-le-Willows WA11,
WA12 . . . . .2 A6
Runcorn WA7 . . . . 49 A8
Vista The M44 . . . . 11 C4
Vista Way WA12 . . . . .2 A4
Viva Way CH65 . . . . 70 A6
Vixen Gr WA8 . . . . .12 F4
Volans Dr WA5 . . . . .7 B2
Volunteer Ave 7 CW5 . . 204 E6
Volunteer Fields CW7 . . 126 C1
Volunteer St Chester CH1 . 237 B2
Frodsham WA6 . . . . 49 D1
Vose CW5 . . . . 15 D6
Vulcan Cl
4 Crow Wood WA8 . . . . . 13 C4
Newton-le-Willows WA12 . . 2 C1
Warrington WA2 . . . . .8 F2
Woodford SK7 . . . . .35 F2
Vulcan Ind Est WA12 . . . . .2 D1
Vulcan Pk Ct 2 WA12 . . . .2 D1
Vulcan Pk Way
Newton-le-Willows WA12 . . .2 C1
Vulcan Village WA12 . . . . . .7 D8
VULCAN VILLAGE 7 C8
Vyrnwy Rd CH4 . . . . 140 D6

W

Waddington Cl WA3 . . . . . .3 F8
Wadebrook Gr 4 SK9 . . 34 D1
Wadebrook Trad Est
CW9 . . . . 104 C8
Wade Cres CW8 . . . . 78 A3
Wade Ct ST7 . . . . 195 A1
Wade Deacon High Sch
WA8 . . . . 13 A2

Wades Field Pl
10 Crewe CW1 . . . . 190 A8
8 Crewe CW1 . . . . 190 A8
WADES GREEN 171 F5
Wades La CW7 . . . . 126 D3
Wadeson Way WA3 . . . . . . .9 B7
Wadham Cl WA7 . . . . 23 C1
Wadsworth Cl SK9 . . . . . . 34 E3
Waggon Cotts ST7 . . . . . 208 E1
Waggs Rd CW12 . . . . 156 C1
Wagg St CW12 . . . . 156 D2
Wagon La WA11 . . . . .1 B6
Waight Cl SK7 . . . . .35 E2
Waine St CW1 . . . . 190 D5
Wain Ho CH1 . . . . 94 A1
Wain Lee ST7 . . . . 195 F4
Wakefield Cl CW1 . . . . . . 189 F7
Wakefield Ct CW9 . . . . . . 104 A5
Wakefield Ho WA5 . . . . . . .15 F6
Wakefield St WA3 . . . . .3 A7
Wakes Mdw CW6 . . . . . . 185 E8
Walden Cl WA4 . . . . 17 D3
Walden Dr CH1 . . . . 93 D8
Waldon Rd SK11 . . . . 112 A5
Waldron Gdns CW2 . . . . . 189 F1
Waldron Rd CW1 . . . . 191 D3
Waldron's La CW1 . . . . . . 173 D1
Walfield Ave CW12 . . . . . 156 D5
Walford Ave CW2 . . . . . . 190 B3
WALGHERTON 220 B6
Walgrave Cl CW12 . . . . . . 156 A3
Walker Brow Rd SK23 . . . .65 B5
Walker Cl CW1 . . . . 191 D4
Walker Dr CW10 . . . . 151 C8
Walker La SK11 . . . . 112 E2
Walker Rd CW9 . . . . 78 C1
WALKER'S GREEN 152 D7
Walkersgreen Rd ST5 . . . 210 D2
Walkers La
Ellesmere Port CH66 . . . . . 69 C6
Farndon CH3 . . . . 180 F2
Scholar Green ST7 . . . . . . 177 B2
Tarporley CW6 . . . . 146 D1
Warrington WA5 . . . . .14 E3
Walker St Chester CH2 . . 237 C4
Crewe CW1 . . . . 190 B5
2 Macclesfield SK10 . . . . 112 C8
Warrington WA2 . . . . 16 A6
Walk Mill La CH3 . . . . . . 144 A5
Wallace Ct CW7 . . . . 127 D1
Wallace St
Northwich CW8 . . . . 103 E7
Widnes WA8 . . . . 23 A8
Wallbrook Ave SK10 . . . . 111 E8
Wallcroft CH64 . . . . 68 A7
Wallcroft Gdns CW10 . . . 128 C1
Walled Gdn The CW10 . . . 127 D5
Wallenge Rd CW10 . . . . . 151 D5
Waller Cl CW1 . . . . 191 E5
Wallerscote Cl CW8 . . . . 102 E8
Wallerscote Com Sch
CW8 . . . . 102 E8
Wallerscote Rd CW8 . . . . 102 E8
Waller St SK11 . . . . 112 E6
WALLEY'S GREEN 172 E7
Walleys La CW5 . . . . 203 C7
Wallfields Cl CW5 . . . . . . 204 E7
Wall Fields Rd CW5 . . . . 204 E7
Wallhill La CW11 . . . . 177 D7
Wallingford Rd SK9 . . . . . 34 C5
Wallis Dr WA8 . . . . 13 C3
Wallis St Crewe CW1 . . . . 190 D4
Warrington WA4 . . . . .16 B3
Wall La CW5 . . . . 204 E6
Wallrake CH60 . . . . .40 F7
Walls Ave CH1 . . . . 118 B1
Wallsend Ct WA8 . . . . . . .12 F3
Wallworth's Bank CW12 . 156 E2
Wallworth Terr SK9 . . . . . 59 E8
Walmer Pl CW7 . . . . 149 C6
Walmoor Pk CH3 . . . . . . 119 A1
Walmsley St
Newton-le-Willows WA12 . . .2 D4
Widnes WA8 . . . . 23 C8
Walnut Ave CW8 . . . . . . 102 D7
Walnut Cl Chester CH2 . . 118 D7
Warrington WA1 . . . . .17 E7
Wilmslow SK9 . . . . 60 E8
Walnut Cotts LL13 . . . . . 196 D8
Walnut Croft CH3 . . . . . . 180 F6
Walnut Dr CW7 . . . . 127 A1
Walnut Gr CH66 . . . . 70 A1
Walnut La CW8 . . . . 103 A5
Walnut Rd M31 . . . . 11 D3
Walnut Rise CW12 . . . . . . 156 B2
Walnut Tree La
Bradwall Green CW11 . . . . 153 A4
Warrington WA4 . . . . .26 F4
Walpole Cl CW1 . . . . 191 C5
Walpole Gr WA2 . . . . .8 C2
Walpole Rd WA7 . . . . 49 C6
Walpole St CH1 . . . . 237 A4
Walsh Cl WA12 . . . . .2 C5
Walsingham Dr WA7 . . . . 24 D2
Walsingham Rd WA5 . . . . .14 F5
Walter St Chester CH1 . . . 237 B4
Warrington WA1 . . . . .16 E7
Widnes WA8 . . . . 13 D1
Walters Wood SK23 . . . . . .65 F5
Walthall St CW2 . . . . 190 C2
Waltham Ave WA3 . . . . .5 C7
Waltham Ct WA7 . . . . 24 E4
Waltham Dr SK8 . . . . .35 B6
Waltham Pl CH4 . . . . 141 A6
Walton Ave WA5 . . . . 14 E5

Walton Gr ST7 . . . . 210 C8
Walton Hall & Gdns ★
WA4 . . . . .25 C7
Walton Heath Dr SK10 . . . .87 B4
Walton Heath Rd WA4 . . . 16 B1
Walton La WA3 . . . . .9 E5
Walton Lea Rd WA4 . . . . . 26 A7
Walton New Rd WA4 . . . . 26 B8
Walton Pl CH1 . . . . 117 C4
Walton Rd Culcheth WA3 . . .4 F3
Warrington WA4 . . . . 26 C8
Walton St 13 WA7 . . . . . . 23 A2
Waltons The CH4 . . . . . . 141 E6
Walton Way ST7 . . . . 210 C8
Wandsworth Way WA8 . . .22 F5
Wansfell Pl WA2 . . . . .8 A3
WARBURTON 19 C8
Warburton Bridge Rd WA13,
WA3 . . . . 11 A1
Warburton Cl
Altrincham WA15 . . . . 32 D6
Barnton CW8 . . . . .77 F4
Lymm WA13 . . . . 19 A4
Warburton Dr WA15 . . . . . 32 D6
WARBURTON GREEN 32 D6
Warburton La M31, WA13 . .11 E2
Warburton Rd SK9 . . . . . . 34 D4
Warburton St WA4 . . . . . . 16 D1
Warburton View WA3 . . . . 11 A2
Ward Ave WA5 . . . . 88 A8
Ward Cl WA5 . . . . .7 B1
Ward La SK12 . . . . 38 F4
Wardle Ave CW5 . . . . 187 C2
Wardle Cotts CW5 . . . . . . 187 C7
Wardle Cres SK11 . . . . . . 111 E1
Wardle Dr CW9 . . . . 104 C6
Wardle Ind Est CW5 . . . . 187 A4
Wardle Mews CW10 . . . . . 151 D8
Wardle St 7 SK11 . . . . . . 112 D7
Wardley Rd WA4 . . . . 16 B1
Wardour Cl 6 SK11 . . . . . 111 F7
Wardour St WA5 . . . . .15 E6
WARDSEND 37 A1
Wards La CW12 . . . . 179 C8
Ward's La CW11 . . . . 153 C5
Ward's Terr CH2 . . . . 118 F3
Wareham Cl Haydock WA11 . .1 C7
Warrington WA1 . . . . 17 C8
Wareham Dr CW1 . . . . . . 190 B8
Wareham St SK9 . . . . 60 B7
Warford Ave SK12 . . . . . . 37 A2
Warford Cres SK9 . . . . . . .84 B7
Warford Hall Dr SK9 . . . . .84 B6
Warford La WA16 . . . . 59 B1
WARFORD PARK 58 E1
Warford Terr WA16 . . . . . . 59 B2
WARGRAVE 2 D3
Wargrave House Sch
WA12 . . . . .2 C1
Wargrave Mews WA12 . . . . .2 C1
Wargrave Prim Sch WA12 . .2 C1
Wargrave Rd WA12 . . . . . . .2 C2
Warham Gr 7 CW7 . . . . . 125 F2
Waring Ave St Helens WA9 . .1 B2
Warrington WA4 . . . . .16 F5
Warkworth Cl WA8 . . . . . . 12 C3
Warkworth Ct CH65 . . . . . 70 E3
WARMINGHAM 173 D7
Warmingham CE Prim Sch
CW11 . . . . 173 E8
Warmingham Ct CW10 . . . 151 D7
Warmingham Grange La
CW11 . . . . 173 D7
Warmingham La
Middlewich CW10 . . . . 151 D5
Sandbach CW11 . . . . 174 B8
Warmingham Rd CW1 . . . 173 D4
Warnley Cl WA8 . . . . 12 D3
WARREN 111 D1
Warren Ave
Knutsford WA16 . . . . 56 E2
Lostock Gralam CW9 . . . . . 80 A3
Warren Cl Knutsford WA16 . .56 F2
Middlewich CW10 . . . . 151 B7
Poynton SK12 . . . . 36 B4
Warren Croft WA7 . . . . . . 50 D7
Warren Ct
Ellesmere Port CH66 . . . . . 69 D3
Frodsham WA6 . . . . 74 D6
Warren Dr
Altrincham WA15 . . . . 32 D7
Broughton CH4 . . . . 139 A3
Ellesmere Port CH66 . . . . . 69 E7
Newton-le-Willows WA12 . . .2 F4
Warren SK11 . . . . 111 D1
Warrington WA4 . . . . 26 D8
Warren Gr SK11 . . . . 111 D1
Warren Hey 2 SK9 . . . . . . 60 E8
Warren La Bebington CH62 . .43 F8
Hartford CW8 . . . . 103 A4
Warrington WA1 . . . . 17 D8
Warren Lea SK12 . . . . 36 E5
Warren Rd
Warrington WA4 . . . . 26 C7
Warrington, Orford WA2 . . . .8 D1
Warren The
Cuddington CW8 . . . . 101 D5
Newton-le-Willows WA12 . . .2 A3
Warren Way CW6 . . . . . . 168 D8
Warrilow Heath Rd ST5 . . 210 C1
WARRINGTON 16 E2
Warrington Ave
Crewe CW1 . . . . 190 C6
Ellesmere Port CH65 . . . . . .70 C6
Warrington Bank Quay Sta
WA1 . . . . 15 F4
Warrington Bsns Ctr WA2 . 16 A6
Warrington Bsns Pk WA2 . .8 C1

Warrington Central Sta
WA2 . . . . .16 B6
Warrington Collegiate
WA2 . . . . .8 B1
Warrington Hospl WA5 . . 15 F6
Warrington La WA13 . . . . 19 E2
Warrington Mus & Art
Gallery ★ WA1 . . . . 16 A4
Warrington Rd
Bold Heath L35, WA8 . . . . 13 D7
Comberbach CW9 . . . . 78 D7
Cronton L35 . . . . 12 E8
Cuddington CW8 . . . . 102 A5
Fowley Common WA3, WN7 . .5 C5
Golborne WA3, WA12 . . . . . .3 A6
Hatton WA4 . . . . .25 F4
Little Leigh CW8 . . . . 77 A5
Lymm WA13 . . . . .18 B4
Mere WA16 . . . . 56 B7
Mickle Trafford CH2 . . . . . 119 E7
Northwich CW9 . . . . .53 E1
Runcorn, Castlefields WA7 . . 24 B4
Runcorn, Manor Park WA7 . . 24 B4
Warrington WA5 . . . . .11 A3
Warrington, Risley WA3 . . . .9 E7
Widnes WA8 . . . . 13 A5
Warrington Trad Est WA2 . 16 A6
Warrington & Vale Royal Coll
CW7 . . . . 126 E1
Warton Cl Bramhall SK7 . . 36 A7
Warrington WA5 . . . . 15 A3
Warwick Ave
Newton-le-Willows WA12 . . .2 E2
Warrington, Bewsey WA5 . . 15 F7
Warrington, Great Sankey
WA5 . . . . 14 D7
Warwick Cl
Kidsgrove ST7 . . . . 195 A3
Knutsford WA16 . . . . 57 C1
Macclesfield SK11 . . . . . . 111 F6
Neston CH64 . . . . 66 E5
Warwick Ct
Ellesmere Port CH65 . . . . . .70 E2
Warrington WA1 . . . . .16 E7
Warwick Dr SK7 . . . . 36 D8
Warwick Gate CW5 . . . . . 217 C2
Warwick Gr 1 WA7 . . . . . 23 F1
Warwick Mews SK11 . . . . 111 F6
Warwick Pl CW7 . . . . 149 C6
Warwick Rd Blacon CH1 . . 117 F5
Irlam M44 . . . . 11 D5
Macclesfield SK11 . . . . . . 111 E6
Warwick Wlk SK11 . . . . . . 111 F6
Wasdale Gr CW1 . . . . 173 B1
Washburn Ave CH65 . . . . . 70 B5
WASH END 4 C8
Washford Cl CW12 . . . . . . 156 F5
Washington Cl
Biddulph ST8 . . . . 179 C2
Cheadle SK8 . . . . 34 F8
Widnes WA8 . . . . 12 F3
Wash La Allostock WA16 . . 106 E3
Warrington WA4 . . . . 16 E3
Wasley Cl WA2 . . . . .8 F3
Waste Hill Rd CH3 . . . . . . 184 B6
Waste La Cuddington CW8 . 101 E3
Delamere CW8 . . . . 123 F6
Kelsall CW6 . . . . 122 F4
Watch La CW11 . . . . 174 A6
Waterbank Row CW9 . . . . 103 E7
Waterbridge Ct
2 Lymm WA13 . . . . 18 C3
Warrington WA4 . . . . 26 D8
Waterbridge Mews WA7 . . 24 A2
Waterfoot La SK23 . . . . . . 65 D6
Waterford Dr CH64 . . . . . . 67 A7
Waterford Pl SK8 . . . . 34 B8
Waterford Way WA7 . . . . . 50 C6
Waterfront WA4 . . . . 50 F6
Waterfront Dr
1 Grappenhall WA4 . . . . . 17 B3
Warrington WA4 . . . . 17 B3
Watergate Row N CH1 . . . 237 A2
Watergate Row S CH1 . . . 237 A2
Watergate Sq CH1 . . . . . . 237 A2
Watergate St CH1 . . . . . . 237 A2
Watergrove Cres 1 WA5 . 14 D8
Waterhouse Ave SK10 . . . .87 F8
Water La SK9 . . . . 60 A7
Waterlily Gr 1 CW5 . . . . . 205 B3
Water-Lode CW5 . . . . 204 E5
Waterloo Cl 5 CH65 . . . . . 70 C5
Waterloo Cotts WA6 . . . . . 99 F8
Waterloo Gr ST7 . . . . 195 A2
Waterloo Ho 15 CW8 . . . . 103 F8
Waterloo La WA6 . . . . 74 F1
Waterloo Rd Bramhall SK7 . 35 F8
Chester CH2 . . . . 118 C4
Haslington CW1 . . . . 191 D4
Northwich CW8 . . . . 103 E7
Poynton SK12 . . . . 37 A2
3 Runcorn WA7 . . . . 22 F2
Widnes WA8 . . . . 23 A5
Waterloo Street W SK11 . 112 D8
Watermead Dr WA7 . . . . . .50 F5
Watermill Dr SK11 . . . . . . 112 F7
Watermill La CH2 . . . . 96 F2
Watersedge WA6 . . . . 49 D2
Waters Edge
Anderton CW9 . . . . 78 D3
Chester CH1 . . . . 118 B2
Waters Edge Mews
CW10 . . . . 151 C8
Watersfield Cl SK8 . . . . . . 34 F8
Waters Gn SK11 . . . . 112 D8
Waterside Disley SK12 . . . . 38 E7
Furness Vale SK23 . . . . 39 E3

Waterside *continued*
Macclesfield SK11 . . . . . . 112 E7
Warrington WA4 . . . . 26 D8
Waterside Cotts CW5 . . . 216 E5
Waterside Ct WA7 . . . . 22 E3
Waterside Dr WA6 . . . . . . 49 D2
Waterside La WA5 . . . . . . 22 C5
Waterside Mews CW11 . . 174 F3
Waterside Rd SK12, SK22 . .38 E7
Waterside View
Chester CH1 . . . . 237 B3
Northwich CW9 . . . . 104 E6
Waterside Way CW10 . . . . 128 B2
Waters Rd CH65 . . . . 70 D6
Waters Reach SK12 . . . . . .36 F5
Water's Reach SK6 . . . . . . 37 E7
Waters Reams CH3 . . . . . 142 B8
Water St Bollington SK10 . . .88 B8
Macclesfield SK11 . . . . . . 112 C8
Newcastle-under-Lyme
ST5 . . . . 210 D2
Newton-le-Willows WA12 . . .2 C4
Northwich CW9 . . . . 104 A7
Runcorn WA7 . . . . 23 A3
Widnes WA8 . . . . 23 A6
Water Tower (Mus) ★
CH1 . . . . 118 B2
Water Tower Rd CH64 . . . . 41 E1
Water Tower St CH1 . . . . . 237 A3
Watertower View CH2 . . . . 118 F2
Waterway CH3 . . . . 143 B5
Waterway Cl CW5 . . . . . . 204 C6
Waterways WA5 . . . . 15 D6
Waterways Ave SK10 . . . . 112 E6
Waterwheel Way SK10 . . . .87 F8
Waterworks Cotts WA12 . . .2 F4
Waterworks La
Ellesmere Port CH66 . . . . . .68 E8
Hooton CH66 . . . . 43 E1
Winwick WA2 . . . . .8 B7
Watery La Astbury CW12 . . 178 C5
Frodsham WA6 . . . . .74 E6
Winwick WA2 . . . . .7 E6
Watkins Ave WA12 . . . . . . .1 F3
Watkinson Way WA8 . . . . 13 C5
Watkin St Sandycroft CH5 . 116 A3
Warrington WA2 . . . . .16 B7
Watlands Rd ST7 . . . . 209 E2
Watling Cres CW4 . . . . . . 141 E7
Watling Ct Chester CH3 . . 119 C2
Cuddington CW8 . . . . 102 B2
Watling Dr CW6 . . . . 123 C6
Watling St CW9 . . . . 103 F8
Watson Dr 6 CW7 . . . . . . 150 A8
Watson's Cl CH4 . . . . 139 C3
Watton Cl WA4 . . . . 17 C3
Wavell Ave WA8 . . . . 22 D8
Waveney Dr SK9 . . . . 34 D2
Waverley Ave WA4 . . . . . . 26 D8
Waverley Cl SK10 . . . . 113 A8
Waverley Ct 1 CW2 . . . . . 190 D2
Waverley Dr SK8 . . . . .35 B7
Waverley Terr CH2 . . . . . . 118 E4
WAVERTON 143 B4
Waverton App CH3 . . . . . 164 E6
Waverton Bsns Pk CH3 . . 142 F4
Waverton Cl Hough CW2 . . 206 E2
Northwich CW9 . . . . 103 E4
Waverton Com Prim Sch
CH3 . . . . 143 A5
Waverton Mill Quays
CH3 . . . . 143 B5
Waverton Pk CH3 . . . . . . 143 B5
Waverton Rd CH66 . . . . . . .69 E5
Wavertree Ave
Scholar Green ST7 . . . . . . 194 E7
Widnes WA8 . . . . 23 A8
Wavertree Ct CH66 . . . . . .69 F7
Wavertree Dr CW10 . . . . . 151 B7
Wavertree Rd CH1 . . . . . . 117 C5
Waybutt La CW2 . . . . 221 D8
Wayfarers Ct CW9 . . . . . . .79 F7
Wayfarers Dr WA12 . . . . . . .2 E2
Wayford Cl WA6 . . . . 49 B1
Wayford Mews WA7 . . . . . .49 B1
Way's Gn CW7 . . . . 149 E8
WAY'S GREEN 149 E8
Wayside Cl WA13 . . . . 18 D2
Wayside Ct CH2 . . . . 119 F8
Wayside Dr SK12 . . . . 36 C4
Wayside Linley ST7 . . . . . 193 F2
Wayside Rd SK10 . . . . 112 F8
Waystead Cl CW9 . . . . . . 103 F4
Waywell Cl WA2 . . . . .8 F3
Weald Dr CH66 . . . . 69 A6
Wealstone Ct CH2 . . . . . . 118 E5
Weal Stone La CH2 . . . . . 118 E6
Wearhead Cl WA3 . . . . .2 F7
Weaste La WA4 . . . . 17 C2
Weates Cl WA8 . . . . 13 F3
Weathercock La CW12 . . . 157 E3
Weatherstones Cotts
CH64 . . . . 67 D8
Weatherstones Mews
CH64 . . . . 67 C8
Weaver Bank CW5 . . . . . . 204 D5
Weaver Brook Way CH5 . . 216 E4
Weaver Cl Alsager ST7 . . . 193 A3
Biddulph ST8 . . . . 179 D1
Sandbach CW11 . . . . 174 E7
Weaver Cres WA6 . . . . 49 D1
Weaver Ct SK11 . . . . 112 C6
Weaverdale Pk CW8 . . . . . 77 A6
Weaver Gr
Mickle Trafford CH2 . . . . . 119 F8

Weaver Gr continued
St Helens WA9 . . . . .1 A3
Winsford CW7 . . . . 126 E1
Weaver Grange CW9 . . . . 126 E8
Weaverhall La CW7 . . . 150 B5
WEAVERHAM 77 C2
Weaverham By-Pass
Bartington CW8 . . . . .77 B2
Weaverham CW8 . . . . 102 B7
Weaverham High Sch
CW8 . . . . 102 C8
Weaverham Rd CW8 . . . 102 B4
Weaverham Way SK9 . . . .34 E4
Weaver Ho 18 CW8 . . . . 103 F8
Weaver La WA6 . . . . .49 B2
Weaver Park Ind Est WA6 . 49 D2
Weaver Prim Sch The
CW5 . . . . 204 E3
Weaver Rd Culcheth WA3 . . .5 A2
Ellesmere Port CH65 . . . . . .70 C2
Frodsham WA6 . . . . .49 D1
Moulton CW9 . . . . 126 F2
Nantwich CW5 . . . . 204 E6
Northwich CW8 . . . . 103 E7
Runcorn, Heath WA7 . . . . . .49 A6
Weavers Cotts 3 CW12 . 156 D3
Weavers Fold WA1 . . . . . . .16 C6
Weaverside CW5 . . . . 204 E2
Weaverside Ave WA7 . . . .49 F4
Weavers La SK7 . . . . .35 D6
Weaver Square Sh Ctr 22
CW9 . . . . 103 F8
Weaver St Chester CH1 . . 237 A2
Winsford CW7 . . . . 126 E1
Weavervale Pk CW8 . . . . .77 A6
Weaver Valley Rd CW7 . 126 F3
Weaver View
Audlem CW3 . . . . 229 E3
Church Minshull CW5 . . . . 172 A6
Northwich CW8 . . . . 103 F7
Weaverham CW8 . . . . .77 D1
Weaver Way CW9 . . . . . . .78 F1
Webb Dr WA5 . . . . .6 F6
Webb's Cl CW9 . . . . 103 F7
Webb's La CW10 . . . . 128 C2
Webbs Orch SK23 . . . . . . .65 D8
Webster Cl CH4 . . . . 139 C3
Webster Ct Kingswood WA5 . .7 B2
Warrington WA5 . . . . .7 B2
Websters La CH66 . . . . . . .69 F2
Weddell Cl WA5 . . . . .15 D7
Wedge Ave WA11 . . . . .1 A5
Wedgwood Ave ST7 . . . . 210 A1
Wedgwood Dr
Widnes WA8 . . . . .13 B4
Wilderspool WA4 . . . . .16 C3
Wedgwood La ST8 . . . . . 179 C2
Wedgwood Rd ST7 . . . . . 210 D7
Wednesbury Dr WA5 . . . . .14 F6
Weedon Ave WA12 . . . . .2 B5
Wee La WA16 . . . . .58 A6
WEETWOOD COMMON . . 122 C2
Weighbridge Rd CH5 . . . .92 A4
Weint The WA3 . . . . .11 B3
Weir Gr ST7 . . . . 195 B2
Weir La WA1 . . . . .17 E6
Weir St Northwich CW9 . . . 103 F7
Warrington WA4 . . . . .16 A1
Welbeck Ave WA12 . . . . . . .2 D2
Welbeck Cl CW10 . . . . . . 128 B1
Welford Ave WA3 . . . . .3 C7
Welford Cl 7 SK9 . . . . . . .60 E8
Welford Gdns 1 WA5 . . . .14 E8
Welland Cl CW11 . . . . 174 C5
Welland Gdns WA12 . . . . . .2 C1
Welland Rd SK9 . . . . .34 E2
Well Ave SY14 . . . . 213 B3
Well Bank CW11 . . . . 175 B6
Well Bank Cotts WA16 . . 108 C8
Wellbank Cl CW12 . . . . . . 156 E2
Well Bank La WA16,SK11. 108 C7
Wellbrook Cl WA7. . . . . . . .50 C5
Well Cl Neston CH64 . . . . . .67 A4
Shavington CW2 . . . . 206 B5
Wellcroft Cl CW2 . . . . . . 206 B7
Wellcroft Gdns WA13 . . . .19 A2
Weller Ave SK12 . . . . .36 D2
Weller Cl SK12 . . . . .36 D2
Wellesbourne Cl
Macclesfield SK10 . . . . . . .86 F1
Neston CH64 . . . . .66 D6
Wellesley Ave
Ellesmere Port CH65 . . . . . .70 C5
Haslington CW1 . . . . 191 C4
Wellesley Cl WA12 . . . . . . .2 B5
Wellesley Cres CH3 . . . . 142 C5
Wellesley Wlk 6 CH65 . . . .70 C5
Welles St CW11 . . . . 175 B6
Well Farm Cl
Malpas SY14 . . . . 213 B3
Warrington WA1 . . . . .17 D8
Wellfield Runcorn WA7 . . . .50 E5
Widnes WA8 . . . . .13 A3
Winsford CW7 . . . . 127 A2
Wellfield Cl WA16 . . . . . . .80 A7
Wellfield Rd WA3 . . . . .4 F4
Wellfield St WA5 . . . . .15 E5
Wellfield Way SY13 . . . . . 225 F1
Wellingford Ave WA8 . . . .22 B5
Wellington Cir SK10 . . . . . 112 E8
Wellington Cl
Congleton CW12 . . . . 156 D4
3 Ellesmere Port CH65. . . .70 C5
Knutsford WA16 . . . . .57 C4
Newton-le-Willows WA12 . . .2 A3

Wellington Cl continued
Warrington WA2 . . . . .8 F2
Wellington Gate L24 . . . .21 E2
Wellington Gdns WA12 . . . .2 A3
Wellingtonia Dr 3
CW12. . . . . 155 E5
Wellington Pl CH1 . . . . . . 237 B3
Wellington Rd
Bollington SK10 . . . . .87 F8
Broughton CH4 . . . . 139 B4
Ellesmere Port CH65 . . . . . .70 B4
Hazel Grove SK7 . . . . .37 B8
Kidsgrove ST7 . . . . 195 A1
Nantwich CW5 . . . . 204 E4
Wellington Road N CH65 . . 70 C5
Wellington St
15 Macclesfield SK11 . . . . 112 D8
Newton-le-Willows WA12 . . .2 A3
Northwich CW8 . . . . 103 E7
3 Runcorn WA7 . . . . .23 A3
Warrington WA1 . . . . .16 C5
Widnes WA8 . . . . .23 A6
Wellington Street Ind Est
WA8 . . . . .23 A6
Wellington Street Wrkshps
4 WA1 . . . . .16 C5
Well La Alsager ST7 . . . . . 193 C3
Antrobus CW9 . . . . .53 A4
Biddulph ST8 . . . . 179 D3
Chester CH2 . . . . 118 E5
Heswall CH60 . . . . .41 B6
Kingsley WA6 . . . . .75 C2
Little Budworth CW6 . . . . . 147 F7
Macclesfield SK10 . . . . . . .88 B2
Manley WA6 . . . . .98 F3
Mollington CH1 . . . . .94 F2
Neston CH64 . . . . .66 F5
Prestbury SK10 . . . . .87 C8
Stretton WA4 . . . . .52 E8
Warrington WA5 . . . . .14 F3
Weaverham CW8 . . . . .77 C1
Wells Ave
Haslington CW1 . . . . 191 D5
Lostock Gralam CW9 . . . . . .80 B2
Wells Cl
Ellesmere Port CH66 . . . . . .94 E8
Gatley SK8 . . . . .34 C7
Mickle Trafford CH2 . . . . . . 119 F8
Warrington WA1 . . . . .17 B8
WELLS GREEN 205 F8
Well St Malpas SY14 . . . . 213 B3
Mow Cop ST7 . . . . 195 D7
New Mills SK22 . . . . .39 B8
Winsford CW7 . . . . 126 C1
Wellswood Dr CW2 . . . . . 205 F7
Wellswood Rd CH66 . . . . .69 E7
Welsby Cl WA2 . . . . .8 F3
Welshampton Cl CH66 . . .69 D2
Welsh La CW7 . . . . 149 D6
Welshmen's La CW5 . . . . 204 C7
Welshpool Cl WA5 . . . . . . .7 D2
Welsh Rd
Connah's Quay CH5 . . . . . 116 A7
Ellesmere Port CH66 . . . . . .68 E4
Maes Gwyn CH5 . . . . .93 A1
Woodbank CH1 . . . . .93 C6
Welsh Road Cotts CH1. . . 93 D8
Welsh Row
Nantwich CW5 . . . . 204 D5
Nether Alderley SK10 . . . . .84 F6
Welton Cl SK9 . . . . .59 F4
Welton Dr SK9 . . . . .59 F4
Welton Gr SK9 . . . . .59 E4
Welwyn Cl WA4 . . . . .17 C3
Wem Gr ST5 . . . . 210 E2
Wemyss Rd CH1. . . . . 117 D4
Wendover Cl WA11 . . . . . . .1 D7
Wenger Rd WA8 . . . . .13 B5
Wenlock Cl
Macclesfield SK10 . . . . . . .87 B2
Newcastle-under-Lyme
ST5 . . . . 210 E2
Warrington WA1 . . . . .17 A8
Wenlock Gdns CH66 . . . . .69 F2
Wenlock La CH66 . . . . .69 F2
Wenlock Rd WA7. . . . . .50 A4
Wenlock Way CW4 . . . . . . 140 F6
Wenning Dr 3 CW9 . . . . . 104 C5
Wensleydale Ave
Bebington CH62 . . . . .43 E5
Congleton CW12 . . . . 157 A5
Wensleydale Cl WA5 . . . . .14 F8
Wensley Dr SK7 . . . . .36 D7
Wensley Rd WA3 . . . . .3 E7
Wentworth Ave
Macclesfield SK11 . . . . 111 F6
Warrington WA1 . . . . .17 B7
Wentworth Cl
Northwich CW9 . . . . 104 E7
Widnes WA8 . . . . .13 A5
Wentworth Dr
Bebington CH63 . . . . .43 C5
Bramhall SK7 . . . . .36 A7
Kidsgrove ST7 . . . . 195 C3
Wentworth Gr CW7 . . . . . . 126 A2
Werburgh Cl WA13 . . . . . .19 C8
WERETON 209 C1
Wereton Rd ST7 . . . . 209 D1
WERVIN 96 A4
Wervin Rd CH2. . . . . .96 A3
Wesleyan Mus * ST7. . . . 195 D7
Wesley Ave Alsager ST7 . . 193 D4
Haydock WA11 . . . . .1 F7
2 Sandbach CW11 . . . . . 175 B6
Wesley Cl
11 Macclesfield SK10. . . . . .87 B2
Nantwich CW5 . . . . 204 E5
Neston CH64 . . . . .66 D8

Wesley Ct
Congleton CW12 . . . . 156 D2
Winsford CW7 . . . . 126 F1
Wesley Gdns 7 ST7 . . . . 195 A2
Wesley Pl Crewe CW2 . . . . 190 D2
4 Northwich CW9. . . . . . 104 A8
Wesley St ST7 . . . . 210 A1
Wessex Cl
Shavington CW2. . . . . 206 C3
Warrington WA1 . . . . .17 E7
Wessex Dr CW9 . . . . 104 C6
Westage La CW9 . . . . .79 B8
West Ave Crewe CW1 . . . . 190 B4
Kidsgrove ST7 . . . . 194 C1
Middlewich CW10 . . . . . . 128 C2
Northwich CW9 . . . . 104 D7
Warrington WA2 . . . . .16 B8
Weston CW2 . . . . 207 B5
WEST BANK 23 A4
West Bank
Alderley Edge SK9 . . . . . . .85 A8
Chester CH2. . . . . 118 C4
West Bank Dock Est WA8 . .22 E5
West Bank Prim Sch WA8 . 23 A4
West Bank Rd SK10. . . . . . .87 B1
West Bank St WA8 . . . . . . .23 A5
West Bond SK10 . . . . 112 C7
Westbourne Ave CW1 . . . 190 A6
Westbourne Dr 16 SK9. . . . 34 D1
Westbourne Ho CW12 . . . 156 B2
Westbourne Mews
CW12. . . . . 156 B2
Westbourne Rd
Blacon CH1 . . . . 118 A4
Warrington WA4 . . . . .26 B7
Westbridge Mews 3
WA1. . . . . .16 F7
Westbrook Ave WA4 . . . . . 16 D2
WESTBROOK CENTRE 7 B1
Westbrook Cres WA5 . . . . .7 B2
Westbrook Ctr WA5 . . . . . .7 C1
Westbrook Dr SK10 . . . . . 87 C1
Westbrook Old Hall Prim Sch
WA5 . . . . .15 D8
Westbrook Rd WA6 . . . . . . 75 B2
Westbrook Way WA5 . . . . .7 B1
Westbury Cl Crewe CW2. . . 206 C7
Middlewich CW10 . . . . . . 151 B8
Warrington WA1 . . . . .17 A8
Westbury Ct SK11. . . . . . . 112 A7
Westbury Dr SK11 . . . . . . 112 A7
Westby Way CH4 . . . . 140 F6
Westby St SK7 . . . . .36 A7
West Cheshire Coll
Chester CH1. . . . . .69 C1
Chester CH4. . . . . 141 D7
West Cl SK10 . . . . .87 F7
Westcliffe Ct WA8. . . . . . . .13 B4
Westcliff Gdns WA4 . . . . . .26 E3
West Courtyard SK10. . . . .85 A3
Westdale Rd WA1 . . . . .17 A7
West Dr Heswall CH60 . . . . .41 A7
Neston CH64 . . . . .66 E6
Warrington WA5 . . . . .15 B4
Winsford CW7 . . . . 127 A2
West Dudley St CW7. . . . . 126 F1
West End CH3 . . . . 121 E7
West End Cotts CW12. . . . 156 C2
West End Ct LL13. . . . . 196 D8
West End Gr WA11 . . . . .1 A6
West End Rd WA11 . . . . . . .1 A6
Westenra Ave CH65 . . . . . .69 F6
Westerham SK10 . . . . .87 B2
Westerhope Way WA8. . . . .12 F3
Westerings The CH62. . . . .43 C6
Western App CH2 . . . . 118 E4
Western Ave Blacon CH1. . . 117 D4
Macclesfield SK11 . . . . . . 112 C5
Milton Green CH3. . . . . . . 165 C2
Nantwich CW5 . . . . 204 E4
Western Ave Sh Mall 7
CH1. . . . . 117 D4
Western Ct CH2 . . . . 118 E4
Western Dr SK11 . . . . 112 C4
Western Pk CW11 . . . . . . 191 F8
Western Way
Northwich CW8 . . . . 103 C8
Winnington CW8 . . . . .78 C1
Westfield Ave ST7. . . . . . . 209 C2
Westfield Cl Chester CH4 . 141 B7
Winsford CW7 . . . . 149 C5
Westfield Cres WA7 . . . . . .22 E1
Westfield Dr
Knutsford WA16 . . . . .56 E1
Willaston CW2 . . . . 205 E8
Westfield Gr CW8. . . . . . . .77 F4
Westfield Mews WA7 . . . . .22 F1
Westfield Prim Sch WA7 . . 22 E1
Westfield Rd Cheadle SK8. . .34 F8
Mow Cop ST7 . . . . 195 C7
Northwich CW9 . . . . 104 B7
Runcorn WA7 . . . . .22 E1
Westfields WA15. . . . . .31 F8
Westfields Ave SK10. . . . . .87 B1
Westfields Rise CW3 . . . . 232 C1
Westford Rd WA4 . . . . .16 D2
Westgate Widnes WA8 . . . . .22 B7
Wilmslow SK9 . . . . .60 A5
Westgate Ave CW7 . . . . . . 126 A5
Westgate Pk CW2 . . . . 206 E2
West Gn CH5 . . . . 116 A6
West Gr Alsager ST7. . . . . . 193 E4
Heswall CH60 . . . . .40 F8
West Hall Ct WA16 . . . . . . .29 C5
Westhay Cres WA3 . . . . . . 10 A5
WEST HEATH Congleton . . 156 A4

WEST HEATH continued
Crewe 221 E8
West Heath Gr WA13 . . . . . 18 C4
West Heath Sh Ctr
CW12. . . . . 156 A3
Westholme Cl
Congleton CW12 . . . . 156 C3
Crewe CW2 . . . . 206 C8
Westholme Ct SK9 . . . . . . 60 A2
Westhouse Cl CH63 . . . . . .43 C5
West House Ct SK10. . . . . . .86 E1
West Hyde WA13 . . . . .18 C3
West La Cuddington CW8 . . 101 F3
High Legh WA16 . . . . .29 C6
Runcorn WA7 . . . . .49 F8
Westland Ct CW12 . . . . . . 156 C2
Westland Dr WA2 . . . . .8 E2
Westlands ST7 . . . . 209 F2
Westlands Cl CH64 . . . . . . .41 F1
Westlands Rd CW10 . . . . . 128 B1
Westlands The CW12 . . . . 156 C2
Westlea Prim Sch CW2. . . 118 E7
West Lorne St CH1 . . . . . . 237 A3
West Mains L24 . . . . .21 A3
Westmere Cl CW2 . . . . . . 207 B5
Westmere Dr CW1 . . . . . . 190 F2
Westminster Ave CH4 . . . 141 B7
Westminster Cl
Middlewich CW10 . . . . . . 128 B1
9 Northwich CW8. . . . . . 103 C5
Warrington WA4 . . . . .17 C2
Widnes WA8. . . . . .22 B8
Westminster Ct CH2. . . . . 118 E7
Westminster Dr
Bebington CH62 . . . . .43 D7
Cheadle SK8. . . . . .35 B6
Haydock WA11 . . . . .1 F7
Wilmslow SK9 . . . . .60 A4
Westminster Gn CH4 . . . . 141 D7
Westminster Gr
Ellesmere Port CH65 . . . . . .70 C6
8 Winsford CW7. . . . . . . 149 A8
Westminster Ind Pk CH65 . .69 F6
WESTMINSTER PARK 141 B6
Westminster Pl 1 WA1. . . .16 F5
Westminster Prim Sch
CH65. . . . . .70 B6
Westminster Rd
Broughton CH4. . . . . 139 B3
Chester CH2. . . . . 118 F3
Ellesmere Port CH65 . . . . . .70 C6
Macclesfield SK10 . . . . . . .87 C1
4 Macclesfield SK10. . . . 112 C8
Westminster Ret Pk CH65. 70 D6
Westminster St
Crewe CW2 . . . . 190 C2
14 Macclesfield SK10. . . 112 C8
Westminster Terr CH4. . . . 141 C7
Westmoreland Cl WA14 . . .31 B8
Westmorland Ave
Talke ST7 . . . . 210 F7
Widnes WA8. . . . . .13 B1
Westmorland Cl SK10. . . . .86 F2
Westmorland Rd M31 . . . . . 11 E2
Westmorland Terr CW4. . . 130 B3
WESTON Crewe. 207 C5
Macclesfield 111 F8
Weston Cl
Middlewich CW10 . . . . . . 151 C7
Northwich CW9 . . . . 103 F5
Weston Cres WA7 . . . . .49 A6
Weston Ct Runcorn WA7 . . . .48 F7
Shavington CW2. . . . . 206 C5
Weston Ctr The CW1 . . . . 190 E1
Weston Gr Chester CH2. . . 118 E2
Halewood L26 . . . . .21 A6
Weston La CW2 . . . . 206 E5
Weston Link WA7 . . . . .49 D6
WESTON POINT 48 D7
Weston Point Com Prim Sch
WA7 . . . . .48 E7
Weston Point Expressway
Runcorn WA7 . . . . .22 E2
Runcorn, Rocksavage WA7. . .49 B5
Runcorn, Weston WA7 . . . . .48 E6
Weston Prim Sch WA7. . . . 49 A6
Weston Rd Crewe CW1 . . . 190 F1
Runcorn WA7 . . . . .48 E7
Weston CW1, CW2. . . . . . 207 B7
Wilmslow SK9 . . . . .60 E6
Weston Sq SK11 . . . . 111 F7
Weston View WA7. . . . . . . .49 D4
WESTON VILLAGE 48 F6
Weston Village Prim Sch
CW2 . . . . 207 C5
Westover Rd WA1 . . . . .16 F8
West Park Ave SK12 . . . . . .36 A4
West Park Dr 7 CH66 . . . . .94 F8
West Quay Rd WA2 . . . . . . .7 F3
West Rd Congleton CW12. . . 156 C3
Ellesmere Port CH65 . . . . . .70 C3
Hooton CH65 . . . . .44 C4
Runcorn WA7 . . . . .48 D7
Weaverham CW8 . . . . .77 B1
Westrees CW8 . . . . 101 D5
West Side Ave WA11 . . . . . .1 A6
West St Alderley Edge SK9 . . 60 A1
Chester CH2. . . . . 237 C4
Congleton CW12 . . . . 156 D3
Crewe CW1 . . . . 190 B5
Haslington CW1 . . . . 191 C5
Macclesfield SK11 . . . . . . 112 B8
Middlewich CW10 . . . . . . 128 C1
Mount Pleasant ST7 . . . . . 195 B6
Warrington WA2 . . . . .16 B7
West Vale CH64 . . . . .66 E6
West View Antrobus WA4 . . 53 A5
Ellesmere Port CH66 . . . . . .69 A8

West View continued
Northwich CW9 . . . . 104 B8
Warrington WA3 . . . . .9 A1
West View Rd WA6 . . . . . . 101 A4
Westville Dr CW12 . . . . . . 156 A2
Westward Rd
Chester CH3. . . . . 142 B8
Wilmslow SK9 . . . . .59 F6
Westway CH60 . . . . .40 F6
West Way
Holmes Chapel CW4. . . . . 130 B3
Sandbach CW11 . . . . 174 F4
Shavington CW2. . . . . 206 C3
West Wing The CW10 . . . . 127 D5
Westwood WA7 . . . . .24 C1
Westwood Cl CW2 . . . . . . 207 B1
Westwood Ct CH64 . . . . . . .41 E2
Westwood Rd SK8. . . . . . . .34 B8
WESTY 16 F5
Westy La WA4 . . . . .16 F4
Wet Gate La WA13. . . . . 19 E4
Wetheral Rd SK10. . . . . . . .87 B2
Wetherby Cl Chester CH1 . 118 B2
Newton-le-Willows WA12 . . .2 C5
Wetherby Way CH66. . . . . .69 B5
Wet La Hobb Hill SY14. . . . 198 D2
Kidnal SY14 . . . . 212 F7
Wetreins La SY14, CH3 . . . 197 D2
WETTENHALL 170 F7
WETTENHALL GREEN 170 F6
Wettenhall Rd CW5 . . . . . 188 B4
Wetton La CW8 . . . . .76 E4
Wetton Way SK11 . . . . 113 D2
Wexford Ave L24. . . . . .21 D2
Wexford Cl WA11 . . . . .1 D7
Weybourne Ct CW4 . . . . . 140 E5
Weybridge Cl WA4 . . . . . . .26 E7
Weybridge Dr SK10 . . . . . .87 B3
Weygates Dr WA15. . . . . . .32 C7
Weymouth Cl WA7 . . . . . . .50 E6
Weymouth Rd WA5. . . . . . . .6 F1
Whaddon Dr CH4 . . . . 140 F4
WHALEY BRIDGE 65 D7
Whaley Bridge Prim Sch
SK23. . . . . .65 E7
Whaley Bridge Sta SK23 . . .65 E8
Whaley Ct CH1. . . . . 117 A8
Whalley Ave WA3 . . . . .5 C7
Whalley Dr CW6 . . . . 147 B3
Whalley Gr WA8 . . . . .13 D3
Whalley Hayes SK10. . . . . 112 C8
Whalley Rd CW9 . . . . 104 A8
Whalley St WA1 . . . . .16 C6
Wharams Bank CW11. . . . 176 F5
Wharburton Cl CW8 . . . . . 101 F2
Wharf Ct SK23 . . . . .65 E7
Wharfdale Ave CW1 . . . . . 173 B1
Wharfdale Cl WA5 . . . . . . .15 A7
Wharfe Cl CW12. . . . . 156 F1
Wharfedale Ave WA7. . . . . .50 B6
Wharfedale Dr CH62 . . . . .43 F5
Wharfedale Rd CW12. . . . 157 A5
Wharfe La CH65. . . . . 70 A7
Wharf Ind Est The WA1. . . . 16 C4
Wharf La CW12 . . . . 178 B3
Wharf Mill CW12 . . . . 156 F1
Wharford La Runcorn WA7 . .24 F3
Runcorn WA7. . . . . .24 F3
Wharf Rd
Collins Green WA12. . . . . . . 1 E2
Whaley Bridge SK23. . . . . .65 E7
Wharfside Ct 6 WA4 . . . . . 16 E1
Wharf St WA1. . . . . .16 C4
Wharf The Chester CH1. . . 118 B1
Runcorn WA7 . . . . .50 F6
Wharmby Rd WA11. . . . . . . .1 E6
WHARTON 127 A2
Wharton CE Prim Sch
CW7 . . . . 126 F1
Wharton Ct CH2. . . . . 118 F2
Wharton Gdns CW7 . . . . . 127 A3
Wharton Gn CW7. . . . . 127 A4
WHARTON GREEN 127 B4
Wharton Hall CW7 . . . . . . 127 A3
Wharton Ind Est CW7 . . . . 126 F2
Wharton Park Rd CW7. . . . 126 F2
Wharton Rd CW7 . . . . 127 A2
Wharton Ret Pk CW7. . . . . 126 F3
Whatcroft Cl WA7 . . . . . . .49 D6
Whatcroft Hall La CW9 . . 104 F1
Whatcroft La CW9. . . . . . . 127 E8
Whatcroft Way CW10. . . . 151 D5
Wheatcroft Cl WA5. . . . . . .15 C6
Wheatfield Cl
Barnton CW8 . . . . .78 A3
Ellesmere Port CH66 . . . . . .69 C3
Macclesfield SK10 . . . . . . .87 C3
Wheatfield Dr CW1. . . . . . 173 A1
Wheatfield Rd WA8 . . . . . .12 C5
Wheatland Rd CH60 . . . . . .41 C7
Wheatlands WA7 . . . . .23 E1
Wheatley Ave WA12 . . . . . .2 C5
Wheatley Rd CW1 . . . . . . 190 E6
Wheat Moss SK11 . . . . .84 B3
Wheatsheaf Cl SK23 . . . . . .65 E6
Wheatsheaf Rd SK23 . . . . .65 E6
Wheelman Rd CW1. . . . . . 190 A7
WHEELOCK 174 F4
Wheelock CW11 . . . . 174 E3
Wheelock By Pass CW11. . 175 B4
Wheelock Cl Alsager ST7 . . 193 A3
Handforth SK9 . . . . .34 D1
Kingsmead CW9. . . . . 103 F6
Wheelock Ct CW11 . . . . . . 175 A2
Wheelock Dr CW7 . . . . . . 126 B2
WHEELOCK HEATH 192 A4
Wheelock Prim Sch
CW11 . . . . 175 A4

Wheelock St CW10 . . . . . . 128 C1
Wheelock Way 2 ST7 . . . . . 195 B2
Wheldon Cl CH2 . . . . 118 E8
Wheldon Rd WA8 . . . . .21 F7
Wheldrake Cl CH66 . . . . . . .69 B5
Whernside WA8. . . . . 12 C3
Whetstone Hey CH66 . . . . . 69 D5
Whetstone Rd ST8 . . . . . . 179 C2
Wheycroft Mews CW1 . . . . 190 C5
Whickham La WA4 . . . . .12 F3
Whimbrel Ave WA12. . . . . . .2 C3
Whimbrel Cl WA7 . . . . .49 F5
Whinchat Ave WA12 . . . . . . .2 C4
Whinchat Cl WA3 . . . . .3 E7
Whinchat Dr WA3 . . . . .9 F3
Whinfell Gr WA7 . . . . .49 E5
Whipcord La CH1 . . . . 118 B2
Whirley Cl CW10 . . . . 151 C7
WHIRLEY GROVE 86 D3
Whirley La SK10 . . . . .85 F1
Whirley Prim Sch SK10 . . . 86 D1
Whirley Rd SK10 . . . . 86 C1
Whirlow Rd CW2 . . . . 206 B7
WHISTERFIELD 109 D3
Whisterfield La SK11 . . . . . 109 E3
Whiston Cl
  Macclesfield SK11 . . . . . . 112 B4
  Winsford CW7 . . . . 127 A4
Whiston Mews SK11 . . . . . 113 B4
Whistons La SK11 . . . . 113 D1
Whiston St SK11 . . . . 112 C7
Whitbarrow Rd WA13 . . . . . 18 C4
WHITBY 70 A4
Whitby Ave Chester CH2 . . 118 D5
  Warrington WA2 . . . . .8 D2
Whitby Cl Crewe CW1 . . . . 190 B8
  2 Newton-le-Willows WA12 . .1 F2
  Poynton SK12 . . . . 36 D4
Whitby Dr CW8 . . . . 78 C1
WHITBYHEATH. 70 B3
Whitby Heath Prim Sch Cty
  CH65. . . . . .70 B3
Whitby High Sch The
  CH66 . . . . 70 A2
Whitby La CH1 . . . . .95 B6
Whitby Park Nature
  Reserve★ CH65 . . . . .70 B3
Whitby Rd
  Ellesmere Port CH65 . . . . . 70 C5
  Runcorn WA7 . . . . 23 A1
Whitby's La CW7 . . . . 126 B1
WHITCHURCH. 226 A1
Whitchurch Cl WA1 . . . . . . 17 A8
Whitchurch Gr ST5 . . . . . . 210 E2
Whitchurch Rd
  Audlem CW3 . . . . 229 C3
  Beeston-brook CW6 . . . . . 168 D3
  Broxton CH3 . . . . 183 A3
  Chester CH3 . . . . 119 B1
  Christleton CH3 . . . . 142 E7
  Edge Green SY14, CH3 . . . 199 B4
  Handley CH3 . . . . 182 D8
  Milton Green CH3 . . . . . . 165 C4
  Newhall CW5, SY13 . . . . . 228 A6
  Royal's Green CW3, SY13 . . 228 C2
  Sound CW5 . . . . 217 E3
  Waverton CH3 . . . . 143 A3
Whitchurch Way WA7 . . . . . 49 D7
White Ave CW2 . . . . 189 F4
Whitebarn Rd SK9 . . . . . . .85 B8
Whitebeam Ave 5 CH66 . . .69 F1
Whitebeam Cl
  Lower Heath CW12 . . . . . 156 E5
  Newcastle-under-Lyme
  ST5 . . . . 210 D1
  Runcorn WA7 . . . . 24 C1
Whitebeam Row CW8 . . . . 102 E7
White Bear Yd 18 WA16 . . . 57 A2
White Broom WA13 . . . . . . .19 B4
White Clover Sq WA13 . . . . 19 A2
Whitecroft Ct SK10 . . . . . . .87 E2
Whitecroft Heath Rd
  SK11 . . . . 109 B3
Whitecroft Rd CH66 . . . . . 69 A6
Whitecroft Villas M31 . . . . 11 E2
WHITECROSS 15 E6
Whitecross Rd WA5 . . . . . . 15 E5
Whitefield WA13 . . . . 19 A4
Whitefield Ave WA12 . . . . . .2 E2
Whitefield Cl Golborne WA3 . .3 A8
  Lymm WA13 . . . . 19 A5
Whitefield Ct WA3 . . . . .4 F2
Whitefield Gr WA13 . . . . . . 19 A4
Whitefield Rd WA4 . . . . . . .26 B8
Whitefields CH2 . . . . .72 B3
White Friars CH2 . . . . .12 F3
Whitefriars Wlk 2 M22 . . . .33 D8
WHITEGATE. 126 A7
Whitegate Ave WA3 . . . . . . .4 F2
Whitegate CE Prim Sch
  CW8 . . . . 125 F7
Whitegate Cl CW10 . . . . . . 151 C6
Whitegate Fields LL13 . . . . 180 D1
Whitegate La CH3 . . . . 121 E7
Whitegate Rd CW7 . . . . . . 125 F3
Whitegates CW12 . . . . 179 D4
Whitegates Cl CH64 . . . . . .42 E1
Whitegates Cres CH64 . . . . 42 E1
Whitegates Ho CW2 . . . . . 189 E2
Whitehall Ave ST7 . . . . 194 F2
Whitehall Cl Barnton CW8 . . 78 A4
  Wilmslow SK9 . . . . 60 A5
Whitehall Ct 3 CW5. . . . . . 204 D5
Whitehall Dr CW8 . . . . 103 C5
Whitehall La WA6 . . . . 124 E1
White Hall La CW11 . . . . . . 151 E1
White Hall Pl 5 WA6 . . . . . .74 B8
White Hart Gdns CW8 . . . . 102 F4

White Hart La CW2 . . . . . . 205 E8
Whitehaven La CW5 . . . . . . 203 A7
Whitehaven Rd SK7 . . . . . . 35 C5
WHITE HILL 195 B2
Whitehill Rd ST7 . . . . 195 B2
White House La WA11 . . . . . .1 B6
White House Dr WA1 . . . . . .17 E7
Whitehouse Expressway
  WA7. . . . . 50 A1
Whitehouse Ind Est WA7. . . 50 E4
Whitehouse La
  Nantwich CW5 . . . . 204 F7
  Partington WA14 . . . . 20 D8
  Plumley WA16 . . . . .80 F5
Whitehouse Rd WA16 . . . . . 30 B3
White Iris Pl 3 CW5. . . . . . 205 A3
White La CH3 . . . . 142 D8
Whiteleas Rd SK23 . . . . . . 65 D3
Whiteleggs La WA13 . . . . . .19 B1
WHITELEY GREEN 62 E2
White Lodge Cl CH62 . . . . . 43 D5
White Lodge Mews CW8 . . . 102 A3
Whitemere Ct CH65 . . . . . . 70 C7
Whitemore Rd CW10 . . . . . 151 C6
Whitepark Cl CW10. . . . . . . 128 D2
Whiteridge Rd ST7 . . . . . . 195 B2
Whitesands Rd WA13 . . . . . 18 C4
Whiteside Rd WA11 . . . . . . .1 B6
Whites La CW2 . . . . 207 B6
Whites Mdw CH3 . . . . 142 A7
Whitesmead Cl SK12 . . . . . 38 D5
White St
  Macclesfield SK11 . . . . . . 112 D6
  Warrington WA1 . . . . 16 A5
  Warrington, Stockton Heath
  WA4 . . . . 16 C1
  Widnes WA8. . . . . 23 A5
Whitethorn Ave WA5 . . . . . 14 F5
Whitethorn Way ST5 . . . . . 210 E1
Whitethroat Wlk WA3 . . . . . 9 F3
Whitewell Cl CW5 . . . . 204 F5
Whitewood La SY14 . . . . . . 212 D7
White Wood Rd 11
  CW11. . . . . 175 D7
Whitfield Ave WA1 . . . . . . .16 F7
Whitfield Dr SK11 . . . . 112 B4
Whitfield Gr WA11 . . . . . . .1 A6
Whitfield Rd ST7 . . . . 195 B2
Whitfields The SK10 . . . . . . 87 A1
Whitley Ave Barnton CW8 . . 78 B3
  Warrington WA4 . . . . 17 A4
Whitley Cl
  Middlewich CW10 . . . . . . 151 B7
  Runcorn WA7 . . . . 48 F8
Whitley Dr
  Broughton CH4. . . . . 139 D4
  Hartford WA8. . . . . 103 A4
Whitley La WA16 . . . . .55 B8
Whitley Pl CW1 . . . . 190 D8
WHITLEY REED 53 D8
Whitley Village Sch/Sch
  House WA4. . . . . 52 A4
Whitlow Ave CW5 . . . . 204 F4
Whitlow La CW9 . . . . 126 F8
Whitney Croft SK10 . . . . . . 113 A8
Whitson Cl WA16. . . . . 29 C4
Whitstable Pk WA8. . . . . . . 12 E4
Whittaker Ave WA2 . . . . . . .8 D2
Whittaker Cl
  Congleton CW12 . . . . 156 E5
  Crewe CW1 . . . . 190 A7
Whittington Gdns CW9 . . . 104 A2
Whittle Ave Haydock WA11. . .1 A5
  Warrington WA5 . . . . 15 A7
Whittle Cl CH5 . . . . 116 A3
Whittle Hall La WA5 . . . . . . 14 F6
Whittlewood Cl WA3 . . . . . 10 A5
Whitton Dr CH2 . . . . 118 E5
Whitwell Cl WA5 . . . . 14 D7
Whitworth Ct WA3 . . . . . . .9 E3
Wicker La
  Altrincham WA15 . . . . 32 C8
  Guilden Sutton CH3 . . . . . 120 A4
Wickson La CH3, CW6 . . . . 167 D3
Wickstead Cl CW5. . . . . . . 205 A4
Wicksten Dr WA7 . . . . 23 C2
Widdale Cl WA5. . . . . 14 F7
Widgeon Cl SK12. . . . . 36 B4
Widgeons Covert CH63. . . . 41 F5
WIDNES. 22 E7
Widnes Rd
  Cuerdley Cross WA5, WA8 . .13 F2
  Warrington WA5 . . . . 14 C3
  Widnes WA8. . . . . 23 B8
Widnes Shopping Park 1
  WA8. . . . . .23 B8
Widnes Sh Pk 15 WA8. . . . 23 B8
Widnes Sta WA8 . . . . 13 A3
Widnes Trade Pk WA8 . . . . 23 C8
Widnes Waterfront WA8 . . . 23 C7
Wiend The CW8 . . . . 118 D4
Wigeon Rd CW2. . . . . 189 E1
Wigg Island Nature
  Reserve★ WA7. . . . . .23 E4
Wight Cl CH65. . . . . 70 C1
Wightman Ave
  Hurdsfield SK10. . . . . 87 C1
  Newton-le-Willows WA12 . . .2 C5
Wigland Hall La SY14 . . . . 224 C6
Wigmore Cl WA3. . . . . 10 A6
Wigsey La WA13 . . . . 19 A7
WIGSHAW. 4 D2
Wigshaw La WA3. . . . . .4 D2
Wigwam Cl SK12. . . . . 36 C4
Wilbraham Cl Acton CW5 . . 204 A7

Wilbraham Cl continued
  Mickle Trafford CH2 . . . . . 119 F8
Wilbraham Rd
  Acton CW5 . . . . 204 A7
  Congleton CW12 . . . . 156 F3
  Weaverham CW8. . . . . . . .77 C1
Wilbrahams Way ST7 . . . . . 193 D4
Wilbraham's Wlk ST7 . . . . 209 D2
Wilcock Rd WA11 . . . . .2 B8
Wilcote Cl WA8 . . . . 13 C4
Wilcott Dr SK9. . . . . 59 F4
Wild Arum Cl 8 WA3. . . . . . 3 E8
WILDBOARCLOUGH 137 E6
Wilderhope Cl CW2 . . . . . . 206 C7
WILDERSPOOL 16 C2
Wilderspool Cres WA4 . . . . .16 B1
Wilderspool Cswy WA4 . . . . 16 C3
Wild Flower Cl 5 CW5 . . . . 205 A3
Wild Goose Ave ST7 . . . . . 195 D3
Wilding Ave 8 WA7. . . . . . .23 B2
Wilding Bsns Pk CH3 . . . . . 119 C4
Wilding Dr CW1. . . . . 190 D7
Wildings Gr CW9. . . . . 103 F2
Wildings Old La WA3 . . . . . .9 A8
Wilding St CW1. . . . . 190 E4
Wildmoor La CH3 . . . . 97 D1
Wildwood Gr WA1. . . . . . . .17 B7
WILKESLEY 233 F7
Wilkesley La SY13 . . . . . . 233 F7
Wilkin Croft 5 SK8. . . . . . . 34 E8
Wilkins La SK9. . . . . 33 E5
Wilkinson Ave WA1 . . . . . . .16 F6
Wilkinson Cl WA8 . . . . 23 A5
Wilkinson Ct CW7 . . . . 149 B6
Wilkinson St
  Ellesmere Port CH65 . . . . . 70 C6
  Warrington WA2 . . . . 16 C7
Wilkinson Street Mews 1
  CH65 . . . . 70 C6
Wilkinson Street N CH65. . . 70 C6
Wilkinson Way CW7 . . . . . . 149 B7
Willan Rd CH1 . . . . 117 D4
WILLASTON Ellesmere Port . . 68 A4
  Nantwich 205 D8
Willaston CE Prim Sch
  CH64. . . . . .67 F8
Willaston Dr L26 . . . . 21 A6
Willaston Farm CH64 . . . . . .67 F8
Willaston Green Mews
  CH64 . . . . .67 F8
Willaston Hall Gdns
  CW5. . . . . 205 C6
Willaston Primary Acad
  CW5 . . . . 205 D6
Willaston Rd CH63, CH64 . . 42 D4
Willaston Way 8 SK9. . . . . . 34 D5
Willbank La CW5. . . . . 202 D5
Willerby Cl 1 SK10. . . . . . . 112 C8
Willeymoor La SY13 . . . . . 225 D8
William Barker Ct 10
  . . . . 175 B6
William Beamont Com High
  Sch & Specialist Sports
  Coll WA2 . . . . .8 C1
William Ct CH64. . . . . .41 F2
William Dykes Cl 3
  CW1. . . . . 191 D5
William Foden Cl CW11. . . . 174 D7
William Higgins Cl ST7 . . . 192 F4
William Johnson Gdns
  CH65 . . . . 70 C6
William Penn Cl WA5. . . . . .14 E5
William Rd ST7 . . . . 195 A2
Williams Ave WA12. . . . . . . .2 C5
Williams Cl CH2. . . . . 118 C4
Williams Dr
  Shavington CW2. . . . . 206 B5
  Stud Green CW11. . . . . . . 152 C2
Williamson Cres SK23 . . . . 65 D8
Williamson Dr CW5 . . . . . . 204 C5
Williamson Rd SK23 . . . . . 65 D8
William St Chester CH1 . . . 237 B3
  Congleton CW12 . . . . 157 A4
  Macclesfield SK10 . . . . . . 112 F8
  6 Northwich CW9 . . . . . . 104 B8
  Widnes WA8. . . . . 13 C1
  Winsford CW7 . . . . 126 E1
William Stockton Cl
  CW2 . . . . 206 D4
William Stockton Com Prim
  Sch CH65. . . . . .70 B5
Williams Way
  Frodsham WA6. . . . . 74 A8
  Henbury SK11 . . . . 111 C8
William Wild Dr CH1 . . . . . 117 F7
Willington Ave CH62 . . . . . .43 E3
Willington Cnr CW6 . . . . . . 122 E2
Willington La
  Duddon CW6 . . . . 145 E7
  Kelsall CW6 . . . . 122 D4
Willington Rd
  Duddon CW6 . . . . 145 B7
  Kelsall CW6 . . . . 122 C4
Willis Cl CH3. . . . . 119 E5
Willis St WA1. . . . . 16 D6
Willmer Cres ST7 . . . . 195 B6
Willotts Hill Rd ST5 . . . . . 210 D1
Willoughby Cl WA5. . . . . . . .7 C1
Willow Ave
  Newton-le-Willows WA12 . . .2 E4
  2 Widnes WA8 . . . . .13 B2
Willoway Rd CH3. . . . . 119 B2
Willow Bank Cheadle SK8. . . 35 A6
  Helsby WA6 . . . . 73 D2
  Nantwich CW5 . . . . 204 F6
Willowbank Dr SK10. . . . . . 88 C8
Willow Bank Est WA12. . . . .2 F4

Willowbrook CH5 . . . . 116 B4
Willowbrow Rd CH63,
  CH64 . . . . 42 D3
Willow Cl Chester CH2. . . . 118 D8
  Lymm WA13 . . . . 18 E4
  Newcastle-under-Lyme
  ST5 . . . . 210 D1
  Paddockhill WA16 . . . . . . .59 B5
  Poynton SK12 . . . . 36 E3
  Runcorn WA7 . . . . 49 C7
  Winsford CW7 . . . . 126 D3
Willow Cres Chester CH2 . . 119 A4
  Crewe CW2 . . . . 189 F2
  Moore WA4 . . . . 25 A7
  Warrington WA1 . . . . .17 B8
Willowcroft Way ST7 . . . . . 195 E4
Willow Ct Alsager ST7 . . . . 193 E4
  Connah's Quay CH5 . . . . . 91 D1
  Higher Kinnerton CH4 . . . . 161 A7
  Macclesfield SK10 . . . . . . .87 B2
  Middlewich CW10 . . . . . . 128 C2
  Nantwich CW5 . . . . 204 F7
  Newton-le-Willows WA12 . . .2 D4
  Warrington WA2 . . . . .7 F3
  Winsford CW7 . . . . 127 B2
Willowdale WA1 . . . . .17 B8
Willowdale Way CH66 . . . . .94 F8
Willow Dr Blacon CH1 . . . . 117 D5
  Bunbury CW6 . . . . 185 E8
  Handforth SK9 . . . . 34 D3
  Sandbach CW11 . . . . 175 E7
  Warrington WA4 . . . . .16 E1
Willow Gn Knutsford WA16 . 56 F3
  Weaverham CW8. . . . . . . 102 D8
Willow Gr Barnton CW8 . . . 78 B4
  Chester CH2. . . . . 119 B4
  Ellesmere Port CH66 . . . . . 95 A8
  Elton CH2 . . . . 72 A3
WILLOW GREEN 77 B5
Willow Green La CW8 . . . . .77 B5
Willow Hayes CH3. . . . . . . 121 F7
Willowherb Cl CH3 . . . . . . 142 A6
Willow La Goostrey CW4 . . . 107 E1
  Thornton Hough CH63,
  CH64 . . . . 42 D3
  Warrington WA4 . . . . .26 E4
Willow Lea CH1 . . . . 94 F2
Willowmead Dr SK10 . . . . . 87 A5
Willowpool WA13 . . . . 19 C1
Willow Rd Chester CH4 . . . 140 F6
  Haydock WA11 . . . . .1 E7
  High Lane SK6 . . . . .37 F7
  Newton-le-Willows WA12 . . .2 E4
  Partington M31 . . . . 11 E2
Willows The
  Frodsham WA6. . . . . 74 C8
  Higher Wincham CW9 . . . . .79 F6
  Newton-le-Willows WA12 . . .2 D4
  2 Northwich CW9 . . . . . . 103 E6
  Partington M31 . . . . 11 F3
  Sandbach CW11 . . . . 175 B7
  Warrington WA5 . . . . 14 F5
Willow Stream SK22. . . . . . 39 D8
Willow Tree Ct WA8 . . . . . . 13 D2
Willow Tree Gr ST7 . . . . . . 193 F7
Willowview Sch CW1 . . . . . 173 D2
Willow Way Bramhall SK7. . . 35 D7
  Broughton CH4. . . . . 139 B3
  Prestbury SK10 . . . . 87 A5
Willow Wood Com Prim Sch
  CW7 . . . . 127 A2
Wilmere La WA8 . . . . 13 A6
Wilmot Ave WA5 . . . . 14 F6
Wilmot Dr WA3 . . . . 2 F7
WILMSLOW. 60 D7
Wilmslow Acad The SK9. . . 34 E1
Wilmslow Ave CH66 . . . . . .69 E5
Wilmslow Cres WA4 . . . . . .17 D4
Wilmslow Ct SK9. . . . . 34 D3
Wilmslow Dr CH66 . . . . . . .69 E5
Wilmslow Grange Prim Sch
  SK9 . . . . 34 C4
Wilmslow High Sch SK9 . . . .60 B6
Wilmslow L Ctr SK9. . . . . . .60 B7
Wilmslow Old Rd
  Mottram St Andrew SK10. . .61 A2
  Wythenshawe M90. . . . . . 33 A6
WILMSLOW PARK 60 D7
Wilmslow Park N SK9 . . . . 60 D7
Wilmslow Park S SK9. . . . . 60 C7
Wilmslow Prep Sch SK9 . . .60 B7
Wilmslow Rd
  Adlington SK10 . . . . 61 D6
  Alderley Edge SK9 . . . . . . 60 A4
  Gatley SK8 . . . . 34 D7
  Gatley SK8, SK9 . . . . 34 C6
  Handforth SK9 . . . . 34 D4
  Mottram St Andrew SK10. . . 61 A3
  Mottram St Andrew, Greendale
  SK10. . . . . 86 D8
  Woodford SK7 . . . . 35 C1
  Wythenshawe M90, SK9,
  WA15 . . . . .32 F5
Wilmslow Sta SK9 . . . . 60 C7
Wilmslow Way SK9. . . . . . . 34 F4
Wilmslow Wlk 13 SK11 . . . . 112 E6
Wilsbury Grange CW8 . . . . 103 A5
Wilsden Rd WA8 . . . . .12 B1
Wilson Cl Warrington WA4 . . 17 D3
  4 Widnes WA8 . . . . 13 D1
Wilson Cres CW9. . . . . .80 B3
Wilson Dr CW9. . . . . 126 F7

Wilson Patten St WA1 . . . . 16 A4
Wilsons La CH65 . . . . 70 A3
Wilson St
  Warrington, Bewsey WA5 . . 16 A7
  Warrington, Birchwood WA3 . 9 E5
Wilton Ave SK8 . . . . 34 C7
Wilton Cl
  Ellesmere Port CH66 . . . . .69 B5
  Northwich CW9 . . . . 103 E4
Wilton Cres
  Alderley Edge SK9 . . . . . . .59 F2
  Macclesfield SK11 . . . . . . 111 E6
Wilton Dr WA15 . . . . 32 C8
Wilton La WA3 . . . . .4 B5
Wiltshire Cl
  Macclesfield SK10 . . . . . . .86 E2
  Warrington WA1 . . . . 17 D6
Wiltshire Dr CW12 . . . . . . 156 E4
Wiltshire Rd M31 . . . . .11 E2
Wiltshire Wlk SK10. . . . . . . .86 F2
Wilwick La SK11 . . . . 111 F7
Wimberry Dr ST5 . . . . 210 D1
WIMBOLDSLEY 150 F4
Wimboldsley Ave CW10. . . . 151 D5
Wimboldsley Com Prim Sch
  CW10 . . . . 150 F4
WIMBOLDS TRAFFORD 96 F6
Wimborne Cl WA5 . . . . . . .15 C5
WINCHAM 79 D3
Wincham Ave CW9 . . . . 79 D3
Wincham Bsns Pk CW9 . . . 79 D3
Wincham Com Prim Sch
  CW9. . . . . .79 F5
Wincham La CW9 . . . . 79 D3
Wincham Park (Witton
  Albion FC) CW9. . . . . 79 C2
Winchester Ave
  Ellesmere Port CH65 . . . . . 70 C4
  Warrington WA5 . . . . 15 C5
Winchester Cl
  Shavington CW2. . . . . 206 B3
  Wilmslow SK9 . . . . .59 E5
Winchester Ct CW2 . . . . . . 207 E3
Winchester Dr SK10 . . . . . 111 F8
Winchester Ho 12 SK10 . . . 111 F8
Winchester Pl WA8. . . . . . . 22 C8
Winchester Sq CH4. . . . . . 140 F5
WINCLE 160 A7
Wincle Ave SK12 . . . . 36 F2
Wincle CE Prim Sch
  SK11 . . . . 136 F1
Wincle La SK11 . . . . 136 E6
Windermere Ave
  Chester CH2. . . . . 119 A6
  Warrington WA2 . . . . .8 D3
  Widnes WA8. . . . . 13 B4
Windermere Cl CH64 . . . . . .66 F7
Windermere Dr
  Alderley Edge SK9 . . . . . . .59 F1
  Congleton CW12 . . . . 156 A2
Windermere Rd
  Crewe CW2 . . . . 189 E2
  Ellesmere Port CH65 . . . . . 70 C2
  Handforth SK9 . . . . 34 C4
  Haydock WA11 . . . . .1 B6
  High Lane SK6 . . . . .37 E8
  Winsford CW7 . . . . 126 C2
Windermere St WA8 . . . . . . 13 B4
Windess Sh Pk 15 WA8. . . . 23 B8
Windfields Gdns CH66 . . . . 69 D7
Windgather Rd SK23 . . . . . 90 A7
Windings The CW10 . . . . . 128 B2
Windle Ct Neston CH64. . . . 41 E2
  Warrington WA3 . . . . .9 C4
WINDLE HILL 67 C7
Windlehurst Ct SK6 . . . . . . 37 D5
Windlehurst Rd SK12. . . . . 37 D8
Windmill Cl Buerton CW3. . 230 E4
  Warrington WA4 . . . . 26 C6
Windmill Dr CW3 . . . . 229 F3
WINDMILL HILL 24 C1
Windmill Hill Ave WA7. . . . . 24 D2
Windmill Hill Avenue E
  WA7. . . . . 24 D1
Windmill Hill Avenue N
  WA7. . . . . 24 D3
Windmill Hill Avenue S
  WA7. . . . . 24 D2
Windmill Hill Avenue W
  WA7. . . . . 24 C2
Windmill Hill Prim Sch
  WA7. . . . . 24 C2
Windmill La
  Bollington SK10 . . . . .88 B6
  Christleton CH3 . . . . 142 D8
  Hankelow CW3. . . . . 230 F4
  Preston on the Hill WA4 . . . 51 A6
  Warrington WA4 . . . . 26 C6
  Warrington, Penketh WA5 . . 14 E5
Windmill Rise CH2 . . . . . . 118 D7
Windmill St
  Macclesfield SK11 . . . . . . 112 E6
  Runcorn WA7 . . . . 23 B2
Windscale Rd WA2 . . . . . . .9 C2
Windsor Ave Crewe CW1 . . 190 B6
  Newton-le-Willows WA12 . . .2 D2
  1 Tarporley CW6 . . . . 146 D1
  Wilmslow SK9 . . . . .34 F4
Windsor Cl Bollington SK10. .87 E6
  Cuddington CW8 . . . . 101 F4
  Middlewich CW10 . . . . . . 151 D7
  Poynton SK12 . . . . 36 D4
Windsor Ct Chester CH1 . . 237 B1
  1 Warrington WA4 . . . . . . .16 E1

Windsor Dr Alsager ST7 . . **192** F4
Altrincham, Bowdon WA14. . .**20** F1
Broughton CH4. . . . . **139** A3
Ellesmere Port CH65 . . . . . . **70** A3
Faddiley CW5. . . . . **202** E7
Haydock WA11. . . . .**2** A7
Helsby WA6 . . . .**73** B2
Warrington WA4 . . . .**17** B2
Winsford CW7 . . . . **149** C5
Windsor Gr Cheadle SK8 . . . .**34** F8
Runcorn WA7. . . . .**49** B8
Windsor Ho
5 Northwich CW8. . . . . **103** C5
Talke ST7 . . . . **210** D6
Windsor Pl CW12 . . . . **156** F2
Windsor Rd Chester CH4. . **140** F6
Golborne WA3 . . . .**3** C8
Widnes WA8 . . . . **13** A4
Wistaston CW7 . . . . **205** E8
Windsor Sq SK11. . . . . **112** D4
Windsor St WA5 . . . .**15** E6
Windsor Way WA16 . . . .**56** F2
Windways CH66. . . . .**69** D7
Windy Bank Ave WA3. . . . .**3** E8
WINDYHARBOUR **109** C1
Winfield Way WA8 . . . .**23** B8
Winfrith Rd WA2. . . . .**9** A2
Wingate Rd CW62 . . . .**43** E5
Wingfield Ave SK9. . . . .**59** E6
Wingfield Dr SK9. . . . .**59** E6
Wingfield Pl CW7 . . . . **149** B6
Winghay Rd ST7 . . . . **195** B2
Winifred St WA2 . . . .**16** C7
Winkwell Dr CH4. . . . . **141** A5
Winlowe **18** SK11. . . . . **112** E7
Winmarith Dr WA15 . . . .**32** D7
Winmarleigh St WA1 . . . .**16** A4
WINNINGTON **78** D1
Winnington Ave CW8. . . . . . **103** C8
Winnington Ct **13** CW8. . . . . **103** F8
Winnington Hill CW8. . . . . . **103** F8
Winnington La CW8 . . . .**78** D1
Winnington Park Prim Sch
CW8 . . . . **103** D7
Winnington St
Northwich CW8 . . . . **103** F8
Winsford CW7 . . . . **126** E1
Winnows The WA7 . . . .**23** D1
Winscar CI WA5. . . . .**14** E8
Winscombe Dr CH3 . . . . **119** C2
Winsfield Rd SK7. . . . .**36** E8
WINSFORD **126** E2
Winsford-Bypass CW7 . . . **150** A8
Winsford CI WA11. . . . .**1** F7
Winsford Cross Sh Ctr
CW7 . . . . **126** D1
Winsford Dr WA5 . . . .**6** E7
Winsford E-ACT Acad
CW7 . . . . **126** C1
Winsford Gr CH66. . . . .**69** C3
Winsford High Street Com
Prim Sch CW7 . . . . **126** D1
Winsford Ind Est CW7 . . . . **127** C3
Winsford Lifestyle Ctr
CW7 . . . . **149** D8
Winsford Rd CW7 . . . . **170** F6
Winsford Sta CW7. . . . . **127** C1
Winsford Way CH1 . . . . **117** F2
Winslow CI WA7 . . . .**50** D8
Winstanley CI WA5. . . . .**15** C5
Winstanley Ho WA16 . . . .**56** F2
Winstanley Ind Est WA2. . . . . .**8** B1
Winstanley Rd CH64. . . . .**66** E5
Winston Ave Alsager ST7 . . **193** C5
Newton-le-Willows WA12 . . . . .**2** C3
St Helens WA9 . . . .**1** B2
Winston Ct CH2 . . . . **119** A5
Winterberry Way CW5. . . . . **205** A3
Winterbottom La WA16. . . . . .**55** E8
Winterburn WA5. . . . .**14** C6
Winterford La CW6. . . . . **147** B2
Winter Gr WA9. . . . .**1** B3
Wintergreen Wlk **3** M31 . . .**11** F3
Winterlea Dr L26. . . . .**21** A6
WINTERLEY **191** F7
Winterside CI ST5. . . . . **210** D1
Winterton Way SK11 . . . . . . **112** D3
Winton Gr WA7 . . . .**24** D1
Winton Rd WA3. . . . .**3** E6
WINWICK **8** A6
Winwick CE Prim Sch WA2. . . .**8** B6
Winwick La WA3 . . . .**3** E3
Winwick Link Rd WA2, WA3. . .**8** C6
Winwick Park Ave WA2. . . . .**8** A5
WINWICK QUAY **8** A3
Winwick Quay WA2 . . . .**8** A3
Winwick Rd
Newton-le-Willows WA12 . . . . .**2** F1
Warrington WA2 . . . .**8** A2
Winwick St WA2 . . . .**16** B6
Winwick View WA5. . . . .**1** D1
Wirksmoor Rd SK22 . . . .**39** B7
Wirral CI WA3. . . . .**4** E4
Wirral Cres CH64. . . . .**66** F5
Wirral Ctry Pk★ CH64. . . . . . .**67** C4
Wirral Way The CH60. . . . .**40** D8
WIRSWALL **226** A5
Wirswall Rd SY13 . . . . **226** C8
Wisbech CI WA7 . . . .**24** E1
Wisdom Wlk CW11 . . . . **174** D7
Wisenholme CI WA7. . . . .**49** E5
WISTASTON **205** D8
Wistaston Ave CW2 . . . . **189** F2
Wistaston Church Lane Prim
Sch CW2 . . . . **205** E8

WISTASTON GREEN. **189** D2
Wistaston Green CI CW2. **189** E2
Wistaston Green Prim Sch
CW2. . . . . **189** D2
Wistaston Green Rd
CW2. . . . . **189** E2
Wistaston Pk CW2 . . . . **189** F1
Wistaston Rd Crewe CW2. **190** C3
Wistaston CW5 . . . . **205** E6
Wistaston Road Bsns Ctr
CW2 . . . . **190** B4
Wisterdale CI CW2 . . . . **206** A7
Wisteria Way WA9 . . . .**6** A1
Witham CI CW2 . . . . **206** A8
Witham Way ST8. . . . . **179** E1
Withens CI CW8. . . . . **102** D8
Withenshaw La SK11 . . . . . . **136** E5
Withens La CW8. . . . . **102** D8
Withers Ave WA2 . . . .**16** D8
Wither's La
High Legh, Primrose Hill
WA16 . . . .**28** C6
High Legh, Rowlinson's Green
WA16 . . . .**28** B4
Witherwin Ave WA4. . . . .**26** F7
Withington Ave WA3 . . . .**5** A3
Withington CI
Northwich CW9 . . . . **104** A6
Sandbach CW11. . . . . **175** C7
WITHINGTON GREEN. **108** E3
Withinlee Rd SK10 . . . .**86** D6
Withins Rd Culcheth WA3 . . . . .**4** F3
Haydock WA11. . . . .**1** F8
Within Way Hale L24 . . . .**21** E1
Weston Point L24. . . . .**48** A8
Withnall Dr CW2 . . . . **206** B4
Withy CI WA6 . . . .**74** C8
Withycombe Rd WA5. . . . .**14** E4
Withy Croft CH3. . . . . **142** B7
Withyfold Dr SK10. . . . .**87** E1
Withy La CH3 . . . . **183** A1
Witney Gdns WA4 . . . .**26** E6
Witney La SY14 . . . . **213** D8
Wittenham Ho SK9 . . . .**34** D2
Wittering La CH60. . . . .**40** D7
Witterings The CH64. . . . .**41** E1
Witton Church Walk CE VA
Prim Sch CW9 . . . . **104** A8
Witton Lake WA5 . . . .**14** D8
Witton Pk CW9 . . . . **102** F4
Witton St CW9 . . . .**79** A1
Witton Wlk **5** CW9 . . . . **103** F8
Witt Rd WA8. . . . .**23** A7
Wivern Pl WA7 . . . .**23** B3
Wob The WA6 . . . . **100** F7
Woburn Ave WA12 . . . .**2** D2
Woburn CI Haydock WA11. . . . .**1** F7
Macclesfield SK10 . . . .**87** C2
Northwich CW9 . . . . **103** E5
Woburn Ct SK12 . . . .**36** F4
Woburn Dr Chester CH2 . . . **118** F7
Congleton CW12 . . . . **179** B8
Cronton WA8 . . . .**12** D6
Woburn Rd WA2 . . . .**8** A4
Woking Rd SK8 . . . .**35** A7
Wolfe CI
Grappenhall Heys WA4. . . . . .**27** A8
Knutsford WA16. . . . .**57** C3
Wolstanholme CI CW12.. **156** F1
Wolstanholme Elmy Way
Radnor CW12. . . . . **155** E5
West Heath CW12 . . . . **156** C6
WOLVERHAM **70** D4
Wolverham Prim Sch
CH65. . . . .**70** D4
Wolverham Rd CH65 . . . .**70** D3
Wolverton Dr
Handforth SK9 . . . .**34** D1
Runcorn WA7 . . . .**24** D1
Wolverton Ho **11** SK9 . . . .**60** A1
Wolvesey Pl CW7 . . . . **149** B6
Woodacre Gr CH66. . . . .**69** F8
Woodacre Rd CH66. . . . .**69** F8
Woodacres Ct SK9 . . . .**59** F6
Woodale Cl WA5 . . . .**14** E7
Woodall Ave CH4 . . . . **140** E6
Woodall Dr WA7 . . . .**23** B1
Woodavens Gr CW3 . . . . **229** A2
WOODBANK **93** F6
Woodbank SK9 . . . .**60** A2
Woodbank CI CW2 . . . . **206** A7
Woodbank La CH1 . . . .**93** D5
Woodbank Rd
Ellesmere Port CH65 . . . .**70** B2
Warrington WA5 . . . .**15** A4
Woodbine Ave M44 . . . .**11** D4
Woodbine Rd WA13 . . . .**19** B4
Woodbourne Rd SK22 . . . .**39** A5
Woodbridge CI WA4. . . . .**26** E4
Woodbrook SK23. . . . .**65** E8
Woodbrook CI SK23 . . . .**65** E7
Woodbrook Rd SK9 . . . .**60** C1
Woodburn Dr CH60. . . . .**40** F6
Woodchurch La CH66 . . . .**69** E6
Woodclose CH60. . . . .**44** A1
Woodcock La ST7 . . . . **195** C6
Woodcock's Well CE Prim
Sch ST7 . . . . **195** C6
Woodcote Ave CH65. . . . .**70** B1
Woodcote CI WA2. . . . .**8** D1
Woodcote Pl CW11 . . . . **191** F8
Woodcotes The CH62. . . . .**43** D6
Woodcote View SK9. . . . .**34** F1
Woodcott Ave CW7 . . . . **126** B1
Woodcott CI CW2 . . . . **206** E2
Woodcott Gr **3** SK9. . . . .**34** E1
Woodcotthill La CW5 . . . . . . **217** B3
Woodcroft ST7 . . . . **210** A1

Wood Croft CH3 . . . . **119** F4
Woodcroft Gdns WA4 . . . .**26** E6
Wood Dr ST7 . . . . **193** A4
WOODEND. **38** E8
Woodend WA7. . . . .**50** E7
Woodend CI CW10 . . . . **151** C6
Wood End Ct WA8. . . . .**13** D2
Woodend Farm La CH3 . . . . **183** E1
Wood End La
Hollins Green WA3. . . . .**10** D2
Mobberley WA16 . . . .**58** E8
Wood End La
4 Barrow's Green WA8. . . . .**13** E4
Burton CH64. . . . .**67** E4
Woodend Rd CH65 . . . .**69** F6
Woodfall CI CH64. . . . .**67** A6
Woodfall Gr CH64. . . . .**67** A6
Woodfall La CH64. . . . .**67** B6
Woodfall Prim Sch CH64. . . .**67** A6
Wood Farm CW2. . . . . **189** B4
Wood Farm CH3 . . . . **119** E5
Woodfield CI CH4 . . . . **139** A3
Woodfield Gr CH2. . . . . **119** B5
Woodfield Ho CH2 . . . . **119** A5
Woodfield Rd Cheadle SK8. . .**35** B7
Ellesmere Port CH65 . . . .**70** C5
Woodfield Road N **2**
CH65. . . . .**70** C5
Woodfields CH3 . . . . **142** E7
Woodfin Croft SK11. . . . .**84** A3
WOODFORD **35** E2
Woodford Aerodrome
SK7. . . . .**36** A1
Woodford Ave WA3 . . . .**3** D7
Woodford CI Crewe CW2 . . **189** F2
Helsby WA6 . . . .**73** B2
Runcorn WA7. . . . .**49** B6
Warrington WA4 . . . .**17** C3
Woodford Court Ind Est
CW7 . . . . **149** A8
Woodford Ct CW7. . . . . **149** A7
Woodford Dr WA8. . . . .**13** C4
Woodford La
Prestbury SK10 . . . .**61** D7
Winsford CW7 . . . . **149** B8
Woodford Lane W CW7 . . . **149** A7
Woodford Lo SK12 . . . .**36** C4
Woodford Lodge Cty High
Sch CW7 . . . . **149** A7
Woodford Lodge Cty High
Sch **2** CW7 . . . . **149** A7
Woodford Lodge Sports Ctr
CW7 . . . . **149** A7
Woodford Mews WA3. . . . .**34** D4
Woodford Park Ind Est
CW7 . . . . **148** F8
Woodford Rd Bramhall SK7 .**35** E4
Poynton SK12. . . . .**36** B6
Wilmslow SK9 . . . .**61** B8
Woodgate Ave ST7. . . . . **194** A5
Woodgate Farm La CW6 . . **148** A1
Woodgate La CW7 . . . . **170** A8
Wood Gdns SK9. . . . .**60** B2
Woodgreen La CW5 . . . . **171** D5
Woodhall CI Bramhall SK7 . . .**35** E3
Warrington WA5 . . . .**15** A8
Woodhall Rd ST7. . . . . **195** C3
Woodham CI
Northwich CW8 . . . . **103** C5
9 Stud Green CW11 . . . . . **152** C2
Woodham Gr CH64. . . . .**66** F5
Woodhatch Rd WA7. . . . .**50** B5
Wood Heath Way CH62 . . . . . .**44** A7
WOODHEY GREEN. **202** B6
Woodhey Hall La CW5 . . . . **202** B6
Woodhey La CW5 . . . . **202** C5
Woodhouse CI WA3. . . . .**9** F3
WOODHOUSE-END. **135** C8
Woodhouse End Rd
SK11. **135** C8
WOODHOUSE GREEN **158** D2
Woodhouse La
Biddulph ST8 . . . . **179** F2
Buerton CW3 . . . . **235** D8
Partington WA14 . . . .**20** C4
Warren SK11. . . . . **111** E1
Wythenshawe M90. . . . .**33** D7
Woodhouse Mid Sch
ST8 . . . . **179** E2
Woodhouse Rd M22. . . . .**33** D8
WOODHOUSES. **73** E4
Woodhouses La WA6. . . . .**73** E5
Woodhouses Pk WA6. . . . .**73** F5
Wood La
Bradwall Green CW10,
CW11 . . . . **152** E3
Broughton CH4. . . . . **139** B4
Burton CH64 . . . .**67** C2
Duddon CW6 . . . . **145** E7
Goostrey CW4 . . . . **107** C1
Neston CH64 . . . .**41** D2
Partington M31 . . . .**11** D3
Runcorn WA7. . . . .**24** A1
Runcorn, Brookvale WA7 . . . . .**50** C6
Sutton Weaver WA7 . . . .**49** F4
Tattenhall CH3 . . . . **167** A1
Warrington WA4 . . . .**26** E8
Weaverham CW8. . . . . **102** E8
Wilmslow WA16. . . . .**32** D1
Woodlan Ct CW6 . . . . **146** B6
Woodland Ave
Crewe CW1 . . . . **190** F4
Lymm WA13 . . . .**19** A2
Nantwich CW5 . . . . **205** A5
Newton-le-Willows WA12 . . . . .**2** F3
Widnes WA8. . . . .**12** F1
Woodland Bank CH2 . . . .**96** F1
Woodland CI SK11 . . . .**84** A3

Woodland Ct ST7 . . . . **193** D4
Woodland Dr WA13 . . . .**19** A2
Woodland End SK11. . . . .**84** A3
Woodland Gdns CW1. . . . . . **190** D6
Woodland Rd
Ellesmere Port CH65 . . . .**70** B2
Rode Heath ST7 . . . . **193** E8
Woodland Rise
Kelsall CW6 . . . . **122** E5
Newtown SK12. . . . .**37** A4
Woodlands CW8 . . . . **103** B5
Woodlands Ave
Chester CH1. . . . . **118** B4
Congleton CW12 . . . . **156** D4
Kidsgrove ST7 . . . . **194** D1
Woodlands CI
Cheadle SK8. . . . .**35** A8
Cotebrook CW6 . . . . **147** A8
Neston CH64 . . . .**66** D8
Woodlands Ct
Alderley Edge SK9 . . . .**85** A8
Knutsford WA16. . . . .**57** B2
Woodlands Dr
Chester CH2. . . . . **118** E4
Chorlton CW2. . . . . **207** C3
Goostrey CW4 . . . . **107** E1
Knutsford WA16. . . . .**57** D3
Warrington WA4 . . . .**17** D3
Woodlands Gr CW8 . . . .**77** F3
Woodlands Ind Est WA12. . . .**2** C6
Woodlands La CH3 . . . . **119** A2
Woodlands Pk
Congleton CW12 . . . . **156** C3
Newton-le-Willows WA12 . . . . .**2** C6
Woodlands Prim Sch
CH66. . . . .**69** F2
Woodlands Rd
Chester CH4. . . . . **141** A7
Handforth SK9 . . . .**34** E3
High Lane SK12 . . . .**38** A6
Huntington CH3 . . . . **142** A6
Macclesfield SK11 . . . . **112** C6
Neston CH64 . . . .**66** D8
New Mills SK22 . . . .**39** A8
Northwich CW8 . . . . **103** C5
Wilmslow SK9 . . . .**33** F1
Woodlands Road E **1**
CW8. . . . . **103** C5
Woodlands The
Chelford SK10 . . . .**84** E3
Higher Wincham CW9 . . . .**80** A6
Kidsgrove ST7 . . . . **194** E3
Winnington CW8 . . . .**78** E1
Woodlands Way CW6. . . . . . **146** D2
Woodland View
Ellesmere Port CH66 . . . .**69** B8
Horwich End SK23 . . . .**65** F2
Woodland Wlk
Bebington CH62 . . . .**43** C8
Runcorn WA7 . . . .**24** A1
WOOD LANE **210** A1
Wood Lane E SK10 . . . .**63** B8
Wood Lane N
Fourlane-ends SK10. . . . .**63** B8
Wardsend SK10 . . . .**37** B1
Wood Lane Prim Sch **1**
ST7. . . . . **210** A1
Wood Lane S SK10 . . . .**63** B7
Wood Lane W SK10. . . . .**63** A8
Woodlark CI CW7 . . . . **150** A8
Woodlea Ave CH2 . . . . **118** F7
Woodlea CI CH62. . . . .**43** D5
Woodlea Ct CW8 . . . . **103** D7
Woodlea Dr SK10 . . . .**87** E8
Woodleigh Ct SK9. . . . .**60** A2
Woodley Fold WA5 . . . .**14** F4
Wood Memorial Prim Sch **4**
CH4. . . . . **140** E6
Woodnoth Dr CW2 . . . . **206** C5
Wood Orchard La CW3 . . . . **230** A2
Woodpecker CI WA3 . . . .**9** F4
Woodpecker Dr
Northwich CW9 . . . . **103** F4
Packmoor ST7 . . . . **195** E1
Woodpecker Pl CW12 . . . . . **154** F6
Woodridge WA7 . . . .**24** C1
Woodrow Ct **4** WA5. . . . .**15** C7
Woodrow Way Irlam M44. . . . .**11** F8
Newcastle-under-Lyme
ST5. . . . . **210** F1
Woodruff CI ST7. . . . . **195** F1
Woodruff Wlk **7** M31 . . . .**11** F3
Woods CI CW7 . . . . **126** E2
Wood's CI WA16 . . . .**82** F6
Woods Ct WA12. . . . .**2** A3
Woodsfin La CH3. . . . . **183** F7
Woods Gr SK8 . . . .**35** B7
WOODSHUTTS **194** F1
Woodshutt's St ST7 . . . . **194** E1
WOODSIDE **99** C2
Woodside
Ellesmere Port CH65 . . . .**70** C2
Knutsford WA16. . . . .**57** B1
Lawton-gate ST7 . . . . **194** E4
Poynton SK12. . . . .**36** F4
Siddington SK11. . . . . **110** A3
Wilmslow/Alderley Edge
SK9 . . . .**59** C7
Woodside Ave
Alsager ST7 . . . . **193** E4
Crewe CW2 . . . . **189** F2
Frodsham WA6. . . . .**74** D7
Kidsgrove ST7 . . . . **195** A1
Woodside Cotts ST7 . . . . . . **195** D7
Woodside Ct CH2 . . . . **118** C4
Woodside Cty Prim Sch
WA7 . . . .**49** D2

Woodside Dr
High Lane SK6 . . . .**37** F7
Sandbach CW11. . . . . **175** C6
Woodside La
Crewe CW2 . . . . **189** F1
Lymm WA13 . . . .**19** B1
Poynton SK12. . . . .**36** E4
Woodside Rd Blacon CH1 . **117** C5
Haydock WA11. . . . .**1** F1
Warrington WA5 . . . .**14** F6
Woodside St SK22. . . . .**39** B6
Woodside Terr CW9 . . . . **104** B4
Woods La SK8 . . . .**35** B7
Wood's La CW8 . . . . **101** C5
Woodsome CI CH65 . . . .**70** B1
Woodsome Dr CH65. . . . .**70** B1
Wood Sorrel Way WA3 . . . .**3** E8
Woods Rd Hartford CW8 . . . **103** D4
Irlam M44 . . . .**11** F8
Wood St Audley ST7 . . . . **209** E3
Congleton CW12 . . . . **156** D3
Crewe CW2 . . . . **190** D2
Golborne WA3 . . . .**3** D3
Macclesfield SK11 . . . . **112** D7
Mow Cop ST7 . . . . **195** D7
New Mills SK22 . . . .**39** B7
Sandycroft CH5 . . . . **116** A2
Warrington WA1 . . . .**16** D6
Widnes WA8. . . . .**13** C1
Woodstock Ave
Cheadle SK8. . . . .**35** A7
Newton-le-Willows WA12 . . . . .**2** D2
Woodstock CI SK10 . . . .**87** A2
Woodstock Dr CW10 . . . . . . **151** C6
Woodstock Gdns WA4 . . . .**26** F6
Woodstock Gr WA8 . . . .**12** D2
Woodthorn CI WA4. . . . .**24** F4
Woodvale CI WA2 . . . .**8** E1
Woodvale Rd
Ellesmere Port CH66 . . . .**69** D6
Knutsford WA16. . . . .**82** A8
Wood View ST7 . . . . **210** A1
Woodview Cres WA8 . . . .**22** A8
Woodview Rd WA8 . . . .**22** A8
Woodville Ave SK9 . . . .**59** C7
Woodville Pl WA8 . . . .**12** D1
Woodville Rd SK9 . . . .**59** C7
Woodward CI **2** SK10 . . . .**87** E5
Woodwards Cotts CH64. . . . . .**66** E7
Woodward St CW8 . . . .**77** D1
WOODWORTH GREEN **186** B8
Woodyatt Way **1** WA13. . . . . .**18** F1
Woodyear Rd CH62 . . . .**43** E7
Woolacombe CI WA4 . . . .**16** D2
Woolam Ave CH65. . . . .**70** C5
Woolaston Dr ST7. . . . . **193** D3
Woolden Rd M44, WA3 . . . . . .**11** B8
WOOLFALL **230** E6
Woollam Dr CH66. . . . .**69** D7
Woolley Ave SK12 . . . .**36** D2
Woolley CI WA6 . . . .**49** D2
Woolmer CI WA3. . . . .**10** B6
WOOLSTANWOOD **189** E3
WOOLSTON. **17** C4
Woolston Ave CW12 . . . . **157** A2
Woolston CE Prim Sch
WA1 . . . .**17** D8
Woolston Com High Sch
WA1 . . . .**17** B7
Woolston Com Prim Sch
WA1 . . . .**17** C7
Woolston Dr CW2 . . . . **206** E2
Woolston Eyes Bird Reserve
The★ WA1/WA4 . . . .**17** D5
Woolston Grange Ave
Warrington WA1 . . . .**9** D1
Warrington, Woolston WA1 . .**17** F8
Woolston Hall WA1 . . . .**17** D7
Woolston L Ctr WA1 . . . . **17** D7
Woolston Rd WA11. . . . .**1** C7
Woolton Ct CH66. . . . .**69** F8
WOORE **232** B1
Woore Prim Sch CW3. . . . . **232** C1
Woore Rd CW3. . . . . **230** D3
Worcester Ave WA3 . . . .**3** B8
Worcester CI Talke ST7. . . . **210** D7
Warrington WA5 . . . .**15** C5
Worcester Ct WA7 . . . .**23** C1
Worcester St CH65 . . . .**70** C6
Worcester Pl CH1 . . . . **118** A4
Worcester Wlk **6** CH65. . . . .**70** C6
Wordsworth Ave
Warrington WA4 . . . .**16** B2
Widnes WA8. . . . .**22** F8
Wordsworth CI
Crewe CW2 . . . . **189** F1
7 Sandbach CW11 . . . . . . **174** D6
Wordsworth Cres CH1. . . . . **118** A5
Wordsworth Dr CW1 . . . . . . **190** F4
Wordsworth Ho SK10. . . . .**86** F1
Wordsworth Mews CH1. . . . **118** A5
Wordsworth Sq CH1. . . . . . . **118** A5
Wordsworth Way
Alsager ST7 . . . . **193** D4
Ellesmere Port CH66 . . . .**69** E1
Works Cotts WA7 . . . .**49** E3
Works La CW9 . . . .**79** E1
World Freight Terminal
M90. . . . .**32** F7
World Way M90. . . . .**33** B8
WORLESTON **188** F5
Worleston CI CW10. . . . . **151** C6
Worley Ct CH3 . . . . **183** A8
Wornish Nook CW12 . . . . . . **155** F8
Worrall St CW12 . . . . **156** E3
Worsborough Ave WA5. . . . . .**15** B5
Worsdell CI CW2 . . . . **190** E1

Worsley Ave
Saughall CH1 . . . . **117** A8
Warrington WA4 . . . .**16** F4
Worsley Cl WA7 . . . . **24** A2
Worsley Dr CW12 . . . . **157** B1
Worsley Rd WA4 . . . .**16** B1
Worsley St Golborne WA3 . . . .**3** A8
Warrington WA5 . . . .**15** F7
Worth Ct SK12 . . . . **36** D2
WORTHENBURY **211** A1
Worthenbury Rd
Caldecott Green CH3 . . . . . **197** C4
Shocklach SY14 . . . . **211** D6
Worthing St CW9 . . . . **104** C8
Worthington Ave 9 M31 . .**11** F3
Worthington Cl
Henbury SK11 . . . . **111** C8
Nantwich CW5 . . . . **205** A5
Runcorn WA7 . . . . **50** A7
Worthington Ct CH2 . . . . . . **118** D4
Worthington Pl SK9 . . . .**60** F8
Worth Prim Sch SK12 . . . .**36** F2
Wrekin Ho 8 CW8 . . . . . . **103** C5
Wrekin Way CH4 . . . . **140** F6
Wren Ave CW4 . . . . **129** C2
Wrenbury Cl ST5 . . . . **210** D1
WRENBURY **216** F4
Wrenbury Dr 3 CW9 . . . . **103** E5
WRENBURY FRITH **216** C6
Wrenbury Frith CW5 . . . . . **216** B7
Wrenbury Green CW5 . . . . **216** E4
Wrenbury Hall Dr CW5 . . **217** A5
WRENBURY HEATH **217** B5
Wrenbury Heath Rd
CW5 . . . . **217** D5
Wrenbury Ind Est CW5 . . **217** A3
Wrenbury Prim Sch
CW5 . . . . **216** F4
Wrenbury Rd Aston CW5 . . **217** B3
Chorley Bank SY14 . . . . **201** D1
Marbury SY13 . . . . **226** E8
Wrenbury SY13, CW5 . . . . . **216** B1
Wrenbury Sta CW5 . . . . **217** A3
Wrenbury Wood CW5 . . . **216** D5
Wren Cl Macclesfield SK10 . . **87** A1
Runcorn WA7 . . . . **50** A6
Warrington WA3 . . . .**9** F4
Wren Dr CW1 . . . . **190** F6
Wrenmere Cl
12 Elworth CW11 . . . . **174** E8
Sandbach CW11 . . . . **174** E8
Wrens Cl CW5 . . . . **204** F3

Wrenshot La WA16 . . . . **29** D4
Wrexham Cl Biddulph ST8 . **179** D1
Warrington WA5 . . . .**7** E1
Wrexham Ind Est/Ystad
Ddiwdiannol Wrecsam
LL13 . . . . **196** A1
Wrexham Rd
Bickerton SY14 . . . . **200** A8
Bulkeley SY14, CW6 . . . . . . **184** E1
Burland CW5 . . . . **203** C8
Chester CH4 . . . . **141** B4
Faddiley CW5, CW6 . . . . . . **202** D6
Holt LL13 . . . . **196** B7
Malpas SY14 . . . . **212** E2
Pulford CH4 . . . . **162** E5
Roughhill CH4 . . . . **140** F1
Worthenbury SY14 . . . . **211** C1
Wright Ave CW9 . . . . **104** D6
Wright Cres WA8 . . . . **23** A5
Wright Ct CW5 . . . . **204** F5
Wright Lodge 6 CW5 . . **204** F5
WRIGHT'S GREEN **27** A6
Wright's La Burtonwood WA5 **6** F3
Sandbach CW11 . . . . **175** D6
Wright St ST7 . . . . **194** D1
Wright Tree Villas M44 . . **11** D5
Wrigley La SK10 . . . .**86** B3
Wrigley Rd WA11 . . . .**1** E6
Wrinehill Rd CW5 . . . . **220** E7
Wroxham Cl Chester CH2 . **237** B4
Helsby WA6 . . . .**73** B4
Wroxham Rd WA5 . . . . **14** E6
Wrynose Rd CH62 . . . .**43** E8
Wybersley Rd SK6 . . . . **38** A8
WYBUNBURY **220** A8
Wybunbury Delves CE Prim
Sch CW5 . . . . **220** B7
Wybunbury La CW5 . . . . . **205** E3
Wybunbury Moss National
Nature Reserve ★ CW5 . . **206** B1
Wybunbury Rd
Willaston CW5 . . . . **205** D4
Wybunbury CW5 . . . . **220** B7
Wyche Ave CW5 . . . . **204** D5
Wyche Cl CW9 . . . . **104** E6
Wyche La CW6 . . . . **185** F8
Wychelm Rd M31 . . . .**11** F3
Wyche Prim Sch The
CW5 . . . . **204** E6
Wyche Rd CW6 . . . . **185** F8
Wych House Bank CW5 . . **204** D5

Wych-House La CW10 . . . **128** C1
Wych La SK10 . . . . **62** D5
Wychwood Ave WA13 . . . . **18** C3
Wychwood Pk CW2 . . . . . . **207** C1
Wycliffe Ave SK9 . . . . **60** A7
Wycliffe Ct CH2 . . . . **119** A2
Wycliffe Rd
Ellesmere Port CH65 . . . . . .**69** F3
Haydock WA11 . . . .**1** E7
Runcorn WA7 . . . . **23** C1
Wye Cl CW4 . . . . **130** D2
Wyedale CH65 . . . .**70** B3
Wyedale Rd WA11 . . . .**1** C6
Wykeham Chase 8
SK11 . . . . **111** F7
Wyncroft Cl
Ellesmere Port CH65 . . . . . .**70** B3
Widnes WA8 . . . . **22** C7
Wyncroft Ct CW8 . . . . **77** C1
Wyncroft Rd WA8 . . . . **22** C7
Wyndham Cl
Bramhall SK7 . . . .**35** E7
Northwich CW9 . . . . **103** F5
Wyndham Cres CH66 . . . . .**69** E2
Wyndham Rd CH1 . . . . **117** C4
Wynd The CW6 . . . . **122** C4
Wynfield Ave M22 . . . .**33** F7
Wyngate Rd WA15 . . . . **31** F8
Wynnstay Rd CH4 . . . . **139** C4
Wynter Cl SY14 . . . . **198** B3
Wynter La SY14 . . . . **198** B3
Wythburn Gr WA7 . . . .**49** E5
Wythens Rd SK8 . . . . **34** B8
Within St CW6 . . . . **168** D1

Y

Yardley Ave
Meadowbank CW9 . . . . **126** F8
Warrington WA5 . . . . **15** F8
Yarmouth Rd WA5 . . . .**14** E6
Yarrow Cl CH4 . . . . **139** C3
Yarwood Cl CW8 . . . . **103** F7
Yarwoodheath La WA14 . .**30** E7
YATEHOUSE GREEN **128** D6
Yatehouse La CW10 . . . . . **128** D7
Yates Cl WA5 . . . . **15** C5
Yates Gr SK9 . . . . **59** C5
Yates Rd New Mills SK22 . . . . **39** C7
Thornton-le-Moors CH2 . . . .**71** E1
Yates St CW2 . . . . **190** C2

Y Berllan Geirios/Cherry
Orch LL13 . . . . **196** D8
Yeald Brow WA13 . . . .**18** B3
Yeardsley Ave SK23 . . . . . . **39** D3
Yeardsley Gn SK23 . . . . **65** D8
Yeardsley La SK23 . . . . **39** D3
Yearsleys La WA6 . . . . **101** A5
Yeld La CW6 . . . . **122** E8
Yellowhammer Cres 1
Yeoman Way CH66 . . . .**69** F1
Yeovil Cl WA1 . . . . **17** C8
Yerburgh St CH2 . . . . **118** D4
Yew Cres CW12 . . . . **155** E4
Yewdale Dr CH66 . . . .**69** F1
Yewlands CW8 . . . . **101** D5
Yewlands Dr WA16 . . . . **57** C2
Yew Tree Ave WA12 . . . .**2** A4
Yew Tree Ave/Lon yr Ywen
CH1 . . . . **116** F7
Yew Tree Bank CW6 . . . . . **145** B5
Yewtree Cl SK23 . . . . **66** F7
Yew Tree Cl
Broughton CH4 . . . . **139** C3
Bulkeley SY14 . . . . **184** D2
Little Budworth CW6 . . . . . **147** F7
Lymm WA13 . . . .**18** E4
Macclesfield SK11 . . . . **112** A6
Middlewich CW10 . . . . **128** B2
Prestbury SK10 . . . .**87** B7
Thornton-le-Moors CH2 . . . .**71** E1
Widnes WA8 . . . .**22** B8
Wilmslow SK9 . . . . **60** D7
Yew Tree Ct Alsager ST7 . . **193** E2
Chester CH4 . . . . **163** B2
6 Heswall CH60 . . . . **41** A8
Wimboldsley CW10 . . . . . . **150** F3
Yew Tree Dr
Barnton CW8 . . . .**78** B3
Nantwich CW5 . . . . **204** D5
Yew Tree Farm Trad Est
WA11 . . . .**2** A8
Yew Tree La
Appleton Thorn WA4 . . . . . . **27** C5
Astbury CW12 . . . . **178** C3
Bridgemere CW5 . . . . **232** A6
Poynton SK12 . . . . **36** B3
Yew Tree Park Rd SK8 . . . . .**35** B6
Yewtree Rd WA16 . . . . **80** F3
Yew Tree Rd
Wardsend SK10 . . . .**37** B1
Wistaston CW2 . . . . **206** A8

Yew Tree Way
Golborne WA3 . . . .**3** B7
Prestbury SK10 . . . . **87** C6
Yew Wlk 1 M31 . . . .**11** E2
Y Llwyfenni SY14 . . . . **222** F5
Yonne The CH1 . . . . **237** A2
York Ave Culcheth WA3 . . . .**4** F2
Warrington WA5 . . . . **14** E7
York Cl Biddulph ST8 . . . . . **179** C2
Talke ST7 . . . . **210** D7
York Cres SK9 . . . . **60** D8
York Ct 2 WA4 . . . .**16** E1
York Dr
Mickle Trafford CH2 . . . . . . **119** E8
Warrington WA4 . . . . **17** A2
Winsford CW7 . . . . **149** D6
Wythenshawe M90 . . . .**32** F7
York Gdns Midway SK7 . . . . **36** A2
Woodford SK7 . . . . **35** F2
York Ho 4 CW8 . . . . **103** C5
York Pl WA7 . . . . **23** A2
York Rd Connah's Quay CH5 . **91** C1
Ellesmere Port CH65 . . . . . . **70** C5
Irlam M44 . . . . **11** D5
Warrington WA4 . . . . **17** A2
Widnes WA8 . . . . **22** C8
Yorkshire Rd M31 . . . .**11** E2
York St Chester CH1 . . . . . . **237** B3
Macclesfield SK10 . . . . **112** E8
Runcorn WA7 . . . . **23** A2
Warrington WA4 . . . . **16** C4
Yorston Lodge Sch WA16 . . **56** F1
Ysgol Borderbrook SY14 . **222** F5
Ysgol Derwen Prim Sch
CH4 . . . . **161** A7
Ystad Ddiwdiannol Wrecsam/
Wrexham Ind Est LL13 . . **196** A1

Z

Zan Dr CW11 . . . . **175** A3
Zan Ind Pk CW11 . . . . **175** A3
Zara Ct WA11 . . . .**1** C7
Zinnia Dr M44 . . . .**11** E8
Zion St 3 CW8 . . . . **103** E7
Zurich Ave ST8 . . . . **179** E1